THE FAMILY ENCYCLOPEDIA OF HEALTH

DR. RAJENDRA SHARMA

Dr. Rajendra Sharma *is Medical Director of the world-renowned Hale Clinic. He is associated with practices in Europe and the United States, where he blends the culture and medical techniques of East and West. Dr. Sharma has studied with specialists in most alternative medical fields. While his particular interest is in working with cancer, HIV/AIDS and other serious and chronic illnesses, Dr. Sharma is considered by many to be their family doctor.*

THE FAMILY ENCYCLOPEDIA OF HEALTH

THE COMPLETE FAMILY REFERENCE GUIDE TO ALTERNATIVE & ORTHODOX MEDICAL DIAGNOSIS, TREATMENT & PREVENTATIVE HEALTHCARE

DR. RAJENDRA SHARMA

ELEMENT
BOSTON, MASSACHUSETTS • SHAFTESBURY, DORSET • MELBOURNE, VICTORIA

First published in the U.K. in 1998 by
Element Books Limited
Shaftesbury, Dorset SP7 8BP

This edition published
in the U.S.A. in 1999
by Element Books, Inc.
160 North Washington Street, Boston,
MA 02114

NOTE FROM THE PUBLISHER
Any information given in *The Family Encyclopedia of Health* is not
intended to be taken as a replacement for medical advice.
Any person with a condition requiring medical attention
should consult a qualified medical practitioner or suitable therapist.

Cover design by Slatter-Anderson
Design by Andrew Sutterby
Illustrated by Michael Courtney, Deborah Maizels,
Anthony Warne, Michael Cole and David Woodroffe
Typeset by Dorchester Typesetting Group Ltd
Printed and bound in the U.S.A.

Library of Congress Cataloging in Publication
data available

ISBN 1 86204 426 0

Contents

To
My reasons for being—
Emily, Liam, and Madeleine,
and others yet to come.

Acknowledgments

Thank you to my late father, Chandra, who was and is the greatest teacher I will ever have and to my mother, Rosemary, for always being there, supporting and believing in me. Thank you to Justin (my loving and much-loved brother) and Frankie (and Vivian) for their love and grounding effect.

No Emily, no book. My wife has transcribed and turned this work into a readable form, while keeping our home and children swathed in love. Thank you so much.

Thank you to my friends who encouraged and supported my writing, especially Tibs' friend (Alon), who will, I know, be the literary giant he deserves to be. Thanks also to Ian Fenton who bothered to find me, and to Matthew Cory at Element Books who did all the hard work.

Thank you to those who inspired and taught me, especially Dr. Issac Mathai Nooranal, Dr. Harald Gaier, Dr. Anthony Soyer and Laurens Holve.

A special thank you to the colleagues I have worked with over the years and from whom I have learned so much—especially the 101 Group of Practitioners. Thank you to Fiona Harrold for her support throughout my career. Thanks also to my newer colleagues from the Hale, Castle Street, and Kailash Clinics. Thanks to my American support, especially Dr. Woodson Merrell (and, of course, Gaye), Dr. Timothy Lynch, Laura Gabbe, and Kathy Dunn.

A special thank you to John Piper (and Becky) and Malcolm for keeping me sane.

A very big and special thank you to my team: Chan and Mary (and their support team Wendy, Debbie, and Jim) for protecting me, and to Robin for helping to set it all up. Thank you to those friends who believe in me and help me escape from medicine sometimes, particularly Tina Turner, David Pugh, Kevin and Susie, John Vos, Richard Berenson, and the Arsenal football team!

I am indebted to James and Sheelagh Colton, Dr. Stephen Davis, Dr. Julian Jessel-Kenyon, Agnes Kernan, Professor D. Schweitzer and Annette Wilkinson for providing material for use in this book, and also to the Science Photo Library for permission to use their photographs.

Finally, an apology to those patients who find information or instructions in this book that I failed to give to them in consultations. I have learned a lot in the last three years while preparing this book, and if you saw me before the information had come to me, it would not have filtered through to you. Thank you for helping me to learn.

Foreword

Health care has undergone dramatic changes in the last decade. On the stressful side, national and private health care systems have put a significant crimp in many patients' ability to receive quality care. All too often the physician's time allotment per patient has dwindled to the point that only cursory care can be provided, with attention only given to immediate problems. Emphasis on preventative and early intervention is wilting, despite insurance company pronouncements to the contrary.

On the positive side, there is increasing realization by patients that there is more to health care than immediate symptom alleviation. The rise of alternative/complementary medical studies and access to data through print media and the Internet has revolutionized our possibilities for achieving healing instead of disease management. Increased access to information, and generally heightened public awareness of preventative and alternative/complementary therapies have encouraged patients to take greater control of their own health care. In fact there is so much information available that it can be a daunting task to weed out the useful from the spurious.

Until the last few years, there had been only a handful of credible, responsible clinicians who were able to combine the best of conventional medicine, with the wisdom of their ancestors and with modern complementary methods. Too often "alternative" practitioners have utilized poor guesses founded on inadequate information to formulate treatments for their patients that were expensive, usually unhelpful, and occasionally downright dangerous. It has been the quest of a few of us to correct this condition, and practice and teach a medicine that is humanistic, safe, efficacious, well-studied, and inclusive of all healing traditions.

One of the early pioneers in this field has been Rajendra Sharma. I first met Rajendra back in the 1980's, shortly after his beloved father had passed away. Dr. Sharma's father was one of the most revered homeopathic physicians in the history of the discipline. When I met Rajendra, he had just finished mastering "Western" medicine and had begun incorporating homeopathy and other complementary modalities into his practice. He had been spoiled. He had been raised by one of the masters. He described to me that at the end of his father's practice, he was not even sure what the "remedies" had to do with the patients' healing—so many of the patients said they felt better just by being in Dr. Sharma Sr's presence. Quite a gauntlet was thrown to Rajendra. His father would be very gratified to see that, as this book makes very evident, the son has taken much of the best from the father, improved it, and moved on to synthesize newer possibilities into his armamentarium.

Dr. Sharma currently heads the largest alternative/complementary care clinic in Europe. He teaches and sees patients throughout Europe and receives patients from all over the world. I have many patients who have traveled to London to be treated successfully by him.

Over the last four years there has been an explosion of books on alternative/complementary medicine. Why is this one special? You will see that the accumulated wisdom of two generations, and one of the world's busiest and most successful alternative/complementary practices of the last 20 years has resulted in a treasure trove of knowledge. The structuring of the information by stages of life is unique and especially useful. The specific chapters on sex and fertility, nutrition and alternative therapies are exhaustive. The entire book takes very complex issues and presents them clearly, with a remarkable blending of traditional medical information and treatment with alternative/complementary therapies. It also teaches us to assess our health and infirmities in a much wider manner. Not everyone may agree with all that is discussed in this book; some of it is controversial or may seem too "folk." However, most of it is based on careful study and long personal experience. As with any book of recommended healings, you take from it what speaks to you.

The depth to which Dr. Sharma understands his patients' problems is remarkable—from the spiritual, emotional and physical levels. The range of preventive and curative remedies which he recommends is inspiring. The book reads as though your wise uncle is sitting with you and compassionately working through your problems and their solutions. Whatever page you turn to you will be in for a medical treat.

Woodson Merrell, M.D.
Assistant Clinical Professor of Medicine
Columbia University College of Physicians and Surgeons
Executive Director
Center for Integrative Medicine
Continuum Health (Hospital) Systems
New York City

Introduction

This book has come about because of the need for an easy-reference first-aid book that deals with the problems we are all likely to come across in our lives. The book discusses, illnesses such as cancer (one in three people will have to deal with this in their lifetime), AIDS, diabetes, and psoriasis, but attention is also paid to options for treatments for conditions that we may all face through our lives.

There is a myriad of books about orthodox, complementary, and alternative-medical first-aid, but they are specifically drawn towards one type of treatment, such as homeopathy, herbal treatment, or dietetics. An individual requires a veritable library of books to have a reasonable overall knowledge, and selecting the best treatment for a specific problem is not easy. I hope this book will simplify matters.

A Unified Approach to Health

I am the first to admit that to try to encompass a working knowledge of all complementary and orthodox therapies would be beyond even the most sophisticated computer, but to be aware of the existence and the possibilities that each therapy can offer is both feasible and enjoyable. Over the years, I have come into contact with therapists in most fields of medicine and through discussion and reading about the specialty have learned enough to know when to recommend treatment, and which are the appropriate therapies to recommend.

The clinics in which I work have experts in the various fields that I believe have credibility. Such truly holistic practices offer patients a complete understanding of their health and the availability of any treatment necessary to restore their well-being. Using this book will allow the reader to share my experience.

In no way should this book be seen as a replacement for doctors and practitioners. It must be used as a guide to the appropriate courses of treatment. However, it may help not only the reader, but also the physician or practitioner whose care the patient is under. Information gleaned from these pages can be presented to your carer for assessment of its use. Do not assume your practitioner knows all the possible treatment routes—all practitioners are constantly learning and should be happy to discuss other therapies apart from their own.

WHAT IS HOLISTIC MEDICINE?

Before the advent of "modern science" in the West about 150 years ago, medicine and healthcare were based predominantly on trial, error, and observation.

Physicians had no more real knowledge than an experienced grandmother. A lack of knowledge concerning viruses and bacteria meant that hygiene was little understood, and therefore health was poor and life expectancy was short. As science took hold, the "art" of medicine became less studied, and the birth of modern medicine took us away from some of the gentler skills and techniques that had accrued over centuries.

Thousands of years of traditional knowledge from the Tibetans, Chinese, Ayurvedic (Indian), and other long-established cultures were put aside as the Western world developed. The necessary balance between the modern scientist and the traditional healer was lost, and the pendulum swung more towards manufactured drugs and high-technology methods.

Now, however, the pendulum is swinging back and hopefully will settle midway, allowing a balanced attitude towards healing to come to the fore. There is a place for the surgeon's knife and antibiotics, alongside the hands of the faith-healer and the brews of the herbalist.

The names "alternative" and "fringe" medicine have largely been replaced by "complementary" medicine. This was an attempt by the practitioners in nonscientific medical art to try to persuade the mighty physician that they were suitable assistants to orthodox medicine. There is no doubt that this attitude was required to create the necessary change, but as we see more and more failures within the modern medical system, the complementary medical practitioner has now suggested a new term—integrated medicine—to try to achieve a level of equal importance with orthodox medicine. It is, in my opinion, as erroneous of an acupuncturist to suggest that he has a higher level of knowledge as it is for a Professor of Surgery to assume an air of superiority.

The term "holistic" (derived from the Greek *holos*, meaning "whole") is the closest to the direction in which I believe medicine and healing must go. Unfortunately the term has been associated with quackery and mysticism, and thus is not one that an orthodox physician would willingly be labeled.

We all have to learn that there can no longer be any differentiation. The art of healing must draw from all philosophies and all schools of teaching to create a single healthcare system. Divisions will be required, because no one individual can retain and use all the available treatment options, but there has to come a time when doctors have as broad a knowledge of the availability of treatments as possible so that they can recommend the most effective and fast-acting repair process to their patients. A doctor today should be aware of treatment options such as acupuncture or osteopathy, and a homeopath should be knowledgeable about the potential use of antibiotics, for example. We have, at present, a divisive system that has to change. I hope that this book will help to achieve this.

Health and Healing Today

The doctors of today—let alone the untrained population—appear to know only a smattering of the simple, nondrug treatments that have much value in treating our common ailments.

In no way do I wish to belittle the work of us Western-trained doctors. More and more patients are, however, becoming disenchanted and alarmed at the advice they receive from their doctors and hospital specialists when seeking advice for general health and nonlife-threatening conditions.

CASE HISTORY

Mrs. J. B., age 62 years and an active grandmother and homemaker, suffered a stroke three years prior to coming to see me. The stroke had severely affected her speech and the left side of her body had retained less than 10 percent of its function. Over the three-year period, she had regained most of her speech through invaluable speech therapy but, despite physiotherapy, had only managed to regain about 30 percent of the movement and strength in her left arm. Mrs. J. B. had high blood pressure (until the stroke, when it "miraculously" reverted to normal) and she had been given, theoretically, adequate blood-pressure control medicine for several years.

After I had examined her I suggested that she try Chinese herbal medicine in conjunction with some osteopathy and acupuncture. Within two months, Mrs. J. B. was able to walk more than 200 yards, as opposed to the 20 yards that had exhausted her before. Her mood had elevated beyond recognition, and she was able to play with and enjoy her grandchildren far more.

When she returned to the doctor who had been sympathetic over the previous years, his attitude was not one of surprise and interest—in fact, quite the opposite. He warned Mrs. J. B. about the dangers of herbal medicine, and told her that acupuncture was unproved and osteopathy was dangerous.

Apart from the fact that all these statements are untrue, as these therapies had been given by correctly qualified people, the doctor managed to frighten Mrs. J. B. and create a negative reaction towards treatments that in two months had done more to help her than three years of the orthodox approach.

This, I think, is typical of the state of healthcare or healing available in the West at the moment. Scientifically trained doctors who have had no teachers to advise them to stay in touch with their instincts, and who have been taught to accept nothing if it does not have a scientific explanation, are losing touch with the principles of healing. This case history is typical of the Western doctor's approach to health and healthcare.

Doctors are trained to memorize facts and stay within specific boundaries or protocols, until time and studies prove new techniques and treatments to be safe and effective, or until they are shown to be dangerous. This often allows today's orthodox doctor to be completely without responsibility, leaving much to the pharmaceutical industry who are not professional carers (in fact, one might say that they do not care at all) but money makers.

The most notorious example of this is the drug thalidomide. Doctors were told that prescribing thalidomide throughout pregnancy was safe, but this proved not to be true. After the damage was done, all the prescribers held up their hands and said "Do not blame us, not our fault, we did as we were told." If the doctors had read the facts, or even questioned the safety tests, a major disaster might have been averted. This scenario is being repeated constantly—at the time of writing, in the last year alone, seven types of contraceptive pill have been shown to be hazardous. In the summer of 1996 a common cardiac drug was scrutinized for safety and failed. In 1995, the efficacy of AZT in the treatment of AIDS was disproved, and the year before that, two of the three available measles vaccines were withdrawn. The third vaccine is currently under scrutiny. The list goes on and on.

Of course, the consideration of using any treatment outside the parameters of "scientifically" proven, and therefore "safe" (whether or not it has been used for thousands of years), is actively discouraged.

Good health has been defined by the World Health Organization (WHO), and I paraphrase,

The Three Levels of Health

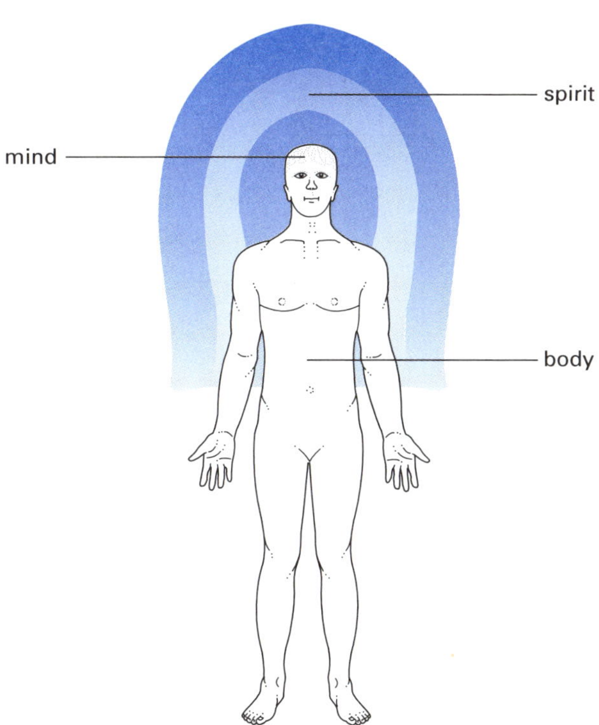

The well-being of an individual depends not only on the health of the mind and body, but also of the spirit, here represented by an aura around the head.

"a level of health that is not only free from illness, but also includes the well-being of an individual in physical, emotional and spiritual terms." In principle, the WHO is stating that good health requires a level of contentment on the following planes:

- the physical/physiological/biochemical level
- the psychological/conscious level
- the spiritual/subconscious level.

For thousands of years, physicians, practitioners, and healers in many disciplines have worked on the principle that health must be considered at all three levels. We are reaching a time when there is too much knowledge for any one physician to retain. Specialization is a necessity, but not only with respect to the physical plane. We need advice on all three levels. We have reached a point where the *life-saving* doctors must work in tandem with the *health-saving* practitioners.

Holistic medicine is about understanding how to deal with all three levels, and doing so in simple and effective ways. We all need to have an understanding of the simple processes of health maintenance and repair, with a knowledge of how to use the many disciplines—both orthodox and alternative—that are available.

This body, mind and soul "stuff" is not some ethereal mumbo-jumbo, either. Doctors today are not told about much of the evidence of a strong, scientific nature that supports mind/body concepts. The most striking example is that of the psychiatric patient with multiple personalities reported by Drs. Braun and Goldman. This patient, not unusual in having multiple personalities, was found to exhibit different diseases depending on who she was at any one time. One personality had diabetes, and when this character was in control, the patient's sugar levels were very high. As soon as the personality changed, away went the diabetes. Another character developed hives in reaction to certain substances, and these also came and went with this persona.

The hypothesis that living cells contain a vital force is one that is present in many medical philosophies throughout the world. The West has lost sight of this because of an overdependence on science. This is even more strange, because the foundations on which this science is based are very flimsy. Chemistry is founded on physics. Physics has worked itself down to fundamental particles, atoms, electrons, quanta, quarks, and so forth, but ask a physicist "How did it begin?" or "What is the force holding electrons together or the force that we call gravity?" and there is no definitive answer. We can measure the effects, but the vital force is unknown. If a rock falls to the ground, the vital force is gravity, and this is accepted, yet if a tumor disappears by the influence of the vital force of a healer, it is unacceptable.

STAYING HEALTHY

It is much easier to keep someone healthy than to get them better. The bulk of this book is concerned with repair, but ideally I hope that the reader will not have recourse to look at these sections. The best way to avoid this is to maintain a healthy lifestyle, and the following tips may give some guidance on how to do so.

The 24 hours in a day should be divided into the following:

Sleep	8 hours
Enjoyable, productive work	8 hours
Exercise	40 min–1hour
Meditation	1–2 hours
Basic hygiene	0.5–1 hour
Preparing and eating food	1½–2 hours
Having fun	The rest of the time

Of course, all these time suggestions are variable: 10 minutes of exercise is better than none, and the same could be said for meditation.

Sleep should not be cut out for the benefit of any of the other time allocations because sleep is essential for repair and well-being.

A Healthy Day

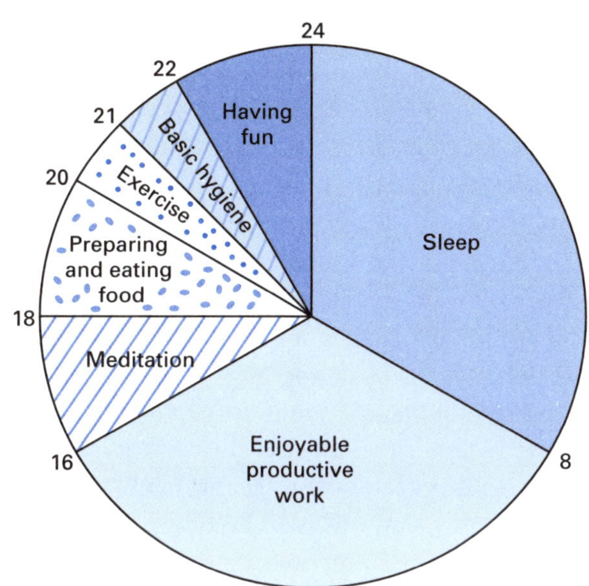

Wherever possible, work should be enjoyable, and serious consideration given to changing employment that is not so.

Exercise and meditation are discussed in their own sections in this book, but must make up a part of every day. Eating and the preparation of food is discussed in chapter 7 on nutrition.

Basic hygiene is very often overlooked in the West, but is integrated into the social and religious philosophies of Eastern and Middle Eastern cultures—for example, a Hindu would not consider eating before ablutions. All parts of the body should be considered, starting with a cleansing of the skin and hair, emptying of the bowel and bladder, and the cleaning of our VIPs (very important places!), which include the oral cavity, genitals, ears, nostrils, and anus. Special attention should be paid to the feet, which are often neglected until a problem sets in.

In an attempt to make life simple, I suggest to my patients that they draw themselves the following chart.

I suggest that each day, individuals give themselves marks out of five for each of these subjects, aiming to score over 40 points and ensuring at least three points in each category.

If sex is not available, score another five points with some other enjoyable activity!

ACTIVITY	0	1	2	3	4	5
• Basic hygiene						
• Doing something creative						
• Eating						
• Exercise						
• Fun						
• Prayer or meditation						
• Sex						
• Sleep						
• Socializing						
• Work						

ILLNESS, DISEASE, AND HEALTH

Principally, there is a big difference between being ill and lacking health.

Being Well and Staying Well

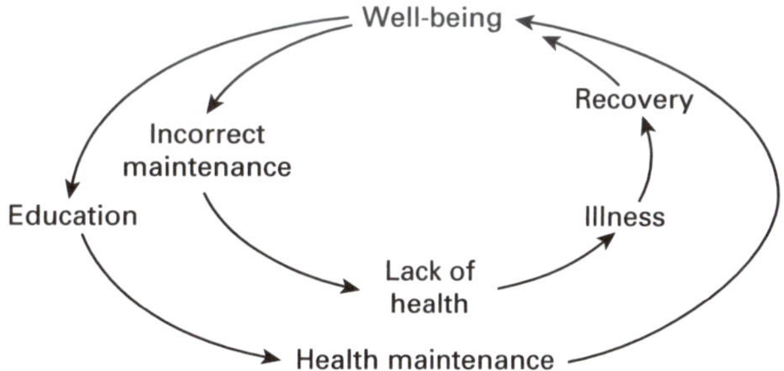

When we lose control or if we are poorly educated about how to maintain our health, then unhealthy living will lead to a lack of health, which is quite distinct from illness. A lack of health can be corrected merely by re-education and rearrangement of our lifestyles, whereas illness generally requires intervention or treatment. A broad example would be that of a smoker. Inhaling 20 cigarettes a day will initially lead to an increase in the likelihood of coughs, colds, sinusitis, or sore throats, which may indicate a lack of health and can be corrected by not smoking. If these early warning signs are ignored, then the destruction of lung tissue is inevitable, and conditions such as chronic bronchitis, emphysema, and cancer may (and usually do)

set in. This is illness, and requires intervention rather than simply refraining from smoking.

Being well and staying well is a matter of correct education. If we know what we are doing and how to encourage those around us to do the same, then staying well is not that difficult. Persuading those close to us may be relatively easy, but when dealing with large corporations, government, and industries, keeping ourselves from pollutants and toxins is—unfortunately—much harder to do. This book will do its best to help you avoid some of the poisons that are fed into our food and atmosphere.

The human being responds to ill health in three ways.

- **Elimination:** a process that throws things out of the body. Mucus production during a cold, vomiting, diarrhea, sweating, and persistent urination are all elimination reactions.
- **Reaction:** when the body produces symptoms that do not seem to be throwing anything out. Skin rashes such as eczema, asthma, abdominal colic, or cramps are a few examples.
- **Retention:** when the body holds onto problems by forming lumps and bumps, or stones in the gall bladder or kidney.

Good health is about a balance of all three, although individuals tend toward one type more than another.

It is not "more healthy" or better to exhibit any one of these three response types, because different conditions will be more dangerous in different response groups. A retentive type of person is more likely to be able to deal with problems that stay in the body, and will handle cancer cells more effectively than, say, an eliminator, who is more geared to throwing things out. Furthermore, food poisoning or a condition such as cholera, which encourage fluid loss through vomiting and diarrhea, may be far more devastating to a body that habitually throws things out than to one that is geared to holding things in. In contrast, an infection in a retentive type is liable to stay in the system for longer than it would in that of an eliminator.

Reactions are usually warnings and the initiation of a repair process depends either on an elimination or the body being able to deal with the problem internally.

Individuals should establish their type and tendency, and use this knowledge to enhance any treatment choices. Establishing your body type will also relieve anxiety. If you are a retentive sort, then most lumps and bumps are not likely to be cancerous. If you are an eliminative type, a stomach upset should not last very long because the "bug" will be thrown out rapidly.

GETTING BETTER

This book is about healing, which in turn is about getting better. The body responds to not being well by producing symptoms that fall into one of three categories.

- Warning Symptoms.
- Repair Processes.
- Loss of Control.

The first two categories are the body healing itself, and the third is when the body is failing to do so.

The important factor in helping to heal is being able to differentiate between the three categories of symptoms.

WARNING SYMPTOMS

The body may create certain symptoms to advise the patient that a particular action is liable to lead to problems. A good example is the following case history.

CASE HISTORY

Mr. N. F., age 38 years, had been told that he had a stomach ulcer. On close questioning, it became clear that his upper-abdominal pain was made worse by drinking coffee. If he did not drink coffee, he did not have the pain. Interestingly, on further questioning it became clear that Mr. N. F. was very sensitive to caffeine, which would keep him awake for up to 4 hours if he drank it after his evening meal.

In this simple example, Mr. N. F. was being warned by his stomach that the continual use of caffeine was overstimulating his system, which would lead to more serious complications in the future. Most pain is a warning, and if the warning is heeded, the problems should be healed.

RECOMMENDATION

- *Do not ignore symptoms. They are the body, mind, and soul's way of advising you.*

REPAIR PROCESSES

Quite often, symptoms are created to repair the body. A cut that hurts, falls into the warning category, telling the individual to protect that area of damaged skin. However, the pain is also sending information to the nervous system, which in turn sends information back, opening up blood vessels and attracting more white blood cells, scar tissue-forming cells, and nutrients necessary for repair to rush into the damaged area. In this example, the pain is not only warning but also encouraging repair. Taking a painkiller, therefore, can not only allow further damage to occur, because we become less conscious of the damage, but also interfere with the reflex-repair process.

Healing response

One problem with any self-help text associated with alternative medicine is the concept of the healing response. Orthodox medicine is very much geared towards removing unpleasant symptoms, regardless of the effect on the underlying disease. Holistic medicine is about curing the problem, thereby alleviating the symptoms from a deeper, nonsuperficial aspect. Many treatments in the complementary medical field will trigger reactions that may be initially unpleasant, or worsen the symptoms that the treatment is supposedly curing. It is vital to have an understanding of this, and I believe that the case history below illustrates the matter clearly.

CASE HISTORY

Mrs. J. D., age 22 years, came to see me with a history of persisting and recurrent "cold" symptoms. She was very precise about her symptoms, and discussed with me at our first meeting the fact that she would sneeze between 10 and 20 times per hour, have a fever that never raised itself above 98°F, and was able to take warm fluids through her sore throat, but when her symptoms were at a peak, she was unable to swallow solids. She was in my consulting room at the zenith of her current cold, and told me that the problem would take another week of slow improvement before it disappeared, but that she would probably be ill again within the month.

I took her medical history, performed a full examination, and initiated the appropriate treatment. I neglected to advise Mrs. J. D. on the principles of the healing reaction, and three days later I found her back in my consulting room: "I don't know what you gave me doctor but I am now sneezing over 30 times an hour, my temperature reached 100°F, and I am now unable to swallow even fluids."

I explained that all her symptoms had worsened because the virus was being thrown out quicker by the sneezing; the inflammation in her throat was due to more blood in the area, bringing with it more white blood cells to kill the virus; and that *she* can live at 100°F, but many viruses cannot! Such healing responses should, therefore, shorten the time of the illness. I explained that her immune system was now fighting a stronger battle, and that this indicated that the treatment was working. Mrs. J. D. did improve over the next 24 hours, and has since suffered only two "colds" each year during the last five years.

RECOMMENDATION

- *Do not suppress or cover up symptoms—they may be healing you.*

The Five Reactions of Healing

There are five reactions worth noting as part of the repair process. These are particularly relevant for anybody going through a homeopathic treatment course, but are also relevant to any naturopathic healing process.

- As mentioned above, symptoms may get worse before they get better.
- Despite symptoms getting worse, an individual will feel better on a psychological level before the physical symptoms resolve. This is an extremely important factor in the healing process while waiting for physical effects to take place.
- Problems often leave the body in a downward motion: for instance, a headache may become a backache; an upset stomach may eliminate as diarrhea; a rash on the chest may leave via the feet.
- Problems will resolve from inside, outwards: internal illness may expel itself as a rash as in the case of measles or chickenpox; food poisoning may cause vomiting; toxins may come out through the hair or nails.
- An illness may regress through symptoms previously suffered. This is described as "present conditions go to past conditions." In an acute disease such as pneumonia, the patient rarely wakes up with pneumonia, but first goes through cold symptoms, flu-like symptoms, and a mild chest infection; conversely, a patient with pneumonia rarely wakes up suddenly feeling wonderful, but goes through symptoms of a mild chest infection, flu symptoms, a cold, and then feeling well again. Chronic conditions may do the same, even though there may be no direct or obvious connection. For example, someone, aged 30 years, with rheumatoid arthritis may find that the condition improves, and at the same time they have a rash that reminds them of a problem they had when they were 15 years old. Very often that rash was suppressed, the condition went deeper, and is now being resolved. This scenario may occur many years into the future.

It is important to understand these facts, because reporting to the complementary medical practitioner can be made more accurate by including any symptoms within these parameters, and will also allow the individual to feel confident despite a slow improvement.

LOSS OF CONTROL

When the body loses control of its symptoms, then the situation demands medical intervention. A cancer can grow unnoticed in a major organ, showing no signs or symptoms until it is too late to be treated. Other "silent" conditions, such as AIDS and diabetes, may not present until the disease process is very far gone. It is a sign of ill health to have a disease process and show no symptoms, which is ironic because a bad cold will bring the patient to a practice complaining that they are "ill" or at "death's door" when in fact their variety of symptoms is repairing them. Conversely, someone attending for a check-up who feels fine and "full of the joys of spring" may be discovered to be ravaged by cancer, or slowly damaging their arteries with arteriosclerosis.

RECOMMENDATION

- *Do not assume that a symptom-free life is a healthy one. Visit a health practitioner regularly and consider having relevant screening annually.*

ABOUT THIS BOOK

This book has arisen from my experience of helping individuals search for guidance toward optimum healthcare techniques. Until the time comes when all practitioners of medicine are encouraged to broaden their outlook, this book will enable people to understand the available techniques—both modern and traditional—to be well.

The speed with which medical treatments, both orthodox and complementary, are being thrown out to the eager public suggests that by the time you have read this sentence, new ideas and concepts for treatment will have manifested themselves. The subject is so large that I may not have included all possible treatment avenues despite my extensive research. I invite any practitioners or individuals who have had success with treatments not mentioned in this edition to have no hesitation in writing to me with references so that I can continue to update this book in the future.

This book is indexed to allow easy access to any particular condition. Each subject has a brief explanation from both an orthodox and an Eastern-medical perspective, where appropriate, and the most effective treatments are mentioned. I have chosen only to list those medicines and therapies that are easily available, and where I make reference to a particular need to see a practitioner or doctor, this is because many other treatments are available, but may be difficult to obtain or require skilled judgment in prescribing.

I hope that this book will enable individuals to look after themselves and find safe treatments swiftly, by helping them to choose the best option rather than experimenting until the right formula is found. I also believe that this book may be an invaluable companion for doctors, hospital specialists, and complementary/alternative practitioners whose training—I am sure they will agree—does not necessarily illustrate the available options from specialties other than their own.

The purpose of this book is to provide a first-aid reference and a mini-encyclopedia for both the initiated and for newcomers to complementary medicine. It would not be possible to cover all health matters in one single volume, and nor is it necessary. There are many books that can provide in-depth details of specific health problems.

I give many recommendations for all the common ailments that we may come across in our personal or family lives. It would take another book of this size to give all the references. One resource center told me that they have over 40,000 references for papers and trials on complementary medicine. Where I have given advice, be assured that it is from personal experience or from other reputable sources. I have also not given all the reasons why certain compounds may work on a particular condition. While fascinating, this is not the reason for this book, which should act as a reference for home medicine and suggest suitable treatment courses, both orthodox and alternative, and give an understanding of what practitioners are doing, and why.

USING THIS BOOK

This encyclopedia follows a format in which ailments that occur *commonly* at particular times of life are discussed. For instance, I write about the best nutrition for pregnancy in the section about pregnancy and childbirth. However, some conditions span many age groups. Eczema can occur at any stage of life, but is initially discussed in the section on childhood, since this is when eczema most commonly presents itself to a physician. After the discussion of any particular condition, I suggest under the heading RECOMMENDATION(S) the appropriate actions that may be taken.

RECOMMENDATION

- *Check in the index at the back of the book for any specific complaint when using this book as a reference. You may be directed to a different age group, but the treatment will be the same for your own.*

COMPLEMENTARY MEDICINE

The complementary medical advice given for any condition is at best curative, and at worst ineffectual. Specific treatments may have effects that are unpleasant, and "healing responses" (*see* **Getting Better**) may occur as the body repairs. Certain illnesses, such as meningitis, can develop rapidly and must be treated by doctors. *Do not ignore the advice in the text if it supports orthodox treatment.*

RECOMMENDATION

- *For any condition where self-help is initiated, discuss the matter with a professional if improvement is not apparent within 24hr, or sooner if the condition worsens. If in any doubt, consult a professional practitioner immediately.*

REMEDIES

When homeopathic remedies are mentioned, be aware that the list may not include the best remedy for you. Homeopathy is best prescribed by looking at the totality of symptoms, both pleasant and unpleasant, in an individual. The typical, modern approach of selecting *one* remedy for *one* symptom is incorrect and most often unsuccessful. However, it is unlikely that any negative reaction will occur by using an incorrect remedy. Probably nothing will happen at all. Using a recommended remedy is therefore safe.

RECOMMENDATION

- *Most medication and therapies mentioned are general, but when homeopathic remedies are listed, please be aware that correct selection depends on a specific symptom picture and reference to a homeopathic manual is highly recommended.*

DOSAGES

When no specific dosage is given for a homeopathic remedy, assume that it should be taken as either four pills (round), two tablets (disc shaped), or four drops every two waking hours until improvement is seen, then reduced to every four hours. Stop the remedy 24 hours after the condition has gone.

When I recommend a herbal extract, you will see the amounts and dosages. If I recommend a therapy, the length of treatment will be decided by the patient's response and the therapist.

FURTHER INFORMATION

Any questions, omissions, corrections, or criticisms (constructive only, please) should be directed to the attention of:

Dr. Sharma
Medical Director
The 101 Group
87 North Road
Parkstone
Poole
Dorset BH14 0LT
UK

YOUR MEDICINE CABINET

This book covers the most common conditions, and describes treatments that are either easily or readily obtainable. Where feasible, treatment recommendations are given that include the amounts and potencies that should be taken. However, certain recommendations include nutrients, vitamins, and minerals that are obtainable from food, and these foods have not been listed. I also frequently mention the need to refer to "Your preferred Homeopathic Manual." There are many good books, but I take the liberty of mentioning those that I think should sit next to the medicine cabinet, and I list these at the foot of the following page.

THE MEDICAL KIT

There is a benefit in having certain naturopathic and homeopathic remedies easily at hand in the house. The following is my recommendation for the contents of a first-aid cabinet. Most of these should be available in good health-food stores and pharmacists, but if not, they are available through mail order from:
c/o Best of Both Worlds,
13123 Eastbrooke Avenue,
Downey, CA 90242, U.S.A.

Lotions
Arnica-Fluid Extract
Calendula-Fluid Extract
Hypericum-Fluid Extract
Euphrasia-Fluid Extract

Creams
Arnica Cream
Calendula Cream
Any cream containing both of the above

Essential oils
Clove oil
Lavender oil
Mullein oil
Olbas Oil
Peppermint oil

Homeopathic remedies
The following should be kept at potencies of 6 and 30:

Aconite
Agaricus muscarius
Agnus castus
Allium cepa
Argentum nitricum
Arnica
Arsenicum album
Baptisia
Baryta carbonica
Belladonna
Bellis perennis
Berberis
Bryonia
Calcarea carbonica
Calcarea phosphorica
Calendula
Cantharis
Carbo vegetalis
Caulophyllum
Causticum
Chamomilla
Chelidonium
China arsenicum
Cimicifuga
Coffea
Drosera
Euphrasia
Ferrum phosphoricum
Gelsemium
Hepar sulfuris
Hypericum
Ignatia
Ipecacuanha
Kali bichromicum
Kali bromatum
Kali carbonicum
Lachesis
Lycopodium
Magnesia carbonica
Magnesia phosphorica
Mercurius corrosivus
Mercurius solubilis
Natrum carbonicum
Natrum muriaticum
Natrum sulfuricum
Nitricum acidum
Nux vomica
Pertussin
Phosphorus
Phytolacca
Pothos foetidus
Pulsatilla
Rhus toxicodendron
Ruta graveolens
Secale cornutum
Sepia
Silica
Spongia
Staphysagria
Streptococcus
Sulfur
Thuja
Urtica urens
Veratrum album

- **The Family Guide to Homeopathy,** Dr. Andrew Lockie, *Hamish Hamilton Ltd., London, 1992.*
- **The Vitamin Bible,** Earl Mindell, *Warner Books, New York.*
- **The Encyclopedia of Pregnancy and Birth,** Janet Balaskas and Yehudi Gordon, *Little Brown & Co.*
- **Toddler Taming,** Dr. Christopher Green, *Vermilion, London, 1992.*

For those interested in more complex homeopathy or for practitioners of homeopathy, the following are a must:

- *The Encyclopedic Dictionary of Homeopathy,* by Harald Gaier—published initially by Harper Collins and republished by Michael O'Mara, U.K. and by Avery, New York, U.S.A..
- *The Homeopathic Materia Medica,* with repertory by William Boericke, MD, is a must for those who intend to use homeopathy accurately.

INVESTIGATIONS

In the text, there are indications of suitable investigations or tests that should be available through your doctor, practitioner, hospital or health clinic. If not, then you may contact: *c/o Best of Both Worlds, 13123 Eastbrooke Avenue, Downey, CA 90242, U.S.A.*

Practitioners may liaise with a sympathetic doctor or may contact the above address to ask about tests.

A list of addresses where further information may be sought is placed at the end of this book.

Part One

Chapter 1

Sex, Fertility, and Conception

Chapter 1

Sex, Fertility, and Conception

"Children are Nature's longing for itself."

So wrote Kahlil Gibran in his magnificent work, *The Prophet*. Nature wants us to conceive. However, nature does not want unhealthy or weak genes, and will therefore go to great lengths to weed out all but those that are the strongest and most likely to survive.

One Eastern philosophy believes that the spirit of a child will select its parents. If this is the case then the physically healthier and psychologically more secure the parents, the more likely the infant spirits will be to vie for these parents and, through natural selection, the most healthy and psychologically adjusted child will develop from the parents' union. From a more-grounded and less-ethereal point of view, it is clear that the healthier the parents, and the more psychologically ready and spiritually secure they are, the more likely it is that the child will be born healthy.

CHOOSING A PARTNER

There are two extremes in choosing a partner. The Eastern philosophy of arranged marriages lies at one end, and the Western romantic notion of falling in love at the other. At the first end is the conscious appraisal by elders of two youngsters' attributes and what they would bring to a partnership or to the respective families. At the other end is the emotionally charged, "love is blind" method. As in most matters, the balance probably lies in between.

I am not seeking to change religious or ethical inclinations, but feel strongly that choosing a partner is such an important decision that neither should it be left solely to others nor left entirely to the vagaries of our emotional states.

On the following pages are a list of questions that should be answered by a prospective couple at some stage through their decision to have a baby. If you wish, you may photocopy these pages and send them to *c/o Best of Both Worlds, 13123 Eastbrooke Avenue, Downey, CA 90242 U.S.A.*, and a relationship counselor will assess the answers and advise you on areas that may prove problematic.

THE MISCONCEPTIONS OF CONCEPTION

The reasons why we have sex are manifold. The sensory pleasures that are derived from interacting in a sexual way with another human being give both pleasure and comfort. Most people enjoy sex and those who do not, often instead use sex to derive respect or security, or to derive some other gain. When all is said and done, however, the one-, two-, and three-play that leads up to foreplay and sex are all social distortions of our necessity to create the next generation of our species.

The large majority of women will, at some time in their lives, consider whether they wish to become pregnant. If they did not, we would not be here. The decision is reached when the correct physical age is attained, and it is decided that it is time psychologically and spiritually to be a parent.

There are over 750,000 births per year in the U.K. and five times that number in the U.S.A. It is estimated, however, that as many as two out of every five pregnancies fail to reach maturation (be delivered). This means that there are possibly 2.5 million conceptions in the U.K. and 12.5 million in the U.S.A. each year. Most are not even noticed. The fertilized egg fails to implant in the womb or fails to survive for reasons such as faulty genes in either the sperm or in the egg, or because of problems with the health of the mother. The fertilized egg is then shed imperceptibly, usually at the next period. Problems of conception, however, are not only due to failure once an egg has been fertilized. Many couples failing to conceive do so because the male and female sex cells do not even meet. Problems either with the production of the egg from the ovary, or inadequate amounts of sperm, or nonviable sperm, can also cause infertility.

A minority of the 10 million women in the U.K. and 50 million in the U.S.A. who could conceive at any particular time may have problems in doing so, but what advice and treatment is currently available to those who are unsuccessful? In the U.K. approximately 30,000 women—either alone or with their partner—attend clinics or specialists each year, because they have not been able to conceive. Approximately 14 percent of couples in the U.S. are infertile which equates to over 3 million infertile couples. This is six times the estimated rate in the U.K. which is an interesting figure that, perhaps, needs serious research.

Earlier this decade the orthodox medical establishment stated that only 15 percent of infertile females respond favorably to orthodox treatment. This figure has probably doubled due to scientific advances. It was also established that various alternative methods gave much the same response. Holistic medicine, effectively being the use of both orthodox and alternative treatments, may, arguably, double the chances of a couple having a child.

The problem of infertility, as with any health matter, should be studied and treated at the three levels of well-being: body, mind, and spirit. The actual causes of infertility can be divided into problems arising from the male or the female, but many factors are shared.

GETTING THE TIMING RIGHT

The average menstrual cycle is 28 days. There is, of course, much variation—some females can have a cycle as long as 40 days, while others may have periods every three weeks. As a rule, the egg is ready for fertilization approximately 14 days before the next period is due. For women with a regular cycle, this can be calculated quite simply, but for others, tests of the urine or the vaginal secretions can accurately suggest the time to get their partner into bed. Kits for such tests can be obtained from your local drugstore. Another common method is to measure the half-degree rise in body temperature, which can be used with some confidence toward its accuracy. Simply measure and record your temperature every morning by placing a thermometer under your tongue. Put the result on a large-scale chart and watch out for a half-degree rise (*see the example below*).

Couples must remember that not every period and not every month necessarily means the eviction of an egg from the ovary, and they should not be distressed if the tests show negative during some months.

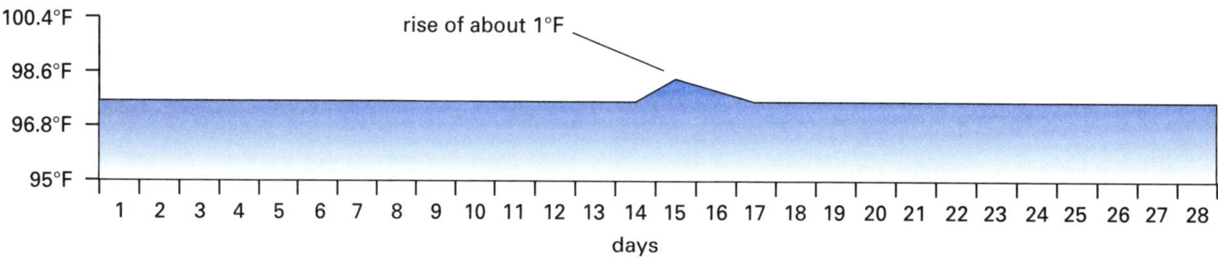

A woman's temperature rises when an egg is ready for fertilization.

NAME (please print) ....

ADDRESS ....

....

GENERAL

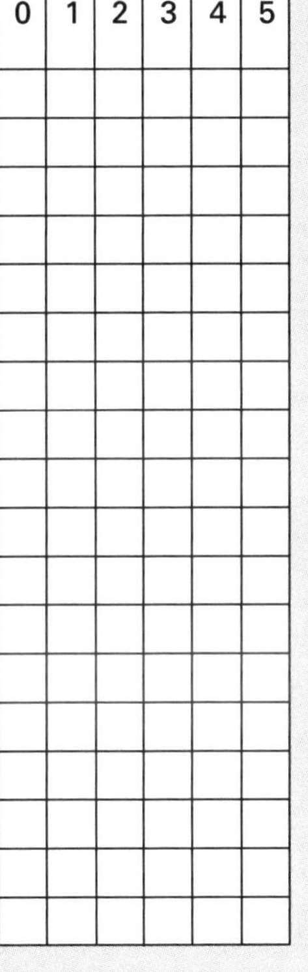

- I am satisfied with the ways we resolve our differences.
- I am confident about our physical and mental health.
- I agree with my partner on our involvement in running our home.
- I agree with my partner's goals and plans.
- I wish to be with my partner and I am not being forced.
- I never have doubts that we are right for each other.
- I share similar interests with my partner.
- I am happy to talk with my partner.
- I am happy with what my partner expects of me.
- I am confident with the compatibility of our education and intelligence.
- I find it easy to express my feelings to my partner.
- I would worry if I thought that we would not be together.
- I feel that we have the same ideas about lifestyle.
- I agree with my partner on how to decorate and furnish our home.
- Our jobs are not interfering with our relationship.
- There are no objections to our being together.
- I understand the circumstances that could end our relationship.
- We agree on when and whether to get married.

HABITS AND HOBBIES

0	1	2	3	4	5

- My partner does not place too much emphasis on neatness.
- My partner does not worry me about his/her use of alcohol/tobacco/drugs.
- My partner is not too busy for us to do enough things together.
- I am not uncomfortable on occasions with my partner's behavior.
- My partner does not need more outside activities.
- Our leisure activities are compatible.

FAMILY/FRIENDS

0	1	2	3	4	5

- My partner's spiritual beliefs are acceptable to me.
- My partner's spiritual beliefs are acceptable to my family.
- Our families have similar cultural/social/economic/ethnic values.
- We share attitudes about values.

	0	1	2	3	4	5
• We share attitudes on children and the attitudes we would like them to have.						
• I like my partner's friends.						
• I am happy for my partner to spend time with his/her own friends.						
• I am happy to spend time with my partner's friends.						
• I do *not* worry that either of our families will cause friction between us.						
• We have the same feelings about pregnancy, childbirth, and adoption.						
• We agree on our roles as parents in raising children, if we have them.						
• I believe that my partner will make a good parent if we have children.						
• We agree on whether to talk about our problems with close friends.						
• I believe that we should talk about our problems with each other.						
• We agree on whether to talk about our problems with our families.						
• My partner is not too dependent on his/her family.						
• My partner's family is not too dependent on him/her.						
• My family agrees with my choice of partner.						
• My partner's family likes me.						
• I am comfortable when I am with my partner's family.						
• We agree on whether to have children.						
• I do *not* worry that my own childhood will badly affect my relationship with our children, if we have any.						

PERSONAL

	0	1	2	3	4	5
• My partner is not depressed and does not have major mood swings.						
• My partner is very unlikely to hurt my feelings.						
• My partner and I have a similar sense of humor.						
• My partner is a good companion.						
• My partner expresses feelings well.						
• My partner does not have a problem with his/her temper.						
• I have no doubt my partner has made the right choice in me.						
• I have no doubt that I have made the right choice in my partner.						
• My partner does not have prejudices that upset me.						
• Most of the time I am satisfied with life.						
• I find that I feel comfortable with my partner most of the time.						
• I try very hard to avoid disagreements with my partner.						
• My partner tries very hard to avoid disagreements with me.						
• I always feel safe with my partner.						
• My partner handles personal problems well.						
• My partner is not too possessive.						
• I do not get annoyed with any of my partner's mannerisms.						

	0	1	2	3	4	5
• I am never embarrassed by my partner's behavior.						
• My partner is not stubborn.						
• My partner is there for me when I am down.						
• I am comfortable with my partner's moods.						
• My partner is a good listener.						
• We are able, when necessary, to talk over problems when we disagree.						
• My partner is not too aggressive.						

SEXUAL COMPATIBILITY

	0	1	2	3	4	5
• I feel good about my sexuality.						
• I feel good about my partner's sexuality.						
• We agree on the process of lovemaking and intercourse.						
• I like the way I look.						
• I do not think that sex is the way to sort out our problems.						
• I am not embarrassed by sexual contact with my partner.						
• I am happy with how sex is initiated.						
• I am not worried about being unable to satisfy my partner sexually.						
• I am not worried about being unsatisfied by my partner sexually.						
• I can trust my partner with members of the opposite sex.						
• I am happy in the way we show affection for each other.						
• I am not worried that I might be sexually impotent or frigid.						
• I am not worried that my partner might be sexually impotent or frigid.						
• I understand that if I were unfaithful it could ruin our relationship.						
• At times I need my personal space and my partner gives it to me.						
• I can discuss sex with my partner.						
• My partner and I have the same views on premarital sex.						
• The method or absence of birth control is not a problem between us.						
• At times, if my partner does not want sex or to be touched, it is all right with me.						

RECOMMENDATION

Where the couple have differing or opposing views, the points should be discussed among themselves or their friends and family. If resolution is not forthcoming, then I strongly advise a session with a relationship counselor or, in the case of religious disagreements, a suitable spiritual advisor.

PHYSICAL PREPARATION FOR CONCEPTION

The Eastern philosophies of medicine all categorically state that the use of drugs, alcohol, and tobacco, or any compound that effects the nervous system, will alter the levels of energy through the meridians or energy channels and, if not directly affecting the conception, will affect the pregnancy. Toxins specifically decrease the body's kidney Qi or Chi—pronounced "chee"—which is thought to be the body's energy store and the main supplier of energy at times of conception and pregnancy. Each individual may have particular likes and dislikes, intolerances or even allergies that should be excluded prior to conceiving (*see* **Chinese and Oriental medicine**).

Successful conception relies upon a healthy sperm meeting a healthy egg. The nutritional status of both partners is paramount. The number of known toxins to both sperm and eggs is limited, namely: tobacco, alcohol, and drugs (recreational or prescribed, including the contraceptive pill).

Tobacco

Tobacco is a known teratogen (capable of altering cell structure). Many studies have shown that infants of mothers who smoke are often preterm deliveries and underweight. There is no exception and no quantity that is safe. If you smoke, your baby will be affected to some extent, and this effect may take place at any stage during conception and pregnancy. An intended father who smokes may actually cause more birth defects than a smoking mother-to-be by damaging the sperm before it leaves him. The motility (movement) of the sperm is also adversely affected.

RECOMMENDATION

- *Women should not smoke for at least one cycle before attempting conception and men should abstain for at least ten days.*

Alcohol

I copublished a study in 1984 concerning the Fetal Alcohol Syndrome, which suggested that this potentially lethal and devastating effect by alcohol on fetuses is often underdiagnosed and may be caused by a small amount of alcohol. Throughout this book I will touch upon the dangers and joys of alcohol, and principally will not support abstinence. When aiming to conceive and through the early part of pregnancy, however, I am a strong advocate of abstinence. In the male partner, alcohol adversely affects the motility of the sperm.

RECOMMENDATION

- *Do not drink alcohol for at least ten days before attempting conception.*

Drugs

Drugs are harmful in any case, but more so in pregnancy. There are very few orthodox, doctor-prescribed drugs that have been shown to have any level of safety during pregnancy. Very little evidence is available on the effects of drugs during conception, but we do know a lot about the dangers of drugs during early pregnancy.

Studies on recreational drugs have clearly stated that they are dangerous. They can alter the genetic material and affect the mother's ability to nourish the child. Drugs also adversely affect the motility of sperm.

RECOMMENDATION

- *Do not use a drug, unless absolutely essential, for at least one month before attempting conception.*

DETOXIFICATION PRIOR TO CONCEPTION

Once the ovulation cycle and the days when fertility is at a premium have been determined, I recommend a detoxification diet.

RECOMMENDATION

- *See the* **Detox** *(3-day) and* **Semi-fast** *(7-day)* **diets** *in chapter 7. These should be considered at least one week before the period is expected and continued until ten days before the next period is due. The Hay diet (see chapter 7) can be followed in between attempts to conceive so that the body remains predominantly alkaline- and toxin-free.*

Vitamins and supplements

Principally, a good diet should provide individuals with all the vitamins and supplements they need. There is no specific advice for males other than healthy eating, unless a couple are not conceiving. Women, on the other hand, should add some supplements to their diet for at least one month prior to conception.

RECOMMENDATIONS

- *Folic acid (400mg daily) has been shown to reduce the number of neural-tube defects (problems with the formation of the spinal column).*
- *A natural multivitamin and multimineral complex should be used to avoid any problems that we may not yet be aware of due to deficiencies of the trace elements.*
- *Visit a nutritionist to establish a clear-cut dietetic regime to follow after the Detox and Semi-fast diets recommended above.*
- *Visit a doctor for a thorough, orthodox check-up.*
- *Visit a homeopath to establish a constitutional pattern (see* **Homeopathy***).*

THE ENERGY OF CONCEPTION

The vessel of conception and the governing vessel, according to the Chinese, are terms for an energy flow that passes through or over the pituitary and thyroid glands, the pancreas, and the uterus. I discuss this vessel in more detail later (*see* **The vessel of conception**). If a woman who is intending to become pregnant has a mother who has had problems with the thyroid, diabetes, or the uterus, then she should see a Tibetan or Chinese practitioner for acupuncture, with or without herbal treatments. A weakness in any of these organs may represent a weakness in this midline energy flow, and this may mean that the intended mother has a weakness and a predisposition to developing diabetes or hypothyroidism during a pregnancy.

SEXUAL POSITION AND TECHNIQUE

Physically speaking, the art of lovemaking is important in a successful conception. The male orgasm indicates a successful ejaculation, and an improper technique can lead to faulty "firing." The woman's orgasm is associated with an increased flow of blood to the genital tract prior to orgasm, which ensures that everything is primed prior to reception of the sperm. The orgasm causes the blood to disperse, which decongests the area and allows the sperm to travel more easily. It is therefore preferable, when trying to conceive, to time a mutual orgasm.

Mutual orgasms are not a prerequisite to successful conception, but they are liable to help. Orgasms are moments of physical, psychological, and spiritual bliss, so if both partners can share this at a time when a new life is being created, then it is a better start from a spiritual, energetic point of view.

On a more practical note, the position of intercourse may be of vital importance. Human beings (and some fish) are the only animals to copulate facing each other. Most intercourse takes place with the female on all fours and the male supplying the semen from behind. As the human being developed an upright stance, nature had to establish some changes to allow the sperm a

UTERUS—Normal and Retroverted

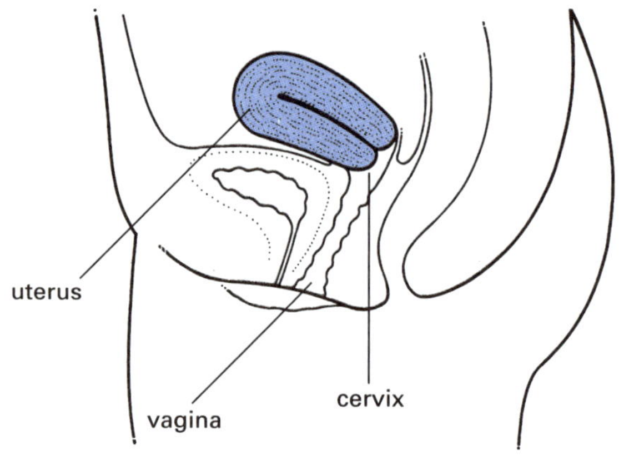

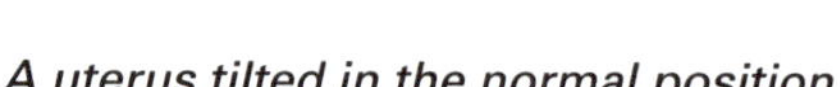

A uterus tilted in the normal position.

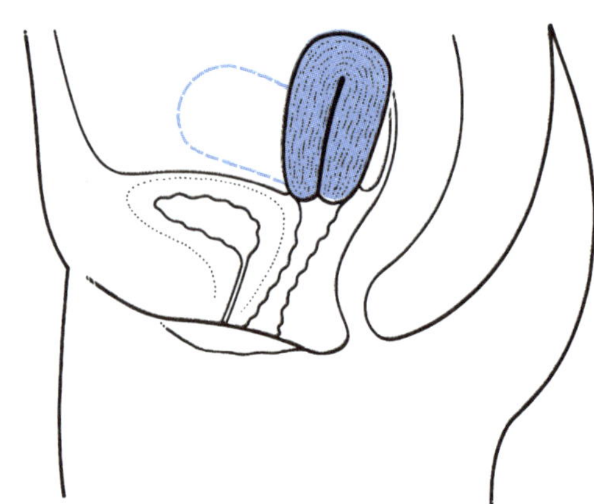

The almost vertical position of a retroverted uterus.

greater chance of getting to the egg. The only female of any species to experience an orgasm is the human being, as it is nature's intention to tire out the woman and keep her lying flat for at least a few minutes. This places the uterus on a horizontal plane, and the sperm do not have to fight against gravity, as they would if she were to get up immediately afterwards.

There is a surprisingly common condition called a retroverted uterus. In this condition, the body of the uterus tips or is held backwards towards the spine. The cervix—the opening to the uterus—automatically pushes forward, and can push into the front wall of the vagina. During intercourse, the semen is fired from the penis at speeds of up to 80 miles per hour. If this hits the cervix directly, the sperm obtain quite a head start on their travel from the opening of the cervix to the egg. If the uterus is retroverted and the cervix is pushed forward, then the sperm can be fired into the posterior fornix and then have to swim around, find the cervix and travel a much greater distance. Amazingly, during female orgasm, the cervix "dips" into the pool of semen to help the sperm on their journey, but even so the sperm are disadvantaged.

The uterus can also have a tendency to tip to the right, to the left, or forward, and in each case can cause the cervix to be pushed against any of the sides of the vaginal wall. A basic examination by a qualified doctor can clearly illustrate the position of the cervix. If the cervix is pushing into one of the sides of the vagina, then the woman should take up a position during intercourse that moves the uterus through the pull of gravity, thus moving the cervix away from the vaginal wall.

CASE HISTORY

Mrs. J. O. came to see my late father over 15 years ago. She was from the Cameroon, and had undergone tests for infertility there, in Switzerland, and in London, all to no avail. She came to see a complementary practitioner as a last resort, and was very surprised when my father, after a full examination, gave her a basic homeopathic remedy and told her to lie on her right-hand side whenever she and her husband were trying to conceive. I now look after her and her family of four children, all conceived at times when she was lying on her right-hand side.

For the reasons I have described above, a long penis can find itself passing the cervix and ejaculating into the top of the vagina. At times of attempted fertilization, it is wiser to try to keep only two or three inches in the vagina in an attempt to ejaculate onto the cervical opening.

INFERTILITY AND MEN

The following advice is really relevant only after a year of unprotected and well-timed intercourse has been attempted, although the concepts hold true at any time.

Approximately 30 percent of infertility arises from inadequacy of the sperm. Sperm are created in the testicles, and passed into seminal fluid that is produced in another part of the testes and the prostate gland. This fluid provides nutrition for the mobile unit carrying the male's genes (correctly known as the spermatozoa). In addition, rare pathological problems—such as testicular tumors and hormonal imbalances—can occur in a man, and infection may sometimes cause decreased sperm production and motility.

Genitals—Male

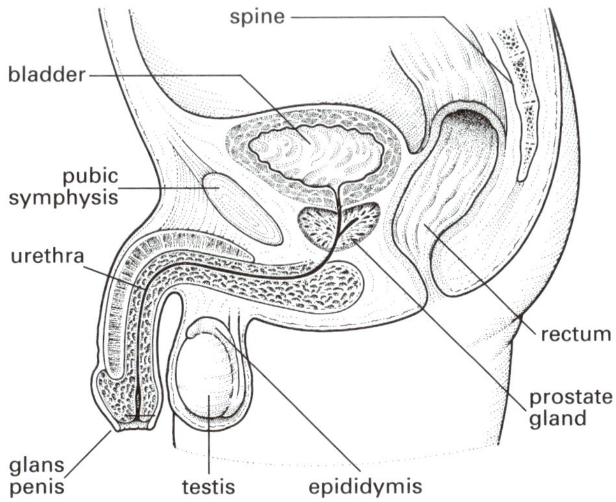

The first line of treatment in the case of any infertile couple is to check the male out and assure that his sperm count is good. The tests are noninvasive and fast to perform. The male provides a semen sample, and a blood test may be taken to check the hormonal situation if the sperm count or motility is low. If something is wrong, the following can be of help.

RECOMMENDATIONS

- *Provide a sperm sample after three days of not ejaculating.*
- *Ensure that loose boxer shorts and trousers that are not tight-fitting are worn.*
- *Korean, Chinese, or Tibetan ginseng (2g twice a day).*
- *Believe it or not, half a dozen oysters, lean red meat, and crab may help. They all contain a high level of zinc, which is essential for motility and production of sperm. Alternatively, try 5mg of zinc per foot of height before sleep at night.*
- *The following may be taken daily with food, in divided doses per foot of height: beta-carotene (3000iu), vitamin C (1g), and vitamin E (100iu).*
- *Stress reduction (see* ***Stress****). Adrenaline reduces sperm production.*
- *Reflexology can be of benefit. Gentle pressure should be applied to areas on the feet representing the testes, and adrenal and pituitary glands.*
- *Allow for lengthy foreplay before ejaculation.*
- *Infertility beyond one year should be assessed and treated by a complementary medical practitioner with knowledge of the subject.*

Assuming that all is well with the male, then the investigations turn to the female.

INFERTILITY AND WOMEN

As with men, do not become overly worried until conception has not occurred for a year of unprotected and well-timed intercourse. If you are trying to conceive after the age of 38 years, then seek advice after six months.

Women have much the same potential difficulty in producing viable eggs as men do in

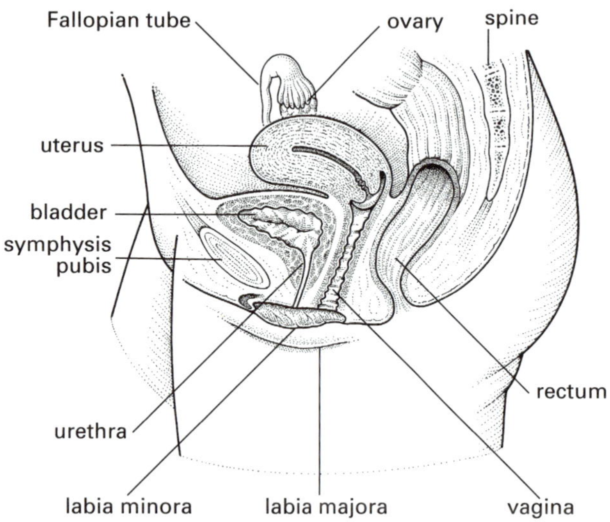

creating sperm. Girls are born with a finite number of eggs in each ovary. These lie dormant as the ovary and the rest of the female matures. Around the time of the menarche (the starting of the periods), the chemical changes that occur with young girls at that age cause eggs to mature and ripen. Due to a particular chemical "cut-out" method, usually only one egg matures each month from either ovary and is released into the opening of the Fallopian tube. Many reasons can account for failure of an egg to ripen: nutritional factors, infections, stress and unhappiness, hormonal imbalances, and ovarian pathology.

Practical matters can be a hazard too. Once the egg has passed into the Fallopian tube, it has to travel the equivalent of a human being walking from Los Angeles to Salt Lake City. The egg is assisted by peristaltic waves pushing the packet of female genes toward the uterus. Most fertilization occurs in the outer one-third of the Fallopian tube, requiring the more motile sperm to travel a much greater distance. As you can clearly see, there is much scope for structural problems causing a barrier between the two gametes. Previous infections can scar up the Fallopian tubes, and difficulties such as endometriosis (misplacement of uterine tissue around the Fallopian tubes onto the ovaries or in the abdominal cavity) can bar the movement of the microscopic egg and sperm.

HORMONAL MATTERS

Once the basic health of the couple has been checked, the physician may move onto more specific tests. In women, problems such as diabetes

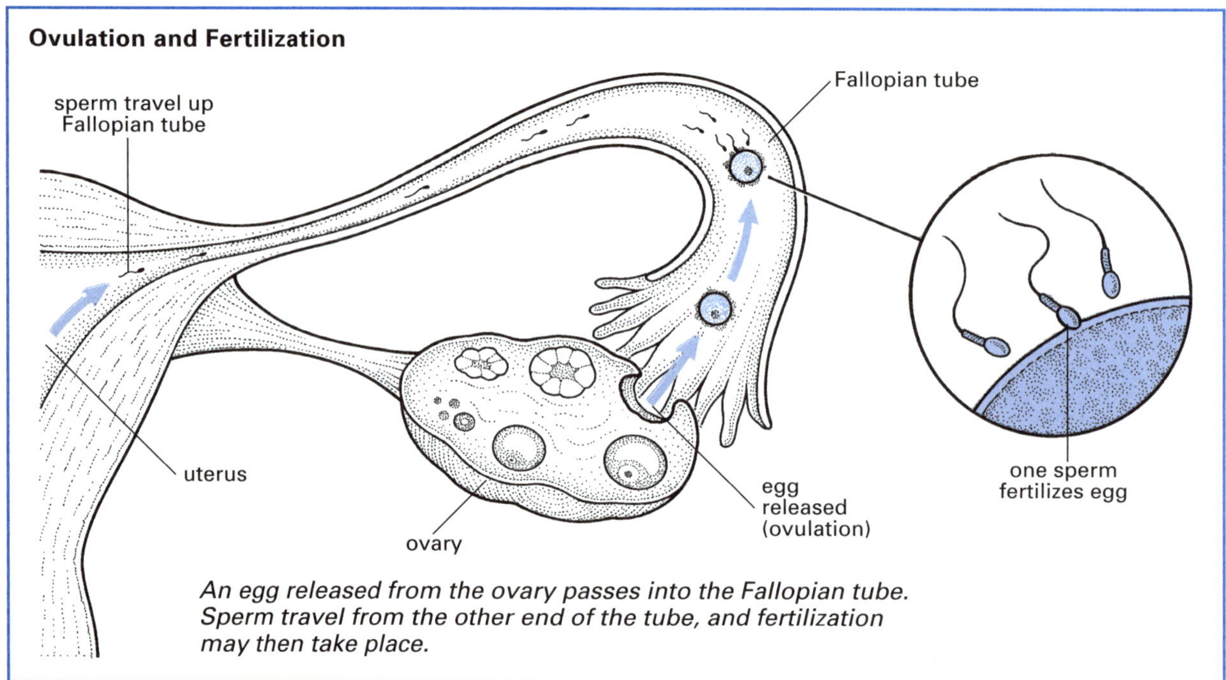

An egg released from the ovary passes into the Fallopian tube. Sperm travel from the other end of the tube, and fertilization may then take place.

and thyroid imbalances can alter the picture, and generally a complete blood screen is performed to check hormone levels. If nothing is found to be wrong, then blood tests are taken at particular times of the cycle to get an idea of the hormonal pattern. The hormones checked are:

- estrogen and progesterone
- follicle-stimulating hormone (FSH)
- luteinizing hormone (LH)
- prolactin.

Estrogen and progesterone are necessary for the preparation of the uterus to allow the fertilized egg to implant. Follicle-stimulating hormone (FSH) causes an egg within the ovarian tissue to mature and ripen, and the luteinizing hormone causes the shell of the ovary to open and allow the egg to be released into the Fallopian tube. Prolactin is formed to prepare the breasts for lactation; an excess of prolactin, usually due to a noncancerous tumor in the pituitary gland, can prevent pregnancy, which is why lactation and breast feeding may prevent pregnancy.

RECOMMENDATIONS

- *Established hormonal problems should not be treated without guidance from specialists in this field, both orthodox and complementary.*
- *Any hormonal problems need to be monitored by a gynecologist.*
- *Nutritional, herbal, and homeopathic medicine can help (see chapter 9). Ensure the practitioner has knowledge of natural estrogens and natural progesterones, both transcutaneous (passed through the skin) and oral.*
- *Visualization and meditation can be useful.*
- *If stressed or anxious, see a counselor.*

BLOCKAGES

One of the more common causes of infertility is a blockage in the Fallopian tubes, so the specialist's first step is usually to perform a laparoscopy. This is an operation that usually requires a general anesthetic. A small incision is made underneath the navel and a thin flexible scope is passed through, enabling the surgeon to have a look at the ovaries, Fallopian tubes, and surrounding structures. A dye is passed through the cervix and the flow is watched from the two open ends of the Fallopian tube. This is called a hysterosalpingogram. The discovery of a blockage can be cured by operation, as can polycystic ovaries (a condition that can run in families, where the ovaries have multiple fluid-filled cysts that act as a blockage as well as sometimes being associated with hormonal imbalance).

Ideally, before this invasive stage is reached, I would recommend that alternatives are assessed. Without the tests, you cannot be certain of the diagnosis of a blockage, although a history of infection may point to this. Good pulse-readers claim to be able to diagnose a blockage, as can Kerlian photography (*see* relevant sections).

RECOMMENDATIONS

- *Tibetan and Chinese herbs prescribed by experts may help.*
- *Silica 30, twice a day for 14 days only, may reduce blocking scar tissue over a three-month period.*
- *Use visualization of a small person with a pick-axe traveling down the Fallopian "tunnel."*
- *Osteopathy is a must to try.*
- *Polarity therapy and Alexander technique can theoretically affect posture and relieve blockages.*

Orthodox Methods for Infertility

One should always allow a few months for the results of any technique to be conclusive, but if the couple remain infertile, then they should resort to the orthodox methods with some increased success, because all holistic techniques automatically improve the general health of the individual and the area to be treated by drugs or surgery.

Any structural difficulties, such as scarred tubes or blockages, can sometimes be dealt with operatively. As our scientific techniques become more elaborate, so do our techniques for unblocking the microscopic lumens of the Fallopian tubes. Hormonal imbalances can be corrected chemically, and fertility drugs such as clomiphene can be administered, usually with side effects, but with some success. Most women react unpleasantly to these drugs, and I view them as a last resort rather than first choice. In any case, complementary methods can be beneficial in reducing the unwanted side effects.

RECOMMENDATION

- *If orthodox drugs are to be used, ensure a visit to a naturopathic physician of any discipline to receive advice on how to avoid side effects.*

ARTIFICIAL FERTILIZATION

Once initial treatments have failed and the specialist feels that the individual is suitable for artificial techniques, then the "test-tube baby" concepts come into play. The tried and tested technique of *in vitro* fertilization (IVF) is one option. This technique requires the removal of mature eggs from the female's ovaries through a specialized laparoscopic procedure after drug inducement of the ovary to produce eggs. The mature eggs are then fertilized under laboratory conditions by the father's or donor's sperm. The fertilized eggs are then replaced in the uterus, and hopefully nature takes its course. The uterus is prepared to receive the implant through a program of administering hormones.

Another successful method is called gamete intrafallopian transfer (GIFT), which once again entails the removal of an egg from the ovary; the egg is then placed back into the Fallopian tube with an amount of donor sperm. If fertilization occurs, the fertilized egg is then moved down the Fallopian tube naturally into the uterus for implantation.

The success of these techniques varies greatly from one clinic to the next. There is a 15–20 percent fertilization rate and one in seven pregnancies that result from artificial fertilization ends with a live birth. I feel sure these figures will improve as the techniques get better.

There are always risks with any procedure, and the most debilitating (and potentially fatal) is a condition known as ovarian hyperstimulation. This occurs because of the influence of the drugs that stimulate egg production, which causes swelling of the abdomen and vulva, abdominal pain, and (a serious sign) vomiting.

RECOMMENDATIONS

- *Try complementary medical techniques, as discussed above, before considering artificial fertilization.*
- *Please consult with your preferred complementary practitioner while going through orthodox fertility treatment to ensure the best level of health possible.*
- *Before any invasive procedure, see* **Operations and surgery**.

THE PSYCHOLOGY OF CONCEPTION

When deciding to have a baby, there are many psychological factors which should be faced and dealt with. For either the male or the female to make a decision to have a baby and a family is a true "coming of age." We are stepping away from being the child of our parents to being the parents of a child. We all have to deal with increased responsibility, a loss of freedom, a loss of choice, and financial constraints. We also have to face a lifetime of commitment, not only to the child but also to our partner.

Follicle-stimulating hormone (FSH) and luteinizing hormone (LH), which control the ovulation cycle, are produced by a small, walnut-sized gland next to the brain, the pituitary gland, so it is perhaps anatomically acceptable that the emotion centers surrounding this gland feed into it chemicals that can block the production or release of FSH and LH. Long-term unhappiness, such as that produced by an unhappy relationship or marriage, can put persistent pressure on this gland and hamper its normal production. Stress in males, similarly, can also cause problems. So, the simple experience of being happy with your partner can chemically affect your chances of becoming pregnant.

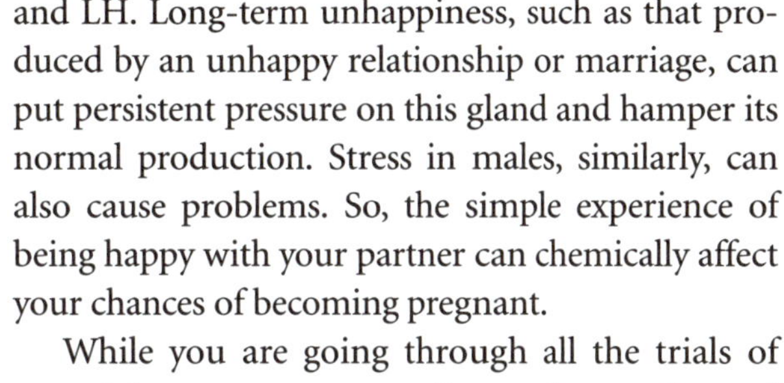

While you are going through all the trials of conceiving, you must not forget that at the end of the day, no one is really sure what makes the whole event happen. What is the vital force that gives life to any particular cell? Hindus believe that spirits choose their parents, or more scientifically, that a life force enters a fertilized egg. I often see couples where one or both are so full of anger or misery that I find myself asking if I would really want these two as my parents. It is important, I feel, when inviting a spirit into a family unit, that the environment is conducive. I always encourage peace and harmony in any infertile situation. Too many marriages and families break up because the parents were not suited, and how many relationships struggle on with the idea that the baby will make things "right"? It is vitally important for all involved to be content and happy. Choosing and being with the right partner is discussed at the beginning of this chapter, and elsewhere, but my experience makes me believe

THE VESSEL OF CONCEPTION

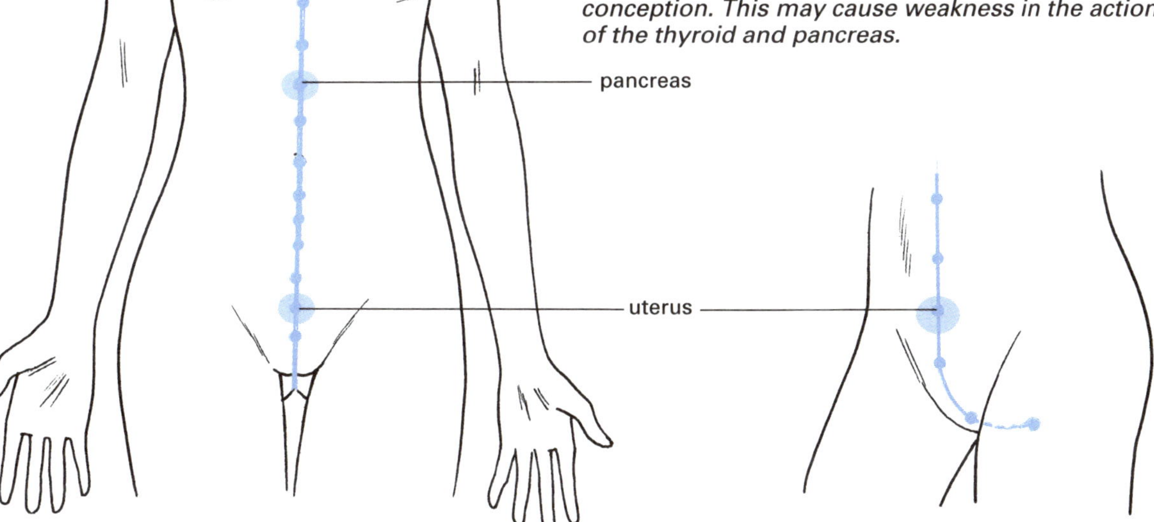

Pregancy may draw vital energy from the vessel of conception. This may cause weakness in the action of the thyroid and pancreas.

that being with the right or best partner alters conception problems favorably.

RECOMMENDATIONS

- *If, at any stage, negative emotions enter the scene in either partner, visit a counselor.*
- *Do not try to conceive when surrounded with negative energy.*
- *Learn a meditation technique and spend a suitable amount of time each day practicing this.*

THE VESSEL OF CONCEPTION

All philosophies of medicine that include an energy flow through the bodily system describe a mid-line channel, or meridian. The Chinese call this the "vessel of conception", among other terms. It is so called because of the establishment, over thousands of years, of an energy flow from the pituitary gland (the hormonal controller of the female cycle) to the uterus. This energy line travels through or over the thyroid and the pancreatic glands. It is interesting, is it not, that pregnancy can induce both diabetes and hypothyroidism with no accepted scientific reasoning? This line then travels through the uterus (or the testes in the male) to complete this energy channel.

My view is that a pregnancy draws energy into the uterus, thereby diminishing the vital force necessary for the correct maintenance of health within the thyroid and the pancreas. I believe that the vessel of conception receives energy from those close to us. Parents, in particular, pass energy from their vessel of conception to their offspring, and energy is also received from lovers and best friends.

A weakness in the relationship between any of our close contacts, partners, and parents will lead to a weak vessel of conception. Energy is passed from both father and mother to their offspring, and if the vessel of conception is not initially well supplied or refueled along the way, then each pregnancy will drain the parents' meridian, leading to problems with subsequent children.

It is essential to have a strong relationship with the partner when conception is considered, and the connection between the intended parents and their parents should also be strong and positive.

RECOMMENDATION

- *Clear up any misunderstandings, mend any rifts and involve both your parents—especially your mother—in decisions concerning conception and pregnancy.*

SPIRITUAL MATTERS

Eastern philosophies are much more spiritual in their consideration of pregnancy, and use many techniques (including acupuncture) to relieve energy blocks, which in turn interfere with fertility. The West, through its dependence upon science, has lost touch to a great extent with the spiritual aspect of conception. Religions consider a birth "a blessing", but little, if any, forethought goes into the preparation of starting a new life. Eastern medical philosophies differ substantially.

Mr. J. G. Bennet, a philosopher and student of Gurdjieff, discussed the existence of spiritual genetics. He defined this as an energy that exists on an (as yet) immeasurable plane that travels with individuals, and at the time of conception this energy is passed, along with the physical genetic material, into the embryo. Whether this occurs at the moment of conception or at some stage during the pregnancy is open to debate, and whether it is the same thing as "vital force" or the spark of life, or whether it is a state of consciousness that may enter the fetus at a later stage, are all philosophical points. It is wise, however, to ensure that, when trying to conceive, both partners:

- are in a nonaltered (alcohol- and drug-free) state
- want a child
- love each other.

These are the three emotional components that traditional Eastern philosophies believe the human spirit can offer, and to this you may add the contribution of whichever religion you may follow.

RECOMMENDATIONS

- *Sit with your religious advisor and talk.*
- *Those of us who do not have such a teacher should find an Ayurvedic- or Tibetan-trained practitioner to draw on the medically associated aspects of correct spiritual preparedness.*

ASTROLOGY

Lastly, but only because of the scant evidence of accuracy, why not look at astrological patterns? If the Sun and Moon can shift huge bodies of water several miles, as the tides all over the world testify, why shouldn't the small influences of Pluto and Jupiter cause changes in the microscopic amounts of fluid in the egg and sperm?

It is worth checking out whether you and your partner's astrological charts are compatible, and when the best time for a child's birth would be. It is an interesting point that the time between conception and delivery is the same time it takes for the planets to reverse their aspects in the heavens. Perhaps charts should be drawn up at the time of conception rather than delivery. Might this rule out the inaccuracies that can occur?

CHAPTER 2

PREGNANCY AND CHILDBIRTH

Chapter 2

Pregnancy and Childbirth

Pregnancy

Pregnancy is not a disease process that requires medical intervention. Three out of every five of pregnancies in the world will be managed by unqualified personnel, friends and relatives, commonsense, and nature.

In the West, due to a lack of nutritional understanding, toxins being knowingly or unwittingly introduced into the body and poor physical preparedness, pregnancies can be uncomfortable and problematic, although are safe in comparison to other countries. Problems in these other countries occur mainly due to malnutrition, poor sanitation, and negligible emergency services, although pregnancies are generally treated in a more natural manner. As usual, neither the highly-developed countries nor the poorest nations have an ideal situation. The most comfortable and successful pregnancies will have a blend of the best from both. There is a need to mix the high technology of modern science with the intuition and experience of traditional medicines.

DISCOVERING A PREGNANCY

Provided that you are trying, expecting, or happy to become pregnant, the revelation is a time of mixed emotions and feelings. The joys of having conceived are tempered with the anxieties of something going wrong. In a first-time pregnancy, the fear of the unknown is tempered with the spirit of adventure. The physical symptoms of early pregnancy usually mingle with a profound sensation of well-being. But not always!

Most couples discover that they are pregnant when an expected period is missed. A woman may or may not feel:

- nausea
- mood changes
- aches and pains
- swollen feet and hands.

Nausea

At some point in the day nausea, is caused by reaction to human chorionic gonadotrophin (HCG), a chemical essential for the survival of the fertilized egg.

RECOMMENDATIONS

- *Ginger: as cookies (two or three eaten before rising from bed in the morning); as tea (quarter-inch thick, chopped fresh in hot water); as juice (quarter-inch slice with apple, liquidized).*
- *Avoid low-blood sugar: eat small, healthy snacks at regular intervals (see* **Hypoglycemia***).*
- *Acupressure (see* **Nausea***).*
- *Place a drop of peppermint oil on a sugar cube and suck slowly. You cannot use this if you are using a homeopathic remedy, because mint of any sort will inhibit the action of the remedy.*
- *A crushed stick of fresh cardamom in yogurt.*
- *Homeopathic remedies Ipecacuanha 6, Nux vomica 6 or Cocculus indicus 6 taken every 15min.*
- *Failing the above, both acupuncture and reflexology can be curative.*

Mood changes

Mood changes can be either positive or negative. Do not fight the elation! Negative moods may be alleviated by talking, so do so with friends, relatives, and even your partner!

RECOMMENDATIONS

- *If depressed, tearful, fearful, or angry, use a carefully selected remedy, ideally chosen by a homeopath. Remedies are best given at high potency, and many are not recommended during pregnancy.*
- *Depression or anger may respond to D, L-phenylalanine (100mg per foot of height, three times a day).*
- *Massage works wonders.*
- *A drop of rose oil on your collar.*
- *Sesame oil rubbed into the feet for 5min before washing it off.*
- *Keep your blood-sugar levels up with healthy snacks.*
- *Practice or learn a suitable meditative technique. Self-hypnosis is useful before, after, or at delivery.*

Aches and pains

Aches and pains are caused by hormonal effects on ligaments, even this early on in the pregnancy.

RECOMMENDATIONS

- *Comfortably hot baths with chamomile, lavender, or rosemary essential oils.*
- *Vitamin B_6 (50mg daily) and copper (2mg daily) for up to five days.*
- *Massage—especially Shiatsu.*
- *Polarity therapy is good at all stages of pregnancy.*
- *Yoga. The earlier in pregnancy that yoga is learned and practiced, the better.*
- *Arnica 6 or Magnesia phosphorica 6, four times a day for up to five days.*

Swollen feet and hands

Swollen feet and hands are a side effect of the hormones of pregnancy but may be helpful because of a diluting down of the chemical effects on the body tissues. Diuretic treatments should be avoided. If the male partner is experiencing "sympathetic pregnancy," he may find the following recommendations useful as well. These are all normal and can be alleviated.

RECOMMENDATIONS

- *Place swollen hands or feet in hot and cold water alternately.*
- *Natrum muriaticum 6 can be used four times a day for three days.*
- *Increase your protein intake at each meal.*
- *Lymphatic drainage massage is tremendous.*

SYMPATHETIC PREGNANCY

Male partners often experience similar symptoms to pregnant women. These are known as symptoms of sympathetic pregnancy. The male partner may find all the previous recommendations useful. Why this phenomenon occurs is uncertain, and may be purely psychological, but possibly pheromonally (inhaled chemical) induced.

PREGNANCY TESTS

Today pregnancy tests are 98 percent accurate. Two tests having the same result is usually conclusive. The options are:

- home testing
- a test at your local drugstore or pharmacy
- a test by your doctor or local medical society.

Wherever it is done, testing produces the same degree of accuracy. A drop of urine is placed on a small pad, or a small sample of urine is shaken with a chemical that measures the presence of human chorionic gonadotrophin (HCG). A color change or the appearance of a line indicates a positive pregnancy test.

A pregnancy test can be carried out as soon as two weeks after fertilization is thought to have occurred. The earlier the test, the greater the chance of a "false" negative or positive result, so it is probably best to wait for two weeks after a missed period.

Home testing for pregnancy

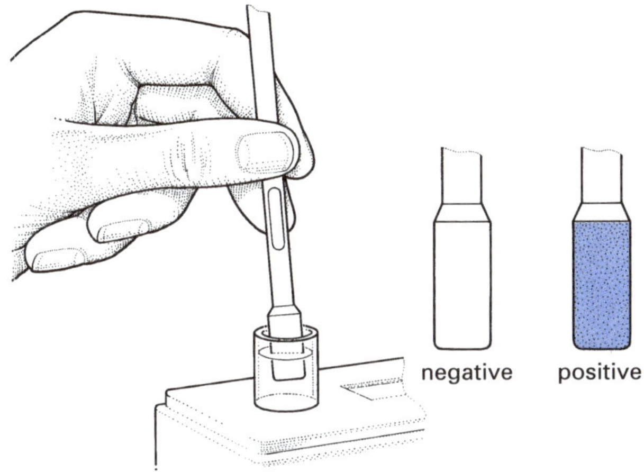

There are many different home-testing kits, and they mostly work on the same principle—a particular color or line indicating the presence of human chorionic gonadotrophin (HCG).

ESTIMATING THE EXPECTED BIRTH DATE

The estimation of a delivery date is always a "best guess," and not an exact science. Assessing the delivery date is considered in the West to be a mathematical problem. The simplest technique is to add seven days to the first day of your last period, and take off three months. For example, if the first day of the last period was 14 July, add seven days to make 21 July and subtract three months. The delivery date is 21 April. You will then be told that the delivery could occur anywhere around that date.

The moon is considered to be very influential in the female hormonal cycle, especially with regard to childbirth. It is worth assessing the stage of the moon around the expected time of conception. If you conceived on a full moon, then delivery is more likely to be around the full moon. Conversely, a new-moon conception will support a new-moon delivery.

CHOOSING YOUR MEDICAL SUPPORT

Pregnancy and childbirth is one of your most exciting and rewarding life experiences. As with any event, it is usually better if it is shared. The choice of your medical caregivers is important, because they will be sharing this marvelous time with you. If you do not get along with them, much of the enjoyment can be spoiled in much the same way that a prime cut can be ruined at a shared meal with an ardent vegetarian!

It is essential to visit your maternity unit and meet as many of the nurse-midwives as possible. Any one of them could be on duty when you deliver. The obstetrician is, hopefully, not going to be particularly involved unless things go awry, but it helps to get on well with the specialist, although not to the same degree as with the nurse-midwives.

Ensure that your views concerning position of delivery, water birth and pain relief are shared with the nurse-midwives, otherwise friction and doubts can manifest.

To a lesser extent, partners should be happy with the team because they too will be part of the event. There are good and bad in all professions, and it is very hard for patients (or, for that matter, doctors) to be able to isolate the jokers in the pack. A conversation with your doctor or complementary medical practitioners will probably make the selection process a lot easier.

CHOOSING YOUR HOSPITAL

Ideally, each maternity unit would have a blend of the best in orthodox technology with the comforts of your own bedroom. The unit would be staffed by experienced medical personnel with the personal touch of your closest friend and relative. An emergency unit would be next to the birthing unit, and your God would be in the waiting room in case anything went wrong. This is not the case, and until it is, we have to adjust the situation to our best advantage. I am not a great believer in the safety of home births, and certainly not for a first pregnancy and delivery. For latter pregnancies when no complications have arisen before, the home nurse-midwife and OB/GYN are very experienced, and emergency facilities are close by, then perhaps the risk is negligible.

I prefer to look upon childbirth as an unusual part of life and not a household activity. In contradiction to this last statement, I feel that if the local hospital facilities are not "homely" enough, then a home delivery may be preferable as long as easy access to the emergency facilities is available. As will be mentioned many times throughout this book, each case should be judged on its individual merits.

The place of delivery should preferably be in a room with a comfortable atmosphere for the parents. A bed at the correct height which allows Mom to place her feet on the floor and keep her backside on the edge is needed, and also a large tub or bath that can allow her and her birthing partner to relax comfortably with clear access from the sides for the midwives. Full medical facilities should be available within moments in case anything goes wrong.

Such hospitals are few and far between, although their numbers are increasing dramatically. Access to such units is becoming increasingly available in big cities, but still remains out of reach for those in rural areas.

RECOMMENDATIONS

- *Search out the ideal maternity unit in your area. This can be located by contacting your doctor or the American Board of Obstetrics and Gynecology. Always check that medical personnel are board-certified.*
- *If this hospital is more than 30min away (judged at rush hour), then a nearer hospital should be advised of the possibility of your arrival in case your labor comes on unexpectedly or the delivery be rushed.*

CHOOSING AND USING A COMPLEMENTARY MEDICAL CLINIC

In an ideal situation, your doctor and your obstetric team will have a liaison with a complementary medical clinic or practitioners. If this is the case, then you simply follow the guidelines set down by your now complete team.

Unfortunately, it is rare to find a unit that has all the available options from a complementary point of view. The choice of a clinic is best made by asking friends who have had dealings with clinics in your local area, or practitioners within striking distance of your home or place of work. The complementary clinic should have at its disposal the following therapists, practitioners, and techniques.

Acupuncturist

Acupuncture can be most beneficial for morning sickness, aches and pains, mood changes, and

MORNING SICKNESS—Acupuncture Points

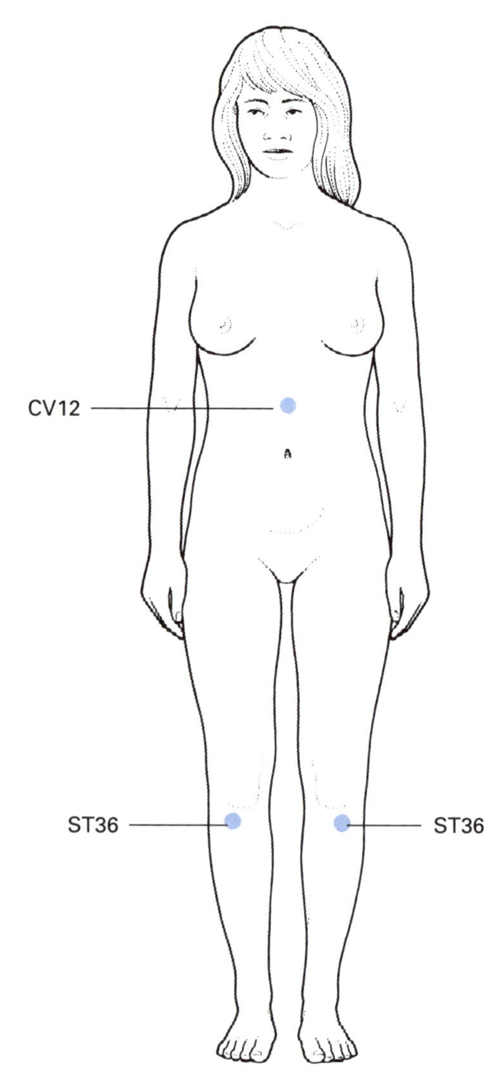

Acupressure or acupuncture treatment at Conception Vessel meridian point 12 (CU12) and Stomach meridian point 36 (ST36) may help alleviate morning sickness.

other symptoms during pregnancy. In the right hands, acupuncture can also be of benefit at the time of delivery by speeding up the process and reducing pain.

Bodywork

Bodywork should be an integral part of pregnancy. Any massage technique is liable to be relieving, especially for the inevitable backaches associated with carrying extra weight. Muscles which go into spasm can be relieved through massage. Shiatsu massage is even more beneficial, since it uses acupressure points and meridian stretches, as well as muscular pressure. It is useful for the mother-to-be's partner to learn some basic pressure points, as these can be useful at the time of delivery.

RECOMMENDATIONS

- *A local masseur or one who can visit your home should be found, and a weekly massage from three months onwards is ideal. It helps to keep the muscles supple, and also creates an amount of endorphin release that is mentally soothing to both the mother and the baby. Partners should be taught some basic massage techniques for use on a daily basis.*
- *Shiatsu massage is of great benefit. Not only is it soothing, but it can be useful by teaching the partner specific acupressure points that may help delivery. There are certain Shiatsu techniques and pressure points that should not be used during pregnancy, but be assured that any registered and qualified Shiatsu practitioner will know the places to avoid.*
- *Other techniques of body work, such as polarity, osteopathy, and chiropractic can all be used if aches and pains come to the fore.*

Homeopathy

There has been much anecdotal evidence over the last 150 years to support the use of homeopathy both in the treatment of problems in pregnancy and in aiding the delivery of the baby. Because of the unknown constitution of the fetus/baby, I only recommend the use of this form of medicine under the guidance of a practitioner but, having said that, there is no evidence whatsoever to suggest any dangers to mother or baby with the use of homeopathy. There are many remedies that can encourage the contraction of the uterus, among them Caulophyllum and Secale cornutum. These may be taken at potency 30 as soon as contractions start. Secale cornutum may also be used after the delivery of the baby to encourage the third stage of labor. There are many remedies that can be used for problems associated with pregnancy such as backaches, nausea, discharges, and painful breasts. Having a homeopath as part of the "team" is an extremely useful idea.

Hypnotherapy

An excellent study was concluded in the 1980s and published in the *Journal of Obstetrics and Gynaecology*. It showed that hypnotherapy can reduce the length of labor by as much as one-third and the need for analgesia by up to 50 percent.

Different hypnotherapists use different techniques, but my recommendation is a course of self-hypnotherapy taught two or three months before delivery to help the sleep pattern, which is often disturbed by the discomfort of late pregnancy and the delivery itself.

Nutritionist

The importance of correct nutrition has been discussed in the section **Physical preparation for conception.** *See* also **Nutrition in pregnancy.**

Psychotherapist or counselor—*see* **The psychology of conception** and **The vessel of conception.**

Yoga or polarity—*see* **Exercise in pregnancy.**

All the above may not necessarily be required, but access to them all is preferable just in case. All the above techniques have specific uses at times during normal and complicated pregnancies.

CASE HISTORY

Mrs. E. B., age 38 years: "My first attempts at becoming pregnant were half-hearted, and started at the age of 24 years. After several months of not conceiving, I visited my doctor and was told not to worry until I had not conceived for over a year. When that time came, I went back and was promptly pushed through the orthodox system, and both my husband and I ended up having a variety of tests, culminating in a laparoscopy under general anesthetic six months later. At no stage was I advised on my diet, possible nutritional deficiencies, or the use of alternative medicines, although I was offered a heavy drug regime that I took for three months before the side effects were too much for me to bear. I was unable to conceive for no obvious reason until the age of 32 years when, following a very uncomfortable pregnancy, I delivered a very low-birthweight daughter. After that, I miscarried twice a year, and was able, two years later, to produce a little baby boy successfully, who was also of markedly low birthweight.

Two years ago, on the advice of a friend, I attended a complementary medical clinic, and was found to be mineral-deficient, and have a tilted pelvis that the Shiatsu practitioner felt would compromise the blood flow to the pelvic organs. I was also treated with homeopathic remedies to encourage my ability to absorb and avoid further deficiencies. During the next pregnancy, I used a hypnotherapeutic technique because I was so shocked from my previous adventures. I received counseling and a couple of lessons in yoga that helped me to relax and perform better through the delivery. My third baby was born after five hours of labor and was at the top end of the normal-weight scale. I had no problems during the pregnancy, and may well decide to have another child in the near future."

Most complementary medical clinics will have a manager or head therapist who will be able to discuss your particular requirements. Your own physician may have some insight, and the next few pages will cover a lot of the ground.

INVESTIGATIONS

Your doctor or hospital will run routine urinalysis and blood-pressure checks, and at later stages of the pregnancy will check your hemoglobin levels for anemia.

I encourage my patients to have their hemoglobin checked early on in the pregnancy, and if there is any drop in the level, then this should be compensated for. The orthodox approach is to maintain the hemoglobin level within "normal limits", and supplemental iron may not be administered until the level drops below 10mmol/l. Each person is an individual and if your hemoglobin starts at 14mmol/l, then that is where it should stay. All patients should have a routine antibody screen for:

- rubella
- toxoplasmosis (especially for anyone with a household containing cats)

They should also have a hair analysis or other test for deficiencies (*see* **Bioresonance** and **Hair analysis**). Minor mineral and vitamin deficiencies can be quite devastating to a healthy pregnancy.

Ultrasound scans are not completely safe. Research in the early 1990s suggested that more than eleven ultrasound scans in a pregnancy can lead to a low-birthweight baby. For some reason, the ultrasound waves inhibit growth. The orthodox world considers that up to ten scans is therefore safe. My experience and common sense do not agree. I feel that the benefits of ultrasound in being able to diagnose problems is enormous, but try to confine ultrasounds to a maximum of three per pregnancy, unless problems exist. A scan at around 11–16 weeks to confirm a viable fetus, around 20–24 weeks for defects, and around 30–34 weeks to check for correct growth is ample investigation.

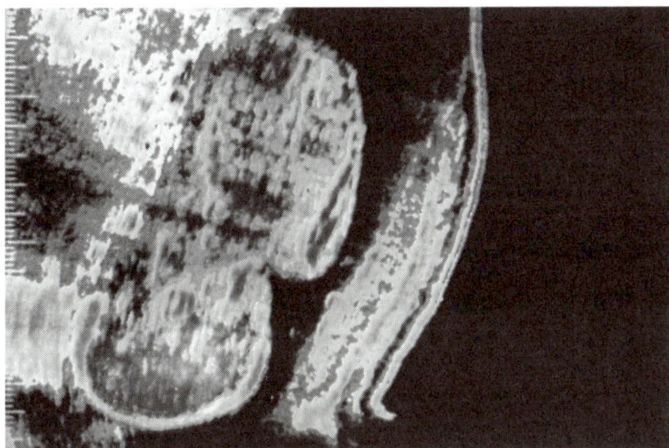

Fetal ultrasound scan.

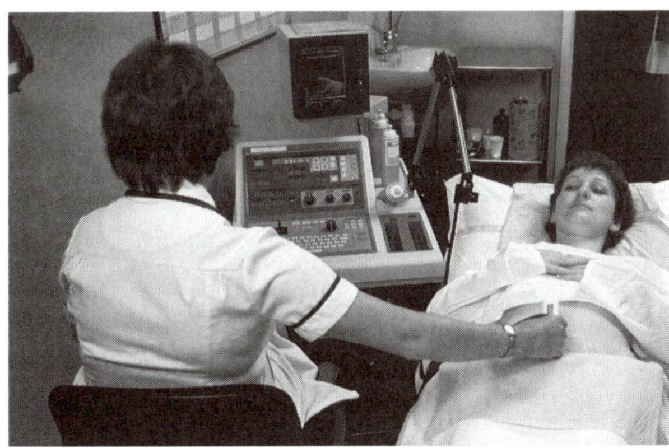

Ultrasound scanning.

OTHER ORTHODOX INVESTIGATIONS

Amniocentesis

Amniocentesis (the insertion of a needle and withdrawing of the fluid surrounding the fetus) has its place, but not in routine pregnancy care. Much information can be gleaned from analysis of the fluid, including a diagnosis of Down syndrome and other chromosomal abnormalities. There is now, however, a blood test that is becoming more available and accurate, although not as accurate as the amniocentesis. Amniocentesis carries a 2 percent complication rate (1 in 50 such investigations may cause a problem), whereas the blood test is harmless.

Amniocentesis

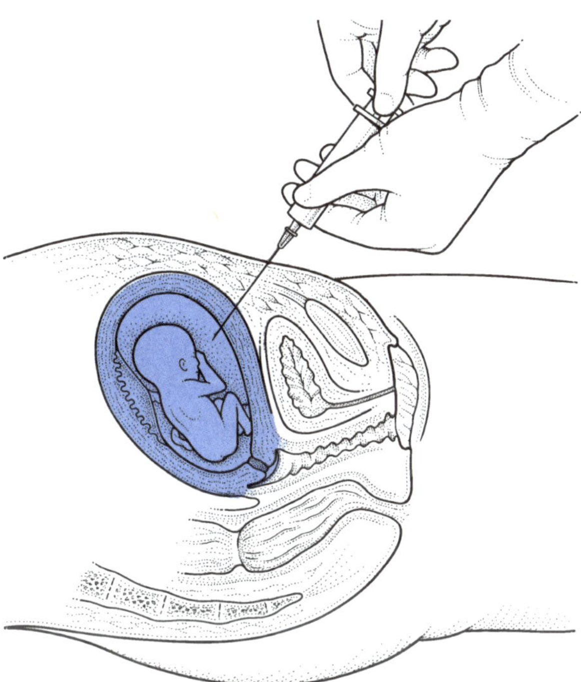

Amniotic fluid, extracted by syringe through the abdomen, is used to diagnose for genetic abnormalities.

RECOMMENDATIONS

- *Discuss any suggestion of this procedure with more than one obstetrician, and ensure that there is a need for such a process. Would you have a termination (an abortion) if something were wrong?*
- *Chorionic villus sampling (CVS). The chorionic villi are on the fetal side of the placenta. The cells are therefore derived from the genetic components of the fetus, and a biopsy or sample of this tissue can be extracted to test for congenital or hereditary defects. The complications and problems are the same as for amniocentesis.*

THE ENVIRONMENT

Please follow these recommendations with regard to the home environment when pregnant.

RECOMMENDATIONS

- *Never—pregnant or not—sit nearer than eight feet away from a television.*
- *Avoid VDUs (visual display units). There is evidence that they increase the chances of miscarriage. If you have to use one or are near any, avoid the back or sides. Do not sit at one for more than 20min without a 20-min break, avoid old machines, obtain low-radiation units, and do not trust the "screens"—they are next to useless.*
- *Loud music will detrimentally affect the fetus. Apparently, classical music is good, especially Mozart!*
- *Get outside as much as possible, and walk barefoot on the grass where safe and possible. If you are a town dweller, make a point of going to the country as often as you can.*

NUTRITION IN PREGNANCY

Once you have established that you are pregnant, the first (and possibly the most) important thing to do is to ensure that your diet is adequate and that you are supplemented correctly. A well-balanced diet will probably not need any extra nutrition, but for those under pressure, with any form of illness, or who are regularly missing meals, or are subjected to fast food or inadequate nutrition, then supplements should be utilized.

There is no set diet for pregnancy, and intuition is extremely important. The stories of odd cravings are possibly an indication of the body's requirements. The not-so-unusual cravings for charcoal or chalky substances are suspected to be due to the body's increased requirements for calcium and other minerals. The brain is good at knowing that it needs something, but it does not always get it right.

RECOMMENDATIONS

Many of the requirements have been discussed earlier, in chapter 1, and the nutritional requirements throughout your planning to conceive should continue during pregnancy, specifically:

- *Folic acid (400mg) can be taken daily, although the requirement is most important while trying to conceive.*

Most other recommendations are not categorically proven. I think it best, however, to err on the side of caution, and anyone who is not well-versed in eating a specifically well-balanced diet should take supplements to allow for the increased demands by the baby and the mother's metabolism, therefore:

- *Multivitamins—most obstetricians and doctors who disagree with additional supplementation do so on the grounds that it is an unnecessary expense, and not because taking extra supplements could harm the mother or baby. Having said that, an excess of anything may, of course, be harmful, as recently suggested by the vitamin-A scare from pregnant women eating too much liver.*
- *A trace element and mineral compound specifically to cover zinc, manganese, and copper.*
- *Remember to go with your instincts, but only if your cravings are for healthy food. If you are yearning for foods that you know are not necessarily healthy, such as French fries, specific flavors of potato chips, and processed foods, then examine the food groups (see* **Hay diet***) and select out healthy items from that food group, eat some, and see if the unhealthy craving diminishes.*
- *It is not advisable to change your diet dramatically. Being vegetarian or eating more meat is neither beneficial nor necessary. Aim at a balance.*
- *Specific foods that you should add to your diet include occasional meals rich in soya or tofu, half-raw/half-cooked vegetables at some time during the day, seaweed every now and then, and ginger.*

- *A tablespoon of honey should be eaten per day.*
- *Avoid nuts, filberts, and oats because they may contain alpha-toxins or promote their production, which can cause fetal damage.*

Avoid extra vitamin A

In direct opposition to the need for supplementing the diet with folic acid to avoid birth defects, it is important not to take an excess of vitamin A for exactly the same reasons. Vitamin-A content in food does not cause a problem, although eating an excess of liver or carrots may be harmful. It has been shown that more than 10,000iu of vitamin A can increase the risks of developmental problems and should not be taken.

EXERCISE IN PREGNANCY

It is extremely important to maintain a level of fitness and suppleness during pregnancy. A pregnant woman will be carrying extra weight, which will put pressure on joints, ligaments, and muscles. The fitter and stronger the muscular framework, the easier the extra weight is dealt with.

RECOMMENDATIONS

- *Stretching is extremely important, and will allow for a much easier delivery.*
- *Do not commence a heavy exercise program because you find yourself pregnant. If you are already active, then there is no reason why you should stop unless your exercise is a contact sport such as soccer or rugby (many women now play these sports), or a sport that results in jolting the body. Games such as squash where you place your feet down heavily and bounce off walls, and activities such as jogging, where the downward force on the lower abdomen and pelvis is quite marked, are best avoided.*
- *Preferably use aerobic exercise, such as walking and especially swimming. Dancing is an excellent exercise, but avoid your local rave! Many ancient cultures have incorporated dance techniques into the pregnancy period, and intuitively moving your body to your favorite piece of music will not only have a beneficial effect on your structure, but also be soothing to the baby.*

Nothing more needs to be done, but:

- *I highly recommend learning some basic Alexander techniques to ensure correct posture. Polarity is equally effective.*
- *Yoga is, in my opinion, the best form of exercise in pregnancy. Yoga incorporates deep breathing and relaxation techniques, stretching and muscular strengthening, along with postural exercises. Certain yoga techniques should not be used during pregnancy, and it is best to have a private session or two with a yoga teacher to ensure that you are practicing the best techniques.*

PSYCHOLOGICAL ASPECTS

Pregnancy should be a time of great joy, but almost invariably at some stage during the puerperal (the time you are pregnant) period, feelings ranging from ambivalence and indifference, through depression, to anger and anxiety are all commonplace.

Often it is not suitable to use your partner—however close you may be as a couple—for expressing these emotions, but express these emotions you must. Feeling guilty about a state of mind is almost as detrimental to health as the negative emotion itself. Partners, however, are undergoing their own "crises," and are caught between giving you the best advice and the advice that they think you want to hear. It is an unfair situation to be put in, and quite often beyond the intuitive expertise that partners can have.

It is better to face your dilemmas with a "professional friend" and bring your conclusions to the attention of your partner. Do not hide your feelings from those close to you, but do not expect them to have answers. Counselors are available through any obstetric unit, general practice, complementary clinic, or recommendation by friends.

Yoga Exercises in Pregnancy

Yoga techniques for relaxation, as well as stretching and muscular strengthening, are the best form of exercise in pregnancy.

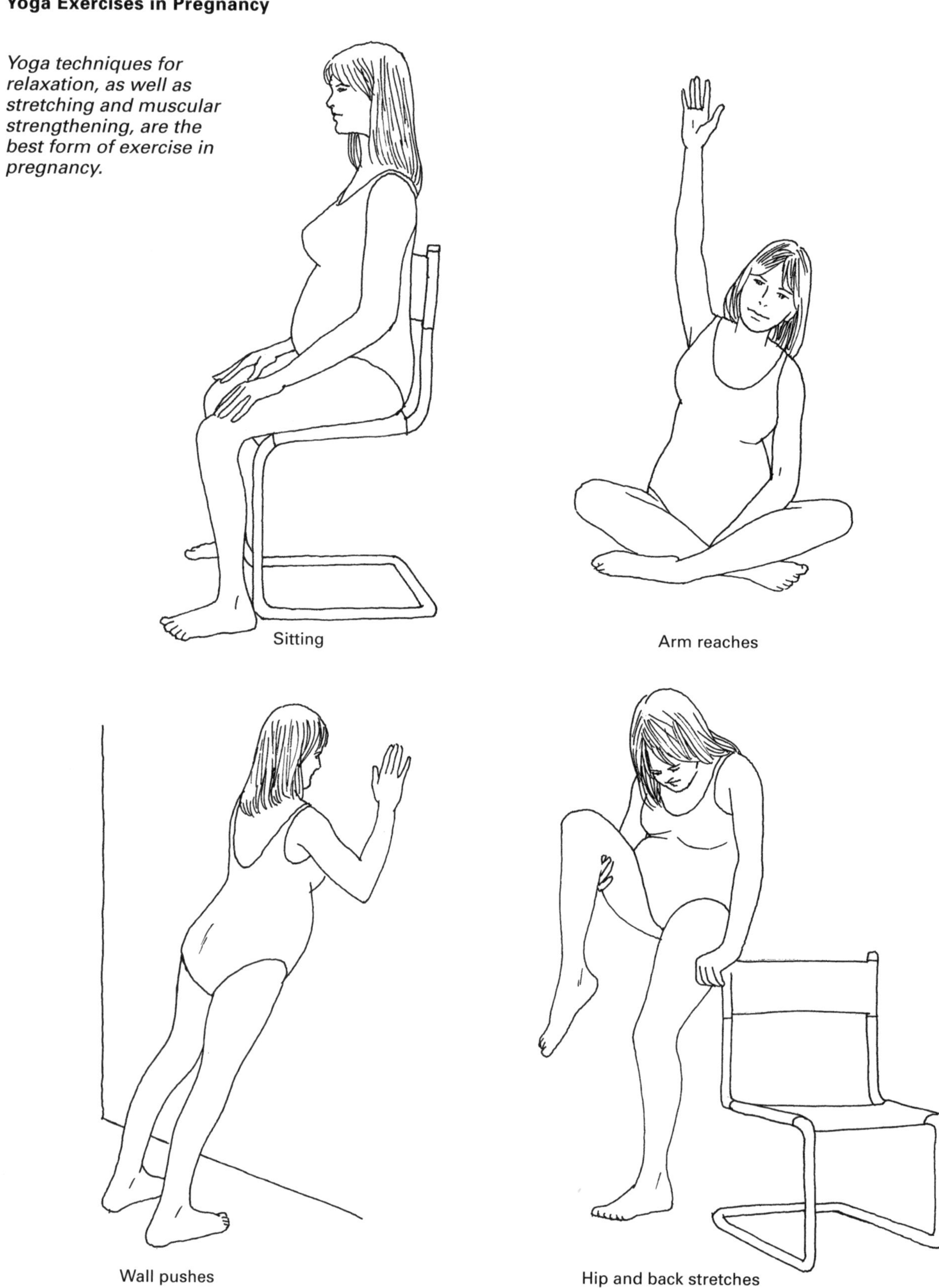

Sitting

Arm reaches

Wall pushes

Hip and back stretches

It is best to deal with a woman psychotherapist who has been through pregnancy because you will have both the professional and the personal opinion.

Do not be ashamed to ask for support—pregnancy is a time of great change, and the psychological help of the extended family is fast dwindling here in the West. It can only be beneficial to be nurtured.

RECOMMENDATIONS

- *See a counselor.*
- *Drink strong camomile tea. This is a great psychological relaxant and can make problems far easier to solve.*
- *Specific essential oils, such as rosemary, chamomile, and lavender, can be used as massage oil, in the bath, or on the collar.*
- *Homeopathic remedies worth looking up in your preferred homeopathic manual are: Aconitum if fear is the main component; Aurum metallicum if sad and despairing; Ignatia if your sense of freedom is lost and your sense of responsibility too great; Pulsatilla if your mood is very tearful, although this remedy should not be taken for longer than three days because it may encourage contractions. Other remedies can be of great benefit, and your homeopath would be best suited to choose the correct one. All may be taken at potency 30.*
- *The Bach flower remedies are marvelous, and a specific book should be reviewed or a therapist's opinion sought to establish the best choice.*

COMMON PROBLEMS ARISING DURING PREGNANCY

Pregnancy is a natural process, and not one that requires medication as a rule. Some conditions can arise, however, that may need treating.

ANEMIA IN PREGNANCY

Anemia is the medical term given to a range of conditions that are all associated with a lack of the oxygen-carrying compound hemoglobin, found in the red blood cells. Assessment of normal levels of hemoglobin vary from laboratory to laboratory around the world, but principally the amount we carry in our bloodstreams is 11.5–17mmol/l.

Anemia is not uncommon in pregnancy, due to the baby using up the mother's supply of iron or folic acid. The symptoms of anemia range from tiredness, lethargy, shortness of breath, and irritability to palpitations and fainting. The signs are a pale skin, a pallor under the fingernails, and sometimes tingling in the hands and feet. The only way to be certain that anemia is the cause is by having a blood test which shows your hemoglobin level to be low.

RECOMMENDATIONS

- *The orthodox world considers a person to be anemic only if their hemoglobin level drops below the "normal" levels. I believe it to be more relevant to have your hemoglobin level checked at an early stage of pregnancy, and if your level drops from that figure and any of the aforementioned symptoms are present, then consider yourself in need of treatment.*
- *Increase your input of green-leaf vegetables, especially spinach and collard greens, and enjoy a little more lamb. Molasses should be used instead of sugar.*
- *The homeopathic remedy Ferrum phosphoricum 30 should be taken twice a day for 10 days.*
- *Using blood tests, establish the cause of an anemia. Most often it is due to lack of iron, folic acid, or vitamin B_{12}, but it may be an amino acid or other vitamin. Once established, replenish with natural food supplements, and seek advice from a complementary medical practitioner concerning the correct amount to take.*
- *Strawberry tea with half a teaspoon of thyme per mug may taste a bit earthy, but helps if taken three times a day.*

- *If symptoms persist, acupuncture and especially moxibustion can be administered by a healthcare practitioner who will advise you further.*

BLEEDING IN PREGNANCY

Bleeding from the vagina during pregnancy requires immediate discussion with your doctor or obstetric team. Bleeding before the 28th week is classified as a threatened miscarriage, and after that week is called an antepartum hemorrhage.

Very often, a small bleed lasting a short time is nothing to worry about, and is probably due to a burst vein or changes to the vagina or cervix due to the new hormone levels.

RECOMMENDATION

- *I do not recommend any home care, although treatments from a homeopath or a herbalist can be used to great effect, but only after a doctor has been consulted.*

BREAST PROBLEMS

Many changes will occur to the breasts in response to the hormonal changes of pregnancy. They will feel more sensitive, heavier, and more tender, almost to the point of being painful.

The area around the nipples—the areola—may produce little bumps called Montgomery's tubercules, which produce the necessary secretions to help the nipples prepare for breast feeding. The areola may darken and the nipple may enlarge out of proportion to the rest of the breast. This is all normal, and requires no treatment.

RECOMMENDATIONS

- *Milk ducts may become blocked and hard, painful swellings may arise within the breast tissue. Apply alternate hot and cold compresses and gently massage the lump in the direction of the nipple. The lump may become slightly red, but if it becomes deeply red or inflamed, or streaks of red appear, move onto the next recommendation.*
- *If the breast lump becomes red or inflamed, use Belladonna 6 every 15min for three doses and then every 2hr until the matter settles. If it does not settle after 24hr, talk to a healthcare practitioner, but avoid antibiotics as a first-line treatment.*
- *Ensure that correct-fitting, cotton bras are obtained. Spend as much time as possible with the breasts exposed to air and sunlight.*
- *Comfortably hot baths can be very relieving for painful breasts.*

CONSTIPATION

Constipation occurs for several reasons: the direct effect of the hormones on the bowel musculature, the body naturally slowing down the transit time (the time taken for food to travel from the stomach to the rectum) to allow more digestive process and absorption; reduced activity, dehydration, and the taking of iron supplements.

Commonsense approaches, such as drinking more water and maintaining activity levels, are essential. If the problem continues, the following recommendations can help.

RECOMMENDATIONS

- *Reduce dairy products, meat, and eggs. Increase your fiber intake (see chapter 7), and ensure that you are taking multivitamins because deficiencies in several vitamins can worsen the problem.*
- *Lactobacillus acidophilus—two million bacteria with each meal will encourage the bowel flora to break down the feces.*
- *Four ounces of yogurt, two teaspoonfuls of olive oil, and a clove of garlic, mixed and eaten with wholegrain pita bread.*
- *A mildly spicy vegetable dish (Indian, Thai, etc.).*
- *Massage in general, but abdominal massage in particular can be very relieving.*

- *Pure licorice comes as a soft bar, and is distinct from the children's sweetened rubbery licorice; 10–20g eaten before bedtime will help.*
- *Molasses instead of other sweeteners is a help, or it can be taken as 2 dessertspoonfuls before bed.*
- *Drink at least 8 ounces of water per foot height per day.*
- *Laxatives are not an option. If constipation continues despite the measures mentioned above, bring the problem to the attention of a complementary health professional.*

CRAMPS

RECOMMENDATIONS

- *Increase water input.*
- *Drink strong camomile tea.*
- *Calcium (500mg daily), copper (2mg daily), zinc (15mg at night), and magnesium (400mg daily) should all be taken for up to one week. If the problem persists, speak to your health professional.*
- *Massage, Shiatsu, and yoga techniques will all relieve cramping.*

DIABETES IN PREGNANCY

Diabetes mellitus is caused by an insufficiency of naturally-occurring insulin from the pancreas. It causes a rise in the sugar level in the blood, which is detrimental to most organs and systems in the body.

Diabetes, like thyroid problems, can occur during pregnancy despite not being a problem in the same person when they are not pregnant. The Chinese have a meridian or energy line that travels from the top of the head down the midline of the body. This meridian is called the vessel of conception, or the directing vessel, and is of paramount importance in the reproductive systems of both men and women. The orthodox world considers problems in the pancreas or the thyroid to be due to chemical overdemand, but all Eastern medical philosophies have an energy line such as the vessel of conception, which connects the pituitary gland (control of the cycle), the thyroid gland, the pancreatic gland, and the uterus (*see* **The vessel of conception**).

Weakness in this energy channel is brought on by poor health throughout the system, but also by a lack of energy received from the relationship of the pregnant woman with her partner and her parents.

RECOMMENDATIONS

- *Discuss diabetes situation with a nutritionist to adjust the diet correctly.*
- *Because of the association of diabetes with the vessel of conception, see a Chinese or Tibetan practitioner for acupuncture and possible herbal treatment.*
- *Once a nutritionist has adjusted your diet, you may use dandelion (Taraxacum) fluid extract (five drops in water) 10min before each meal.*

HYPOTHYROIDISM

Hypothyroidism occurs infrequently in pregnancy. The orthodox world has some belief that this is caused by an excessive demand, or by some suppression of the thyroid gland by chemicals produced by the baby or by the mother herself. The Eastern philosophies consider that the energy is being pulled down into the uterus, leaving less for the organs associated with the vessel of conception (*see* **The vessel of conception**).

Any symptoms of hypothyroidism—especially excessive tiredness, feeling cold, dulled concentration, and excessive water retention—should all arouse suspicion. Most pregnant women like to sleep more, but an excessive sleep requirement in association with tiredness regardless of the rest received should also arouse suspicion.

RECOMMENDATIONS

- *Please obtain the opinion of your doctor or OB/GYN and complementary medical practitioner.*
- *Please follow the advice and recommendations given in the section in this book on hypothyroidism.*

MISCARRIAGE

Sadly, some pregnancies do not reach a satisfactory conclusion. One Eastern philosophy believes that a pregnancy that ends in a miscarriage is a tremendous blessing for the parents, who had vested upon them a spirit requiring a very short incarnation that is usually associated with an Advanced Soul. However, this information does not take away the devastating sadness of the loss of a baby. If a miscarriage takes place, please follow the recommendations below.

RECOMMENDATIONS

- *To try to help avoid a miscarriage once it is suspected to be likely, contact your complementary medical practitioner for a reference to someone in the alternative medical field who has some knowledge of this subject. That person or your own practitioner may be able to help, but your home medical kit is unlikely to be enough.*
- *Visit a counselor, however well you feel that you are dealing with the event.*
- *The sudden change in hormonal structure is best dealt with by a health professional. Please see your complementary practitioner.*
- *If a miscarriage has occurred and bleeding continues, use the homeopathic remedy Phosphorus 6 or Secale cornutum 6 (four pills every hour) until the bleeding and discharge stops. Once this has occurred, take Arnica 200 (one dose twice a day for five days).*
- *The male partner should take Arnica 200 (one dose twice a day for five days) and would also benefit from a counseling session.*

PRE-ECLAMPSIA AND ECLAMPSIA

Pre-eclampsia refers to a rising blood pressure and the presence of protein in the mother's urine. These two parameters are constantly checked, because the development of eclampsia can be extremely dangerous. Eclampsia is characterized by convulsions due to the effects of swelling in the brain.

RECOMMENDATIONS

- *A pre-eclamptic condition must be monitored by a gynecologist and a doctor.*
- *A naturopathic physician should be consulted, and homeopathy, herbal medicine, acupuncture, and meditation/relaxation treatments can be effective, reducing the risk of hospitalization. Delivery is usually by Cesarean section if the pre-eclamptic condition is not controlled.*

DIZZY SPELLS AND FAINTING

Dizziness and fainting are usually due to lowered blood-sugar levels, nutritional deficiencies, and just plain exhaustion. If the following recommendations do not help with dizziness within a few days, or if you have more than one faint, take yourself along to your health practitioner and advise your doctor that you are doing so.

RECOMMENDATIONS

- *Eat small snacks in between meals if dizzy spells or a single faint should occur (see **Hypoglycemia diet**).*
- *Consult a nutritionist to establish correct dietetics.*
- *Ensure that clothes are not too tight around the waist.*
- *Use the homeopathic remedy Aconite 6 (four pills every 15min). If the fainting or dizziness is associated with a flush, use Belladonna 6, and if the dizziness is noticeable when rising from bed or a chair take Bryonia 30, one dose three times a day for five days.*

NAUSEA AND HYPEREMESIS GRAVIDARUM

Hyperemesis gravidarum is the Latin terminology

for severe nausea in pregnancy. The most effective treatments that I have come across are mentioned at the start of this chapter under the heading "Discovering a Pregnancy," but if they do not work consider the following.

RECOMMENDATIONS

- *Regular visits to an acupuncturist to obtain a suitable acupressure technique.*
- *Severe nausea and vomiting can lead to malnutrition, and may need to be controlled by orthodox drugs via your doctor.*

POLYHYDRAMNIOS

Polyhydramnios is the presence of too much amniotic fluid, and can be associated with twins or diabetes. Symptoms are abdominal pressure and distension, in association with a tense and larger-than-expected abdomen.

RECOMMENDATIONS

- *I have not seen alternative techniques correct this situation, although bed rest and massage can be relieving.*
- *Do not be tempted to use herbal treatments, because anything that can affect the production of amniotic fluid is liable to affect the fetus.*
- *A gynecologist can drain excess fluid under ultrasound guidance, which is a comparatively safe and effective procedure.*

SWELLING AND EDEMA

This has been discussed earlier in the chapter but if the recommendations do not ease the problem, then visit your health practitioner for their expert advice. *See* **Polyhydramnios** and **Swollen feet and hands.**

URINARY-TRACT PROBLEMS

Infections

During the pregnancy, urine tests will be performed. While looking for sugar to show diabetes, the urine will also be checked for the presence of protein or nitrites. Evidence of either of these leads to a suspicion of a urinary-tract infection, and the orthodox world is divided as to whether to treat this finding with antibiotics or not. You must not allow a bladder infection to travel into the kidneys, which can lead to spontaneous abortion. On the other hand, one does not want to give antibiotics, which can affect the normal bowel bacteria and lead to absorption problems.

Urine Analysis	
pH	7.0
Protein	+ (0.30g/l)
Glucose	Negative
Ketone	Negative
Blood	+
Microscopy	
WBCs	>100/HPF
RBCs	Not seen
Casts	Not seen
Epithelial cells	+
Crystals	Not seen
Organisms	++
CULTURE	No bacterial growth

Example of the results of urine analysis showing the chemistry and biology of the urine sample.

RECOMMENDATIONS

- *If proteins or nitrites are found in the urine sample, insist that the sample be sent to a laboratory for culture and sensitivity. This means that any bacteria will be grown and tested against antibiotics so that a correct drug is given if the need arises.*
- *Any discomfort in the bladder or in the lower back (the kidney area) must be brought to the attention of your medical caregiver.*
- *In the early stages of a mild discomfort, you may use cranberry tablets or powder, as directed by a practitioner or pharmacist. There is no standard strength for cranberry preparations. Do not use the sweetened cranberry juices; the sugar content will encourage bacterial growth.*
- *Juniper or Berberis vulgaris fluid extracts (ten drops four times a day in water) may be curative.*

- *Depending on the symptoms, the following homeopathic remedies should be reviewed: Cantharis, Pulsatilla, Equisetum, Staphysagria, Phosphorus, and Mercurius.*
- *Apply reflexology to the bladder and kidney points on your feet (see* **Reflexology***).*
- *Add 20 drops of eucalyptus and sandalwood essential oils to a hot bath.*
- *Drink one glass (5–6 oz) of water or herbal tea every hour, and put half a teaspoonful of sodium bicarbonate (baking soda) into every other glass (maximum of 32 ounces of water per day).*

Frequency and urgency

The need to pass urine and having difficulty in holding a full bladder are symptoms that can occur very early in pregnancy, but will definitely occur as the pressure on the bladder increases with the growth of the baby.

RECOMMENDATIONS

- *Yoga and pelvic floor exercises are essential.*
- *Try not to drink a lot within 2hr of going to bed.*
- *Two less-well-known remedies, Chimaphila umbellata 6 and Linaria 6, can be taken at a dosage of four pills every 4hr but if you find no relief after five days, stop.*
- *Acupuncture, craniosacral therapy, and osteopathy can all make an appreciable difference.*

Vaginal discharges

Vaginal discharges are common, usually due to the hormonal changes affecting the cells lining the walls of the vagina. Any bloody or brown (stale blood) discharges should be discussed with a doctor or gynecologist but other minor discharges should be left alone and assumed to be normal.

If the discharge is irritating, copious, colored or bad smelling, then a simple douche technique as described below is acceptable. It may well be a thrush infection, so *please see* the section in chapter 4 that deals with this problem.

Concern is sometimes expressed about cleaning the vagina when pregnant, because this may introduce infection. To an extent this is true, but since intercourse is permissible with the resultant introduction of another person's bacteria and body fluids, I do not see why the following antiseptic technique is not perfectly safe.

RECOMMENDATIONS

- *Obtain a 20ml or 50ml syringe, leave it in recently boiled water for 5min. Mix one tablespoon of live yogurt with a large mug of boiled water cooled to a warm temperature, and draw the milky solution into the syringe. Insert the syringe no more than two inches (5cm) into the vagina, and gently depress the plunger. Thoroughly flush the vaginal vault, and perform this each morning for seven days. The procedure should be repeated at night using a tablespoon of cider vinegar in a large mug of warm water.*
- *The following homeopathic remedies may be helpful: Hydrastis 6 if the discharge is thick and tenacious; Mercurius 6 if greenish yellow, smarting, with some swelling and worse at night; and Stannum metallicum 6 for a white, mucousy, profuse discharge, especially if the back aches. As always, refer to a good homeopathic text for a more accurate prescription.*

SKIN PROBLEMS

Skin changes occur in all pregnancies, usually for the better. Sufferers of eczema and psoriasis frequently find that their condition improves, which is good news because the drugs used in psoriasis, and the steroid creams used in eczema should be stopped if possible. If you are under any treatment for psoriasis that involves taking oral medication, this should be stopped several months before pregnancy is planned (*see* chapter 1).

Stretch marks

The stretching of the skin can lead to shiny streaks over the breasts and abdomen.

RECOMMENDATION

- *Apply a high-dose vitamin-E cream, or mix vitamin E (1,000iu emptied from capsules) into a tablespoonful of olive oil, and massage in twice a day.*

Itching skin

All too frequently, at some point during a pregnancy, itching skin will become a problem. The cause is uncertain, although there are two possibilities: altered hormone levels and a histamine release in the skin due to the waste products produced by the baby.

RECOMMENDATIONS

- *Change your soaps, bath products and laundry detergent to unmedicated hypoallergenic products. Make sure you only wear natural material, such as cotton or wool, avoiding synthetics.*
- *Add camomile extracts, coconut oil or almond oil to your baths. Camomile extracts are very often successful.*
- *Borage oil can be applied either directly or through the bath.*
- *Use Evening Primrose Oil 1g three times a day for five days. Licorice extracts can be remarkably soothing when applied to the skin.*
- *Calamine lotion can be used if the above compounds do not work.*

CHILDBIRTH AND AFTER

The most important aspect of the Eastern philosophy of medicine is the concept of the balance of energy flowing through and contained in the body. The Chinese refer to Yin and Yang as being opposite, yet complementary, factors. Here are some examples of Yin and Yang.

YIN	YANG
Inferior	Superior
Front (abdomen)	Back
Interior organs	Exterior organs (skin)
Structure	Function
Water	Fire
Quiet	Noise
Wet	Dry
Slow	Rapid
Storage	Distribution
Curled up	Stretched out

From these examples you can see that the process of development in the womb is predominantly influenced by Yin. Life, however, is one of balance, and leading up to the delivery, the balance is redressed by the more Yang-dominated energy of delivery.

It is best, therefore, to support the promotion of Yang as we move towards the latter part of pregnancy, because a deficiency may create the problems that can be associated with delivery.

Yin/Yang circle depicting the dynamic relationship between Yin and Yang.

ONE MONTH BEFORE LABOR

One month before labor, there is going to be a strong desire to get this business over! In some

U.S. clinics, weights are attached to the husband's abdomen and chest, and they are asked to wander around like that for a short time. We men are not aware of the strain and effort that goes into the later stages of pregnancy. A pregnant mother will be fed up with the restrictions but, hopefully, will have enjoyed the health that is usually associated with pregnancy.

It is around this time that thoughts turn to the preparation for delivery. A lot of intervention is not needed, of course, but certain preparations can be made to try to reduce any delays with the delivery.

RECOMMENDATIONS

- *The pain-relieving techniques taught through hypnotherapy earlier in the pregnancy should be practiced regularly.*
- *Ensure that, by now, your partner has a grasp of the Shiatsu pressure points; if not, send him off to the practitioner to learn.*
- *Daily yoga, however uncomfortable it may be, should be continued to ensure good muscular tone.*
- *Ensure relaxation, breathing techniques, or meditation is continued to engender a sense of calm leading up to the event.*
- *Contact your preferred complementary medical practitioner to glean any advice.*
- *Ten days prior to the expected delivery date, take the homeopathic remedy Caulophyllum 30 for seven days before bed, and for the last three days before the delivery date, use Caulophyllum 200 before bed. This higher potency can be used for up to one week if the delivery date is passed.*

ALTERNATIVE TECHNIQUES FOR INDUCEMENT OF LABOR

There is rarely a good reason to induce a delivery, but if there is no sign of labor two weeks after the expected date (remember that the date calculated from the last period and the day suggested by the scans during pregnancy may differ due to the length of the mother's monthly cycle), then pressure may be applied by the nurse-midwives and OB/GYN. The reasons are simple and sound: the baby may grow to a size that may make it difficult to fit through the pelvic rim; and the placenta may be unable to sustain the baby's nutritional and oxygen requirements.

Provided that the obstetrician and the ultrasound scans agree that the baby is the correct size, then alternative techniques for induction of labor can be employed ten days after the expected delivery date.

RECOMMENDATIONS

- *The homeopathic remedy Secale cornutum 30, four pills every 3hr.*
- *Acupuncture or specific acupressure (Shiatsu) points can be activated. These are illustrated in the diagram opposite, along with the areas that should not be massaged under normal circumstances at any stage during pregnancy. The specific points are:*

  GB21 (gall bladder 21)—on the highest point of the shoulder where a perpendicular line drawn from the nipple crosses the top of the shoulder;

  LI4 (large intestine 4)—in the center of the flesh before the first and second metacarpal bones (in the hand);

  LIV3 (liver 3)—in the depression up the foot from the big toe and the second toe.

  BL67 (bladder 67)—on the lateral side of the small toe at the base of the toenail;

  SP6 (spleen 6)—three thumb-widths above the tip of the inner ankle bone and backwards to the edge of the bone;
- *Fluid extracts of Pulsatilla or, if available, Caulophyllum can be taken, ten drops in water every three hours.*
- *Raspberry-leaf tea, one tea bag in a mug four times a day.*
- *Reflexology can be utilized on the uterine and pituitary points on the feet.*

- *A brisk walk.*
- *Sexual intercourse.*

Shiatsu Points for Inducing Labor

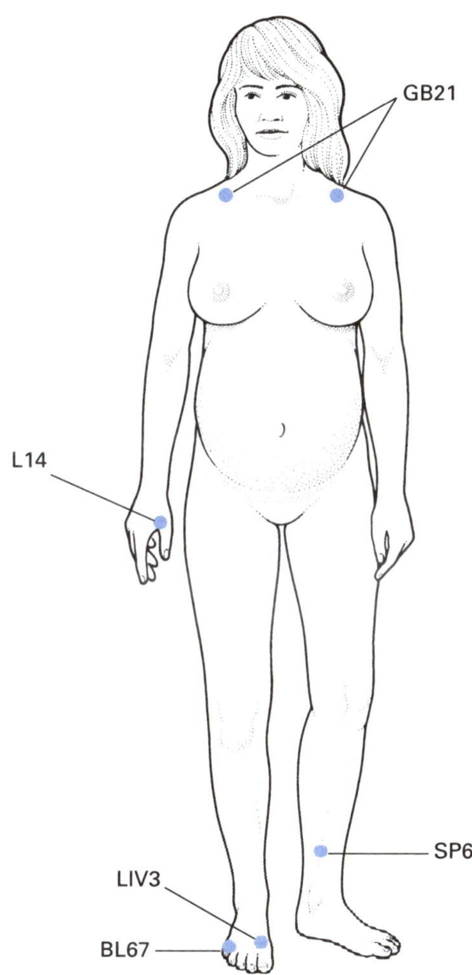

Nutrition

There is no need to alter the diet, particularly if all has gone well through the first eight months of a pregnancy. Always consider your intuition and cravings as being the best guidelines. You may encourage Yang energy building up towards the expected delivery date by adding the following foods into the diet. They should not be taken in excess, nor too early in the pregnancy because, as explained above, the uterine environment is predominantly Yin, and excess Yang may cause problems. The foods to increase are:

- lamb
- lobster and shrimps
- basil, dill, sage, cinnamon, thyme, nutmeg, clover, garlic, ginger, and fennel.

Exercise

RECOMMENDATIONS

- *Ensure that stretching exercises are practiced regularly throughout the day. The act of squatting with your knees as far apart as possible and the back supported by your partner or a wall is excellent.*
- *Practice holding certain positions that you may choose at the delivery, and hold these postures for as long as you can.*
- *Walk and swim: 15min of swimming and 40min of walking (provided that your back is all right) is a sensible plan.*

Medication

It is not necessary to consider the use of medication for, or leading up to, delivery. However, certain treatment protocols can be used if mild problems or symptoms are arising. These should be dealt with according to the symptoms, and in consultation with your health practitioner.

RECOMMENDATIONS

- *See earlier in this section for the use of Caulophyllum.*
- *Pulsatilla fluid extract—1 teaspoonful in water four times a day, starting the day before delivery is expected.*
- *Apply a combination cream of Arnica, Calendula, and Urtica to the outer aspects of the vagina, the perineum, and around the anus. Do so three or*

four times a day to prepare the area for the stretching that it will undergo. Arnica or Calendula creams will suffice, as will olive oil, if the combination is not readily available.

BRAXTON HICKS

These contractions, named after the gynecologist who felt that attention should be drawn to them, can occur any time from six weeks before the expected date of delivery. They tend to be infrequent, which differentiates them from the contractions of the first stage of labor, although Braxton-Hicks contractions may be very powerful, and can lead to the concern about early labor.

RECOMMENDATIONS:

- *If you have any doubts, be reassured by your doctor or gynecologist.*
- *If the contractions create anxiety, you may use Aconite 6, four pills every hour for three doses.*

DELIVERY (LABOR)

I prefer to use the word "delivery" because it has the connotation of the arrival of a wanted gift. The term "labor," while accurate, has a somewhat negative ring to it! Delivery is divided into three parts: the first, second, and third stages of labor. Before discussing the details of these, let us cover one or two other points.

At the onset

When delivery seems imminent—by the "show," the breaking of the waters, or by frequent contractions—the following can be recommended.

RECOMMENDATIONS

- *Walk around. The Yang energy is encouraged by movement.*
- *Increase the glucose levels in preparation for expending energy by eating light meals, preferably of complex carbohydrates (wholegrain bread, brown rice, honey).*
- *Sleep as much as you can, especially in the breaks between contractions.*
- *Cry if you wish, and be open to demanding love and support at a notoriously insecure time.*

Placenta previa

Placenta previa is the medical term for the positioning of the placenta within the uterus in such a

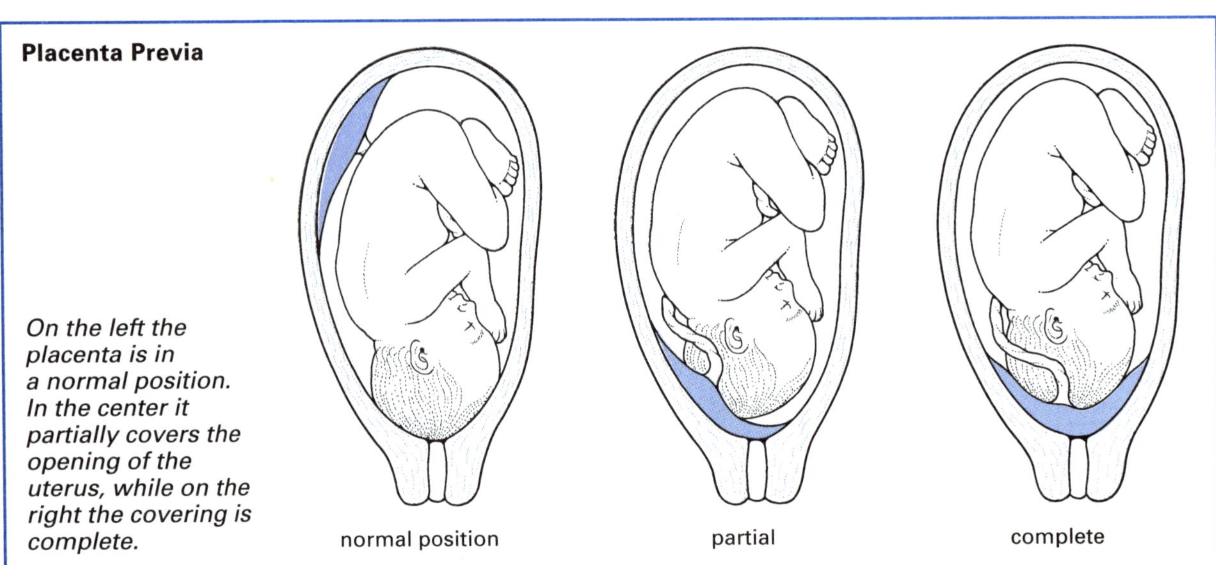

Placenta Previa

On the left the placenta is in a normal position. In the center it partially covers the opening of the uterus, while on the right the covering is complete.

way that it covers the opening from the uterus through the cervix into the vagina.

A full placenta previa has never been corrected by a complementary medical technique in my experience, although many times I have seen a partial placenta previa "move" after therapies. It should be mentioned that this may occur in any case as the uterus enlarges.

RECOMMENDATIONS

- *Osteopathy, in combination with Tibetan or Chinese acupuncture and herbal treatments, has most often proved successful.*
- *Do not allow an excess of ultrasound investigation to be performed. Once a scan has identified a placenta previa, do not have repeated tests; have a rescan one month before delivery, and if things have not changed, then consider orthodox management (see* **Ultrasound***).*

Water birth

The use of water has been much publicized. A recent appraisal of the popularity of delivering in water has suggested that many mothers prefer to be in water for the first part of labor but over 50 percent choose to deliver out of the pool.

There is no advantage or disadvantage to delivering under water, although some questions are being broached by pediatricians concerning the hygiene of underwater deliveries. In a healthy clean environment, I do not believe that they will find any problems.

Laboyer

Frederick Laboyer focused on the commonsense attitude that the impersonal atmosphere of hospital delivery rooms was not conducive to healthy or comfortable delivery. This point of view has flourished since the early 1970s in the West, although it has been a principle of delivery throughout the Eastern philosophies for thousands of years. Choose your music, lighting, and aromas in the delivery suite or room.

DELIVERY—FIRST STAGE OF LABOR

The first stage of labor includes the "ripening" (softening) of the cervix and the first 2 inches of dilation. At this time a "show" may occur, which is the exiting of the mucus plug that has been a major protective factor in the cervical "os" or opening. The "waters" (the protective, amniotic-fluid sack) may break before the first stage of labor or in the early part. This natural lubrication is an important indication of delivery, and excessive drying of the fluids should be avoided. Contractions should be occurring at 10–20-minute intervals and lasting up to 30 seconds.

Dilation from 2 to 5 inches can take a matter of minutes or several hours. The recommendations below can help to shorten this timespan. During this dilation, contractions will last for 20–90 seconds, be profoundly intense and painful, and can occur anywhere between 10 minutes and 30 seconds apart.

Your natural instinct with regard to breathing, and the training you will have received through your antenatal care and yoga classes is never more important than at this stage. The desire to push down and expel the baby is at its strongest, but pushing too early can tear the cervix and lead to difficulties. Your nurse-midwife will be very experienced and supportive, leaving you with little doubt as to how your breathing should be. Do not worry!

Pain relief

Delivering babies is painful. Pain is relative, and some mothers are better equipped anatomically and physiologically than others to handle the discomfort. But nobody has a painfree birth unless they have a very high-level meditation technique!

RECOMMENDATIONS

- *Do not be ashamed or embarrassed to ask for pain relief.*
- *Use the self-hypnotherapy techniques taught to you for the pregnancy. Use acupressure techniques (see over).*

BL31 (bladder 31)—a tender spot at the base of the spinal column, approximately one hand-width above the buttocks in the midline. Please note that the use of these pain-relief points may shorten contractions, and therefore should be used only at the point in time when pain is most severe, otherwise labor may be prolonged.

ST36 (stomach 36)—four finger-widths inferior to the knee cap, and one finger outwards.

BL60 (bladder 60)—in the depression half-way between the outer ankle bone and the Achilles tendon, level with the most prominent point of the ankle bone;

- *Use Chamomilla 6 (four pills every 15min) for intolerable pains, especially associated with the back. If fear or shivering is present, consider Aconite 6 (four pills every 15min).*
- *Use the "gas" (nitrous oxide) as much as you like.*
- *If these measures are not effective, then do not hesitate to ask for an epidural. It may take some time for the anesthetist to arrive, so make your request sooner rather than later!*

Shiatsu Points for use through Delivery

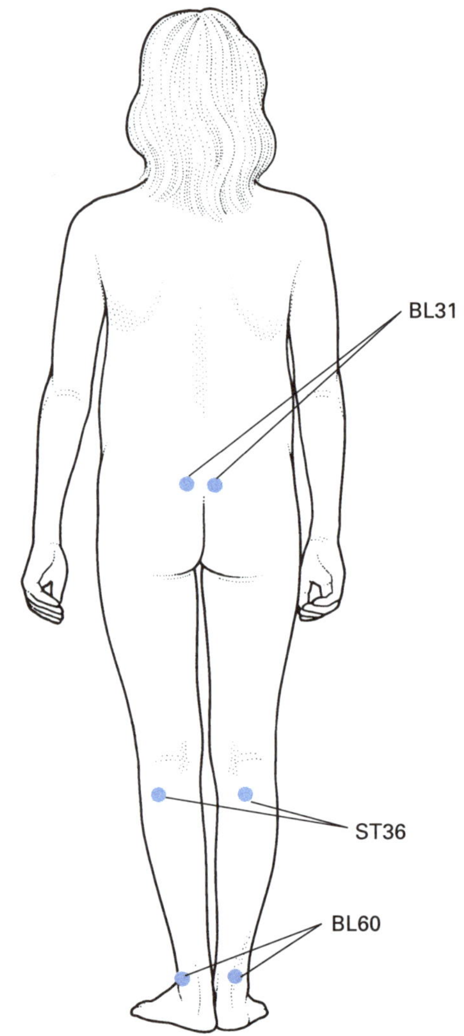

Have your partner apply pressure to the above acupressure points.

The delivery of the head is the most difficult and time-consuming part of this second stage. Hopefully, the process will be swift, but delays can occur.

If any difficulty is expected in the birth, such as when a baby is in the complete breech position (aligned in the pelvis bottom-first, with knees flexed), a Cesarean section will be automatically

Stages of Delivery

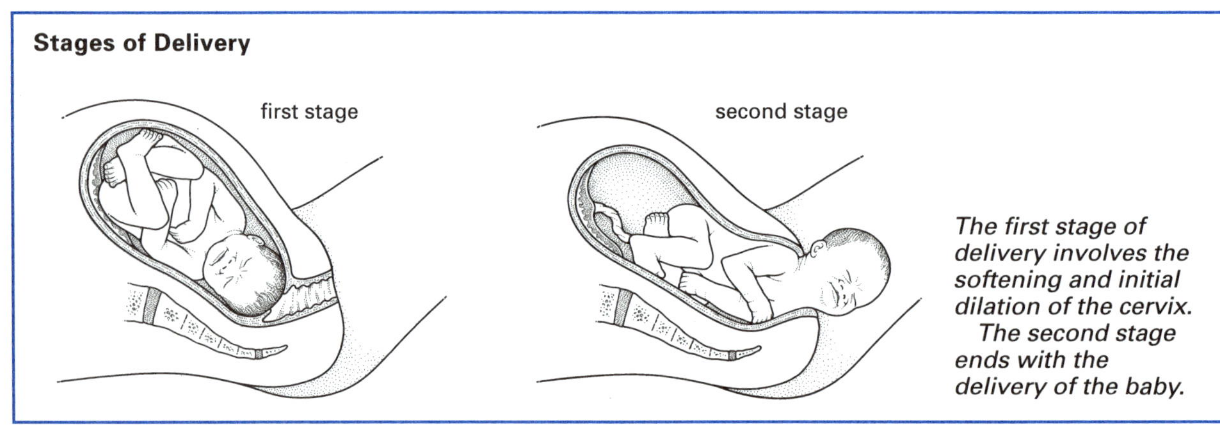

The first stage of delivery involves the softening and initial dilation of the cervix.

The second stage ends with the delivery of the baby.

Delivery Positions

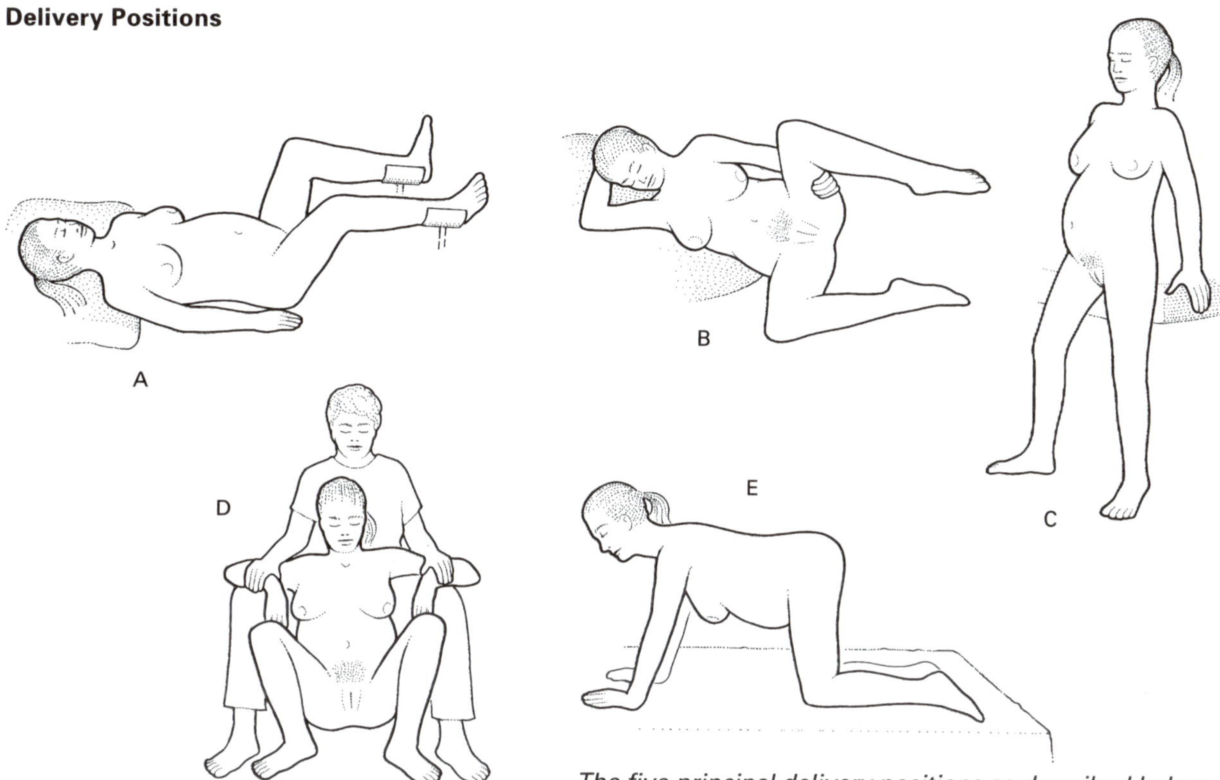

The five principal delivery positions as described below.

performed. "C-Sections" are performed in about 20 percent of all U.S. births, largely because they do guarantee a safe delivery of the baby, and thereby any litigation against the hospital, obstetricians, surgeons or nurse-midwives involved in the birth.

The most unpleasant aspect is the sensation that the perineum (the area between the vagina and the anus) is tearing. This is not often the case, and the use of the mixed Arnica, Calendula, and Urtica cream beforehand generally reduces the risk. The midwife will be applying considerable pressure in this area to avoid tears.

RECOMMENDATION

- *Make sure that the midwife is aware of the sensations you experience, and encourage her to give more support or apply more pressure.*

DELIVERY—SECOND STAGE OF LABOR

Now we are getting down to it, the waiting is nearly over. There may be a break between the first stage and second stage, especially in a first pregnancy, and if this is the case, rest.

The second stage starts when the cervix is fully dilated, and ends with the delivery of the baby.

Delivery position

There is no correct or incorrect position to deliver a baby. Instinct combined with particular and individual anatomy will make this decision for you (*see* above). The principal options are:

A Lying semiprone on your back, with feet together and knees apart or feet in stirrups;
B Lying on either side with the upper leg raised;
C Standing with buttocks supported against the bed;
D Squatting, using your partner's knees and thighs as an "armchair" support;
E On the knees leaning against the bed, or on all fours.

Any of these positions can be utilized, and changes from one to the other will be determined by how you are feeling.

RECOMMENDATIONS

- *Choose your atmosphere. There is no right or wrong.*
- *Be comfortable with those in attendance. If grandmother, mother, sister, or milkman provide you with the most support, then invite them to be present. Do not crowd out the midwife, however!*
- *Unless there is a medical reason, avoid monitors. The presence of modern, medical technology creates the perception of the possibility of something going wrong. Both Mom and Dad already have their fears, especially in a first delivery, where they are launching into the unknown, and asking the midwives to use equipment only when essential is not risky but better for the psyche.*

DELIVERY—THE THIRD STAGE OF LABOR

Birth ends when the placenta is expelled in this, the third part of delivery. Occasionally, bleeding may persist and the midwife may push down hard above the pubic bone. If this does not stop the bleeding, a drug derived from a natural plant extract called ergotamine may be injected into the mother's arm. This causes the uterus to contract and applies pressure to the bleeding vessel, thereby stopping the hemorrhage.

Umbilical Clamp

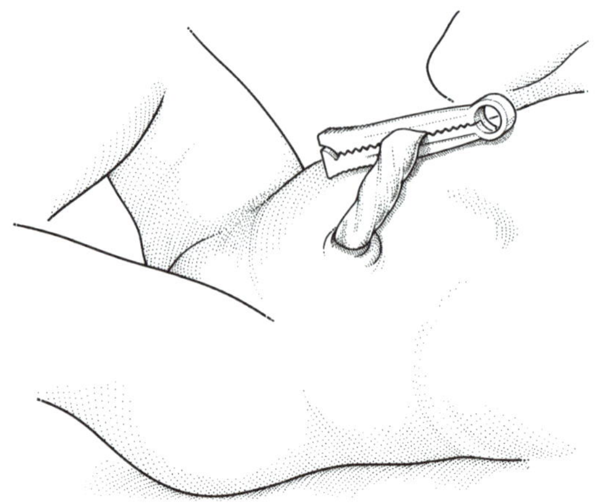

Umbilical clamp in place.

The midwife will gently push any blood that is in the umbilical cord towards the baby, and within a couple of minutes the cord—which actually pulsates—will come to rest. At this time the midwife will cut the cord by placing two clamps near the baby's tummy and cutting in between. The clip nearest the baby will remain in place anywhere up to 24 hours or so before the cord closes off completely, and the remnant drops away, leaving a sealed umbilicus or belly button.

RECOMMENDATIONS

- *Follow the midwife's instructions, and if any problems have arisen, let the professionals get on with their tasks.*
- *The remedy Secale cornutum 30 should be taken every hour for three doses to encourage uterine contraction.*
- *Rehydrate as soon as it is comfortable to drink water. Any persisting soreness should be treated with Bellis perennis 30 every 3hr.*
- *Arnica 200 should be taken every 12hr for six doses, to deal with the inevitable physical and mental strain.*

The baby

Instinct will take control for both mother and baby. The baby will either rest or seek the nipple, and the first feed is extremely important because it provides a special type of milk called colostrum, which aids digestion. Baby's breathing will be very smooth and natural, and is stimulated by the cooler temperature so will not need the much-heralded slap on the bottom. This is not a nice way to start life, and the midwife should be asked not to do this. Nowadays, most midwives wouldn't consider it, but some die-hards may habitually use the technique!

The First Feed

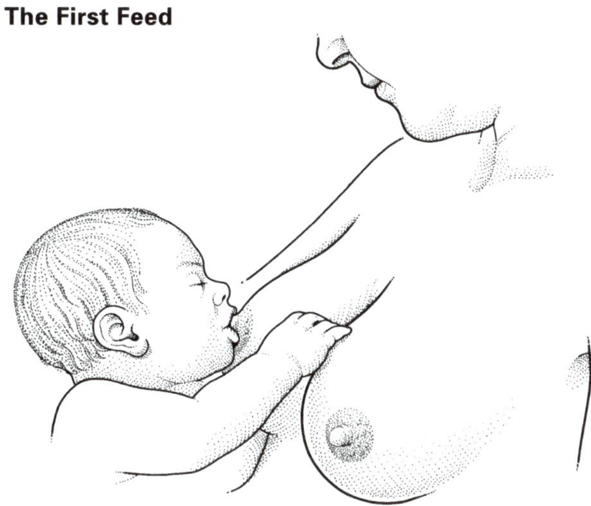

The baby should be allowed to suckle as soon as possible after birth.

RECOMMENDATIONS

- *Allow baby to suckle as soon as possible, but do not force the point.*
- *Refuse antibiotics in the baby's eyes and, in preference, when baby has finished his first feed, squeeze a few drops of breast milk into the eyes to cleanse them.*
- *Until all controversy has passed, do not give the vitamin-K injection. There may be some problems with this vitamin in injectable form, and it can promote a tendency to jaundice.*
- *The baby will have bonded with his mother well before delivery, and possibly even with the father through hearing his voice. Time spent together at this early stage is very worthwhile.*

PHYSICAL PROBLEMS AFTER DELIVERY

Most physical problems that might arise because of pregnancy are covered in this book under their own heading because they may occur at other times as well. For example, mastitis is more common through lactation, but because it can occur elsewhere it is covered in its own section. A few problems are specific to postpregnancy, and these are mentioned below.

Episiotomy

Occasionally, tears will occur in the perineum, simply because the baby is fractionally too large and the stretch of the vagina is too little. There is not much that can be done at the time, although the repair process afterwards can be hastened, and the appropriate techniques are mentioned below.

Iatrogenic—"caused by the physician" or, in this case, the midwife—episiotomy is sometimes required. The process involves injecting local anesthetic (although this is frequently not required) and a surgical incision is made back from the vagina towards the anus. It is a messy and bloody procedure that can be quite a shock if the delivering mother and attending partner are not aware of this. Done properly, the area is stitched up after the delivery, and does not cause complications. It is sometimes safer to have an iatrogenic episiotomy rather than allow nature to create its own tear, although a natural tear is thought to heal quicker. Should an episiotomy of any sort occur, the following recommendations should be followed after the delivery.

RECOMMENDATIONS

- *Splash alternate hot and cold water over the area for 2min four times a day until healing is complete.*
- *Apply Arnica or Calendula creams to the area and flush the vaginal vault with a dilute solution of Arnica or Calendula fluid extract.*
- *Use the homeopathic remedy Bellis perennis 6 (four pills four times a day) until healed. If the wound has not completely resolved, or discomfort or discharge prevail after five days, then bring the problem to the attention of your gynecologist, medical caregiver, and complementary health practitioner.*

Painful nipples

While this can happen through chafing at any stage of life, painful nipples are most commonly associated with suckling.

RECOMMENDATIONS

- *A tablespoon of olive oil with the juice of half a lemon can be applied four times a day (but wash off before feeding) at the first hint of nipple soreness. If the nipples have a tendency to crack, this should be done twice a day as a prophylactic.*
- *Cracked nipples will benefit from the homeopathic remedy Graphites or Silica, potency 6, taken every 2hr at the onset and reduced to every 4hr once healing has started.*
- *It may be necessary to express milk by hand or pump to give the nipple time to heal away from baby's mouth.*
- *Nipple guards (transparent, plastic covers) may be used until the problem has resolved.*

Abdominal muscles

More than anything, a pregnancy causes abdominal muscles to stretch. In an ideal situation, a pregnancy would be started with good abdominal musculature, because this will return much more easily to its prepregnancy state.

RECOMMENDATION

- *Exercise as frequently as possible through the early part of pregnancy, with gentle abdominal exercises, and return to these as soon as you are capable after the delivery.*

Engorged breasts

Engorged breasts occur for two reasons: because the production of milk exceeds the demand and use, and because of engorgement of the breast tissue by excess fluid, encouraged by the persisting high levels of female hormones.

RECOMMENDATIONS

- *Ensure that the baby gets all the milk he or she desires; any excess should be expectorated by hand or pump, and kept for up to 12hr in the fridge. This might allow Dad the opportunity of a feed and give Mom a rest.*

Engorged Breasts

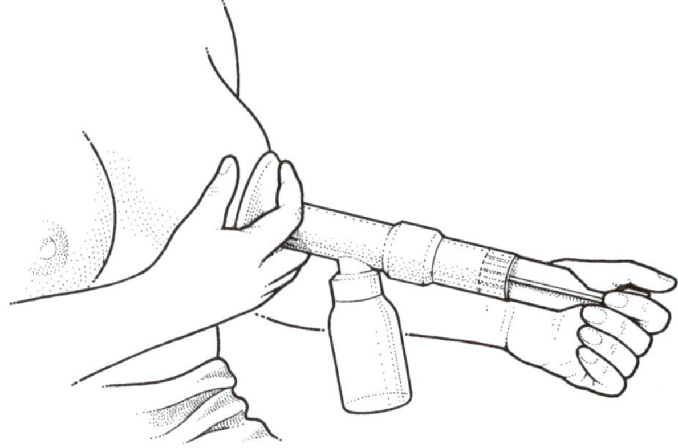

Expressing milk using a pump.

- *Soak the breasts in a hot bath, or apply hot flannels or heat pads. Occasionally, ice wrapped in a wash cloth may benefit if heat does not.*
- *Supplements may help breast-fluid retention, and can be taken without unduly influencing mother's milk. The mother should use the following: Vitamin B_6 (50mg), Evening Primrose Oil (1,000mg two or three times a day), and zinc (15mg before going to sleep).*
- *The homeopathic remedies Phytolacca 6 or Natrum muriaticum 6, taken every 15min may help.*
- *Acupuncture and herbal treatments may be of benefit in recurrent problems, and a practitioner could be consulted.*
- *The use of Tylenol, or Tylehol with Codeine is acceptable as a last resort, but should be taken after the baby's feed so that the body can metabolize it before the baby's next meal.*

Stretch marks

The increased size of the abdomen through pregnancy can stretch the skin and create a scar-like appearance.

RECOMMENDATIONS

- *Prevention is the best bet, and application of olive oil with lemon juice (half a lemon squeezed into a tablespoonful of pure virgin olive oil) may make a difference.*
- *Gentle, regular, massage may increase blood flow and recover the overstretched elastin fibers.*
- *Returning to abdominal exercises as soon as the baby is delivered and Mom is up to it will help.*
- *A Calendula- and Arnica-based cream (if a mix is not found, use one of each) applied four times a day.*
- *Vitamin-E oil may also benefit if applied regularly.*

Breast-feeding

Many women find it difficult or unpleasant to breast-feed, and I am reluctant to make the statement "breast is best" for the sake of those mothers who may take on an element of guilt or unworthiness. But . . .

Nature has been at breast-milk formulation for millions of years, as opposed to the pharmaceutical industry, who have done a good job over the last 40 years. Breast milk contains a variety of nutrition that is well balanced for a human baby. Formula preparations come close, but most use cow's milk as their matrix, which is harder to digest and, despite complex formulation, does not contain everything that breast milk does.

The breast milk also contains high levels of immunoglobulins, which are part of the baby's first line of defense against infection, and breast milk is not capable of creating an allergic or intolerant response. Eczema, asthma, and hay fever are less common in breast-fed babies, and studies have shown that there may be a slight increase in the breast-fed baby's IQ. Colic is often associated with an allergic response, and therefore breast-fed babies may suffer less.

Mother and baby may bond slightly more if the child is suckled, and breast-feeding is much more convenient as far as traveling and the need for equipment is concerned. Sterility is not a problem, of course. An even greater advantage for the mother may be that there is a decreased risk of breast cancer in mothers who continue to feed their babies by the breast longest.

Not enough breast milk

It is not unusual for a mother to find that her baby is still hungry after a feed. This is often because there is not enough milk. This may be due to dehydration or deficiencies in the mother's diet, or simply because of exhaustion.

RECOMMENDATIONS

- *Ensure a water intake of at least 12 ounces per foot of height, to be drunk throughout the day.*
- *Ensure a well-balanced diet, or discuss suitable supplements with a complementary medical practitioner.*
- *Try to get as much sleep as possible.*
- *The herb Galega officinalis may be used: a teaspoonful of fluid extract three times a day in milk sweetened with a teaspoonful of honey. (Galega may bring down sugar levels.)*

Weaning

There is no set time to wean (introducing foods other than breast milk), but a good guideline is when the child is not getting enough from mother's milk, which is recognized by the child failing to put on weight or remaining hungry after a feed.

The breasts will still produce milk and engorge if the milk is not expressed. This can make weaning an uncomfortable period.

RECOMMENDATIONS

- *If the choice is available, breast-feed for at least four months after the birth.*
- *Cut down by one feed per 24hr over one week*

- *See* **Engorged breasts.**
- *Try to obtain some jasmine: in fluid extract, essential oil, or even from the garden. Three drops of the extract or oil should be rubbed into the breasts, or the flowers should be steeped in water for 24hr and a teaspoonful drunk three times a day.*

THE FATHER AND SIBLINGS

Fathers will at some stage realize how useless they are during a delivery. Massaging and pushing a few acupressure points does not really seem like sharing the burden and the pain that the mother is suffering. Fathers, please do not be too disheartened. Every little bit helps, and "being there" means a lot.

Many deliveries nowadays have older siblings present, the benefit of which very much depends upon the character of that child. A timid or young child who may not understand the process should not be involved, because the apparent anguish of their mother will be very hard to comprehend. Remember that children are very self-centered, and a young child will assume that the mother is in pain because of something that he or she is doing.

However, it is important to introduce the newborn to a sibling as soon as possible. It is hard to conceive that love is not a finite emotion, and siblings may fear that the more people there are, the less Mom can love each one. Logic sticks its oar in and it is extremely important that a sibling feels that the baby is as much a part of them as it is a part of Mom and Dad. Bonding should actually start early on in pregnancy, and children should be introduced to the baby as soon as possible. There will inevitably be some jealousy, and it is important not to criticize an older sibling for this emotion.

RECOMMENDATIONS

- *Involve family members from the start of the pregnancy, and especially at the birth, where possible.*
- *Do not involve timid or young children, who may not understand what is going on.*
- *There is plenty of love to go around. Continue to distribute it evenly.*
- *Baby is going to take plenty of knocks in life, so do not be too critical of a sibling's apparent rough handling. Baby has just come through quite a trauma, and it can handle a push and a poke.*

AFTER DELIVERY

The first month or so after delivery is an exhausting time, both psychologically and physically. Although it sounds harsh, one must remember that pregnancy is in fact a parasitic infestation, and the baby will have drained a lot of nutrients from the mother while growing, and will continue to extract goodness through her breast milk. Mother, meantime, is having her sleep disturbed and is having to adjust to a completely new lifestyle. Whether it is the first or twenty-first child, the situation will be no different.

RECOMMENDATIONS

- *Talk to friends and relatives who have been through the situation before.*
- *Read as much about newborn babies as possible. You will discover that the experience is well-documented, and that anything you are going through has been gone through before, and there is someone out there with experience enough to help.*
- *High-dose multivitamins, preferably natural-food-state, along with a strict adherence to five portions of fresh, organic fruit and vegetables daily, should replenish the system within two weeks. Discussions with your complementary medical practitioner may be needed if recovery has not been achieved by then.*

POSTNATAL DEPRESSION

There is a marked drop in hormone levels as soon as the baby is delivered, and the subconscious will register this and notice that there is something "wrong." In fact, things are simply different, but the brain will translate this into an anxiety or a depression. There is also a certain sense of anticlimax when parents realize that the delivery was in fact the start of a lifelong commitment, and not just the end of a nine-month event. Tears will come easily; anger and irritation will be prominent, but often counteracted with bouts of great joy and the tears that also go with that. Dad will feel this as well, but most definitely will suffer the brunt of Mom's depression and mood swings.

All this should pass within a few days, and it is only if it does not pass, that a condition known as postnatal depression needs to be considered. Unrecognized or untreated, this condition may go on for years. I have had patients who have gone through several pregnancies and spent decades in a postnatal depression without realizing that this was the case.

RECOMMENDATIONS

- *Always feel free to speak to a counselor with regard to any unwanted emotional state, but especially so after a birth. Friends and family will try to say what they think you want to hear, and resolution of depression is much slower if dealt with that way.*
- *Never accept that "she should be over it by now." Chemical shifts may be permanent unless readjusted.*
- *Consult a homeopathic physician for a suitable remedy.*
- *Consider using Bach flower remedies, paying particular attention to Larch, Pine, Elm, Sweet Chestnut, Willow, Star of Bethlehem, Oak, and Crab Apple. These are all excellent for despondency or despair. If the emotion seems to be about responsibility, consider Chicory, Vervain, Vine, Beech, and Rock Water. Take a few minutes to read about these in a suitable booklet, and pick the most appropriate.*
- *Take a multimineral/vitamin supplement at twice the daily recommended dose because depression may be associated with deficiencies.*
- *Take phenylalanine (an amino acid) at three times the recommended dose on any proprietary package for three days, and reduce it to twice the dose for up to two weeks.*
- *Persistent depression should be dealt with by a complementary medical practitioner and counselor: definitely one who has had children, and preferably a woman.*
- *Artificial estrogen has been shown to be beneficial when taken sublingually. Before trying this, make sure that other avenues have been explored, and consider the use of natural estrogens first.*

Chapter 3

Infancy and Childhood

CHAPTER 3

INFANCY AND CHILDHOOD

All things being equal, children, and infants in particular, have remarkable powers of recovery if left to themselves. Medical intervention should be sought in only a few of the common childhood conditions. Conversely, a sick child can deteriorate very rapidly. The skill of good parenting is to know which conditions should be treated at home and when you should seek expert consultation.

I hope that all alternative practitioners will agree when I say that our training with regard to children is generally poor. I am very grateful that I spent large chunks of time, when I was in medical school and after, in pediatric wards. The principles with which a child is treated are much the same as those of an adult, but children are much more sensitive—especially to complementary medicines—and can go downhill at a rapid rate. Practitioners who have not had children themselves, and who lack teaching or experience in dealing with children, can underestimate the speed with which a child can develop a serious problem. This creates a paradox for parents. We would like our children brought up as drug-free as possible, but we need to be wary that an alternative practitioner may not have the experience to deal with our child. We wish to avoid medication, but do not wish to miss a diagnosis.

RECOMMENDATIONS

- *Do not hesitate to obtain the opinion of an experienced family practitioner or pediatrician if your child is not well.*
- *Once you have established that the child is not seriously ill, utilize alternative treatments for 24hr before subscribing to orthodox medicines.*

RECOGNIZING AN ILL INFANT

Parents, especially first-time parents, often have the preconception that symptoms represent illness and not repair. A whining infant may be uncomfortable but, as a general rule, is not ill. Infants with conditions that require treatment are generally:

- floppy
- sleeping a lot
- not interested in their food
- motionless
- persistent with their symptoms.

A child who may be screaming and fractious, interspersed with periods of normality, is generally likely to recover quickly. Fevers up to 100°F, blocked and running noses, coughs, and most rashes may seem aggressive and worry the parents, but if the child is up and about, rarely does this indicate a severe condition.

RECOMMENDATION

- *If you have any doubts whatsoever, obtain your doctor's opinion.*

GENERAL

ACCIDENTS

An accident, by definition, is supposedly out of our control and is an event that occurred purely by chance. This may not always be the case. An accident-prone child may have medical conditions that are treatable. For example, more road traffic accidents occur in the early hours of the morning and 2 hours after lunch. This strongly suggests that tiredness and hypoglycemia (low blood-sugar) are instrumental. Certain diets predispose to hypoglycemia, and accident-prone children may well have too much refined sugar in their diets.

Children who feel under pressure to perform may also overextend their capabilities and bodies to impress demanding friends and family, and this can be dealt with from a psychological angle.

Hyperactivity—usually diet-related—brings to mind the adage "act in haste, repent at leisure." This is often the case with injuries to overactive children. Poor concentration may result in accidents, and may be directly related to dietary deficiencies and food intolerances.

RECOMMENDATIONS

- *Reduce sugars and obtain dietetic advice from a nutritionist for any accident-prone child. Food intolerance/allergy testing may be required.*
- *If diet is not in question, seek the opinion of a child psychologist or art therapist.*
- *Suspect additive/preservative sensitivity leading to hyperactivity in accident-prone children.*

The treatment of individual accidents should be undertaken by reference to specific injuries elsewhere in the book.

ASPHYXIA

Asphyxia is the inability of an individual to breathe due to obstruction of the airways. *See* **Resuscitation of infant or child.** This is a procedure that all adults should learn.

BIRTH DEFECTS (CONGENITAL ANOMALIES)

The tragedy of the arrival of a child with an unexpected birth defect is indescribable. Fortunately, prenatal (during pregnancy) techniques using blood tests and ultrasound now make this unexpected surprise less frequent. However, the diagnostic abilities of modern science have simply shifted the dilemma to an earlier stage, and the problem still has to be faced.

Defects that are life-threatening may lead to a discussion on terminating the pregnancy (*see* **Termination of pregnancy**) or create a discussion on the difficulties (or blessings) of all that will arise.

There is little that complementary or alternative medicine can do to alter the physical structure of a child, but support can be given to the shocked psyches of parents, especially mothers. Holistic beliefs would hold that defects that were forged at conception would have been created by defective sperm or eggs, and avoidance of such defects is encouraged by being in good health before fertilization occurs. This is discussed in the section, **Physical preparation for conception**, in chapter 1. Defects formed after fertilization are due to the condition within the womb throughout the pregnancy, and are predominantly caused by what is taken in by the mother—specifically, ingested toxins, which include smoking, alcohol, drugs (both prescribed and recreational), insecticides, pesticides, and household-cleaning chemicals. Orthodox medicine, on the other hand, can now perform intricate operations while the fetus is developing within the uterus, and structural anomalies may be correctable.

Biochemical defects, neurological deficits, and problems associated with that part of the pregnancy or delivery after ultrasound has stopped being used, are unlikely to be detected until the infant is born.

Conditions such as Down syndrome (*see* opposite), spina bifida, and others are discussed in their own sections in this book. Chromosomal abnormalities that cause physical growth or mental retardation are so numerous (and thankfully rare) that they are beyond the scope of this book. However, the orthodox world often describes the symptoms and explains to the parent the percentage chance of progression to a variety of symptoms.

For example, the rare condition known as Angelman's syndrome (caused by a chromosomal defect) will cause epilepsy in 80 percent of sufferers in children around the age of two years.

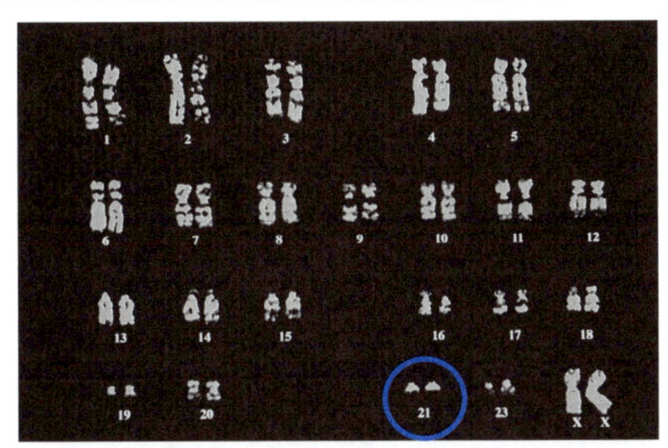

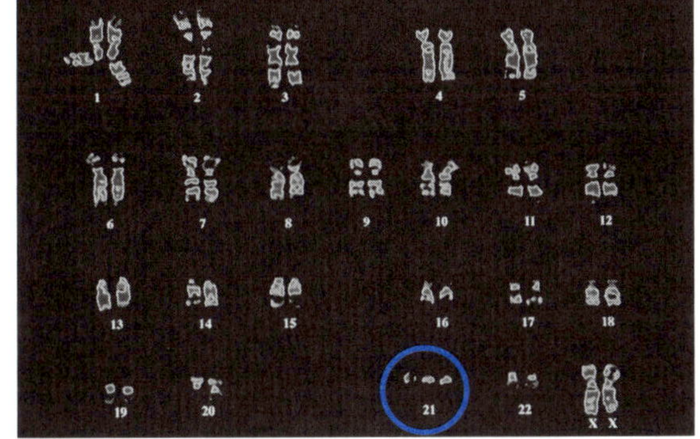

Down syndrome is caused by the presence of an extra chromosome (circled above).

Hyperactivity is another major symptom. The orthodox world offers no suggestions, but a more holistic view may surmise or hypothesize that as the child grows and receives more sensory input, the nervous system may become overloaded. If the child has a tendency to hyperactivity in any case, this may be the cause of epilepsy. Presumably, the 20 percent of children who do not have fits have some neurochemical mechanism that suppresses this hyperactivity. No studies can prove this suggestion, but perhaps homeopathy, herbal medicine, and supplemental medicine, to encourage the production of serotonin, dopamine, and other brain-calming chemicals may benefit the child and keep him or her from having fits.

The Eastern philosophies, particularly the Hindu religion, consider the concept of karma. It may be necessary for an individual to suffer neurological or structural handicaps in order to learn lessons that bring them closer to their God. In the same way that a spontaneous miscarriage may be a blessing conferred by a spirit who needed only a short incarnation, a handicapped child may teach parents many emotional lessons, from dealing with shock, disappointment, anger, and frustration to a deeper level of understanding, responsibility and—most surprisingly—joy. So often, the more severe the handicap, the more the individual is surprisingly free of negative emotions such as anger, hatred, or guilt. It may take many lifetimes to achieve the state of joy and innocence that the mentally handicapped can take as a norm.

RECOMMENDATIONS

- *Always undergo the safe investigations of pregnancy. Ultrasound and blood tests are essential, because forewarned is forearmed.*
- *Consult a professional with experience in dealing with parents of congenitally compromised children. There is so much support, love, and expertise out there that this battle need not be fought alone.*
- *Consult with an experienced complementary medical practitioner to ensure that nutrition during pregnancy and the nutrition of the infant are at an optimum, because many conditions are exacerbated by deficiency or toxicity.*
- *Homeopathic remedies both for the parents and the child can have a profound effect on psychological as well as physical problems.*
- *Spend time with a spiritual or religious teacher, and remember to glean the most from the difficulties that are associated with a child with birth defects. Lessons come in many guises.*
- *Check for pesticides and other toxins in the bloodstream of both parents to determine whether this may have been the cause of a defect that might affect future pregnancies.*

CHICKENPOX

Chickenpox is created by a member of the herpes viral family known as *varicella*. It is a self-limiting disorder (meaning that it will clear itself up without medical intervention), and shows itself as a red rash with characteristic, clear or yellow-fluid-filled pimples. There is usually an associated mild fever, general malaise, and loss of appetite, but the worst symptoms are generally the irritation and itch.

The holistic consensus of opinion is that chickenpox, along with measles and possibly mumps, is a useful childhood infection triggering responses in the immune system that help to fight more serious infections at a later stage.

The incubation period (the time when someone is infectious) is generally thought to be one week prior to the arrival of the rash and for the first five days thereafter.

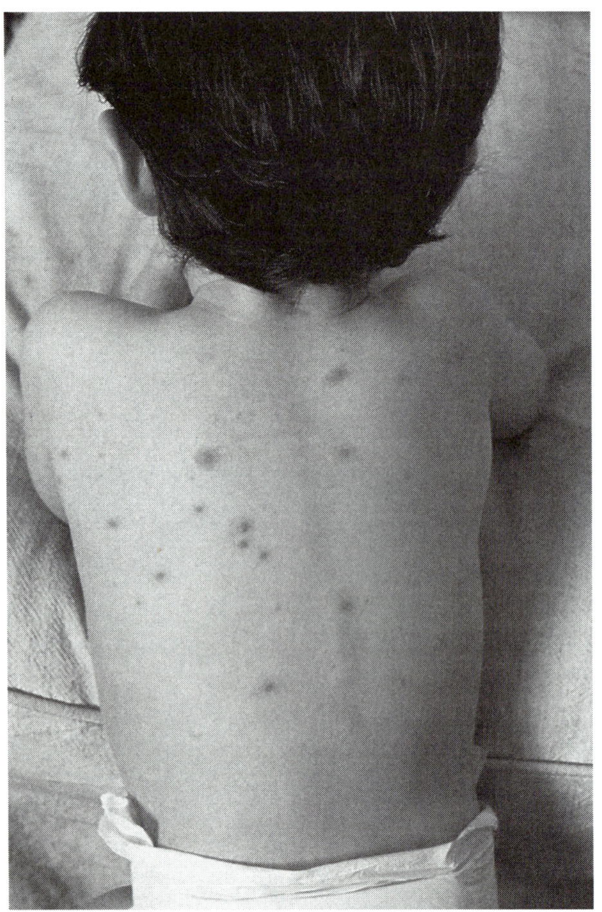

Chickenpox on the back of a two-year-old child.

RECOMMENDATIONS

- *If in doubt about the diagnosis, or if the pimples and rash are very aggressive or persistent, contact your complementary medical practitioner or doctor for advice. Unfortunately, the orthodox world has little to offer other than antihistamine-like topical applications.*
- *Add one tablespoon of baking soda to 16 ounces of water and apply with a silk material to the irritated areas. You may concentrate this, if there is no response, to as much as three tablespoons per 16 ounces of water, but ensure that there is no stinging effect by trying it out on any small cut or scratch you may have before applying it to a child. If the child is old enough to talk, you can apply it directly and ask!*
- *Consider the homeopathic remedies Rhus toxicodendron or Pulsatilla. A simple technique is to try first one and then the other (potency 6 every 2hr) until improved, and then reduce to every 4hr until the rash goes.*
- *If a lesion becomes infected, apply Arnica, Calendula, or Hypericum cream.*
- *A cool bath with ten tablespoons of baking soda can be relieving.*
- *The following supplements can be administered per foot of height: Beta-carotene (1mg), vitamin C (500mg in divided doses throughout the day), and zinc (2.5mg before bed).*
- *Antihistamine compounds can be used to reduce the itch if complementary techniques are not beneficial.*
- *Severe cases should be dealt with by a doctor or specialist in complementary medicine who has experience of this condition.*
- *See* **Herpes**.

COLDS

A cold, supposedly so named because of the incorrect assumption that they occur because of cold weather or being cold, is in fact an infection caused by any of around 120 viruses known as rhinoviruses (after the Latin *rhinus* for nose).

There is, in fact, no such thing as a cold; it is a collection of symptoms: headache, sinus pain, running nose, blocked nose or sore nose, sore throat, cough, aching, general lethargy, and tiredness. The cold is therefore a combination of a number of these symptoms.

We are further away from finding a cure for the common cold than we are for cancer, and I suspect that this will continue to be the way because the cold viruses mutate and change, and our immune systems are not capable of keeping up with the speed of alteration, so we cannot fight these viruses easily. Interestingly, as we get older our colds become less frequent as we build up our immunity to the 120 rhinoviruses.

Colds rarely need medical intervention, although advice from a homeopath as to the correct remedy and the attention of your doctor for too frequent or recurrent colds (to rule out anything underlying or nasty) may be required.

Colds are often the body's method of triggering its seasonal defense mechanism, and we should all expect and "enjoy" a cold at the start of winter and at the arrival of spring.

RECOMMENDATIONS

- *Review from your favorite homeopathic manual the following common homeopathic remedies: Allium cepa, Gelsemium, Bryonia, Pulsatilla, Dulcamara, and Mercurius. Once the correct remedy is selected, use potency 6 every 2hr.*
- *Consider the use of high doses of vitamin C, vitamin A, bioflavonoids, zinc, and magnesium at doses twice those recommended on the packaging and taken with food. Zinc should be taken at a dosage of 5mg per foot of height before bed.*
- *The herb Echinacea can be taken in doses recommended on packaging.*
- *Ginger drinks (with honey and lemon) made from fresh gingerroot (half-inch/1cm chopped up) and hot water should be drunk and the steam inhaled.*
- *Avoid heavy exercise. The concept of sweating out a cold is not correct.*
- *Ensure good hydration by drinking twice as much water as you normally do. The mucus and sweat will double your insensible water loss.*
- *Good old chicken-broth soup replenishes fluids and provides protein for repair. The chicken cartilage may actually have an antiviral effect as well.*
- *"Starve a fever and feed a cold" is an accurate adage and, provided your cravings are healthy, go with them.*
- *Nasal washing with mild salt-water solutions can speed up the process of decongestion and the removal of the virus.*
- *Do not consider the use of decongestants, either topically sniffed or taken orally, because this will stop the immune system's destruction of the virus and increase the chances of more serious infections, such as middle-ear infections, labarynthitis, sinusitis, and even meningitis.*

COMPUTERS AND VISUAL DISPLAY UNITS (VDUs)

With the advent of computers reaching every child, either in the home or at school, we must be wary of problems that may be associated with them and are, as yet, not well documented.

Like televisions, computers emit a radiation that may be harmful. The intensity of the emotions and the time spent at the computer are known to induce problems with eyesight, headaches, and psychological symptoms such as depression, lack of concentration, and insomnia.

The radiation from computers is emitted from all around the machine, not just the screen. The use of a protective shield may be beneficial to the user, but of no consequence to those sitting close by.

RECOMMENDATIONS

- *Ensure that the position of the screen is suitably set in relation to the chair in which you sit, to avoid structural and postural problems.*
- *Ensure that natural light hits the eyes by placing the computer with its back toward the windows.*
- *Use a screen that cuts down the computer's emissions.*
- *Try to use the computer only in short bursts of up to half an hour, with at least a 10–15min break before returning.*
- *Place a screen between yourself and the back of any other computer in your proximity.*
- *Allow as much distance between the computer and yourself as your vision will comfortably allow.*
- *Persistent users of computers should take suitable antioxidant supplements daily to counteract the mild, free-radical production that radiation will create.*
- *See* **Radiation**.

Child with Down syndrome.

DOWN SYNDROME

Down syndrome is named after a physician in the 19th century who recognized a syndrome of mental retardation, atypical faces, and various other physical changes, including a single palmar crease. Children with Down syndrome can resemble the Mongol race, thus the outdated term Mongolism.

This genetic condition is caused by an extra gene being present from conception. A medical term for Down syndrome is, therefore, Trisomy (three) 21, because it is this 21st chromosome that is trebled (*see* page 57).

A pregnant woman, especially if over the age of 35, will be offered or actively encouraged to have certain tests performed to rule out abnormalities, predominantly Down syndrome. These tests include a blood test known as the "Triple Test," which is checking for particular proteins in the bloodstream that, if found, can give strong evidence that further investigation is required. The Triple Test is not, by any means, definitive in itself. Further investigations include ultrasound where, specifically, a pad of fat is sought on the back of the embryo's neck. More invasive procedures such as amniocentesis (where a needle takes a small sample of the fluid surrounding the baby) or chorionic villus sampling (a similar procedure taking some cells from the baby's side of the placenta) are accurate, but carry up to a 2 percent risk of introducing infection or causing abortion. It is of paramount importance for parents to establish whether or not they would seek the termination of a Down pregnancy. The risks of the test procedures and the negative attitude of many towards Down babies makes these tests unnecessary intrusions if parents would not choose to abort.

I have had the privilege of looking after many Down children through my years of practice. While different, Down children are generally happy and loving participants of any family unit. Many have IQs capable of functioning in society and few have aggressive or unpleasant tendencies. I wish I could say the same for all "normal" children.

There is increasing evidence that Down children are not fatalistically destined to a poor-quality life by their gene malformation. Nutritional and dietetic supplements, alongside naturopathic medicine—both herbal and homeopathic—may make a profound difference on both cognitive and physical development.

What seem to have been overlooked for decades are the subtle biochemical and metabolic changes that may lead to ill health, poor mental and physical abilities, and growth. Now, researchers are finding that Down individuals have specific deficiencies and certain enzymes that make them less capable of dealing with compounds that we may look upon as mild toxins or even as nutrients.

RECOMMENDATIONS

- *Once a pregnancy is recognized, establish whether a termination would be your preferred choice should your baby have Down syndrome. If not, then avoid the investigations.*
- *All Down children should be under the care of a pediatrician specializing in this condition. Surgical or orthodox drug intervention may be necessary early on because defects in the heart, lungs, and other organs may need to be corrected.*
- *Contact your local Down Syndrome Association and obtain more information from, probably, the world's leading alternative-thinking Down syndrome specialist: Dr. Jack Warner, The Warner House, 1023 East Chapman Ave, Fullerton, CA 92631. Tel: (714) 441-2600.*
- *Establish as soon as possible, by working with a complementary medical practitioner with expertise in this field, the functioning of the thyroid and thymus.*
- *Establish through a complementary medical practitioner the levels of stomach acid and digestive enzymes.*
- *Establish any food allergies. Pay special attention to gluten found in wheat, cow's products, and specifically lactose (milk sugar).*
- *Isolate and replenish any deficiencies, paying special attention to minerals (including zinc) and amino acids.*
- *Avoid fluoridated water, smoked foods, smoke from cigarettes, algae supplements, and Ginkgo biloba. These compounds affect the Down genetics in a variety of ways, but specifically by suppressing the thyroid and the body's defense systems.*
- *Cranial osteopathy, osteopathy, physiotherapy, and, when the child is old enough, the Alexander technique, polarity therapy, and yoga will all be markedly beneficial, both physically and mentally.*
- *A constitutional homeopathic remedy should be chosen and changed as the child develops through consultation with a homeopath. The homeopathic remedies of Thymus and Thyroidinium, both at potency 3 or 6 given daily in conjunction with a constitutional remedy, should prove to be highly beneficial.*

DREAMS AND NIGHTMARES

Dreams and nightmares occur at all ages but I have put it in the "Childhood" chapter because of the frequency with which a child will bring a nightmare to the attention of its parents. They can be particularly disturbing and interfere with sleep patterns, but, to an infant or young child, this may not be so damaging, because sleep will be caught up. For adults, whose life structure may not allow them to sleep as much or as long as they would like, frequently disturbing dreams or nightmares may be a health hazard.

Dreams, pleasant or otherwise, are neurological impulses that pass into the conscious center from the sensory receptor areas of the brain. The speed with which the brain can transmit these impulses is very rapid and an epic dream lasting several hours may actually be imprinted through the conscious centers within seconds.

A dream may be the brain's attempt at reflecting upon an event or trauma, and may be used by the subconscious to help sort out problems.

A frightening movie before bed may create images as the brain tries to sort out whether it should be concerned at the recently raised levels of "fear chemicals" such as adrenaline.

Past-life therapists may consider dreams to be carried over, and their relevance may be of great import in certain therapeutic techniques. Although much study has been made of dreams, their significance is still poorly understood, both from an orthodox scientific or an Eastern philosophical point of view. From a health stance, their only relevance is if they are disturbing sleep.

The contents of a dream do not necessarily reflect an underlying angst. It is hypothesized, for example, that dreaming of death will represent a marriage or birth. These associations are not strictly founded on any scientific studies, but on the anecdotal evidence of people who have studied dreams for years. It is more likely that the brain will try to create either an answer or an escape for the consciousness. Ayurvedic physicians from India would consider the dream from the point of view of its *dosha–vata* (space and air), *pitta* (fire) and *kapha* (earth and water): a pitta nightmare may often be violent or heat-filled; tidal waves or drowning may represent excess kapha; and flying may be a vata excess. A tidal wave may also represent being overwhelmed by events beyond the individual's control, and may give a pointer to the area of the psyche that needs to be confronted.

RECOMMENDATIONS

- *Review your life structure and change stress patterns.*
- *Counseling by a psychotherapist with an interest in the relevance of dreams may be of great use if no obvious anxiety is apparent.*
- *Avoid stimulating foods or compounds that affect the nervous system, for at least 6hr before going to sleep. These include caffeine, alcohol, cigarettes, and other drugs. Foods containing amines, such as chocolate and cheese, are also culprits.*
- *The flower remedy Rockrose and good old Rescue Remedy are both useful if taken 1hr before bed-time.*
- *There are hundreds of homeopathic remedies associated with scores of different dream/ nightmare subjects. The best remedy is chosen by reference to a homeopathic Materia Medica or a homeopathic prescriber. The remedies Aconite, Arsenicum, Belladonna, and Nux vomica should all be reviewed for children who are having nightmares. Potency 30 before bed for five nights should do the trick. Please refer to your preferred homeopathic manual for the best remedy.*

DYSLEXIA

Dyslexia is an impairment of an individual who once knew or would be expected to know how to read or understand letters and/or numbers. A normal IQ differentiates this difficulty from those who have, say, brain damage or a low IQ.

Dyslexia is commonly overlooked. It ranges from a mild inability to differentiate between, say, the letters "p" and "q", or the numbers 6 and 9, to the transgressional dyslexia between the letter E and 3. Speech is normal, but written words or letters may be transposed.

In itself, dyslexia is not necessarily a great problem, but its social consequences—especially if not detected—can be devastating. A child may find himself/herself ridiculed in class and create an abhorrence of letters and numbers. This not only affects the child's academic standards, but can lead to social withdrawal and difficulties in making friends. Children who are ridiculed in class may choose not to participate in sports for fear of more humiliation. Therefore, early motor skills may be denied, adding to a further sense of inadequacy.

Any parent who finds their child overly shy, withdrawn, reluctant to participate in group activities, fearful of school, or avoiding books and numbers should immediately consider dyslexia. The human being is remarkably adaptable, and will often find defense measures—such as becoming unruly at school—a useful tool in avoiding facing up to dyslexia. Because of this, dyslexia may not be discovered until a later age, possibly even into adulthood. I mention this because it is never too late to use the available treatments with great success.

RECOMMENDATIONS

- *Discuss the matter with the child's teacher or school superintendent, who should have good knowledge of this condition.*
- *There is strong evidence that certain deficiencies may cause or enhance dyslexia. Discuss with a nutritionist any suitable dietetic changes and supplements: use more zinc, lecithin, and amino acids, which are used in neurotransmission; above all, beware of dehydration.*
- *There are well-established remedial techniques and, in severe cases, special schooling that will enable a dyslexic to function perfectly normally in society.*
- *Any child who avoids letters and numbers and is particularly shy, antisocial, or falling behind in school should be investigated for dyslexia. Any association of these characteristics with clumsiness should also be investigated.*
- *Referral through your doctor or a local dyslexia organization to a specialist psychologist in this area is a prerequisite.*
- *Specialized training programs, remedial exercises, and training techniques can be practiced in special units, and also taught to parents to perform at home.*
- *Homeopathic remedies, chosen according to the constitution of the child, are potentially beneficial.*

FALLS

A fall can occur at any age, of course, but I have chosen to mention it in the childhood chapter because persistent or frequent falls may be due to deeper problems of lack of concentration, poor coordination, and a general tendency to be accident prone (*see* **Accidents**).

A fall may result in a bruise, fracture or emotional shock, all of which may be associated with blood loss and internal organ damage. Each of these areas needs to be reviewed in the specific section in this book.

Conditions such as diabetes, hypoglycemia and the use of drugs (prescribed or otherwise) may be a reason for an individual to fall.

RECOMMENDATIONS

- *Any obvious injury, loss of consciousness, or change in character of an individual who has fallen needs to be reviewed by a doctor.*
- *Any injury can be treated with the homeopathic remedy Arnica, at potencies 6–12, every 2hr.*
- *An osteopathic opinion should be obtained following any serious fall, because other parts of the body may take the strain off an injured part, leading to problems at a later date.*

FEVER

Fever in a child requires a little more attention than it does in an adult, because a persisting or very high fever may cause febrile convulsions (*see* **Convulsions**). Normal body temperature for all ages is around 97.6°F.

Understanding the cause of a fever is a prerequisite to its treatment, but you must remember that fever is a friend. Most bacteria and viruses are inhibited by high temperatures: certain defensive chemical reactions occur in the body at a faster rate in the presence of fever, and it is established that the chemicals produced create the fever. Suppressing a fever from within is therefore unwise, and you should only attempt to keep the body cool externally without stopping the actual chemical reaction, as this is less likely to hamper the immune system.

Fever may be an early warning for a serious, underlying infection. Children old enough to express themselves may give some clues, but infants with a persisting high fever need to be assessed by a physician.

RECOMMENDATIONS

- *Any persisting, recurrent, or very high fever should warrant a medical opinion. Specific treatment against, say, an infection should be initiated either from a complementary or orthodox point of view.*
- *Keep the child in light cotton if sweating or remove clothing if dry.*
- *Apply cold compresses to the neck, stomach, and ankles.*
- *It is not advisable to use herbal remedies in children unless you are absolutely certain of their strength and quality. Orthodox preparations such as Tylenol for children should be employed if the temperature rises above 101°F. By this stage, however, medical advice should have been sought.*
- *Remember that a fever is generally a friend, whether it is curing or warning, and should be treated as such.*
- *Homeopathic treatment needs to be aimed at the symptoms, and reference to your preferred homeopathic manual is required. Pay specific attention to the remedies Aconite, Arsenicum, Belladonna, Gelsemium, and Mercurius.*

Rheumatic fever

Rheumatic fever is characterized by pains in the joints, fever, and general malaise following a streptococcal infection, usually of the throat. The pains in the joints occur because of a reaction (antigen-complex reaction) between the bacteria and the body's defense mechanism.

The body recognizes the infection and sends out antibodies to attack the bacteria (the antigen), and in some cases this triggers an inflammatory response that affects the joints and frequently the heart valves. The complexes can affect the delicate tissues of the kidney, and a sore throat with associated kidney symptoms (*see* **Sore throats**) must be treated as urgent.

The orthodox approach is to use antibiotics at the first sign of a streptococcal sore throat, but alternative measures initially may be just as effective. If heart or kidney effects are suspected (associated chest pains, irregular heartbeats or heart sounds) then treatment must be considered as urgent. Prolonged use of penicillin is still considered by many orthodox practitioners to protect against reinfection of damaged heart valves. Antibiotics will also be encouraged if any operative procedure, including dental work, is to be performed.

RECOMMENDATIONS

- *Sore throats—and streptococcal sore throats in particular—should not be taken lightly, and complementary medical treatment should be initiated swiftly. See* **Sore throats**.
- *If rheumatic fever is confirmed, consult a homeopathic practitioner, but initiate the use of the remedy Streptococcin 30 every 4hr.*
- *Commence the child on the following supplements in divided doses throughout the day: vitamin A (1,000iu per foot of height) or beta-carotene (2mg per foot of height); vitamin C (500mg per foot of height); vitamin E (150iu per foot of height); and zinc (5mg per foot of height before bed).*
- *Use Echinacea (dried root) 200mg per foot of height. Please note that dry powdered extract is not the same as dried root and should be given at quarter the dose.*
- *Ensure good hydration, especially if there is any kidney involvement.*
- *At any suggestion of chronic damage to the heart valves (this is diagnosed by a doctor), seek advice from a complementary medical practitioner with regard to homeopathic or herbal cover through adolescence as an alternative to*

daily use of penicillin. More than two attacks, despite alternative or complementary treatment, warrants the use of prophylactic antibiotics to protect against serious damage. Consult a complementary specialist to get advice concerning the side effects of these drugs (see **Antibiotics***).*

Scarlet fever

Scarlet fever is so called because of the bright-red appearance of an individual with a fever. This is caused by a streptococcal infection, and is often associated with a sore throat. As the risk of this condition developing into rheumatic fever is slight, but nevertheless real, my recommendations are found under the section on rheumatic fever.

GROWTH

DELAYED GROWTH

Delayed growth in a child can occur at any stage and is defined by falling below a set height or weight, as shown in the charts (overleaf).

It is very important to note that a child's size may be dependent upon their genetics, inherited from their parents. A child with small or light parents may not necessarily be underdeveloped, and it is important for each individual to be assessed from this point of view. Growth is governed by good nutritional input and also by a variety of hormones. Specifically, growth hormone (from the pituitary gland), thyroxine, and insulin levels must all be in balance. Malabsorption or malnutrition will deprive the child of proteins, vitamins, minerals, and trace elements, all of which are essential to correct growth.

RECOMMENDATIONS

- *If worried about developmental failure, or if your child does not correspond to the charts, then please consult your doctor.*
- *Once serious underlying conditions such as pituitary problems, diabetes, and thyroid or malabsorption problems have been ruled out, consider the advice of a nutritionist.*
- *The homeopathic remedy Silica, potency 30 twice a day for three weeks (or a higher potency as prescribed by a homeopath), encourages absorption, and therefore growth, in cases of poor nutritional intake.*

GROWING PAINS

This nonmedical term has crept into use because of its accuracy in describing the symptoms. Pains are constantly felt by children as their muscles and ligaments stretch in response to the growth of their bones. Growing pains may also be related directly to muscular cramps, and some adjustment of dietetics, hydration, and supplementation generally deals with the problem.

Pain may be located and persistent at the part of the bone that actually grows. This is usually at either end of the bones. It is rare for these pains to be indicative of anything serious, although severe or persistent pain should be reviewed.

Children who grow too rapidly are prone to growing pains, and a markedly rapid growth may indicate underlying hormonal dysfunction that will need to be reviewed by a physician or pediatrician.

RECOMMENDATIONS

- *Massage, heat, or ice (depending on which soothes) and the application of Arnica cream should be relieving.*
- *Increase the calcium and magnesium intake through sesame seeds, nuts, vegetables, fish, and chicken, or supplement with a suitable calcium/magnesium compound supplying the recommended daily allowance (RDA).*
- *Depending on the symptoms and their site, a homeopathic remedy should be chosen from your preferred manual or via a homeopath.*

Growth Assessment

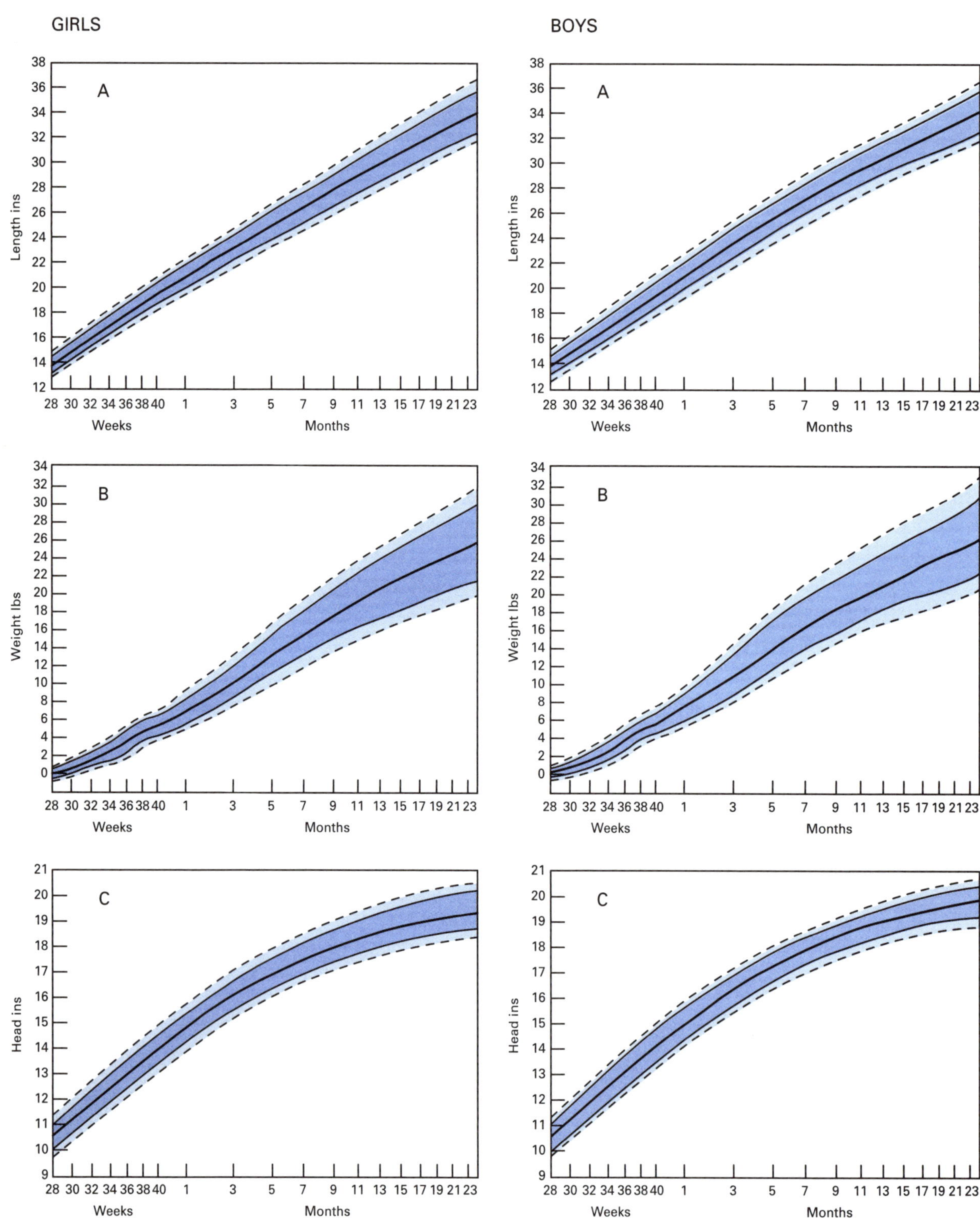

The charts show the ideal length (A), weight (B), and head size (C) of girls and boys over the first two years.

- *Persistent discomfort should be reviewed by an osteopath, and brought to the attention of a doctor only if osteopathic care and advice does not help.*

HYPERACTIVITY AND ATTENTION DEFICIT DISORDER (ADD)

I am sure that parents have noticed hyperactivity in their children ever since the Homo Sapiens erected onto two legs. Parents today will notice periods where their children are more active or overexcited than at other times. Learning appropriate responses takes time, and is the cause of the "terrible twos."

I believe that we must be careful not to label a child overactive when the problem may be parental intolerance. Overactivity must be disruptive, persistent, and preferably recognized by a third party such as a teacher. There is a strong correlation, especially in America, between hyperactivity and attention-deficit disorder (ADD). Attention-deficit disorder may be present without hyperactivity, and is characterized by a short attention span, poor concentration, an inability to finish projects, and an ease of distraction. It is important to differentiate between this and the absences seen in petit mal epilepsy (*see* **Epilepsy**).

It is worth noting that both hyperactivity and ADD may continue beyond childhood, and when it does so it is termed "residual attention-deficit disorder." The causes are much the same, and are well researched. It is thought to affect approximately 3 percent of the population, although—and this is why it is very important to establish diagnosis—some studies have suggested hyperactivity in up to 20 percent of the population.

Food additives—of which, believe it or not, there are over 5,000 in the U.S.A.—have been clearly cited as a cause for these syndromes. It is important to understand that the term additives includes not just colorings, but also thickeners, preservatives, flavorings, and many others. Artificial "antioxidants" are being confused by the public as being healthy additives, because antioxidants have come to prominence in dealing with cardiovascular and cancer problems. Please do not be fooled. Individuals buying foods primarily from supermarkets may be ingesting up to 15g of additives per day.

Low blood-sugar (hypoglycemia) is a major contributing factor to hyperactivity and ADD, predominantly caused by taking in refined (white) sugars that are absorbed rapidly, and which cause a large insulin response that in turn lowers the blood-sugar level. Any hyperactive child who behaves in such a way an hour or so after eating is probably taking in too many carbohydrates.

Food allergies are a major consideration and an individual correlation between poor behavior and specific foods can be made by keeping a list, noting any changes with particular foods.

Lead poisoning has been shown to be responsible for bad behavior, and therefore this and other metal or environmental toxins should be considered as possible causes of ADD.

RECOMMENDATIONS

- *Discuss the matter of a hyperactive or suspected ADD child with teachers, a counselor experienced in these matters, or a local group.*
- *Remove refined carbohydrates (especially white sugar) and all processed foods from the diet.*
- *Consider food-allergy testing, or keep a very clear diary of foods eaten and the child's behavior.*
- *Consider the possibility of nutritional deficiencies. It is possible that deficiencies in certain amino acids (tyrosine, tryptophan, or phenylalanine), as well as a lack of certain minerals such as zinc or iron, may all be contributing factors, if not the cause.*
- *Consider the possibility of metal poisoning, or other toxins such as pesticides.*
- *Consider art therapy if the problem persists, and assessment through an art therapist who specializes in problems with children.*

- *A medical opinion may be necessary if none of the above considerations work but, because orthodox medicine is pharmaceutically oriented, a first-line treatment may be a drug such as methylphenidate hydrochloride, known as Ritalin. This option should be used as a last resort. Ritalin might, although I have no evidence to support this, go on to show itself as an addictive drug that requires persistent use. If so, in later life it could lead to a dependency on tranquilizers.*

JAUNDICE OF THE NEWBORN

See **Jaundice** in chapter 5.

Jaundice of the newborn is frequently seen within the first five days of life. It usually clears within the first two weeks, and is due to the incomplete development of a chemical pathway within liver cells, which results in a decreased ability to bind bilirubin (one of the breakdown products of blood cells) with a particular acid. Normally, once this binding has taken place, the waste products are passed into the gall bladder and expelled into the bile, which gives the stool its normal brown color. If this process does not take place, the amount of bilirubin rises and flows back into the bloodstream, is deposited around the system, and causes the yellow discoloration of the skin.

The condition is usually mild and self-limiting without any unpleasant symptoms for the infant, but occasionally the problem can persist. Premature infants may be more prone to a longer-lasting, more severe deposition of bilirubin, which can lead to a condition known as kernicterus. This condition can result in severe neurological deficit or even death, caused by degeneration of the nerve cells in the brain due to irritation by the bilirubin.

Another serious condition that causes jaundice in the newborn is erythroblastosis fetalis. This occurs when the blood of the infant contains an antibody from its mother that attacks the infant's own red blood cells.

RECOMMENDATIONS

- *A jaundiced infant is usually spotted before he/she leaves hospital. For those who develop jaundice after they arrive home or after home deliveries, it is imperative that a pediatrician is advised of the situation.*
- *Treatment is unnecessary unless the condition is serious, in which case an experienced, medically-trained homeopath should be consulted.*
- *A child who is born yellow or jaundiced may have been suffering with blood incompatibility. The pediatrician at the hospital will diagnose this through a blood test. Treatment is rarely necessary, but the child will be kept in hospital and a blood transfusion may be required.*
- *Ensure a full discussion with the pediatrician before a subsequent pregnancy is undertaken.*
- *The infant should be given the homeopathic remedies Lycopodium 30 and Ferrum metallicum 30 in fluid form alternately every 3hr through the initial illness and twice a day for two weeks after a recovery is made.*
- *A healer may help speed up the process of a return to normality.*

ABO and Rhesus-blood incompatibility

A child may be born jaundiced and the parents may be told that the child and mother have incompatible blood types. This is caused by two conditions known as ABO and Rhesus incompatibility; it is triggered when the baby's blood cells are different from those of its mother's womb, and some of the baby's blood cells escape through the placenta into the mother's bloodstream. The mother's defense mechanism recognizes this as a foreign body and forms antibodies against it. These pass back through the placenta and attack the baby's blood cells. Interestingly, the effect is not a big problem in the first child, but any subsequent baby with a blood group foreign to its mother will find that it enters the womb of an

Blood-Group Compatibility

	A	B	AB	O
A	✓	✗	✗	✓
B	✗	✓	✗	✓
AB	✓	✓	✓	✓
O	✗	✗	✗	✓

individual whose immune system is primed to attack its red blood cells. This is why it is important to know the blood group of a mother.

Most people know about the blood groups A, B, and O. Making a complicated situation simpler, if you are blood group A, you will have antibodies to blood group B, and vice versa. If you are blood group O, you are said to be a universal donor, meaning that you can give your blood to anyone. Group O does have antibodies to both A and B, but the amount given to someone in a transfusion is minimal. There is another group, AB. People who are blood group AB are universal recipients because they have no antibodies to either group A or group B.

To make it even more complicated, there is another major, red blood-cell protein known as Rhesus factor. You either have this (Rhesus positive) or you do not (Rhesus negative). If a baby has Rhesus factor but the mother does not, the mother will form antibodies against this blood-cell protein and, as I have mentioned above, will attack it. Rhesus incompatibility is a more common finding and is treated by giving the mother a large injection of Rhesus protein after the infant has been born. The mother's antibodies attack the protein and effectively get "mopped up." This injection, known as antiserum D, may be given prior to or early on in subsequent pregnancies in an attempt to protect the unborn infant. It is generally a successful technique, although problems may arise.

RECOMMENDATION

- *Please discuss the matter of antiserum D with your midwives and pediatrician. There is some concern that the manufacturing process does not guarantee injections free of infections such as the "mad cow disease" organism, HIV, or hepatitis. This association has only recently been considered, but may become more prominent in the near future.*

MEASLES

Measles is a highly contagious disease, typified by fever and a red rash with raised spots. Measles very often causes a cough, runny nose, lethargy, and tiredness, and—depending on the areas that the virus attacks—conjunctivitis and irritation in and around the genitals. Typically, spots are seen in the mouth; these are known as Koplik's spots, which usually turn up on day two or three of the infection. The rash usually appears on the fourth

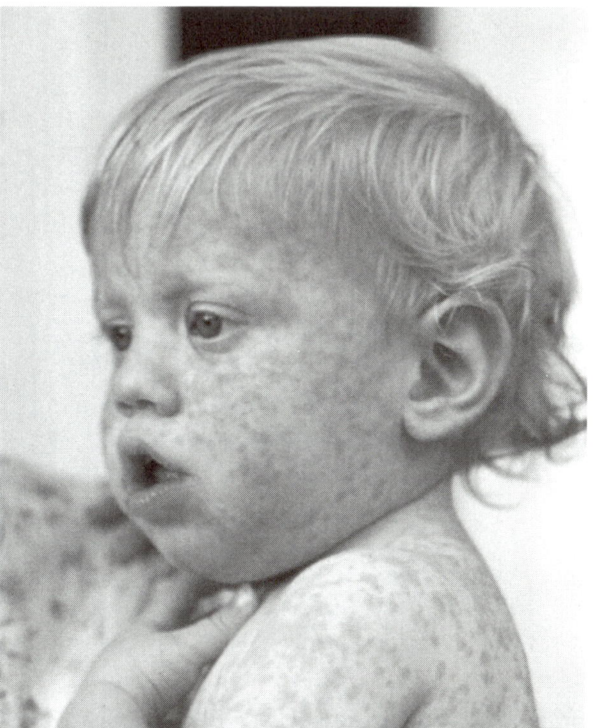

The red rash and raised spots symptomatic of measles are clearly visible.

day, often starting on the neck and spreading to other areas. The rash may persist for two to four days.

In itself, measles is rarely a serious condition, although children who are immunosuppressed may find the condition fatal due to the secondary conditions and complications. Undernourished children, or those with underlying immune weakness, may contract bronchitis, pneumonia, otitis media, and a rare form of encephalitis (inflammation of the brain). It is these serious conditions that have encouraged the Western world to put a strong emphasis on vaccination programs.

At this time I am uncertain as to the safety of automatic vaccination of all children. *See* **Vaccinations**, where I discuss the measles vaccine in detail.

RECOMMENDATIONS

- *Diagnosis is made clinically, although blood tests may be used in more serious cases. Interestingly, because of the vaccination programme, many doctors may qualify and enter a General Practice without having seen measles. Consult Grandma!*
- *See* **Vaccinations.**
- *The irritation of the rash will be soothed by applying a sodium-bicarbonate solution. Add one tablespoon of sodium bicarbonate (baking soda) to 16 ounces of water. Iced water may be more soothing.*
- *The homeopathic remedy Pulsatilla 6 can be given every half-hour, and in particularly irritating cases, the remedy Rhus toxicodendron 6 can be given at the same frequency.*
- *Beta-carotene (1mg per foot of height given with a meal or in a child's bottle up to three times a day) is protective of infection of mucus membranes, such as in the eyes and the lungs. It should certainly be used if any symptoms of conjunctivitis, vaginitis, or bronchitis are present.*
- *Discuss the matter with a complementary medical practitioner, especially if the symptoms are severe or the child is particularly unwell.*

MOTION SICKNESS

Motion sickness can occur at any age, but is most troublesome in children. Humankind was not designed to travel at speeds greater than a run, and so the advent of the use of animals and machinery to take us at far greater speeds is not ingrained in our nervous system. The movement of objects passing us, in combination with irregular movements within the vestibular canal or balance center in the inner ear, creates an unusual and unexpected neurological impulse state within the brain. The response is to attempt to stop us and a very good way to do this is to make us feel sick. As we age and become more used to traveling, our brain accepts that this is not a dangerous situation and therefore the need for nausea diminishes.

RECOMMENDATIONS

- *See* **Nausea.**
- *Persevere with the travel because the body and brain will adjust eventually.*
- *The homeopathic remedy Cocculus indicus 6 can be taken every 15min while in motion and every 2hr prior to the intended journey, starting the day before. Other remedies include Tabacum and Rhus toxicodendron.*
- *Avoid strong smells of food or tobacco while in transit, and ensure adequate fresh air.*

MUMPS

Mumps is a viral infection that affects glands throughout the body, but predominantly the salivary glands under the jaw and the parotid gland in front of the ear. It is an infectious disease spread by coughs, sneezes, and physical contact; it is more common in hot weather and is sometimes associated with a fever. Lifelong immunity is usually conferred after an attack. In a healthy individual, mumps is a short-lived problem, usually lasting about ten days, through which time the individual is infectious. Unfortunately, mumps takes two to four weeks to develop, and the child has probably been spreading the infection throughout this period.

Rarely do complications occur, but the older the individual, the more likely the possibility of infection of the testes, brain, or pancreas, which can lead to very serious conditions.

Vaccination is routine and encouraged by the orthodox world, but consideration for vaccinations in general should be made before these are given (*see* **Vaccinations**).

RECOMMENDATIONS

- *See* **Fever**.
- *The homeopathic remedies Belladonna, Aconite, Mercurius, Hepar sulfuris calcarium, and Phytolacca should all be considered via your preferred homeopathic manual. Potency 6 should be taken every 2hr through the acute phase.*
- *If an individual has been exposed to mumps, protection may be afforded by taking the homeopathic remedy Parotidinum 30, twice a day for two weeks.*
- *Avoid flavorsome food that encourages salivation and thus increases pain.*
- *A multivitamin—vitamin C and Beta-carotene—should be given at three times the RDA for the age or size of the individual.*

POLIO

Polio is the abbreviation for the disease known as poliomyelitis. It is a common viral disease that usually runs an asymptomatic or mild course, characterized by upper-respiratory or gastrointestinal symptoms. The virus may progress to involve the central nervous system, and result in either a nonparalytic or a paralytic form of the disease. Poliomyelitis is endemic (meaning that it lives within populations) and has epidemic flare-ups (there is a maximum frequency for this from July to September in temperate zones). As with most transmittable diseases, it is spread by coughing, but also by the oral–fecal route (a carrier with polio in the bowel may prepare food without washing off the virus after their last visit to the toilet). Fecal contamination of water and flies are other vectors.

Immunization against polio is available for those in the Western world, but for the majority, their own immune system is their only defense. As with all contagious diseases, the health of the individual is the deciding factor on whether polio will come and go, and confer a lifelong immunity or strike and create the feared neurological result.

Subclinical polio occurs in 95 percent of those infected. The immune system fights the battle, and the infection may not have been recognized. This form is a mild, nonspecific illness causing cough or flu-like symptoms, or a gastrointestinal disturbance such as diarrhea.

The nonparalytic form is a meningitis-like illness (*see* **Meningitis**) causing fever, headache, and a stiff neck. Less than 1 percent of individuals infected may have the paralytic form, which starts with a headache, general illness, and muscular pains. Fever, neck stiffness, and muscle tenderness may be present. This then leads to severe muscle pains, an inability to move the parts affected and, if the brain is contaminated, difficulty in swallowing and talking. At worst, respiratory paralysis may occur in 5 percent of these rare cases, usually due to complications of respiratory paralysis. Patients showing even very severe paralysis may make a reasonable recovery over two years. Only in occasional instances does a permanent paralysis remain.

RECOMMENDATIONS

- *See* **Vaccinations**.
- *See* **Influenza** *and* **Herpes simplex**, *because the basic antiviral advice given for these conditions should be followed for polio.*

- *If meningitis is the outcome, see* **Meningitis**.
- *Recovery will benefit from constitutional homeopathic repair, and as soon as a diagnosis is made use the remedy Lathyrus 30, four times a day, until a more suitable remedy may be chosen.*
- *Through the recovery phase, osteopathy, chiropractic, Rolfing, and Feldenkrais have been shown to benefit.*
- *If any residual paralysis remains, the Alexander technique, polarity therapy, yoga, or Qi Gong (Chi Kung) should be studied.*
- *Marma therapy and neurotherapy, branches of Ayurvedic physical therapy, can be used also.*

PUBERTY

Puberty is the period at which the sexual organs become capable of exercising their function of reproduction. Increases in androgens (male hormones, the most well-known of which is testosterone) and the female hormones (predominantly estrogen and progesterone) create character changes. A boy will find that his voice deepens and muscle development increases, around the shoulders, in particular. Erections become more frequent, and seminal discharge will accompany orgasm. Girls will start their periods and develop a rounding of features, especially over the hips. The breasts will start developing at a faster rate.

Delayed puberty

The timing of these events is generally one year before or after the age at which the parent of the same sex went through their puberty. A delay beyond two years and an absence of puberty after the age of 15 years is considered a delayed puberty. Small children and those who are undernourished may find their puberty delayed. Chronic illness and the use of steroids in conditions such as asthma may also prevent puberty.

RECOMMENDATIONS

- *If puberty has not occurred by the age of 15 years, consult with a physician, who may refer the child to a pediatric specialist.*
- *Consult a homeopathic practitioner for a suitable constitutional remedy.*
- *If no underlying disease is apparent, test for nutritional deficiencies through blood and hair analysis under the care of a naturopathic specialist, and correct any nutritional deficits.*
- *Consider some form of counseling, preferably art therapy, because a delay may create a marked lack of self-confidence at a very important time of the development of the psyche. Regardless, be extremely supportive as a parent, and do not dismiss the child's anxieties.*

Precocious puberty

Should symptoms of puberty occur early, some concern may need to be dispelled. Using arbitrary cut-off figures, puberty in girls before the age of 8 and in boys before the age of 10 should be referred to a pediatric specialist. We come across those children who are mature beyond their years, both mentally and physically, and this may simply be a normal but early development. Musical and mathematical "geniuses" may simply be children who have developed faculties before the expected age. These are not to be considered a disease process. Social chastisement may occur, however, and this needs to be addressed.

Extremely rarely, tumors of the pituitary gland may produce hormones that stimulate early periods or excessive growth (*see* **Gigantism**), but these can be ruled out by blood tests and, if necessary, brain scans.

RECOMMENDATIONS

- *Excessive growth or other early developmental milestones should be assessed by a suitably qualified practitioner or pediatrician.*

- *Moral support must be given by parents to support a child who may be "different" to his or her peers. Counseling, preferably art therapy, can be utilized.*
- *Early periods may lead to a tendency to iron and protein deficiency, which may inhibit growth. Increased growth or development usually corresponds to an increased appetite, but nutritional foods containing proteins, vitamins, minerals, and trace elements must be encouraged, and supplements given if the child is a pernickety eater.*
- *Consult a homeopath for a constitutional remedy.*

RUBELLA (GERMAN MEASLES)

Rubella, or German measles, is an innocuous infection causing a mild fever, lethargy, and a characteristic rash. This rash initially starts on the face and neck, spreads to the trunk and limbs, is characteristically bright red and is often accompanied by rose-colored spots on the palate and the throat. The rash usually lasts a few days, and may be associated with stiff joints and swollen glands. The true diagnosis can only be made through confirmation of a blood test, but most doctors are experienced enough to make a clinical diagnosis. The virus may be contracted and incubated for 14–21 days, and the patient is infectious for about one week before and up to one week after the appearance of the rash. In principle, however, German measles is not a problem to an individual.

The danger with rubella is that, more than most viruses, it has an ability to cause malformation in the developing fetus. This makes it a dangerous infection to contract while pregnant. The orthodox world, with its predilection for vaccination and its disregard of the possibility of risks or dangers associated with this form of treatment, used to encourage all teenage girls to have a rubella vaccination. Recently, in a vain attempt to eradicate the disease, all children between the age of five and 15 years are automatically being given rubella vaccinations in combination with measles and mumps. This MMR vaccine is discussed and vilified in the section on vaccinations (*see* **Vaccinations**).

RECOMMENDATIONS

- *Seriously consider the need to vaccinate your children but, for rubella in particular, girls reaching the age of procreation can have a blood test to check for immunity (very often the infection is contracted unknowingly in earlier years), and if natural immunity has been formed, no further action need be taken. If not immune, then the vaccination should be considered (see* **Vaccinations***).*
- *Treatment for the symptoms of rubella is similar to that of measles (see* **Measles***).*

SLEEPLESSNESS

A full discussion on insomnia may be found in chapter 5 (*see* **Sleep problems**), but in children sleeplessness is rarely a disease process.

Most infants and children will sleep as required, although the pattern may not fit in with the parents. A baby may feed every 2–3 hours through the night, and by sleeping in bursts for 2–3 hours through the day, has its necessary sleep quota (anywhere up to 16 hours) and is perfectly all right. This may leave parents in tatters, and very often convinced that their child does not sleep.

Sleeplessness is influenced by colic and the inadvertent ingestion of stimulants, due either to food allergy or drinking mother's milk, which may contain caffeine or other stimulants such as drugs of abuse if the mother partakes.

RECOMMENDATIONS

- *Accepting that the most common causes for an infant's disturbed sleep pattern are hunger, colic, or discomfort from, say, a soiled diaper, then change, feed, and comfort the child.*

- *Ensure that the environment is neither too hot nor too cold, and that the child's bed covers are suitable for the temperature. A quilt in summer or a sheet in winter may be inappropriate.*
- *Remember that infants and children are learning constantly, and overattention to the slightest complaint will teach them an inappropriate way of attracting attention. If a child seems to be exploiting the parents' anxieties, leave him/her to cry for 5min, then give comfort until settled, and leave the room. Next time, wait for 10min. Repeat this process, and you may find that the child falls asleep while whining. Experience will quickly develop, and most parents will be able to differentiate between an attention-seeking wail and a cry associated with a true problem.*
- *Parents should feed their baby, even if it means waking the baby, before they go to bed.*
- *Paradoxically, an infant or child may sleep poorly because of overtiredness. Try putting baby to bed 15min earlier, and you may find that baby sleeps longer. If this trick does not work, try the commonsense approach of allowing the child to stay up later.*
- *An irritable baby will be soothed by the homeopathic remedy Chamomilla, especially if the child is teething. Coffea 6, three doses on the hour starting 1hr before bedtime may help an overexcited child.*
- *For children over the age of two years, Nux vomica 200 on three consecutive nights followed one week later by one dose of Sulphur 200 can be magical! If the child responds after any of the doses of Nux vomica, hold off on the sulfur until the pattern is once again disturbed. This process may be repeated up to once a month, but if it does not work consult a homeopath for a more specific remedy.*
- *A camomile tea sweetened with very little honey, if necessary, may be soporific.*
- *Avoid putting the child to bed within 2hr of the last meal (in the case of an infant or a child that falls asleep after eating, do not awaken the child of course) and avoid exciting or vigorous activity within that time.*

SPEECH

The ability to speak is a combination of anatomical and neurological coordination in conjunction with learned responses. From as early an age as possible, parents must "teach" children by correlating objects with words. The intricacies of language develop as the child grows, and concepts such as verbs and adjectives come into play.

Development of speech

In the first month, baby communicates using guttural sounds and crying. By the second month, the child will start to vocalize, making cooing noises and vowel sounds, but continues to communicate mostly by crying.

The third month will bring an attempt at communication by squealing and focusing on an individual. Consonant sounds start, and the child may repeat combinations of syllables. At this point, the child will derive some pleasure from vibrations felt in the lips, and be enthusiastic about his/her gurgles.

In the fourth and fifth months, the child will be having long "conversations" by combining vowel sounds with consonant sounds. Babbling will increase, especially if the child is spoken to.

The sixth and seventh months will bring a marked increase in phonetics. The child will start to babble while performing a simple task or having things done to him/her, such as being dressed.

By the seventh month the child will be using vocalization to attract attention, and will start talking louder if ignored.

Around the eighth and ninth months, the first words will come forward—"Dada" and "Mamma" are usually the first. (Fathers, do not take umbrage if your partner's name is uttered first! "Mamma" is actually easier to say than "Dada," and is often heard a lot more in the first few months of life.) Between the tenth and fifteenth months, an infant will start to use meaningful one- and two-word sentences: "Dada gone" and "More toast" are common examples.

By 15 months to two years an improvement is seen, to the point that meaningful sentences will come forward. "Look at birdie" and "Pasta on floor" are clear indications of the child using language accurately.

Between the age of two and three years, full sentences are formed, and in the latter stages conversation should be possible.

After three years of age, egocentricity arises and the terms "I" and "Me" increase.

Any problems with hearing or vision will impede development, but it is important to remember that these months are only guidelines, and leeway either side by at least 2–3 months should be allowed before the child is considered to be surprisingly advanced or delayed.

Development of Speech

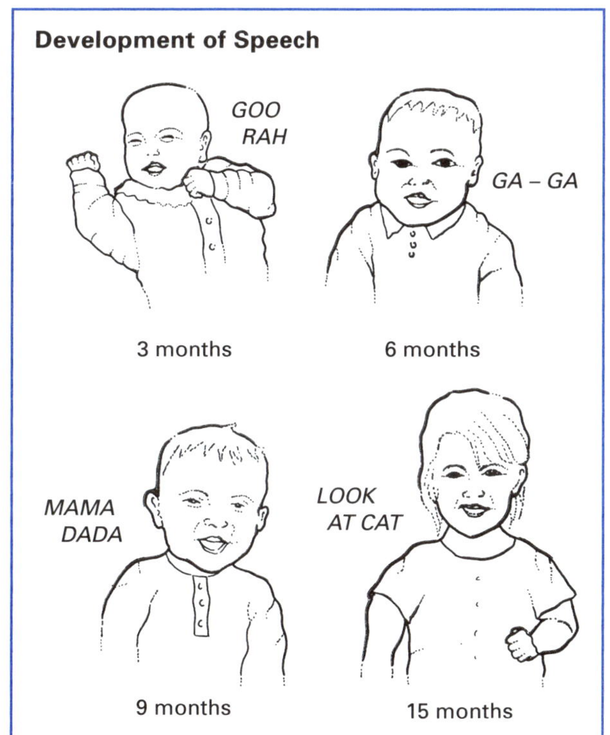

RECOMMENDATIONS

- *If your child is falling outside of these basic guidelines, a pediatric assessment is essential to establish hearing, vision, and mental ability.*
- *The orthodox world may overlook the importance of nutritional deficiencies in development, and a multivitamin/mineral should be considered for children once they are off the bottle or breast.*
- *Ensure that constant communication with both visual and verbal aspects is kept at a maximum through these early formative years.*
- *Do not sound or behave critically if a child is failing to pronounce correctly or is not calling objects by the right name. Criticism can cause introspection and shyness at this early age, much more so than at a later stage.*

Stammering and stuttering

A stammer is one of several irregularities of speech marked by involuntary halting, repetition of words or smaller segments, transposition or mispronunciation of certain consonants, or a combination of any of these defects. A stutter is marked by an intermittent inability to enunciate a phonetic segment of one syllable without repeating it, straining to overcome the block, or both.

Stuttering is common among children until the age of five years, but beyond that the majority of stutterers will carry the difficulty into adulthood. About 1 percent of adults have a stutter or stammer. This tends to run in families, and is more prevalent in males and left-handed people.

If a stammer or stutter starts in a child, the chances are that it is a habit, and is very often associated with stress. An onset in adulthood is generally a sign of an injury or disorder to the central nervous system.

Everybody may stammer under pressure because the neck muscles, and particularly the vocal cords, become tense and less controlled in an embarrassing or awkward situation. This is not a problem unless it is interfering with social life, in which case treatment is required.

RECOMMENDATIONS

- *Adult onset of any speech difficulty should be assessed by a neurologist.*
- *A child may benefit from the counseling of an expert in this field, who should also deal with the parents. At a later age, relaxation and meditation techniques should be taught.*
- *Many homeopathic remedies may be utilized, depending on the type of speech difficulty. Review the remedies Stramonium, Agaricus muscarius, Cuprum, and Arsenicum. Potency 30 three times a day of a suitable remedy taken for one week may make an impact.*
- *Zinc deficiency may be relevant, and can be counteracted by taking 5mg of zinc per foot of height each day before bed for two weeks. If this resolves the problem but it returns, then assume that there is a lack of zinc in the diet, or poor zinc absorption. Seek guidance from a nutritional expert.*
- *Test for metal toxicity. Copper and lead have been shown to be a problem, and other metals have similar effects.*
- *The Bach flower remedy Trumpet Vine is useful for speech difficulties while speaking in public.*

SUDDEN INFANT-DEATH SYNDROME (SIDS or RIB DEATH)

Sudden infant-death syndrome (SIDS), more commonly known as crib death, is the most tragic of occurrences. Approximately three in 100,000 children each year will be found lifeless for no apparent reason. These deaths most commonly occur in the winter months, and usually between the ages of two and four months.

There are several factors associated with crib death that are accepted throughout the orthodox world, and others that are suggested through alternative sources.

Orthodox associations

- Smoking. The association is startling, and it is the most important of all known factors. Maternal smoking during or after pregnancy, and those smoking around a pregnant mother or baby, may cause up to two-thirds of crib deaths.
- Infants sleeping face down in cribs. This may be made worse by certain fire-retarding materials, although the suggestion has not been substantiated.
- Infections, particularly chest infections, whether they are mild or serious.
- Genetic predisposition, creating either a fault in the part of the brain that tells the body to breathe, or enzyme deficiencies that prevent the availability of energy from food.
- Overheating or exposure to cold.
- Excessive caffeine intake during pregnancy.

Alternative possibilities

- Medicines such as those used in treating colic, or decongestants.
- Antibiotics when used to treat infections.
- Food allergy or intolerance.
- Recent vaccination.

Prevention is the key, and as many safeguards as possible should be encouraged.

RECOMMENDATIONS

- *Place an apnea blanket under the child. These are easily obtainable, although expensive, and are special blankets that register the child's movement. If the child stops breathing an alarm sound will go off, which may awaken the child and will alert the parents, provided that an inter-room sounder is utilized if the parents or child's guardian are out of earshot.*
- *Cover all crib mattresses with a plastic sheet.*
- *Ensure an even temperature with fresh air in the child's room.*

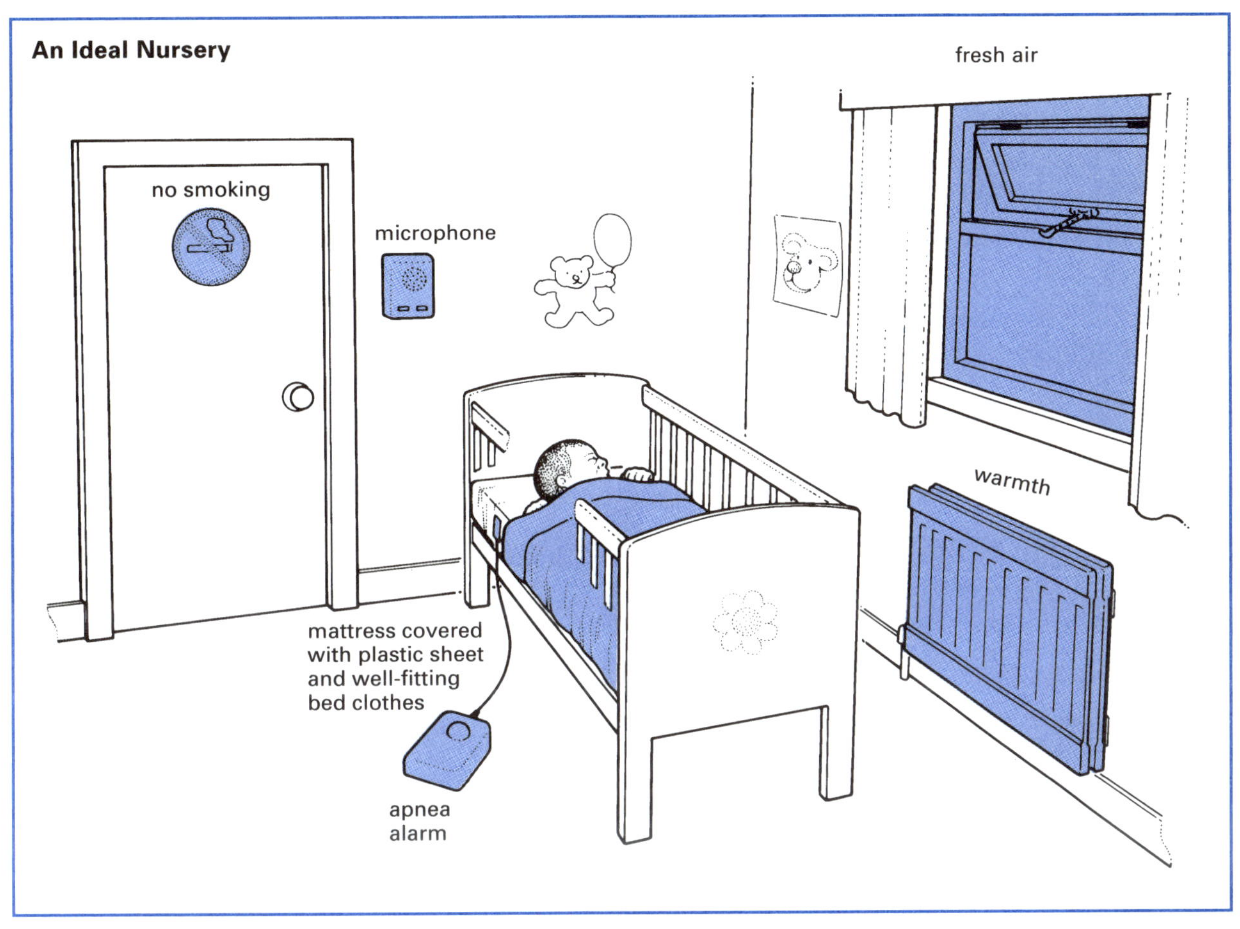

- *Ensure that the child sleeps on his/her back. Even children sleeping on their side have a higher incidence of SIDS.*
- *Clothing and bedding must be well-fitting, because anything loose may slip over the baby's head. Infants should not use duvets until after one year old. Bedding should be securely tucked in.*
- *For this more than any other condition—absolutely* ***no*** *smoking through pregnancy, around the child, or even in the same house as an infant.*
- *Avoid caffeine during pregnancy.*
- *Pay special attention to any child on orthodox medication. If the apnea blanket/alarm system is not utilized, a child with an infection may be best preserved from SIDS by sleeping in the same bed as the parents.*

If this tragedy has occurred within your family or circle of friends, it may be worth considering the Hindu philosophy that we are reincarnated as part of a long cycle of attainment, understanding, and teaching. A spirit that enters the body of a child who does not live for long is considered to be a very advanced soul, who only needed a short incarnation and was principally here to teach sadness and loss to those around. Such a visitation is considered a blessing, and although this cannot touch the pain created by such a tragedy, I have found that it may give some meaning to the pain and sorrow.

VACCINATIONS

There are major confrontations between holistic medicine and modern Western medicine, but none is more contentious than the matter of vaccinations. As usual, there is no right or wrong answer, but particularly in the case of vaccinations, there is no reason to believe that vaccinations are correct and safe for all. When dealing with undernourished and immunosuppressed masses such as in the troubled states of Africa, the vaccination program probably saves millions of lives each year. Of interest, however, is a well-documented report on the use of vitamin A instead of vaccinations against measles, which showed an unequivocal, comparative success rate between the two treatments with regard to preventing undernourished children from developing measles pneumonia, a serious and often fatal condition. This trial has, to my knowledge, not been repeated, basically because vitamin A costs next to nothing, whereas a vaccination costs a substantial amount. Studies cost money, and there is no advantage for pharmaceutical companies to spend money on studies that invalidate the use of their products. All governments are advised by specialists, often on the payroll of pharmaceutical companies, so the truth is hard to get to. Personally, I am unsure of what that truth is.

There is a lot of information on the pros and cons of vaccinations, but the negative information is rarely fed to the overburdened and busy doctor. The subject demands a book to itself, and this section mentions a publication that I recommend be read by all parents and travelers before considering vaccinations.

I make special mention of the measles vaccine later because the government in Britain in 1994 vaccinated eight million children between the ages of five and 15 years with, in my opinion, no true care or concern of the down side. The powers that be boasted that they had saved 50 lives and over 3,000 hospital admissions, but reports that were leaked to the popular press six months later suggested that the expected epidemic (the official reason for carrying out this mass vaccination program) may never have occurred, and there may have been up to 1,500 adverse reactions to the vaccination reported. There have been several reported cases of autism and the same number of a Crohn's-like disease in children that have been directly attributed to the measles vaccination. These are only the reported cases, and may represent the tip of the iceberg because doctors might not yet be correlating the onset of these conditions with the measles vaccination. At the time of writing there is a powerful and contentious debate going on between a research fellow at the Royal Free Hospital, London, and senior scientific colleagues. There has been a study of 12 cases of autism that suggest a direct correlation with the MMR vaccination and this adds substance to the reports mentioned above.

The principle of vaccination is the administration of a very small amount of either dead or nonfunctioning virus, which causes the body to respond by forming antibodies. If an individual comes into contact with the live virus, the body will have memorized it as having been present before, and the antibodies will attack the invading agent and kill it. Usually vaccines are given by injection (the exception is one of the polio vaccines, which is given orally). Theoretically, this is a sound method of defense.

There is, however, a consensus of opinion in the holistic medical world against the use of vaccines. There is some concern that the process of manufacturing these vaccines allows entry into the body of proteins that, being similar to our own, cause the body to form antibodies against ourselves. There is also the hypothesis that by stimulating the body in this artificial way, the natural response is in some way diminished. Introduction of these infections directly into the bloodstream by injection also bypasses primary defenses found in the mucus membranes and skin. The body, therefore, produces an antibody defense, but none other.

Add to this the fact that vaccinations caused problems when they were first used and, even up to 1992, when two of the three types of measles vaccine were taken off the market because of adverse side effects, vaccinations have proved to be risky. Until 1995, I advised parents, and those considering traveling, to utilize vaccines, but also to take homeopathic remedies at the same time in an attempt to counteract any adverse effects, and also stimulate the body to a better response against the agent in the vaccine. I have, however, recently read a considerable amount about the matter of vaccination, and my advice now is different. Please read on.

I have, at this time, chosen not to vaccinate my children and, unless more information comes my way, I will avoid their coming into contact with vaccinations.

These are my views; they may be right or wrong. Please may I ask everyone to obtain and read *The Vaccination Handbook* (published by WHAT DOCTORS DON'T TELL YOU) and make their own judgments. Copies may be obtained through me or my clinics, or by calling WDDTY on (44) (0171) 354-4592 with a credit card number. This publication gives an overview that I think is very accurate.

Basically, there is strong evidence that vaccines:

- do not work as well as we are told.
- have greater risks attached than we are told.
- may be more dangerous than the disease itself in well-nourished, healthy children.

If asked by a parent or intended traveler about vaccinations, I ask them to read *The Vaccination Handbook*, and then I support whatever they decide to do, including using homeopathic remedies either with or without regular vaccination.

I do not recommend an individual to take or avoid vaccinations, but I do state that **I will not be vaccinating my own children, and neither will I take or prescribe vaccines, except under unexpected circumstances, in the future.**

Should I vaccinate my child?

This question boils down to a parent asking themselves the following question: is my child or my child's place in society more important? If vaccinations are carrying an unexpected and unassessed risk, then they should be avoided. However, statistically it can be argued that vaccinations do reduce the incidence of disease when given to large populations. The view I take is that children who are liable to be susceptible to infections need vaccinations, whereas those who are healthy do not.

A parent, I think, should be able to give an affirmative ("yes") to the following questions, and if they can they should not vaccinate their child. On the other hand, if any of these questions bring forward a negative ("no") answer, then the child should be vaccinated.

- Is my child well nurtured, in a clean and hygienic environment, and likely to stay in such an environment?
- Is my child well nourished, and am I aware of his/her nutritional requirements?
- Is my child in good health, and genetically predisposed to stay that way?
- Am I an observant parent with the time and knowledge to notice a depreciation in my child's state of health?

United States law prohibits children from entering school without being vaccinated. This legal requirement makes the following comments of interest but, at this time, the option not to vaccinate is not there. The author has decided to retain this section in the American version of this book since he feels the following information should be known.

RECOMMENDATIONS

- *If an individual or a parent feels that they cannot fulfil the above recommendations, or if the individual or child is in an immunocompromised state or will be unavoidably subjected to infection, then I feel that the use of a vaccination is less likely to cause a problem than the contraction of a disease, and vaccinations should be taken.*

- *Ensure that an individual or a child has no underlying condition that may predispose him or her to the effects of childhood illnesses.*
- *Visit a nutritionist to establish good individual and family nutrition.*
- *Discuss matters of hygiene with a complementary medical practitioner.*
- *If considering the use of vaccinations, ensure that there have been no previous reactions to other vaccines, or eggs, and that there is no current serious illness. Vaccinations may cause reactions or provoke a reduced immune response.*
- *If taking regular vaccines, use the homeopathic remedy that corresponds to the disease process. This should create a body response to the infection, should it be introduced by a faulty vaccine (see* **Homeopathic inoculations***).*
- *If vaccines have been given in the past, take three doses of Thuja 200, one each night. If a vaccination has actually caused a reaction, use the remedy Natrum muriaticum 30 four times a day for one week. Both of these remedies are reported as being able to deal with the "ill effects of vaccinations."*
- *A bi-yearly visit to a holistic practitioner and a regular doctor to establish good health.*

If you decide to vaccinate

If an individual chooses to take a vaccination or to give them to his/her children it may, theoretically, be best to prepare the body beforehand. The following recommendations may prevent the individual from overreacting to the vaccination, prepare the individual for the invasion of animal proteins used in the manufacture of the viral vaccines, and also avoid the reaction of a vaccine to which the individual may be allergic.

RECOMMENDATIONS

- *Ensure that the individual is in good health with no underlying acute problems, such as a cold or fever, before giving a vaccination.*
- *In the case of children, delay the vaccinations until six months old, allowing the immune system some time to develop before a potent immune stimulant is administered.*
- *Use the homeopathic remedy Thuja 200 prior to any vaccinations, along with specific homeopathic preparations for the vaccine itself (see* **Homeopathic inoculations***).*
- *Try to find a physician who will give one-tenth of the dose of the vaccine two weeks prior to giving the vaccine proper. Theoretically, this allows the body to prepare for the more major reaction and will preempt any aggressive reaction.*
- *Give vaccinations as single doses, ie do not give Measles, Mumps, and Rubella all at once, but separately. Leave at least two weeks between taking vaccinations, and preferably three months, so that the body is not subjected to "overload."*

Homeopathic inoculations

There is no such thing as a homeopathic vaccination. At best, homeopathic remedies may create a response lasting a few months, but certainly not a lifetime. Remedies tend to protect the body against particular infections, and if you are subjected to that particular infection then by taking the equivalent homeopathic inoculation your body may well produce a strong immunity.

There is no good scientific evidence that homeopathic remedies confer immunity. However, some studies have been done, largely on the Indian subcontinent. These studies show that certain remedies create immune responses, but we cannot be certain that the antibodies against these diseases did not form simply because the individual children were exposed to the infection because it was endemic (prevalent in the area). Government statistics (not truly acceptable scientific evidence) do show that homeopathic remedies can act as vaccines, and there is evidence of lower levels of infection in groups that have received the correct homeopathic treatment.

I hypothesize that the use of a remedy in a child who will come into contact with the natural infection will bolster his or her immune system at that time. A remedy will not cause an immunoglobulin (antibody) response. However, if an individual contracts an infection within, say, one month of taking a suitable homeopathic remedy, the immune response may be much swifter and more effective, and therefore set up a lifelong immunity without the child even knowing the infection had been contracted. I must stress that this is all theoretical. If I extend this hypothesis, then the use of homeopathic remedies just prior to taking orthodox vaccinations may create a better response and, possibly, protect against the potential side effects or an immune system overload.

The chart below gives the suggested remedies for childhood infections. (A similar chart can be found for the homeopathic equivalent support for travelers' vaccinations in the section on travel.)

Condition	Remedy*
Diphtheria	*Diphtherinum* 200
Hepatitis (A, B, and others)	*Lycopodium* 200 and *Chelidonium* 200
HiB (*Hemophilus influenzae* B)	*See* **Meningitis**
Meningitis	*Belladonna* 200 and *Iodoformum* 200
MMR (Measles, mumps, and rubella)	*Pulsatilla* 200
Polio	*Lathyrus* 200
Tetanus	*Hypericum* 200
Tuberculosis	*Tuberculinum* 200
Whooping cough (pertussis)	*Pertussin* 200

*All these should be taken five days apart, starting one month before the first vaccination is given.

The measles vaccine

I make special mention of the measles vaccine because of the recent mass vaccination program that took place in Britain in 1994.

Interestingly, but not surprisingly from a financial point of view, the powers that be are recommending that the vaccination program is repeated, because more than the estimated numbers of children have not shown a positive response and have not developed immunity. I discuss below a strong argument against continuing these mass vaccinations.

At the moment, if an epidemic were to strike the country, approximately 50 children would be expected to die, and over 3,000 would be hospitalized with serious complications. (I mention here that there is no correlation between the health of the child and the type of child who may succumb to measles. All children—the well-nourished, nurtured, and loved, as well as the less fortunate—are bracketed together.)

In 1994, eight million children were vaccinated. Four million of those were girls between the age of 5 and 15 years. The number of children who did not respond to the vaccine is estimated at 10 percent. This means that 400,000 girls are not immune to measles. Over the next ten years, these 400,000 children are unlikely to come across measles because it has been eradicated from 90 percent of their peer group. They will therefore not be able to develop natural immunity.

Let us assume that over the next ten years, 25 percent of those children not immunized will bear their own child; 100,000 infants will therefore be born to mothers who carry no immunity to measles. The antibodies (immunoglobulins) that defend against measles pass from the mother's bloodstream into their baby's while still in the womb, and will protect infants for up to six months. Breast-fed babies will also receive antibodies, but in the 100,000 infants born to mothers who are not immune, no measles protection will be conferred.

Most pediatricians will tell you that measles in an infant is far more serious and potentially far more lethal.

There may be a 90 percent reduction in the chances of contracting measles because we have vaccinated the herd, but are we protecting the interests of those 100,000 infants in the generations ahead?

As a final note, after all the orthodox pressure applied to parents, the number of cases of measles in children who were vaccinated doubled in 1994.

RECOMMENDATIONS

- *Pay heed to the notes above.*
- *Breast-feed as long as possible.*
- *Vaccinate as late as possible.*
- *Only consider "measles parties" if the original child has a mild case and your child is healthy.*
- *Remember that many infections, such as rubella, can be tested for by a simple blood test.*

The Head and Neck

THE EARS

CARE OF THE EARS

The ears do not require a lot of care and concern because, generally, they are adequately protected. It is important to keep the ears warm and covered as they have little protection from the cold or excessive sun and, as the blood vessels to the ear are very small, damage may take time to repair. Sunburn and gangrene are not uncommon in extremes of weather, and the use of protective coverings such as sun-block and ear muffs should always be considered.

The ear canal is lined by small hairs called cilia, which meticulously flick outwards dirt and debris that enter the canal. Different people will create different amounts of secretion, which, if in excess, can block the canal and is known as ear wax (*see* **Ear problems**).

Cleaning of the ear should be done daily using mild soap and water, cleaning only the external or pinna part of the ear. The use of Q-tips (small balls of cotton on the end of sticks) may cause more harm than good. The insertion of anything into the ear can push dirt, wax and infection deeper into the ear, and is unlikely to be of any great benefit because the cilia will do the job.

The need for the protection of the ears from loud noises is becoming more apparent as younger people are experiencing auditory loss (deafness) at an alarmingly increasing rate. This has been associated with the advent of loud popular music, but more so with the widespread use of personal stereos. Loud noises cause vigorous vibrations that in turn cause small abrasions around the ear ossicles, which slowly but surely scar and reduce the mobility of these middle-ear bones. Conductive deafness is the outcome, and may not be repairable (*see* **Conductive deafness**).

EAR PROBLEMS

Problems with the ear can occur at any age, but they are most frequently associated with children. The reason for this is probably twofold. Firstly, the middle ear (the most common area to cause problems) is much smaller and therefore easier to affect and, secondly, children are more prone to mucus production and coughs and colds, which can block the narrow Eustachian tube (the channel between the middle ear and the throat).

Anatomically and medically speaking, there are three parts to the ear:

- The pinna and outer canal make up the outer ear.
- The middle ear, including the stapes, incus, and malleus (the ear bones or ossicles).
- The inner ear, comprising the cochlea, which contains the fluid through which sound waves are transmitted to the auditory nerves.

Problems must therefore be divided according to

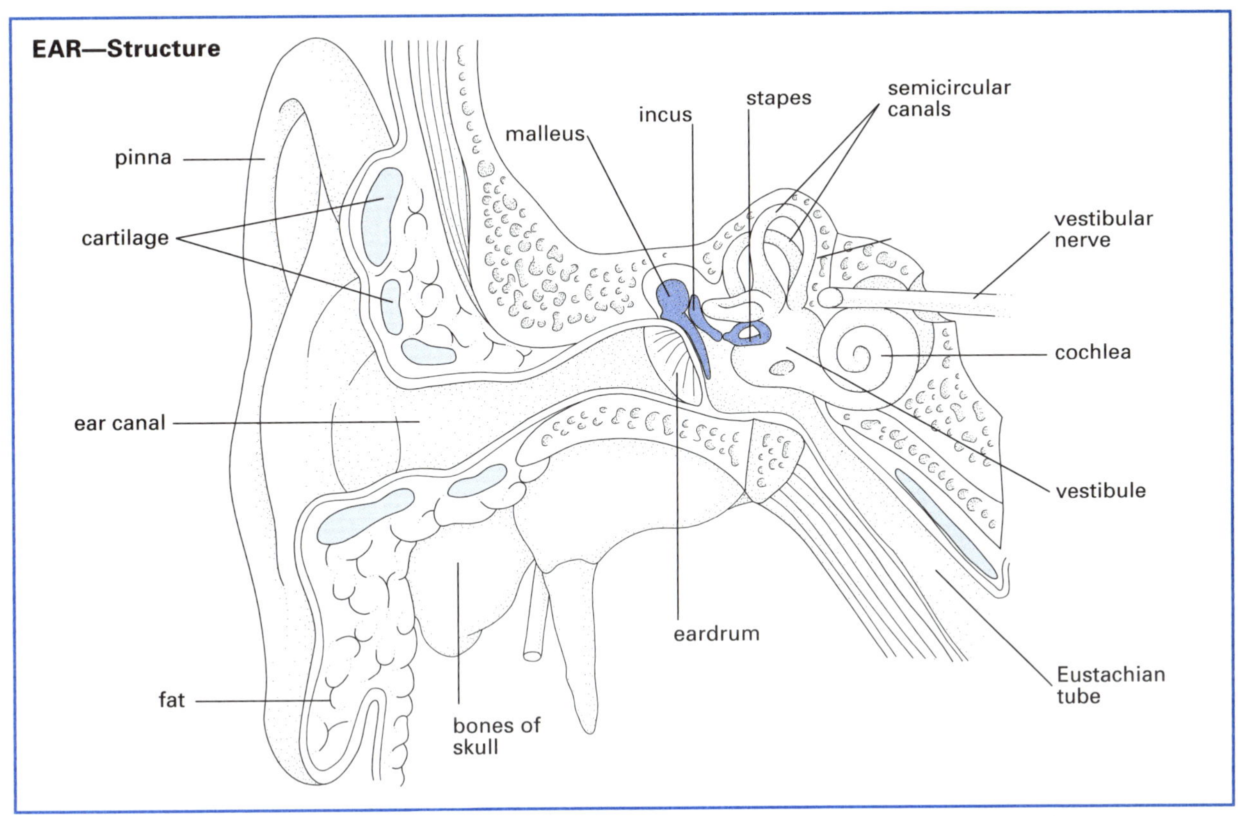

which part of the ear is affected, and the appropriate treatment followed.

ACHES AND PAINS

Outer ear

Pains in this part of the ear are usually caused by the cold, trauma, infections, or foreign bodies. Eczema of the external ear may often lead to infection, and treatment of this dry skin is necessary. Common sense is the initial treatment, including warming of the pinna, removal of foreign objects (*see* **Foreign body in the ear**), and application of soothing balms.

RECOMMENDATIONS

- *Apply common sense, especially with regard to the removal of foreign objects (see* ***Foreign body in the ear****).*
- *Topical application of Arnica or Calendula creams may be curative.*
- *An inflamed external ear associated with cold wind may be successfully treated with Aconite 6, one dose every 2hr.*
- *Review the remedies Petroleum and Graphites if there is eczema associated with the external-ear discomfort.*

Middle ear

Aches and pains in the middle ear are usually associated with infection or trauma caused by loud noises.

It is well accepted throughout the orthodox medical world that approximately 50 percent of ear infections are caused by viruses. The pain is the same, but the use of antibiotics (ineffective against viruses) should be limited to infections that are caused by bacteria. The persistent use of antibiotics in ear infections leads to resistant strains and recurrent infections. I recommend that antibiotics are used only when a problem is very severe, and preferably after the doctor has taken a swab of any discharge and sent it to a laboratory for confirmation of the presence of bacteria. The use of an antibiotic may weaken the individual's immune system and prolong the problem (*see* **Antibiotics**).

RECOMMENDATIONS

- *Earache that is severe or persistent should be assessed by a doctor. If the doctor recommends an antibiotic, ask if it is possible to take a swab (it may not be feasible if there is no discharge) and ask the doctor's opinion on whether he/she is convinced that it is not viral.*
- *One or two drops of mullein oil can be instantly relieving and potentially curative. This can be repeated every 3 or 4hr if required.*
- *If there is discharge associated with the pain, while awaiting the laboratory report on the swab that should have been taken by your doctor or practitioner, consider reviewing the following homeopathic remedies: Pulsatilla, Hepar sulfuris calcarium, Chamomilla, Silica, and Belladonna.*
- *If there is discharge, keep the outside of the ear as clean as possible, but do not attempt to clear the ear canal.*
- *Earache without discharge requires reviewing the following homeopathic remedies: Allium cepa, Gelsemium, Belladonna, Magnesia phosphorica.*
- *With or without discharge, opening of the Eustachian tube is beneficial because it allows drainage of any catarrh in the middle ear. This is best achieved by inhalations of Olbas or lavender oil (one drop in a bowl of steaming water) or inhaling the steam from a ginger tea (chop half-inch of gingerroot in hot water).*

Inner ear

Pain emanating from the inner ear is difficult to assess, and an infection of this part of the ear requires specialist attention.

RECOMMENDATIONS

- *Follow the advice of an ear, nose, and throat specialist.*
- *Gain the advice of a homeopath based on these symptoms.*

BLEEDING FROM THE EARS

Bleeding from the ear is potentially a serious matter that requires a medical opinion to illuminate the cause. A small, visible scratch with a little blood loss is not relevant, and can be treated with common sense, but any bleeding that comes from within the canal or deeper, and is not caused by an external cut, must be seen by a physician.

RECOMMENDATION

- *All bleeding from the ear must be dealt with by a physician (unless from a visible, accessible cut).*

EARWAX

See **Care of the ears.**

Certain children have a predisposition to wax build-up. Regular review by parents, gently pulling the earlobe down and forward will allow visual access. If in doubt, please ask your doctor to have a look.

RECOMMENDATIONS

- *Reduce mucus-forming foods such as dairy produce, refined foods, and especially white sugar.*
- *Do not attempt to clear out the ear by inserting any objects.*
- *Proprietary earwax-softening solutions available from drugstores are safe, and more effective than naturopathic compounds. Warm olive oil may be used, however, with some effect.*
- *Persisting wax may need to be "washed out," which should be done only by experienced medical practitioners, especially in the case of children. Before this, you may have success with*

proprietary drops and supporting the child's head in a comfortably hot bath with the ears below the water line.

- *Please do not use earwax candles at any age, and especially not in children.*

FOREIGN BODY IN THE EAR

It is not uncommon for small children, in particular, to lodge small objects in the ear canal. If these are not easily removed, do not attempt to do so without medical attention.

RECOMMENDATIONS

- *An easily visible and removable object can be dealt with by fingers or blunt tweezers. If there is any resistance, either from the child or the object, take the child to hospital.*
- *One or two drops of castor oil, olive oil, or even vegetable oil, on the way to the hospital may alleviate the problem sooner.*

"GLUE" EAR

Glue ear is not strictly a medical term, although it has entered the vocabulary. It is characterized by a thick mucus/catarrh that coagulates within the middle ear and is then unable to travel down the Eustachian tube. This thick syrup prevents the ear bones or ossicles from vibrating in response to sound waves, and therefore leads to conductive deafness. The problem is compounded in youngsters who may not hear their teachers, parents, or peers, and therefore it can lead to poor academic standards, disobedience, and poor sociability. A child may be incorrectly labeled "retarded" in extreme cases.

The thickened catarrh can also act as a medium for the growth of bacteria and fungi, thereby predisposing the child to recurrent infections. Glue ear is most frequently associated with:

- poor hydration (allowing the catarrh to become thick and tenacious).

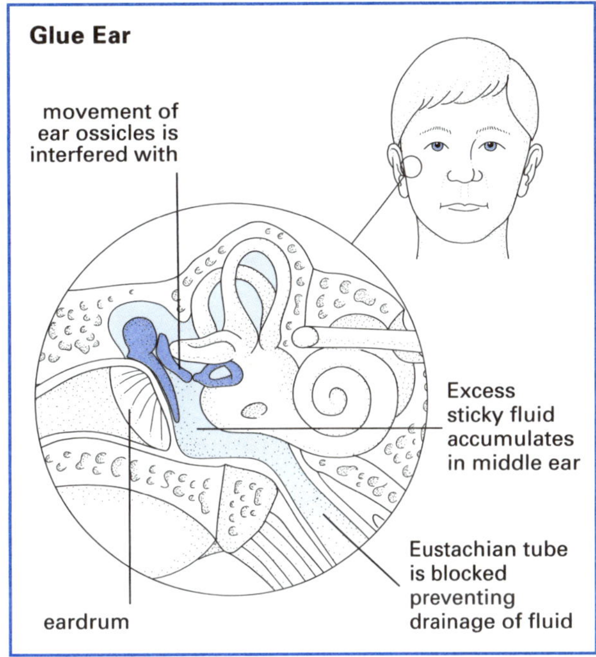

- excess mucus production (associated with mucus-forming foods, such as white sugar).
- poor immune-system response (encouraging the production of mucus as a defense process).
- food intolerance/allergy (particularly dairy products).

One of the most important causes is passive smoking. A child living in a home where a parent smokes is 50 percent more likely to have glue ear. Parents, please note that even if you do not smoke in the presence of your child, it may still be a problem because the cigarette toxins settle on carpets, curtains, and furniture and are then inhaled when the child moves around the room.

RECOMMENDATIONS

- *The diagnosis of glue ear needs to be established by a practitioner looking at the external eardrum and seeing a level of fluid in the ear. Try the following alternatives before using decongestant or operative options.*
- *Consult a complementary medical specialist to ensure that the child has a sound and effective immune system.*

- *Remove mucus-forming foods, such as dairy products, refined foods, and especially white sugar. Food intolerance/allergy testing by bioresonance or blood analysis is recommended.*
- *If the child is catarrhal, use the homeopathic remedy Allium sativa. For chronic catarrh associated with ringing or noises in the ear, consider Causticum, Chenopodium or Calcarea carbonica. All these homeopathic remedies can be used at potency 6, three doses a day for two weeks, in association with the necessary restrictions discussed in the previous recommendation.*
- *Ensure that adequate water is being drunk. Aim at 16 ounces of water per foot of height per day. Juice and other fluids are not the same as water.*
- *The use of Olbas or lavender oil inhalations as a decongestant may open the Eustachian tube, and in conjunction with good rehydration, making the catarrh less viscous, may allow the "glue" to drain.*
- *If treatment is not effective, then the placing of small plastic tubes (grommets) through the eardrum under anesthetic is a surgical option. See* **Operations and surgery** *if this is required. Prior to this, a doctor may recommend decongestants, but I have not seen these work well.*
- *Do not allow the child anywhere near an environment where smoking has occurred.*
- *See* **Otitis media** *and* **Catarrh.**

INFECTIONS OF THE EAR

Middle ear (Otitis media)

Diagnosis of a middle-ear infection can only be made with the use of an otoscope in the hands of an experienced professional. If the doctor diagnoses an ear infection, ask the following questions.

- Can the doctor see fluid behind the eardrum?
- Does the doctor have strong grounds for believing that the infection is bacterial?

General practitioners are becoming less swift to prescribe an antibiotic for what may be a viral infection, but this does often occur unnecessarily (*see* **Antibiotics**). A red eardrum with no fluid behind it is not likely to burst, nor have any permanent damage done, and naturopathic treatments could be employed for 24 hours before an antibiotic is used. An eardrum that has burst and allowed the fluid to discharge is *not* a permanently damaging event, in most cases. The infection will be able to leave the body, and usually the eardrum heals perfectly.

RECOMMENDATIONS

- *If you suspect an ear infection (the infant is pulling at the ear), visit your doctor.*
- *If the doctor recommends antibiotics, ask the reasons why a bacterial infection is suspected.*
- *If the doctor is ambivalent regarding whether the infection is bacterial or viral, ask the doctor if waiting 24hr may be dangerous.*
- *If the doctor is not insistent, then apply two drops of mullein oil or warm olive oil, four times a day, to both ears.*
- *Homeopathic remedies are often very effective. The most commonly prescribed are Aconite, Belladonna, Pulsatilla, and Silica. Refer to a homeopathic manual to select the best treatment.*

If the problem has not resolved over 24 hours, consult a naturopathic practitioner; and if 24 hours later the problem persists, then consider using antibiotics.

Outer ear (Otitis externa)

Occasionally the outer ear may become irritated, red, or scaly.

RECOMMENDATIONS

- *Two drops of mullein oil four times a day.*
- *Bring any persistence to the attention of a naturopathic physician.*
- *Keep the outer part of the ear clean.*
- *Give the child the herbal remedy Echinacea at a dose recommended for children on the packaging, or obtain advice from a local pharmacist or naturopathic practitioner.*
- *Select a homeopathic remedy, dependent upon the symptoms from your preferred homeopathic manual. In the meantime, give Pulsatilla 6, two pills every 2hr.*
- *Avoid antibiotics. General practitioners are still too quick to prescribe these for what may be a viral infection. Many reports in top medical journals suggest that antibiotics should only be used after a definitive diagnosis of a bacterial infection has been made.*

RUPTURE (PERFORATION) OF THE EARDRUM

Rupture of the eardrum, also known as perforation, is associated most commonly with middle-ear infection or trauma. Middle-ear infection causes pressure outwards, which is markedly painful until the eardrum bursts and the pain is relieved. Discharge and small amounts of blood are the characteristic symptoms. Trauma, usually from loud blasts or a slap with an open hand, causes the eardrum to burst inwards, which is characterized by a very severe and sharp pain, followed by a dull ache.

Hearing may or may not be affected, depending on the cause, size of the tear, and associated damage to the ear ossicles.

RECOMMENDATIONS

- *Any suggestion of the above symptoms should be taken for review to your doctor.*
- *Small tears or perforations will generally repair without problem, but larger tears may require the expertise of surgical repair.*
- *In the case of rupture caused by infection, antibiotics may need to be used because homeopathic or naturopathic therapies may work too slowly, and the infection may worsen the rupture or destroy the eardrum. It may be easier for a complementary practitioner to deal with the side effects of the antibiotics than to repair a potentially serious eardrum injury.*

THE EYES

CARE OF THE EYES

The eyes, like most organs in the body, do not need particular attention because they are capable of maintaining their own well-being. However, the eyes are less well-protected than many other organs in the body, and much more open to the environment. They are remarkably delicate and sensitive, and therefore demand a little more respect than other organs.

RECOMMENDATIONS

- *Ensure adequate sleep and rest.*
- *Avoid the use of eye drops unless specifically required. Tears are the eyes' best cleanser and protector.*
- *Consider the use of corrective lenses (glasses or contact lenses) for any visual defects.*
- *Rest the eyes through the day by using the palming technique (see* **Palming***).*
- *Each morning and evening, splash the eyes 20 times with hot water and 20 times with cold water to encourage fresh blood flow.*

BLACK EYE

A black eye is not strictly a problem of the eye, but of the surround. The skin of the face attaches around the eye socket (orbit), such that any bruising that occurs cannot drain farther than around the eyes. Trauma to any part of the head from the lower part of the orbit upwards and backwards that causes bleeding will gravitate downwards, and form blue/black rings around the eyes.

RECOMMENDATIONS

- *Any head trauma that leads to damage or pain of the eye or concussion must be reviewed by a doctor.*
- *The homeopathic remedy Arnica, potency 6 or 12, can be used every hour for three doses and then every 4hr until discomfort is relieved.*
- *The long-established practice of placing raw steak over a black eye generally seems to reduce the severity and the longevity of discoloration, but I know of no scientific reason why this should be the case!*
- *Swelling in association with a black eye will be relieved by ice packs. Avoid prolonged contact with excessive cold to the eyeball itself.*

CONJUNCTIVITIS

Conjunctivitis can occur at any age, but is most commonly found in children because of their frequent touching of eyes and eyelids, and the highly infectious nature of most of the bacteria and viruses that cause conjunctivitis.

Conjunctivitis is characterized by redness, grittiness, or burning, and occasionally swelling of the lining of the eyelids.

See **Blepharitis.**

RECOMMENDATIONS

- *Bathe the eyes in milk, preferably breast milk if available.*
- *Consider the use of Euphrasia (eyebright) mother tincture by applying one drop to an eggcup full of water (preferably boiled and then cooled). This can be placed in an eye bath or applied with a dropper. Bathing the child's eye with cotton wool soaked in this solution, and then gently but firmly prising open the eyelids, will allow some of the fluid to enter.*
- *Review the homeopathic remedies Rhus toxicodendron, Staphysagria, Arsenicum album, Aconite, and Mercurius.*
- *Beta-carotene (2mg per foot of height) in divided doses through the day will speed recovery.*

DISCHARGES FROM THE EYES

The eyes of babies are frequently associated with discharge. A not-infrequent reason is a blocked duct that drains the tears from the eye through a small tube into the nose. Sometimes this nasolacrimal duct remains closed, and requires surgical opening. A persisting watery or discharging eye should be looked at by a specialist.

Lacrimal Gland

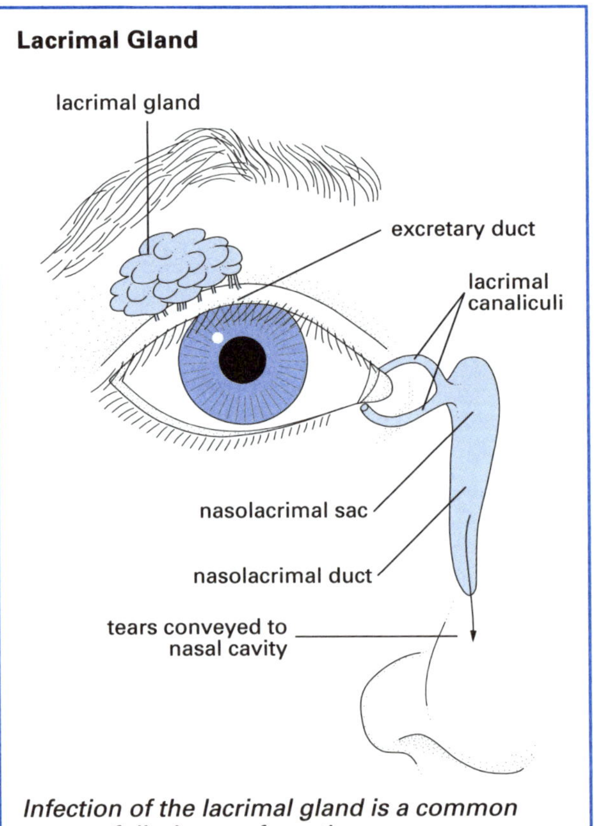

Infection of the lacrimal gland is a common cause of discharges from the eyes.

Mild redness of the eyelids, red veins in the white of the eye, a discharge that is colored (yellow or green usually), or persisting crusting can be treated initially at home.

A discharge from the eye usually represents a conjunctivitis (*see* **Conjunctivitis**), or infection of the lacrimal gland or ducts. More rarely, it is caused by an embedded foreign body in the eyeball.

RECOMMENDATIONS

- *Breast milk, carrying natural immunoglobulins, can be dropped into the eye four times a day. Standard cow's milk can also be used in the same way.*
- *Do not use chemical preparations or naturopathic herbal solutions without the support and advice of a naturopathic practitioner, although a weak solution of camomile tea can be tried, and is soothing and effective.*
- *The homeopathic remedy Rhus toxicodendron 6, one pill every 2hr, can be administered.*
- *Any eye condition persisting for longer than 24hr should be seen by a professional.*
- *Persisting eye infections may be an early indication of allergies or food intolerances, and this possibility should be mentioned to your naturopathic physician.*
- *Any painful or persistent discharge should be reviewed by a doctor.*
- *Cleansing the eyes with a diluted Euphrasia (eyebright) solution can be employed.*
- *Specific homeopathic or herbal treatment can be used, depending on the cause. Remedies to review are Pulsatilla, Kali bichromicum, and Mercurius.*

DOUBLE VISION

See **Double vision** in chapter 4.

Establishing double vision in an infant or child before he/she can speak or show signs, such as bumping into door frames or trying to pick up an object by grasping the air beside it, is nearly impossible. Any suggestion of a visual defect, which also includes responding to Mom's face while looking at her ear, should be brought to the attention of a physician or optometrist immediately.

See **Squint** if you notice that your child's eyes point in different directions.

RECOMMENDATION

- *Please obtain professional guidance on any visual problem in an infant.*

DRY EYES

Chronic dry eyes may represent underlying disease, such as sarcoidosis and other autoimmune conditions. These need to be treated appropriately after diagnosis from a doctor or eye specialist.

Acute dry eyes may be treated with the recommendations below, provided that relief and cure are forthcoming within a short period of time.

RECOMMENDATIONS

- *Persisting or painful dry eyes must be reviewed by a doctor.*
- *Avoid artificial tears, which contain chemicals, and in preference use milk or Euphrasia eye drops.*
- *Ensure good oral hydration by drinking at least 48 ounces of water per day.*
- *Avoid eye make-up or, if this is unavoidable, ensure that it is thoroughly washed off as often as possible, and certainly do not leave eye make-up on through the night.*
- *Persisting cases may respond to homeopathic remedies, and the following should be reviewed: Sulphur, Petroleum, Silica, and Causticum.*

EXCESSIVE WATERING OF THE EYES

The lacrimal glands produce tears that should drain through a small hole and tube in the corner of the eye that leads into the nasal passage.

Up to 50 percent of children may be born with a blockage in this duct, and less than 2 percent have a permanent blockage requiring surgical intervention. Older children and adults may have a foreign body or inflammation from infection or trauma creating a blockage.

RECOMMENDATIONS

- *Trauma, injury, or infection should be reviewed by a complementary medical practitioner with knowledge in this area, and an eye specialist's opinion should be obtained if treatment does not resolve the problem within a matter of days.*
- *Trauma to the side of the nose or infection may require more urgent treatment, and a medical opinion should be obtained, although antibiotics should be avoided until alternative measures have failed.*
- *The homeopathic remedy Silica is effective in dealing with infected or blocked drainage ducts. Silica 6 should be taken every 2hr.*
- *Gentle massage from the corner of the eye down the side of the nose may relieve the blockage.*

EYELIDS

The eyelids are a remarkably important part of the body. They are protective and busy (blinking every 5–8 seconds).

They are colored to attract attention, and similarly this may reflect the health of an individual. Darkened or swollen lower eyelids are a reflection of anything from tiredness through water retention to kidney problems. Many people are born with darkened or swollen eyelids, and will maintain them through their lifetime and this is not an indication of ill health, but a development of "bags" under the eyes should be reviewed by a complementary medical practitioner initially. The Eastern philosophies of medicine correlate the color under the eyes with our energy stores, specifically kidney energy.

Inflammation

Inflammation of the external eyelid is a common site for eczema (*see* **Eczema**).

Inflammation of the internal aspect of the eyelid is conjunctivitis (*see* **Conjunctivitis**).

RECOMMENDATIONS

- *See* **Eczema** *and* **Conjunctivitis**.
- *Resist applying any make-up to this area until a treatment course has been set.*

Lumps

Lumps on or in the eyelids may simply be a reflection of the skin condition, such as a wart or a pimple, but are best reviewed by a physician because of the potential spread of infection into the eye, and also because of conditions such as skin cancers that may appear anywhere. Lumps that are specific to the eyelids are meibomian cysts or xanthelasmata.

Meibomian cysts (Chalazions)

Meibomian glands are found in the rim of the eyelids, and produce a secretion that contains many immunoglobulins and protective immune factors. These glands have small ducts that can become blocked, which leads to the secretion being unable to leave, and causes a swelling along the eyelid rims. Rarely are these painful, but they do have a tendency to become infected and may develop into styes (*see* **Styes**).

Very often, meibomian cysts will reabsorb, but if not, treatment may be required.

RECOMMENDATIONS

- *The homeopathic remedies Staphysagria or Thuja can be used at potency 6, four pills every 3hr for five days.*
- *Surgical intervention by ophthalmic surgeons is rarely required, but a growing, cosmetically unacceptable or painful meibomian cyst should be seen by such a specialist.*
- *See* **Styes** *opposite.*

Stye on Eyelid

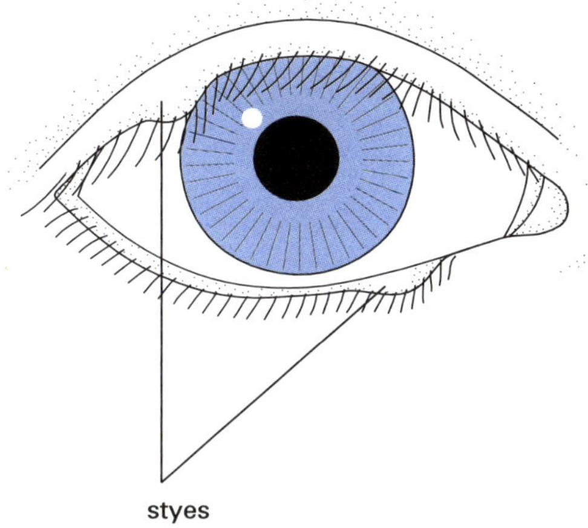

Styes

Styes usually occur as a red, itchy, or painful swelling caused by bacteria proliferating in an eyelash-root cell or a meibomian cyst.

Styes are usually self-limiting, but recurrent infections may require medical examination for underlying problems such as diabetes or other immunosuppressant conditions.

Styes commonly found in children are often to do with mild malnutrition, and occur during growth spurts.

RECOMMENDATIONS

- *Bathe the eye in milk.*
- *Hot and cold compress application can bring the boil to a head, and allow easier discharge.*
- *Euphrasia eye drops can be used.*
- *The homeopathic remedies Pulsatilla, Rhus toxicodendron, Apis, and Staphysagria should all be reviewed.*
- *Ensure correct hygiene by washing your hands because styes tend to be very easily transmitted.*
- *A multivitamin/mineral supplement should be administered to a child who is not eating at least three portions of fruit or vegetables each day.*

Twitching eyelids

A twitch anywhere is representative of a trapped, irritated, inflamed, or damaged nerve. This may occur in the central nervous system (brain or spinal column) or at the neuromuscular junction. Most twitches are short-lived and of no consequence, but others may be a warning or a result of nerve damage or, more commonly, deficiencies.

RECOMMENDATIONS

- *A persisting twitch should be reviewed by a complementary medical practitioner initially and then, if no improvement is forthcoming, a neurological specialist.*
- *Consider any deficiencies that may have arisen, specifically calcium, magnesium, copper, and B-complex vitamins, all of which are necessary for the correct and smooth functioning of nerves and their muscular connections.*
- *Gentle massage around the eyelid, and also the nape of the neck, may be relieving.*
- *Cranial osteopathy, craniosacral therapy, and acupuncture may be employed, once more serious causes have been eliminated.*
- *A nervous twitch brought on by stress is best dealt with through hypnosis and counseling.*
- *The homeopathic remedy Agaricus 6 taken hourly may be of benefit, as may the remedy Codeinum.*

FOREIGN BODIES AND SUBSTANCES IN THE EYE

Foreign bodies

A foreign body that is not easily removable by flushing the eye with fluid from a dropper bottle, or blinking in water in an eye bath or the palms of the hand, or by a clean piece of tissue paper, must be taken to a doctor. Any object that is embedded in the eyeball or is causing bleeding in the conjunctiva, and is not removable by fingers, must, once again, be dealt with by a medical practitioner.

EYE—Structure

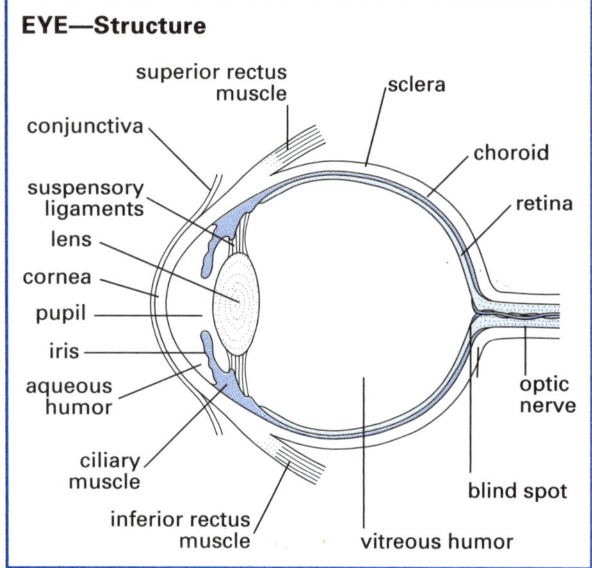

It is unwise to use instruments such as tweezers, because the sensitivity of the eye makes the patient very jumpy and further damage probable.

RECOMMENDATIONS

- *Seek medical attention if the object is not easily removable.*
- *Commence the patient on Aconite 6, two tablets every 10min, and gently massage the other eyeball through the eyelid, because the eyes move in conjunction with each other and the gentle movement may dislodge the object.*

Foreign substances

RECOMMENDATIONS

- *Identify the foreign substance that has infiltrated the eye, keeping any bottles available for inspection by a doctor if necessary.*
- *Regardless of the acidity or alkalinity of the compound, the eye should only be flushed with water under a gently running fawcet, or with water or saline from a dropper bottle.*
- *After a thorough flushing with water, any remnants of an acidic substance should be counteracted by bathing the eye in milk. An alkaline substance should only be washed out with water.*
- *The homeopathic remedies Apis and Belladonna, potency 6, can be given every 15min until the discomfort is settled or medical advice is sought.*

INFLAMMATION OF THE EYES

Inflammation of the eyelids is known as conjunctivitis (*see* **Conjunctivitis**). Inflammation of the eyes themselves falls into two divisions: iritis (inflammation of the iris) and scleritis (inflammation of the whites of the eyes).

Both iritis and scleritis may be associated with underlying conditions such as autoimmune disease or venereal disease, and a persistence in either of these problems must be investigated fully as soon as possible.

Iritis

The symptoms of iritis are pain and redness around the central, colored part of the eye.

This is often associated with visual disturbance, such as blurring, photophobia, aching eyes or headaches. Persistent iritis requires medical attention because the inflammation can cause a blockage of the channels between the anterior and posterior "humors" (fluids), which can lead to an increase in pressure known as glaucoma. Damage to the iris may affect vision (very rarely causing blindness) and encourages the development of cataracts.

RECOMMENDATIONS

- *Very severe or prolonged (longer than 4hr) iritis should be seen by a doctor.*
- *Bathe the eye with milk or Euphrasia eye drops every hour.*
- *Use the homeopathic remedy Aconite 6 every 15min at the onset of an attack.*
- *Consider the homeopathic remedies Euphrasia, Mercurius corrosivus, Rhus toxicodendron, Arnica, and Hamamelis by referring to your preferred homeopathic textbook.*

Scleritis

Scleritis is a less-serious condition than iritis, although if left untreated, this red, dull aching of the white of the eye may run the risk of affecting the retina at the back of the eye, or even perforating it, running the risk of the loss of fluid from the eye or allowing infection in.

RECOMMENDATIONS

- *A persisting scleritis or one that is particularly painful should be reviewed by a physician.*
- *Aconite 6 should by taken every 2hr.*
- *Use milk or Euphrasia eye drops as frequently as every 3hr.*
- *Food allergy and allergy to airborne matter must be excluded if the problem persists.*

INJURIES TO THE EYE

See **Black eye** and **Foreign bodies and substances in the eye**.

Injury to the eye occurs from a direct blow, from penetration of the eyeball by a foreign object, or from foreign matter on the surface.

Any crush or penetrating injury must be tended to by an eye specialist. Injuries that cause leakage of fluids from the eye into the bloodstream can trigger an antibody response that could cause the body to attack the other eye. This may lead to blindness, and needs to be considered and treated immediately.

RECOMMENDATIONS

- *If common sense and simple procedures can remove a foreign object from the eye, then proceed. If not, seek medical attention immediately.*
- *The injured eye should be covered and gentle pressure applied if there is marked bleeding. Avoid pressure if a foreign body has penetrated the eye.*
- *Ice wrapped in a wash cloth may be applied if it is soothing.*
- *Bathing the eye in milk or Euphrasia may be relieving.*
- *A patch or blindfold over both eyes may prevent the non-injured eye from moving quite so much. Because the eyes move in unison, as little movement as possible is preferable.*
- *Any persistence of discomfort or visual disturbance should, once again, be examined by an eye specialist.*

Pain in the eyes

RECOMMENDATIONS

- *Any pain that does not have an obvious cause or does not fall into any of the categories mentioned must be reviewed by a doctor.*
- *Use Aconite 6 every 10min for an eye pain while awaiting diagnosis.*
- *Once a diagnosis has been established, treat accordingly.*

Palming

Palming is one of the Bates' eye exercises designed to give the eyes a rest. The eye muscles, perhaps more so than any other muscles in the body, are constantly in action, and therefore tire more easily. This is why when we are tired we find it difficult to keep the eyes open.

The technique of palming allows the eye muscles to relax thoroughly because the technique prevents any light entering the eyes, thereby allowing complete dilation of the pupil, which is equivalent to full relaxation of the pupillary muscles.

- Keeping the eyes open, place the palms of the hand over the eye sockets.
- Move the palms until no cracks of light can be seen around the edges.
- Stare straight ahead for 3 minutes, blinking as required.
- After 3 minutes close the eyes, remove the palms and open the eyes, taking care not to look directly into bright light.

Palming the Eyes

Palming the eyes allows the eye muscles to relax thoroughly.

SQUINT OR STRABISMUS (LAZY EYE)

The definition of strabismus is an abnormality of the eyes in which the visual axes do not meet at the desired objective point. Put more simply, it means that one eye will be fixed on an object while the other is looking elsewhere. This is due to uncoordinated action of the extrinsic ocular muscles, which control eye movement.

A squint in an infant is hard to assess because very often the eyes move independently for the first three months. If a child has apparently got convergent or divergent eyes after three months, then a specialist opinion is recommended. At a young age, two visual pictures will be sent to the ocular part of the brain, and this is very confusing. The brain will select one, not the other, and the eye whose vision is being rejected will effectively become useless. This is known as a lazy eye, and is the reason why expert advice is needed.

A squint developing at a later age (including those that develop in adulthood) may be associated with more serious conditions, such as diabetes, neuromuscular conditions like myasthenia gravis, or even brain tumors.

RECOMMENDATIONS

- *Any suggestion of a squint should be reviewed by an ocular specialist.*
- *Techniques such as patching the eye may be less common with the advent of more accurate eye surgery. This includes tightening or releasing the muscles around the eye to allow a better control.*
- *Specific eye exercises, such as Bates' methods, can be utilized before surgery is contemplated.*
- *The homeopathic remedies, Gelsemium, Hyoscyamus, Belladonna, Stramonium, and Zinc may all be useful at high potency over a period of two weeks. Prescribing should be done by a homeopath for the most benefit.*

THE NOSE

Nasal congestion occurs in infants because they have no concept of "blowing their noses." Unless the child is too wriggly, the very careful use of a Q-tip can relieve congestion from the lower part of the nostrils. Infants spend a lot of time lying flat, which allows gravity to pull the catarrh to the back of the nose. Prop the baby up as much as possible.

RECOMMENDATIONS

- *Leave well alone. The problem will resolve by itself, despite the apparent discomfort the child is suffering.*

- *In severe cases, hold the child on your lap by a table. Place a few drops of lavender oil, elder flowers, Euphrasia, or a mixture of rosemary and thyme in a bowl of steaming water, and place a towel over yourself, baby, and the bowl. Stay there for a few minutes while the steam and oil act as a decongestant.*
- *Two drops of lavender oil or camomile oil on the pillow may be effective, or one of the orthodox decongestants can be used, but if the child is taking a homeopathic remedy this will be nullified if the preparation contains camphor, menthol, or mint of any sort.*
- *Nosebleeds in infants should be checked by a pediatrician or suitably qualified practitioner.*

CATARRH

Catarrh is the medical term for mucus found in the upper respiratory tract—sinuses, nose, and throat. Catarrh is an essential part of good health because it contains antibodies and white blood cells that attack invading viruses, bacteria, and fungi. Catarrh is also produced when the body is trying to rid the membranes of toxic substances such as pollutants or excess dust, and in response to foreign proteins such as plant pollen. The orthodox approach to troublesome catarrh, usually associated with colds, is to try to suppress this useful excretion, whereas the holistic approach is to encourage its production so that the cause of the excess mucus can be eliminated.

RECOMMENDATIONS

- *Try to encourage the production of catarrh if the symptoms are mild.*
- *Excess catarrh can be reduced by eliminating dairy products, alcohol, and sugar from the diet until the condition has improved.*
- *Homeopathic remedies can encourage the production of catarrh and, depending on the color, consistency, amount, and time of day of production, a suitable remedy can be most beneficial. There are over 200 remedies that have a catarrhal effect, and specific assessment is required from your favorite homeopathic manual.*
- *The following vitamins and supplements can be of benefit if taken as prescribed, with food, per foot of height: vitamin A (1,000iu), vitamin C (500mg), and zinc (2·5mg).*
- *Persistent catarrh may be an allergic response. See* **Allergies**.
- *Ensure good hydration, drinking at least 16 ounces of water per day per two feet (61cm) of height in addition to your normal fluid intake. This dilutes the catarrh, making it easier for the body to blow or cough out.*

NOSEBLEEDS—*see* Epistaxis (Nosebleeds)

THE MOUTH

COLD SORES—*see* Herpes simplex

HARELIP (CLEFT PALATE)

Harelip is the nonmedical term for a failure of fusion through embryonic development of the hard palate at the top of the mouth.

From an orthodox point of view, the cause of cleft palate is uncertain, although nutritional deficiencies and infections are occasionally cited for any developmental problems.

Deformities, although psychologically damaging, may or may not have a physical difficulty associated with them. Surgical repair is now at such a high standard that a deformity may be hardly noticeable. Technology is advancing, and repair of serious cleft palates can be done *in utero* (with the baby still in the mother's uterus). Severe deformities can lead to problems with speech and, more seriously, with the inhalation of food that is difficult, if not impossible, to chew. Such deformities must be repaired.

Upper Respiratory Tract—Catarrh

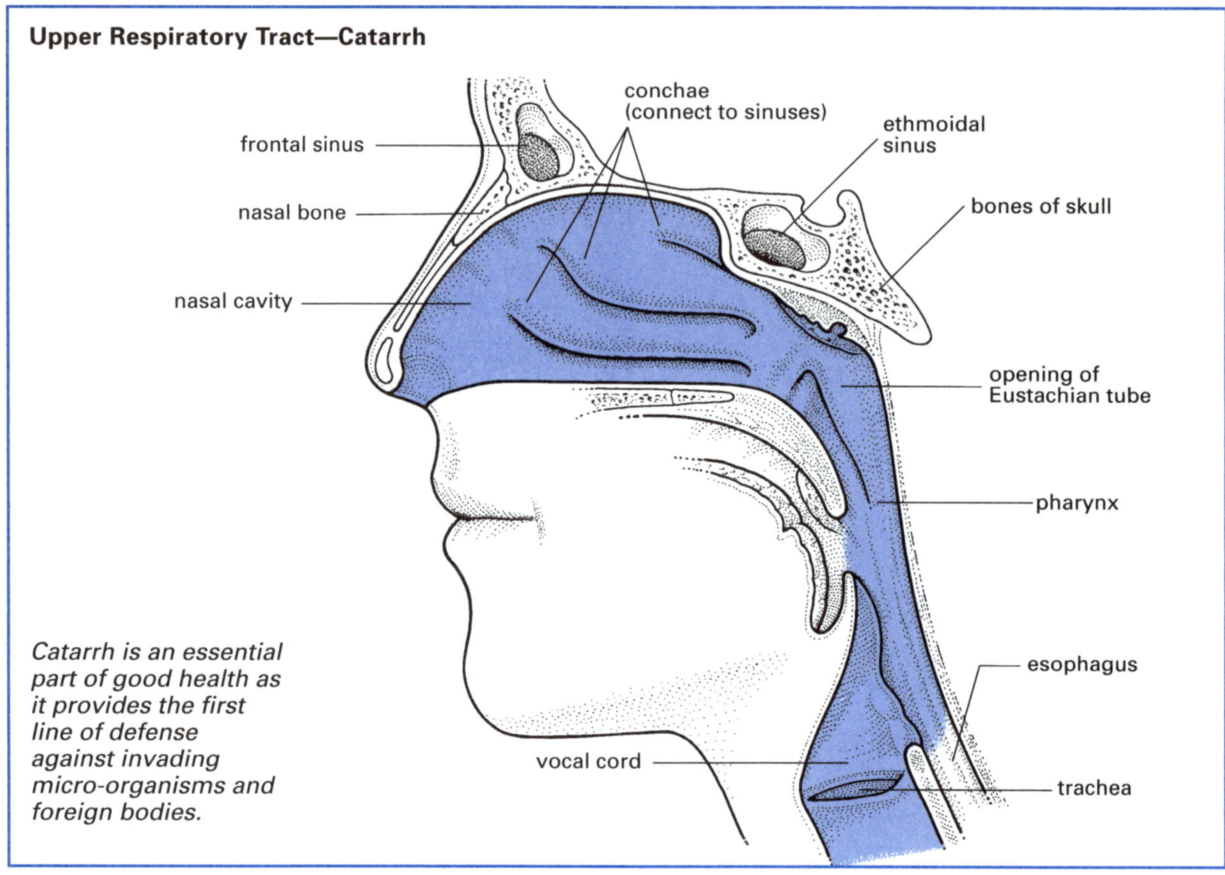

Catarrh is an essential part of good health as it provides the first line of defense against invading micro-organisms and foreign bodies.

RECOMMENDATIONS

- *Cleft palate is diagnosable through ultrasound of the fetus in utero. Discuss the possibility of surgical repair as soon as possible.*
- *See* **Surgery and operations**.
- *Have a consultation with a nutritionist to discuss the possible deficiencies that may be present in any developmental abnormality.*
- *All individuals with a cleft palate must see a speech therapist, and referral through your doctor will advise on the time to start. Generally, it is as soon as a child is able to understand commands (around 18 months to two years).*
- *Cranial osteopathy will help postoperative healing and also correct any imbalances in the cranial bones.*

MOUTH ULCERS

Mouth ulcers can occur at any age, but most commonly are a bother to children. The main cause is trauma, usually created by biting the tongue or cheek. Nutritional deficiencies, especially of vitamins A and C or the mineral zinc, can be the cause, and this tends to occur in individuals who are reluctant to eat, or not given, fruit and vegetables.

Poor dental hygiene, irregular teeth, or oral braces may all be traumatic, and an excess of mercury fillings may irritate via absorption into the saliva. Metabolic disorders such as diabetes and malabsorption syndromes can be indicated by recurrent and persistent mouth ulcers, and in smokers or tobacco chewers, a mouth ulcer may be the sign of an oral cancer.

Food allergy or intolerance may trigger any inflammatory or degenerative process, and may need to be considered; sharp, acidic, or spicy foods may aggravate rather than cause problems.

RECOMMENDATIONS

- *Ensure good dental hygiene and regular check-ups from the dentist.*
- *Do not eat quickly, and avoid talking while eating as this encourages biting of the tongue or cheeks.*
- *Mouthwashes with warm salty water with or without Calendula fluid extract will speed up healing.*
- *Clove oil applied to the lesion will sting, but will give considerable relief. Dilute in olive oil if the initial application is unpleasant.*
- *Aspirin-containing gels may be used in the short term quite effectively.*
- *The homeopathic remedies Mercurius and Arsenicum should be reviewed, although other homeopathic remedies may fit the symptoms. Reference should be made to your preferred homeopathic manual.*
- *Persistent ulcers should be brought to the attention of a complementary medical practitioner, who should check for diabetes, malabsorption syndromes, leaky-gut syndrome, food allergies, and specifically, oral candidiasis (thrush), which is not uncommon in bottle-fed infants and individuals who are run down.*

THE TEETH

The tooth is made up of an outer, hard, enamel coating, below which is a layer of dentine, which forms the bulk of the tooth and is a hard, elastic, yellowish-white substance. This is embedded in a cement that resembles bone in structure and whose action is to anchor the tooth. The cement is attached to periosteum tissue (that covers the jawbone).

The tooth is divided into the crown (above the gum), the neck (at the level of the gum), and the root (embedded in the jaw).

TEETH and GUMS—Structure

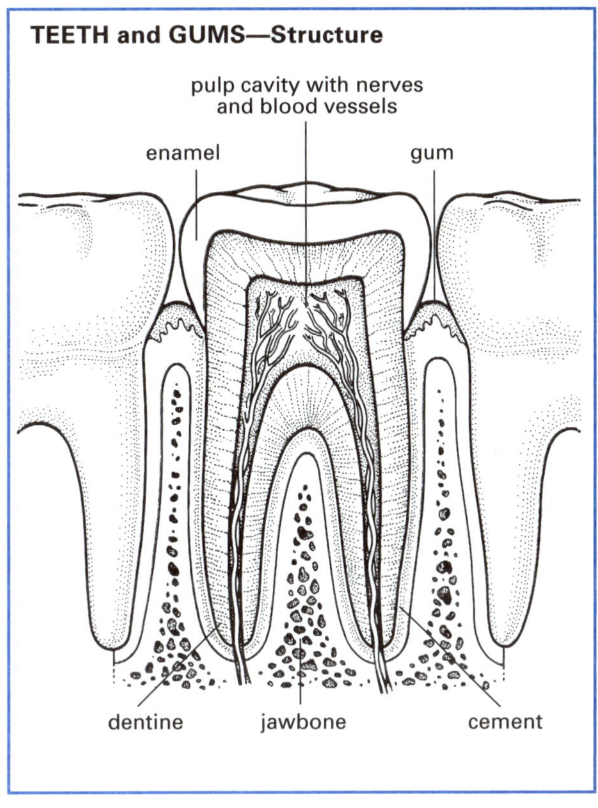

CARIES

Avoidance of caries (holes in the enamel of teeth) is dependent upon good oral hygiene and dietetics. Caries are produced by trauma or because of production of acid from bacteria that exist in the mouth. This acid breaks down the hard enamel and dentine, and reaches the inner pulp. It is this that causes toothache, because the pulp contains the nerve fibers.

RECOMMENDATIONS

- *Regular brushing and cleaning of teeth is essential. A fluoride toothpaste should only be used once a day (see* **Fluoride***).*
- *Good calcium intake through dairy products, meat, chicken, fish, nuts, and particularly sesame seeds, is required from an early age.*
- *Chewing on raw fruit and vegetables helps to prevent caries.*

- *Most importantly, avoid refined sugars and foods containing them.*
- *Persistent caries, despite following the above advice, should be reviewed by a nutritionist or naturopath to assess if the saliva has lost its protective function.*
- *Removal of the infection and sealing the hole with a non-mercury filling, performed under local anesthetic by a dentist.*
- *See* **Toothache**.

FILLINGS

Dental fillings can be required at any age, but the risk of fillings and the potential number are both increased in childhood.

There is much controversy about the use of mercury in tooth-cavity-filling substances called amalgams. At present, the British Dental Association refuses to accept that mercury from fillings is a problem, but most physicians associated with environmental or nutritional medicine consider mercury to be a problem (*see* **Mercury poisoning**).

Cavities in the teeth need to be filled with non-mercury fillings.

RECOMMENDATIONS

- *Ensure six-monthly visits to the dentist, and have any fillings repaired.*
- *Prior to the visit, regardless of whether any dental work will be done, take homeopathic remedy Arnica 6 four times a day, starting the day before the visit.*
- *If fillings are known to be required, insist on nonmercury fillings, and, if this is not possible, change your dentist.*
- *If mercury fillings are in place, visit a practitioner who uses a bioenergetic diagnostic device such as a Bicom or Quantum CI computer (see* **Bioresonance***) to establish whether mercury is a problem within your system. Alternatively, a red blood cell mercury level can be obtained. If toxicity is the case, then a sympathetic dentist needs to be found who will remove all amalgam fillings and replace with a nonmercury composite.*

FLUORIDE AND FLUOROSIS

Fluorosis is the medical term given for fluoride poisoning. Ingesting or inhaling any compound containing fluorine is potentially lethal. Very small amounts can be handled by the body, but not so well by bacteria. This is the reason why individuals in Western societies are forcibly—and without option—fed fluoride. Fluoride is placed in our water reservoirs, our processed foods, and even our vitamin supplements. Most famously, it is advertised as an important additive to our toothpaste. This latter addition is encouraged because of the association of decreased dental caries when fluoride was initially introduced at higher levels into our food chain.

Unfortunately, studies have shown that tooth decay diminished at the same rate in areas where water was not fluoridated. Consider the healthy teeth of young Caribbean children who have not been introduced to enforced fluoridation. One might like to note that these children often chew constantly on wild cane, which does not have the same decaying effect on the teeth that our Western refined sugar has.

The argument that fluoride destroys bad bacteria is correct, but unfortunately it is not specific and creates considerable damage to our own beneficial bacteria. The amounts that are forced upon us do not take into account the levels of fluoride that we take in through our food, and therefore, potentially toxic levels of fluoride may affect all of us. Some individuals have a specific allergy or an oversensitivity to fluoride, and they are particularly susceptible to conditions such as fluorosis of the teeth or bones, causing increased caries or tendency to fracture. Fluoride has also been noted (and the information suppressed by the big businesses that provide fluoride and introduce it into our food chain, such as food manufacturers and water suppliers) to cause biochemical changes in the body, birth defects, and cancer.

Toxic levels may be created by taking in water that contains ten parts of fluoride per million parts of water. The recommended dosage for "good dental health" is four parts per million. A fractional error in contaminating our water supply may lead to poisoning, and no mention is made of those people who may have a higher level of fluoride in their diet from such foods as tea, seafood, some meats, and green vegetables. Children often enjoy the taste of toothpaste and swallow it, and many vitamins may have fluoride as part of their constituents.

It should be noted that few areas in the UK have the water supply fluoridated, but it is worth asking about your area.

RECOMMENDATIONS

- *An individual who has a well-balanced diet, including seafood and tea, and who uses fluoride-containing toothpaste should have a reverse-osmosis water filter installed to remove the excessive fluoride from tap water.*
- *An occasional drink of tap water will quite adequately provide the flouride we need.*
- *Use a fluoride-containing toothpaste once a day only.*
- *Ensure good exercise to maintain bone-density strength.*
- *Consider a bi-yearly use of the homeopathic remedy Fluoricum acidum 200 (one dose) to encourage the body to fight against excess fluoride.*

GRINDING TEETH (BRUXISM)

Teeth grinding occurs for two reasons, neither of which are confined to childhood, but it is most frequently noticed at this age. This predisposition most commonly occurs in those under stress. The masseter (jaw) muscles are very sensitive to stress, as is shown by the obvious clenching of those who are concentrating or are angry. Most frequently, this occurs at night.

The second reason is not well supported by scientific evidence, but is anecdotally accepted as a possible calcium deficiency. The body is aware of the calcium levels in the teeth, and tries to make it available by grinding. Most commonly, this occurs in children rather than adults, and during sleep rather than while awake. Teeth grinding can be associated with threadworms, and any symptoms such as an itching anus or excessive appetite with no weight gain should be noted.

RECOMMENDATIONS

- *Establish any emotional causes and deal with them appropriately. Basic counseling may be most beneficial.*
- *Add in a calcium supplement or take sesame seeds and dairy products, provided that there is no allergic or intolerant association.*
- *The homeopathic remedy Arsenicum album 6, four pills before bed, can be most effective. Also refer to the remedies Zinc, Phytolacca, Calcarea phosphorica, and Silica.*
- *If bruxism is associated with threadworms, use the homeopathic remedy Cinchona 6.*
- *Use chelated zinc (3mg per foot of height) before bedtime.*
- *A consultation with a cranial osteopath may relieve tension in the jaw muscles.*
- *A dentist's opinion may be required if grinding is persistent, and may suggest a protective cover put on at night to prevent wearing down the teeth.*
- *If the tendency is persistent, please review the individual case with a complementary medical practitioner.*

ORAL HYGIENE

It is best to start an infant's oral hygiene as early as possible. A small gauze pad or soft cloth should be wrapped around your finger, moistened, and used to massage the gums. This helps teeth break through, and gets the baby used to teeth cleaning.

Infants should not have fatty foods or refined sugars introduced to their diet. In fact, it is quite feasible to avoid artificial sweeteners until the child attends the home of a less-conscientious parent, which may not be until the age of two or three years. Refined sugars encourage bacterial growth, and if a sweet food is ingested, a gentle gum or teeth rub with camomile tea will encourage salivation and wash the sugars out.

PLAQUE AND TARTAR

Plaque is a collection of bacteria that adheres to the enamel of teeth, and tartar is a build-up of a calcium compound that itself adheres to teeth. The plaque lives within tartar, and slowly but relentlessly eats away at the gum, encouraging infection, tooth decay, and loss of teeth.

RECOMMENDATIONS

- *Proper dental hygiene and regular descaling by a dental hygienist is essential.*
- *Using specialized brushes that get between the teeth or dental floss is good hygienic practice. This is even better if started at a young age before gaps clearly form between the teeth where food can stick and encourage bacterial growth.*

SENSITIVE TEETH

Sensitivity to hot or cold is a common manifestation, and is generally caused by the exposure of nerves in the gum or the pulp of the tooth.

RECOMMENDATIONS

- *Ensure that general care is taken as advised above to avoid tooth or gum damage.*
- *Regular dental check-ups (at least every six months) and specific attention to a sensitive area may seal the exposed nerves.*
- *Application of clove oil directly onto the area by dipping a Q-tip into the essential oil may help. Be careful not to allow too much clove oil onto the area because this will irritate the tongue. Application twice a day over a period of ten days will, potentially, numb the nerve permanently.*
- *The homeopathic remedy Natrum muriaticum 6 can be taken four times a day. Sensitivity to cold may respond better to Silica 6, four times a day.*

TEETH DISCOLORATION

The overuse of fluoride through toothpaste, water, and tablets was a common factor, especially in the children of dentists, 30 years ago. Nowadays, fluoridation is controlled, and this mottled appearance is no longer seen commonly. The same effect may be produced by the use of tetracyclines (aggressive antibiotics). Smoking, chewing tobacco, and excessive ingestion of red wine (not all that common in young children!) may stain teeth at an older age.

The most common cause of discoloration is the yellowing that occurs from teeth that are not cleaned. Certain infections may cause a gray-white patchy discoloration, the most common of which are whooping cough and measles.

RECOMMENDATIONS

- *Ensure that regular cleaning takes place.*
- *Regular visits to the dentist or the dental hygienist for removal of debris will benefit.*
- *The discoloration from infection may be removed by using the nosodes (homeopathic remedies made from the causative agent) Pertussin for whooping cough and Morbillinum for whooping cough and measles respectively. Use potency 6 or 12 twice a day for one week.*

TEETHING

Teething is a term that describes the arrival of the milk teeth (the first set of teeth) in an infant. This usually occurs anywhere from before birth to the age of three years. Typically, the first tooth will arrive at around six to eight months, and the full set will be exposed around the 30-month mark. The breaking of the gum is a painful experience, and it is not surprising that infants are often inconsolable as they go through this period. There is usually marked excessive salivation and, less frequently, a red rash that resembles the after-effects of a smack on one or both cheeks. A fever may be noted, either by the child feeling hot or by a thermometer, and a general malaise or lethargy may be observed. Diarrhea is often associated.

Gently feel the gums for protrusions and, if possible, look for any redness or swelling. If there is no evidence of teething, do not assume that any symptoms are due to teething, but consider other possible problems.

A teething fever is generally mild. A temperature over 100°F is unlikely to be caused by teething.

RECOMMENDATIONS

- *Give the child something hard to chew on, preferably a carrot or a piece of apple but otherwise an artificial "teether." The colder these objects are, the more relieving it will be.*
- *Gentle massage around the jaw may reduce inflammation.*
- *The use of the homeopathic remedy Chamomilla 6, one dose every halfhour if the child is particularly upset, otherwise twice a day throughout the period of teething.*
- *Do not hesitate to use a childhood antipyretic (antifever) if the child is not sleeping.*
- *Two drops of clove oil in eight drops of olive oil applied to a ruptured gum is very soothing. Test it on your own tongue. It should tingle, not burn. Dilute with more olive oil if necessary.*
- *Catnip, lime flowers, or camomile teas throughout the day can be very soothing.*

TOOTHACHE AND DENTAL PAIN

Toothache is created by exposure of nerves either in the gum or the pulp of the tooth. Cleansing and debriding (removing) of tartar and plaque (*see* **Plaque and tartar**) is essential to remove the base of the bacterial infection responsible for the acid that has decayed the area.

RECOMMENDATIONS

- *Visit a dentist at the earliest opportunity to cleanse the area and isolate the inflamed nerves.*
- *The remedies Arnica 6 or Hypericum 6 may be taken every halfhour if the discomfort is bad, before the dentist is seen.*
- *Prepare a mouthwash from a cup of water with a teaspoon of salt and a teaspoon of Arnica fluid extract. Force this through the teeth at a temperature that is soothing or comfortable.*
- *The application of clove oil via a Q-tip dipped in the essential oil and applied just to the sensitive area. Do not use too much clove oil, because this will cause stinging of the surrounding tissue.*
- *Please refer to your preferred homeopathic manual for a more suitable remedy based on the type of toothache, the site and its sensitivities.*
- *A persistent toothache may be associated with sinusitis, or an osteopathic lesion in the neck or jaw that may be pinching the trunk of the nerves supplying the jaw. An osteopath may be very effective.*

THE GUMS

A lot of dental work is needed, not specifically because of the teeth, but due to poor health of the gums. The gums are a specialized, tough mucus membrane that covers the jawbone and lower aspects of the teeth. Maintenance of the integrity of the gums is essential to avoid tooth decay and jawbone problems.

CARE OF THE GUMS

Infections of the gum are often difficult to treat because the bacteria can find their way into deep

Dental Hygiene

brushing with a circular motion

flossing with an up and down motion

mouthwashing with salt water

recesses around the tooth root, well-protected from the mouth's natural antibodies found in the saliva and also from oxygen, which is often detrimental to bacterial growth.

Plaque is a thin, transparent film of bacteria on the surface of the teeth. The bacteria live comfortably despite the body's natural defense mechanisms, and slowly but surely eat into the gum tissue. It is this plaque that needs to be destroyed.

RECOMMENDATIONS

- *As early as possible, teach your child to brush the teeth with a circular motion, ensuring that the bristles travel between the teeth.*
- *The toothbrush should be as hard as the gums will accept without bleeding.*
- *Toothpaste (without fluoride) or baking soda can be used as a tooth cleanser, although the brushing action with lightly-salted water is the most beneficial aspect of gum care.*
- *Avoid refined sugars or ensure teeth brushing and gum cleaning (the same thing) after any sweet meal. Natural sugars do not have the same bacterial support, as is noticed by the healthy teeth in Caribbean children whose sweeteners come from raw cane rather than refined sugar.*
- *Regular mouthwashes with salt water being forced between the teeth is highly recommended.*
- *Avoid the use of a mouthwash. The antibacterial action kills the good bugs as effectively as it kills the bad bugs, and has little effect on the hard barrier of protection of the plaque. The outcome is the loss of good bacteria rather than the bad.*
- *Ensure regular chewing of raw vegetables or hard fruit, which encourages blood flow into the gums.*
- *Chewing on licorice sticks (fresh, not sweetened) is most beneficial.*
- *Regular flossing between the teeth with cord or a wooden stick is recommended.*
- *The gums, like all body tissues, are dependent upon good nutritional and vitamin intake. The gums are particularly sensitive to vitamin C deficiency.*

Bleeding gums

Gums bleed due to overenthusiastic brushing, poor hygiene (not cleaning the teeth and gums), deficiencies and diseases such as diabetes, those effecting blood clotting, and other rarer conditions. The term "gingivitis" is given to gums that are inflamed, spongy, and tend to bleed easily.

RECOMMENDATIONS

- *See* **Care of gums***.*
- *Consult a complementary medical practitioner or nutritionist to ensure that you are not missing any vital nutrients.*

- *It may be necessary to investigate this through blood, sweat, or hair analysis.*
- *Ensure that your toothbrush is neither too hard nor too soft.*
- *Persisting bleeding of the gums, despite the above measures, requires investigations by your doctor or a holistic-minded dentist.*
- *Use a toothpaste with homeopathic Arnica or Calendula twice a day. Use an Arnica or Calendula fluid extract—1 teaspoonful in a cup of water already containing half a teasponful of salt. Use this as a mouthwash and forcibly push this through the teeth.*

Gingivitis

The medical term for inflammation of the gums. For treatment *see* **Bleeding gums.**

Gum infections

Pockets of bacteria, fungi, yeasts, and viruses can settle deep in the gums and cause problems, both to the oral cavity and, if swallowed or absorbed into the bloodstream, throughout the body. Regular review by your dentist is essential to avoid this.

RECOMMENDATIONS

- *Gentle brushing around the area and dental flossing of the gap above the infection (very gently) in association with a salt-water mouthwash will often clear up gum infections.*
- *Toothpaste containing myrrh, cloves, cinnamon, and bee propolis (avoid if you have allergic reactions to bee or wasp stings) can be curative. If the toothpaste is not available, application of the essential oils can be useful in both clearing the infection and reducing the pain. Painful infections are particularly relieved by clove oil.*
- *Suitable doses of vitamin C, zinc, and magnesium should all be taken with any gum infection.*
- *The remedies Hepar sulfuris calcarium, Belladonna, and Calcarea fluorica should all be reviewed.*
- *See* **Care of the gums.**

THE THROAT

SORE THROATS IN INFANTS

Sore throats are difficult to diagnose in infants. If, when the child is crying, a light can be shone to the back of the throat, redness or discharge (pus) may be visible.

RECOMMENDATIONS

- *Try the child on warm or cold drinks to see if either is soothing.*
- *Breast milk must be encouraged.*
- *A multivitamin, preferably recommended by a health practitioner, can be administered.*
- *The homeopathic remedies Aconite, Baptisia, Kali bichromicum, Kali muriaticum, Mercurius, and Phosphorus should all be referred to. One pill of potency 6 every 2hr will often clear up a sore throat in an infant.*

ADENOIDS AND TONSILS

The adenoids and tonsils are lymphatic glandular tissue found at the back of the nose, at the top of the throat. They should be there. They are the home to numerous white blood cells that kill infections. Children are particularly prone to nasal and throat infections, and the adenoids and tonsils are a main part of the defense mechanism.

Until the 1970s, it was commonplace for the adenoids and tonsils to be removed, quite often for no reason. Nowadays, most ear, nose, and throat specialists and pediatricians agree that removal should be a last resort.

Recurrent inflammation and an excess of thick mucus result in enlargement of these glands, leading to snoring, a nasal-sounding voice, and sometimes partial asphyxia. The problem is not the adenoids and tonsils, but the child's immune system being ineffective and allowing persistent or recurrent infections.

Adenoids and Tonsils

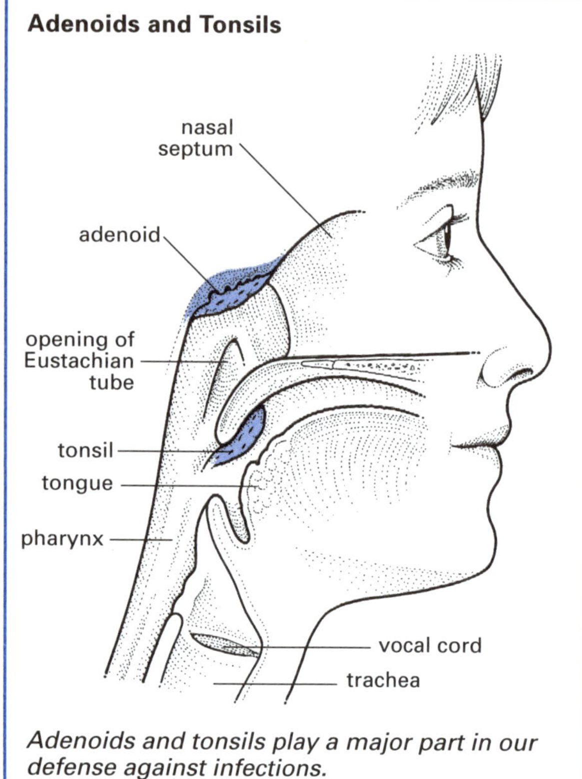

Adenoids and tonsils play a major part in our defense against infections.

RECOMMENDATIONS

- *Reduce or remove white sugar and excessive sweet things from the diet. These thicken the lymph which blocks the glands.*
- *Ensure good water intake. This thins the mucus.*
- *Ensure good diet and supplement with multivitamins if the child has persistent infections. Obtain naturopathic advice before resorting to antibiotics and operations.*
- *Review the following homeopathic remedies through your manual: Belladonna, Calcarea carbonica, Hepar sulfuris calcarium, Pulsatilla, and Silica.*

CHOKING

An inhaled object or incorrectly swallowed food may block the trachea (windpipe), leading to choking, which, if fully obstructive or persistent, can be fatal.

Choking in an infant or child

- As soon as evidence of choking occurs, try to remove the object with your fingers from the back of the throat. Do not waste time trying to view the object.
- If you cannot reach the object, pick the child up by the feet, and while upside down, apply firm slaps with the palm of the hand between the shoulder blades. If the child is too heavy, then place him/her head down over your knee or thigh, and repeat the slaps.
- If this fails, then the Heimlich maneuver should be employed (*see* **Heimlich maneuver**).

QUINSY (PERITONSILLAR ABSCESS)

The tonsil is a collection of lymphatic tissues within a capsule at the back of the mouth. An infection that does not drain may become an abscess, which has been named "quinsy" after the surgeon who first described it.

A patient will complain of a severe sore throat usually associated with fever and, on examination, a tonsil (it is usually one-sided) will appear enlarged and inflamed. There is usually swelling around the area, and a mass may be seen (although often it is not because the abscess may be tucked behind the tonsil).

RECOMMENDATIONS

- *A quinsy should be treated with antibiotics once diagnosed. This condition may obstruct the airways or eat into the close-lying carotid artery if left unattended.*
- *Take twice the recommended dosage of a good-quality acidophilus (yogurt-bacteria tablets) product for five days longer than the antibiotic.*
- *See* **Sore throats** *for complementary treatments.*

"STREP" THROAT

A streptococcal sore throat is a frequent diagnosis that can actually only be made accurately once a swab is taken of any discharge from the tonsils or back of the throat, and found to be growing the bacteria *Streptococcus*.

The symptoms, which are most common in childhood but can occur at any age, are: sore tonsils and back of the throat; difficulty in swallowing; and, if the tonsils are particularly enlarged, difficulty in breathing. Fever (either dry or sweating) loss of appetite, lethargy, and swollen, external neck glands are all part of the picture.

RECOMMENDATIONS

- *Request a throat swab, especially if the individual is being threatened with a course of antibiotics.*
- *See* **Sore throats** *and* **Tonsillitis**.
- *Pay attention to the homeopathic remedies Hepar sulfuris calcarium, Belladonna, and Streptococcus by referring to them in your preferred homeopathic manual.*

TONSILLITIS

Inflammation from infection of the tonsils is dealt with in chapter 4.

THE CHEST

ASTHMA

Asthma is the broad term given to shortness of breath caused by narrowing of the bronchial tree (the main airways in the lungs) due to contractions of the muscles in the tubes and by excess excretion of the normal mucus production. This mucus is often thicker than normal, and causes plugs in the already narrowed airways. Asthma can be acute or chronic, and range from mild to severe. Minor upper-respiratory-tract infections can cause temporary asthma and simply may last for the few days of infection. Asthma attacks may be triggered by other lung irritants, such as airborne pollution, fog, and humidity, as well as certain intolerances to food, which can be very specific. Common triggers include caffeine, chocolate, cow's milk products, wheat, oranges, nuts, and eggs.

There has been a sixfold increase in childhood asthma in the last 20 years. Many hypotheses are put forward, and I suspect that a genetic

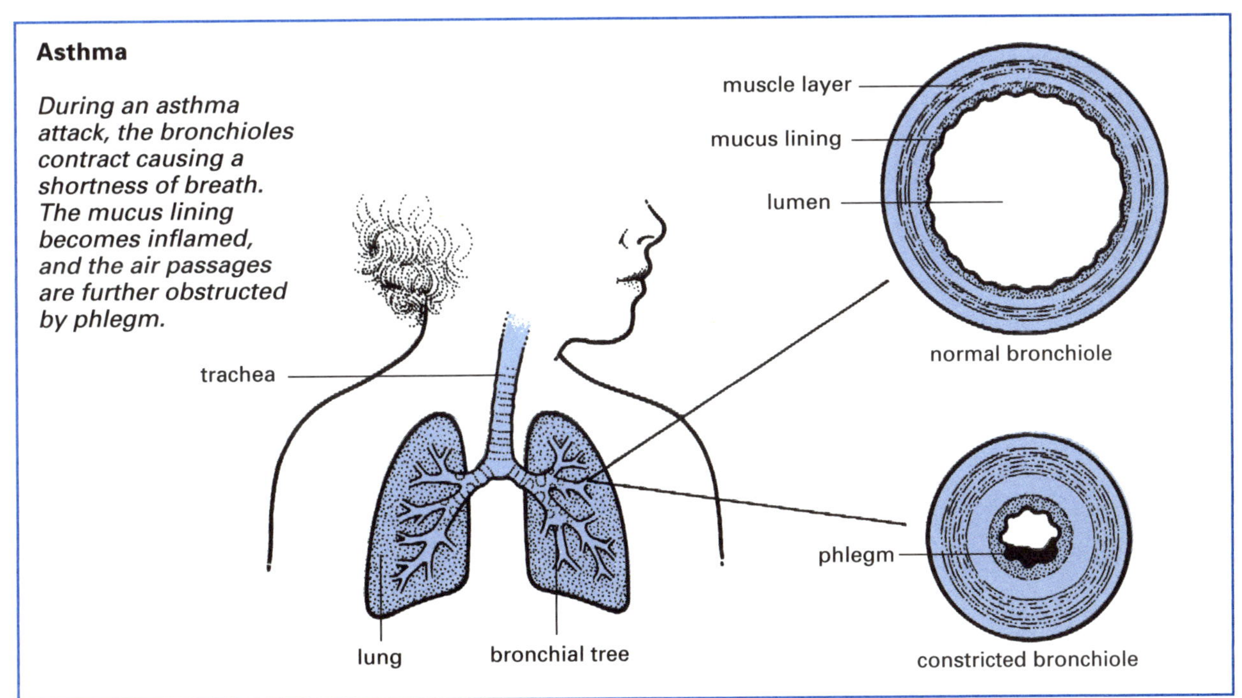

Asthma

During an asthma attack, the bronchioles contract causing a shortness of breath. The mucus lining becomes inflamed, and the air passages are further obstructed by phlegm.

predisposition must be triggered by several factors, including air pollution, food (pollutants such as preservatives, additives, and pesticides), an increase in our refined-sugar intake, our increased use of vaccinations and antibiotics, and climatic changes such as the loss of the ozone layer. Asthma must never be underestimated. It is a lethal condition and can come on very swiftly, causing fatal airway obstruction, especially in children. Doctors are very swift to diagnose asthma and encourage the use of bronchodilators (drugs that relax the muscle spasm and reduce mucus production), such as salbutamol.

Recognizing asthma

The power of pulling air into the lungs through the diaphragm and intercostal (ribcage) muscles is much greater than the power available to exhale. Asthma is actually most often caused by an inability to remove the carbon dioxide from the lungs rather than a difficulty in getting air in.

In mild-to-moderate asthma, therefore, you will see individuals pursing their lips in an attempt to blow out the trapped air. This and a respiratory rate of more than 15 inhalations per minute are the immediate tell-tale signs. A rattling in the chest, most easily heard through a doctor's stethoscope, is usually present as the air is forced past the mucus plugs. However, asthma does not demand rattling. Wheezing is much more common, again caused by air being forced past the mucus obstruction.

Moderate-to-severe asthma will have all these signs, plus a noticeable amount of panic on the part of the sufferer. Any suggestion of dizziness, blacking out, or blueness around the mouth needs to be treated as a medical emergency.

Self-help for asthma is limited, but works on the following principles:

- removing triggers
- learning breathing techniques
- dealing with acute attacks.

Removing triggers

It is important to keep a journal or list of attacks. This should include times and recent events, foods and drink taken in the previous 24 hours, and stress factors. If asthma attacks are occurring in conjunction with any particular input or event, these can be eliminated. Triggers such as coughs and colds require a naturopathic opinion on why the immune system is behaving incorrectly.

Learning breathing techniques

These are not applicable until the child is old enough to understand and learn different patterns. This is discussed in chapter 4.

Dealing with acute attacks

RECOMMENDATIONS

- *At any sign of asthma, bring the patient to the attention of your doctor. In mild-to-moderate cases, resist the immediate use of bronchodilators until you have consulted with a naturopath.*
- *At any suggestion of a moderate-to-severe asthmatic condition, take the drugs and obtain a complementary medical view afterwards.*
- *Take the homeopathic remedy Aconite, potency 6, 12 or 30, two to four pills every 10min, if the attack comes on suddenly; take Arsenicum album 6, four pills every 15min if the child is better with warm drinks, for attacks between midnight and 3am that are associated with restlessness; take Carbo vegetalis 6, four pills every 15min, if worse for talking and associated with a cough; take Natrum sulfuricum 6, four pills every 10min, for attacks that come after 3am and when the child is holding the chest.*
- *Mix and keep aside the essential oils of lavender and camomile. Place a few drops in steaming water and apply to the collar of the child, or use as a steam inhalation.* *See* **Nasal congestion** *for the technique.*

- *Ensure that any child with an asthmatic tendency is taking extra vitamin B_6, vitamin C, magnesium, and zinc. The amount is variable, depending on the child's size, and is best prescribed by a naturopath.*
- *If attacks are occurring in association with stress situations, then a child psychologist, preferably an art therapist, should be consulted.*

COUGHS

(The following advice applies for adults as well.) Coughs and colds in infants are usually self-limiting and require little, if any, treatment. Remedies should be considered if a cold persists for longer than three days or the child is particularly unwell, in which case a physician should be consulted.

A cough, while distressing to listen to, is the body's way of eliminating unwanted substances from the bronchial tree (the pipes leading to the lung tissue) and the alveoli (the lung tissue).

Cough with a sudden onset

The sudden onset of a cough may be caused by the inhalation of a foreign object. If the child is having difficulty in breathing, becoming red in the face, or even blue, assume that an object has been inhaled.

RECOMMENDATIONS

- *Have somebody call an ambulance.*
- *Gently but firmly open the child's mouth by applying a pincer pressure to the jaw muscle and shine a light into the throat.If an object can be seen, try to extract it using your fingers. The use of an instrument such as tweezers should only be used if the child is asphyxiating (unable to breathe) or is blacking out.*

Loose coughs

A cough that sounds catarrhal is usually associated with the production of excess mucus, and is related to a cold. Unless the child is asthmatic, these coughs may last for weeks, especially through the winter season, but are associated with a healthy, happy and functional child, and should not be taken too seriously.

RECOMMENDATIONS

- *Avoid cow's products and refined sugars because these encourage mucus production.*
- *Avoid dehydration by encouraging water intake because this keeps mucus from becoming too thick or tenacious.*
- *A few drops of the oil of aniseed, cinnamon, or hyssop can be used as an inhalation. See* **Nasal congestion** *for the technique.*
- *Fresh ginger or thyme can be chopped and used as an inhalation as above.*
- *One drop of lobelia per year of age (up to 15 drops maximum) in water or diluted juice, three times a day, can be most beneficial.*
- *Refer to the remedies Antimonium tart, Sepia, Nux vomica, or Pulsatilla, although others may be indicated.*

Dry coughs

Dry coughs may indicate more serious problems, such as whooping cough, laryngitis, croup, and tracheitis. A dry cough of sudden onset should alert one to the inhalation of a foreign object. Most dry coughs are viral and can be treated as follows.

RECOMMENDATIONS

- *Steam inhalations with flaxseed, licorice, or mullein oils, using the technique described for nasal congestion.*
- *Vitamin C, 100mg per foot of height three times a day.*
- *Vitamin A, 300iu three times a day (for children aged six months or older). Give 100iu three times a day until six months old.*

- *A homeopathic remedy should be chosen from all the symptoms. Initially, however, the following remedies are masters at the quick cure: Aconite for a hard barking cough of sudden onset in a restless infant: Belladonna if the child is red, hot and has bursts of coughing that distress it particularly; Drosera if the child is being sick with the cough; and Sticta if the cough has a ring to it and is worse at night. Any of these should be given at potency 6 every 15min for 1hr and, if improvement is forthcoming, every 2–3hr until the child is better.*

CROUP

A dry cough that persists for longer than three days or disturbs the child's sleep for more than two nights should be brought to the attention of a health practitioner. Croup is a spasm of the vocal cords, and will improve if steam inhalations are encouraged. Boiling a kettle in the child's nursery is an effective initial treatment. The dry cough of croup is alarming and inhibits the child's breathing, and *must* be brought to the attention of a physician *immediately*. A croupy cough is always associated with breathing difficulties, and sounds like the call of a crow. It has a vibrant, ringing quality, almost as if the child is calling while coughing.

RECOMMENDATIONS

- *Give Aconite 6, Hepar sulfuris calcarium 6 and Spongia 6 in rotation every 5min. If the child is not improving within half an hour, call the doctor or take the child to casualty.*
- *If the child settles, contact your health practitioner as soon as possible, continuing to alternate the Hepar sulfuris calcarium and the Spongia every half-hour.*
- *Avoid giving the child anything by mouth in case an anesthetic has to be given to pass an intubation tube.*

SUFFOCATION

Suffocation is the interference with the entrance of air into the lungs, which, if it persists, will result in asphyxiation.

Resuscitation of Infant or Child

Heaven forbid one ever should have to perform this technique, but all adults should know the procedure. The following steps are worth practicing on a large doll or teddy bear:

Resuscitating a Child

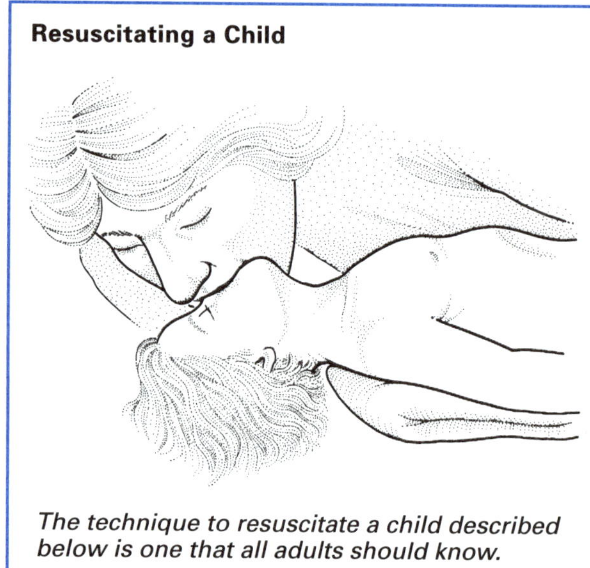

The technique to resuscitate a child described below is one that all adults should know.

(a) Lie the child flat.
(b) Gently tip the chin back until the throat is stretched straight.
(c) Ensure that any obstruction at the back of the throat is removed.

If the child has not responded to this, then proceed to step (d):

(d) Place your mouth over the infant's mouth *and* nose.
(e) Look at the child's chest.
(f) Breath until the child's chest expands. *Do not blow hard or for too long because this will overexpand and possibly damage the child's lungs.*

(g) Count to three and repeat, stopping every five breaths to see if the child has started to breathe spontaneously.

If the child has not responded after five inhalations, proceed to step (h):

(h) Place two fingers to the side of and just above the Adam's Apple. A pulse should be felt. If there is no pulse, place the forefinger and middle finger of one hand onto the child's breastbone (sternum).
(i) Apply pressure until firm resistance is felt, and repeat five times.
(j) Repeat steps (d) to (f) five times, and then return to pushing the sternum five times. Alternate this until the child revives or the ambulance arrives.

Once the child has revived, give him/her one pill of Arnica 6 every 10 minutes. Nothing else should be given by mouth in case the child requires an anesthetic.

RECOMMENDATIONS

- *Pay special attention to the covering of a child, ensuring that it cannot entangle bedclothes around the head.*
- *Be wary of pets, especially cats, that may rest on the warmth of the baby's body.*
- *See* **Asphyxia**.

WHEEZING

Wheezing is a high-pitched sound created by inhaling or exhaling through a narrow tube. The narrowing may be caused by muscular contraction such as in asthma or by an inflamed mucous membrane as in asthma, bronchitis, and pneumonia. If associated with crackles, the narrowing may be due to mucus production or fluid secondary to pulmonary edema.

RECOMMENDATION

- *See* **Asthma** *earlier in this chapter and in chapter 4 for tips on how to open the tubes and breathe more freely.*

WHOOPING COUGH

Whooping cough is characterized by spasmodic coughing bouts that can last up to a minute. As the child draws in breath there is the recognizable "whoop," which is often associated with the expectoration of thick mucus and often vomiting. It is caused by a highly infectious bacterium known as *Bordetella pertussis*, which causes an inflammatory process within the air passages.

Whooping cough is a prolonged illness that develops over a two-week period and lasts up until six weeks. It is not a particularly dangerous condition unless contracted in the first year of life, when the coughing spasms not only interfere with feeding but are exhausting. A prolonged spasm may result in an inability to breathe, causing asphyxiation with brain damage or death. This is extremely rare and can, of course, happen with any infection.

Whooping cough is associated with the production of much mucus, which may plug airways, rendering them ineffective or causing the lung tissue beyond to collapse.

A diagnosis is made by hearing the characteristic whoop, but this is not necessarily present. Culture can be made from a swab or sputum, and antibodies may be measured.

There is no orthodox antibiotic that attacks this unusual organism so treatment is based on treating the symptoms, although the orthodox medical world would give antibiotics to prevent a secondary infection. One holistic concern is that by taking out some of the necessary healthy body bacteria, we are reducing the competition and the ability to digest and absorb, thereby leaving the individual with a reduced immune system capacity.

Whooping cough is known to occur in

epidemics, and when it does, it is generally quite aggressive because through our use of vaccinations we have been breeding more difficult strains to attack. The vaccination question is particularly relevant in the case of pertussis because, like all vaccinations, there is a positive and a negative aspect. The pertussis vaccine developed in the 1960s had a very high incidence of causing epileptic fits and, potentially, brain damage. Many doctors at that time quite rightly became reluctant to administer the vaccine, and this fear was passed onto generations of parents and doctors taught by this group.

The pharmaceutical industry has gone to great lengths to purify the vaccine, and claims that it is quite safe now. The evidence suggests otherwise. There are many reports of continued problems, and strong evidence to support the ineffectiveness of the vaccine. Some studies and plenty of anecdotal evidence, including comments from pediatricians, suggest that children vaccinated against whooping cough will actually fare worse than those who are not, should they contract the infection. It appears that the immunization is only partially effective, but it convinces the body that it already has a defense mechanism, and thereby delays the immune response. This continues to be a controversial subject, but then so were the side effects of the measles vaccine until strong evidence of high risk was finally brought to light in July 1997.

Whooping cough needs to be treated aggressively, and home treatment is not necessarily the best form. However, the help of a complementary medical practitioner is invaluable, because if the condition persists, it can lead to a weakened lung, which may give rise to problems throughout life.

RECOMMENDATIONS

- *See* **Coughs**, **Colds**, **Pneumonia,** *and* **Fevers**. *Treat appropriately.*
- *Administer the homeopathic remedy Drosera 30 every 2hr if a whooping cough is suspected.*
- *Use Drosera 200 as soon as symptoms alleviate, one dose each night for five nights. This potency may also be administered nightly for five nights if whooping cough is known to be in the area or your child's school.*
- *If Drosera does not seem to be controlling the situation, the next remedy to try is Pertussin 30 given every 3hr. It would be best to consult a complementary medical specialist with homeopathic and herbal knowledge sooner rather than later.*
- *Lobelia-fluid extract, one drop per foot of height in a small amount of warm water, should be given three times a day and a teaspoonful placed in steaming water for inhalation.*
- *Comfrey root, mouse ear, and sundew (Drosera) are all established herbal treatments, and should be discussed with a herbalist for the correct dosages. It is not wise to dose a whooping child without expert guidance.*
- *If the child (or adult) is old enough and can appreciate the teaching of a breathing technique, a yoga, Qi Gong (Chi Kung), or meditation teacher should be able to give instructions.*
- *Bed rest is essential, along with good nutrition, and the supplements recommended for coughs or pneumonia should be reviewed (see* **Coughs** *and* **Pneumonia***).*
- *The child should not return to school until well, even if there is a likelihood of falling behind. Firstly, the child may be contagious and, secondly, running around will make things worse and probably lead to more chest infections over the next formative years, leading to more missed school time.*

THE DIGESTIVE SYSTEM

ABDOMINAL PAINS

It is very difficult to determine which part of an infant's body is in pain, although babies have a tendency to pull or touch areas that hurt. Once children can communicate, life is a lot simpler. Abdominal pain is very often the culprit. In a non-talking child, wait for a quiet moment and gently push on the abdomen. A painful tummy will usually trigger crying again. Persistent crying requires a doctor's opinion, but once abdominal pain is diagnosed, the following tips may be helpful.

RECOMMENDATIONS

- *If the following alternative suggestions do not resolve an infant's or child's abdominal pain within a few hours, contact a general practitioner. If there is any severe pain, or if the child is clearly unwell, do not delay but get a medical opinion immediately.*
- *Weak camomile tea can be used at all ages, but if the problem is not resolved through such a drink, stop administering anything in case an anesthetic is required.*
- *Refer to a homeopathic manual and consider the remedies Arsenicum album, Chamomilla, Carbo vegetalis, Coloccynthsis, Nux vomica, and Silica.*
- *"The Colic Carry." Place the baby on your forearm, chest down, and legs either side of your elbow, with the head in the palm of your hand. Walk around. Honestly, this makes a big difference!*
- *Tummy patting. Cup your hand and gently pat baby's tummy. Trapped wind is often the cause, and a few moments of this followed by burping the baby over your shoulder will help.*
- *Consider a consultation with a cranial osteopath.*
- *Pharmaceutical colic medicine and Tylenol may be used as a last resort, although there is some level of toxicity created by these compounds and a possible association with SIDS (crib death).*
- *Assume a food intolerance. breastfeeding mothers should cut out spices, caffeine, onions, and excess white sugar. If this does not seem to help, then specific food intolerances, including dairy produce, should be eliminated (see* ***Food intolerance****). Older infants and children should be considered for food restrictions (see chapter 7).*
- *High-dose homeopathy should be considered, and a consultation arranged.*

Abdominal migraine

Migraines are generally associated with headaches. The cause of most migraines is dilation of the blood vessels in the brain, and this can occur in the abdomen, especially of children. Usually associated with food intolerance or stressful situations, the advice relating to head migraines is also suitable here.

Mild viral infections that cause lymphatic-gland activity (as is commonly felt in the neck of patients with infections) can occur in the large number of lymphatic glands in the abdomen. A stomachache associated with glands in the neck, under the arm or in the groin should be suspected as inflamed lymph glands.

RECOMMENDATIONS

- *Refer to a homeopathic manual and consider the remedies Belladonna, Calcarea carbonica, Kali carbonicum, and Phytolacca, all good glandular remedies.*
- *See* ***Abdominal pains*** *and* ***Migraine****.*

Appendicitis

The appendix is thought to be vestigial (a part of the body no longer a necessary organ). It is, in fact, a collection of lymphatic tissue about the size of your own little finger. It probably plays a minor role in the defense mechanism of the bowel. In some unfortunates, the appendix can become inflamed and cause appendicitis.

Appendix

The function of the appendix is uncertain, but it probably acts as a defense against infection in the bowel.

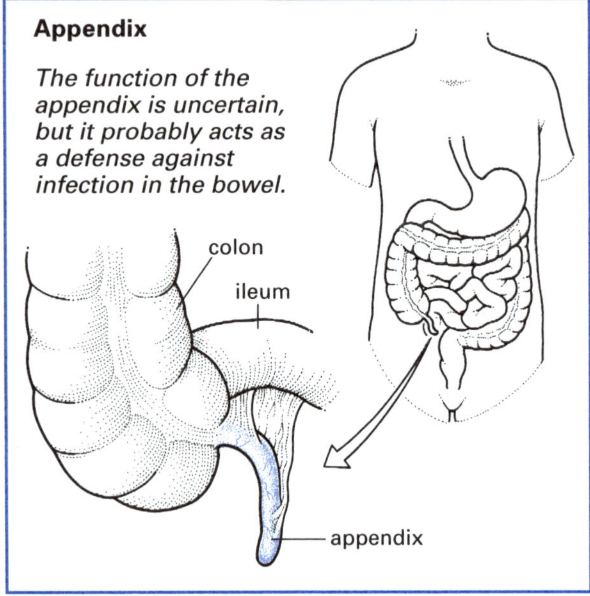

Appendicitis is characteristically a sharp pain on the right lower abdomen. It is characterized by "rebound" tenderness. If you push on the tender area, there is not as much pain pushing in as when you let go. This sign is pathognomonic for an inflamed lining of the bowel, and requires immediate hospital attention. Appendicitis can start with a pain around the tummy button, but usually migrates down into the right iliac fossa, as that area is medically termed. There is often a mild fever, and the individual will be off their food and may have diarrhea.

RECOMMENDATIONS

- *With any persistent stomachache or any suggestion of rebound tenderness, have the child seen by a doctor.*
- *If appendicitis is suspected, do not try to treat it without an operative procedure.*
- *See* **Operations and surgery**.

Intussusception

Intussusception is a surgical problem found more commonly in boys than girls, and usually around the first eight months after birth. For some reason, the bowel folds in on itself much like a telescope.

The characteristics are a limp child who screams with pain at intervals, associated with the contractions of the bowel. A child with intussusception is ill. In between bouts of pain, they are likely to be floppy and inert. Vomiting may occur, but a characteristic red, jelly-like stool is almost diagnostic. A hard lump may be felt in the child's abdomen, most commonly in the lower right quarter, and the child will be distressed if any pressure is applied to this point.

Intussusception

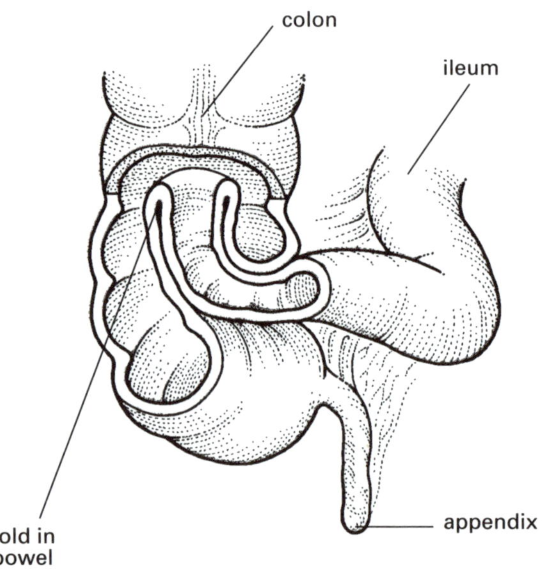

RECOMMENDATIONS

- *Any child with severe pain from no obvious cause must be seen by a doctor.*

- *If intussusception is suspected, do not give the child anything to eat or drink, but on the way to the doctor give the homeopathic remedy Rhus toxicodendron 6, two crushed pills every 15–20min under the tongue.*
- *An experienced casualty doctor or pediatrician may be able to manually manipulate the bowel back into working order, although there is a slight risk of the problem recurring. Frequently the child may need to have an operation and, if this is the case, see* **Operations and surgery**.

CELIAC DISEASE

Celiac disease is characterized by weight loss, undigested greasy stools, and any disorders showing deficiency such as stunted growth, poor learning ability, and recurrent infections. Diagnosis of this condition is, however, only made through very specific blood tests and a biopsy of part of the small intestine called the jejunum. This process requires the patient to swallow a metal capsule on the end of a wire, and when the capsule is in the right part of the small intestine, as defined by x-ray, the capsule is opened, grabs part of the mucosal lining, is closed, and withdrawn with the biopsy sample. It is not a particularly unpleasant test, other than you have to sit there with a wire hanging from your mouth and the discomfort of the instrument hanging down your throat. It may take several hours for the capsule to reach the jejunum, but usually this occurs within one or two.

The condition is caused by a sensitivity to one of the proteins in gluten called gliadin. This protein, found predominantly in wheat, but also in rye, oats, corn (corn), buckwheat, rice, and millet, causes a type of inflammation in specific individuals that makes the small intestine swell and become incapable of proper absorption.

The condition is most commonly genetic, being passed down family lines. The genetic fault seems to be created by an incorrect defense or immune response affecting the lining of the bowel that comes into contact with gliadin. The need to treat this condition is paramount, because there are associated problems with the thyroid, rashes, and psychiatric disturbances such as schizophrenia. More disturbingly, there is a higher incidence of diabetes and cancer in untreated celiac patients.

RECOMMENDATIONS

- *Celiac disease can only be diagnosed in a specialist unit, but any suspicion must be referred through your doctor for investigation.*
- *Once a diagnosis of gluten sensitivity has been established, all gluten-containing foods must be avoided. The list above gives the main foods in question but millet, corn, and rice should only be avoided until the problem has settled because their level of gliadin is negligible.*
- *Milk and milk products should be eliminated initially because the condition is often associated with milk intolerance.*
- *Keep a very close eye on pre-prepared foods or on foods eaten out, because many foods, such as sauces, ice cream, soups and alcoholic beverages, contain gluten products.*
- *Celiac societies in your area can be found through your doctor, and they can help with diet programming and finding support groups.*
- *Intravenous nutritional supplementation is of benefit in severe cases, and can be utilized initially because the exclusion treatment may take several weeks to prove effective.*
- *High-dose oral antioxidants, particularly beta-carotene, may correct nutritional deficiencies swiftly.*
- *See* **Food intolerance**. *Any small intestinal inflammation can lead to poor digestion and the absorption into the bloodstream of large molecules, which in turn lead to an immune response. It is worth having a food*

allergy/intolerance test performed through blood investigation or by the use of Vega/bioresonance computers.

- *Herbal treatments and homeopathic remedies should be prescribed by an expert in those fields.*
- *The compound papaine, found in papaya, specifically digests wheat gluten, and up to 1,000mg taken with meals may allow those with mild celiac disease to tolerate small amounts of gluten.*

DIARRHEA

Diarrhea in childhood is not an uncommon ailment while infants develop their bowel flora and habits. Also, children have a tendency to put anything and everything into their mouths. One must never underestimate the effects of serious, profuse, or chronic diarrhea because malabsorption, malnutrition, dehydration, and infection may all be associated.

In principle, diarrhea should not be considered a bad thing. Most often, diarrhea represents the body's attempts to throw out some toxin—either a food that disagrees or a bacterium or virus, the most common of which is *Campylobacter*. Allowed to run its natural course, a few bouts of diarrhea with or without abdominal pain will clear within a matter of hours or a couple of days, and nothing needs to be done other than a simple homeopathic remedy and ensuring good hydration by keeping up the water intake.

Persisting diarrhea in an infant may be associated with conditions such as celiac disease (allergy to wheat) or other food allergies. The orthodox world, while having a clear definition and picture of wheat allergy, seems reluctant to accept that other foods may cause the same problems. It is worthwhile remembering this and obtaining a complementary medical practitioner's suggestions before ending up following a drug-orientated orthodox approach. Incorrect bowel flora can show itself as persistent diarrhea, and often follows the use of an antibiotic, immediately or up to six months later. Unfortunately, much of our food, especially meat, is treated with antibiotics and chemicals, and gut dysbiosis (alteration of our bowel flora) can occur quite unwittingly due to the ingestion of these chemicals.

RECOMMENDATIONS

- *Severe, persistent, bloody, or mucousy stool is an indication that a doctor's opinion is required.*
- *Any diarrhea that persists beyond 48hr or is associated with pain, pallor, or a change in the character of the child, should be reviewed by a doctor.*
- *Ensure good rehydration. The smaller the child, the quicker dehydration can set in. Rehydration should occur with a mixture of fluids to ensure glucose and nutrient intake. Alternating some water, then half an hour later some diluted fruit juice, water, then some soup, then water with a pinch of salt in rotation should do the trick. Try to match any output (including any water loss through sweat, if fever is associated) with the amount taken in. Avoid milk and other cow's produce except live yogurt, which may be of benefit.*
- *Avoid anything too sweet as this will pull water into the bowel and make the diarrhea worse.*
- *A weak camomile tea can be very soothing and replenishing. Stir in a teaspoonful of honey per 8 ounces of fluid and a pinch of salt (it should not be possible to taste this) to replenish some glucose for energy and for salts that invariably have been lost.*
- *Allow the child to eat by instinct. If the appetite is good then try to encourage foods that will "mop up" poisons, such as wholegrain bread, pasta, and rice, but avoid anything with refined sugar, caffeine, or an excess of "binding" foods, such as eggs.*

- *Refer to your preferred homeopathic manual and pay attention to the remedies Chamomilla, Carbo vegetabilis, Nux vomica, Mercurius, and Arsenicum album. These can all be used safely at potency 6, two tablets every 1–2hr.*
- *Use probifidus as a live-yogurt culture to encourage the growth of the body's normal bowel flora.*
- *Estimate the amount of diarrhea, and replenish with the same quantity of fluids. Dilute juices are acceptable, but water is best.*
- *Obtain the opinion of a complementary medical practitioner with a knowledge in nutrition, homeopathy, and/or herbal medicine before taking orthodox medicine.*

GASTROENTERITIS

See **Gastroenteritis** in chapter 5.

Gastroenteritis in children can be particularly serious, because the fluid loss due to diarrhea in small beings may be rapid and cause dehydration and biochemical changes to occur rapidly.

A typical causative organism is *Campylobacter*, which can be fatal in undernourished children, although is usually not severe in well-nourished Western children.

RECOMMENDATIONS

- *Any persistent diarrhea or vomiting should be referred to a physician, who should be encouraged to check the stool for Campylobacter urgently. Severe cases should be treated with antibiotics, and a complementary medical practitioner consulted to deal with the effects.*
- *Follow the guidelines in chapter 5 on gastroenteritis, and diarrhea in this chapter.*

ITCHY ANUS (PRURITUS ANI)

Not an uncommon problem in children, this can occur at any age. The principal causes are the laying of eggs by parasitic infestations, usually worms (threadworms, roundworms, or tapeworms). Candida (thrush) infection, especially for infants still in diapers, trauma, eczema, or piles (hemorrhoids—very unusual in children) may all be responsible.

One commonly overlooked possibility is that of food allergies.

RECOMMENDATIONS

- *Examine the anus first thing in the morning because eggs are laid at night. See* **Worms**.
- *Persistent itching should be reviewed by a physician for a clear diagnosis, and reference made to the relevant sections in this book.*
- *The homeopathic remedy Aesculus 6 may be taken four times a day.*
- *Hamamelis fluid extract diluted in iced water and applied to the rectum may be very soothing.*
- *Calendula cream may be of benefit, but only applied for a few minutes each day.*
- *Keep the area dry with nonmedicated talcum powder.*

LEAKY-GUT SYNDROME

If we assume that the derivation of the word malabsorption includes the French word for bad—*mal*—then leaky-gut syndrome is part of malabsorption. The small intestine acts like a selective sieve, allowing through into the bloodstream only the breakdown products of digestion. Larger proteins, carbohydrates, and fats are rejected, permitting only the amino acids and peptides from proteins, single- or double-sugar molecules from carbohydrates, and small chains of fatty acids from fats. Anything larger may be recognized by the body as an invading particle, and an immune response is set up. In leaky-gut syndrome, this sieve mechanism fails. Foods that are not fully digested are absorbed, and the body sets up an allergic or immune response that will from that time on, if not treated, recognize basic foods as bacteria or viruses, and set up an attack.

The cause of a leaky gut varies from any food that may inflame the bowel; a parasitic, fungal or yeast, bacterial or viral agent; the use of antibiotics that diminish the bowel's natural flora; chemical toxins such as pesticides, preservatives; and additives; or even stress, which produces adrenaline that cuts down the oxygen supply by reducing blood flow and thereby creating an unhealthy bowel. The absorption of incompletely digested foods is distinctly a malabsorption. Leaky gut may be the cause of many conditions, and should be considered in *all* conditions that are unresponsive to treatment.

Leaky-gut syndrome may account for most food allergies that may change within a few days because of new, undigested molecules being absorbed.

RECOMMENDATIONS

- *See* **Malabsorption**.
- *See* **Gut permeability testing**.
- *Start on a good acidophilus supplement until you can see an experienced complementary medical practitioner.*

MALABSORPTION

The orthodox medical world recognizes malabsorption as an "all-or-nothing" syndrome that occurs at any age, but is most often seen in children. It is due to deficiencies in enzymes or oversensitivity of the immune system. An example of the former is lactose intolerance, where the body does not form the correct enzyme to break down milk sugar. Oversensitivity occurs in conditions such as celiac disease where the body attacks gluten found predominantly in wheat and most other grains.

I believe that there is a considerable gray area where many individuals may not absorb a variety of nutrients from the bowel, usually because of food intolerance creating inflammation in the small intestine.

Any symptoms ranging from mild tiredness and depression through to major malabsorption syndromes will cause failure to thrive or grow and decrease learning abilities. Physical illnesses will follow, but are generally not the symptoms that bring malabsorption to a parent's or physician's attention.

Malabsorption may occur because of a failure of the body to produce the right digestive juices. Achlorhydria is an accepted orthodox condition describing an inability of the stomach to produce hydrochloric acid. In fact, diminished production of this acid may have a profound effect on absorption. The alternative medical world is aware of this not-uncommon problem, and specific tests can be done to establish if low-acid concentration is present. Most digestion occurs because of enzymes produced by the pancreas. A deficient pancreatic exocrine function (an exocrine gland is one that produces a substance that does not pass directly into the bloodstream) is another factor well recognized by complementary practitioners, and will also cause malabsorption due to a poor ability to break down the foods.

RECOMMENDATIONS

- *Any developmental delay or failure to thrive must be reviewed by a pediatrician. Specific blood tests can be obtained to establish which foods or nutrients are not being absorbed.*
- *Replenishment of deficiencies may make a difference if high-strength supplements are given, but this may not make a difference if the body is incapable of absorbing. Intravenous administration is rarely required, but may be considered.*
- *Genetic deficiencies in enzyme production are unlikely to be treatable, but constitutional homeopathic prescribing by an experienced homeopath may make a difference.*
- *Any history of antibiotic use or bowel disturbance may suggest leaky-gut syndrome. Specific treatment under the care of an experienced complementary medical practitioner to deal with allergic responses and to correct the imbalance in the bowel is required.*

- *Enquire about noninvasive investigations of hydrochloric acid and pancreatic enzyme production (see* **Gastrograms** *and* **Pancreatic exocrine tests** *in chapter 8).*
- *If required, or if noninvasive tests are not available, try a hydrochloric acid supplement a few minutes before each meal. If a warm glow occurs, then reduce the amount or strength of the acid supplement.*
- *There are two types of naturopathic pancreatic supplement that may be tried if noninvasive investigations are not available: the first stimulates the pancreas to produce more enzymes, and is generally made out of a selection of herbs; the second is usually an extract from the pancreas of an animal, and acts directly on foodstuffs. Follow the instructions on the packaging as instructed by the practitioner.*
- *The homeopathic remedy Silica encourages absorption, and should be taken at potency 30 twice a day for two weeks. If a response is noted, increase the potency to 200 for three nights, and repeat monthly if the effect wears off.*
- *Please note that hydrochloric acid and pancreatic supplementation should only be administered to children under medical supervision.*

PYLORIC STENOSIS

Food is mixed with acid in the stomach and is passed through a valve known as the pylorus into the duodenum, the start of the small intestine. Some children are born with a congenital thickness of this valve, which causes a narrowing (stenosis).

A child or infant will show a characteristic projectile vomit due to the stomach compressing harder in order to force food through the stenosis but, in fact, pushing food up past the much weaker esophageal stomach valve. The vomit is generally fermented food. The infant will not be growing, and will be persistently hungry, therefore

Pyloric Stenosis

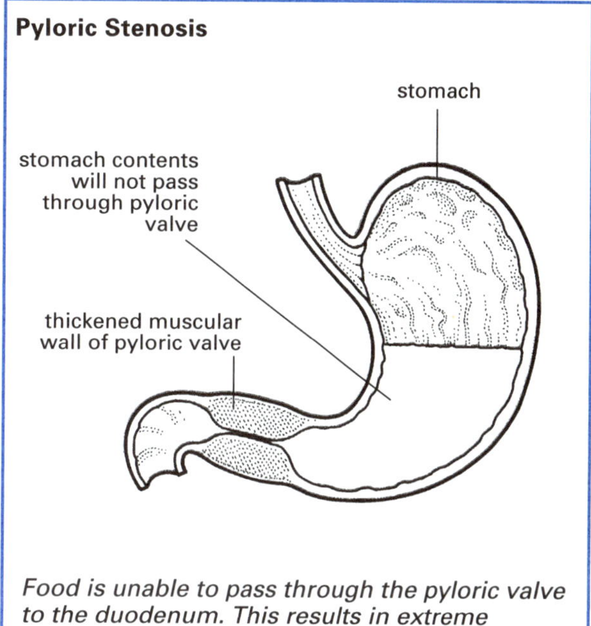

Food is unable to pass through the pyloric valve to the duodenum. This results in extreme discomfort and vomiting.

whining. The child may only want very small feeds because discomfort occurs if the stomach is filled, and a diagnosis of constipation may be falsely suggested because the child only passes small amounts infrequently.

On occasions, a knot may be felt in the upper part of the abdomen below the sternum (chest bone).

RECOMMENDATIONS

- *Any failure to thrive or a persistently uncomfortable child must be reviewed by a doctor or pediatrician.*
- *Pyloric stenosis requires an operative procedure (see* **Operations and surgery***).*
- *Nutritional deficiencies may have set in, and a consultation with a nutritionist postoperatively is recommended to ensure a well-balanced, high-calorific diet.*

STOMACH UPSETS—*see* Gastroenteritis, Diarrhea, and Abdominal pains

Volvulus

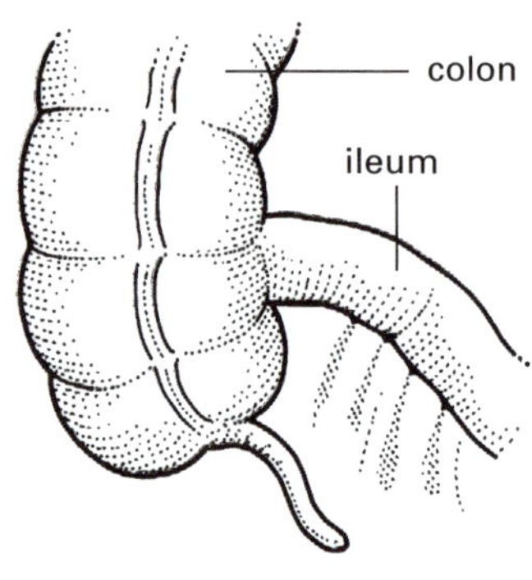

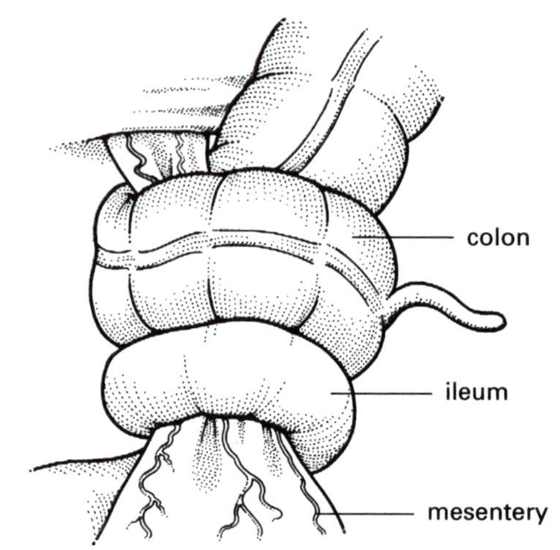

In cases of volvulus, the bowel may twist around itself, causing constriction.

VOLVULUS

When the bowel develops, a mesh known as the mesentery is attached to the 30 feet of intestine. This provides blood vessels to and from the bowel walls, and also contains the nerves and lymphatic systems. This mesentery should be a fairly tight sheet, but in rare cases may develop loosely, thereby not functioning as a fixator of the bowel. This allows the bowel to twist upon itself, and may occlude the lumen, the space inside the intestine, and in severe cases, this will compromise its circulation. This most commonly occurs in the sigmoid colon (lower part of the bowel), and can occur at any stage of life. Pain and symptoms of obstruction, such as bloating and constipation, arise, and if not fixed quickly, can result in bowel ischemia and gangrene.

RECOMMENDATIONS

- *Any abdominal pain that is severe or persistent must be reviewed by a doctor.*
- *Volvulus requires surgical repair (see* **Operations and surgery***).*

WORMS

Infection of the intestine in human beings is a mild problem in the U.S. and other Westernized countries, but can be chronically debilitating in the tropics.

Roundworms (nematodes) and threadworms (pinworms)

These white worms can grow up to half an inch long, and are found specifically in children all over the world. They live in the colon and rectum, and travel down to the anal margin to lay their eggs, usually at night. The result is an itchy anus, which is the principal symptom. Irritability and insomnia are other factors.

Worms may be seen in the feces, or even protruding from the anus, and a simple diagnostic procedure is to place a piece of adhesive cellophane (such as clear tape) across the anus and, folding the adhesive sides together, take this sample to a laboratory or doctor's office for examination under a microscope. The eggs may be visible.

Worms

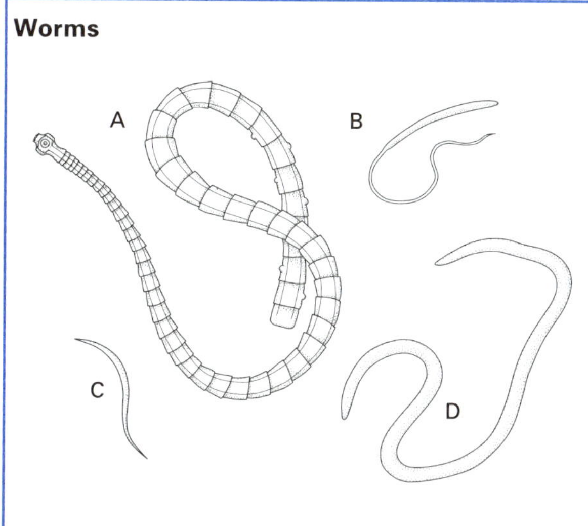

A *Pork tapeworm* (Taenia solium, *up to several feet in length*);
B *Whipworm* (Trichuris trichiura, *5 inches*);
C *Threadworm* (Enterobuis vermicularis, *1/4–1/2-inch long*);
D *Roundworm* (Ascaris lumbricoides, *3 inches*).

Whipworms

These are very common parasites, with the worms growing up to one sixth of an inch in length and tending to attach themselves to the first part of the large bowel. Symptoms are extremely uncommon unless a child is malnourished, when bloody diarrhea or rectal prolapse may actually occur.

Toxocariasis

This is not to be confused with toxoplasmosis, which is a parasitic infection also contracted from cats and specifically dangerous in pregnancy.

This condition is an accidental infection from cat or dog feces. The worms do not develop in humans, but if the larvae are ingested they travel via the bloodstream into major organs, where they die, causing obstruction of blood vessels.

Tapeworms (cestodes)

Tapeworms normally share two hosts: the worm living in the intestine of one organism and the larvae normally in the muscles of another. In human beings, the most common tapeworms are *Taenia saginata* and *Taenia solium*. The former exists in beef and the latter in pork.

These worms may grow into a parasite up to 26 feet long over a three-month period. Symptoms are often absent, but weight loss, disturbed appetite, and vague abdominal pains may accompany the passage of segments of the worm noted in the stool.

Other worms

Ascaris, Trichinosis, and Filoariasis are less common, predominantly being found in hotter countries, and are beyond the scope of this book.

RECOMMENDATIONS

- *Any symptoms suggestive of worm infestation should be discussed with a physician, who should check the anus and take samples via the tape method and stool samples.*
- *Treatment with orthodox antihelminthic drugs is safe and recommended. Remember that the whole family group, and possibly the school class should be treated as well.*

THE UROGENITAL SYSTEM

BALANITIS

Balanitis is the medical term for inflammation of the head of the penis and, more commonly, the foreskin. The term is also occasionally used for inflammation of the clitoris and the sheath surrounding it. Often associated with poor hygiene, balanitis can also occur through trauma (the penis–zipper entrapment syndrome—as it sounds!), infections including herpes (although this is rare in infants) and, most importantly, make sure diabetes mellitus can be ruled out. In this latter situation, sugar in the urine allows bacteria and yeasts to multiply rapidly, causing irritated inflammation.

RECOMMENDATIONS

- *Ensure that the area is clean and that diapers or underwear are dry. Use nonmedicated talcum powder in abundance.*
- *Slowly but surely retract the foreskin as the child ages. Do not force the retraction, but by the age of nine months the foreskin should be fully retractable. Then clean this VIP (very important place) every bathtime.*
- *Ointments containing Calendula can be very soothing. Being careful and tender, try to introduce some of the cream or lotion under the foreskin if it is not easily retractable.*
- *The homeopathic remedies Apis, Mercurius and Causticum can be reviewed and given every 2hr at potency 6.*
- *Persistence of inflammation should be reviewed by a doctor, and in rare circumstances circumcision may need to be considered (see* ***Circumcision****).*

BED-WETTING

Urinating in the bed is only a problem if it occurs beyond a certain age. This age is very variable. About 10 percent of children will still be wetting the bed at five years of age, and intervention and treatment should only be considered if the child is still wetting the bed after the age of seven or eight years. Occasional bed-wetting can occur in association with fevers and urinary tract infections in children and adults of all ages. Incontinence associated with old age is discussed elsewhere (*see* **Incontinence**).

Children should understand the concept and feeling of a full bladder at about the age of two years. Control and requesting to go to the toilet should occur by three years of age, and control at night follows on from that.

Most commonly, bed-wetting is associated with stress. This may be apparent or subconscious, and may be associated with the child or the atmosphere in the home or school. Children are extremely intuitive, and problems between parents, however well disguised from the child, may often be the cause. Infections (bacterial or parasitical, such as worms), diabetes, and food intolerance can all be physical causes, and need to be ruled out before psychological causes are assumed.

RECOMMENDATIONS

- *Have a urine sample checked by your local doctor.*
- *Provided that there is no obvious physical cause, consider the following homeopathic remedies by referring to your homeopathic manual: Plantago, Equisetum, and Kreosotum. A less well-known remedy and therefore difficult to read about is Ilex paraguayensis. Use potency 6, four pills nightly for three weeks, and if improvement is not persistent, obtain higher potencies until resolution is achieved.*
- *Ensure that the child does not drink too much fluid within 2hr of bedtime.*
- *Ensure that the child urinates before bed, and awaken the child to go to the toilet again prior to your going to bed.*
- *A visit to the osteopath, chiropractor, or craniosacral therapist can be instantly curative if there is any structural imbalance in the lower spine or pelvis, which in turn puts pressure on the nerves to the bladder.*

CIRCUMCISION

Male circumcision

Circumcision is the removal of the loose skin (known as the foreskin) found at the head of the penis. The medical reasons for circumcisions include a narrow opening (*see* **Phimosis**), balanitis (*see* **Balanitis**), or trauma such as the penis–zipper entrapment syndrome (self-explanatory!). There are no other medical reasons to perform this traumatic surgery. There is no benefit with regard to cleanliness, provided that good hygiene is followed and the foreskin is retracted at bathtime. There is no sexual enhancement one way or the other, although an uncircumcised penis may be slightly more sensitive.

Religious reasons need to be respected, although some of the techniques of circumcision are only little short of barbaric, and run high risk of complications, which at worst can lead to penis amputation and enforced gender changing in children. To perform circumcision without good hygienic preparation, preferably in a surgical unit, or without anesthetic, is medically and, in my opinion, morally unacceptable. The concept that infants do not remember pain is unproved, and the effects on a child's psyche when pain is created, apparently with parental approval, may have much deeper and more profound effects in the long term.

Circumcision for cosmetic reasons, like any self-mutilation on narcissistic grounds, should be considered only after time spent with a counselor, and assessment of the effects that social pressures, usually from advertising, have created. I am considerably against circumcision for anything other than medical reasons without available alternatives.

The foreskin is a protective sheath that may be of use if left attached, and its removal can offer no benefit. The argument that the foreskin allows the harboring of potentially infectious material such as human papilloma virus (genital warts) or other infectious agents is not acceptable, provided that good hygiene is followed.

RECOMMENDATIONS

- *Unless recommended by a doctor, do not circumcise.*
- *If circumcision is to go ahead, then prepare the area by applying an Arnica or Calendula (or both) cream at least three times a day five days prior to the operative procedure.*
- *See* **Operations and surgery**.
- *If any complication whatsoever or however mild appears, such as swelling, bleeding, or redness, please contact your doctor without hesitation.*

Female circumcision

Certain cultures remove the protective hood from around the clitoris and, unbelievably, remove the clitoris itself.

This barbaric act is unconscionable and potentially extremely risky both from a health point of view and a psychological one.

RECOMMENDATIONS

- *Endeavor to do your best to avoid this operation.*
- *If unavoidable, ensure that the poor individual is prepared for an operative procedure by following the guidelines in this book.*

PHIMOSIS (NONRETRACTABLE FORESKIN)

Occasionally, children are born with a constricted foreskin that does not allow for retraction. This can cause constriction over the exit of the urethra, which can create an obstruction to the outflow of urine. This can create a ballooning under the foreskin, with a high-pressure stream through the small, narrowed outlet.

RECOMMENDATIONS

- *The situation should be reviewed by a specialist because an operative procedure, including circumcision, may be required.*
- *Do not try to force back the foreskin, because this will lead to tears and potential infection.*
- *If an operation is considered, see* **Circumcision**.

UNDESCENDED TESTICLE

The testes develop within the abdominal cavity through the fetal stage. They travel down into the scrotum either just before birth or within the first few weeks after. As they descend, they bring with them blood vessels, lymphatic vessels, and nerves, and travel down the inguinal canal.

In some cases, for no known reason, the testes

fail to descend. This is sometimes associated with short vessels that do not stretch, thereby impeding descent.

The testes hang away from the body and the scrotum because they function at a lower temperature than the body would provide. Failure to descend, or entrapment within the inguinal canal, will prevent maturity and the ability to produce sperm.

RECOMMENDATIONS

- *Undescended testes by the age of one year may be treated by the homeopathic remedy Clematis 200, one pill each night for three nights. If there is no effect over the next month then use the remedy Aurum Metallicum 200, one dose each night for three nights.*
- *Surgical intervention may be necessary and this is usually performed after the age of three years. See* **Operations and surgery** *if this avenue is to be taken.*

STRUCTURAL MATTERS

ACHES AND PAINS

All children have aches and pains. The term "growing pains" is often bandied around, and refers to the stretching of tendons and ligaments created by the child's growth. There is rarely anything to worry about although persisting discomfort, especially around joints, should be brought to the attention of a physician. Certain deficiencies and dehydration can cause mild problems, and need to be corrected.

RECOMMENDATIONS

- *Do not underestimate the power of a kiss on the injured part.*
- *Gentle heating and massage of the area will help.*
- *Dehydration is a common cause of aches and pains. Ensure that your child is drinking enough water, very diluted juice, or herbal teas. Aim at 8 ounces per foot of height per day.*
- *Camomile tea can be very soothing.*
- *Minor deficiencies of calcium, magnesium, zinc, and copper can all be culprits for aches and pains. A good diet should be adequate, but sometimes mineral supplementation is beneficial.*
- *Persisting pain without an obvious cause should be reviewed initially by an osteopath or chiropractor. If relief is not forthcoming, then a pediatrician should be approached.*

Please note that any aches and pains that are altering the child's gait (walking) should be assessed by an osteopath or other body worker specializing in children.

BROKEN BONES AND FRACTURES

See chapter 4 for the principal information on fractures.

Children heal quickly, but have a tendency to misbehave while having a broken bone, which can lead to a delay in repair. It is important to maintain a watchful eye. Fractures that occur near the growing points of bones need to be monitored by orthopedic specialists. Definitely see an osteopath to encourage alignment to take the pressure off the opposite side of the body. Remedies can be used as for young-adult fractures, but *do not* administer a comfrey remedy to a child.

THE FEET

CARE OF THE FEET

The feet may be considered phenomenal when one reflects on exactly what they do and the way we treat them. We cram them into tight socks,

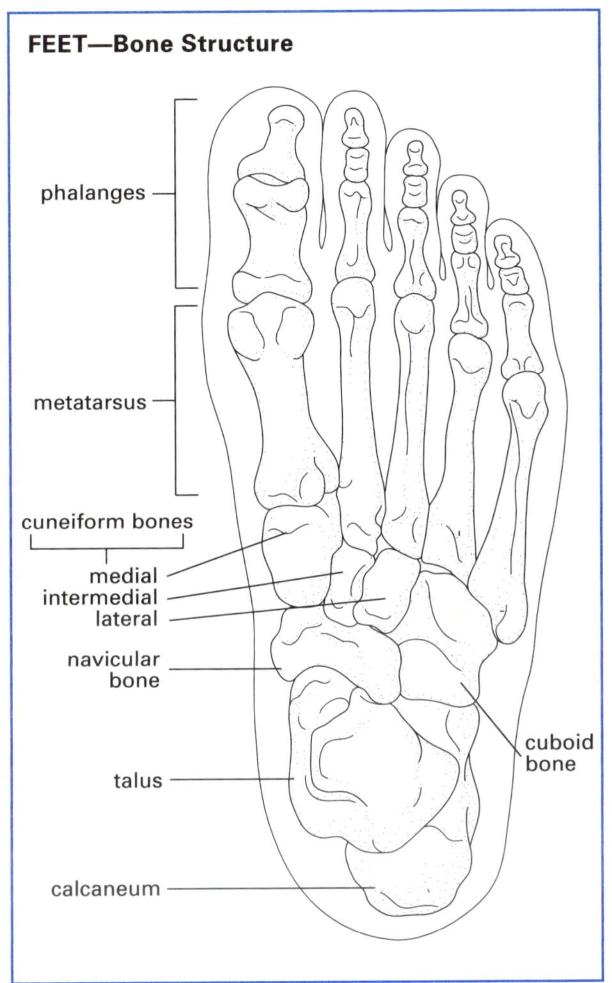

shove them into often ill-fitting shoes, and pay scant regard to their hygiene, despite their use and tendency to sweat in their cramped environment. We then stand on them, walk with them, and with each step place our entire body weight on the three square inches that we call the ball of our feet. The feet contain small blood vessels that, when we are standing, have the effect of gravity pulling blood into them, and then we get surprised when our feet swell! The bones and muscles, despite the weight they carry, tend to be very resilient and rarely cramp, but infrequently do we spend any time relaxing these hard-working parts of our body.

The Eastern philosophies also consider the feet to be our connection with Mother Earth, but rarely do we spend time with our feet directly on the ground. I find it interesting that the masters of yoga will spend time upside down and in the lotus position with the soles of the feet facing the sky, thereby creating a potential connection between our "soles" and heaven.

Any diseases of the arteries through smoking, diabetes, or a genetic predisposition to cold feet require special attention to the feet, because the blood vessels are small, and any occlusion, as found in the above conditions, can discourage healing. Diabetics in particular may have neurological deficits, and therefore not be aware of damage to their feet; special attention must be paid to this area.

RECOMMENDATIONS

- *Spend as much time as possible in bare feet, preferably with some of that time allowing contact with the earth.*
- *Ensure that socks and shoes are loose fitting.*
- *Ensure cleanliness of all parts of the body, but pay special attention to the feet and between the toes. This is a very comfortable area for warmth and moisture to encourage bacterial and fungal growth.*
- *Careful cleaning and drying, especially between the toes, is essential. The use of nonmedicated talcum powder is encouraged if the feet are sweaty or if any length of time is to be spent in socks and/or shoes.*
- *If possible, spend a few minutes each day with the soles of the feet exposed to direct sunlight.*
- *Any injury should be treated with respect. The blood vessels in the feet are small, and injuries may not receive a good blood supply.*

ATHLETE'S FOOT

Athlete's foot is characterized by a red, itching, and peeling skin, generally between and around the gaps in the toes. This is created by a fungus usually (*see* **Tinea versicolor**), although secondary bacterial infection can make the condition worse.

Most commonly contracted from damp changing-room or swimming-room floors, the condition usually responds to good foot hygiene.

RECOMMENDATIONS

- *Treatment is often unnecessary if the basics of foot hygiene are followed (see* **Care of the feet***).*
- *Always keep the feet dry, and use nonmedicated talc.*
- *Spend as much time barefoot as possible, keeping in mind that these fungal infections are transmittable.*
- *Tea tree oil, applied in a concentrated oil and then dried with a hair dryer, is beneficial.*
- *Rub crushed garlic onto the affected areas, leave for 20min, wash off, and dry thoroughly. Calendula ointment can be used similarly.*
- *For resistant infections, apply grapefruit extract twice a day for one week.*
- *Avoid orthodox preparations if possible. They can lead to resistant strains of fungus that are harder to clear up.*

CLUB FOOT—*see* Talipes

FLAT FEET

The inner, middle aspect of the foot is supposed to have an arch. There is no particular amount of arching that is healthy or unhealthy, but if this part of the anatomy rests flat on the ground, then the individual has flat feet. This is not a problem unless there are pains in the feet, a persistence or occurrence of discomfort in other parts of the body—especially the lower back and lower limb joints—or if running is painful or ungainly.

The arch of the foot is created by the muscles and ligaments around that part of the anatomy. As these tighten and develop, the arch is raised. A child's foot is very often flat, and the arch will develop once the child is walking.

RECOMMENDATIONS

- *Treatment for flat feet is not required unless any of the above criteria for discomfort are apparent.*
- *Correct-fitting shoes with a raised arch will be fitted and prescribed by podiatrists, who should be consulted.*
- *Discomfort will be relieved by reflexology, and a cranial osteopath, osteopath, or chiropractor should by consulted if there are pains elsewhere.*
- *Walking barefooted and specific foot exercises can be discussed with the podiatrist.*
- *If there is any alteration of gait when walking or running, then a visit to an Alexander technician to discuss posture is recommended.*

FUNGAL INFECTIONS OF THE FEET
—*see* **Athlete's foot**

HOT OR BURNING SENSATIONS IN THE FEET

This is a surprisingly common symptom, often found in individuals who have had the symptom all their lives and take it for granted. Indeed, there may be no particular disease process associated, and it may simply be an awareness on the part of these individuals.

Certain diseases, such as multiple sclerosis, other neurological conditions, and diabetes may all create neurological damage that sends impulses to the brain, indicating heat in the area, even though there may not be anything excessive.

Burning feet may be an indication of nutritional deficiency, particularly folic acid, vitamin B_{12}, and other vitamins within the higher complexes.

Eastern philosophy may consider that heat in the feet is an indication of a block in the lower chakras, thereby causing excess energy to remain in the lower limbs.

RECOMMENDATIONS

- *Persisting heat or burning sensations in the feet should be assessed by a medical practitioner to rule out serious, underlying conditions.*
- *Sometimes, but rarely, cold applications on a persistent basis may make a difference.*
- *Discuss the problem with a homeopath, because many remedies have burning feet as part of their symptom picture, but correlation with the individual's constitution as a whole is more likely to find the right remedy.*
- *Take three times the daily recommended dose of any zinc and B complex (ensure that it contains vitamin B_{12}) for at least three weeks.*
- *If the above treatments do not relieve the situation, then some form of energy release under the hands of a healer, acupuncturist, or Shiatsu practitioner may release a block in the pelvis, allowing the energy to flow more freely and relieve the pressure on the feet.*

SHOES

The selection of shoes is extremely important, as is ensuring that socks are not too tightly fitting. Tight-fitting shoes will alter the very delicate bone structures in infants' feet, and the same can be said up until growing has stopped at the age of 20 years or so. Shoes should be measured both for length and width, be comfortable, and lined with natural material to avoid sweating.

Many persistent backaches, whether neck or lower back, are created by malalignment of the pelvis, which in turn can be created by one leg being longer than the other. This is corrected by accurately fitted inner soles, or additions to the heel and external soles of shoes.

RECOMMENDATIONS

- *Ensure that shoes are fitted by accurate measurement of a child's feet and not by fashion consciousness.*
- *Ensure, to the best of your ability, that shoes are made out of natural materials, and that the inner lining allows "breathing" and sweat absorption.*

SWEATY FEET

Sweaty feet, like hot or burning feet, are not necessarily an indication of ill heath, and may simply be a genetic predisposition.

RECOMMENDATION

- *See* **Hot or burning sensations in the feet**.

TALIPES (CLUB FOOT)

This condition is present at birth and is characterized by one foot or both feet being angled inwards

Talipes

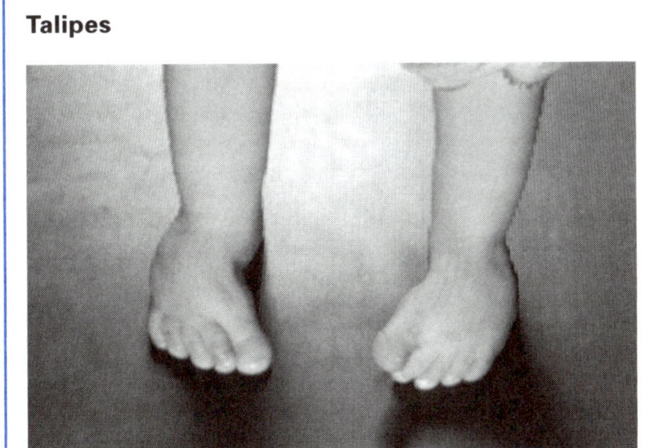

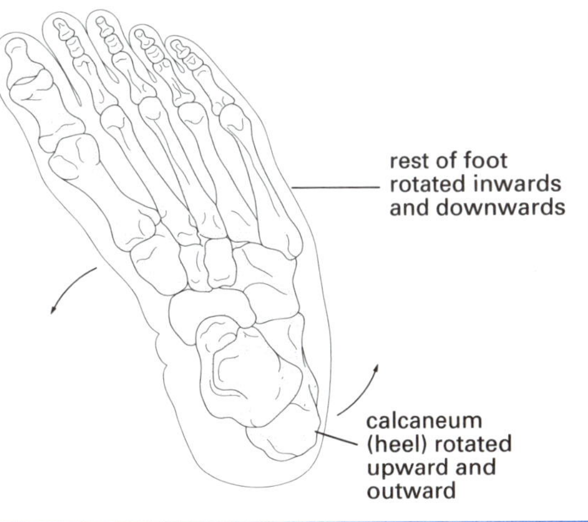

and pointing downwards. Medically speaking, club foot can also represent an outward and upward deformity of the ankle and foot.

RECOMMENDATIONS

- *Assessment is best made by an orthopedic surgeon.*
- *Doctors, chiropodists, and some osteopaths and chiropractors will be able to show parents massage techniques that may correct this condition. The use of Arnica cream while using this technique is beneficial.*
- *Splinting may be necessary.*
- *Surgical intervention is sometimes required. If so, see* **Operations and surgery**.

THE SKIN

BITES

Human and animal

It is not uncommon for anyone to be subjected to the bite of an insect, animal, or human being. I talk about bites in the chapter on childhood because bites tend to occur more often at this age. Treatment is, however, similar for all age groups.

A bite is of no consequence unless it breaks the skin. Once this has occurred and the outer protection of the body has been breached, however minor the abrasion may appear, treatment is essential. Human bites are particularly problematic because the mouth carries many viruses and parasites that are extremely aggressive. The same can be said for animal bites, the most infamous of which is the bite of an animal carrying rabies. Insect bites (as opposed to stings—*see* **Stings**) may well inject poison into the area at the same time. Reptilian (snake) bites and their associated venom vary appreciably in danger, but all need medical attention.

RECOMMENDATIONS

- *Any bite that breaks the skin should be assessed by an orthodox physician, preferably in an accident-and-emergency department.*
- *With any bite, flush the area immediately with running water and soak the injury in a heavy salt-water solution (five tablespoons per 16 ounces of water) with any available antiseptic, but preferably five teaspoonfuls of Calendula and/or Hypericum lotion.*
- *Human bites are notorious, and must be flushed out immediately. The same can be said for other animal bites.*
- *If bitten by an animal or insect, try to capture it or at the very least, memorize close details of it. Antivenom serum is very specific, and being able to remember the markings on a snake is of vital importance to the emergency team.*
- *In dealing with a snake bite, ignore everything that you have seen in cowboy movies. Do not use a tourniquet, and if you are going to suck the poison out of the wounds, do not cut it first, and do not consider this procedure if you have any obvious cuts or sores in the mouth. Keep the victim resting, because activity will increase the heart rate and move the poison around the body quicker.*
- *If there is any suggestion that the animal is rabid, obtain the homeopathic remedy Hydrophobinum, potency 30, 12, or 6, and take one dose every 10min as soon as it is obtained. Do not delay going to the hospital, however.*
- *Apply Arnica, Calendula, and/or Hypericum or Urtica creams.*
- *You will be advised to have a tetanus injection, and whether you do or do not have one, use the remedy Hypericum, potency 30, 12 or 6, four pills every 15min for the first hour and then every 2hr for three days.*

BURNS

Burns are liable to occur at any time, but are most worrying in children. A six-inch square area of a burn on an adult may represent 2 percent of skin damage, but on an infant it may represent up to 20 percent. The skin is essential for many processes, including protecting from germ invasion and holding fluid in the body. Loss of skin through burning can allow fluid loss very rapidly. The greater the area of skin that is damaged, the greater the fluid loss and the larger the risk to the individual.

Burns are described as:

- **First-degree** when only the superficial layer of skin is damaged.
- **Second-degree** when the superficial and middle layers are involved, but the deep layer where reproduction of the skin occurs is still intact.
- **Third-degree** when the skin, including its basal layer or skin manufacturing layer, is destroyed.

Third-degree burns, if they are small, may have skin growth from around the area, but if they are too large they will require skin grafting.

Skin Percentages

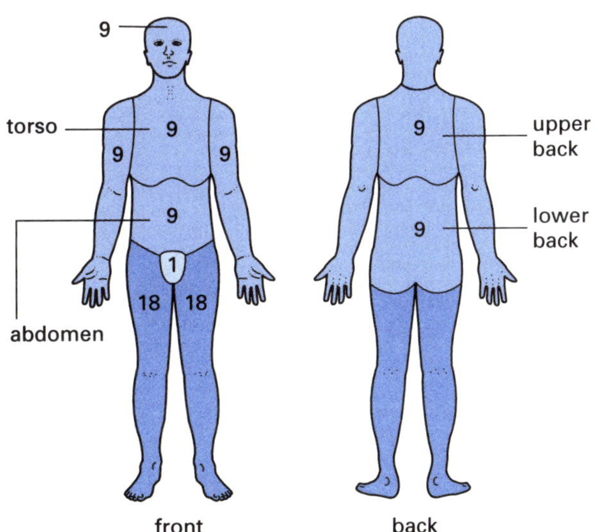

The "rule of nines" gives the percentages of the surface area of skin for each section of the adult body. However, the results are not the same for children, due to their differential growth rates.

RECOMMENDATIONS

- *Any burn that breaks the skin or weeps should be assessed by a doctor.*
- *Any burn greater than 3 percent of the body area should be viewed in an emergency department.*
- *Apply cold water immediately.*
- *Contrary to many old-wives' tales, do not apply butter or oils (the area will fry), and do not burst blisters.*
- *Arnica, Calendula, or Hypericum fluid extracts should be applied, three tablespoons to 16 ounces of water.*
- *Do not remove clothing from a burned area unless it falls away easily.*
- *Consider the remedies Arnica and Urtica urens for superficial burns, Arnica and Kali bichromicum for second-degree burns, and Causticum and Hypericum if the pain of the burn persists. Take potency 6 of any of these every 10min.*
- *Apply Aloe vera, Calendula, Hypericum or Urtica gels or lotions continuously.*
- *See* **Sunburn**.

CHAFING

Although chafing can occur at any age, it is most commonly found in children because their intolerance of cold when they are playing outside seems to be greater. Chafing is a medical term for the breakdown of the superficial layers of the skin, allowing dryness and cracks to appear due to a combination of dryness and cold.

RECOMMENDATIONS

- *Avoid using moisturizers, chapsticks, etc., because this leads to a dependency in that part of the body. In severe conditions where the elements are unavoidable, such as when skiing or sailing, then short-term use is acceptable.*

- *Skin is best moisturized and healed from within, so ensure good hydration and suitable nutritional intake in the form of fruit and vegetables.*
- *If damage has occurred, administer the following supplements in the dosage suggested per foot of height: vitamin A (1,000iu), vitamin C (500mg), vitamin E (100iu), and zinc (2.5mg). These should be given in divided doses with meals.*
- *The use of Arnica or Calendula creams for short periods is effective and acceptable.*

CHILBLAINS

Chilblains are painful swellings usually found on the extremities, such as toes and fingers. In severe cases, the swelling may cause the skin to break down and secondary infection may compound the problems.

Chilblains are caused by poor peripheral (capillary) circulation, and are brought about by the affected part becoming cold. The skin is more likely to break down if the area is damp as well. Principally, this is a problem with the circulation as a whole, and topical intervention may be of benefit, but a deeper look at the miasm or chronic tendency of the individual and their ancestors to have poor circulation is a much more profound treatment.

RECOMMENDATIONS

- *In acute cases, ensure that the area stays warm. It is a fallacy to believe that socks and shoes necessarily keep the feet warm. Tight-fitting footware will actually impede circulation and make the problem worse. Loose, woolly socks in slightly oversized shoes are a must for sufferers.*
- *Gentle warming with warm hands or other dry, warm applications can be most relieving.*
- *Rotating the arm at the shoulder, or the foot at the knee, will pull blood into the peripheries.*
- *In persistent or mild conditions of poor peripheral circulation, high doses of cayenne-pepper extract and then lowered-maintenance doses can be beneficial if taken over three months or more.*
- *In adults only, a tot of alcohol daily can increase peripheral circulation. An excess of alcohol will create a rebound effect causing initial increase in circulation, but a later and prolonged decrease.*
- *The homeopathic remedies Petroleum 6 and Agaricus 6, one dose every 2hr, may be beneficial in acute cases, but prolonged or chronic conditions require a homeopathic prescription based on the individual as a whole.*
- *If the chilblains are causing itching when warmed, a cream containing Calendula, Arnica, and Urtica can be most soothing.*

CHONDYLOMATA—*see* Warts and verrucas

COLD SORES—*see* Herpes simplex

CRADLE CAP

Cradle cap is characterized by crusty patches on the scalp created by an overproduction from the scalp (and skin) of the natural oil known as sebum. The sebum dries over and under the skin, which is why picking or trying to remove the unsightly condition will inevitably lead to bleeding and the possibility of secondary infection.

RECOMMENDATIONS

- *Frequent shampooing (even if there is not much hair) will speed up the process. If there is hair, do not shampoo more than three times a week, because this will take out the natural oils.*
- *One teaspoon of lemon juice in two tablespoons of olive oil applied to the scalp twice a day may help.*
- *Do not pick.*
- *Gentle massage and brushing with soft bristles will encourage faster flaking.*

CUTS AND ABRASIONS

These can occur at any age, of course, and the treatment is much the same.

RECOMMENDATIONS

SEVERE CUTS

- *Remove any debris or dirt with fingers or tweezers as soon as possible.*
- *Heavy bleeding should be stemmed by applying a clean material to the wound with suitable pressure. Medical assistance and assessment should be obtained as soon as possible.*
- *Rarely, if localized pressure is not stemming the blood flow, then occlusion of the artery higher up the limb may be considered by tying any material tightly. This should not be done except in exceptional circumstances.*

MINOR CUTS

- *Clean the wound with water, preferably previously boiled, but tap water or stream water is perfectly acceptable.*
- *If bleeding is persistent, obtain a medical assessment in case a stitch is required.*
- *Apply a Calendula-based cream. Take Arnica potency 6 every halfhour for three doses and then every 3hr until pain has resolved.*

DIAPER RASH

All children will develop rashes in the area of the groin and buttocks at some point. Indeed, if an adult were to spend time in moist underwear, as is often the case after a workout at the gym or other exercise, rashes and the associated irritation or discomfort would become apparent all too soon.

Diaper rash is a red, irritating, and occasionally spotty condition found in and around the areas covered by the diaper. It is caused by ammonia in the urine, and digestive juices from the feces irritating the skin.

It is important to differentiate this common rash from more persistent and irritating conditions, such as *Candida* (thrush), or bacterial, viral, or fungal infections. Occasionally, secondary infection from normal skin bacteria or skin fungi will worsen the situation. Infection by *Candida* (thrush) is not uncommon.

A persisting or frequently recurring rash may be indicative of more serious conditions, such as diabetes.

RECOMMENDATIONS

- *Any rash that does not respond to the suggestions below after 48–72hr should be seen by a physician for a firm diagnosis.*
- *Allow the baby to spend as much time as possible without a diaper on.*
- *Change diapers frequently, and ensure that the area is cleaned three times a day using water or simple, nonchemically treated soaps.*
- *Use nonmedicated talc liberally before bed and with every other diaper change throughout the day.*
- *Treat a rash as soon as it appears using a zinc or caster-oil cream before applying a diaper, especially at night. Try Arnica or Calendula creams. These may make the area more inflamed, because the principle of a herbal treatment is to pull blood into the area to allow healing to occur more quickly. If this is the case, desist from use. Clean the creams off at these times when you are able to expose the baby's skin to the air.*
- *Most irritant rashes will benefit from the application of zinc-oxide creams. These should be used with the knowledge that they are barrier creams, and a generous application is required. These creams do not need to be rubbed in, but are left on the surface.*
- *The use of creams containing benzyl compounds is acceptable if natural products are not dealing with the problem.*
- *The homeopathic remedy Anacardium 6 can be used every 2hr if the child is irritable, Bovista if the rash is associated with diarrhea and is worse in the morning, Hepar sulfuris calcarium if recurrent, Rhus toxicodendron if the area*

appears swollen, and Urtica urens if the rash resembles a nettle sting.

- *Persisting recurrence may be related to diet or the mother's intake if the baby is breastfed, and a nutritionist could be asked for advice.*

ECZEMA (DERMATITIS)

Eczema is a simple term for what is a complicated condition. Many people have their own idea of what eczema is but, medically speaking, it is characterized by irregular skin patterns with various characteristics. Eczema may be nothing more than a dry, scaly patch of skin, or it may be characterized by redness, swelling, cracking, and dry or exudative lesions. This damaged skin is more open to infection, and therefore there may be associated pimples or pus.

Contrary to popular belief, eczema is not always a longstanding or chronic condition, and may occur as an acute condition arising as quickly as it may disappear. By definition, eczema has no recognized orthodox cause and, strictly speaking, any rash that resembles eczema that has a known cause, such as topical irritants, staphylococcal infections, or food/drug-allergy reactions, should be referred to as dermatitis. Very often, lay-medical books will refer to dermatitis and eczema as the same thing.

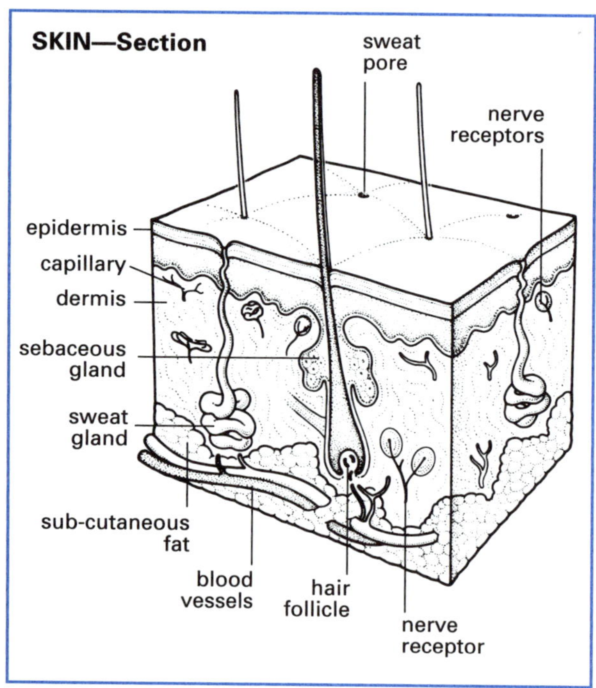

Despite eczema occasionally being exudative of clear fluid (serum), the main characteristic is dryness and redness. Eastern medical philosophies consider eczema to be a condition of excess heat, although the serum may be an attempt to correct the problem, in which case this form of eczema would be considered to be "damp heat." Alternative therapies are therefore geared towards finding the cause of this excess heat and removing it. There may be genetic predispositions to eczema (as there is in asthma and hay fever), and in these cases, the eczema is known as *atopic* eczema.

Hahnemann, the father of homeopathy, formulated the medical belief of the presence of deep-seated tendencies or problems he called miasms (*see* **Homeopathy**). One of these miasms was known as the psoric or psora, which is manifest by skin eruptions, and Hahnemann believed that seven eighths of all chronic illnesses were ascribed to suppression of skin conditions. Indeed, in the centuries before the advent of the suppressive effects of steroids, many diseases showed themselves initially through the skin. As homeopaths fervently believe in the transmission of a disease process from one generation to the other until treated effectively, skin conditions (and particularly eczema) are looked at as a problem of the internal working of the body rather than as an actual problem with the skin, and frequently "passed on" from generation to generation.

The skin is certainly a remarkable organ, having many functions. It is directly or indirectly related to most other organs and systems in the body, and therefore when dealing with a skin problem, one must look closely at the body as whole. The skin acts as protection, and contains many of the facets of the immune system; it can absorb and excrete, performing functions similar to the lung and the kidneys (sweat and urine are very similar in composition); and the skin can transform sunlight into chemicals that are both protective and essential to our well-being, such as melanin (our tanning process), and the production of vitamin D (essential for our survival).

The skin is also a reflector of our emotional state, becoming, for example, pink with embarrassment, red with anger, and white with fear. The skin, therefore, according to Eastern philosophies, reflects the inherent energy of the heart, lung, liver, and the nervous system, because all of these organs have associated emotional states.

When the skin misbehaves, therefore, the answer may be an associated, underlying condition affecting any of our organs.

RECOMMENDATIONS

- *Eczema must be treated holistically, and as far as possible without suppression. Very often, the condition is so severe that steroids or natural equivalents are necessary, but they should be used only in conjunction with a complementary medical view, and then only sparingly.*
- *Review eczema with a homeopathic practitioner in conjunction with a Chinese or Tibetan doctor. Remember, however, that many herbal treatments, although effective, are plant-steroid-based, and may be suppressive.*
- *In acute eczema, the homeopathic remedies Psorinum, Calcarea carbonica, and Graphites can be used at potency 6 every 2hr until your complementary medical specialist is consulted.*
- *A tablespoon full of baking soda in 16 ounces of warm or cool water (depending on which is most soothing) may reduce the itch.*
- *Dry eczema can be treated and protected from infection by the use of Calendula or Urtica creams, vitamin E cream, or nonmedicated petroleum-jelly extracts.*
- *A base massage oil may have Roman camomile, lavender, or neroli essential oils added, which can be soothing if not curative.*
- *The following vitamins and supplements should be taken in amounts recommended by a specialist: vitamin A, vitamin E, copper, flax seed, and gammalinoleic acid.*
- *Ensure that no chemicals, including medicated soaps or shampoos, come into contact with the skin. Water, glycerine soaps, or aqueous cream should be the only cleansers.*
- *The close connection of the psyche with the skin requires that stress-management techniques are employed. If the patient is old enough, then psychotherapy, hypnotherapy, or techniques such as neurolinguistic programming (NLP) should be instigated. If the child is too young, then massage techniques should be employed. It is important to understand that a child's stress may be a reflection of the anxiety levels within the house, and that unhappy parents or siblings may need counseling in order for the child's skin to clear up.*
- *Eczema may be a reflection of food intolerance or allergy. Assessment through Vega or bioresonance computers, as well as blood tests, is recommended in resistant cases.*
- *Low levels of hydrochloric acid in the stomach, i.e. hypochlorhydria, is a common finding in patients with eczema. This decreased ability to break down foods may lead to the absorption of larger food molecules, leading to allergic responses. Tests to check for hydrochloric-acid secretion are available through a complementary medical practitioner, and should be checked.*

IMPETIGO

This bacterial infection, usually caused by a staphylococcal bacteria, is most commonly found in children, but can occur at any age. It is generally an indication of a weakened immune system, because staphylococcal bacteria are usually commensal (they live on us without any harm being caused). Use of antibiotics or antiseptic creams and lotions can lead to resistant strains that are tougher for the body to deal with, and often result in a staphylococcal or impetigo infection.

It is important to recognize these blisters, which appear in a red rash, burst, and form a brown crust, because impetigo is highly contagious and can spread rapidly. It is most often seen on the face, but can occur anywhere.

RECOMMENDATIONS

- *Any aggressive, painful, or fast-spreading rash should be assessed by a complementary medical practitioner, and then reviewed by a doctor if the condition does not respond to complementary medicine. Antibiotics may need to be used.*
- *Insist upon a skin swab, and consider using the homeopathic nosode (the remedy made from the bacteria), potency 30, every 2hr until improvement is seen, and then four times a day until better.*
- *Apply a Calendula lotion to the area every 2hr. Do not use an oil-based cream, because the bacteria prefer a moist environment. Do not use antiseptic solutions such as TCP, which will kill off the good bacteria around the lesion that are competing with the bad bacteria.*
- *Specific homeopathic remedies can be chosen depending on the symptoms, and a constitutional remedy should be administered via a homeopath.*
- *The following supplements should be given per foot of height in divided doses throughout the day with meals: beta-carotene (2mg), vitamin C (1g), and vitamin E(100iu). Zinc should be given at a dose of 5mg per foot of height before bed.*
- *Remember the highly contagious nature of impetigo, and ensure good hygiene and that the infected party uses separate towels. No school until the infection has completely cleared.*

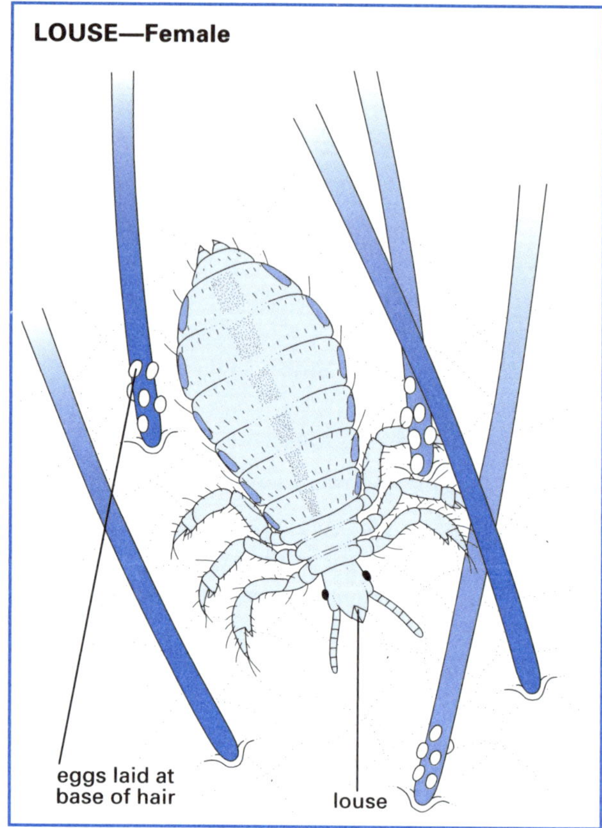

LICE

Lice are parasites found predominantly in children, contracting it from classmates, but they can be found in all age groups. Different types live in different parts of the body, such that the head louse is a different species to the pubic louse (crabs). These parasites lie flat on the skin, attaching to small capillaries, and cause itching, redness, and occasionally bleeding because of aggressive scratching.

Lice lay their eggs at the base of body hairs, and attach them with a tenacious cement.

RECOMMENDATIONS

- *Alternative therapies may be beneficial, and should be considered before the use of any proprietary solutions. Recent government health and safety laboratory tests have shown that the active ingredient, malathion, is readily absorbed into the system by the scalp, and may affect developing nervous systems.*

- *Take 100ml of almond oil and put in 10ml each of lavender, eucalyptus, and bergamot. Apply to the scalp and hair, and cover with a shower cap overnight. Wash out thoroughly the next morning, and follow the combing instructions below.*
- *Comb with a metal nit-comb twice a day for a period of two weeks. Electric nit-combs are now available, which cut down on the time involved since the lice are killed on contact.*
- *All members of the family or close social group (such as classmates) should be treated.*

RINGWORM

Ringworm is an infection of the skin, hair, or nails by a variety of fungi, although most commonly one called *Tinea*. These produce a red, circular lesion with raised borders and a normal or slightly pale-colored center, which is in fact healed skin. It is this ring-like appearance that gives the condition its name, because there are no worms involved!

If the condition affects the scalp, alopecia (bald patches) can occur; *Tinea* is also one of the skin fungi that cause athlete's foot, groin rashes, and other lesions in moist areas.

Ringworm has no species preference, and will pass through pets as easily as through human beings. It is quite contagious and, left to its own devices, may persist and irritate for weeks.

RECOMMENDATION

- *See* **Fungal infections**.

Ringworm

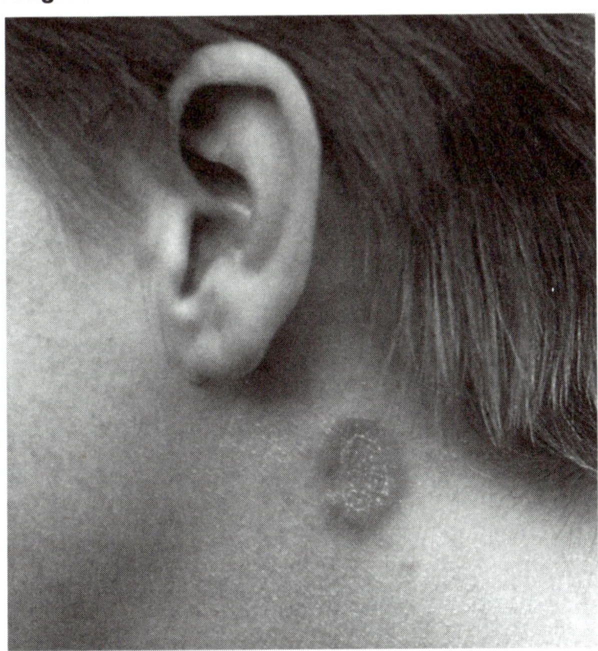

SCABIES

This is a contagious disorder that is caused by a little mite, and is characterized by intensely itching lesions that can take many shapes. The itch is often markedly worse at night, because the female insects burrow beneath the skin to lay their eggs, which causes the irritation.

Areas of the body most commonly affected are the wrists and the webs between the fingers, but it can appear anywhere.

Identification is by recognizing the characteristic burrows, which are a fraction of an inch to half an inch long, wavy and with a little lump at one end. The body mounts an immune response

Scabies

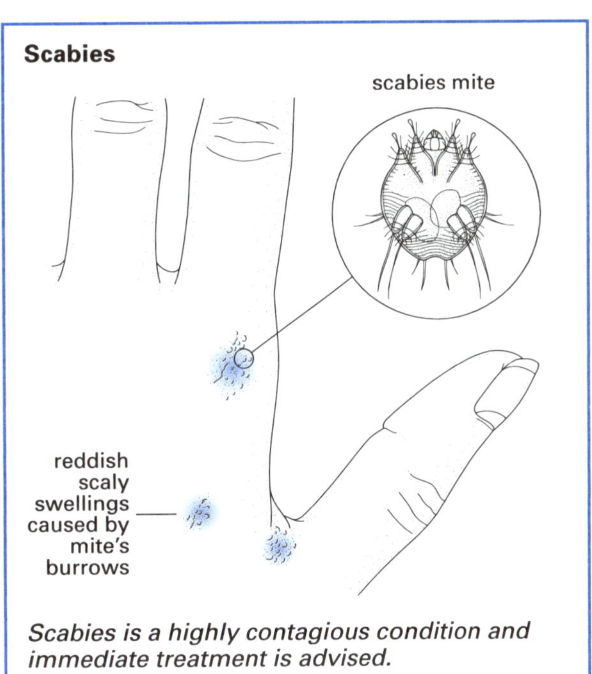

Scabies is a highly contagious condition and immediate treatment is advised.

against this mite, as it would to any other infection, and therefore the more often an infection is contracted, the more aggressive the response can be. A patient who has never had scabies before may remain symptomless for anywhere up to one month, by which time a large area may be infected.

Unrecognized, the irritation may continue, and the itching will lead to the possibility of secondary infection, an eczema-like condition, and a persisting and profoundly irritating rash.

Investigation is usually done by a doctor, who will recognize the characteristic lesions and may be able to spot the mites with a magnifying glass. It is possible to remove a parasite from a burrow with a pin and look at it under a microscope. Skin scrapings may also be examined in this way.

RECOMMENDATIONS

- *Orthodox lotions are effective and, if the skin is not particularly damaged, are unlikely to be absorbed at a rate that a healthy body could not deal with. Treatment is swift and efficient, although repeated use of the chemicals might be necessary while the remaining eggs hatch.*
- *Lavender oil is a well-established and longstanding treatment, probably working in the same way as proprietary drugs. A quantity in the bath or directly applied if the area infected is small may do the trick, but it needs to be repeated twice a day for five days at least.*
- *All clothes need to be thoroughly cleaned if they have been worn within a week. Mites generally do not live longer than 3–4 days away from the skin and one week is allowing a good safety margin.*
- *The homeopathic remedy Sulphur 6, taken four times per day, is often effective, although it may exacerbate the irritation and cause a flare-up of any other underlying skin conditions.*
- *Please note that all members of a family, and possibly a school group, should be treated.*

SCALDS

A scald is damage to the skin caused by hot fluids and should be treated as for any burns (*see* **Burns**).

SPLINTERS

A splinter is a small shard of any material that embeds itself in the skin. These are generally painful, and are worse if the area where the splinter has embedded has any pressure applied to it.

RECOMMENDATIONS

- *Any puncture wound may have debris or a splinter beneath the skin surface that may be invisible. Any puncture wound that continues to hurt should be examined by a doctor.*
- *X-ray investigation is only beneficial if the splinter is made of metal, because most other materials will not appear radio-opaque (visible on x-ray).*
- *Any attempt to remove a splinter should be done with the correct implements, such as a pair of fine tweezers. The use of a needle to break the skin over a splinter to allow access for the tweezers is acceptable if the splinter is not buried too deep. All equipment should be sterilized in boiling water over a naked flame for at least 1min. (Do not hold the other end of the metal instrument while sterilizing it.) Alternatively, a dilute solution of a disinfectant may be used, but this needs to be washed off with boiling water before applying to the skin.*
- *Use an Arnica- or Calendula-based cream before and after.*
- *Squeamish children (or adults!) may try applying the adhesive part of a sticky Band-Aid to a visible splinter. Leave on for 48hr. The body will eject the foreign object at the rate of skin growth, and this may adhere to the sticky plaster which, when removed, will pull the splinter out.*
- *Do not hesitate to visit a doctor, who will have all the equipment to remove a splinter and be able to offer a local anesthetic as well.*

STINGS

A sting is usually delivered by an insect, and differs from a bite by injecting a chemical that causes burning, pricking or . . . stinging! Most commonly, stings are given by wasps, bees, and the mosquito group, which includes gnats. Less common are the more dangerous stings from hornets. Certain marine animals, such as jellyfish and types of coral, may also impart a sting.

The injected irritant directly affects the nerve endings, but also breaks down cells that release histamine-like chemicals that attract blood into the area. Rubbing and scratching the site tends to spread the poison and make the situation worse.

RECOMMENDATIONS

- *The best treatment is avoidance and the use of insect repellent in areas of infestation.*
- *Apply a cold or ice compress as soon as possible.*
- *Vitamin B_6 (50mg at dusk) may repel mosquitoes, and the application of pyrethrum solution will ward off most insects.*
- *Remove any residual part of the insect or its sting as quickly as possible, using sharp fingernails or tweezers. Do not use teeth or suck out the toxin, as a more aggressive reaction may take place in the mouth. Remember that certain insects will leave a sting and the poison sacs pumping in the wound.*
- *Stay inside and apply directly to the sting any of the following tinctures: Calendula or tea tree oil for gnat and mosquito bites; Arnica or lavender for bee stings; and Arnica or Ledum for wasp or hornet stings.*
- *If the above are not available or do not work, try applying the juice from a potato by pressing a freshly cut potato over the area. If this has not worked within 2min, use an onion.*
- *The homeopathic remedies Ledum or Apis mellifica can be taken at potency 6 every 5min. The more red and inflamed the sting, the more the preference would be for Apis.*
- *In multiple or aggressive stings, papain or bromelain supplements should be taken at three times the recommended product dosage for three days.*

WARTS AND VERRUCAS

A wart is an overgrowth of skin triggered by a viral infection in the basal (growth) layer. Depending on where they are, a wart may be soft and fleshy (such as in the vagina), or firm (as found on hands and feet). A verruca is a wart found in the hardened tissues of the soles of the feet.

RECOMMENDATIONS

- *At the onset or arrival of a wart, increase your vitamin A and zinc intake via orange and green vegetables, or through supplements (twice the recommended dosage).*
- *Apply Thuja tincture, garlic, or caster oil for several days underneath a bandage. If this is impractical, then apply the compounds frequently through the day. Ask a complementary medical practitioner if the wart is internal.*
- *Liquid nitrogen may be applied by a doctor to freeze off the warts, and preparations may be available over the counter at a pharmacy, but should only be used if other treatments have failed because the chemical treatments damage the surrounding skin and lead to a higher incidence of recurrence.*
- *Homeopathic remedies are beneficial and, depending on the type, should be selected from Thuja, Nitric acid, Dulcamara, and Causticum.*

THE NERVOUS SYSTEM

CEREBRAL PALSY

Cerebral palsy is a disorder of movement originating *in utero*, in infancy, or in early childhood. Most often the damage to the brain that causes this problem occurs during birth due to a lack of oxygenation or, more rarely, by infections of the brain, seizures, or maternal drug-abuse during pregnancy.

The extent of the brain damage varies, and may be mild or may leave the infant incapacitated, unable to communicate, and possibly unaware of his/her surroundings. Uncontrolled movements, aggressive behavior patterns, blindness, deafness, and an inability to speak are some of the more serious problems.

Eastern philosophies consider the birth of an incapacitated child to be part of that individual's soul karma. We all, at some point in our cosmic cycle, have to go through a period of incapacity and dependency on others. The karma of the parents is also that of a lifetime of servitude to a distressed physical body and mind. I find that it helps to discuss the inevitable trauma that befalls the family of a cerebral-palsy victim by discussing matters from a more ethereal and spiritual angle. Very little pleasure can be derived from the necessity of caring for a severely debilitated child, but then a connection between two souls is not dependent upon physical or material means, and caring for a soul in a distressed body can be a very loving and enlightening experience. To give is often considered a greater pleasure than to receive, and if one can focus on this, then caring for a cerebral-palsy case should be considered a blessing.

RECOMMENDATIONS

- *Contact a local cerebral-palsy group to share with other families your grief, joys, and experiences.*
- *See* **Paralysis** *and* **Birth defects**.
- *Ensure that cranial osteopathy or craniosacral therapy is tried for at least six to ten sessions, since profound changes in an individual can be seen.*
- *Consult with a nutritionist and a homeopath, because correct supplementation and homeopathic medication can be of great benefit, although not curative.*

CONVULSIONS

Convulsions, commonly termed "seizures" or "fits," are an involuntary occurrence of muscular spasm or contraction. There are two types of convulsion: clonic (characterized by alternate contraction and relaxation) and tonic (a continuous contraction or spasm).

Convulsions can occur due to any insult on the nervous system, which leads to it sending out massive impulses instructing the muscles to behave incorrectly. Convulsions are most commonly associated with a loss of consciousness.

Occasionally, convulsions will occur in association with high temperatures, most commonly in young children below the age of two years. Other causative factors are epilepsy, infections such as meningitis or encephalitis, an adverse drug reaction or food allergy, or lesions such as tumors in the brain.

RECOMMENDATIONS

- *Have somebody call an ambulance. This request can always be canceled if the convulsions are minor and/or short-lived.*
- *One convulsion or fit does not represent a serious condition in most cases, but all fits should be reported and examined by a doctor. Referral to a neurological specialist is sometimes required.*
- *Do not restrict someone having a convulsion. Instead, clear the area of solid objects and protect the patient by surrounding with cushions or other soft objects.*
- *If blood is seen to be coming from the mouth, this may be due to biting of the tongue, and firm but careful opening of the jaw with an instrument surrounded by a handkerchief or cloth is acceptable.*
- *Upon recovery, administer Aconite, potency 30 or lower, every 10min until recovery is complete or medical attention arrives.*

Cranial Osteopathy

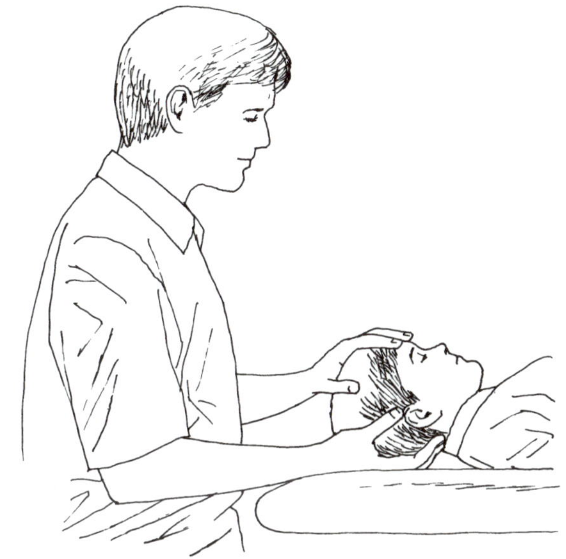

frontal occipital hold

palpation of splenoid motion

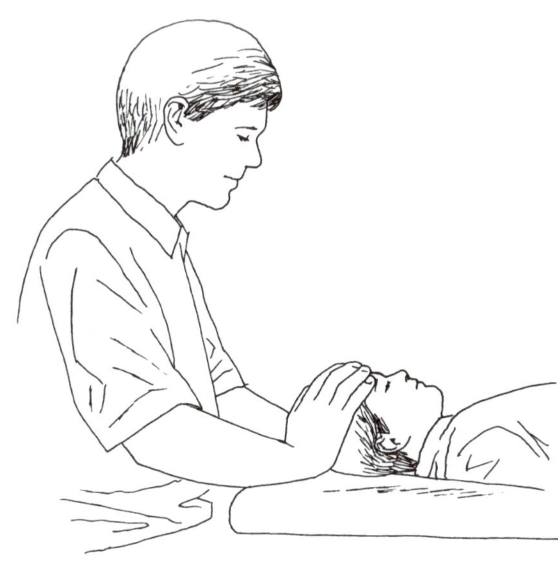

frontal base hold

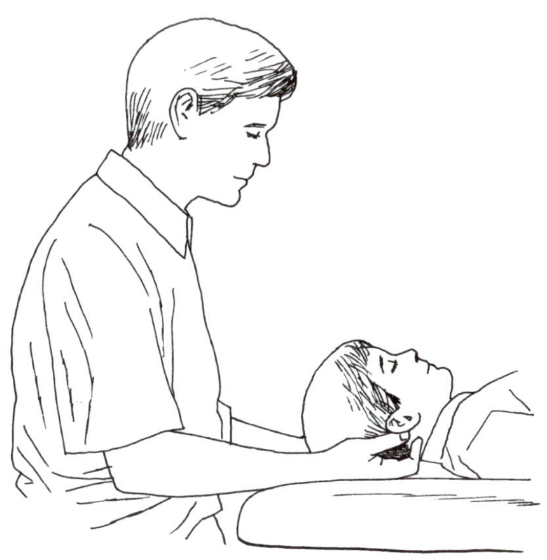

cranial-base release

Cranial osteopathy is a gentle technique in which the bones of the skull are manipulated. It is especially useful with children, and can help treat a wide range of symptoms.

- *If associated with fever, use cold compresses or a lukewarm bath to lower the temperature (see* ***Fever****).*
- *Recurrent fits must be assessed by a doctor. If no serious underlying cause is present, then an assessment from a complementary medical practitioner is recommended, with special attention being paid to diet, food allergy, craniosacral malalignments, and deep psychological-stress factors.*
- *After any convulsion, see a cranial osteopath or craniosacral practitioner at the earliest opportunity.*

EPILEPSY—*see* Convulsions

Epilepsy is not specifically a childhood condition and may occur at any age, but is most frequently spotted, especially if there is any genetic predisposition, at this age. Treatment is similar for any age group.

Epilepsy is a disorder created by excessive nerve discharges in the brain. These manifest episodes of dysfunction in movement, perception, or understanding, and may be associated with unconsciousness or convulsive movements. There are many types of epilepsy that may affect up to five people out of every thousand.

Grand-mal epilepsy

Grand-mal epilepsy is the common perception of a seizure: loss of consciousness and uncontrolled muscular spasms, which can include the risk of tongue biting and the head being slammed against the floor.

Petit-mal epilepsy

Petit-mal epilepsy is characterized by a blank or vacant moment when the individual, most frequently a child, is unresponsive. Repetitive movements may be apparent.

Temporal-lobe epilepsy

This must be considered if there is a temporary loss of awareness, confusion or disorientation, and auditory or visual hallucinations.

Focal epilepsy

As the term suggests, this is a loss of control of one part of the body.

Grand-mal and temporal-lobe epilepsy may be preceded by unusual sensations of smell, vision, or sound, known as an "aura."

Epilepsy may occur for a variety of reasons: trauma or injury to the brain tissue; chemicals, including prescribed and recreational drugs; food allergy; infection; arterial disease; or other causes of a lack of oxygen or glucose reaching the brain. Brain tumors are a serious cause, and other areas that are less well-established that may trigger epilepsy include mercury poisoning (from dental materials), strong electrical currents, and stress. Stress may trigger epilepsy through chemical effects of adrenaline and other catecholamines, but may also tighten the muscles around the skull leading to cranial osteopathic lesions of the jaw and other skull joints.

Epilepsy is not *cured* by orthodox treatment. Complementary therapies may be far more efficacious, and should therefore be used as early as possible. The danger with epilepsy arises from *where* the person has the fit rather than from the fit itself. However, falling downstairs, driving a car, or having a fit when in charge of potentially dangerous tools or instruments require that epilepsy be *controlled,* and therefore orthodox treatment is essential. Any fit should be reviewed by a doctor, with referral to a neurological specialist if required, and thereafter monitored by the medical profession, with anti-epileptic drugs utilized until the doctor recommends withdrawal.

RECOMMENDATIONS

- *Any suggestion of epilepsy needs to be fully investigated by a specialist in neurology to rule out any serious cause.*

- *Supervision and the avoidance of any dangerous situations, such as cooking or operating machinery, must be avoided until the problem is solved.*
- *Orthodox medical treatment should be utilized if fits have become frequent, although one fit does not make epilepsy. Alternative treatments may be considered following diagnosis of the cause, but should not exclude the possible benefits of orthodox drug treatment.*
- *A set diet from a nutritionist with knowledge of this area is essential. Avoidance of sugar, caffeine, alcohol, and artificially sweetened food (saccharine and aspartame) should be strictly adhered to. Canada is currently pioneering a specific nutritional treatment known as the Ketogenic diet, which may become an essential aspect of the treatment of epilepsy.*
- *The brain produces many anticonvulsant chemicals, the most prominent of which is adenosine. This is blocked by theophylline-containing drugs often used by asthmatics. Tea should also be avoided therefore.*
- *To encourage the body's natural anticonvulsants, an alternative practitioner should be consulted to prescribe the correct dosages of specific amino acids, namely taurine and gamma-aminobutyric acid. High-dose vitamin-B complex is also necessary.*
- *Herbal treatments are available as anticonvulsant therapy, but today's drugs are well-established, generally safe and probably better to use.*
- *Constitutional homeopathic remedies are essential, and a homeopath should be consulted.*
- *Craniosacral work, the Alexander technique, and polarity therapy should all be considered.*

MENINGITIS

Infection of the lining of the brain known as the meninges can be characterized by a mild, persistent headache through to violent pain with coma and, if not treated swiftly, death. There is often an associated photophobia (dislike of or pain from light), and an almost characteristic neck stiffness that differentiates meningitis from migraines and other headaches.

Recognizing meningitis in an infant may be impossible without medical expertise. An inconsolable child clearly in pain that is worsened by attempting to dip the chin onto the chest, or a child who is markedly fevered, or becomes floppy or unresponsive, must be considered possibly to have meningitis and rushed to the hospital.

One particular type of aggressive meningitis is caused by meningococcal bacteria, which can have a very swift effect. Meningococcal meningitis can kill a child within four hours. A headache associated with a rash that does not blanch when a glass is pressed onto it is meningococcal meningitis, and must be treated by antibiotics via a hospital or doctor immediately. This rash characteristically appears on the thighs.

Meningitis can occur at any age, but I mention it in the childhood chapter because of the swift and severe nature should it strike at this age. Most meningitis is caused by viral infection, and tends not to be particularly dangerous. The pain is hard to control, but the condition is usually self-limiting, and rarely leaves any sequela. Bacterial or fungal meningitis is much more serious, and can lead to persistent neurological deficits.

RECOMMENDATIONS

- *Any persistent or severe headache must be reviewed by a doctor or accident-and-emergency department.*
- *A lumbar puncture will be required for a firm diagnosis, along with blood and urine examination. More intense investigations, such as CAT scans, may be required, and none of these should be refused.*

- *Viral meningitis will not respond to an antibiotic but secondary infection may make the situation worse and, especially in a child, orthodox medication should not be refused.*
- *Contact your complementary medical practitioner for advice on treating with alternative medicines alongside orthodox treatment, rather than trying to deal with this problem without expert guidance.*

MENTAL DISABILITY

The term mentally disabled refers to those individuals who, for any reason, have damage to the brain, causing a marked debility in mental function. There are several scales used throughout the world to measure mental handicap, and these finer definitions are best left to the experts.

Mental disability affects two parties: the individuals who, very often, are quite unaware or disturbed by the abnormality; and those who care for them. Most helpful advice needs to be given to the latter, who may have had no training or expectations—only fears—of being placed in such a position.

Mental disability can vary in severity from mild—as is often the case in conditions such as Down syndrome (*see* **Down syndrome**)—to severe. Those who have severe disabilities, such as cerebral palsy, post-traumatic injury, or the sequela of infections such as meningitis, may be further hampered by physical inabilities or sensory loss. All levels of disability can benefit from complementary medical treatment to some degree.

RECOMMENDATIONS

FOR THE INDIVIDUAL

- *Ensure that hygiene and sanitation are at a premium. Those who cannot care for themselves are more likely to contract infections.*
- *Consult with a nutritionist, because minor deficiencies can cause major problems, and correct supplementation may dramatically alter the general well-being of the mentally disabled.*
- *Consult a homeopath to assess a suitable constitutional remedy, which can enhance a sense of well-being and, theoretically, prevent infections.*
- *Do not isolate anyone with a mental disabilities. Social interaction, kisses, and hugs have a profound effect on the biochemistry and psychology of all individuals.*
- *Ensure that the highest-quality accessories are made available. In particular, pay attention to the mattress, seats, or wheelchairs. Sores are notoriously difficult to heal in individuals who may scratch or play with an injury, or who are confined to a position that applies pressure to the damaged area.*
- *Never underestimate the level of understanding of a mentally-disabled individual. As there is a fine line between genius and insanity, the mentally disabled may have a marked sensitivity to negative emotions and, as much as any of us, need to be surrounded by laughter, joy, and music. Children make excellent companions for the disabled, because they are before the age where we adults have introduced prejudices.*
- *Frequent cranial osteopathy or craniosacral therapy, along with healing, may make a profound difference, especially if the individual is in any way aggressive or seems disturbed.*
- *Ensure that exercise is undertaken where possible. Swimming is best and most swimming pools will have set times and facilities for the disabled.*
- *Regular massage or Shiatsu is essential for those who are incapacitated by their disability.*

RECOMMENDATIONS

FOR THE CARER

- *Remember that you are not alone. There are many in your situation and many groups in all areas of mental disability. Individual discussion with counselors or group therapy is essential.*

- *Ensure that you have home help if possible, and that you spend time away. Feelings of guilt for leaving the individual will only reduce well-being on both sides, and encourage feelings of guilt in the disabled person. Remember that emotions are perceived at not only a mental level, but also a spiritual one.*
- *Ensure that regular exercise is taken. All too often, one forgets to allow time in which to maintain physical well-being.*
- *Have consultations with a homeopath or naturopath, whose remedies will help to maintain the spirits through difficult times. The use of constitutional remedies, good nutrition, and Bach flower remedies can be beneficial in both the short and the long term.*

TETANUS

Tetanus is a disease caused by a poison produced by a bacterium known as *Clostridium tetani*. It is characterized by severe, painful muscle spasms, often noticed initially as difficulty in chewing, discomfort in the jaws, and aching in the neck and back. These symptoms led to its common name "lockjaw." If untreated, the problem may lead to difficulty in breathing and swallowing. *Clostridium tetani* forms spores, which are found in soil and particularly in the feces of animals. This bacterium is very resistant to climatic changes, and will survive drought or flood.

The bacterium will enter the body through an injury, which may be no more than a scrape, and multiply locally. The toxin from *Clostridium* enters the bloodstream and travels to a specific part of the nervous system that normally blocks muscular activity. With this inhibition diminished, muscles tense up.

The symptoms develop any time from two days to several weeks later, and if left untreated may last up to ten weeks. Complications can arise because of a loss of respiratory muscles, and the effect the toxin may have on the heart muscle and the muscles within the arteries.

Treatment of tetanus is difficult, because the antibiotic (usually penicillin) may kill the bacteria, but does not remove the toxin. Tetanus immunoglobulins are available in serious cases. These are antibodies taken from other humans that are specific against tetanus. The prognosis in cases of tetanus is dependent upon the well-being of the individual and the medical care available. Most cases of tetanus are mild, but some may be fatal.

Vaccination against tetanus— *see* Vaccinations.

Tetanus vaccine is usually given in combination with diphtheria and pertussis (whooping cough), and is known as DPT. There are reports of convulsions, collapse, sudden-infant-death-syndrome (SIDS), and even encephalitis and anaphylaxis. In the U.S., legal requirements may prevent an individual, or the parents of a child, deciding whether or not to vaccinate against tetanus. The holistic consensus of opinion would be that an individual with a good immune system would not have a problem in fighting tetanus, and the chances of contracting tetanus must be put into the equation. Picking up *Clostridium* in cities, for example, is rare. One must balance what is called the risk–benefit ratio, considering that adverse reactions do occur with the vaccine.

RECOMMENDATIONS

- *A cut or graze at risk of Clostridium infection should be thoroughly cleansed and debrided (dead tissue removed). A hospital may be necessary for this to be done completely. Any dirt in a wound needs to be removed.*
- *Immediately apply a solution of Hypericum at a dilution that just tingles, but does not sting. This should be repeated every 15min for 1hr.*
- *Give the homeopathic remedy Hypericum 30 every hour for 3hr and then every 4hr for three days. Following this, take one dose of Hypericum 200.*

- *Antitetanus serum should be given by a doctor.*
- *Consider systemic penicillin if the wound was inflicted where animal feces are liable to be found.*
- *A tetanus vaccine will be offered by any orthodox physician, but will have no benefit for at least two or three weeks.*

PSYCHOLOGICAL MATTERS

AUTISM

Autism is childhood schizophrenia. It is characterized by a collection of psychological symptoms ranging from body rocking, withdrawal from social situations, little if any language development, and repetitive (often self-damaging) actions.

The cause of autism is poorly understood from an orthodox point of view. Chemical imbalance is certainly an aspect, although early parental deprivation and fears can be very relevant. Recent research has shown that low levels of sulfates may interfere with the metabolism of certain proteins and have a particular effect on autistic children. Sulfur-containing foods should be encouraged. The best sources are beans, fish, eggs, cabbage, and beef.

There are many techniques being used with a variety of success in autism. Art therapy, music therapy, and specific learning techniques are constantly being developed and are available by contacting the Autism Society of America.

In 1997 a researcher at the Royal Free Hospital in London noted that children who had been given the Measles, Mumps, and Rubella (MMR) vaccination were at increased risk of developing an inflammatory-bowel condition similar, if not actually, Crohn's disease. This has been associated with an increase in autism. The complementary medical world had been aware of this association for quite some time. (*See* **Vaccinations.**) A change in character of a child, or any signs or symptoms of autism developing within a few months of an MMR vaccine, should arouse suspicion.

RECOMMENDATIONS

- *Discuss the matter with your doctor, an art therapist, and the Autism Society of America.*
- *Homeopathy should be utilized, but requires a specialist prescription.*
- *Ensure that the child is on a high-dose multivitamin tablet that includes zinc and manganese.*
- *Introduce the child to a cranial osteopath.*
- *All autistic children should have their sulfate-containing food input increased.*
- *If a vaccination is considered a possible cause, discuss high-potency Thuja and Natrum muriaticum (both homeopathic remedies that may have an effect on the adverse effects of vaccinations) with a homeopath.*

BEHAVIORAL PROBLEMS

It is very difficult to define a badly-behaved child. So much depends on the objective attitude of the parents and their view of their child. To establish if a child has a behavioral problem requires the following criteria to be met.

- The parents, close friends and, if the child is of school age, a teacher must all express concern.
- The child must display some antisocial or self-harming behavioral patterns, such as aggression or self-inflicted wounds, inappropriate behavior with regard to a particular situation, excessive crying or irritability, poor food intake, or cruelty to animals.

Bad behavior may not be a psychological problem. It has been established that many deficiencies and some toxicities can create a problem. Studies in the prison population have shown that slight alterations through the use of supplemental medicine can have a profound effect on the behavior of prisoners, and this hypothesis has been supported by several small studies on children.

Toxins, especially lead, and therefore, by inference, other heavy metals such as mercury, may cause an effect. Refined sugars and other aspects of poor nutrition may lead to hypoglycemic states, which can create irritability and therefore poor behavior. All of these aspects must be taken into consideration.

RECOMMENDATIONS

- *See* **Hyperactivity** *and* **Attention deficit disorder**.
- *Many psychological problems are created by deficiencies. Ensure that the child is getting the following supplements in divided doses each day in combination with a well-balanced diet: zinc (2mg per foot of height); multi-B complex as recommended by a nutritionist or pharmacist; vitamin C (1g per foot of height); and any trace element supplement as recommended for the weight and age of your baby by the health food store or pharmacist.*
- *Homeopathy is marvelous if the correct remedy is chosen. It is preferable to be accurate, and therefore the use of a homeopath is required.*
- *Remove processed foods: foods containing a high sugar or salt content, additives, preservatives, and caffeine.*
- *Rule out dyslexia. See* **Dyslexia**.
- *If a behavioral problem is established and the matter is not one of ill-discipline, then I recommend art or music therapy for all child psychological problems.*
- *If response is not forthcoming with the above treatments and therapies, there are specialized behavioral clinics with which the child psychologist or your doctor will be able to put you in touch.*

LEARNING DIFFICULTIES

There are a broad range of reasons why a child may present with difficulties in learning. The age at which the child appears deficient is also very relevant. An infant who is slow to talk or perform expected tasks may have an unnoticed deficiency in hearing or eyesight, or may be exhibiting mental disability. Not achieving developmental landmarks needs initially to be assessed by a pediatric psychologist.

In older children, disabilities and autism (childhood schizophrenia) should be apparent, and need to be dealt with appropriately. If obvious causes are not apparent, then conditions such as dyslexia, attention deficit disorder (ADD), and poor nutrition need to be considered. Deficiencies in B complex, zinc, and various amino acids can impair learning ability. Most of us have some hidden talent and, taking this concept to an extreme, all of us may be a genius at something if given the time, space, and training. If your child is proving slow at languages but adequate at mathematics, then education and not medicinal support is required.

RECOMMENDATIONS

- *As a parent, do not try to diagnose your own children. Seek help from a child psychologist if you have any doubts about your child's development or learning abilities.*
- *Ensure that the child's diet is well balanced, and if you have a pernickety eater, give daily supplements for those food groups that may be missing.*
- *If you have any doubts about the child's nutrition, talk with a dietician.*
- *If a problem is diagnosed, then treat appropriately, but slow learning may be improved by cranial osteopathy and art or music therapy.*
- *Without doubt, the correct homeopathic constitutional remedy will benefit, and should be selected by a trained homeopath.*

TOILET TRAINING

Toilet training may be a messy matter, but it is rarely an illness or a disease process that requires treatment. Girls tend to potty train quicker than boys, but each individual will come out of diapers at his or her own rate. A problem should only be considered if a child is still soiling after the age of about four years.

The usual cause of delayed toilet training is because the child does not feel uncomfortable in a wet or soiled diaper. There is very little that can be done about this, other than gentle persuasion. Criticism or punishment will only help to delay matters further, be used as an attention-seeking device, or cause the child to withhold and become constipated.

RECOMMENDATIONS

- *Toilet training should start as soon as the child is old enough to understand verbal instructions.*
- *Aim for daytime potty-use initially, and then moving on to the toilet thereafter.*
- *Urination should be trained first, and defecation afterwards.*
- *Night-time training should follow in reverse order, encouraging the child not to soil the diaper, but expect a wet diaper each morning. When the child is old enough, try to have them pass urine before bed, when the parent goes to bed (which necessitates awakening the child), or if the child awakes in the night.*
- *Thoroughly congratulate the child on successful use of the potty or toilet, but never criticize them for failing. Explanation of the situation as the child gets old enough to understand is ample critique.*
- *Bedwetting is usually not a training problem, and is discussed in its own section* *(see* **Bed-wetting***).*

Chapter 4

Young Adult

Chapter 4

Young Adult

General

ALLERGIES

See also **Food allergy and intolerance** and **Food-allergy testing.**

An allergy is an inflammation triggered by the interaction of a foreign substance (called an antigen) with the body's defense system. The body has specific white cells that produce chemicals called immunoglobulins, which attach to an antigen and make them recognizable to other defense cells, which then envelop or destroy them. This reaction is constantly going on throughout the system, and is only termed an allergy when the body, by mistake, is overreacting.

The word allergy is commonly used to refer to the running, itching, and red nose of a hay-fever sufferer. This is correct, but allergic reactions can cause symptoms depending on the area of the body the inflammation is affecting. A reaction can be triggered by an antigen or allergen being inhaled, ingested, or coming into contact with the membrane. Symptoms can occur anywhere in the body; these include skin rashes, asthma, gastrointestinal problems, mood swings, lethargy, and tiredness. In fact, any set of symptoms anywhere in the body *may* be created by allergy. There are four types of allergic reaction as defined by medical science.

- Type 1 is called *immediate-onset allergy reaction*. Here, immunoglobulin E attaches to an allergen and causes several body defense reactions. These include the release of histamine, free radicals, lysosomal enzymes, and other complicated chemicals. These compounds are produced to attack a foreign substance, but they unfortunately and inadvertently damage the local host tissues. The symptoms are felt because these chemicals and reactions cause digestion of cells, increase the blood flow, and make capillaries more "leaky" to allow the defense system to get to the area affected. These chemicals also cause constriction of the blood vessels leaving the area in order to stop further spread of the foreign substance, close down the bronchial (lung) tree, and increase mucus production.
- Types 2 and 3 are reactions differentiated by *biochemical* changes, and do not have the same immediate or aggressive effect as type 1. They develop within a few hours, and may show up as anything from a mild rash or wheeziness to not being noticed at all.
- Type 4 is known as *delayed-onset allergy*, and may take up to 72 hours to develop. Being delayed does not reduce the severity, and this allergic response may be as severe as immediate onset, but is more commonly noticed as a mild reaction or not noticed at all. Delayed onset or type-4 allergy is commonly associated with foods, and may well give rise to chronic conditions such as cancer or diabetes, although this hypothesis has not been fully established.

There is a holistic consensus of opinion that allergy will occur when the body is already primed to fight something else. Everybody comes into contact with pollens and house dust-mites, but not everybody overreacts. There are certainly genetic tendencies, but many families will have some allergy sufferers when other members have no problems, even though they share the same genetic traits. The overresponsive system is generally battling a condition elsewhere, knowingly or otherwise. Hay-fever sufferers (who may also have eczema or asthma, as this triad is not uncommon) may struggle because they have an allergy to some food or other input without which they would not react to pollen.

There is strong evidence to suggest that allergies are linked to the psyche. In a well-known study of a psychiatric patient with multiple personalities, the allergies would change as each personality took control. Another example was illustrated by an artificial flower triggering hay fever. Hypnosis can achieve the same effect.

You may often hear the term atopic used in conjunction with allergic responses, such as atopic eczema and atopic asthma. This simply refers to the predisposition or genetic tendency for that individual to have allergies.

Atopic allergic reactions have been considered to have a genetic element, but recent developments have suggested that atopy may also be associated with exposure to common childhood infections. Recent studies have shown that men with antibodies to viral infections and those who had older siblings (leaving them more prone to being introduced to childhood infections) had fewer atopic allergic responses. This suggests that the more the body learns to fight infections when younger, the less likely it is to overreact as in the case of allergic responses. The prevalence of allergies such as hay fever, asthma and eczema has greatly increased over the last 30 years. This, interestingly but not surprisingly to a holistic practitioner, coincides with the increased use and advent of vaccinations, which has possibly reduced the body's need to activate an immune response early in life, thereby increasing allergic tendencies. This may mean that we need to reconsider the automatic vaccination of children against measles, mumps, and rubella, for example, because the lives we save or improve by protecting against measles may not compensate for the damage and deaths caused by asthma at a later age.

Treatment is, therefore, to illustrate any sensitivities or toxins specific to that sufferer, and also to alleviate the symptoms. Never underestimate the potential danger of an allergy. We have all had contact with or heard of people having anaphylactic reactions—sometimes lethal—to eggs, peanuts, or bee stings.

Tests for allergies

Testing for allergies can be performed using the following routines:

- Skin testing
- Hair analysis
- Blood allergy testing
- Bioenergy computer techniques
- Avoidance and restrictions.

Skin testing

Small or dilute amounts of suspected allergens are pinpricked under the skin's surface. The body's allergic response will occur if immunoglobulins are present in the system. Dilutions are made of the reactive substances to give an idea of how strong the allergic response is. A technique of desensitization (enzyme-potentiated desensitization) can be used once this diagnostic process has isolated the culprits (*see* Recommendations opposite).

Hair analysis

This is a poorly proven way of testing for allergy, but the principle is sound. If the body has poisons in the system, it may well choose to eliminate them by combining them with the inert keratin that makes up hair. By taking a hair sample and combining it with immunoglobulins against particular foods, for example, reactions will take place that can be studied under the microscope or in a more sophisticated manner by computer. One may hypothesize that if there is a reaction to the compound in the hair, there may well be a reaction in the body, because the body seems to be throwing this particular substance out.

Be wary of hair-allergy testing that uses radionics (a pendulum technique), since this has not been shown to be accurate and can lead to aggressive restrictions that have no scientific basis. This does not mean that radionics are not accurate, but that they need to be put into the context of a broader and more established allergy assessment.

Blood-allergy testing

See **Food-allergy testing** in chapter 8.

This is generally performed using accepted and scientifically proven techniques, the most available and sensitive being Enzyme-Linked Immunosolvent Assay (ELISA). It is a complicated technique involving competition between the body's antibodies and specially "labeled" antibodies. In principle, your blood's serum will be mixed with a laboratory solution and then passed through a special machine that checks for the presence of a fluorescent dye, which will attach itself to the serum if an antibody/antigen (allergy) reaction has occurred. Many of these tests are qualitative (i.e. will tell us whether there is any reaction), but a few are quantitative (i.e. will tell us how strong the reaction is), and the latter are very helpful in determining which foods may be troublesome. This method of testing can be used for inhaled pollutants, but having this information may not alter any treatment program, because it is often not possible to change the air that we breathe other than by moving to a different location.

Bioenergy computer techniques

Computers such as the Voll and Vega machines have now been surpassed by Bioresonance, Bicom, and Quantum computers, all of which are capable of measuring electromagnetic changes in the system in response to stimuli such as specific foods and airborne allergens. The individual is attached to the computer, a small electromagnetic current is passed through the system, and either different compounds are added to the circuit via the computer, or the computer has within its own structure the energetic resonance or vibrations from the electrons from a multitude of substances. These techniques are becoming more available and, although not accepted by the orthodox scientific world, I believe they are very accurate and effective investigations.

Avoidance and restrictions

This is not strictly a test, but may prove to be a very clear and concise manner of illustrating the foods to which you may be allergic. To try this, make a list of any foods you suspect make you feel unwell, any foods you crave, and any foods you eat frequently. Eliminate all of these and set up a five-day dietetic plan that does not repeat any of the foods you are going to eat. Stick to this rotation diet for one month, and then introduce one of the "forbidden" foods every five days to see if there is a reaction. If your list of suspected allergens is long or you seem to be cutting out a major food group, then this technique should only be undertaken with the supervision of a nutritionist.

Causes of a predisposition to allergy

As I have mentioned, there certainly are genetic tendencies within families, but many substances act as a trigger that can predispose any of us to allergic responses.

Principally, the problems of allergy will arise when foreign matter, usually protein, gets onto mucus membranes, or into the bloodstream, or the body is battling some other problems, and therefore—being already primed—acts overzealously in defending itself. Very often, proteins that should be broken down by the digestive enzymes into smaller peptides or amino acids are absorbed into the bloodstream due to a "leaky" gut. Something, somehow, affects the mucous membrane in the intestinal tract to allow larger molecules to be absorbed, which are then recognized in the same way as bacteria or viruses. This "leaky-gut syndrome" can occur through infestation with *Candida*, parasites, or chemical insult from eating contaminated foods. Poor secretion of the stomach acids and intestinal enzymes, alcohol, and certain drugs such as aspirin, antibiotics, and nonsteroidal anti-inflammatory drugs can all have a detrimental effect. *See* **Leaky-gut syndrome.**

RECOMMENDATIONS

- *For any allergic condition other than a mild one, place yourself under the care of a complementary practitioner. The cause of most allergies is often deeply buried, and needs expert guidance to illustrate.*
- *Avoid orthodox medication, except in severe cases, until alternative treatments have been*

used and failed. Orthodox treatments such as antihistamines block the effect of the body's attempts to cure itself.

- *Have a food-allergy test, and eliminate all foods to which you react strongly.*
- *Do your best to avoid the allergens that cause your problems. Look broadly and consider fabrics, metals such as nickel, aerosols, and the cosmetics you should not be using.*
- *Visit a homeopath for an accurate prescription. Minor ailments can be alleviated by considering the use of the following remedies: Allium cepa, Sabadilla, Euphrasia, Apis, Urtica urens, and Arundo taken as potency 6 every 2hr.*
- *High-dose vitamin supplementation may be effective: vitamin C (1g for every foot of height in divided doses with each meal), vitamin B_6 (20mg for every foot of height), and vitamin B_5 (100mg for every foot of height).*
- *Quercetin (150mg per foot of height) taken with breakfast, and hydrochloric acid tablets and pepsin with meals are beneficial.*
- *Ensure that you are drinking 16 ounces of water per foot of height per day. Correct hydration is essential for proper immune response, but diluting the system can also dilute the allergen and reduce the response.*
- *Acupressure and reflexology points. A point in the web between the thumb and index finger can help to relieve nasal symptoms.*
- *A nasal washing technique taught by a yoga teacher can be very beneficial for nasal symptoms (see* **Nasal washing***).*
- *Be fastidious about the vacuuming of carpets, mattresses, and pillows. Curtains should be washed frequently, as should all bed linen. Use allergy covers for mattresses and pillows.*
- *Visit a hypnotherapist, or preferably a neurolinguistic practitioner, to remove any psychological element.*
- *Enzyme-potentiated desensitization. This technique is performed by few practitioners, but can be very effective, and should be considered if other therapies have not worked.*

ANEMIA

The diagnosis of anemia is made through a blood test. It is defined as a lack of hemoglobin or red blood cells.

Symptoms arise from having a lack of oxygen delivered from the lungs to the body tissues. The symptoms of anemia can be very subtle, but include pallor, general weakness, lassitude, and inability to fulfil a normal day's function, unexpected exhaustion on exercise and, less commonly, recurrent infections and nausea.

Normal and Anemic Blood Samples

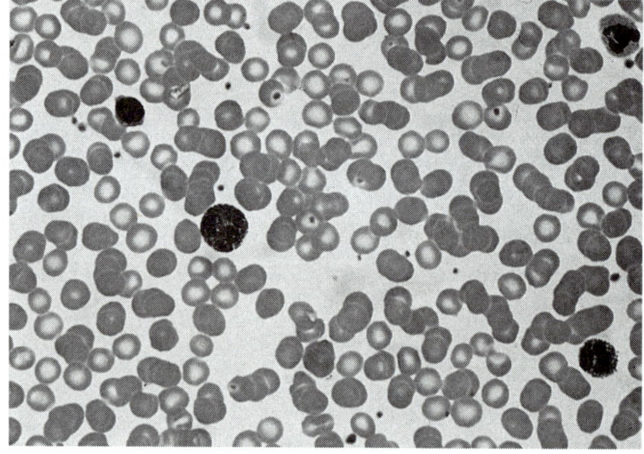

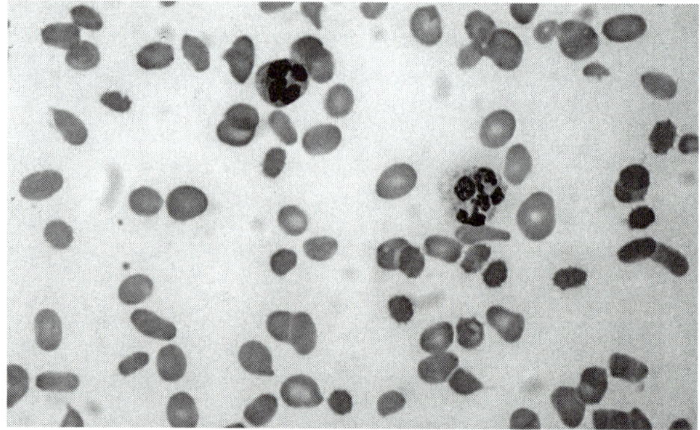

The anemic blood sample (bottom) shows a much lower number of red blood cells. Many of the remaining cells are deformed. Consequently, the oxygen-carrying capacity of this blood is drastically reduced.

Causes of anemia

- Blood loss: trauma, ulcers, heavy periods, hemorrhoids, and other internal injuries.
- Inability to make red blood cells or hemoglobin: disease of the bone marrow and toxins, such as drugs.
- Disease process: cancer and other chronic diseases.
- Malabsorption: disease of the bowel, malnutrition, and food allergies.
- Physiological: pregnancy and the first few periods.

All food groups are needed to maintain red blood cell production, including amino acids, vitamins, and trace elements. Certain compounds are particularly important and are needed in quantity. These are:

Iron: offal, red meat, oysters, eggs (principally the yolks), dried peaches, nuts, beans, asparagus, molasses, and oatmeal.

Vitamin B_{12}: offal, red meat, pork, and dairy products.

Folic acid: deep-green, leafy vegetables, carrots, liver, beans, rye, and cantaloupe melon.

RECOMMENDATIONS

- *Establish a cause after a blood test has confirmed anemia. Many conditions mimic anemia, and a clinical diagnosis is not always accurate.*
- *A pot of plain yogurt with a teaspoonful of turmeric is an Ayurvedic treatment, and is best eaten on an empty stomach any time of the day before the late afternoon.*
- *The homeopathic remedies Ferrum metallicum and Ferrum phosphoricum can help iron-deficiency anemia, and remedies such as Veratrum album, Arsenicum album, Carbo animalis, and Cinchona arsenicum should be reviewed to help the symptoms.*
- *Ensure good intake of the foods listed above.*
- *Blood tests can identify the cause of anemia through deficiency and, having established this, supplements can be taken.*
- *Ensure a minimum vitamin C intake of around 1g per meal to encourage iron absorption.*

BODY ODOR (BO)

Everybody has their own specific body odor. The smell should be neither obtrusive nor offensive, but nevertheless distinctive. The smell emanates from the sweat pores, and is dependent upon the content of sweat and other matters. This is not an unusual problem for many teenagers, due to body odor being associated with poor hygiene after exercise, bacterial activity in association with changing hormones, and the predilection of this age group to use chemical deodorants that damage the body's natural flora and allow bad bacteria to produce their toxins and odors on the skin unchallenged. Persistent bad body odor may represent the presence of certain systemic diseases.

Sweat is similar in composition to urine, except for the presence of urea, a nitrogen-based protein waste product. The blood is generally cleansed by the kidneys, and rarely has to resort to eliminating through the skin, but dehydration and certain drugs and diseases affecting the kidney can lead to the utilization of sweat as a waste product, and thereby alter its smell.

Eating an excess of pungent foods such as garlic or spices may simply overload the system, and the sweat absorbs the product with no pathology being present in the system.

Skin bacteria should produce little, if any, odor, but certain strains, especially those that have been altered by the use of antibiotics, can produce noxious gases that are experienced as BO. The more sugar in the diet and the moister the environment in which the bacteria live, the more they multiply and these increased numbers create increased odor.

Some hormones have their own smell, such as adrenaline (the smell of fear), and female cyclical hormones actually encourage bacterial growth, which in turn may encourage body odor.

RECOMMENDATIONS

- *Use only unmedicated soaps, and avoid deodorants other than topical applications of essential oils, preferably to the undergarments.*
- *Observe any changes on a daily basis in association with certain foods. Foods such as garlic and onions can create a body odor, and individuals may be susceptible to particular foodstuffs. Keep a journal, and ask a family member or close friend to monitor changes over a period of a few weeks. Correlate this to foods eaten, and avoid any suspect foods.*
- *Bad bowel bacteria can produce toxins that find their way into the sweat. Use high doses of Lactobacillus acidophilus and Probifidus shortly before each meal. Chlorophyll can be utilized similarly.*
- *Zinc (30mg each night) should be tried.*
- *Poor digestion can lead to an abundance of foods for bacteria, which multiply quicker and produce more toxins. Use hydrochloric acid and digestive enzymes in the amounts recommended on the packet.*
- *Wear natural fibers that absorb sweat more effectively, and change clothes regularly if necessary.*
- *Ensure good hydration by drinking at least 16 ounces of water for every foot of height in divided doses throughout the day. Ensure that more water is drunk if exercising or drinking alcohol and caffeine, as these dehydrate the body.*
- *Ensure good hygiene, and regular washing and changing of clothes.*
- *Review the homeopathic remedies Calcarea carbonica and Silica and use potency 6 three times a day for ten days.*

CHRONIC-FATIGUE SYNDROME (CFS)

Inexcusably, this condition (also known as myalgic encephalomyelitis (ME) and postviral fatigue syndrome (PVFS)) has only been officially recognized by the medical profession in the U.K. since the summer of 1996. Other countries have been a little bit more open, but a large percentage of doctors refuse to accept that this syndrome exists.

The definition of CFS is initially a "diagnosis of exclusion." This means that other medical causes must be investigated and eliminated. The symptoms must include fatigue or lethargy causing a 50 percent loss of physical and social function for at least six months. Four of the following symptoms must also be present:

- **Physical:** sore throat, persistent infections, swollen and/or sore lymph nodes, headaches, and pain in muscles or joints.
- **Psychological depression:** impaired memory or concentration, excessive sleep requirement, appetite loss or gain, and agitation.

Very often these symptoms worsen with the slightest exertion. It is important to differentiate this from the persistent fatigue that is felt by 20–50 percent of the population in association with incorrect lifestyle or stress, as this is quite separate from this condition.

For many years, the orthodox world has been searching for a specific cause, and the term postviral fatigue syndrome was popular because it suggested that this condition occurred after viral infections. This is simply not the case; CFS can occur with no previous or obvious illness preceding it.

In principle, any stressful event, be it physical, psychological, personal, or social, can trigger this syndrome, but generally it occurs in those who already have a weakened energy or constitution. The Eastern philosophies believe in an energy store (the Chinese call it kidney Qi) which can be depleted by life's events or habits. With this energy-level low, any event may trigger CFS.

Specific imbalances in the energy and

Herbal Remedies for Chronic-Fatigue Syndrome (CFS)

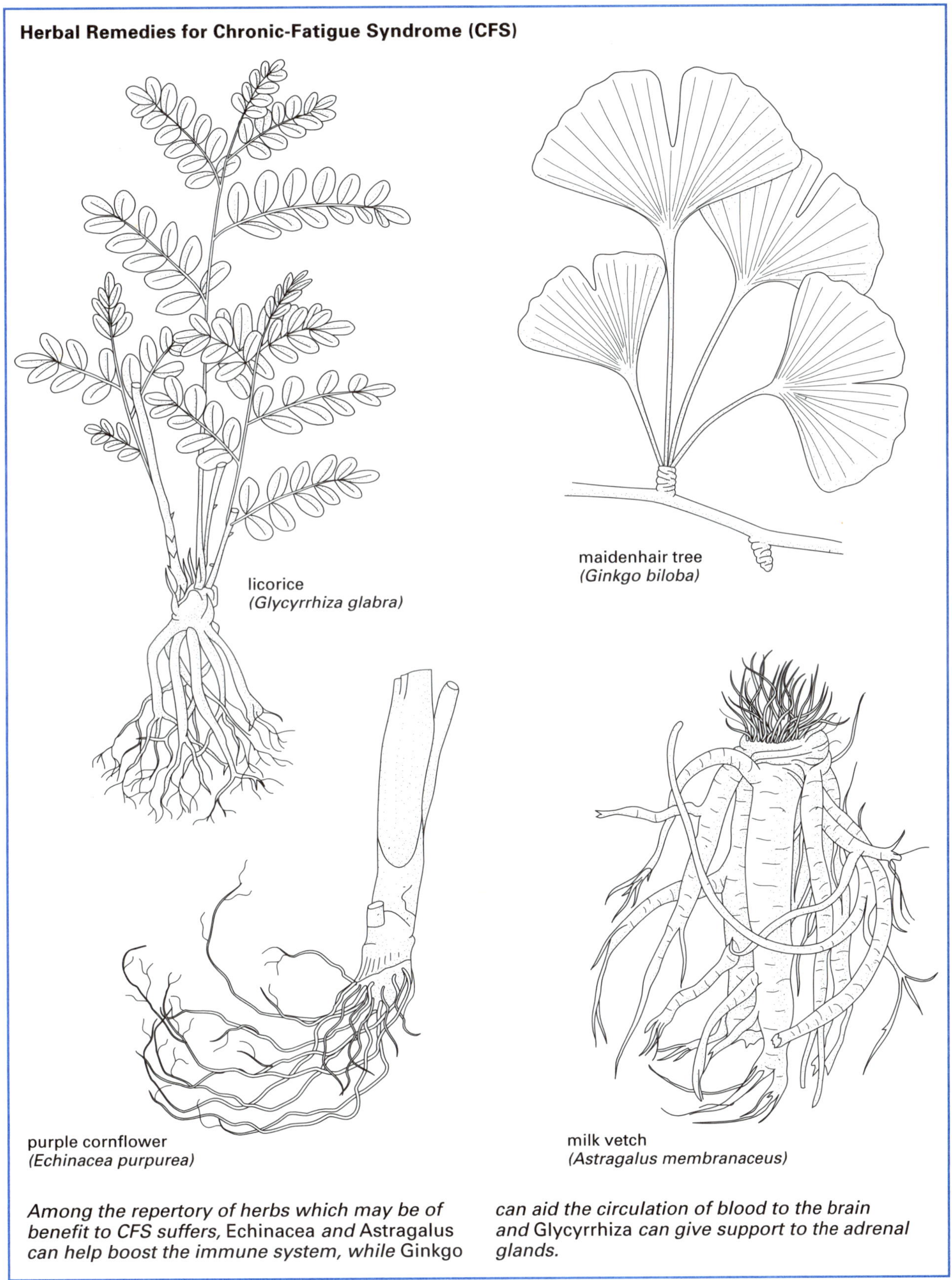

Among the repertory of herbs which may be of benefit to CFS suffers, Echinacea *and* Astragalus *can help boost the immune system, while* Ginkgo *can aid the circulation of blood to the brain and* Glycyrrhiza *can give support to the adrenal glands.*

functioning of the pituitary gland or the parts of the nervous system that produce serotonin have been found in some cases, but not in all. The pituitary gland and serotonin are involved in stress controlling the adrenal gland to a great extent.

There are no tests that confirm a diagnosis of CFS, although approximately 60 percent of sufferers will have a specific protein in their blood called viral protein 1 (VP1). Treatment must be geared towards both the physical symptoms and the psychological or neurological components of this condition. The use of drugs such as antibiotics or anti-inflammatories that may create a leaky gut can predispose to food allergy development that may turn out to be a much underestimated cause of Chronic Fatigue Syndrome.

RECOMMENDATIONS

- *Rule out any other cause for your symptoms by visiting your doctor initially.*
- *Do not push your body beyond its limits. Unlike trying to get fit, for example, working beyond your body's endurance only makes the condition worse.*
- *Remember that the condition is both physical and physiological due to the chemical changes that occur in the neurological system. Advice should be sought both from a complementary medical practitioner and psychological specialists, such as neurolinguistic programmers, counselors, or meditation teachers.*
- *Ensure that your diet is suitable for yourself (see chapter 7). Test for food allergy/intolerance through blood test or bioresonance techniques.*
- *Remember that the problem stems not from an incident, but from a depleted energy store prior to the commencement of the symptoms. Review your lifestyle, stresses, and habits, and endeavor to remove any contributing habits such as cigarette smoking, drug taking, and lack of exercise.*
- *Consider an initial detoxification program (see chapter 7), and remember that you may feel an exacerbation of your symptoms as your body starts to repair.*
- *Homeopathy can be most effective, depending on your symptoms, and referral to your preferred homeopathic manual, or a session with a homeopath to choose a remedy for the symptoms and your constitution is an excellent first step.*
- *Take twice the recommended daily allowance of the following compounds in divided doses with breakfast and a late afternoon snack (not with your evening meal): beta-carotene, a multi-B complex, vitamin C, and zinc.*
- *Maximum recommended doses of adrenal extract and thymus-gland extract should be taken.*
- *Ginseng and licorice may be supplemented with some success.* *See* **Herbal remedies** *on previous page.*

If you have no response with these supplements within one month, then contact your preferred complementary medical specialist.

CIGARETTES

An entire book could be written about the toxic effects of cigarettes. My experience is that many people do not know a fraction of the detrimental effects that cigarettes can cause, merely assuming that you either get cancer or you do not. Everybody knows somebody in their eighties who has smoked 40 cigarettes a day. This is indeed true, but for every one person who tolerates cigarettes and their poisons, there are 1,000 who do not. Whichever way you look at it, cigarettes are highly toxic, and very few of us have the constitution that will allow us to smoke and not develop some disease process, be it mild or terminal.

There are over 3,000 recognized compounds in cigarette smoke. We have no idea of the effect of many of these compounds on the system, but we have recognized 16 compounds known to cause cancer, and recently (beyond the dispute of the tobacco industry and their friends) one compound, a bendrofluoride, has been shown to trigger cancer changes in lung tissue. The tar in which these compounds are contained is a breeding ground for bacteria and, as the tar coats the delicate lung tissues, it allows the bacteria to destroy the air sacks where oxygen is absorbed.

Nicotine is a most highly addictive compound, proving even more difficult to withdraw from psychologically than heroin.

Conditions that are smoking-related include:

Sinusitis	Anosmia (loss of smell)
Ear infections	Catarrhal conditions
Taste loss	Recurrent coughs and colds
Conjunctivitis	Poor facial skin
Tooth and gum decay	Laryngitis
Pharyngitis	Recurrent sore throats
Acute bronchitis	Chronic bronchitis
Emphysema (loss of lung tissue)	Heart attacks
Strokes	Gangrene
Stomach and duodenal ulcers	Esophageal ulcers
Ulcerative colitis	

Cancer is not the most common medical condition created by smoking, but of the following list, smoking is implicated in increasing the chance of contracting this cancer, or is directly related to its onset: cancer of the mouth, tongue, throat, larynx, bronchial tree (lungs), esophagus, stomach, large intestine, skin, and the ovaries.

It is worth remembering that the lungs do not finish growing until we are in our early twenties. Smoking before this time will damage the foundations of the lung, and the earlier cigarettes are started, the worse the prognosis.

Passive smoking (inhaling other people's smoke) carries equal risks for those who are sensitive or reactive.

RECOMMENDATIONS

- *Do not smoke.*
- *Do not be around smoke.*
- *Do not smoke indoors. Smoke lingers.*
- *Do not smoke anywhere near children, or where they live or play.*
- *Do not smoke in front of children—they mimic.*
- *See* **Smoking**.

CLUSTER HEADACHES—*see* Migraines

DEHYDRATION

Dehydration can occur in both an acute and a chronic state: the former is easy to identify and fairly easy to remedy; the latter is insidious, overlooked and, I believe, the cause of many of today's illnesses and conditions.

Acute dehydration

This occurs most frequently in younger adults who overexercise in hot or humid conditions. The athletes we see failing in their excursions due to cramp are usually doing so because of dehydration. The symptoms are obvious in some cases, but in others require a little thought.

A sensation of thirst, dry mouth and lips, is fairly obvious, but overlooked are tiredness, muscular fatigue and cramps, dry skin, or cessation of sweating. Later signs of acute dehydration will include dizziness or fainting, rapid heartbeat, and confusion or delirium. This usually only occurs when dehydration is very severe, as can be seen in desert movies!

RECOMMENDATIONS

- *Avoid dehydration! If you are in a hot climate or performing exercise, ensure a regular or persistent intake of water.*
- *If dehydration has occurred, replenish water slowly. Alternate with salty or sugary solutions, or use specially prepared electrolyte solutions in conjunction with water to replace the lost salts and glucose. Use natural sugars, not refined.*
- *In more severe cases, place the body in a bath or wet cloth and, of course, remove from heat where possible.*

Chronic dehydration

Chronic dehydration does not have the same immediate or acute symptoms as described above. It occurs over a period of time when most individuals slowly but surely drink less water than they require, and the body adjusts by losing its sensitivity to thirst and learns to live with dry lips, dry skin, muscular aches and pains, and a variety of other symptoms described below. This lack of sensitivity is a tribute to the human body's ability to adjust to its circumstances, but it may be that this adaptation has led us to deal with an increase in many of the symptoms that plague us, especially in the Western world. These include cancer, asthma, arthritis, eczema, digestive problems, and susceptibility to infections.

The biochemistry of the body requires water in most, if not all, of its reactions. Most of these reactions go on within cells that will be reluctant to give up water if less-than-adequate amounts are taken in regularly. Every cell in the body will protect itself by taking up cholesterol, other fats or lipids, and proteins to create a lipoprotein layer around itself. This prevents water leaving the cells, but also inhibits water from entering the cells. The biochemical processes continue but, like a stagnant pond, will eventual use up some of the natural energy provided in molecules that can interchange with each other and, although the processes will continue, the natural energy associated with them may not. Meanwhile, the water we take in is not absorbed fully into the cells, our tissues can become bloated, and the bloodstream mildly diluted, telling the brain that we do not need water, and thereby reducing our thirst and perpetuating the dehydration cycle.

The cholesterol, fats, and proteins that are required for this protective process are made by the liver. The liver works overtime and has less availability to deal with the body's general requirements for metabolism, both in breaking down toxins and building up the compounds that we need. More energy is required to keep the liver functioning, and therefore less energy is available elsewhere, so that tiredness and fatigue become common initial symptoms. The lack of breakdown of toxins puts pressure on the kidneys, and poisons get deposited around the body. Much of this poison is taken up by fat stores, which also accommodate the extra fats that the liver is constructing for the benefit of the protective layer of the cells, and so the fat stores increase, as does your weight. Toxins are dissolved into the fat stores, and more water is pulled into these tissues to dilute down these toxins. This again increases the body's retention of water in areas where it should not be held.

The slightly higher metabolic rate created by dehydration encourages the production of free radicals, known to promote atheroma, which leads to heart attacks, strokes, and also cancer.

Lacking water, the body generally concentrates its fluids. The hydrochloric acid in the stomach and the digestive juices throughout the intestine become more concentrated and, while this may help digestion overall, it challenges the lining of the bowel, leading to inflammation and ulcerative conditions, and this inhibits the correct production and multiplication of the body's natural bowel flora.

The higher concentration of acidity is absorbed into the bloodstream, and can cause: arthritic conditions; conditions in the skin, such as psoriasis or eczema; and concentration of other fluids, such as in the gallbladder, leading to gallstones.

Need I go on ... ?

Put simply, the argument could be made for dehydration affecting many—if not most—medical conditions in the body. Dehydration is insidious. You must remember that we are losing approximately 32 ounces of water each day in our urine, approximately the same through sweat, and about 16 ounces through nasal mucus and stool. This has to be replaced, otherwise we fall into a dehydration pattern.

RECOMMENDATIONS

- *Any persistent or recurrent condition of a lack of health, or an illness, requires a review of the body's hydration.*
- *There is no strictly accurate amount that suits everybody. If you are a thirsty person, ensure that your thirst is quenched by water, and that any other fluids (tea, coffee, alcohol, juices, etc) are taken for pleasure or effect, rather than to quench the thirst.*
- *If you are not a thirsty person, then a minimum of 8 ounces of water per foot of height should be taken throughout the day.*
- *Do not confuse the intake of fluid with the intake of water. You are not rehydrating yourself using anything but water or the most dilute of juices.*
- *Tea, caffeine and sugars (both refined and natural, such as fruit juices) are all potentially dehydrating. Each time any of these are enjoyed, a glass of water should follow within 15min.*
- *Avoid sink water where sanitation is poor or the water is fluoridated (see* **Fluoride***). The installation of a reverse-osmotic filter or the use of mineral water should be balanced with one glass per day of sink water in fluoridated areas, unless the fluoride intake through the diet is known to be adequate, or fluoride toothpaste is used.*
- *Vary your mineral waters because some are higher in some components than others.*
- *Water should be drunk at room temperature or warmer, especially if rehydrating. Iced drinks, while enjoyable, are not good for the body, and should be limited.*

DIABETES MELLITUS

Diabetes mellitus, commonly shortened to diabetes or sugar diabetes, is a complex condition that arises because the body's metabolism of sugar is impaired, faulty, or absent.

Diabetes is often discovered through the simple symptoms of passing urine too frequently and having a persistent thirst. This is caused by too much sugar in the blood being passed through the kidneys into the urine, and water following due to osmotic attraction. Because the individual is passing so much urine, the body recognizes dehydration and drinks more. Excessive sugar in the bloodstream can lead to problems in any organ or system in the body, predominantly by causing arteries to clog up. Unrecognized diabetes can therefore cause blindness, kidney failure, strokes, heart attacks, and a myriad of neurological symptoms. The problems may take years to develop and therefore a regular screen of the urine and blood is a wise precaution, especially if there are any diabetics in the family. (Diabetes has a strong genetic tendency.) The tests are simple and accurate. Testing for raised sugar levels (above 140mg/dl or greater than 10mmol/l) is done simply, and the same blood sample can measure a particular type of hemoglobin known as HbA, which can be monitored to establish the severity of the diabetes.

There are several types of diabetes, which I classify as follows.

Temporary diabetes

This can occur during pregnancy, and is known as gestational diabetes (*see* **The vessel of conception**). Temporary diabetes can also be associated with a variety of ailments, such as viral infection, malnutrition, eating disorders, and pancreatic disease. Several commonly used drugs can induce diabetes. Most of these conditions will be short-lived, or respond when the causative factor is removed.

Non-insulin-dependent diabetes mellitus (NIDDM type-2 diabetes)

The onset of this type of diabetes is usually in adulthood, and is caused either by a mild deficiency in production of insulin from the beta cells in the pancreas, or by cells in the body not responding to the insulin that is being produced, possibly even at high levels. The reasons for this loss of sensitivity are not well established, but it is known that being overweight seems to desensitize the individual to insulin levels; chromium deficiency is also implicated.

Insulin-dependent diabetes mellitus (IDDM type-1 diabetes)

This type of diabetes usually has its onset at a young age. It is possible to be born with this hereditary lack of beta cells in the pancreas, or they may be destroyed by virus, autoimmune attack, or drugs (either medical or from food).

The Eastern philosophies of medicine consider the pancreas to lie under the vessel of conception (*see* **The vessel of conception**), and it may also be the area for the solar plexus, a central yogic chakra. The vessel of conception is an energy line provided for by the parents, and therefore a weakness would be, in Western terms, genetic. During pregnancy, the uterus (another organ on this midline meridian) pulls energy into itself to feed the child, therefore further depriving the pancreas and thyroid of their energy. These two organs control sugar and thyroxine levels, both of which can fall, inexplicably, during pregnancy.

Recognizing diabetes

I mention above that the most common symptoms are those of excessive urination and thirst. Increase in appetite, weight loss despite eating, frequent infections, and slow healing of simple wounds are all warning signs.

More serious complications, such as blindness and stroke, occur after years of uncontrolled diabetes, and are generally discovered by taking the problem to a physician.

If the basic blood and urine tests are equivocal, then a glucose-tolerance test is performed: a 75g dose of a sugar solution is given orally, and blood samples are taken just before and at half-hourly intervals after ingestion. If the levels of sugar in the blood exceed those expected, then a diagnosis of diabetes is made.

Diabetes is not a condition to be confronted without professional support. Monitoring by your doctor or hospital is essential. Consultations with a complementary medical practitioner with training in nutritional medicine should run alongside orthodox monitoring. Uncontrolled diabetes can cause coma and death fairly swiftly, and if treatment is required with insulin, the same outcome may occur if too much insulin is injected. Insulin has to be injected because it would be destroyed by the acid in the stomach if taken orally. There are several types of insulin, including those made artificially and those extracted from animals such as the pig. There is some controversy as to which is the best type, but your individual specialist will have his or her own protocol, and this should be followed until the scientists come up with complete answers. Insulin comes in quick-acting, intermediate, and long-acting forms, and generally insulin-dependent diabetics will require a mixture.

Do not underestimate diabetes as a disease. It effects over 4 percent of the Western population, and this number is rising. There is a strong correlation between diabetes and diets high in refined sugar, such as those found in the West. Type-2 diabetes or NIDDM is usually well-controlled through diet and supplementation, and very often complementary medical practitioners will help an individual avoid the insulin-lowering drugs that are all too quickly prescribed by many diabetologists.

RECOMMENDATIONS

- *Monitor urinary and blood-sugar levels through your doctor or hospital specialist. They will explain home-monitoring options, usually by pinpricks of blood, nowadays monitored by small computers kept by the bedside. Do not shirk this responsibility.*
- *Consider the Pritikin diet (see* **Pritikin diet***) early after a diagnosis of non-insulin dependent diabetes.*

- *If you are overweight, lose it. Obtain as much help or support as you need, but obesity may cause or adversely affect diabetes.*
- *Discuss dietetics with a well-qualified and experienced nutritionist. Ensure that the following areas have been covered: eat low-fat, low-sugar, whole foods, and avoid refined sugars, flour, and any additives, preservatives, or other chemicals; avoid cow's-milk products, which may be directly responsible for promoting diabetes in some genetically susceptible individuals.*
- *Discuss with your nutritionist the correct amounts of chromium, zinc, magnesium, and other trace minerals, all of which have an important cofactor relationship in sugar-level balancing.*
- *Until glucose levels are stable (and there is strong evidence that the stability is more important than the level) use high-dose antioxidants and follow the advice in the section on atheroma (see* **Atheroma***) in an attempt to protect the arteries from clogging up.*
- *Ensure a daily intake of gammalinoleic acid and omega-3 and omega-6 fish oils.*
- *Enjoy garlic, onions, and fenugreek in your diet, and discuss with a herbalist suitable amounts of anthocyanoside from blueberry or blackberry sources.*
- *Quercetin, 100mg per foot of height twice a day, should be added to the use of high-dose antioxidants if there is any suggestion of cataracts, eye, or neurological problems.*
- *Formulate a personal exercise program that includes daily yoga. Excessive exercise may cause fluctuations in sugar levels from too low to too high, but yoga has actually been shown to be of benefit to diabetics. Aerobic exercise at the right level is essential to enhance cardiovascular strength, as well as being part of a weight-control program.*
- *Reduce stress. Stress creates chemicals such as adrenaline and cortisol that raise blood-sugar levels, and again, techniques such as meditation have been shown to lower blood-sugar levels and give diabetics better control.*
- *Homeopathic remedies aimed at the individual's constitution will help, but they need to be given at specific, high potencies, and will only be beneficial if prescribed by an experienced homeopath.*

DIABETES INSIPIDUS

This condition is characterized by excessive passing of dilute urine and excessive thirst. It is created by the lack or blocking of antidiuretic hormone made in the pituitary gland.

The causes range from tumor, drug intake (medical, drugs of abuse, or others yet to be established), infections, and blood loss. It is sometimes associated with heavy bleeding after delivering a child.

RECOMMENDATIONS

- *Excessive urination and thirst must be assessed by a physician, and if diabetes insipidus is diagnosed, follow orthodox treatments.*
- *Complementary medical treatment should be based on the symptoms, but acupuncture, Shiatsu, and yoga are considered to strengthen the midline energy that is part of all Eastern philosophies of medicine (see* **The vessel of conception***).*

ENLARGED SPLEEN

Any examination of the abdomen will require the physician to push under the ribs on the left side of the body. We are checking for the possibility of an enlarged spleen.

The spleen is basically an organ full of lymphatic tissue and blood vessels. It works as a store for blood, and breaks down old or useless red blood cells. Lymphatic tissue, acting like a large

Self-checking the Spleen

The blue line indicates the potential area of spleen enlargement.

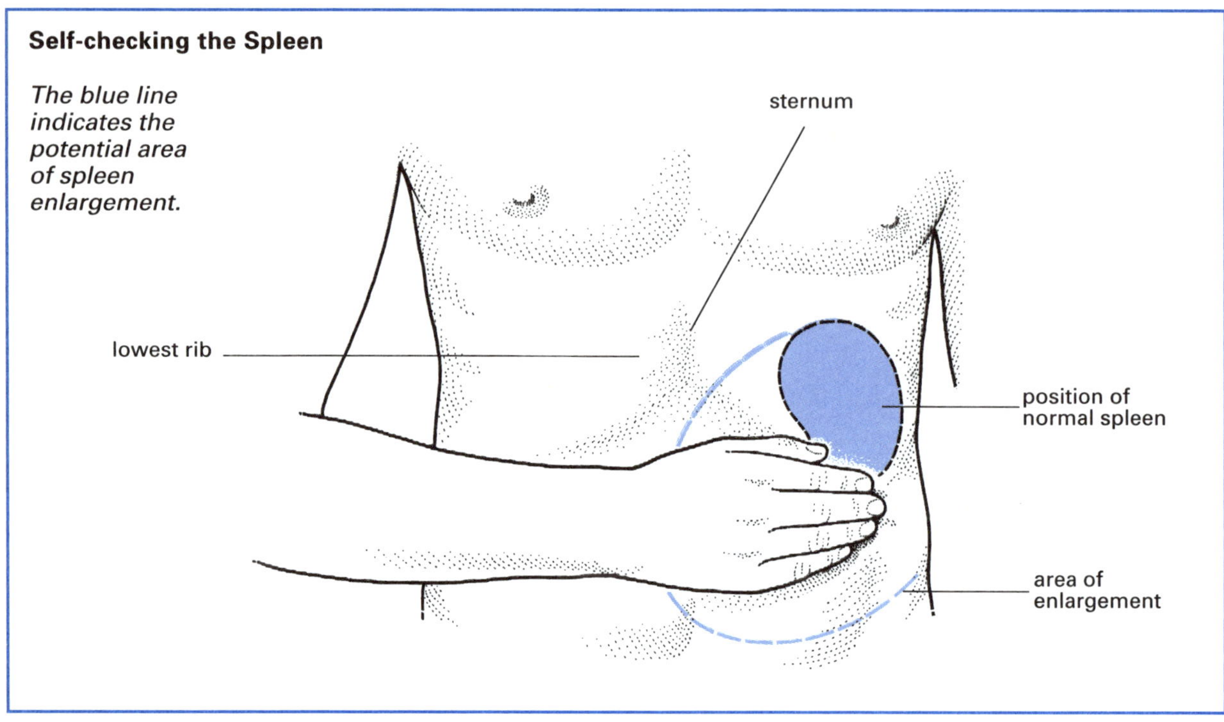

lymphatic gland, will swell with infection, or any process such as leukemia that involves the increased production of white blood cells.

An enlarged spleen, therefore, can represent nothing more than a bad viral infection, but may be associated with disorders of the bloodstream and, at worst, cancer.

RECOMMENDATIONS

- *Self-examination for an enlarged spleen is difficult, but any noticeable lump on the left upper abdomen under the ribs, or a persisting pain in that area, should be referred to a physician.*
- *The considerations of a complementary medical practitioner are warranted once a firm diagnosis of the cause of an enlarged spleen has been made.*

EXAM NERVES—*see* Nervousness

EXERCISE

Exercise is one of the most important factors in maintaining health. The human being has evolved over millions of years as an ambulatory (walking) creature, and anthropologists suggest that "man" probably walked for 6–8 hours a day, much like the period we may work in today's Western culture. Much of the body design is geared towards walking, with short bursts of high energy (running or fighting). Exercise is necessary to maintain physical as well as psychological well-being. During exercise, the body burns up stress chemicals that can inhibit concentration, and it has been demonstrated that exercise can enhance creativity and reduce depression.

Western culture has provided an abundance of food and this, combined with our natural survival instinct of storing food in our body, leads to a tendency to obesity. Our ancestors had to work hard to produce, gather, or catch their food, and calorific input and output seemed to balance. Nowadays, this is not the case, and with the advent of telephones and carry-out food we could exist with very few physical demands.

The outcome of all this is a need to exercise. As a general rule, the male metabolic rate, at rest, uses up approximately 2,200 calories, and the female approximately 1,700 calories. If you consider that a bowl of cereal, and two pieces of toast with butter and marmalade, replace up to 800 calories, and a shrimp cocktail, meat, and two vegetables followed by apple pie with cream can add up to over 1,500 calories, you can see that we are generally out of balance. To redress this, we need to exercise.

The best form of exercise

There is no best form of exercise! Everybody should find their preferred technique and enjoy it. Daily exercise is preferable, but three or four times a week is acceptable, provided that it is of the right sort. Half an hour a day or 3 hours per week is a sensible goal.

"The problem with exercise is that it is hard work, is time consuming, and there is no immediate benefit." If I were to ask an individual to do anything that included these three factors, should I be surprised if there is a reluctance? These three objections are in fact an indication of misunderstanding exercise rather than appreciating the truth of the matter.

Exercise should not be hard work. The amount of time spent on exercise should not interfere with lifestyle and, provided the right exercise is employed, it should be fun and thereby of benefit immediately. Let me try to point you in the right direction.

What is exercise?

Exercise is defined as muscular exertion for the purpose of preservation or restoration of health or the development of physical prowess or athletic skill. This occurs through many mechanisms, both physical and psychological.

Physical benefits

Exercise burns up calories. The body is extremely good at taking in what it needs, and it is only when we consciously fight our own instinctive ability to balance our physical exercise with our food intake that exercise can be harmful. By staying within certain boundaries, as described below, exercise controls excess.

When we exercise, our body uses up stress chemicals such as adrenaline and cortisol. Too much stress created by our daily life is thus taken out of the system, benefiting health as a whole. Exercise also produces the body's natural opiates, known as endorphins and enkephalins. These reduce pain and create a sense of well-being, even euphoria, and benefit the body as a whole. The heart beats faster and the respiratory rate increases because of the demand by the muscles for oxygen and nutrients. Other parts of the body, especially the vital organs, benefit from this increased flow of oxygen and nutrients, thereby establishing a greater level of health and longevity. The heart strengthens and the body's blood vessels become more open. Fat and cholesterol are actually reduced and obesity avoided. Many other metabolic benefits are derived, some of which can reduce the chances of conditions, such as stroke and high blood pressure.

Psychological advantages

"Look good, feel good" is most accurate. Our body and self-image are extremely important in directing our confidence, which in turn helps us to achieve. This simple argument alone supports the encouragement of exercise, but in fact the production of the body's natural opiates and the reduction in adrenaline and other stress chemicals has a profound effect on our state of mental well-being. Depression is alleviated, anxiety is reduced, addictive tendencies are transferred, and sleep patterns are corrected.

Choosing an exercise

The benefit of exercise will only be noticed if around 30 minutes of a suitable standard is undertaken at least three times a week. This is strictly for maintenance; if you are trying to improve your level of fitness, more exercise is required.

The exercise chosen should raise the heart rate to a level of approximately 75 percent of the individual's maximum heart rate. This is calculated by subtracting your age from 220. A 20-year-old should exercise to a level of 75 percent of 220 minus 20, which is equal to 150. A 60-year-old should reach a heart rate of about 120. Heart rate should not exceed 80 percent of the maximum level.

Exercise needs to be enjoyed, otherwise enthusiasm will wane rapidly. Those who are competitive by nature will benefit from competitive sports. Those who are not should choose noncompetitive pastimes. Brisk walking is not likely to strain the body, but is time consuming and it may not take the heart rate to its optimum level, but if an enjoyable environment can be found, then an exercise-paced walk may be most stimulating and relaxing. It is better to aim at an exercise that fits in with the individual's lifestyle. A mother may benefit by taking her young children to the swimming pool. A busy professional might find 20 minutes on the local gymnasium's treadmill quicker and more convenient.

Do not forget exercises such as dance and cycling which can fit into your entertainment or travel sections of the day. Yoga, Qi Gong, Tai Chi, and techniques learnt in a local aerobic class can be used in convenient breaks in the working schedule at home, in the office, or while travelling. A small floor space can act as effectively as a thoroughly equipped gymnasium, once the techniques are understood. Ten minutes three times a day may not be as beneficial as a straight half-hour, but it is better than nothing. Twenty minutes each working day supplemented by 45 minutes at the weekend can transform a body within a month.

A gym instructor will be able to set a suitable program, and specific machines or gymnasium techniques such as Pilates can help an individual to reach fitness at a rapid rate.

Swimming is heralded as the best form of exercise and, for those who enjoy it, it probably is. It is not weight-bearing and, provided that there are no neck problems, it rarely puts a strain on any part of the system. Swimming, more so than other exercises, helps to control breathing, and can be very useful in lung disorders such as asthma.

The body is very much geared towards survival. If weight reduction is necessary, then the body will do its best, provided that it is not fed incorrectly. A diet containing the recommended 10–15 percent fat of its total recommended input (approximately 70 percent carbohydrate and 20 percent protein make up the whole – *see* **Nutrition**, chapter 7) will comfortably return a body to its preferred weight. Removing fats and carbohydrates completely will dramatically lead the body into thinking that it is deficient, and it will therefore go into storage mode. The next time any amount of fat or carbohydrate is eaten, it will be swiftly converted into fat storage. The biochemical adage is that "fat burns in the flame of carbohydrate." To break down the fat stores requires energy. In fact, two units of energy are required to release six units of energy stored in fat. If we do not feed ourselves with a certain amount of carbohydrates, then fat stores will not diminish. The body can convert protein into energy, but this is not as easy as carbohydrate conversion.

Exercise should be divided into two categories.

Meditative exercise

Clearing the mind while exercising allows a balance of the mind–body connection. The body automatically does this as it supplies oxygen to the active muscles, thus decreasing the availability of oxygen in the brain. It is difficult to concentrate or be creative through exercise, therefore. On a busy day, when our consciousness spends most of its time from the neck upwards, the strain and mild pain that the body should feel when exercising allows the consciousness to move down and distribute the Qi. Techniques such as Yoga, Qi Gong, Tai Chi, martial arts, calisthenics, and simple stretching release blocked energy while exercising the muscles. (To stretch a muscle group, a joint must be extended or flexed, and this is only created by the work of an opposing, contracting muscle group. Exercise!)

Aerobic exercise

Aerobic exercise is a term coined to describe the increased utilization of air. For aerobic exercise to be most beneficial, the heart rate should not exceed an individual's age plus 100, and the respiratory rate must not prevent the ability to answer a question. Of course, both of these parameters will be exceeded in a competitive moment, or if pushing the body to achieve a new limit of endurance, such as might be expected from professional athletes, but for the rest of us, exercising within these parameters is wise.

I am a great believer in eliciting expert opinion initially, but this is not necessary. A sensible program starting, if you are unfit, with a brisk walk is perfectly acceptable. Any sport, competitive or otherwise, should be considered, but do not go back to five-a-side football when you are 40 years old if you have not played for 20 years. The mind will remember your previous abilities, but the body will have a markedly reduced capability. Any such desire should be reviewed by a coach or gym instructor, and a certain level of fitness should be achieved first.

I think that modern gymnasiums are excellent starting points, with their electronic gadgetry combined with basic weights and floor exercises. Any gym instructor will set up a suitable program that should leave the new exerciser feeling that they have achieved and want to do more. However, it is wise not to carry on, but instead come back tomorrow.

Weight-bearing exercise (especially for women) because of its antiosteoporosis effect, must take up some of the week's exercise. Floor exercises (most commonly used for abdominal and back strengthening) and swimming are excellent forms of exercise, and should be considered a part of the program, but only a part.

RECOMMENDATIONS

- *Like so many things in our lives, getting motivated and remaining enthusiastic are often the hardest parts. Have a look in the mirror. Are you satisfied? Visit your preferred health carer and ask for a basic assessment. Are you jeopardizing your health? Can you keep up with your friends/children? Ask whatever question it takes but initiate a decision to reach an optimum level of health.*
- *Choose a date upon which you will start. For the week prior to this, cut out as many bad habits as possible: smoking, drinking, and overeating should be reduced, if not stopped, and a healthy diet initiated.*
- *Ensure that rehydration is at the top of your list by drinking at least 16 ounces per foot of height per day.*
- *Establish a routine and be as disciplined towards this as towards a work routine.*
- *Do not put pressure upon your work or social time. Exercise within your acceptable parameters.*
- *Partake in an exercise that is enjoyable. If none obviously fall into that category, look around and ask friends for their opinion. Golf may be boring until you have a try. Visit a local gym and try the various machines, or resurrect an old school sport if possible. Experiment with different exercises.*
- *Half an hour a day or 3hr a week is an optimum amount of time to be spent on exercise. More should not be considered until a peak of fitness is reached.*
- *There is no preferred time of the day to exercise, and each individual should choose by instinct the period of day that suits them. It is not wise to exercise within 1hr of eating, because the body is in assimilation mode.*
- *If you have a competitive nature, make a plan of what you want to achieve or take on individuals of your own caliber. Do not overestimate your abilities. Fitness will come quicker than you think, and will remain longer if you achieve a high level more slowly.*

- *Do not hesitate to use a professional guide or teacher initially. Never feel embarrassed about asking a physical-fitness instructor about setting a plan. They too have their masters.*
- *Regardless of what exercise is chosen, have a lesson or two in yoga, Qi Gong, or Tai Chi. They will enhance your abilities in any sport by improving your balance and strength and, more ethereally, helping to control Qi. Enjoy both meditative and aerobic exercises.*
- *Start slowly and build up. As with anything, stop while you are enjoying the event rather than pushing yourself through a pain barrier. This is a sure way to remove the enthusiasm and feel degraded.*
- *Stretching before and after exercise is extremely important. The before bit is well established but, even experienced athletes underestimate the importance of stretching after as a "warm-down." Keep warm, and do not rush the postexercise shower or bath.*
- *Do not exercise in a state of dehydration. It is better to drink 16 ounces of water approximately 40min before exercise, and the same amount over a period of 1hr after exercise.*
- *The meal eaten before exercise should be predominantly carbohydrate and light.*
- *Wear only absorbent, natural materials when exercising.*
- *Use bodywork techniques such as Shiatsu and massage regularly, especially through the initial weeks of starting an exercise program.*

FACIAL FLUSHING

Facial flushing may occur because of a medical condition such as fever, a skin condition such as eczema, and the taking of certain drugs, including steroids, but in young adults it is most commonly known as blushing. High blood pressure and alcoholism may also create a red face, but this tends to be permanent rather than fluctuating.

A blush is a facial arterial response to the hormones created by the nervous system, generally in response to embarrassment. This is a physiological condition, and need not be treated unless severe.

A flush of the face may also occur in response to adrenaline-like substances produced with anger. This too is a physiological response, and does not warrant treatment.

RECOMMENDATIONS

- *Unless particularly severe and causing social difficulties, this is not a condition requiring medical treatment.*
- *There is no orthodox treatment, and heavier facial make-up may be recommended as a last resort.*
- *Blushing through embarrassment may benefit from the homeopathic remedies Lachesis or Baryta carbonica, taken at potency 200 nightly for seven nights and allowing one month for the full effect to take place.*
- *Hypnotherapy, meditation techniques, and counseling, including the use of neurolinguistic programming, may all reduce the amount of hormone produced in response to embarrassment or, in the case of anger, bring out any underlying subconscious reasons for this overreaction.*

FAINTING

Feeling faint is a weakness or lack of strength, but actual fainting is a temporary loss of consciousness. Generally caused by a lack of oxygen to the brain, fainting may also be induced by low blood sugar, toxins in the bloodstream, such as drugs, occasionally food to which the individual is allergic, or shock.

Evolutionarily, a faint was a survival mechanism. Lying completely still or feigning death apparently encouraged the predator to ignore the "carcass" in favor of the individual still alive. We are rarely confronted by such life-and-death situations in modern Western life, but we still have the tendency in response to sudden shocks or prolonged anxiety, such as before exams or public speaking.

RECOMMENDATIONS

- *An occasional faint may just be a characteristic of an individual and, provided that there is an obvious trigger, no further action need be taken.*
- *Frequent or repeated fainting requires investigation by an orthodox medical practitioner. Attention should be paid to hypoglycemia, arterial occlusion, and input of drugs or alcohol.*
- *The homeopathic remedies Aconite, Arsenicum album, Sepia, and Veratrum album should all be reviewed in a homeopathic manual.*
- *Repeated faints without any obvious pathological cause as defined following full medical investigation should be reviewed by a homeopath, nutritionist, and cranial osteopath.*

FEVER (PYREXIA)

See **Fever in children.**

Fever should be considered a friend. Fever itself is unlikely to cause any problems to an adult, but it is important to assess the underlying cause because a fever may be a symptom of problems such as meningitis, pneumonia, or kidney infection.

A normal temperature lies in the range 96.8–98.6°F.

RECOMMENDATIONS

- *A persistent or very high temperature (above 104°F) should be reviewed by a medical practitioner.*
- *Refer to the relevant section in this book for the treatment of any established cause of a fever.*
- *Ensure good water intake, increasing normal consumption by at least 32 ounces of water per day. A fever with sweating may need more. Avoid cold water, preferably drinking room-temperature or warm water.*
- *Refer to your preferred homeopathic manual for suitable remedies, paying special attention to Aconite, Arsenicum album, Belladonna, Bryonia, Gelsemium, and Phosphorus.*
- *Herbal remedies include extracts from elderflower and peppermint as an equal mix, or camomile by itself or with yarrow, as an infusion taken four times a day.*
- *Cold compresses on the forehead, neck, abdomen, and ankles will bring the discomfort down while leaving the core temperature raised to encourage the immune-system response.*
- *Fever diminishes appetite and the saying "starve a fever, feed a cold" is true for short periods of time. Eat by instinct.*
- *Avoid alcohol, caffeine, and other stimulants.*
- *Exercise should be kept to the minimum of a short walk in fresh air if the patient feels like it.*

GERMAN MEASLES (RUBELLA)

See **Rubella.**

Attention should be paid by pregnant women who do not know if they have had a previous exposure to or infection by German measles.

RECOMMENDATIONS

- *See* **Rubella** *in chapter 3.*
- *All women intending to become pregnant should have a blood test for previous exposure and current immunity to German measles. If negative, vaccination should be considered (see* **Vaccinations***).*

GUILLAIN-BARRÉ SYNDROME (GBS)

The Guillain-Barré syndrome (GBS) is a neurological condition that is characterized by symptoms ranging from lethargy and muscle weakness to paralysis. In severe cases, paralysis of the respiratory muscles may prove fatal. The etiology (cause) is unknown, and the condition is diagnosed by excluding other causes of the symptoms. There is a strong association between GBS and previous, recent viral infections and recent vaccinations, particularly the measles and polio vaccines.

I believe that this potentially devastating syndrome is multifactorial, and will only be triggered if the underlying nervous system is weak. This weakness can be created by persisting physical causes such as food allergy, drug abuse, and other unhealthy lifestyles. I believe that stress, leading to excessive adrenaline production over a period of time, can "strain" the nervous system and leave it open to such problems as GBS.

RECOMMENDATIONS

- *Any persisting neurological problem, or one involving any form of paralysis must be reviewed by a physician or a neurological specialist. Any problems with breathing make this a medical emergency.*
- *Besides life-saving first-aid, the orthodox world can only offer palliative treatment for GBS. Consult a complementary medical practitioner with experience in this field.*
- *Consider osteopathic or Marma therapy.*
- *Polarity therapy, cranial osteopathy, yoga, and the Alexander technique have, in my experience, all been beneficial.*
- *Ensure that food-allergy testing is performed (see* **Food-allergy testing***).*
- *Homeopathic remedies based on the symptoms should be prescribed by a homeopathic specialist. If vaccinations have been taken prior to the onset of GBS, consider using the homeopathic remedy Thuja or Natrum muriaticum, potency 200, morning and night for one week.*
- *Strictly review lifestyle, because any toxin may be responsible for the underlying weakness. Smoking, excess alcohol, and drug abuse may all be culprits.*
- *Sit with a counselor to discuss any obvious or subconscious anxieties and stresses.*
- *See* **Paralysis**.

HANGOVERS

This is a section often looked at in health books by the fit and healthy male! It is not that females do not have hangovers, but their health conscientiousness seems to be in the right place. Sorry to disappoint you, but there is no magic cure, despite my reading of the subject, especially during parts of my misspent youth.

It is important to understand that a hangover is a "good thing." Alcohol in excess is a toxin that can damage many parts of the body, particularly the liver, heart, pancreas, kidney, and nervous system. Alcohol is associated with high blood pressure, low blood sugar and diabetes, cirrhosis, and neurological problems such as blindness, to mention but a few. The hangover is the body's attempt at warning of our overindulgence and risk. As we age, our liver produces more chemicals to break down alcohol, which is why our tolerance increases, but unfortunately our body also adapts, and therefore loses its hangover. This is not a good thing, because we may be unaware of the damage we are doing and the extra work that our livers are having to perform.

The hangover sensations of headache, lethargy, muscle weakness, diminished concentration, photophobia, and an upset stomach are all associated with dehydration and the breakdown product of alcohol and aldehydes.

I do not think it appropriate for a doctor of holistic medicine to give any of the numerous tips he or she may have to reduce a hangover, because a successful treatment may encourage people to overindulge with the knowledge that they will not feel the pain. My recommendations are therefore based on helping the body to clear out, thereby minimizing the damage, but not necessarily reducing the discomfort.

RECOMMENDATIONS

- *Drink 5 ounces of water for every measure of alcohol (8 ounces of beer, one glass of wine, or one measure of spirits).*

- *Eat before drinking alcohol, even if it is only a small amount. Avoid drinking on an empty stomach.*
- *Do not mix your alcoholic drinks at any session.*
- *The homeopathic remedy Nux vomica potency 6 can be taken every hour. A more specific remedy choice may be made depending on the symptoms, and remedies such as Aconite, Chamomilla, and Pulsatilla should all be reviewed.*
- *Avoid the popular use of "the hair of the dog." While making some impact on well-being, it enhances the potential damage. Coffee is also a poor idea because it enhances the dehydration.*
- *An individual who indulges and creates frequent hangovers should consider the daily use of a liver support, such as milk thistle or other herbal concoctions, such as Liv 52.*
- *Joking apart, frequent hangovers may be an indication of a mild form of alcoholism (see* **Alcohol***).*

HEAD INJURY—*see* Concussion

HUMAN-IMMUNODEFICIENCY VIRUS (HIV) INFECTION and ACQUIRED-IMMUNE-DEFICIENCY SYNDROME (AIDS)

There are some basic facts to establish:

- Having HIV does not mean having AIDS.
- Human-immunodeficiency virus is not proven beyond doubt to be the sole cause of AIDS.
- Having HIV in the system may not need to lead inevitably to AIDS.

Taking these three points into account, it is worth examining potential treatments against HIV and AIDS. The HIV is not a particularly aggressive or fast-replicating virus. It affects different people in different ways, which is why some people can contract the virus and die rapidly, while others are alive and healthy 15–20 years later. The state of the individual's immune system appears to be very relevant to this observation. Carrying HIV is asymptomatic (without symptoms), but the effects of HIV can be minor or profound.

The virus finds a comfortable home in a subset of the body's white-cell defense mechanisms, which are commonly known as T-helper cells. They are so called because they are produced in the thymus and help other white cells to be active in the destruction of other invaders such as bacteria, fungi, and viruses. Destruction of these cells allows minor infections that would normally not bother the system to become lethal. Once two or more of these infections are present, then the criteria for a "syndrome" are satisfied and a diagnosis of AIDS is made. If the symptoms are not particularly severe then another term, AIDS-related complex (ARC), is used to describe the symptoms, thus creating a syndrome that is not in itself life-threatening.

Acquired-Immune-Deficiency Syndrome, on the other hand, is a life-threatening condition. Symptoms can occur throughout the body, but most commonly affect the lungs (*Pneumocystis carnii*), the skin (Kaposi's sarcoma and wart infections), the bowel (*Campylobacter*, *Candida*), and the nervous system (a variety of infections). It is found all over the world, very often in people with no HIV infection. This is a pedantic point, because the majority of AIDS patients have their condition as a result of the association with HIV.

Many scientists and doctors from all over the world, some very eminent, believe that AIDS is not solely associated with HIV. Very acceptable concepts have been put forward to suggest that AIDS will only manifest when the body's immune system is incapable of keeping the T-helper cells healthy and functional. Human-immunodeficiency virus undoubtedly damages this section of the immune system, but then so do many other factors. It is feasible that HIV will not be lethal unless associated with other components that damage these T-helper-cells. Drugs (both prescription and drugs of abuse), unhealthy lifestyle, infectious diseases such as syphilis, fungi and parasites, and environmental pollutants have all been put forward with enough evidence to create scepticism in some scientific areas. Currently, there are 29 different illnesses that exist independently, any of which in combination are labeled AIDS, but are these secondary infections possibly part of the cause of the immune-system failure?

Many government departments and "independent" watchdogs are financially supported by the pharmaceutical industry, who would like to find a compound or compounds that would kill HIV. This means that authorities and the pharmaceutical industry, generally, do not emphasize the concept of personal health being relevant in fighting AIDS.

Human-immunodeficiency virus is transmitted through some body fluids more than others. Theoretically, HIV can survive in most body fluids but, in reality, blood and semen appear to be the main transmitting factors. If transmission has occurred through saliva, sweat, or other discharges, it is extremely rare and not well documented. The virus needs to be transmitted directly into the recipient's bloodstream, which occurs through punctures and abrasions in the skin and mucous membranes.

The term "HIV-positive" does not refer to having AIDS. It has been established that there are two viruses (although many others are suspected), namely HIV-1 and HIV-2, both of which have detrimental effects on the T-helper-cell population. The phrase "HIV-positive" refers to the presence in the bloodstream of antibodies against these viruses. This phrase does not refer to the presence of HIV. It infers that HIV has at some time been present in the bloodstream because the immune system has produced a defense against them. This is of vital importance, because it is a qualitative result (a "yes" or "no" to infection), and not a quantitative test (how much virus is in the system). More accurate tests, such as the polymerase chain reaction (PCR), measure the amount of virus. The PCR is not routinely done because of the expense and the controversy concerning its accuracy. Measurement of the T-helper-cell and specifically the CD4 levels indicates the amount of damage to the immune system, but is not a good predictor of prognosis because the cell count can rise or fall independent of HIV, but is very dependent on the other factors that alternative practitioners and many scientists think are relevant to the disease process.

One often hears of the CD4/CD8 ratio. The CD8 T-cells are immune-system inhibitors. They are equally important in normal health because they prevent an overreaction in the immune system. Unfortunately, if the normal balance between the CD4-helper cells and the CD8-inhibitor cells is disturbed, then ill-health will arise.

A most fascinating point of interest is that the speed with which HIV multiplies, infects, and then destroys T-helper cells is much slower than the normal replication speed of the T-helper cells themselves. One eminent authority has likened the process to chasing an airline jet on a pedal cycle. As this is the case, how the orthodox world continues to assume that HIV is solely responsible belies logic.

The carriage of HIV and AIDS is not a homosexual disease. The practice of anal intercourse allowing infected semen directly into the bloodstream through the inevitable abrasions in the rectal mucosa has allowed the spread of HIV to move rapidly in this section of society. The virus, which probably originated in Africa, having mutated from a harmless virus, is also transmitted heterosexually and through accidental injury. The vaginal mucosa is much tougher and less prone to abrasions, and the vaginal secretions are much more antiviral than many other fluids. Once the "epidemic" was established and accepted, the "safe sex" practices of male homosexuals stemmed the increase in transmission in many educated parts of the world. Educated or otherwise, the increase in the spread amongst the heterosexual population is now the world's largest problem.

Those who understand about the epidemic have been poorly educated into understanding that heterosexual sex is a danger, and in uneducated areas, people simply know no better. Contraception is not easily available in many parts of the world, and anal intercourse is practiced to avoid pregnancy throughout Africa and Asia. The increase of heterosexual HIV carriage is quite alarming in these parts of the world.

Despite hygiene and education being the most likely treatments to work, the orthodox world continues to follow its "germ" theory, and spends billions of dollars researching into drugs that can inhibit the growth of HIV. The drugs AZT and, more recently, DDI and DDT are highly toxic chemotherapy agents that aim at killing the cells in the immune system on the assumption that this will not allow the virus to survive. Most patients placed on AZT will come off the drug because of its side effects, and the main study—the Concord Trial—showed that patients using AZT fare worse than those not taking it. It is disturbing that the authorities who allowed such a treatment to be practiced are the same people who block the use of naturopathic treatments for exactly the safety reasons that they bypassed for these far more profitable drugs.

Despite the poor outcome of AZT trials, the pharmaceutical industry continues to attack the virus while ignoring the commonsense approach, which would be to stimulate the human-immune system. Having found that the destruction of infected T-helper cells does not prolong the life of AIDS patients, two new drug-groups were focused upon: nucleosides inhibiting HIV production and protease inhibitors blocking the chemical process by which HIV enters new T-helper cells, as well as blocking viral replication. Currently, all AIDS and HIV-carrier patients are being "strongly" advised to use "triple therapy," which includes taking AZT with drugs from both of these new groups several times a day. Those who can tolerate this chemical cocktail certainly show good results initially. I say "initially," because long-term studies have not been completed, and we must remain sceptical because the initial findings of AZT were equally promising.

Most importantly, before I discuss the options for treatment, be very aware that there are documented cases of HIV infection clearing up. This has been noted in children, and was reported most recently in the *New England Journal of Medicine*, March 30, 1995:

> A baby boy born prematurely at eight months was diagnosed as having asymptomatic HIV-1 infection. The child contracted the infection from his mother, who had had intercourse with a former intravenous-drug abuser. The infant was not well, due to his prematurity, but showed no evidence of AIDS. Blood tests were done on separate occasions, and showed the child to be infected with the virus. Blood tests were repeated at frequent intervals, and at the age of 1 year, the tests proved negative. They could find no evidence of HIV. The child and his immune system had destroyed and removed all evidence of the HIV. The case was finally reported when the child was aged 5 years, and when he continued to remain free of disease.

I believe that AIDS is not caused by HIV alone. Without a doubt, this virus is detrimental to the immune system and speeds up the process of disease, but is not solely responsible for the ill health associated with AIDS. More relevant is long-term abuse of the body through poor nutrition, environmental toxins in the air and food chain, the chemicals produced by stress, drugs (both prescription and those of abuse), and frequent exposure to infections and the antibiotics with which they are treated.

Treatment recommendations are based on dealing with all these factors.

RECOMMENDATIONS

- *Avoid risks. Whether you have contracted the HIV already or not, have "safe sex." Oral sex cannot be considered safe if an individual is carrying HIV.*

- *If you have unhealthy habits or lifestyle, make a change.*
- *Do not fight this battle alone. Find a complementary practitioner with knowledge of AIDS, and a group or counselor specializing in this area.*
- *Discuss with either of the above, or a nutritionist, a suitable diet plan. This is absolutely essential to your well-being.*
- *Remove toxins from your life in the form of drugs (including tobacco and excess alcohol), and foods containing steroids or antibiotics (most meats). Spend time in the fresh air, out of the cities. Do not ignore this good advice, it is essential.*
- *Ensure food allergy/intolerance testing is undertaken through blood tests, or by an experienced bioresonance computer technician.*
- *Deal with or come to terms with the stresses in your life. Excess adrenaline is poisonous to the immune system. Do not underestimate the importance of this factor.*
- *Try to avoid antibiotics—steroids in particular because they damage the immune system. All infections should be given the opportunity to be treated from an alternative angle.*
- *Do not be surprised if alternative practitioners offer a treatment that they claim may be curative. Ensure with a medical practitioner that the treatment is not in itself poisonous, and give it a try. It cannot be as harmful as orthodox drugs.*
- *The use of the "triple therapy" should be considered if good health is not being maintained or blood counts are dropping to low levels. Until long-term studies have been done, I consider these chemicals toxic, and they should be used only as a last resort.*

Dealing with HIV and AIDS is a team process, and there is an answer, as in the case described above. Do not give into the orthodox view of inevitable demise, because there is plenty of evidence to suggest that treatment and possible cure are available.

HYPERVENTILATION

Hyperventilation is not specifically defined as an illness, but refers to a tendency to overbreathe. There is a natural, instinctive tendency to control breath in times of stress. If very frightened, we may hold our breath, but with moderate levels of anxiety we may have a tendency to overbreathe. This is very often a necessary physiological response and not a problem, as is shown in exercising.

Without wishing to blind the reader with science, the need to hyperventilate or alternatively hold the breath is governed by the level of carbon dioxide in the bloodstream, which is measured in a part of the brain known as the respiratory center. It is all based on a chemical equation:

$$H_2O+CO_2 \rightleftharpoons H_2CO_3 \rightleftharpoons 2H^{+}+CO_3^{2-}$$

Keeping it simple, this equation shows how water (H_2O) and carbon dioxide (CO_2) react to form a chemical chain of two hydrogen ions ($2H^+$) and a carbonate ion (CO_3^{2-}). The hydrogen ions are kept at a particular level to allow the body's biochemical function. Any disturbance requires this equation to flow one way or the other. For example, when we exercise, our muscles produce more CO_2 as a waste product. This CO_2 is blown off by our breathing more swiftly. Because we are throwing out more CO_2, the equation moves to the left and the number of hydrogen ions in the body diminishes. This is a "good thing" because we are also producing more lactic acid from our muscle use, and if we did not get rid of the hydrogen atoms in our bloodstream, we would become too acidic and many of our biochemical functions would fail.

If you have managed to follow this so far, then the relevance and importance of hyperventilation will be apparent. Hyperventilation most often occurs when we are frightened. We blow off the carbon dioxide, causing a loss of hydrogen ions, and what is known as a respiratory alkalosis

Hyperventilation

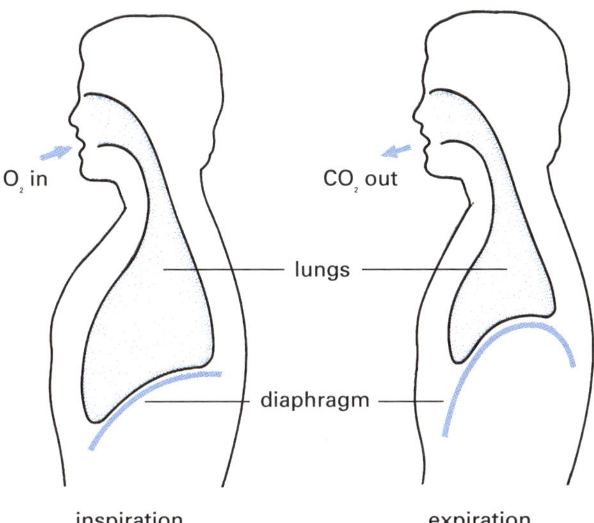

During inhalation, the diaphragm contracts, making the lungs expand. When exhaling, the diaphragm expands forcing air out of the lungs.

occurs, which makes us feel dizzy and faint. The time-honored tradition of breathing in and out of a paper bag causes us to inhale our exhaled carbon dioxide, thereby reducing the loss of hydrogen ions and rebalancing our blood acid/alkaline levels (pH). This in turn returns our biochemistry to normal, and we stop feeling odd.

The important point of all this is the tendency of many of us to hyperventilate without realizing it. Being under pressure or stress, which so many of us are, constantly causes us to hyperventilate not at a level that causes dizziness and fainting, but at a level that alters our blood pH. Living at a persistently mild-alkaline level affects the biochemistry of the body, and can have profound effects, particularly on the cardiovascular system and lungs. Asthma, heart attacks, and stroke are the most researched problems, but it is possible that other conditions, including cancer, may result from a persistent state of hyperventilation.

It is difficult to assess whether an individual is hyperventilating, because breathing 14 or 15 times a minute is only wrong if you should be breathing 12 times a minute, and symptoms and problems may develop only after many years.

Recognition of chronic hyperventilation is not possible from a clinical standpoint. Orthodox blood tests are of little value, because modern science has shown that the biochemistry of the body will take place at a set, narrow band (a pH of 7.34–7.48). The body is very good at maintaining these levels, but may be putting a considerable strain on the tissues and cells in controlling this. It is this strain that may cause chronic and serious illness. The use of the Humoral Pathological Laboratory Test and bioresonance techniques may disclose an alkalosis or acidosis, and such tests must be considered in chronic illness (*see* **Humoral Pathological Laboratory Test** and **Bioresonance**).

RECOMMENDATIONS

- *Acute hyperventilation from a shock, fright, or an acutely anxious situation can be dealt with by placing a suitable container such as a paper bag over the mouth and nose, and rebreathing the exhaled carbon dioxide.*
- *There will be a tender point either side of the shoulders between the neck and the shoulder tip. Gentle pressure on these will help. There will also be tender points 2 inches either side of the chest bone, and 2 inches below the collarbone. Gentle application to these will also help.*
- *Everybody should have training in breathing techniques (see* **Breathing***). Yoga, Qi Gong, and Buteyko methods are appropriate.*

HYPOGLYCEMIA

This is the medical term for low blood sugar. The condition of *hyperglycemia* is better known as diabetes, and much is known about this condition. Hypoglycemia, on the other hand, is poorly documented, and is not considered a problem by the orthodox world unless somebody overdoses on insulin or some other form of blood-sugar-lowering agent when treating themselves for diabetes.

The holistic consensus of opinion is that hypoglycemia is far more prevalent and, in my experience, I must agree.

The symptoms of an acute hypoglycemic attack are dizziness, confusion, blurred or double vision, poor balance, nausea, sweating, muscular lethargy and, at its extreme, fainting. In the case of a diabetic who has overdosed on a blood-sugar- lowering agent, the symptoms can come on very rapidly. Individuals who have low blood sugar may find that symptoms are mild, persistent, and/or recurrent. They most commonly occur about 1 hour after eating or first thing in the morning.

The main reason for low blood sugar is an overproduction of insulin. The pancreas, under the control of very sensitive sugar-level-monitoring systems in the nervous system, produces more insulin when sugar levels rise. Refined or white sugar is absorbed very rapidly, and therefore the insulin production is equally rapid, causing blood-sugar levels to drop. Having a persistent low blood-sugar level or tendency towards hypoglycemia can cause metabolic changes, especially in the membranes of the body. A low blood-sugar level can cause an excess of mucus production and a tendency for muscles to spasm. When this occurs in the lungs or the bowel, problems, including asthma and irritable-bowel syndrome (IBS), can ensue. Any persisting membrane problem that does not respond to other areas of treatment should be considered as being possibly caused by hypoglycemia.

Other than an excess of insulin, some conditions within the system can use up blood sugar rapidly. The biggest culprits are infections, especially abnormal bowel bacteria and yeast infections such as *Candida*. Symptoms of hypoglycemia or chronic diseases of membranes in association with bowel problems may well be *Candida*-related.

It is also worth noting that hypoglycemia may be physiological, not pathological, as is the case when natural processes use up the available blood sugars in pregnancy and after exercise. More sinister conditions such as cancer, which can also burn up sugars, have to be considered and ruled out.

Some Eastern philosophies place a central energy point or chakra on the midline at the top of the abdomen. This coincides with the pancreas, and an energy block that prevents the vital force from moving through that area can interfere with digestion and insulin control.

RECOMMENDATIONS

- *A glucose-tolerance test, most often used in establishing diabetes, can be used to diagnose hypoglycemia (see* **Glucose-tolerance test***).*
- *A diet high in fiber and low in refined carbohydrates and sugars is essential.*
- *Frequent small snacks throughout the day are better than three larger meals.*
- *Several homeopathic remedies may match the symptoms, and a reference to your preferred homeopathic manual should include reviewing the remedies Phosphorus, Aconite, Veratrum album, and Carbo vegetabilis.*
- *Herbal treatments may be of benefit, but should be taken only under the expert guidance of a holistic practitioner. In the case of bowel-bacteria problems, a one-week course of 2 billion acidophilus premeals is indicated, along with the consideration of the use of caprylic acid under the care of a complementary practitioner.*

INFECTIOUS MONONUCLEOSIS (MONO) OR GLANDULAR FEVER (EPSTEIN-BARR VIRUS)

Infectious mononucleosis, otherwise known as glandular fever, is associated with swollen glands in the neck, axilla, and groin (although glands in the abdomen and thorax will also be enlarged, but not palpable) in association with a fever. This condition is often recurrent because the causative agent, Epstein-Barr (EBV) virus, is resilient, and may hide intracellularly, especially within the liver. (It may cause hepatitis.)

Mono usually appears as a sore throat, fever,

malaise, and lethargy in association with the above findings. In a healthy individual, the problem will last less than two weeks. Recurrence, however, may be every couple of weeks, or it may in fact lie dormant for several months. Known in the past as the "kissing disease," Epstein-Barr virus is disseminated by kissing, sneezing, coughing, and mouth-to-hand-to-mouth contact (shaking the hand of someone who may have licked their fingers). Unless one is already immunocompromised, as is the case in AIDS, Epstein-Barr virus is not generally a serious infection, although it can cause a nonchronic hepatitis.

Epstein-Barr virus may be responsible for chronic-fatigue syndrome (postviral-fatigue syndrome) but most frequently appears as a sore throat, muscle pain, loss of concentration, and depression with the aforementioned glandular swelling.

RECOMMENDATIONS

- *A blood investigation known as the Paul Burnell test should be performed on any persisting, resistant, or recurring fever. A positive result may be indicative of acute or past infection.*
- *Epstein-Barr virus (EBV) is a member of the herpes group of viruses (see* **Herpes***).*
- *Recurrent infections should be treated with Echinacea or Hydrastis by taking, per foot of height, 100mg of powdered solid extract, or three drops of fluid extract in water in divided doses throughout the day.*
- *Persisting affliction requires a complementary medical opinion, because it is usually indicative of a suppressed immune system.*

INFLAMMATION

Inflammation is the body's response to damage of tissues. If an injury occurs, the body will attempt to repair the damage by sending more blood into the area. The blood carries scar-tissue-forming cells, oxygen, and nutrients necessary for repair and is therefore a "good thing." Unfortunately, the increased blood flow puts pressure on the nerves, which are already injured, and therefore the inflammation is painful. In severe injuries, there will be a reflex reaction of a severed artery to close off, in which case inflammation does not take place, and eventually gangrene sets in.

Inflammation is controlled by the nervous system, which opens or closes blood vessels by a reflex action that may include pathways through the spinal column. The nerves are stimulated by special tissue factors that are released from damaged cells, and also by chemicals released from white blood cells that are pulled into the area by the initial nervous reflex. Orthodox drugs generally work by closing down the blood vessels or blocking the chemical reactions of these tissue factors or those within the nervous system.

The orthodox world considers only the symptoms, and therefore does its best to suppress inflammation. There are a myriad of lotions and potions that pronounce themselves anti-inflammatory, ranging from aspirin and other nonsteroidal anti-inflammatory drugs to steroids. Topical creams made from these drugs are also freely available. These treatments have their place when pain is unbearable, but they are in principle slowing down the healing process.

RECOMMENDATIONS

- *Inflammation is a healing process and should not be suppressed unless out of control. The holistic principle of encouraging the process will lead to a speedier recovery in most cases. This advice must be ignored if the inflammation is of a major organ, such as the brain (i.e. meningitis), heart, or kidney. Persistent inflammation may be associated with infection, and reference should be made to the relevant section in this book.*
- *Application of ice in a towel or wash cloth will relieve symptoms, but will not prevent the purpose of inflammation.*

- *Arnica creams for deep tissue inflammation, Calendula cream for skin reactions and Urtica creams for very superficial inflammation can all be used.*
- *Reference to your preferred homeopathic manual so the selection of a remedy based on the predominant symptoms can be made, with special attention to Apis, Belladonna, Rhus toxicodendron, and Urtica urens.*
- *Persistent inflammation can be treated with high-dose vitamins and herbal remedies, but should be done under the guidance of a complementary medical practitioner.*

LUPUS—*see* **Autoimmune disease** and **Systemic lupus erythematosus** (SLE)

MASTURBATION

When religion sets down a doctrine, it usually has a basis in some health or social foundation. I fail to see why religion is almost universally against masturbation. There are no serious health disadvantages and, if anything, it will enhance the desire for sex, thereby increasing the likelihood of procreation. It is interesting, however, that all higher levels of spiritual attainment generally involve celibacy, and do not condone masturbation.

The Eastern philosophies, coinciding with Freudian concepts, suggest that sexual energy is a lower form than spiritual energy, and perhaps there is some basis in avoiding masturbation and orgasm if trying to attain a higher spiritual level. I actually believe that an orgasm is the pinnacle of both spiritual and physical pleasure, and therefore masturbation, in leading to an orgasm, is a simple technique of achieving a glimpse of Nirvana.

Excessive masturbation may cause bruising to the penis or clitoris, and masturbation at inappropriate times or places may be an indication of psychiatric disorder, but otherwise, from a medical point of view, there are no pros or cons.

RECOMMENDATIONS

- *There is no medical reason not to masturbate.*
- *Avoid excessive masturbation that can cause bruising, and avoid the incorrect use of instruments to enhance pleasure.*
- *Bruising can be helped by the use of the homeopathic remedy Arnica 6 every 2hr, and an Arnica-based cream applied two or three times a day.*
- *Excessive or inappropriate masturbation should be reviewed by a counselor in case an underlying psychiatric disorder is associated.*

MIGRAINE

A migraine is a recurrent headache that is probably created by changes in the level of dilation of the blood vessels in the brain. Migraines vary in intensity, frequency, and duration. They commonly start on one side of the head, spreading to other areas, and are often associated with nausea, vomiting, visual disturbances or other neurological sensations, weakness and even paralysis, and mood disturbances. Migraines are often found to run in

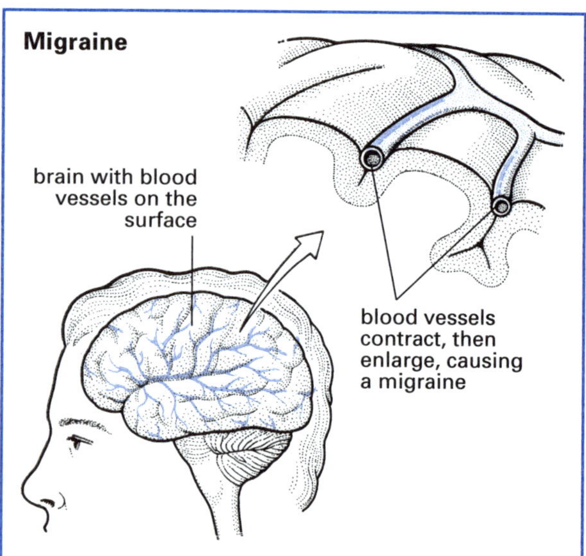

After an initial narrowing of the arteries in and on the brain, they then dilate and this causes the symptoms associated with migraine.

families, and they therefore have a genetic factor.

A classic migraine may last up to 24 hours, and 50 percent of sufferers have warning symptoms known as auras, which can be anxiety, fatigue or any of the neurological symptoms mentioned above that occur before the pain comes on. A type of migraine known as "cluster headaches" are migraine-like pains that usually localize around one eye and tend to occur in clusters of up to three or four headaches a day over a few days, but only recurring every few months.

Interestingly, one in five men and one in four women will suffer from migraines at some time in their lives. Very often the onset is in childhood. Most migraines start between the ages of 20 and 35 years, and generally disappear as we get older.

The jury is still out on deciding which of several possible mechanisms is responsible for causing migraine. Even with the technically advanced use of specialized tests, there is still some debate. There are thought to be several main factors that can trigger a migraine, however.

Stress chemicals such as adrenaline and catecholamines

Stress chemicals cause the release of a chemical called serotonin from specialized blood cells called platelets. This chemical causes blood vessels to constrict, resulting in a reduced oxygen flow to parts of the brain. A rebound-defense reflex occurs that causes an increase in blood flow, causing pressure on the nerves, and also a release of a substance that triggers pain, known cleverly as substance P.

Food and other allergens, including pollutants

Food intolerance and other toxins may trigger a stress-chemical response as described above. A specific group of proteins known as amines that are found in alcohol, chocolate, and cheese can all trigger attacks by directly causing vasoconstriction (narrowing of blood vessels). The list of foods that have been found in many trials to cause problems is very long, but isolating each individual's food "triggers" is necessary.

Structural

Any problem that can affect cranial blood flow may be relevant, and malposition of the cranial bones, especially the jaw joint (known as the temporomandibular joint), is common.

Hormonal and other causes

Hormonal changes found in a normal female cycle, tiredness, weather changes, and eye "strain" can all precipitate migraines, as can withdrawal from drugs that cause vascular changes. A withdrawal syndrome may occur within a few hours of smoking a cigarette or drinking a cup of coffee, and does not always refer to stopping a drug to which an individual is addicted or takes a lot of.

RECOMMENDATIONS

- *Keep a concise journal over a period of time that covers at least three migraines. This must include food intake, stress levels, times of the attacks, and hours asleep. Try to isolate and alter any obvious causative factors from those mentioned above.*
- *Consider food-allergy testing, but specifically eliminate caffeine, cheese, and chocolate.*
- *Learn a relaxation technique through yoga, Qi Gong, or meditation.*
- *Counseling, hypnotherapy and biofeedback techniques are all beneficial.*
- *Consider cranial osteopathy or craniosacral work to correct any malalignment of the cranial and neck bones.*
- *Polarity therapy and Alexander techniques to maintain posture may be relevant.*
- *Acupuncture and acupressure (Shiatsu) have been shown to be very effective in reducing the frequency of attacks.*
- *Homeopathic remedies should be chosen based on the symptoms, but pay special attention to the following homeopathic remedies that could be tried, one at a time, at potency 6 every half-hour in the "aura" stage, or every 10min if a migraine starts: Thuja and Spigalia for left-sided*

onset; Sanguinaria, Rhus toxicodendron, and Iris for right-sided onset. Accurate prescribing based on the symptoms is essential, and referral to your favorite homeopathic manual or a homeopathic prescriber is preferable.

- *The following supplements may be beneficial, and should be taken in divided doses throughout the day at the recommended dosage per foot of height: niacin (vitamin B_3), 10mg; Magnesium 100mg; Quercetinn 100mg.*
- *The herbal medicines capsicum, taken at 5mg per foot of height in divided doses throughout the day, and feverfew, taken at the same levels, may be beneficial.*
- *For symptomatic relief, see* **Headache**.
- *Orthodox drugs are available that work specifically against migraines. These need to be prescribed by a medical practitioner, and should be considered only when alternative therapies have failed. Always try to take a minimum dose of a drug, and even experiment by halving the dose recommended, just in case you need less.*

Nasal Polyps

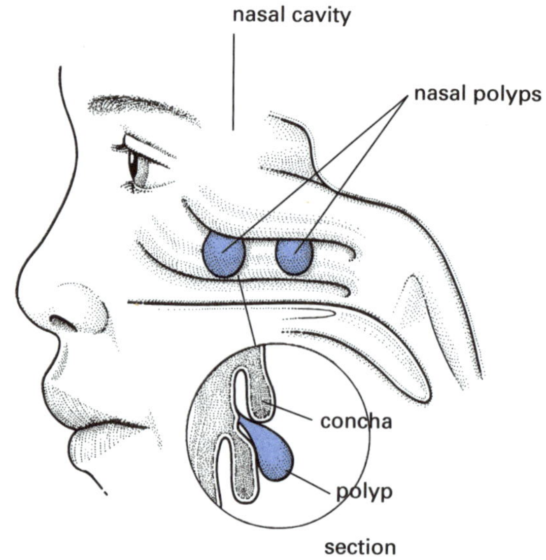

Polyps are most commonly found in the nasal lining, although they may be present on most mucous membranes. Usually they are benign.

POLYPS

A polyp is a smooth, round, or oval projection from a membrane surface. Polyps may be broad-based or on a stalk. They rarely cause any sensations, and are usually discovered on routine examination.

RECOMMENDATION

- *Treatment is dependent upon the site of the polyp, i.e. nasal polyp (see below), bowel polyp, or cervical polyp (see relevant section, depending on the site of the polyp).*

SEXUAL PROMISCUITY

There is no right or wrong concerning sexual promiscuity, but from a holistic and medical point of view, the subject needs to be broached. The definition of promiscuity is dependent upon both peer and social boundaries. One country may differ markedly from another, governed predominantly by the strength of its religion. Within any geographical distribution, peer groups exert an enormous amount of pressure on an individual. The availability of suitable partners, sex, and personal attractiveness or, at least, personal self-confidence are all factors in deciding the number of partners that an individual may have.

Medically speaking, promiscuity is defined arbitrarily, but in the West it usually encompasses four or more partners within 12 months.

Physical considerations

The higher the number of partners, the higher the risk of contact with a sexually-transmitted disease (STD). Viral infections cover both ends of the medical spectrum. Human papillomavirus (genital warts) and herpes are rarely life-threatening, although the former may trigger cervical cancer in women. On the other hand, human-immunodeficiency virus (HIV) is clearly associated with AIDS. Bacterial infection such as gonorrhea is rarely a problem, provided that adequate treatment is available, whereas syphilis is becoming more resistant to antibiotics and, once again, is on the increase. Other infections such as Pelvic Inflammatory Disease (PID), *Candida*, *Chlamydia*, and *Trichomonas*, the latter two being responsible for the majority of nonspecific urethritis (NSU), are also more prominent in the promiscuous.

RECOMMENDATIONS

- *Promiscuity is a risk, and reducing the number of partners is medically advisable.*
- *Safe sex needs to be practiced, principally by using nonpenetrative sex or correct use of condoms.*
- *Prompt attention to any genital irregularity is to be recommended.*
- *A social conscience that inhibits promiscuity by those that have infections must also be encouraged.*

Psychological considerations

The psychology of sex is a vast subject, and beyond the scope of this first-aid book. Sex, designed to be an act of procreation, is used by the human species to reflect many underlying emotions. Anger, aggression, and frustration through rape, love and adoration through making love and, arguably, low self-esteem and loneliness may be reflected by promiscuity, which temporarily placates the latter and, through peer adoration, raises the former. Sex is used as a recreation, and our sexuality is pinpointed by many forms of advertising as a way to sell products. Our subconscious is constantly alerted by sexuality. Sex is pleasurable, and the psyche is geared towards seeking pleasure. Sex is not always exactly what the individual requires, but may be the inevitable end-point of the hug or kiss that was.

RECOMMENDATIONS

- *Focus on the reason that sex is being sought and performed.*
- *Reflect, especially if alcohol or drugs are required to enjoy the act. Altered senses usually give altered signals of requirement.*
- *Remember that sex is not the inevitable outcome of any relationship where attraction is manifest. Most long-standing and supportive relationships succeed on other foundations.*
- *Never be ashamed to sit with a professional to discuss any problems of sexuality.*

Spiritual considerations

Spirituality and sexuality in combination create a fascinating subject. Religion, proclaiming in different guises to be the height of spirituality, generally chastises the sexually promiscuous. Spirituality, without religion, generally accepts sexuality as a part of a "being," and in the case of Tantric yoga, actively encourages male promiscuity within certain spiritual confines. If we accept the concept of unity with all living creatures that is expounded by the native Indian peoples of North and South America, we must tie our sexual/spiritual sense to our animal instincts. Many of these cultures believe that we all have a connection to an animal spirit, and universally across the animal kingdom, sexual promiscuity is a method of promoting natural selection and the strongest genes for the species.

The most satisfying aspect for the soul is the experience of oneness, wholeness, or union. It looks like you unite with another, but it is in fact the removal of the "sense of oneness" that makes us feel separate, that makes us seek to reunite. If sexual activity leads only to a heightened awareness of separateness or loneliness, it is not being used properly.

Our spirituality governs or *is* our being. Suppression of any aspect will lead to a suppression of our physical and psychological selves, so clarity of thought and an understanding of our deeper spiritual/sexual selves is essential for good health.

RECOMMENDATIONS

- *Spend time in meditation or discussion on the underlying beliefs and energies that motivate a choice of partner or partners.*

- *Consider the concept of a "soul mate" and ask the question "do many partners increase or decrease my chances of finding one?"*

SHYNESS

To be shy is a character trait that is not necessarily abnormal. Our personality and upbringing will determine the levels of shyness, and it is only if our timidity causes social or personal problems that it needs to be considered worthy of treatment. Most people will suffer some shyness, but if an inability to socialize or perform occurs, then treatment is recommended.

RECOMMENDATIONS

- *Consult a homeopathic Materia Medica and choose a remedy that most matches other psychological and physical attributes of the individual. Pay special attention to the remedies Baryta carbonica, Coca, and Pulsatilla.*
- *Copper or zinc excess or deficiency may encourage timidity. A hair sample should be taken and deficiency supplemented. If there is an excess, it is necessary to isolate the foods that may be putting too much into the system and remove them.*
- *Behavioral modification techniques through counseling or neurolinguistic programming may benefit, but commitment to the course is necessary.*
- *Bach flower remedies, specifically Buttercup and Pink Monkey Flower, may be tried.*

SMOKING AND HOW TO STOP

See **Cigarettes.**

Among the 3,000 or so chemicals found in cigarettes lurks nicotine, a strongly addictive substance. Within a few weeks of smoking, most people will find their nervous system in need of nicotine to maintain a sensation of well-being. While this is the main reason for addiction to cigarettes, it is also worth noting that tobacco, being a plant, has many compounds in it that the body utilizes. Examples are nickel and cobalt, both of which are necessary for the absorption and utilization of oxygen in the bloodstream. Therefore, when attempting to stop smoking, not only does the nervous system recognize that it is missing something, but the body may also actually move into deficiency because substances absorbed through the lung are taken in very rapidly, and after a while, saturate the body's requirements, therefore negating the use of the bowel. In other words, if you are getting what you need through the lungs, the bowel does not need to work so hard and stops the chemical processes, such that if you stop smoking there may be a lag phase of several days before the bowel again begins to absorb what you need. This combination of the nervous system recognizing that it is missing something and the bowel not absorbing quickly leads to many people eating more in an attempt to satisfy their cravings. The nervous system lives off glucose, so the cravings tend to be for sweets or carbohydrates, and therefore people put on weight. This factor is very relevant when it comes to helping people to stop.

Stopping

Many different techniques have been employed over the years to help people stop smoking, and most have an element of success. My view, and perhaps the truly holistic view, is to utilize whichever treatments may work, and use them in combination. Determining whether somebody is psychologically or physically (or both) "hooked" leads us to the suggested treatment course.

Psychological treatments

Counseling

It is necessary to establish whether a smoker "wants" to stop smoking or "wants to want" to stop smoking. Most failed treatments occur because the individual has no real desire to stop. This must be confronted, and a counselor may be necessary to help decide which level the smoker is at. Counseling or other psychological measures (*see* below) must be utilized to move the smoker into the "wants to stop" bracket.

Hypnosis

There are two techniques of using hypnosis, which may be used individually or in combination. I have called them suggestive hypnosis and "part" hypnosis.

Suggestive or suggestion hypnosis involves the individual being hypnotized into a deep state of relaxation, and a suggestion that smoking is an uncomfortable or distasteful habit is placed in the subconscious. On returning from the deep, relaxed state, hopefully the smoker will dislike cigarettes. Allow three or four sessions of this type of hypnotherapy. Success in helping to stop smoking occurs in 10–30 percent of patients.

Part hypnosis takes the smoker into a hypnotized state and, while there, the hypnotherapist will have a conversation with the subconscious "part" of the person's psyche that is encouraging the habit. Very often, smoking starts at an age where acceptance into a group apparently requires cigarette smoking. Not having a cigarette with the "gang" may lead to being an outcast, and the subconscious quickly correlates the nicotine buzz with being accepted and being socially adequate. It is a small step to find that the cigarette is your best friend, and will indeed substitute for the group, especially if you did not like the group in the first place! Nicotine, by creating a sense of well-being, may mask sadness, guilt, or fear, which is pushed into the subconscious and can be avoided by using the drug. Again, the underlying psychological pull needs to be established and dealt with before smoking can be taken away, otherwise it is similar to removing the crutch from an individual with an injured leg.

Physical therapies

Supplementation therapy

This much-underused technique is based on the principle that when we stop smoking, the body craves some of the useful compounds that we may absorb through the cigarette smoke. High-dose supplementation may make the availability of these trace elements greater, therefore taking away some of the craving. More useful is the use of intravenous-supplementation therapy, which bypasses the slower bowel absorption.

Diet

The use of detoxification-diet techniques (*see* **Detox diet**) helps rid the body of the nicotine that will have settled in the nervous system and in fat stores. The quicker the nicotine is out of the system, the quicker the cravings diminish.

Exercise

It is essential in nearly every case to introduce an exercise program that helps to control breathing and increase oxygen consumption. Smoking reduces the lung capacity and the body's oxygen utilization, which, when increased, will make the individual feel better. Techniques such as Qi Gong, yoga, Tai Chi, and basic aerobic exercises are most beneficial.

Breathing techniques

Until recently, techniques of breathing through yoga or Qi Gong were the best methods of retraining the lungs and bloodstream into accepting and enjoying oxygen without toxins. These techniques are still very beneficial if practiced correctly but, more recently, a Russian doctor named a technique after himself. The Buteyko technique of breathing is, in fact, quite different from yoga techniques. It encourages a shallow breathing that alters the acid/base balance in the body (*see* **Breathing** and **The Lungs**), and seems to remove the craving for cigarettes. This technique is becoming more widely available and, while the teaching requires several hours of attendance, early research shows it to be extremely beneficial.

Bodywork techniques

The use of massage techniques, especially manual

lymphatic drainage or Shiatsu, helps in removing the nicotine levels that have settled into the tissues, which, in turn, helps to maintain the cravings.

Acupuncture

When used in conjunction with other therapies, acupuncture is an extremely beneficial method of removing the craving. Even used by itself, it has proven effective. The acupuncture may be general or auricular (needles in specific parts of the ear).

Nicotine replacement

Nicotine patches, chewing gum, or implants are beneficial in nonresponsive cases, but it must be remembered that the nicotine is still being pulled into the system with all its neurological and addictive aspects. You are not dealing with the underlying addictive tendency, merely shifting it from one compound to another. Eventually, the replacement stops and the cigarette craving, not having been dealt with, may well return.

RECOMMENDATIONS

- *Establish that you "want" to stop smoking and not that you "want to want" to stop smoking. If you do not "want to want," then visit a counselor or hypnotherapist initially.*
- *Consider the macrobiotic diet (see chapter 7).*
- *Take in high levels of multiminerals, trace elements, and vitamins for at least six weeks. Consider intravenous supplementation.*
- *Use a detoxification diet or even consider a week or two under supervision at a health farm.*
- *Establish, through reading or a visit to a qualified homeopath, your constitutional remedy, and take this at high potency for one month.*
- *Learn a Qi Gong, Tai Chi, or yoga technique. Perform aerobic exercises two or three times a day for 10–15min. If you can find a Buteyko teacher, try this preferentially.*
- *If the going is tough, visit a manual lymphatic-drainage masseur or Shiatsu practitioner regularly.*
- *Acupuncturists can treat you regularly, or place a "stud" needle in the ear for days at a time.*
- *Avoid nicotine replacement if possible.*

STAGE FRIGHT—*see* Nervousness

SYPHILIS

Syphilis is a sexually-transmitted disease caused by a bacterium called *Treponema pallidum.* It is transmitted through any form of intercourse—oral, anal, or vaginal—but is more prevalent in the homosexual population following nonvaginal intercourse. Like most sexually-transmitted diseases, *Treponema* passes into the tissues of the genitals, rectum, or throat via seminal fluid or vaginal excretions entering small abrasions.

There are four stages, at any one of which the body's immune system may overwhelm the infection, or treatment may be applied. The later the stage, the less likely it is that the outcome will be good.

Primary syphilis is characterized by a sore or chancre developing three to four weeks after infection. This sore is hard to heal, but will spontaneously disappear about six weeks later. This is not a fixed-time schedule, and any lesion in the genital or anal area must be regarded with suspicion. Lesions in or around the mouth or throat must also be considered as potentially syphilitic, especially in the promiscuous or in homosexuals.

At this stage, investigation includes a swab that is placed under a microscope, and a technique known as dark-field microscopy is used to identify the bacterium. It is necessary, sometimes, to repeat this as the bacterium may be missed by the swab technique.

Secondary syphilis manifests before the chancre heals, or may be delayed for up to a year. Symptoms of a skin rash, sore throat, headache, and fever in association with a history of a genital sore, must raise suspicion.

Dark-field microscopy is again utilized, and by this stage, blood tests will be positive for syphilis.

Latent syphilis only occurs if an untreated secondary stage continues. This latent phase is symptomless and is due to the bacterium, for some reason, not replicating but lying dormant. Occasionally small lesions may appear, but may not be considered relevant. Blood tests throughout this period of time, which may last a lifetime (the average, however, is 10–15 years), may be negative or only weakly positive.

Tertiary syphilis—the fourth stage—must be suspected in any condition that does not have an- other obvious answer. The *Treponema* generally attacks the mucous membranes, the skin, and arteries, and therefore can pass into any system. Ten percent of untreated syphilis will develop into neurosyphilis, to which it is assumed Henry VIII succumbed, along with many in the years prior to the Second World War, when the introductio of sulphonamide antibiotics offered effective treatment.

Syphilis took a marked decline in frequency after the Second World War, but is now on the rise. Injudicious use of antibiotics has led to resistant strains, and there are reports of *Treponema* strains that are, along with tuberculosis, proving resistant to all known antibiotics. What may be more worrying is a poorly substantiated but nevertheless growing concern that syphilis is directly related to HIV infection.

RECOMMENDATIONS

- *Any genital lesion must be investigated by a doctor, gynecologist, or specialist in this field.*
- *Antibiotic use must only be undertaken once the sensitivity of that particular syphilitic strain is established.*
- *Alternative therapies have been used for centuries, but should only be used in a complementary fashion now, provided that antibiotics are effective (which they still are in most cases).*
- *Choice of treatment should be selected by a complementary medical practitioner using homeopathic and herbal treatments.*
- *Topical treatment is rarely needed because these lesions are generally painless, but applications of Calendula or Hypericum cream may be beneficial.*

TERMINATION OF PREGNANCY (TOP, ABORTION)

The need for the termination of a pregnancy should be based on medical grounds, such as a risk to the mother's health or life, or due to the inevitability of a nonviable fetus—one that will not live beyond a certain point of development *in utero*. In many parts of the West, however, a termination may be considered if the mother might undergo psychological duress or if the child will be born with anything but normality. Many societies do not allow termination at all, and others only if life-threatening physical conditions exist.

Termination of pregnancy is an emotive subject, but from a holistic point of view, it needs to be considered from four angles.

The body aspect

Pregnancy confers a marked change in hormonal profile in women. The well-known female hormones estrogen and progesterone maintain high levels and, as any woman who struggles with premenstrual syndrome (PMS) will tell you, many changes go on throughout the system. A termination suddenly removes the control mechanism, the body goes through a sudden drop, and many of the changes that were taking place will cease, creating some biochemical confusion. These are corrected over a period of time, but a variety of symptoms, such as tiredness, headaches, mood swings, water retention, abdominal pains, and skin changes, may occur.

A termination is generally performed by inserting a vacuum-like instrument through the cervix into the lumen of the uterus and extracting the contents through a sucking action. The embryo or fetus is pulled out with the inner lining of the uterus. The body has to deal with this injury, as well as with the effects of the anesthetic on the nervous system and liver. Repair of all of these areas is necessary, and requires both energy and building materials.

Any operation carries a risk, and a problem with the procedure or the introduction of infection into the uterus may lead to illness and sterility if the uterus or Fallopian tubes become scarred.

The psychological aspect

Every individual is different, and will relate to the concept of a termination differently. Parental values, religious teachings, social status, and peer pressure will all alter the ease or difficulty with which a woman comes to terms with an abortion. Very few women find the decision easy, and this is compounded by the natural fear of a general anesthetic and operative procedure.

The conflict with social and religious doctrines inevitably creates a dilemma, and there is rarely a termination that does not have its supporters and critics.

The spiritual aspect

There is no right or wrong outside of one's beliefs, but most human beings have a high respect for life, and a termination distinctly goes against that innate predisposition. All religions, supposedly derived from spiritual values, will criticize (and in many countries ostracize) a woman who undergoes a termination. A decision must come from the depths of the soul of the individual.

The Hindus profess that a spirit chooses its parents, and that a karmic (vital force) connection is made even before conception. A termination severs this bond and, unless the soul returns in a later pregnancy, that experience and energy will be lost, at least for this lifetime. I do not think that the Hindu spirituality is greater than any other doctrine, but looking at the situation from this point of view may alter the perception that a termination is not a deeply spiritual conundrum. It is.

The partner aspect

Sadly, all too often, the male plants the seed and then he leaves. Men who behave in this way claim that it is a natural response, and that masculine animals have many mates and that they are simply obeying an acceptable male instinct. Absolute nonsense. This is self-denial designed to alleviate the potential for responsibility that most males fear so markedly in comparison with the female of our species. The truth of the matter is that males in the animal kingdom rarely plant a seed without accepting the responsibility of protecting and nurturing their offspring.

Nevertheless, if this attitude happens to be that of a specific partner, then there is little that can be done and, quite frankly, his opinion should be discarded in favor of friends and family who are around to give support; no energy or time should be wasted on chasing the aberrant male.

I would like to think that the majority of partners who find their mate pregnant in a socially unacceptable situation will take an important role in supporting the decision of the woman. A burden shared is a burden halved, they say, and although I do not think that the division is quite 50/50 in the case of a termination, all and any support is beneficial.

RECOMMENDATIONS

- *Closely review the spiritual aspects of termination. Only each individual can do this, and they should not be led by any social doctrines or pressures. If a connection with the life growing inside is there at all, termination should not be considered.*
- *Psychological considerations may be made easier by asking the question: "Do I feel that a termination is the right approach, or do I* think *it is?" Always go with your feelings. It is much easier to look back on a mistake and say "I did what I* felt *was right" rather than have to deal with "I did what I* thought *was right." Remember that suppression of emotion creates illness, but making a mistake does not.*

- *Remember that a possible side effect of a termination is sterilization. Terminating a pregnancy may lead to a life barren of children.*
- *Consult a counselor or health practitioner with whom you have a connection. Discuss your emotional state fully, and ensure that any decision is reached after complete and absolute discussion by looking at the problem from both sides of the fence.*
- *Do not surround yourself with friends who support only one side of the debate. You may be covering guilt by obtaining moral support for a decision that you are not certain about.*
- *A termination may be performed at an early stage of pregnancy by chemical induction with high doses of progesterone-like drugs. These have the side effects of nausea, vomiting, headaches, and other unpleasant symptoms, including abdominal pains, and they work by disrupting the chemical balance required for pregnancy and encouraging contraction of the uterus. Menstruation (a period) is the outcome. If chemical termination is used, see* **Heavy and painful periods** *and follow the advice.*
- *If a termination is to be performed by operative procedure, generally this is necessary after the eighth week of a pregnancy (see* **Operations and surgery**).

TOXOPLASMOSIS

This is an infection by a protozoan (bacteria/viral-like organism) called *Toxoplasma gondii*, which is widely distributed in nature and can cause fetal developmental problems as well as infections within individuals.

Clinical manifestations of damage include enlarged liver and spleen, blindness, cysts, mental retardation, and the development of too large or too small a brain. Problems may be apparent soon after birth, or may develop later on in life. In the acquired form, a fever with a rash, enlarged glands, enlarged liver and spleen, and an inflamed eye may occur. If serious, the infection may affect the brain or the heart.

Toxoplasmosis is spread predominantly by animal feces, and especially those of cats. Owners of dogs and cats should be particularly and specifically wary, especially prior to an intended pregnancy.

In the unfortunate circumstance that a toxoplasmosis blood test shows positive in a pregnant woman, there is a need for further investigation to pinpoint when the infection took place. Toxoplasmosis can have a devastating effect on a fetus in the first trimester. The infection can lead to growth defects, brain damage, and death. Once the placenta has formed (usually by 12–13 weeks), it is harder for the infection to get into the baby, but transmission does occur and can lead to other damage, including blindness, limb-growth retardation, and less-serious brain effects.

Calculating when an infection took place is therefore paramount, because a decision to terminate on medical grounds may be considered. Pinpointing the time of infection is done by taking blood samples from the mother at an interval of at least three weeks apart. A current infection will have a rising level of antibodies against toxoplasmosis, and the amount of antibodies and the speed with which it is being produced give a clue as to when infection took place. The level of antibodies, known as the titer, will remain stable if the infection was from some time ago, but will rise if the infection was more recent. If toxoplasmosis is suspected, ultrasound will give a clear definition of any obvious brain damage or limb defects, but cannot illustrate conditions such as blindness.

It is currently not common practice in Britain to test pregnant women for toxoplasmosis as a general rule. I think this is wrong, and any woman who owns or has been in contact with animals, especially domestic cats, should be tested for antibodies before conception and at the end of the third trimester.

RECOMMENDATIONS

- *Prior to becoming pregnant and during a pregnancy, a blood test should be done to test for the presence of Toxoplasma.*
- *If any of the main symptoms are present in conjunction with a positive blood test for toxoplasmosis, an antibiotic treatment should be taken.*
- *Consult a complementary medical practitioner for treatment to run alongside orthodox antibiotic care (see* **Antibiotics***).*
- *If pregnant and a positive test is found, but no symptoms are present, then consult your obstetrician and ask to be put in touch with the area or national specialist for toxoplasmosis. He/she will be able to advise you on the chances of a problem, and also as to the best treatment.*
- *Your preferred complementary medical practitioner should be consulted to boost the immune system and deal with the possible use of antibiotics and, if you are pregnant, to advise you on the best counselor for the inevitable anxiety that will be present.*

YEAST INFECTION

Yeasts are a subgroup of fungi in the big scheme of categorization. It seems less emotive to discuss the potential for infestation by yeast rather than suggesting that somebody is infected by a fungus!

The most-common fungal infection is thought to be *Candida*, although many other fungi and yeasts live in or on the body surfaces. In their natural place they act as symbionts (both taking and giving some benefit from the host), principally by attacking other—perhaps more dangerous—organisms, and also eating available sugars and thereby reducing the amount for other organisms, which, in turn, have their growth inhibited.

Yeast infections are most commonly associated with the vaginal vault, and discharges, discomfort, odors, and diseases may result.

Normal and fungal blood samples

The blood above is a healthy sample while strands of fungi are clearly visible below in this Humeral Pathology Laboratory Test.

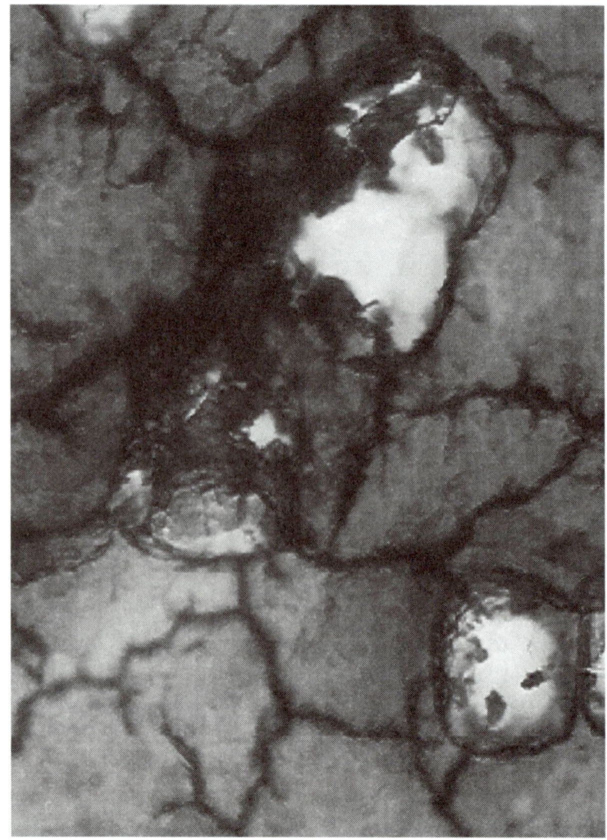

Yeast may flourish in the bowel, but generally it causes no problems unless the normal bowel-flora are reduced and a population overgrowth occurs. The yeasts and fungi of the body tend to produce chemicals that we find toxic, and if these increase, then symptoms ranging from malaise and tiredness to chronic-fatigue syndrome and cancer may evolve.

Yeasts or fungi should not travel around the body, and if they are found in the bloodstream, they are usually killed off rapidly or filtered out by the liver and kidney. If they do survive, they may travel to major organs and cause serious complications. This is much more apparent in those with an immunocompromised status, such as AIDS.

RECOMMENDATIONS

- *The orthodox world very rarely takes into account the presence of yeasts and fungi, and persistent problems should be assessed by a complementary medical practitioner, who should be reminded of the possibility of yeast infection.*
- *Orthodox cultures of urine and stool rarely look for yeasts, and sometimes it is worth specifically asking a laboratory to do so.*
- *A Humoral Pathological Laboratory test (examination of blood samples under high-powered microscopy) may show fungal or yeast spores in any body fluid or excreta, or the reaction by red blood cells to the presence of fungal toxins.*
- *Treatment depends on the problem (see* **Candida** *and* **Fungal infections***).*

YELLOW FEVER

This is an acute viral disease transmitted to human beings by mosquitoes and characterized by fever, jaundice, bleeding tendencies, and a slowing down of the heart rate, and other neurologically associated problems if the condition is severe.

Vaccination is recommended for those who are liable to come into contact with the infection but, like any vaccine, it has its risks, and the benefits must be weighed against these.

RECOMMENDATIONS

- *See* **Vaccinations**.
- *Follow orthodox advice for this extremely dangerous and contagious condition; for complementary medical support, see* **Fever**.

THE HEAD AND NECK

DANDRUFF

Dandruff, unless very severe, is more of a cosmetic nuisance than a medical problem. Characterized by a flaking of the scalp, dandruff is of no medical consequence unless it is disturbing an individual's social lifestyle or irritating the scalp.

Occasionally associated with more-aggressive skin conditions—such as psoriasis or dermatitis (eczema)—the cause is either a minor fungal infection, an excess of heat in the system (from an Eastern point of view), or is associated with a lack of water intake (dehydration) and an excess of heat-creating foods or adrenaline-producing stress.

RECOMMENDATIONS

- *Wash the hair with a selenium-containing shampoo not more than three times a week for three weeks.*
- *Take a vitamin B complex, five times the recommended daily dose for one week. Take zinc (5mg per foot of height) each night for two weeks and flaxseed oil (1 teaspoonful per foot of height) in divided doses with meals.*
- *Flaxseed oil can be applied directly to the scalp with gentle massage.*
- *Standing on your head will increase blood flow, and should be performed for 10min per day.*
- *Consider chronic dehydration and correct this by drinking 8 ounces of water per foot of height per day.*

- *Persisting dandruff should be reviewed by a complementary medical practitioner with experience in herbal treatment, who may consider several herbs including camomile, figwort, rosemary, and willow. Shampoos made from any of these may be curative.*
- *Severe dandruff may be associated with underlying skin diseases, and dandruff of sudden onset or not resolving swiftly should be reviewed by a doctor.*

ENCEPHALITIS

The word encephalic means affecting or involving the brain; "itis" on the end of any word means inflammation. Encephalitis is inflammation of the brain, which is an extremely serious condition and is not one to be dealt with at home. This can occur at any age.

Severe headache and any neurological symptoms, such as visual disturbance, numbness, tingling, unsteadiness, dizziness, or feeling faint, may all represent an encephalitis, and any such symptoms that persist or are associated with drowsiness, loss of consciousness, or even coma must be considered.

RECOMMENDATIONS

- *Any unexplained neurological symptoms should be assessed by a doctor immediately, especially if loss of consciousness or pain is associated.*
- *Use Aconite 30 every 15min on the way to the physician.*

INTRACRANIAL BLEEDS

Extradural hemorrhage

There are several linings to the brain, the outermost of which is called the dura. A bleed, usually caused by trauma but occasionally by disease of blood vessels or an infection, is known as an extradural hemorrhage.

As with any bleeding vessel, the flow of blood may be swift, in which case neurological symptoms, loss of consciousness, and headache may be apparent. A slow bleed, however, may take up to six weeks before symptoms as mild as a change of character may be noticed.

RECOMMENDATIONS

- *Any injury or blow to the head, persistent headache, or neurological symptoms should be reviewed by a physician.*

Extradural and Subdural Hematomas

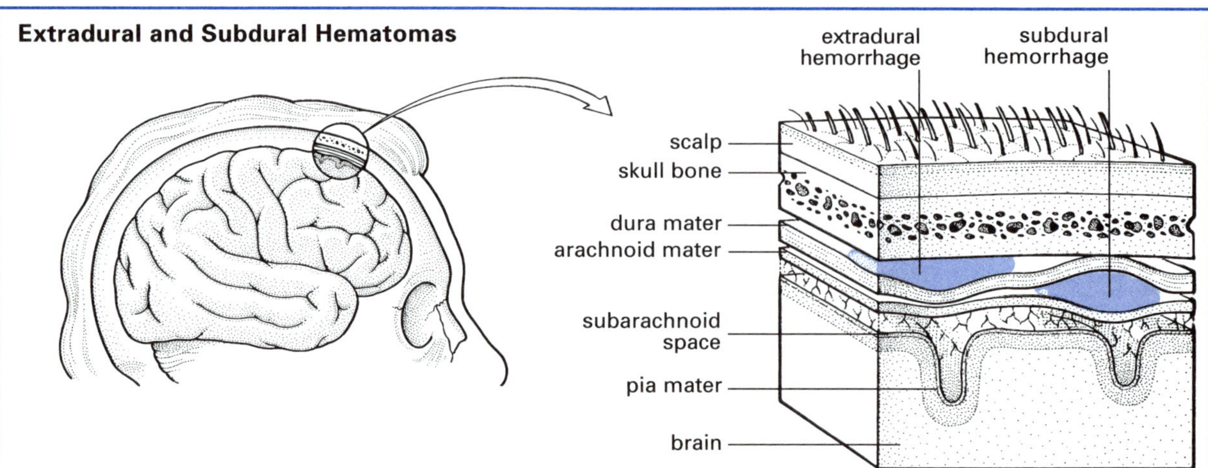

Extradural and subdural hematomas may form blood clots that put pressure on the brain. The symptoms described in the ***recommendations*** *should be watched out for in anyone who has suffered a blow to the head.*

- *A telltale sign of an intracranial (within the skull) bleed is one pupil (often on the other side from the injury) being dilated or constricted—but definitely different from the other side and potentially unresponsive.*
- *Any suspicion of a bleed must be examined by a CT scan for safety.*
- *Following a head injury, ensure that friends and relatives keep an eye on behavior patterns. A change in character anywhere up to six weeks following a blow to the skull needs to be treated as an emergency by a hospital.*
- *The homeopathic remedy Natrum Sulphuricum potency 6 can be used every 15min on the way to the hospital following any head injury. Natrum sulphuricum 200, taken each night for three nights, can be used following a head injury.*
- *Orthodox treatment may be as simple as monitoring, but may also include blood-letting following bur-holes in the skull (**see* **Operations and surgery***).*

Subdural hematoma

A subdural hematoma is a bleed underneath the dura. It behaves and requires treatment similar to an extradural hematoma or hemorrhage.

RECOMMENDATION

- *For recommendation and treatment,* *see* **Extradural hemorrhage***.*

THE EYES

CONTACT LENSES

Contact lenses are a remarkable invention that have benefited people with poor eyesight, both near and far, over the last two decades. They come as either hard or soft lenses, which refer to the type of material used in their manufacture and, to some extent, their thickness.

Hard lenses tend to be small and cover the dimension of the pupil (the black part in the center of the eye), whereas soft lenses tend to cover the entire iris (the colored part of the eye). Hard lenses are cheaper and more durable, and can be used for a much broader spectrum of visual problems, but they tend to be less comfortable. The soft lenses wear out more quickly, cost more, and are not so easy to keep sterile.

It is of paramount importance that sterility is maintained when the contact lenses are not in the eye. Following your optician's instructions is extremely important to avoid irritation, inflammation such as iritis and conjunctivitis, and more serious conditions such as chronic blepharitis. Always wash your hands before removing or inserting your contact lenses and, however experienced you may be, do not rush the process. It only takes one misjudged insertion or removal to cause potentially permanent eye damage. Please note that contact-lens cleaners may have an association with chemical damage to the eyes, and must be rinsed off thoroughly.

RECOMMENDATIONS

- *The choice of lens should be made in consultation with an optician specializing in contact lenses.*
- *Do not shirk the responsibility of cleaning the lenses.*
- *Clean hands before touching the lens or eyes.*
- *Always thoroughly wash off any contact-lens cleaning solution because these may damage the eye.*
- *Antiseptic solutions will also kill off the body's normal and useful bacteria found along the edges of the eyelids.*

CORNEAL ULCERS

The cornea is the transparent part of the eyeball that lies over and protects the pupil. Its job is protection, and occasionally it may get scratched or damaged, usually by a foreign object. Infections can attack the cornea, and a not uncommon cause is herpes, which causes a branching effect over the cornea and is known as a dendritic ulcer.

Corneal scratches are very painful, and are made worse by the eyelid rubbing the area as it blinks. Watering and redness are characteristic, and the eye is generally kept shut and still.

The cornea is well supplied by blood vessels, and tends to heal fairly rapidly, but while damaged, it is open to infection.

Ulceration of the cornea (the front part of the eye) is most commonly caused by trauma, but may be associated with rarer diseases and malnutrition. It is a painful and serious condition, insomuch that if it is not dealt with properly, the pain continues and, if it is associated with illness, blindness may result if the ulceration worsens.

RECOMMENDATIONS

- *Any eye injury involving foreign matter should be cleansed with running water, if possible (see* **Foreign bodies and substances in the eye***).*
- *A cold compress over the closed eye may give relief.*
- *Any eye injury, however slight, must be reviewed by a doctor, and accept a referral to a specialist if necessary (see* **Injuries to the eye***).*
- *With any eye injury, take the homeopathic remedy Aconite or Hepar sulfuris calcarium potency 6 or 12, four pills immediately and every 15min until you are seen by a medical person.*
- *An accurate selection of a remedy from your preferred homeopathic manual is recommended should other symptoms set in (see* **Inflammation of the eyes***).*
- *General advice includes patching the eye, although recently it has been advised to keep the eye open to the air to allow faster healing.*
- *Severe damage may heal faster by taking beta-carotene (5mgs) with each meal if you are over the age of 12, or proportionately less (best prescribed by a nutritionist) if you are younger.*
- *Euphrasia (eyebright) lotion, 1 drop in an eggcupful of water, can be very soothing and antiseptic.*

DETACHED RETINA

The retina is the medical term for the layer at the back of the eye where all the visual nerves collect the light that travels through the lens, cornea, and vitreous fluids in the two chambers of the eye.

Detachment usually occurs following injury, surgery, infection, or arterial damage, such as atheroma in the elderly.

Symptoms of retinal detachment are seeing flashing lights, funny shapes, and eventually blindness that starts with the peripheral vision (outer part of your vision) and moves inwards.

Detached Retina

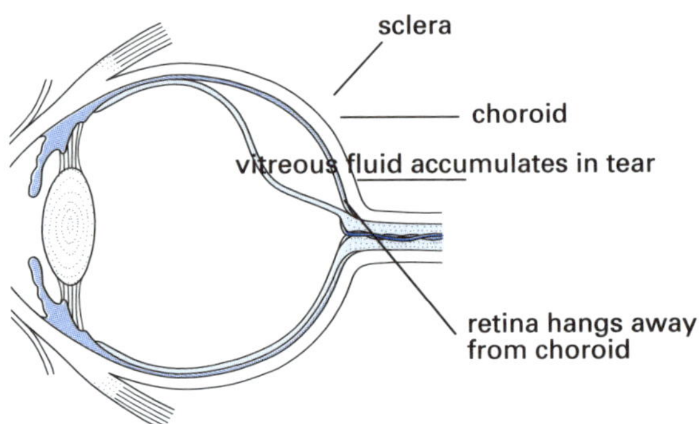

The retina hangs away from the choroid—the rich layer of blood vessels at the back of the eye.

RECOMMENDATIONS

- *Any visual problem should be taken to your doctor or local emergency room immediately. Specific laser treatment may now be used to prevent further detachment of the retina once it starts, and the sooner this treatment is provided the better.*
- *On your way to the doctor, the remedies Apis or Aconite, potency 6, can be taken every 10min.*
- *Recurrent detachment needs to be treated by a complementary medical specialist with experience in this field, who may use specific homeopathic remedies and high-dose supplementation in conjunction with eye exercises. High-dose antioxidants may be used until the consultation (see* **Antioxidants***).*

DOUBLE VISION

Double vision is created by the optical part of the brain receiving two images at the same time. This occurs because the eyeballs are not synchronized or because of extra impulses being incorrectly transmitted through the nervous system.

Problems can occur from the front of the eye, caused by the muscles of the eye pulling the eyeball in different directions, and from neurological problems of the optic nerve leading to the optical part of the brain.

Trauma, infection, damage to the nerve tracts by growths, diabetes, or drugs must all be excluded. More-complicated neurological or muscular diseases also need to be eliminated as possible causes.

Remember that the most-common cause of double vision is a blow to the eye or head, and is liable to be temporary but, as in any visual disturbance that lasts for more than a few minutes, seeking a medical opinion is best.

Conditions such as multiple sclerosis or muscular dystrophy may rarely present as double vision, and therefore I must emphasize the importance of establishing an underlying cause, because naturopathic treatments for even these serious conditions may work better if started early in the course of such diseases.

RECOMMENDATIONS

- *Visit a doctor or emergency room for any visual disturbance.*
- *The homeopathic remedy Arnica should be used if trauma initiated the double vision. Take Arnica 6 every hour until the problem resolves. A persistent double vision caused by trauma that has been examined to rule out any other complications may be treated by Natrum sulphuricum 30, four pills four times a day for five days.*
- *Having ruled out the necessity for orthodox intervention, cranial osteopathy, craniosacral therapy, and specific eye exercises, such as the Bates' eye exercises, will be beneficial.*

DRY EYES

Dry eyes are more of a symptom than a medical condition, although lack of tears can be associated with disease processes such as sarcoidosis or blocked tear ducts. A persistence of this problem needs to be seen by a doctor.

Most frequently, dry eyes are associated with adverse weather conditions or mild conjunctivitis (*see* **Conjunctivitis**).

RECOMMENDATIONS

- *Persisting dryness or dryness without obvious cause needs to be reviewed by a doctor.*
- *Rule out an association of dry eyes with smoking, poor-quality air-conditioning, or allergies to airborne or food antigens. If associated, try to change the situations.*
- *Euphrasia as a diluted fluid extract can be used as an eyebath and as a remedy, potency 6, four times a day.*
- *Artificial tears (available from drugstores) can be used in the short term.*

THE MOUTH

DENTAL OPERATIONS

There is a strong predilection among many dentists to remove the back molar or wisdom teeth automatically. This, along with trauma and decay of teeth and gums through poor hygiene, frequently leads to the need for dental operations. More unusual situations, such as infection in the gums or jaw, may need to be pre- and postoperatively treated.

Most dentists would encourage the use of antibiotics in any surgical procedure, and especially in people who have a history of heart-valve disease (*see* **Rheumatic fever**) or kidney infections. Studies and trials suggest the use of antibiotics in such situations as being warranted. These studies tend not to look at the sequela, and are probably done on people with a broad spectrum of preoperative health. Antibiotics (*see* **Antibiotics**) are not necessarily harmless or safe, and if they can be avoided they should be. I have always been fascinated by the fact that dentists and doctors are so adamant concerning the use of these antibiotics before dental operations. Very often the bacteria that may be involved in any infection live in the mouth, so why should they only be a problem when an operation is involved? These bacteria are being absorbed into the cuts in the mouth and around the infected area all the time and generally do not seem to cause us any problems.

RECOMMENDATIONS

- *Ensure adequate hygiene by cleaning the teeth and gums two or three times a day as soon as any problem is suspected.*
- *Commence mouthwashes preoperatively using Arnica and Calendula lotions or fluid extracts diluted in water. Ensure that the solution is forced through the teeth and not just rinsed around the mouth. This should be done four times a day, preferably starting one week before the dental work, but even one wash may be beneficial.*
- *Homeopathic remedies should be considered before and after. For operations with no infection, use Arnica 30 four times a day starting three days before the operation. For infections that are deeply embedded or trapped in an abscess or the jawbone, use Hepar sulfuris calcarium 30 four times a day starting as soon as the infection is noted. Immediately after the operation, commence on Calcarea fluorica 30, four times a day until healing is complete. These are basic and general recommendations that might be overridden by a homeopath, who would deal with specific symptoms.*
- *Find a dentist who is open to alternative and complementary medicine in an attempt to avoid the use of antibiotics. Do not go into an operation if you are "under the weather" and consult with your complementary medical practitioner for a constitutional buildup prior to any operative procedure.*
- *The following supplements should be used per foot of height: vitamin C, 1g; argenine, 2g; magnesium, 500mg in divided doses with meals; zinc, 5mg before bed; and regardless of height, five times the recommended daily allowance of a multi-B complex.*
- *It is very worthwhile consulting a cranial osteopath after any dental work, since adjustments to the jaw joint will encourage blood flow to the damaged area and avoid the possibility of jaw strain, which can lead to headaches, migraines, and other complications.*

THE LIPS

Care of the lips

The lips have several functions. They form the opening to the digestive tract and, together with the nostrils, the top part of the respiratory system. They act as a form of communication by forming many of our vocal sounds, and are also an area that we use to attract the opposite sex, hence the use of lipstick! Once attracted, the lips are usually the first point of sexual contact.

The lips contain an intermediate form of cell between that of the skin and those of the mucous membranes. They have sweat or sebaceous glands, and rely upon the moisture of the mouth (saliva) to keep their integrity. Internal moisture is therefore very important, as well as the constituents of saliva.

It is also worth remembering that the lips reflect the internal environment. For instance, dry, cracked lips mean dehydration; pale lips, anemia; red lips, fever or internal inflammation.

RECOMMENDATIONS

- *Dry or cracked lips require an increase in the hydration of the body.*

- *Calendula or Graphites creams should be applied. Avoid moisturizing creams that are geared towards temporary relief, thereby encouraging more use of the compound. Habitual users of chapsticks are habitual users because they use chapsticks.*
- *Avoid application of heat through hot drinks or smoking as much as possible.*
- *Spend as much time as possible without lipstick.*
- *Use a sunblock if in strong sunshine.*
- *A central crack in the lips is a guiding symptom for the homeopathic remedy Natrum muriaticum. Graphites, Calcarea carbonica, and Sulphur are other remedies that should be reviewed in dry lips.*
- *If the lips are pale, see* ***Anemia****.*

WISDOM TEETH

The backmost teeth at both sides of the upper and lower jaw make up the four molar teeth known as the wisdom teeth. They are so called because they finally push through the gum between the ages of 17 and 25 years (but usually around 21 years), a time when our childhood experiences supposedly convert into wisdom.

The emergence of the wisdom teeth should not cause a problem, but in the West we are seeing increasing incidence of impaction (the wisdom teeth not coming out) and infections of the surrounding gum. This is probably caused by a decrease in the amount of chewy, fibrous food, such as raw vegetables and fruit, eaten and a higher amount of softer, refined foods.

Pain may develop from impaction and infection, and teeth that only partially become exposed leave pockets of gum that allow bacteria to breed. Left unattended, erosion of the bone and loosening of these teeth and their neighbors can present a problem within a few years, or later on.

WISDOM TEETH

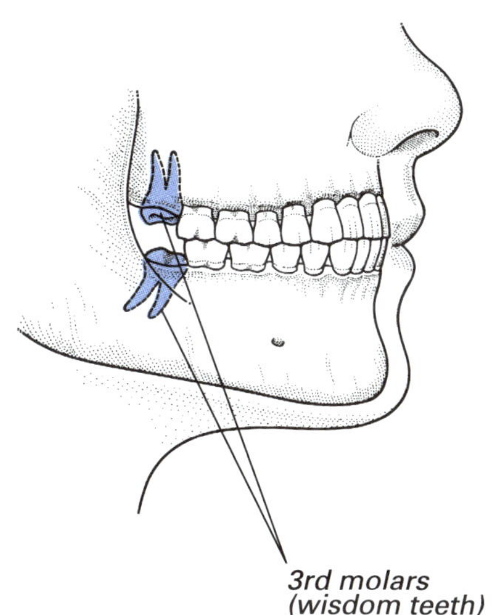

RECOMMENDATIONS

- *Pay special attention through brushing and flossing as soon as these teeth start to emerge. They are not easy to access, and special brushes can be provided by your dentist.*
- *Regular mouthwashes of a teaspoonful of salt and a teaspoonful of Arnica fluid extract in a cup of water is a useful daily treatment.*
- *Cranial osteopathy may be beneficial in impacted wisdom teeth.*
- *Many dentists are very quick to encourage the extraction of wisdom teeth, and a second opinion from a less-invasive professional may be wise before this minor operative procedure is considered.*

The Chest

ASTHMA

See **Asthma** in chapter 3.

Asthma can be triggered at any age, but quite often the teenage years are the starting point. Treatment from this age onward is similar to that of a child.

RECOMMENDATIONS

- *See* **Asthma** *in chapter 3.*
- *Homeopathy can be very effective, but high potencies are required, and a homeopathic consultation is recommended. Acute attacks can be helped by referring to a homeopathic manual with special reference to the remedies: Aconite, Arsenicum album, Calcarea carbonica, Ipecacuanha, and Natrum sulphuricum. Do not stop using orthodox treatments such as inhalers without supervision by an experienced practitioner, and even then, only with your doctor's support.*
- *Eucalyptus oil as a steam inhalation is very effective, but it counteracts homeopathic remedies. Better to use a combination of lavender and camomile oils (four drops of each in a bowl of steaming water).*
- *Acupressure may be used to help relieve an attack. Find the top of the chestbone (sternum) and move outwards along the collarbones on both sides. Move down the edge of the collarbone and find two sensitive spots on either side. Pull the shoulders back and gently apply pressure to the point of pain while inspiring for 3sec and expiring for 4sec.*
- *Relaxation and meditation. It is not easy to relax or meditate in the middle of an asthma attack. However, all asthmatics should practice a daily meditation routine and be able to utilize this technique during an attack.*
- *At the first sign of an asthma attack, take 10mg per foot of height of vitamin B_6 twice a day. Also, per foot of height: 500mg of vitamin C with each meal, 5mg of natural-food-state zinc taken last thing at night, 500mg of magnesium twice a day, 1,000iu of vitamin A twice a day and 100mg of N-acetylcysteine twice a day.*

BREATHING

If there is only one section of this entire book that I would ask everyone to read, it is this short note concerning breathing.

The Eastern philosophies of medicine all have breathing techniques as part of their health maintenance programs. Evidence from all over the world shows that breathing techniques adjust the biochemistry of the body by influencing the amount of oxygen we take in and carbon dioxide that we breathe out. No part of the body functions without oxygen, and all active cells produce carbon dioxide that needs to be eliminated.

For many centuries, it has been established that breathing techniques will aid meditation and relaxation, as well as enhance athletic performance and activity.

There is no specific method of breathing that is best suited for all individuals since each one of us is unique, but basic rules hold steady.

We somehow manage to train ourselves out of good breathing as we age. Infants and children follow simple patterns:

- They breathe more frequently when they are active, and reduce their respiratory rate at rest.
- When active, the depth of breathing increases; when asleep, the respiration is shallow.
- They exhale for a fraction longer than they inhale, and when at rest, they allow a moment before repeating the cycle.
- Children breathe "into their navel."

Western society seems obsessed with being slim, or appearing so, and much effort is spent by people as they age by holding in the abdomen. This causes stress which affects the flexibility of the diaphram—the large muscles that span the area below the lungs and which separate the chest from the abdomen. This leads to shallower breathing, and less oxygenation into the lower and deeper aspects of the lung. Paradoxically, learning to breath abdominally tightens the abdominal muscles and flattens the stomach.

At the time of writing, a major debate is taking place concerning the use of breathing techniques in asthma and many other conditions. It has been thought for millennia that breathing techniques from yoga, Qi Gong, and other exercise/relaxation techniques are the most beneficial for asthmatics. In many cases this is true. Recently there has been some contention brought forward by Western awareness of a Russian technique. Konstantin P. Buteyko, a Russian medical scientist and practitioner, claims that the deep-breathing techniques are compromising the brain and body's understanding of its own carbon dioxide levels that control many biochemical pathways in the body, including those that maintain normal airflow through the lungs. At the time of writing I understand that *The Lancet*, a prestigious British medical journal, is considering publishing an international trial supporting the breathing techniques of Dr. Buteyko. The personal experience of some of my colleagues suggests that his is a technique worth learning if you are an asthmatic. This technique is not widely available yet, but search around.

RECOMMENDATIONS

- *Ensure adequate rest and sleep when the body can govern its own respiratory pattern.*
- *Concentrate through the day on breathing abdominally. Place the hands over an area below the navel and breathe such that you move the hands at least one inch forward.*
- *Spend time concentrating on opening the chest by stretching the top of the head upwards and pulling the shoulder back slightly.*
- *Avoid polluting the lungs with cigarettes, unnecessary perfumes, and noxious fumes. If you are a city dweller, ensure as many trips into the countryside as possible.*
- *Learn a breathing technique from a meditation teacher. Deep breathing is not necessarily good breathing, and a basic rule of thumb is to inhale for 3sec and passively (without forcing) exhale for 4sec. Allow 1sec before repeating the cycle. Practicing even this technique a few times a day will help to retrain the body.*
- *Any conditions such as asthma and bronchitis that interfere with breathing may benefit from the Buteyko method.*
- *Consider learning techniques of Qi Gong, yoga, and Tai Chi, or a martial art, which will automatically teach you better breathing techniques.*
- *Consider using low-oxygen therapy for any condition that affects breathing (see* ***Oxygen therapy****).*

ENDOCARDITIS

Endocarditis is inflammation of the inner lining of the heart, including the valves. It can be caused by viruses, bacteria and, in rare circumstances, autoimmune disease. Endocarditis most commonly follows infection from open wounds, such as teeth extraction or trauma.

It is characterized by cardiac symptoms such as irregular or rapid pulse, shortness of breath, general feeling of weakness, and pain. It is a serious condition that should not be treated without expert medical advice.

Endocarditis can lead to persistent damage of the heart valves, as is often the case after rheumatic fever in childhood. The orthodox world recommends antibiotic cover whenever any major dental work is performed and, in the case of rheumatic fever, long-term antibiotic cover with penicillin is recommended to protect against further heart damage. Any decision to avoid antibiotic cover, whether acute or long-term, should be made only after discussion with a medically qualified complementary practitioner (*see* **Dental operations**).

RECOMMENDATIONS

- *Any persisting symptoms in the chest should be reviewed by a physician.*
- *Complementary therapy should be administered by a medical practitioner or an alternative therapist only in conjunction with a cardiologist.*
- *Once the acute situation has settled, a complementary medical therapist may be consulted for long-term care and repair of damaged endocardial tissue.*
- *See* ***Atheroma****.*

THE LUNGS

Diseases and disorders of the lungs vary in type and severity, and specific conditions are discussed throughout this book in different age groups. The lungs, more so than most other organs, deserve a few words because they are exposed to the outside world more than any other internal organ.

The lungs are the body's quickest method of taking in and expelling products.

Theoretically, it may be possible to breathe through the skin (as an amphibian does) or even through the bowel, but the paper-thin qualities of the alveolar sacks within the lungs make this the fastest and most appropriate method. Excretion of the main waste product of metabolism—carbon dioxide—is performed through the lungs, and the balance of acid/alkali within the body is governed by the lungs and kidneys working in harmony.

Any damage to the lungs will thus prevent the fuel of life (oxygen) from getting in and the toxins from getting out.

I find it amazing that 5,000 years ago, the Eastern philosophies were drawing the same conclusions. All Eastern medical beliefs stem from an understanding that the lungs are the main organ of energy input, as well as being a major elimination center. The scientific knowledge of how the lungs and kidneys control the acid/base balance is reflected by the connection in Eastern philosophies that the lungs pull energy into the body, and the kidney energy is the store.

According to Eastern medicines, the lungs are the organ that represents grief, loss, and sorrow, which is perhaps why we sigh when saddened, and why a few deep breaths can restore a sense of well-being.

The formation of the lungs takes up to 25 years, and persisting infections or the self-assassinating habit of smoking are more damaging the younger

The Lungs

The insert shows the interface between the alveoli and the blood-capillary network, where oxygen is exchanged with carbon dioxide.

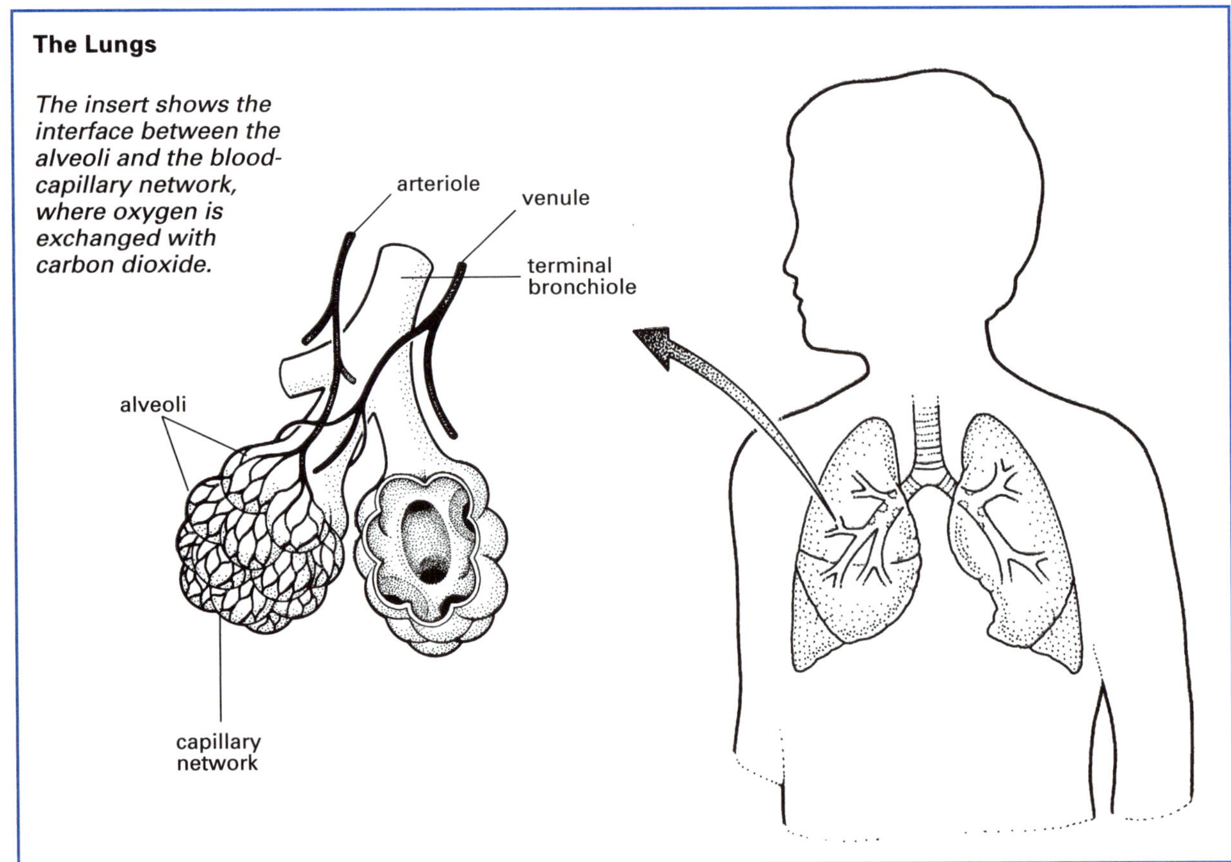

we start. Like a house with poor foundations, any damage to the lungs at an early age will reflect throughout our lives, not only in our breathing and tendency to recurrent infections, but in every aspect of our energy flow. Pollution, including passive smoking by children in the homes of smoking adults, will be taking its toll. Asthma is on the increase, and although no definite scientific evidence has been shown to incriminate air pollution, I am dubious of the trials done to date.

RECOMMENDATIONS

- *Above all other organs, pay the lungs respect from as early an age as possible.*
- *City dwellers should spend as much time as possible in the country, even if it is simply a day trip to the seaside.*
- *Everyone should be taught and should practice a breathing technique, and a yogic nasal-washing procedure should be employed.*
- *Any lung problem, such as an inflammation or infection, should be treated swiftly, especially in those under the age of 25 years.*
- *Carrots, swedes, yams or sweet potatoes and deep-green, leafy vegetables should be eaten regularly for the vitamin A content. Vitamin A has a profound effect on the lung membranes. Supplements should not be needed, but can be used if the diet is poor. Take 1mg of beta-carotene per foot of height as a basic maintenance dose, and treble this at times of lung infections.*
- *Any grief or sadness should be dealt with through counseling as swiftly as possible, because these emotions will drain the lung energy.*

PNEUMOTHORAX AND HEMOTHORAX

A pneumothorax is the presence of air in the space between the lungs and inner chest wall. A hemothorax is the presence of blood in the same space.

Air enters this space either through a puncture wound or through an injury that tears the lungs, allowing inhaled air to pass through the damage. Air is inhaled into the lungs by the negative pressure created by the diaphragm contracting downwards, thereby pulling air in through the mouth and nostrils. A small puncture or tear in the lungs may mean it takes some time for the pleural sac to fill, but as it does, the air causes the lung to collapse. A large hole may create an instant or spontaneous pneumothorax. A spontaneous pneumothorax can occur in apparently healthy individuals, due to asymptomatic lung disease.

The symptoms are of a gradual or sudden onset of shortness of breath, with or without pain on the affected side. Recognition is by failing to hear lung sounds on one side of the chest and a noticeable lack of movement in comparison to the other side. This is not easy to recognize. Confirmation is often required by a chest x-ray, especially if the pneumothorax is developing. A bilateral pneumothorax is, of course, extremely serious if not dealt with rapidly.

Pneumothorax and Hemothorax

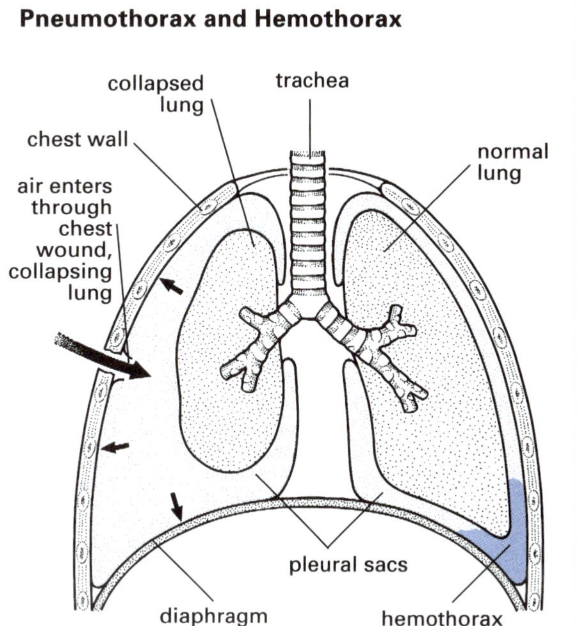

The pneumothorax, shown on the left, is caused by air entering the pleural cavity through a hole in the chest wall. The hemothorax, on the right, is due to blood entering the cavity from broken vessels.

A hemothorax develops in the same way but is caused by a damaged blood vessel pouring blood instead of air into the pleural space. Treatment is a minor surgical procedure, and should be performed at a local hospital.

If this is not available and the individual is moving into respiratory failure, follow the instructions below.

RECOMMENDATIONS

- *An onset—sudden or otherwise—of a shortness of breath must be reviewed by a doctor.*
- *Keep the patient as still as possible, and reassure them that the other lung will deal with breathing as long as they stay calm. This is true for most cases for a short period of time.*
- *If a doctor is not available or a bilateral pneumothorax is suspected, and the patient is in respiratory distress, losing consciousness, or has passed out, an emergency "chest drain" is recommended.*

Emergency insertion of a chest drain

- Do not start this procedure unless the following are available: a sharp blade or instrument; tube or piping at least one foot long; and a container and some fluid.
- With the patient on his/her back, find the lowest rib on the affected side in a line down from the front of the armpit. Count up two rib spaces.
- At this point, insert the blade through the skin, and keeping it on the top of the lower rib, penetrate until any resistance appears to give. The tip of the blade is now in the pleural space.
- Insert the tube. Place the other end in the fluid in the container.
- Secure the tubing and seal, with whatever means possible, any obvious injury that is allowing air to penetrate.

As the patient breathes, the lung will expand and air in the pleural cavity will be pushed out through the fluid. The fluid will act as a valve and prevent air from reentering, and after a few

Emergency Chest Drain

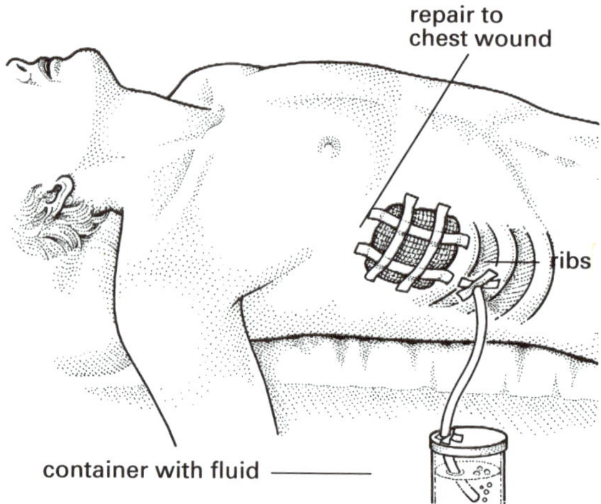

breaths the lung will expand again. If the patient's breathing has arrested, then please follow the instructions for artificial respiration (*see* **Artificial respiration**).

The Digestive System

BAD BREATH (HALITOSIS)

Most halitosis is caused by poor care of the gums, allowing small pockets of infection to breed bacteria that release noxious gases. The smell of fermenting food is combined with decaying flesh in bad cases.

Slow digestion may leave food in the warm acid of the stomach where bacterial action is unlikely, but a certain amount of fermentation does take place. The gas produced may rise up the esophagus, and rarely cause halitosis. More commonly, the lungs will eliminate noxious gases that have been absorbed into the bloodstream, as is apparent when garlic can be smelt on the breath many hours after ingesting the plant. The presence of bad bacteria or yeasts such as *Candida*, which produce gas as part of their metabolism, may reflect halitosis; enzymes may similarly be a reflection of halitosis.

RECOMMENDATIONS

- *Ensure regular visits to the dentist and ask their opinion of your breath. Friends and loved ones may be too embarrassed to mention a problem. Respectfully, ask the dentist to consider the possibility of small pockets of infection and have a triannual cleanse by a dental hygienist.*
- *Obtain an Arnica fluid extract, dilute it one teaspoonful to one cup of water and use as a mouthwash three times a day. Avoid antiseptic mouthwash because this kills good bugs as well as bad, thereby diminishing the competition for food and encouraging bad bacterial growth in the long run.*
- *Take zinc, 5mg per foot of height, daily before bedtime.*
- *If bad breath comes and goes, reflect on the foods eaten up to 24hr previously and avoid any potential culprits.*
- *Obtain a pancreatic enzyme and hydrochloric acid supplement, and a good-quality yogurt bacteria extract, and use at maximum dosage for three weeks.*
- *If none of the above techniques prove successful then consult a complementary medical practitioner to assess general health, because a toxic system or poorly functioning liver may be the underlying cause.*

COLITIS

Colitis literally refers to "itis" (inflammation) of the colon (large intestine). Colitis is not an uncommon feature at any age, and mild forms are created by eating a diet too high in acid or alkali, the ingestion of drugs, allergic foods, and infections caused by bacteria, fungi, and viruses.

Colitis usually presents as a mild pain and some diarrhea and is self-limiting, lasting less than 24 hours. Medical books and some therapists erroneously confuse colitis with ulcerative colitis, which is a much more chronic and persisting condition requiring medical intervention.

RECOMMENDATIONS

- *Any persistence of mild colitis should be seen by a healthcare professional.*
- *If there is a suggestion of ulcerative colitis, see* **Ulcerative colitis**.

CROHN'S DISEASE

This condition, first described by Dr. Crohn in the 1930s, is an inflammatory condition found anywhere from the mouth to the anus, but most commonly in the small intestine, usually before the colon (large intestine) begins. The condition is characterized by pain, diarrhea, bleeding, and weight loss. Flatulence, fever, and lethargy are all associated.

There are genetic predispositions, and the problem usually shows itself between the ages of 15 and 30 years. There is a higher incidence in the Jewish race, and slightly more in the female population.

The causes and treatments are the same as in ulcerative colitis (*see* **Ulcerative colitis**).

RECOMMENDATIONS

- *Review the food eaten over the 24hr previous to the pain or discomfort, and avoid these if there seems to be a correlation.*
- *Take a good form of Acidophilus with each meal for one week.*
- *Do not use colonic enemas in Crohn's disease unless the large intestine (colon) is particularly affected, and only under medical advice.*
- *More so than in ulcerative colitis, a link has been found between Crohn's disease and a bacterium called Mycobacterium paratuberculosis, found in cow's milk and sink water. These two drinks and any cow's milk products should be avoided.*
- *If alternative treatments used for ulcerative colitis (see* **Ulcerative colitis***) do not work, then the antibiotics rifabutin and clarithromycin have shown profound improvements. Complementary therapies to offset the side effects of these strong antibiotics are recommended.*

DIARRHEA

Diarrhea is the passage of loose stool with more frequency than an individual passes stool normally. Therefore, one bout of loose stool is not, necessarily, diarrhea. In most cases diarrhea is not a serious problem and is merely the body or bowel clearing out a toxin. Diarrhea is commonly associated with the ingestion of food that the body rejects or with mild viral or bacterial infections. More serious infection, such as *Salmonella*, will usually show up as diarrhea, abdominal pains, and associated vomiting, and it needs to be treated under supervision. Less than severe cases—those improving over 48 hours or those with no other associated symptoms except perhaps mild abdominal discomfort—can be treated with the recommendations below.

Persisting diarrhea (more than 72 hours) or diarrhea associated with severe symptoms such as pain, vomiting, fever, and debility should be reviewed by a doctor and/or a complementary medical specialist. A change in bowel habit that is persistent may reflect a condition as sinister as a cancer, and other problems such as ulcerative colitis (especially if there is blood and mucus associated with the stool), Crohn's disease, and malabsorption syndromes. It is best to have a definite diagnosis before any self-help or complementary medical treatment is prescribed.

RECOMMENDATIONS

- *Diarrhea that persists longer than 48hr or is nonresponsive to the recommendations below should be reviewed by a doctor.*
- *Once a definite diagnosis has been made, which may include stool sampling, a complementary medical view can be obtained.*
- *Ensure good rehydration because diarrhea can very swiftly lead to dehydration. Replenish any fluid loss, 16 ounces for 16 ounces, by judging the amount lost. Take water every halfhour, alternating with diluted fruit juice, soups, and slightly salted water, but avoid milk, caffeine, alcohol, and any drinks containing refined sugar.*
- *Go with instinct and appetite. If you are hungry, aim at eating foods that "mop up" poisons, such as wholegrain bread and pasta or rice. Avoid "binding" foods such as eggs.*
- *Take a good-quality Lactobacillus acidophilus or equivalent, which must be encapsulated to avoid the acid in the stomach. Live-yogurt culture is useful, but may not survive the acidity.*
- *Consider from your preferred homeopathic manual the remedies Arsenicum album, Carbo vegetabilis, Mercurius, Nux vomica and Sulphur. Take the selected remedy at potency 6 every hour for three doses and then every 2hr until better.*
- *Avoid any medication or herbal treatment that "stops" diarrhea. It is better to obtain complementary medical advice when dealing with persisting diarrhea than stopping the elimination.*
- *Two teaspoons of camomile tea with a teaspoonful of rosemary and a teaspoonful of sage per 16 ounces flavored with honey is a soothing and potentially antibacterial drink that can be used as part of your fluid replenishment.*

DYSENTERY

This condition of bloody diarrhea, abdominal pain, and associated debility is uncommon in areas of good sanitation and hygiene and is generally caused by a bacterium called *Shigella* or by an ameba. It is an unpleasant condition and, if left untreated, may be serious or even fatal. Serious complications occur because of dehydration and electrolyte imbalance caused by persistent loss of body fluids.

RECOMMENDATIONS

- *Any bleeding from any orifice that is persistent or recurrent needs to be reviewed by a doctor.*
- *Diagnosis is made by culture of the stool, and unless the situation is very serious, antibiotics should be refused until a diagnosis of the*

causative organism has been made. The use of antibiotics against ameba is at best pointless and at worst harmful to the body's natural flora, which are competing with the ameba.

- *Ensure constant rehydration with water and salt/sugar solutions.*
- *Dysentery should not be treated without expert help, but the homeopathic remedies Phosphorus, Mercurius, and Baptesia, all at potency 6 and taken every hour, can be considered until further medical or homeopathic advice can be gleaned.*
- *Two billion units of Lactobacillus acidophilus should be taken every 4hr along with live yogurt and polished rice. (This is one of the rare occasions where I encourage the use of a refined food over the harder-to-digest wholegrain foods.)*
- *Specific herbal preparations can be used against both bacterial and amebic infections in the bowel, but these should be taken under the guidance of a herbalist.*
- *See* **Diarrhea**.

FECES

Feces or stool are the correct and polite medical terms for the bowel's waste products. To the practitioner of medicine, the stool can be a mine of information, and some basic knowledge can be a great help in self-diagnosing problems at an early stage.

Blood in feces

The presence of blood in the stool is abnormal and such a finding without a known cause must be investigated by a medical practitioner. The most common cause of blood in the stool is from a hemorrhoid or pile (*see* **Hemorrhoids**). Less common causes, but sadly more sinister, include cancer, ulcerative colitis, Crohn's disease, and benign growths such as polyps. Blood may be mixed with the feces or separate on the outside, in the pan or on the toilet paper, and these factors, along with the color (bright or dark), give the practitioner a clue as to the probable cause. The more the blood is mixed with the feces, the higher up the gastrointestinal tract is the bleeding; the darker the blood, the longer it has been present.

Color of feces

The colour of feces is dependent upon the diet. One should get used to looking at one's stool so that any variation from the norm may be noted.

A very black or tarry stool is known as melena, and is caused by bleeding in the upper-gastrointestinal tract, such as the stomach. The tarry effect is caused by blood being digested and is an indication of potentially serious gastritis or ulcer.

A white or yellow stool is indicative of the presence of undigested fat and may represent liver or gallbladder disease.

A persistent change in color not related to dietetics should be mentioned to a complementary medical practitioner, who should examine you from a broad, constitutional angle to ensure that there is no other digestive or systemic problem.

Frequency

Everybody should have their own bowel evacuation frequency. In other words, we should all go a regular number of times per day. It is acceptable to open the bowels only once every other day provided that this is normal for you. Put simply, there is no correct number, although once a day, in the morning, is preferable.

A change in frequency that persists and is not associated with an infection or a change in diet should be reviewed by a physician, who may choose to perform investigations. A change of frequency or bowel habit is an early and therefore invaluable sign of bowel cancer.

Mucus with stool

Mucus is a clear, jelly-like compound that may be watery or gelatinous. The bowel produces mucus to protect itself from acids and alkalis, but by the time the feces reach the colon it should be mixed in and not noticeable as a separate entity. The presence of noticeable mucus is indicative of some inflammatory response and requires a medical opinion and investigations such as a colonoscopy or barium study.

Mucus may be associated with a temporary bowel infection but would therefore be associated with pain or diarrhea. If this passes then no further action need be taken, but a persistence of mucus production must be investigated.

Texture of feces

See **Diarrhea** and **Constipation.**

The texture of stool is dependent upon the diet and amount of dehydration. A dry, crumbly stool is indicative of a lack of water, whereas a loose stool may represent a diet lacking in fiber.

The presence of undigested food suggests that the diet or the digestive juices are not correct, and a review with a nutritionist is advisable.

A change in the texture of stool, as with its frequency, that persists beyond two weeks and is not associated with a change in diet or recent infection might be an indication of something sinister and should be reviewed by a doctor.

RECOMMENDATIONS

- *As disagreeable as it may be to some, it is advisable to have a knowledge of your regular feces, and occasional glances at them is highly recommended. Any persistent changes should be brought to the attention of your health adviser.*
- *Remember that there is no right or wrong color, texture, or frequency, and everyone is different. It is the changes that need to be registered.*

IRRITABLE-BOWEL SYNDROME (IBS)

Irritable-bowel syndrome is a diagnosis to be considered only when all other reasons for the symptoms have been ruled out.

The characteristics of IBS are persistent and recurrent abdominal pains, usually gripping, but sometimes with sharp or cutting episodes; bloating; irregular bowel habits with diarrhea or constipation; flatulence; and associated nausea, and lethargy. All or some of these symptoms may be present. Some authorities would also consider the passage of mucus a potential sign of irritable bowel, but excess mucus and therefore the passage of it is, in my mind, an association of inflammation or other pathology, and should not therefore be considered part of an irritable-bowel syndrome. There is no inflammation in IBS.

There is no doubt that stress is a principal factor in IBS. Stress chemical or catecholamines, the most common of which is adrenaline, cause blood to move from nonessential organs to the heart, lung, brain, and muscles in preparation for "flight or fight." The bowel loses some of its blood flow, and in extreme cases, a lack of oxygen will cause the bowel to contract and the individual will defecate. For those under a persistent level of stress, a small reduction in blood and therefore oxygen will lead to mild cramping as seen in IBS. Some consideration must be given to IBS being associated with a low-fiber diet because this prevents the bowel muscle from exercising, and therefore it cramps more easily. Some studies have shown that increasing the fiber content may actually make IBS worse, so the jury is out on that possible cause.

A weakened hydrochloric-acid production or pancreatic-enzyme flow may also result in IBS, by leaving undigested foods that may trigger some form of mild and transient inflammation.

More likely is a food allergy or intolerance, infestation of yeast, fungi, or parasites, and the inevitable disturbance of the normal bowel flora. The unwanted organisms cause the production of chemicals that trigger cramping, and poor-quality normal bowel flora leading to an overgrowth of these unwanted organisms.

RECOMMENDATIONS

- *Any persisting abdominal discomfort should be reviewed by a doctor and serious pathology ruled out.*

- *All IBS sufferers must consider counseling and a relaxation technique. Yoga, Qi Gong, Tai Chi, and meditation are all prerequisites to eliminating the underlying cause of the problem, even if a physical reason is found. For those who disbelieve this, please have one session of hypnotherapy to ensure that there is no underlying and subconscious anxiety.*
- *If IBS is diagnosed, a course of capryllic acid (an extract from coconut) and grapefruit seed should be taken in combination. The maximum recommended dose on the product you buy is a guideline for prescribing.*
- *A high dose of a purified Acidophilus (yogurt bacteria) should be taken at a maximum dose as recommended on the packaging.*
- *Avoid eating a lot of meat or dairy produce. Cut out greasy, spicy, and sweet foods. During attacks of discomfort, eat well-steamed vegetables, rice, potatoes, and other soft foods, such as bananas.*
- *If the diet is low in fiber, increase this with fruit and vegetables at each meal, but stop if the discomfort worsens.*
- *Keep a journal and note bad days. Note accurately the foods and drinks you take in and the levels of stress you are under. See if there is any pattern, which may be delayed by 48hr, and try avoiding the possible triggers.*
- *Try 500mg of bromelaine before meals three times a day.*
- *Bach flower remedies Cerato, Gorse, and Vervain can be taken.*
- *Consider a suitable blood test for food allergy, or see a nutritionist who uses a bioresonance technique to isolate intolerances. Applied kinesiology is an alternative choice.*
- *Consider a trial with a pancreatic extract or hydrochloric-acid supplement, again as recommended on the product. Simple, noninvasive hydrochloric acid and pancreatic enzyme-level tests are available.*
- *Shiatsu and basic body massage may be very relieving by addressing the excess of adrenaline in the system, and working on the lymphatic system, and acupuncture meridians. Techniques of abdominal massage associated with manual lymphatic drainage can be instantly relieving, and regular massage treatments can reduce the severity of symptoms.*
- *Herbal treatments such as those in Ayurvedic, Tibetan, and Chinese medicine are all helpful when prescribed by a specialist.*
- *Homeopathic remedies should be chosen on the basis of the symptoms. Pay attention to the homeopathic remedies Natrum carbonicum, Magnesia phosphorica, Carbo vegetabilis, Argentum nitricum, and Ignatia.*
- *Enteric-coated peppermint oil (the oil is enclosed in a capsule that bypasses the strong acids and alkalis of the stomach and small intestine, thus reaching the colon where the spasm most commonly occurs) can be used. This has a strong antispasmodic action and will act to relieve (although probably not cure) the problem.*
- *Two teaspoonsful of camomile, one teaspoonful of rosemary, and one of sage in an infusion taken every 2hr will also act as an excellent antispasmodic.*

STOMACHACHE

The lay use of "stomachache" is of course not medically accurate. The word stomach is used colloquially to cover the entire abdomen.

Abdominal pain needs to be treated depending upon the underlying cause. Most often, the reason is clear and associated with the ingestion of some bad food or a nutrient to which an individual is intolerant. Stomachache in association with other symptoms, such as vomiting or diarrhea, will help the diagnosis.

RECOMMENDATIONS

- *Try to find an underlying cause and refer to that section in this book.*
- *If no reason is apparent, any severe pain or one that lasts longer than a few hours should be referred to a doctor for a further diagnosis.*
- *The homeopathic remedy Aconite can be used at the onset of any condition. Aconite may not only take away the discomfort, but also bring forward other symptoms at a faster rate to help diagnose the underlying problem.*
- *There are two acupressure points that may be gently stimulated; they lie below the edge of the ribcage, the length of the individual's thumb away from the middle of the lower edge of the sternum (chestbone). They can be located easily because they will be slightly painful.*
- *Camomile (two teaspoonsful), rosemary and sage (one teaspoon of each) may be infused in 16 ounces of boiling water, and a cupful drunk every halfhour. This concoction has an earthy taste and may benefit from some honey.*
- *Drink plenty of water, at least 8 ounces per foot of height during the day.*
- *Ginger tea made by chopping up half an inch of fresh ginger root into a mug of hot water, can be drunk and may be soothing.*
- *In children and infants, see* **Colic** *and* **Abdominal migraine**.

ULCERATIVE COLITIS

Ulcerative colitis is an inflammatory condition of the large intestine (colon) that presents with sharp abdominal pains as well as cramps, diarrhea, flatulence often associated with bloating, weight loss, symptoms of malabsorption, and very often with blood in the stool or diarrhea. Small cuts (fissures) are often found around the anus.

This can be an inherited tendency, although the hypothesis of the cause varies: food allergy, infection, autoimmune attack (when the body's immune system attacks itself), poor digestive enzymes, low levels of hydrochloric acid, and psychological stress including anger, sadness and grief.

Diagnosis is made by barium meal or enema, x-rays and colonoscopy.

Ulcerative colitis and its small intestinal colleague, Crohn's disease, can spread through the bowel very rapidly. Do not underestimate these conditions. Full orthodox investigation and, in the first case, steroid treatment are often recommended to settle the acute situation before alternative therapies are employed. Do not stop orthodox treatment until resolution has occurred. Failure to control the inflammation can lead to surgical removal of the colon and/or other affected parts of the intestine in Crohn's disease.

RECOMMENDATIONS

- *Any persisting bowel problem or show of blood from the bowels should be investigated by your doctor with referral to a bowel specialist if required.*
- *Follow through with the orthodox treatment initially, and then contact your complementary medical specialist. Self-help is not recommended, but the following points should be brought up and discussed with your healthcare professional.*
- *During an acute episode, avoid raw or rough foods, preferably having soups and other easily digestible foods. Chew well.*
- *There is evidence that the following foods may be involved in inflammatory-bowel conditions and they should be avoided, particularly when an attack is bad: refined sugars (white sugar), alcohol, caffeine, cow's milk products and any foods known not to be tolerated or to which you are allergic.*
- *Have a food-allergy test.*

- *A placebo study showed conclusively that many sufferers responded favorably to stress management. Relaxation, meditation techniques, and gentle exercise are all mandatory in cases of colitis or Crohn's disease.*
- *Ensure supplementation with zinc, magnesium, and vitamin C. During acute phases of ulcerative colitis and Crohn's disease, malabsorption is common and therefore high levels of multimineral/vitamins, trace elements and protein supplements are all recommended. The amounts should be dictated by a nutritional or complementary therapist.*
- *Flaxseed, slippery elm, and camomile are all soothing.*
- *Deglycyrrhizinated licorice root and bioflavonoids such as quercetin may have healing properties.*
- *Colonic enemas in the hands of specialists can be relieving in acute phases and beneficial in long-term care (not necessarily suitable in Crohn's disease).*

THE UROGENITAL SYSTEM

CHLAMYDIA

Chlamydia is a tenacious bacterium often associated with vaginal irritation and discharge. It is blamed for inflammatory condition in the uterus and Fallopian tubes, and can lead to blockages and therefore to infertility, and should be treated swiftly and effectively.

It is important to treat an infected sexual partner. Since getting a partner to a clinic or doctor's surgery for a potentially uncomfortable, if not painful, swab is difficult, an early morning urine sample collected at home and sent or brought to a laboratory may suffice. It is also worth asking for *chlamydia* to be looked for on routine cervical smears, since infection may be asymptomatic (without symptoms).

RECOMMENDATIONS

- *See* **Vaginitis**.
- *Specifically make up a solution of zinc sulfate by adding 5ml of a 2 percent solution to 16 ounces of water, and use this as a douche. Do not ingest.*

CYSTITIS

Cystitis is inflammation of the urinary bladder. It is usually caused by a bacterial infection, but the possibility of viral or yeast infestation is often overlooked. The orthodox world is very swift to supply antibiotics, never considering the possibility that this might make things worse if a yeast is the problem. Also not considered is the possibility that the bladder is inflamed by toxins filtered from the bloodstream by the kidneys. Chemical compounds and specific food intolerances may also cause inflammation.

Infection is usually introduced via the urethra from outside the body. The urethra in the female is short and organisms do not have that far to travel. The male urethra is longer and has the added advantage of the protective effects of seminal fluid that collect in the prostate, which acts as a valve, before organisms can enter the bladder. Dehydration, being sedentary, and sexual intercourse all predispose to urinary-tract infections. Interestingly, women who do not achieve orgasm easily or frequently tend to have more cystitis, probably due to the fact that pelvic-blood congestion occurs without the orgasmic release. (An orgasm is accompanied by blood flow from the pelvis.) One-fifth of women will have a urinary-tract infection in any year, and most will succumb to this uncomfortable condition at some time in their life. It is rare in men.

The symptoms are generally of pain in the vagina, penis, or lower abdomen, and this may be an ache or a sharp discomfort. Urination usually makes the pain worse. There is generally increased frequency, and the urine may change color, becoming a deeper orange or even red if blood is present. A cloudy urine is not uncommon, and particles (pus or bladder-wall lining) may be visible.

Cystitis itself is not a pleasant condition, but not particularly harmful unless the infection is allowed to travel up the ureters to the kidneys. This occurs in approximately 20 percent of infections, and is characterized by an ache, or worse, in the small of the back. The kidney area may be tender to touch. Renal involvement or recurrence, which may occur because of a general decrease in immunity, obstruction to the outflow, or a bladder that has lost some of its sensitivity and therefore does not empty fully, needs to be treated by professionals. Pregnancy may apply pressure to the bladder outflow, as may a full rectum if the individual is constipated.

Asymptomatic bacteria

Four percent of females carry bacteria in the urine with no symptoms. This is generally a sign of a good immune system. Asymptomatic bacteria increases markedly in pregnancy, and anywhere up to 50 percent of women may, at some time during the pregnancy, carry bacteria without symptoms. As the individual is symptom-free, the discovery of this condition is usually done on routine testing and no treatment need be preferred.

RECOMMENDATIONS

- *At the first sign of cystitis, increase water intake to at least 16 ounces per foot of height in divided drinks throughout the day. In every second 16 ounces add two teaspoonfuls of baking soda. These drinks should be at room temperature.*
- *Pass urine as frequently as is required and especially after intercourse.*
- *Unsweetened cranberry juice or juniper extract (one teaspoonful per glass of water) should be added if the baking soda does not improve the problem within 12hr.*
- *Eat plenty of garlic with meals, or take the maximum recommended dose of any good garlic supplement.*
- *Refer to your preferred homeopathic manual and select a remedy based on the totality of symptoms. Pay special attention to Cantharis, Berberis, and Apis. Staphysagria should be considered if symptoms occur predominantly in association with intercourse.*
- *The herbs Uva ursi and Hydrastis can be considered by taking the maximum dose recommended of a proprietary preparation or after consultation with a complementary specialist.*
- *The following supplements should be added into a predominantly vegetable and fruit diet. All should be taken in divided doses with meals in the following amounts per foot of height: beta-carotene, 1mg; vitamin C, 1g; and zinc, 5mg (if this creates any nausea, take the full dose before bedtime).*
- *Assess the possibility of any toxin if the condition is recurrent. Pay attention to foods eaten, and if necessary, consider food-allergy testing. This is a must in any chronic or recurrent condition.*
- *Ensure good hygiene. Vaginal douching (see* **Vaginal douching***) should be used if the problem is recurrent. Use Sandalwood or Calendula soap for the outer aspects of the vagina, but only clean water for the vaginal vault. Do not use deodorants, and remember to wipe up towards the abdomen after urination and towards the back after defecating. Use only cotton underwear to encourage absorption.*
- *Any cystitis that persists for more than 24hr despite the above measures should be treated by a doctor or an experienced naturopath.*
- *Collect a midstream urine (MSU) sample by letting the first 2sec of urination flow into the pan, collect the urine until nearly completed, and then let the rest go into the pan.*
- *Try to avoid antibiotics, unless a culture and sensitivity test has been performed on the urine sample to ensure that the correct antibiotic is being used.*

- *Persistent or recurrent infections that are not amenable to complementary specialist treatment may require a urologist's opinion. Treatment may include dilating any constricted or blocked urethra, and in severe cases of cystitis (known as interstitial cystitis) may require partial or total removal of the bladder. This is an extremely rare occurrence and should be avoided.*

DYSPAREUNIA

Dyspareunia is the medical term for painful sexual intercourse. Occasionally found in males, it is most commonly associated with females, and diagnosis of the cause needs to be ascertained after consultation with a doctor, or in the case of females, a gynecologist.

Dyspareunia in men

This unusual situation is usually associated with mild inflammation or infection of the foreskin or penis (*see* **Ballanitis**). Urethral inflammation such as caused by gonorrhea or nonspecific urethritis may also be a cause.

More rarely there are congenital deformities in the opening of the urethra (hypospadias), although this does not often cause pain.

RECOMMENDATIONS

- *Establish a firm diagnosis by visiting a doctor or specialist.*
- *Once a diagnosis is made, please refer to the relevant section in this book before embarking on any orthodox treatment, which may often include the use of antibiotics.*

Dyspareunia in women

Pain on the initiation of sexual intercourse is usually due to inflammation of the vaginal opening or the vagina itself. *Candida* and other infections may be the cause, as may trauma from previous vigorous intercourse or masturbation. Self-examination may isolate redness or white, cheesy patches (*see* **Candidiasis**).

Dyspareunia associated with penetrative sex may be caused by inflammation of the cervix, uterus, Fallopian tubes, and ovaries. Occasionally, inflammation in the rectum or bowel may be incorrectly interpreted as dyspareunia. Infection, endometriosis and, very rarely, tumors may be associated, and correct diagnosis is essential via a general practitioner's or gynaecologist's examination, or other specialist and noninvasive techniques such as ultrasound. A vaginal examination is generally recommended.

It is worth going to your doctor armed with the knowledge of when, where, and how the pain is brought on. Different sexual positions may relieve or exacerbate the problem, and this information is helpful in forming a diagnosis.

The vaginal muscles may spasm involuntarily, creating a condition called vaginismus, which can cause discomfort and pain if penetrative intercourse is attempted.

RECOMMENDATIONS

- *Visit your general practitioner, gynecologist, or specialist for an early and sound diagnosis.*
- *Try to avoid the use of antibiotics until complementary methods have been reviewed.*
- *Review the relevant section in this book for specific treatments once a diagnosis has been made.*

EJACULATION PROBLEMS

The most common problem with ejaculation in young adults is that of premature ejaculation (achieving orgasm and ejaculation with minimal or no physical contact). Strictly speaking, this is not a problem of the urogenital tract, it is more to do with psychology. Other problems of ejaculation are due to the rare occasions when individuals may not produce semen or seminal fluid or if the sympathetic nervous system—part of the autonomic, uncontrolled nervous system—is damaged. This may occur around the penis or throughout the spinal column. Injury to the penis itself, or infections that have caused scarring in the tubes from the testes upwards, may all cause problems with ejaculation.

Premature ejaculation

If ejaculation is taking place too quickly, there is rarely a need to bring a doctor into the equation, but if ejaculation is absent, then medical opinion should be sought.

Understand and believe that this is a very common problem faced by most males at some time of their life. It is often associated with early sexual experiments, or erotic partners or situations, and time usually heals the problem.

RECOMMENDATIONS

- *If ejaculation is absent, please see your doctor for referral to a specialist.*
- *If ejaculation is too swift (premature ejaculation), try the following routine:*
  - *(a) Practice, either through masturbation or with your partner, intimacy without genital contact, and conclude the intimacy before an orgasm or ejaculation occurs. Overenthusiasm may occur too often, and it is important to put it down to experience and next time use even less stimulation until an acceptable level is reached that does not cause ejaculation.*
  - *(b) If ejaculation seems imminent, stop the activity and squeeze firmly just below the head of the penis.*
  - *(c) Slowly increase the sexual activity. An individual may find that although premature ejaculation occurs with initial contact, the "second round" will be prolonged and more controlled.*
  - *(d) Consult with a counselor (most of whom will have had training in such matters) if the problem does not resolve within a few weeks. The longer premature ejaculation carries on, the more ingrained a problem it becomes.*

EPIDIDYMAL CYSTS

These are caused by a block in the epididymis (*see* opposite), which has many tubes collecting seminal fluid from the testes. They are noticed as painless lumps behind the testes, which are usually firm but indentable masses. Epididymal cysts are benign, and rarely require treatment. They are generally caused by mild trauma, often unperceived.

RECOMMENDATIONS

- *Any lump in the scrotum must be examined by a doctor.*
- *If an epididymal cyst is diagnosed, it should be left alone unless large enough to cause physical inconvenience.*
- *The homeopathic remedies Apis and Graphites, potency 30, taken twice a day for two weeks have been seen to reduce testicular cysts.*
- *Surgical intervention should be considered only as a last resort, because operations in this area may cause scarring that can block the seminal duct and lead to infertility.*

EPIDIDYMITIS

The tube that leads from the testes to the urethra is known as the seminal duct. The part that lies behind the testes through which the seminal fluid (the nutritious liquid in which the sperm flourish) flows is known as the epididymis. Epididymitis is the inflammation of this coiled, lengthy tube.

Epididymitis, like testiculitis, is generally characterized by a sharp or dull pain, tenderness to the touch, and possibly swelling, and redness of the scrotal sack.

Inflammation may be caused by trauma, infection or, more rarely, an underlying tumor. It is because of this latter possibility that medical advice is essential, but chronic inflammation from infection or unrecognized damage from trauma also makes it preferable to obtain a medical opinion.

Epididymitis

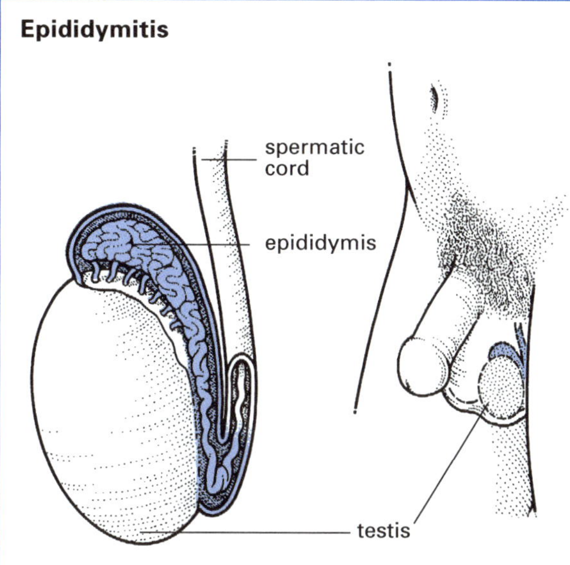

When the coiled tube of the epididymis becomes inflamed, this can be experienced as tenderness, pain, or swelling.

Epididymitis is a very specific diagnosis, and testicular pain may come from other causes such as torsion (twisting), which is a serious medical emergency (*see* **Testicular torsion**) or indeed may be referred pain from another part of the genital tract.

RECOMMENDATIONS

- *Any testicular pain or swelling should be examined by a doctor.*
- *Use the homeopathic remedy Arnica 6 every half an hour until a firm diagnosis has been made. Once a diagnosis has been made, consider the following homeopathic remedies, depending on the cause and symptoms: Belladonna, Pulsatilla, Hamamelis—all at potency 6 every 4hr.*
- *Apply a cold compress if it helps.*
- *If antibiotics are recommended and homeopathic treatment is not working, then consult your complementary medical practitioner without delay and consider using the antibiotics if an alternative treatment is not effective within 12hr. Incorrect or a lack of treatment may lead to sterility, especially if the cause is infection, which may spread to the testes.*

ERECTION FAILURE (IMPOTENCE)

Impotence is the medical term for an inability to raise or sustain an erection. It can be divided into physical and psychological causes. To understand the mechanism of this, it is necessary to illustrate how an erection works.

Under the stimulant of arousal, either physical touch or psychological eroticism, the nerves of the penis cause the arteries to expand and the veins to constrict. This allows more blood to fill the corpus cavernosa, which, like a fluid-filled tire, will harden and erect the penis. Any interference with these mechanisms will lead to impotence. This reaction is caused by the autonomic (uncontrolled) nervous system.

Physical causes

- Trauma to the corpus cavernosa, arteries, or nerves.
- Atheroma clogging the arteries.
- Disease (or trauma) of the central nervous system.
- Toxic effects.
- Certain drugs, including alcohol, amphetamines and cocaine, are a common cause of temporary impotence.
- Several orthodox drugs, including those used for cardiac and blood-pressure problems, can cause temporary impotence.
- Postoperative trauma following prostate or bladder surgery can damage the nerves controlling erection.

Psychological causes

Over 90 percent of erection failure that present to a holistic counselor or doctor are caused by psychological matters.

Evolution has made it very clear that the chemicals and hormones of stress must outweigh the effects of sex hormones. If we were busily procreating when a saber-toothed tiger came into view, then we would need to be more fearful than excited, otherwise we would not, by preference, run away. Those of our prehistoric ancestors whose testosterone levels outweighed their adrenaline flow would stay to finish the job and were presumably killed. Nowadays, we are rarely confronted by wild animals, but the fear chemicals induced by bank managers, employment situations, and domestic difficulties are just the same, and override the hormones and neurological impulses involved with intercourse.

One most frequent cause is fatigue. Chemicals produced in response to tiredness inhibit erections. Anxiety, stress, and phobias all produce large amounts of catecholamines, which directly affect the nervous system and specifically cause dilation in the penile veins, thereby preventing erections. The causes may be superficial, such as anxiety about performance, or they may be more deeply buried. Either way, a counseling session will help to illustrate the need of psychotherapeutic work.

Tiredness, stress, anxiety, fear, and guilt are all, therefore, responsible for erection failure.

RECOMMENDATIONS

- *Establish or rule out any physical cause by having a full examination from a doctor or specialist if in doubt.*
- *Assess and remove bad habits and stress-creating situations wherever possible.*
- *Employ meditation and relaxation techniques through the practice of yoga, Qi Gong, and meditation.*
- *Exercise. This reduces the amount of adrenaline in the system, and enhances endorphins and encephalins, which are sexual stimulants and, paradoxically, stop the tiredness associated with stress.*
- *If the above measures are not easy to comply with, then techniques of counseling, such as neurolinguistic programming, are most often beneficial.*
- *Consider the use of homeopathic remedies: Lycopodium if anticipating problems; Conium maculatum if erection occurs but does not last; and Agnus castus if the erection is not firm enough. These remedies should be taken at potency 30 every night for two weeks. Further consultation with a homeopathic prescriber is well recommended, as there are many remedies that are documented as being useful with erection problems.*
- *Vitamins E and K, the botanical medicines Gingko biloba and Ginseng, and a variety of Chinese, Tibetan, and Ayurvedic herbs can be considered as adjuncts to the necessary treatment to deal with the underlying cause, but they should be prescribed by a complementary medical practitioner if taken above the doses recommended on the packaging that are necessary to elicit a response.*
- *Testosterone may be recommended by specialists if testosterone levels are found to be low. There are many side effects associated with this drug, and I would recommend a visit to an Ayurvedic, Chinese, or Tibetan physician, who will prescribe herbal medicines appropriate to the case. Use testosterone as a last resort.*
- *A new drug, Viagra, is available and has proven through initial studies to enhance erection. As with all new drugs, I recommend waiting for at least two years of its being available on the market, since studies are often flawed and problems only arise after any drug has been used for some time.*
- *Orthodox specialists can teach an individual to inject a drug known as prostaglandin E1 into the base of the penis. This is only used in cases where other treatments have failed, since penile pain and prolonged erection are just a couple of the more common side effects.*

GENITAL WARTS

Genital warts are caused by a group of viruses known as the human papillomavirus (HPV). There are over thirty types of HPV, of which two may be responsible for creating a cancerous condition in the cervix. Most are not serious from a medical point of view, but are highly infectious, disfiguring, and embarrassing.

They are recognized as small, wart-like projections or raised areas found anywhere on the penis or within the vagina, most commonly on the moist surfaces.

As with most infections, the problem may not lie within the area infected but within the immune system as a whole. General health must be encouraged.

Warts very rarely undergo malignant change, but if one is bleeding, itching, growing rapidly, or changing color, then an urgent dermatological opinion is recommended.

RECOMMENDATIONS

- *The best treatment is avoidance, and self-inspection should be encouraged to reduce the risk of spread.*
- *Intercourse with a condom is extremely effective protection.*
- *Specific proprietary topical applications can be used with safety, but pay attention to the warning not to place the compound on the surrounding healthy skin. Also, note that compounds used for warts on other parts of the body are not suitable for genital warts.*
- *See* **Warts and verrucas**.
- *Warts, like any viral infection, are dependent on a depressed immune system. Follow a detoxification program for a few days, and consider a consultation with a nutritionist to discuss diet and lifestyle.*
- *Homeopathic remedies may be considered, depending on the type and place, but particular attention should be paid to Nitric acid and Thuja.*
- *Surgical intervention may be required if warts are disfiguring or spreading. Diathermy (burning), liquid-nitrogen application (freezing) and, very rarely, surgical excision may be required.*
- *Viral warts are not an indication of poor hygiene or promiscuity. They may lie dormant from a sexual contact many years before. Be open about the problem and discuss the matter freely. Remember the safety of using a condom.*

GONORRHEA

This is a sexually transmitted bacterial infection that is characterized by a greenish, creamy discharge, usually from the urethra, but also from the vaginal vault in women. Similar discharge may appear in the pharynx, tonsils, or anus as a consequence of oral or anal intercourse. Most often, the discharge is associated with a sharp, cutting pain and inflammation, although occasionally the discharge may be painless. It is this latter asymptomatic state that leads to inadvertent spread of this highly contagious condition.

Orthodox treatment ranges from a single large dose of a penicillin to longer courses of newer antibiotic generations—past injudicious use of antibiotics thus causing resistant and tougher strains of the gonococcal bacterium.

C. S. Hahnemann, the founder of homeopathy, paid special attention to gonorrhea, which, until the 1940s (and even today if left untreated), was a debilitating, if not fatal, condition. Gonorrhea can be responsible for urethral strictures, leading to potential kidney damage, kidney infection, sterility, local abscesses, and septicemia, leading to infected organs including the brain. Hahnemann felt that a gonorrheal infection, like syphilis, may persist and be passed through generations. His fears may have less-scientific foundation today, although congenital syphilis has certainly been proven to exist and have devastating effects. Gonorrhea, from an orthodox point of view, is not thought of in the same way, although arguments may be made on a hypothetical basis. Traditional homeopaths will invariably ask about sexually-transmitted diseases, and ideally would like to know whether these were contracted by parents and grandparents. Today, were he alive, Hahnemann may well have grouped together other venereal diseases such as *Trichomonas* or *Chlamydia* and registered these as having a deeper or greater significance to overall health than medicine does at the moment. The debate continues.

RECOMMENDATIONS

- *Any discharge, discomfort, or pain in the genitals should be seen by a doctor immediately.*
- *Avoid antibiotic use until a clear diagnosis has been confirmed by a reputable medical laboratory. Swabs need to be taken. In severe cases, an antibiotic may be started, provided that a sample is taken before.*
- *Herbal treatments are effective and, theoretically, homeopathic therapy may solve the problem, but my recommendation is to use antibiotics and a suitable, anti-antibiotic, naturopathic therapy.*
- *Ensure that all sexual contacts are aware of the diagnosis, and use condoms for intercourse until all symptoms and signs of infection have been absent for at least one week.*
- *The homeopathic remedies Mercurius and Cantharis, potency 6, may be considered if infection is a likely cause. Take one dose every 3hr. (See* **Sexually-transmitted disease***.)*

HEMATOSPERMIA—BLOOD IN SEMINAL FLUID

Blood in any body fluid or discharge is pathological, and needs to be watched or investigated. The appearance of blood in the ejaculate is indicative of a bleed anywhere from the tip of the penis to the testes.

Trauma, infection, or tumor are the most common causes.

RECOMMENDATIONS

- *Any blood in the ejaculate should be investigated under the care of a physician or urogenital specialist, unless an obvious cause such as trauma is acknowledged. Even then, if the bleeding persists beyond 24hr or is associated with pain, have the problem checked out.*
- *Note when the blood appears: blood before seminal fluid suggests a problem in the urethra; blood at the end of the ejaculate is likely to be from the testes. Discoloration of the semen or a mix of blood and seminal fluid may indicate a prostate problem.*

HERPES SIMPLEX

Herpes is a group of about 70 viruses, the most common of which are herpes simplex, varicella zoster (responsible for chickenpox and shingles), and the Epstein-Barr virus (EBV).

Each of these is discussed in its own section, but in principle the treatments are as in this section.

Herpes genitalis (HSV-2), occurs most commonly around the entrance to the vagina, the vaginal vault, the cervix, and occasionally up into the uterus. In men it is found on or around the head of the penis and foreskin. Herpes genitalis can, however, occur anywhere in the genital area, and may even spread to the buttocks, lower back, and upper thighs.

The symptoms range from small, painless fluid-filled blisters, through mild stinging with associated redness, to excruciating pain, burning, and marked inflammation. There may be associated fever and inflamed lymph nodes, and most commonly a generalized malaise or lethargy that may be caused by the infection or be part of the depressed immune system that allows the virus to take a hold.

Up to 40 percent of the population are liable to come into contact with herpes genitalis or labialis (HSV-1) (the type of herpes found around the mouth and called a cold sore). Eighty-five percent of people who have an initial attack will deal with the problem and it will not recur. The other 15 percent may have recurrent attacks, and the top 2 percent may have very severe and frequent symptoms. Bearing in mind that most of us will contract chickenpox in our youth, we all have had experience of fighting herpes and, in principle, a healthy body should not end up with recurrent herpetic attacks.

Transmission is by contact with the fluid associated with the viral lesions, and is generally introduced to the next host through small cuts or abrasions (which are common and unnoticed during intercourse), and also depends on the new host having a depressed immune system at that time. By "depression" I am referring to being overworked, undernourished, or with a mild infection such as a cold. Those who have recurrent attacks harbor the HSV in a nerve center known as the ganglia. Herpes tends to lie dormant until an individual runs down with a cold, stress, periods, or allergic reactions to certain foods. Also, sunburn, overexercising, and sexual activity can trigger the recurrence. The virus multiplies, travels back down the nerve—often to the original site of infection—and spreads through the dendrites or branches at the end of the nerve, causing a slightly larger area to be affected.

Combating herpes is carried out on two fronts. The first is to enhance the individual's own defense system, and the second is to weaken the defense that the virus puts up by surrounding itself with an impregnable protein coat that the immune system cannot penetrate. The requirements to enhance the individual's immune system are rather dependent on the person. The recommendations below are specific for inhibiting the reproduction of the herpes virus and also weakening its defense.

RECOMMENDATIONS

- *Increasing lysine and reducing argenine (both amino acids) in the diet is required. Foods to be discouraged through attacks are nuts, chocolate, seeds, and pulses, all wholegrains, pork, sunflower oil, and crustaceans such as crabs and shrimp. Foods to be encouraged through acute attacks are fish (especially halibut), chicken, and turkey, and yeast-containing foods such as raised white bread, potatoes, milk, and lamb.*
- *Recognize the cause of the immune suppression and try to avoid the situation (allergic foods, stress, and lack of sleep).*
- *Through an acute attack, supplement each meal with the following: lysine 1g, vitamin C 2g, bioflavonoids (500mg), zinc (10mg, but if you feel any nausea, then avoid this and take 30mg before you go to sleep), and a thymus extract as directed on the packaging.*
- *In the case of recurrent attacks, the supplements mentioned above for acute attacks should be taken daily as recommended, but only with one meal per day.*
- *The lesion can be treated with the following applications: apply moist coffee grounds four times a day; zinc (0.05 percent) and vitamin E cream (0.1 percent) may be used separately or combined four times a day; or vitamin E can be applied for 15min three times a day.*
- *For lesions that are resistant to the above recommendations, insomuch as attacks continue to be frequent and just as severe, discuss the use of licorice or lithium succinate (8-percent solution) with your complementary medical practitioners. Melissa officinalis (1-percent solution) can be applied four times daily.*
- *Avoid the preparatory applications of the antiviral agent acyclovir because this only deals with the superficial infection, and also has been shown to encourage the development of resistant strains of the virus that are much more difficult to deal with and can lead to much more serious complications, especially in the immunocompromised.*
- *The homeopathic remedies Kali muriaticum, Rhus toxicodendron, Urtica urens, and the nosode Herpes simplex can all be taken every hour for three doses in an acute attack, dropping to every 2hr. In chronic conditions, a constitutional remedy is best selected by a homeopath.*

It is unusual for treatment to be instantly effective, and recovering is often shown by less-frequent attacks of a shorter duration. Sometimes, the more virulent viruses are not destroyed, and a mild attack once or twice a year is the best that we can hope for—thus the concept that herpes, like diamonds, is forever. This is only the case in a very small percentage.

MENSTRUATION AND MENSTRUAL PROBLEMS

See **Uterus** and **Uterine problems.**

Menstruation occurs in women on a cyclical basis. It is the clearing out of the inner lining of the uterus following a cycle, where fertilization of an egg and pregnancy did not occur. The menstrual bleed, commonly known as a period, lasts from one to seven days, the average being a heavier flow of menstrual discharge on days 1–3 with a reduction in the amount thereafter.

The diagram below show the growth of the inner lining of the uterus, known as the endometrium, in relation to the hormones that control the cycle. The Eastern philosophies believe in a central energy that the Chinese call the vessel of conception (*see* **The vessel of conception**). The energy connection between the pituitary gland, thyroid gland, pancreas, and uterus has been well known for over 5,000 years, and an imbalance in this energy can cause problems in any of these organs, and is very often the underlying reason for irregularity in the menstrual cycle. Any stimulants that affect thyroid production, deficiencies, excess refined sugars, or nerve-affecting drugs may alter the cycle.

Amenorrhea

Amenorrhea is the absence of periods. This can be primary—periods never started—or secondary—usually associated with hormone imbalances caused by stress, anorexia/bulimia, and other causes of sudden weight loss. Amenorrhea may also occur following childbirth, coming off contraception such as the coil or the pill, and after diseases affecting other glandular (hormone-

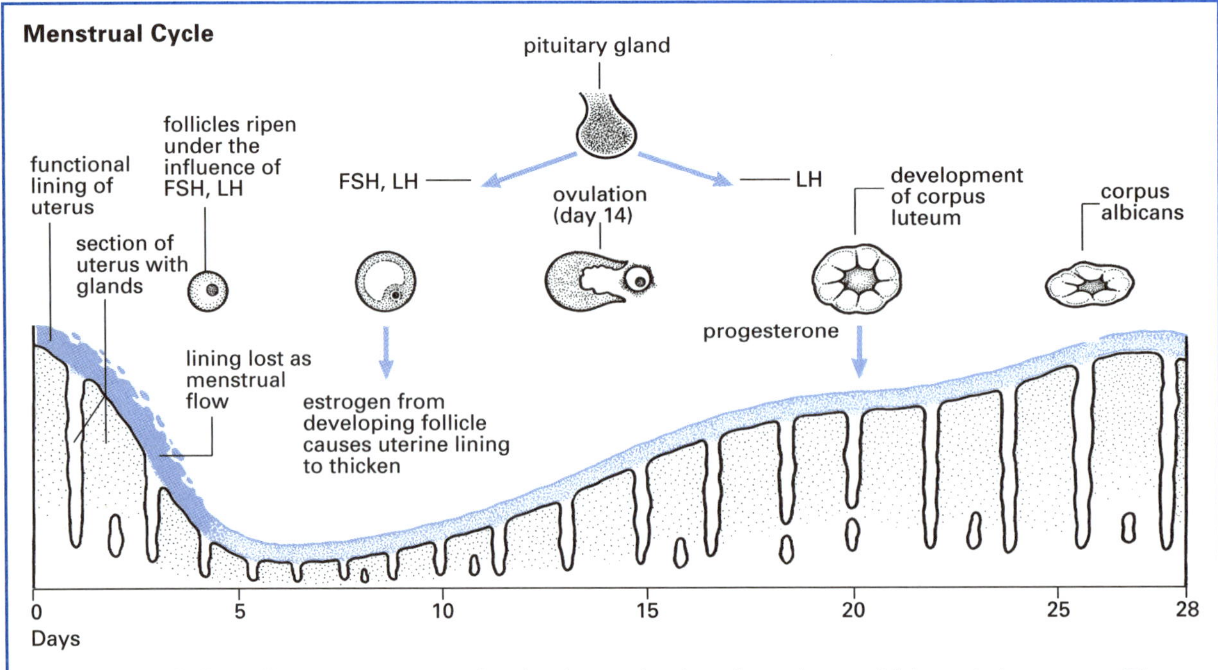

The lower half of the diagram represents the clearing out and regrowth of the uterine lining during the course of the female cycle. Above this, we see the development of a follicle in the ovary, under influence from hormones secreted by the pituitary gland, to the point at which ovulation occurs. The empty follicle then develops into a corpus luteum which secretes the hormone progesterone, causing the uterine lining to thicken. The corpus luteum then degenerates to become a corpus albicans.

producing) organs, or severe illness leading to malnutrition.

The inner lining of the uterus builds up prior to ovulation, and if pregnancy is not an occurrence then this lining is shed. A correct production of estrogen and progesterone, as described in chapters 2 and 3, is required for a normal cycle to occur.

The Eastern medical philosophies include an energy line, the vessel of conception, that travels from the perineum (the area between the vagina and anus) up through the uterus, pancreas, thyroid, and pituitary gland. If deficient, this axis can cause "misbehavior" in any of these organs, including amenorrhea. (*See* **Menstruation and menstrual problems**.)

RECOMMENDATIONS

- *Remember that the most-common cause of amenorrhea is pregnancy. Obtain a pregnancy kit if you have had intercourse, protected or unprotected, up to one month prior to missing a period.*
- *Review any weight loss or appetite changes. If any are present, then speak to a complementary medical practitioner.*
- *If no obvious reason is apparent from those mentioned above, consult a medical practitioner and your complementary therapist when you have missed three periods. Premature menopause and tumors of the pituitary gland are easy to diagnose, and potentially treatable if caught early.*
- *Increase the protein in the diet. Ensure that iron, vitamin B_{12}, and folic-acid levels are normal (see* **Anemia***).*
- *Homeopathic remedies can be most beneficial: Aconite and Arnica if the periods are associated with a shock; Natrum muriaticum or Ignatia if associated with grief or fear; and Sepia if emotionally indifferent or tearful. Consider Ferrum metallicum, Graphites, and Pulsatilla when reviewing a good homeopathic book.*
- *Yoga, Shiatsu, and acupuncture can all remove the energy blocks that can lead to amenorrhea, and they should be considered.*
- *Stress is a principal cause of amenorrhea, and if this is abundant, or there is any evidence of anorexia or obsessive dieting, consider discussing matters with a counselor.*
- *See* **Delayed puberty** *for discussion of primary amenorrhea.*

Delayed, late or infrequent periods

The first two years of menstruation, which can start at any age from 11 years, may be irregular, and a delayed or infrequent period should only be considered as abnormal if this is a new pattern differing from previously regular periods. A delayed or late period may have many causes, and pregnancy must first be ruled out. The hormones that control the cycle are produced by the pituitary gland, which is a small, walnut-sized piece of tissue that sits in the middle of the brain. This gland is very susceptible to changes in the neurotransmitters or brain chemicals, and therefore the cycle can easily be thrown by emotional disturbances. Problems with boyfriends, parents, or impending exams may all trigger a suppression of the pituitary gland's production of follicle-stimulating hormone and luteinizing hormone, both of which are necessary for ovulation to take place and therefore for the period.

Once ovulation has taken place, a period generally follows 14 days later, and most delays or long cycles are caused by an increase in the first part of the cycle known as the proliferative or follicular phase (*see* diagram opposite). The second part of the cycle is known as the secretory or luteal phase, and this is followed (if pregnancy is not an occurrence) by the menstrual phase.

Delayed or late periods may result from overexercising or undereating. There is no firm scientific foundation for this occurrence, but I suspect that it is to do with chemical suppression by exercise-induced hormones such as cortisol or endorphins. These are released when muscles are exercised or because of a lack of nutrients necessary to build up the inner lining of the uterus through the proliferative phase. Whatever the biochemical reason, energy is taken from, or not provided to, the uterus.

Certain metabolic conditions, such as hypothyroidism and polycystic ovaries, may be the cause of delayed or absent periods, and this may need to be checked out.

RECOMMENDATIONS

- *One or two late or delayed periods are generally not a problem. A missed period may represent a pregnancy, and this needs to be tested for.*
- *Ensure that the diet is regular and nutritious. Any alteration in the cycle in association with dieting suggests a deficiency and an incorrect dietetic plan. Remove excess sugars from the diet.*
- *Review psychological stresses and discuss the matter with a counselor if no obvious cause is apparent.*
- *Avoid medication unless prescribed by a complementary medical practitioner experienced in this matter, because alteration of a body's normal cycle, delayed or otherwise, may be injurious.*
- *Persistently late periods that are not altered after discussions with a nutritionist, counselor or complementary practitioner should be viewed by a gynecologist to rule out any underlying metabolic disorder.*
- *Avoid the use of the oral contraceptive pill as a technique of controlling the cycle, except as a last resort.*
- *Consult with a homeopath who will consider the symptoms in light of the individual as a whole, and work from a constitutional standpoint.*
- *Specific deficiencies in vitamins and trace elements may also cause a problem in the formation of the endometrium. Take a protein supplement, Vitamin B_6, Evening Primrose Oil, and zinc at twice the recommended dose for one month.*

Dysmenorrhea (painful periods)

Dysmenorrhea is the medical term for painful menstruation. The start of menstruation, the menarche, occurs between the ages of 11 and 16 in females. There is often a hereditary pattern, and a girl may start her periods at the same age as her mother and grandmother did. A textbook menstrual cycle is 28 days long, with the bleed lasting 2–7 days (on average around 5 days). The first half of the cycle is under the control of estrogens, which prepare the ovary to release an egg. The second part of the cycle still has some estrogen effect, but is predominantly controlled by progesterone, which causes the buildup of the inner lining of the uterus in preparation for the implantation of a fertilized egg.

In the first part of the cycle the amount of estrogen is controlled by the pituitary gland, which sits in the middle of the brain. In the second half of the cycle, the progesterone and estrogen production is produced by the corpus luteum, which is the "shell" of the egg or ovum that has been released from the ovary.

If an egg or ovum is not fertilized, then the corpus luteum dies off, and the progesterone and estrogen levels diminish. These lower levels are a trigger to the pituitary gland to start the cycle all over again, but before it does, the unused, inner lining of the uterus needs to be shed. This is done through menstruation (or a period). The process of removing this inner lining or endometrium is aided by mild contractions of the uterus. These contractions are painful, and the amount of pain depends on:

- the force of the contraction
- the amount of inner-uterine lining
- the pain perception of the individual
- from an Eastern perspective, the amount of energy flowing through and supplying the uterus and female hormonal system. All Eastern philosophies believe in a midline energy flow which, interestingly, corresponds to the hormonal system. The top of the energy line is through or around the pituitary gland, which provides hormonal control for the thyroid and

uterus in females. This energy line, called the vessel of conception (see **The vessel of conception**) in Chinese medicine, actually travels down through the thyroid and the pancreas on its way to the uterus. The pancreas is not directly under the control of the pituitary gland, but insulin levels from the pancreas are related to sugar levels, which in turn are controlled to a great extent by the levels of adrenaline, growth hormone, thyroxine, and natural body steroids, all of which are controlled by the pituitary gland.

It needs to be understood, therefore, that dysmenorrhea is not only to do with the uterus. It is important to establish an underlying cause, which may fall into any of the above categories.

RECOMMENDATIONS

- *Discuss the matter with your gynecologist or doctor and rule out any of the rare, underlying conditions that may cause painful periods by having ultrasound, blood tests for hormonal imbalances, and a full clinical checkup, including a cervical smear and internal examination.*
- *Before commencing any orthodox treatment, discuss the matter with a complementary medical practitioner.*
- *Strength of contraction is dependent upon the body's levels of calcium, magnesium, sodium, and potassium. It is also extremely important to be well hydrated, and many cases of dysmenorrhea are alleviated by taking a mineral supplement and ensuring an intake of 64–96 ounces of water per day.*
- *The amount of endometrium (inner lining of the uterus) is associated with the uterine response to progesterone. Excess progesterone may be counteracted by the natural phyto-estrogens found in soya milk and its products, celery, fennel, rhubarb, and hops. An increase in these foods, leading up to and during a period, may be relieving. Conversely, stimulating the body's own progesterone production with the use of herbs such as Agnus castus or homeopathic derivatives at potency 200, or using natural progesterone through transcutaneous Mexican-yam extracts may be of benefit. The amounts of these supplements and remedies should be decided in consultation with a complementary medical practitioner who has knowledge in these areas.*
- *The perception of pain is exacerbated by stress. Good relaxation techniques and an evaluation of life's problems may be curative. Neurolinguistic programming and hypnotherapy, meditation, yoga, and Qi Gong are all successful in helping to deal with painful periods.*
- *Acupuncture, chiropractic, and osteopathy are all useful techniques, and probably work on the strengthening of the underlying energy weaknesses or tensions that build up in the lower pelvis.*
- *The following supplements may be useful in divided doses: Evening Primrose Oil (1g per foot of height) and Vitamin B_6 (10mg per foot of height) during the day, and zinc (5mg per foot of height) at night.*
- *Homeopathic remedies must be chosen on the type of pain, duration, and associated factors, such as amount of bleeding and the presence of clots. Remedies that could be reviewed include: Magnesia phosphorica, Arnica, Belladonna, Calcarea carbonica, and Cinchona officinalis. All should be taken at potency 6 every hour.*
- *Chinese/Tibetan herbal medicine has much documented evidence of efficacy, and a popular compound is Dong Quai (angelica), which, like most herbs, is best prescribed by a specialist.*
- *If alternative techniques fail, or the underlying cause is not amenable to change, then the use of the oral-contraceptive pill can be considered but, as always with any drug, weigh the potential risks with the benefits.*

- *Provided that there are no contraindications, do not hesitate to use ordinary painkillers such as Tylenol or Tylenol with Codeine. If this is not working well, mefanamic acid is prescribable by your doctor and is a popular pain reliever. Taken over the more painful couple of days, you are unlikely to do yourself any harm while you find the underlying cause.*

Early periods (short cycle)

A short cycle may be considered as the arrival of an early period, but is not a problem if this is the general pattern. A cycle of 20 days is not usually a disease process unless it is a departure from a longer cyclical pattern.

As for delayed periods, psychological matters can have a profound effect by the chemical influence of neurotransmitters from the pituitary gland.

An early menstrual phase is usually due to a shortened proliferative phase, and is therefore commonly associated with a much lighter and shorter period.

RECOMMENDATIONS

- *A short cycle is only a problem if it is a variation from a previously longer pattern.*
- *Psychological stresses and anxieties play a major role, and a consultation with a counselor may start the process of resurrecting the cycle.*
- *Consultation with a complementary medical practitioner, preferably a homeopath, will isolate potential homeopathic treatments.*
- *Early and therefore more frequent periods may lead to anemia secondary to blood loss and any tiredness, malaise, or mild depression may be associated with anemia (see* **Anemia***).*

Heavy periods—*see* Menorrhagia

Menorrhagia (heavy periods)

Menorrhagia is the medical term for an excessive menstrual flow. Many of the principles discussed in the section on dysmenorrhea (*see* **Dysmenorrhea**) are relevant to menorrhagia.

The amount of endometrial tissue discharged is proportionate to the amount that is laid down through the second part of the cycle. This is dependent upon the effects of progesterone on the endometrial growth; however this is not the only influence.

The uterus provides the female with another avenue to eliminate toxins from the body. Each month, new tissue is laid down and provided with a rich blood supply. Toxins in the bloodstream will, therefore, automatically find themselves in abundance in this endometrial tissue. Toxins such as lead from car exhaust fumes are laid down and shed on a cyclical basis. Whether the body is actually intent on doing this is uncertain, and we may argue that the body would protect against allowing toxins to settle in a part of the body where reproduction takes place, but the body is a phenomenally complex system. Assuming that toxins settle there with or without the body's blessing, menorrhagia may be a toxic-excretion technique.

As with dysmenorrhea, in Ayurvedic and yogic medicine, a buildup of vital force or energy in the lower part of the vessel of conception (*see*

The Chakras

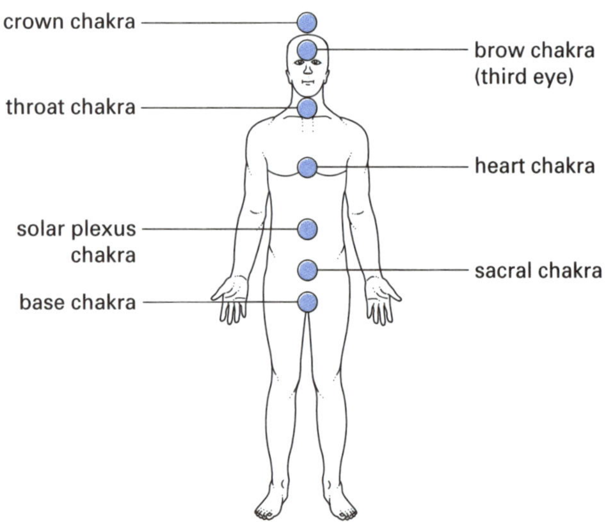

Dysmenorrhea) may be responsible for the overgrowth of endometrial tissue.

Energy must flow smoothly between all the chakras, and an excess in any particular point will cause deficiency above or below. Therefore a block in the abdominal or solar plexus chakra may lead to an excess in the lower chakras, which in turn can cause the overgrowth found in menorrhagia.

Certain deficiencies such as vitamin A, iron, or hypothyroidism may all cause menorrhagia.

Menhorrhagia is rarely a symptom of a more-serious condition. Fibroids, endometrial polyps, and salpingitis (*see* **Salpingitis**) may present initially as menorrhagia, as may endometrial cancer.

RECOMMENDATIONS

- *A full gynecological examination, including ultrasound and hormonal blood tests, is a starting point. Having ruled out a serious condition, consider complementary techniques before orthodox ones.*
- *Examine lifestyle and habits, and eliminate any obvious toxins. Food-intolerance testing through blood tests, Vega, bioresonance, or applied-kinesiology techniques are all recommended.*
- *Furthermore do not underestimate the toxic effects of caffeine, alcohol, tobacco, and other recreational drugs.*
- *Assess the potential for stress, because the pituitary gland, which indirectly controls the levels of progesterone, is centered towards the middle of the brain, and is very much under the influence of the psyche. Techniques of relaxation and stress management should be embraced.*
- *The need to establish free energy flow through the chakras or vessel of conception requires consideration. Emotional, psychological, spiritual, and physical causes may be at work, and a review with an Eastern-thinking complementary practitioner is recommended. Yoga, Shiatsu, and acupuncture may all be curative.*
- *Menorrhagia may lead to deficiencies, particularly in iron and proteins, and supplements of amino acids and a multimineral including iron (which should always be associated with zinc and vitamin C) should be considered. A daily recommended dose of a natural-food state supplement should be taken until the problem is resolved, and this level should be doubled throughout the actual bleeding period. Paradoxically, iron deficiency may cause menorrhagia.*
- *Homeopathic remedies are, again, chosen on the symptom picture of the individual as a whole, but those remedies mentioned in the section on dysmenorrhea (see* **Dysmenorrhea***) may be applicable. If anemia is diagnosed or the individual is particularly pale, then please consider the remedies Ferrum phosphoricum and Borax at potency 30 taken four times a day.*
- *Supplement the diet with beta-carotene, 2mgs per foot of height in divided doses with meals through the day.*

Menorrhalgia (pain in pelvis)

This is the medical term for excessive pain in the pelvic area associated with menstruation but different from the individual's usual period pain.

All the suggestions and recommendations for dysmenorrhea should be adhered to, but your gynecologist and complementary practitioner should consider the possibility of endometriosis (*see* **Endometriosis**).

Painful periods—*see* Dysmenorrhea

NONSPECIFIC URETHRITIS (NSU)

Nonspecific urethritis (NSU) is a term initially provided for symptoms of cystitis (*see* **Cystitis**) that have no apparent cause. It was assumed that NSU was caused by viruses, but in the last two decades the two organisms *Trichomonas* and *Chlamydia* have been thought to be the culprits.

Most commonly, these create vaginal infections that are often asymptomatic. At worst, they may ascend into the uterus and cause salpingitis (inflammation of the Fallopian tube; *see* **Salpingitis**), but they frequently trigger urethritis.

Nonspecific urethritis may also be a pseudonym for "honeymoon cystitis" created by the friction of intercourse. In my opinion, the true definition is somewhat blurred.

RECOMMENDATIONS

- *See* **Cystitis** *for specific symptomatic treatment.*
- *If Trichomonas or Chlamydia are isolated, treatment of the vaginal vault is recommended. Single or combined treatments using pessaries of Tea Tree, Lavender, Hydrastis, and Calendula may be beneficial if used morning and night.*

ORGASM

An orgasm is an intense, diffuse, and pleasurable sensation experienced during sexual intercourse or masturbation. In the male, it is associated with ejaculation (but please note that ejaculation may occur before and after orgasm), and in the female with uterine and pelvic muscular contractions, and a warm, flooding sensation throughout the pelvis.

Orgasms may vary in intensity, depending very much upon the state of the nervous system, both physically and psychologically. Persistent friction on the head of the penis, the clitoris or a small area just inside the upper aspect of the vagina (colloquially known as the "G" spot) sends off nervous impulses to the central-nervous system. An accumulation of these impulses triggers a profound neurotransmitter release that principally affects the pleasure centers, but also blocks both pain and some neuromuscular channels. Coordination is particularly affected momentarily, and heart rate, blood pressure and peripheral circulation can increase.

Achieving an orgasm requires a conscious effort, but the actual nervous reflex is governed by the parasympathetic, autonomic (uncontrolled) nervous system. Damage to these nerves can cause a decrease in intensity or a total loss of orgasm, whereas a hypersensitivity may cause an orgasm to arrive too quickly. Often associated with premature ejaculation, this oversensitivity can be created by natural hormones, excitement, or stimulation, and by the use of certain drugs. Other drugs may have a converse effect: alcohol, amphetamines, cocaine and ecstasy are commonly abused for this purpose (*see* **Ejaculation problems**).

The yogic philosophy believes that energy known as the *kundalini* is stored in the pelvis. Genital stimulation awakens this energy, which flashes up the spinal column and affects the brain. Masters of meditation can release this energy without physical stimulation, and there are reports of telepathy being able to create orgasms in the partners of meditators. Certainly, meditation will remove inhibitory chemicals and lead to easier attainment of orgasm.

Some physical disorders, such as multiple sclerosis or other nerve diseases and problems with the prostate gland, can interrupt the nerve supply and prevent orgasm. Damage to the central-nervous system may also cause a loss. Anxiety, stress, and phobias, often resulting from failed previous sexual experiences or guilt from religious teachings, can affect the ability to have an orgasm or might cause premature ejaculation. These are usually not serious conditions, but may require some time and special counseling.

RECOMMENDATIONS

- *Delayed or absent orgasm may be a process of age, but may also be caused by disease process and should be reviewed by a doctor, gynecologist, or specialist in the field.*
- *Meditation and counseling to alleviate anxieties or phobias may have a profound effect. Sexual counseling may be required.*
- *See* **Ejaculation problems**.

OVARIAN CYSTS

The ovaries are a complex of different types of tissue that harbor the female eggs. These are all produced at the fetal stage of an individual's development. Therefore a 40-year-old woman will have 40-year-old eggs. This is partially why the older a woman gets, the more chance there is of a genetic mishap in conception.

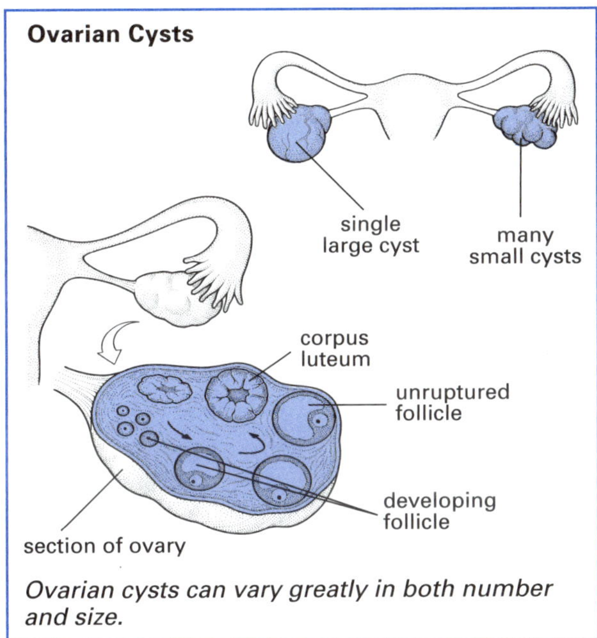

Ovarian cysts can vary greatly in both number and size.

As an egg ripens, it moves to the surface and is released, leaving behind a chemical-producing cell known as the corpus luteum. This produces chemicals, including human-chorionic gonadotrophin (HCG), and other hormones, such as estrogen and progesterone, until the placenta is formed and takes over this role after eight weeks of pregnancy. These corpus lutea are often the site at which fluid can accumulate, creating a cyst. A cyst may form in other parts of the ovary, and may be triggered by infection that travels along the Fallopian tube. A common cause is when the mature egg fails to open or be released by the tougher, outer, fibrous coat of the ovary, and this causes a follicular cyst.

Cysts in general may grow by an excess of fluid or damp in the system, and the Chinese physicians consider cysts to be most commonly associated with an excess of Yin in the diet.

Most often, cysts are symptoms and, without ultrasound techniques, may go unnoticed. Cysts are being found more commonly because of routine pelvic ultrasound, but I do not know of any study that has monitored whether these come and go as a regular occurrence. However, there is a belief that a cyst may be associated with cancer and the percentage chance of this being the case is equal to the age of the patient. Put more simply, a 20-year-old with a cyst has a 20 percent chance of it being associated with cancer, but a 50-year-old has a 50 percent chance.

A cyst may grow to the size of a football, and cause pressure symptoms on the bladder, bowel, or other internal organs. Usually, bloating and a visible swelling would be noticed before any serious effects are created. An infected cyst may burst and lead to peritonitis, with severe pain and associated symptoms. Menstrual-cycle changes may occur, although this is unusual, and the cyst may put pressure on nerves, leading to painful intercourse or back and leg aches.

An increasing number of women are presenting with multiple ovarian cysts not associated with the menstrual cycle and ovulation. Polycystic ovary syndrome has mild or considerable imbalances in the female/male hormonal structure, often associated with excess follicle-stimulating hormone (FSH) or testosterone. The absence of a normal cycle, hirsutism, and lack of libido, are amongst the symptoms of this syndrome.

The orthodox world uses powerful oral-contraceptive pills, many of which create unpleasant side effects, which may or may not be effective. Alternative therapies as mentioned below should be considered, especially the use of natural progesterone, before these are tried.

The apparent increase in the number of women with this condition suggests that there is some environmental, hormonal effect, possibly from estrogens in our food chain, or even the use of the oral-contraceptive pill. More study is needed, more research is not forthcoming.

RECOMMENDATIONS

- *Ovarian cysts are often picked up on routine gynecological examination, and will be confirmed by ultrasound. Do not be rushed into an operative procedure, but consult a complementary medical practitioner.*
- *Some ovarian cancers release a particular chemical known as a marker into the bloodstream, which should be measured if there is any suggestion or risk of an ovarian cancer.*
- *Remove sugar, alcohol, cow's-milk products and caffeine from the diet.*
- *Fruit and watery vegetables should be reduced to a minimum, and Yang foods should be increased (see* **Yang foods***).*
- *Homeopathic remedies should be chosen depending upon the symptoms, but the remedies Apis (right-sided cysts), Colocynthis (left-sided cysts), Oophorinum (cysts associated with menopause), and Kali bromatum (if there is any suggestion of the cyst being associated with a tumor) can all be used at potency 30 three times a day for three weeks.*
- *The following supplements may reduce a cyst and should be taken as follows: vitamin E (200iu per foot of height in divided doses throughout the day with food) and gammalinoleic acid (30mg per foot of height with breakfast). Beta-carotene (1mg per foot height in divided doses) should also be taken to counteract the effect that vitamin E has of draining the vitamin A.*
- *Abdominal massage in experienced hands may remove a cyst.*
- *The use of natural progesterone creams with or without the concurrent use of the herb Agnus castus can be administered, and has been shown to remove ovarian cysts. The treatment must be under the control of an experienced practitioner or physician.*
- *Herbal treatments, especially Chinese, in association with acupuncture have proven successful.*
- *Surgical intervention may be required and is usually performed through a laparoscopy. A small tube is inserted through a half-inch incision just below the navel and passed into the abdominal cavity. Try to find a gynecologist who is willing to remove the cyst rather than the ovary.*

PARAPHIMOSIS

Paraphimosis is the retraction and constriction of the foreskin behind the head of the penis. The event usually occurs after intercourse or masturbation, and is more likely in those whose foreskin is tight, either as an anatomical anomaly or following infections of the foreskin (balanitis).

This retraction impedes the venous blood flow, causing swelling of the head of the penis. This tightens the foreskin even more, and the engorgement causes intense pain.

RECOMMENDATIONS

- *Prevention is the best cure. Make sure that the foreskin is pulled forward after intercourse, and use Vaseline or soap and water as soon as any difficulty in pulling the foreskin forward is noted. The problem is self-perpetuating, and left to its own devices will worsen.*
- *If paraphimosis has occurred, place some ice cubes in soft material such as silk and surround the head of the penis. Apply gentle pressure, and attempt to push the blood from the penile head up the shaft.*
- *Use the homeopathic remedy Apis 6 every 5min, and if the problem is solved, move onto Arnica 6 every 3hr until any residual ache subsides.*
- *If this technique fails, go to the nearest emergency unit as soon as possible. The doctor there will apply a pain-killing gel (which is, unfortunately, only partially effective) and*

squeeze the head of the penis. It is worth taking a painkiller on your way to the hospital, but inform the physician that you have done so.

- *If this technique fails, it is sometimes necessary for an operation under general anesthetic to incise the foreskin. This usually leads to a circumcision.*

PELVIC INFLAMMATORY DISEASE (PID, SALPINGITIS)

Pelvic inflammatory disease (PID) is an infection of the uterus and Fallopian tubes, typically caused by an infection with *Chlamydia* (*see* **Chlamydia**) or *Trichomonas*. Other infections—bacterial, viral, or fungal—may cause PID, which may be recurrent or simply persist as a chronic infection.

The symptoms are of pain ranging from a dull ache to sharp and cutting. This may be felt from the vagina through to the back. A discharge is frequently associated, and is most commonly unpleasant smelling, but not always.

Pelvic inflammatory disease generally occurs following intercourse but any vaginal examination, uterine operation such as a dilatation and curettage (D & C), or a termination may introduce infection.

A severe or persistent infection may lead to damage of the narrow Fallopian tubes, and is a major cause of infertility. Uterine and ovarian infection may lead to abscesses.

Any problem in the pelvis may represent a stagnation or lack of energy in the base chakra. There is a strong correlation between PID and sexual promiscuity, and the reasons for this need to be confronted if the problem is a chronic or repetitive one.

RECOMMENDATIONS

- *Any discomfort that persists or is severe must be examined by a physician.*
- *Ultrasound, vaginal swabs, and full-blood counts to test the level of white cells are recommended before any treatment course is started. In severe cases, these may be done after initiating treatment.*
- *This is one of the few occasions when an antibiotic should be considered a firstline treatment. Failure to treat may lead to chronic, serious complications or infertility. Combination antibiotics for bacteria that breed well in nonoxygenated areas, as well as a broad-spectrum aerobic antibiotic, are usually used. Chlamydia and Trichomonas may require strong antibiotics, and this treatment requires protection of the bowel and other body flora as described in the section on antibiotics (see* **Antibiotics***).*
- *Homeopathic treatments should be chosen from your preferred homeopathic manual depending upon the symptoms. While deciding, use Aconite 6 every half an hour.*
- *Herbal treatments can be used. Echinacea and Golden Seal are particularly useful for any infection, and should be taken in the quantity recommended on a good-quality product or via a naturopath.*
- *If PID is associated with promiscuity, a truly holistic answer must include counseling to confront the need for multiple partners.*
- *Osteopathy and acupuncture are physical techniques to release blocked energy in the pelvis and encourage bloodflow to wash out infections.*
- *Yoga, Tai Chi, Qi Gong, and Polarity therapy techniques should be used in conjunction with other treatments.*
- *If intercourse was the initiating factor, the male partner needs to be examined using a penile swab and urine sample, because many infections are asymptomatic. Urine samples, taken first thing in the morning, may also isolate a causative bacteria.*
- *Chronic, recurrent conditions should be assessed by a complementary medical practitioner with experience in this area.*

PREMENSTRUAL SYNDROME/TENSION (PMS/PMT)

Most women will admit to some decrease in well-being in the 2–14 days prior to menstruation. This is predominantly caused by an increased sensitivity throughout the body because of raised estrogen and progesterone levels. Deficiencies in vitamins and minerals, an excess of stress chemicals such as adrenaline, and physical stress from food allergy may all make matters worse. Premenstrual syndrome is a troublesome and recurrent multisymptom condition that can be anything from mildly disturbing to profoundly debilitating. The symptoms can be divided into categories.

Psychological symptoms

Anxiety, confusion, depression, memory deficit, irritability, mood swings, tearfulness, exacerbated tension, and insomnia occur in 75 percent of PMS sufferers.

Physical symptoms

Headache, lethargy, dizziness, or fainting, fluid retention with associated weight gain, abdominal bloating and breast tenderness will be apparent in about 70 percent of cases.

Studies have shown that the symptoms are directly related to hormonal imbalances. It is important to understand that on the way to making estrogen and progesterone, the body produces many similar chemicals, all of which can have an effect on the system. Some symptoms are created by low levels, while others by high levels. Other hormones such as androgens, aldosterones, prolactin, follicle-stimulating hormone (FSH), and thyroid levels can be affected.

Deficiencies in vitamin B_6 and magnesium can have a profound effect on the production of some of these hormones, as well as affecting brain neurotransmitters such as dopamine, which are responsible for the emotional changes. These two supplements also play a part in the production of a particular hormone known as prostaglandin E_1, the function of which is not well understood, but is often found to be low in women struggling with PMS. Excessive fat intake or deficiencies in omega 6 and omega 3 fatty acids (which are included in extract of Evening Primrose Oil) can cause low levels of this compound. Mercury and lead poisoning may be associated with PMS, as may deficiencies in vitamins A, C, and E, and the minerals selenium, zinc, and iron, in addition to those mentioned above.

RECOMMENDATIONS

- *Premenstrual syndrome is not imagined. There is a lot of scientific evidence to support causes that can be treated without using the antidepressants that are the firstline treatment of the orthodox medical world.*
- *Avoid animal fats, fried foods, and any hydrogenated oils (that includes many margarines), especially during the time leading up to the period. Reduce sugars and increase vegetable sources of proteins such as soya and legumes. Any compound that affects the liver, such as alcohol and caffeine, will reduce its ability to break down hormones and therefore exacerbate some cases of PMS.*
- *Consider a trial of vitamin B_6 or magnesium, or preferably have these levels checked by a competent complementary medical practitioner.*
- *If deficient, for a trial period take vitamin B_6 and magnesium, both at 50mg per foot of height in divided doses throughout the day, starting on day 14 of the cycle and carrying on until the period starts (day 1 is the first day of a period).*
- *Obtain a fish oil or eicosapentenoic acid (EPA) supplement, and take three times the recommended daily allowance (RDA) from day 14 to the first day of the period. Vegetarians may use flaxseed oil—one teaspoonful per foot of height divided with meals through the day.*
- *Beta-carotene (2mg per foot of height) and vitamin E (5iu per foot of height) in divided doses during the day may be of some benefit.*

- *Gammalinoleic acid (GLA), 50mg per foot of height) taken with breakfast may be beneficial. This can be found in Borage, Star Flower, or Evening Primrose Oil capsules.*
- *Licorice taken as a tincture diluted 5:1 with water (1 teaspoonful per foot of height) in divided doses with meals.*
- *Alfalfa contains phyto-estrogens (plant estrogens), and should be considered, but prescribed by a herbalist.*
- *Hair-mineral analysis should be considered if the above are not working.*
- *Bromelain at twice the dose recommended of a good, natural product may help.*
- *A study has shown that osteopathy can reduce the physical symptoms of PMS.*
- *Acupressure and acupuncture are beneficial.*
- *Homeopathic remedies that match the symptoms will be beneficial, and specific attention should be paid to Calcarea carbonica, Sepia, Causticum, Pulsatilla, Ignatia, and Kali carbonicum.*
- *Reflexology, with attention paid to the pituitary and adrenal glands, will help.*
- *If all this fails, consider seeing a complementary medical practitioner, because nearly everyone who practices medicine has some trick up their sleeve! The use of natural progesterone derived from the Mexican yam can be beneficial if the symptoms are created by low progesterone or unopposed estrogen, but this needs to be prescribed by a practitioner with expertise in this area.*
- *Relaxation and meditation techniques through yoga or Qi Gong can be very beneficial.*
- *Resort to the oral-contraceptive pill only if the above measures do not have an effect.*

PRIAPISM

This is an abnormal, persistent, painful erection of the penis which, by definition, is unrelated to sexual desire. It is caused by certain blood disorders, such as sickle-cell anemia that blocks the venous (bloodflow outlet) system or by problems of the central-nervous system that cause contraction of the corpora cavernosa, the blood spaces that fill and cause the hardening of the penis. If not dealt with, impotence may result.

RECOMMENDATIONS

- *The problem must be dealt with by a urogenital specialist.*
- *Complementary treatment is dependent upon the underlying cause.*

PUBIC LICE

Pubic lice are usually transmitted by sexual contact. These small parasites cause itching and appear as small freckles. Watched closely, especially in a bath, movement may be seen and the telltale sign of small, white eggs will be found at the base of the pubic hairs, stuck on with a remarkably tenacious glue. Raising a louse with tweezers will cause a very small pinprick of blood.

RECOMMENDATIONS

- *See* **Lice**.
- *Topical, orthodox preparations are effective, and need to be applied to the affected area, including the lower abdomen, thighs, and hairs around the anus, then covered by underwear and left on overnight. Repeat this process one week later.*

SEXUALLY-TRANSMITTED DISEASES (STD) AND VENEREAL DISEASE (VD)

A sexually-transmitted disease is one that is passed from one sexual partner to another. It is most commonly associated with penetrative intercourse but may be passed through oral sex as well. Transmission can be divided into groups.

Viral infections

Acquired-immune-deficiency syndrome (AIDS) is transmitted by passing the human-immunodeficiency virus (HIV). Herpes around the genitals is caused by herpes-simplex type 2, and the human papillomavirus (HPV) causes warts. These are all discussed in their own sections.

Bacterial infections

The better-known bacterial infections are syphilis and gonorrhea. These are stored in some part of the urogenital system, and transmitted through associated fluid. Bacterial infections from other parts of the body, such as the bowel, may also be transmitted by the act of intercourse. Vaginal, uterine, and bladder infections are commonly caused by a bacterium known as *Escherichia coli*, which thrives in the bowel and is part of the normal bowel flora. If this bacterium finds its way into another organ, it can be quite devastating, and produces very unpleasant symptoms.

Other infections

Some organisms behave more like parasites, existing within cells in the same manner as viruses, but also behaving like bacteria in their metabolism. *Chlamydia* and *Trichomonas* are commonly found in association with nonspecific urethritis (NSU) and typically spread by sexual intercourse.

Pubic lice, or "crabs," as they are colloquially known, are generally spread through sexual intercourse.

Candidal infection, most commonly known as thrush, is typically spread through sexual intercourse.

Safe sex

"Safe sex" is a phrase that has been coined since the rise of HIV/AIDS. It is an extremely accurate definition, and it is becoming more relevant as Western societies become less critical of sexual promiscuity. This attitude is pervading the so-called Third-World countries, where unprotected sex is more common than not because of the lack of availability of condoms. Add to this an apparent increase in homosexual activity and the use of anal intercourse in poorer nations as a form of contraception, and you have several reasons why the importance of practicing safe sex is increasing.

There is some controversy as to whether oral sex is safe sex. Vigorous oral activity that produces small cuts or lesions will allow the transmission of infective agents. Bacterial infections, such as gonorrhea and syphilis, are known to transfer from male ejaculate causing throat and tonsillar problems, as does *Candida* (thrush). It is unlikely that HIV will transfer in this way, but the possibility cannot be excluded. The herpes-simplex type-2 virus (genital herpes) prefers to live in tissue other than that found around the oral cavity. However, in rare instances transmission can occur, and it is best to avoid unprotected oral sex if a herpetic lesion is visible.

RECOMMENDATIONS

- *All of the above conditions are discussed in their relevant sections.*
- *All sexually-transmitted disorders are best treated by avoidance. Sexual promiscuity should be reduced, and safe sex practiced.*
- *Maintaining hygiene and a personal, high level of immune-system activity will decrease the risk of transmission and encourage any infection to be destroyed effectively.*
- *The use of drugs and alcohol reduces the immune-system response and, in conjunction with sexual promiscuity, will increase the risk of an infection taking hold. Keep "abuse" to a minimum.*
- *The use of a condom is effective against diseases which are vaginally transferred or carried in the semen.*
- *Anal intercourse and vigorous vaginal or oral sex will predispose to small (or large) lesions, into which infected agents may travel directly into the bloodstream. Avoid these techniques, or be gentle and use adequate amounts of lubrication.*

- *Wash the genitals before and after intercourse, where possible.*
- *Urinate after intercourse when possible.*

THE TESTICLES

The testes descend from the abdomen and rest in the scrotal sac (scrotum) away from the body because their function and their maturity depend upon being below body temperature. Considering how sensitive they are, they have very little protection other than that the reflexes in that area, which are very rapid, will draw the body around the midriff swiftly.

Sperm are produced at a rapid rate, and each spermatozoon lives approximately five days. If no ejaculation has taken place, the sperm break down and are re-absorbed. Sperm are stored in a collection of tubules known as the vas deferens before passing up into the urethra at the level of the prostate via the vas deferens.

It is here that the sperm mix with the seminal fluid from the prostate. This mildly viscous, sticky, milky compound completes the ejaculate and contains fructose in high quantities, which provide the sperm with food on their journey.

The Testes and Penis

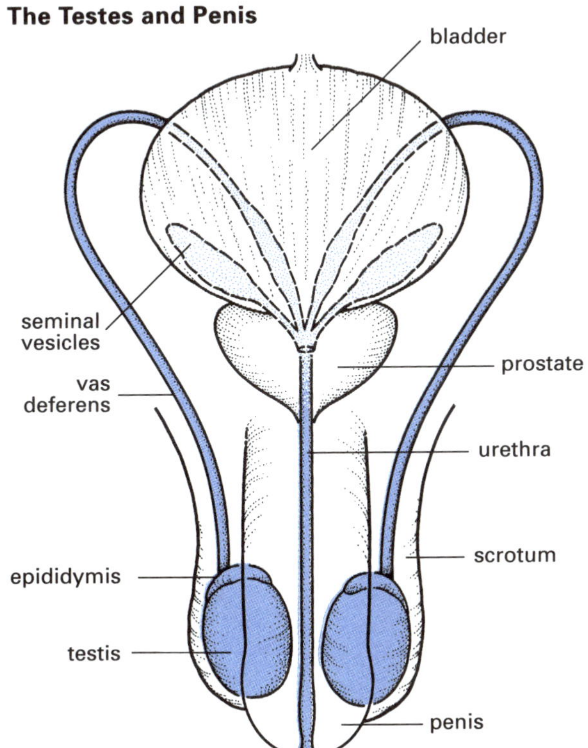

Injury to the testes

Any trauma to the testes is extremely painful because of the high number of nerves in the area. The testes are associated with a complex of blood and lymphatic vessels, and any trauma can rupture these, forming cysts (*see* **Hydrocele**). An injury to a blood vessel may bleed and cause a hematoma (bruise), which, while clotting, may cut off the blood supply and lead to testicular gangrene.

RECOMMENDATIONS

- *Encase the scrotum in an ice-filled towel to relieve the discomfort.*
- *Take deep breaths, pulling energy down into the lower abdomen.*
- *Take Arnica 6 every 10min until the discomfort is relieved, and then every 2hr until the pain has gone completely.*
- *Any pain that is not easing within a couple of hours must be examined by a physician in case a more-serious injury has occurred. Delay may run the risk of the loss of the testicle.*

TESTICULAR TORSION

The testicle hangs in the scrotal sack to be kept away from the heat of the body (the testicle works best at 2°F lower than body temperature). This requires blood vessels and nerves to travel from the body along the spermatic cord from the testes up to the penis. The testicle is anchored into place through fibers that may be congenitally absent, or damaged through trauma. If this is the case, the testes can twist causing occlusion of the blood vessels and an excruciatingly painful pressure on the nerves. If this twist or torsion is not corrected, the testicle will die from a lack of oxygen, and gangrene with its inherent dangers will set in. It is not possible to miss a torsion, except in an infant, since the pain is fierce.

RECOMMENDATIONS

- *Please follow the advice for an injured testicle (see above).*
- *Any pain persisting without remission over 2hr must be reviewed by a doctor.*
- *Repair of a torsion that does not spontaneously untwist is surgical. In an emergency situation, untwisting the testes may be possible, provided that the turn is in the right direction. The pain is such that it is difficult to discern this, as no relief will be immediately noticeable. This procedure must only be undertaken by somebody with experience, who cannot operate immediately, or if medical availability is too far away. In any case, an operation is required because the testes need to be fixed to prevent recurrence.*
- *The remedy Aconite 6 can be taken every 10min while awaiting treatment.*
- *Ice wrapped in a towel and applied may reduce swelling, but the slightest touch may make the pain worse, and therefore even the ice is not desired.*
- *Please accept an anesthetic or an intravenous tranquilizer such as diazepam, despite any alternative medical views of these drugs. The bravest of brave are unlikely to deal with the pain of examination, let alone treatment.*
- *See* **Operations and surgery**.

THRUSH

Thrush is the colloquial name for a *Candida* infection, commonly found in the vagina but also affecting other moist areas such as the anus and oral cavity. Men with foreskins may have an irritation there (*see* **Candida**).

TRICHOMONAS

Trichomonas is a protozoan (an organism that exhibits both bacterial and viral activity) that may be responsible for vaginitis and uterine infections.

RECOMMENDATION

- *See* **Chlamydia** *as treatment is identical.*

URETHRA

The urethra is the tube passing from the bladder down the penis or to the upper aspect of the vagina. At the top end, just below the bladder, are consciously and unconsciously controlled valves (involved with the prostate in the male) that allow urine flow. Bacteria may travel up the urethra from the external skin surface, but these are generally washed away by the flow of urine on a regular basis. The male urethra is a stretchable tube allowing for an erection, but it is quite a long passage for bacteria to travel to infect the bladder. The urethra in women is much shorter, and markedly so in girls, increasing the chances of infection and cystitis.

RECOMMENDATIONS

- *External hygiene is extremely important, and washing the genitals is a must, especially at an early age or after intercourse.*
- *Good hydration leading to frequent urination is an important protective measure.*

Urethral discharge

A discharge from the urethra is usually associated with bacterial infection, although yeast infection such as *Candida* may be a culprit. The color often gives away the causative agent. A yellow/green discharge is usually gonorrhea, which is the most common cause.

RECOMMENDATIONS

- *Immediately start treatment by water intake to flush the system.*
- *Collect a urine sample for the doctor's surgery.*
- *A urethral swab is recommended so that an accurate diagnosis can be made, and the correct antibiotic used if required.*
- *See* **Cystitis** *for the treatment.*

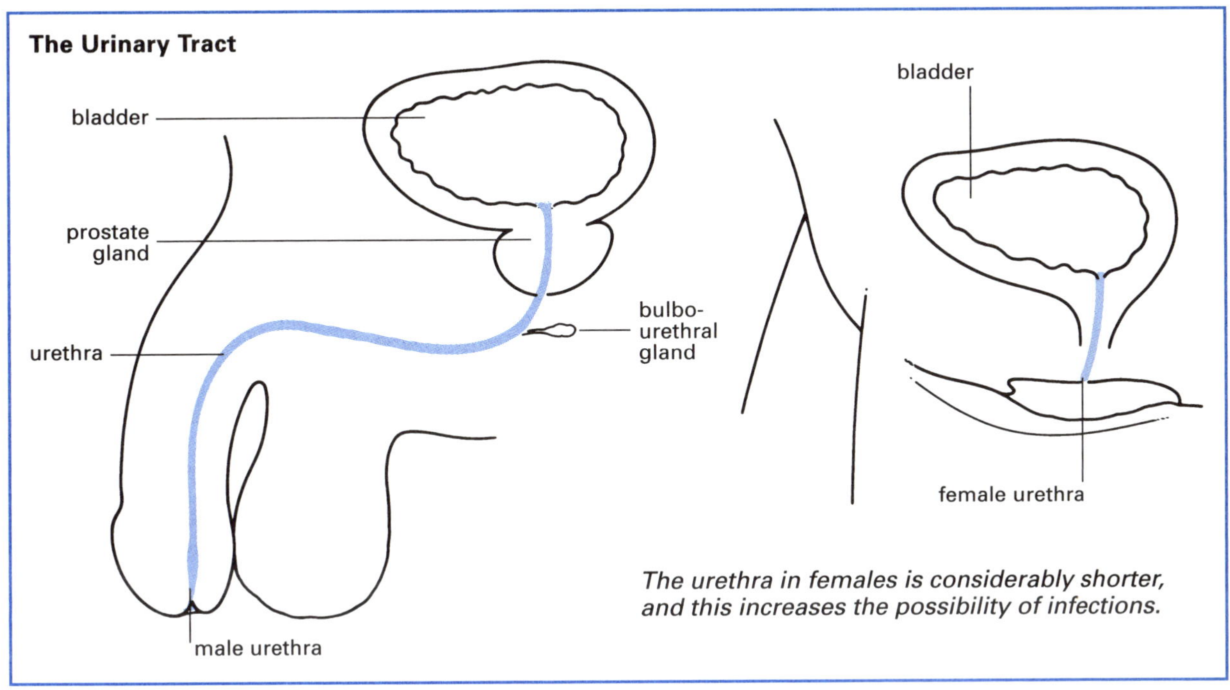

The urethra in females is considerably shorter, and this increases the possibility of infections.

Urethral stricture

A stricture is an obstruction, usually caused by scar tissue. Congenital malformations may account for a small percentage. Scar tissue is usually formed after a severe infection or recurrent problems, and may, if severe, impede urinary flow or cause pain when passing urine.

> RECOMMENDATIONS
>
> - *Any difficulty in the flow of urine must be assessed by a urologist.*
> - *Commence the homeopathic remedy Silica 30 three times a day for two weeks, because this remedy may remove unwanted scar tissue.*
> - *Manual breakdown of the stricture may be required and performed by passing a metal rod into the penis under general anesthetic and surgical conditions. If this is required, see* **Operations and surgery**.

UTERUS AND UTERINE PROBLEMS

Endometriosis

This is a painful condition characterized by discomfort, usually in the pelvis or abdominal areas, and very often associated with cyclical changes of rising estrogen levels just before and during the period.

The condition is caused by the presence of the inner lining of the uterus (the endometrium) existing in abnormal locations such as the outside of the uterus, Fallopian tubes, or ovaries, or

Endometriosis

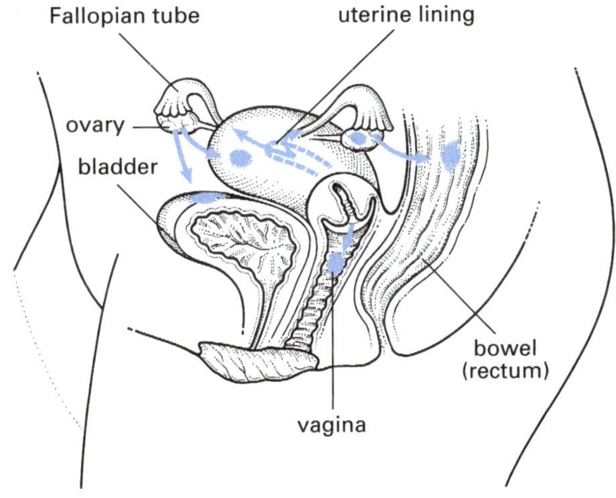

Some of the many possible sites of endometrial growth are highlighted and areas to which endometrial growth might migrate.

attached to the bowel, or other organs such as the bladder or the bowel wall.

The pain occurs because this endometrial tissue behaves towards the estrogen and progesterone levels as does the endometrium within the uterus. It engorges with blood and swells as if it were expecting a fertilized egg; this swelling causes inflammation and pain at the site.

Endometriosis, depending on its site and the amount of displaced tissue, can lead to other problems, such as painful intercourse, infertility, and bowel and bladder problems.

The orthodox approach is to consider blocking the menstrual cycle by using either oral-contraceptive pills or a drug called danazol, which blocks the pituitary gland (which controls the female cycle). Other drugs are being considered all the time. Surgery, either laparoscopic or open surgery, may have to be considered to remove aggressive or larger deposits.

RECOMMENDATIONS

- *Consult a herbalist. Phyto-estrols have a weak estrogen effect, which may block the natural estrogens and therefore lessen the amount of endometrial swelling. Herbs such as dong quai and glycyrrhiza, dandelion root, and others may be considered.*
- *Consult a homeopath. Depending on the symptoms, a variety of homeopathic remedies may be beneficial.*
- *Acupuncture can be useful, both as a pain reliever and potentially as part of a curative protocol.*
- *Deep, abdominal massage by a practitioner with knowledge in this area can break down adhesions.*

Fibroids

Fibroids are an overgrowth of uterine muscle that may develop as a type of polyp into the uterine space (intraluminal), within the uterine wall itself (intramural), or outside of the uterus (extramural). Depending on where they are, the symptoms of a fibroid may differ, although many fibroids are symptomless and will cause no problems. Their size is relevant to the level of discomfort they might cause by adding weight to the uterus, which in turn will push on the sacral and possibly lumbar nerves, causing discomfort and pain.

Fibroids

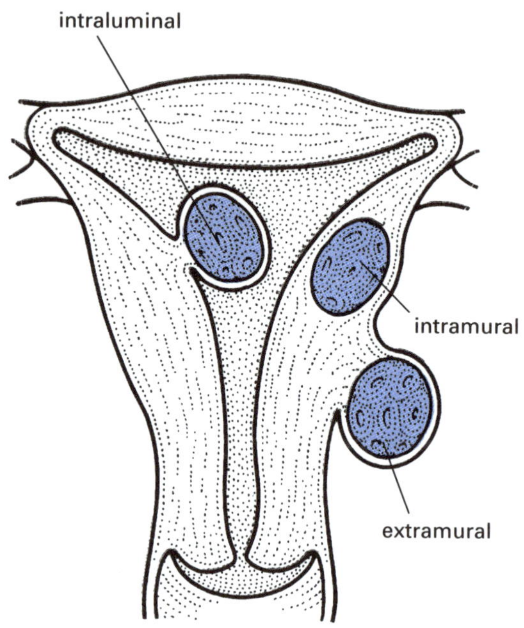

Intraluminal

Symptoms will include increased bleeding (menorrhagia), painful periods (dysmenorrhea), painful intercourse (dyspareunia) and, much more rarely, discomfort.

Intraluminal fibroids are a cause of infertility, and may be discovered when a couple investigate this distressing problem.

Intramural

Fibroids found in the wall of the uterus may create all the problems associated with intraluminal fibroids, and are actually far more common.

Extramural

These fibroids do not carry the same number of complications, although painful intercourse and pressure-induced discomfort are the principal clues to discovery.

The orthodox world is uncertain as to the cause of fibroids, but the consensus of opinion in the holistic medical world is that an excess of energy builds up in the pelvis, uterus, or lower chakra (*see* **Menorrhagia** and **Dysmenorrhea**).

Fibroids are much more under the control of estrogen than endometrial tissue buildup, which is under the control of progesterone. Bear this in mind when referring to the section on menorrhagia. Fibroids often diminish through the menopause (when the estrogen levels drop dramatically), and therefore progesterone treatment may be considered when dealing with fibroids.

RECOMMENDATIONS

- *Please refer to the recommendations in the section on menorrhagia.*
- *Homeopathic remedies should be considered at high potency and, in particular, Calcarea iod and Thuja should be reviewed.*
- *Natural progesterone absorbed into the body through the skin can have very beneficial effects, but often needs to be taken over a 2-year period. This needs to be monitored by a doctor or complementary medical practitioner with experience in this field. Please note that natural progesterone is currently available by extraction from the Mexican yam (no other wild yam has the same proven efficacy), but it cannot pass through the acid in the stomach, and is therefore not available in pill form.*
- *Orthodox treatment is restricted to operative procedures, either dilatation and curettage (D & C) or modern techniques using laser. It is becoming less common, but hysterectomy is still too frequently recommended.*

THE VAGINA

Care of the vagina

The vagina is a remarkably tough area of the body. It is the hallway to the cervix and uterus, and the exit of the urinary system. Urine is constantly passed through it, and the vagina is approximately one inch away from the anus. Intercourse constantly introduces foreign matter, and the act of sex itself can be quite bruising. The vagina has to act as a barrier and protector of the womb while undergoing pressure from all of these external influences.

The vaginal vault has its own protective secretions, in which there live normal body bacteria that attack and compete with invading organisms. The vaginal secretions contain many immunoglobulins and white blood cells in preparation for this activity. The secretions must also be lubricating enough to allow intercourse, and receptive enough not to attack and kill sperm and thereby reduce the chances of fertilization.

The vagina manages all this through a very careful regulating system that keeps the acid/alkaline levels balanced and is very much under the control of the body's hormonal system, especially

The Vagina

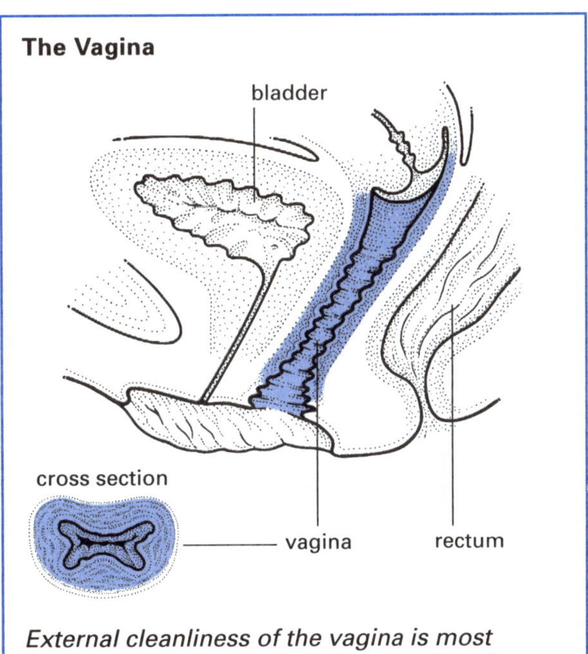

External cleanliness of the vagina is most important, although all medicated cleansing products should be avoided.

estrogen and progesterone. Different times of the cycle will produce different levels of these female hormones, which in turn affect the cellular production of these secretions. These tend to thicken and take on a characteristic viscous feel around the time of ovulation, which is of great benefit to the survival chances of the sperm.

External cleanliness is important, and the wiping of the urethral exit away from the vagina is as important a learned trait as wiping the anus backwards and upwards. Medicated soaps and toiletries should be avoided because these will interfere with the normal bacterial flora, and natural soaps and fresh water should be the only cleansing agents. Vaginal perfumes are not to be encouraged. Any unpleasant odor is generally due to dietetic problems, hormonal imbalances, or infections, and should be treated appropriately. Cleanliness is especially important throughout menstruation. Old blood is a perfect medium for bacterial growth. External pads are theoretically more hygienic than internal tampons, but not so popular, and may give a greater rise to discomfort and odors. Both should be changed frequently, in any case.

Vaginal douching

There is no need for a vaginal douche as a regular cleansing mechanism. The healthy body will produce ample lubrication and immune response to protect the vagina, and a douche should only be used to support this basic cleansing mechanism. Douching should not be performed during a period, because the cervix may be slightly more open and may allow easier access for infection. However, this is generally counteracted by the bloodflow, and therefore douching may be desirable if the vagina is uncomfortable or odorous, or in preparation for sexual intercourse.

RECOMMENDATIONS

- *Douche only when necessary.*
- *Douche bags are available from drugstores or ask your doctor for a 50ml syringe.*
- *Preferably, use boiled water in the preparation of a douche.*
- *A basic cleansing solution may be obtained by adding one tablespoonful of cider vinegar to 16 ounces of water or one tablespoonful of live yogurt to 16 ounces of water. These quantities may be doubled in the case of a vaginal discharge or infection. Douching with these solutions may be done up to every 4hr, and may be very beneficial in infections if used on an alternating basis.*
- *Boric acid (500mg in 8 ounces) of water can be used, but not more than once a week.*
- *Douching solutions can be made from Hydrastis, tea tree oil and zinc sulfate (one tablespoonful of a 2 percent solution to 16 ounces of water), but generally use these only for treatment, rather than for regular hygiene.*
- *Arnica or Calendula lotion may be used at a dilution of one tablespoon per 16 ounces of boiled water.*
- *All of the above can be used up to four times a day in acute infections, but if there is no improvement after five days, then bring the problem to the attention of your doctor or gynecologist.*

Vaginal discharge

A vaginal discharge is due to either excessive secretion or the action of the vaginal defense mechanism. The former is usually associated with sexual excitement, or hormonal or neurological stimulation. The latter is a general reaction in an attempt to flush out any foreign object or organisms that may be causing irritation.

Candida tends to produce a thick, whitish discharge with a typical, yeasty smell, soreness, and itching. Green/yellow discharge is indicative of bacterial infection—*Streptococcus* or *Trichomonas* are the most frequent. A gray discharge is often associated with *Gardnerella*, and *Chlamydia* often produces a clear, runny discharge.

RECOMMENDATIONS

- *Follow the douching instructions in the section above.*
- *Use the homeopathic remedy Kreosotum 6 four times a day if Candida is suspected, and Mercurius 6 for any other infection until a more accurate selection can be made from your preferred homeopathic manual or via a homeopath.*
- *As for any infection, stop caffeine, alcohol, smoking, and other drug intake.*
- *Ensure adequate hydration.*

Foreign objects

A foreign object may well be found in a vagina in children or infants who show a discharge. Adults are less likely to be unaware of the contents of the vagina, but all too frequently, internal tampons may be forgotten. Bacteria have a predilection for living in a blood-soaked tampon, and a syndrome known as Toxic-Shock Syndrome (TSS) is a surprisingly common occurrence. In this condition, bacteria grow at a rapid rate in a forgotten tampon, release toxins, and cause severe poisoning, not infrequently resulting in death.

RECOMMENDATIONS

- *Do not forget that objects have been placed in the vagina—whether for medical reasons or for enjoyment.*
- *Daily washing should include a brief inspection using your fingers, especially around the time of the period.*
- *Any object that is not easily removed should be left in place and taken for medical extraction.*

Irritated or itching vagina

Itching of the vagina is most commonly found on the outer lips (vulva), but can be anywhere. It is generally caused by minor infections or contact dermatitis from irritating creams and deodorants. In older women the menopause leads to a diminution in normal secretions, which automatically encourages dryness and potentially infection. Different stages of the normal menstrual cycle may alter the level of secretion, protection, and normal vaginal flora, and this may lead to an irritation.

The quality of the vaginal secretions is dependent upon nutrition, and deficiencies in nutrients, and excesses of sugar and toxins, such as from smoking and alcohol, can lead to irritants being expressed through secretions. Poor hygiene will lead to mild, infected irritation, and fungal infections by skin fungi can affect the vagina in the same way as athlete's foot.

RECOMMENDATIONS

- *Please follow the above recommendations for the care of the vagina. See* **Vaginal douching** *and* **Vaginal dryness**.
- *Ensure good hydration by drinking 8 ounces of water per foot of height per day.*
- *The homeopathic remedies Sulphur or Graphites, potency 6, may be taken four times a day until a better remedy is selected from your preferred homeopathic manual.*
- *Arnica or Calendula cream or lotion may be applied as frequently as is necessary to reduce irritation.*

Infections of the vagina

Vaginal infections may be asymptomatic (without symptoms), or present as a discharge which may be colored or clear, an irritation or a pain, or may only be discovered during intercourse.

The vaginal vault has a considerable amount of its own normal bacteria, which compete with bad bugs for food, thereby keeping unwanted bacteria at bay. Provided regular hygiene is maintained, vaginal infections are infrequent.

A persisting problem requires a medical examination, whereby a swab may be sent to a laboratory for culture to see if anything is growing.

Antibiotics are the orthodox world's first line of treatment, but should only be used as a last resort.

RECOMMENDATIONS

- *Depending on the symptoms, see **Vaginal discharge** and **Vaginitis**.*
- *Tea tree oil, lavender, Hydrastis or Calendula pessaries or any combination should be considered for use as directed by the practitioner who prescribes them.*
- *Chlamydia or Trichomonas infections may warrant an antibiotic as a firstline treatment. See the relevant sections in this book on these infections.*

Odor

Odor is generally created by a bacterium or yeast infection that has settled into the vaginal vault, despite the body's normal vaginal flora. The normal flora will have a characteristic smell, but should not be offensive.

Vaginal secretions, like any discharge from the body, will reflect the contents of the bloodstream, and diet will have a strong influence on the smell.

RECOMMENDATIONS

- *Consider diet and mild infections as being relevant. Correct the nutrition, and visit a doctor for a swab to isolate any causative organism.*
- *Please refer to the relevant section if an infection is present.*
- *See **Vaginal douching** and use the technique after a sample or swab has been taken.*
- *Do not use vaginal deodorants directly because this will interfere with the normal vaginal flora. Instead, if necessary, deodorize the groin area of the outermost clothes.*

Vaginal dryness

Lubrication is produced by special cells that line the vaginal walls and are under the influence of estrogen and progesterone. These cells themselves are governed by the autonomic (involuntary) nervous system, and both the hormones and these nerves stimulate the production of lubricant in response to sexual stimulus.

General dryness may be due to neurological problems, but most frequently are the result of diminished hormonal activity or production. Menopause is notorious for creating vaginal dryness.

The lack of secretions leads to a diminution in the protection of the vaginal vault, due to a loss of the immunoglobulins and white blood cells that attack invading organisms. The normal vaginal flora also need a moist environment, and this too will diminish. Intercourse becomes painful or irritating.

RECOMMENDATIONS

- *Vaginal dryness for no apparent reason, but often due to age, needs to be reviewed by a complementary medical practitioner and doctor.*
- *Ensure that dehydration is not an aspect by drinking 8 ounces of water per foot of height.*
- *If hormonal imbalances are ruled out and no neurological conditions are found, consider using nonmedicated lubricants. Vaseline® is the best known, although vitamin E creams or olive oil may be used.*
- *Ensure adequate foreplay before intercourse. This is particularly important after menopause when lubrication is physiologically diminished, but still capable of being produced given enough stimulus.*
- *The homeopathic remedies Belladonna, Lycopodium, and Natrum muriaticum should be reviewed, and the most suitable remedy for the individual constitution should be chosen.*

Vaginismus

Vaginismus is a painful spasm of the vagina created by constriction of the muscles within the vaginal wall. It is a nervous condition usually associated with a trepidation of intercourse. Most frequently found in teenage girls, this condition may persist, and can be painful and embarrassing.

RECOMMENDATIONS

- *Vaginismus is not a disease, and is treatable but it requires psychological intervention. Please seek a counselor with experience in sexual dysfunction.*
- *Do not try to force intercourse, but digital insertion may remove some of the anticipation.*

Vaginal warts—*see* Genital warts

Vaginal pain

Pain in the vagina is usually associated with trauma following violent or aggressive intercourse or the traumatic insertion of foreign objects. Inflammation from any cause of vaginitis, especially infection, may cause vaginal pain.

Often overlooked is a lower spinal-nerve entrapment that causes a referred pain; and food allergy has been cited as creating a variation to the normal vaginal secretions, causing irritation and discomfort.

Pain of the vaginal lips (vulvodynia) is occasionally present, with no known cause. This condition is thought to be neurologically based rather than a local problem.

RECOMMENDATIONS

- *Any severe or persistent pain in the vagina that is without obvious cause, must be reviewed by a physician or gynecologist.*
- *If associated with back pain or is persistent, regardless of treatments for specific problems, it may be relieved by osteopathy, especially with the use of ambulatory traction as offered by a lightweight contraption fitted for a few minutes by osteopathic specialists.*
- *Surprisingly, consider food allergy for unexplained and unremitting vaginal discomfort.*
- *The tranquilizer amitriptyline may be of benefit in unrelenting vulvodynia.*

Vaginitis

Symptoms of itching, even pain, discharge, burning, redness, and pain on intercourse can all be symptoms of vaginitis.

The vagina is a resoundingly tough part of the anatomy considering the battering it gets from intercourse and foreign compounds such as sperm, douches, deodorants, tampons, and condoms etc. The vagina also houses many bacteria, most of which are useful and attack bad bacteria but also, amid the colonies, there lurk small amounts of "bad guys" who are no trouble at all until the normal, healthy, vaginal flora are disturbed by the use of antibiotics and other drugs and chemicals, such as perfumes and over-the-counter douches. Hormonal imbalance, often created by oral contraception and the eating of nonorganic meats (which contain estrogens), can all create vaginitis. Excess white sugar and specific allergic foods can also encourage bad bacterial/fungal growth.

RECOMMENDATIONS

- *Maintain good hygiene with daily baths, and clean the vagina after intercourse with water or a natural douche (see* **Vaginal douching***). Ensure that the area between the anus and vagina (the perineum) is cleaned by washing with strokes away from the vaginal opening.*
- *If forced into using an antibiotic or chemical douche, ensure protection through complementary medical means, including natural douches and ingestion of high doses of Lactobacillus acidophilus or an equivalent.*
- *Through any acute episode, avoid refined sugars (white sugar) and foods containing them.*

- *Vaginal pessaries containing one or a combination of the following as instructed on the container or by a complementary practitioner are beneficial: tea tree oil, Hydrastis, Calendula, Pau d'arco.*
- *Any persistence of a problem, despite treatment after five days, should be reviewed by your doctor or gynecologist. If any discomfort appears to be traveling to the uterus or lower abdomen, visit your specialist straight away.*

WET DREAMS

Wet dreams are an essential part of the normality of growing up. There is no pathological cause of ejaculating in the sleeping state. There is no "normal" frequency, and there may be times when wet dreams will occur several times in one week.

STRUCTURAL MATTERS

ACHES AND PAINS

Aches and pains in a young adult that are not associated with exercise must be reviewed by both a medical practitioner and a complementary body worker, such as an osteopath or chiropractor. Diseases of the muscles and joints in young adults are unusual, and may require treatment.

RECOMMENDATIONS

- *Ensure that you are well stretched out before and after exercise.*
- *Ensure that you are well hydrated. Eight ounces of water per foot of height drunk through the day, and an extra amount of water for any extra sweating or the intake of alcohol, caffeine, or excessively sweet foods. All of these are dehydrating.*
- *Ensure that you have a high intake of vegetables of all varieties, because mineral deficiencies can lead to persisting cramps, etc.*
- *Persisting pains with no obvious reason must be brought to the attention of a medical practitioner, orthodox or complementary to begin with.*

ACHILLES TENDON

The Achilles tendon is the lower part of the calf muscle that attaches through a dovetail-like insertion into the heelbone. This tendon is commonly strained, especially in young adults, due to poor stretching before vigorous exercise. It is most commonly strained when playing hardcourt games such as tennis or badminton, and can be extremely painful.

The Achilles tendon can split due to excessive contraction of the calf muscle. This most commonly occurs if the tendon is not stretched before activity, if the body is dehydrated, or if the calf muscle is swollen.

ACHILLES TENDON

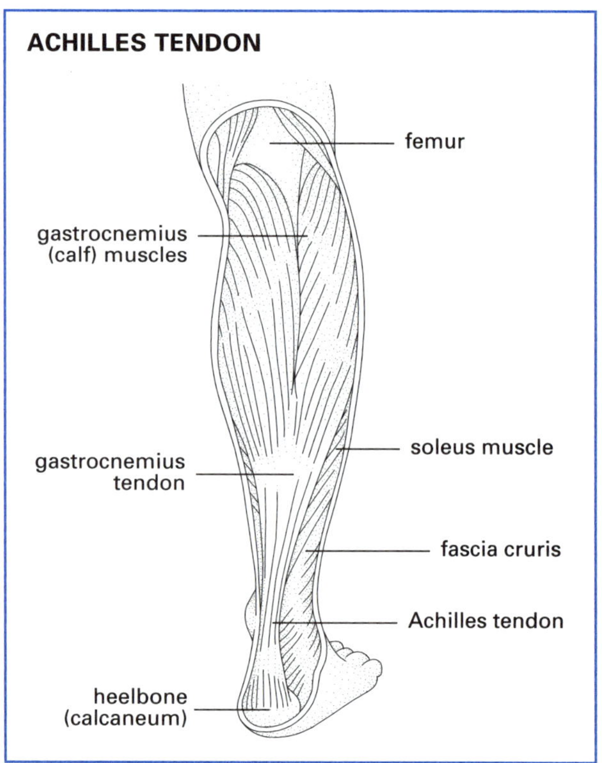

RECOMMENDATIONS

- *Always stretch out before and after exercise.*
- *Apply an Arnica cream to the tendon and calf, if ever there is soreness in that area.*
- *Alternate hot and cold applications via a bucket of hot and iced water.*
- *The remedies Arnica, Rhus toxicodendron, and Ruta should be reviewed.*
- *An Achilles-tendon rupture (which commonly sounds like a gun shot) must be surgically treated.*
- *Persisting discomfort should be reviewed by an osteopath or body worker with knowledge of posture. Incorrectly fitting shoes can be very detrimental.*

BRAS

It may be surprising to come across a section on the bra in a medical book. However, more so than any other garment, the bra can lead to or harbor problems.

Correct fitting is essential. A tight-fitting bra can rub on the skin over a period of time and may lead to slight abrasions that can allow mild infection or *Candida* to set in. Persistent rubbing can lead to skin cancers, and moles that lie underneath the tight-fitting lining of a bra have a higher tendency to develop cancerous changes.

Support is essential, especially for larger breasts in athletic women. Unfettered bouncing can lead to stretching of the ligaments that support the breasts, and this can cause unnecessary sagging in later life.

RECOMMENDATIONS

- *Ensure correct-fitting bras. Bear in mind that breasts may change depending on the time of the month, and it may be necessary to have different-sized bras. Avoid forcing the breasts into cups that are too small.*
- *Spend as much time braless as possible.*
- *Pay special attention to any abrasions or moles that might come into contact with the harder parts of the bra.*
- *Change bras frequently. Despite washing, certain fungi and yeasts can live in bra straps and cause minor irritations.*

BREASTS

Full discussion on care of the breasts is in chapter 5, because more problems arise in that age group.

RECOMMENDATION

- *Read thoroughly the section on breasts in chapter 5, because the sooner you learn how to examine and what to look for, the better.*

COCCYDYNIA

I have yet to meet a nonmedical practitioner who has heard of this condition, although nearly every patient I have ever questioned has suffered from it! Coccydynia or coccygodynia is simply pain in the region of the coccyx, which is the bone at the base of the spine or at the top of the buttock cleft. Most of us will have fallen on it at some point, and this is a major cause of discomfort, although pain can emanate from that area without trauma due to compression of nerves and muscular spasm.

RECOMMENDATIONS

- *As soon as possible, commence the remedy Arnica 6, four pills every hour. Apply Arnica cream and avoid sitting on hard surfaces.*
- *Persisting pain should be examined by an osteopath with knowledge of cranial osteopathy. Chiropractors and acupuncturists may also have an angle on this problem.*
- *Hot baths and hot-water bottles can be instantly relieving.*

DISLOCATIONS

Normally, a joint is made up of two or more bone surfaces opposing each other. They are covered by layers of cartilage, and surrounded and separated by an oily fluid called synovial fluid. The joint is held together by strong fibers known as ligaments, and muscles connect within a few inches either side of the joint via tendons. A dislocation occurs when the two surfaces become unopposed.

A joint may separate and stay unopposed, or it may slip back once having dislocated. This is described as persistent or replaced. If a joint partially dislocates, it is known as a subluxation—these usually spontaneously replace themselves.

Dislocation and subluxation usually occur through injury, although certain conditions weakening the ligaments that hold the joints in place or musculature that give added protection to the stability of joints may be relevant. Dislocations may cause damage to blood vessels, the lymphatic system, and nerve tissues that are associated with the joint, and the pain of a dislocation may cover damage to cartilage or even a fractured bone. It is for this reason that medical attention must be sought whenever a dislocation occurs.

Recognizing a dislocation is often difficult, especially if it has replaced or was a subluxation. A persistent dislocation will show an irregularity of that joint, immobility and considerable pain. A replaced or subluxed joint may not be quite so apparent. The shoulder joint is the most commonly dislocated main joint of the body and is discussed in its own section. (*See* **Dislocation of the shoulder**.)

RECOMMENDATIONS

- *Any suggestion of a dislocation of any sort should be treated as an emergency. Check the part of the body furthest away from the suspected dislocation for bloodflow by checking for a pulse and constantly monitoring the area for coldness or blueness. Obtain medical attention as soon as possible.*
- *Radiography (x-rays) should be considered.*
- *Feel free to use analgesia, especially if the joint has to be replaced.*
- *Use the homeopathic remedy Arnica up to potency 30 every half-hour until the joint has been reestablished and splinted. Thereafter use Arnica 30 and Ruta 30 alternately every 4hr for five days.*
- *Ruta fluid extract, a variety of amino acids, minerals, and multivitamins should all be taken to help speed up the repair process. The amounts vary depending on the individual and the extent of injury. A naturopathic practitioner will advise.*

KNEE—Dislocated and Subluxed

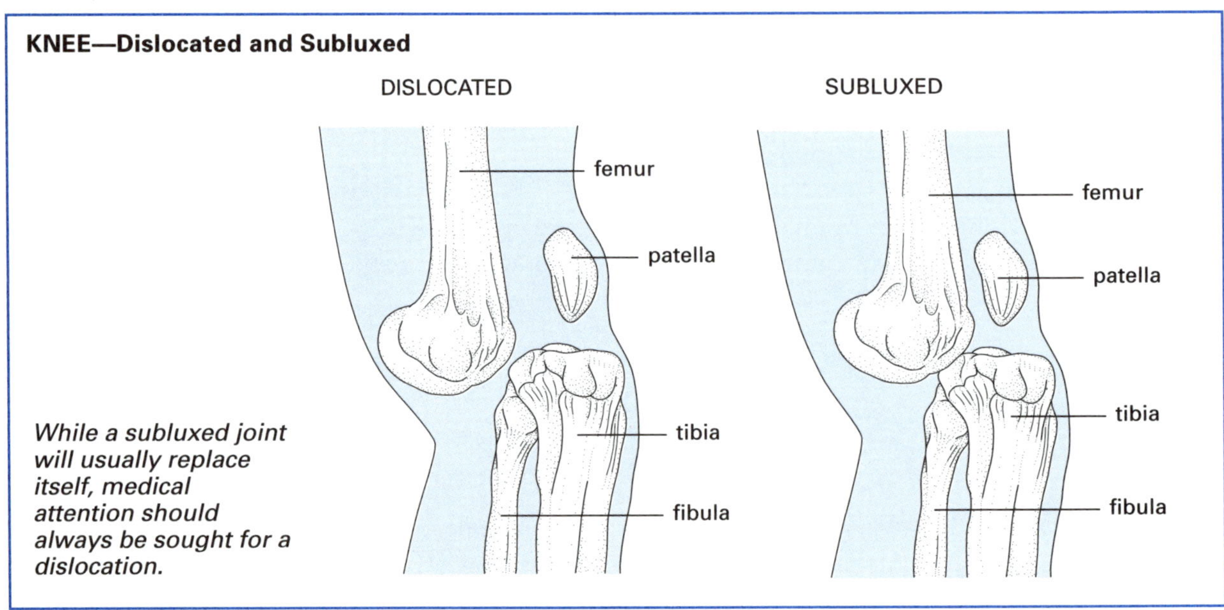

While a subluxed joint will usually replace itself, medical attention should always be sought for a dislocation.

- *Application of Arnica and Calendula creams will draw blood into the area and help healing.*
- *Persisting discomfort will be relieved by acupuncture.*
- *Depending on the joint, a period of time will be advised by the expert dealing with the injury when immobilization is essential. Do not reduce the time of immobility, because this will lead to recurrent dislocation since the tissues will not have had time to repair.*
- *Osteopathic or chiropractic assessment is recommended, because an injury to a joint will inevitably cause extra pressure on the corresponding joint of the body, and also the joints above and below the injury. Backache is not uncommon following any body injury, because of an imbalance in the body's natural fulcrum and structure.*
- *Specialist orthopedic opinion is warranted with any such injury, but if the problem is recurrent, then a surgical procedure may be required.*

FRACTURES OR BROKEN BONES

In medical parlance, a broken bone is referred to as a fracture regardless of its severity. Fractures are divided into simple (the skin is not broken) and compound fractures (the skin and surrounding tissues are damaged). A fracture is considered to be complicated if a blood vessel or nerve has been damaged. Further subdivisions describe the break, such as: complete (where the bone is separated), incomplete (there is just a crack), and multiple (several fragments are visible on X-ray). The term "greenstick" fracture is now used less frequently, but refers to a crack in the bone.

If there has been displacement, there is usually deformity visible, but this is not always the case. Diagnosis of a fracture is difficult without an x-ray, but you must suspect a fracture and seek medical attention in any injury that has:

- swelling
- immobility
- pain
- discoloration from bruising
- an inability to bear weight.

Immediate first-aid

RECOMMENDATIONS

- *If a break is suspected, organize medical attention.*
- *While awaiting medical expertise, immobilize the suspected broken bone by splintering to a piece of wood or similar material or, in the case of the lower limb, the other leg. Fingers and toes can be used similarly.*

Bone Fractures

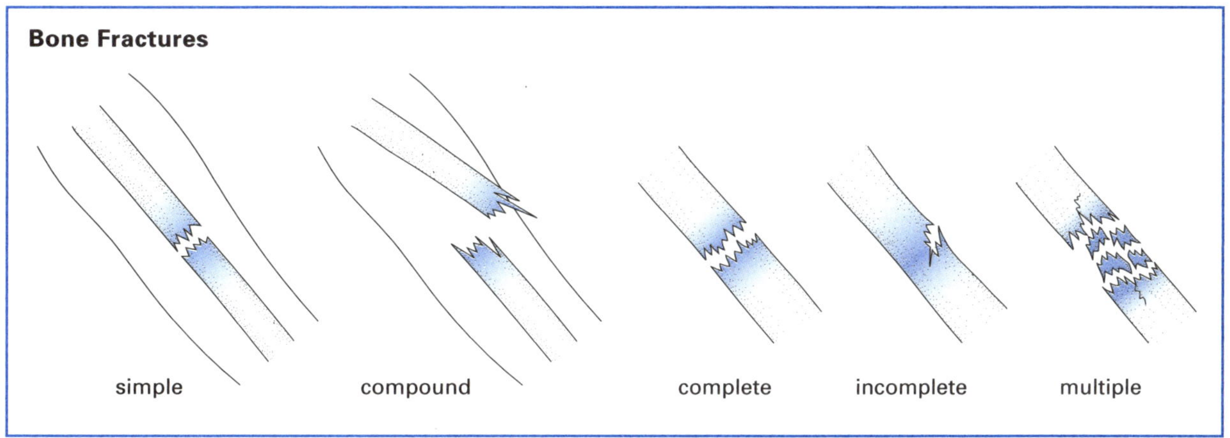

- *Homeopathically, the following routines should be administered: Aconite 6 or 12, four pills every 10min, or Aconite 30 every half-hour for 1hr; then Arnica 30 alternating with Symphytum 30 until the pain has diminished.*
- *Calcium and magnesium supplements should be taken at a maximum dose as recommended on the package.*
- *Increase your protein intake. The calcium in bones is attached to a protein network, and both are required for rapid bone healing.*

After medical treatment

Medical treatment will include assessment, pain relief, and immobilization. If there is much swelling in the area, a plaster-of-Paris "back slab" will be used. This is only a partial-circumference bandage that prevents the swelling from being compressed. After keeping the damaged area raised above the heart (to help decrease the swelling) for 24–72 hours, a full plaster-of-Paris or fiber-glass bandage will immobilize the bone for, on average, six weeks. More aggressive fractures may need to be bandaged for much longer.

While bandaged, the muscles will lose approximately 15–20 percent of their mass, which is usually rebuilt within a few weeks following the correct exercises.

RECOMMENDATIONS

- *Follow your orthopedic consultant's advice. It never pays to shorten the expected healing time, especially if a break is around a joint, because this will lead to an increased risk of arthritis.*
- *The homeopathic remedy Symphytum 30 should be taken three times a day for at least half the length of time you are expecting to be bandaged, and if, following further x-rays, the healing is slow, also use the remedy Calcarea phosphorica 30, twice a day for the remainder of time in the bandage.*
- *The herbal remedy comfrey can be taken as a tea, but not more than one cupful every two days because it may have a toxic effect on the liver if taken in large quantity.*
- *Attend a physiotherapist. The techniques of muscle exercise and ultrasound and electromagnetic therapy can speed up repair.*
- *Ensure that you exercise the joints and muscles that are not restricted by the bandage.*
- *Any injured part will be compensated by its opposite side. This generally leads to an imbalance in the structure, and a visit to an osteopath, Polarity therapist, Shiatsu practitioner, or Alexander technician is advised as soon as the injury has been secured.*
- *Acupuncture can be very beneficial in speeding up long-term injuries. Electroacupuncture is most beneficial.*

FROSTBITE

Frostbite is the nonmedical term for an area that, having been exposed to extreme cold, loses its circulation. Characteristically, the area will be cold, firm, pale, or streaked and, contrary to popular belief, painless. There is initial pain as the cold sets in, but the nerves are numbed by the cold, and pain only returns as the area is warmed. Left untreated, the tissues will die and gangrene will set in.

Individuals with poor circulation are more prone to frostbite, which may occur at higher temperatures than for the rest of the population. Smokers, those with diabetes, and individuals using certain drugs such as beta-blockers may all have a greater predisposition.

RECOMMENDATIONS

- *Do not warm the area rapidly. Apply the affected area to a warm body part, i.e. place the hand in the groin or armpit only.*
- *Common sense prevails: cover the individual with blankets or coats and find shelter.*

- *Administer warm (but not hot) drinks.*
- *Administer painkillers if hospital is not available, and use the homeopathic remedy Apis 30 every 15min as the affected part reheats.*
- *Damaged skin and tissues may respond to the remedy Agaricus muscarius 30 four times a day for five days.*
- *Apply Arnica cream to the area of the injury and above to encourage circulation.*

SHIN SPLINTS

"Shin splints" is a colloquial term for the medical condition "anterior tibial compartment syndrome." The tibia is the shinbone, and on the outer aspect, on the front of the leg, lie the muscles that cause the foot to flex upwards. These muscles are encased in a tough, fibrous sheath known as the anterior-tibial compartment. Pressure and inflammation within this compartment is the cause of a characteristic, dull ache with periods of sharp pain, most commonly associated or worsened by movement.

The term "shin splints" actually has nothing to do with the shinbone, but is caused by small tears in the muscles within this compartment that cause fluid to leak into the tissues, which in turn cause a buildup of pressure in this tightly compacted area. The pressure leads to a diminution in bloodflow, causing ischemia (lack of oxygen), which the nerves register, causing them to send pain impulses to the brain.

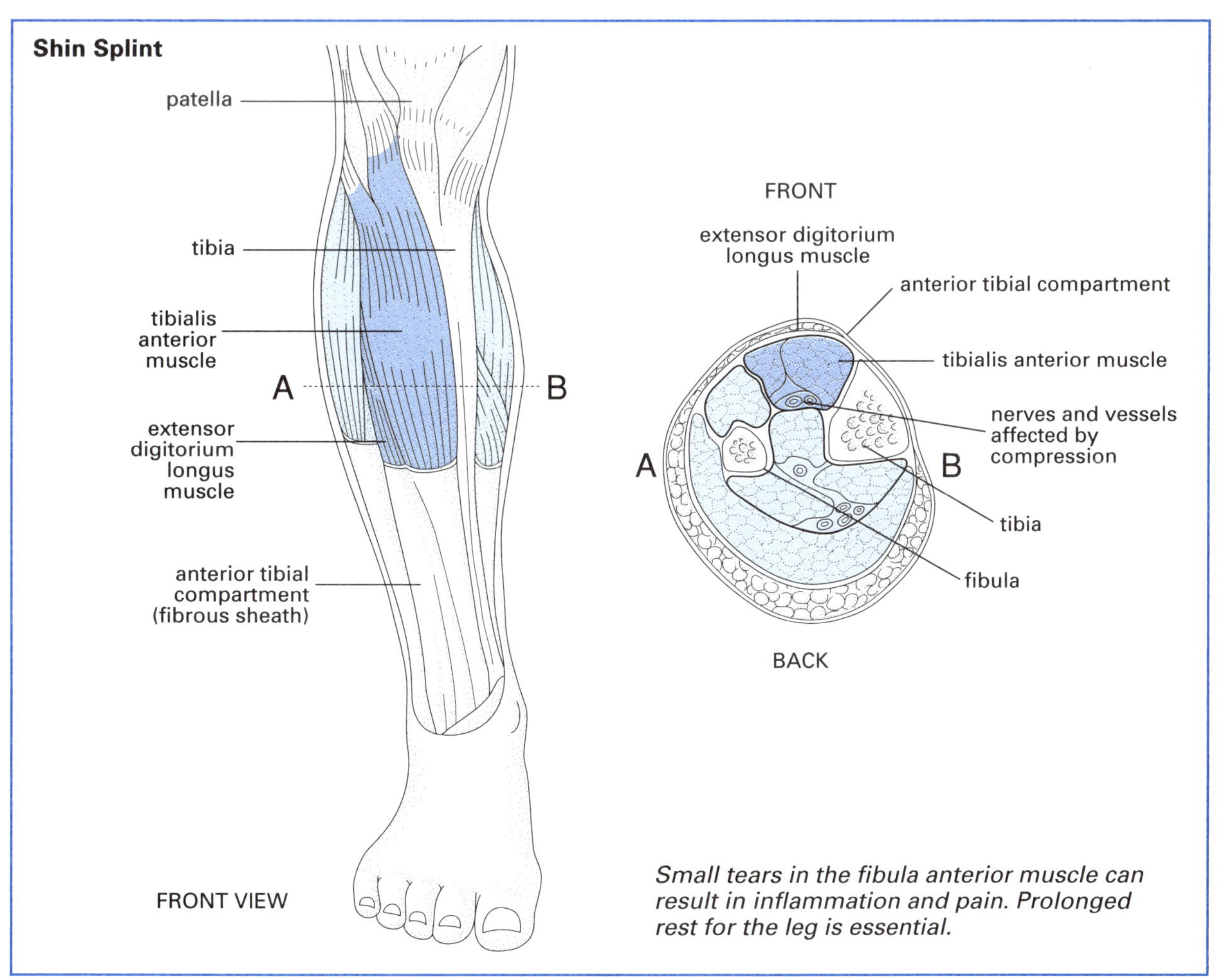

Small tears in the fibula anterior muscle can result in inflammation and pain. Prolonged rest for the leg is essential.

RECOMMENDATIONS

- *At the first sign of this condition, rest is essential. Continuing to exercise the area will worsen the condition and make treatment more difficult. A period of inactivity of up to six weeks may be necessary if the condition is bad.*
- *While warmth may be more soothing, icing the area will reduce the inflammation by decreasing the bloodflow.*
- *Rub in Arnica-based creams several times a day.*
- *Very gentle massage moving the encased fluid up the leg may help the symptoms. If the massage is too aggressive, the bruising will worsen. Massage is important once the condition has settled, because it will prevent recurrence.*
- *Ultrasound or deep-heat treatment is occasionally given by those who do not understand the underlying physiology. This will encourage bloodflow and prolong the condition.*
- *The homeopathic remedies Arnica, Bryonia, Rhus toxicodendron, and Ruta should all be considered through examination of your preferred manual. Take potency 6 every 3hr when the condition starts, and after three days increase the potency to 30, but reduce the frequency to twice a day until the condition has resolved.*
- *Acupuncture may be instantly relieving.*
- *Osteopathy should be considered because manipulative techniques may help the lymphatic drainage, thereby clearing the excess fluid, and also the malalignment that is common because of the other side of the body taking more strain.*
- *When returning to exercise, start slowly and avoid exercise on hard surfaces, such as road jogging, basketball, and tennis.*

THE SHOULDER

This region, where the arm joins the trunk of the body, is formed by the meeting of three bones—the clavicle, scapula, and humerus—that create several joints, all and any of which can cause shoulder pain and varying degrees of immobility.

The shoulder is a complex area and its ball-and-socket joint between the upper-armbone (humerus) and the scapula is the most flexible in the body.

Bone injury

Fractures of any part of the shoulder joint are painful, but specifically difficult to heal if the joint surfaces are involved.

RECOMMENDATIONS

- *Any shoulder injury should be examined by a doctor or osteopath. An x-ray is usually recommended.*
- *Immobility for a minimum of six weeks is recommended in most fractures, or longer if the articular surface has been compromised. Do not shirk on this or try to do too much too soon, because long-term arthritis is the usual outcome.*
- *Fractures of the scapula cannot be splinted, and severe breaks in this area or anywhere in the shoulder joint may require surgical pinning.*
- *The clavicle is more-commonly fractured in contact sports and events like skiing. It may often be left to heal even though the bones may be considerably malaligned.*
- *See* **Fractures**.

Dislocation of the shoulder

Dislocation of the shoulder generally refers to the misalignment between the head of the humerus and the socket aspect of the scapula. If the dislocation occurs forward, it is known as an anterior dislocation, and backwards as a posterior dislocation. The dislocation may repair spontaneously or may stay out of place, in which case it needs manipulating.

To dislocate usually requires a considerable amount of force, because of the strength of the ligaments and muscles surrounding the shoulder joint. Falling on an outstretched arm is the usual cause. Because of the anatomy of the shoulder the

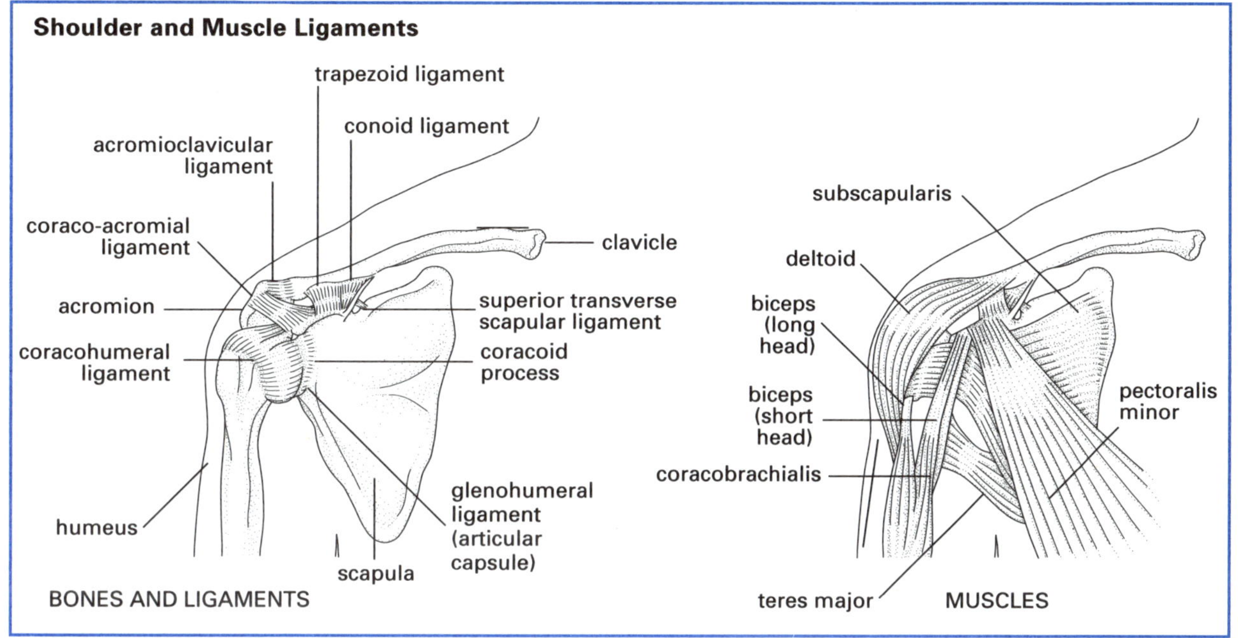

head of the humerus tears through the anterior-synovial capsule four times more frequently than the posterior aspect. Damage to the nerves and arteries running through the armpit is not uncommon, and when replacing a dislocated shoulder, this needs to be borne in mind. A relocation must be done swiftly if the pulse is compromised at the wrist. If numbness or paralysis of the fingers has ensued, then replacement should be done by medically-trained personnel for fear of risking further nerve damage.

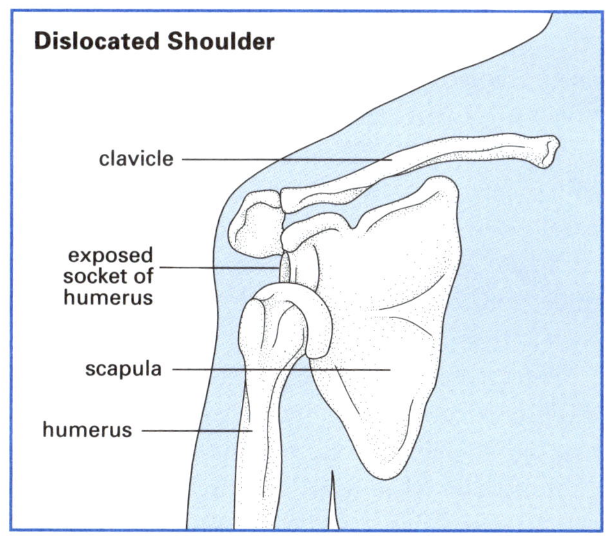

RECOMMENDATIONS

- *See* **Dislocations**.
- *Emergency replacement or relocation of the humerus when no complications are observed should proceed as follows, but only if the joint cannot be stabilized until a professional can do the job:*
  - *(a) The arm will be flexed at the elbow because of the shortening of the biceps tendons, and will automatically be across the chest in an anterior dislocation. Hold the forearm as close to the elbow as possible, and apply gentle, downward traction.*
  - *(b) Move the hand of the dislocated arm outwards, continuing to apply strong-but-gentle traction downwards at the elbow as in (a) above.*
  - *(c) If the shoulder has not realigned, gently pull the elbow towards the other shoulder while continuing the downward traction and keeping the hand rotated away from the body.*
  - *(d) This is a painful process, and should preferably only be done if analgesia is available.*

Frozen shoulder

A frozen shoulder is a chronic or longstanding inflammation of the tendons and synovial capsule around the shoulder joint. It is characterized by pain that gets worse on moving the shoulder. Any motion is limited by this pain.

This lay term has passed into medical parlance and represents a painful tightening of the muscles around the shoulder joint. It is most commonly created by an initial pain causing a lack of movement on a persistent basis, leading to a profound stiffness and worsening of the pain in these muscles.

The causes are generally unknown, but there is increased vascularity, degeneration, and scarring of the fibers within the tendons and synovial capsule. Arthritic conditions and trauma are often associated.

Several meridians or energy channels travel across the shoulder joint or are indirectly connected. These include the large and small intestine, heart, lung, and reproductive organs. The triple heater (arguably the energy line that controls the heat of the body via its influence on the adrenal and thyroid glands) is very much associated with shoulder problems. The triple heater is often weakened in stress situations. Problems such as frozen shoulder that have no obvious causative factor need to be reviewed from this point of view.

RECOMMENDATIONS

- *Osteopathic or chiropractic assessment is necessary for a firm diagnosis.*
- *Manipulative treatment, including work on the neck and spine, is mandatory.*
- *Acupuncture may be instantly relieving, and should be used in combination with osteopathy.*
- *Shiatsu may take the place of both of the above.*
- *The application of heat may pull blood to the surface, reducing inflammation; or holding an ice bag over the area for a period of time may cool the area down. Both techniques may be soothing, but neither are particularly relevant in long-term care.*
- *Ensure good hydration because persistent cramps may be indicative of dehydration: 48 ounces of water on top of current intake (up to a maximum of 96 ounces per day) is necessary.*
- *Ensure that calcium and magnesium supplements are being taken at three times the daily recommended dose on a chelated product.*
- *Homeopathic remedies should be reviewed in your preferred manual, and specific attention paid to Arnica, Rhus toxicodendron, and Ruta.*
- *Arnica 6 can be used every hour if pain and limitation of movement is noticed.*
- *Avoid orthodox practitioners because the treatments of choice are anti-inflammatory drugs and steroid injections, which may give temporary relief and a full sense of well-being that will allow further movement, but longer-term injury and recurrence are not uncommon.*

SPINAL INJURY

An injury to the spine is a serious and potentially grave injury. At best, it may represent a rupture of ligaments or a crack in the vertebrae, but at worst it may mean injury or severance of the spinal nerve cord. The possibility of an injury progressing due to instability of the vertebrae means that all spinal injuries need to be treated the same, and with the utmost care and urgency until a firm diagnosis is made by a qualified medical practitioner or casualty team.

If the casualty is not correctly handled, the spinal cord may be permanently damaged, with paralysis or death resulting.

Spinal injury generally occurs as a result of a direct force, a fall, or hyperflexion or extension, such as in a whiplash injury.

A fracture of the vertebrae will not be known until an x-ray is taken, but a dislodged vertebra may be palpable. If the patient is conscious the pain must be taken into account, but pain is generally a better sign than no pain.

RECOMMENDATIONS

- *If the patient is conscious then remind and insist that he/she does not move.*
- *Assess by asking questions, which should include: "Where does it hurt?," "Can you feel your fingers and toes?," "Can you move your fingers and toes?" The point of asking these questions is simply to reassure and to have an idea of the gravity of the situation. Whatever the answers, the individual must not move until medical expertise has arrived. Brief the medic on his/her arrival.*
- *Cover the individual with a blanket or whatever it takes to keep him/her warm.*
- *If medical aid is not forthcoming or is unavailable, only then should transportation of the individual be considered.*
- *Enlist as much help as possible, and keep the individual's shoulders and pelvis in the position they were in when the casualty was found. Place pads of soft material between the thighs, knees, and ankles.*
- *Tie the ankles and feet together with a figure-of-eight bandage, and tie bandages around the thighs and knees. Make do with whatever material is available.*
- *The casualty is best transported in the face-upwards position, but only if that was the position in which he/she was found. Do not turn the neck to accommodate this.*
- *An unconscious casualty must be supported with blankets, pillows, or any material to avoid movement.*
- *A stretcher must be a stiff board. Consider a door if nothing else is available.*
- *Once the casualty is on the board and supported, strap down around the forehead, shoulders, pelvis, and knees, and then place in the smoothest vehicle available.*
- *Avoid giving anything by mouth.*
- *At all times throughout this procedure, ensure that the airways, breathing, and circulation (ABC) are intact. Commence cardiopulmonary resuscitation (CPR) at any stage, attempting to keep the patient in the correct position.*

STRESS FRACTURE

A stress fracture is a small crack or break in a bone that occurs because of excess pressure or overuse of a part of the body. It is most commonly found in soldiers who march or athletes whose footwear has not protected them from the hard surface they may be exercising on. Basketball players who constantly land on a hard-covered wooden playing area are very prone to stress fractures of the feet.

RECOMMENDATIONS

- *Rest is unfortunately an essential part of healing a stress fracture.*
- *See* **Fractures***.*
- *The use of ultrasound may speed up the process in bone-stress fractures beyond that of most other bone injuries.*
- *Reflexology will speed up healing in most injuries.*

SWELLING

For swelling that is generalized throughout the body, or the swelling of both ankles or legs, *see* **Edema** and **Fluid Retention**. The swelling of one part of the body, such as a leg, arm, hand, or foot, may be due to lymphatic obstruction caused by a trauma, inflamed or infected lymph glands, or tumors blocking lymphatic flow. All of these conditions need to be reviewed independently once a cause is established.

A swelling caused by an injury or infection represents the body's attempt to splint, immobilize, and repair the area. The site of a swelling is also a warning to the conscious mind that protection is necessary, and a similar injury-causing event should be avoided.

Damaged tissue sends a nervous reflex to the spinal column that returns instructions to the surrounding blood vessels to open up and flood the area with more nutrition, oxygen, white blood

ARM—Swelling

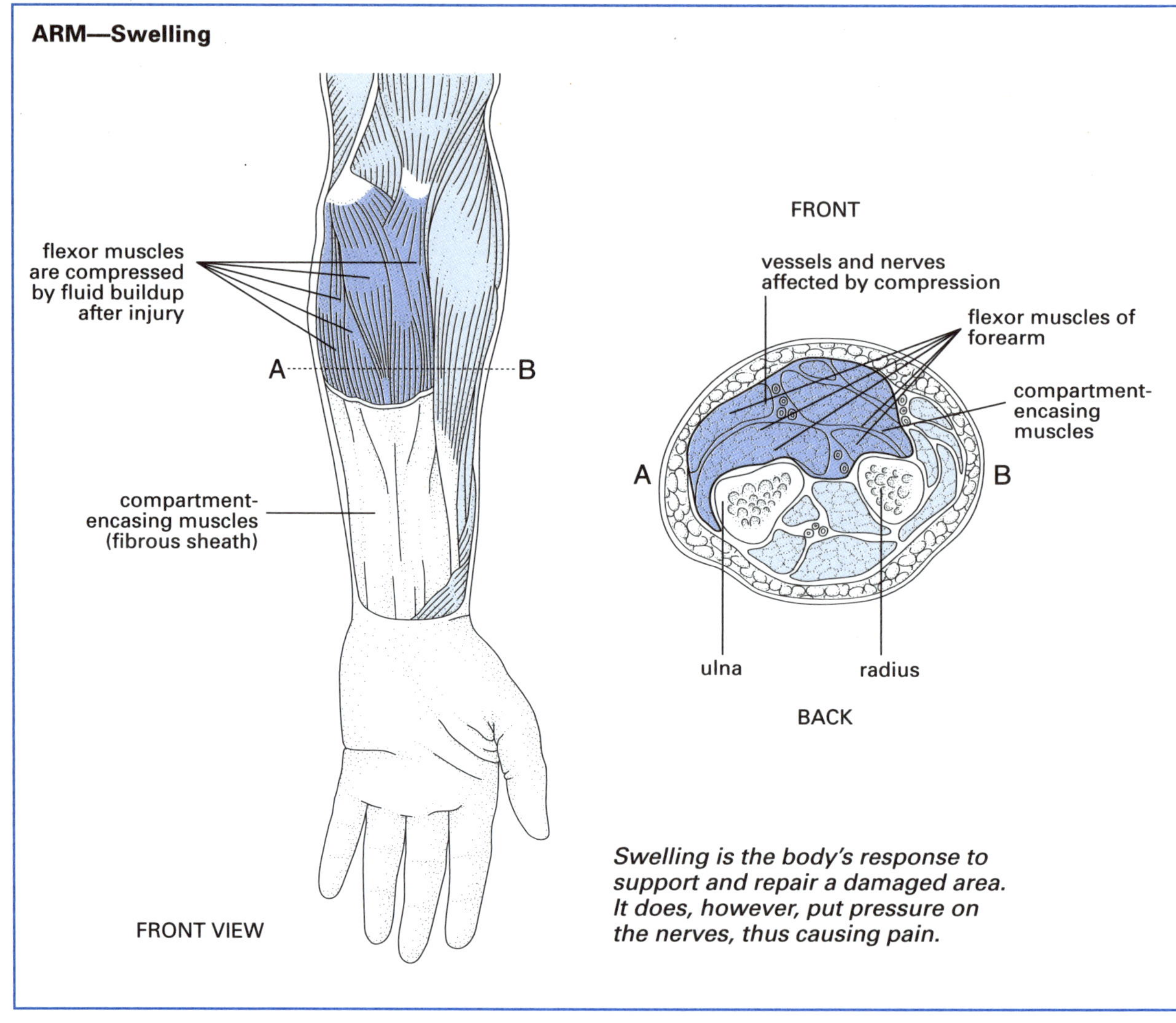

Swelling is the body's response to support and repair a damaged area. It does, however, put pressure on the nerves, thus causing pain.

cells, and scar-forming cells. Blood vessels are also encouraged to open by the release of certain chemicals from injured cells.

In principle, the body should be allowed to get along with its healing, but swelling does apply pressure to nerves and, like inflammation, causes pain. Reduction of swelling will occur automatically as soon as the injured area is given support, and this can be encouraged by applying pressure to the lymphatic and venous flow, thus taking fluid from the area.

RECOMMENDATIONS

- *Application of ice in a towel may relieve swelling.*
- *Ensure that the injured area is immobilized if a joint is involved, has pressure applied to it through bandaging, and is rested.*
- *The homeopathic remedy Arnica 6 should be taken every hour for three doses and then every 3hr until a more suitable remedy is chosen, on the basis of the specifics of the injury. An accurate remedy should be chosen from your preferred homeopathic manual.*
- *Rub in an Arnica-based cream three or four times a day.*
- *Massage, paying special attention to moving fluid towards the heart; any physical-therapy technique will benefit.*

THE SKIN

ACNE

Acne is caused by an excess production of sebum, the waxy substance that our skin produces. The overproduction clogs the skin's pores, leading to blackheads, pimples, and pustules. Nearly everyone at some time will have this problem, but unhappily, it can be very severe in a few of us.

There is some correlation between poor diet or hygiene and acne, and a certain amount of improvement can be made by changes of habit. Very often, the difficulty lies in the sebum being too viscous, and dehydration may be a major factor. Secondary infection by skin bacteria worsens the situation.

Any skin problem may have a psychological basis. Stress causes adrenaline-like substances to be produced that cut down the bloodflow to the skin. This prevents nutrition, protection, and healing from reaching the skin at the necessary levels.

There is a correlation between acne and hormonal changes or imbalances. Acne is most prominent in teenagers going through puberty. The actual mechanism is uncertain, but may be due to the hormonal effect on sebum-producing cells, on skin bacteria, or the effect of hormones on the skin blood supply, thereby encouraging more oxygen and nutrition to either the sebum-producing cells or the skin bacteria.

RECOMMENDATIONS

- *Ensure that you are drinking 8 ounces of water for every one foot of height.*
- *Use nonmedicated soaps and no oil-based cosmetics. Try sandalwood or Calendula soap if available.*
- *Some people will benefit by reducing fried foods, spicy foods, citrus, and all refined (white) sugars.*
- *Tea tree oil (one drop to five drops of olive oil) applied to the skin after cleaning can be curative. Dilute further if this stings.*
- *In moderate-to-severe cases, use a teaspoonful of garbanzo-bean flour with a teaspoonful of almond powder mixed in goat's milk. Apply for a few minutes twice a day.*
- *Try Evening Primrose Oil (1g three times a day), zinc (15mg before sleep), and copper (2mg with breakfast).*
- *Homeopathy can work wonders. Look up the remedies Sulphur, Kali bromatum, and Antimonium tartaricum. A homeopath's opinion is well warranted.*
- *Deal with your stress levels. Learn some basic meditation and visualization techniques. I am often amazed at how swiftly skin conditions, including acne, will clear when anxieties are relieved.*
- *Consider hypnotherapy if basic relaxation has no impact.*
- *Under the supervision of a complementary medical practitioner, try a natural estrogen extract, and if this does not work, try a natural progesterone treatment. The herb Agnus castus can be very beneficial.*

AEROSOLS

Do not use them. They are environmentally unfriendly, and contain innumerable chemicals that are, to some extent, absorbed through the skin. Use natural fragrances in basic oils rubbed onto the skin instead.

BLISTERS

Blisters are caused by fluid leaving damaged blood vessels, generally after a pinch, friction, or excess heat. This fluid contains many of the nutrients that help the repair process, and should be allowed to stay in the area. If the blister becomes too full, it can start to cause pressure on the stretch-sensitive nerves and produce pain. This is the only indication to burst a blister, and it should be done under medical supervision only.

RECOMMENDATIONS

- *Do not burst a blister.*
- *See* **Burns**.
- *Applying gentle pressure to the blister may take away some of the discomfort.*
- *Apply Arnica creams or lotions. If the blister is on the fingers or toes, use Hypericum creams or lotions.*
- *Review the homeopathic remedies Cantharis and Rhus toxicodendron for small blisters.*
- *Recurrent blisters or blisters that occur after no apparent injury may represent an underlying condition that requires medical diagnosis, and this should be assessed by your family practitioner.*

BOILS (FURUNCLES)

A boil is a localized infection of the skin and subcutaneous tissue. It usually starts around a hair follicle and develops into a solitary abscess. An abscess is defined as a collection of pus (the body's dead, white blood cells) that drains to the nearest surface through a single tract. This may be external to the skin or internal to the bowel, lungs, etc.

They are differentiated from pimples by an arbitrary decision on the size.

RECOMMENDATIONS

- *Recurrent, numerous, or persistent boils should be addressed by a complementary medical practitioner.*
- *Application of hot and then cold compresses can draw a boil out.*
- *Soaked oats and wholegrain-bread poultices may be very beneficial.*
- *The homeopathic remedy Hepar sulfuris calcarium 6, four pills every hour, is one of the rare master remedies for a general condition.*
- *Boils should only be lanced under medical supervision.*
- *Application of Arnica creams is encouraged.*
- *Any boil around the anus must be treated by a medically-qualified complementary practitioner immediately. They have a higher tendency to drain inwards, allowing a tract for the feces and related bacteria to travel into the boil/abscess.*

BRUISES

A bruise is caused by damage to capillaries and larger blood vessels, allowing blood to drain into the tissues. The variety of colors that appear in the skin are due to the amount of blood and the contents of the blood cells moving to the surface. Superficial bruises are rarely complicated, deeper bruises can cause extreme pain by cramping muscles, and a bruise underneath the tough lining of bones is excruciating.

If bruising occurs with minor bumps or for no apparent reason, this may indicate fragile capillaries or an underlying deficiency in the body's clotting mechanism.

RECOMMENDATIONS

- *If a bruise is persisting or is extremely painful, obtain an examination from a doctor or osteopath/chiropractor to ensure that no underlying damage is being concealed. A hematologist should be consulted if bruises are occurring too easily.*
- *Apply Arnica and Urtica creams on a regular basis throughout the day.*
- *Hot-and-cold applications can be very relieving.*
- *Fragile capillaries can be improved through nutritional and herbal treatments, but these require a consultation with a complementary medical practitioner.*
- *Large bruises can be dissipated quicker by the use of massage and an unusual aromatherapy oil called Helichrysum. Hyssop or lavender are more easily available and can be equally effective. Place a few drops into five tablespoonsful of extra virgin olive oil and apply.*

- *The homeopathic remedies Arnica and Bellis perennis can be used at potency 6, four pills every 4hr.*
- *If there is no underlying illness for recurrent bruises, then one can administer the following in divided doses with each meal: vitamin C (1g per foot of height per day), vitamin E (100iu per foot of height per day) and vitamin A (1,000iu per foot of height per day).*

CARBUNCLES—*see* Boils

CELLULITIS

The medical term for inflammation is "itis." Cellulitis is, therefore, an inflammation of cells. It presents as a red area, usually around or spreading from an injury or lesion. Cellulitis can occur at any age, but is most commonly found following accidents, allowing bacteria to get underneath the skin and cause infection. The body's response is to send blood into the area carrying white blood cells, and this increase in bloodflow causes redness, swelling, and pain.

Cellulitis is often associated with "tracking," which is seen as streaks of red traveling away from the area of inflammation through lympathic ducts towards the nearest group of lymph nodes.

Cellulitis can spread very rapidly, especially if the infection is a virulent staphylococcal bacteria. Often associated with conditions that reduce the immune system, such as diabetes, use of steroids, AIDS, and nutritional deficiencies, the problem should not be underestimated.

RECOMMENDATIONS

- *Any cellulitis that is spreading rapidly should be seen by a doctor, and antibiotics should be utilized along with complementary medicine to help protect against the unwanted side effects from the antibiotics.*
- *If the cellulitis is mild, then complementary medical care can be used, provided that the condition does not worsen.*
- *Apply hot-and-cold compresses to the area, and clean any associated wound with Arnica, Calendula, or Hypericum solution.*
- *Take some white bread, steep in Arnica, Calendula, or Hypericum solution, apply to the area, and gently wrap with a suitable cloth or bandage.*
- *The homeopathic remedies Apis, Urtica, Belladonna, Calendula, and Hypericum can all be reviewed in your homeopathic manual.*

CHLOASMA

This patchy hyperpigmentation is most often seen on the face, nipples, and down the middle of the abdomen, although it can show up anywhere. The patches may be of varying size, and often become marked during pregnancy, menstruation, and with disorders of the ovaries or uterus, and occasionally in association with tumors.

Very often, the condition has no obvious cause but may be due to the action of sunshine on areas of the skin affected by perfumes and cosmetics, as well as certain hormonal problems.

Chloasma

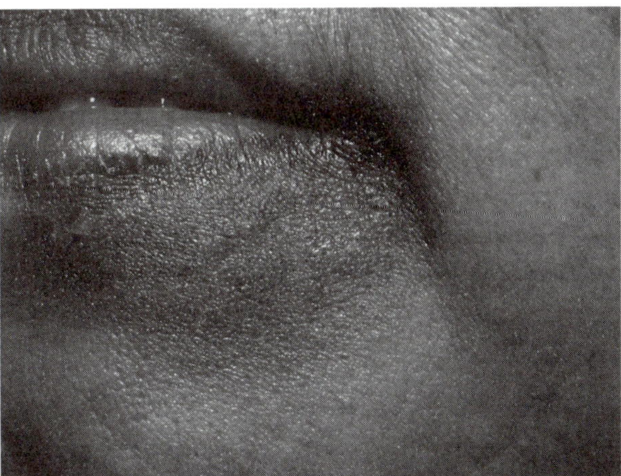

RECOMMENDATIONS

- *A full assessment from a medical practitioner to rule out anything nasty is the first step.*
- *Avoid buying any medicated compounds, cosmetics, or perfumes for use on the areas affected.*

- *Obtain a complementary medical view from a homeopath and/or herbalist, because these two branches of medicine claim to have the highest success rates.*
- *As with all skin conditions, subconscious or underlying psychological conditions must be determined, either through counseling or hypnotherapy.*

CRABS

This very unfortunate term is given to an infestation of small parasites that do, under the microscope, resemble the shape of beach crabs. Generally considered to be a sexually-transmitted parasite, although transmission can occur through any contact (not only sexual), these small parasites tend to live in the pubic hair.

RECOMMENDATION

- *See* **Lice**.

ERYSIPELAS

This is a form of acute streptococcal cellulitis confined to the skin, and having a slightly raised, red area with a well-demarcated, advancing border. There are many types, depending on associated symptoms and the presence of pustules or vesicles. The condition may be very aggressive and spread rapidly, or persist over a period of time. Diagnosis is made by a general practitioner or dermatologist.

RECOMMENDATIONS

- *When a diagnosis of erysipelas is made, treatment should depend upon the speed of spread. If fast and aggressive, then antibiotics must be considered.*
- *A slow or persistent area of erysipelas may be treated constitutionally by a complementary medical practitioner.*
- *See* **Cellulitis**.

FUNGAL INFECTIONS

Fungus is a low form of plant life, most commonly thought of as mushrooms and growths on the side of trees. Similar but different organisms live on and under the human skin, and may even colonize our intestine. Many of these fungi are harmless, and may compete with more aggressive or pathogenic fungi, thereby being protective. This is an important factor when treating fungal conditions, because we do not wish to wipe out our own beneficial flora.

Most fungal infections are noticed because of red, itchy, inflamed areas on the skin. Athlete's foot (*see* **Athlete's foot**) is the most frequent, but fungi will grow in any darkened or moist area such as the groin, under the breasts, armpits, and skin folds, especially in those who are overweight.

Fungi will predominate in those who are immunocompromised and, while not dangerous, can be an indication of a depressed immune system.

Medically speaking, nails are an extension of the skin, and therefore fungal infections of the nails should also respond to the following recommendations. Fungal infections of the nails are characterized by a discoloration (usually yellowing) and thickening of the nail without any discomfort. The fungus is embedded in the growing part of the nail (the nailbed) and is difficult to get at. Orthodox treatment recommends oral antifungal agents that will unfortunately not only destroy the harmful fungus over a six-month period, but will also potentially damage the healthy fungus that we have on our skin and in our bowel. This treatment is not recommended by holistic practitioners, who are more concerned with the underlying deficiency in the immune system that has allowed the fungus to settle.

RECOMMENDATIONS

- *Twice-daily applications of vinegar, selenium-containing solutions, or grapeseed extracts can be applied.*

- *Garlic can be applied, although the smell may be unsociable. Fungal infections under the nail respond well to twice-daily applications of garlic under the nail and around the nailbed.*
- *Tea tree oil applied in a solution as concentrated as the skin will allow (there should be no discomfort) is effective.*
- *Reduce refined sugars and sweet foods.*
- *Aerate the affected areas as much as possible.*
- *There may be an association with yeast infection in the system, and persisting fungal infections should be treated systematically (by looking at the whole body) by a complementary medical practitioner.*
- *If the above techniques fail, then antifungal-drug treatments from the pharmacist can be used, but avoid oral-antifungal drug treatment by seeking complementary advice.*

MOLES

A mole is a fleshy, pigmented lesion known in medical parlance as a nevus. These lesions contain increased amounts of melanocytes, which give the skin its pigmentation. In themselves moles are harmless but disfiguring, and if very obvious or very numerous, can cause social embarrassment and feelings of inadequacy.

Melanoma and Solar keratosis

Melanomas should be distinguished from solar keratosis—a precancerous condition caused by overexposure to the sun.

A mole carries a slight chance of becoming a melanoma (*see* **Melanoma**), and it is therefore important to watch out, for the following signs:

- an increase in size
- a change or variation in colour
- bleeding
- itching.

Moles may appear on meridians or energy lines, and be reflective of underlying weakness in an organ. Multiple moles probably have no relevancy, but a single mole, especially if there at birth or developing in the first few years of life, could be assessed by a Chinese or Tibetan practitioner, who may compare its position with weaknesses in the pulses.

RECOMMENDATIONS

- *Most moles are harmless, but any of the changes mentioned above should raise suspicion, and a doctor or dermatologist should be consulted.*
- *Removal and microscopic examination of the mole is the only sure way of establishing its innocence.*
- *See* **Operations and surgery** *if necessary.*
- *The homeopathic remedy Thuja can be taken at potency 200, one dose daily for three days every three months, as a possible protective measure in individuals with many moles.*

PIMPLES

A pimple is a small pustule or circumscribed elevation of the skin that, by definition, is less than half an inch in diameter. Any bigger than that and it is considered a boil or abscess.

Pimples can be found at any age, but are particularly prominent through the teenage years in response to hormonal activity and increased intake of refined sugar.

RECOMMENDATION

See **Acne** *and* **Boils**.

PITYRIASIS

Pityriasis is a fine, scaly condition of the skin. There are many different types, defined by the position on the body or shape of the lesion. There may be an association with vesicles and pustules, and the condition may even be in the body, such as on the tongue.

Pityriasis rosea

This is a common, self-limiting skin disease of the trunk that usually clears up within three months. It is characterized by a pale-red patch with a fawn-colored center. There may be one or many patches, which usually appear on the trunk and upper arms and thighs.

RECOMMENDATIONS

- *See* **Rashes**.
- *Specific homeopathic treatment should be selected on the symptoms and the person as a whole by a homeopath, but Natrum muriaticum 6 taken four times a day may clear the problem.*
- *Application of Calendula or Urtica-based creams are useful.*
- *Examination of where the lesions are by an acupuncturist or specialist with a knowledge of acupuncture points may be beneficial to discover any underlying weakness in the system that has allowed this condition of unknown origin to occur.*

PRURITUS

Pruritus is an itching or uncomfortable sensation due to irritation of the peripheral sensory nerves, usually caused by inflammatory chemicals being produced from surrounding cells due to infection or external irritation.

Most commonly, pruritus ani (an itchy anus) is seen in childhood and is discussed in chapter 3 (*see* **Pruritus ani**). Other common causes include a cold climate, particularly the dry, cold conditions caused by air conditioning. Pruritus senilis is triggered in the elderly by a lack of sebum (the body's skin-oil). Pruritus vulvae is an intense or mild itching of the vulva and vagina.

The causes may be chemical irritation, mild infections such as thrush (*Candida*) or a contact dermatitis. If left unattended, secondary infection from bacteria may evolve, which will lead to damage of the skin and, in the case of the vulva, possible malignancy.

RECOMMENDATIONS

- *Treatment is dependent upon the cause being removed.*
- *See* **Itching skin** *and* **Itching vagina.**
- *Application of a Calendula or Urtica cream may be curative in pruritus ani or vulvae.*
- *Pruritus senilis may benefit from increased levels of EPA or fish oils, and the levels should be determined by consultation with a nutritionist because digestive processes may be troubled in some cases.*

PSORIASIS

Psoriasis is a skin disease that is characterized by the development of red patches that are covered over with silvery-white scales. The disease affects the scalp and extensor surfaces of the elbows and knees mostly, but can appear anywhere on the body.

The skin grows from a basal cell at the bottom of several layers of cells. These basal cells multiply in psoriasis up to 1,000 times faster than they should. The resulting higher layers cannot shed off quickly enough, and the characteristic appearance results. There are two chemical complexes, called cAMP and cGMP, that inhibit or encourage cell proliferation, respectively. An imbalance caused by a decrease of cAMP or an increase of cGMP results in excessive cell growth.

There are many factors that can imbalance these chemicals. Certain proteins and toxic compounds from bacterial and yeast metabolism in the bowel are known to inhibit cAMP or increase cGMP, respectively. The proteins and toxins responsible are derived from unbalanced bowel flora or digestive incapabilities, and are an essential factor in treating psoriasis.

Toxins are normally broken down by the liver, and any deficiency in liver function will cause or encourage psoriasis. Alcohol and smoking are particularly straining on the liver, as are most drugs. Several studies have shown the damaging effect of alcohol and cigarettes on psoriasis cases.

Deficiencies in certain oils, amino acids, and zinc have all been shown to cause psoriasis. Increased levels of insulin and glucose also seem to have an effect.

There is evidence that stressful events may trigger psoriasis, and certainly stress is an important factor in most skin conditions because adrenaline and other catecholamine levels affect the amount of bloodflow to the skin.

There may be some connection to an autoimmune syndrome (the body attacking itself), because an arthritic condition may be associated with psoriasis. Nails may become characteristically pitted due to fluctuations in the growth rate of the nailbed.

RECOMMENDATIONS

- *The association with bowel toxicity is well documented. It is necessary to remove animal fats, refined sugars, and sweetness in general and yeasty or fungal foods such as bread and mushrooms.*
- *Weight-reducing diets automatically cut out refined foods, and may be beneficial.*
- *Regular bowel motions are necessary to keep the colon cleansed, and increased fiber and water intake is essential.*
- *Oily fish such as salmon, herring, and mackerel should also be added into the diet, along with one teaspoonful of flaxseed oil per foot of height.*
- *Learn a meditation technique, and increase exercise to a substantial level.*
- *Ultraviolet light from sunshine is beneficial. Ultraviolet B is a preferred treatment, although ultraviolet A (PUVA therapy) is offered by orthodox treatment centers. The PUVA therapy may be associated with side effects.*
- *Vitamin D, licorice, comfrey and camomile-based creams or lotions have been shown to be beneficial. Try one at a time, and note any benefits.*
- *Localized heat through electric pads or ultrasound may be effective.*
- *The following supplements should be taken in divided doses with food per foot of height: folic acid (100µg), beta-carotene (2mg), vitamin E (100iu), selenium (40µg), eicosapentenoic acid (1g, and zinc (5mg before bed). All of these should be administered daily for one month, and if improvement is noted, remove one supplement each ten days, starting with the vitamin E. If any deterioration is noted, add back that compound and see if you can isolate the particularly active supplement. Discuss with a nutritionist the foods that may be absent in your diet that contain any culprit.*
- *The herb Sarsaparilla, taken as a dried root should be used (1g per foot of height in divided doses throughout the day).*
- *Milk thistle could be taken. Take twice the advised dose on any product recommended by your local healthfood store or herbalist.*

SHAVING RASH (BARBER'S RASH)

This red, itching, and irritating rash is associated with shaved areas. It is caused by the normal skin bacteria (*Staphylococcus*) accessing the lower levels of the skin due to small abrasions following shaving.

RECOMMENDATIONS

- *Avoid shaving an infected area until the problem has cleared.*

- *The use of aftershave causes a reflex closure of opened pores, and also acts as a mild antiseptic against skin bacteria for a short while. Its use, especially on skins with a tendency to shaving rash, may be painful, but lessens the risk of infection.*
- *Choose an aftershave that is as nonmedicated as possible, and use small amounts because the chemicals used in proprietary types may cause local or toxic problems.*
- *See* **Itching skin**.

SUNBURN

A burn from the sun may be as mild or serious as a burn from any other source of heat. First-, second-, and third-degree burns are all conceivable. Sunburn may be more damaging than other burns, because generally more of the skin is damaged. Sunburn frequently occurs in a relaxed situation where suntanning was intended, or the effect of the sun went unnoticed or was underestimated, perhaps because of being in a swimming-pool or the sea, with its cooling effects.

Sunburn is often associated with heatstroke, and because the damage may be caused by ultraviolet light, not heat alone, a sunburn can penetrate below skin level.

Sunscreens

Increased use is being made of ultraviolet light-blocking chemicals in preparations known as sunscreens. These are expensive, and tend to be improperly used. Their principal function is as a barrier, and if significant amounts are not actually placed on the skin, then the effect is minimal. Most users will rub the lotion in, as opposed to leaving it on the surface.

What is more disturbing is the suggestion, in a recent study, that those who use sunscreens to achieve a tan run an increased risk of melanoma and possibly other skin cancers. This may be because the sunscreen gives a false security that prolonged exposure is safe, or the chemicals are imparting some form of cancer-causing effect.

RECOMMENDATIONS

- *If a burn has occurred, see* **Burns**.
- *Prevention is the best form of treatment. Avoid exposure, and when this is unavoidable or time is spent in the sun with large areas of the skin exposed, use sunscreen compounds efficiently.*
- *Ensure that at least five portions of fruits and vegetables are eaten to encourage higher levels of antioxidants.*
- *If exposure is inevitable or intended, take the following supplements per foot of height in divided doses with food throughout the day: beta-carotene (2.5mg), vitamin E (100iu), and selenium (40µg).*
- *Aloe vera and lemon juice or gels can be soothing.*
- *Calendula or aloe-vera gels will be soothing and potentially healing for any sunburn.*
- *Homeopathic remedy Sol can be taken at potency 30 three times a day, starting three days before the holiday or sun exposure, and continuing until your return.*
- *Strictly avoid any antiseptic soaps or lotions because the loss of skin bacteria will predispose to the secondary infection of a burn.*
- *Many orthodox drugs, especially tranquilizers, antihistamines, and antinausea drugs, all of which are commonly used in holiday situations, may increase the sensitivity of the skin to the sun.*
- *See* **Melanoma** *and* **Moles**.

Sunbeds

As a general rule of thumb, avoid them. If this is not possible, stay well within the recommended time-dose, because many beds are faulty or poorly serviced, and the amount of ultraviolet light emitted is not necessarily accurate.

Please follow the general advice for sunburn above if a sunbed is going to be used.

SUN STROKE—*see* **Dehydration** and **Sunburn**

SWEATING (PERSPIRATION)

We all perspire to some degree. Sweating is an essential bodily function, and should only be considered a problem if absent or in excess.

The primary function of sweat is as a cooling mechanism. For instance, one minute of running produces 10Kcal of heat. This heat has to be removed from the body, and this is done by cooling down the skin's surface. Sweat passes from sweat pores, settles on the skin, evaporates using heat to do so, and thereby cools the skin's surface. This in turn cools the body, and maintains a steady internal temperature. Sweat that drips off the body is not cooling. The sweat glands are under the control of the nervous system, and sweating is the main physiological adjustment to an increased heat load. The control comes from specific centers in the brain that recognize and increase heat in the bloodstream.

A second, less-well-thought-of, reason for sweating is based on the fact that sweat is similar in composition to urine. Urea, a nitrogenous waste product from protein metabolism, does not come out in the sweat, but most other compounds can. The body may use sweating to eliminate toxins or to regulate electrolyte balance by removing salt and other elements.

Anything that heats the body, such as exercise, alcohol, caffeine, smoking, and spicy foods, will increase sweating. Outside-air temperature causes a body-temperature rise and a reflex sweat. High humidity will prevent evaporation and prevent the cooling mechanism. The body sweats more in a vain attempt to encourage evaporation, but may fail to do so. Overheating may occur in a humid climate, and dehydration is also a risk.

The sweat glands are under the control of the nervous system, which in turn responds to stress chemicals such as adrenaline. Nervousness or anxiety can trigger sweating. This is an evolutionary reaction in principle to prepare the body's cooling mechanism if a fight-or-flight reaction is required.

An absence of sweating may be found in individuals who have a genetic predisposition to a warmer core body-temperature, and therefore, cooling is not required. A lack of sweat is most commonly associated with dehydration, and needs to be corrected.

Excessive sweating is also a genetic predisposition, and may not be a sign of ill health. Generally, however, sweating is a sign of a raised body-temperature, usually due to infection or an overproduction of thyroxine or adrenaline. Any situation that creates fear or anxiety can promote sweating; interestingly, an internal-fear mechanism associated with heart conditions and sweating may be an early sign of heart disease.

Obesity (being overweight) puts an insulating layer around the body, which prevents heat from leaving and thus raises the core body-temperature. Sweating is thereby triggered.

Sweat glands

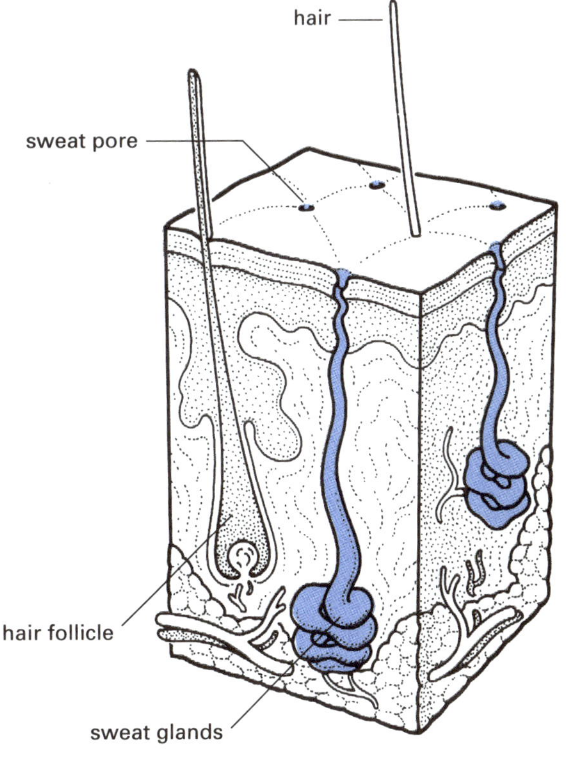

Some unfortunate individuals have a tendency to sweat in particular parts of the body. Our armpits and groins will appear moist with exercise, but some will sweat profusely in these areas with little strain. The hands, feet, and scalp are all areas that may sweat independently of body temperature or anxiety. There is no orthodox reason for this nervous overstimulation of the sweat glands in these areas, but the Eastern philosophies consider the acupuncture meridians as being relevant. The palms of the hand contain points on the acupuncture meridians of the lungs, heart protector, or sexual function, and the heart. All these organs and systems must be examined, and their corresponding psychological and spiritual associations considered.

RECOMMENDATIONS

- *Try to establish a cause and remove it. It may be necessary to lose weight, remove the heat-creating foods mentioned above from the diet, or learn a relaxation/meditation technique to take nervous anxiety away.*
- *Absorbent material such as cotton should be worn, especially in humid conditions, to mop up sweat and aid the evaporative process. It may seem illogical to wear something if you are hot, but in fact a cotton undershirt is cooling for this reason.*
- *Remember that fever is a friend and that sweating in association with infection or disease should not necessarily be inhibited (see **Fever**).*
- *A genetic predisposition to sweat may be difficult to alter, but homeopathic remedies at potency 200 or higher may alter fundamental tendencies. Prescribing is best done by a homeopath, but special attention should be paid to Calcarea carbonica, Hepar sulfuris calcaria, Lycopodium, Psorinum, Silica, and Veratrum album. The place, time of day or night, smell, and other variables will lead to the best choice.*
- *If excessive sweating is creating an unpleasant smell, see **Body odour**.*
- *Excessively sweaty palms may interfere markedly with an individual's social life, and if the above measures do not resolve the problem, surgical intervention to cut the nerves that control sweating can be considered. This is a technically difficult operation for fear of damaging other neurological controls. It is therefore not a particularly successful procedure, and is best avoided.*

THE NERVOUS SYSTEM

CONCUSSION AND UNCONSCIOUSNESS (LOSS OF CONSCIOUSNESS)

From a medical point of view, concussion is actually the state of being shaken or the result of such a jarring. The term has, however, passed into both lay and medical colloquialism, referring only to brain concussion, and so is now used to describe an immediate loss of consciousness, transient in nature due to a violent shaking or agitation of the brain within the cranium (skull). Concussion may be associated with a penetrating injury, but usually it is due to a blunt blow, and is caused by a change in the momentum of the head. What this means is that a blow causes the skull to go in one direction, but the brain, because it is floating in cerebrospinal fluid, stays stationary and gets "hit" by the skull.

Most often, such an injury results in a headache and nothing more, but if a loss of consciousness is associated, then the term "concussion" is used to describe the situation.

Concussion may also be used for a partial loss of consciousness where an individual is clearly unaware of where he/she is, or aspects of reality that relate to that current time.

Associated with concussion may be a shallowness of breathing, a massive adrenaline response leading to pale, cold, and clammy skin, a tachycardia (rapid heartrate), and a drop in blood pressure noted by a weak pulse. Recovery may also be connected with nausea and vomiting, and loss of bowel and bladder control. Upon recovery, a loss of memory is not uncommon.

It is important to remember that concussion is a temporary state, and if it persists, then the term used is "unconsciousness." Further symptoms occur in unconsciousness that are generally not associated with concussion. These include twitching of the limbs or convulsions, a flushed face rather than pallor and, as the patient recovers consciousness, weakness or paralysis may be noted in any part of the body, and the awareness or alertness of the individual may be deficient.

A warning sign that the brain has been damaged and that an intracranial bleed may be occurring is an inequality in pupil size, a bilateral dilation of the pupils, or pupils that are not reactive to light (*see* **Intracranial bleeds**).

RECOMMENDATIONS

- *Whether concussion or unconsciousness is the ultimate definition, emergency first-aid is relevant, and the ABC (airways, breathing, circulation) routine or cardiopulmonary resuscitation (CPR) is the first step.*
- *Once the ABC of resuscitation is performed, establish the probable cause of concussion. If there is any suggestion of spinal injury, ensure that no movement takes place, and follow the instructions for spinal injury (see* **Spinal injury***).*
- *If movement is permissible (no spinal injury is likely and all injuries are splinted), move the patient into the recovery position (described overleaf).*
- *Cover with a blanket and, if possible, also place one underneath the casualty.*
- *Check the patient's wallet and pockets for any medical notification, such as a diabetic card, steroid card, anticoagulant card, or medical-alert bracelet that may be worn.*

Recovery Position

Establish that there is no neck or spinal injury before proceeding (see overleaf).

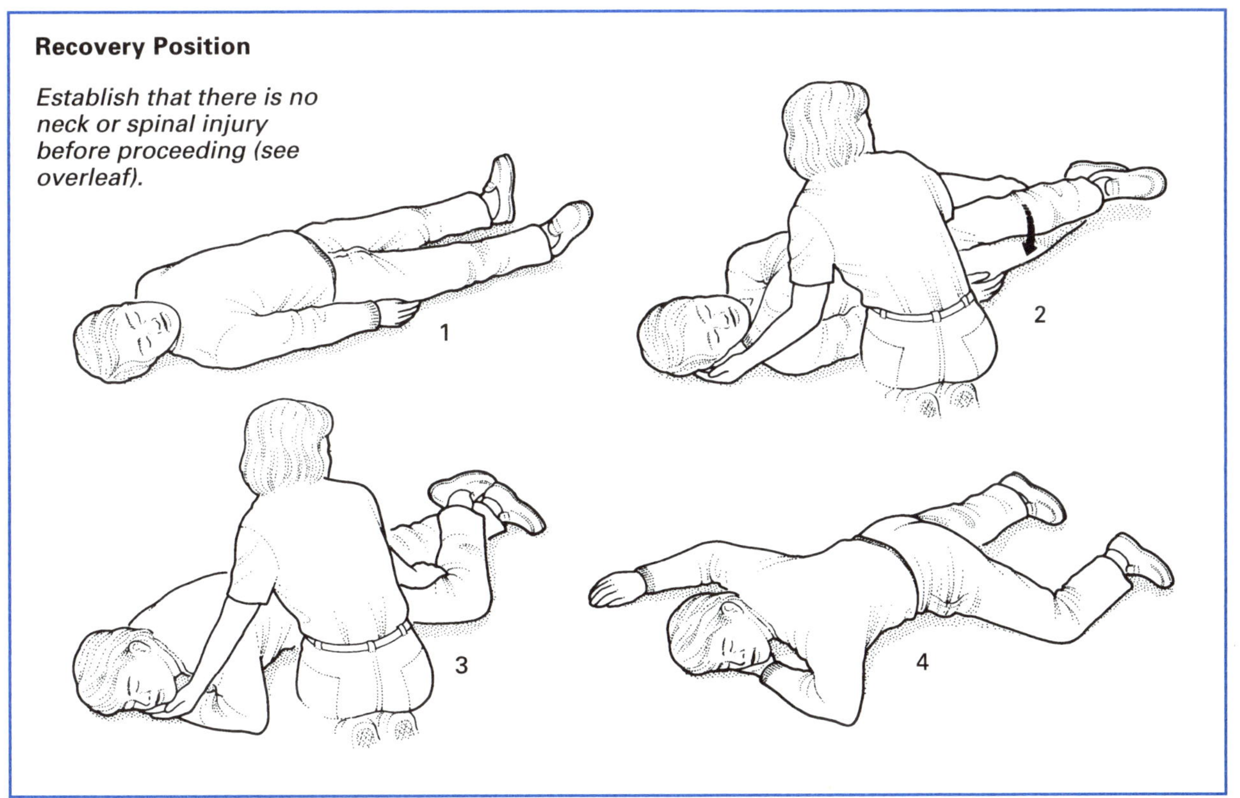

The recovery position

Any unconscious patient should be placed in the recovery position to avoid the possibility of vomiting, which may be inhaled and cause asphyxiation. The positioning of a casualty into the correct position—which used to be known as the coma position—must be preceded by clearly establishing that there is no neck or spinal injury. Moving a patient with such damage may lead to paralysis or death by putting pressure on or severing the spinal cord.

Moving a body safely

If there is no possibility of neck or spinal injury, use the following procedure, as illustrated on the previous page:

1 Place casualty's arms close to the body and straighten the legs.
2 Place furthest arm across chest and draw the palm of the hand outwards to rest against the right cheek. With your hand just above the knee, draw the furthest leg across the nearest.
3 Now roll the casualty towards you, keeping the hand resting against the cheek.
4 Bend the upper leg of the casualty at right angles to the body, and place the furthest arm in a 'stop traffic' position.

This position places the body in such a way that it will be stable and prevent asphyxia (4). The heavier the body, the more difficult this procedure, and it is often easier to do all of the above in a kneeling position beside the casualty.

MULTIPLE SCLEROSIS (MS)

Multiple sclerosis is the medical term given to a condition that strips the nervous system of the sheath that surrounds the neurone, which is the part of the nerve that transmits the impulses. The sheath is called myelin and, therefore, MS is a "demyelinating" disorder.

The orthodox world has postulated a variety of causes for MS, including viral, autoimmune disease (the body's immune system attacking the nervous system), dietary causes, and specific chemical reactions in the nervous system, probably caused by genetic errors. The complementary medical world views the cause as being all of the above, plus the possibility of heavy metal toxicity, food allergy, vaccine reaction, and (arguably) psychological factors.

My experience suggests that anger produces chemicals within the nervous system that have a direct effect on the body's ability to protect the nervous system's myelin sheaths. The anger is usually repressed and stems from childhood, and most often is associated with problems between the child and a parent.

Symptoms of multiple sclerosis are many and variable. They can be divided into sensory symptoms, such as visual disturbance, tingling and numbness, and movement symptoms, such as loss of balance, loss of bladder or bowel control, weakness, and paralysis. Problems usually occur in one part of the body, although they can rarely be bilateral, and may come along for a matter of minutes or last for years. Repeated episodes of neurological disturbance need to be assessed by specialists before a diagnosis can be made. Multiple sclerosis is well known for going into remission. This means that people with neurological conditions may resolve them and not have problems again until many years later. It is this principle of remission that alternative practitioners work on, because it shows that the body is capable of overriding the condition. After all, a permanent remission is the same as a cure.

Diagnosis is made by excluding other causes, and is confirmed by specific visual tests called "visual-evoked response" (if the patient has visual disturbances), magnetic resonance imaging, and on occasions, biopsy.

A multiple sclerosis sufferer by the name of Cari Loder discovered that her problem was alleviated with the use of tricyclic antidepressant in combination with an amino acid, and with regular intake of vitamin B_{12}. There has been no study published to date, but anecdotal evidence

Multiple Sclerosis

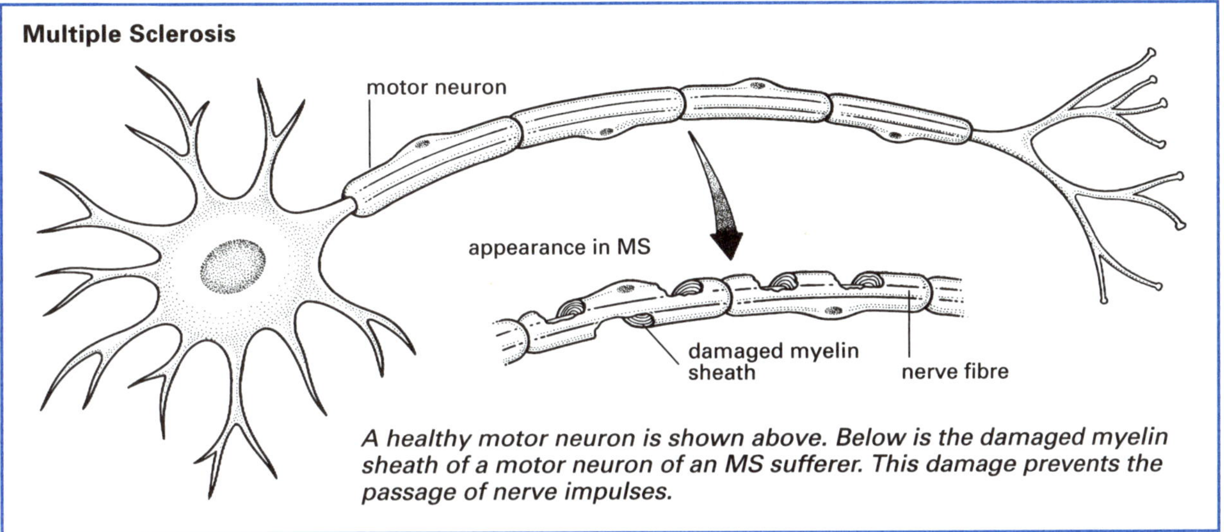

A healthy motor neuron is shown above. Below is the damaged myelin sheath of a motor neuron of an MS sufferer. This damage prevents the passage of nerve impulses.

and support from people who have used her course of treatment is hopeful. While we await results of studies, I see no reason why people should not try the course. Because it involves a drug, a doctor needs to prescribe the antidepressant, and it would be best to have the doctor keep an eye on the situation.

Adrinex—The Cari Loder-suggested treatment:
Morning dose
70mg lofepramine
500mg L-phenylalanine

Midafternoon dose
500mg L-phenylalanine
1000mg vitamin B_{12} given by injection weekly for 10 weeks.

RECOMMENDATIONS

- *Self-help for MS should take the form of informing your health practitioner of the following recommendations, but you should be under the care of an orthodox neurologist.*
- *Orthodox treatments such as adrenocorticotrophic hormone (ACTH) or steroids may be recommended, and should be considered if the following alternative treatments are not effective. The use of beta-interferon is distinctly a last resort.*
- *Have your essential amino acid, copper, calcium, magnesium, and zinc levels checked out, because deficiencies will exacerbate symptoms.*
- *The following supplements should be taken at doses of twice the daily recommended level, and can even be given intravenously, under the care of a doctor with supplemental medicine training: Vitamins B_1, B_5, and B_{12}, folic acid, vitamin C, magnesium, molybdenum, chromium, manganese, zinc, and selenium.*
- *Take D, L-phenylalanine, approximately 100mg per foot of height twice a day.*
- *Establish and remove any food allergies. Specifically, have a very low animal-fat intake (less than 10g/day), and reduce even vegetable fats to less than 50g of polyunsaturated oils. No cow's-milk products, although sheep's and goat's-milk products can be used in small quantities. Absolutely no caffeine or tannin, which therefore means no coffee, tea, or cola drinks. Cocoa needs to be avoided as well, which includes chocolate.*
- *Vegetable proteins such as soya, lentils, and grains should be increased to compensate, and fish should be eaten at least every other day. Salmon, herring, and mackerel are the best.*

- *Supplements that should be taken at levels recommended by a nutritional or complementary medical specialist include cod-liver oil, eicosapentenoic acid (500g twice a day), docosahexanoic acid (300mg with meals), N-acetylcysteine (500mg with meals every other day), zinc, copper, selenium, and vitamin E.*
- *Discuss the use of the herb Ginkgo biloba.*
- *Exercise such as yoga or Qi Gong is essential.*
- *Consider using the Ayurvedic massage technique Marma or Shiatsu on a regular basis.*
- *Bee-venom therapy has some poorly supported evidence of efficacy, and should be considered if other treatments are not helping. Hyperbaric oxygen proved successful in one trial, but this has not been followed up and may therefore not be an effective treatment.*
- *Consult a Tibetan physician and ask about Padma 28, a combination of different herbs that has shown to be an effective treatment in a scientific study.*
- *Lastly, but most importantly, address any anger—conscious or subconscious, present or past, known or unknown—via regular counseling and meditation/relaxation techniques.*
- *Polyunsaturated-fatty acids need to be assessed, preferably by an essential-fatty-acid blood test, and any deficiencies corrected through diet or supplements.*

PARALYSIS

Paralysis is the loss of muscle function with or without loss or diminution of sensation. It is classified in many ways, depending on: the body part involved; the cause; the tone of the muscle—a paralysis can be described as flaccid or spastic; and the distribution, such as monoplegic (one limb) or hemiplegic (one side of the body).

Certain types of paralysis are sometimes called palsies (*see* **Cerebral palsy**).

A partial paralysis is known as paresis. The variety of types and causes of paralysis require different treatments, and it is best to refer to that section in this book concerning the underlying cause. There are, however, certain treatments and techniques that can be used for all those with paralysis.

Paralysis occurs because of damage to the nervous system. This can occur anywhere from the brain to the local nerves controlling the area or part paralysed. Paralysis may be of a digital limb, or may affect the muscles of breathing, in which case the damage is extremely serious and potentially fatal. Paralysis of a part of the body may be caused by a progressive disease, and the cause must be found as soon as possible.

The orthodox medical world will point out that nerve damage is irreparable. This is true to a great extent, although naturopathic techniques may encourage some repair, and they work predominantly to encourage other nerves to take over the sending of instructions to muscles that has been lost by the damage to the original nerve. I consider the possibility of repairing a paralyzed area as being similar to teaching a right-handed person to use their left hand. It requires another part of the nervous system to learn functions that it has not used, but there is a strong possibility that this may occur. A lot depends on the extent of the damage.

RECOMMENDATIONS

- *Identification of the cause of paralysis is paramount, because it will help to decide which treatments are of benefit.*
- *Establish good communication with a physiotherapist, and use the techniques recommended as often as possible. It will make a big difference in most cases.*
- *Ensure full support from "home services." Take advantage of all household gadgets that can make life easier.*

- *Ensure that clothes, footware, wheelchairs, and other accessories are comfortable.*
- *Try to find a practitioner of Marma massage or neurotherapy, which are physicotherapy techniques derived from Ayurvedic medicine.*
- *If Marma or neurotherapy is not available, then consider osteopathy, chiropractic, Polarity therapy, yoga, or the Alexander technique. Any of these structural or energetic treatments may be of benefit.*
- *Definitely utilize acupuncture.*
- *Bioresonance techniques and healing hypnotherapy are useful.*
- *Tibetan medicine encompasses bodywork, nutrition, acupuncture, and herbal treatments, and is probably the best all-round medical treatment if available. If not, an Ayurvedic or Chinese assessment is essential.*
- *Herbal and homeopathic treatments may be of benefit. In traumatic paralysis, Arnica potency 6 or 30, given every 15min may make a difference in the long term. A homeopath or herbalist would be required for more specific prescribing according to the symptoms.*
- *Cranial osteopathy or craniosacral therapy should be tried for at least six to ten sessions because marked benefit may occur.*
- *Please undertake some training in a meditative technique in association with counseling. Great benefit will be derived if an inner peace and understanding of what has happened can be reached. For those with a strong religious faith, then time spent with your spititual advisor will also prove invaluable.*

SEIZURES—*see* **Epilepsy** and **Convulsions**

PSYCHOLOGICAL MATTERS

ADDICTION

It is arguable that all of us are addicts. Problems only arise when the addiction is detrimental to health. It is also arguable that the "abuse" of a healthy action or substance in an addictive manner may in fact be beneficial. Frequent visits to a church, temple, or mosque could be considered an addiction, especially if it changes one's life. Provided that religious fanaticism does not set in, this could be considered a nondestructive addiction. Can we extrapolate this to the use of alcohol? Do two or three gin-and-tonics each evening to shrug off the day and engender a relaxed feeling for the evening constitute addiction? We may argue that if it is felt to be beneficial, then it may be an addiction, but is not one that is harmful. On the other hand, would we do better without the toxins, but then the issue becomes to "do better" or to be more content?

You can see that the discussion is tricky, with tangent after tangent proffering itself for philosophical discussion. I feel that treatment for addiction depends very much on establishing whether one is addicted or not. If the answer is "yes" to any of the following questions, then my recommendations should be studied.

- Is there anything that you do or take that you wish you did not?
- Is there anything that you do or take that others wish you did not?
- Is your life negatively affected by something you do or take?
- Is somebody else's life negatively affected by something you do or take?
- Is your health or fitness affected by something you do or take?
- Have you had to debate any of the above questions to reach the conclusion "no"?

If you have answered "yes" to any of the above, then you are probably an addict, and would benefit from changing.

RECOMMENDATIONS

- *There is no simple answer to breaking an addiction, and fighting the battle by yourself is slow and often ineffective.*
- *Establish a rapport with a counselor you like. There are no "good or bad" points to look for when choosing a psychologist. If you get along with the professional, you have your initial starting point.*
- *Consult a Bach flower-remedy manual to establish the best remedy to keep in your pocket at all times.*
- *Use the following homeopathic remedies depending upon your addiction: for alcohol addiction—use Lycopodium 200 nightly for one week; for tobacco addiction—use Tabacum 200 nightly for two weeks. For the following addictive substances, obtain homeopathic potency 200 of the recommended remedy and use nightly for seven nights. Further recommendations must come from a homeopath: cannabis addiction, take Cannabis indicus; cocaine addiction, take coca; heroin addiction, take Morphinum; addiction to ecstasy, LSD, and other manufactured drugs requires a high potency of the corresponding remedy, available through homeopaths or homeopathic pharmacies.*

Eastern philosophies regard reincarnation to be an important aspect of health. With regard to addiction, the philosophy is the same. To reach nirvana, one must free one's spirit of all shackles. Addiction is a tie to the mental and physical plane, and must be dealt with to be "free" or enlightened. This is not a religious concept, more a spiritual one, but even strong religious dogmas such as Christianity will place an abuser in "Hell," suggesting as usual a strong tie-in between Eastern and Western theology.

RECOMMENDATIONS

- *Do not fight addiction alone. Get help from a specialist, a support group (including Alcoholics Anonymous and Narcotics Anonymous), and a complementary medical practitioner.*
- *When dealing with addiction, learn a meditation technique that is suitable for you. This may be transcendental, a personal technique taught to you, or an active form such as yoga, Tai Chi, or Qi Gong. Dealing with the mental and physiological aspects is only two-thirds of being released from addiction.*

Dealing with an addict

Living with an addict, being related to an addict, befriending or loving an addict is a situation that requires help in itself. Addiction is not just about the addict. There are one million registered alcoholics and drug addicts in the U.K. If each one has a parent, a lover, a child, a brother, or sister and a best friend, we can estimate that five million people are directly influenced by an addict. If you consider that only one in five people registers or realizes they are an addict, we have anywhere from 5 million to 25 million (nearly half the population) influenced by addiction. You can multiply these figures in the U.S.A. by five!

An addict without a will to change and the support structure to do so, will continue to be socially disruptive by being deceitful, untrustworthy, violent, changeable, vindictive, and hateful. Addicts will lie, cheat, and steal, all beyond their control, and all with a self-hatred that overpowers the care and love that those affected can offer.

RECOMMENDATIONS

- *Do not try to solve this yourself. Professionals fail, so you probably will.*
- *Seek help for the addict if they wish but, importantly, contact a support group for yourself via your doctor or complementary clinical therapist.*

ASSERTIVENESS

A lack of assertiveness must be differentiated from shyness and timidity, both of which are character traits. A lack of assertiveness is sociologically unacceptable, leading to difficulties with social or professional life.

RECOMMENDATIONS

- *Self-help is difficult, and a consultation with a psychologist is highly beneficial to differentiate between acceptable and unacceptable levels of poor assertiveness.*
- *Homeopathic remedies can have a profound effect on areas of psychology, and special interest should be paid to the remedies Baryta carbonica, Pulsatilla, Gelsemium, and Petroleum.*
- *Martial-arts training is excellent at increasing assertiveness, especially Qi Gong.*

CLAUSTROPHOBIA

This condition is characterized by acute anxiety in enclosed spaces or in areas where immediate escape is not evident, such as in a crowd.

The symptoms may range from a mild discomfort to profound anxiety, including panic, uncontrolled tears or screaming, sweating, palpitations and fainting.

RECOMMENDATIONS

- *The homeopathic remedy Aconite 6 should be kept in the pocket and used every 10min if a situation that may encourage claustrophobia is liable to occur. Argentum nitricum 6 may also be tried.*
- *If the condition is affecting well-being, then neurolinguistic programming, hypnotherapy, or other behavioral modification techniques are usually beneficial.*
- *Eye-movement desensitization, a new branch of psychotherapy, may be very effective.*

EATING DISORDERS

The term "eating disorder" is extremely broad. It may represent a food phobia leading to deficiencies and illness, excessive eating leading to obesity, or the conditions of anorexia or bulimia.

Any of the eating disorders may be mild, moderate, or severe, and move from one category to another. Severe and prolonged eating disorders will lead to ill health and be potentially fatal. With anorexia, which strikes most usually in young females (20 girls to 1 boy) below the age of 25 years, 1 in 10 will be admitted to hospital, and 1 in 10 of these will die.

Eating disorders are rarely caused by physical conditions, although any eating disorder can lead to pathology. It is unusual for a food allergy to create anorexia or bulimia, but it may well create a phobia towards a food or to overeating leading to obesity.

More commonly, eating disorders are in fact an imbalance of energy or a matter of psychological concern. The Eastern philosophies consider the stomach to be the energy meridian responsible for the intake and absorption of food. The small intestine and heart meridians are involved in absorption and distribution, and the liver meridian is concerned with energy for the processing. Imbalance in any of these meridians can lead to the apparent condition of an eating disorder.

The orthodox world will most often cite emotional disturbance as the cause. Suppressed or unrecognized anger, depression, low self-esteem, or psychosexual crises are all found in association with eating disorders.

In my practice, I have noted a tendency for those with eating disorders to fall into a category that I define as the "pretty-person syndrome." At some point in a child's development, usually at a psychologically susceptible age (often around puberty), the child has found him/herself in a situation where physical appearance or beauty has taken on a profound sociological meaning. Very often, this stems from overadoring parents or finding oneself in a social group that places too much emphasis on prettiness or ideal body measurements. The correlation between being sociably acceptable and being thin is very much a Western development, as indeed are eating disorders. The association, therefore, between the perfect body and not eating is clearly seen.

At some point in our development, we consider our own inner self-worth. If our society (parental or social) focuses on our outward appearance, then the inner self or soul questions whether it is loved for itself or the shell in which it is encased. By shutting off that part of our consciousness that truly sees the shape of the body and by focusing on the "unattractiveness" of fat, the subconscious can feel confident that if someone likes the individual, then it is because of them and not because of the way they look. There are many holes in this argument as being the underlying cause of eating disorders, particularly anorexia, but it may account for why the disfigurement of anorexia is not seen by the individual, and why a large number of sufferers are often young and attractive, and can be found in the modeling, acting, or singing professions.

RECOMMENDATIONS

- *Establishing an eating disorder requires not only the individual's perception, but also the input from those around, because the patient may not be aware.*
- *Ten to twenty percent of body-weight loss must be apparent in association with dieting or irregular eating patterns before an eating disorder should be considered as a diagnosis.*
- *Self-help is usually inadequate, and counseling from psychotherapists and nutritionists is advisable: the former to deal with the cause, and the latter to deal with the inevitable imbalances that occur.*
- *Biochemical changes, such as depression and cessation of periods, are often associated with dehydration. Ensure that 64–96 ounces of water are taken per day, regardless of any other intake.*
- *Mineral deficiencies, particularly zinc, are associated, whether as a cause or an effect is uncertain.*

Anorexia nervosa

Anorexia is the medical term for a loss of appetite. Anorexia nervosa is a severe condition whereby individuals starve themselves because they incorrectly view their body as overweight. This psychological pathology occurs 20 times more frequently in girls than in boys, and can range from mild obsession to being a fatal condition.

RECOMMENDATIONS

- *If you or someone close recognizes that your dieting is encroaching into your lifestyle, sit down with a counselor and discuss the matter. There may be an early sign of anorexia nervosa.*
- *If you disagree with other people's image of your body, go to see a counselor.*
- *Do not assume that this problem will go away by itself. Go to see a counsellor.*
- *Having seen a counselor, you may consider sitting with a nutritional expert to establish whether any supplementation is necessary to replace deficiencies.*
- *See a homeopath to obtain a constitutional remedy.*

Bulimia

This is a nonmedical term for an insatiable appetite with excessive food intake. It is in common use for the correct medical term Bulimarexia, where an individual will alternate bingeing or gorging with self-emptying by enforced vomiting, prolonged fasting, or self-induced diarrhea, usually under the influence of laxatives.

Bulimics are not as obvious as anorexics, because their body features may not change. Bulimia, unlike anorexia, does not focus itself in young adults only, and has quite an even distribution of ages.

Bulimia is less inclined to lead to physical pathology, although vomiting can tear the esophagus and cause biochemical imbalances, and is considered much more of a psychological problem occurring in young, affluent women who have low self-esteem, a history of rejection, or a fear of failure.

RECOMMENDATION

- *Constitutional prescribing by a qualified homeopath is highly recommended.*

FRIGHT AND FEAR

Fright is an essential emotion for survival. Those of our prehistoric ancestors who did not respond to a fearful situation with fright generally did not run away or fight, and their gene line will have stopped abruptly. Adrenaline and other similar hormones called catecholamines are produced in response to frightening situations, and prepare the body for action by moving blood into areas such as the heart, lungs, muscles, and brain, and removing it from non-essential areas such as the skin, bladder, and bowel.

A severe fright or shock can produce such a surge of adrenaline that the sudden change in the position of blood in the body can cause a faint or temporary paralysis. This faint mechanism was another survival technique, namely "playing dead."

Fright, like fear, is not a disease process and does not need specific treatment unless it is persistent and socially disruptive. In this case, the condition is known as a phobia (*see* **Phobia**).

RECOMMENDATIONS

- *Learn a relaxation–breathing technique if you have a tendency to be fearful.*
- *Keep the remedy Aconite 6 at hand, and use up to every 15min in the case of a sudden shock.*
- *Keep a rescue remedy (a Bach flower remedy) at hand, and use two drops every 15min if required.*

FRIGIDITY

Frigidity refers to an unwillingness to have sexual relations, and needs careful consideration as to whether or not this is a pathological situation. It is neither right nor wrong to have a high or low sex drive, and discussion is essential to establish whether or not frigidity is actually a problem. Social pressure nowadays encourages young adults to have sexual relations at an ever-decreasing age. Nature did not intend us to have an interest in or indulge in sexual intercourse until we were in our mid-to-late teens, and therefore it is important to differentiate between the absence of our natural sexual drive and frigidity.

RECOMMENDATIONS

- *Discuss the matter openly with parents or friends to establish whether the emotional block is within normal parameters. If you feel uncomfortable with this, then a counselor should be able to give guidance.*
- *If a problem is identified, then counseling is an essential aspect of treatment, starting as soon as possible and continuing in weekly sessions for as long as is necessary.*
- *Constitutional homeopathic remedies can be chosen by a homeopath with experience.*
- *Do not confuse frigidity with a difficulty in intercourse, such as vaginismus (see* **Vaginismus***). A physical discomfort (dyspareunia) that creates a dislike of sexual intercourse is not frigidity.*

HYSTERIA

Hysteria is commonly envisaged as "that screaming woman" in a Hitchcock movie. While this is an extreme example of sensory hysteria, it is important to understand that you can also have motor hysteria. Sensory hysteria is an inability to control an emotion, most often fear. Usually associated with stress, hysteria can present as a continuous babbling in association with a loss of awareness of what is being said around them. Motor hysteria refers to a loss of function of the body, the most dramatic of which is hysterical paralysis.

Whatever the type of hysteria, the effect is caused by an overload of adrenaline and catacholamine chemicals into the nervous system. The brain loses its normal neurotransmitter control, and nervous system failure ensues.

Hysteria is usually short lived, resulting in a self-limiting event such as a faint, or it can take some time to pass, as is often the case in hysterical paralysis. In very rare events, hysteria can persist and lead to a deep psychotic event or persisting paralysis.

RECOMMENDATIONS

- *If in attendance of a hysterical individual, use a calming voice and any necessary, commonsense advice to placate the panic.*
- *A slap on the face is potentially injurious, and a safer technique is to apply pressure to the tissue at the base of the thumb and first finger. Try it now, and you will appreciate how painful that point can be.*
- *Hyperventilation often associates with hysteria, and is often the cause of worsening panic (a respiratory alkalosis affecting the brain—see* **Hyperventilation***) and paralysis (due to alkalosis preventing muscular action). The homeopathic remedy Aconite, potency 6 or higher, can be given every 5min until the situation is completely under control. One dose is often enough to placate the individual.*
- *A recurrent hysteria needs to be treated by a counselor with knowledge in specific relaxation and breathing techniques.*

NERVOUSNESS

Nervousness is not so much a medical term, but in common parlance, covers milder forms of anxiety and fearfulness. Nervousness is divided into two levels: acute and chronic.

Acute nervousness

Acute nervousness or anxiety is generally brought on by events that are real or imaginary. Public speaking, pre-exam nerves, or pre-event anxiety are all common, and will be faced by most of us.

Symptoms include a rapid heartbeat (tachycardia), "butterflies" in the abdomen, a desire to defecate—even as diarrhea, a desire to urinate, trembling, and muscular tension that can lead to headaches. Nausea and vomiting may also be present. These are all acceptable symptoms, provided that they are controlled and pass once the event has started or concluded.

RECOMMENDATIONS

- *If the following tips do not help, or the symptoms are severe enough to be disruptive, then a complementary medical opinion should be sought.*
- *Take three times the recommended daily dose of a vitamin-B complex, starting three days before any event that may be causing the "nerves."*
- *Use D, L-phenylalanine (100mg per foot of height) with each meal, starting three days before the event.*
- *Regardless of appetite, ensure that the diet includes at least four portions of fresh fruit or vegetables, and complex carbohydrates (wholegrain foods) for at least three days prior to the event.*
- *Ensure a good breathing technique, preferably by learning one in association with a relaxation technique through yoga, Qi Gong, Tai Chi, etc.*
- *Ensure at least six hours of sleep per night, avoid caffeine and other stimulants (the brain does not memorize as well under such adrenaline-like affects), and exercise daily for at least half an hour to reduce the buildup of adrenaline compounds.*
- *The following homeopathic remedies can be taken at potency 30 four times a day, starting three days before the event, and at potency 6 every hour on the day of the event: Argentum nitricum if you are unable to concentrate or*

memorize, and are suffering from abdominal upsets such as nausea, vomiting, diarrhea, or abdominal pains; Lycopodium is ideal for a nervous individual who is full of bravado and has a tendency to do well regardless of the strong anticipation of failure; and Gelsemium is a master stage-fright remedy for when the body becomes weak or borders on paralysis, and the mind goes blank.

- *In uncontrolled cases, your doctor may recommend beta-blockers, which will temporarily deal with physical symptoms. Before you advance to this level of drug treatment, consider using a teaspoonful of Passiflora or Valerian-fluid extract diluted in a cup of water four times a day.*

Chronic nervousness

Persistent anxiety or fearfulness can be most disruptive, and at its extreme can be considered a phobia. This is the case if the nervousness focuses on a particular theme or object, such as not wishing to go outside, or a fear of spiders.

Longstanding nervousness arguably stems from early childhood experiences, psychological trauma such as accidents, or relationship problems, and may simply be a character trait that does not require treatment. If, however, the nervousness is affecting lifestyle or well-being, advice should be sought.

Nervous dispositions may be created by improper intake. Drugs (both prescribed and those of abuse), alcohol, and tobacco (which are all potentially depressive), and nutritional deficiencies such as zinc, the amino acids tryptophan, tyrosine, and phenylalanine, and vitamin B complex may all cause nervousness.

RECOMMENDATIONS

- *Counseling should be sought for an initial discussion on the options available. Hypnotherapy and neurolinguistic programming may be of benefit in isolating underlying causes at a faster rate than psychotherapeutic or psychoanalytical techniques.*
- *A homeopathic consultation to establish a constitutional-remedy treatment is essential.*
- *Establish any nutritional deficiencies through a consultation with a nutritionist or specific blood and/or bioenergetic tests.*
- *Embark upon a course of meditation. The release of endorphins (the body's natural painkillers and calmants), let alone the connection with your higher spiritual being, may be curative on its own.*
- *Avoid tranquilizers like the plague. They cover the symptoms, encourage dependence and, from the onset, are not curative. Herbal preparations are available, but should only be taken on the advice of an experienced herbalist.*

SCHIZOPHRENIA

Schizophrenia is actually a group of problems and not a single psychotic disorder. It often starts in the teenage years, and is characterized by an alteration in the ability to form concepts, with misinterpretation of reality. This affects behavior and the intellect in varying degrees. The most-common disorders are a tendency to withdraw, ambivalence, inappropriate responses, and irregular moods; difficulty in maintaining a stream of thought and; in severe cases, hallucination and delusion.

This condition is not necessarily easy to establish if symptoms are mild, so the term "borderline" schizophrenia is often used when symptoms are mild, but nevertheless noticeable. Symptoms of schizophrenia in childhood are termed autism (*see* **Autism**), but a shy, withdrawn, overly nervous adolescent may be all of those things, or may be borderline schizophrenic. As the individual grows up, these tendencies may be assumed to be normal, and the underlying psychiatric disorder not noticed and therefore not treated.

Terms such as *hebephrenic* (childish behavior and markedly disorganized thoughts), *paranoid* (a conviction of persecution), and *catatonic* (completely cut off from the outside world, often associated with rocking in the fetal position) are all types of schizophrenia. The underlying cause, from an orthodox point of view, is an imbalance of brain chemicals. Holistically, it is well established that certain nutritional deficiencies, environmental hazards, and heavy-metal poisoning are associated on the physical plane. There is always a fine line between "genius and madness," and there may be a strong spiritual link to those labeled schizophrenic and those a step closer to God. The Eastern philosophies would assume that a chemical imbalance in the brain could be created by an excess-energy flow in the higher chakras and therefore spiritual or emotional effects, especially in childhood, may be at work.

Diagnosis is generally made by a psychiatrist using a variety of tests. Other tests include checking for deficiencies in all the B-group vitamins, checking the mineral levels, and assessing from other physical symptoms the possibility of deficiencies in essential-fatty acids. Amino acids may be deficient, and investigation of any specific absence may be relevant. Schizophrenia has been associated with celiac disease, which is an oversensitivity of the bowel to gluten, and other gliadins and glutenins found in wheat, rye, corn, and (to some extent) in all other grains and starches. Most naturopaths with experience in this area would support the view that other food components may also trigger psychiatric problems.

Schizophrenics are more likely to harm themselves than others, but their presence can be extremely disruptive, both to family life and society. Correct professional treatment is necessary.

RECOMMENDATIONS

- *Assessment by a psychiatrist for a definitive diagnosis is essential before any treatment is undergone.*
- *Perform nutritional deficiency tests under the care of a complementary medical specialist with experience in this area.*
- *Test for heavy-metal poisoning and, regardless of the results, remove mercury from the mouth and aluminum from the kitchen. Specifically, look for copper levels (via red blood cells, not hair only).*
- *Chelation therapy is recommended if toxicity is found.*
- *Test for food allergy and eliminate any allergens.*
- *Consult with a homeopath. There are many remedies when used at potencies above 200 that will have a profound effect on the psyche. Self-prescribing can be considered in acute schizophrenic episodes, when the remedy Stramonium 6 can be given every 10min. Paranoia may be helped by Hyoscyamus 30 given every 10min, and should be kept or carried by an individual or their families or partner, especially if traveling away from home.*
- *Family therapy is essential for both the individual and home life. Any illness within the household will affect all members. Individual psychotherapeutic sessions are a must for children or adolescents because early recognition and counseling can have a profound effect in the long run.*

CHAPTER 5

ADULT

CHAPTER 5

ADULT

GENERAL

ANAPHYLAXIS

Anaphylaxis is the term used to describe an over-allergic reaction. The body becomes flushed and sweaty, the patient feels strong palpitations, becoming short of breath because of narrowing of the airways. The mouth, tongue, and lips can swell, and there is usually considerable fear associated with the symptoms.

Anaphylaxis can occur from bee/wasp stings, ingestion of certain foods (especially peanuts and eggs), and the use of drugs (both prescription and those of abuse). *See* **Cardiopulmonary resuscitation**, and learn the technique.

RECOMMENDATIONS

- *At any suggestion of a shortness of breath or chest pains—call an ambulance.*
- *While waiting for the ambulance, administer Aconite 6 or Apis 6, four pills every 10min.*
- *Apply pressure to acupuncture points one inch below the middle of the clavicle (collarbone) on both sides.*
- *Place a few drops of Olbas or lavender oil in steaming water and encourage the patient to do some inhalations.*
- *If the patient loses consciousness, check for breathing and pulse, and if necessary commence cardiopulmonary resuscitation.*

ARTERIOSCLEROSIS OR ATHEROSCLEROSIS (ATHEROMA)

This short section of the book is the most important. Arteriosclerosis (AS) is the highest cause of death in the Western world, claiming one in three lives. It is the underlying cause of heart disease, strokes, and high blood pressure.

Arteriosclerosis is the clogging of the body's arterial system. It is part of the natural aging process, and arterial wall changes have been noted in babies as young as one year old.

The inner lining of all the arteries in the body should be smooth. Anything that causes damage to this delicate layer predisposes to AS. Infections, drugs, radiation, and free radicals formed from the ingestion of toxins such as pesticides, insecticides, smoking, and alcohol all actively damage the arterial wall. The body automatically tries to repair this by releasing chemicals that attract platelets (a specialized type of red blood cell), scar tissue-forming cells and nutrients. Nearly every cell in the body has cholesterol as part of its cell structure, and this is one of the main nutrients pulled into the damaged area. All these different components knot together to create an irregular patch in the arterial wall, which then grows by trapping other passing molecules such as cholesterol and platelets.

Arteriosclerosis is a silent condition that will not show up until occlusion of the artery creates a

Arteriosclerotic artery

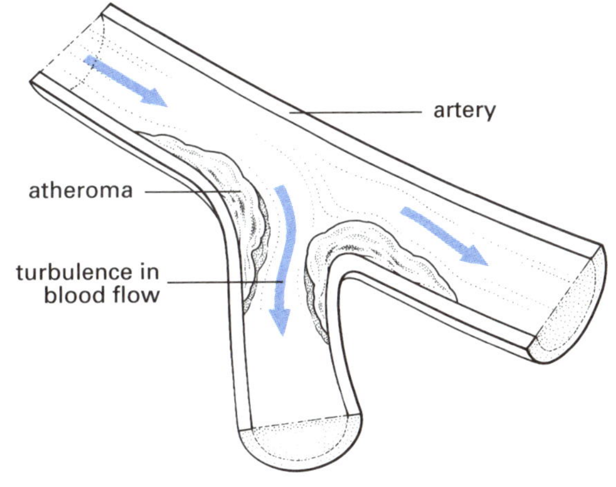

Arteriosclerotic artery, showing the buildup of atheroma on the inner lining.

problem for the tissues being supplied. The build-up of debris within the artery is known as a plaque. This will finally obstruct the bloodflow, cutting off oxygen and nutrients. The plaque may also become loose and travel to a more-narrow part of the artery, causing the blockage at a distant point. This moving plaque is known as an embolus (*see* **Embolism**). The occlusion of arteries to organs such as the brain or heart can have an instant and potentially fatal effect. Occlusion to one kidney may not be fatal, because the other will take over and, as another example, the blockage of part of the liver-blood supply will still leave plenty of liver cells elsewhere to carry on normal function. The plaque also hardens the arteries, making them less responsive to the neurological control that governs their diameter. This "hardening" of the arteries causes the blood pressure to rise, which in turn leads to a further risk of strokes and cardiovascular disease.

It is feasible that most disease conditions associated with age are caused, or contributed heavily to, by AS. A decrease in oxygen or nutrition will lead to disease, and is the main cause of "aging" and its characteristics.

Assessment and investigation

Arteriosclerosis is a difficult condition to assess without being invasive. The following observations may be made to assess the level and potential risk of AS.

Pulses

A pulse can be felt easily in arteries at the neck, wrist, on top of the foot, and behind the inner-ankle bone. Weak pulses in the feet may be indicative of a genetically poor bloodflow, and cannot be used to assess AS if the individual has had cold feet for most of their life. However, anyone with "poor circulation," as exhibited by cold feet and hands, must be especially careful not to encourage AS.

Practitioners may often "roll" their fingers backwards and forwards over the pulse in the wrist (the radial pulse) to feel the texture and tension within this superficial artery. An individual may do the same on their own pulse, but a comparison is needed, and because AS develops slowly this is a difficult technique to use. The harder the artery the more likely AS is involved.

Listening to bloodflow (auscultation)

A practitioner may place the stethoscope over the carotid arteries (beside the Adam's apple) or over the femoral arteries (in the groin) to listen for a gentle buzz. This is known as a "bruit" (French for noise) and is caused by turbulence within the artery, in turn caused by blood flowing over the roughened artery. This is similar to the gentle rumble of rapids. The louder the bruit, the greater the damage.

Fundal examination

The back of the eye is known as the fundus. A practitioner can look with an ophthalmoscope through the front of the eye, and examine the blood vessels at the back of the eye. Arteriosclerosis reflects the light more brightly, and damaged arterial walls will show up like two shining railway tracks either side of a central core of bloodflow.

Ear Crease

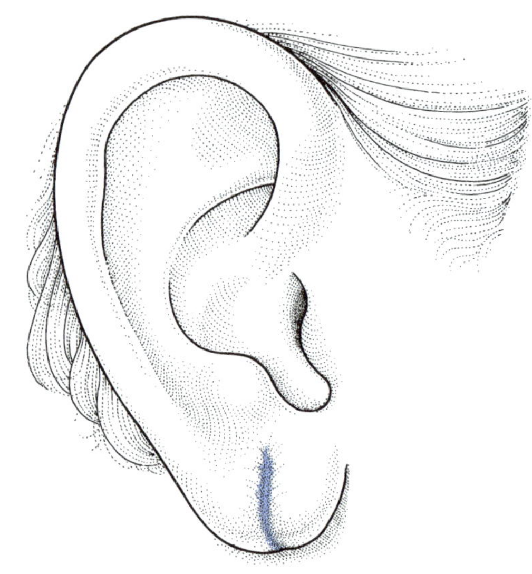

Crease in earlobe indicating the occurrence of AS. The deeper the crease, the worse the AS.

Earlobe crease

Perhaps the easiest technique of assessing AS is by examining the earlobe. Many studies have shown and correlated the development of a crease running down the earlobe. The deeper the crease, the worse the AS. The development is created by clogging of the arteries to the ear. Anybody with a crease needs to take preventive action to avoid the almost inevitable development of AS.

Blood tests

A blood sample can be sent to the laboratory for assessment of total cholesterol, high-density lipoprotein (HDL) and low-density lipoprotein (LDL) levels. These can be correlated as mentioned below in the section on cholesterol, and a risk level obtained.

Doppler examination

The Doppler test is a noninvasive, sound-related investigation that tells the patency of arteries (*see* chapter 9).

Arteriograms

This invasive procedure carries a small risk and should only be used as a last resort; it is also important to bear in mind that the accuracy of this investigation has been questioned. *See* **Radiography** in chapter 8.

Risk factors

Cholesterol

Cholesterol levels are the highest risk. There are different types of cholesterol, and their functions are discussed in chapter 7 (*see* **Cholesterol**). It is extremely important to read that part of the book.

Several factors are very relevant in AS with regard to maintaining lowered cholesterol levels. Refined sugars and all fried foods and saturated fats (*see* **Fats**) raise the LDL "bad" cholesterol. Deficiencies in calcium, copper, and chromium, as well as an excessive level of zinc in the bloodstream, can all create too much LDL, and decrease the good HDL.

Remember that cholesterol will be drawn into any area of damage, and the lower the levels of the LDL cholesterol, the less likely it is that plaques will form. Although I discuss this in the cholesterol section, it is worth reiterating the importance of knowing whether one has good or bad cholesterol in abundance. The best measure of this is the total cholesterol:HDL ratio. This should be below 5 in males and below 4·4 in females. A high-cholesterol level does not necessarily mean that an individual will have a problem.

Toxins

Any compound that may cause damage to the arterial wall must be considered a toxin, and removed from the diet or lifestyle. The biggest risks are smoking and free radicals. Cigarettes contain over 3,000 chemicals, any of which may be responsible for damaging the inner lining of the arterial wall. Smoking also creates free radicals along with high-fat, sugar, and red-meat diets. Anything that stresses the liver will prevent the breakdown of toxic substances, so alcohol and drugs (prescribed and those of abuse) are all liable to predispose to AS.

A special mention needs to be made of coffee. Coffee has a direct effect on the liver, as well as on the cholesterol levels. It is worth noting that tea does not have the same detrimental effect, and therefore it is not only the caffeine, but other compounds within coffee that cause the problem. Caffeine itself may not act directly, but its effect on blood pressure may exacerbate the effects of AS.

The platelets

These specialized red blood cells are an important part of the blood-clotting mechanism (*see* **Blood clots**). They have a structure that allows them to adhere to damaged tissue, and they also release chemicals to attract "healing" compounds, such as white blood cells, scar-tissue-forming cells and nutrients. Platelet stickiness is increased by a lack of vitamins B6 and E, excess saturated fats, or a lack of omega-3 and omega-6 oils, deficiency in the amino acid methionine (found predominantly in vegetable proteins), and deficiencies in the minerals magnesium and selenium.

Aspirin is known to decrease platelet stickiness, and is therefore the orthodox world's choice of basic prevention of AS-related diseases such as stroke and heart attacks. The use of correct diet and naturopathic supplements are, probably, more effective than aspirin, and carry a low risk of side effects (*see* **Diet** below).

Arterial-muscle condition

The arteries have muscles within their walls that contract or relax, depending on neurological and hormonal instructions. Magnesium or calcium deficiencies will lead to poor muscular control, thereby making the clogging of arteries more dangerous.

Exercise

Exercise increases HDL, encourages arterial dilation, and thereby increases arterial patency (openness). A good exercise program is extremely important in reducing the risks of AS.

Stress control

Many studies have shown that the endorphins released through meditation and relaxation techniques reduce cholesterol levels and increase arterial patency. A good meditation and relaxation program is essential for all of us, but more so for those with AS.

Diet

The diet controls the amount of nutrients we absorb and, as can be seen from reading the above, many components can have a direct effect on AS.

The ideal diet for those at risk of AS or those who would like to avoid this condition developing is simply a vegetarian diet with oily fish such as herring, salmon, tuna, and mackerel, eaten four times a week. Vegetables carry fiber that binds with cholesterol in the gut, and also contain vegetable proteins that are known to lower cholesterol levels. Methionine is the best example. A compound called carnitine, manufactured in the liver, is made up from lysine found in lamb and poultry, but is more prominent in vegetable proteins. Vitamin B_6, co-enzyme Q_{10}, beta-carotene (synthesized into vitamin A), chromium, and selenium are all found, along with calcium, copper, and magnesium, in most vegetables.

Onions, garlic, and especially ginger, act by decreasing platelet stickiness. The protein lecithin from soya beans binds with cholesterol in the gut and bloodstream. It is worth pointing out that eggs are often criticized for having high cholesterol levels. There is a rule in nature that insists upon balance, and the white of an egg contains lecithin that binds with much of the cholesterol in the yolk, rendering eggs less dangerous than advertised. An occasional egg for anyone at risk from AS is not a big problem.

The oily fish contain the "good" oils omega 3 and 6, as well as eicosapentenoic acid. Vegetarians can find these in flaxseed and cold-pressed olive oils.

Water is the best fluid for reducing AS risks by diluting toxins, but specific treatment may be obtained from the Asian green tea. A small amount of alcohol on a daily basis may be beneficial. Do not drink particularly sweet drinks, and even fruit juices may be harmful if taken in excess. Sixteen ounces of juice a day is an acceptable level, but should be diluted and taken in divided doses.

RECOMMENDATIONS

FOR AVOIDANCE OF AS

- *Consider being assessed by a complementary medical practitioner on a yearly basis.*
- *Consider the Ornish or Pritikin diets (see chapter 7).*
- *If at risk (or otherwise), consider a vegetarian diet, supplemented with some oily fish and fowl. Avoid fried foods and red meat.*
- *Consider using the macrobiotic diet (see chapter 7).*

- *Avoid all lifestyle risk factors such as smoking, heavy drinking, drug use, and coffee.*
- *Establish a good exercise program.*
- *Learn and practice a good meditation and relaxation technique.*

RECOMMENDATIONS

FOR THOSE WITH AS

- *Follow the recommendations of avoidance above.*
- *Discuss the matter with an experienced complementary medical practitioner.*
- *Take the following in addition to a good diet. The doses prescribed are per foot of height and, should be taken in divided doses throughout the day with food.*

Beta-carotene	*2mg*
Vitamin C	*500mg*
Vitamin E	*100iu*
Vitamin B_6	*10mg*
Methionine	*200mg*
Carnitine	*200mg*
Flaxseed oil	*1 teaspoonful*
Eicosapentenoic acid	*1g*
Ginkgo biloba	*200mg*
Lecithin	*500mg*
Cysteine or N-acetyl cysteine	*50mg*
Zinc	*5mg (taken before bed)*
Copper	*0·5mg*

These dosages should be considered for six months following an AS-related event such as a heart attack or stroke, and then reduced to half the amount thereafter. I would encourage lifelong use.

- *With the guidance of a practitioner, consider the homeopathic remedy Crataegus.*
- *Chelation therapy. This is described in chapter 9.*

ARTERITIS

Arteritis is the inflammation of an artery. It most commonly occurs in the temporal arteries at the side of the forehead, and is an extremely dangerous condition.

Temporal arteritis can occur as a sudden pain or one of gradual onset. It is very severe, unrelenting, and rarely affected by mild painkillers. The temples may or may not be sensitive to touch. This condition is associated with arterial supply to the eyes and brain, and if not suppressed, can lead to blindness or death.

RECOMMENDATIONS

- *At any suggestion of symptoms as described above, go immediately to an emergency department. They may recommend steroids—take them.*
- *Once the condition is under the care of an orthodox physician, refer yourself to a cranial osteopath and naturopathic physician.*

AUTOIMMUNE DISEASE

Autoimmune disease is the term used when the immune system turns on the body itself. Through complex and poorly understood biochemical mechanisms, the immune system recognizes its own body parts. When foreign matter enters the body, the immune system recognizes it as being alien and destroys it. The reasons why this recognition system fails are not well understood. The Eastern philosophy considers the immune system to be overburdened by defending against infections, food allergies, and pollutants, and certain body tissues get caught up in the battle.

Principally, the immune system recognizes its own and foreign proteins, and the introduction of these into the system can trigger a self-attack response. Viruses, bacteria, drugs, and pollutants all fall into this category. The most common autoimmune diseases are rheumatoid arthritis and systemic lupus erythematosus (SLE).

Autoimmune disorder is a complex matter, and signifies the failure of the immune system after prolonged ill health, even if it has been symptom-free. Autoimmune disease can be very serious, and even fatal. Most cases, however, are treatable with complementary and orthodox therapies, and many are self-limiting, lasting only a few years.

RECOMMENDATIONS

- *Consult a complementary medical practitioner with a knowledge in homeopathy, herbal medicine, and nutrition. All these areas must be reviewed.*
- *Any lifestyle habits such as smoking that are clearly polluting the body should be avoided.*
- *Any foods that are known to cause reactions should be eliminated, and food-allergy testing can be of great benefit.*
- *Please refer to any specific condition in this book.*

Systemic lupus erythematosus (SLE)

This condition, commonly termed Lupus, is a surprisingly common autoimmune disease. The orthodox world is uncertain of its cause, but most complementary practitioners with experience in this field would consider it to be an aggressive oversensitivity by the body's immune system as a whole, and the underlying reasons that cause it may be multiple.

Systemic lupus erythematosus is characterized by inflammation of any tissue in the body, and is often referred to as a "mimicker." The condition must be suspected in any persisting joint pain, fever, and general malaise, but is often associated with a "butterfly" rash, which shows as a red lesion covering the forehead and cheeks (the wings of a butterfly). The rash may cover the entire body and may be associated with any number of symptoms.

Diagnosis is generally made after other conditions are excluded, and there are specific blood tests that show positive in over 90 percent of cases.

Orthodox treatment is steroids, pain relief, and drugs aimed at any of the multitude of symptoms that may appear. The complementary medical world must look at any autoimmune disease, as discussed in the section above, but special attention must be paid to diet, food intolerance/allergy, stress levels and, environmental toxins, all of which can trigger an overreactive immune system.

RECOMMENDATIONS

- *This is a condition that should be treated by an experienced complementary medical therapist, who should coordinate treatment with a homeopath, herbalist, and nutritionist.*
- *Stress management through counseling or meditation teaching is a prerequisite.*
- *Pain associated with SLE may be due to a magnesium deficiency. This should be checked by a blood test for intracellular magnesium, and replenished if the test is positive.*
- *The Ayurvedic technique of drinking the first morning urine may be of benefit, although techniques of extracting the sediment from the urine and taking this in drop form (somewhat more appealing) may be available through an experienced complementary medical practitioner.*
- *The roots and stem of a plant called Tripterygium wilfordi at a dose of 10–15g three times a day was shown to be effective in a study reported in China. The side effects of abdominal discomfort, nausea, and loss of menstruation in women all disappeared after a few days of treatment or within six months of stopping.*

BLEEDING—*see* Hemorrhage

Bleeding from trauma

Loss of blood is pathological in all instances. Bleeding from cuts and trauma needs to be controlled as soon as possible. The arteries have an inbuilt spasm mechanism should an artery be cut. Interestingly, the cleaner the cut—i.e. the less trauma to the vessel—the less the constrictive response. The more traumatic the injury, the more spasm is likely. This accounts for the fact that a swift cut with a knife will bleed more than an amputation.

RECOMMENDATIONS

- *If an injury does not stop bleeding in 10–15min, then seek medical attention. This should be sought sooner if blood loss is heavy, or in children as they have less blood in the body.*
- *Apply compression to the wound, and only consider constriction of a bleeding vessel above the site of the injury if medical attention is close at hand and compression itself is not working. Occlusion of an artery can cause permanent damage to a limb within half an hour.*
- *Do not attempt to stitch a wound without medical supervision, except in extreme circumstances.*
- *Arnica 6, four pills every 10min is a master remedy.*

Bleeding from areas other than the skin

Bleeding from an orifice such as the anus, penis, vagina, or from sensory organs such as the eyes, ears, and nose, is *always* pathological, except for a female's period.

RECOMMENDATIONS

- *Such bleeding must be investigated by a medically qualified professional.*
- *Sudden onset of bleeding can be treated with Aconite 6, four pills every 10min; slower but persistent bleeding noticed over 24hr can be treated with Phosphorus 30 every hour until medical advice is sought.*

Internal bleeding

Injuries such as road-traffic accidents or trauma with a blunt instrument can cause bleeding inside the body. Diagnosis can only be made by experienced medical personnel, but the signs to look for are:

- Dizziness, visual disturbance, and headaches for head injuries.
- Pain, dizziness, and difficulty in breathing for chest injuries.
- Pain, nausea, vomiting, and bloating for abdominal trauma.

Anybody who faints after receiving a blow from a blunt instrument must be rushed to an emergency room.

RECOMMENDATIONS

- *You may administer Aconite 6, four pills every 10min, if there is any suggestion of internal bleeding on your way to the hospital.*
- *Once a diagnosis has been made, please refer to the relevant section for complementary treatments.*

BONE-MARROW DISORDERS

The bone marrow found predominantly in the long bones (arms and legs) and the sternum (chestbone) is responsible for the production of the blood cells. Those that we all know about—the red blood cells (erythrocytes) and the white blood cells (leucocytes)—are manufactured along with others including the platelets, a modified type of red blood cell very important in the mechanism of blood clotting.

The bone-marrow function can fail in one of two ways. It may cease to produce any of these cells, or it may produce too many of them. Specific conditions such as polycythemia rubra vera (increase in red blood cells and, usually, white blood cells) and thrombocythemia or thrombocytosis, are conditions marked by an absolute increase in the number of platelets (throbocytes is the medical name for platelets). Thrombocytopenia is a lack of platelets.

Excessive production of white blood cells in the bone marrow form myeloid leukemias, which are covered in their own section.

Certain drugs, radiation, and viral infections are all associated with bone-marrow disorders, but who will succumb to this group of disorders is not known. There may be some genetic predisposition, but these problems tend not to run in families.

I have a theory. Stress releases adrenaline and cortisol, which are the stress chemicals (*see* **Stress**). To counteract this, the body will try to make calming chemicals such as serotonin. The platelets are cells that contain and release serotonin when the body is under stress. I hypothesize that at certain levels of stress, the platelet–serotonin-release function may increase, and the body may be tempted to make more platelets due to some chemical response. If the stress is persistent, this mechanism may trigger a permanent effect, leading to thrombocytosis. If the stress persists, perhaps the controlling chemical may run out, therefore the stimulation to make platelets may be reduced leading to thrombocytopenia. These are rare conditions, and I have only treated a few cases, but in each there has been a noticeable, stress-related time period prior to the condition forming.

The condition is often found only on routine blood test, but may also be discovered because of symptoms related to clotting difficulties. Unexplained bruising and bleeding, or conditions such as stroke may occur because of excessive clotting.

RECOMMENDATIONS

- *This condition is potentially life-threatening, and needs to be monitored by a hematologist.*
- *As we are uncertain about the causes, consider food allergy, deficiencies, and environmental toxins as possible triggers.*
- *Obtain the opinion of a medically qualified complementary practitioner for assessment of the above and treatment through homeopathy, herbal, and supplemental therapies. None are documented as being effective, but they may help.*
- *Learn a meditation technique, and sit with a counselor to discuss problems and anxieties.*
- *Do not refuse orthodox treatment, which may include steroids, bone-marrow-suppressing drugs, radiation, or surgical treatments. Look at the alternatives, which may reduce the amount or the level of intervention.*

CANCER

Before I discuss cancer and its treatment from a holistic point of view, I would like to discuss exactly what it is and some of the salient facts.

Cancer cells have three characteristics:

- They are cells in the body that have lost their growth regulatory system. Each cell of the body contains chromosomes, which divide to form other cells. Part of these chromosomes are known as telomeres. Each time a cell divides, some of these telomeres are cleaved off, and once their number falls below a certain level, the cell can no longer multiply. In cancer cells, these telomeres are not cleaved.
- Cancer cells infiltrate adjacent tissue, and this differentiates them from benign tumors.
- Cancer cells can spread through the lymphatic or blood system. These are known as metastases.

The causes of cancer

The orthodox world has few treatable causes of cancer, but does accept that the following are relevant:

- Poor nutrition and excess calorific intake in childhood.
- Genetic factors.
- Infections—probably by viruses. Those known to cause problems are the human papilloma virus, hepatitis-B virus, certain herpes viruses, and HIV.
- Chemical compounds—such as asbestos, metals, hydrocarbons, chemicals known as olefins in solvents, *N*-nitroso compounds in tobacco smoke, and certain natural substances such as aflatoxins (mold that grows on foods, especially stale grains).

- Deficiencies—specifically vitamins A, C and E, the mineral selenium, and dietary fiber.
- Radiation—ultraviolet, gamma and x-ray.
- Persistent irritation.
- Defects in the immune system.
- Age—due to a natural failing of cell division.
- Psychological causes. It is known, for example, that women are more likely to develop breast cancer if they have had a serious shock, such as a bereavement or divorce within the previous two years.

The holistic world accepts all of the above causes, but also considers the possibility of parasitic infection, persistent food allergy/intolerance, the possible carcinogenic effects of food preservatives, additives, and organophosphates used as crop sprays, as well as certain amino-acid deficiencies, in particular methionine and cysteine. While psychological shocks have been established, the complementary medical world looks at longstanding suppression of emotion or stress to be potentially capable of causing cancer.

Staging of cancer

The medical world has tried to simplify passing information from one physician to another by creating a clinical classification of tumors. The most commonly used classification is the TNM system.

T (stands for tumor size)
T—primary tumor
Tis—carcinoma *in situ* (confined to an area)
T0—no evidence of a primary tumor
T1–4— an arbitrary description of the local size
Tx—location and size unknown

N stands for lymph node involvement
N—regional lymph nodes involved
N0—no evidence of regional lymph-node involvement
N1–4—arbitrary differentiation of the number of lymph nodes involved
Nx—cannot be assessed

M stands for metastases
M—distant metastases
M0—no evidence of distant metastases
M1—distant metastases present
Mx—cannot be assessed

Certain tumors have their own terminology, such as stage or grade, that generally can be thought to substitute for T and N as described above.

Prognosis

One of the big questions that anybody is faced with when dealing with a cancer is the chance of cure or surviving the disease. It is difficult nowadays to assess the outcome of patients who are not treated, because anybody with a cancer is generally subject to orthodox treatment. What is more, the orthodox world does not seem to differentiate for the lay person the difference between "cure" and five-year survival rate. The table below shows this survival rate as published by the American Cancer Society. I was unable to locate comparable figures for cases before modern intervention came into play, but statistics suggest that in the last 30 years, there has been little if any change in the overall cure rate, despite aggressive intervention.

Site of malignancy	5-year survival rate
Pancreas	3%
Bronchi (lung tubes)	13%
Leukemia (all sorts)	34%
Ovary	48%
Ear, nose, and throat	52%
Colon and rectum	52%
Cervix	67%
Prostate	70%
Breast	75%
Urinary bladder	75%
Melanoma	80%
Uterus	85%
Testes	87%

The orthodox world does not ask why certain people do less well than others, but I am convinced that it is to do with the individual and their immune system, rather than the cancer itself.

Cancer is a chronic condition that arises because of a multitude of factors, ranging (as I have mentioned above) from genetic to environmental. Orthodox treatment against cancer takes strides forward every day, but the majority of cases still end up with poorer results than they should because complementary treatments are not considered.

There are thousands of reports of spontaneous regression and alternative cures for cancer. Many of these have scientific validation, and are not in common or orthodox use, simply—but sadly—because trials are not completed due to financial and political considerations. Also, the necessity to stand up to double-blind, placebo-controlled studies is not, and will never be, an acceptable method of testing for alternative treatments. This does not mean that they are not effective or in common use —as the art of surgery shows. No surgical technique has ever been proven double-blind in a study.

Treatment

Working against cancer requires the consideration of six different areas:

- establishing and removing the cause
- the use of orthodox treatment
- the activation of the immune system
- psychological and spiritual aspects
- dietetics and nutrition
- alternative, anticancer treatments

Establishing and removing the cause

Some cancers have a clear cause. Lung cancer and smoking, bowel cancer and low-fiber diets, and skin cancers with excessive exposure to the sun are examples. Many cancers are being shown to have a genetic predisposition, and I am sure that over the next decade, genetic reasons and answers will be found to fight cancer. At the moment, a hereditary trait puts most cancers beyond our control. The use of complementary diagnostic techniques (*see* chapter 8) in association with orthodox screening techniques should be used to clarify an individual's health on a regular basis, and also to establish the origin of the tumor. The cause of cancer can range from psychological and stress-related causes to food intolerance and environmental pollutants. The need to look at an individual holistically and consider their mind, body, and soul is clearly as relevant in this disease, as in all chronic illnesses. The orthodox world is advancing at an enormous speed as far as diagnostic capabilities go. The advent of computers with x-rays, magnetic-resonance imaging (MRI), and other visualizing techniques can pinpoint, to within a fraction of an inch, the location of a tumor buried deep in the body. Unfortunately, none of the billions of dollars that is spent on diagnostic research appears to go towards predicting or forecasting the development of cancer. The smallest of masses may be isolated once formed, but we seem unable to predict where or when this might happen. However, there is hope.

Over the last 50 years, research has gone into proving that the body contains energy channels that can be measured using sensitive, electromagnetic transmitters and receivers. These basic machines have now been developed into sophisticated computers known as bioresonance computers. These machines are capable of measuring the normal flow of energy through an individual, and can differentiate any irregularity in the system. Cancer cells have a particular resonance that will differ from normal tissue, and this can be measured.

A simple blood test, known currently as the Humoral Pathological Laboratory Test, examines a dried drop under a high-powered microscope, and compares what is seen with samples of known conditions or samples taken from people who have gone onto develop certain conditions. Blood changes rapidly, and is extremely sensitive to deficiencies and toxins, and can therefore—theoretically—predict the presence of a cancerous tendency. For example, red and white blood cells behave in a particular way in the presence of free radicals: negative ions that can trigger cancerous changes in the nuclei (the brain center) of cells.

It is becoming clear that chemicals within our food chain—often placed there through crop spraying or actively injecting livestock—can cause cancer within our system. A recent study showed over 12 cancer-causing compounds in a basic three-course meal—shrimp cocktail, meat and two vegetables a dessert—provided in a popular, chain-type restaurant. Removing these chemicals from the body may not be easy, but homeopathic principles may work alongside detoxification diets.

There is some evidence that food allergy may be relevant to certain tumors, and possibly (by inference) to all cancer. Establishing food-allergy response is essential in all chronic conditions, but especially in cancer, because correct dietetics may be curative (*see* **Dietetics and nutrition** overleaf).

All the above investigations are becoming more available and are discussed more fully in chapter 9, Alternative Therapies.

The use of orthodox techniques

Orthodox medicine has come a long way in the treatment of cancer, and should rarely be discounted in a holistic treatment course. The surgeon's knife is curative, and chemotherapy and radiation treatments are improving constantly. The side effects of these treatments continue to be a problem, and orthodox treatments are often toxic to the system. Full and frank discussions in consultation with medically-qualified orthodox practitioners, and thereafter alternative practitioners with experience or specialization in the treatment of cancer, are essential. Very often, an attempted cure may be pointless or even worse than the disease. It is arguable that a slow-growing tumor in someone elderly should be left alone because the body will wear out before the cancer can affect it. Complementary treatments to prepare the body for these procedures, treatments to speed healing after surgical and radiation damage, and the correct alternative therapies to protect the body from the toxic effects are all essential.

The orthodox world is experimenting to find a vaccine for cancer, and while the possibility is not close at hand, I believe this to be a very important area of research.

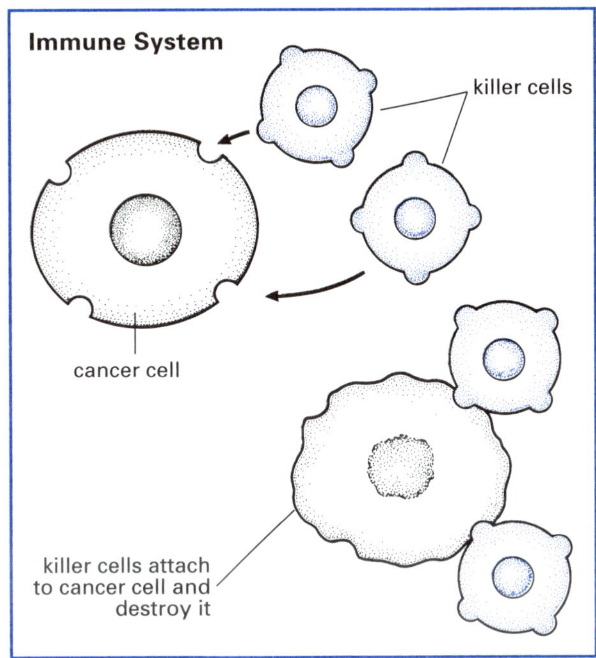

Activation of the immune system

Cancer may be created (and certainly proliferates) due to a failure of the individual immune system. The body has specific anticancer cells named "killer" cells, and produces chemicals that act as antioxidants to remove the free radicals that cause or promote cancer-cell growth. Cancer is the proliferation of a particular type of cell. This means that the normal multiplication rate has been lost, and the cell is replicating too fast. There are certain genes called telomeres that are cleaved off each time a cell multiplies. When all these have been removed, the cell can no longer multiply and eventually dies. In cancer, this cleavage does not occur. The reasons for this, I am sure, will soon be illuminated by science. Whatever the cause, the fundamental energy that keeps these cells healthy is absent, and part of the body's defense mechanism has gone wrong. This, too, needs to be corrected, and working on this energy plane is as important a part of supporting the immune system as promoting the effects of the killer cells.

Psychological and spiritual aspects

The field of psychoneuroimmunology has recently come to prominence. The ability of the psyche to affect the neurones (the nerve cells), which in turn send out chemicals to the entire central nervous system, is well established. This affects all parts of the body, including the immune system, and stimulates other areas that are essential for dealing with illness or maintaining health. Breast cancer has now been correlated with sudden emotional shocks, and the holistic consensus of opinion is that tension, stress, and long-term anxiety can also create cancer.

There are many examples of prayer curing cancer, and whether a religious or purely a spiritual attitude is concentrated on, this is an area that must not be overlooked in dealing with the fight. The use of antistress techniques, counseling, hypnotherapy, visualization, and meditation techniques must all have a place in the treatment of cancer.

Dietetics and nutrition

There is much evidence to support the use of strict dietetics in both preventing and hindering the growth of tumors. Some researchers have shown—although not to double-blind scientific levels—that diet may cure cancer. I believe that dietetics have an important role to play alongside most other forms of treatment. The best-known anticancer regimes are based on the works of the physician Max Gerson in the early part of this century and the philosophy of the macrobiotic diet. A review of individual nutrition is mandatory in the treatment of cancer.

Alternative anticancer treatments

There are a myriad of claims and much anecdotal evidence supporting alternative medical treatments. I have read books, spoken to their authors, worked with healers, and been involved with patients, all of whom have an answer to cancer. There are many potential cures out there, presently being destroyed by the advance of humankind into tropical rainforests, with the associated destruction of dozens of curative plants each day. Of treatments that are available and discussed, the following should be reviewed by the individual with a complementary specialist, and should not be taken without a full understanding of their "unproven" effects. They are, however, not toxic if taken as recommended, which cannot be said for orthodox regimes.

High-dose antioxidant therapy (AOT)

There is much high-level scientific research and study done on the effects of antioxidants on cancer. Antioxidants are vitamin-based molecules that neutralize negatively-charged particles found in the bloodstream, known as free radicals. These free radicals cause changes in normal cells to allow cancer to develop. There is scientific proof that antioxidants can prevent the development of cancer, and research is ongoing to confirm studies that suggest that AOT is potentially curative.

In advanced cases, those patients undergoing radiation or chemotherapy, those patients due for or recovering from surgery, and any patients who are found to have high levels of free radicals, will possibly be recommended to have initial treatment by intravenous administration of antioxidants.

Native legend tea (Essiac)

Essiac is a combination of herbs used as a basic "tea" by the North American Ojibway Indians in the Canadian–U.S.-border region near Lake Superior. Doctors noted that the number of cancer cases in the tribe were far below those expected, and did some basic studies on the Essiac tea. No acceptable scientific studies have been performed on Essiac, and the evidence is purely anecdotal at this time. It is worth noting, however, that a highly esteemed and established physician who looked after the Kennedy family has written a letter endorsing this product based on the evidence to date.

Yeastone

A doctor discovered the effectiveness of a yeast extract on cancer cells through some basic research. He took his findings to Aston University, where a first-level trial supported Yeastone's efficacy against cancer cells. Trials were performed on rodents with impressive results. Yeastone has been used on humans with some good results. It comes as a strong, yeast-flavored drink that needs to be taken three times a day. Yeastone is not pleasant to drink, but this is only a minor disadvantage.

Iscador

Iscador, a mistletoe extract, has had a lot of research performed on it, with some considerable success, via the Cancer Research Society in Switzerland. It is administered by injection, sometimes as frequently as daily, depending on each individual case. Iscador may be taken orally, but this is not as effective.

Ukrain

Ukrain is an extract from the celandine plant. It has been shown over the last 15 years to have an anticancer effect. Attempts to organize trials have been ongoing for 15 years under a medical professor in Vienna, Austria. Scientific evidence is strong, and case histories have been very promising.

Ukrain is administered intravenously (it can be given intramuscularly, but is painful) at least twice a week. This may be inconvenient. Although your family practitioner or a local physician could be asked to administer the compound, very often orthodox practitioners are resistant to unlicensed therapy, even though they are entitled to administer it. The cost of Ukrain is also prohibitive.

Hydrazine sulfate

This is an extract from rocket fuel that was initially found (goodness knows how!) to be beneficial for patients who were cachectic (losing weight). Cachexia is a prominent feature in many cancer cases, and through experimentation on cachectic-cancer cases, there has been a suggestion that hydrazine sulfate may have an anticancer effect. The compound comes in easy-to-take capsules, and is considered in any case where weight loss is relevant.

Shark cartilage

There are at least three proteins found in shark cartilage, all of which have weak, anticancer effects due to the inhibition of the development of new blood capillaries needed to feed a fast-growing tumor. When put together, the effects seem to be enhanced, and multicenter trials are currently under way. The Federal Drugs Administration (FDA) have approved shark cartilage for second-level trials, which is a considerable achievement for any naturopathic compound. Early trials have been very encouraging. On average, a patient needs to take around 0.03oz of this powdery, fish-tasting compound per 2.2lb of their own body weight. Treatment is divided into three doses per day. This is not easy to take, which is a slight disadvantage.

Chelation, hydrogen peroxide, ozone, and chelox therapy

There is some evidence to support the use of a compound called ethylene diaminetetraacetic acid (EDTA), and the use of hydrogen peroxide or ozone in treating cancer.

Chelox is a combination of EDTA, oxygen therapy, and high-dose vitamin/antioxidant therapy administered intravenously.

Bioresonance techniques

Forty years of practitioner experience has shown that inserting small electromagnetic waves transmitted by healthy cells into cancerous tissue can prevent cancer growth, and even act in breaking down the cancer cells. There is poorly documented scientific evidence, but impressive amounts of anecdotal evidence. This treatment requires a visit to a bioresonance practitioner on a weekly basis, and is both noninvasive and easy to apply.

Other treatments

There are several other potential treatments, the most well known being an extract from almond called Letrile, which showed remarkable results in the hands of the alternative practitioners who initially used it over 40 years ago. The governments and pharmaceutical industries removed this as well as other potential products from the market. The reason was not the poor efficacy or the dangers of the compound, but the lack of substantial evidence through scientific trials. These were only unavailable because governments and the pharmaceutical industry would not pour the necessary millions of dollars into the research, as the compounds are natural and therefore cannot be patented. The finding of a simple, naturopathic cure for cancer or, for that matter, any disease process, would cost the pharmaceutical industry billions of dollars. These billions, that are received and circulated through universities, laboratories, government departments, and pharmaceutical employees, make it largely undesirable for a cure to be found. When confronted by:

- a pharmaceutically-backed clinical laboratory asking for funds for research;
- a trial on a manufactured compound that has much evidence to support its efficacy; or
- a single physician who has worked on a compound in his garden shed;

where would you distribute the millions of dollars collected from the well-caring public? We are, at this point, at an impasse when dealing with the funding of cancer research.

RECOMMENDATIONS

- *Cancer is cured by the individual, with help from external measures. Decide to be cured.*
- *Discuss with a medically-qualified complementary practitioner the various investigations that might be recommended. Biopsies and x-ray investigations may be more harmful than they are beneficial (see specific sections in this book).*
- *When confronted with a treatment program, get a second opinion from a physician who will not be associated with your treatment. If there is no profit motive or conditions laid down by hospital-ethics committees, you may find that a less-aggressive but equally effective treatment is suggested.*
- *Always consult a complementary practitioner. The orthodox world will pay no heed to helping the body deal with the tumor.*
- *Establish a preparatory program before therapy, and a detoxifying program during and after chemotherapy.*
- *If radiotherapy is offered, see* **Radiotherapy** *for techniques to reduce the side effects.*
- *Do not underestimate the effect of positive attitude and counseling, and relaxation techniques; they are mandatory.*
- *Diet has been shown to be curative in itself. A full dietetic program should be set up through work with a nutritionist.*
- *Use all alternative diagnostic techniques to understand where the disease has its origin. Treatment is pointless if the cause is not clear.*

CARDIOPULMONARY RESUSCITATION (CPR, ARTIFICIAL RESPIRATION)

All adults should know the technique of CPR. Thousands of lives a year could be saved if oxygen is fed into the blood and the heart is kept pumping while awaiting emergency services.

It is important not to move anyone who has been involved in an accident because of possible damage to the spine and neck. However, if there is no pulse or respiratory movement, the patient will need to be moved. The first step, therefore, is to establish whether breathing is occurring and the heart is beating.

Artificial Respiration

- Watch the chest. If there is no movement, place your ear by the nose and mouth and listen. The mirror test (placing a mirror or glass by the nose and mouth to see if it mists) is an ancient but effective technique.
- To establish if the heart is beating, place two fingers—index and third—on the patient's Adam's apple, and push gently but firmly to one or the other side. The carotid artery is easily felt pulsating below your fingers. You can also try the pulse in the wrist, which is found less easily one inch up the arm from the wrist on the side of the thumb.

The first aspect is to remember ABC—Airway, Breathing, Circulation.

RECOMMENDATIONS

- *Ensure that the airway is clear. Pushing with one hand on the jaw muscles will open the mouth. With your other hand, push one finger to the back of the throat and ensure that there are no obstructions. Look also. Remove any false teeth.*
- *Place the patient flat on the ground. Tip the chin upwards, which will automatically open the mouth and straighten the trachea (the airway tube).*
- *Place a handkerchief or piece of material over the patient's mouth. Clamp your mouth over the patient's mouth through the material.*
- *Take a deep breath, and breathe into the patient's mouth, holding the chin up with one hand, and with your other hand on their forehead.*
- *Look at the chest to see that it is rising. If it is not, double-check that there is no obstruction in the upper airway.*
- *Perform this twice before commencing cardiac massage.*
- *Cardiac massage. Place yourself on your knees next to the patient. Place one hand on the sternum (breastbone) and the other hand on top of the first. Rocking forward and applying firm, downward pressure, imagine compressing the sternum onto the heart lying below. Successful cardiac massage may result in broken ribs. This is not a pleasant sensation or sound, but is an indication that the massage is efficient. Judgment is required, because you do not want to push too hard for fear of pushing a rib into the lungs.*
- *Repeat this five times before repeating the breathing technique.*
- *Carry on until the emergency services arrive or the patient starts to breathe spontaneously.*
- *It is important to stop occasionally to check for a carotid pulse or chest movements. Cardiopulmonary resuscitation is not beneficial if the heart is beating and breathing is occurring.*

I recommend that everybody take a first-aid course and practice this technique on a dummy. Do not practice this technique on patients who do not have an arrested heart or breathing.

CHOLESTEROL, HIGH—*see* Cholesterol

DEEP-VEIN THROMBOSIS (DVT)

Deep-vein thrombosis is most commonly associated with the formation of a blood clot in the lower legs, and is characterized by pain in the calf. Simply put, deep-vein thrombosis can occur in any deep-lying vein. Most commonly found in the calf, they also appear elsewhere in the legs, pelvis, and abdomen.

Deep-vein thrombosis is a dangerous condition due to the not-infrequent movement of the clot from the site of origin through the larger blood vessels to the heart. From the heart, these clots are pumped into the lungs, causing a blockage and a pulmonary embolism.

The characteristics of DVT are localized pain, swelling and discomfort caused by an inability of blood to pass the blockage, and associated redness. These symptoms must be taken to your doctor and treated as an emergency if there is any suggestion of chest pain or shortness of breath.

Deep-vein thrombosis is often associated with superficial varicose veins, although clots in this area are not dangerous because they are unlikely to travel into the larger veins leading to the heart. Any conditions thickening the blood (including dehydration), and any condition that may block the venous bloodflow, such as pregnancy, injury, obesity, or estrogen drugs (found in the oral contraceptive pill and HRT) may predispose to DVT. Individuals who are restricted by sedentary jobs, driving, air travel, or those confined to wheelchairs may also compromise the bloodflow from the legs, and therefore be predisposed to DVT. Anyone in this group should be wary of any characteristic symptoms, and bring them to the attention of a doctor immediately.

RECOMMENDATIONS

- *The possibility of a DVT should be treated as a medical emergency, reviewed by a doctor, and if necessary, treated in the acute phase with anticoagulants such as heparin or warfarin.*
- *Establish the most probable cause and discuss this with a complementary medical practitioner with experience in this condition. Homeopathy, herbal medicine, and dietetics are all beneficial.*
- *Establish a good exercise regime to encourage bloodflow generally.*
- *Consider regular massage or Shiatsu as part of your lifestyle.*
- *In an acute situation, while awaiting the doctor's opinion, use the homeopathic remedy Lachesis 6 every 15min.*
- *Ensure that you drink 64–96 ounces of water per day.*

DIZZINESS, GIDDINESS, AND VERTIGO

In common parlance, these three words are often taken to be synonymous, but medically speaking, the difference in symptoms between the three definitions following is very useful to the practitioner trying to isolate the cause.

- Giddiness is an unpleasant situation of losing your relationship to surrounding objects.
- Vertigo actually reflects the sensation that the world is revolving about you (objective vertigo), or that you are moving in space, although you know that you are stationary (subjective vertigo).
- Dizziness is a mixture of both, combining a difficulty in relating to objects, with feelings of rotation or whirling. Very often weakness, faintness, and unsteadiness is associated.

Depending on your symptoms, an experienced practitioner or doctor will be able to isolate whether the problem is occurring because of sensory input (vision or problems with the pressure receptors in the feet, if standing) or motor control (loss of control of the body through nervous or poor muscular coordination). The other reason that dizziness, etc. may occur is because of problems in perception actually within the central nervous system or brain. The causes can be as serious as brain tumors and other space-occupying lesions, or less serious, such as low blood sugar not providing the brain with enough energy.

Dizziness, giddiness, and vertigo may be initial symptoms of the presentation of atherosclerosis (AS) causing clogging of the arteries, and therefore reducing the blood supply and oxygen to parts of the brain. The intake of any drugs or specific food allergens may also affect the perception of the brain, sensory input, or motor control of the body. Except when an obvious cause has created dizziness, such symptoms should be reviewed by a doctor.

Eastern philosophies consider dizziness to be a deficiency in being "earthed" or an excess of space/air. Treatment is therefore based on centering or earthing the body and, according to the Chinese, nourishing or working on the stomach meridian is useful.

RECOMMENDATIONS

- *For any persistence of dizziness, please visit a doctor. The practitioner will need to check your sugar levels through your blood and urine, and if examination does not reveal anything, may suggest further investigations such as computed-axial tomography (CAT or CT scans) of the brain to rule out anything bad. Follow through with these investigations, as treatment is dependent on accurate diagnosis.*
- *Once a diagnosis has been established, review the situation with a complementary medical practitioner.*
- *In an acute situation, try drinking a small glass of fruit juice, water and some nonrefined carbohydrate, such as a slice of wholegrain bread. (This will raise the blood sugar and feed the stomach meridian.)*
- *Pressure can be applied to stomach-meridian points; the most well-used is stomach 36, situated four finger-widths below the kneecap in a small dent found on the shinbone. Apply gentle pressure for about 2min at least.*
- *The following homeopathic remedies may be of benefit, if taken at potency 6 every 15min until the problem relieves itself or medical attention is sought: Kali carbonicum—if worse for movement or concentrating on something, or if the individual is better in the open air or by an open window; Conium maculatum—if symptoms are worse for lying down; Gelsemium—if the dizziness is associated with weakness and feeling shaky.*
- *Avoid alcohol, caffeine, or refined sugars.*
- *When the cause of the sensations such as hypoglycemia and arteriosclerosis has been isolated, please refer to the relevant section in this book.*

EMBOLISM

Embolism is the medical term for the occlusion of a blood vessel by matter that is foreign to the bloodstream, such as a blood clot, air, tumor, fat, bacteria, or a foreign body that may have entered the bloodstream through an injury.

Symptoms of an embolism depend on the size and position of the artery that has been occluded. The body forms small clots constantly, which are destroyed by the anticlotting mechanism in the bloodstream and specific, white blood cells that attack any foreign matter. Occlusion of small vessels will therefore go completely unnoticed.

An embolism that obstructs a major artery can lead to a stroke if it is in the brain, a heart attack if a cardiac artery is obstructed, or neurological symptoms such as pins and needles, numbness, and coldness if the artery that is blocked is supplying a limb or digit. Occlusion of a bowel artery or other internal organ may give sudden and severe symptoms.

One of the main causes of embolism comes from deep-vein thrombosis (*see* **Deep-vein thrombosis**), and dislocation of a clot from the deep leg veins can lead to the more-serious complication described below.

Pulmonary embolism

A commonly heard term is that of pulmonary embolism, where a clot—very often following an operation in the lower part of the body, such as a hip replacement—dislodges and blocks the artery to the lung. This blockage prevents blood from reaching the lung tissue, resulting in poor oxygenation and a major stress on the heart. Symptoms of sudden breathlessness and chest pain, a bloody cough, and faintness or fear following an operative procedure or trauma that has affected the lower part of the body, should all warn of the possibility of a pulmonary embolism.

RECOMMENDATIONS

- *Any symptoms resembling an embolism must be treated as a medical emergency and reviewed at the nearest hospital.*
- *Decoagulation with drugs, and possibly even operative procedures, may be required, and these should be followed through without hesitation.*
- *The homeopathic snake remedies Bothrops and Lachesis, potency 6, can be taken every 15min en route to the hospital.*
- *Vitamin E, certain herbal preparations, and relevant dietetic changes, especially increasing water intake, should all be discussed with a complementary medical practitioner as soon as any emergency has passed.*

FLUID RETENTION (EDEMA)

Fluid retention describes an excess of fluid in the tissues, caused by an incorrect leakage from the blood vessels, especially the capillaries. Fluid in the body exists in three compartments: in the cells (intracellular), in the tissues (interstitial), and in the blood vessels. There is constant interchange between these three compartments, and they are all "fed" by fluid taken in from the bowel. The balance is maintained by osmosis (where water molecules follow larger molecules through blood-vessel and cell walls), and by chemical messengers that increase or decrease the size of the pores in the blood vessels and cell walls.

There are many reasons why fluid will build up in the interstitial compartment, but in principle, this is either because protein leaks from the capillaries, pulling water with it, or the fluid cannot enter the cells because of a protective fat/protein layer that is laid down around the cells. Specific areas of the body may become edematous because of a blockage in the drainage system (the lymph system), which can occur through infections causing elephantiasis, trauma, or tumor.

Many conditions affect capillary permeability, but hormone imbalance is one of the most common. Low thyroid levels and imbalance between estrogen, progesterone, and hormones produced by the kidneys and nervous system, all affect the size of blood vessels and their permeability. Water is attracted into tissues by osmosis. Osmosis is a physiological reaction caused by molecular electromagnetic attraction that, simply put, pulls water through a membrane until there are equal numbers of water molecules either side. A similar situation will occur if there is a lack of sodium or potassium, and other electrolytes and minerals within the bloodstream. Excess salt or sugar in the tissues will pull water into them, as will toxins. This latter process is an attempt by the body to dilute down the potentially poisonous effects.

Simple back pressure caused by obstruction to venous flow or heart failure will literally force fluid through the capillary pores. Symptoms of edema or water retention are dependent on where the fluid has settled. The biggest complaint concerns water that settles in the ankles and lower legs, hands, and fingers, around the face and jaw, and the midriff. The more-serious places for edema to occur are within the vital organs, such as the brain and lungs. The latter two are associated with medical complications, and need urgent attention.

Fluid in the lower limbs is often associated with venous obstruction, and is commonly found in pregnancy and obesity. More-serious conditions, such as heart failure and diseases of the liver (through which the main vein of the body—the vena cava—passes) causes back pressure and forces fluids into the tissues.

More generalized edema is often noted with hormonal fluctuation, and premenstrual syndrome is notorious for having this as one of its most-awkward symptoms. Shoes become tight to wear, and rings obstruct circulation to the fingers.

Dietary deficiencies will lead to poor electrolyte, amino-acid, and mineral content, allowing water to move cosmetically into the tissues, and a food allergy may create a toxic state within the tissues that causes water to be pulled in for dilution. Other toxins, such as alcohol and its breakdown product, aldehyde, cigarette byproducts, and other drugs of abuse may all cause a toxic state requiring dilution, as well as creating a chemical effect directly on the permeability of the capillaries. Orthodox drugs may well induce edema for the same reason.

One of the major causes of water retention that is commonly overlooked is, paradoxically, dehydration (*see* **Dehydration**). Although it is not immediately obvious why not drinking enough water may cause an excess of water in the tissues, the mechanism is simple. If not enough water is ingested, the individual cells in the body recognize dehydration. They attract fluid into themselves, and when replete, will surround their outer walls with a waterproof-lipid/protein protection. This cover is generally a cholesterol-based compound manufactured in the liver, and is a cause for raised cholesterol levels in the bloodstream.

Despite the cells being hydrated and therefore normal metabolic function progressing without illness forming, the body will recognize the dehydration and give instructions to hold water in the system because there is not enough. The bloodstream will provide fluid to the body tissues, particularly to the fat stores, thereby creating edema and the midriff effect so commonly associated with PMS. This leaves the bloodstream concentrated, triggering further reflex-water retention.

Another less-respected cause of water retention is the buildup of toxins in the system. The body will often hold water to dilute poisons that may be found in the interstitial and cellular compartments, thereby rendering the concentration less dangerous. The characteristic bloating often found after drinking or abusing drugs is caused by a combination of dehydration and toxic buildup.

RECOMMENDATIONS

- *It is important to rule out underlying hormonal or biochemical changes that may be due to conditions such as hypothyroidism and diabetes. Diseases of the heart, liver and kidney—the former two leading to venous back pressure and the latter to electrolyte disturbance—all need to be ruled out.*
- *Review any drug prescription via the doctor who prescribed it in case one of its side effects is water retention. It may need to be changed or removed.*
- *Review the diet. Restrict salt and processed foods, which are inevitably high in sodium content.*
- *Consider testing for food allergies. Whether this is required may be established by using a Detox diet or fast for three days, ensuring adequate water intake. If an improvement occurs, food allergy is probable.*
- *Drink plenty of water. As described above, the mechanism is paradoxical, but the more water that is drunk, the less the retention is maintained. Normal input should be 8 ounces per foot of height at the least, but in cases of water retention, this should be doubled. Water intake may need to be restricted in cases of fluid retention caused by heart, liver, or kidney problems. Discuss this with your practitioner.*
- *Water retention associated with the hormonal cycle may benefit from vitamin B_6 (20mg per foot of height divided into two doses) taken with breakfast and supper.*

- *The homeopathic remedy Natrum muriaticum 30 taken four times a day for five days may shift the problem, and can be repeated up to twice a month.*
- *Herbal treatments such as Uva ursi, Herberus, and juniper can be utilized, but should be considered as a drug or a diuretic, and should be prescribed by a herbalist rather than taken as an over-the-counter remedy.*
- *Any retentive disorder (one that forms lumps, bumps, or cysts), including water retention, may be a bodily reflection of a mental or spiritual attitude. Water retention associated with depression or an inability to express is literally "holding it in" and it is necessary to confront these emotions. Counseling is invaluable in water retention that does not seem to have an underlying physical illness associated with it, or does not respond to the naturopathic recommendations above.*

GEOPATHIC STRESS

The earth carries magnetic and electrical fields, and lines that travel in different directions depending on an area's relation to the north and south poles. The movement of water, the position of the sun and the moon, and "manmade" electrical-power stations all affect this natural electromagnetic status.

The human body is known to have electromagnetic energy traveling through its system, from both an orthodox point of view as well as that of Eastern philosophies, which conclude that all health is created through these meridians or channels.

The subject of geopathic stress is enormous and is poorly documented, although there is much evidence of disease and illness being created through interfering with these lines.

RECOMMENDATIONS

- *See* **Feng Shui.**
- *See* **Radiation.**

GIGANTISM (ACROMEGALY)

This is a chronic disease due to excessive secretion of growth hormone by the pituitary gland. It causes overgrowth of bone and tissues, but has a particular effect on the hands, feet, face, and head. It is a rare condition, and does not particularly jeopardize longevity, although specific problems caused by moving an excessively large frame around may be apparent as muscular strains, including that on the heart muscle.

RECOMMENDATIONS

- *The reason for excess growth-hormone production needs to be eliminated. Consult an endocrinologist.*
- *Complementary treatment is dependent upon any particular problems associated with acromegaly.*

THE GLANDS

Glands are a special type of tissue that produce chemicals which travel through the bloodstream and affect cells in other parts of the body. These chemicals are called hormones, and they are extremely potent, being produced in very small amounts but having profound effects. The true meaning of gland is "tissue that secretes hormones," but the term is also used for tissues that secrete products that travel locally.

ADRENAL GLANDS

These sit on top of the kidneys, and are divided into two parts: the outer cortex, which makes steroids; and the inner medulla, which produces adrenaline in response to nervous control from the central nervous system. Some consider the adrenal glands to be governed by an energy meridian called, in Chinese medicine, the "triple heater," and the adrenal glands in turn govern the *pitta* or fire energy in Ayurvedic beliefs.

Stress, both physical and psychological, will drain the adrenal glands of energy, leading to biochemical–chemical imbalances caused by poor

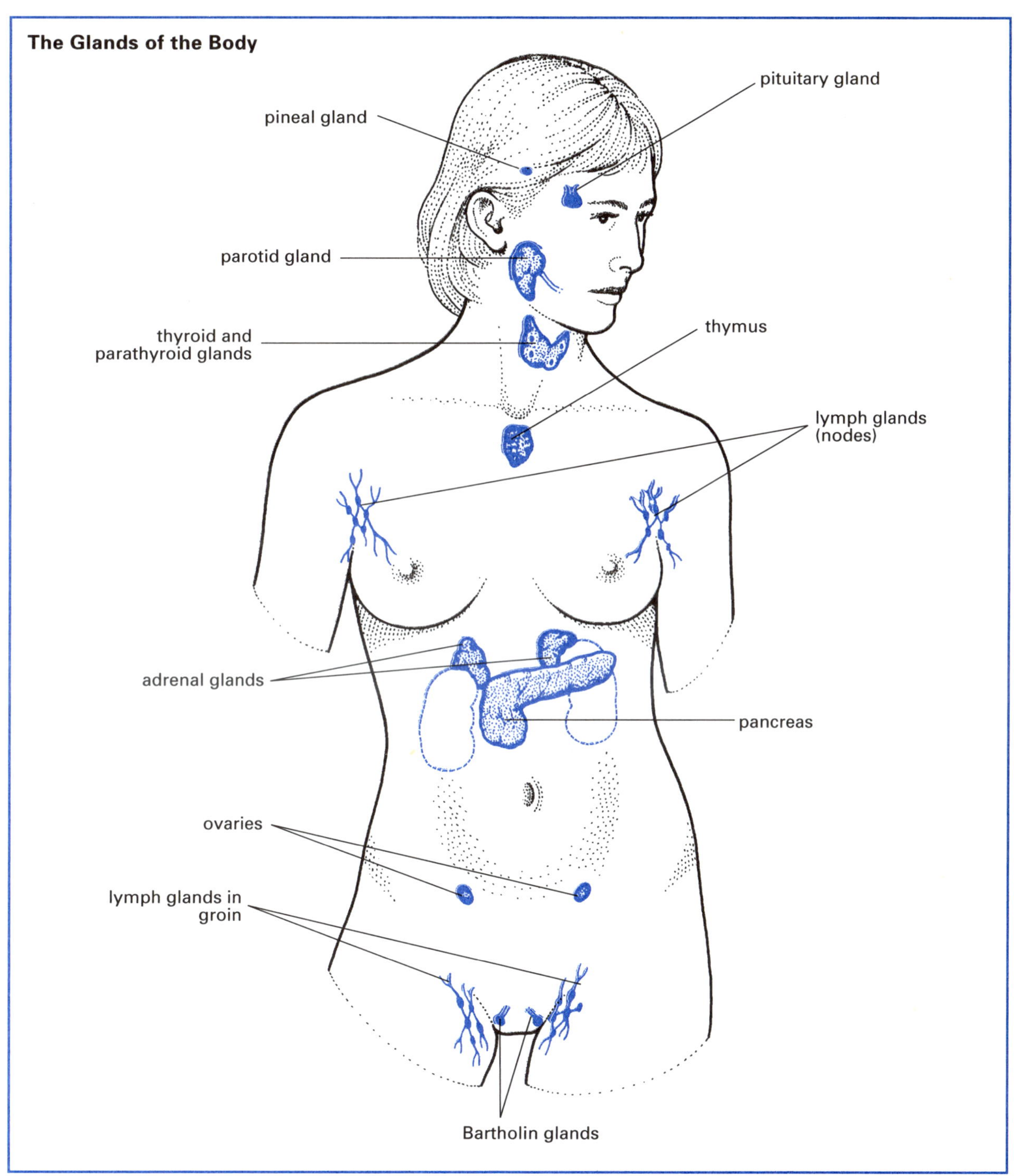

steroid production, as well as general malaise and tiredness from the lack of adrenaline. Tumors may arise in all glands, but the most common in the adrenal glands is pheochromocytoma, which is a tumor of the adrenal medulla that causes an excess of adrenaline, which in turn can cause rapid heart rate, a rise in blood pressure, weight loss, and sweating. This is a serious condition that mimics hypothyroidism; it requires immediate medical attention and probably surgery.

BARTHOLIN GLANDS

These are not truly glands, because they do not secrete a hormone. They are small amounts of tissue found in the labia on either side of the vagina that secrete a lubricating and cleansing fluid. A blockage in the duct from these so-called glands leads to Bartholin cysts (*see* **Bartholin Cysts**).

LYMPHATIC GLANDS

In the truest sense of the word, these are not strictly glands. They are a mesh of protein found in the lymphatic system. After the goodness from blood has left the blood vessels and fed the tissues, it is collected with waste product in the lymphatic system, and drained through a complex of vessels that match the arteries and veins for quantity and length before going back to the bloodstream in the chest. Along the way, the lymph, which will be carrying bacteria, viruses, and any other foreign matter, will pass through lymph glands. Caught in the meshwork are white blood cells that devour the foreign matter and break it down before releasing it back into the lymph flow.

These glands can swell in the presence of infection, and this is generally a good sign, showing that the body's defense mechanism is active. Unfortunately, if the body is overreacting or out of control, such as in leukemia or lymphoma, the numbers of white blood cells increase, get trapped in the lymph glands, and these swell excessively.

Cancer can also drain from its primary site into lymph glands, which then harbor the cancer cells which help to prevent their spread around the body. Temporary swelling in the lymph glands in association with an obvious infection can—and should—be left alone, but any persistence or pain within glands should be reviewed by a health practitioner.

PARATHYROID GLANDS

These small glands are found in the middle of the thyroid tissue in the neck. They are responsible for the balance of calcium, and thereby magnesium, in the body tissues.

Problems with the parathyroid glands are a potentially serious medical condition, and are often found by routine blood screening showing incorrect levels of calcium. Any persistent swelling in the neck should be reviewed by a physician (*see* **Thyroid**).

PAROTID GLAND

This gland is found at the side of the face in front of the ears and overlying the jaw joint. It is a salivary gland with a tube passing down the side of the cheeks to a small opening. The parotid gland produces saliva, helping digestion and cleanliness of the mouth.

The parotid gland is surrounded by a tight capsule, and infection or inflammation that causes swelling can be very painful and should be treated urgently. Tumors in the parotid gland are not uncommon, and may be dangerous if left unattended. Stones may form in the parotid duct, leading to a blockage and swelling. This too needs to be attended to swiftly.

If anyone has occasionally noticed a sharp but transient pain in the side of the cheeks when putting anything sour or tart-tasting in the mouth, they may be interested to know that this is because of the immediate response of saliva production from the parotid gland, which causes a restriction within the muscles of the parotid gland tubes that is like a cramp. It is a physiological response, and nothing to worry about.

PINEAL GLAND

This small gland is found towards the front of the brain, and corresponds in Eastern philosophy to the third eye. Its function is not fully understood, but it is known to produce the natural hormone melatonin, which controls our circadian rhythms and sleep patterns. There is probably some control over our mood and, as I notice that science slowly but surely finds support for ancient Eastern philosophies, we will find that the pineal gland has something to do with our intuition or sixth sense (thereby corresponding to the third eye).

Diseases or problems with the pineal gland are rare, and usually only found on investigations such as CT scans.

PITUITARY GLAND

This is probably the most-complex gland in the body. It is found in the middle of the brain tissue, and is divided into two parts, anterior and posterior, that control most of the other glands in the body.

The hormones produced control the thyroid gland, growth (especially in children), the female hormonal cycle and ovulation, water content in the body, steroid production from the adrenal glands, and other functions throughout the body. This walnut-sized gland may cause a variety of problems if it does not function as it should. Tumors of the pituitary gland initially may be noticed as visual disturbance, because it sits close to the route of the optic nerve. Diagnosis of pituitary malfunction requires a physician's expertise, although many minor problems may be associated with the pituitary gland and its relevance to Eastern medical philosophy.

I find it fascinating and not coincidental that all Eastern philosophies believe in a central energy point at the top of the head, the crown chakra. This corresponds to the superficial point of the

PITUITARY GLAND—Hormones

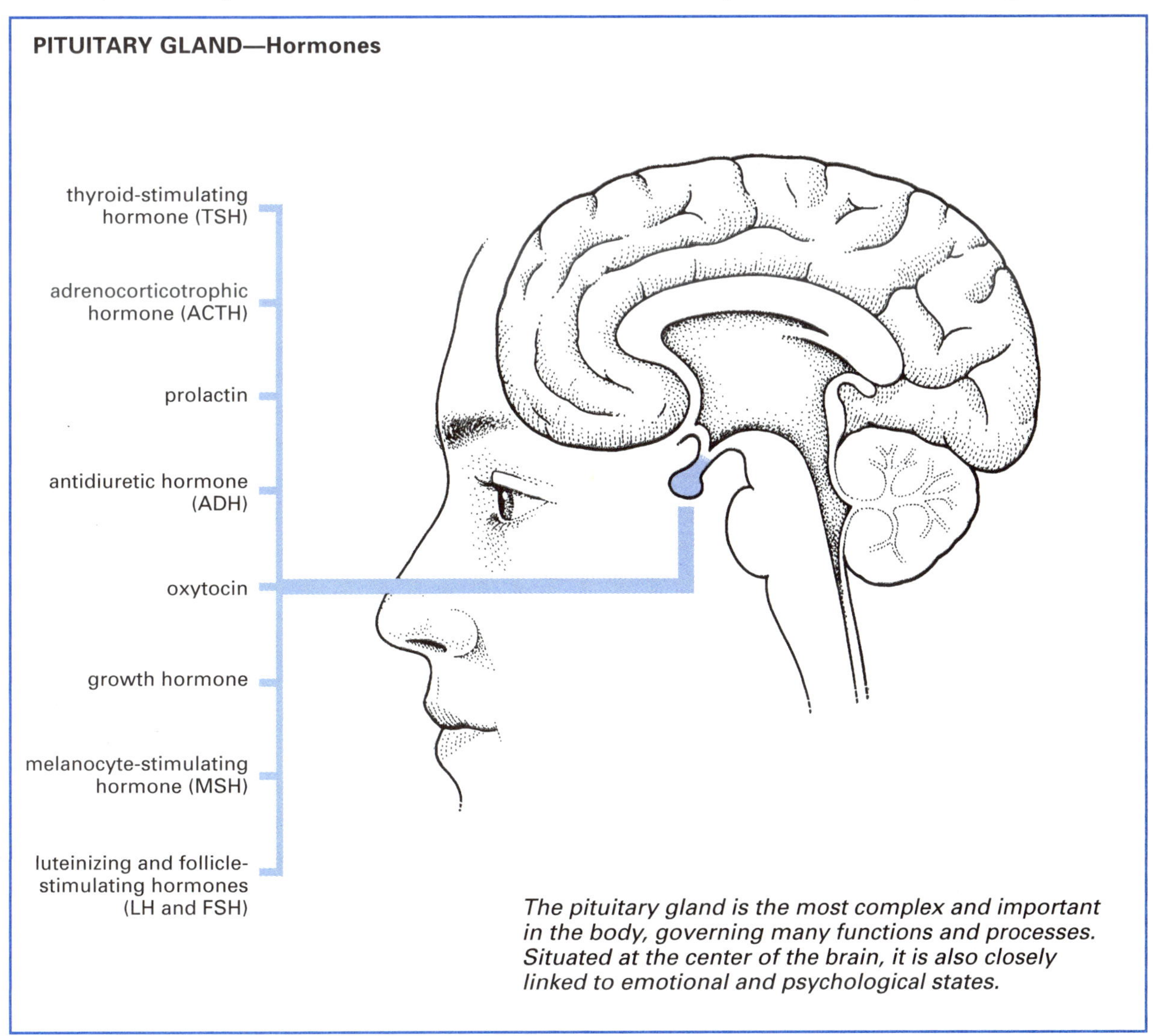

The pituitary gland is the most complex and important in the body, governing many functions and processes. Situated at the center of the brain, it is also closely linked to emotional and psychological states.

pituitary gland. It is interesting that for over 5,000 years, this point has been documented as being a master control point of the entire system. This belief has since been supported by modern science and its findings over the last 100 years, as we have unraveled the complex control function of the pituitary gland.

The principle of a psychological effect on the pituitary gland is not well accepted by the orthodox world. It is accepted that stress and anxiety can cause hormonal fluctuations, and the holistic consensus of opinion is that the psychology of an individual produces chemicals from the brain or transmits energy to the pituitary gland that have a negative effect. The most obvious symptoms are those suffered by young females, in particular, who under pressure may throw their cycle. The pituitary has a connection to a part of the brain that registers and recognizes smell, and it may be this sensitivity to pheromones (airborne chemicals) that induces a coinciding of hormonal cycles in women who live in close proximity.

PROSTATE GLAND—*see* Prostatitis

SALIVARY GLANDS

Salivary glands (which include the parotid gland) are distributed around and under the jaw line. They produce saliva, which contains enzymes to start the breakdown of food; fluid to moisten what we eat; and different types of immunoglobulins to help protect and clean the mouth. Saliva is mildly alkaline, which accounts for its extra production in association with gastric problems that may cause an excess of acid production.

The control of salivation is through neurological reflexes, and some neurological problems—such as motorneurone disease and tumors of the salivary gland—can produce excess salivation. It is necessary to bring any persistent excess salivation or pain in the soft tissues underneath the jaw line to the attention of a physician. A dry mouth may be caused by disease of these glands or a stone in the duct (*see* **Saliva**).

SEBACEOUS GLANDS

Sebaceous glands are found in the skin; these produce sebum, which is the characteristic moistening and protective compound necessary for healthy skin. Excess sebum production leads to oily skin, and blockages in the ducts from these microscopic glands can be the cause of pimples, acne, and sebaceous cysts (*see* the relevant sections).

There are rare genetic conditions that prevent the sebaceous glands from functioning, leading to persistent dry skin open to infection. Dehydration may affect the constituency of sebum and the function of sebaceous glands, and this needs to be corrected by increased intake of water (*see* **Skin**).

THYMUS GLAND

This small amount of tissue is found behind the sternum (breastbone) and is responsible for the production of T cells. These T cells are a vital part of the body's white-blood-cell immune system.

Problems with the thymus gland are rare, although it corresponds with the heart chakra, and therefore is influenced by the emotional state of an individual. A recent hypothesis suggests that the thymus gland may store parasites that may be released on contact with petrochemical pollutants in the atmosphere. Release of these parasites causes destruction of the T cells, which may be instrumental in the ill health of HIV/AIDS patients (*see* **AIDS**).

THYROID GLAND

The thyroid gland is an H-shaped structure about the size of a palm situated along and under the Adam's apple. It is made up of cells that are concerned with the synthesis of thyroid hormones, the most prominent being thyroxine (T_4) and Triiodothyronine (T_3). These are both made up from iodine and the amino acid, tyrosine. (The thyroid gland also contains a small amount of tissue known as the parathyroid, which produces a hormone called calcitonin that controls calcium levels in the body.)

The thyroid hormones are responsible for

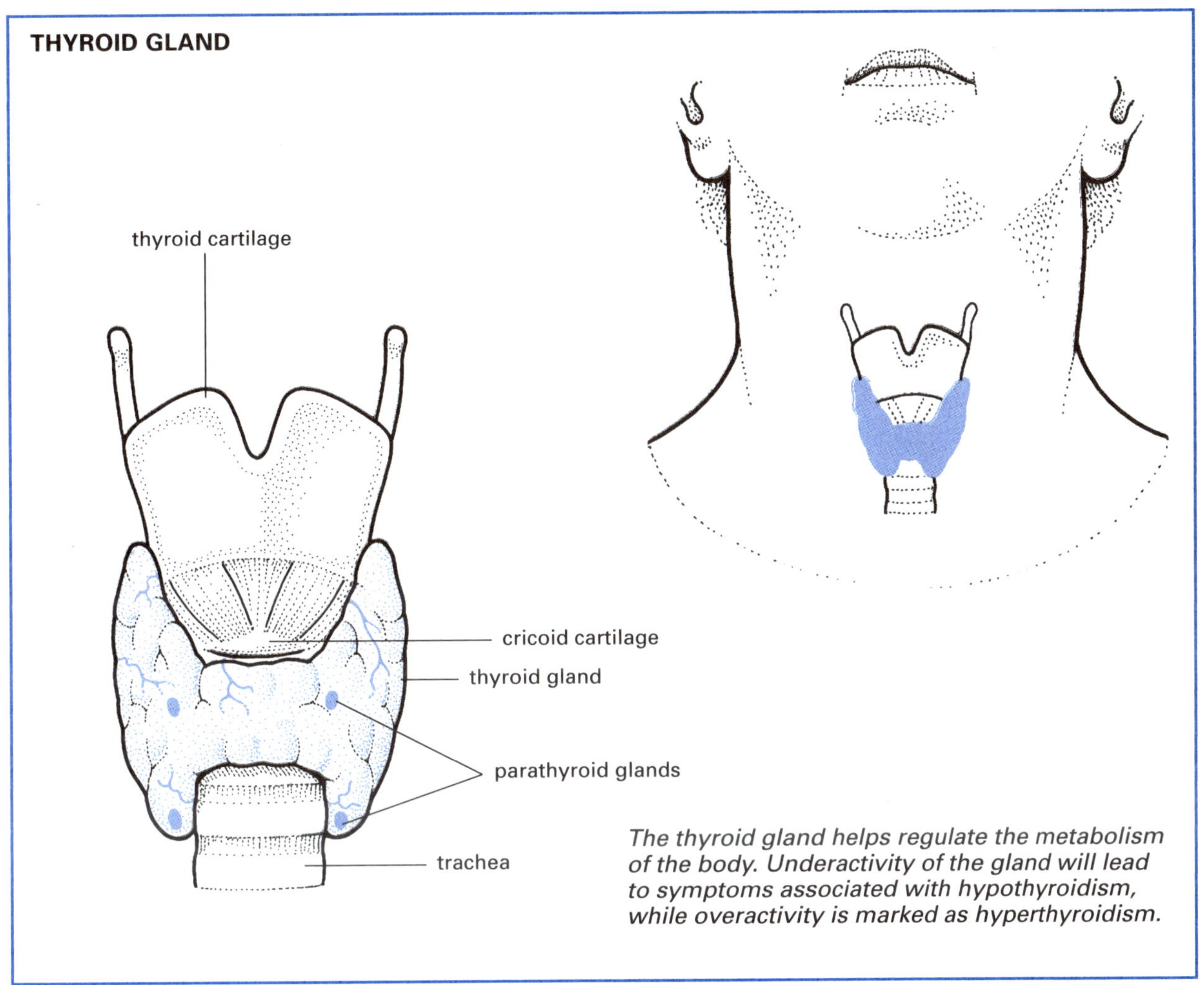

The thyroid gland helps regulate the metabolism of the body. Underactivity of the gland will lead to symptoms associated with hypothyroidism, while overactivity is marked as hyperthyroidism.

regulating the metabolism of cells throughout the body. The amounts in the body are controlled by a chemical released from the pituitary gland, known as thyroid-stimulating hormone (TSH). This itself is controlled by another hormone called TSH-Releasing Hormone (TRH), which comes from a part of the brain known as the hypothalamus. This is a prime example of a biofeedback mechanism. An increase in the level of thyroid hormones depresses the production of TRH, which is not available to stimulate the production of TSH, which, thereby, does not stimulate the thyroid gland unless T_3 and T_4 are made. This cycle attempts to maintain a constant level of circulating hormone within a suitable range.

Blood tests are now freely available, but the normal ranges are only guidelines. For example, one laboratory has a normal range of 44–143nmol/l. Somebody with a figure of 50nmol/l would therefore be considered normal. If that individual should, however, have a level around 120 then they are, in reality, hypothyroid.

High or low figures should not be considered by themselves. It is better to evaluate thyroid status by measuring the basal body temperature (BBT), which gives us some indication of the metabolic rate of the cells of the system. This, in combination with the blood tests and symptoms of hypo- or hyperthyroidism, provides a much better guideline. Individuals may have T_3 or T_4 levels in the low part of the normal range and be considered "euthyroid" (normal for thyroid function), but in reality their levels should be, say, 120.

The orthodox medical world would consider the thyroid to be functioning normally, but in fact the person is considerably hypothyroid.

Basal body temperature (BBT)

To measure the BBT, place a thermometer beside your bed before sleeping, and then first thing on awakening, place the thermometer under the tongue while remaining in bed for at least 5 minutes. It is best to repeat this test on ten successive days, and take the average temperature. Normal body temperature is between 97.6°F and 98.2°F.

A BBT below the norm in association with thyroxine levels in the lower half of the normal range is much more indicative of a hypothyroid state than just a blood figure. Numbers at the other end of the scale may indicate hyperthyroidism.

I have described elsewhere in this book the principle of the vessel of conception described by Chinese acupuncturists. If you refer to that section (*see* **The vessel of conception**) you will see that the thyroid may well be controlled not only by hormones from the pituitary and hypothalamus, but also by a direct energy flow. Problems—either biochemical or energetic—with these parts of the brain may therefore strongly influence the entire body by affecting the thyroid.

GOITER

A goiter is the term used for *any* enlargement of the thyroid gland.

Goiter is therefore the definition of a symptom similar to jaundice, rather than a condition itself. A cancer or inflamed thyroid may show up as a goiter. Bacterial infections causing an acute thyroiditis are very uncommon, but a viral infection such as mumps is a little more frequent. These are known as subacute thyroiditis, and generally present as a tender thyroid with severe pains throughout the neck.

A goiter can be described as nontoxic or toxic. A toxic goiter is a swelling associated with hyperthroidism, discussed in that section.

A nontoxic goiter is caused by the thyroid gland enlarging in an attempt to trap more iodine to make more thyroxine. This occurs in people who are not taking enough iodine into their system through diet, or who have a glandular defect (*see* **Hypothyroidism**).

The goiter in hypothyroidism therefore tends to be diffuse, with an equal growth throughout the gland. Hyperthyroidism may exhibit a diffuse growth, but also appears in a uninodular or multinodular pattern. Frequently, a rumble may be heard if the gland is listened to through a stethoscope because of the increased vascularity.

Most goiters are asymptomatic (without symptoms) but, if they grow too much, local pressure effects may be noted, particularly a tightness around the neck, a persistent irritation of the throat, or a change in voice due to pressure on the vocal cords.

Physiological goiters may occur at puberty and pregnancy. This is due to the influence of estrogen and progesterone.

RECOMMENDATIONS

- *Any swelling in the neck should be reviewed by a physician for a firm diagnosis. This may include investigations via ultrasound and blood tests.*
- *Please refer to the relevant sections on hypo- or hyperthyroidism, depending upon the cause or effect of the goiter.*

GRAVES' DISEASE

Named after an Irish physician in the early 19th century, this disease is characterized by a diffuse swelling of the thyroid gland—known as a goiter, and a bulging of the eyes, known as—exophthalmos. The cause of the disease is unknown, although it tends to be hereditary, and most commonly affects women. The thyroid gland is overactive, and symptoms of hyperthyroidism are prominent; the condition has a specific symptom of circumscribed lesions under the skin over the shinbone (this is known as pretibial myxedema).

RECOMMENDATIONS

- *Any suggestion of a swelling in the neck or development of bulging eyes, with or without symptoms of sweating, palpitations, weight loss, insomnia or overactivity, should be reviewed by a doctor to check that hyperthyroidism is not the diagnosis.*
- *See* **Hyperthyroidism**.

HYPERTHYROIDISM

The symptoms of hyperthyroidism are principally:

Weight loss	Heat intolerance
Increased sweating	Warm and moist skin
Shortness of Breath	Palpitations
Tachycardia	Flushing
Increased blood pressure	Irregular heartbeat
Weakness	Tiredness
Anxiety	Irritability
Insomnia	Occasional psychosis
Tremor	Diarrhea
Irregular periods	Miscarriages

Left untreated, a characteristic bulging of the eyes known as exophthalmos develops, and is known as Graves' disease (*see* **Graves' disease**). The causes of hyperthyroidism are little understood. The thyroid gland becomes overprotective throughout the tissue, through multiple nodules, or occasionally a single "hot" nodule. Frequently, a chemical known as long-acting thyroid stimulator (LATS) is found in the system. This is an immunoglobulin, and is being produced somewhere, for some reason, by the body's immune system. It may well be in response to some other factor, and its effect on the thyroid is purely a side effect. A group of antibodies known as the thyroid-stimulating antibodies (TSAbs) can be demonstrated in the serum of thyroid-toxic patients, and these seem to attack the receptors in the thyroid for THS, thereby stimulating the activity and causing the thyroid to produce too much T_3 and T_4. There is some suggestion that there is an autoimmune (the body attacks itself) stimulus, but holistic physicians look more at toxicity, potentially parasitic or fungal infection of the thyroid, food allergy, and vital-force imbalance, then at the vessel of conception or midline chakra points.

Naturopathic treatment is remarkably ineffective against hyperthyroidism, in my experience. Severe hyperthyroidism is a potentially swift, lethal condition, and needs to be treated with the appropriate respect. Mild hyperthyroidism may respond to naturopathic treatment, but all cases must be monitored carefully.

RECOMMENDATIONS

- *Establish a baseline of thyroxine levels in comparison to the BBT. If very high, do not hesitate to follow orthodox treatment; if only just outside the normal scale, monitor the situation frequently, and pay attention to the worsening of any symptoms.*
- *Add goitrogens (foods that inhibit thyroxine production) to the diet by increasing the intake of broccoli, cabbage, turnips, spinach, collard greens, brussels sprouts, soya products, peanuts, pine nuts, and millet.*
- *Try the following herbal tinctures in divided doses three times a day: lycopus, five drops per foot of height; cactus, five drops per foot of height.*
- *The homeopathic remedy Thyroidinium 200, one dose nightly for one week.*
- *Specific symptoms may be relieved by a correctly selected homeopathic remedy. A homeopath should be consulted.*

HYPOTHYROIDISM

The thyroid hormones affect the whole body. The symptoms of hypothyroidism may be seen in any part of the body, and should be considered if one of the following symptoms appears, persists, or is combined with two or more other symptoms.

Depression	Insomnia
Anxiety	Poor concentration
Loss of memory	Numbness or tingling
Dizzy spells	Carpal-tunnel syndrome
Poor vision, especially at night	Weight gain
Fatigue	Sensitivity to the cold
Water retention	Hoarse voice
Slow speech	Abnormal rhythms
Slow heartbeat	Increased number of cold symptoms
Palpitations	Decreased appetite
Constipation	Infertility or miscarriages
Irregular periods	Muscle cramps
Absent periods	Brittle hair
Dry skin	Ridged nails
Hair loss (notably, eyebrows)	
Irritability	

There are also other less-common symptoms.

If left uncontrolled, the above symptoms will continue, and a condition known as myxedema may develop. This term is derived from the deposition of a fatty material around the body that causes an edema-like swelling all over the body. If myxedema is profound, then a coma may be the outcome, associated with very low body temperature and damage to other organs through low oxygen supplies.

Hypothyroidism may be divided into primary or secondary.

Primary hypothyroidism

In primary hypothyroidism there is a failure of the thyroid to develop, and if severe or not spotted, will lead to a marked inability, known as cretinism. There are many causes.

- Iodine deficiency—which occurs in specific parts of the world where iodine is not in the food chain to any great extent. Seafood, in particular, is high in iodine, and mountainous areas that may not consider fish as part of their regular diet are more prone to iodine deficiency. Damage to the thyroid by foods known as goitrogens, which contain substances that prevent the utilization of iodine, is another cause. This list includes soya bean, peanuts, millet, turnips, cabbage, and mustard. It is worth noting that cooking usually inactivates goitrogens.
- The stress hormone, cortisol, is known to block the production of T_3.
- Rarely, thyroid levels may be normal (or even raised), but symptoms of hypothyroidism continue. This may be due to the cells of the body not recognizing thyroid hormone. Metal toxicity may be relevant in this condition.
- Destruction of normal thyroid-glandular tissue by tumors, operations, or radioiodine. The latter two are more frequent, because these are common treatments for hyperthyroidism.
- Autoimmune thyroiditis (Hashimoto's disease) most commonly affects middle-aged women, and is due to antibodies being formed against different constituents of the thyroid gland. Simply, the body attacks its own thyroid.
- Drug-induced hypothyroidism may be caused by certain prescribed drugs, including those used for heart arrhythmias, some tranquilizers, and antiepileptic drugs.

Secondary hypothyroidism

Secondary hypothyroidism is created by reduced TRH or TSH caused by afflictions of the pituitary gland by the hypothalamus.

The treatment for hypothyroidism is generally replacement with thyroxine, which replenishes the blood levels but does not attempt to isolate or treat the cause. Holistic practitioners may try to restimulate the thyroid once they have removed any possible underlying causes of hypothyroidism, but may have to resort to thyroxine replacement because restimulation is frequently not achieved. The following recommendations should be tried for a short time, and thyroid function tests and symptom assessment should be made very objectively. Many patients are reluctant to consider having to use a "drug" for the rest of their lives, but need to be reminded that it is simply a replacement of what the body naturally produces. Completely natural thyroid is available, although the pharmaceutical form is much purer, and a physician knows exactly how much is being given.

RECOMMENDATIONS

- *Rule out any changeable cause of hypothyroidism, such as iodine deficiency or drug-induced deficiency.*
- *Remove the goitrogens mentioned above from the diet.*
- *Check for nutritional deficiencies, specifically tyrosine (the amino acid), iodine, zinc, copper, iron, and selenium, all of which are necessary for thyroid function.*
- *Practice a relaxation or meditation technique regularly, and sit with a counselor to discuss and attempt to resolve underlying stress-creating conditions.*
- *Check mercury, lead, and other chemical contamination through blood and hair samples and treat accordingly (see* **Poisoning***).*
- *Add the following nutrients into your diet, regardless of blood results, because the system may simply need more thyroxine to function normally. The following should be taken with breakfast at the recommended dosage per foot of height: iodine (50µg), selenium (50µg), copper (500µg), and tyrosine (100mg); and zinc (5mg per foot of height) should be taken before bed.*
- *Acupuncture can be used to try to stimulate the thyroid.*
- *Yoga or Qi Gong should be used, because exercise may stimulate thyroid production, and the techniques move the energy through the chakras, thereby potentially relieving blocks or deficiencies in the throat chakra, that overlies the thyroid.*
- *Thyroxine replacement through orthodox preparations should be used if symptoms of hypothyroidism are troublesome. The above recommendations may still stimulate the thyroid and brain centers, regardless of the presence of thyroxine in the bloodstream. Taking thyroxine will diminish symptoms swiftly.*
- *Desiccated, natural thyroid can be used, although I see no advantage. Whichever is taken, ensure that blood levels and BBT are taken every three weeks until normality is achieved and symptoms have regressed.*

TUMOR AND CANCERS OF THE THYROID

Single or multiple benign growths in the thyroid are common, and frequent in areas where iodine intake is low. These are harmless, and have no greater tendency to become cancerous than normal thyroid tissue.

Cancer of the thyroid should be suspected in any thyroid with a single nodule. Initial testing is done by scanning the gland after administration of radioactive iodine. Overactive thyroid tissue will pick this up, and is termed a "hot" nodule. This may be an indication simply of an overactive area of the thyroid, and nothing more than a hyperthyroid state, but it can also indicate cancer. Benign nodules do not pick up the radioiodine to any great extent, and are known as "cold" nodules.

RECOMMENDATIONS

- *Any swelling in the throat must be examined by a physician.*
- *Do not avoid investigation of thyroid nodules, because early detection increases the chances of a better outcome.*
- *A "hot" nodule may need a biopsy or even a lumpectomy, and this should be undertaken, usually under general anesthetic, with your permission to remove the thyroid if cancer is found.*
- *Treatment of a goiter is dependent upon the cause and the associated symptoms.*

- *Do not shirk from investigation for fear of a bad result, because most goiters are innocent and easily proven so.*

HAIR

Hair is an evolutionary remnant of our ape ancestry. Intended to keep us warm and protected from the elements, the use of protective clothes encouraged natural selection to remove our fur. Hair has remained on our heads, our armpits and groins in greater abundance. That on the scalp I can understand as a protective factor, but armpits and groins ... ? If anybody knows, do please write in with the answer!

Hair is principally made of keratin, which is a protein, and may accurately be described as a "dead" material. However, the follicle from which the hair grows is very much alive, and is considered by complementary practitioners to be a useful eliminatory cell, and the hair itself to be a reflection of health. Many conditions, such as hypothyroidism, will be reflected by dry, brittle hair, and hyperthyroidism may actually cause hair to fall. Some less-well-proven food allergies/intolerance tests examine the hair for molecules of food that have become enmeshed with the keratin structure, in the belief that the follicle will remove toxins or compounds less-well tolerated by the body, which can therefore be measured.

Most cultures consider the hair to be an adornment worthy of spending much time keeping attractive. This is an important factor in "mate" selection, and care of the hair should be looked upon as a necessity, not a vanity.

Care of the hair and the scalp

Medicated hair products detract from the ability of the scalp to maintain its hair in good condition. If you look at the hair of healthy children, you will see that very little needs to be done if the individual is in good health.

The hair follicles and sweat glands act as elimination organs, and the more toxins in the system, the more the hair will contain debris, and the more the sweat will coat the hair with poisons. Dehydration, excess fats, refined foods, additives, and preservatives will all take the shine and gloss out of the hair.

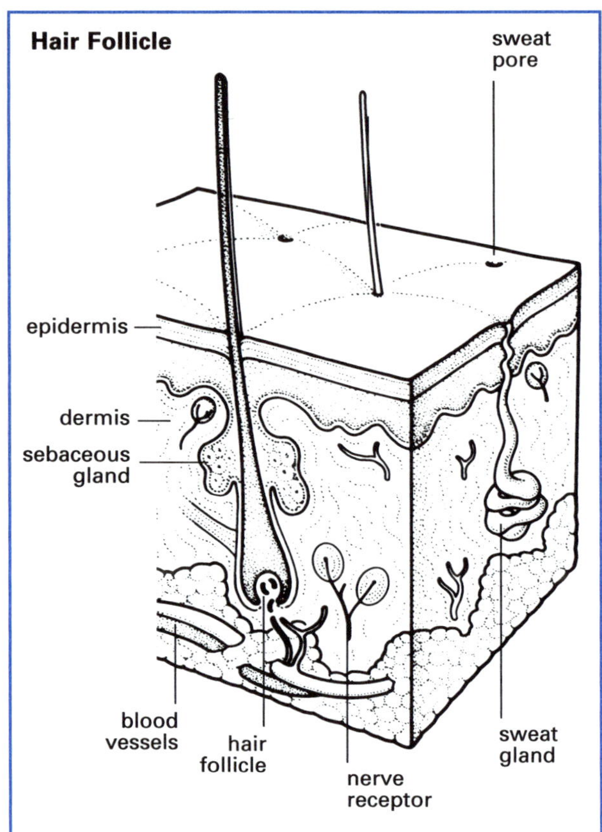

The hair itself is dependent upon the production of a protein called keratin, which demands an amino-acid supply in the diet. The easier the protein is to digest and break down, the easier it is for hair to be formed. Therefore, amino acids from vegetable proteins and light meat (fish, chicken) will be better for the hair.

Remember that the skin absorbs compounds, albeit at a slow rate, and the highly vascular scalp is an effective route of entry for compounds into the body. Certain plant extracts are less toxic than chemicals, and will adhere to the hair just as efficiently. The more natural the hair product, the less likely it is to create a toxic environment in the system. The scalp in which the hair follicles live is a very active part of the skin surface. Sweat, sebum, and hair are constantly produced, and diseases of the scalp, which include dandruff and alopecia, are best prevented rather than treated. Stress will affect the condition of the hair. When under pressure or stressed, the body produces more adrenaline, which cuts down the blood supply to the skin in order to provide more oxygen and nutrients to essential organs for a fight-or-flight reaction. This 10 percent reduction in bloodflow may not be noticeable, but will cut down the nutrient and oxygen supply to the hair follicle, sweat, and sebum glands, and thereby diminish the amount of essential nutrients reaching the hair follicle.

RECOMMENDATIONS

- *Do not wash the hair more frequently than is necessary. If your hair is losing its luster or appearing dirty every day, then reflect on your diet, not your hair products. Daily washing removes the natural oils, which in turn diminishes the quality and condition of the hair.*
- *Do not use medicated shampoos. Shampoos with plant extract such as jojoba are perfectly safe, and just as beneficial as most chemical additives.*
- *Hair that is dry may benefit from a weekly application of olive oil and lemon juice. Mix one tablespoon of olive oil with one teaspoon of lemon juice, and apply until all the hair is covered. Leave this on for 15min, and then wash off with a natural shampoo. Dry hair generally suggests dehydration (see* **Dehydration***).*
- *Avoid medicated conditioners, again using natural products instead.*
- *Scalp massage either by yourself, a professional, or a partner will encourage bloodflow, and potentially promote healthy hair.*
- *A multimineral supplement may be beneficial if hair growth is slow.*
- *Meditation or relaxation techniques are an essential aspect of healthy-looking hair in those who are stressed or under pressure.*
- *Persisting lacklustre hair may be a reflection of poor diet or underlying ill health. A trichologist and/or a complementary medical practitioner should be consulted.*

Gray hair

There are several hypotheses for the physiological reaction that allows hair to gray, but in principle, the color of hair is genetically predisposed, and is to do with the way light reflects off the protein structure in the hair, rather than any additive to the hair matrix. Gray hair is often found to run in families, although the Eastern philosophies believe that gray hair is an indication of a lack of fundamental energy, especially when associated with youth (premature graying). There is no doubt that shock (an excess of adrenaline) can cause the hair to gray, and persistent pressure or stress (persistent production of adrenaline) will encourage graying. The mechanism is described in the section above on hair care.

RECOMMENDATIONS

- *Be proud of your hair color rather than fighting it.*
- *Reduce stress and alter lifestyle to avoid persistent pressure.*
- *Correct diet and mineral supplementation may affect hair color.*
- *Hair dyes should not be used, because the products will be absorbed to some extent by the scalp, but if the use is considered necessary, then try to obtain as natural a product as possible.*

Hair dyes

Changing the color of the hair stems from an evolutionary need to camouflage or attract attention, either for courting purposes or making the appearance more aggressive before going into battle. The latter use is not so much required any more, although the brightly colored hair of some younger people may be making a form of social statement!

Dyes will be absorbed to some extent by the highly vascular scalp, and may create a toxic reaction, major or minor, within the system.

RECOMMENDATIONS

- *Use only the most natural of hair colorants because the body will deal with natural herbs much better than artificial chemicals.*
- *Medically speaking, avoid hair dyes. Be comfortable with yourself, and possibly consider sitting with a counselor if you have a strong need to appear as that which you are not.*

Hair loss

Losing hair may be a physiological or a pathological response. A certain amount of hair loss will occur when the weather becomes warmer, through pregnancy and lactation, and with aging. Pathological causes may vary from overwashing, medicated or poor-quality shampoos, persistent use of hair dryers, especially in association with the current hair design or cutting and possibly from overuse of hairsprays or gels. More-serious conditions can cause hair loss, such as hypothyroidism and other metabolic diseases. Skin fungus—most often responsible for dandruff—may cause hair loss, and toxins such as excess alcohol, drugs of abuse, steroids, and anticancer drugs can all cause the hair to fall.

Nutritional deficiencies of minerals (especially sulfur), proteins, and vitamins may all cause hair to thin; and stress, as discussed in the section above on hair care, will also have an effect.

RECOMMENDATIONS

- *Feel assured that if hair loss is associated with physiological causes, the hair will regrow.*
- *Whether physiological or pathological, increase vitamin and mineral intake through fresh fruit and vegetables (at least five portions a day), or take a multivitamin/multimineral supplement at twice the daily recommended dose.*
- *Persistent hair loss with no obvious cause requires a studious examination of hair care and the products used, or, preferably, an initial consultation with a complementary medical practitioner or a trichologist.*
- *Persistent hair loss should be considered by a general practitioner with possible referral to a endocrinologist.*

Excess hair

Excess hair is usually only considered a problem if it is facial. Excessive growth is usually an ethnic or genetic predisposition, although certain, rare metabolic conditions and drugs may encourage hair growth. Hormone imbalance, particularly excess testosterone and other male hormones (androgens), is a cause in women.

RECOMMENDATIONS

- *If no ethnic or genetic reason is apparent, then a consultation with a trichologist and a general practitioner will be in order.*
- *Discuss naturopathic estrogen and progesterone treatments before using orthodox drug approaches to blocking androgen effects.*
- *If no metabolic or drug problems are the cause, then hair removal can be considered. Both chemical and electrical techniques can be used, although the latter is less likely to create a toxic response.*

HAY FEVER

Hay fever or allergic rhinitis is characterized by itchy nose, throat, and palate, congestion and/or runny discharge from the nasal passages, itching, or stinging eyes. These symptoms are often associated with tiredness, lethargy, and sinus-type headaches. Hay fever is caused by the body producing chemicals, including histamine, in response to pollens from plants attaching themselves to membranes in the nose and throat.

The orthodox treatment is the use of antihistamines, which temporarily blocks the effects of histamine. Other types of decongestant can be used concurrently. These treatments do not offer cure, only temporary relief, and it is worth trying alternative treatments, which can be very effective.

Complementary practitioners may look at hay fever as being an inappropriate response to pollens or other inhaled particles, due to an oversensitivity created within the body by food allergy or intolerance. Treatment for hay fever is therefore a complex, all-body concern, and not one that demands a topical therapy.

RECOMMENDATIONS

- *See* **Allergies**.
- *Nasal-washing techniques. The easiest to use is a yogic technique called Jala Lota, which employs a salt solution and a little watering can. You pass the solution from nostril to nostril by holding the head in a downward position; the solution washes off the pollens, and the salt solution helps the congestion. Pots are available through many health-food stores, but it is best to be trained by a yoga practitioner.*
- *Gencido ointment and injections are a Swiss-made pollen-based homeopathic preparation that can be applied to the nostrils or, in more-serious conditions, injected. This needs to be prescribed by a doctor with knowledge of the compound.*
- *Vitamins C, A, and zinc have all been shown to desensitize membranes and relieve hay fever. These supplements should be taken in the following amounts per foot of height in divided doses with food throughout the day: vitamin A (1,000iu), vitamin C (1g), and zinc (5mg just before bedtime).*
- *The homeopathic remedies Allium cepa, Pollen, and Arundo can be taken at potency 6, four times a day, as can the various hay fever homeopathic combinations.*
- *Herbal preparations are useful, but need to be prescribed by a specialist in that field.*
- *Avoid alcohol, caffeine, refined sugars, and cow's-milk products, all of which encourage mucus production and make congestion worse.*
- *The holistic consensus of opinion is that hay fever suffers generally have an overaggressive immune system, attacking things like pollen that should not cause a problem. This is often caused by persistently eating or drinking foods to which the individual is allergic. Food-allergy testing is recommended through blood tests or bioresonance techniques.*
- *Desensitization with specific homeopathic remedies for that type of pollen can be beneficial. It is possible to check the bloodstream for immunoglobulins for airborne pollens in order to isolate which ones are the culprits.*
- *Enzyme-potentiated desensitization (EPD) is a specific desensitization technique being studied by the John Radcliffe Hospital in Oxford, England. Only a few doctors around the world have the equipment to use this new-but-effective treatment in severe cases.*

HEATSTROKE—*see* Dehydration and Sunburn

HEMORRHAGE—*see* Bleeding

The term hemorrhage is generally reserved for a serious bleed, and not the inevitable scratches and cuts obtained in the garden and kitchen.

Hemorrhages that occur through trauma may be external or internal, the latter being more serious as symptoms may not appear immediately. A fractured femur (thighbone) can cause severe blood loss, and yet show no signs of swelling because of the powerful sheath around the leg muscles. A ruptured spleen or liver can bleed into the abdominal cavity, which will be painful if the patient is conscious, but may not show if the patient is not.

Bleeding from specific areas such as the nose, ears, or bladder should be reviewed in the specific sections in this book.

RECOMMENDATIONS

- *Any trauma or injury, especially of the head, must be reviewed by a doctor to rule out the possibility of internal bleeding.*

- *External bleeding should have firm compression over the area that is bleeding. Do not tie a ligature around a limb unless compression is not preventing the bleeding, or an amputation has occurred. Even then ensure that the ligature is loosened every 15min to allow profusion of the tissues above the serious injury. Send someone for or obtain medical assistance as soon as possible.*
- *Homeopathic remedies Arnica 6 and Phosphorus 6 should be alternated every 10min until medical advice is obtained.*

HICCUPS

A hiccups is caused by the spasmodic contraction of the diaphragm. This causes a jolt of the upper body, and is in itself quite harmless. A hiccup can only be considered a problem if it is persistent.

Hiccups occur because of an irritation or inflammation of the diaphragm. Psychological stress can cause a mild cramp, and ingestion of a compound that may irritate or inflame the esophagus or stomach, which in turn touches the diaphragm, can also cause the problem. Rarely, the irritation of the phrenic nerve in the neck can cause problems, because this controls the diaphragm.

RECOMMENDATIONS

- *Try a couple of old wives' tales: drinking a glass of water with the head between the knees, or dropping a cold object down the back of the collar while holding the breath. Each of these techniques causes the diaphragm to spasm, which can take away the irritation.*
- *The homeopathic remedies Ratanhia and Sulfuric acid are first-line remedies, but they are unusual; you may find Nux vomica in your medical chest, and this can be tried initially. Take potency 6 every 10min.*
- *Ginseng taken with meals at twice the dose recommended on any over-the-counter product may be beneficial.*
- *A persistence of hiccuping may indicate an underlying, sinister cause of an irritation to the diaphragm, such as a tumor or abdominal-cavity abscess, and needs to be investigated by a doctor initially.*

HIGH BLOOD PRESSURE (HYPERTENSION)

Any tube with a fluid in it will exert a pressure. Like the garden hose, the amount of water being pushed through it and the flexibility of the tube will affect the pressure in the same way as a thumb held over the end. The more of the opening that is obscured, the faster the water spurts out of the end. This is an indication of increased pressure. The arteries in the body act on exactly the same principles.

The heart pumps blood out into the aorta, exerting a pressure known as the systolic blood pressure. The aorta and other major arteries expand because more blood is pushed into them, and the contractile muscles around the artery constrict for the same reason as a stretched rubber band will contract. The pressure exerted by these constricting arteries is known as the diastolic pressure. When your blood pressure is taken, reference will be made to two figures. For example, 120/80 represents a pressure of 120mmHg due to the systolic push of the heart, and a pressure of 80mmHg due to the diastolic constriction of the arteries.

Blood Pressure Chart

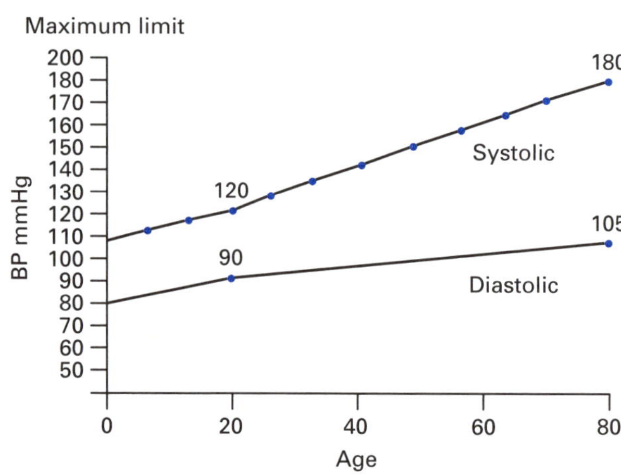

The typical systolic and diastolic blood pressures rise as the age of the individual increases.

A rule of thumb for normality is an individual's age plus 100 (give or take 20mmHg) for a systolic pressure, and a figure below 90mmHg for a diastolic pressure.

High blood pressure may be variable. "White-coat" blood pressure is well established, and describes the rise in blood pressure that occurs when an individual is subjected to a visit to the doctor. Persistently high blood pressure on repeated visits needs treating, but any fluctuation can be checked by a 24-hour ambulatory blood-pressure monitor, which may show that the blood pressure rises only in situations of stress. This is extremely relevant to ensure that unnecessary treatment is not undertaken.

High blood pressure occurs for several reasons:

- The development of atheroma in aging arteries, those who smoke, or those who have high-cholesterol levels, leads to inflexibility in the arteries, which decreases the arteries' ability to expand, and also narrows the lumen. Liken this to placing half of your thumb over the end of a hose pipe, and see how much further the water will squirt.
- Increased weight requires the heart to beat with more strength to get the blood around the increased amount of tissue. The fat also constricts major arteries and causes the muscles to have to work harder, which requires more oxygen, again encouraging the heart to beat harder to pump more blood through. Carrying too much weight also increases the amount of insulin produced, which in turn increases sodium, which is known to increase blood pressure.
- A lack of exercise or a sedentary lifestyle will cause a blood-pressure rise. Exercise reduces adrenaline, oxygenates the body, and works in several other biochemical ways to reduce blood pressure.
- Adrenaline, thyroid hormones, and the body's natural steroids all control blood pressure, and both dietary and stress factors that increase these will raise the blood pressure.
- Dietetic factors such as salt, alcohol, and caffeine all raise the blood pressure, and a reduction or cessation of the use of these can bring the blood pressure down to normal limits.
- Toxins or poisons such as cadmium and lead are known to raise the blood pressure, probably by a direct action on the center in the brain that monitors and tries to control blood pressure by increasing or decreasing the heart rate, and opening or closing blood vessels around the body. Food allergies have been researched and shown to cause hypertension.

Recognizing high blood pressure

High blood pressure may cause symptoms ranging from headaches, dizzy spells, nose bleeds, throbbing in the ears or tinnitus, or it may be asymptomatic (no symptoms at all). Many people who do not check their blood pressure regularly may exist with high blood pressure, and have no problems at all, and have no increased risk of heart failure, heart attacks, or strokes. A high blood pressure may indicate that the heart is working too hard, therefore heart failure or a heart attack may ensue; a raised pressure may fracture small or damaged arteries to cause bleeds, which if occurring in the brain will result in a stroke, but other factors need to be present also.

It is important to put high-blood-pressure risks into perspective. You will read that high blood pressure increases the risk of a cardiovascular accident by anywhere from two to six times. This sounds like a great risk. However, if the chances of a heart attack or a stroke at a young age are 1 in 1,000, and high blood pressure may increase that to 6 in 1,000, then the odds are still low. In my opinion—and this will be hotly argued by most doctors and pharmaceutical companies—high blood pressure, while potentially dangerous, should not be made into the evil that it currently is. Basic, naturopathic treatments can and usually do make a profound difference, and drug medicine should be used only as a last resort. Long-term studies have shown that individuals with hypertension who control the pressure but do not take orthodox, blood-pressure-lowering medicine do much better than those who take prescription drugs. I am sure this is because blood pressure, like most signs or symptoms in the body, is a warning about some aspect of lifestyle. Even those who have a genetic predisposition to high blood pressure may be found to have a specific trigger that needs to be eliminated. Simply dealing with the high numbers is not dealing with a cure. What a surprise to find that no orthodox drug for high blood pressure is intended to cause a cure, but merely lowers the figures, ignoring any underlying factor. The intricate control that the body shows in controlling blood pressure through centers in the brain, the delicate balance of sodium and other electrolytes in the kidney, the strength of the heart, and the nervous control of the vessels all suggest that the body may know what it is doing when adjusting blood pressure. It may be that an individual needs to have a raised blood pressure for specific functions, and it is only the persistently very high or sudden hypertensive (a condition known as malignant hypertension) that needs to be treated.

Secondary hypertension

"Secondary" hypertension is found in approximately 6 percent of all high blood pressure cases, and is due to some underlying disease process such as a tumor, which produces adrenaline or thyroxine, or kidney tumors, which affect specific chemicals from the kidney that act to control blood pressure. Certain metabolic conditions, pregnancy, and drugs such as the oral contraceptive pill may raise the blood pressure. Theoretically (but I think somewhat outside the definition of secondary hypertension), you might consider alcohol and tobacco to be a cause of secondary hypertension, because these compounds do cause the problem. The volume of blood within the arteries will also be relevant to the blood-pressure reading. The higher the salt content, the more water will be present through the process of osmosis.

Primary hypertension

Most high blood pressure has no orthodox disease causing it. It is called primary or essential hypertension, and is generally treated immediately by physicians with an orthodox drug. Such drugs are diuretics (which remove water from the bloodstream, and thereby—like turning down the tap on the hose pipe—lower the blood pressure, but they do nothing to explain why the blood pressure was raised in the first place); beta-blockers (which slow the heart rate or prevent arterial contraction); calcium-channel blockers (which stop arterial muscle contracting); or antiangiotensins (drugs that block controlling hormones that come from the kidney). Other drugs are slowly but surely being prepared, but they all aim at lowering the figures without dealing with underlying causes.

High blood pressure does run in families, but as I mentioned above, there is probably some form of environmental or lifestyle trigger. It is important to note that geographical studies show that high blood pressure is far more prevalent in Western societies than in others. A prime example is the Afro-American race, who have far higher blood pressure than Caucasians when living in the U.S.A., but in Africa, high blood pressure is negligible. Studies have shown conclusively that the Western diet, high in refined sugars, caffeine, and alcohol, is directly responsible.

Generally speaking, complementary or alternative methods of treating this condition can bring the diastolic pressure (the one that is most often raised and the figure that is most often monitored to see if treatment is helping) down by 10–15 points.

RECOMMENDATIONS

- *Lose any excess weight through a slow, steady dietetic plan.*
- *Remove salt completely from the diet.*
- *Stop smoking, and drinking alcohol or caffeine until the blood pressure is normal, and then reintroduce slowly, keeping a close eye on the pressure rise.*

- *Increase exercise. Yoga has been shown to help control hypertension, and is a must, regardless of any other aerobic-exercise regime.*
- *Investigate the possibility of cadmium or lead poisoning through specific blood or hair analysis.*
- *Check for food allergies using a bioresonance technique or accurate blood test.*
- *Stress reduction through biofeedback, hypnosis, and counseling will all help to lower blood pressure.*
- *Calcium and magnesium taken in divided doses throughout the day as follows may help: calcium (200mg per foot of height) and magnesium (150mg per foot of height). These should be taken in the form of citrates or aspartame.*
- *The integrity of the arterial vessels may determine the danger of hypertension, and the recommendations in the section on arteriosclerosis should be reviewed (see* **Arteriosclerosis***).*
- *If blood pressure is proving resistant, consider herbal treatment in the hands of a specialist. Crategus and Viscum album should be discussed.*
- *Antihypertensive drug treatment should be considered only when the above measures have failed, and only if blood pressure is shown through 24-hr monitoring to be persistently high, especially if the individual has a family history of stroke or cardiovascular disease, smokes, remains overweight, or is taking the oral-contraceptive pill.*

HOT FLUSHES

Hot flushes usually occur in women who are going through the menopause. The sensation occurs because the peripheral blood vessels expand and allow more warm blood from the center of the body to reach the peripheral-nerve endings, thus creating a sensation of heat. The dilation of the blood vessels occurs because of a dimunition of ovarian estrogen and the fluctuating amounts made to compensate this loss by the adrenal glands. Estrogen has exerted some control over the contraction of blood vessels since the start of the indivudual woman's periods.

Hot flushes that occur away from the menopause are most commonly associated with anxiety. Nervous conditions, diseases of the liver, and problems associated with an excess production of thyroxine or adrenaline may also be associated.

RECOMMENDATIONS

- *Hot flushes not associated with the menopause or anxiety should be investigated by your doctor.*
- *Avoid caffeine, alcohol, spicy foods, and smoking, all of which can cause hot flushes in themselves, and will certainly exacerbate the situation.*
- *Wear only natural fibers next to the skin.*
- *Increase the following foods in the diet: fennel, celery, rhubarb, and any soya product (this may be contraindicated if the individual has a thyroid deficiency—please consult your complementary medical practitioner).*
- *Try the following supplements at the recommended doses per foot of height in divided doses throughout the day with food: vitamin B_6 (20 mg), zinc (5mgs; if this makes you feel nauseous, take the recommended dose in one go before sleeping at night), and Evening Primrose Oil (500mg).*
- *The herb Agnus castus can be used by following the maximum dose recommended on a good brand. Phytoestrogens (plant-derived estrogens) that have a mild estrogenic effect can be used with safety, except in those who are known to have an estrogen-dependent cancer, and even then it is best to discuss this with a practitioner.*
- *The following homeopathic remedies may be suitable, and any one of these can be taken at potency 30 every 3hr for one week. If there is no*

improvement, please try the next remedy. If an effect is found, then reduce the dose of that remedy until the flushes return, step up in frequency, and maintain on that level for one month: Belladonna, Agnus castus, Amyl nitrate, Lachesis, Pulsatilla, and Sulfuric acid.

- *Persisting flushes may require the consideration of hormone-replacement therapy (HRT). Before orthodox drugs are used, try natural progesterone in combination with natural estrogen. This needs to be prescribed by a practitioner with experience in this area.*

HYPERLIPIDEMIA

Hyperlipidemia is the medical term for an excess of fats in the bloodstream. There are many types, but basically the two that are measured are cholesterol and triglycerides. These two compounds are essential for the integrity of cell membranes, and are involved in many biochemical processes.

An excess of triglycerides without a rise in cholesterol levels is generally associated with the eating of a fatty meal, and should not be considered a particular risk.

INFLUENZA (THE FLU)

Influenza is most commonly abbreviated to the word "Flu." There are a variety of symptoms, ranging from mild to severe, all created by specific viruses.

The symptoms range from head- and eye aches, sore throats, coughs (dry or productive), glandular swelling, and pains that can often create abdominal cramps in children, aching limbs, lethargy, malaise, and depression. Secondary infection from a bacterium is not uncommon, and is often the cause of serious complications, especially in the elderly, very young, or those who are immunocompromised.

The flu generally lasts 4–5 days, as opposed to a cold that can linger for 10 days or more. This often surprises people, who think that flu is longer lasting.

RECOMMENDATIONS

- *Please refer to the relevant section in this book with regard to the specific symptoms being suffered.*
- *Rest, preferably in bed.*
- *Any underlying illness may be worsened by an influenza virus, and your health practitioner should be contacted if you are asthmatic, diabetic, or carrying the human-immune-deficiency virus (HIV).*
- *The following supplements should be started for each foot of height in divided doses: beta-carotene (2mg), vitamin B complex (10mg) taken with breakfast only, and vitamin C (1g).*
- *Please refer to your preferred homeopathic manual for a suitable remedy, depending on your symptoms. Consider Bryonia, Gelsemium, and Arsenicum album initially.*
- *Acupuncture and Shiatsu can be useful if breathing is compromised or congestion is prominent.*

IRON DEFICIENCY

A deficiency in iron is often associated and thought of as anemia. Indeed, a deficiency in iron can be one of the many causes of anemia, but iron is required for many functions in the body, and problems such as dermatitis, neurological problems, general lethargy and tiredness, and muscular weakness can all be caused by iron deficiency. Problems in the uterus, such as fibroids or polyps may be associated with low iron levels.

As ever, the orthodox world suggests that there is a normal level within the blood, and tests can be beneficial. It is always worth remembering that blood levels do not necessarily correspond to the levels in the tissues, and that iron deficiency may be a problem despite normal levels. It is better to correlate blood analysis with the Humoral Pathological Laboratory Test (*see* chapter 8), or if this is not available, hair analysis.

Vegetarians and vegans are more likely to become iron-deficient because of the lack of red meat in their diet. Vegetable sources include green, leafy vegetables, with particular interest paid to spinach and collard greens. Parsley is a good source, but large amounts need to be eaten regularly, as do dried peaches, nuts, beans, asparagus, molasses, and oatmeal. Heavy periods are a most-common cause of iron deficiency and, paradoxically, anemia can actually encourage heavy and painful periods.

A French study has shown that 15 percent of children are iron-deficient. This is due to poor iron intake through breast milk, formula milks, and the types of foods given early in life. This may be the cause of tiredness and lethargy, with persistent coughs and colds in children under the age of five.

RECOMMENDATIONS

- *Iron deficiency should be recognized by specific cellular iron levels, and not simply by blood levels.*
- *Replenishment should be made using iron in chelated combination with gluconate, citrate, fumerate, or peptonate at a level of approximately 50mg per foot of height in divided doses with meals. Do not use ferrous sulfate. This should be carried on until symptoms alleviate, and then the dose should be halved for two weeks.*
- *Ensure an increase in the sources listed above.*
- *Vitamin C at approximately 250mg per foot of height in divided doses with meals should be taken to enhance iron absorption.*
- *Elemental iron should not cause constipation, but if this occurs, pay special attention to increasing the fiber in the diet, or temporarily adding bran or psyllium husks throughout the day.*
- *The plant extract of broom can be used under direction from a herbalist if iron levels are not rising, or if constipation is unavoidable.*
- *Persisting iron deficiency or iron deficiency without an obvious cause should be reviewed by a doctor, because it may indicate unrecognized bleeding, malabsorption syndromes, or even more-serious conditions such as cancer.*

JAUNDICE

Jaundice or, as it used to be known, icterus, is a yellowing of the skin, mucous membranes, and secretion due to hyperbilirubinemia—an excess of bilirubin in the blood. Bilirubin is a breakdown product of old blood cells that is formed in the liver, and should be excreted in the bile. If there is any obstruction to the bile flow, an absence of enzymes in the liver or the liver cells are diseased or inflamed, bilirubin cannot be processed correctly, and backs up and flows into the bloodstream instead of the bowel. Once traveling in the blood, the yellow pigmentation will settle all over the body, thus causing the yellow appearance.

Jaundice, therefore, is actually a symptom and not a disease. It can occur at any age and is commonly seen in the newborn within the first five days of life (*see* **Jaundice of the newborn**). The causes of jaundice are numerous, with hepatitis, gallstones, and tumors of the head or the pancreas (which surrounds the lower part of the bile duct) being potentially serious conditions.

A false jaundice may be noticed by those who have an excessive amount of beta-carotene. Carrot juice in excess is a very typical cause of a mild yellowing of the skin.

RECOMMENDATIONS

- *Any sign of jaundice must be reviewed by a doctor and a firm diagnosis made.*
- *Please refer to the relevant section in this book once the underlying cause is isolated.*

LEGIONNAIRE'S DISEASE

This is a pneumonia that is caused by a bacterium called Legionnaire's bacillus. It is so called because it was first recognized at a convention of the American Legion in 1976. It is a dangerous pneumonia because it affects the kidneys, the bowel, the liver, and the nervous system.

The Legionnaire's bacillus lives comfortably in air-conditioning units and is spread through airborne transmission.

RECOMMENDATIONS

- *See* **Pneumonia**.
- *Ensure that all filters in air-conditioning units are changed frequently.*

LEUCOPLAKIA

This is an abnormal thickening and whitening of the lining of an internal body cavity. The mouth and vagina are the most common. It is uncertain what creates this thickening of the epithelium of mucous membrane, although smoking and persistent friction (as from a pipe) may be responsible for leucoplakia in the mouth. An ill-fitting dental bridge may also be a cause. Viral infection is another probable cause. Leucoplakia may indicate a precancerous condition.

Leucoplakia on the tongue may be isolated to particular areas, and be representative of disease in part of the body, according to Eastern philosophies of tongue reading. The condition arising in the vagina is probably a viral creation, but effectively lies on the vessel-of-conception meridian, and an individual needs to look at their relationship to their parents and loved ones.

RECOMMENDATIONS

- *Any white patches need to be reviewed by a physician.*
- *Stop smoking and remove any item that may be causing friction.*
- *See a complementary medical practitioner for a review of lifestyle and general health because there may be a precancerous tendency or condition lurking.*

LEUKEMIA

Leukemia is a definition of any disease of the blood or bone marrow that is characterized by an uncontrolled multiplication of white blood cells. The term "uncontrolled proliferation" is the same as cancer. Leukemia is classified on the basis of the speed with which the white cells will multiply, specifically being known as acute, subacute, or chronic. Further differentiation is made by naming the type of white blood cell that is out of control, and lastly by the difference in the cells themselves. The more varied the white blood cells, the more dangerous the cancer.

White blood cells are initially made in the bone marrow with further production and modification in the lymphatic system. White-blood-cell proliferation in the lymphatic system is known as lymphatic leukemia, whereas that in the bone marrow is known as myeloid leukemia. The latter condition can overwhelm the bone marrow, and the production of normal cells becomes diminished, leading to symptoms of anemia. An acute situation can come on within a matter of weeks, and be triggered by viruses, radiation, and, possibly, agrochemicals/pesticides. The chronic forms may not be noticed for months, if not years, but if left untreated the outcome will be the same.

Symptoms depend on the type of leukemia. Those affecting the bone marrow will lead to lethargy, paleness, lack of appetite, shortness of breath, and a rapid heartbeat, whereas the lymphatic leukemia will lead to enlarged lymph glands, liver and spleen; in both acute and chronic leukemia, eventually there is a marked decrease in immune function. Leukemia can strike at any age, with the acute lymphatic leukemia most commonly affecting children.

RECOMMENDATIONS

- *See* **Cancer** *and* **Anemia**.
- *Leukemia—chronic more so than acute, and lymphatic more so than myeloid, appears to be susceptible to chemotherapy, radiotherapy, blood- and bone-marrow transfusions. Do not necessarily refuse these, but use complementary medicine alongside.*

LIBIDO (SEXUAL DRIVE)

Sexual drive is governed by the sex hormones: testosterone in males and estrogen/progesterone in females. Testosterone has an added aspect of aggression. Both men and women have levels of all three major sex hormones, and (as always in nature) it is about balance.

It is rare for a physician to come into contact with patients who complain of too high a sex drive. Nymphomania, which is defined as an excessive sexual desire on the part of a woman (it is interesting that there is no male counterpart!) is more often a psychological problem rather than a chemical one. Excessive sexual desire on the part of a male is hard to define because men do not have an estrus cycle, and are therefore, "on heat" all the time. Women are primarily, from an evolutionary point of view, geared towards procreation, and therefore reach sexual peaks under the influence of luteinizing hormone (LH) and follicle-stimulating hormone (FSH), which are produced around the time of ovulation, when the woman is at her most fertile. The definition of a sexually-aggressive male is generally used inaccurately. Sexual abuse and rape are very little to do with sex, and mostly to do with sociopathic-aggressive behavior.

Most complaints about libido are to do with a low sex drive, and the most common causes are linked with stress. Evolution made it very clear as to whether adrenaline (the fear chemical) or the sexual hormones should be more dominant. A couple copulating and faced with a saber-toothed tiger needed to feel fear above sexual excitement to stand a chance of surviving. Those of our ancestors who found sex more titillating than fear would attempt to finish the act and were in all probability killed. Natural selection did the rest. While we are rarely confronted by wild animals, we do have to put up with other stressful situations. Adrenaline is produced in response to these with the same suppressing effect on our sex drive.

Longer-standing and deeper-seated anxieties stemming from our childhood, relationship with parents and siblings, and our early sexual encounters are all relevant to the amount of adrenaline and other stress chemicals that we produce and can therefore have a detrimental effect on our sexuality.

I find it interesting that the Eastern philosophies consider sexuality to be a source of energy. On reflection, it is understandable that because life is created from intercourse, sex is really the fountain of vital force. Indeed, the more tired we are, the less sexually active we feel. The yogics believe in *kundalini*, which can be thought of as a coiled snake lying in the pelvis. Sexual arousal is the same as the uncoiling of the snake, and an orgasm can be thought of as the rapid strike of the cobra. The serpent launches itself up the spinal column and spreads its cheeks to embrace the brain. A strikingly accurate analysis, considering that 5,000 years ago the understanding of neuroanatomy and physiology was nonexistent. The Chinese and Tibetans, while using a different language, reflect sexuality in much the same way. A weakened libido is therefore a combined physical and psychological problem stemming from present and past conditions, and needs to be reviewed holistically by considering physical, mental, and spiritual well-being.

The use of stimulants is only of temporary benefit, and will inevitably lead to a longer-lasting and more difficult problem to deal with. Alcohol, cocaine, and marijuana all act by lowering inhibitions and heightening the senses. At the time, this is not a problem, and on occasion is fine and should be considered only as a treat. The difficulty arises when the mind and soul lose contact, and the memory of the pleasures of sex for sex's sake. A French fry with a sprinkling of salt may not be a healthy enjoyment, but a pleasure all the same. Once that chip has been dipped in catsup, many people find it hard to go back to having their minor sin, without the red sauce embellishing the product. Sex "under the influence" can very rapidly lead to a dependency upon a drug, without which the act is no longer enjoyable.

It is also important to remember that a decrease or lack of libido may simply be an aging process. As we age, we move away from the more material needs, and our spiritual and mental requirements become more important. Nature does not particularly want us to sire or mare offspring at an older age when we are less likely to be able to protect them. The universe prefers that as we age, we use our experience to teach the younger generation, and our usefulness becomes more cerebral and spiritual. It is not illness to be lacking or to enjoy a level of sexuality at any age, but one must be careful not to try to conform to what society expects, but instead to look inside and ensure that we perform at a level that is satisfactory to ourselves.

RECOMMENDATIONS

- *Remove any stressful stimuli such as alcohol, caffeine, and other drugs of abuse. Smoking is a notorious neurological depressant, and often overlooked in weakened sexuality.*
- *Remove stress chemicals such as adrenaline by increasing physical exercise and reducing levels of anxiety.*
- *Meditation minimally, through counseling and then to active spiritual practices such as Tantric yoga (a branch of yoga using specific sexual positions and practices), should be considered, learned, or studied.*
- *Homeopathic and herbal treatments, especially Chinese, Ayurvedic, and Tibetan, can be utilized to increase both masculine and feminine energies.*
- *Time spent toning the body will release the body's natural opiates (which are natural aphrodisiacs), reduce adrenaline, and simply make us look better and therefore feel more attractive, and is a simple process of raising the libido.*
- *Ensure that you are getting enough sleep. Introduce variety into the sexual act. Monotony is a notorious damper of libido.*

LOW BLOOD PRESSURE (HYPOTENSION)

Some authorities would consider low blood pressure to be a problem that requires treating. Doctors in Germany are quite active in raising blood pressure although there is little, if any, evidence to suggest that this is necessary. A low blood pressure should only be treated if symptoms of fainting, dizziness, depression or persisting lethargy are associated with a blood pressure that has a systolic level below 80 or a diastolic level below 50. (Systolic pressure is that of the heart beating, and diastolic is the pressure exerted by the arteries, *see* **High blood pressure.**) So nonplussed appear the authorities that I was unable to find any reference to treatment for non-emergency hypotension in the English language.

Low blood pressure will occur when the heart fails to pump correctly, there is marked blood loss or the blood vessels dilate, usually in response to some toxin, most probably a hypertension drug such as a beta-blocker. Hypotension that occurs suddenly should therefore be considered a medical emergency and be treated accordingly.

RECOMMENDATIONS

- *A sudden drop in blood pressure must be assessed by a doctor and treated accordingly. Ensure that any blood-pressure-lowering drugs are not being taken in excess. Different people have different sensitivities.*
- *Low blood pressure without symptoms should be left alone.*
- *If symptoms are present, try increasing water and protein intake to enhance the volume of blood.*

LUMPS AND BUMPS

Lumps and bumps come and go, and those that persist need a diagnosis, because rarely they may turn out to be something nasty.

Most lumps are completely innocent, being formed by trauma, which can cause cysts or scar tissue, or hormonally related, such as breast lumps, which could be encouraged by estrogen or progesterone production.

Putting it simply, there are three different body types, just as there are 12 astrological signs. The description is more fully embellished in the introduction, but basically the body should be a balance of elimination, reaction, and retention. Lumps and bumps are a tendency to be too retentive, suggesting some form of lifestyle inbalance. Frequent formation of lumps and bumps tends to suggest that a consultation with a complementary practitioner to review lifestyle, diet, and exercise would be beneficial.

RECOMMENDATIONS

- *Any lump that arises anywhere without cause, or a lump that persists despite a known causative event, should be seen by a doctor.*
- *Consider ultrasound and magnetic resonance imaging (MRI) before radiological investigation (x-rays), but do not shy away from investigations.*
- *Surgical lumpectomies should be a last resort, but again, not ignored as an option of diagnosis, especially if the lump is associated with the breasts or genitalia.*
- *Please refer to the relevant section in this book once the underlying diagnosis of lump has been made.*

LYME DISEASE

This is an acute, transient form of arthritis that is accompanied by a fever and skin lesions, transmitted by the bite of a deer tick. It is so named because it was first observed near a town called Lyme in Connecticut in 1974. The condition is now spreading and, although rare, is found throughout Europe and the British Isles.

The symptoms, while debilitating, are not particularly dangerous, but the parasite is now known to attack major organs, especially the nervous system. The condition should be suspected if an individual has been in an area where deer are found. Any sort of insect bite that has a clear center and red circles of inflammation surrounding it must raise suspicions. The tick may not be felt, and a close inspection of the body after a walk through deer country is important because if the tick is removed within 36 hours, the chance of contracting Lyme disease is reduced. Symptoms such as fever, stiff neck, and painful joints usually appear within four weeks.

RECOMMENDATIONS

- *If you think that you have been bitten by a tick, please see a doctor with knowledge of Lyme Disease. Prophylactic antibiotic treatment may be offered, and is probably a wise precaution, especially if the tick has been on the body for more than 24hr. A blood test for Lyme disease can be performed, but not for around three weeks after the bite, by which time early, interventional antibiotic treatment is still possible but may not be as effective.*
- *The use of antibiotics is necessary because alternative treatments may not be effective, and any delay in destroying this bacterium can have long-term effects.*
- *See* **Antibiotics**.
- *See* **Arthritis** *if the disease process has taken a hold.*
- *The homeopathic remedy Ledum 30 should be taken twice a day for one month while undergoing any orthodox treatments. If possible, potency 6 should be taken every 15min if a tick bite has been noticed, for five doses.*

MALARIA

Malaria is one of the world's most frequently fatal diseases. It is endemic (meaning part of the natural system) in Africa, the southern half of Asia, and South America. The entire population of sub-Saharan Africa will contract malaria and suffer to some degree. Those with strong constitutions and good immune systems may suffer from infrequent mild fevers and chills with general malaise, while those who are weaker may have severe symptoms, and at worse, suffer severe anemia, immune collapse, and renal failure.

The malarial parasite, of which there are many types, has a group name of *Plasmodium. Plasmodium falciparum* is the most aggressive, and has probably developed to become so dangerous because of resistance to antimalarial drugs that have been used over the last 20 years. *Plasmodium falciparum* can infect the nervous system, giving rise to severe neurological symptoms, including paralysis and coma.

Antimalarial agents have recently been given a bad name, because one particular compound, mefloquine, was reported as causing neurological symptoms. While this is true, most people who used this aggressive drug had no problems, and were protected against *P. falciparum*. There is always resistance to having to take a drug, but if you weigh the risks of malaria against the risk of a serious side effect, the ratio is negligible. Alternative antimalarial medicines derived from herbs have been used both in treatment and prevention for thousands of years, derived from plants from all parts of the world where malaria is found. In principle, these are fine to take, but they probably act in the same way as the manufactured drugs. The advantage of a pharmaceutical preparation is that doctors know exactly how much of what they are giving. Herbal preparations vary greatly in their constituents, and we may be under- or overdosing.

The drug treatments are very effective prophylactically, and less so as a treatment, but nevertheless, have made a profound difference on the prognosis. Ideally the scientific community needs to concentrate its efforts on controlling the *Anopheles* mosquito that transmits, the malarial parasite. Much work is being done in this field but, as always, nature is very tenacious, and mosquitoes resistant to insecticides are developing at the same speed as the malaria parasites are becoming immune to antimalarial drugs.

Preventing being bitten is probably the best treatment. The use of drug repellents runs the risk of absorbing these chemicals, which may have a detrimental effect on general health, but at this time, again, the risk of malaria is greater than the hypothetical dangers of insecticide poisoning. Natural repellents are undoubtedly safer but, in my experience, tend not to work so well. Individuals have a greater or lesser predisposition for attracting mosquitoes and, other than levels of vitamin B_6 in the bloodstream, there is no evidence to suggest why this is.

RECOMMENDATIONS

- *Unless a specific intolerance or symptoms develop to antimalarial drugs, these should be used as directed by the World Health Organization (WHO), who advise all pharmacists of the best drugs for the area to be visited.*
- *Mefloquine should be avoided wherever possible because of its neurological side effects.*
- *If you are pregnant or unwell, avoid traveling to malaria-endemic areas. If this is inevitable, discuss the matter with your doctor.*
- *Antimalarial drugs should be started at least one week before traveling, and continued for at least three weeks after leaving the malaria-endemic area, because the parasite may lay its eggs in the red blood cells, which may not hatch for at least two to three weeks. The drugs are ineffective unless the parasite is swimming freely in the bloodstream outside of the red blood cells.*
- *The best treatment is prevention. Use mosquito repellent sparingly, but effectively.*
- *The use of vitamin B_6 at a level of 10mg per foot of height taken with breakfast and before dusk can have a profound, antimosquito effect.*
- *If prevention fails and the fevers, shakes, sweating, fatigue, and headache of malaria are suspected, then a blood test for diagnosis is usually available, and needs to be taken at the*

peak of the fever, if possible. Orthodox drug treatment with quinine derivatives is usually initiated immediately, and should be taken alongside alternative treatments.

- *Only if you react badly to the drugs should you consider the use of Peruvian bark (Cinchona succirubra): either one teaspoonful of the bark per cup of boiling water that has simmered for 30min, drunk three times a day; or 1–2ml of the tincture three times a day.*
- *Burberry (Berberis vulgaris): put one teaspoonful of bark in a cup of cold water, bring to the boil, leave for 15min, and drink three times a day; or take 2–4ml of the tincture three times a day.*
- *The above concoctions may be used as a treatment if orthodox drugs are failing, or at the same time.*
- *Some unsubstantiated homeopathic sources suggest that the homeopathic remedy Natrum muriaticum can be taken, potency 6, three times a day, and has a protective effect against malaria. An individual is taking a risk if relying on this alone.*
- *If malaria is contracted, review the homeopathic preparations of Cinchona, known as China, or two of its derivatives, Cinchona arsenicum or Cinchona sulfur. These should be taken as potency 6 every 2hr through the fever, and every 4hr between bouts.*

MEDITATION

Throughout this book, I will advise people to learn a technique of meditation for physical, psychological, and spiritual benefits. With respect and with the assumed consent from the few teachers I have come across, I will paraphrase their teachings.

What is meditation?

Meditation is many things to many people. To some it is a concept as alien as a holiday on Mars, and conjures up visions of portly Indians levitating cross-legged in orange robes and sandals. Fair enough. Meditation may be like that, but in the broader sense, meditation is whatever it takes to allow an individual to recognize his part in the big scheme of things.

The Eastern philosophies believe that every molecule within our body is connected with all others, both within the self and the surrounding environment and universe by an (as yet) unmeasurable energy. Attempting to achieve a connection with this energy source is what meditation is about.

Most of us achieve some contact, either through prayer or formal meditative techniques, and all of us achieve a glimpse of meditation when we drift into sleep. At that time, most of us, provided that we have not taken any extreme anxieties to bed, and even then, find that those moments before sleep are blissful.

A more orthodox view suggests that meditation is a technique that stimulates relaxing chemicals within the brain, which takes us to a happier place. In reality, both the orthodox and alternative views are accurate, and actually the same.

Maharishi Mahesh Yogi has probably done the most to bring meditation to the Western consciousness. His association with the superstars of the 1960s attracted much media space and time and made a distinct change in Western consciousness. However, the Maharishi simply spread to the West those techniques that had been formalized thousands of years ago, but have probably been practiced since our higher mental state developed. "Since" might actually be unfair to primates, who, for all we know, meditate at a very high level.

Why meditate?

There is no reason why anybody has to meditate. But then again, there is no reason why anybody should exercise or eat correctly. It is simply how an individual's consciousness may choose to exist—healthily or unhealthily, that is the option. Meditation can be looked upon as the aerobics of the mind, and whether one takes the orthodox approach to the production of calming chemicals, or the Eastern philosophy of connecting with the "whole," the benefit is better than not meditating at all.

Meditation positions

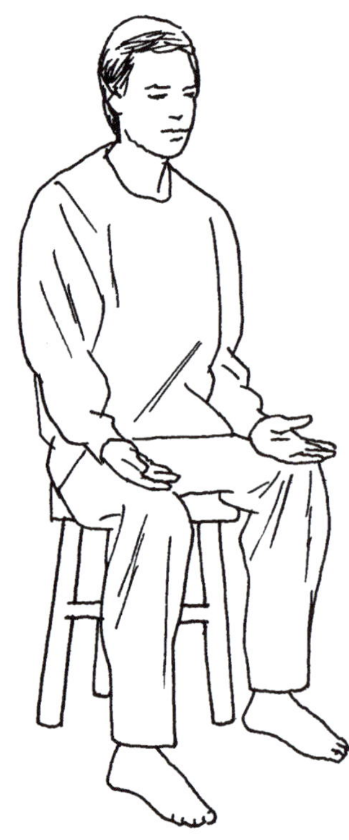

There is no "right" meditation position. While the two shown above are popular, experiment and see what works for you.

How to meditate

Meditation may be a silent, passive event, or found in prayer, chant, or nonaerobic exercise. The body's energy (Qi) or neurochemistry can be influenced by all and any technique. The important thing is to find the avenue that you feel most comfortable with.

Personally, I have had the privilege of befriending or being in the presence of some of the world's greatest meditators. I have never felt comfortable in a passive, stationary, meditative technique. I have found it easy enough to learn, but difficult to continue at my current level of spiritual development. I think I need and hope to get to a point where passive meditation is accessible to me, but for now the use of Qi Gong seems perfect. The breathing techniques, stretches, and positions in association with the conscious practice of finding the time can lead me into a state of relaxation within 10–15 minutes.

Twenty minutes twice a day is an acceptable minimum in order to benefit from meditation, but 5 minutes a day is better than none. I suggest that a human being is geared towards 8 hours of sleep, 8 hours of work, 6 hours of play, and 2 hours of meditation within a 24-hour cycle to balance the body's energies. It is difficult to imagine contriving a lifestyle that allows this, but I believe that we should all have this goal.

I considered describing a basic meditative technique that I have found benefits most people, but somehow I felt that it would defeat the object of this short section by creating a finite technique. An individual may find that it is perfect, but most may demand an alternative and be put off by attempting the wrong concept—a bit like trying to learn tennis, not enjoying it, and therefore considering all racket sports anathema.

RECOMMENDATIONS

- *Ask around and see if any of your friends or acquaintances practice an art of meditation. Very often, those within your social circle may share your preferences.*

- *Do not give up if one particular type of meditation does not suit. Try others. See if yoga, Qi Gong, Tai Chi, or a martial art attract your attention rather than a more passive form.*
- *If you find one that you enjoy but get bored, persevere and keep returning to the practice, even if it is only for a few minutes, days, or weeks apart. The body, mind, and soul will appreciate even a few moments of meditation. Can you think of anything that you have achieved that you have not had to work at? Meditation is the same.*

OPERATIONS AND SURGERY

Surgery carries risks, but at the end of the day, is the most curative aspect of modern medicine. This is a debatable point, because removing a lump may indeed rid the individual of the symptom, but will not necessarily answer the cause. However, a cancer that is taken out may not spread, and therefore it is arguably true to say that the problem is cured.

Any holistic approach to health must include surgery as part of its whole. Ayurvedic, Tibetan, and Chinese medicine all have surgical techniques—some of them extremely sophisticated considering the lack of technical knowledge—entrenched in their roots. Modern medicine, by using incredibly sophisticated scientific techniques, has made surgery much safer than it was even ten years ago. Techniques include the use of laser instead of scalpels, "keyhole" endoscopic surgery instead of open surgery, and robotic techniques. Surgeons can work using x-rays and magnetic-resonance imaging (MRI) without actually visualizing the organ on which they are operating. All in all, the techniques are fascinating, and not to be discouraged when required.

Plastic surgery

A special mention, I feel, should be made of elective (optional) operations, and most of these fall into the category of cosmetic surgery, or—as it used to be known—plastic surgery.

While surgical techniques have much improved, there is still a 1 in 500 chance of having a severe adverse reaction to an anesthetic. A bad reaction may even include death. Surgery itself may entrap nerves or create scar tissue that irritates and hurts well past the healing of the wound, and I feel that all of this must be taken into account. I also feel that much cosmetic surgery is done for the wrong reasons; principally, as we age, we should not try to compete with those younger than us, but accept that wrinkles and wisdom—being saggy, sage and eroding while gaining experience—are inextricably linked.

RECOMMENDATIONS

- *Always ask the questions, "Does this procedure need to be done?" "Does this procedure have a medicinal alternative?"*
- *A physician should decide if a surgical procedure should take place. Surgeons cut, that is what as a profession they do, therefore that is what they will recommend.*

Pre- and postoperative care

Sometimes, when the body fails to heal itself, it is necessary to resort to mechanical repair, in other words, surgery.

Preoperative preparation

Leading up to an operation is invariably an anxious time, whether it is sprung upon you through an emergency or planned, elective surgery. As soon as anxiety starts, we produce adrenaline, which speeds up the body's metabolism, and certain compounds may run into deficiencies. Combine this with the inevitable "nil by mouth" instructions at least 6 hours before an operation, and it generally means that an individual is going into a damaging process with poor nutrition. Preparation to avoid this should start two weeks before an operation by building up stores of vitamins, minerals, trace elements, and water.

Suggestions for medication prior to an operation are given in the recommendations below.

The operation

When having an operation it is necessary to view the patient from four angles:

- psychological
- repair of operated area
- liver toxicity
- nervous system shock

Psychological aspects

Going in for an operation can be a very harrowing experience, and a full explanation by a physician, a surgeon, and if necessary, a counselor should be provided. This explanation of the procedure and its side effects must be clear to the patient. People who are particularly anxious should be introduced to techniques of relaxation and meditation, thereby often negating the need for a premed (a drug given to keep you calm on your way to the surgical ward) and thus reducing the drug effect on your body.

Many operations can leave individuals disfigured, and psychological support for operations leaving visible signs such as amputations or mastectomies is often very necessary.

Repair of the operated area

When operating, the skin or membrane is cut, the underlying tissues are damaged, and the surrounding blood vessels and deep tissue all need repairing. The repair process requires scar tissue formation, as well as many other biochemical reparative processes, all of which use proteins, vitamins, trace elements, and other nutrients. Before an operative procedure, therefore, a check-up with your health professional is recommended, and supplemental advice should be offered to ensure that the body has a pool of required nutrients, etc. to enable the body to heal without hindrance. Supplementation can be given orally or preferably intravenously, and this should be discussed with your health professional.

Liver toxicity

An anesthetic is a powerful drug. As with any medication, the liver is instrumental in its breakdown and removal from the body. The effects on the liver are mild in nearly all cases, but the liver is nevertheless poisoned and requires support. Supplements, herbal medicines, and homeopathic remedies should be utilized to strengthen the liver.

Nervous-system shock

An anesthetic works by preventing the vibration of electrons within nerve tissue. While this very rarely damages the nerves permanently, it gives the central nervous system quite a shock. As far as the brain is concerned, unconsciousness has occurred for no reason. The chemicals within the nervous system that activate us are instructed to awaken us, and there is quite considerable activity on that level as the anesthetic effect wears off. As with the liver, the nervous system needs to have its building blocks in abundance to allow it to repair itself rapidly, and supplementation and homeopathic remedies are useful in this area.

RECOMMENDATIONS

- *Inform your complementary medical practitioner of any operation—major or minor—involving a general or a local anesthetic, preferably two weeks before the procedure. The following recommendations should be administered by a professional, preferably. Operations should not be undertaken unless as good a standard of health as is feasible—considering that a surgical operation is required—is achieved. Do not go under anesthetic with a upper-respiratory or chest infection.*
- *Be absolutely certain that you are comfortable about having the operation, and understand the need and probable outcome. Do not hesitate to consult your doctor, surgeon, or a counselor if you have any doubts or insecurities.*
- *Ensure that the risks and side effects are clear.*

- *Ensure that you are taught a technique for relaxation, and thereby reduce the need for a "pre-med."*
- *Avoid any junk food at least one week before an operation. Ensure that five portions of fresh fruits or vegetables are taken every day for that period, and at least ten days after. These will not be provided by hospitals, and should be organized from outside.*
- *Good hydration is essential, because no water will be allowed for several hours prior to, during, and while recovering from an operation. The day or so before an operation, drink at least 12 ounces per foot of height throughout the day, and start drinking water as soon as it is permissible after the operation. This is important to dilute down the anesthetic toxins and encourage the biochemistry of healing.*
- *Three days before the operation, take the following supplements as directed below and continue until healing is complete: vitamin C, 1g per foot of height in divided doses with meals; zinc, 5mg per foot of height taken before bed; and argenine (an amino acid), 5g with each meal. Argenine may not be tolerated, and may cause digestive upset, in which case halve the dose and see if this can be tolerated, If not, take the minimum amount to avoid problems. Please note that argenine may trigger viral herpes attacks, and carriers should not attempt to use this supplement.*
- *Nux vomica, potency 30, should be taken four times a day starting the day before an operative procedure, and carried on at hourly intervals on the day of operation. After the anesthetic use Arnica, potency 200 three times a day for three days, and then potency 30 four times a day until repair is complete.*
- *A herbal liver cleanser, available in most healthfood stores, should be taken at twice the daily recommended dose. If this is not available then milk thistle at twice the recommended dosage can be used. Either should continue for one week postoperatively.*
- *See* **Wounds** *and* **Cuts** *for supplemental advice and start supplements at least one week before the operation.*

PARASITES, COMMENSALS, AND SYMBIONTS

Organisms that live off the cells or fluids to the detriment of another organism are known as parasites. Those that feed off or within a host but do not do harm are known as commensals. Some commensals actually benefit their host, and these are known as symbionts.

A common example of a symbiont is the bowel bacteria; a commensal is *Candida*; and a parasite is malaria. The human being benefits so much from bowel flora that without them we would actually die. We provide food and shelter, they provide essential nutrients and digestive processes. *Candida* is a yeast that generally lives in small colonies in many of us, doing little good, but relatively little harm. An excessive growth of *Candida* will lead to a problem, and this is often the case in those who are immunocompromised through conditions such as AIDS, or in people who are forced to use steroids. Parasites actually do harm. Theoretically they may kill. Generally, parasites are single-celled organisms that have a lifecycle, such as malaria and ameba, but they may also be complex organisms such as a tapeworm, which may grow up to several feet in the intestine of those infected.

Parasitic infections may be asymptomatic or create reactions in the area that is affected. Bowel infections frequently create diarrhea, liver infestation may cause jaundice, but most will cause malaise and fatigue. A tapeworm may eat vital nutrients and leave an individual deficient.

As an interesting philosophical discussion point, try to place a fetus during pregnancy into one of these categories!

Blood Parasites

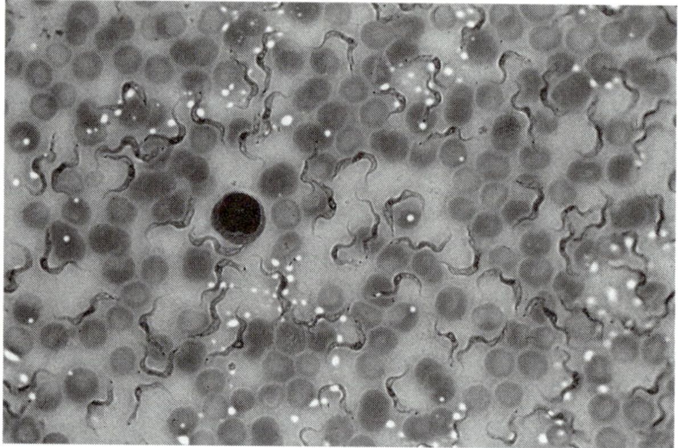

This blood sample contains the blood parasite that causes the serious tropical disease sleeping sickness which is spread by the bite of the tsetse fly.

RECOMMENDATIONS

- *Diagnosis of a parasite, commensal or symbiont is by discovery following investigations for any number of symptoms.*
- *High-magnification blood analysis, known as the Humoral Pathological Laboratory Test, may show up parasitic infestations within the system, either by isolating an organism in the bloodstream or by showing changes that are reflected by the blood cells caused by the chemicals produced by the parasite. This is not a fully accepted orthodox test, but it is available and, in my opinion, accurate.*
- *Parasitic infection is best dealt with by a suitable orthodox drug with concurrent, protective, alternative treatments prescribed by a complementary practitioner.*
- *For those who are reluctant to use orthodox medicine, herbalists with experience in this field may be able to offer a treatment. There are hundreds of years of reported success of treatment through botanical means.*
- *Orthodox treatment for parasites in the gut is generally effective, and rarely produces side effects. Treatment against parasites in the bloodstream or organs, such as malaria or ameba, often requires courses of antibiotics (see* **Antibiotics***).*

POISONING

Poison is a substance that impairs health or kills if introduced into the body. Some substances are instantly toxic, whereas others may require large or protracted ingestion before they cause a problem. I classify poisoning as either accidental, intentional, doctor-induced (iatrogenic), or environmental.

This emotive term reminds us of the serial killers such as Crippin in the early 20th century in England, but unfortunately poisoning is taking place most of the time either unintentionally or by governments and industry turning a blind eye. There is very little that an individual can do to avoid environmental poisoning, but supporting the charities and bodies that lobby on our behalf against such pollution is, I think, everybody's duty.

We hear about the ozone layer and the pollution of our atmosphere, the disposal of toxic products into our rivers and streams, thereby polluting our rivers and seas, but we do little to recognize the toxification of our livestock, and the application of pesticides and agrochemicals is not criticized or closely monitored.

Many homes have lead in their pipes, aluminum in their cooking pans, and we are subjected to fluoride in our water, and chlorine and its derivatives in most of our detergents. We have a suggestion that fumes from our babies' mattresses may be involved in crib deaths; there is radiation from our televisions, microwaves, and computers; and very little is said to the masses who smoke in their houses leaving cancer-causing residues in the carpets, curtains, clothes, and bedding that our children are fully exposed to.

It is a wonder that we survive, and no wonder that most chronic disease processes are increasing. We survive them better because of the miracles of emergency medicine, but we need to do something to protect ourselves individually and *en masse*. Different sections in this book deal with individual toxic problems and how best to remove them from the system.

Environmental poisons

Metal poisoning

There are many types of metal found in our environment, all of which can cause a poisonous effect. Those I have listed below are the most common.

Iron

The clinical features of iron poisoning are vomiting and bloody diarrhea within a couple of hours of ingestion; 6–8 hours later, dizziness, confusion, fainting, and even coma may ensue. The pulse will be rapid and weak, and if blood pressure is measurable, it will be very low. This is due to iron having a direct effect on the cardiovascular system, causing peripheral dilation. The individual may appear flushed at some point. If left untreated or if the levels are not high enough to cause the above collapse, then liver necrosis, renal failure, and gut spasms can all occur.

RECOMMENDATIONS

- *Acute ingestion is a medical emergency, and hospital treatment is required. This will include gastric aspiration and lavage (washing), and the use of a compound called desferrioxamine, which will bind with the iron in the gut, thus preventing absorption. This compound may be used intravenously if blood levels are found to be high.*
- *The homeopathic remedy Ferrum metallicum should be given, potency 30, every 20min if poisoning has taken place at a single incident, or twice daily if the poisoning has been over a period of time.*

Lead

This is difficult to diagnose because the ingestion of lead is usually via cooking in lead pots or by those working in smelting and refining factories. Absorption used to be common through lead-based paints, either by painters and decorators or children who would chew on lead-painted toys. Rarely, lead can be ingested by drinking home-brewed wine or beers that were made and stored in earthenware pots, and an unsuspecting vagrant may drink lead in an antiknock compound.

Lead poisoning can cause fits, anemia, colic, and constipation. Lead has recently been shown to be responsible for bad behavior in children. Specific toxicity of the nervous system can cause weakness, specifically a weak wrist. This causes a characteristic sign called "wrist drop." Another specific sign for lead poisoning is a blue line forming on the gums.

RECOMMENDATIONS

- *Investigate lead levels in the blood for a firm diagnosis.*
- *An intravenous administration of a compound called EDTA binds with most heavy metals.*
- *The homeopathic remedy Plumbum metallicum can be given, potency 30, every hour in an acute poisoning, or twice a day over three weeks if the toxicity has been over a longer period.*

Mercury

Most commonly ingested by a child who chews on a mercury-filled thermometer, this metal used to be the cause of "Hatter's shakes" because hatmakers would paint mercury nitrate onto felt—thus the term "Mad as a hatter." The features include anxiety/depression, an imbalanced walk, tremors that affect the face and limbs, blushing, and excessive salivation.

Mercury poisoning may come about because of the use of mercury for filling teeth caries.

RECOMMENDATIONS

- *Chelating agents, especially one called dimercaprol, are administered in hospital.*
- *The remedy Mercurius 30 should be given every 15min in an acute poisoning and twice a day over three weeks if the poisoning has been over a prolonged period.*
- *See* **Fillings**.

Agricultural chemical poisoning (pesticides)

There are approximately 5,000 different, frequently used pesticides and other agrochemicals that affect all the foods provided to us that are not strictly organically grown. The intention of these is to stop the growth of fungi, yeasts, bacteria, and viruses. They do an effective and excellent job, and will continue to do so in our system unless we are able to wash them off. Unfortunately we need our fungal, yeast, bacterial, and viral populations to maintain our health. This is not so easy, because many of the chemicals are actually designed to penetrate into the food substance. This is especially the case when agrochemicals are used in animal produce such as beef, lamb, pork, chicken, and fish.

We are also exposing ourselves to chemicals through the use of insect repellents, weedkillers, lawn fertilizers, pet sprays, and household-cleaning agents.

The orthodox medical world claims that the levels that we ingest are negligible and cannot cause problems, but these are also the same scientists who tell us that they have no idea why we have increasing asthma, eczema, irritable bowel syndrome, cancer … shall I go on? There is no doubt that these compounds do cause serious conditions such as cancer, because numerous studies have shown that individuals who are exposed to these compounds—especially from youth—are more prone to have serious problems. It is possible that pesticides can actually cause genetic damage, and therefore are particularly able to create illness in pregnancies and children. The effect of phosphate-based chemicals on the brain of children is known to create aggression, emotional problems, and even schizophrenia. We also know that these chemicals can attack the nervous system, causing multiple sclerosis, muscular dystrophy, and Guillain-Barré-like syndromes. There are hypotheses that chronic fatigue syndrome and allergic responses may also be worsened—if not caused—by these compounds.

This may not be a problem for the human race in the long run, because there is a strong correlation between declining sperm counts and agrochemical poisoning. There has been a marked and noticeable decline in sperm counts in the Western world over the last 20 years, which coincides with a far-greater increase in the use of these chemicals. If we continue we shall become an infertile race and, pesticides or no pesticides, health books or no health books, the problem will become academic!

RECOMMENDATIONS

- *All sufferers of chronic diseases and persistent or serious illnesses, and everyone who has been brought up with or exposed to agrochemicals, should be tested for levels in their bloodstream. To find a laboratory in the U.S., check with the U.S. Department of Agriculture.*
- *The use of homeopathic remedies derived from any specific poisons should be administered at potency 30 twice a day for at least three weeks.*
- *Wherever possible eat only organically grown foods.*
- *These compounds tend to be stored in fats, so maintaining a lean weight is markedly beneficial, especially for those who work in the farming industry.*
- *Discuss the matter with a complementary medical practitioner, who may be able to set up a specific detoxification regime to be used on a regular basis, and should also be able to provide a liver tonic.*

Iatrogenic (doctor-induced) poisoning

One hopes that it is never the intention of a doctor to poison a patient, but unfortunately this does occur all too often. Rarely is this due to a doctor's mistake; more commonly it occurs because an individual does not tolerate a particular drug or the prescription label is misprinted or misread. Many drugs are taken as over-the-counter preparations, and therefore are not actually doctor-prescribed but doctor-encouraged. I believe I read in a nonmedical journal that over 2,000 deaths in 1994 were attributable to over-the-counter prescriptions being taken incorrectly.

The effect of poisoning may vary from a mild

nausea to diarrhea, vomiting, and sweating. Persisting lethargy, tiredness, malaise, or any physical symptom that does not clear up may be a gradual onset of poisoning. In any case, whether the symptoms are mild or marked, or the medicine was taken intentionally or unintentionally (say, by a child), any symptoms that may be associated with drug ingestion should be dealt with immediately.

Complementary medical practitioners are not blameless. Incorrect or overdosed prescribing of herbal medicines (or, very rarely, supplements) may also be toxic to the system.

RECOMMENDATIONS

- *If an acute or serious poisoning has occurred, contact your local doctor or hospital for the telephone number of the Poison Control Center in your area. Ideally, you should have this in your telephone book.*
- *Discuss any possibility of poisoning with the prescriber of the medication or, if you have doubts, get a second opinion.*
- *Unless the medication is life-preserving—as in an antibiotic in a life-threatening disease, or a cardiac or epileptic drug—stop taking it, preferably after consultation with your doctor. Remember that steroids suddenly stopped may lead to a life-threatening crisis, and these too should not be stopped without medical supervision.*
- *Use a homeopathic remedy Nux vomica 6 every hour until the acute symptoms of poisoning have subsided.*

RADIATION

When most of us consider radiation we think of medical investigations like x-rays, and those "our government would never let us take a risk" stories about leakages from nuclear-power stations. These situations are very true to life, and I personally have no faith in either the medical technological industry or the governments advising us of safe levels. We are also constantly exposed to radiation by:

- The sun—and the diminished protective ozone layer.

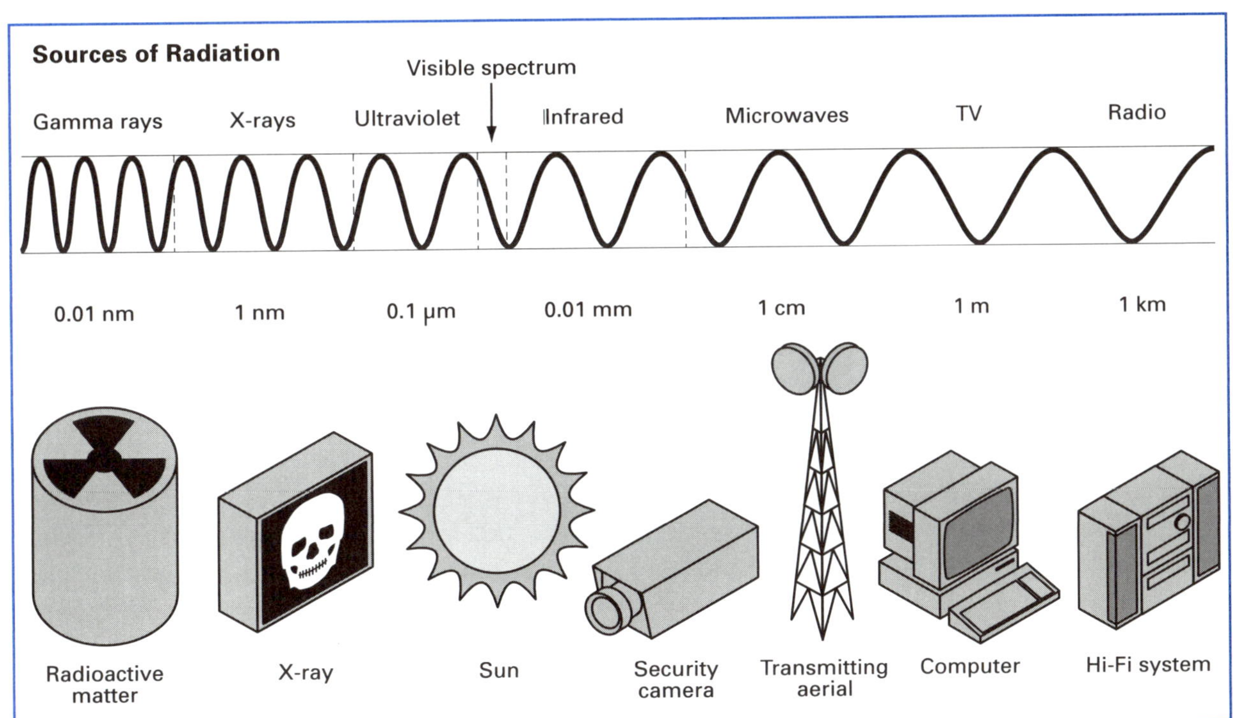

- Air travel—being closer to the sun increases our exposure to x-rays.
- Microwaves and car phones—leak emissions, and these appliances emit low-level microwaves that have been shown to affect our DNA (genetic material). Asthma, neurological symptoms, and skin problems have all been reported, and much more-serious diseases may be being triggered by the DNA effect.
- Computers and visual-display units (VDUs)—these create minor symptoms such as tiredness, headaches, and skin and eye problems, but also have been shown conclusively to increase the risk of miscarrying, and may even create birth malformations.
- Pulsed and static fields—created by our everyday appliances and the wiring within houses, thus changing the electrical and magnetic fields within our environment. These emissions may have the same effect as electromagnetic radiation.
- Electromagnetic waves (EMR) from power lines—strong correlation with leukemia. (Televisions emit EMR.)
- Radioactive material—this is being dumped into our rivers from hospital waste, especially as radioactive iodine.
- Ultrasound radiation—considered absolutely safe until it was found that more than 11 scans during pregnancy created small-for-dates babies. Does that make ten scans safe?

Not all radiations are necessarily bad, and the body is very capable of dealing with exposure most of the time. Indeed, radiation keeps us alive. Without sunlight we would not exist. The ethereal energy that we term vital force or Qi is also radiation. Used correctly, it may block the harmful effects of the "manmade" energies. I wonder if our attempts and dabblings in the realms of physics are some deep or subconscious attempt to attain a better understanding of the vital-force energy that we understand and utilize so little? Radiation is being used to "purify" our food, and in the process of killing the unwanted bacteria, is hypothetically altering the natural energy within molecules. Food has an energy, and the way it is prepared is vital to the availability of this life force. Radiation acts at the core level of an atom, and must be having some effect, surely.

However the radiation gets into the system, the areas that it is most likely to damage are the chromosomes (affecting processes such as cancer), the nervous system, and the more-delicate organs such as the back of the eye (retina). Investigations such as x-rays and radiotherapy are meant to target certain areas of the body. The accuracy is now marked, especially with computerization, but what the orthodox world seems to overlook is the blood in the area when the x-ray exposure is conducted. The blood cells become irradiated and "carry" radiation to other areas of the body. This is partially why even pinpoint radio therapy may create radiation sickness, and feelings of tiredness and malaise.

This is an incredibly difficult and sensitive subject. We need some very clear studies, and a move away from the greed culture that promotes money-making above the potential for health damage. I do not see this happening in my lifetime. We receive the same assurances that the scientists gave in the 1950s when using radiation to perform tonsillectomies and allowing our soldiers to stand a few unprotected miles away from atomic-bomb experiments. We did not know the damage we were causing then and, giving the authorities the benefit of the doubt, perhaps we do not know the dangers now. We need to heed the warnings that many trials are showing that any radiation may be harmful.

It is not easy to avoid radiation in the Western or Westernized environments that are spreading throughout the entire planet, but both small measures and major lifestyle changes may be possible for all of us, and the options need to be considered.

RECOMMENDATIONS

- *Keep household electrical appliances to a minimum.*
- *Avoid sitting within ten feet of a television. This is extremely important in the case of children. Furniture should be situated away from any electrical source, wherever possible.*
- *Avoid microwave emissions by limiting or avoiding the use of microwaves, and mobile phones should be used hands-free wherever possible. The proximity to the brain may be detrimental.*
- *Use protective screens with VDUs and computers, remembering that emissions from the side and from behind are often greater than from the screen. Pregnant women should be even more wary.*
- *Avoid keeping electrical appliances in the bedroom as you may spend one third of your life there.*
- *It is possible to have the electrical fields in your home measured. You may hire or buy a magnetometer and, apparently, your local power company may offer to come out and test. They won't do this at night, but a daytime reading is attainable. The difficulty is believing the current guidelines on safety levels, but if your environment is overcharged, take action to reduce it.*
- *It is not ridiculous to avoid or refuse housing near "risk" sites. Nuclear-power stations and electricity substations may make a profound difference to your health, and especially that of your children, and one must never counteract health with convenience. Pay attention to overhead power lines, and move away from them if possible. More difficult to assess is the possibility of power lines under the house, but your local electricity company should be able to tell you.*
- *Diviners, with their now-very-sophisticated instruments, and practitioners of radionics, who often use pendulums to assess radiation fields, may be able to isolate areas within the house that are energetically incorrect. Beds, and once again, especially our children's beds, should not be close to these areas.*
- *If radiation is unavoidable within the home environment, powerful magnets placed around the areas that are liable to be injurious may create a specific field that will block other radiation. The question is: might these be harmful?; at this stage, I can find no evidence either way. We watch and wait for further evaluation.*
- *Radiation may have an effect on the body by producing free radicals, and daily use of antioxidants can only be beneficial. See* **Free radicals** *for treatment values, and reduce these by half for a daily supplemental dosage. Increase your intake of natural, organic fruit and vegetables.*
- *A dose of the homeopathic remedy X-ray 200 every three months may protect, and should be considered on a monthly basis by any frequent flyer.*
- *Lastly, but probably most importantly, consider the possibility that the vital force or Qi is the most potent form of radiation, although little understood. Meditation techniques and active Qi control through Qi Gong, Tai Chi, and yoga are principally the best defenses we have. Daily use, especially in those who are confronted by radiation professionally, is essential.*

SALMONELLA (INCLUDING TYPHOID FEVER)

Salmonella is a group of bacteria of which there are hundreds of types. They cause generalized fevers and illnesses, acute gastroenteritis and, if severe, can multiply in the bloodstream causing septicemia, which may affect every part of the system.

One of the most dangerous types is *Salmonella typhae* (or *typhosa*), commonly contracted in hot climates and characterized by fever, headache, a cough, rose-like spots on the skin, and a generally toxic state. The bacteria can cause ulceration and inflammation in the bowel and lymphatic system, and may be characterized by an enlarged spleen (found under the left, lower ribs and extending into the upper abdomen). Other common salmonella poisonings are known as paratyphoid, of which there are different types (A, B, and C), the most frequent of infections being "food poisoning." This may be caused by a variety of bugs in the salmonella group, ranging in symptoms from mild diarrhea and cramps to potentially fatal events.

RECOMMENDATIONS

- *If a diagnosis of salmonella poisoning is made, see* **Poisoning**.
- *Typhoid should be treated by antibiotics if a complementary practitioner with experience has not controlled the problem within 24hr.*

SHOCK

The term shock is used very loosely by the lay person to denote a strong element of surprise, but in medical terms it is the clinical manifestation of a failure of blood to return to the heart. The consequence of this is that the heart has less to beat upon, and circulation diminishes.

The most common cause of shock is blood loss, which may be visible or invisible. Internal injuries in the chest or abdomen may allow a bleed of some quantity to occur without any external appearance. The abdomen can hold most of the blood in the circulatory system, and the severing of a major artery such as the aorta or one of its main branches can lead to a state of shock within seconds.

The neurological system can induce medical shock by a sudden or severe surprise, but it more usually occurs with fear. Fainting is often caused by a sudden drop in blood pressure, caused by nervous impulses preventing the right amount of blood from reaching the brain. The nervous system may affect the arteries, as may toxins such as drugs or chemicals produced by certain bacteria. The effect is to cause marked dilation of the blood vessels, thereby reducing blood pressure and, again, preventing bloodflow to the heart. Strictly speaking, a heart attack or any condition that affects the beating of the heart can lead to shock.

Recognition of shock is important, because rapid intervention may be necessary to save a life. Any bleeding must be stemmed, and any suspicion of internal bleeding must rapidly be dealt with by a doctor. First-aid techniques are necessary until such intervention is available. The signs are pallor, weakness, and a rapid heartbeat accompanied by sensations of dizziness, confusion, nausea, and a need to sit or lie down. If a blood-pressure-recording instrument is available, a low blood pressure is usually found.

RECOMMENDATIONS

- *Lower the head below the heart by placing it between the knees in a sitting position or lying flat with the legs raised.*
- *Remember the ABC (Airways, Breathing, Circulation) of emergency resuscitation, and move to stem any bleeding, if visible.*
- *Avoid giving anything by mouth, especially if internal bleeding is suspected, because this may interfere with any necessary medical intervention.*
- *Keep the individual warm, using body contact if necessary.*
- *Despite the recommendation above, it is acceptable to give a few drops of Rescue Remedy or a few drops or pills of Arnica 6 or Aconite 6 under the tongue. Do this every 10min until medical attention is received.*

Electric shock

A high-level electrical jolt most commonly will have an effect by interfering with the electrical conductivity of the heart and stopping it temporarily or, sadly, permanently. Electric shock also has an effect on the nervous system through creating peripheral blood-vessel dilation, so that all of the blood pulls into the surface vessels, thereby reducing the cardiac flow.

RECOMMENDATIONS

- *Do not touch a body that has received an electric shock unless you are certain that it is out of contact with the source.*

- *Use a nonconducting instrument such as a plastic broom handle to knock out any flex from the wall or pull the carpet from under the individual.*
- *Please follow the recommendations for shock as listed on the opposite page.*

Emotional shock

As described above, the word shock is not actually a medical term for an emotional state (*see* **Fright**).

SICK-BUILDING SYNDROME (SBS)

The advent of modern offices geared towards high utilization of space and profits has done away with the more natural and healthy working environment. Sick-Building Syndrome was a phrase coined in the late 1970s, following a boom in the use of computers and high-tech communications.

Symptoms

Individuals working in these offices may find themselves suffering from the following symptoms:

- headaches
- visual and eye problems
- dry throat and nose (including nosebleeds)
- congestion
- asthma
- skin irritations
- generalized aches and pains
- neurological symptoms, such as numbness and tingling
- lethargy and fatigue
- sleep problems

This syndrome is not well recognized, although more companies, especially in the U.S.A., are accepting that more modern working conditions do not necessarily mean healthier working conditions. The problems arise from a variety of different areas within the building, and the following only scratches the surface of the problem.

Air

Most offices contain a "soup" of substances in the atmosphere known as volatile organic compounds (VOC). These arise from the cleaning fluids from the carpets, the dry cleaning substances from our clothes, and the chemicals released from the computers and VDUs, such as ozone, negatively charged radicals, and gold (yes, gold; it is used to coat certain components within computers), all mixed with our own aftershaves and perfumes. These compounds are absorbed, and act as free radicals within the system, as well as direct irritants and allergens.

Lighting

Ultraviolet light does not penetrate glass. Light is necessary for the skin to produce vitamin D, which, in turn, balances calcium and phosphate levels in the system, both of which are essential for the normal functioning of many biochemcial pathways. Muscles in particular are affected by an imbalance, causing a tendency towards aches, pains, and strains. The brain chemicals that switch on and turn off our levels of activity (including naturally produced melatonin) are all dependent upon amounts of ultraviolet light. An absence created by being in an environment with no natural light, especially in the darker winter months, leads to fatigue and sleep disturbances.

Noise

Noise from extractor fans, air-conditioning units, traffic, the buzz of computers, and the raised voices of colleagues not only continually activates the brain, but sets up vibrations that affect the nervous system and increase the release of VOC from machines.

Sitting position

Chairs are increasingly designed with the user in mind, but these are often expensive, and most offices are furnished with chairs that encourage bad posture. Stooping over a desk closes up the chest cavity, therefore impeding breathing and applying compression to nerves as they leave the spinal column. This, in conjunction with a lack of exercise and calcium imbalances caused by a lack of natural light, leads fairly swiftly to structural problems. Repetitive strain injury is encouraged by all of this.

Poor nutrition

Many larger offices have canteens where the food may be bought in bulk to save costs and thereby is liable to be nonorganic, processed, and full of additives. It is likely to be microwaved in its preparation, thereby removing some of the vital force (*see* **Microwaves**).

Other factors

See **Geopathic stress**, which may come into play, depending on the position of the office building itself.

RECOMMENDATIONS

- *Insist upon fresh air, using suitable filters if necessary.*
- *Insist upon natural light, preferably through open windows or, as a last resort, through natural-light bulbs.*
- *If noise cannot be avoided, spend some time in silence when away from the office. Even relaxing music is stimulatory.*
- *Get outside as much as possible (through breaks or at lunchtime), spend time looking at the sky (not directly at the sun), and remember to take off any spectacles.*
- *Ensure that a part of your day is spent at exercise.*
- *Ensure an adequate diet (see chapter 7).*
- *A weekly (at least) session with a masseur or Shiatsu practitioner is sensible.*
- *Consider inviting a practitioner with a knowledge of Sick-Building Syndrome to visit, along with a Feng-Shui practitioner (see* **Feng Shui***).*

SLEEP PROBLEMS

Sleep is described as a transient, reversible, and periodic state of rest in which there is diminution of physiological activity and consciousness.

The human sleep-cycle generally progresses through five stages, with stage 1 being light sleep and stage 5 deep sleep. Following this deep stage, there is an interlude of rapid-eye movement (REM), and then the cycle repeats. This REM stage is named after the characteristic bursts of rapid-eye movement, which also coincides with the facial muscles becoming floppy and, if one were attached to an electroencephalogram (EEG), a pattern of "desynchronized" brain waves. It is assumed that most dreams occur in the deeper stages of sleep and in association with REM.

There is a marked decrease in activity throughout the body when asleep. Cell function continues and does not appear to need rest, but the diminution in nervous system activity decreases the level and number of commands to stimulate cell metabolism. Why the nervous system needs to sleep is poorly understood. Scientists know the chemicals that are produced in abundance to put us to sleep, but why they are produced is not recognized. I have a theory.

Nature is in balance. For every rain shower there is a sunny spell, for every ice cap there is a desert. Activity and rest are simply the night and day of the natural human balance. Sleep is the closest that most people get to a meditative state, and it is well established that meditation has a profound effect on well-being if practiced properly. Scientists tend to look for a chemical/biological necessity for sleep, but in fact it is to do with a spiritual requirement and connection to the source of vital force. Without sleep, we die very quickly due to the nervous system's loss of control over vital functions such as digestion and heart rate. There is no neurochemical basis for why rest would "recharge" nervous-cell activity, so the answer will be found when we can better assess the spiritual plane. Sleep is the body's attempt to connect with its God. That moment just prior to falling asleep, if not influenced by our conscious mind, is a very happy moment. I hope this is how we would all feel coming into contact with our "maker," whatever our beliefs. Awaking from our dream state is often unpleasant.

Narcolepsy

Narcolepsy is a disorder of the body's normal circadian rhythm (body clock) with regard to sleep. Narcolepsy is characterized by uncontrollable attacks of drowsiness or falling asleep in the daytime, a sudden loss of muscular power often associated with emotional experiences, sleep paralysis (*see* **Sleep paralysis**) and frequent vivid hallucinations during sleep.

It is important to differentiate narcolepsy from occurrences such as hypoglycemia, which may have very mild forms of the same symptoms. Narcolepsy may well be created by damage to the brain through infection, toxins, or physical damage. Acute or chronic dehydration may alter the electrolyte balance within the cerebrospinal fluid (the solution that the brain receives its nutrition from). Many cases of narcolepsy have no anatomical or chemical basis, and one must return to the spiritual concept and ask why an individual is shutting out their consciousness. We must ask the question why does the sufferer need to escape reality.

RECOMMENDATIONS

- *Try to isolate the cause by removing obvious toxins such as cigarettes, alcohol, and other drugs. If the condition started at a particular point in time, review the events of the previous three months and see if any change in diet (food allergy) or close contact with an environmental pollutant may be relevant (see* ***Poisoning*** *and* ***Radiation****).*
- *Ensure that narcolepsy is not being confused with excessive tiredness due to a lack of sleep at the appropriate times.*
- *Ensure good hydration by drinking 8 ounces of water per foot of height as a minimum daily intake.*
- *Take a multivitamin/multimineral supplement at three times the daily recommended dose (RDA) for three weeks and see if there is an effect.*
- *Review any orthodox drugs, as many have a narcoleptic effect. Antihistamines, tranquilizers, and hypnotics are all very relevant.*
- *Consult with a qualified homeopath to select a suitable constitutional remedy.*
- *Consult a physician for a diagnosis if the above measures have not succeeded.*

Sleep apnea

Sleep apnea is the cessation or suspension of breathing. Its reversibility separates it from asphyxia, which is effectively suffocation. However, for the few seconds that apnea occurs, the physiology is moving towards respiratory failure.

The cause is uncertain, but for some reason the nasopharyngeal area of the throat (that part behind the nose and mouth) closes up. If the problem is associated with an infection, treatment should be followed as for a common cold, but if it occurs separately and without reason, treatment should be attempted.

Rarely is sleep apnea a problem for an adult, although partners of those who share a bedroom with the condition often have very disturbed sleep. Symptoms that are characteristic are grunting, snoring, and restlessness as the individual attempts to pull air in past the obstruction. Cessation of breathing may occur for several seconds, followed by an apparent sleep-state panic, which includes the noises mentioned above, plus marked restlessness and an eventual gasp. The individual rarely wakes up, and settles to repeat the cycle within a few moments. Periods of sleep apnea occur throughout the night, rather than remaining persistent.

Sleep apnea in children below the age of two years may lead to asphyxia, and is known as sudden infant-death syndrome (SIDS) or crib death (*see* **Sudden Infant-Death Syndrome**).

RECOMMENDATIONS

- *Please look up in this book any concurrent problems, such as the common cold, if sleep apnea is transient.*
- *A constitutionally chosen homeopathic remedy should be selected by a homeopath.*

- *The Bach flower remedy Vervain should be taken before bed.*
- *See* **Snoring**, *because apnea may be an extension of this condition.*

Sleep paralysis

A most disturbing occurrence is experienced by most people at some time. On awakening, the body is unable to move. This condition rarely lasts for more than a few seconds, but can continue for a moment or so. Quite simply, the body is unable to move due to some lack of coordination between conscious thought and neuromuscular control. As the condition is sporadic, it is not possible to do studies on this matter, but the assumption is made that a chemical disturbance occurs within the cerebellum at the base of the brain, an area that controls coordination.

RECOMMENDATIONS

- *The problem is transient, and is probably due to an excess of sleep chemicals not being removed from a part of the brain that controls coordination.*
- *If the problem persists, see a neurological specialist.*

Sleep patterns

The biochemistry of the brain is controlled by chemicals that are stimulated by the level of oxygen, glucose, and probably other nutrients in the bloodstream. On top of this, the brain responds by producing chemicals such as melatonin in response to sunlight and darkness.

The human being has evolved as a daytime animal, and principally we should sleep when the sun goes down and arise at dawn. Our evolutionary ancestors benefited by sleeping longer hours and keeping their metabolic rate low in winter when food was less abundant, but could enjoy longer periods of wakefulness through the summer, when nature produced its bounty.

The Eastern philosophies had noticed a time clock and brought it into their medical philosophy well before science discovered chemical

Chinese Energy Clock

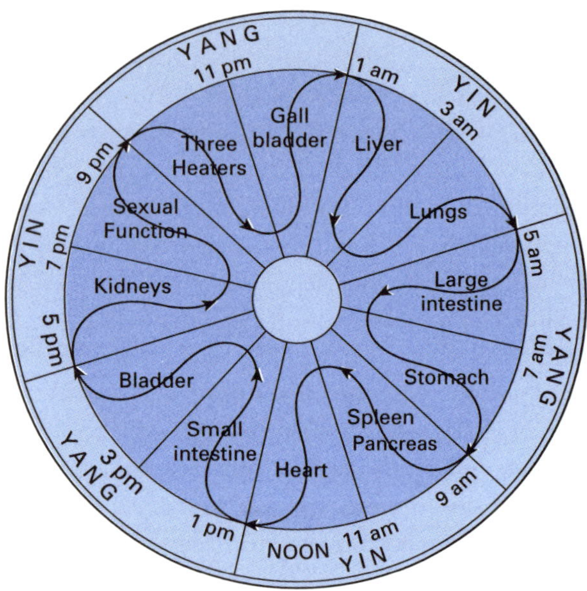

"circadian" rhythms. The diagram above is one suggested time clock, which shows when various organs are energized. Sleep is a very active process, as far as energy flow is concerned (*see* **Insomnia** below).

Insomnia

Insomnia needs to be divided into those who cannot get to sleep (sleep induction) and those who awaken (sleep interruption). The causes may overlap, although psychological stress factors are more likely to stop someone from sleeping than wake them up. Disturbed sleep is the result of a poor production of sleep chemicals (particularly serotonin), an overproduction of stimulating hormones such as adrenaline, cortisol, and glucagon (the antagonist of insulin), or external disturbances.

The causes of insomnia may be divided into the following categories.

Psychological factors

Any cause of stress, fear, anxiety, or tension needs to be assessed and dealt with. As with any problem, if it cannot be solved, then the individual must learn how to come to terms with it through counseling or relaxation techniques. Other factors include an unfavorable or noisy environment, a change in sleeping venue, or a snoring partner. Psychological anxieties may lead to nightmares, sleepwalking, restlessness, and sleep talking, which will disturb sleep and potentially awaken the individual.

I have often noticed that an individual may be deprived of sleep if their mind or body is trying to sort out a problem that sleep does not have an answer for. Do not go to bed with an unanswered question, wherever possible, but if this is unavoidable, then ensure that 15–20 minutes of a relaxation technique or meditation time is taken to counteract the adrenaline created by the unresolved problem.

Toxins

There are obvious stimulants, such as amphetamines and cocaine, that keep people awake. Caffeine has some effect on most people, and may be hidden in foods such as a bedtime cup of chocolate or tea, as well as coffee and coffee-flavored ice cream. Less well-known are the arousing effects of nicotine, cheese, red meat, alcohol, and marijuana. The latter two are often a surprise to the uninitiated, who may confuse passing out with going to sleep. As the alcohol is denatured, a stimulatory effect is created and sleep is disturbed.

Bad habits

Other than those that come under the heading of toxins, such as smoking or drinking coffee, it is worth noting that a lack of exercise will inhibit sleep patterns. Regular exercise for as little as 20 minutes per day will use up excess adrenaline and release endorphins—the body's natural opiates. Having a large meal at night will create a large insulin response, to be followed at some point through the night by a reflex hypoglycemia. When the brain registers a low-glucose level, it will instruct the body to release adrenaline, glucagon, and steroids to raise the blood-sugar level, but at the same time it will overstimulate itself and thereby disturb sleep.

Ley lines

The earth has energy lines known as ley lines, created by the production of positively and negatively charged particles produced by the flow of water. These ley lines can interfere with our own intrinsic electromagnetic pattern, and can be very disturbing to sleep. Those with unrelenting insomnia may consider the proximity of water, especially streams, which may be underground. The regional geological Survey Departments or local water companies may be able to furnish you with maps. Treatment is available by moving the bed so that the energy lines move in harmony with the body, rather than contradicting it.

Do not resort to botanical or supplemental medicines unless all the potential causes have been removed, because in the long term, symptoms will only be suppressed and will then show up in another way later on. If the mind does not want to sleep, help it by removing the cause rather than suppressing it. The use of over-the-counter sedatives (usually an antihistamine-type drug) or prescribed sedatives or hypnotics should really be avoided except for very short-term use.

Sleep disturbances

Many conditions, both physiological and pathological, can disturb sleep: pregnant women; weak bladders; men suffering with prostatism; breathing difficulties from conditions such as asthma or hay fever; vivid or bad dreams.

Simple matters, such as ineffective curtains, an uncomfortable mattress or pillow, need to be considered, more unusually, the atmospheric ionic (positive or negatively charged air) effects of nearby or subterranean waterflow. If you are near water or there is a suspicion of a subterranean stream, try moving the bed for a few nights to see if there is any benefit (*see* **Ley lines** above).

Other factors

The Eastern philosophies believe that specific organs and systems are energized at different times of the day and night. The diagram above in the section on "Sleep Patterns" describes different times when different organs are fed with the vital force. The triple heater, which controls the adrenal and thyroid glands, is at its weakest at the end of the day, and is replenished between 9pm and 11pm.

The gallbladder and the liver are replenished between 11pm and 1am, and 1am and 3am, respectively, having spent the day helping digestion and processing toxins.

Between 3am and 5am, the lungs receive their energy, so they may be fully active during the day. The energy to the large intestine is replenished between 5am and 7am, which is why we generally evacuate our bowels at that time. Any disturbance to these organs will correspond to a greater or lesser demand for energy, which disturbs the general flow and in turn disturbs sleep.

As we age, we need less sleep. There is no orthodox scientific reason for this, although certain chemicals are known to diminish as our cells deteriorate, which may have some effect. The Eastern principle considers the diminution in "vital energy" (life force) to be pertinent. The vital force we have requires less replenishment, and sleep is the time when this most occurs. We require less because we use less by lowering our levels of activity.

There is a condition known as nocturnal myoclonus which is characterized by a muscle group contracting while asleep. Like snoring, the perpetrator is unlikely to be aware of the condition, and a sleeping partner usually initiates the diagnosis. This condition is similar to the restless-legs syndrome (*see* **Restlessness**), and treatment may be needed.

RECOMMENDATIONS

- *Eliminate all stimulants from the diet and lifestyle. Once a sleep pattern returns, introduce these stimulants early in the day, and monitor whether they disturb sleep. If they do, they have to be cut out permanently.*
- *Assess any stress and deal with this, or learn and practice a good relaxation/meditation technique.*
- *Look back 6hr from the time of awakening, and register what was eaten or drunk. This may be a specific intolerance, and should be eliminated.*
- *Do not eat a heavy meal late at night, and avoid refined sugars at the evening meal.*
- *Ensure that the sleeping environment is comfortable, quiet, and dark. The reclining Buddha is always seen lying on his right with the right hand under the head. This position encourages the energy flow needed for sleep, and should be practiced by everyone.*
- *The following supplements and extracts can be used in doses as recommended below per foot of height approximately 1hr before going to sleep. Try one of the compounds at a time, and add in the next if the effect does not become apparent after five nights: niacin (20mg), vitamin B_6 (10mg), and magnesium (60mg).*
- *The amino acid tryptophan can be taken at 75mg per foot of height, but is difficult to obtain because there is some controversy over the possibility of a toxic effect. Medical practitioners may have access to this amino acid. This should be taken 1hr before sleeping, with water and no other food or drink.*
- *Valerian, Passiflora, and Chamomilla can all be taken, but should be administered by a herbalist or knowledgeable complementary practitioner. Over-the-counter supplements may be tried, but take care not exceed the recommended dosage.*
- *There are many homeopathic remedies that have insomnia or sleep disturbance as part of their symptom picture. Accurate selection is necessary, but pay attention to the remedies Aconite, Lycopodium, Coffea, and Arsenicum. The remedy Opium should also be reviewed, but may not be easy to obtain without a homeopath's prescription. All of these remedies should be*

taken at potency 200 for three consecutive nights, and a result may occur immediately or within ten days. Be patient.

- *Ensure that 20min of exercise is performed each day, and for bad insomnia try doing this again in the evening.*
- *Melatonin is being well-hyped as a safe "supplement." I put this word in inverted commas because this hormone comes under the licensing of a supplement, but is in fact being touted as a medicine. It may well be safe, but there is scant evidence to support this. Melatonin is best left alone or used as a last resort under medical supervision.*
- *If the individual is awaking at a particular time, please review the possibility of an energetic disturbance in the organ or system that corresponds to that time of night (see the diagram above).*
- *Move the bed 90° in case ley lines are relevant.*

SNORING

Snoring is a rough, audible sound caused by vibration of the soft palate at the back of the roof of the mouth during sleep. Anything that influences the tension, weight, or size of the soft palate will influence snoring. This part of the roof of the mouth is very important in the formation of sound and swallowing, and therefore has many muscular connections.

When we sleep, our muscles relax. The deeper the sleep, the more the relaxation, and therefore a deep sleeper may well relax the soft-palate muscles to such a point that it vibrates through normal breathing. The use of sleep-inducing drugs and—most frequently overlooked—alcohol will relax the tension in this area, and cause snoring.

Fat settles around the soft palate and its muscles, and an excess will alter the weight of the palate and predispose to snoring. Any condition that may inflame the area, such as the common cold, hay fever or other causes of rhinitis and—very importantly—smoking, can cause snoring.

Noisy breathing through sleep that is not actually soft-palate-created snoring may occur with any nasal obstruction. Rhinitis, the common cold, nasal polyps, sinusitis, and enlarged adenoids may all produce a snoring sound. The use of the nose to abuse drugs such as cocaine, amphetamines, and heroin by "snorting" will create inflammation and worsen snoring.

RECOMMENDATIONS

- *Temporary snoring associated with a common infection may benefit from treatment directed at rhinitis (see* ***Hay fever****).*
- *Persistent snoring may be stopped by losing weight, and giving up smoking, alcohol, and excessively sweet foods.*
- *The position in which a snorer sleeps may influence the noise. Generally speaking, sleeping on the back makes the problem worse.*
- *The homeopathic remedy Opium (often available only on prescription, especially in the U.S.A.) can be taken at potency 200 each night for one week.*
- *The Bach flower remedy Vervain, four drops before bed, may also influence snoring.*
- *L-Tryptophan, an amino acid that is difficult to obtain, may well be beneficial if taken in moderate doses because the nervous system turns it into serotonin, which enhances muscular tension.*
- *The orthodox world will offer steroid nasal sprays; these show some efficacy, but need to be used continually.*
- *There are devices called mandibular-advancement devices (MADs), which prevent the lower jaw from falling back, thereby pulling the tongue forward and away from the soft palate.*
- *Continuous positive-airways pressure (CPAP) units actually pump air at high pressure into the airways, which may strengthen the musculature.*
- *Surgery may be offered as a last resort. Avoid, if at all possible.*

SPEECH PROBLEMS—*see* Stammering and Dysphasia

TINNITUS

Tinnitus is the medical term for a persistent noise heard in the head, or in one, or both ears. Very often, tinnitus will disappear if there is background noise, but in severe cases, it will override even that.

Tinnitus is caused by stimulation of the nerves and structures leading to the auditory centers in the brain, and can therefore be triggered by inflammation or damage from the eardrum through the ear ossicles (bones) found in the middle ear, through the delicate nerve endings in the inner ear, and damage along the nerve pathways into the brain. Continuous noise and very loud noises (such as an explosion), infections, head injuries, and arthritic conditions of the ear ossicles can all be potential causes. Irritation of the eardrum by earwax can be an innocent and easily treatable problem. Certain mineral deficiencies may also trigger the problem.

RECOMMENDATIONS

- *Take magnesium and potassium replacements at twice the recommended dose given, or eat six bananas per day (two with each meal).*
- *Vitamin B complex (50mg) or vitamin B_6 (50mg) may help to remove fluid in the middle ear.*
- *Ginkgo biloba, around 50–60mg a day for an adult, taken in divided doses with breakfast and supper may be beneficial.*
- *The homeopathic remedies Salicylic acidum, Cannabis indicus, and Kali iodatum should be reviewed to see if the symptoms are suitable.*
- *Reduce saturated fats and cholesterol in your diet, and avoid aspirin.*
- *If the above do not help over a few days, then a visit to your doctor to rule out an obvious and visible cause should be undertaken.*
- *Chiropractic, craniosacral, and cranial osteopathic treatment can all be instantly effective, although a few sessions may be necessary.*

Tinnitus—Ear and Nerves

The vestibular nerve transmits extraneous stimuli to the auditory centers in the brain, which we experience as tinnitus.

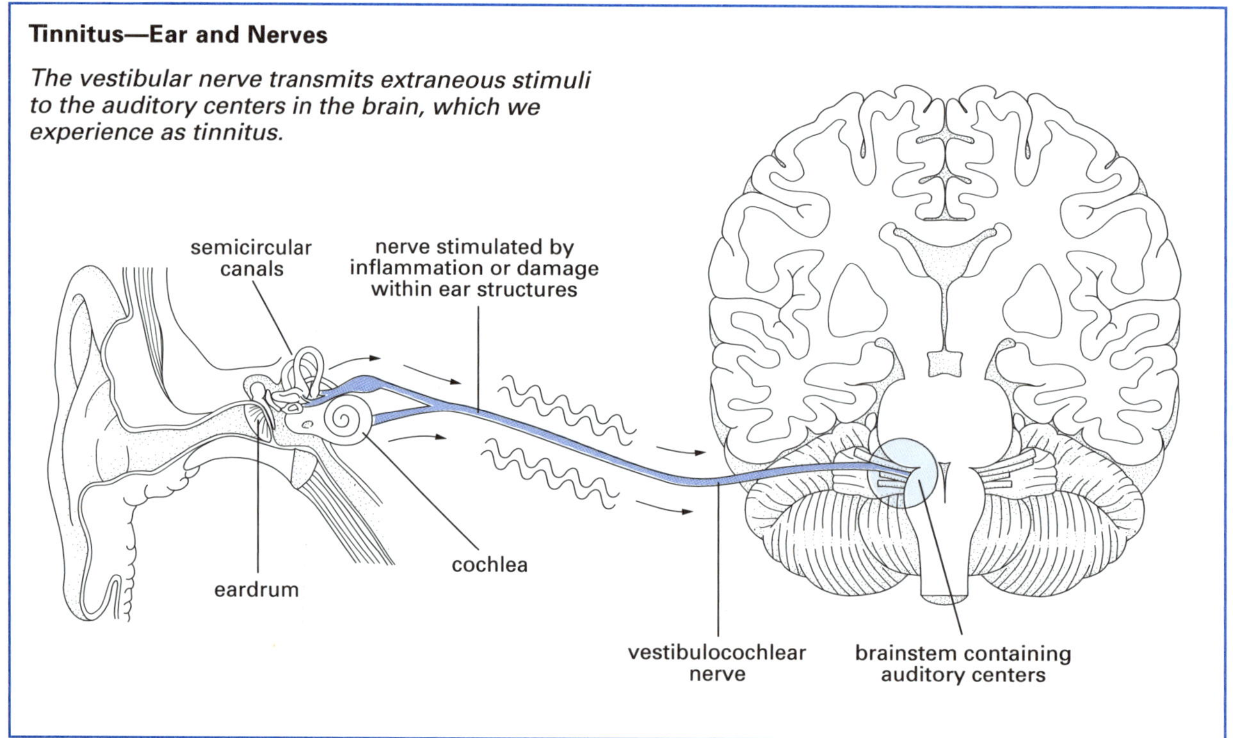

- *It is also wise to remove the amalgam (mercury) from your teeth and ensure that you are not taking in metals from aluminum pans. A metal-toxicity test may be beneficial here.*
- *If tinnitus persists after these measures, then a referral to a neurologist and CT or MRI scanning is advisable to rule out the (rare) serious causes of this problem.*
- *Provided that there is no serious problem, try hypnotherapy if it persists.*

TRAVEL

Traveling has become an extremely accessible pastime because of the advent of high-speed airplanes, trains, cars, and fast sea-faring vessels which allow us to get to parts of the world that would otherwise be inaccessible. What took Dr. Livingstone seven years and cost him his life can now be achieved in a matter of days, with a lot more safety. The subject of travel from a medical point of view is enormous, but few books have been written about it. The basics are as follows.

Preparation for travel

When booking tickets and organizing your foreign currency, it is worth looking at general and basic health preparation and precautions. When traveling, we are exposing ourselves to different temperatures, the sun, pollution, foods, and hygiene standards, and our ability to adapt is extremely important. Adaptability is very much geared toward our basic level of health, and the more extreme the travel or adventure, the healthier we should be. Those lacking in health should not risk travel to countries that are very different from their own.

RECOMMENDATIONS

- *Avoid traveling when your health is below par.*
- *Travel to tropical areas when there is lower risk of infections, such as avoiding the monsoon season in malaria-endemic areas.*
- *A basic check-up with a complementary medical practitioner is a useful starting point; follow their suggestions to achieve and maintain a good level of health.*
- *Take suitable medical supplies as described below.*

Medical supplies for travel

I recommend that the following homeopathic and supplemental remedies are taken and used as described, as well as certain supplements and

Medical Supplies for Travel

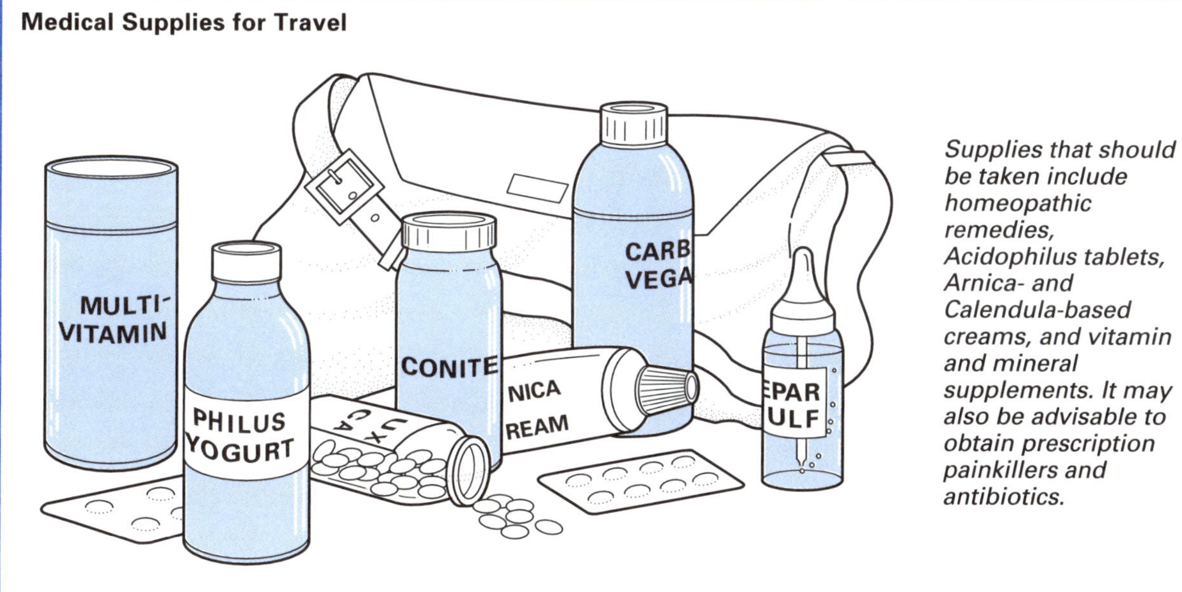

Supplies that should be taken include homeopathic remedies, Acidophilus tablets, Arnica- and Calendula-based creams, and vitamin and mineral supplements. It may also be advisable to obtain prescription painkillers and antibiotics.

topical creams. All remedies should be bought at potency 6 and taken up to every 15 minutes if acute symptoms arise. As the problem resolves, reduce the dose to every 2 hours, and stop 24 hours after the condition has settled. Always contact a physician if symptoms worsen or do not resolve within a few doses of a homeopathic remedy.

RECOMMENDATIONS

- *Aconite—for any condition that comes on suddenly, and any problem that is associated with fear or agitation.*
- *Apis—for any sting, bite, red, or hot area on the skin or in any joint. Bites from unidentified snakes or spiders must be dealt with by a doctor, although Apis may be used prior to consultation.*
- *Arnica—for any shock, psychological or physical. It can be used for any bruise or sprain until a better choice of remedy is available.*
- *Carbo vegetabilis—for diarrhea associated with pain and flatulence. Any upper-abdominal symptoms such as heartburn or reflux may benefit from this, and Carbo vegetabilis is a good remedy for a stomach upset that is associated with a chest infection. Use this remedy if bowel-habit changes because of the type of food eaten, rather than for food poisoning.*
- *Hepar sulfuris calcarium—this remedy is useful for any topical infections, such as an abscess or earache, and infections that are associated with glandular swelling, including tonsillitis. It is always wise to use a specific remedy, but Hepar sulfuris calcarium is an excellent first-aid choice.*
- *Nux vomica—this is useful in dysentery or diarrhea following food poisoning. Frequent visits to the toilet, or diarrhea alternating with constipation suggest Nux vomica.*
- *Acidophilus—High-potency yogurt bacteria tablets should be taken with any sort of abdominal upset. Acidophilus needs to be refrigerated, and therefore may survive only a few hours in the heat. Aircraft holds are below freezing temperature, so Acidophilus exposed to nonrefrigeration on the way to the airport and on arrival, until the mini-bar or a kitchen can be accessed, should be fine. Adults should take two tablets three times a day, preferably just before eating something, and children should take one tablet at the same frequency.*
- *An Arnica-based cream should be taken up to four times a day for any penetrating injury or bruises, sprains, and ligament or bone injuries.*
- *A Calendula-based cream should be used up to four times a day on any cut, scrape, bite, burn, or superficial injury.*
- *A multivitamin/multimineral supplement should be taken at twice the daily recommended dose, because travel usually exposes individuals to processed foods, and is unlikely to provide the recommended five daily portions of fresh fruit or vegetable. A change in diet often alters absorptive capacity until the bowel readjusts, and a natural-food-state multivitamin should compensate. Once the normal diet has been resumed, drop the supplements to just the recommended doses.*

Orthodox drugs for travel

If the travel will be taking the individual out of reach of immediate medical care, then the following prescriptions should be obtained from a doctor and packed with the luggage.

RECOMMENDATIONS

- *A Tylenol or Tylenol with codeine mix as a moderate painkiller.*
- *A powerful painkiller (a step below opiates), such as mefenamic acid.*
- *The antibiotic amoxicillin, a broad-spectrum antibiotic which should be used only if an*

infection has settled in and naturopathic treatments are not working. Use this for any general infection, such as a sore throat, tonsillitis, or chest infection.

- *The antiobiotic metronidazole. This is useful in infections by bacteria that do not require oxygen to breed, and therefore is potentially useful for severe bowel infections, dental infections, sinus infections, or a deep wound.*

Ensure that the doctor or pharmacist labels the maximum allowable dosages of all of these compounds.

Travel vaccinations

I am principally against the use of vaccinations, which I think may be more dangerous than protective in some individuals, unless the traveler is immunocompromised (has a low immune system) or is unlikely to be able to avoid coming into contact with a condition. Most parts of the world only recommend vaccination, although some require it as a prerequisite for obtaining a visa. *See* **Vaccinations** after finding out your requirements through a local pharmacist or a major airline's medical section.

If you choose (having read the information in this and other publications) not to use vaccinations for traveling, you may use the following homeopathic remedies, bearing in mind that their efficacy is not scientifically accepted, despite government statistics to the contrary. Alternatively, you may take these remedies before regular vaccinations because they may prevent unwanted side effects from the orthodox drugs.

It is acceptable to take all of these together, but it would be better to space them out. Start all homeopathic prophylaxis one week before departure.

Malarial prophylaxis is not a vaccination, and I generally recommend the use of these drugs if exposure to malaria is probable (*see* **Malaria**).

Travel tips

RECOMMENDATIONS

- *If traveling outside of developed countries, drink only bottled water. Even in "First-World" countries, water safety can be suspect. Mediterranean countries and others with hot climates may still*

Condition	Remedy	Frequency
Cholera	*Camphora* 200	Weekly
Hepatitis (A, B, and others)	*Lycopodium* 200	Weekly
	Chelidonium 200	Weekly
Japanese encephalitis	*Belladonna* 200	Weekly
Malaria	*Natrum muriaticum* 12	Morning and night while away, and for one week after returning
Meningitis	*Belladonna* 200	Weekly
	Iodoformum 200	Weekly
Polio	*Lathyrus* 200	Weekly
Rabies	*Hydrophobinum* 30	Weekly
Tuberculosis	*Tuberculinum* 200	Every two weeks
Typhoid	*Baptisia* 30	Weekly
Yellow fever	*Arsenicum album* 200	Monthly

The homeopathic remedies that correspond with the infections commonly vaccinated against when traveling. (See ***Travel vaccinations****.)*

carry risks. Sterilization tablets should only be used in circumstances where bottled water is not available, because these compounds kill all bugs, including the normal bowel flora.

- *Avoid foods that have been washed in sink water, such as salads and fruits with edible skins. Peel these, and they should be okay.*
- *Try to eat foods that you have seen being cooked. These should be served fresh, and not allowed to sit for any length of time. Restaurants in top-class hotels are also permissible dining venues, but even these are not likely to be as safe as the street seller with a boiling vat of lentils.*
- *Consider going vegetarian, as many dangerous infections are transmitted more easily in meat.*
- *Consider the cleanliness of the cook or chef. If you have any doubts, do not risk him transmitting disease through the oral–fecal route.*
- *Bottled and carbonated drinks are generally not good, but two or three a day in a hot climate will replace sugars and salts that are lost through sweating. These should be taken with water to avoid the dehydrating effect.*
- *"Chai" or "Chaa" is a milky, sweet tea with cardamom and other spices, commonly served on the streets in India and other hot countries. This acts as a marvelous antiseptic for the bowel, and the high (unfortunately refined) sugar content replenishes energy that is used up by the sweating process. It tastes nice, too.*

Jet lag

Jet lag is a most disturbing aspect of long-distance travel. It is caused by the alteration of the body's internal clock, which throws the chemical, sleep, hydration, and elimination patterns out of synchronization. The nervous system adjusts slowly, and the trick in avoiding unpleasant patterns is to readjust to these at a quicker pace.

RECOMMENDATIONS

- *No alcohol for 24hr prior to departure.*
- *If you are crossing more than four time zones (4-hr difference), start adjusting a few days before by going to bed earlier or later, and getting up at the time the sun rises at your destination.*
- *Try not to travel if you have a cold or ear problems. See a health practitioner if you have.*
- *Avoid the aisle seats. You are invariably going to be disturbed by passengers and staff walking by.*
- *Consider ordering the vegetarian meal—proteins demand more energy to digest.*
- *Ensure that you drink 16 ounces of water for each 3hr on the plane.*
- *Take healthy snacks with you, and eat them at the meal times of your destination.*
- *Homeopathic remedies. People who have trouble during take-off should consider the use of Spongia 6, four pills four times a day prior to the flight, and every hour starting 3hr before take-off. Those who have trouble during landing should consider the remedy Borax 6 at the same frequency. Other remedies that can be reviewed are Arnica, Aconite, Cocculus indicus, Rhus toxicodendron, and Nux vomica.*
- *Calendula cream is the moisturizer of choice.*
- *Broad-spectrum light (BSL) stimulation. BSL stimulates the production of melatonin and, if used at the times specified on specialized charts, can maintain the circadian (normal body) rhythm.*
- *Pituitary—light stimulation—visors. There is now a computerized, high-tech visor available that delivers a suitable dose of broad-spectrum light. The flight times and appropriate stimulation are delivered via the computer, which sits comfortably in a sport-like sun-visor on the forehead. This stimulates the pineal and pituitary gland to produce natural melatonin, and markedly reduces jet lag. These are invaluable to a frequent traveler, and may be bought or hired.*

Skin, hair, and eye care

RECOMMENDATIONS

- *Calendula-based creams can be used as a moisturizer.*
- *Euphrasia (eyebright), one or two drops of a diluted solution, can be dropped into the eye during and after a flight. It may be very helpful for "red-eye."*
- *Hair should be washed and conditioned before and after a flight with a nonmedicated shampoo.*

Relaxation techniques

RECOMMENDATIONS

- *Some airlines now have a video or audio channel set aside for passengers who are frightened of flying, or who wish to have an audible aid to meditation while in their seat. Use this.*
- *A session with a yoga or Tai Chi teacher can give you a personal plan suitable for you to use during and after flights.*
- *Massage. Those lucky enough to fly first class with certain airlines may be offered an in-flight massage. Accept it. For the rest of us, basic self-assisted massage using acupressure, stretch techniques, and Shiatsu can be taught by a Shiatsu practitioner to help circulation in muscles and lymphatic drainage. Many travelers find that they catch colds and sore throats on long flights. This is partly caused by the air conditioning and the close proximity of infected passengers, but also by the lack of lymphatic flow caused by neck stiffness.*

Treatments and remedies

Several homeopathic remedies and supplements can be utilized, depending upon the individual and their anticipated problems. It is best to discuss matters with a homeopath, but the following suggestions can be used safely.

RECOMMENDATIONS

- *I currently advise against the use of the new drug melatonin (discussed in chapter 10). It is probably safe, and works by mimicking the body's natural melatonin, which puts us to sleep. The trouble is that there has not been enough research to state categorically that it is safe, and any drug that takes over from a natural function of the body may in some way inhibit normal function. Some people also have side effects such as headaches.*
- *If you are fearful of flying, take Aconite 30 every 4hr, starting the day before travel and every half-hour after checking in.*
- *If you suffer from travel sickness, try Cocculus indicus 6, starting half an hour before boarding, and taken every half-hour if necessary through the flight.*
- *If you are frightened of landing or nauseous during downward movement, try Borax 30. This remedy should be taken every 2hr once on the plane, and every 15min as soon as the descent is commenced.*
- *If you are frightened by taking off or frightened of heights, use Spongia 30. Start 6hr before the flight and take a dose every 2hr, increasing this to every 15min once on the plane. Once cruising altitude has been reached, take Spongia as infrequently as the fear arises.*
- *Lavender oil, two drops on a handkerchief or the collar of a shirt, is essential if any congestion is being suffered in order to avoid ear and sinus pain. One drop in hot water (provided by the cabin staff) can be used as an inhalation.*
- *A whole amino-acid tablet taken with each meal on the day of the flight and the following day supplies the essential amino acids that will help the body to produce its own relaxation and sleep chemicals. This is not a tranquilizer of any sort, because you could take the entire bottle and not have any neurological effect. It simply provides the body with the amino acids that it needs to produce its own sleep chemical when it tries to.*

TUBERCULOSIS

Tuberculosis is caused by a bacterium known as *Mycobacterium tuberculosis*. There are two strains, one human and one bovine (cow), which are spread by inhalation of infected sputum in the case of the former, and by drinking infected milk in the case of the latter.

Tuberculosis is generally overcome by an intact immune system, but anyone with a lowered resistance from conditions such as malnutrition, diabetes, and drug use (including alcohol or smoking, or drugs taken for immuno-suppression, as in HIV and AIDS) are more likely to succumb if this disease is contracted. Anybody with lung infection or disease is also more prone.

The incidents of tuberculosis remain high in overcrowded and Third-World countries, but until recently tuberculosis was on the wane in the Western world. Unfortunately, injudicious use of antibacterial agents has led to resistant strains developing, which are now defeating even the strongest of antibiotics. We appear to be coming full circle (as with syphilis), and returning to a time when individual health and a strong immune system is going to prove of more benefit than drug treatment.

This condition used to be known as consumption because of the symptoms of malaise, weight loss or failure to grow, and a persisting cough with the development of shortness of breath. Many other features are known to physicians, and would be looked for at an examination, if necessary.

Left alone, the great majority of those who contract the condition will simply defeat the bacteria and leave a characteristic calcified area noted on x-rays. This is formed by the body's attempt to wall in the infection. Tuberculosis may continue to live within this cavity, and may escape at times when the individual is run down, causing a reactivation of the symptoms.

Investigations include chest x-rays with lesions that usually appear in the upper part of the lungs. Some blood changes may be found, but a definitive diagnosis is generally made by culturing sputum or urine samples, depending on where the infection is, and growing them in special culture mediums.

In a severely ill person, treatment with antibiotics may need to be started before a firm diagnosis is made, and before it is known whether the antibiotics being used are in fact going to affect this type of bacteria. Complementary medical treatment may be of benefit in less seriously ill people while they await the sensitivity reports so that accurate antibiotic treatment may be given.

RECOMMENDATIONS

- *Any persistent illness needs to be checked by a doctor, and it is worth reminding physicians in the West who may not come across tuberculosis to consider it as part of their differential diagnosis.*
- *If tuberculosis is diagnosed, do not rush into drug treatment unless symptoms are causing marked problems. Instead, consult a complementary medical practitioner with experience in this field. Self-treatment may not necessarily be the best.*
- *Ensure that a change in lifestyle is made to eliminate all factors that may be reducing immunity, especially bad habits such as smoking and excess alcohol. Any drug of abuse will reduce the body's immune-system response.*
- *While awaiting specific treatment protocols, use the homeopathic remedy Tuberculinum 200 nightly for three nights.*
- *Prevention is generally the best form of treatment, so ensure that health is at an optimum level before visiting areas where tuberculosis is endemic. If optimum health is not present, then see* **Vaccinations** *to decide whether such an inoculation should be used.*

Miliary tuberculosis

If tuberculosis spreads through the blood, it can land in any tissue anywhere. Widespread symptoms may occur, and the above treatment recommendations should be considered, bearing in mind that this condition is far more aggressive and likely to have a poorer prognosis.

TYPHOID—*see* Salmonella poisoning

ULCERS

An ulcer can be described as an interruption of an internal or external surface which is associated with an inflamed middle or base. Ulcers are usually due to some traumatic event, or to some toxin directly applied or produced by a disease process.

RECOMMENDATIONS

- *Treatments for ulcers vary, depending on the epithelial surface that is damaged.*
- *See the relevant ulcer section in this book, such as* **Mouth ulcers** *or* **Peptic ulcers**.

WATER RETENTION—*see* Fluid retention

WEIGHT LOSS AND OBESITY (OVERWEIGHT)

The word obesity is used by doctors to label those in the population who are 10 percent above the average. This can be 50 percent of the population in some parts of the world and, distressingly, is becoming more common in our children. Being overweight is not as simple as having a set ratio of height/weight, because some people with large muscle mass may be overweight, but should not be considered clinically obese. Obesity is only a problem if it affects an individual psychologically or is creating a strain on the body. This stress may be a structural one, affecting the joints and circulation, or affecting vital organs such as the heart, which has to beat harder to move the blood around the increased size of the system.

Interestingly, most of the charts that doctors use to help an individual determine an ideal weight are based on a population of those who have taken out insurance and remained in good health over a period of years. As most people who take out insurance come from a higher-income bracket and are more likely to pay attention to their health, this standard may be incorrect. It may be better to determine obesity by comparing fat with lean weight. This can be done by:

- Skin-fold callipers. This simple piece of equipment measures the thickness of a fold of skin, most commonly measured below the navel, just below the shoulder blade, above the hip bone,

Height and Weight Chart

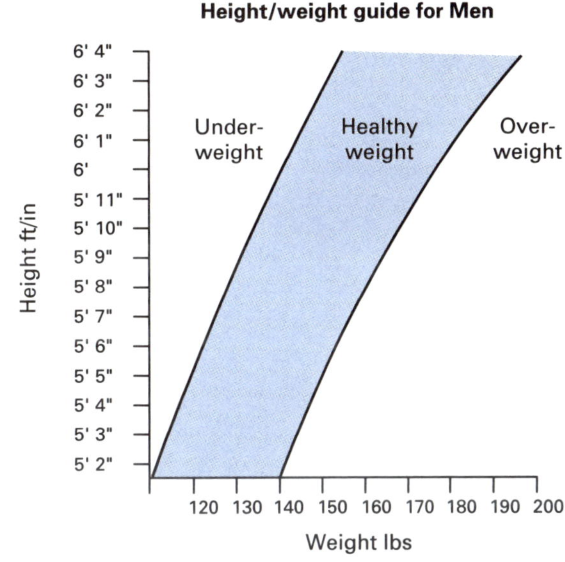

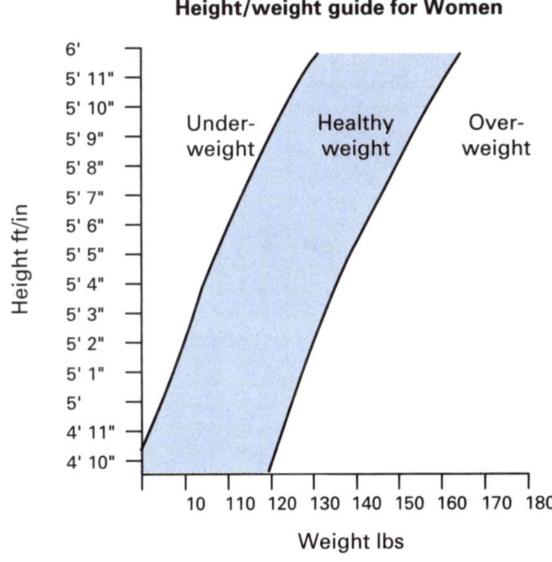

While there is no one, ideal weight for men and women of certain heights, the above tables show the weight ranges we should aim to maintain.

and behind the upper arm, by the use of specialized callipers.
- Computers are now available in most gymnasiums or diet clinics that calculate the speed of electrical flow, which is different through fat than through lean tissue. By entering height and age into the computer, an extremely accurate lean-body: body-fat ratio can be calculated.

Obesity is actually governed by the size and number of fat cells. Somehow, the cells seem to have a target minimum size that increases with age. If this size is not met, then hormones are sent to the brain by the fat cells themselves telling the nervous system that it is hungry. Cravings ensue and increased input results. The biochemistry of this metabolic system is not yet fully understood, but we watch with interest because it will inevitably lead to options in treatment.

There are two types of fat cell: white fat cells that store, and brown fat cells that control storage. Those individuals with more brown fat cells are able to eat large amounts and rarely put on weight, whereas those with little brown fat may behave extremely well dietetically, and yet increase in weight. Certain diseases, such as diabetes, hypothyroidism, and liver disease may all act through hormonal or metabolic mechanisms to increase fat cell deposits. Food allergens and other toxins may be taken out of the system by being stored in fat deposits, and chronic dehydration will certainly cause water to be stored in fat tissues, falsely increasing their size, but nevertheless causing the scales to show increased figures and clothes to become too tight.

The psychology of weight

There is a strong psychological aspect, which is both conscious and subconscious. Consciously, some people may not accept the social or medical rules and may choose to eat in excess. These people may also shy away from exercise and, provided that their obesity is not harming their health and they are happy, there is no reason for them to change their attitudes. The subconscious, however, may not necessarily be making them happy or healthy.

We respond to external stimuli such as the sight, smell, and taste of food, which can trigger almost addictive tendencies to eating. We are constantly bombarded by advertising, and one of the biggest culprits is television. Around meal times, advertisers promote their fast-food products, which trigger memories of sweet, fat, and other stimulatory tastes. Interestingly, television watching is specifically linked to obesity, not only because of its reduction in physical activity, but also because it has a trance-like effect that leaves the brain thinking it needs something and, not knowing exactly what it wants, it decides that food is the easiest answer.

We also have a tendency to reward with food. A visit to Grandma or an outing to the cinema, fun fair, or sporting event is usually "rewarded" with a sweet drink, refined sugar, or processed meat snack. This association of food with good times leaves us feeling empty if we are relaxing but not imbibing.

Weight and our habits

At the end of the day, when all is said and done, an increase in fat and weight is due to an excess of calorific input over calorific expenditure. A pound of human fat is equivalent to 3,500 calories, and weight reduction can only be obtained if output is greater than input to that degree. In more realistic terms, a negative output/input balance of 500 calories is needed per day to lose one pound of weight per week. Running a mile at your top speed will burn up approximately 400 calories, but a fast-food hamburger will put on over 450. A large gin-and-tonic will add over 200 calories, which would take nearly 15 minutes at a fast pace to burn off on an exercise machine. Evolution and nature have remembered days gone by when food was not easily available, and the storage mechanisms in the human system were important survival factors, but have not yet adapted us to our more affluent lifestyles.

I find it interesting to note that obesity is much more a problem in the developed countries of the world. Primitive cultures that remain untouched by modern advances and refined foods are not overweight. So-called Third-World countries that are affected by refined and high-fat foods have much greater levels of obesity, and a corresponding shorter life expectancy. Kenya is an interesting example. The Africans who live within the cities tend to be overweight, and indeed a culture has developed that regards obesity as an attractive asset. However, the native, indigenous peoples not affected by unnatural foods tend to maintain a healthier, lower weight.

Weight and Qi

The Western world has concerned itself entirely with calories when it comes to obesity. A more-holistic viewpoint is that food carries an energy. It is the same vital force that exists in every living cell, and is possibly a reflection of the way in which electrons, surrounding their nuclei, move and resonate. The presence or absence of electrons alters the function of any atom, and thereby gives it many of its characteristics. This vibration is transmitted to other substances that it may come into contact with. Food created by nature's humors—air, light, water, and earth—will carry specific vibrations and building blocks from which we have evolved. Our need to store is less pronounced when nature's balance is allowed to run its course. The vital force within a food substrate may be more relevant than we realize.

Many gurus and their disciples who meditate for many hours of the day require little if any sleep, and often exist on very small amounts of water and food. Their metabolic rate is reduced, but even that cannot account for the reduction in the amount of nutrients and calories upon which they need to survive. The hypothesis put forward by those who have studied meditation is that energy is actually absorbed from the cosmos through the art of meditation. On a more tangible note, I have wondered why individuals expending the same amount of calorific output and living in similar climates may have such disparate ranges of weight. For example: the population living in Florida are much fatter than people of a similar socioeconomic group who live in, say, Calcutta. I have drawn the conclusion that processed foods and nutrients that have been attacked by preservatives, additives, and microwave energy lose their vital force. Although the calories and nutrients are available, the vital force is missing, and therefore much larger amounts need to be eaten to create a level of satiety. Natural and fresh foods do not lack this energy, and create a "fullness" more swiftly. Ask somebody to eat three bananas, and they would be struggling. The equivalent amount of calories would appear in a donut or a small bar of chocolate and, more often than not, one is not enough.

Fat storage may therefore not simply be a calorific matter, but revolve around a quest for energy. Fat stores are not just holding calories, but are an attempt to contain a vital force that is not coming into the system regularly or naturally. Stagnation of this Qi is a well-accepted Eastern philosophy, and may be to do with a lack of electron movement in "dead" calories.

Weight and deficiencies

If the body is deficient in a particular nutrient, instructions will be sent via nerves or hormones to the brain advising it to imbibe the missing factor. Instincts and cravings are very accurate in children, but alter as we age, mostly by psychological factors. As I have mentioned, the reward and comfort eating of sweet and fatty foods registers in memory banks, and the brain correlates these high-calorie foods with types of reward and happiness. We train our children at a very young age by rewarding and congratulating them with sweets, chocolates, French fries, and carbonated sweet drinks, rather than fruit or other natural sweeteners. This tendency is very much appreciated by the brain which, after its structure is in place, utilizes only glucose to function. Refined foods, sweet foods, and fats provide a swiftly absorbed source of glucose that the brain can utilize at a quicker rate than a complex carbohydrate or protein. When a nervous or hormonal instruction is sent to the brain, intending to register a deficiency in a nutrient, the brain cannot differentiate whether this is a need that is easy to fulfil or one suggesting a period of starvation. The brain triggers a response that basically says "eat," and as the brain itself prefers sugars, our tendency is to eat sweet foods. Refined starch comes a close second, and fats third, because these provide sugars as mentioned above. A deficiency in, for example, chromium, may therefore lead to a sugar-and-starch craving, and it is often only by good fortune that the original deficiency is plugged.

Weight loss

Losing weight is achieved by dealing with the following four areas.

Correct diet

This needs to be balanced between protein, carbohydrate, and fats, and contain the correct amounts of essential trace elements and minerals, vitamins, and supplements. A correct dietetic plan may need to be followed, and guidelines are set out in chapter 7.

Exercise

When all is said and done, calories and fat cannot be stored if the output of the body is greater than the input. The correct exercise plan is dependent on an individual's body type, and the natural tendency to avoid exercise as we age needs to be borne in mind (*see* Exercise).

Psychological factors

Incorrect attitude and education is the principal cause of obesity from a psychological point of view. Being socially advised, through peer pressure and advertising, to alter body weight leads to weight swings that can alter the body's natural mechanism for achieving satiety when enough calories have been taken in. Reprogramming the consciousness and subconsciousness, and removing the reward aspect of calorific foods, is extremely important.

Stagnation and deficiency of Qi

This leads not only to obesity, but also to disease processes. Poor dietetic-energy input must be evaluated and corrected. This is a concept that is perhaps best taught by meditation teachers, and yoga and Qi Gong masters.

RECOMMENDATIONS

- *A sudden onset of weight gain or obesity without obvious reason should initially be reviewed by a physician who should check for metabolic disorders such as hypothyroidism and diabetes. The liver is very responsible for much of the body's fat metabolism. Alcohol in particular, and other liver-stressing drugs including orthodox medication, can affect the liver metabolism, and thereby encourage obesity. This clearly needs to be reviewed, but may require a complementary medical practitioner's assessment as well. Poor digestive capabilities through a lack of hydrochloric acid or pancreatic enzymes may also need reviewing by a nonorthodox practitioner.*
- *Simple analysis of whether obesity is in fact a problem should be undertaken before any attempts are made to lose weight. Trying to keep the body below its preferred size is difficult, and will be an uphill and, ultimately, losing battle.*
- *Establish a suitable diet by reviewing or sitting with a nutritionist.*
- *See* **Exercise***, or discuss matters with a gym master. A personal exercise program should be set up, which should minimally include 20–30min of aerobic exercise at least three times a week, and should balance the amount of calorific input.*
- *Depression, anxiety, and other strong emotions may lead to comfort eating. Review and analyze*

attitudes to food with friends and family or discuss the matter with a counselor. Neurolinguistic programming and hypnotherapy may be of great benefit if craving tendencies are marked.

- *Do not underestimate the role of Qi or the vital force in weight gain. Techniques of yoga, Qi Gong or Tai Chi, and even ballet or martial arts, can offer both an exercise program and techniques for moving energy through the system.*
- *Marked weight fluctuation is probably water retention, and the most common causes for this are hormonal, cyclical changes and dehydration. Do not confuse obesity with water retention, and ensure that at least 16 ounces of water is drunk per foot of height per day.*
- *Decrease television watching. More so than other stagnant activities such as reading, viewing of the television has been shown to have a pronounced effect on obesity through factors other than decreased activity. Do not eat in front of the TV.*
- *Acupuncture may be useful in helping to decrease appetite, but should only be used in a program aimed at dealing with the underlying causes of obesity.*
- *The Buteyko breathing technique changes the acidity of the blood, creating a weight-reducing biochemical effect. If available, learn the technique.*
- *Certain weight-reducing diets may advise gentle exercise after a meal. I believe they are wrong. Exercise will interfere with digestion.*
- *Increasing fiber in the diet will suppress appetite without any side effects by swelling the stomach and giving the sensation of fullness. Fiber will also bind to fats and cholesterol in particular, holding them in the bowel for excretion through the feces. Strictly avoid appetite-suppressant medication. There is inevitably a rebound effect, because deficiencies are inevitable, and there are serious risks including heart attacks and strokes.*
- *Avoid crash diets or total fasts as a means of weight reduction. The body registers starvation and will hold onto its fat stores, preferring to break down protein (muscle) to provide energy. Some fat stores will, of course, diminish, but these will be replaced before the muscle. Weight reduction can only be obtained if carbohydrates and a small amount of healthy fats are absorbed. An ideal weight reduction program will not encourage weight loss beyond two to three pounds per week.*
- *Weight loss may be quite marked in the first week or two, because of an initial removal of water stored in the tissues. Do not be downheartened if weight loss seems to tail off. You are now losing fat and not water.*
- *Gauge weight loss by the comfortable fitting of clothes and a personal impression of the body in a mirror rather than on a scale, because exercise may build up muscle mass, which is markedly heavier than fat. A review of the body-fat: lean-weight ratio is the best guide.*

THE HEAD AND NECK

BALDNESS

I have not come across any particularly successful treatment for male baldness in the world of alternative medicine. Some people have had some benefit by taking high-dose mineral supplements, oxygen therapies, scalp massage, and yogic headstanding techniques, but never to any great degree. If you are genetically predisposed to losing your hair, orthodox noninvasive, surgical, and drug treatments are your only option.

RECOMMENDATIONS

- *See* **Hair** *for initial advice.*
- *Visit a trichologist for supplemental advice, and the latest methods of hair replacement and weaving.*
- *The drug minoxidil has been hailed as effective.*

It works for approximately 12 percent of people, but needs to be used continuously; 50 percent or so have some success, and the remainder obtain no benefit. Minoxidil was a hypertensive drug (until withdrawn from the market) that created hirsutism (increase in hair growth), and was experimentally applied topically. It has many side effects, including water retention, weight gain, and tachycardia, and should only be considered in full knowledge of these effects.

- *If baldness is detrimentally affecting your life, counseling and hypnotherapy may allow you to come to terms with the problem, even though they do not solve it.*

Alopecia

Baldness occurring in patches or throughout the scalp, as opposed to male-pattern baldness, is called alopecia, and is associated with:

- fungal infections
- stress
- drug taking, such as anticancer drugs
- trauma
- mineral and protein deficiencies

Hair is dependent upon a good blood supply to the hair follicles. Stress can cut down the blood supply to the scalp; mineral and protein deficiencies can prevent the follicle from forming the hair; and drugs poison the follicles. Trauma and fungi inhibit the follicles as well.

RECOMMENDATIONS

- *Visit a complementary medical practitioner to establish a cause.*
- *Replenish the body with high-dose mineral and essential amino-acid supplements.*
- *Stop using medicated shampoos unless instructed by a qualified practitioner. Certain medications may inhibit folic activity.*
- *Gentle massage and yogic headstanding techniques can be beneficial, but need to be taught. Too much rubbing may be detrimental.*
- *Homeopathic and herbal treatments are available, but are best prescribed by practitioners because they must aim at the underlying cause.*
- *As in all conditions where stress is relevant, consult with a stress-management advisor.*

SKULL FRACTURES

Trauma or, extremely rarely, diseases such as Paget's disease or cancer may cause a fracture to the skull. Treatment is very much dependent on where the fracture has occurred. Diagnosis is generally made by medical consultation, examination, and radiographs (x-rays), and generally hairline or thin fractures are left alone. Care must be taken to observe an individual in case an intercranial bleed (*see* **Bleeding**) has occurred.

Depressed fractures where the skull bone may be pushing down on the brain tissues or fractures which are causing malalignments may need to be corrected surgically.

RECOMMENDATIONS

- *Any blow to the head must be examined by a doctor immediately.*
- *Do not refuse x-rays or even CT scans if the doctor is uncertain.*
- *Skull fractures may not be dangerous in themselves, but may cause damage to the blood vessels underneath, which if they continue to bleed, may cause pressure on the brain and create symptoms up to two months later (see* **Subdural hemorrhage***).*
- *Use the homeopathic remedy Arnica 6. Take four pills every 15min, until symptoms such as pain have resolved.*

THE EARS

LABYRINTHITIS

The labyrinth is a part of the inner ear that contains specialized nerve fibers that send impulses to the brain, giving information about the head's position. If the head is tipped, the fluid level within the labyrinth moves, and some nerves have more pressure applied, while others have less. This combination tells the brain exactly what position the head is in. It assumes that the rest of the body is following suit!

Inflammation of this area causes symptoms of dizziness, nausea, and vomiting, which can last anywhere up to one month, although the first few days are generally the worst. The infection is generally caused by a viral infection, although dehydration and an acid/alkaline imbalance may also be relevant.

RECOMMENDATIONS

- *See* ***Dizziness****.*
- *It may be necessary to take time off work and stay lying flat, because labyrynthitis may cause an individual to fall over and potentially risk injury.*

MENIERE'S DISEASE

This is a disease of the inner ear that is characterized by deafness, vertigo, nausea, and often vomiting. Tinnitus (the perception of a buzzing or ringing in the ears) and an involuntary movement of the eyes from side to side may also occur.

The cause is uncertain, although infection is possible. There is some evidence for an allergic reaction being the cause, but so may dehydration or electrolyte imbalances which cause more fluid to pass into chambers within the body, instead of staying in the tissues or blood vessels.

RECOMMENDATIONS

- *See* ***Dizziness****.*
- *Check for food allergies (see* ***Food-allergy testing****).*
- *Reduce salt intake.*
- *Ensure good hydration by drinking at least 8 ounces of water per foot of height.*

THE EYES

If you study a horizontal section of an eyeball, you will see the complexity of the eye, and perhaps like me, wonder why more things do not go wrong. Light has to travel through the conjunctiva and cornea (the covering layers of the eyeball), through a variety of channels and fluids to affect the retina, which is a collection of nerve endings and light-sensitive cells which are at the end of the fibers which join together and become the optic nerve. These, in turn, transmits the impulses to the optic centers at the back of the brain. Problems anywhere along this pathway will lead to visual disturbance. Neurological diseases such as multiple sclerosis (MS) may show up as double vision, and specific problems are discussed in this book under their own title.

The function of the eye is to bring the rays of light that enter to a sharp focus on a layer of light-sensitive receptors at the back of the eye, known as the retina. Light rays are bent towards the retina mostly as the light passes through the cornea and the anterior and posterior chambers of the eye, which are fluid-filled. However, part of the

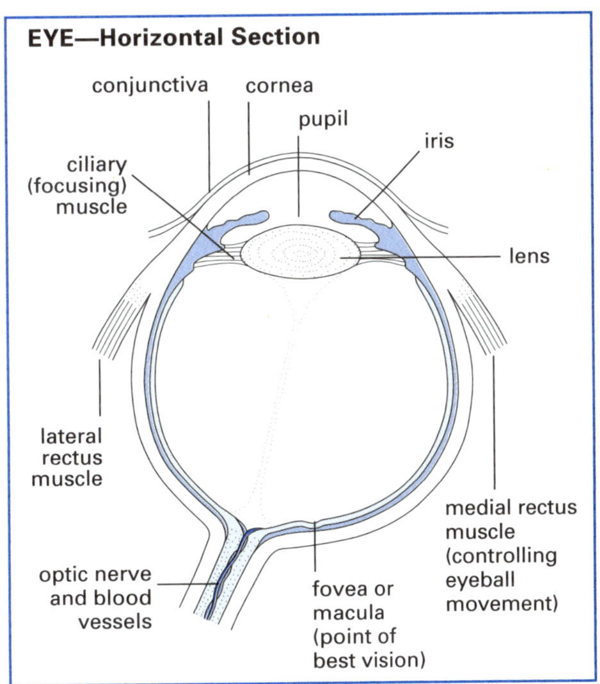

adjustment occurs through the lens. The lens is itself contractible, controlled by the ciliary muscles. This ability to change the width of the lens is known as accommodation. In our youth the lens is elastic, and objects can be sharply focused by accommodation, but from the age of eight years onwards and usually by middle age, the elasticity of the lens becomes reduced, and the unaided eye can no longer see objects as clearly. This condition of diminishing close accommodation is known as presbyopia. At some point, it is most common for adults to require reading glasses, for fine print in particular.

BLEPHARITIS

Blepharitis is inflammation of the eyelids. This often presents as redness associated with discharge, and treatment is similar to that for conjunctivitis.

RECOMMENDATIONS

- *See* **Conjunctivitis**.
- *Consider the remedies Graphites, Sulfur, Apis, and Euphrasia from your preferred homeopathic manual.*
- *The fluid extract of Euphrasia (eyebright) can be used in a dilution of two drops to one eyebath of water.*
- *Avoid topical antibiotics if possible, because these will kill the good bugs as well as the bad, and allow the possibility of a difficult bacterium to enter the eye.*

BLURRED VISION

A blurring of vision may be created by faulty accommodation, but things tend to come back into focus either in the distance or close up, depending on the type of problem. Blurred vision at any distance is liable to be either traumatic or due to a disease process affecting the neurological pathways, and should initially be dealt with by a specialist.

RECOMMENDATIONS

- *Any problem with vision, whether acute in onset or gradual, should be reviewed by a specialist for a firm diagnosis.*
- *Eye exercises may make a profound difference, especially those known as Bates' eye methods. In principle, Bates' and other eye-training techniques teach the brain to "see," not "look," by a series of exercises. The techniques are best taught, although books can be found on the subject, but time and patience are required.*
- *Stress and tiredness cause changes in muscle tension, and may therefore affect the shape of the lens, thereby altering an individual's ability to accommodate. "Eye strain" does not actually exist, but persisting anxiety and tiredness may come close to creating something along those lines.*
- *The use of spectacles and contact lenses should be considered (see* **Contact lenses***).*
- *Take beta-carotene (3mg per foot of height) in divided doses throughout the day, and review the diet with a nutritionist to find out why the deficiency has occurred.*
- *Blurred vision or problems not corrected with spectacles or contact lenses must be reviewed by an ophthalmic specialist.*

EXOPHTHALMOS

This is a medical term for protruding eyeballs. Genetic or hereditary protrusion is, of course, not a medical problem, but the development of exophthalmos usually indicates some pathology. Sadly, the common cause is emaciation of the face, through starvation, but this is not true exophthalmos, because it is really only a relative widening of the eyes in comparison to the surrounding tissues.

Unilateral exophthalmos is usually associated with tumor growth in the orbit or eye socket, but by far the most common cause of exophthalmos, typically bilaterally, is Graves' disease. This is a condition of hyperthyroidism at its extreme. The raised levels of thyroxine, and in particular another hormone called long-acting thyroid stimulator, encourage the small amount of fat that lies behind the eyeball in the orbit to grow excessively. This increased fatty tissue pushes the eyeballs forward.

RECOMMENDATIONS

- *The development of exophthalmos requires a medical opinion.*
- *Once a full diagnosis has been made, a complementary medical practitioner may be able to offer treatment for the underlying condition but, unfortunately, exophthalmos is not reversible.*
- *In extreme circumstances, operative procedures may be feasible.*

FLOATERS

Floaters are small black dots of irregular shape that are visible by all of us if we look. They are caused by small amounts of debris in the vitreous humor of the eye. Floaters are usually not noticed, but trauma or diseases of the retina may cause larger fragments, which become disturbing.

RECOMMENDATIONS

- *An increasing number of floaters should be viewed by an eye specialist.*
- *Sadly, I have not come across any alternative or orthodox therapies that can help with floaters. They are often broken down and reabsorbed by the body, and may not therefore be a persistent problem.*
- *Hypnotherapy may be beneficial in helping to ignore the visual annoyance.*

GLAUCOMA

Glaucoma is an increase in pressure within the eye, usually caused by an obstruction to the outflow of the fluid in the eye. There is, rarely, an increase in production of this fluid, which is not drained quickly enough, and this results in an imbalance.

There may be some correlation between longstanding glaucoma and the amount of a type of protein called collagen found in the tissues of the body, which acts as a type of scaffolding. An excess of collagen may block the outlet, as may abnormalities in the tissues at the back of the eye. There are two types of glaucoma:

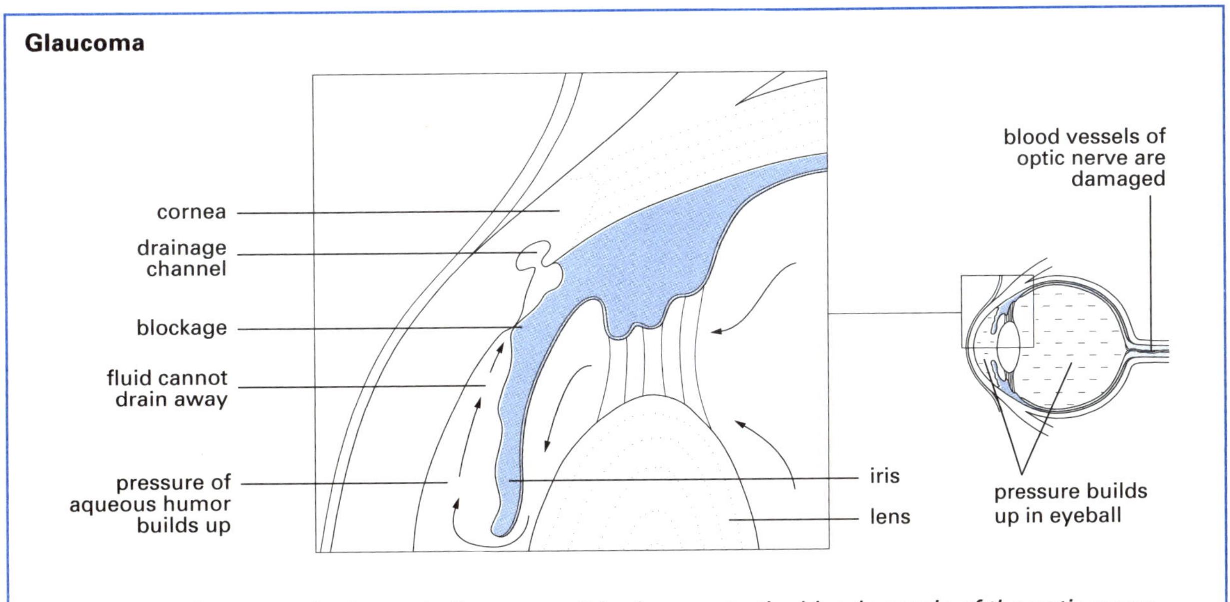

The buildup of pressure in the eyeball may result in damage to the blood vessels of the optic nerve.

Acute (closed-angle) glaucoma

Acute glaucoma presents with a severe pulsating pain in the eye, blurred vision and, commonly, nausea or vomiting. The pupil will be dilated and fixed, and does not respond to light as it should. Acute glaucoma can occur in one eye only.

Chronic (open-angle) glaucoma

This may have no symptoms until the condition has been present for several years. It is noticed as a gradual loss of peripheral vision, and if left untreated, will result in tunnel vision, which is exactly as it sounds. If no action is taken, then pain, blurring, headaches, and nausea will eventually result. I have one patient whose eyeball pressure rose at times of stress. This is not a well-recognized factor, but it may be that stress can cause glaucoma.

RECOMMENDATIONS

- *Acute glaucoma is a medical emergency. If untreated, the pain will be excruciating and blindness will ensue. Rush to an emergency department, as any therapy needs to be started within 48hr.*
- *Any disturbance of vision must be checked initially by an optician. He or she will refer you to your family practitioner, who will decide on whether a specialist is required. Do not delay, because many conditions can progress rapidly to blindness.*
- *Many studies support the belief that allergy may play a major part in chronic glaucoma. Food-allergy testing is a highly recommended procedure.*
- *Vitamin C is known to reduce inner-eye pressure, and in chronic glaucoma should be used at a dose of 1g (1,000mg) per 22 pounds of body weight in divided doses with meals through the day. One gram of vitamin C can be taken every 15min in acute glaucoma, and every hour once treatment has been initiated. Take natural-food-state vitamin C, otherwise at these levels you are guaranteed to upset your digestion.*
- *Blueberry extract—anthocyanoside, 15mg per foot of height taken three times a day initially may be used in chronic glaucoma. Continued use of this compound should be monitored by a complementary practitioner with experience in this area.*
- *Learn a relaxation/meditation technique.*
- *Homeopathic remedies may be chosen based on the symptoms, but the remedies Spigelia and Phosphorus should be reviewed initially. Spigelia 6 should be taken every 15min on the way to the hospital in acute glaucoma.*
- *Do not refuse orthodox eyedrop treatment, regardless of trying alternative therapies.*

MYOPIA (SHORTSIGHTEDNESS) AND HYPERMETROPIA (LONGSIGHTEDNESS)

A normal eye produces a sharp image on the retina of an object at a distance by not bending—or accommodating—the lens at all. However, not all eyes are the same. Some are too long from front to back, and the focus forms in front of the retina, causing a blurred vision (myopia). This can be corrected by providing the individual with a concave (known in optical circles as a negative) spectacle or contact lens.

Other eyes are too short, in which case they form the positive image behind the retina, once again causing blurring (hypermetropia). This problem is corrected by a convex or positive spectacle or contact lens.

Not all blurred vision is created by defects of light refraction, and disease or damage to the retina or optic nerves may be the reason. Vitamin C and nutritional deficiencies can also cause problems, as can tiredness and stress.

Any visual problem can reduce confidence and, in the case of shortsightedness, close the world around an individual. Simple pleasures like going to the theater, a football match or taking part in field sports become more difficult, and a vanity concerning wearing glasses or contact lenses can often lead to mild but repairable psychological difficulties. Children, in particular,

Sight—Long and Short

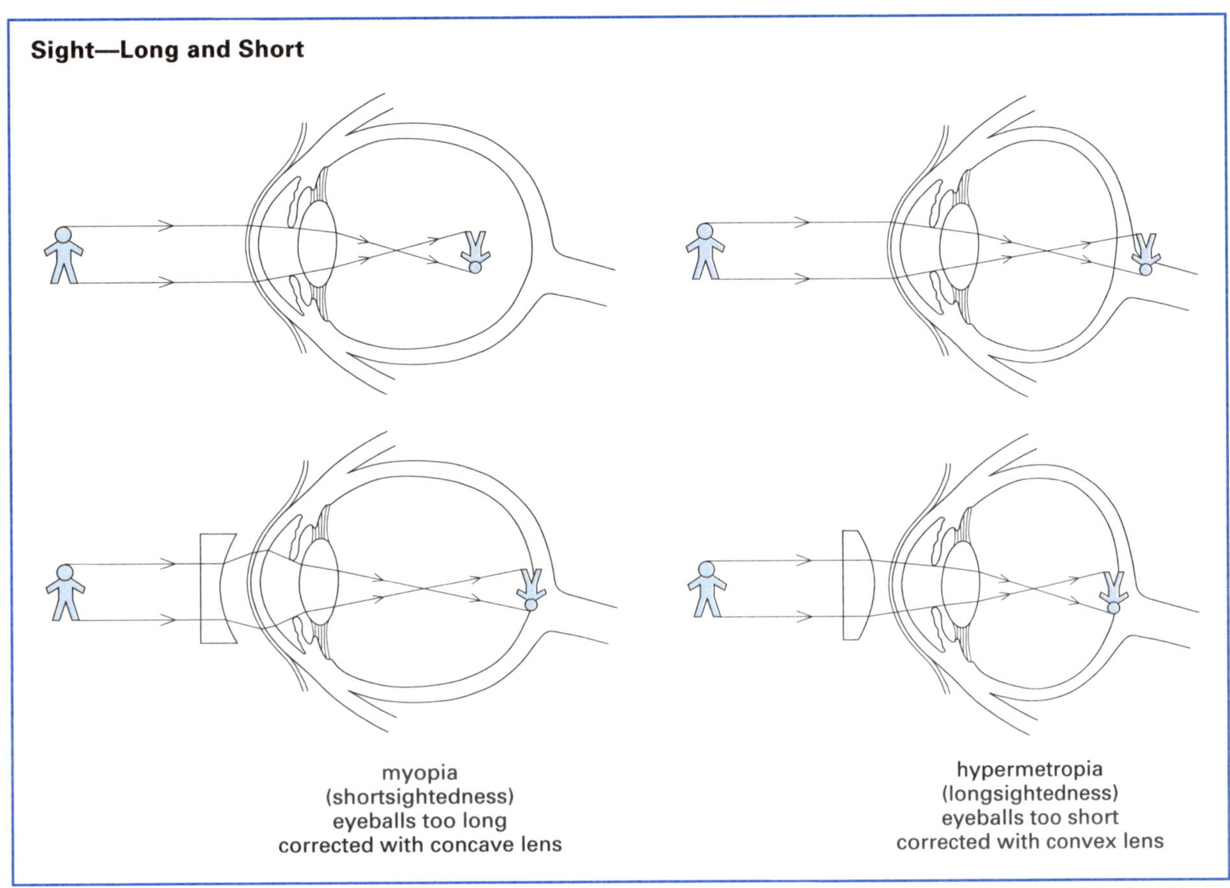

myopia
(shortsightedness)
eyeballs too long
corrected with concave lens

hypermetropia
(longsightedness)
eyeballs too short
corrected with convex lens

may not wish to disclose their "failing" and an eye test is advisable for any child who is failing at school or is becoming less sociable. A change in hand–eye coordination may well be a visual problem.

One must always ask the question when confronted with a visual problem: "what do I not want to see?"

NIGHT VISION

Difficulty in seeing at night or in a darkened environment may be a matter of becoming shortsighted (myopic). However, deficiency of a chemical called rhodopsin, which is found in association with vitamin A, may stop the specialized pigment cells in the retina (back of the eye) from working properly. Other causes include glaucoma and decreased circulation to the retina. The symptoms may be most noticeable when driving at night.

RECOMMENDATIONS

- *Any problem with vision should be checked by a physician or ophthalmic specialist.*
- *Ensure that your glasses or contact lenses are correct.*
- *Increase the intake of yellow/orange and deep-green vegetables such as spinach, collard greens, broccoli, carrots, pumpkin and squash. Supplementation may be made by taking 1mg of beta-carotene or 2,000iu of vitamin A per foot of height in divided doses throughout the day.*
- *Anthocyanidin extract from blueberry can be taken at 20mg per foot of height in divided doses.*
- *The homeopathic remedies Belladonna and Nux vomica may be useful if taken at potency 30 each night for ten days. Other remedies can be chosen for poor nighttime vision, but these should be selected based on your constitution as a whole by a homeopath.*

- *Tobacco can affect night vision, and smoking should be stopped.*

THE NOSE

The nose is the preferred entrance for air to enter the lungs. It is a longer route than breathing through the mouth, and thereby the air is warmed and cleansed more effectively by the nasal hairs. The nasal membranes are sensitive to pollutants, and produce mucus to trap foreign material and protect the delicate lung tissues. The sinuses—air spaces within the skull bones—are mucous-membrane-lined cavities that drain fluid into the nasal passages.

CARE OF THE NOSE

The nose is very much self-repairing, and provided that it is not damaged, will look after itself. Damage can occur from trauma and, becoming more common, from the inhalation of drugs of abuse such as cocaine, heroin, and amphetamines. Smoking is highly injurious to the nasal mucous membrane, hairs, and sinuses.

Nasal-washing techniques are popular in the East, and little watering cans known as Neti Lota pots are used in a cleansing technique known as Jala Lota. These pots are available through outlets, but the technique is best taught by a skilled yoga practitioner or complementary medical practitioner with experience. Techniques of inhaling water without these watering cans are commonly practiced, but definitely need to be taught (*see* **Nasal washing**).

ANOSMIA (LOSS OF SMELL)

At the top of each nostril is a yellow-brown epithelium, which contains millions of receptors that join together to form the olfactory nerve responsible for smell. This runs to a receptor area in the brain, which is able to differentiate an immeasurably large number of odors.

Unlike vision or taste, which have a variety of components made up from primary colors (red, blue, and yellow) or taste (sweet, sour, bitter, salty, spicy), smells cannot be made up from a few components. Each olfactory receptor may have its own specific odor molecule to recognize, and it may mean that thousands have to be activated before the brain recognizes a smell.

As an aside, smells may be unrecognized, but nevertheless noticed. Insects in particular are known to give off pheromones (airborne chemicals) that attract members of the opposite sex. It is probable that human beings recognize or pick up airborne chemicals from others without registering them consciously as a smell. The phenomenon whereby women placed in a dormitory or in close proximity will all eventually have their periods at the same time suggests a pheromone activity. (Either that, or there is a nonmeasurable energetic transmission from some part of the brain, probably the pituitary gland, or an area that is considered by Eastern philosophies to be the center of the highest chakra.)

A loss of smell occurs due to any interference with the transmission of impulses from the receptor to the brain including its olfactory center.

Transient or temporary loss is often noted with colds or inflammation of the nasal membranes. Conditions such as hay fever or nasal polyps, whereby the mucous membranes swell and may engulf the olfactory receptors, may appear permanent until the season changes or the polyps are cured. A more permanent anosmia will occur if the olfactory receptors are damaged, as they are by pollution, smoking, and the inhalation or "snorting" of narcotics such as heroin, cocaine, and amphetamines. Glue-sniffing is a sad and rapid cause of olfactory-receptor damage. Trauma or infection such as meningitis or encephalitis can damage both the olfactory nerve and the brain center, as can tumors.

RECOMMENDATIONS

- *A transient loss due to an obvious cause should be treated as per the recommendations in the appropriate section in this book.*
- *A gradual or persistent loss of smell should be examined by a doctor with referral to a nose specialist or neurologist. Testing will be carried out by asking an individual to smell coffee, almond, tar, and lemon, all of which are generally pungent and easily recognized. Foul-smelling compounds, such as asafetida, which possesses a smell so unpleasant that the nose will wrinkle uncontrollably, are used to determine whether anosmia is complete or not.*
- *In chronic cases, food allergy must be considered, and blood testing to isolate culprits is recommended. Ingestion of allergens may create a permanent inflammation in the membranes, which envelop and block the olfactory receptors.*
- *Homeopathic remedies may be of use, and should be chosen based on the constitution of an individual by a homeopath.*
- *The Eastern philosophies, especially Tibetan medicine, believe that the loss of one of our senses is an indication of a very deep disorder. It does not mean that it is particularly life-threatening, but simply that treatment may be difficult and require much discipline and therapy. Referral to a Tibetan physician is recommended, but if none are available, then Chinese or Ayurvedic physicians may help.*

BROKEN NOSE

A broken nose is a common injury, especially in people who play a lot of sport. It is a painful occurrence, and very often the softer cartilage at the front of the nose is itself fractured or fractures away from the bone. The nasal bones may be broken, and very often the swelling will hide any marked deformity. Radiographic examination is often required but, because little is done to treat a broken nose until the swelling has subsided, this may not take place for a couple of days. The nose is a highly vascular area, and bleeding is often very profuse.

RECOMMENDATIONS

- *If a broken nose is suspected, it should be reviewed by a physician or accident-and-emergency doctor.*
- *Administer the homeopathic remedy Arnica 6 every 10min for five doses, and then every 2–3hr for 2–3 days. If the damage is severe, alternate the Arnica with Symphytum 6 every 3hr for one week.*
- *Apply an Arnica-based cream around the damaged area.*
- *An operative procedure may be necessary (see* **Operations and surgery***).*

EPISTAXIS (NOSEBLEEDS)

The cause of nosebleeds is often trauma, such as a direct blow or persisting inflammation in the nasal passages caused by infection or irritants, which may be as innocuous as pollen in hay-fever sufferers.

Rarely is a nose bleed serious, although it can be associated with diabetes and hypertension. Sinusitis and nasal polyps are less serious conditions, but also need to be considered. Problems with the clotting system may often show up as more bleeds.

In children, ensure that there is no foreign body in the nose, and do your best to stop any picking!

RECOMMENDATIONS

- *Sudden, unexpected, persistent (more than 25 minutes) or bright-red bleeding should be examined by a physician, since cauterization (sealing of a blood vessel by heat) may be necessary.*
- *Remove any foreign object, if necessary.*
- *Keep the head tipped forward and apply pressure to the soft, lower part of the nostril or nostrils.*
- *Apply a cold compress on the bridge of the nose and the back of the neck. This may help to stem the flow by decreasing bloodflow.*

NASAL PASSAGES

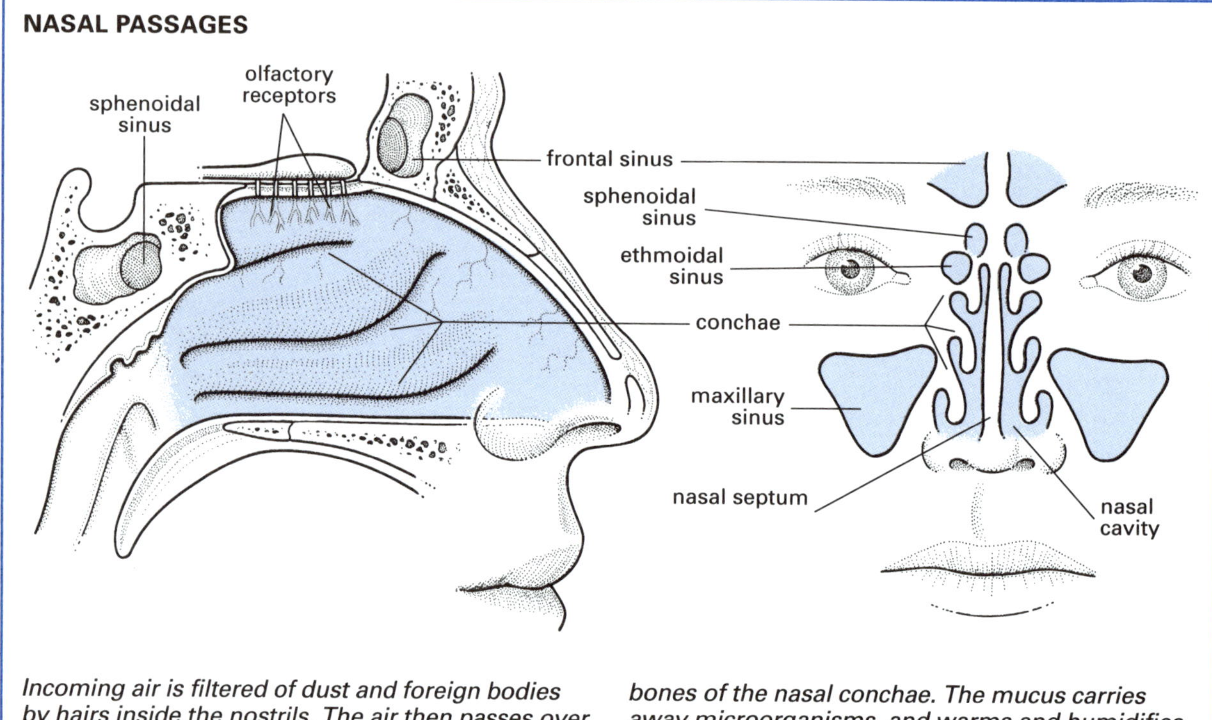

Incoming air is filtered of dust and foreign bodies by hairs inside the nostrils. The air then passes over the mucous membranes in the sinuses between the bones of the nasal conchae. The mucus carries away microorganisms, and warms and humidifies the air before it passes into the lungs.

- *Avoid swallowing blood by spitting out.*
- *The following homeopathic remedies can be employed and taken every ten minutes at potency 6. Bright red blood—Phosphorus; bright blood with steady flow—Ferrum Phos; following injury—Arnica.*
- *Recurrent nose bleeds, with no established serious cause, should be treated with treble the recommended dose of a multimineral and vitamin supplement. Beta-carotene (2 mgs per foot of height) should be taken in divided doses through the day. Recurrent nosebleeds should also be examined by an ear, nose, and throat specialist to isolate any defective or weak blood vessels, or other underlying health problem.*
- *If no obvious cause is apparent, consult a complementary medical practitioner, and check for vitamin and mineral deficiencies.*

NASAL BLOCKAGE

The nose can be blocked by a foreign object, inflammation, growths, or polyps. Inflammation is most commonly caused by pollutants, including smoking or drugs of abuse, or infections such as the common cold.

RECOMMENDATIONS

- *See the appropriate section once the underlying cause of an obstruction is established.*
- *A foreign body may be easily removed, but if not, see a doctor.*

NASAL POLYPS

Nasal polyps are actually fluid-laden, mucous-membrane "sponges," usually created by persistent irritation from an external pollutant, such as pollen, mechanical fumes, or drugs of abuse. Smoking in particular is a major cause. There is a correlation with hay fever, asthma, and other allergic responses, and it may be triggered by food allergies. Hypoglycemia encourages membrane swelling and mucus production, and is often an overlooked reason for polyp production. There is some hereditary predisposition. The nasal passages swell in response to tears, and emotional suppression is another overlooked cause of polyp growth.

Nasal polyps are most often protruding from the sinuses, especially the ethmoid and frontal sinuses. Their presence causes nasal obstruction, mucus excess, and diminution in smell and taste.

RECOMMENDATIONS

- *Any persistent discharge or congestion should be examined by a doctor.*
- *Avoidance of any nasal pollutants, including smoking, should be encouraged.*
- *Diets high in sugars and refined foods should be adjusted. Spicy foods and alcohol should also be avoided.*
- *Specific food-allergy testing should be undertaken to identify any negative response.*
- *A nasal-washing technique should be learnt (see* **Nasal washing***).*
- *Homeopathic remedies should be considered, in particular Calcarea carbonica and Teucrium. These should be taken at potency 30 twice a day for two weeks.*
- *Herbal treatments may be of benefit, but should be prescribed by a specialist. These include nasal sprays of herbal and homeopathic remedies. Try them—they may work.*
- *The following supplements should be taken in divided doses throughout the day at the following levels per foot of height: beta-carotene (1mg), vitamin C (1g), chromium (twice the daily recommended dose of a good-quality product), and zinc, 5mg taken before going to sleep). These levels should be tried for one month in conjunction with homeopathic remedies.*
- *Any repression of sadness or tears needs to be brought to light, and neurolinguistic programming or hypnotherapy prior to counseling may be curative.*
- *Steroid drops prescribed by a doctor and taken without fail four times a day for one month may be curative if the underlying cause is removed. At the very least, steroids will be effective at relieving the congestive symptoms. Do not exceed the recommended two drops per nostril, because some absorption will take place through the membranes, and a considerable amount may be swallowed unless the head is in the correct position. This requires an individual to kneel and place the vertex of the skull on the floor, and stay in that position for a couple of minutes. Do not sniff and swallow afterwards; instead, preferably blow the nose gently.*
- *Refined endoscopic techniques are now available for surgical polyp removal and should be insisted upon if other treatments do not work and surgery is required. Bear in mind that 40 per cent of polyps will recur and that the procedure is an uncomfortable one and should really be left until other avenues have failed.*

Nasal washing

Nasal washing is best done by the use of a Neti pot (a small watering can available at many health-food stores and clinics) and the technique from yoga known as Jala Lota.

For Jala Lota prepare a saltwater solution using a teaspoonful of salt in a cup of warm water. Fill the Neti pot and, standing by a sink or a bath, place the top of the head pointing directly down. Breathe through an open mouth slowly, and pour the water through the Neti nozzle up one nostril and out of the other. Ensure a continuation of breathing, as this creates a negative pressure, and may help to pull the fluid into the sinuses. Repeat this technique up to four times a day.

POSTNASAL DRIP

A postnasal drip may be recognized as a sensation of fluid at the back of the nose, but is often unrecognized. While upright and awake, a postnasal drip tends to be swallowed or coughed out, but at night when asleep or in a horizontal position, the trickle may descend into the lungs, causing a nighttime cough. If the postnasal discharge is infected, then sore throats, loss of voice, and bronchitis may be created. Most postnasal discharge comes from the sinuses.

RECOMMENDATIONS

- *See* **Sinusitis**, *but bear in mind that sinus discharge is not necessarily associated with infection, and therefore may not be painful.*
- *Adenoids (lymphatic glands at the back of the nose) may also become inflamed and create mucus, as may the nasopharnyx mucous membrane. If sinuses are not a problem, see* **Coughs** *and* **Colds**.
- *Pay special attention to food intolerances, cow's-milk products, alcohol, and sweet foods, as all these encourage mucus production.*

SINUSITIS

The skull bone is extremely heavy, and if it were not for the air-filled cavities known as sinuses, it would be too heavy for the neck to support. These hollows are lined by mucous membranes that produce secretions to protect the bones from infection and trap airborne invaders. If these membranes become inflamed, the condition of sinusitis occurs.

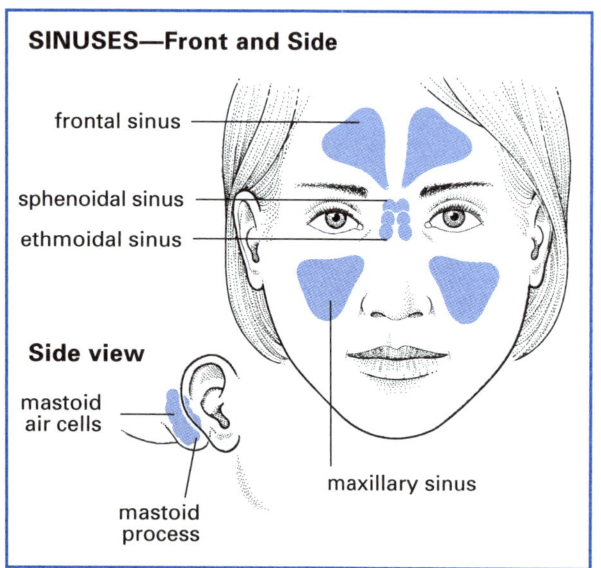

Sinuses can be very extensive and travel back into the skull bones. They interconnect, and all the sinuses drain into the nasal cavity, except for the mastoid sinus, which drains into the middle ear. Inflammation of the drainage channels can lead to back pressure, which is extremely painful. Diving, or rising or descending in a poorly controlled pressurized aircraft leads to a differentiation of pressure, which can cause pain. The Valsalva movement (pinching the nose and blowing) is most commonly used to free any blockages in the Eustachian tube, but can be used to open up the passages to the sinuses.

Sinus infection may be either acute or chronic. Pain is usual in chronic sinusitis, but is not always present, and the site is dependent on which sinus is affected. Most commonly, infection will trigger inflammation, with viral and bacterial being more common than yeast or fungal, but the latter two are often overlooked. The maxillary sinuses may, one time in four, be inflamed because of inflammation in the upper teeth, gums, or jaw.

Inhalation of noxious substances, which include smoking, inhaled drugs of abuse (such as cocaine and amphetamines), strong industrial fumes, pollution, and even the chlorine from swimming pools, may all trigger a noninfected inflammation. Fatigue, fever, and discharge are associated, and a yellow or green mucus is usually indicative of a bacterial infection.

Frontal sinus headaches have a peculiarity of developing midmorning. I am uncertain why this occurs, but it seems that there must be some body-clock mechanism. Nostrils tend to fluctuate in their patency due to vasoconstriction altering throughout the day, and Ayurvedic philosophy suggests that more energy is absorbed through the left nostril than the right. (This is why all effigies of Buddha in a reclining position have him on his right side.)

Rhinitis created by allergies is a frequent initiator of acute sinusitis, and the chronic state may be encouraged by food or airborne allergies. Low blood-sugar levels trigger mucous membrane inflammation and mucus production, so any factor affecting or causing hypoglycemia must be taken into account. Toxic bowels can often induce sinus irritation.

The diagnosis of sinusitis is frequently clinical, but investigations such as CT scans or fiber optic endoscopy can be utilized. Sinus x-rays are frequently useless, and provide a dose of radiation that is not likely to be of benefit.

RECOMMENDATIONS

- *Attempt to soothe sinus inflammation with inhalations of lavender, camomile, or Olbas by putting two drops of the essential oil into a bowl of steaming water.*
- *Attempt to keep the mucus thin and less viscid by ensuring good hydration, by drinking plenty of water (8 ounces per foot of height a day), and avoiding dry atmospheres such as air conditioning.*
- *Hot showers or hot compresses over the inflamed area will be beneficial.*
- *Homeopathic remedies can be used in both acute and chronic conditions. Selection of a remedy should be based on the site and type of pain, type of discharge, and other associated symptoms.*
- *In acute infections, see* **Colds** *for treatment.*
- *Chronic infections may benefit from using the following supplements in the following dosages per foot of height in divided doses throughout the day: beta-carotene (2mg), vitamin C (1g), chromium (20µg), and zinc (5mg before bed).*
- *The following may be used to thin mucus and act as anti-inflammatory agents: N-acetylcysteine and bromelaine, each at 400mg per foot of height in divided doses throughout the day.*
- *Infectious causes may benefit from Echinacea and Golden Seal taken at twice the recommended dose on a proprietary brand.*
- *If problems continue, nasal-washing techniques may be of use. Sniffing salt water by blocking one nostril and inhaling water until it reaches the back of the throat and blowing it out can clear the nasal passages, but does not encourage the solution to enter the sinuses. It is better to use a small watering can device (known as a Neti pot) often available at healthfood stores. This technique is called Jala Lota (see* **Nasal washing***).*
- *Establish any food allergies by exclusion diets or food-allergy testing, and avoid any allergens.*
- *See* **Allergies** *and* **Postnasal drip**.
- *Consider counseling and hypnotherapy to remove underlying or suppressed sorrow or grief.*
- *The orthodox use of painkillers is sometimes necessary because sinus pain can be most debilitating. Steroid drops and sprays, with or without antibiotics, may be offered, and are usually used if the sinusitis is related to polyps (see* **Nasal polyps***).*
- *Persisting problems may result in an orthodox offer of an operative procedure. This may either be a sinus wash or mucous-membrane removal performed through a small tube known as a sinus endoscope. The procedures are not pleasant, and there is a 40 percent chance of recurrence over the next two years. This procedure should be used only as a last resort.*

THE MOUTH

GLOSSITIS (SWOLLEN TONGUE)

Glossitis refers to inflammation of the tongue. This generally appears as a swollen tongue rather than a painful or red tongue, although these may be in association.

It is important to remember that the mouth is the top end of a 30-foot tube that ends at the anus. Like a hose pipe, holes may occur anywhere along its length, but the two ends receive most of the attention, and can reflect the integrity of the whole pipe.

The Eastern philosophies of medicine pay special attention to the tongue, and a swollen tongue may be very helpful in diagnosing any underlying conditions.

The tongue will swell in response to trauma, such as accidental biting or bee stings. Allergic reactions can cause the tongue to swell to such an extent that it may obstruct breathing, and very rapidly this may become a serious medical emergency. The tongue may also swell in rare medical conditions. A swollen tongue is viewed by holistic practitioners as being an indication of swelling elsewhere or throughout the bowel. This may occur in any inflammatory problem, such as ulcerative colitis, Crohn's disease, or peptic ulcers. The bowel may also swell when absorption is poor, as a reflection of more blood being pushed into the bowel in an attempt to absorb more nutrients. Swelling of the tongue may show as indentations along the edge, caused by long-term pressure on the teeth.

RECOMMENDATIONS

- *A rapidly swelling or persistently swollen tongue needs to be reviewed by a doctor, as a potential emergency. It may only take a few minutes or even seconds for the tongue to swell to a level that obstructs breathing.*
- *Review any intake, such as food or drugs recently imbibed, before swelling was noticed. Particularly salty or acidic food may be a cause.*
- *Rinse the mouth with a strong salt solution, but do not swallow. Gargling, provided that it does not cause retching, is beneficial, because the tongue starts halfway down the throat.*
- *The homeopathic remedy Aconite 6 should be taken every 10min with an acutely swollen tongue, or Apis 6 every 10min for a tongue swelling secondary to an insect bite or sting.*
- *A more-persistent swollen tongue should be reviewed by a complementary medical practitioner with knowledge in either herbal or homeopathic medicine.*

SALIVA AND SALIVATION

Saliva is a secretion from specialized glands around the jaw that should be clear, tasteless, and slightly acidic. The functions of saliva include moistening and lubricating the food before swallowing, initiating digestion (it contains an enzyme called ptyalin, which breaks down starch to simple sugars), and acting as an antiseptic. Saliva enhances the taste of food by its initial breakdown action on sugars, making the molecules more available for the taste buds.

Salivary and Parotid Glands

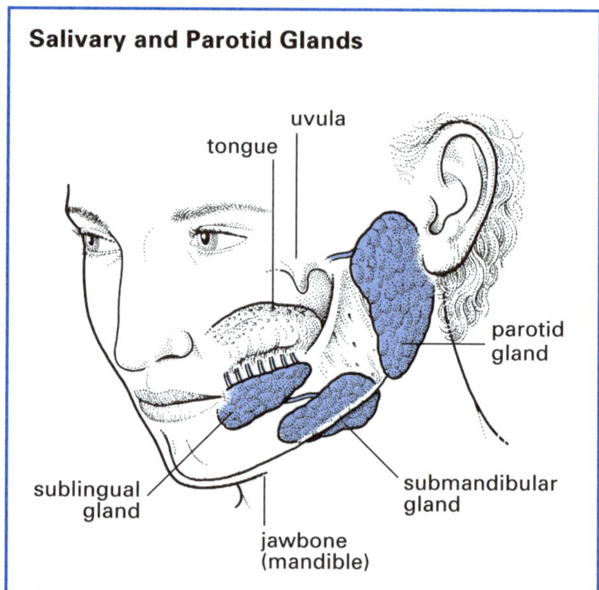

Saliva is produced in the parotid, submandibular (below the jaw), and sublingual (below the tongue) glands. Two little holes (punctae) in the cheeks are the end points of the parotid duct, and may be isolated by gently sucking and feeling the slightly cool saliva entering the oral cavity. Two little fronds are felt at the front of the mouth under the tongue, which are the end points of the other glands. The glands are under the control of the nervous system, which may be stimulated by the sight and smell of food, and even by the sound of cooking. This is a conditioned reflex much studied by Pavlov (the scientist who noted that a dog salivated more when he rang the dinnertime bell, regardless of whether the dogs were fed or not). Once food is in the mouth, other nerve reflexes continue saliva production.

Hypersalivation (excess salivation)

Excess salivation is most commonly associated with a hypersensitivity of smell and taste. This commonly occurs with fevers and in pregnancy, due to heat or to hormones sensitizing the nervous system. Injury or pain in the mouth, such as in teething in infants or disease at a later age, will also initiate hypersalivation. Any disease of the nervous system that causes impulses to be poorly controlled may also stimulate salivation. Such conditions are most commonly seen in Alzheimer's and motorneurone disease. Dyspepsia (burning pain in the upper abdomen) and other digestive problems may increase secretions throughout the gut, including the mouth.

Taste and smell may be diminished by habits such as smoking or persistently eating too-spicy or too-sweet foods. The taste buds get used to a potent chemical effect, leaving less powerful tastes unobserved. Stopping these habits will allow the taste buds to regain their sensitivity within a matter of days, but in the process, the overstimulation from these rediscovered tastes may lead to excessive salivation.

RECOMMENDATIONS

- *Any persistent, excessive salivation should be reviewed by a physician or specialist to isolate an underlying cause that may be treatable.*
- *Occasional bouts may be relieved by the homeopathic remedy Mercurius 6, four pills four times a day for three days.*
- *More intensive homeopathic work or herbal treatments for excess salivation should be prescribed by a complementary medical practitioner once the diagnosis is known, because suppression of the symptom by a "drying" action may suppress an early symptom of a condition better treated in its early stages (i.e. gum disease).*
- *Certain drugs, especially chemotherapeutic drugs, can create hypersalivation through their effects either on the nervous system or on the blood supply, causing an overstimulation of the salivary glands.*
- *Pseudosalivation may occur not because of an excess production, but because the saliva cannot be swallowed. This is usually associated with neuromuscular conditions that may be very difficult to treat.*
- *Acupuncture may relieve symptoms, but should be used in conjunction with herbal treatments as prescribed by a complementary specialist.*

Hyposalivation (lack of saliva)

Hyposalivation occurs because of damage to the salivary glands or a diminished nerve or blood supply to them. This may occur through age or disease as the nerves become less sensitive, especially those of taste. Disease processes such as sarcoidosis may directly affect the salivary gland tissue, as may viral infection. Diuretics, antihistamines, certain heart drugs, and most drugs that affect the neurological system (including drugs of abuse) can have an effect, although usually temporary.

Adrenaline and other catecholamines—the stress chemicals—all suppress bowel activity, including the production of saliva. This is very marked in moments of extreme fear, when the mouth can become parched, but it will have a general effect to some degree in people who are nervous or anxious.

Dehydration will, of course, lead to a dry mouth, and this is part of the first recognition mechanisms (*see* **Dehydration**). Please note that smoking may have a drying effect, as may the intake of any "heat"-increasing compounds, such as spicy food. High sugar levels will encourage a dehydrating effect, and saliva may thicken, causing a dry effect without any actual diminution in production. We all notice a dry mouth after sucking on a piece of candy or eating an ice cream.

RECOMMENDATIONS

- *Isolate the cause by discussions with a complementary medical practitioner or a doctor. Treat the underlying cause, bearing in mind that the cessation of doctor-prescribed drugs may be dangerous.*
- *Ensure adequate hydration. Drink 8 ounces of water per foot of height per day.*
- *There are many homeopathic remedies for a dry mouth, and the correct one should be selected on general symptoms. While assessing the underlying cause, try Nux moschata 30 four times a day.*
- *Learn and practice a relaxation or meditation technique, or consider counseling if anxiety is a notable aspect of the personality.*

SWOLLEN TONGUE—*see* Glossitis

THE THROAT

DYSPHAGIA

This is the medical term for a difficulty in swallowing. If it should occur for no particular reason, or it is persistent, then see a physician, or go to the hospital emergency room immediately.

Dysphagia can occur for either a physical or mental reason. The throat is a central chakra point in Eastern medicine and, whatever the immediate cause of the dysphagia might be, one must ask whether there is a buildup or deficiency of energy in that area, causing a blockage or an inability for the esophagus (food pipe) to swallow.

Physical causes may include inflammation of the esophagus causing the food pipe to close up, external pressure from, say, an enlarged-thyroid or lymphatic gland, but more-sinister obstructive causes such as tumors need to be excluded where there is persistent difficulty in swallowing.

Many people with dysphagia may have an associated eating disorder or a strong subconscious ability to stop a food allergen entering the system. Anxiety in general may create difficulty in swallowing, as may excitement or fear.

RECOMMENDATIONS

- *Persisting dysphagia for no apparent reason must be examined by a general practitioner and possibly a specialist.*
- *The homeopathic remedies Aconite and Stramonium, at potency 6, can be taken every 15min in an acute episode or while on the way to the doctor.*
- *Emotional causes of dysphagia should be dealt with by a counselor.*

DYSPHASIA

Dysphasia is the medical term for difficulty in the ability to use language; aphasia is the complete loss.

In reality, laryngitis may be classed as a dysphasia, as indeed may any condition ranging from inflammation, infection, or even tumor that affects the vocal cords and throat. It is wiser, however, to rule out any serious illness of the area or of the nervous system when dealing with an inability to speak.

Dysphasia may be created by damage to the nervous system, in particular to the speech centers, by events such as stroke, encephalitis, meningitis, and diseases of the nervous system such as motor-neurone disease. These need to be established.

RECOMMENDATIONS

- *Any dysphasia that persists or does not have an obvious cause should be reviewed by a doctor.*
- *Follow through with specialist investigations, including CAT and MRI scans, to rule out or establish the cause. A complementary medical practitioner can then be contacted once a firm diagnosis has been made.*

HOARSENESS

A coarse voice caused by inflammation of the vocal cords is responsible. *See* **Sore throats** and **Loss of voice**.

LARYNGITIS AND PHARYNGITIS

The larynx lies protected behind the Adam's

VOCAL CORDS—Section of Throat

The vocal cords or larynx lie behind the thyroid cartilage. Inflammation or damage to the larynx or associated nerves may cause a sore throat and a loss of voice.

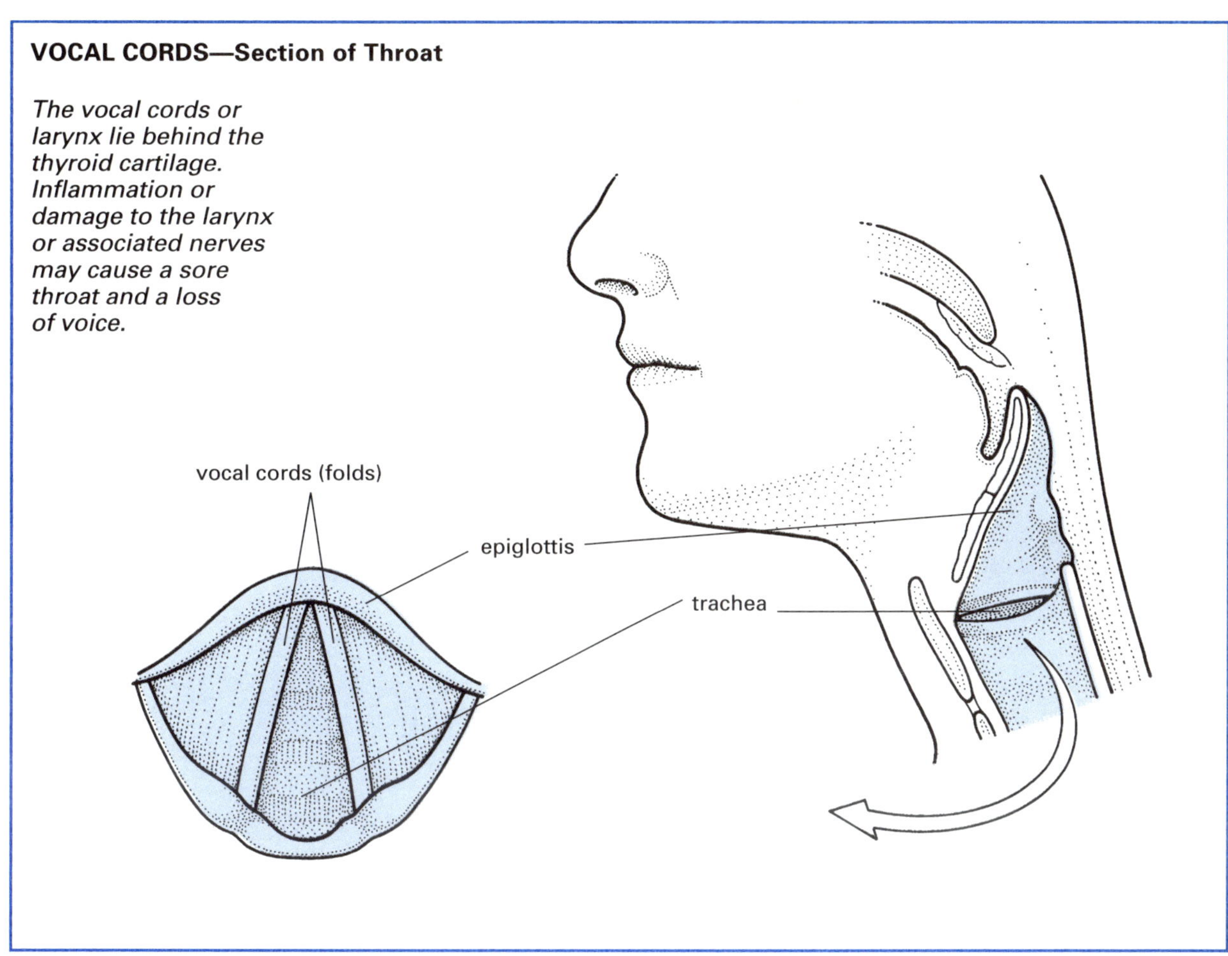

apple. The area above this, leading up to the tonsils, is known as the pharynx. Inflammation in these areas causes a sore throat, and can lead to hoarseness and loss of voice.

RECOMMENDATION

- *See* **Sore throats**.

LOSS OF VOICE

The loss of the voice is most commonly associated with laryngitis (*see* **Sore throats**). The larynx is colloquially known as the voice box, and is protected by cartilage, which can be felt superficially as the Adam's apple. The larynx is composed of two leaves of mucous membrane containing muscle that is very finely innovative and controlled by different laryngeal nerves that are branches of the vagus nerve. A loss of voice may therefore be caused not only by infection and inflammation, but by any damage to these nerves. Trauma, tumors and nerve disease may all result in the loss of voice. Any condition that may apply pressure to the larynx must also be considered, especially an enlarged or inflamed thyroid gland. A loss of voice may be a sign of hypo- or hyperthyroidism. Toxins such as pollution and smoking may also create inflammation, leading to a loss of voice.

RECOMMENDATIONS

- *Isolate the cause. Recurrent or persistent sore throats that do not appear to be associated with inflammation or infection may be an early sign of an underlying disorder, and a doctor's investigations are required.*

- *A loss of voice caused by infection should be treated by referring to the section on sore throats (see* **Sore throats***).*

SORE THROATS

A sore throat can, of course, occur at any age, from a variety of causes. There may be acute (sudden) and chronic (longstanding) sore throats, and they can, broadly speaking, be internal or external. Most sore throats are caused by bacterial or viral infections affecting the membranes (an *internal* sore throat) or affecting the tonsils and neck glands (an *external* sore throat).

Trauma, tumors, tonsillitis, and diseases of the thyroid gland can all be the cause of a sore throat. Laryngitis (inflammation of the voice box) and pharyngitis (the area between the tonsils and the larynx) are simply medical terms to isolate the exact whereabouts of inflammation in this area.

In the case of chronic sore throats, a cause is usually apparent, such as smoking or the overuse of the vocal cords in singers, but is sometimes overlooked, as in the case of people who have many hot drinks throughout the day. Alcohol and fizzy drinks may also be culprits. Persisting sinusitis may lead to a postnasal drip, causing sore throats. This is quite common in smokers. Persisting sore throats that do not have an obvious answer need to be examined by a doctor to rule out less-common and more-dangerous causes. Remember that the throat contains a lot of organs, not just the food and windpipes, and there are also residual pouches, such as the brachial and pharyngeal pouches that exist as little pockets where infection can sit very tenaciously. These pouches have no apparent use, but are present because of our evolutionary development, a bit like the appendix.

RECOMMENDATIONS

- *Remove any obvious cause of a sore throat, such as smoking, shouting, and excessive hot drinks.*
- *Use saltwater gargles if the throat is sore at the back of the mouth. Do not swallow this.*
- *Chop up some fresh ginger root into a hot mug of water, and sip at a comfortable temperature. Honey and lemon may be added if the ginger is an unpleasant taste. You may gargle with this solution before swallowing it.*
- *The ginger solution mentioned above, lavender, or a mix of cloves and cinnamon can be placed in steaming water, and inhaled in the case of a sore throat secondary to sinusitis. This tip is useful in cases of laryngitis or voice loss.*
- *Both internal, but especially external, sore throats may be soothed by wrapping around a silk scarf.*
- *Take comfortably warm or iced drinks of camomile tea as preferred.*
- *A teaspoonful of turmeric powder in 8 ounces of skimmed milk with a half teaspoonful of butter, and a teaspoonful of honey brought to a simmer, then drunk when at a comfortable temperature, may be instantly soothing and curative of sore throats.*
- *The following homeopathic remedies may be beneficial: Aconite 6 every 2hr for sudden onset of a sore throat regardless of the symptoms; Spongia 6 for a dry, barking cough associated with loss of voice; Aconite, Hepar sulfuris calcarium or Nitric acid, potency 6, every 2hr for splinter-like pains on swallowing; Lachesis for a sore throat resulting from overuse of the voice.*
- *There are many different homeopathic remedies that may be chosen, depending on the specific symptoms, such as if it feels better after hot and cold drinks, feels worse in a draft, or has an associated cough. Please refer to your preferred homeopathic manual.*
- *See* **coughs** *and* **colds** *if the sore throat is so associated.*
- *For any inflamed membrane, use beta-carotene (2mg per foot of height) in divided doses throughout the day.*
- *A persistent sore throat or one without obvious cause needs to be reviewed by a physician to rule out more serious, underlying reasons.*

THE CHEST

BREASTS

General care

There has been some recent controversy on the efficacy and necessity of breast self-examination. Whatever the statistical evidence eventually shows, I am of the firm opinion that care and attention paid to the breasts makes a substantial difference to their well-being. I am not a great supporter of the mammogram (*see* **Mammograms**), and I have therefore encouraged self-examination throughout my career. Many lumps have been found and dealt with, including cancers, which when caught early can mean the difference between health and illness.

The breasts are very much under the influence of the female hormones, and there are nervous and hormonal reflexes associated with touching the breasts that may contribute to keeping them healthy. Love and attention from both the individual and partners may have a profound effect.

Self-examination

Self-examination should be performed on a regular daily basis.

In the bath or shower, imagine a line drawn from the middle of the collarbone down through the nipple to the lower rib, and another line bisecting this perpendicularly across the chest at the level of the nipple. We have now imaginarily divided the breast into four quadrants. There is a fifth section that requires attention called the "wing." This is the section from the upper, outer quadrant stretching back to the armpit or axilla.

Using the palm of the hand in a rotating motion, examine the left breast with the right hand, and vice versa. Place the palm in the middle of each quadrant initially, but move the palm so that it covers the entire area. Repeat this in all four quadrants. Lumps are very noticeable in the palm of the hand, and cannot slip between the gaps in

BREAST—Four Quads and Axilla

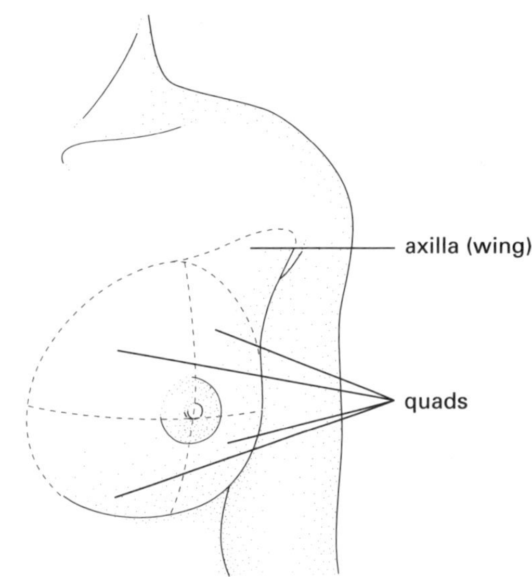

between fingers. The same should be done with the wing of the breast, although fingers must come into play nearer the armpit. Special attention should be paid after this initial examination to the nipple and areola. Gentle palpation with the fingertips all around and directly below the nipple is recommended.

All breasts have lumps. Examining the breast daily will allow the individual to get an idea where these lumps are and whether they change at different times of the cycle.

Breast tissue is very often granular, either generally or at particular times of the cycle when the breast is most under estrogen effect (two weeks prior to the period). Establishing a knowledge of what your breasts feel like will remove the likelihood of your missing an unusual, textured lump or of worrying unnecessarily. I encourage partners to examine the breasts regularly to offer a second opinion. The use of doctors and gynecologists is essential, but should not be considered a completely safe option. While doctors may have more experience, a yearly all-clear does not take into account the lump that develops two months after the examination. A clear examination is not complete security for the year.

Remember that most lumps are harmless, and that bringing a lump to the attention of the doctor does not usually return a verdict of cancer. Developing the "ostrich syndrome" by burying your head in the sand and ignoring a possible cancer can lead to a poor outcome. Breast cancer, if caught early enough, is treatable and curable.

RECOMMENDATIONS

- *Self-examination should be done daily.*
- *Note lumps and bumps mentally, or keep a note if necessary and compare at different times of the month.*
- *Bring any hard or persistent (present for more than one month) lump to the attention of your doctor.*
- *Bring any nipple changes or breast shape changes (unless in both breasts and associated with the cycle) to a doctor's attention.*
- *Cancer lumps generally do not alter on a cyclical basis, although the tissue around them may. A lump that comes and goes is not likely to be dangerous. Do not worry, but get it checked.*

BREAST CANCER

The U.K. has the highest incidence of breast cancer in the world. More than 25,000 women receive a diagnosis of breast cancer each year and 15,000 die from it. It is the leading cause of death among women aged 35–54 years. The devastation to family life is enormous. The figures in Europe and the U.S. are lower but still dramatic, whereas Japan has a strikingly low incidence of breast cancer. These statistics and other evidence indicates that nutrition and environmental pollutants are very likely to be relevant. Women who smoke have a higher incidence of breast cancer, and those with low-fat and higher-antioxidant intake have lower incidence.

There is also an increased rate in those who suffer from constipation. This may be due to an unexplained, raised estrogen level, or a simple increase in body toxins.

The breast is made up of several types of tissue. Cancers can occur in any of these, and treatments and considerations are dependent on which site the tumor has developed in. The two more-common terms are adenocarcinoma (the bulk of the breast tissue) and intraductal carcinoma (within the milk ducts).

Cancer is suspected because of three major, tell-tale signs:

- An unexpected lump, which is most often harder than other lumps found in the breast, and is occasionally immobile.
- Retraction or inversion of the nipple.
- Discharge or blood seepage from the nipple.

Any of these signs must be brought to the attention of a doctor, who has preferably also qualified as a complementary practitioner. I say this because of the current attitude of most specialists to use the mammogram as the principal diagnostic tool.

Investigations

If a breast lump is found that does not disappear at certain times of the cycle, is hard, seems to be fixed to the underlying rib cage or is distorting the skin or nipple area, investigations are warranted.

Medical examination

Most gynecologists will have vast experience in examining breasts, and will be able to give a "best guess." If the specialist is not suspicious, then neither should you be. Most will err on the side of caution, and may suggest further investigations.

Blood tests

There is a compound that can appear in some breast cancers known as CA_{153}. The presence of this "marker" in the bloodstream is indicative of a breast cancer, but unfortunately the reverse is not necessarily true, because many cancers do not produce this chemical. A negative test, therefore, does not mean that the breast is clear.

The Humoral Pathological Laboratory Test—high magnification of blood cells—should be considered if available. This test can show changes in the red and white blood-cell patterns in the bloodstream and, although not well substantiated through scientific experimentation yet, is a useful addition to the equation.

Ultrasound

As ultrasonography is becoming more accurate, this test is a noninvasive and harmless investigation. A small probe is run over and around the breast tissue, and sound waves are bounced off the regular breast tissue and any lumps. A computer will rearrange the sound waves into a picture and, in the hands of an experienced technician, the density and consistency of the breast lump should be easily noted. Any suspicion should lead an individual into further investigations, such as magnetic-resonance imaging (MRI) or lumpectomy.

Magnetic-resonance imaging (MRI)

Details of this test can be found in chapter 8. Magnetic-resonance imaging is a highly sophisticated, non-x-ray technique that at this time has less evidence of being dangerous than an x-ray. It is my preference, at this time, to recommend MRI before mammograms (*see* below). This technique can image a lump and give a clear indication of the possibility of a cancer, and can also be used to test the axillary (armpit) nodes for the possibility of spread.

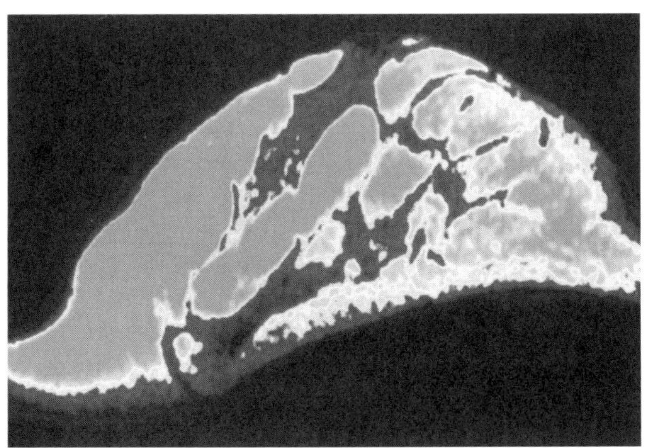

MRI of healthy female breast.

Mammography

I am fearful that mammograms may be more harmful than beneficial, and I suspect that doctors and the public are not being given all the information concerning their efficacy and safety. Despite sophisticated technology, mammograms are not faultless. The machinery may emit far higher levels of radiation than necessary, and give a dose above that which is safe.

The images may suggest a cancer that after operative procedures proves to have been wrong. There is considerable evidence of inaccuracy. This may be partially because of misreading, but also because dense breast tissue is hard for the x-rays to penetrate.

There is no doubt that radiation is toxic and can cause cancer. The amount of radiation in a mammogram is unlikely to trigger this, but radiation has a cumulative effect. Twice the amount of radiation emitted in a mammogram is obtained in a transatlantic flight; however, regular flying and mammograms may build up radiation within the system. Up to 3 percent of the population carry a particular gene, the ataxia-telangiectasia (AT) gene, which is seemingly extremely sensitive to radiation, and can alter into a cancerous state. The AT gene can be tested for, although at about $600/650, the cost is prohibitive, and the test is not easy to obtain. Perseverance through a private laboratory may provide an answer, for those who can afford it.

Statistically, the orthodox world will point out that mammograms do spot cancerous lumps sooner than women who only self-examine. I could find no study that compared mammograms with ultrasound, however. If a mammogram does find a cancer, if the woman is below the age of 50 years it is unlikely to make a difference to the outcome. Put another way, a cancerous lump found by mammogram will receive treatment sooner, but will have little effect on the rate of survival of a woman who discovers the cancer through a self-examination if she is under the age of 50 years. Once over 50 years, there is some statistical significance but, again, the studies have flaws because they do not take into account the overall health of the individual, nor do they compare a group of women whose breast cancers were found by ultrasound.

Mammography is an aggressive and uncomfortable technique. The breast is squashed quite tightly between two x-ray plates, and then held in that position for a few moments. It is well established that crushing and manipulating a tumor lump may encourage its spread, and while the orthodox world is very swift to condemn the use of massage in cancer patients (quite unjustly, as qualified masseurs would not massage a cancerous lump nor lymph nodes that may be involved), they have no criticism of applying pressure to a potentially cancerous lump.

Biopsy

A biopsy of a lump is an outmoded diagnostic technique, but is still used by some practitioners. A needle is passed into the suspicious area, and a sample of tissue taken. The needle may miss the lump altogether, or hit a part of the lump that does not have any cancerous cells. This will provide a false negative result. Alternatively, if the needle does pass into a cancerous area, as it is withdrawn, cells may be seeded into a higher level of the breast or even into the skin, where the spread may be much more profound. I do not support biopsies, and think that further investigations should be done through lumpectomy.

Lumpectomy

A lumpectomy is the procedure of removing a lump. It can occur anywhere in the body, but is commonly used for the removal of breast lumps. This usually requires a general anesthetic, although smaller lumps may be done under a local anesthetic. The lump is isolated and tissue about half an inch around the lump is taken out with it. Very often, this is sent down to the laboratory immediately, while the patient is still under anesthetic, and if a cancer is found, a wider excision or mastectomy takes place. This is always discussed with the patient before the operation.

Lymph-node sampling

At the time of the lumpectomy, or separately, any enlarged or suspicious lymph nodes may be dissected and sent away for examination to see if any cancer has spread through the lymphatic system. This procedure often leaves the lymph drainage of the arm compromised, and can cause swelling (lymphedema) and damage to the nerves in the area, leading to partial paralysis and persistent pain. These side effects are rare, but must be taken into account when giving permission for an operative procedure.

Studies are currently underway to support the excision of one principal lymph node in the axilla area that is thought to collect all the lymph draining from the breast before it distributes this solution to other nodes. A cancer will spread to this node first, and therefore may prevent more-aggressive or more-numerous lymph-gland removal. This procedure is not in common use, and will not be until further trials have taken place, which may take 2–3 more years.

RECOMMENDATIONS

- *Perform self-examination.*
- *Obtain a medical opinion.*
- *Routine screening through blood tests as described above is sensible.*
- *Ultrasound examination on a yearly basis is safe and sensible.*
- *Any suspicious area found on ultrasound should be examined by MRI.*
- *Any continued suspicion after MRI should lead to a lumpectomy. Do not biopsy.*
- *You will note that at no point do I suggest that mammography should be undertaken.*

Treatments

The wide variety of cancer treatments and preventative measures are discussed in the section on cancer (*see* **Cancer**). Breast cancer is preventable and is treatable but, as in most serious conditions, requires the best line of treatment to be decided in consultation with a complementary practitioner.

RECOMMENDATIONS

- *See* **Cancer** *and follow the advice described there.*
- *Broccoli contains a sulfur compound which has been shown to protect against breast cancer in animal studies. Regular intake may help.*
- *Some breast cancers are estrogen-dependent. This means that they grow quicker in the presence of estrogen. There is some debate at the moment about whether plant estrogens act by stimulating cancer growth or by blocking the estrogen receptors on the cancer cells, thereby preventing estrogen from influencing the growth rate. Until this debate has been resolved, all women with estrogen-dependent tumors should avoid plant oestrogens and the foods in which they are contained, such as hops, soya products, celery, fennel, and rhubarb. Those with breast tumors that are not estrogen-dependent should use phyto-estrogen supplements as they may hinder breast tumor growth.*
- *The use of natural progesterone cream should be encouraged, but prescribed by a complementary medical practitioner with experience in this area.*
- *Orthodox treatment—apart from the use of mammography, the orthodox approach to breast cancer has been proven to be very effective over the last two decades. The treatment protocols include:*

  (a) Surgery includes removal of the lump (lumpectomy), removal of part of the breast (partial mastectomy), and total mastectomy. Lymph glands in the armpit (axilla) are often removed, which can lead to the side effect of poor lymph drainage causing limb swelling, but radical mastectomy (total removal of the breast and all lymph glands) is now rare. Some studies have suggested that an operation on a breast cancer is less likely to recur if it is performed in the two weeks before the next period. The higher progesterone levels at this time may have a protective influence.

  (b) Radiotherapy. Certain types of tumor are susceptible to radiation, but first you should insist on genetic testing for the ataxia-telangiectasia (AT) gene, which makes people more sensitive to cancer formation from radiation.

  (c) Chemotherapy. The advent of estrogen receptor-blocking drugs has so far proved to be effective in tumors that are estrogen-sensitive. These drugs, such as tamoxifen and Megace, have side effects and block all estrogen effects, thereby leading to menopausal-type symptoms and improved survival rates, although they are not, so far, proven to be curative by themselves. Other chemotherapy protocols are available in abundance. One major criticism is that despite the liaison and ability of breast-cancer specialists, there are currently over 50 different protocols, none of which seem to be more or less favorable than the others. Clearly, some unity is needed.
- *Establish the percentage success rate of any treatment you are offered. Correlate this with the lifestyle changes and toxicity of the course you are recommended, and in consultation with a medically qualified complementary practitioner, discuss your options. One year of normal life with a possibility of a complementary treatment may be better than two years in and out of treatment centers with all the associated side effects.*
- *Please refer to the various sections in this book discussing complementary therapy alongside the treatments (see* **Operations and surgery**, *and* **Radiotherapy***).*

- *Always obtain a second or even third opinion.*
- *Visit the library and bookshop, and read a couple of books on the subject from a complementary angle.*

BREAST DISCHARGES

Discharge from the nipple at any time other than when breastfeeding—and even then, only breast milk should be leaking—is a sign of pathology, and must initially be assessed by a doctor or gynecologist.

Breast discharge may be related to:

- hormonal fluctuations
- inflammation and infection
- mastitis and abscesses
- intraductal carcinoma

RECOMMENDATIONS

- *Book an appointment with the doctor who deals with your gynecological matters.*
- *Once a cause has been established, see relevant section in this book.*
- *While awaiting diagnosis, a discharge of pus can be treated with Silica 6 (four pills every 3hr); a discharge of blood with Phosphorus 6; and a milky discharge with Calcarea carbonica, at the same potency and frequency.*

BREAST ENLARGEMENT OR REDUCTION

I do not support cosmetic surgery for the sake of vanity, but if an individual's life is being negatively affected and counseling cannot change this, then augmentation or removal of breast tissue is to be considered as an option.

SILICONE IMPLANTS

At the time of writing, silicone breast implants have been banned in the United States after 20 years of use. There is strong evidence to suggest that these implants may promote autoimmune disease, although this has yet to be proven conclusively. There has been some correlation between silicone implants and cancer. New implants containing other compounds are available, and discussion with at least two cosmetic surgeons should be considered before a decision is made.

RECOMMENDATIONS

- *Ensure that the plastic surgeon is a specialist in this area.*
- *Following a recent scare of the potentially cancerous or immune-suppressing effects of implants made from silicone, consider other implant options until this debate is concluded and silicone is found to be harmless.*
- *See* **Operations and surgery**.
- *See* **Plastic surgery**.

MASTITIS AND BREAST ABSCESS

"Mast" is the abbreviation for one of the medical terms for breast, and "itis" means the inflammation of. Mastitis presents as an area of redness, heat, pain, and tension. There may be associated streaks as the inflammation travels along the lymphatic vessels to the lymph glands in the armpit (axilla). If left untreated, this may lead to an abscess.

Mastitis more commonly occurs during lactation and a breast duct becomes clogged, but it may occur away from breastfeeding, when the cause is either trauma or—more commonly—an infection that has tracked up from the openings in the nipple. Mastitis is rarely a presentation of cancer.

RECOMMENDATIONS

- *Apply hot and cold compresses to the area.*
- *Place cabbage leaves from the fridge or freezer over the inflamed area.*
- *Gently massage in an Arnica-containing cream. Do not massage too hard or frequently, as this may increase inflammation.*
- *Consult your homeopathic manual and consider remedies such as Belladonna, Hepar sulfuris calcarium, Apis, and Bryonia. Phytolacca is a master remedy if the mastitis is associated with a lump or lumps.*

- *Phytolacca (pokeweed root)—one teaspoonful in a mugful of water, simmered for 15min and taken three times a day, or 0.5 ml of the tincture with water three times a day—is worth trying before an antibiotic is taken.*
- *Persistence or any associated nipple discharge other than breast milk should be brought to the attention of your doctor. If you are breastfeeding, express the milk from the affected breast, but do not feed it to the child.*

BREAST LUMPS AND SWELLINGS

Breast lumps are most commonly caused by swelling of the breast tissue in response to the hormone estrogen, and are known as breast mice, fibroadenomas, or fibrocystic disease. They are generally harmless, and have no greater tendency to become cancerous than regular breast tissue, but cancer needs to be ruled out (*see* **Breast cancer**).

Generally speaking, these lumps are symptomless, but they can be tender and even painful, especially close to a period. Provided that they come and go, and your doctor and gynecologist (with confirmation by an ultrasound) consider the lump or lumps to be innocent, the following basic recommendations can be beneficial.

RECOMMENDATIONS

- *See the section on "General Care and Self-examination."*
- *Vitamin B_6—(100mg with breakfast), zinc (30mg before bed), Evening Primrose Oil (1g with each meal), and vitamin E (400iu) twice a day can all be utilized until the lump or lumps diminish.*
- *Avoid coffee and caffeine in general—they cause breast lumps.*
- *Reduce dietary fat if the fibroadenomas are sensitive, or preferably before they are due to become so if there is a cyclical pattern.*
- *One teaspoonful of ginger, dong quai, licorice root, and four teaspoonfuls of Pau d'Arco (all readily available in healthfood stores) made up in a 16 ounce of water, simmered for 20min and a cupful drunk when cool is a worthwhile concoction.*
- *The homeopathic remedies Bryonia, Phytolacca, Silica, and Calcarea carbonica should all be reviewed.*

PAINFUL BREASTS (MASTODYNIA)

Painful breasts are not uncommon, leading up to a period. All the advice given in the section on mastitis can be utilized.

RECOMMENDATIONS

- *See* **Mastitis**.
- *Soak in a hot bath.*
- *If you are taking any hormonal replacements such as the pill or HRT, consider this to be relevant if not the cause.*

NIPPLE PROBLEMS

Nipples can become painful, sore, and cracked for reasons of friction, infection, trauma, and skin disorders such as eczema and psoriasis. Breastfeeding is notorious, and special attention should be paid to the nipples during this period.

RECOMMENDATIONS

- *If breastfeeding is painful, express the milk and feed the child from a formulary milk bottle with a suitable nipple. Sprinkle cornflower or slippery elm onto the nipples prior to breastfeeding if the pain is not so severe so as to stop the process. Use nipple shields until the problem has resolved, but ensure that the baby latches on well. Do not hesitate to seek advice from your nurse-midwife when altering breastfeeding habits.*
- *Avoid bras and tight clothing.*
- *Spend as much time as possible with the breasts exposed to the air, and dry them thoroughly after washing.*
- *Calendula-containing creams or the tincture*

(5 drops to an eggcupful of water) are relieving and curative.

- *Burning and itching nipples can be treated by Arsenicum album or Sulfur, potency 6, four pills every 2hr. Cracks, fissures, and ulcerations require selection from your homeopathic manual, taking into consideration the remedies Arnica, Croton tiglium, and Graphites. Generalized soreness can be relieved by Chamomilla, Conium Maculatum, and Phytolacca.*

BREATHLESSNESS—*see* Shortness of breath

BRONCHITIS

Bronchitis is inflammation of the bronchial tree (the tubes to the lungs). It can be acute (short term) or chronic (long term).

Acute bronchitis

Often created by viral, or bacterial infections, acute bronchitis can be associated with colds and flu. The symptoms are irritation, with cough and often pain. The bronchitis may be dry or productive and, as a rule of thumb, if the sputum is clear the problem is viral, and if it is colored, it is bacterial or fungal. Please note that this is not always the case.

LUNGS—Bronchitis

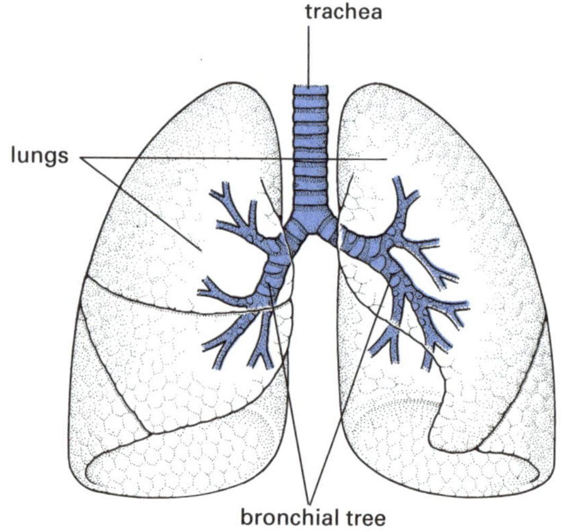

RECOMMENDATIONS

- *Beta-carotene, 2mg per foot of height in divided doses with three meals per day.*
- *Vitamin C, 2g with each meal.*
- *Zinc, 15mg at night.*
- *Consult a homeopathic manual for the best remedies concurring with your symptoms.*
- *With persistence of symptoms over a week, symptoms that disrupt sleep or your lifestyle, and any sign of blood in the product, please go to see your complementary practitioner.*
- *Avoid the use of antibiotics unless a sputum culture is carried out. This is because many bronchitis attacks are viral, and antibiotics may make the situation worse.*
- *Herbal drinks or steam inhalations with the essential oils of the following can be very beneficial: hyssop, mullein, thyme, squill, and especially lobelia. Seven drops of any of these in water may be drunk and can be most relieving. Make sure first that the product is suitable for internal use.*
- *Acupuncture can be instantly relieving.*

Chronic bronchitis

Chronic bronchitis is usually associated with persisting lung infections, often found in smokers or people subjected to industrial airborne pollutants such as asbestos. Here the inflammation has become deep-seated, and usually, bacterial infection abounds. The true definition of chronic bronchitis is a productive cough lasting for more than three months.

RECOMMENDATIONS

- *All the aspects of treatment in acute bronchitis can be utilized.*
- *In addition, learn a breathing technique, and consider regular treatment from a physiotherapist for air-passage clearing, and a Shiatsu practitioner for chest-opening bodywork.*

- *The practice of yoga and Qi Gong is very rewarding.*
- *See* **Breathing**.
- *Homeopathic and herbal treatments must be based on your constitution, and best selected by specialists in that area.*

CARDIOMYOPATHY

This is the medical term for a pathological problem with the cardiac muscle. It is a specialist diagnosis.

RECOMMENDATION

- *There is no self-help for this condition, and consultation with a complementary medical therapist will help you find the better treatment courses using homeopathy, herbal medicine, diet, and exercise.*

CHOKING

Choking occurs if an inhaled object or food travels down the trachea (windpipe).

RECOMMENDATIONS

- *Try to remove the obstruction with your fingers. If you cannot reach it, move to the next step.*
- *If by yourself, punch yourself one inch below your sternum (chestbone). This will be painful, but will throw the diaphragm into spasm, which in turn causes a strong exhalation of air that may force the obstruction out. If somebody is with you, indicate the need for a slap between the shoulderblades hard, three or four times.*
- *If the above procedures do not work, try the Heimlich maneuver.*

Heimlich maneuver

Move behind the person and interlock your fingers. Place your encircled arms over the head and shoulders until the knuckles are facing towards the person, about one inch below the sternum (chestbone). Pull inwards and upwards sharply, three or four times. This will cause the diaphragm to spasm, and force the obstruction out of the airway.

Heimlich maneuver

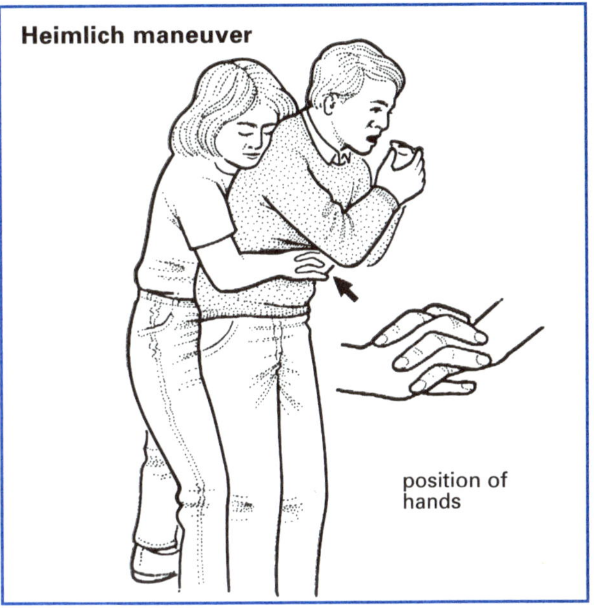

Do not practice this technique on those not choking. If the patient has lost consciousness at any point, then once the obstruction is removed, put into the recovery position and initiate artificial respiration if breathing or the heart has stopped.

Self-Heimlich maneuver

Move to the corner of a table. Swiftly place

Self-Heimlich maneuver

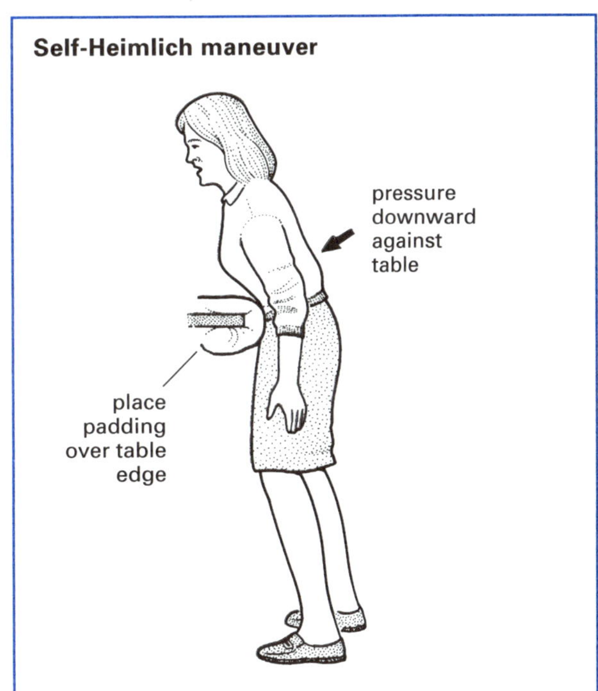

something soft and thick (such as your sweater or sweatshirt) over the corner. Lower yourself to a suitable height, placing the corner one inch below the diaphragm, and lean forward heavily. Repeat this three or four times, using enough force to expel the air in the lungs swiftly.

Do not employ this technique if somebody else is around to perform the above procedure.

EMERGENCY TRACHEOTOMY

A tracheotomy is the formation of an opening into the trachea generally performed under medical supervision when obstruction to breathing has occurred because of trauma to the trachea or mouth above the level of the Adam's apple. In an emergency situation where medical help is not available and an individual is not breathing because of obstruction, it may be necessary to undergo the following emergency procedures.

This technique should only be employed in exceptional circumstances—after other options, such as the Heimlich maneuver, have failed, and if medical personnel are not present. The individual must be completely unable to breath as shown by no movement of the chest, blueness around the lips or cardiac arrest.

Ensure that someone has called the ambulance or emergency service.

- Obtain a tube, such as the outer casing of a pen, and a sharp instrument.
- Lie the patient flat on the floor, and extend the neck by tipping the chin backwards.
- Locate the Adam's apple; below the prominent notch there will be a noticeable dip, approximately half-an-inch wide in an adult.
- While applying adequate pressure, insert the sharp object through this cricothyroid membrane horizontally and, once through the thickened membrane and into the trachea, turn the object vertically.
- There may be a surprising amount of blood.
- As swiftly as possible, insert the tube in the gap either side of the sharp object and, when in place, remove the sharp object.
- Bubbling should be heard as air enters the lungs through the tube and also through the inevitable blood in the trachea.
- If this is not heard, ensure that respiration is taking place and commence artificial respiration, using the tube instead of the mouth.
- Attempt to stem any bleeding with gentle pressure.
- Clean the area as well as possible and tape the tube into place.
- Breathe into the tube if artificial respiration is needed.
- Transport the individual to a medical center as soon as possible.

RECOMMENDATIONS

- *Do not perform a tracheotomy unless it is absolutely essential, and this should be based*

Emergency Tracheotomy

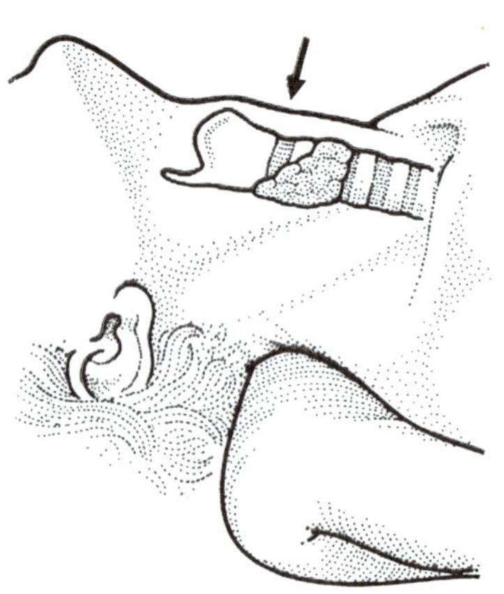

In an emergency tracheotomy, as described in the recommendations above, a tube is inserted into the trachea to allow breathing.
This procedure should only be carried out when absolutely essential.

on the fact that there is no respiration despite attempts at mouth-to-mouth resuscitation.

- *Do not perform a tracheotomy unless you are certain that medical intervention is not forthcoming.*

THE HEART

The heart is, from an orthodox point of view, a four-chambered muscle that pumps the blood around the system. Despite every author and poet being aware that a broken heart is an inevitability for most of us at some time in our life, no credibility is given to the emotional aspects that surround it.

Eastern philosophies describe heart energy as both a distributor and a seat of emotion, particularly of love and understanding. Blood nourishes all parts of the body, providing nutrients and oxygen which are the material manifestations of the "energy" that the Eastern philosophies have spoken about for 5,000 years. Once again, it is interesting to see how modern science is slowly but surely reaching the same conclusions that have been around for millennia.

Heart attack

A heart attack is the lay person's term for a pathological cessation of the normal function. If the heart stops beating, the blood (life force?) can no longer circulate, and death will ensue within two minutes due to a deprivation of oxygen to the brain. The heart will stop for only a few reasons:

- a fault in the electrical conduction system, the causes of which are emotional shock, electrical shock, certain drugs, and diseases. There is little that can be done to prevent the sudden shocks, but a close look at drug use and cardiac disease may prevent the situation.
- disease of the heart muscle. This is unusual, but can be brought on by an excess of alcohol or by bacterial/viral infections affecting the heart valves in particular, but also the muscles. There is an overlap with oxygen deprivation (*see* below) since disease of the blood vessels (atheroma) will limit bloodflow.
- a lack of oxygen to the heart muscle cells. Arterial occlusion can build up over many years or, less commonly, be caused by a clot forming in the coronary vessels. These are the most common causes of heart attacks. Spasm of the coronary arteries may also cause a lack of oxygen to reach the heart muscle, and the reasons for this range from shock to toxins. If a coronary artery becomes blocked by a clot, it is known as a coronary thrombosis. If an area of the heart is deprived of oxygen for more than a few seconds, the cells will die off, and that area is said to have infarcted. The terms coronary thrombosis and myocardial infarction are often used synonymously with heart attack, but may only reflect a couple of the causes.

Rarely are heart attacks symptomless. The stories that we hear of an individual in the prime of life suddenly dropping on the tennis court are unusual. A heart attack is usually preempted by a severe gripping pain in the chest, often radiating to the neck and down the left arm. Discomfort through to the back and down the right arm is less common. Dizziness and nausea are frequent, and all of these symptoms are associated with a shortness of breath. Many other reasons for chest and upper abdominal pain may mimic mild heart attacks, and an interesting differentiating point is the marked fear that is most frequently mentioned by those who have had heart attacks. The orthodox world offers no explanation, but if one assumes that the center of emotion sits in the heart, then perhaps the Eastern philosophies do explain the presence of fear with a heart attack.

RECOMMENDATIONS

- *Without emergency medical intervention, survival from a major heart attack is unlikely. Minor heart attacks have a better prognosis, but are dire warnings for a probably imminent major attack. Seek medical advice immediately.*

HEART—External View

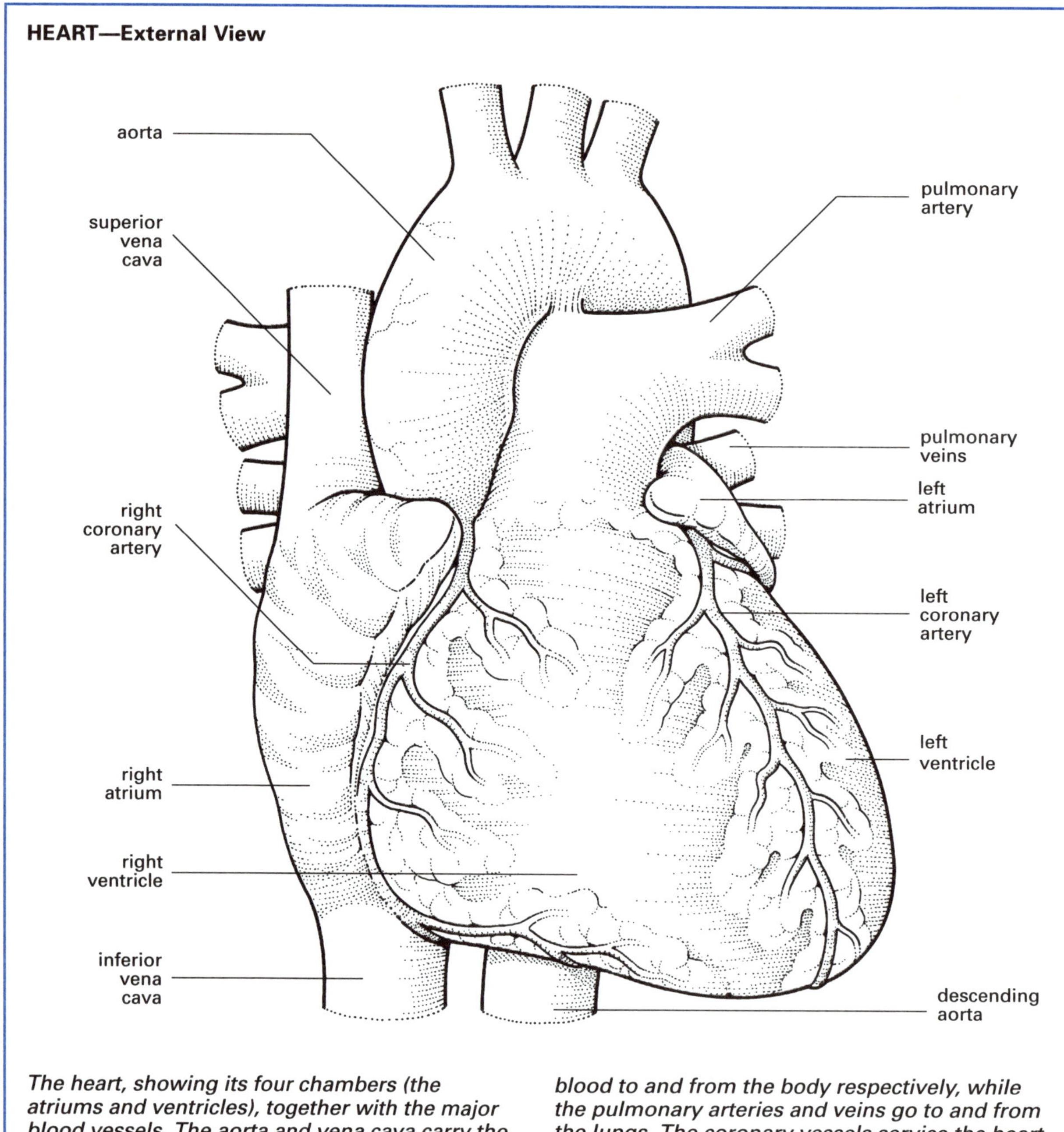

The heart, showing its four chambers (the atriums and ventricles), together with the major blood vessels. The aorta and vena cava carry the blood to and from the body respectively, while the pulmonary arteries and veins go to and from the lungs. The coronary vessels service the heart.

- *Once orthodox medical care has been obtained or the individual is on the way to the hospital, give the homeopathic remedy Aconite, potency 30 or lower, every 15min.*
- *See* **Cardiac arrest**.

I think it is imperative that we are all educated in emergency resuscitation, and I believe this should be part of all school curricula. Sadly, it is not, and therefore I hope the description in this book on emergency resuscitation and cardiopulmonary resuscitation (CPR) will be ample in providing a basic description. I would recommend that everyone, especially parents, spend some time on a first-aid course, or at the very least practice this technique on a large teddy bear! Do not practice emergency resuscitation on a well person.

Recognizing a cardiac arrest

The individual may collapse suddenly or collapse after initial mild or severe complaints of chest pain, shortness of breath, or total inability to breathe, or pains into the neck or down the arm.

Resuscitation concerns ABC (Airways, Breathing, Circulation):

A—Check that there is no visible obstruction in the mouth or the throat.
B—Watch the chest for no more than 10 seconds to see if there is any movement. You may also listen to the mouth and nose for any air-passage sounds.
C—Place three fingers in the space between the Adam's apple and the strap muscle of the neck (the sternocleidomastoid). Move the fingers around a little bit while applying moderate, but not strong, pressure to see if you can feel any pulsation in the carotid artery.

You may then proceed to the following steps.

RECOMMENDATIONS

- *Send somebody for medical assistance, but do not go yourself if you are alone. Hopefully, someone will turn up. The delay you may create by going for help may cost the individual's life.*
- *Follow clearly the instructions to establish whether emergency resuscitation is required.*
- *Follow the instructions for CPR in chapter 4.*
- *Once the patient has been resuscitated, you may give Aconite 6, four pills under the tongue, but nothing else. (A physician may well administer an injection of an anticlotting compound called streptokinase, or give oral aspirin.)*

Heart failure

There are two functional sides to the heart: the right side collects blood that has been around the body prior to pumping it into the lungs, and the left side receives the oxygenated blood prior to pumping it through the aorta to the rest of the body.

The term "heart failure" means just that. If severe, it may be life-threatening but, if mild, symptoms occur depending on which side of the heart is failing. Right-sided failure will lead to a backup of blood in the venous system, leading to water retention, and—most commonly—edema in the legs. Left-sided failure will not allow oxygen to reach the part of the body and this, in combination with the lungs not being able to empty, will cause shortness of breath (dyspnea), lethargy, and tiredness. Persistent, left-sided failure will eventually lead to right-sided congestion, and a failing on that side as well.

Heart failure is a consequence of heart-muscle disease, heart attacks, infections, pollution, deficiencies, and certain drugs. High blood pressure, heart-valve disease, and congenital defects, such as "hole-in-the-heart" can all cause heart failure.

RECOMMENDATIONS

- *Symptoms suggestive of heart failure need to be reviewed by a physician and a cardiac specialist.*
- *Treatment for heart failure should be under the care of an experienced complementary medical practitioner.*
- *Undergo blood tests to isolate deficiencies, particularly in iron and its carrier-protein ferritin, calcium, magnesium, and potassium. Also, check for environmental pollutants through blood and bioresonance techniques.*
- *Discuss with your healthcare provider the use of herbal treatments such as Crategus, and other herbal mixtures. Homeopathic remedies such as Digitalis, Cactus, and Aurum metallicum are among those that have a strong cardiac*

influence. Selection must be accurate to be effective, and a homeopath should be consulted.

- *Avoid straining the heart, but ensure that correct exercise programs are undertaken. Yoga, which pays special attention to the concept of a heart chakra, is essential.*
- *Correct diet must be low salt, low alcohol, and include no caffeine.*
- *Spend time with a meditation teacher or religious advisor to establish the underlying causes of emotional blocks. Suppressed emotion and rage are two underlying factors for the heart to fail.*

HEART—Conduction System

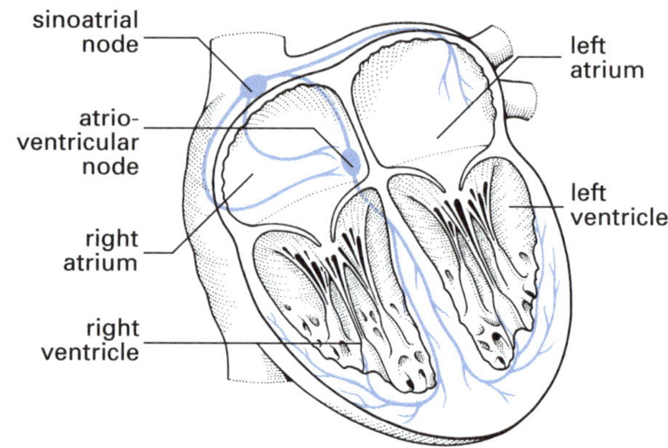

The electrical conduction system of the heart.

Heartbeat—irregular or blocked (arrhythmia)

Arrhythmia is the medical term for an irregular heartbeat. The heartbeat is generally not felt, but at times of stress, whether physical from exercise or mental from anxiety, the tension in the diaphragm and chest muscles, and the increased frequency and strength of the heart itself, can lead to the beat becoming noticeable. "Irregularity" can be noted on inspiration when the heart rate slows, and on expiration, when it may speed up. This is a physiological (normal) variation, and not considered an arrhythmia.

Arrhythmias can take the form of increased beats, decreased rate or missed beats. Please learn how to take a pulse. Place your middle and index finger on your wrist below the creases of the wrist on the side of the thumb. Apply gentle pressure, and you will feel the radial pulse. This should be beating at a rate of 60–75 beats per minute, although a rate of 50 is acceptable in very fit athletes, and up to 85 if anxious or having mildly exercised. A rate outside this range should be considered too slow (bradycardic) or too fast (tachycardic).

The heart has a comparatively simple electrical system that initiates and controls the beating. A small section of tissue known as the sinoatrial node builds up and releases a charge at around 70 impulses per minute. This spreads through electrical conducting tissues known as Purkinje fibers, which travel to the atrioventricular node before distributing to all of the heart muscles. This atrioventricular node also has an intrinsic beat of around 40 impulses per minute, and acts as a fail-safe device should the sinoatrial node fail. The autonomic (uncontrolled) nervous system sends impulses through the vagus nerve from the brain, controlling the heart rate acccording to our oxygen demand, in other words whether we are at rest or exercising.

Any interference with this electrical system will cause an irregularity in the beat. Anxiety and fear will stimulate a faster rate by blocking the suppressive action of the vagus nerve. Hormones or other chemicals such as drugs can have a direct affect on the sinoatrial node. Trauma, such as an electrical shock and disease processes including myocardial infarction, can lead to interruption or disturbance of the electrical system.

If overstimulation occurs, then palpitations and a fast heartbeat can be registered or, alternatively, if the action of the interference is suppressive, then a slower beat or a heart block may occur. There are many types of heart block, depending on whether the individual is simply missing one beat every five, for example, or depending on which fibers are blocked. One may have right- or left-heart fiber bundle-branch block, which are simply medical terms to indicate the area of obstruction.

Symptoms of heart block are varied. Some may not be noticed unless a routine (electrocardiogram) is performed, whereas others are severe enough to cause heart failure or even a heart attack.

RECOMMENDATIONS

- *Orthodox medical investigation is essential, and avoidance of any obvious causes a must.*
- *Complementary treatment must only be initiated by an experienced complementary practitioner, because many herbal treatments prescribed in the wrong way may be dangerous.*
- *Diet is important, and the restriction of alcohol, caffeine, and other neuro-affecting substances are all very important.*
- *Yoga is essential because it works on the heart muscles from an aerobic point of view, and also because of its effect on any heart-chakra weakness or excess. It is best to have an exercise program set by a cardiologist if more-aggressive exercise is desired.*
- *Any heart problem is frightening. Talk about your fears with your doctor.*

Tachycardia

Tachycardia is excessive beating of the heart at a rate above that expected for the level of activity. Exercise may raise the heart rate to above 200 beats per minute, but it should lower swiftly. If it does not, then a tachycardic state is said to exist (*see* the above section on **Heartbeat—irregular**).

Palpitations

Palpitations are the experience of feeling the heart beating in the chest. There are a variety of sensations, some of which are physiological and not to be worried about. Heavy exercise can induce a fast heart rate (tachycardia), which is felt because of tension in the diaphragm and chest-wall muscles. Palpitations must be considered pathological if the sensation is one of an irregular nature. The heart should beat rhythmically at varying speeds, depending on the level of oxygen requirement, but an irregular heartbeat is inevitably pathological. This does not mean that it is dangerous because several conditions, such as atrial fibrillation (*see* **Fibrillation**), can create an irregular heartbeat that may be recognized as a palpitation without it being life-threatening.

The rate of the heart is controlled by nerve tissues within the heart, which are in turn controlled by two nerve centers known as the sinoatrial and the atrioventricular nodes.

Further control is exerted by the autonomic (involuntary) nervous system, through the sympathetic (speeds up) and parasympathetic (slows down) nervous system. The sinoatrial node sends out impulses that cause the heart muscles to contract at a rate of approximately 70 beats per minute. Should this node fail for any reason, the atrioventricular node will cause the heart to continue to beat, but at a slower rate. Any disease or traumatic condition that affects the nodes or conducting system, the central nervous system or the hormones that have an effect on nervous tissue, such as adrenaline and thyroxine, can create an irregular beat. Thyroxine, in particular, can trigger atrial fibrillation, producing an irregular palpitation.

Diseases of the heart muscles, often created by a lack of oxygen following a heart attack or by the buildup of atheroma, can cause areas of heart muscle to release their own impulses, triggering contraction of the whole heart.

The autonomic nervous system can be affected by anxiety, phobias, and depression, all of which can create a palpitation, either by directly interfering with the heart rate or by creating tension within the thorax (chest). The heart and nervous system are sensitive to toxins, and a variety of drugs, such as caffeine, nicotine from cigarettes, amphetamines, cocaine, and other drugs of abuse may trigger palpitations. Thyroxine replacement and other doctor-prescribed medication may also have an effect. Hypertension (high blood pressure) may lead to palpitations because of an increased heart-muscle size or the need for the heart to beat with more strength to get the blood past obstructive blood vessels.

The actual sensation of a palpitation is created by tension within the chest, therefore any levels of anxiety or nervousness may make an individual aware of the heartbeat.

As with any heart problem, according to Eastern philosophies the difficulty is not with the heart itself but with the energy to the heart. Heart energy reflects fear and emotions usually associated with relationships, and these aspects must be addressed for any other treatments to be effective and permanent.

RECOMMENDATIONS

- *Any sensation of an irregular heartbeat that is not associated with exercise or a sudden shock, and palpitations that are persistent, must be seen by a doctor.*
- *If a palpitation occurs that is irregular in nature or is associated with shortness of breath or chest pain, this must be treated as an emergency. On the way to hospital, apply gentle pressure with two fingers just to the side of the Adam's apple where the pulse in the carotid artery can be felt. There are two nerve centers either side of the Adam's apple, which, if stimulated, can slow down the heart. This technique should not be employed if the palpitation is noted to be slow.*
- *Aconite 6 should be taken every 5min until medical attention is received.*
- *An ECG will trace the electrical system's effects on the heart and, occasionally, if the palpitations are sporadic throughout the day, a Holter monitor may be employed. This measures the electrical system throughout a 24-hr period.*
- *Try to isolate any causative factor such as a food, drink, or drug that may create palpitations. Food-allergy testing may be required.*
- *If no reason for palpitation is found, consult a complementary medical practitioner with experience in pulse, tongue, or other diagnostic techniques.*
- *Palpitations may be created by conscious or subconscious anxiety, and a meditation or relaxation technique would be preferable. Counseling may be required.*
- *For palpitations that are irregular, see* **Heartbeat —irregular**.
- *The homeopathic remedies Crategus, Digoxin, and the snake poisons Naja or Lachesis may be reviewed. Any heart problem should be dealt with by professionals, and a homeopathic opinion is best sought.*
- *Self-prescribed herbal treatments are best avoided, but in the hands of an expert herbal treatments may be used with comparative safety.*
- *Chinese or Tibetan herbal medicine may be associated with acupuncture. Masters in the art may actually insert an acupuncture needle that will touch the heart. Be very wary!*
- *Cardiac drugs or other medication, depending upon the cause, are generally effective and potentially life-saving. These should not be ignored or avoided if prescribed.*
- *Rarely, cardioversion using electrical shock may be required, or a pacemaker may need to be fitted. The latter is a small, electrical device that instructs the heart and nervous system to beat at a set rate. Surgery is infrequently required for palpitations.*

Heart transplant

This life-saving interventional surgery is one of the major successful advances in modern medicine. There is, obviously, no alternative treatment, but *see* **Atheroma** and **Cholesterol** to avoid congesting the new heart's blood vessels. There are causes other than coronary thrombosis that lead to the requirement of a heart transplant, and again, prevention is the best cure.

RECOMMENDATIONS

- *See* **Atheroma** *and* **Cholesterol**.
- *See* **Operations and surgery**.

LUNG DISEASE

Pulmonary edema

Pulmonary edema is a medical term describing buildup of fluid in the lung tissues caused by a back pressure from a failing left side of the heart. Fluid is pushed out of the blood vessels, causing the lungs to become like a sponge, thus inhibiting breathing. The symptoms are breathlessness and a cough, which initially may be dry and will produce a frothy, pink sputum. Valvular disease and heart attacks are the most-common causes.

RECOMMENDATIONS

- *Any sudden onset of shortness of breath must be reviewed by a physician.*
- *See the relevant section in this book with regard to the treatment of the underlying cause.*
- *A sudden onset may be helped by Aconite 6 or*

HEART and LUNGS—Cardio Pulmonary System

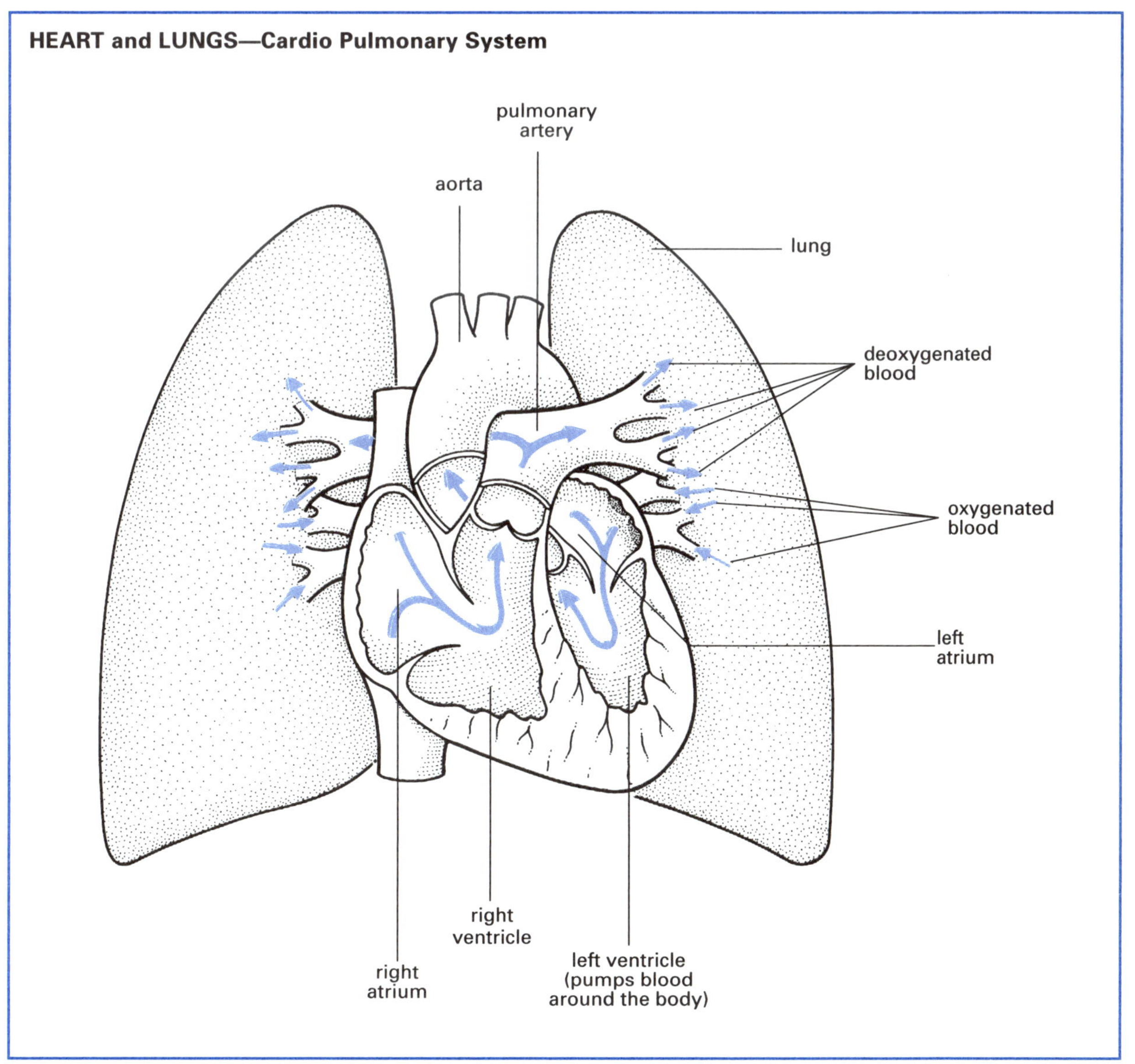

Arsenicum album 6 homeopathically while medical attention is sought.

- *Utilize a breathing and relaxation technique if one is practiced normally.*

- *Specialized tests are necessary to recognize this condition.*
- *Treatment should be dependent on the symptoms (see* **Heart failure** *and* **Bronchitis***).*

Pulmonary hypertension

Pulmonary hypertension is the term used to describe an increase in pressure in the blood vessels of the lung. The right side of the heart pumps blood into the lungs which, once oxygenated, will flow into the left side of the heart to be pumped out through the body.

Any condition that diminishes oxygenation of the blood will encourage the body to send out impulses to the right side of the heart to make it beat faster and harder. This increased flow of blood to the lungs raises the pressure. Conditions that do this are diseases causing anemia, diseases affecting the lung tissue (such as pneumonia, bronchitis, and emphysema) and valve disease, whereby the left-sided valves become stiffened (stenosis) causing a back pressure.

If pulmonary hypertension continues, the blood vessels thicken, the work done by the heart becomes too great, and heart failure sets in. This leads to a failure of oxygenation and bloodflow, leading to edema (water retention in the tissues, especially in the legs), shortness of breath, a blue tinge around the lips, and general malaise and weakness.

Living at a high altitude where oxygen supply may be diminished will naturally create an increase in the blood pressure within the lungs, but rarely does this cause a problem. High-altitude living is not necessarily the best advice for those with lung conditions, contrary to popular belief.

RECOMMENDATIONS

- *Pulmonary hypertension is only diagnosed by specialists in respiratory medicine, although any of the aforementioned symptoms must raise suspicions in an individual who should then seek advice.*

SHORTNESS OF BREATH

Shortness of breath can occur for four reasons.

The lungs

Any disease process that damages the lungs or the blood supply (to and from) will lead to shortness of breath. Obstruction of the upper airway through trauma, asthma, bronchitis, pneumonia, emphysema, or lung collapse (pneumothorax) are the most-common causes of lung-induced shortness of breath.

The heart

Any failure of the heart will lead to poor blood supply and decreased oxygenation, or a buildup of fluid in the lung tissue inhibiting gaseous exchange.

Oxygen demand

Failure to meet increased oxygen demand, exercise, or any increase in adrenaline created by anxiety or fear will increase the body cells' demand for oxygen, which may not be met without increasing the respiratory rate. Very often in moments of concentration, we forget to breathe (a common occurrence if running upstairs), thereby leading to the recognition for a need to breathe quicker. Deficiencies that create anemia also mean that the cells do not get the oxygen they require, and this too is recognized by a demand for an increased respiratory rate.

Failure of the respiratory nerves and muscles

Stroke and brain injuries, or infections such as meningitis and encephalitis, may affect the respiratory center and inhibit the autonomic (uncontrolled) breathing response. Certain metabolic disorders such as kidney failure may alter the levels of electrolytes in the bloodstream, which in turn alter the brain's recognition of oxygen requirement. Muscular or neuromuscular conditions, such as advanced polio or motorneurone disease, may affect the muscles of respiration, thereby making breathing difficult.

RECOMMENDATIONS

- *Isolate the underlying cause of the shortness of breath, and treat appropriately.*
- *See* **Breathing**.

THE DIGESTIVE SYSTEM

ACID REFLUX (HEARTBURN)

Acid reflux is caused by a weakness in the musculature at the lower end of the food pipe (esophagus) and in the stomach being weak. There is actually no valve *per se*, as there is for example in the bladder or at the other end of the stomach before the duodenum. The muscles of the esophagus act as a partial valve. If the acid in the stomach travels up the esophagus, it is due to either a hiatus hernia (*see* **Hiatus hernia**), an over-filling of the stomach, or intra-abdominal fat putting pressure on the stomach contents.

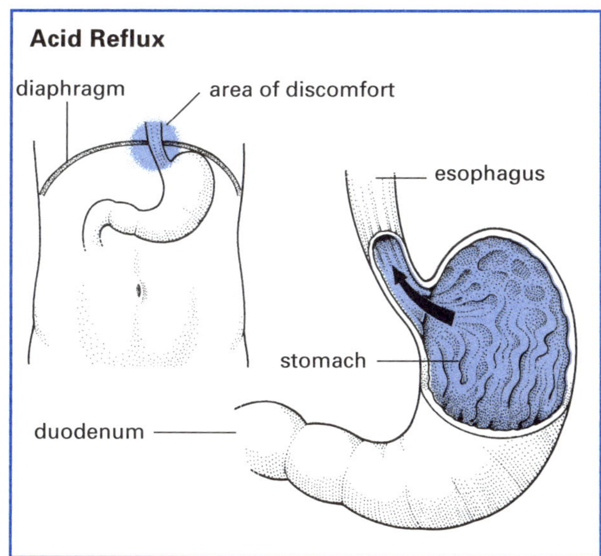

Acid reflux occurs when acid from the stomach travels up the esophagus. The resulting burning sensation is known as heartburn.

The symptoms are usually a burning sensation or, less commonly, a tightness felt at the top of the abdomen or behind the sternum. The burning can extend into the throat.

RECOMMENDATIONS

- *See* **Hiatus hernia**.
- *Consult your doctor if the symptoms persist.*
- *The occasional use of antacids is not unwarranted.*
- *The homeopathic remedies Nux vomica, Carbo vegetalis, Lycopodium, and Arsenicum album should be reviewed in your homeopathic manual.*
- *Milk may give immediate relief, but it stimulates acid production, and can worsen the condition if taken persistently.*

BELCHING

Belching or burping is the release of gas from the stomach through the mouth. There is generally an air bubble floating at the top of the stomach contents, kept in by the weak valve at the base of the esophagus (food pipe), and the tightness created by the diaphragm where the esophagus passes through it. It is perfectly normal to belch, and only needs to be taken as a pathological problem if it is excessive or foul smelling. Eighty-five percent of air in the gut is swallowed, and the other 15 percent is created by bacteria or the release of gas from food fermentation.

RECOMMENDATIONS

- *Try not to talk while you are eating or, more accurately, prior to swallowing.*
- *Cut back on foods that contain air, such as leavened bread, fizzy drinks, and pulses.*
- *If the belching is foul-smelling, see* **Bad breath**.
- *Diaphragmatic tension can squeeze the air bubble at the top of the stomach, so excessive stress can cause belching.*

- *Very rarely, an irritation in the stomach lining can create a sensation of needing to belch.*
- *Belching can also be a habit, which may require hypnotherapy or analysis to resolve.*

BOWEL POLYPS

A polyp is a smooth, round, or oval mass that projects from the bowel membrane. These may be broad-based, but are generally on a stalk. There is a genetic trait in some cases, and then this condition is known as familial polyposis coli when numerous polyps are found throughout the bowel. There is an inevitable change in polyposis coli from a benign to a malignant polyp in this condition, and treatment is currently considered to be a total colectomy (removal of the colon). Most polyps in the bowel are not dangerous except in this condition. Found in the colon on investigations such as colonoscopy or barium enemas, polyps are often removed because of a risk of malignant change.

Investigation is usually initiated because of blood or mucus found in the stool or a change in bowel habit. Polyps may be found quite coincidentally, or may be the cause of these symptoms. It is rare, but they may enlarge to a point that obstructs the bowel, creating symptoms of bloating, constipation, and painful distension.

Bowel polyps are considered by the holistic world to be created through poor diet and a tendency to a retentive body type, which holds toxins in the system and encourages irritation of cells, which then proliferate.

RECOMMENDATIONS

- *Any change in bowel habit or the presence of blood or mucus should be investigated by a doctor and a specialist if necessary.*
- *A polyp is best removed because of its potential for change into a bowel cancer.*
- *A polyp is a warning of lifestyle and diet faults. Increase fiber and water intake and reduce smoking and refined foods.*
- *Homeopathic and herbal treatments may be considered, and attempts to remove the polyps without surgery are possible, but they require expert treatment from a homeopathic practitioner for constitutional prescribing and from an experienced herbalist.*
- *Polyps are generally an indication of a retentive tendency, and psychological and spiritual changes to encourage a more outgoing personality and expansive spiritual belief must be encouraged.*
- *Pre- and postoperative care should be followed (see* **Operations and surgery***).*

CANDIDIASIS

There are shelves of libraries full of books containing evidence of the ill effects of *Candida*, and a myriad of treatments against this yeast. The most common form is *Candida albicans*, which lives within most of us. Fifty percent of women will house *Candida* in the vagina. *Candida* is not a particularly virulent organism, thriving only when our own immunity is low. When this occurs, however, *Candida* can be most devastating in its effects.

Orthodox medicine does not consider it to be a particularly relevant aspect of ill health. The alternative bandwagon has enjoyed portraying *Candida* as the potential cause of many and variable ailments. As always, the answer lies in a balance between the two extremes. It is important not to get drawn into the "germ theory" that the orthodox approach portrays so fully. *Candida* itself is not particularly troublesome; it is the lack of immune system response and generalized ill health within the system that makes it more aggressive.

Very often, a diagnosis of exclusion (ruling other causes out) is the only way to diagnose this condition. *Candida* in the system may not pass out through the urine or stool, and may not be found floating freely in the bloodstream via blood tests. Diagnosis is often made by:

- experienced diagnosticians
- bioresonance techniques
- exclusion of other causes

The symptoms of candidiasis are so varied that to list them would inevitably lead to missing some out. Any organ or system can be affected, either directly by the presence of *Candida* or by the toxins that *Candida* produces. Mental symptoms such as tiredness and lethargy may be produced by the poisonous effects of a small colony of *Candida* existing in the colon. More commonly, symptoms such as vaginal thrush, rashes in infants, diarrhea, and itching may result from direct infection. A persistent presence of *Candida* in the bowel may activate the immune system in such a way that it overreacts to other things, and can therefore be an indirect cause of allergies.

RECOMMENDATIONS

- *Ensure an accurate diagnosis by some form of investigation. Many alternative practitioners have jumped on the bandwagon, suggesting that Candida is the cause of all problems, and sadly often overlooking simpler and more easily treatable conditions.*
- *Swabs from the vagina, and stool and urine tests may isolate Candida. Blood tests may show antibodies to Candida. If these orthodox investigations prove negative, then consider the Humoral Pathological Laboratory Test or bioresonance—see chapter 8.*
- *In principle, Candida is not a problem to the body unless the immune system is low, and bacteria that compete with Candida for food are run down. The use of antibiotics and laxatives, which affect the normal bowel flora, will allow Candida to flourish because of greater availability of food.*
- *Candida, more than other organisms, flourishes on high levels of sugar and carbohydrates, and these foods should be reduced, if not cut out, once a diagnosis has been made.*
- *Avoid foods containing yeasts, such as bread and live cheeses. Many yeasts excrete compounds that help yeast growth.*
- *If over the age of 14 years, take 30mg of zinc each night. Below that age, discuss the matter with a complementary medical practitioner.*
- *The fluid extract of broom or berberis—one teaspoonful 20min before each meal in a glass of water—or a low iron supplement (5mg) can be taken daily.*
- *Caprylic acid (approximately 700mg) can be taken 15min before each meal, and Lactobacillus acidophilus (2 billion organisms) can be taken with the meal.*

Anti-*Candida* diets and treatments

There are many anti-*Candida* diets on the market. My experience is that they are difficult to follow, and the above recommendations often work without ripping into an individual's lifestyle and preferred dietetics.

I do *not* recommend the use of anti-*Candida* drugs such as nystatin. Like most drugs, they kill the majority of the *Candida* colony, but encourage the breeding of resistant strains, which will then multiply because nothing has been done to encourage the bowel bacteria or immune system. This gives a false sense of security, making the individual feel better for a short time, but inevitably leading to a recurrence. The recurrence will be with a much tougher strain of *Candida*, which can lead to worse symptoms or new problems.

The same can be said for colonic irrigation. While this does not confer the likelihood of resistant strains, it is often a temporary measure, and should only be used in conjunction with anti-*Candida* therapy, as recommended above.

CHOLECYSTITIS

Cholecystitis is the medical term for inflammation of the gallbladder and its main ducts. This inflammation is caused by blockage of the tube leading from the gallbladder to the duodenum, causing an increase in pressure, or directly by infection that tends to occur in association with a drainage blockage. Blocking of the bile ducts usually occurs due to small gallstones, but can occur because of more sinister conditions, including cancer of the pancreas.

The symptoms of chronic cholecystitis are a dull but persistent ache on the right side of the abdomen underneath the ribcage. This ache has acute exacerbations, which can be incredibly severe and unrelenting. Very often, these pains are brought on by eating, most commonly, fatty foods.

Acute cholecystitis (sudden and severe) may require an emergency operation to relieve the pain, so any suggestion of aches and pains in that area needs to be investigated thoroughly.

GALLBLADDER—Cholelithiasis

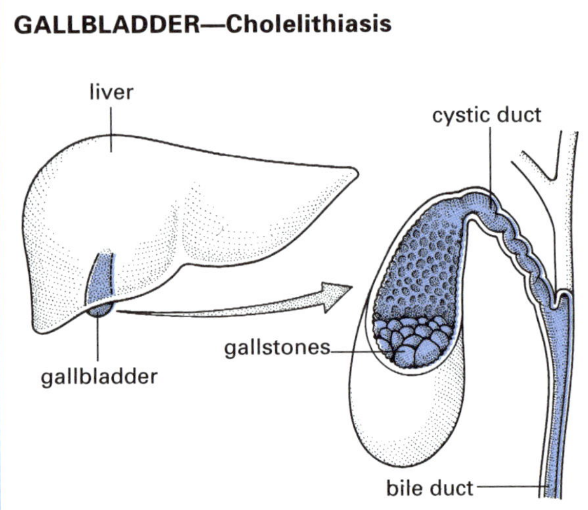

Gallstones are commonly found in the gallbladder, and cause few problems. However, they may be the source of much discomfort if they become lodged in the bile duct.

RECOMMENDATIONS

- *See your doctor who will examine you and organize blood tests and an ultrasound, at least.*
- *Having ruled out more sinister problems, see* **Cholelithiasis**.
- *The discomfort can be markedly relieved by squeezing two teaspoonfuls of lemon juice into warm water and drinking.*
- *Until the problem is diagnosed and treatment initiated, do not eat any fatty foods.*
- *Stop taking any fat-soluble vitamins such as vitamins A and E, cod-liver oil, and Evening Primrose Oil.*
- *The homeopathic remedies Berberis vulgaris 6, Chelidonium 6, and Lycopodium 6 can be taken every 10min, and may relieve the discomfort.*

CHOLELITHIASIS (GALLSTONES)

Gallstones are found in approximately 1 in 5 women in the West, and 1 in 10 men. They are generally made out of cholesterol, liver breakdown products known as bile pigments, calcium, and other minerals or, most often, a mixture of the above. They are generally asymptomatic, sitting in the gallbladder quite innocuously.

Gallstones develop when the bile (the compound made by the liver that is responsible for the breakdown of fats) becomes too concentrated. This may also occur because too much cholesterol and pigment is being made. The former indicates excess activity by the liver on dealing with toxins in the system, and the latter indicates dehydration (*see* **Cholesterol** and **Dehydration**).

Symptoms, if they occur, are caused by the stones moving from the gallbladder into the bile ducts, causing obstruction and pain as they travel down the tubes. The absence of bile in the bowel because of the obstruction will lead to poor digestion, causing abdominal distension, burping and flatulence, nausea, and potentially vomiting. The discomfort is usually in the right side of the abdomen, although it can radiate to the back, which is sometimes a tell-tale sign of gallbladder disease or gallstone obstruction. An experienced physician will be fairly accurate about the diagnosis, but firm assurance can be obtained by using ultrasound.

Prevention of gallstones is much easier than treatment. Principally, this is because a gallstone in the gallbladder is not a problem, and the larger it is, the less likely it will escape into the narrow bile-duct tube. Treatments that reduce gallstones are therefore potentially hazardous and best left in the hands of complementary medical practitioners who can support and monitor the situation. As a rule of thumb, therefore, I recommend that anyone who has a diagnosis of gallstones through a screening test (ultrasound) or who has had one attack should endeavor not to reduce their gallstones, but to prevent further gallstone growth or formation.

Those who have recurrent or frequent attacks, and who are being threatened with surgical procedures, should come under the care of an experienced complementary practitioner, who will use specific treatments to reduce gallstones, and at the same time encourage the patient to maintain a low-fat (not fat-free) diet, thereby inhibiting any aggressive contraction by the gallbladder (in response to fatty foods), which may dislodge a gallstone. It is because of the need to be monitored that I have chosen not to mention the details of specific treatments, which, if effective, may reduce the size of the gallstone and lead to the potentially serious medical condition of a blocked bile duct and cholecystits.

There is a popular gallstone treatment called the olive-oil liver flush. There are variations of this, but they all revolve around an olive-oil mix with lemon juice. Patients have proudly presented, saying that they found green stones in their stool. This is not the case. What has been produced is a complex of minerals, fats, and acid that forms within the gut. The treatment is *not* a good idea. The extra oil can cause the gallbladder to contract, and the oleic acid in olive oil may be a cause of gallstone formation.

RECOMMENDATIONS

- *See* **Cholecystitis**.
- *For recurrent, chronic, gallstone-related problems, consult an experienced complementary medical practitioner for specific therapies.*
- *Reduce the input of foods containing saturated fats, refined sugars, cholesterol, and fried foods. Animal protein should be kept to a lean minimum. Increase the intake of fiber through fruits and vegetables.*
- *Perhaps most importantly, ensure good hydration so that the bile is not encouraged to become concentrated (see* **Dehydration***).*
- *Check for food allergies (see* **Food-allergy testing***). Eggs, pork, onion, dairy produce, and caffeine are all documented as being relevant to gallstone formation.*
- *Vitamin C and vitamin E deficiencies have been noted as increasing gallstone formation: vitamin C (500mg per foot of height in divided doses) and vitamin E (50iu per foot of height in divided doses) should be taken.*
- *If an individual has had one attack or falls into the risk categories mentioned above, then the following compounds should be taken prophylactically on a daily basis per foot of height: phosphatidylcholine (100mg), choline (200mg), and L-methionine (200mg).*
- *When discussing the situation with your complementary practitioner, ensure that the following herbs are considered in the treatment: Taraxacum, Cynara, Scolymus, and Silymarin.*
- *There are pharmaceutical medications that can dissolve some types of gallstones, but this has to be discussed with your doctor, and only as a last resort because it does not deal with the underlying cause or tendency.*
- *Surgical intervention may be required and, at the time of writing, laparoscopic gallbladder removal is the favored method. This avoids major abdominal incisions and reduces the length of time an individual needs to stay in hospital. Ensure that the procedure is performed by a surgeon with experience in this area.*

- *One may be offered lithotripsy, a sound-wave procedure that shatters the gallstones. This is losing favor in some parts of the world because the small particles tend to reform into a larger number of gallstones. This would certainly be the case if the underlying causes of the predisposition, such as dehydration or overactive liver function, were not dealt with. Keep this technique at arm's length.*

CIRRHOSIS

This is the medical term given to the replacement of damaged liver tissue by scar tissue. This tissue is nonfunctional, and blocks the liver-cell ducts and the blood supply. The most popular concept for the cause of cirrhosis in the West is alcoholism, but worldwide, the most-common cause is malnutrition and hepatitis. Drugs and heart failure (causing a back pressure of blood on the liver) are also causes.

The liver is a phenomenal organ, and the body may notice very little change in its well-being until 80 percent of the liver is nonfunctional. It is this principle that is paramount in complementary medical treatment, because medicine has no method of preventing cirrhosis from spreading through the liver once it has started. Helping the healthy and unaffected cells of the liver to work at their hardest encourages both well-being and longevity.

Diagnosis of cirrhosis is made by liver biopsy, which is usually performed after your doctor has established that there are incorrect liver-function tests. These are performed after an individual presents with excessive tiredness, jaundice, digestive problems, nausea, vomiting, or a combination of any of these. Cirrhosis is not a painful condition, unless associated with inflammation of the liver, such as in hepatitis.

RECOMMENDATIONS

- *Any jaundice or suspected liver problem should be assessed by a family practitioner initially.*
- *Cessation of any liver-insulting habits, such as the use of alcohol and drugs, smoking, bad diet, and stressful living, is essential.*
- *The use of magnesium, zinc, and multitrace-mineral supplement and a vitamin-B complex is beneficial, but correct dosage is best assessed by a naturopath. The liver is the main chemical factory of the body, and too high a dose of any of the necessary compounds can be a strain on the healthy liver cells.*
- *Beta-carotene rather than vitamin A should only be used after recommendation by a naturopath.*
- *Homeopathic remedies based on the individual's constitution can be taken, but special attention should be paid to Berberis vulgaris, Natrum sulphuricum, and Lycopodium.*
- *Do not add salt to food; absolutely no alcohol, no fat from red meat and no dairy products, although fish oils and vegetable oils are essential.*
- *Remember that the liver, according to Eastern philosophies, represents indecision and irritability, and so these emotions may well be prominent after cirrhosis sets in, but are more likely to have been present to allow cirrhosis to have occurred and must, therefore, be confronted through counseling.*
- *Detoxifying regimes (see chapter 7) are most beneficial, and should be used on a monthly basis.*

CONSTIPATION

Constipation is a condition in which the bowels are evacuated at long intervals or with difficulty. The body will do this for several reasons:

- because the bowel does not contract well enough;
- because the bowel is moving more slowly to allow longer for food and water absorption;
- because the stool lacks bulk;
- because the stool is too large or hard to pass through the anus without pain.

There is no ideal number of times to evacuate the bowels. Everyone has a rhythm, and it is important to keep that stable. A change in bowel habit that persists needs to be reviewed by a doctor. Everybody will go through constipation and other bowel changes on occasions, and treatment should only be considered if the problem persists or is uncomfortable.

A lack of fiber in the foods we eat causes stool to become soft, so that when peristaltic waves in the colon try to flush the feces towards the anus, some of the stool will pass in the opposite direction. If the body is deficient, it may slow down the movement of food through the small intestine to allow more time for absorption to take place. This can appear to be constipation, simply because there is nothing to pass out. The colon (large bowel), which makes up the last four feet of the bowel, is where most of the water is absorbed from our food and drink. If we are dehydrated, and I think most of us spend our lives in a state of partial dehydration, the colon will move more slowly to allow more time for water absorption.

Because constipation may be due to body deficiencies or dehydration, and involve soft stool or hard stool, there is no single treatment that will benefit all patients. It is important to know the cause of the constipation so that correct treatment can be chosen. Problems not relieved by the following recommendations should be taken to a nutritionist or herbal-medicine practitioner. Ayurvedic and Tibetan practitioners have a very good grasp of this matter.

RECOMMENDATIONS

- *A change in bowel habit that persists must be referred to a doctor for assessment.*
- *Ensure that you are drinking 32–48 ounces of water per day away from food.*
- *Avoid dehydrating conditions, such as exercising without fluid intake, alcohol, caffeine, and an excess of spicy or sweet foods. The latter pulls water into the bowel and prevents the tissues from receiving it.*
- *Ensure that you have adequate fiber in your diet (see chapter 7).*
- *Gut bacteria are essential to the digestive process. Poor diet and the use of antibiotics, directly from pills or indirectly through eating foods containing such drugs, can alter the bowel flora and lead to constipation. Correct this with a good-quality Acidophilus (2 billion organisms with each meal) for at least one month.*
- *"Natural" laxatives are available at healthfood stores, and may be used if constipation is infrequent, but having to use a natural laxative more than three times in any month requires investigation with your complementary medical practitioner.*
- *Stool softeners and stool bulk-formers should be used only as a last resort.*
- *Do your best to avoid regular laxatives, which can have a long-term debilitating effect on the colon and its musculature. Long-term laxative abuse is treatable under the care of a nutritionist, herbalist, or homeopath.*
- *Colonic irrigations are fine on occasions, but they should not be considered as a treatment for constipation.*
- *Please establish, by reading chapter 7 or by having a consultation with a nutritionist/dietician, that your diet is satisfactory.*
- *Three finger-widths below the navel is the Sea-of-Energy acupuncture point, which if you gradually apply more pressure on it for 2min while you are lying down may be beneficial if practiced twice a day.*
- *Try six drops of rosemary oil in half a cup of olive oil, rubbed in a clockwise motion around the abdomen, twice a day.*
- *Constipation following cessation of smoking is treatable by herbalists, who will replace the nicotine effect on the bowel contraction with a healthier herb, which they will reduce over a period*

of time. You may try taking one teaspoonful of Cascara sagrada 1hr before going to bed.

- *Two apples freshly squeezed, in combination with a teaspoonful of fresh ginger juice diluted with a little water, taken three times a day before meals, can be effective.*
- *Two grams of vitamin C with each meal can act as a natural laxative, and can be used for short periods if a problem persists. Children below the age of 14 years need to take half that amount.*

DUODENAL ULCERS AND DUODENITIS

—*see* **Peptic ulcers**

DYSPEPSIA (HEARTBURN, INDIGESTION)

Dyspepsia is a medical term for disturbed digestion, but is generally used to describe a burning or acid sensation in the upper abdomen or lower chest that often radiates up the throat. Generally, dyspepsia—also known as heartburn and indigestion—is caused by inflammation in the lower part of the esophagus (reflux esophagitis), the stomach, or duodenum. All these conditions can be precursors to peptic ulcers (*see* **Peptic ulcers**).

As a rule of thumb, pain occurring after a meal is gastritis, discomfort associated with bending down or lying down is acid reflux (often associated with a hiatus hernia) or, if occurring 2–3 hours after a meal or around 2am, is duodenitis.

It is commonly assumed that the problem is caused by an excessive amount of stomach acid, although the exact opposite may also be true. A paucity of acid (hypochlorhydria) prevents food from leaving the stomach because it has not been broken down, and this persistence causes an irritation in the stomach lining. Yeast and (more recently discovered) *Helicobacter pylori* and other bacterial infection may colonize the stomach, and cause problems.

Anxiety and tiredness will lead to a tightening of the diaphragm, which may pinch the top part of the stomach and force acid up into the esophagus (*see* **Acid reflux**).

RECOMMENDATIONS

- *A persistent or severe dyspepsia should be examined by a doctor to rule out any serious condition.*
- *Recognize and remove any foods that commonly cause problems, specifically alcohol, caffeine, and refined sugars.*
- *Persisting problems may require food-allergy testing via bioresonance techniques or blood tests. Consult your preferred complementary medical practitioner.*
- *Licorice root, Aloe vera, and slippery elm are all soothing, and can be used at the maximum dose recommended on any proprietary product.*
- *Avoid mint or peppermint, despite its effectiveness, because this will render homeopathic treatment useless.*
- *Homeopathic remedies need to be chosen based on the symptoms and reference should be made to your preferred homeopathic manual, paying attention to the remedies Aragonite, Carbo vegetalis, Calcarea carbonica, and Nux vomica initially.*
- *Calcium carbonate tablets are freely available, and should be used, as long as they do not contain any aluminum. Only use half or even a quarter of a tablet at a time, because this can often be sufficient.*
- *Discuss with your holistic-health practitioner the use of hydrochloric-acid tablets, with or without pepsin (a protein enzyme), because low stomach acid may be the cause. I recommend taking a minimal dose before one meal (if any worsening of symptoms occurs, then do not consider this as a treatment). Slowly increase the frequency to before each meal, and then increase the amount over a period of two weeks. Suddenly using a large quantity of hydrochloric acid can create discomfort or worse.*

ESOPHAGEAL PROBLEMS

Esophageal achalasia

This is a condition whereby the nerves controlling the rhythmic peristalsis that allows food to travel down the esophagus are absent or diminished. This causes food to stick in the esophagus, which leads to pain.

The orthodox world has no specific cause for this isolated symptom, although it can be associated with serious neurological problems such as multiple sclerosis or motorneurone disease. Vitamin E-deficiency may be related.

The Eastern philosophies consider this to be a severe loss of energy in the throat chakra, usually caused by a block in the lower energy centers. Severe emotional stress is often associated, although it may be deeply buried and require hypnotherapy to illuminate.

In itself, the condition is unpleasant, leading to pain and halitosis (bad breath), but if not treated, the individual will lose their appetite, and malnutrition will ensue. Orthodox treatment includes investigation with barium swallows and endoscopy, often associated with special dilating techniques, cutting of the esophageal muscles at the lower end of the esophagus, or even removing part of the tube. Before this, antispasmodic drugs will be recommended, and should only be used after the alternative recommendations have failed.

RECOMMENDATIONS

- *A sudden or persistent inability to swallow or esophageal pain should be reviewed by a throat or gastric specialist.*
- *Persistent ingestion of food allergens (foods that the body does not like) may cause a mind–body reaction, leading to the esophagus refusing entry into the system. Food-allergy testing by bioresonance or blood testing might well be appropriate.*
- *Consider underlying stresses, especially anger, and if none are apparent, consider hypnotherapy to illustrate the cause and to help relax the spasm in the muscles.*
- *The homeopathic remedy Cimicifuga 6 every 15min may be of benefit in an acute case. Higher potencies may be recommended, but such conditions should be treated by a competent holistic practitioner.*
- *If surgical treatment is necessary, see* **Operations and surgery**.

Esophageal pain

Pain in the esophagus can occur simply from swallowing a solid bolus of food, such as a hard-boiled candy; the esophageal muscle then cramps, but this pain passes swiftly. If a tear or cut occurs, the pain may be persistent. Unlike tears in other parts of the body, the pain is often described as a cramp rather than a sting. This can be very severe, and may even mimic more serious problems, such as a heart attack.

A persisting pain with no obvious reason needs to be investigated, because conditions such as cancer may give rise to this discomfort. Esophageal spasm can occur through anxiety or persisting esophageal reflux (*see below*).

RECOMMENDATIONS

- *Esophageal pain without an obvious reason needs to be examined by a throat or bowel specialist, who may choose to use a scope.*
- *The homeopathic remedies Magnesia phosphoricum or Cuprum, both at potency 6, can be taken every 15min in an acute spasm.*

Esophageal reflux

The refluxing of stomach acid into the lower part of the esophagus may occur from overeating, but most frequently is associated with a hiatus hernia. For treatment of this condition, *see* **Hiatus hernia** and **Acid reflux**.

Esophageal stricture

Stricture of the oesophagus presents as pain or an

inability to swallow. A buildup of mucus, or vomiting immediately after swallowing food or drink may be an early sign. Strictures may be acute, caused by a spasm of the esophagus that is in turn often caused by swallowing something too hard, which causes a small tear in the esophageal membrane. More serious conditions of stricture occur as a result of cancer or long-term reflex esophagitis, secondary to a hiatus hernia.

RECOMMENDATIONS

- *See* **Dysphagia**.
- *Persistent or sudden discomfort must be reviewed by a throat or gastric specialist.*

FLATULENCE

Flatulence is the passage of gas (flatus) from the intestine through the anus. Individuals of all ages should pass wind between 5 and 15 times a day. There is no right or wrong concerning the amount that is passed from a health prospective. In the West, passing gas is arguably not socially acceptable. Healthwise, it is not a serious matter to withhold the passage of gas, but this often leads to abdominal aches and pains. Eighty-five percent of gas in the intestinal tract is swallowed and 15 percent is produced by bacteria. The swallowing of air is most commonly associated with eating rapidly and talking while masticating (chewing). Most food has air as part of its cellular components or structure, and chewing crushes this out. Poor chewing, therefore, allows air to pass into the stomach and thereafter into the rest of the intestine.

Bad bacteria (those that are not commensal—i.e. meant to be with us) often produce more gas and are the cause of an excess in a few percent of cases. Our natural bowel flora produce gas, and the rate at which they do so will be dependent on the contents of the colon. Higher sugar levels will increase the bacteria's metabolic rate, thereby increasing their gaseous biproduct. Bacterial gas accounts for the characteristically unpleasant smell, which will vary depending on the food eaten and its enhancement of bacterial activity. Flatulence is not a medical problem unless it is associated with bowel pain, is sociably unacceptable, too frequent, or bad smelling.

RECOMMENDATIONS

- *Eat food more slowly, chew well, and avoid talking while masticating and swallowing.*
- *Review the diet in association with the amount or odor of the flatus, and see if specific foods can be isolated as a cause of any problem. Cut down on refined sugars and excessively sweet foods.*
- *Avoid overeating or eating late at night.*
- *Yogurt-bacteria tablets such as Lactobaccillus acidophilus or Probifidus can alter the bowel flora in the colon and have a mild effect on unpleasant flatus.*
- *Review the amount of fibrous foods, and ensure that the diet is not too heavily weighted in foods that are hard to digest, such as raw vegetables.*
- *Consider the use of hydrochloric-acid tablets with a pancreatic-enzyme supplement since poor digestion may allow undigested foods to reach the bacteria in the colon, which then feast. If things improve with this treatment, consider visiting a complementary medical practitioner for a discussion on why the digestive process is lacking.*

FOOD POISONING

Food poisoning is a broad definition, little used by the medical profession. It is most commonly created by the ingestion of bacteria from the *Salmonella* group, but may also be created by other bacteria, viruses, yeast, and fungi. Symptoms may vary from mild nausea through to severe vomiting, diarrhea, and abdominal pain. The severity is often associated with the amount and type of toxins that the bacteria produce while in the bowel. Local inflammation may be caused by the bacteria affecting the walls themselves, but any form of systemic condition—such as fever or rashes—is due to these enterotoxins. Fungi, in particular, including yeasts like *Candida*, may produce chemicals known as aflatoxins that have mild or severe toxic effects, ranging from fevers to nervous collapse and paralysis. Chronic-fatigue syndrome (CFS) may often be associated with these infections.

RECOMMENDATIONS

- *Avoidance is the best treatment. Do not eat food that may have been unrefrigerated or prepared in unhygienic conditions. If you have any doubts, throw the food away.*
- *Food poisoning creates many symptoms, and reference to the various symptoms in this book, such as fever, vomiting, and diarrhea, should be reviewed.*
- *If the causative agent is known, then the homeopathic preparation at potency 30 (such as Salmonella 30, Escherichia coli 30) should be taken every 3hr.*
- *It is important to drink at least 16 ounces of water per foot of height to help flush the bowel, keep toxins diluted, and avoid dehydration.*
- *Remember to replenish normal bowel bacteria by using high doses of Acidophilus or other yogurt-bacteria supplements during and after any food poisoning.*
- *See* **Gastroenteritis,** *below.*

GASTRIC ULCERS AND EROSIONS
—*see* **Peptic ulcers** and **Dyspepsia**

GASTRITIS—*see* Dyspepsia

GASTROENTERITIS

Gastroenteritis is inflammation of the inner lining of the stomach and the intestines, which can occur at any age for a variety of reasons. Symptoms may be mild or severe, and range from abdominal aches and nausea to vomiting and diarrhea; all may be with or without fever. These "tummy upsets" can be very serious in children, the elderly, or the infirm, because associated fluid loss from vomiting and diarrhea can lead to dehydration and biochemical changes. Gastroenteritis can be caused by:

- viruses and bacteria that are ingested;
- drugs (especially antibiotics which destroy the bowel's normal flora);
- alcohol;
- excessively spicy foods;
- even a change of diet, for those particularly sensitive;
- stress, which causes an excess of acid production in the stomach and can lead to inflammation through the entire intestinal tract.

RECOMMENDATIONS

- *Any persisting abdominal complaints or symptoms that are sudden or severe must be reviewed by a physician to rule out any other cause.*
- *Ensure adequate replenishment of water and fluids with natural sugars and salts. Over-the-counter electrolyte-replacement fluids are fine, but natural alternatives include thin broths and soups, diluted fruit juices, and herbal teas.*
- *Avoid foods that are hard to digest, such as proteins, fats, and fried foods. Milk, alcohol, and caffeine should all be avoided.*
- *A hot drink made of two teaspoonfuls of camomile and one teaspoonful each of rosemary, sage, and honey in 16 ounces (500ml) of boiled hot water, a cup of which should be drunk every 15min to half an hour, is of benefit.*
- *Half a tablespoonful of fennel seeds with dried peppermint leaves and a pinch of baking soda may be relieving, but cannot be used if a homeopathic remedy is employed.*
- *Berberis fluid extract (1 teaspoonful in a cup of water) can be drunk four times per day.*

- *Homeopathic remedies are beneficial, but need to be selected based on the symptoms. Please review the sections in this book on whichever other symptoms are prominent, or refer to your preferred homeopathic manual.*
- *Yogurt-bacteria tablets (preferable to live yogurt, which may not survive the acid and alkaline environment in the intestine) may be beneficial. Take 250,000 units of any Acidophilus or derivative per foot of height three times a day.*
- *Ensure that the individual washes the hands after going to the bathroom, because transmission of the causative organism in gastroenteritis is quite common.*

HEMORRHOIDS OR PILES

A hemorrhoid, also known colloquially as a pile, is a vein or veins that become dilated, engorged, inflamed, painful, and occasionally thrombosed or clotted. Symptoms range from mild itching to severe pain or bleeding. There is a thin line where the skin of the buttocks meets the membrane of the anus, known as the anorectal line. Hemorrhoids that originate below this line are called external hemorrhoids, and those above the line are called internal hemorrhoids. Internal hemorrhoids may well extend down past the anorectal line.

A breach or weakness in the anal muscular wall is the cause of a hemorrhoid. Weakness may occur through a lack of dietary fiber, deficiencies (particularly of vitamin C, bioflavonoids, and proteins) that reduce the strength and amount of the connective tissues in the muscular walls, and through trauma from a penetration of the anus. Medical conditions that can cause hemorrhoids are a buildup of pressure from straining, constipation, and an obstructed bladder outlet. Pregnancy, obesity, and an increase in pressure in the veins from obstruction in the abdomen or an enlarged liver blocking the main vein of the body, the vena cava, are also causes. Sitting on a cold surface can cause constriction of the muscle, and straining after this may push a vein through the wall, or prolonged sitting or sitting on a warm surface may draw blood into the veins, which may then pass through weakened muscle walls. Treatment and avoiding recurrence requires consideration of all these factors.

HEMORRHOIDS—Internal and External

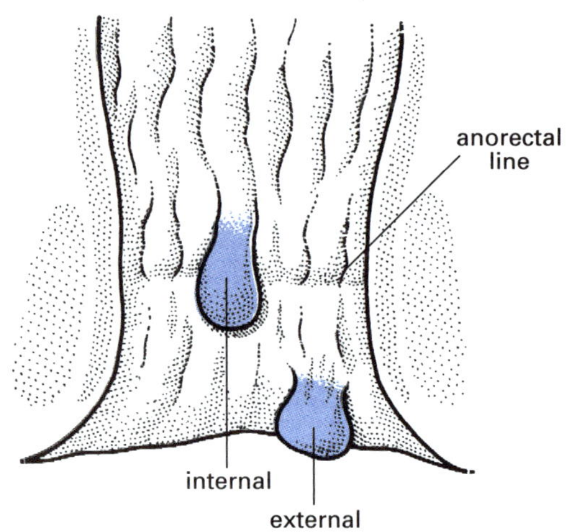

A pile may bleed gently and appear only as a smear on the toilet paper, or may bleed more aggressively and may show as bright blood in the toilet. Provided that the bleeding stops, neither is a serious condition, although a persistently heavy-bleeding pile may require surgical treatment.

RECOMMENDATIONS

- *Any bleeding from the back passage must be reviewed by a doctor, with the possibility of a referral for proctoscopy or colonoscopy because bleeding may represent colitis or even cancer.*
- *Ensure an increase in dietary fiber by eating more fresh fruit and vegetables, lightly cooked. At the time of the pile, one or two teaspoonfuls of psyllium husks twice a day, shaken vigorously with 8 fl oz of water and drunk immediately, will help prevent constipation.*

- *Ensure that 16 ounces of water per foot of height is drunk, spaced throughout the day. Avoid drinking water around meal times.*
- *Avoid caffeine and alcohol until the problem has resolved. These substances dehydrate, and therefore increase the risk of constipation and also weaken muscular walls.*
- *Core out an index-finger-size portion of raw potato and insert as a suppository before bed, five nights in a row.*
- *Peppermint oil (1 drop in 10 drops of olive oil; dilute further if stinging occurs) can be applied with a clean finger.*
- *Soak a wash cloth in witchhazel or Hamamelis-fluid extract (diluted one teaspoonful to three tablespoonfuls of boiled water), wrap it around an ice cube and apply to the anus.*
- *A cream containing Arnica or Calendula (or both) should be applied before and after each stool and before bed (before inserting the potato strip).*
- *Homeopathic remedies may be of benefit. Aesculus 6 four times a day for itching, Hamamelis 6 for bleeding with a bruise sensation, and Capsicum 6 if the sensation is of burning. Other remedies may be chosen, depending on the variety and severity of symptoms.*
- *Sitting in a bath of water at around 103 °F may offer relief.*
- *Hemorrhoids are a varicose vein; see* **Varicose veins** *for further medicinal treatments.*
- *Surgical treatment may be required, but before this takes place, see if you can find a practitioner who uses monopolar direct-current therapy, which can be applied with local anesthetic. Operative procedures may include banding, where an elastic band is placed around the base of the engorged vein, or injecting with a sclerosing fluid (a chemical irritant that produces an inflammatory reaction with subsequent scarring) that causes the vein to collapse and stick together, thereby not allowing blood into the protruding area. If either technique is not convenient or suitable, then a hemorrhoidectomy (removal of the vessel) and surgical sealing of the vein may need to be carried out (see* **Operations and surgery***).*

HEARTBURN—*see* **Dyspepsia** and **Peptic ulcers**

HEPATITIS

Hepatitis is inflammation (itis) of the liver (hepar). There are a multitude of causes of hepatitis, the most common of which is viral. Hepatitis can be, however, caused by drugs, alcohol, bacteria, tumors, heart problems, and food allergy or intolerance. Hepatitis may cause jaundice (yellowing of the skin), but does not necessarily need to do so.

Symptoms of hepatitis may be nothing more than a general ache in the upper-right abdomen, but may also include fevers, gastrointestinal symptoms such as vomiting, and an inability to eat, fatigue, and jaundice. With jaundice, dark urine and pale stools may be symptoms, along with a yellowing of the whites of the eyes.

Hepatitis A

This virus is caught by ingesting food that has been contaminated. This contamination usually comes from food containing fecal matter, often from the unhygienic, unwashed hands of people preparing food. Transmission through water is possible if people have defecated in the source of the water in question. It takes two to six weeks to cause the physical symptoms—this is termed the incubation period.

Hepatitis A in a healthy being is an uncomfortable and unpleasant illness, but rarely serious or fatal. It never becomes chronic, although it can leave the individual unable to tolerate alcohol or fats for up to one year.

Hepatitis B

Hepatitis B is transmitted through infected blood, saliva, and sexual secretions such as vaginal or seminal (sperm) fluids. This is the type that is transmitted through sexual intercourse, particularly anal intercourse, intravenous-drug use, and transfusions. The incubation period is six weeks to six months; the infection is serious, causing death in around 1 percent. In 10 percent of cases, the infected person may not destroy the virus completely; it then settles into the cells of the liver and persists in causing no or only mild problems. This medical situation is called a chronic carrier state, and leaves the individual potentially capable of infecting others and also with a 10 percent risk of developing cirrhosis over the following 30–40 years.

Hepatitis C

This is similar in its transmission to hepatitis B, although up to 40 percent of those infected can develop the chronic-carrier state. This type of hepatitis is found more commonly in patients who have had blood transfusions. The incubation period is thought to be between two weeks and five months, and some studies have suggested that acute hepatitis C may actually have a fatality rate of 10 percent.

Hepatitis D, E, and others

There are many more rare forms of viral hepatitis, probably mutated from the other three. Little is known about them, and more is being discovered regularly. From the point of view of classification, Epstein-Barr virus, more commonly associated with glandular fever, is a cause of a hepatitis similar to hepatitis A. Cytomegalovirus is another uncommon but established cause.

Vaccinations for hepatitis

Hepatitis A is treated with a gamma globulin (an artificial chemical compound based on the body's natural immunoglobulin production that attacks hepatitis A) that is often called a vaccination even though it is not.

Hepatitis B has a vaccination that is encouraged by governments and health officials to be used by those at risk, such as hospital and care-workers. Vaccinations and treatments for other types of hepatitis causing viruses are not yet established.

Investigations

Anyone suspecting that they have hepatitis should be investigated by their doctor and will be tested for raised-liver-function tests (chemicals found in the bloodstream), a variety of tests for different parts of the hepatitis-causing viruses, such as the Australian antigen in hepatitis B, and urinalysis to establish what liver functions are not being performed. Those interested may choose to have a bioresonance or humoral blood test to help establish liver-cell damage.

RECOMMENDATIONS

- *Any liver-area pains that persist, or any suggestion of yellowing of the skin or sclera (the whites of the eyes), must be taken to a general practitioner or other doctor for full evaluation. Remember that you may be transmitting and passing on a dangerous virus unwittingly.*
- *Once hepatitis has been established, consult your complementary medical practitioner, because self-help is not generally enough.*
- *See* **Vaccinations**.
- *Avoid alcohol, caffeine, saturated fats (butter, lard, and animal fats), additives, preservatives, and overeating. Remember that the liver is the chemical factory of the body, and everything you eat passes through it before reaching any other part of the body.*
- *A period of fluid fast or following the basic Detox diet in chapter 7 should be considered if the appetite is poor or vomiting is preventing ingestion (see* **Detox diet**).

- *The liver is required for the manufacture of several essential compounds, and therefore the following should be taken in doses recommended by your specialists: vitamin-B complex, vitamin C, coenzyme Q10, and all amino acids, particularly methionine, choline, and lipoic acid, (100–200mg three times a day for most adults in this case). Specific treatments should include the use of milk thistle, Cheledonium (Celandine), the Ayurvedic herb Phyllanthus amarus, and the widely available Ayurvedic formula called Liv 52.*
- *Intravenous vitamin supplementation can be of great benefit, but needs to be administered by a doctor. The liver may not be processing correctly, and direct introduction into the bloodstream of necessary nutrients can be very rewarding.*
- *Avoid strenuous exercise, lack of sleep, and undue stress. The liver breaks down adrenaline, and the more you produce, the harder the liver has to work.*
- *Those with hepatitis A should not cook for others, and should be particularly careful with their hygiene. Those with other forms of hepatitis should avoid unprotected intercourse until the incubation period is over and they are assured that they do not have a carrier status, which can only be assessed through blood tests.*
- *Constitutional homeopathic remedies with specific remedies against hepatitis are beneficial, and an eminent naturopath recommends a particular homeopathic remedy that is specially made up: two drops of the patient's first morning sputum, two drops of the first morning urine, and two drops of blood, all added to 34 drops of water and successed down to potency 6. Four drops are then given nightly.*
- *A relaxation or meditation technique must be practiced daily.*

HERNIA—Direct (hiatus) and Indirect

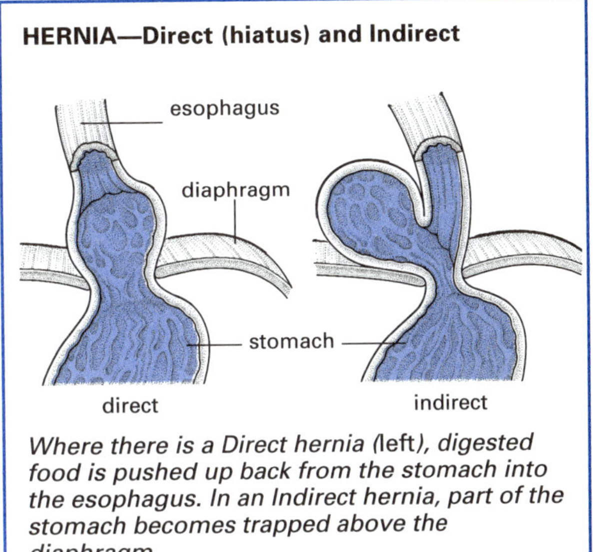

Where there is a Direct hernia (left), digested food is pushed up back from the stomach into the esophagus. In an Indirect hernia, part of the stomach becomes trapped above the diaphragm.

HIATUS HERNIA

The definition of a hernia is an abnormal protrusion of a part of an organ through the containing wall. The hiatus (a space or opening) in this case is in the diaphragm muscle, where the esophagus passes from the chest to the abdominal cavity. There are two types. In the first, the diaphragm is simply weak, and when the stomach contracts to push the digested food through into the duodenum, it refluxes back up into the esophagus (*see* **Acid reflux**). The second situation is one where the upper part of the stomach becomes trapped above the esophagus, either permanently or temporarily; the diaphragm tightens, and the acid flows into the lower part of the esophagus directly.

Treatment must vary, depending on the individual situation. Toning of the diaphragm is vitally important, and very often overlooked by the orthodox world. A diaphragm that is too tight because of hyperventilation and stress requires relaxation techniques, whereas a diaphragm with a weakened opening needs some tightening. Fortunately, yoga-breathing techniques with specific relaxation teaching will cover both angles by toning the diaphragm. Excess acidity may also be a cause, as may obesity. The amount of fat visible on the outside of a body is often reflected within, and fat in the abdominal cavity will push upwards on the stomach, encouraging acid to flow the wrong way and the stomach to be forced through the diaphragm.

Persisting discomfort may require an

endoscopy, and will follow unsuccessful orthodox treatment using antacids and, specifically, calcium carbonate with a compound called algenic acid, which sits on the top of the stomach acid, like algae on a pond. Acid reflux is then prevented from touching the esophageal sides by the oil-like layer.

Diagnosis of a hiatus hernia can only be made through an endoscopy, but the symptoms that are suggested are those of dyspepsia (*see* **Dyspepsia**). The following recommendations can be used if a hiatus hernia is suspected prior to endoscopy.

RECOMMENDATIONS

- *Learn a yogic-breathing technique and meditation exercise.*
- *Any suggestion of being overweight—try to lose it.*
- *Do not stoop preferably; learn to pick things up by bending at the knee. Raise the head of the bed by placing two bricks at the head end—this will allow gravity to pull the stomach and contents downwards.*
- *Avoid antacids as much as possible, and certainly do not use anything containing aluminum. Algenic acid is a godsend in acute or nighttime situations, and can be used until other techniques bear fruit.*
- *Use slippery-elm compounds or pure slippery elm (one teaspoonful mixed into a thin paste with water) before bed, after meals, and if uncomfortable, up to a maximum of six times per day.*
- *Alcohol, smoking, caffeine, and refined sugars all increase stomach-acid production and will worsen a hiatus hernia. Specific food intolerance may be noted, and food-allergy testing through bioresonance or blood tests is recommended. Food allergies can weaken musculature, and may be the underlying cause of the failure of the diaphragm to work as an effective valve.*
- *Do not eat late at night or lie down within 2hr of eating. Siestas should be had in an upright position if this is your custom.*
- *Operative procedures may be necessary in severe cases when the above recommendations, along with both naturopathic and orthodox drug treatments, have failed. If so, see* **Operations and surgery**.

INDIGESTION—*see* Dyspepsia and Peptic ulcers

NAUSEA AND VOMITING

Nausea is the brain's way of telling us that we have taken in something potentially toxic, as in food poisoning, or a warning that we are doing something that may be injurious. In the case of taking an exam where our adrenaline levels may be too high, this is a fair but unnecessary warning. Motion or travel sickness is an unnecessary warning (*see* **Motion sickness**). Nausea is the most common early-warning symptom issued by the brain to inform us of an incorrect situation. Diseases of any part of many major organs, such as the kidney, liver, gut, or even the heart, may be heralded by nausea. Persisting nausea may represent cancer. Obstruction by stricture, inflammation, or tumor anywhere in the gastrointestinal tract can lead to, and be a cause of, vomiting.

In principle, any toxin in the system, whether it is created by, say, a failing kidney or liver, the ingestion of bacteria (such as in food poisoning or excess alcohol) will cause nausea or potential vomiting.

The act of vomiting generally suggests that the body has reached a toxic state, and is trying to rid itself of a poison. Vomiting is often associated with sweating—another eliminatory process—and may be accompanied by a need to urinate or defecate. If the toxin is in the stomach or the upper part of the intestine, then the vomiting may be curative, but very often the poison lies in the bloodstream, has influenced the vomit centres in the brain, and is therefore of no direct use. Vomiting without an obvious cause, or a persistence of vomiting, must be assessed by a physician.

Another of the most-common causes of nausea is low blood sugar. Often associated with hunger, low blood-sugar levels can trigger nausea. This is an odd paradox, because nausea usually reduces appetite. I suspect that nausea is a more-aggressive way for the brain to attract attention to the need for food when hunger pangs have failed. The feeling of an impending vomit is not necessarily a digestive problem. However, the emptying of the stomach contents is.

RECOMMENDATIONS

- *Nausea or vomiting without any obvious cause that is sudden, copious, or persistent must be reviewed by a doctor to rule out a more serious underlying cause.*
- *Once the cause has been established, certain techniques listed below can be utilized, but the principal treatment should be against the underlying cause.*
- *Half an inch of fresh gingerroot chopped into a mug of boiling water may be drunk when the temperature is acceptable.*
- *A combination of camomile tea (two teaspoonfuls) with a teaspoonful each of sage and rosemary per 16 ounces of boiling water can be very soothing if drunk every 15min.*
- *The homeopathic remedies Ipecacuanha, Nux vomica, and Carbo vegetabalis may help. Try one of these remedies at potency 6 every 10min, and if there is no response after three doses, try the next.*
- *There is an acupressure point that may be very beneficial in nausea or vomiting. Place three fingers up the forearm starting at the wrist crease. The third finger will lie over a sensitive point, which should have pressure applied to it for approximately 1min.*
- *If the nausea is associated with not having eaten for several hours or following a particularly sweet meal (there is inevitably a reflex low blood sugar or hypoglycemic state), eat a piece of fruit and see what happens.*
- *Correlate with the possibility of a food intolerance or allergy if the nausea is sporadic.*
- *See* **Motion sickness** *if relevant.*
- *Persisting nausea despite the above recommendations should result in a consultation with a complementary medical practitioner.*
- *Orthodox antinausea drugs should be used only when conditions are not responding to complementary treatment.*

OBSTRUCTION OF THE BOWEL

An obstruction anywhere from the throat to the anus is not a matter of self-help unless it is caused by an easily reachable foreign object. Specific conditions should be referred to in this book and include cancer, toxic colon, volvulus (a twist in the gut) and hernia. Intussusception and foreign objects are the most-common causes in infants and children.

The symptoms are pain and bloating, usually associated shortly after with vomiting and, of course, an absence of bowel motions. An inability to pass wind in association with these symptoms must immediately arouse suspicion.

RECOMMENDATIONS

- *Any suggestion of a bowel obstruction must be examined by a doctor.*
- *Please refer to the relevant section in this book to deal with the cause of obstruction.*
- *Do not try any form of laxative, because this will make things worse.*
- *Do not eat or drink anything until a diagnosis has been established.*
- *The homeopathic remedies Carbo vegetabalis or Cinchona can be considered at potency 6 every 10min until a doctor is seen, and thereafter a suitable remedy should be chosen by a trained homeopath.*

THE PANCREAS

The pancreas is found as an axe-shaped organ behind the upper part of the abdomen, behind the small intestine and the stomach.

It has two principal functions, both glandular. As an endocrine gland (passing a hormone into the bloodstream), the pancreas produces insulin from special cells known as the islets of Langerhans. Insulin controls the sugar levels in the bloodstream. The exocrine (production of chemicals *not* into the bloodstream) function is to produce digestive enzymes that pass into the small intestine. These juices pass down the pancreatic ducts and join the common bile duct before entering into the duodenum.

The pancreas sits in that part of the body often referred to as the solar plexus. It lies under main acupuncture points along the vessel of conception and is tied into a theoretical axis running from the pituitary through the thyroid itself and down to the uterus and prostate. This axis is sensitive, and a problem with any one organ may lead to a problem with another. Pregnancy is a prime example of triggering both thyroid and pancreatic deficiencies for no orthodox reason. These problems must therefore be viewed from a deep, energetic angle as well as the practical, scientific one.

PANCREAS

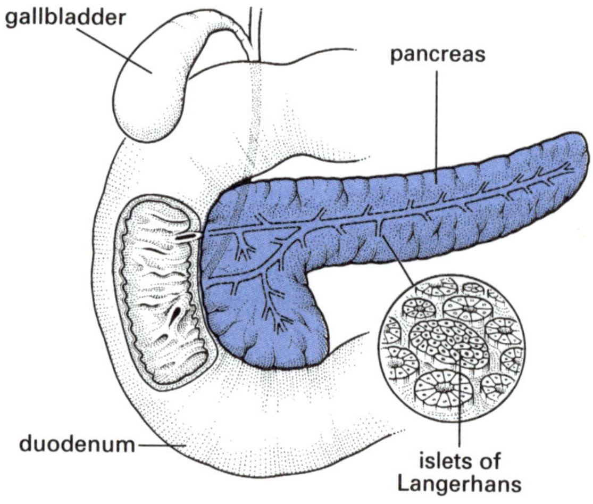

The islets of Langerhans produce insulin, which controls sugar levels in the blood. The pancreas also makes enzymes to aid the digestive process.

Pancreatitis

Inflammation of the pancreas is an extremely serious condition. It can damage the insulin and glucagon (anti-insulin hormone) cells and cause metabolic chaos. More acutely, the enzyme-producing cells may break down, release the digestive juices into the pancreas, and cause considerable destruction. Pancreatitis is, therefore, self-perpetuating, and can be rapid in its development. Pancreatitis is extremely painful and difficult to treat because of this process. Usually triggered by alcoholic excess or viral infections, the symptoms may be the gradual onset of upper-abdominal discomfort or a sudden, severe pain. Nausea and vomiting are often associated with profound lethargy.

RECOMMENDATIONS

- *Pancreatitis must be diagnosed and treated by doctors. A specific blood test for a compound known as amalyse is diagnostic, along with the symptoms of pancreatitis.*
- *Follow the advice given by the hospital and specialists accurately.*
- *Consult with a complementary medical practitioner with experience in this area for homeopathic treatment. Only the most experienced of naturopaths should be allowed to treat prancreatitis with medication.*
- *The pancreas is associated with the vessel of conception, and therefore any energetic form of treatment is liable to be beneficial. Consider acupuncture initially.*
- *Yoga and polarity therapy will affect the central energy store or chakras, and benefit the condition.*

Pancreatic cancer

This is a most serious cancer because it produces the complications of malignant disease, but also pancreatitis at some stage. Cancer of the head of the pancreas can obstruct the flow of bile from the liver and gallbladder, and therefore one of the initial symptoms may be jaundice.

RECOMMENDATIONS

- *See* **Cancer**.
- *See* **Pancreatitis** *above*.

PEPTIC ULCERS

The word "peptic" is derived from the Greek term meaning "pertaining to or promoting digestion." It is the medical term for ulceration that occurs in the mucous membranes of both the gastrum (stomach) and duodenum.

Treatment of peptic ulcers therefore also covers gastric ulcers, duodenal ulcers, and the precursors to this condition: gastritis and duodenitis. Some inflammations and ulcers in this area are "silent" —have no symptoms—but these are rare, and because they are not spotted early, are usually serious. Most ulcerative and preulcerative conditions in this area present as a burning sensation in the upper abdomen radiating occasionally through to the back. The pain may also radiate into the chest and give rise to symptoms similar to heart pains. (The reverse is true, and symptoms suggestive of bowel disease are often found to be emanating from the heart.) Silent ulcers are generally due to the inflammation or erosion not affecting the nerve endings. These ulcers may eat into blood vessels, causing bleeding that, if profuse, may cause vomiting of blood (hemetemesis) or if not so profuse, a black, tarry stool called melena created by the digestion of red blood cells.

The stomach is lined by cells that produce a thick mucus, which protects the stomach lining from the very aggressive hydrochloric acid, produced to break down our food. A failure to produce this mucus, or an overproduction of acid, will lead to inflammation and potential ulcer formation. The duodenum is bathed in a strong alkaline solution,

Peptic Ulcer

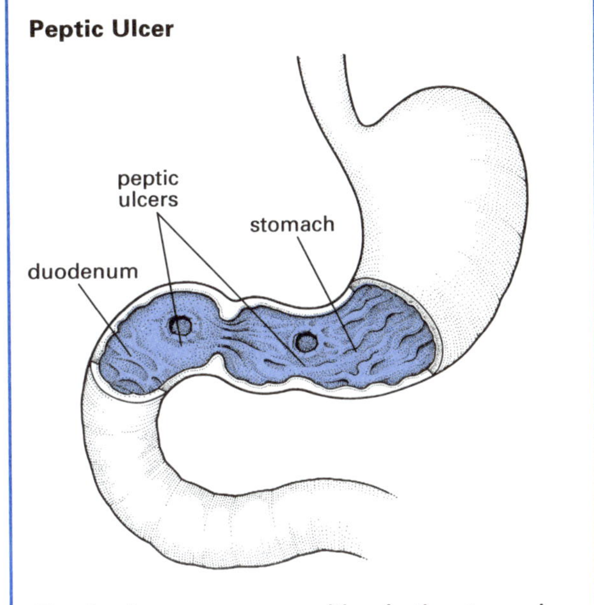

Peptic ulcers may occur either in the stomach or the duodenum.

which neutralizes the small amounts of acid that are released through the pyloric sphincter, but the small intestine also has a protective mucus layer against the strong alkaline that it comes into contact with from the pancreatic juices. Excess acidity passing into the duodenum will override these defensive measures and, again, cause inflammation and the predisposition to ulcer.

Excessive hydrochloric acid is often produced in response to food allergy/intolerance, alcohol, caffeine, tobacco, and excess adrenaline created by stress. Damage to the protective mucosa, and thereby a reduction in the protective mucus, can occur through any of the above, plus excessive eating or the embibement of hot and spicy food. Aspirin, nonsteroidal, anti-inflammatory drugs, steroids, and other less-commonly-utilized drugs can all predispose to preulcer conditions.

Helicobacter pylori

Recently, a specific bacterium called *Helicobacter pylori* has been associated with a higher chance of ulcerative and preulcerative conditions. Indeed, most individuals with ulcers will have *H. pylori,* in attendance, but by no means all. Conversely, many people carry *H. pylori* and have no problems with ulcerative conditions. A holistic practitioner should therefore continue to ignore the persistence of the orthodox world which supports the "germ" theory, and instead understand that *H. pylori* may exacerbate a situation, but is probably not the cause. Treating *H. pylori* is effective, but recurrence usually occurs if the underlying weakness or dietetic problem is not dealt with. This is, of course, a good thing for the pharmaceutical industry, who encourage the frequent and costly use of two antibiotics with a powerful antacid.

RECOMMENDATIONS

- *Persistent burning or discomfort in the upper abdomen, chest, or surrounding area should be considered a preulcerative condition, and treated accordingly.*
- *Keep a diary of foods in association with the discomfort, and isolate and eliminate any causative substances.*
- *Keep the same diary for times of stress.*
- *Specifically avoid hot, spicy, fried, and refined foods. Avoid alcohol, caffeine, and refined sugars until the condition settles, and then keep a close eye on which of these brings the symptoms back.*
- *Foods that are hard to digest, such as raw vegetables, abrasive foods like nuts and nonsoaked wholegrains, wholemeal bread, and oats should be avoided until the condition settles, despite their nutritional value.*
- *Aim at more-easily-digestible foods such as soups, diluted fruit juices, soaked grains, fish, and chicken. Cook your vegetables for slightly longer than would normally be encouraged.*
- *Avoid milk. It may give a temporary relief due to its alkaline properties, but this causes a rebound acid production, and the casein in the milk is hard to digest, which also encourages more acid production.*
- *If the above measures are not effective, then consider some basic treatments, as follows:*

(a) Make fresh cabbage juice, and drink one glass before meals for two weeks. It contains vitamin P, which is shown to help the healing of ulcers. Do not use this technique if you suffer from a hyperthyroid condition.

(b) Take the following supplements, which are known to help membranes heal, in the following amounts per foot of height in divided doses with meals: beta-carotene (2mg) or vitamin A (5000iu); vitamin E (100iu) and buffered vitamin C (1000mg); also take zinc (5mg per foot of height) before bed.

(c) Slippery elm or compounds containing this should be taken as prescribed on the package (it very much depends on the percentage of the compound).

(d) Licorice is healing, and should be taken as prescribed on the package.

(e) A half-tablet of an indigestion compound can be used while the above measures are employed, although, as with milk, there will be a rebound hyper-acidic effect. Aloe-vera juice is soothing, and does not encourage hydrochloric-acid production in the same way.

(f) Meditation and the associated breathing techniques that gently massage the stomach are essential when the excess acidity is stress-associated.

- *Persisting discomfort or any difficulty in breathing should be reviewed by a physician, who may refer the individual to a surgeon for a gastroscope or barium studies. These should be considered only in acute situations, or in persistent cases where the above measures have not helped, because the treatment will inevitably be drug-induced antacid treatment with medications such as ranitidine, cimetidine, or omeprazole. If H. pylori is found, then triple therapy—two antibiotics and bismuth— will be employed, which may be curative, but very often is not for the reasons described above.*

PILES—*see* Hemorrhoids

PROLAPSED ANUS

This is the extrusion of the lower part of the intestinal tract through the sphincter of the anus. This condition is generally created by a weakness of the anus through trauma or marked intra-abdominal pressure. Severe infections such as cholera, which may create marked weakness within muscles and frequent diarrhea, may cause a prolapse. Pressure from a tumor or strain from chronic constipation may cause an anal or even rectal prolapse.

RECOMMENDATIONS

- *Any suggestion of a prolapse of the anus must be reviewed by a doctor.*
- *Conscious pulling up of the anus is a method of strengthening the anal sphincter, and may relieve a prolapse created by internal pressure derived from constipation.*
- *See* **Hemorrhoids**.

The Urogenital System

BARTHOLIN CYSTS

Bartholin glands are found on both sides of the lateral vaginal walls. They generally secrete part of the vagina's protective lubricant. Occasionally, the gland can become inflamed and/or the duct that carries the secretions out can become blocked.

Bartholin cysts present as painful (though not always) swellings or pea-like lesions on either side of the vaginal opening. These are often noticed on intercourse.

RECOMMENDATIONS

- *Any swelling in the genital area that does not respond to basic treatment after 48hr should be viewed by a doctor or gynecologist.*
- *Apply hot and cold compresses to the area.*
- *The homeopathic remedy Hepar sulfuris calcarium 30, four pills every 2hr, can be utilized.*
- *Intercourse should be avoided.*
- *Avoid pressure on the area. Squeezing will not release the blockage.*
- *If the problem persists, the orthodox world would encourage the use of antibiotics, but before you use these, consult a complementary medical practitioner for herbal or homeopathic alternatives.*
- *An operative procedure is rarely required, but if it is, then pre- and postoperative precautions should be taken (see* **Operations and surgery***).*

Bartholin Cysts

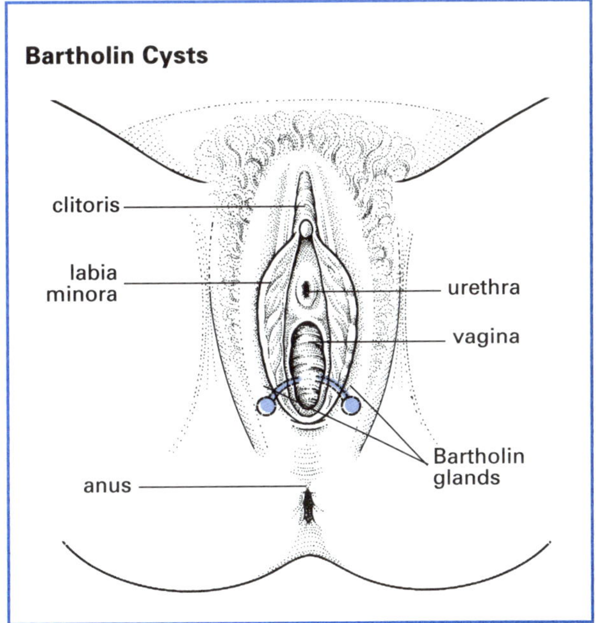

BLADDER PROLAPSE

Bladder prolapse appears as a bulge of the front aspect of the vagina, usually with marked protrusion of the urethra. It is associated with increased frequency of urination, incontinence, and, frequently, cystitis symptoms. It is generally caused by a weakening of the ligaments that hold the bladder in place, and these are generally compromised by pregnancy or pelvic tumors.

RECOMMENDATIONS

- *Pelvic-floor exercises from yoga, Qi Gong, or basic physiotherapy may help a mild prolapse.*
- *Avoid allowing the bladder to overfill with urine by urinating frequently.*
- *Vaginal pessaries are rarely beneficial, and operative procedures are frequently required (see* **Operations and surgery***).*

CANDIDA AND THRUSH

See **Candidiasis.**

Thrush is an irritating, itching condition of the vagina. There may be an accompanying cheesy, white, or pale-yellow, creamy discharge that clings tenaciously to the vaginal walls. There may also be an associated slight, fishy smell, but generally this is not caused by the thrush, but by other organisms. The irritation may be bad enough to cause scratching, which leads to bleeding, and also the *Candida* itself can cause superficial cuts that bleed.

Some women will notice some or all of the symptoms mildly leading up to their periods. The vaginal flora is sensitive to the changes in estrogen and progesterone levels.

As discussed more fully in the section on candidiasis, thrush is encouraged by a decrease in the normal vaginal flora. Antibiotics, poor diet, excess white sugar, and poor hygiene all encourage this condition.

RECOMMENDATIONS

- *Visit your doctor, family-planning clinic, nurse-midwife, or gynecologist to establish a firm diagnosis.*
- *Wear loose clothing around the groin.*
- *Avoid refined sugars throughout the time of irritation.*
- *Teatree pessaries with or without lavender can be used nightly for seven nights.*
- *If available, Calendula and/or Hydrastis pessaries can be used for three nights in succession, and then one week later for three nights again.*
- *Avoid deodorants or medicated soaps in that area, or generally if bathing.*
- *Obtain a douche bag or 1.5fl oz syringe. Mix one tablespoonful of cider vinegar in a mug of water, and douche each evening before bed. One tablespoonful of live-yogurt culture mixed thoroughly in one mug of water should be used as a douche each morning. If no improvement is forthcoming after one week, please see your healthcare provider.*
- *Obtain a homeopathic remedy after consultation with a homeopath, and/or a herbal treatment from a herbalist. Self-prescribing is somewhat hit and miss, although you can review the homeopathic remedies Sepia, Arsenicum album, Lilium tigrinum, Calcarea carbonica, and Silica.*
- *Unless all else fails, avoid strict-dietetic advice, because this is troublesome and not generally effective.*
- *If antibiotics have to be used, ensure vaginal douching with live-yogurt culture as described above.*
- *Adding one cupful of sea salt to bath water may prove soothing.*
- *See* **Vaginal douching** *and* **Candidiasis***.*

CERVIX

The cervix is the name given to the part of the uterus found at the top of the vagina, in which there is an opening (the os), up which the sperm travel into the uterus in search of an egg.

Cervical cancer

Cervical cancer is an aggressive tumor if left untreated, and a regular Papanicolaou (named

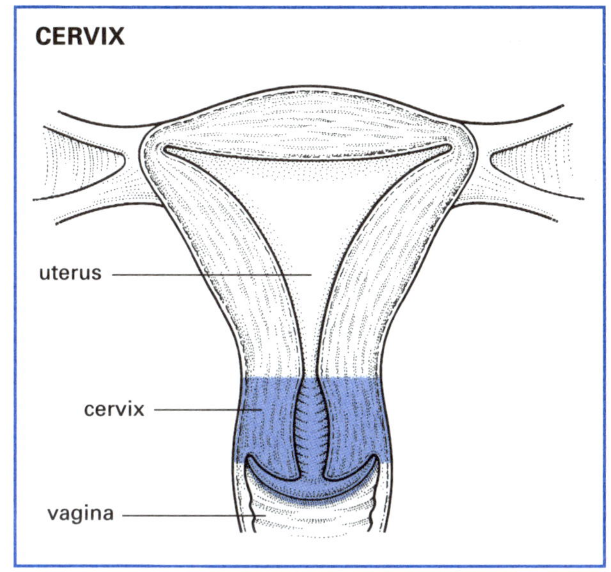

after an American anatomist) test, more commonly known as a Pap smear or simply a smear, is essential.

In the U.S., Pap smears are performed once a year, or more frequently, if there is a specific problem. I recommend that a woman has a smear every year after she has lost her virginity, and every six months if she changes her sexual partner during that time.

The medical world divides changes in the cells of the cervix into precancerous and cancerous cells. Precancerous cells are further divided up into dyskaryotic cells—cells that look, under the microscope, unusual but not cancerous—and cervical interstitial neoplasia (CIN) I, II, and III cells with premalignant changes. The numbers I, II, and III represent the depth to which the precancerous changes are occurring in the walls of the os from where the smear is taken.

If any unusual cells are found, then a further investigation called a colposcopy is performed. This is a specialized scope that can travel into the opening of the cervix (the os) and take biopsies to establish the severity of the changes.

There is an association between two types of human papilloma virus (HPV) and cervical cancer. These viruses are commonly transmitted through intercourse, making this cancer a potentially transmittable one. Like any internal cancer it is often "silent," giving no symptoms. But unlike other cancers, a regular checkup can find precancerous cells or early cancer well in advance of there being any major risk. A specific gene may have recently been found which predisposes a woman to cervical cancer. Over the next few years, this gene may be routinely tested to highlight those women at risk. Cervical cancer is more common in women sexually-active for this reason.

RECOMMENDATIONS

- *Have regular checkups and, if you can afford it, ensure that the smear is examined by a pathologist as well as a laboratory technician.*
- *Consider using a barrier method of contraception with new sexual partners.*
- *Infrequent but regular douching (see* **Vaginal douching***) will encourage the health of the cervix, and help fight viral infection. If changes are noted, consult a medically-qualified practitioner in homeopathy immediately. Follow the advice of your gynecologist as well.*
- *If a cancer is discovered, see* **Cancer**.

Cervical incompetence

The cervix is the lower part of the uterus, found at the top of the vagina. In the center of the cervix lies an opening called the os, which allows access for the sperm to the eggs traveling down the Fallopian tube into the womb. The os is generally closed, except at childbirth, and under hormonal and nervous controls during intercourse.

Cervical incompetence can occur for traumatic reasons, and represents the condition of a persistently open and loose cervical os. This is in no way a problem until childbearing is required, when a patent (open) os may allow the product of conception to fall out of the uterus.

RECOMMENDATIONS

- *If you are advised that your cervix is incompetent, then a gynecological opinion must be sought. There is no complementary or orthodox treatment other than surgical treatment, where a Shirodkar stitch is placed around the opening and tightened.*
- *As with any operation, see* **Operations and surgery**.

Cervical interstitial neoplasia (CIN)

Cervical interstitial neoplasia is a term that describes a precancerous change in the cervix. Cervical smears should isolate these changes, which are more likely to become cancerous than dysplasia, and should be treated accordingly.

Cervical interstitial neoplasia is divided into groups I, II, and III. They do not represent the severity of the changes, but merely the depth to which the precancerous cells are buried in the walls of the os (the opening to the uterus).

RECOMMENDATIONS

- *A precancerous change should be dealt with by a complementary medical practitioner with experience in this area.*
- *Unless there is a reduction in the CIN number, i.e. from CIN III to CIN II, within two months of complementary medical treatment, then the orthodox treatment of laser therapy should be considered. If there is a change, then continue with treatment, and test again.*
- *To avoid this situation in the first place, and certainly if a condition of CIN has been described, condoms or a cap should be used when having intercourse.*
- *High-dose antioxidants and a health diet must be discussed with your practitioner.*
- *See* **Vaginal douching,** *and replace the cider vinegar with a teaspoonful of Arnica- and Calendula-fluid extracts.*

Cone biopsy

This operative procedure removes a cone-shaped wedge around the cervical os opening to remove the precancerous changes that have occurred. This technique has been superseded by the use of laser therapy, and is only used in certain circumstances.

Cervical polyps

Polyps are overgrowths of mucous membrane, and those that protrude through the cervical opening are termed cervical polyps. They have a slightly increased chance of becoming cancerous, more so than any other part of the mucous membrane, and they may bleed, which can cause concern.

Cervical polyps are generally discovered on a routine examination because they are usually symptomless. Gynecologists and physicians will have a tendency to suggest their surgical removal, and this should only be considered if complementary medical techniques fail to resolve the problem. Any polyp is considered to be an excess of damp in the body, and correct dietetics, and homeopathic and herbal treatments are often effective.

RECOMMENDATIONS

- *Obtain a gynecological opinion but avoid surgery except as a last resort.*
- *Consult with a complementary medical practitioner with experience in this area.*
- *Discuss with your preferred practitioner a low refined-sugar diet, and ensure that you are not dehydrated. Consider the homeopathic remedy Thuja 30, one dose three times a day for two weeks, or preferably seek advice from a homeopathic prescriber.*
- *Consider following the Hay diet (see chapter 7).*
- *Ayurvedic, Tibetan, and Chinese medicine may be successful in removing the excess damp that creates polyps.*
- *If the above recommendations do not solve the problem, then surgical intervention should be considered, because a polyp may represent a higher risk of uterine cancer.*

Cervical smears (Papanicolaou, Pap smear)

A cervical smear is a simple, although invasive procedure. The cervix is one of the more-common areas for cancerous changes to take place, and examination of this part of the uterus is a recommended process.

In the U.K., bureaucracy has governed that a cervical smear should be performed every 3–5 years, depending on where the woman lives and the habits of the general practice. I believe this to be too long a gap. A cancer may develop overnight, and in three years will certainly spread. Sexually active women should have a cervical smear every year, and virgins or nonsexually active women every 18 months. After menopause, a two-year gap is acceptable. In the U.S., yearly cervical smears are available for all women, including those who are postmenapausal. I recommend a cervical smear within three or four months of changing a sexual partner. Women with more than one sexual partner should have a cervical smear every six months.

Dysplasia

Dysplasia is the medical term for abnormal cells. It is not a precancerous condition, although it may require more frequent examinations to ensure that precancerous changes do not occur (*see* **Cervical cancer**).

GENITAL HERPES—*see* Herpes

INTERCOURSE (PAINFUL)—*see* Dyspareunia

INTRAUTERINE DEVICE (IUD)

This contraption is more commonly known as the coil. These multishaped devices are inserted by a doctor or gynecologist into the cavity of the uterus. They set up a mild inflammatory response simply by irritating the inner lining of the uterus, which creates an environment in which a fertilized egg is not likely to implant. The fertilized egg will therefore pass out through the cervix or be expelled at the next period, although nature may override this inflammation, and pregnancy can take place.

IUDs

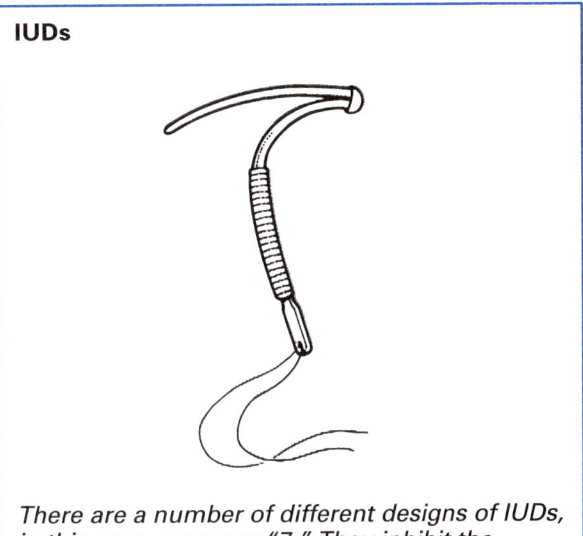

There are a number of different designs of IUDs, in this case, a copper "7." They inhibit the implantation of a fertilized egg in the uterus.

IUD in position

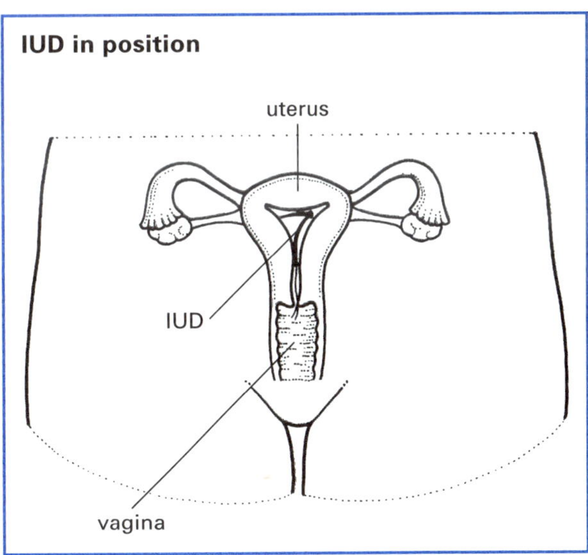

It is important to note that if fertilization of an egg does take place, and if religious doctrine or personal beliefs do not allow the intentional cessation of life, then this form of contraception should not be considered.

There are other reasons why a coil or IUD should be used as a last resort. Infection may enter with the insertion of a coil, or settle around this foreign object. Should the infection travel down the Fallopian tubes, it may block them and create sterility. Very often, insertion is not recommended until the woman has had as many children as she wishes.

A common concern of alternative practitioners, although dismissed out of hand by the orthodox medical world, is the use of copper in coils. This encourages the inflammatory response, but may allow some absorption of copper. Copper poisoning can lead to muscular and neurological conditions, even as severe as epilepsy. There is no scientific evidence to suggest that a coil may create such toxic levels, but minor effects may be created that we are unaware of.

RECOMMENDATIONS

- *The coil should only be considered as a form of contraception once the woman has had as many children as she wishes.*
- *Insist on a noncopper coil.*
- *Ensure that the coil is changed every two years.*

KIDNEY (RENAL) DISEASE

The kidneys are the filtration system for the bloodstream, as well as being the producer of hormones that govern the amount of red blood cells we make, and the level at which blood pressure is maintained. The filtration system balances the level of water and electrolytes (positive- and negative-charged chemicals, such as potassium, calcium, and sodium), and thereby controls our levels of hydration, blood pressure, and toxic excretion. This is a miracle of evolution, especially for an organ that would fit comfortably in the hand.

KIDNEYS—Position in relation to other organs

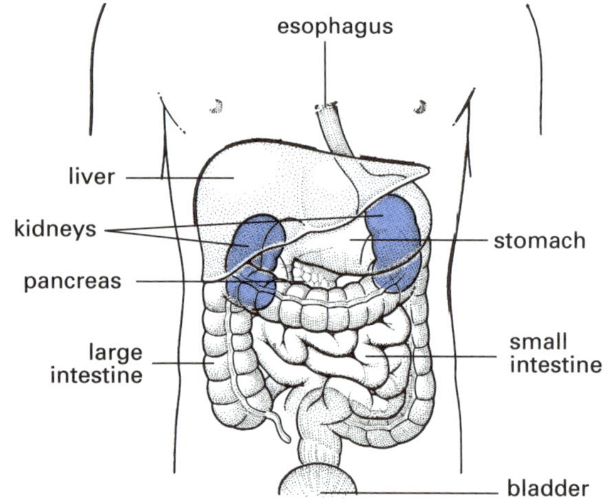

The kidneys act as a filtration system, removing toxins from the bloodstream, together with excess water. They also maintain the balance of acidity and alkalinity of the blood and control levels of salts and minerals.

For some reason, the translation from Eastern to Western understanding has labeled the body's energy store as the "kidney" energy or meridian. The organic function of the kidneys and the Eastern philosophy of kidney energy are not compatible, but nevertheless, the term "kidney energy" is often used by those who follow the principles of energy flow. When a practitioner of complementary medicine says that your kidney energy is weak or in excess, this does not necessarily represent a disease process within the organs themselves. Interestingly, however, disease of any organ is likely to leave the individual tired, but an incapacity of the kidneys seems to result in a much greater weakness within the system as a whole than most other organ problems.

Glomerulonephritis

Glomerulonephritis is an inflammatory disease of the kidney affecting the glomeruli—part of the filtering system. Symptoms may vary from severe pain, blood in the urine, water retention, and headaches in an acute inflammation, to no symptoms at all as the process slowly but surely damages the kidneys.

RECOMMENDATIONS

- *A tell-tale sign is froth in the toilet bowl that persists for more than 60sec (caused by protein in the urine) or blood. Straight to the doctor, please.*
- *Persisting water retention or edema or the discovery of high blood pressure will lead to your doctor checking your urine, as protein and blood may be present, but not obviously visible.*

- *This condition may lead to permanent kidney damage, and should not be treated without expert advice. After initial treatment or advice from an orthodox kidney specialist, discuss the matter with a complementary medical practitioner with experience in the area.*
- *Consider consulting a homeopath, nutritionist, or herbalist before taking orthodox treatment, which will include antibiotic or even steroid use. Complementary naturopathic treatment should run alongside these drugs and, in the hands of a medically-qualified complementary specialist, may even help avoid the use of orthodox drugs.*

Infection of the kidneys—*see* Pyelonephritis

Inflammation of the kidneys —*see* Glomerulonephritis

Kidney stones (renal calculi) and renal colic

Sudden and severe (often described as excruciating) pain that strikes anywhere from the small of the back, around the sides, and down into the groin or vagina/penis/testes may be renal colic, and is most likely to be caused by the passage of a stone. These are usually composed of calcium, oxalic or uric acids, and phosphates. These compounds normally remain in solution, but a change in the acid/alkaline status of the urine, or the presence of a foreign body, may cause these to precipitate out and start a stone or "calculus" formation. If the stone is small, it will travel out of the kidney, down the uretha, through the bladder, and out, but if it lodges in one of the fine tubules in the kidney, it will slowly grow in size.

A calculus forming within the kidney may grow to a very large size before it will cause any problems, and even these may not be noticed, because the pressure, while destroying that kidney, will have no effect on the other one, which will deal with the filtration of the body quite happily without its partner. For some reason, nature has made the urethra a very sensitive passage, and if a stone moves, the pain has been likened to the dragging of a small rock across an eyeball.

This severe pain will be associated with nausea, if not vomiting, generalized weakness, and the characteristic fevers and rigors of kidney problems. It is estimated that 6 percent of the Western population will develop kidney stones. This is much higher than in other parts of the world. The inevitable conclusion is an association with some part of the Western lifestyle, although orthodox renal specialists will not hear of there being any association with diet. This is because a couple of trials have removed the major foods containing calcium and uric acid, and found no appreciable difference. Of course they will not, if other factors such as dehydration, deficiencies, and heavy-metal poisoning are not also taken into account. Studies have shown that vegetarians have a decreased risk of developing stones, as also have those with reduced sugar intake (insulin is very relevant to calcium levels through indirect metabolic pathways) and the presence of low levels of citric acid (from oranges, grapefruits, lemons, and limes). An excess intake of milk and alkali foods including antacids can cause stones. This condition is known as the milk–alkali syndrome. An excess of vitamin D (not uncommon in countries such as the U.S.A., where milk is fortified with vitamin D) is also a risk, because this increases the absorption of calcium, thereby causing an increase in urinary calcium.

Several serious medical conditions can cause an excess secretion of calcium, oxylate, and uric acid, and all these need to be reviewed if a stone is passed.

RECOMMENDATIONS

FOR AN ACUTE ATTACK

- *If a sudden excruciating pain should occur, and a stone is suspected, ensure that all urination is done through a sieve to catch the calculus.*

- *Visit your doctor, preferably with the passed stone. If the stone has not yet left the body, admission into hospital will be preferable for adequate pain relief. Full metabolic investigations must be undertaken, and renal x-rays should be undergone, including those using special x-ray opaque dyes to ensure that the passing stone was not part of a larger calculus.*
- *The homeopathic remedies Aconite and Hypericum, both at potency 6, should be alternated every 10min until the stone has passed or adequate pain relief has been given, usually through an injection of pethidine.*
- *A castor-oil pack on the front, side, and back of the side that is hurting may be beneficial. It is worth remembering that a pain anywhere from the kidney to the tip of the urethra may be reflected from the stone being anywhere along that passage. The brain is not good at isolating the exact point of urogenital pain.*
- *Beta-carotene and vitamin C should be taken as follows to help the healing of the damaged kidney and urethra: beta-carotene (2mg) and vitamin C (500mg), both per foot of height in divided doses with food throughout the day.*
- *Lobelia tincture (three drops in warm water) every hour may make a considerable difference. A tea made from the leaf of Uva ursi (available from herbal shops) can be drunk to relieve the pain, and it also acts as a mild diuretic. Ensure that plenty of water is taken.*
- *A stone may lodge in the urethra due to spasm. A herb known as kella was used 4,000 years ago by the Egyptians in the treatment of kidney stones. Dosage depends on the purity, and it is best prescribed by a herbalist. More easily available are Aloe-vera products, which may actually reduce the size of a stone if taken at a level high enough not to cause diarrhea.*
- *If the presence of kella, Aloe vera, and high-water intake do not remove a lodged stone, the orthodox world will suggest the use of a ureter basket to remove it. This is a specialized instrument that is passed into the bladder via the urethra and up the ureter. At the level of the stone, a small nylon net is ejected from the end, passes around the stone and, when tightened and withdrawn, will bring the calculus with it. This method has now been surpassed by the use of ultrasound, which shatters the stone, but this is not available in all hospitals.*

RECOMMENDATIONS

FOR PREVENTION OF STONE FORMATION

- *There is an increased chance of a stone or calculus reforming unless the following lifestyle changes are considered.*
- *Ensure that someone analyzes the type of stone you have produced, because dietary restrictions will be recommended around the type of compound that created the calculus.*
- *Remove high-protein foods, fat, and refined sugar from the diet. Eliminate caffeine, alcohol, and manufactured soft drinks, which generally contain phosphoric acid.*
- *Do not cook with aluminum pans.*
- *Avoid beets, spinach and collard greens, nuts, cabbage, and rhubarb. Special mention should be made of cranberry and sesame seeds, both of which are considered to be "healthy" for kidney problems, but are contraindicated in renal calculi.*
- *Vitamin B_6 (10mg) and magnesium (50 mg), both per foot of height in divided doses throughout the day, can reduce oxalic acid.*
- *If the stone has calcium involved with it, increase the intake of wheat bran, corn, potatoes, bananas, avocado, brown rice, soya products, oats, and rye, all of which have a high magnesium/calcium ratio.*

- *Ensure that you are not taking any regular vitamin-D compounds, and watch out for those fortified foods.*
- *Aloe-vera—take the daily dose as recommended on your chosen product.*
- *Discuss with a complementary medical practitioner the correct doses for the use of vitamin B_6, vitamin K, glutamic acid, magnesium, and potassium.*

Nephrotic syndrome

Nephrotic syndrome is characterized by the finding of protein in the urine, with consequential low protein levels in the bloodstream that lead to a tendency for edema or water retention within the tissues. Other findings include high-fat levels in the blood. There are often no symptoms, and other tests including blood pressure are normal. This condition results from damage to a part of the kidney that allows proteins to leak through when they should not.

Nephrotic syndrome may occur for no apparent reason in pregnancy, but is probably associated in nonpregnant patients with an asymptomatic infection or toxic intake, such as chemicals, additives, pollutants, smoking, alcohol, and other drugs.

RECOMMENDATIONS

- *This condition is usually diagnosed by a simple urine test, and the physician who performed this is liable to do extensive tests on the kidneys because protein in the urine may represent more sinister conditions such as infection or tumors. It is important to rule out any other condition.*
- *Follow strictly the advice of a kidney specialist. There is some debate whether a high- or low-protein diet should be followed, but whichever belief your kidney expert expounds, the protein intake should be organic and pesticide-free.*
- *See recommendations for the prevention of kidney stone formation.*

Pyelonephritis

Pyelonephritis describes infection of the kidney, and is derived from nephron (a minute filtering structure in the kidney) and pyelo (meaning pus within). An infection may be acute following bacterial infection up from the bladder, or invading the kidney via the bloodstream. Direct trauma may also cause an acute infection. Chronic pyelonephritis is the same situation, but usually with less-aggressive bacteria, and simply means a prolongation of the initial infection. A chronic condition may flare up repeatedly, and can be created due to a weakness at the valves in the bladder end of the urethra, which allows bacteria to travel up.

The symptoms are of tiredness and pain in the small of the back, usually one-sided, but often bilateral. There is often a waxing and waning of fever, and an almost characteristic condition known as "rigors," which are simply uncontrolled shivers. Kidney infection is usually associated with cystitis, and therefore painful urination and blood in the urine are often seen (*see* **Cystitis**).

RECOMMENDATIONS

- *The kidneys can be damaged very swiftly and, if untreated, renal failure is a possibility. If the alternative medical suggestions below do not seem to have an impact within the first few hours of treatment, then a medical opinion, including the use of antibiotics, should be considered, with appropriate complementary medical care aiming at preventing antibiotic effects or a condition becoming chronic.*
- *Take a sample to your doctor for culture, microscopy, and sensitivity (CMS).*
- *While awaiting the results of the CMS, ensure good hydration. Start antibiotics if kidney pain is present while awaiting urine sample report. Drink 16 ounces of water per foot of height in divided doses throughout the day.*
- *Follow the recommendations in this book for cystitis (see* **Cystitis***).*

- *While awaiting the outcome of the urine investigations, use Aconite 6 every 2hr. A more-specific remedy may be chosen by consulting your preferred homeopathic manual.*
- *See recommendations for the prevention of kidney stone formation.*

Renal failure

The failing of the kidneys is an extremely serious condition that requires emergency medical attention. Complementary medicine can only be of benefit in supporting the technical expertise of the nearest hospital with facilities to deal with such an emergency. If the kidneys shut down, the body's metabolism will become out of balance within a couple of hours, and death will ensue within two to three days.

The symptoms of renal failure are nausea, vomiting, drowsiness, confusion, water retention, headaches, diarrhea, itching skin, and eventually, coma. These are created by metabolic changes and the failure to excrete the natural-waste products of our normal metabolism. Urine is named after its main component, urea, a nitrogen-containing compound derived mostly from a breakdown and utilization of proteins. An increase in the amount of urea in the blood leads to a condition known as uremia, which is toxic to the functioning of the nervous system and brain.

Acute renal failure

A sudden drop in blood pressure, usually resulting from trauma or peripheral blood-vessel dilation following a toxic ingestion, will lead to a sudden, acute renal failure. A less-common cause is the formation of a blockage to the urethra, by a stone, tumor, or trauma, which causes a back-flow of urine up the urethra into the kidneys, with resulting severe dilation and pressure necrosis. A severe infection may also cause a sudden shutdown of the kidneys.

Chronic renal failure

Chronic renal failure may exhibit all the signs and symptoms as mentioned above, but tends to develop more slowly. A partial obstruction may lead to a partial hydronephrosis, but recurrent infection or slow-growing tumors may also cause this problem. Untreated or unrecognized high blood pressure or diabetes will damage the bloodflow to the kidneys, and slowly but surely cause renal failure.

The insidious onset of chronic renal failure will create an imbalance of electrolytes, and thereby create new diseases or worsen current ones. An inability of the body to control its sodium levels will lead to higher blood pressure, and calcium and iron deposits will settle around the system because the kidney cannot remove these. As I mentioned above, the kidney also has functions in directly controlling blood pressure through a hormone called angiotensin. Another hormone called erythropoietin is a controlling mechanism for the amount of red blood cells we make. Raised blood pressure and anemia are two of the more-common conditions associated with renal failure.

RECOMMENDATIONS

- *The recognition of renal failure, either acute or chronic, is made by a general practitioner. Emergency orthodox medical treatment must be followed.*
- *Utilize alternative or complementary medical techniques, depending on the underlying cause, symptoms, and treatments.*
- *See recommendations for the prevention of kidney stone formation.*
- *Do not underestimate the speed with which a kidney problem can deteriorate, and do not try to treat renal failure without expert complementary medical guidance. Medically-qualified nutritionists, homeopaths, and herbalists are the only people who should be involved initially.*
- *Acupuncture and healing can be utilized once under proper, orthodox medical care.*

- *If acute renal failure is recognized, use the remedy Aconite 30 every 20min for the first 2hr, and then drop it to every 4hr until a suitable homeopathic remedy has been chosen by a practitioner.*
- *Do not hesitate to use renal dialysis. This may require your visiting a hospital for attachment to a specific machine, but nowadays, special small machines are being used at home, with training for an individual to attach themselves to the life-saving device every 6–8hr. This is known as ambulatory dialysis.*
- *Specific diets will be recommended by the nutritionists or dieticians associated with the renal unit. Follow these guidelines strictly, even if they go against your preferred or previously recommended dietetics.*
- *End-stage renal failure is the gruesome term used to describe exactly that. Sadly, 75 percent of those with chronic renal failure will succumb unless a renal transplant is possible. Dialysis may only be usable for a few years, because certain toxins cannot be removed, and kidney functions just cannot be replaced. The use of the homeopathic remedy Arsenicum album 30, four times per day, will ease the passage from this life to the next.*

THE TESTICLES

As far as the genes and natural selection are concerned, the body is a life-support system for the testicles or testes! Their function is to produce sperm, which, when transmitted through sexual intercourse, will continue procreation. Failure of the testes to develop may lead to a lack of puberty and maturation (*see* **Undescended testes**), and it is possible, following the work of a professor in Zurich, to assess the chances of hypogonadism by comparing the size of the testes to a string of increasing-sized beads known as an orchidometer.

Sperm counts are, apparently, falling, possibly due to pollution and toxins within the food chain, and it may be that the size of the testes will diminish accordingly. Our professor in Zurich will keep an eye on this.

TESTICULAR SWELLING

In the same way that women should be encouraged to examine their breasts on a regular basis, so should males examine their testes through the scrotal sack. Testicular tumors (using the word tumor in its broadest sense—swelling) are most often benign, but an unrecognized and untreated cancer is dangerous.

"Cele" is the medical term for lump, and is prefixed by whatever has caused it. Hydro- (fluid), spermato- (sperm), varico- (a swelling of a vein) or hemato- (blood filled) are all examples. Most often, these fluid-filled sacks are caused by trauma, but many arise spontaneously or with associated diseases such as infections or cancers.

A testicular swelling may prove to be a cancer. There are different types, some of which are more aggressive than others, but orthodox medicine has a good success rate if a testicular tumor is caught early.

Testicular Swelling

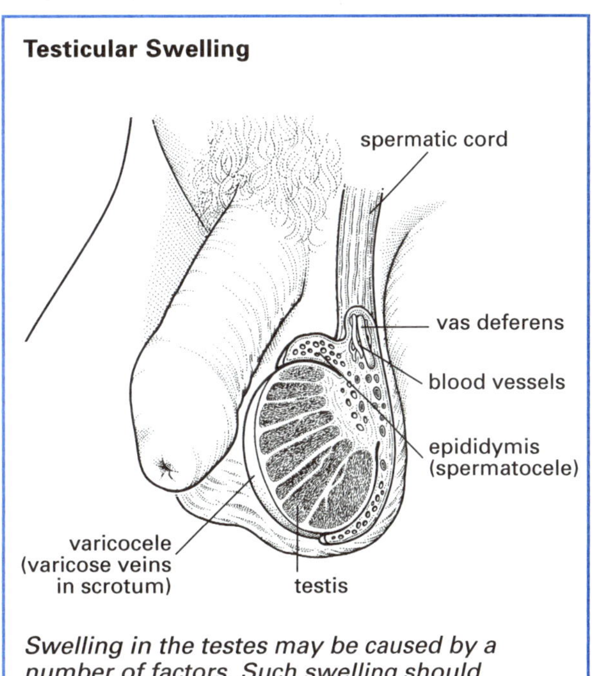

Swelling in the testes may be caused by a number of factors. Such swelling should always be investigated by a specialist.

RECOMMENDATIONS

- *Any testicular swelling must be investigated by a specialist. Ultrasound or endoscopic investigations will be carried out, along with urine, sperm, and blood analysis.*
- *Topical applications are pointless but, as a general rule, loose-fitting underwear and trousers are more comfortable, and less likely to create problems.*
- *Homeopathic remedies are listed, and can be found by reference to your preferred homeopathic manual under the heading of "testicular swellings" or "tumors."*
- *Most swellings can be left alone once a firm and safe diagnosis has been reached, but if this is not the case, then an operative procedure, including the removal of a testicle, may be necessary. Needle drainage of a large, fluid-filled cele is a less-aggressive therapy.*
- *If a swelling is a cancer,* *see* **Cancer**.

URINE AND URINATION

Urination is the product of the passage of blood through the kidneys, which acts as a filtration system, taking out most toxins. Urine is predominantly water, with a variety of minerals and compounds known as electrolytes, which include sodium, potassium, hydrogen, and chloride. These, more so than the minerals such as calcium, magnesium, and sulfates, are sacrificed in an attempt by the kidneys to keep the blood at a balanced level of acidity:alkalinity. Urine obtains its name from the presence of urea, a nitrogenous waste product of the body's metabolism.

Because the body generally produces acid in its metabolic pathways, the urine removes this, and is therefore usually mildly acidic. This is an important factor, because many bacteria prefer an acidic environment, and changing the pH to make it more alkaline may be an effective treatment for bladder and urinary problems.

Urination is the outflow of this waste product, and can amount to between 28 and 72 ounces in a normal, healthy adult. The more we drink and the more diuretics we take in the form of caffeine, alcohol, and refined sugars, the more we pass urine.

The need to urinate is governed by stretch receptors within the bladder wall. A full bladder will take the stretch of these neurones beyond a threshold, and an impulse will be sent to the brain saying "empty." Our consciousness registers a discomfort, and we generally make our way to the bathroom. Stretch receptors may be influenced by pressure from outside of the bladder as well as from inside. Any "growth" in the lower pelvis may trigger the desire to urinate. Pregnancy, enlargement of the prostate, and obesity are common factors. A full rectum or lower "sigmoid" colon can apply pressure, as can an enlarged prostate. More-sinister causes include nerve damage from diseases such as multiple sclerosis and tumors, either benign (such as fibroids in the uterus) or cancerous.

The urethra has sensitive nerves, that if irritated, can send impulses to the brain recommending urination. The intention is to have a flow of urine pass over the irritated area to try to wash out any causative agent.

Urinary System

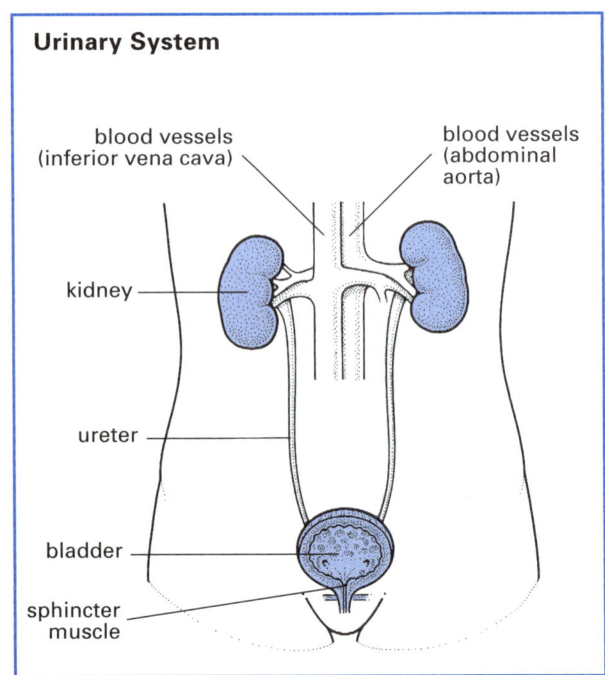

RECOMMENDATIONS

- *An excessive desire to urinate, while usually representing a mild condition, may be an indication of metabolic disease such as diabetes or pelvic pathology, and should always be reviewed by a doctor or gynecologist.*
- *Please refer to the relevant section in this book once an underlying cause has been established.*

Incontinence

The inability to hold urine is known as incontinence. An overfilled bladder in association with increased abdominal pressure from sneezing or laughing may cause a natural incontinence. Attention should be paid if a mild rise of abdominal pressure by coughing, laughing, or sneezing creates a leakage. This is known as stress incontinence. Pregnancy and pelvic tumors may cause pressure that overwhelms the valves, causing incontinence. Inflammation of the urethra or bladder, as in cystitis, will encourage urinary flow to flush out any irritant.

Neurological problems may affect both the voluntary and involuntary valves, and in men, inflammation or enlargement of the prostate may alter the valve control. Incontinence is part of the picture of prostatitis (*see* **Prostatitis**). Women may have weakness of the muscles and ligaments that hold the uterus in place, especially due to overstretching in pregnancy or to the diminution in estrogen levels following menopause. If the uterus should drop down, it puts pressure on the bladder, thereby encouraging incontinence. The bladder itself may lose its supports for the same reasons, and a bladder prolapse may also be a cause.

Anxiety and nervousness may trigger bladder emptying by a mechanism described in the section on stress (*see* **Stress**). Very often, this may create such an impulse to urinate that a dash to find a toilet is inevitable. This is known as urgency incontinence. (*See also* **Incontinence** in chapter 6.)

RECOMMENDATIONS

- *Obtain the opinion of a urologist specialist if urination or incontinence is a problem.*
- *If a specific cause is isolated, try to remedy it by following the instructions in the appropriate section in this book.*
- *The homeopathic remedies Ferrum phosphoricum or Causticum, potency 30 taken four times a day, may be beneficial until a more-specific homeopathic remedy is selected.*

Painful urination

Urination should never be painful. Elimination from the body is usually an enjoyable experience, and a mildly pleasant sensation is usually associated, although not noticed until it is pointed out! The body likes to have its toxins removed, and the nervous system generally says “thank you”.

Painful urination must thereby be considered an important warning. Generally, inflammation in the bladder or the urethra is the cause, but tumors and neurological diseases need to be excluded if the problems do not resolve under basic medical care.

RECOMMENDATIONS

- *Painful urination that does not respond to the advice given in the section on cystitis must be reviewed by a general practitioner initially (see* **Cystitis***).*
- *Homeopathic remedies Berberis, Juniper, and Cantharis may be used at potency 6 until a definite diagnosis has been made, and more-specific homeopathic remedies are chosen on the symptoms as a whole.*

Retention of urine

Retention of urine is the inability to pass the bladder contents. A desire to urinate usually occurs when the bladder is holding approximately 16 ounces of urine. Pain will increase if the bladder is not emptied when approximately 24 ounces is retained. The bladder can stretch and accommodate up to 80 ounces of urine, but then the pain becomes excruciating.

The reason is due to outlet obstruction, and needs to be treated as an emergency, because the back pressure from the full bladder up the ureters (the tubes from the kidneys) will lead to the kidneys developing hydronephrosis (kidneys filled with urine), that in turn will damage the kidney function.

Obstruction may slowly develop due to an enlarged prostate in males, or an increased worsening of bladder or uterine prolapse in women. Strictures from a chronic infection or acute inflammation of the urethra and prostate may all obstruct the flow. Rarely, but more frequently in children, foreign objects may impede urine flow. Trauma to the urethra from external injury, or internally from operative procedures or catheterization, may anatomically block the flow or encourage inflammation. Tumors at the neck of the bladder or (very rarely) in the urethra, may be a problem.

RECOMMENDATIONS

- *An inability to pass urine must always be seen by a doctor immediately. A catheter may need to be passed.*
- *If retention is noted, stop drinking until attention is sought and found.*
- *The unusual remedy Tarantula cubensis 6 can be used in a dose every 10min, and may relieve the situation. If Tarantula cubensis is not available, try Ignatia or Arnica at the same potency and frequency.*
- *See* **Prostate**.

Urine quality

The urine should have a clear-yellow color. The presence of any opacity (cloudiness) or a darkening or redness of the urine is abnormal. The color and viscosity (dilution) is dependent on the food eaten, and those who take vitamin-B complexes will note that their urine may appear a much darker yellow, or even a light orange. A reason for color change must be obvious, otherwise it should be assumed that blood is present, and this is pathological. Colorless urine is associated with overdilution, and is triggered most frequently by drinking diuretics such as alcohol and caffeine. Provided that an obvious reason for this color deficiency is apparent, then no further action needs to be taken.

RECOMMENDATIONS

- *Any change in color of the urine that is not clearly related to a dietetic change must be reviewed by a physician.*
- *At any sign of orange, brown, or pink blood in the urine, bleeding within the urogenital tract must be assumed, and investigated.*
- *Always take a first-morning urine sample, and refrigerate if the appointment with your physician is not within 3hr. In any case, collect the next urine sample after any abnormality is noted.*
- *Until a firm diagnosis is made, any suggestion of blood in the urine should be treated by the remedy Phosphorus 6, one dose every hour.*

Urinary urgency

Urinary urgency is an uncontrollable desire to empty the bladder. It is a sensation unlike any other, and is controlled by information from the nerves in the area. The brain can sense urgency because of an overstretched bladder, inflammation of the bladder or urethra, or by injury or stimulation of the nervous system between the bladder and the brain.

Inflammation caused by infection will encourage the bladder to empty in an attempt to flush out the invading organism, but often irritation from trauma, or overly acidic or alkaline urine may have the same effect. In males, an enlarged prostate will push up on the bladder exit, and send false information about the bladder fullness to the brain. A tilted pelvis or misaligned lower spine may pinch the sensory nerves of the bladder, telling the brain that the bladder is full when it is not. Spinal injury or problems within the brain itself may also do this.

When nervous or under stress, the body produces adrenaline, which moves blood to areas such as the muscles, heart, and lungs in preparation for fight or flight. This blood has to come from somewhere, and will be taken from the skin (we go pale), the bowel (we feel butterflies in our abdomen), and the bladder (we need to pass urine). Stress and anxiety will encourage the desire for urination, and may be the cause of urgency. The brain is sensitive to habit, and once a problem with the bladder has been triggered, the consciousness is concentrated on this area, and an individual becomes even more sensitive.

RECOMMENDATIONS

- *Ensure good hydration, because a concentrated acidic or alkaline urine will trigger urgency.*
- *Isolate the possibility of any psychological stress or nervousness and use relaxation, meditation, or counseling techniques to remove this.*
- *If the problem is sporadic, consider a food-allergy or intolerance test (see* **Food-allergy testing***).*
- *If problems persist, take a first-morning urine sample to a doctor and ask for an assessment and examination.*
- *Please refer to the relevant section in this book if any underlying cause is discovered.*
- *Please refer to the following homeopathic remedies in your preferred homeopathic manual: Cantharis, Kreosote, Petroselinum, and Sulphur. If the desire is nocturnal, consider Causticum, Graphites, and Pulsatilla, as well as those above.*
- *Any undiagnosed situation or one that is associated with back pain should be seen by an osteopath or chiropractor to assess the structural position of the lower back and pelvis.*
- *Hypnotherapy may be of benefit if no physical or obvious psychological cause can be isolated.*

Weak urinary flow or stream

A weak flow is an indication of nerve damage to or from the bladder muscle or a partial obstruction, which may be due to a developing stricture, inflammation, or tumor, but is most frequently associated in men with an enlarging prostate. The enlargement narrows the urethral lumen.

RECOMMENDATIONS

- *Attention should be paid to any cause of a weak flow; if uncertain, please see a doctor or urologist.*
- *Please treat the underlying cause by following instructions from the relevant section in this book.*

UTERINE PROBLEMS

Hydatidiform mole

A hydatidiform mole is a benign (it does not spread) tumor that forms in the part of a fertilized ovum, which attaches to the uterine wall that will become, or already is, the placenta. Hydatidiform moles can mimic pregnancy (by being initially discovered because of a missed period and a positive pregnancy test), and may be dangerous because of the potential for a serious hemorrhage. If caught early (by ultrasound scan), treatment is by dilatation and curettage (D and C), but those that are not noticed may require a hysterectomy. Clearly, this is a devastating condition to have, and I believe one that should be dealt with by modern medicine.

RECOMMENDATIONS

- *A hydatidiform mole is likely to be spotted only by an experienced physician or an ultrasound. Follow orthodox advice.*
- *Consult a complementary medical practitioner for constitutional support.*
- *See* **Operations and surgery***.*

Uterine prolapse

A prolapse is the falling or sinking of a part or the whole of an organ.

Normal and retroverted uterus

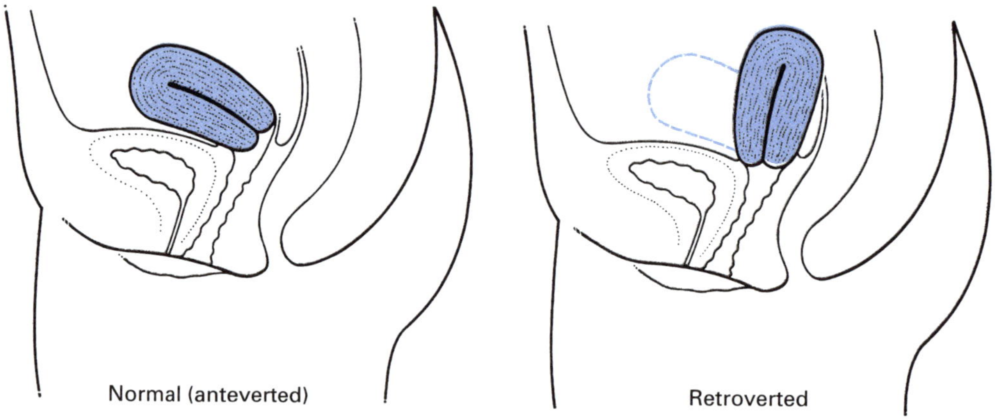

Normal (anteverted)

Retroverted

The illustration on the left shows the uterus tilted in the normal position. On the right is the almost-vertical position of a retroverted uterus.

Uterine prolapse is the displacement of the uterus downwards through the vagina. A mild prolapse may not be noticed, and is quite common after several pregnancies, but may descend to fill the vaginal vault, and even become exposed. The latter produces several problems, as the cervix and the lower part of the uterus will be exposed and lose its moist, protective environment. As the uterus descends, it puts pressure on the bladder, causing a frequent desire for urination and incontinence. Pain may be formed by the pressure.

Prolapse is usually the outcome of a weakening of the ligaments that hold the uterus in the pelvis. This may be due to an overstretching following pregnancy, or through a diminution in the tensile strength because of a loss of estrogen. Prolapse is therefore more common following multiple pregnancies or menopause.

RECOMMENDATIONS

- *Any discomfort or symptoms in the vagina or pelvis that do not resolve need to be examined by a gynecologist.*
- *Pelvic-floor exercises taught through yoga, Qi Gong, or basic physiotherapy may support and correct a mild prolapse.*
- *More-severe prolapses may be corrected by the insertion of a ring pessary that is fitted and placed at the top of the vaginal vault by a gynecologist.*
- *Surgical repair may be necessary, and this is performed by tightening up the uterine ligaments, or, radically, by a hysterectomy.*
- *Before any operative procedure is considered, please see a complementary medical specialist with an interest in herbal medicine and acupuncture, because the two in combination may tighten up the ligaments more so than exercises alone.*

Uterine retroversion/anteversion

When standing erect, a woman should find her uterus in a position with the cervix pointing downwards, but the top of the uterus pointing forwards.

This antiverted position of the uterus to some extent prevents gravity from pulling down the fertilized egg, and has been enhanced through natural selection during human evolution. Many women, however, have a uterus that is more erect in its position, and this condition is called a retroverted uterus. It is an anatomical anomaly and not a disease condition, and only rarely causes problems, such as pressure on the sacral nerves leading to discomfort in the lower back, pelvis, and legs, or infertility. It is caused by a tightness or shortness of the supporting ligaments.

I recommend that all women have a gynecological examination specifically to ascertain the position of the cervix in relation to the uterus. Ultrasound may be very beneficial as well. Unexplained back pains may be associated with this, and prolonged and invasive techniques for investigating infertility may be avoided. As you can see from the diagram, if the cervix is pointing too far forward then there is a strong suggestion of a retroverted uterus. Conception may prove difficult because the sperm will pool at the back of the vagina, and not have easy access to the cervical opening, the os. In such cases, sexual intercourse with the female on all fours or face down will allow the weight of the uterus to fall forward, therefore bringing the cervix more into a midline and available area. It is also worthwhile for the woman to sleep on her front after intercourse in order to maintain the position of the os (*see* **Conception**).

In unusual cases, the uterus may be lying to the left or right in the pelvis, and the cervical opening will be pushed into the left or right side of the vagina. Again, if this situation is established, then corrective positioning through intercourse may well deal with prolonged cases of infertility. (*See* **Sexual position and technique.**)

RECOMMENDATIONS

- *Obtain a gynecological assessment to recognize the uterine position.*
- *Strengthen pelvic-floor muscles through yoga or Qi Gong techniques, because this may pull the uterus into a less-retroverted position.*
- *In infertility, consider using a variety of positions, both for intercourse and for sleeping after sex.*
- *For backache, etc. consult an osteopath/chiropractor, and use in combination with yoga or Qi Gong.*
- *In extreme cases and where necessary, consider operative procedures (see* ***Operations and surgery****).*

VASECTOMY

A vasectomy is the voluntary surgical interruption of the vas deferens from both testicles. It is a simple procedure whereby a surgeon will create a small opening in the scrotum, locate the spermatic cord, isolate the vas deferens (the tube up which the sperm travel), and remove a section. Both ends are sealed, and from then on, any sperm produced cannot gain access to the seminal fluid and prostate, and will be reabsorbed by the body.

Sperm and testicular function are unaltered, although there have been some recent studies suggesting that vasectomies may cause cancer. These have been further researched and refuted.

Vasectomy is generally performed on a man who has established his family arrangements, having had enough children. It is certainly safer for a man to be sterilized than it is for a woman, and it is an effective form of contraception (allowing for a short period of time after the operation, when sperm may still exist in the upper part of the vas deferens or the urethra).

The downside is that a man may be able to father a family well into his dotage, and a vasectomy must be considered irreversible (depending on the amount of tube that is removed, reconnection may be possible, but it is very rare that such a reversal operation is successful). There is no reason to believe that a vasectomy will alter libido or sexual drive one way or the other, and a lot depends upon the psychology of the individual and the reasons why a vasectomy was performed. I have come across no spiritual justification for interrupting a man's fertility.

RECOMMENDATIONS

- *The operation is under local anesthetic, and therefore the insult to the system is reduced.*
- *Prepare the scrotum by applying an Arnica-based cream twice a day for five days before the operation.*
- *Please follow the pre- and postoperative suggestions (see* ***Operations and surgery****) to help healing, because this is a tender operation, although discomfort is generally held at bay by the use of Arnica 6 and a painkiller.*

STRUCTURAL MATTERS

ANKYLOSING SPONDYLITIS (AS)

This is an autoimmune disease affecting the joints between vertebrae. It generally starts in the lower spine, and presents as backache and stiffness, with referred discomfort such as chest pain, leg pains, and sometimes breathing difficulties.

RECOMMENDATIONS

- *Osteopathy and acupuncture are essential for both pain relief and potential curative treatment.*
- *Specific herbal treatments, especially Chinese and Tibetan, can be most beneficial.*
- *Homeopathy needs to be considered, and specific remedies should be based on the type of discomfort. The remedy Calcarea fluorica 30 taken every 2hr can be very beneficial in acute attacks.*
- *Daily exercise is essential to keep the muscles from going into spasm. Yoga and the Alexander technique should be considered.*
- *Regular visits to a Shiatsu or Rolfing practitioner are most relieving, as is basic massage and physiotherapy.*
- *As with any back problems, ensure that you sleep on a hard mattress. Practice the neutral position (head raised on one or two telephone directories, and the knees raised until the small of the back is flat on the ground) several times a day.*
- *See* **Autoimmune disease**.

BACKACHES

Backaches will affect most people at some time of their lives. It is most commonly associated with years of incorrect posture while sitting or walking, and also with poor abdominal musculature. If you consider the trunk of the body as a tube, and imagine cutting out the lower half of one side, you have a good description of a human body with weak abdominal muscles. The strain is all placed on the back muscles, which invariably maintain a level of tension that is much easier to strain or pull.

Structural abnormalities, such as retroverted uterus or kidney inflammation, are a cause, and more-chronic conditions such as arthritis of the spine, ankylosing spondylitis, and ruptured disks must be ruled out, but for basic backaches that are not recurrent or persistent, certain rules can be used.

RECOMMENDATIONS

- *Apply heat in the form of a hot-water bottle wrapped in a towel, or hot baths.*
- *Homeopathic remedies to be considered are Arnica, Magnesia phosphorica, Rhus toxicodendron, and Ruta. These are a few common remedies among the vast array. Refer to your preferred homeopathic book.*
- *Herbal treatments such as strong camomile tea, aniseed (which cannot be used in conjunction with homeopathy), caraway seeds (chew three teaspoonfuls, or infuse in a mug of hot water), and Passiflora (30 drops in water every hour) are a few of the antispasmodic herbs.*
- *Regular body work is recommended. Massage can work wonders. Polarity therapy, the Alexander technique, yoga, and Qi Gong are all useful to correct posture if backaches are recurrent.*
- *Debilitating backaches should be assessed by an osteopath or chiropractor.*
- *Persisting problems not amenable to osteopathy or chiropractic should be referred to Rolfing or Shiatsu practitioners, and have some relief.*
- *Use common sense. If you have a weak back, do not pick up heavy objects, and do not spend time in a stooped position.*
- *Sleep on a hard mattress, preferably face up, without a pillow.*
- *Avoid orthodox painkillers, because removing the pain will allow a continuation of the bad posture or injury, which may therefore worsen.*
- *Assessment from an orthopedic specialist is a last resort.*

BUNIONS

A bunion is the swelling of a small sack that is lined with synovial membrane. Synovial is the medical term for the inner lining of all the sacks that surround the joints in the body. The term bunion is usually associated with a swelling at the base of the great (big) toe, and is associated with a thickening of the overlying skin and a forcing of the great toe across the other toes.

It is usually created by prolonged use of tight footwear, including socks, and if not noted early and treated correctly, surgery is the only option.

RECOMMENDATIONS

- *Avoid wearing tight, pointed shoes.*
- *Spend as much time in bare feet as possible, especially if a bunion is appearing.*
- *Place cotton wool balls between the big toe and the adjacent toe to try to correct the angle for as much of the day as possible.*
- *Apply Arnica creams frequently.*
- *If inflammation sets in, use the homeopathic remedy Apis 6, four pills four times a day; if things do not settle within five days, or if the problem worsens, consult a complementary medical practitioner.*
- *Have your blood checked for levels of uric acid by your doctor, in case you have gout.*
- *Try eicosapentenoic acid and Bromelain at twice the recommended daily dose of a good, natural product.*
- *If an operative procedure is necessary, see* **Operations and surgery**.

BURSITIS

Bursae are the small sacks that surround the joints in the body. They contain a nutrient and lubricating fluid called synovial fluid, and the inner lining of these bursae is known as the synovial membrane.

Bursitis is inflammation of this membrane, and is usually caused by injury or persistent use of the tendons that lie above the bursae. "Housemaid's knee" is the most famous condition, although sportsmen and women can develop inflammation here as well.

RECOMMENDATIONS

- *Submerge the inflamed area in hot and cold water, 2min in each for 20min. Repeat this process three or four times a day.*
- *Apply Arnica creams to the area.*
- *Rest the area. You may need to immobilize the area with a bandage or sling for anywhere from 10 days to 6 weeks. In the case of a bursitis in the knee, avoid kneeling.*
- *A red, swollen, hot joint will benefit from the homeopathic remedy Belladonna 6, four pills every hour, but a persistent discomfort requires a specific remedy, and you should refer to your homeopathic manual, paying attention to the remedies Apis, Bryonia, Pulsatilla, Rhus toxicodendron, and Ruta.*
- *A persisting bursitis should be seen by an acupuncturist/osteopath for very effective and swift treatment.*

CARPAL-TUNNEL SYNDROME

The carpal-tunnel syndrome (CTS) is the most common of the repetitive strain injuries. It is usually brought about by overuse of the wrists in an incorrect position, and therefore found commonly in typists, computer users, and keyboard players. It is less-frequently found in workers who use their wrists and hands in a repetitive manner.

Carpal-tunnel syndrome may be associated with conditions such as rheumatoid arthritis and other autoimmune diseases; hypothyroidism; calcium deficiencies; certain drugs (especially the oral contraceptive pill and HRT); and (not uncommonly) pregnancy. These conditions lead to a deficiency of vitamin B_6, which is relevant to the condition.

The condition is characterized by pain, "pins-and-needles," and a loss of sensation in the thumb, index, and third finger, as well as the palm and, to some extent, the back of the hand and the wrist. A diagnostic technique is to flex the wrist (pull the hand back) for about one minute, which should bring on or intensify the symptoms, and then extend the wrist to relieve the symptoms.

Carpal-tunnel syndrome is caused by swelling of the tendons that control the flexion of the wrist and fingers. Overuse causes extra blood to be pulled into the area to supply the muscles with oxygen, and this swelling puts pressure on the median nerve that nestles in between these tendons. All of these—along with other nerves, veins, arteries, and the lymphatic system—are sheathed in a tight covering that does not allow the swelling to move outwards, and therefore causes pressure directly applied to the nerve.

RECOMMENDATIONS

- *A persistence of this problem needs to be checked by a doctor to rule out any underlying condition such as those mentioned above.*
- *Ensure that the position of your chair (when at a computer, typing, or at a keyboard) is such that your wrists are at a slightly higher level than the keyboard.*
- *If you are taking any drugs, check that they do not cause vitamin-B_6 or calcium deficiency.*
- *Avoid oral contraception or HRT, any colorings in foods, and an excess of protein in the diet, all of which can reduce vitamin-B_6 levels.*
- *Supplement your daily diet with vitamin B_6 (50mg) and calcium (400mg) at each meal.*
- *Use a teaspoonful of turmeric (the Indian spice haldi) mixed with 8 ounces of skimmed milk, four times per day.*
- *It may be necessary to avoid the repetitive action that triggered the problem for up to six weeks, which may be inconvenient for many professions. A persistence of the problem will require this as a medical necessity, and if not heeded, can lead to permanent damage that will require surgical intervention.*
- *Acupuncture and osteopathy in combination is most often curative.*
- *Chinese, Tibetan, and Ayurvedic herbal medicines can be of benefit, and should be used before considering surgery.*
- *Homeopathic remedies Magnesia phosphorica, Hypericum, and Nitric acid can all be used at potency 6, one dose every 2hr for three days during an acute attack, and then one dose twice a day for ten days.*
- *Hot and cold applications around the wrists and up the arm, and also gentle massage of Arnica cream, can be swiftly relieving and even permanently curative.*

GANGRENE

Gangrene is an emotive word that, quite rightly, strikes a note of fear.

Gangrene arises in tissues that have been deprived of oxygen due to a loss of circulation as a result of, for example, frostbite, trauma, diseases that compromise the circulation (such as Buerger's disease in smokers, and diabetes), and age-related conditions such as arteriosclerosis. Blockages in arteries, known as emboli, are also a common cause. Prior to gangrene setting in, the tissues become painful, and if not treated immediately, will turn black, and mercifully numb. This situation is known as *dry gangrene,* so called because it is not infected. *Wet gangrene*, which has a "wet" appearance, is created when anaerobic (not requiring oxygen) bacteria invade the dead tissue. If these produce a foul-smelling gas, then the condition is known as *gas gangrene.* Wet and gas gangrene produce toxic chemicals that will lead to septicemia (blood poisoning) and shock.

RECOMMENDATIONS

- *Seek medical attention immediately.*
- *Refer to the sections in this book to treat any underlying condition.*
- *The homeopathic remedy Bothrops or Lachesis, potency 30 taken every 15min, can be used for dry gangrene while awaiting further medical intervention.*
- *Echinacea and Tarantula cubensis can be used at potency 30 every 15min for wet or gas gangrene (again, while obtaining medical treatment).*
- *Surgical debridement and possible amputation may be necessary, along with antibiotics and medical wound-treatment.*

GOLFER'S ELBOW—*see* Tendonitis

HAMSTRING INJURY

The hamstrings are the large muscles found below the buttocks, behind the thigh bone that causes the knee to flex. These immensely powerful muscles are frequently injured by athletes, who will be seen suddenly pulling up, usually after a sudden movement. Ironically, the more finely tuned the athlete and the stronger the muscle, the more likely the fibers are to tear. Hamstring injury is generally very painful, and if the muscle is ruptured, a lump will be felt. Relief is obtained by relaxing the leg, and the pain is made worse by trying to flex the knee.

RECOMMENDATIONS

- *Avoid hamstring injury by stretching out thoroughly before and after exercise. Place the outstretched leg on a support at hip height, or sit on the ground with the leg splayed. Keep the knee slightly bent, and aim at placing the forehead on the knee. Do not bounce, but apply gentle pressure, count to eight and return to an upright position. Repeat this process eight times.*
- *Apply heat or ice, depending on whichever is soothing, for relief of the immediate pain. If the injury is due to cramp, then heat will be of benefit; if the muscle has torn and inflammation has set in, then ice will be the choice.*
- *If an injury has already been sustained, apply an Arnica-based cream regularly to the entire muscle, paying special attention to the area around the injury.*
- *Apply ultrasound via a physiotherapist or body worker with suitable equipment.*
- *Acupuncture, Shiatsu, and massage techniques will all speed healing.*
- *Osteopathy and chiropractic may be of benefit, but must be considered if the injury is longstanding. Extra weight will be placed on the other leg, and pelvic misalignment is inevitable, but easily adjusted.*
- *The homeopathic remedy Arnica 6 should be taken immediately every 15min. Consider Ruta and more Arnica on a four-hourly basis, depending on the symptoms of the injury.*
- *The fluid extract Ruta should be taken (one teaspoonful in water) three times a day until the injury has healed.*

HERNIAS—*see* Hiatus hernia.

A hernia is the protrusion of an organ from its own cavity or space into another. This usually occurs through muscle, but can also occur through any membrane.

There are over 170 areas where a hernia may occur. The most common are inguinal hernias (groin), a hernia following pregnancy down the midline of the abdomen, and incisional (postoperative) hernia. All these occur because of a weakening of the abdominal muscles, with a protrusion of the bowel or the omentum—the fatty tissue that carries all the blood vessels, nerves, and lymphatic system to and from the bowel itself. These are all, effectively, external hernias. Internal hernias may be just as common, as in a hiatus hernia, which is a protrusion of the stomach through the diaphragm.

Most hernias are repairable, usually by surgery, and more rarely by exercise techniques and naturopathic medicines that strengthen musculature. Hernias only become serious if the organ that is herniating is a vital one, such as the brain, which can herniate down through a membrane that effectively divides the brain into an upper and lower part. Hernias that obstruct or pinch an organ, thereby compromising its normal function or blocking its bloodflow, can lead to gangrene, which can be fatal if not treated.

Inguinal hernia

The inguinal hernia deserves a special mention because it is the most common and the most commonly referred to. There are two types: *indirect* and *direct* inguinal hernias.

The indirect inguinal hernia occurs because of a weakening at the top end of a small canal, down which the testicle descends from the abdomen into the scrotal sack in the latter stages of fetal development or the early part of life. A membrane forms, but this can be torn with excessive internal pressure, often created through pregnancy, excessive coughing, or strain.

The direct hernia occurs usually because of a muscular strain, often by incorrectly picking up an object that is too heavy. Here, the abdominal wall tears and the gut protrudes through. In both cases the hernia may be reducible or not, depending on whether the lump can be reduced. The danger signs are a nonreducible lump that becomes painful, apart from the initial tear that may occur with the strain. This suggests a compromised blood-flow, and must be treated as an emergency.

RECOMMENDATIONS

- *All lumps and bumps that are unexplained, persistent, or painful should be reviewed by a doctor. Surgical intervention may be necessary (see* **Operations and surgery***).*

- *A small muscular tear may repair, but at least six weeks of very careful nonexertion of the muscle group must be maintained.*
- *Applications of Arnica creams four times a day to the area may be beneficial.*
- *If the initial strain is painful, use Arnica 6 every 15min for up to 2hr.*
- *Discuss options for strengthening the muscle group with an osteopath or a sports-injury physiotherapist.*
- *Acupuncture may speed up the healing.*

HIP PROBLEMS

Arthritis of the hip

Arthritis of the hip deserves special mention, simply because of its prevalence in our elderly population. Treatment at any stage of the disease may be effective, but very often, a replacement is in order.

The operative procedure for an arthritic hip is very successful, and recent changes in surgical technique encourage the patient to be up and out of bed within 48 hours. Complications are rare, but poor fixing of the ball and/or socket components does occur, and this operation is notorious, especially if the individual does not get out of bed swiftly, for producing blood clots that can lead to pulmonary emboli. These risks are small, however, and the techniques are improving. Twenty years ago it would be necessary to consider replacing a replacement within 5–7 years but now, with techniques and components at a much-higher standard, a hip may last up to 20 years.

RECOMMENDATIONS

- *See* **Arthritis** *for information on how to avoid the necessity of an operation.*
- *If an operation is required, see* **Operations and surgery**.
- *Ensure that good physiotherapy, osteopathy, and yoga are all employed before and after any*

operation. Strengthening the muscles around the hip joint and ensuring realignment of the inevitably dislodged pelvis speeds healing, and will maintain the joint at a better level of health.

Hip fracture

Gravity has a profound effect on everything, and the calcium in our bones is no exception. As we age, the protein matrix in which the calcium sits in bones diminishes—in part due to lack of exercise, decreased estrogen and, especially, progesterone levels and, for many reasons, the Western diet. The outcome in the longest bone in the body—the femur or thigh bone—is that the top end (the hip) becomes less dense. For a variety of reasons, including a loss of control in the balance centers in the brain and weakening muscles, elderly people have a greater tendency to fall, and this, in combination with the weakened neck of the femur, makes hip fractures one of the two most-common breakages in the elderly (the other being a Colles' fracture of the wrist).

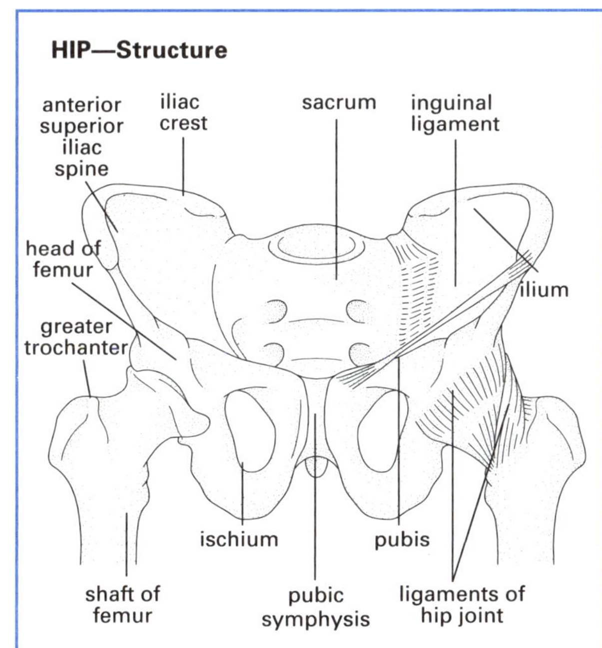

A hip fracture may sever the artery leading to the head of the femur which, having cut off the blood supply, will cause a necrosis (death) of the top part of the bone. This can become extremely painful eventually, and can also lead to gangrene, which could be fatal.

RECOMMENDATIONS

- *Any trauma that leads to an immobile or painful hip must be reviewed by an accident-and-emergency department, and x-ray investigation should be undertaken.*
- *See* **Operations and surgery** *if surgery is required.*
- *The homeopathic remedies Arnica and Symphytum at potency 30 should be taken every 2hr, decreasing to every 4hr after medical intervention has ceased.*
- *See* **Arthritis of the hip** *for recommendations and pre- and postoperative care.*
- *Prevention is the best form of medicine. Unfortunately, bone density is often determined in our teens, and by the time a hip threatens to fracture, interventional treatment is necessary (see* **Osteoporosis***).*

LUMBAGO

Lumbago describes backache in the lumbar or lumbosacral region of the lower back. It is very important to differentiate any underlying cause of lower backache, and lumbago is simply a definition of a symptom rather than a condition in itself. Lower backache may be the outcome of poor posture, muscular strain, structural misalignment, referred pain from abdominal or pelvic organs, or a disease processes within the bones, such as osteoporosis, (rarely) tuberculosis, or even cancer.

In Ayurvedic medicine, sexual energy lies in the pelvis at the base of the spine, and is known as kundalini. Spiritual or psychological problems involving sexuality may lead to persisting lumbago. Chinese practitioners consider the lower back as representing many acupuncture points on the bladder meridian. Bladder Qi is strongly affected by fear, suspicion, and jealousy, as well as being an organ that removes "dirty" fluid waste.

Any of these emotions may be related to lumbago, and need to be assessed in a holistic treatment.

Excessive abdominal weight or pregnancy, in association with weak abdominal musculature, will put extra pressure on the back muscles, and allow either muscular strain or misalignment in the lumbosacral area. The fused joints between the hip bones and the sacrum—known as the iliosacral joints—are often slightly misaligned. In pregnancy and during menopausal changes, raised or lowered estrogen levels will alter the flexibility of the pelvic ligaments (the more estrogen, the more supple), which can alter the pelvic-bone positions. Inflammation can occur in the lower back joints through osteoarthritis, rheumatoid arthritis, ankylosing spondylitis, and certain infections, all of which have to be assessed before a correct treatment can be established.

"Neutral" position for back

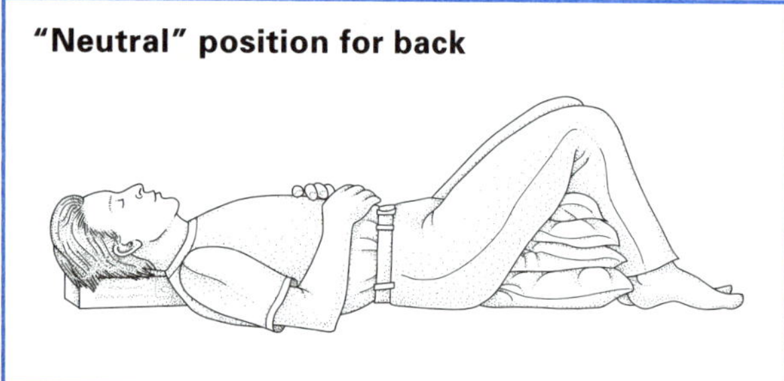

RECOMMENDATIONS

- *Use simple measures such as the application of heat or ice (whichever feels relieving), and spend time in the "neutral" position: with the head raised by a telephone directory (two if you live in a small country!) and four pillows under the knees.*
- *Gentle stretching exercises (best taught by a body worker or gym master) may be relieving.*
- *A visit to an osteopath or chiropractor for a diagnostic consultation should be considered if problems persist.*
- *Polarity therapy, the Alexander technique, yoga, and Qi Gong should all be considered as part of a long-term preventative package.*
- *Back pain through pregnancy or menopause may be hormonally related, and should be treated by a complementary medical practitioner with an understanding of naturopathic treatments affecting hormones. Homeopathic remedies will be of benefit, and should be chosen depending on the symptoms. Arnica, Bryonia, Rhus toxicodendron, and Ruta should all be considered.*
- *Shiatsu and massage will be relieving, if not curative, as may acupuncture in association with other body work.*
- *Please review the relevant sections in this book if a specific condition is causing the lumbago.*

NAILS

Care of the nails

The nails are scaled-down versions of claws, which were once very necessary for survival. They are created by uniting the epithelial or surface cells, integrated with a protein called keratin. The nail grows from the nailbed, which is a very vascular part of modified skin. The half-moon is paler in color because it is less vascular, but is nevertheless an important, growing, part of the nail. It takes approximately 3–4 months for a nail to grow from its base to the loose distal border in the finger, and about 6–8 months in a toenail.

The nail is derived from a modified type of skin surface or epithelium, and therefore any compounds that can benefit the skin can benefit the nails and their strength. Keratin is derived from amino acids, so any deficiency in protein intake is also liable to cause skin problems. Although the function of the nails has diminished as we have developed over the ages, their use as an ornament in women is well respected by the cosmetic industry, and indeed, a well-manicured finger has its attractions, and can reflect a subconscious attitude of the owner for neatness or tidiness. Bitten or chewed nails may show a nervous disposition, and dirty nails may be a comment on personal hygiene (with apologies to those farmers and mechanics whose profession may not allow an alternative to dirty nails!). Health is certainly reflected by deformities, ridges, the nails being brittle, and the color of the nailbed.

NAILS—Structure

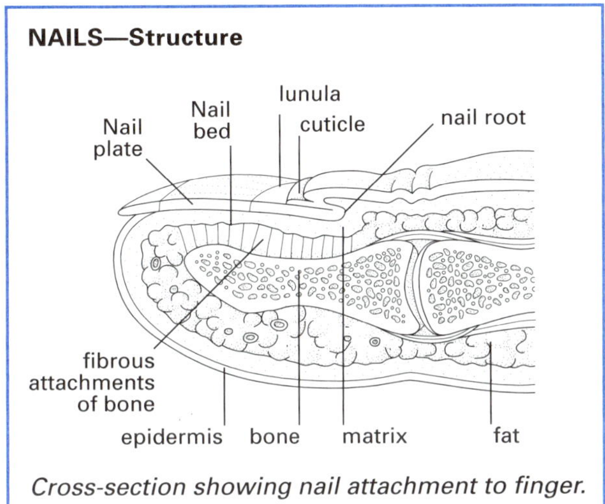

Cross-section showing nail attachment to finger.

Nails grow forward on a flat plane, unless the nailbed has been damaged or infected. Keeping the nails trimmed to the level of the end of the fingers offers protection to a very sensitive part of the body, and protects against injury. Compression of toes can cause the soft pulp around the nails to overgrow or cut into the nail, which will be painful and lead to infection. When cutting nails, it is best to create a small V-shape in the middle section (*see* **Ingrowing toenail**) to encourage growth forward rather than sideways.

There is no health risk or disadvantage in using nail varnish or strengthener, provided that the nailbed and its surround are not infected.

Abnormal nails

An abnormality in shape, color, or texture of the nail can be indicative of underlying disease or deficiency.

Biting the nails

Biting the nails is not a problem, although it usually includes nibbling at the surrounding skin and cuticle. This needs to be stopped if it is painful or predisposing to infections. Nailbiting does suggest an underlying anxiety or nervous disposition, which will benefit from a relaxation or meditation technique. Hypnotherapy and counseling may also be required.

Deformed nails

Deformed nails usually occur because of damage to the nailbed through injury.

Discoloration of the nails

Discoloration of the nail itself usually occurs because of fungal infection, which tends to make the nail yellow. Rarely, toxins in the system will be eliminated in the nails, creating a change in color. Little black specks are indicative of a condition known as bacterial endocarditis, and represent small clots. This is a serious condition, and needs to be dealt with by a physician immediately. White patches are indicative of deficiencies in calcium, zinc, or vitamin A. These are not uncommon in growth spurts in children, but in adults usually represent dietary deficiency or drug-induced calcium loss.

Changes in the color of the epithelium underneath the nail can show anemia if pale, jaundice if yellow, and the rare condition of excess iron ingestion if brown. A bruised nail will appear purplish or black.

Fungal infection

Fungus has a propensity to settle in nailbeds, causing deformity by either killing off the growth area or causing a faster rate of growth leading to thickened nails (*see* **Fungal infections**).

Ingrowing toenail

This painful condition is caused by the edges of the toenail growing downwards, and thereby cutting into the soft pulp of the toe. It is most commonly found in the big toe, and is predominantly created by injury or persistent compression through tight-fitting footwear.

An ingrowing toenail that is uncared for will minimally inflame, but may also create an area of infection that, if left untreated, could jeopardize the toenail or possibly allow gangrene to set in.

RECOMMENDATIONS

FOR INGROWING TOE NAILS

- *Ensure from an early age that loose-fitting shoes are worn, and that as much time as possible is spent barefoot. Remember that tight-fitting socks can be just as compressing.*
- *See* **Feet, care of.**
- *Any injury involving a toenail should be reviewed by a podiatrist or chiropodist.*
- *Ensure that the toenails are kept cut short. Do not cut back too far the area of the nail that is cutting into the toe, because this may, paradoxically, encourage further growth at a faster rate. It is better to cut a small, V-shaped wedge in the middle of the toenail.*
- *Soak some cotton-wool pads, and compress in an Arnica or Calendula lotion, then wedge gently under the nail.*
- *Apply an Arnica or Calendula cream around the inflamed area.*
- *Review your preferred homeopathic manual, paying specific interest to Arnica, Hypericum, and Calendula.*
- *Any persisting problem, or one that is inflamed or infected despite the above treatments, should be seen by a podiatrist or general practitioner, who may remove part or all of the nail under a local anesthetic.*

INGROWING TOENAILS—Treatment

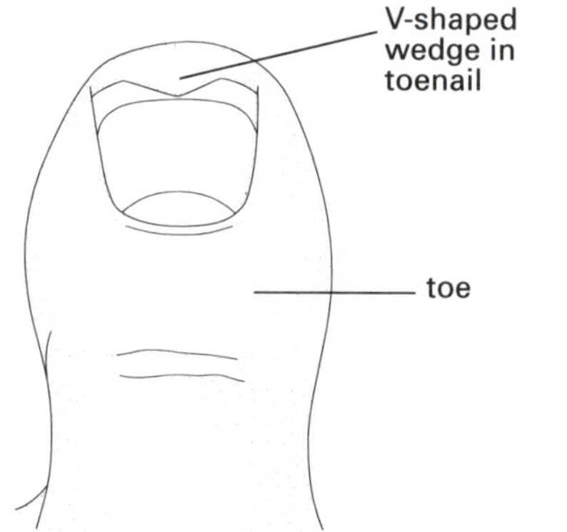

Do not cut back the problem-nail area too far. Cutting a V-shaped wedge will encourage growth away from the affected area.

Infection around the nail (whitlows, paronychia)

Medically termed paronychia or whitlows, or colloquially known as Mother's Blessing, this is a painful, red, or pus-filled infection occurring at the side of the nails, and extending underneath on occasions. These infections are painful, usually because of the pressure buildup, and treatment is recommended at an early stage, as described in the recommendations below.

Ridging of the nails

This can represent deficiencies in the vitamins A, B complex, and D, calcium, zinc, and essential fatty acids.

RECOMMENDATIONS

- *When cutting the nails, create a small V-shape in the middle to encourage forward growth.*
- *Avoid tight footwear, which will encourage the nail surround to be cut by the edges of the nail.*
- *Discoloration of the nail without an obvious cause should be presented to a doctor for diagnosis.*
- *Brittle, ridged, or cracking nails are usually indicative of deficiency or heavy-metal toxicity, and a suitable blood and hair analysis should isolate the specific compound, which should then be replenished. You can try supplementation of the nutrients mentioned above but, because any of them may be the problem, and an improvement may not be seen for 3–4 months (the time it takes for a nail to grow), this is an expensive method of correcting the fault.*
- *A bruised finger may be painful because of the pressure built up under the inflexible nail. Place the digit in ice water in an attempt to take down the swelling. Application of an Arnica-based cream may be beneficial. It may be necessary for a doctor to pierce the nail to release the blood underneath. If a doctor is not available, place a sewing needle in boiling water for a few minutes, remove it, and hold the needle over an open flame (ensuring not to*

burn your own fingers, because both ends of the needle will heat up). While the needle is still hot, apply gentle pressure through the nail, making sure that the needle does not penetrate into the very sensitive epithelium below. Ensure that the nail is thoroughly cleaned, preferably with alcohol, before inserting the needle. The homeopathic remedy Arnica 6 should be taken every hour for three doses, and then every 3hr until better.

- *Paronychia or whitlows should be immersed in hot and then ice water alternately for about 5min. An Arnica- or Calendula-based cream can be applied, and the homeopathic remedy Hepar sulfuris calcarium 6 should be taken every hour. A persistence should be seen by a complementary medical practitioner.*
- *Any injury to the nail or fingers will benefit from the homeopathic remedy Hypericum 6, either taken every hour or alternating with the remedies mentioned above.*
- *Nail biting may benefit by applying an unpleasant-tasting substance around the nails, or may be stopped by hypnosis.*
- *Ridging may represent deficiencies that should be assessed by a complementary practitioner.*

NECK PROBLEMS

The neck is notorious as a site for aches and pains, which can occur at any age. There are numerous neck muscles that control the movement of the head, and the skull, being a heavy object, demands much effort on these muscles. The cervical spine is flexible and, more than any other part of the spinal column, undergoes a lot of movement.

The neck muscles are constantly under tension to pull the skull up, and anxiety and nervousness tighten them more. This makes the muscles more prone to being strained than others, and aches and pains are therefore frequent. The constant movement within the cervical vertebrae leads to a tendency for arthritis to set in, more readily in older age.

The Eastern philosophies consider that several meridians travel through the neck muscles. The large and small intestine, bladder, gallbladder and triple heater all have acupuncture points along the surface of the neck muscles. Weakness in any of these organs or systems can lead to dysfunctional muscles, and thereby problems. I find it fascinating that the triple heater—which may represent the adrenal gland and therefore represent stress—should pass through the neck and over the shoulders. I believe that this accounts for why we

NECK—Muscles, Ligaments, and Cervical Spine

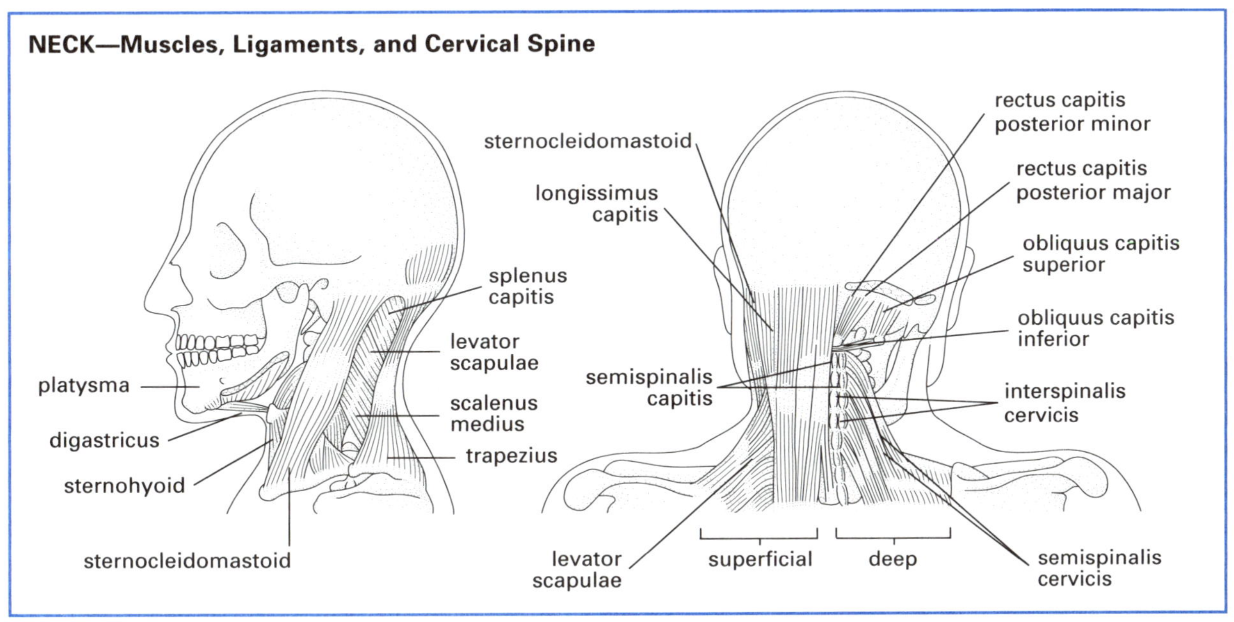

feel tension in these muscles, and benefit so readily from a shoulder rub rather than other muscles such as the thigh, buttocks, or lower back, which carry far more weight and should theoretically tire out much more easily.

RECOMMENDATIONS

- *For specific spinal problems, see the appropriate section.*
- *Neck pains associated with any trauma, such as a road-traffic accident or sport injury, must be seen by a doctor initially, in case the spinal column is damaged.*
- *Injury, especially whiplash, may be investigated by radiography (x-ray). Avoid this unless injury to the spinal column is suspected, or the problem is persisting.*
- *Apply heat or ice, depending on which is most soothing and does not leave the neck in a worse state of spasm.*
- *Spend as much time as possible in the neutral position; the head supported by two telephone directories and the knees raised so that the small of the back is flat on the floor (see* **Lumbago***).*
- *Consider a neck brace if moving the neck is painful, although there is some debate whether neck braces should be used. Discuss this with your health professional.*
- *Use the remedy Arnica 6 every 15min after the injury for three doses, and then every 2hr for the next 24hr. Thereafter take Arnica 30 every 6hr until the discomfort is relieved. Massage in an Arnica-based cream, three or four times a day, and any gentle massage offered should have a downward motion.*
- *Osteopaths, chiropractors, craniosacral therapists, Shiatsu practitioners, and other masseurs who have experience in this field will all have techniques to resolve neck injuries.*
- *Acupuncture may be instantly relieving.*
- *Neck problems with no obvious cause may be related to acupuncture meridians, and a consultation with a complementary medical practitioner with expertise in this area may lead to a diagnosis of weakness within the large or small intestine, gallbladder, bladder, adrenal, or thyroid glands.*

HEAD AND NECK—Acupuncture Points and Meridians

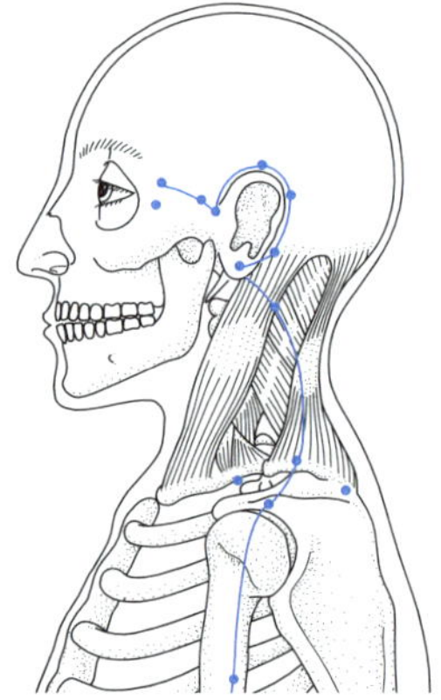

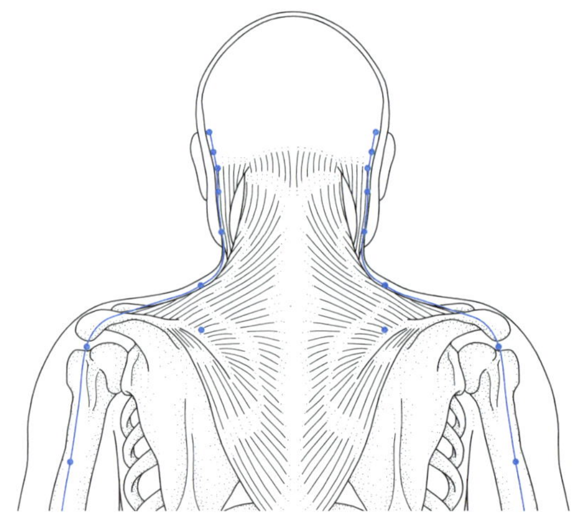

The large and small intestine, bladder, gallbladder, and triple-heater meridians have acupuncture points on the head and neck.

Broken neck

The term "broken neck" is a broad term that may indicate a crack within a vertebra or the severance of the spinal cord.

RECOMMENDATIONS

- *Any neck injury that has any neurological symptoms associated with it—such as numbness, tingling, loss of sensation, odd sensations, or paralysis—must be reviewed by a doctor.*
- *Immediately immobilize the neck (see* **Spinal injury***).*
- *Please refer to the relevant section, depending upon the injury, such as fracture, pain, or paralysis.*

Whiplash

Whiplash is a syndrome that includes headache, pain, and tenderness of the neck and the supporting muscles of the head and neck. Whiplash is a hyperflexion of the neck, usually caused by traveling in a vehicle that suddenly stops, or is hit from behind or in front. The forward motion of the motor vehicle encourages the head to travel in that direction at that speed, and any interference will cause the neck to flex. Most commonly, when hit from behind, the car seat pushes the body forward, leaving the head behind and thereby creating a whip-like movement and injury. The damage is usually caused by a strain on the muscles holding the vertebrae together and the other neck muscles that tense in an attempt to protect movement. Trying to move the head against these cramped muscles causes pain, as well as the strained vertebral muscles.

Other than the pain, neurological symptoms may be present if the spinal column was bruised in the incident. This may range from tingling and numbness through to partial or even total paralysis, which is usually transient.

RECOMMENDATIONS

- *Apply heat or ice, whichever feels more soothing, as soon as the injury has occurred.*
- *Take the homeopathic remedy Arnica 6 every 15min for 1hr, and then every 2hr for three days.*
- *Radiographic (x-ray) investigation is advisable if pain is severe or neurological symptoms are marked.*
- *Osteopathy and acupuncture should be administered as soon as possible.*
- *Massage should also be considered.*
- *There is some controversy about the use of a neck brace. At the moment, the evidence is equivocal, and I think that during the first three days a neck brace should be used, and after that, gentle movements should be encouraged. A neck brace at night is probably a good idea to prevent sudden and unexpected movements.*
- *Any neurological injury that persists should be treated by reviewing the section on nerve injuries and inflammation (see* **Nerves***).*

PROLAPSED ("SLIPPED") DISC

A vertebral disc is a wedge of two types of material between the cartilagenous plate that lies on the surface of adjacent vertebrae.

The peripheral part of this disc is made of a dense protein tissue, and is called the *anulus fibrosus.* Inside the anulus fibrosus, much like a jam doughnut, lies a gelatinous material called the *nucleus pulposus.* The anulus fibrosus is tightly attached to the vertebrae through the cartilage plate, and is the main reason why the vertebrae can only move by small degrees. The elasticity of the disc absorbs a large part of any strain put through the vertebral column. If a stress is greater than the strength of this disc, the anulus fibrosus may rupture, and the nucleus pulposus may herniate. This is described as a prolapsed or slipped disc.

There is usually excruciating pain, and any movement makes the situation worse. The characteristic "locking" in a bent position is because a disc usually slips when a heavy weight is lifted, and the strain is taken at the vertebrae, rather than at the knees as in a straight back lift.

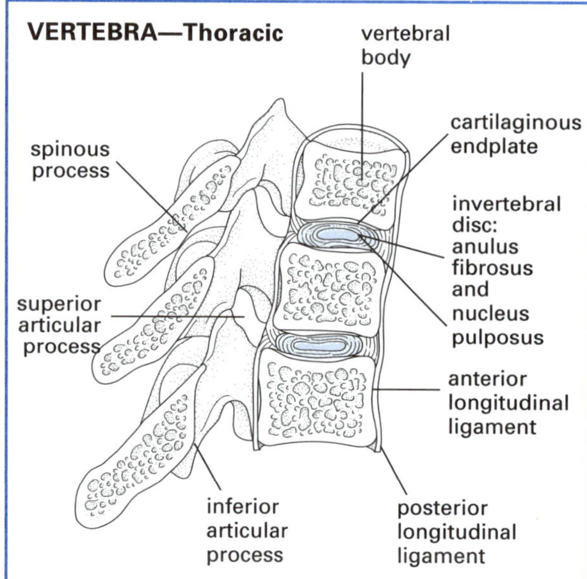

A disk may "slip" if excess strain is put on the spine. The dense, outer layer of a disc, the anulus fibrosus, *may rupture, allowing the gelatinous inside layer, the* nucleus pulposus, *to herniate.*

The spinal column, in Eastern philosophies, represents an anatomical signpost for the major flow of energy through the system. This is especially true in Tibetan medicine. A weakness in a disc, therefore, is not only associated with a bad injury, but is also a fundamental weakness in the energy as a whole. It may take an incorrect lifting position to trigger the event, but the underlying weakness is the reason why the injury occurs. This is particularly relevant if the injury is recurrent or chronic.

A slipped disc may be difficult to diagnose, because pulled muscles and nerve entrapment may mimic the symptoms. An experienced osteopath or chiropractor is likely to be able to differentiate, but sometimes an x-ray is required.

RECOMMENDATIONS

- *Application of heat through a wrapped-up hot-water bottle or heat pad may be instantly soothing. Settle into the most comfortable position and get the opinion of an osteopath, chiropractor, or experienced Shiatsu practitioner.*
- *The immediate use of Arnica 6 every 10min is a homeopathic essential.*
- *Osteopathic, chiropractic, or Shiatsu treatment may supersede physiotherapy in alleviating discomfort and the associated muscle spasm that follows a ruptured disc.*
- *Acupuncture may be instantly relieving.*
- *Any nerve entrapment or associated injury should be dealt with by referring to the section on nerve injury (see* **Nerves***).*
- *Always pick up heavy objects with the back straight, taking the weight on the knees.*
- *Regular exercise and stretching will keep muscles toned and limbered.*
- *Yoga and Qi Gong are essential to prevent recurrence.*
- *Avoid painkillers, because more damage will be done if movement is continued.*
- *A doctor can administer an injection by local anesthetic.*
- *Surgical intervention is a last resort. Techniques are now performed under fiber-optic conditions (a small tube is passed in through the back and the operation is done as "keyhole" surgery), although major operations may be required. In extreme cases, the disc is removed and the vertebrae fused so that the joint becomes immovable.*

REPETITIVE STRAIN INJURY (RSI)

—*see* **Tendonitis**

SACROILIAC PAIN

Of all backaches, this requires a brief but special mention. The pelvis is surrounded by several bones (*see* diagram of pelvis, opposite). Where the iliac bone connects with the sacrum is known as the sacroiliac joint.

This joint is fused, but has enough flexibility to dislodge itself and become misaligned, which it does frequently. Even slight movements can strain the ligaments, and the result is either a short period of discomfort, or longer-lasting and more-severe pain. The inner aspect of the joint is associated with a muscle that bends up the thigh at the hip, known as the psoas. Through and around the psoas travel most of the nerves from the lower lumbar and sacrospinal cord. Any inflammation of the sacroiliac joint may cause inflammation in this muscle or these nerves, leading to a variety of symptoms, including sciatica. Abdominal discomfort and hip pain, as well as pains and neurological symptoms throughout the legs, buttocks, and lower back, are all associated therefore with the sacroiliac joint.

PELVIS—Structure

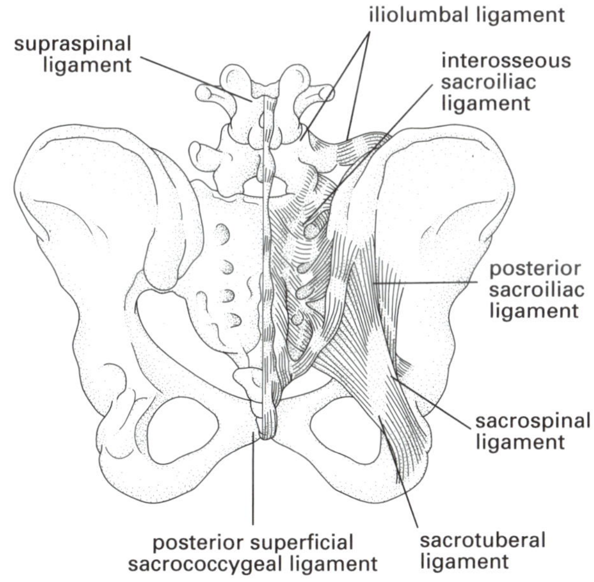

The ligaments of the pelvis are very much under the influence of estrogen, which will loosen them, especially in preparation for pregnancy. Women are therefore prone to sacroiliac displacement when estrogen levels are high during the monthly cycle, and are more prone to straining the joint as the ligaments tighten during menopause. Certain activities, especially if muscular stretching has not been undertaken beforehand, or if heavy weights are lifted without the back being straight, will all entice sacroiliac strain.

RECOMMENDATION

- *See* **Backache**.

SCIATICA

Sciatica is the medical term for a pain that travels from the lower back down the back of the leg, through the calf, and to the outer aspect of the foot. It is caused by inflammation of the sciatic nerve, which is the largest nerve in the body, the main nerve of the lower limb, and has branches coming from the spinal column from the spaces between lumbar vertebrae four and five (L4–5), all the way down to sacral outlet three (S3).

Depending upon which part of the nerve is inflamed, a pain may be felt anywhere along the sciatic nerve line, such that a discomfort in the foot or calf may be a sciatic inflammation. The diagnostic test is to lie down and pull the toes backwards which stretches the sciatic nerve. A worsening is probably sciatic discomfort. The same will occur if the leg is raised with the knees straight.

The cause is usually a misaligned vertebra or inflamed muscles, through which the sciatic nerve passes. A prolapsed disc or arthritic condition may be responsible and, rarely, viral and supplemental defiencies can trigger inflammation.

RECOMMENDATIONS

- *Apply heat through a wrapped hot-water bottle or heat pad to the area.*
- *The homeopathic remedies Colocynthis or Lycopodium may be used if the discomfort is in the right leg, and Carboneum sulphuricum if the pain is on the left. Take potency 6 every hour. A more accurate selection of remedy should be made, depending on the symptoms, from your preferred homeopathic manual.*
- *Osteopathy, chiropractic, Shiatsu, and acupuncture may all be instantly relieving, and perhaps preferable to physiotherapy initially.*
- *Any one of yoga, Qi Gong, Alexander technique, and Polarity therapy may be considered to train*

and strengthen the back muscles to protect the sensitive nerves.

- *Use Vitamin B_1 (15mg per foot of height) with the next meal after the problem starts. Then take 10mg per foot of height with each meal for three days maximum. Any nausea or dizziness associated with taking this compound is an indication to stop.*
- *Bromelaine (150mg per foot of height in divided doses) with meals is a very good, naturopathic anti-inflammatory.*
- *A teaspoonful of turmeric in 8 ounces of full-fat milk (and honey to taste) should be simmered for 10min. A mouthful should be swallowed every half hour until the 16 ounces are drunk.*
- *Two handfuls of white bread mixed with a heaped tablespoonful of cayenne pepper and enough water to make a dough-like consistency can be placed over the lower back and held on by a wraparound. Remove this after 20min because it may burn the skin, but if it is effective, then repeat every 6hr.*
- *Avoid orthodox painkillers if possible, because a removal of the pain may encourage movement, which will further damage an inflamed nerve.*
- *Steroid injection or nerve block is a last resort, but is useful if no other treatment is proving beneficial.*

SEVERED TENDON

See **Achilles tendon.**

The partial or complete severance or rupture of a tendon is a painful and serious condition. It most commonly occurs with the Achilles tendon behind the heel. When this tears, a severe and marked pain is suffered, and if the tendon ruptures, there is often a loud crack, and an individual feels as if somebody or something has hit the back of his leg. The foot becomes flexed if the entire tendon is ruptured, or only a limited amount of extension is possible if some of the fibers are still intact. Tendon rupture elsewhere may not be all this dramatic, but is equally painful.

RECOMMENDATIONS

- *Any injury that immobilizes an area should be reviewed by a doctor.*
- *Please use all of the recommendations for tendonitis (see* **Tendonitis***).*
- *A surgical repair is most often required for Achilles tendon rupture, and this is followed by a period of immobility in a cast. This may be only six weeks, but is often longer. Other tendons may simply be immobilized.*
- *If an operation is required, see* **Operations and surgery***.*

SLIPPED DISC—*see* Prolapsed disc

SPINAL CURVATURE

As the diagram opposite shows, the spine has a natural curvature that is principally controlled by the muscles running alongside and in between each vertebra.

This natural curvature can be disturbed by disease processes such as tuberculosis, ankylosing spondylitis, and osteoporosis, but most usually is affected by bad posture.

Little or no training is given in the West to good posture, whereas the Eastern philosophies—either through the martial arts or simply by a differing view of etiquette—encourage us at a younger age to keep the back erect. Hard mattresses (or the floor) have been replaced by soft ones, and only in the last decade or so has the concept of an orthopedic mattress been recognized in helping bad backs. Poor spinal curvature and lack of good muscular support is the cause of most backaches, whether initiated by trauma or not.

Lordosis

This is a forward curvature of the lumbar (lower) spine. This increase in the concave natural bend is usually created by carrying excess weight in the abdomen in association with poor abdominal musculature.

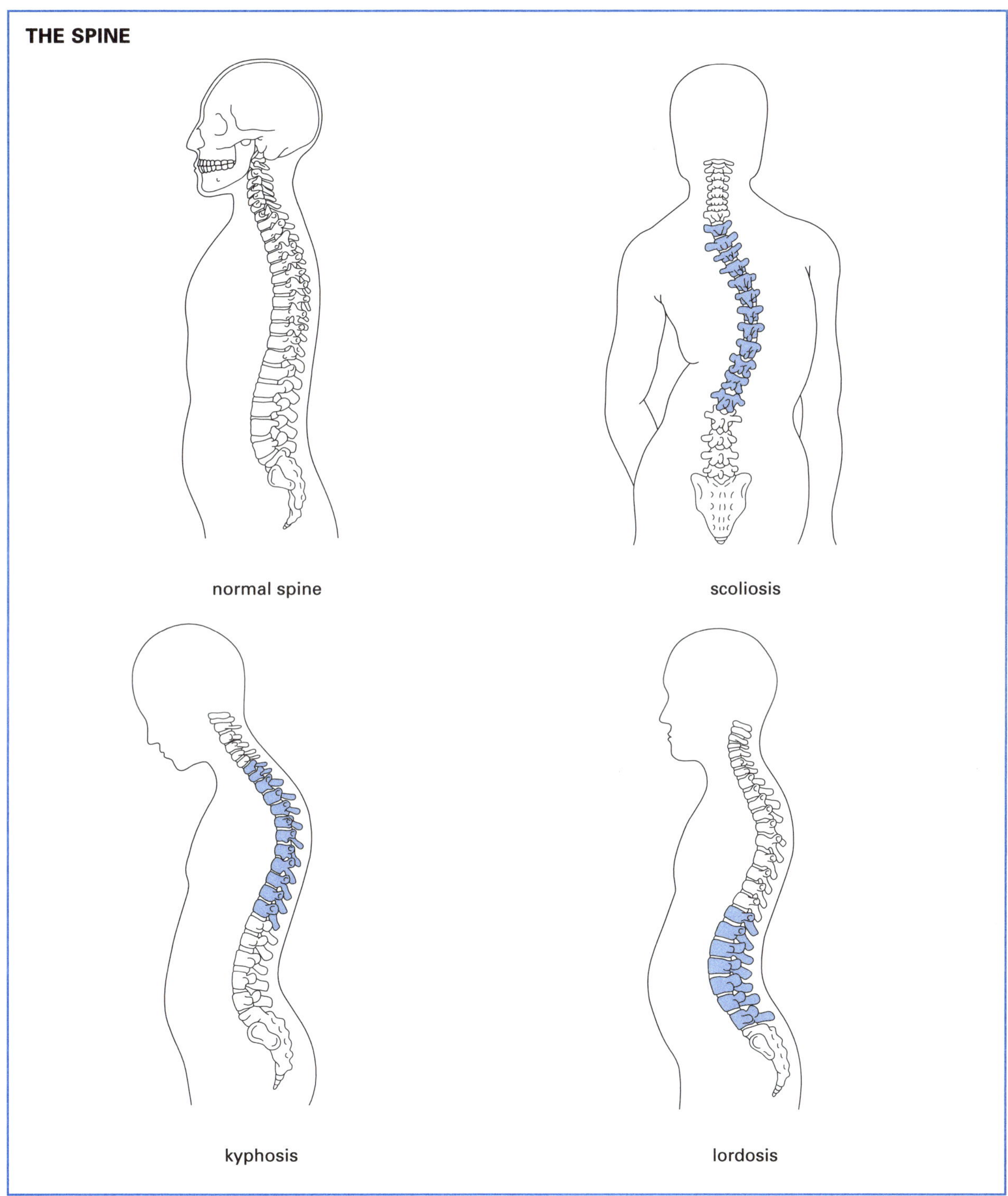

Kyphosis

Kyphosis is a forward bending of the spine in the thoracic (mid-back) area, involving a few or many vertebrae. Our literary friend Quasimodo, the Hunchback of Notre-Dame, is an extreme example of kyphosis, which is more often seen in elderly women with osteoporosis. Again poor posture through our youth is a more common cause of mild kyphosis, which can be a persistent cause of aches and pains in the upper back and shoulders. It is interesting to note that kyphosis is more common in left-handed people.

Scoliosis

This is a lateral curvature of the spine, which is named according to the location and direction of the convexity (the direction in which the bending is occurring). Unlike other curvatures in the spine, scoliosis may be genetically inherited, or caused by trauma that allows a misalignment that is not corrected. Disease processes such as osteoporosis may also cause this problem.

All Eastern philosophies consider the spinal column to be associated with the main flow of energy through the system. A correctly positioned spine is therefore essential for the free flow of energy.

RECOMMENDATIONS

- *A spinal curvature is not in itself a problem, unless discomfort or neurological symptoms are noticed. Be wary that problems may develop if curvatures are not corrected.*
- *The earlier that correction can be attempted, the better the prognosis.*
- *It is never too late to correct posture, and parents should be vigilant of "slumping" children.*
- *Learning the basics of the Alexander technique at an early age is beneficial. Yoga, Qi Gong, and Polarity therapy can also be reviewed; the first two are more active so may be more enjoyable, especially for children.*
- *If a curvature is causing problems, osteopaths, chiropractors, and Shiatsu practitioners can correct problems.*
- *General lethargy, malaise, and depressions that have no obvious underlying cause may respond to correction of an imbalanced spine by affecting the energy flow through the system.*

SPRAINS

A sprain is the wrenching of a joint, producing a stretching or laceration of the ligament. A ligament holds one bone in association with another, and is made of flexible, tough, dense, white, fibrous connective tissue.

The most-common sprains occur in the ankle, fingers, and toes. A mild sprain may require rest for a few days, but a serious tear may require an operative procedure. Ligaments are strongly connected to the bones that they attach, and a tear may actually cause a splinter or a chunk of bone to be fractured as well.

It is difficult to differentiate clinically between a sprain and a muscular strain. Both are painful, although ligament damage is often more so. Swelling and limitation of movement will occur in both injuries, but the latter is generally more painful than a ligament injury. (The term "more painful" is rather subjective, and only experience might help us differentiate here.)

A sprain (or strain) is liable to become recurrent if not healed properly. The recurrence may be associated with a weakness in the underlying energy or meridian line, and this needs to be looked at. The mind–body connection should also be considered.

RECOMMENDATIONS

- *Immediately apply ice to the area, and restrict movement using a splint or bandage if this is felt necessary.*
- *Administer the homeopathic remedy Arnica 6 every 10min for 1hr, and then use Arnica 30 alternating with Ruta 30 every 4hr for one week. If available, drink the fluid extract of Ruta (one tablespoon per foot of height in 16 ounces of water) in divided gulps throughout the day.*
- *Rest is essential. There is no set time, but diminished movement until the area has stopped hurting is necessary. I recommend at least one week of rest for any sprain that immobilizes the joint for longer than 24hr.*

- *Consult an osteopath, who may recommend x-rays to establish that there is no fracture.*
- *Acupuncture will help healing.*
- *Any tendency for the injury to recur, or pain still present after a week, should be reviewed by an orthopedic surgeon who may recommend splinting the joint or putting it into plaster.*
- *Avoid painkillers, except at night, because an absence of pain will encourage movement.*

TEMPOROMANDIBULAR JOINT (TMJ) SYNDROME

This condition is hard enough to say, and attempting to would make any sufferer worse. The TMJ is where your lower jaw (mandible) joins the skull, and is operated by one of the most powerful muscles in the body, the masseter muscle. Any misalignment of the joint or spasm of the muscle will create a pain that affects the jaw, the temples, the teeth, and the cheeks. The discomfort can extend down the neck and around the skull, being a cause of headaches and migraines.

Clicking of the jaw joint may be an indication of the development of TMJ dysfunction, or may be associated with discomfort. The cause is generally an improper alignment of the teeth or injury to the area. Problems with the parotid gland may cause inflammation, creating a tension within the masseter that will pull the jaw out of place; age-related arthritis (osteoarthritis) is another rare cause.

RECOMMENDATIONS

- *See a cranial osteopath as a primary referral.*
- *Relaxation and meditation techniques to take the tension out of the masseter is recommended, and for a few days try to eat soft foods only. Please note that a lack of chewable foods in the diet may give rise to the problem in the first place.*
- *If there is a painful spot just forward of the angle of the jaw, gentle pressure may relieve the discomfort.*
- *The application of heat to the area may relieve the symptoms.*
- *Homeopathic remedy Arnica 6 can be taken every hour in an acute situation, and four times a day to continue treatment once relief is obtained.*
- *Acupuncture may be added to any of the above if the problem persists.*
- *Persistence may be due to an orthodontic difficulty, and dentists who specialize in this condition should be consulted. It might be necessary to alter the bite or remove molar teeth that may have erupted incorrectly.*

TENDONITIS

Tendonitis is the medical term for inflammation of the part of a muscle that attaches to bone and is known as a tendon. (Ligaments attach bone to bone.) The most-common forms of tendonitis are tennis elbow, golfer's elbow, and Achilles tendon. Repetitive-strain injury (RSI) is also included within tendonitis—this being inflammation of the tendons of the forearm muscles that control the fingers.

The symptoms are usually that of a sharp pain, associated with a persistent ache. The pain is worse on movement—the more work being done, the more pain being expressed.

A persistent tendonitis that is resistant to treatment may be associated with the overlying meridian or energy channel. An assessment by a complementary medical practitioner with a knowledge in this area is of use.

Tenosynovitis

Around most joints lies a nutrient and lubricating fluid called the synovial fluid. This is encased by a membrane known as the synovial membrane. Very often, when a tendon or a joint area becomes inflamed, the synovial membrane follows suit. This condition is known as synovitis, and when in conjunction with an inflamed tendon, is termed tenosynovitis.

Trigger finger

Trigger finger is a condition in which the flexion or extension of a finger is at first obstructed, but suddenly accompanied by a jerk or a sweep that is usually painful. It is due to a chronic tendonitis.

RECOMMENDATIONS

- *Either ice or heat will relieve discomfort. Try both to see which is best.*
- *Rest the area as much as possible. Do not work the muscle beyond endurance.*
- *Select a vitamin-B complex, and take the daily recommended dose with each meal for three days. For those aged 14 years or more, manganese (20mg) and vitamin C (1g) should be taken with each meal. An Arnica cream can be applied three times a day to the injury, and if this is not available, take one teaspoonful of cayenne pepper to two tablespoonfuls of a vitamin-E cream (or simply olive oil), mix thoroughly, and apply to the area once a day, leaving it on for 20min. Wash this off and be careful not to allow the compound to enter cuts, because it will sting.*
- *Consult your preferred homeopathic manual and pay attention to Arnica, Bryonia, Rhus toxicodendron, and Ruta.*
- *Both acupuncture and acupressure can be curative, especially in association with osteopathy. Tendonitis can lead to a poor use of that muscle group, leaving the other side of the body more dependent and therefore leading to structural misalignment.*
- *Before resorting to anti-inflammatory drugs, you might consider bee-venom injections. This requires a specialist to administer, and be careful if you have any form of sensitivity.*

TENNIS ELBOW—*see* Tendonitis

VARICOSE VEINS

A varicose vein is most commonly found in the calf and thighs, and appears as blue-tinged lumps or streaks. These are vessels that have become abnormally dilated and tortuous due to a weakness in their walls or, more commonly, the valves within their lumen. The outcome is that blood that is being gently returned to the heart under low pressure falls downward due to gravity, pools, and stagnates. The expansion of the vein makes it visible and, because of the loss of surrounding tissue, it is more prone to being injured, and thereby becoming inflamed. If the bloodflow is stopped, then a clot may occur, leading to a venous thrombosis. Strictly speaking, hemorrhoids (piles) are varicose veins, also.

Statis and clotting are generally not problems in superficial veins, but can be fatal if they occur in a deeper vein. This condition has its own section (*see* **Deep-vein thrombosis**).

The cause of varicose veins is generally multiple. A hereditary weakness is usually exacerbated by long periods of standing, or increased abdominal pressure through pregnancy or heavy lifting. Poor-protein intake may weaken the wall structure, and toxins that affect the structure of surrounding tissues may be relevant.

Although varicose veins are principally an anatomical defect, alternative or complementary medical treatments may be of benefit.

RECOMMENDATIONS

- *Increase the fiber in the diet, along with vegetable proteins to ensure good muscular-wall and surrounding-tissue strength.*
- *Avoid the possible causes of increased abdominal pressure, such as straining, standing, and compression on leg veins through sitting with the legs over a hard edge.*
- *Increase any exercise that involves the leg muscles, particularly the calf muscles, which encourages squeezing of the veins and the upper movement of bloodflow.*
- *The herbal intake of Aesculus (horse chestnut) may be beneficial because it has anti-edema and*

anti-inflammatory properties. Take the extract of the root three times a day, at a dose of 200mg per foot of height.

- *Bioflavonoids from blueberries, cherries, and other blue/red-colored berries may be beneficial. Supplements at a dose of 150mg per day per foot of height in divided doses with meals will increase the strength of the vein walls.*
- *Bromelaine (100mg per foot of height) three times a day, but not with food, reduces fibrin breakdown. Fibrin is one of the proteins that holds veins within their tissues.*

WATER ON THE KNEE

The term "water on the knee," also known as "housemaid's knee," is actually an inflammation of the fluid pads that protect the knee joints. It is triggered by trauma, usually by prolonged rubbing, as was found in servants who scrubbed floors (*see* **Bursitis**).

WOUNDS

A wound is a broad term for any injury, but usually refers to a cut or penetrating injury.

RECOMMENDATIONS

- *See* **Cuts**.
- *Other wounds, especially deep-penetrating ones, need to be treated by a medical practitioner, but the basic complementary therapies are the same as for a cut.*

THE SKIN

The skin is a multifunctional organ, the primary function of which is to encase and protect tissues and organs of the body. The skin also provides sensory information, and in its waterproof and insulating capacity, acts to keep the external environment out and warmth in.

SKIN—Structure

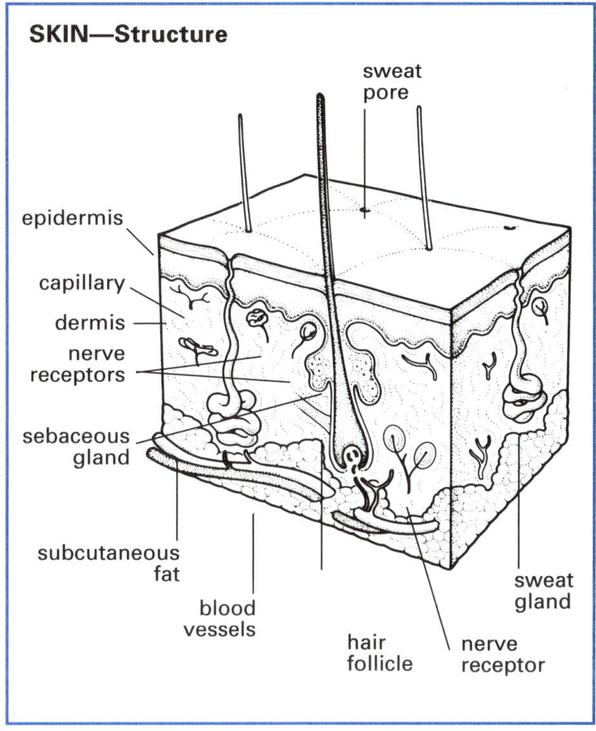

The skin contains two types of glands: the sweat glands (*see* **Sweating**) and sebaceous glands (*see* **Sebaceous cysts**).

The basal layer of cells grows and moves towards the surface, becoming thicker as a protein known as keratin is laid into and between the cells. This keratinized layer is thicker on the feet due to persistent pressure from the weight of the body. It is this layer that offers the greatest protection from the elements. Within the deeper layers lie the sweat glands, involved with cooling the body and eliminating toxins, and the sebaceous glands, which produce the oily secretion that helps keep the skin moist and contains immunoglobulins to fight infection.

There are certain cells in the skin known as melanocytes that contain a chemical called melanin, which darkens in the presence of sun. This darkening is triggered by absorbing what would otherwise be harmful rays of the sun, in particular ultraviolet light. The more melanocytes, the darker the skin, and the better the protection.

Disease or dysfunction of the skin may be a topical condition, or reflect systemic or internal problems. The skin is dependent on good nutrition and hygiene, more so than the many other parts of the body that it protects. Specific problems are discussed throughout this book, and should be looked up according to the disease process.

Through the layers just below the skin travel the major energy lines or meridians that the Eastern philosophies of medicine consider to be integral to health. A weakness in these energy lines by disease processes of particular organs or systems may reflect through the skin. Conversely, damaged skin may lead to a block in the energy flow, and thereby cause disease.

CARE OF THE SKIN

RECOMMENDATIONS

- *Keep the skin as clean as possible. Most of the world will achieve this with water, but if soaps are available, unmedicated types are the best. The skin pores will react to medication by assuming that it is a foreign body and, even if there are no symptoms, energy is expelled defending itself. Except in circumstances where skin may be sullied following sport or by dirt from the workplace, the skin should only be washed once a day. More frequent washing will lead to a loss of the natural skin oils (in the sebum), and diminish quality and the skin's immune response.*
- *Avoid applications of deodorants and make-up, beyond that which are socially necessary.*
- *Remember that the surface of the skin is only one of many layers, and that skin integrity is dependent on nutrition, hydration, and oxygenation from within.*
- *A well-balanced diet is essential for the skin's well-being, and nutritional lack may well show up in a variety of skin conditions initially.*
- *High levels of refined sugars and fats will find their way to the skin, providing surface bacteria with excess nutrients, and will cause an increased rate of growth. Sugar will also attract moisture, and therefore prevent correct distribution of fluid to the skin tissues.*
- *The integrity and tension of the skin is dependent upon nutrients to form elastin and collagen—the tissues underneath the skin that prevent wrinkling. As we age or damage the skin through sunlight and chronic dehydration, these fibers diminish, causing the characteristic changes of wrinkled skin and cellulite.*
- *Massage, saunas, and exercise all have a closing effect on the skin by either increasing bloodflow or encouraging natural excretion. All these should be practiced frequently.*

SKIN CONDITIONS

Dry skin

The skin maintains its moisture by protecting itself through the outer epidermal layer and by producing sebum from sebaceous glands. Sebum is composed of fat, proteins, keratin and hyalin, and cellular debris. The production of this compound is dependent upon the quality of oxygenation and nutrition supplied by an adequate bloodflow to the sebaceous glands in the deeper layers of the skin. Poor nutrition or oxygenation will prevent sebum production, and lead to dry skin.

The sebum travels up the hair follicle from the sebaceous gland, and any blockage by dirt or infection prevents the natural moisturizer from reaching the surface layers. Without it, essential defense immunoglobulins are absent and infection is more likely to set in.

Excess heat externally will dehydrate the sebum, and a lack of water intake will do the same. The Eastern philosophies would express the view that anything that heats the body—such as stress, excessive exercise, hot drinks and spicy foods—will also dehydrate the sebum, and may result in dry skin.

RECOMMENDATIONS

- *Consider rehydrating from within, rather than applying topical moisturizers. A skin that is dry but falsely moistened will not send out reflex nervous responses to try to pull more fluid into the area. (This is most commonly noted by those who use chapsticks for dry lips. The more you use, the more you need.)*
- *Ensure an adequate supply of fats and oils in the diet. Low-fat diets are notorious for causing dry skin.*
- *Remove heating foods such as hot drinks, alcohol, pepper, chilies, and other spicy foods.*
- *A cigarette burns at over 530 °F. This heat is absorbed into the bloodstream rapidly through the lungs, and heats the body. It is a potent dehydrator, and a commonly overlooked cause of dry skin.*
- *Avoid any contact with oils or chemicals that may block the skin pores. This includes most roll-on and spray deodorants.*
- *Do not use antiperspirants.*
- *Homeopathic remedies may be very beneficial, and those that should be reviewed in your preferred homeopathic manual are Calcaria carbonica, Graphites, Petroleum, Silica, and Sulphur. Use low potencies for an acute condition, six or twelve four times a day, or higher potencies 30 and 200 less frequently, if the condition is longstanding.*

Wrinkles

The fullness and turgor of skin is maintained by the level and quality of the interstitial tissues (the connective tissues), made up of protein and fats. Special tissue components known as collagen, fibrin, and elastin give the tissues of the body its support and elasticity. These tissues are dependent upon good oxygenation, nutrition, and hydration. Absence of the first two will lead to a breakdown of the protein structure, and lack of water will damage the cells; the outcome will be similar to a grape becoming a raisin, or a plum becoming a prune.

Wrinkles are therefore not strictly a skin problem, although the effect is reflected on the outer layer. Anything that dehydrates or depresses nutrition and oxygenation to the tissues will result in wrinkling.

Wrinkles are a natural part of aging and are in no way a disease condition. They are generally only noticed by those who feel that their looks are suffering. Naturopathic attempts at repair or skin rejuvenation may have an effect, but it is unlikely that the skin will ever return to its former glory. With wisdom comes wrinkles, and hopefully the reverse is also true.

RECOMMENDATIONS

- *Repair of wrinkled skin is much more difficult than prevention.*
- *Encourage a persistently good blood supply by avoiding those conditions that block arteries. Avoid smoking, high-fat foods, and a lack of exercise.*
- *Please use the supplemental recommendations for atherosclerosis (see* **Atheroma***) at reduced rates, depending upon the amount of fresh fruit and vegetables eaten. Five portions of fruit or vegetables should not require any supplementation, and add in one-fifth of the recommendation for every portion not eaten each day.*
- *Encourage oxygenation by frequent exercise. Yoga and Qi Gong are appropriate, but should be supplemented at least three times a week by aerobic exercise.*
- *Ensure that a breathing technique is practiced; this will be enhanced by using a meditative or relaxation technique.*
- *Ensure a daily intake of vegetable protein through beans, lentils, nuts, or soya.*
- *Do not avoid fatty foods, but ensure that they are vegetable-based, polyunsaturated fats.*
- *Massage will encourage bloodflow, and specific Ayurvedic facial massage using acupressure*

points is particularly useful because it is wrinkles on the face that create the most despair.

- *The use of Arnica- or Calendula-based creams may be of benefit, because this will attract blood and nutrients into the area.*
- *Perhaps most importantly, ensure that at least 8 ounces of water per foot of height is drunk as a general rule, and increase that by 50 percent when actively dealing with skin problems.*
- *Sunlight is damaging only if taken in excess, and exposure should not be discouraged but monitored carefully.*
- *Avoid cosmetic creams, because they tend to increase fluid levels below the area to which the cosmetic is applied. They have an artificial "de-wrinkling" effect, which diminishes once the product is stopped. While using such products, the body may stop nutrition and fluid moving into that area, because it apparently does not need it. This creates a dependency upon the application.*
- *Surgical repair (plastic surgery) is an option that may be very effective.*

BASAL-CELL CARCINOMA (RODENT ULCER)—*see* Cancer of the skin

CANCER OF THE SKIN

There are three forms of skin cancer.

- basal-cell carcinoma (rodent ulcer)
- squamous-cell carcinoma (SCC)
- melanoma

Recognizing skin cancer

Skin cancer may be present if any of the following simple observations are noticed:

- any lesion that grows;
- any lesion that changes color or has different colors within it;
- a persistently itchy or painful lesion;

Skin cancers

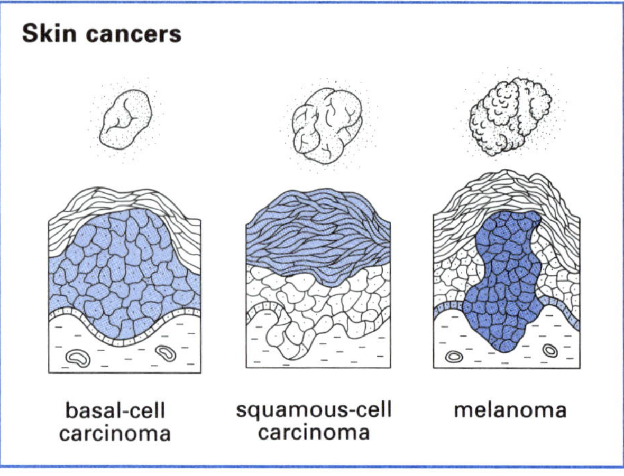

- a lesion that bleeds;
- any lesion that recurs.

Basal-cell carcinoma

Basal-cell carcinoma, or rodent ulcer, develops from the lowermost level of the skin, and tends to be slow growing, and does not spread. A rodent ulcer can be recognized as a rough or scaly bump, or as a small ulcer. They generally form where skin meets membrane at the corner of the eye or mouth. This flesh-colored, painless lesion rarely grows beyond three-eighths of an inch in diameter without being noticed and dealt with.

Squamous-cell carcinoma

Squamous-cell carcinoma (SCC) usually arises due to skin damage from heat, ultraviolet light, chronic infection, or compromised blood flow, such as in association with arteriosclerosis or venous ulceration. This tumor is invasive to local tissues, ulcerates easily, and appears as a friable lesion that bleeds easily. Squamous-cell carcinoma does metastasize (spread), and can settle in the lymph glands and other parts of the body.

Melanoma

Melanoma is discussed in its own section (*see* **Melanoma**). Basal-cell and squamous-cell carcinoma are named after the cell from which the cancer initially developed.

However, SCC is less dangerous than melanoma because it is slower growing and less apt to spread, and usually tends to produce some local symptoms. It is also amenable to chemotherapy and radio therapy if the need should arise.

RECOMMENDATIONS

- *Pay attention to the above-mentioned criteria, and have any such lesion removed. However experienced a practitioner might be, only the microscope can discern a cancerous cell.*
- *Any skin lesion that does not resolve easily must be considered to be a type of skin cancer, and excised.*
- *Squamous-cell carcinoma and melanoma must be treated with respect, and the advice given for general cancer should be adhered to (see* **Cancer***).*
- *Basal-cell carcinomas need only local treatment, but a tendency to recurrence suggests an underlying cancer that may exhibit itself elsewhere in a more-serious form.*

CELLULITE

Cellulite is not strictly a medical term, but has entered the domain of medicine through plastic and cosmetic surgeons who are faced with an increasing number of individuals, 95 percent of whom are women, who struggle with this deforming condition.

Cellulite is a rippling formation in the deeper layers of the skin, found predominantly in areas where fat is deposited. Cellulite can be symptomless and simply disfiguring, or may cause discomfort, a feeling of tension or tightness, and (rarely) pain.

Below the superficial (epidermis) and dermal layers of the skin lies a layer of fat. This is more prominent in women of any age, and therefore the condition is more common in this sex. The fat cells are kept apart by a type of tissue called connective tissue, which literally connects the different types of tissues throughout the body. Certain foods and conditions cause this connective tissue to degenerate, pushing the fat cells together in an irregular shape and closer to the surface of the skin.

Cellulite is divided into three groups:

- Stage one—the skin is smooth until it is pinched, when the pitted effect become visible.
- Stage two—the pitting becomes visible on tensing the underlying muscle or on standing.
- Stage three—the pitting is visible at all times.

RECOMMENDATIONS

- *Reducing the fat content in the body will reduce the fat layer under the skin, which then, in turn, reduces the cellulite effect.*
- *Strengthening the muscles underneath the area where cellulite is prominent will increase bloodflow and maintain or even repair the loss of connective tissue in that area, thus reducing the fat stores as mentioned above.*
- *Massage of the area—both professionally and by the individual—will help to break down some of the fat conglomeration, and also increase bloodflow and support the connective-tissue structure.*
- *A compound called Centella asiatica, an extract from a plant, can be taken by adults at a strength of 30mg with food three times a day. This plant extract helps to restructure connective tissue, and is the only botanical treatment with reasonable scientific evidence.*
- *An interesting paradox: there is a compound called Cola vera that contains 14 percent caffeine. Applied in a solution up to 1.5 percent locally, it can be beneficial. However, caffeine has been cited as being a cause of cellulite if taken orally, and it is important for anyone fighting a cellulite battle to avoid coffee, tea, caffeine-containing canned drinks, and chocolate.*
- *Many cosmetic preparations are based on hydrating the area, which simply pushes water into the pitted skin, causing it to swell and lose some of its unsightly appearance. Once you stop using the application, the problem will return within a few days.*

CORNS

A corn, medically known as a clavus, is usually a cone-shaped area of hardened skin with an associated growth of a horny substance, found most commonly around the toes. It is caused by frictional pressure.

RECOMMENDATIONS

- *At the earliest sign of a change in skin texture on the feet, review your footwear, and avoid any tight-fitting shoes and socks.*
- *Regular applications of Arnica, Calendula, or Urtica (or all three) creams may soften and eventually reduce the corn.*
- *Chiropodists, dermatologists, or plastic surgeons will all be able to remove these efficiently, but ensure that the above creams are used before and postoperatively to prevent infection and reduce the risk of recurrence.*

FISSURE AND FISTULA

Fissures are cracks in the skin or ulcers that form on mucous membranes. Fistulas are small fissures. In medical parlance, these are most commonly referred to when painful (and occasionally bleeding) lesions occur around the area of the anus.

Fissures and fistulas are most often caused by trauma. This may be from the outside (as in anal intercourse) or caused by passing hard stools, often associated with straining as in constipation. This latter tendency often associates fissures with hemorrhoids.

There are certain conditions, such as Crohn's disease, that can have an association with anal fissures, and therefore a persisting irritation or discomfort should be investigated. Fissures and fistulas can occur at any age, although adulthood is the most common time. Any such injury in a child, however, must unfortunately bring to mind the possibility of abuse, which must be addressed immediately.

RECOMMENDATIONS

- *Consider the probable cause, and avoid the trauma.*
- *If persistently constipated, see* **Constipation**.
- *Application of Arnica, Calendula, or Hamamelis ointments should clear the problem.*
- *Consider the homeopathic remedies Aesculus, Ratanhia, Peonia, and Graphites.*
- *If the problem does not relieve itself within a few days, then consult a doctor, who needs to rule out any underlying condition. Surgical intervention, specifically anal dilation, which causes the small tear to open and thereby be healed more aggressively, may be required.*

HIVES

Hives are an allergic reaction characterized by a red, raised, itchy, or irritating, circumscribed lesion that appears anywhere on the body, usually in groups, but occasionally isolated.

Hives are a response caused by the release of histamine and similar chemicals, which cause small blood vessels (capillaries) to leak, thus causing swelling of the tissues. These substances also encourage the opening of the small arteries, causing more blood to flow in because the body has sensed a "foreign" invader, and is trying to flush it away.

Hives may be triggered by allergies, which in turn may be caused by any number of things, ranging from toxins, the foods we eat, the drugs we take, and infections, such as yeast or fungi. It is well documented that stress can cause a hive reaction, and needs to be considered if more material causes cannot be illustrated.

RECOMMENDATIONS

- *Pay attention to possible triggers, especially drugs such as antibiotics that may appear in processed meats.*

- *See **Allergies** for treatment.*
- *Try applying ice, onion juice, or an Urtica (nettle) solution.*
- *An Acidophilus supplement may be curative if the problem is a reaction to one's own bowel-yeast population.*
- *Quercetin (500mg per foot of height) in divided doses with food throughout the day may be effective.*
- *Homeopathic remedy Urtica urens 6 taken every 15min may remove the irritation.*
- *Ensure to sustain a high intake of water to flush the system.*

INFECTIONS OF THE SKIN

The skin has a very strong, protective ability. It is water-resistant, and therefore bacteria and other ineffective agents find it difficult to penetrate. The top layers of the skin are dead cells, and therefore viruses cannot live within them. The skin surface is a precarious habitat because our own bacterial flora competes for food with harmful bugs, and attacks them directly. The sebum contains immunoglobulin A, a defense chemical that attacks foreign bodies. The deeper layers of skin are packed full of white blood cells, and the basement membrane on which the skin basement cells grow is another fairly impenetrable barrier of fat and protein.

For infection to set in, damage must first be made to the integrity of these barriers or the protective secretions. Once an infective agent penetrates, it can set up home and feed off the nutrients in the blood. Infections will benefit by the sugar content in the bloodstream, which is promoted by ingestion of refined sugars and fats.

If the body's defense mechanism is low, or an infection is left untreated, abscesses and boils may form. Infections within the bloodstream may be expelled through the skin, as in chickenpox, measles, or more serious infections caused by bacteria in the bloodstream (septicemia). Staphylococcal and streptococcal infections may cause a condition called impetigo.

RECOMMENDATIONS

- *See **Care of the skin** to avoid infections and assess why an infection has set in.*
- *Please refer to the specific section in this book for conditions such as abscesses, boils, and impetigo.*
- *Review and pay attention to general nutritional status, because the skin may reflect any deficiencies before other organs.*
- *Persisting skin infections need to be assessed by a doctor to find underlying causes, although treatment is best offered by complementary medical practitioners.*
- *Use Calendula-based creams on the site of infection.*
- *Ensure good hydration by drinking 16 ounces of water per foot of height throughout the day to ensure dilution of sebum, which may thicken, especially if there is fever.*
- *Avoid topical antibiotics, which will kill off the good skin bacteria as well as the bad, and may encourage resistant strains.*
- *Avoid steroid applications, which may take down the level of inflammation, but in the process, remove the body's defense mechanism.*

ITCHING SKIN

An itch, medically speaking, is a low level of pain. It is created by some irritation in the nerve endings that is not enough to send a pain impulse, but enough to act as a warning. The nerve endings are affected by any obvious external irritant, including chemicals; inflammation through trauma or infection; irritants that have been eaten and are coming out through the sweat; histamine release from a food allergy or insect sting; or a metabolic disorder such as jaundice and eczema, or dermatitis.

RECOMMENDATIONS

- *Isolate the cause, or consult with a complementary medical practitioner initially to diagnose an underlying condition. Remove the cause where possible.*
- *Persistent itching should be reviewed for diagnosis by a doctor or dermatologist.*
- *Hot or cold applications may be very beneficial.*
- *In isolated or small areas, the application of either a potato or an onion may be relieving.*
- *Bathing in water containing a tablespoonful of almond oil may help. Do not rub off the oil, but preferably dab or air dry.*
- *Please refer to your preferred homeopathic manual, and isolate one of the many remedies associated with itching.*
- *Herbal treatments may be utilized, but because they act as a type of antihistamine, they are best taken under the instruction of a herbalist.*
- *Many cases of itching skin are allergy related (see* **Allergies***).*
- *See* **Pruritis***.*

KELOIDS

A keloid is an overgrowth of scar tissue. Most commonly found following trauma or surgery, the formation of excess scar tissue has uncertain origins. Generally, the body has a mechanism by which it prevents an excess of scar tissue being created, and this mechanism is faulty in those who develop keloids. It is most often found in black-skinned people. I have yet to find any complementary therapy that can alter this defect, which is probably genetic.

A silicone derivative applied to an adhesive gel sheet has been developed that is claimed to work by flattening, softening, and fading red and raised scars. This has been shown to work in scars up to 20 years old, and (as usual) is declared to have no risks. Its action is by hydrating the scar area, which helps to reduce the size and redness of a scar, and can improve elasticity of the tissue. The compound is traded as CICA-CARE.

RECOMMENDATIONS

- *Surgical treatment of a keloid may offer temporary relief, but a keloid will form around the scar created by the operation.*
- *The use of injected steroids may be of benefit, and the experience of individual plastic surgeons or dermatologists is the guiding light.*
- *If a trauma occurs or an operative procedure is inevitable in a keloid-forming individual, then consider using the homeopathic remedy Silica 30 twice a day, starting one week before the operation, and continuing for three weeks after the procedure or any trauma.*
- *A Calendula cream may be of benefit, and can be applied frequently to a keloid-susceptible site.*
- *Please consider the use of CICA-CARE.*

MELANOMA (MALIGNANT MELANOMA)

Malignant melanoma, more commonly known simply as melanoma, is a cancer that is initiated in the melanin-containing cells in the lower layer of the skin. It is characterized by a brown or black mole-like lesion. Like any skin cancer, ominous signs to help recognize this condition are an increase in size (usually expansive rather than raised), a darkening or variation in the color of the lesion, itching, bleeding, or an associated lump in the closest lymph-gland group (usually found at the nearest joint).

Unfortunately, melanomas do not always fall into this category, and can be pale and quite unnoticeable. These are, however, rare. Individuals who have many moles have no greater risk of any mole becoming a melanoma, but have more moles and therefore have more lesions to be wary of.

A malignant melanoma may remain localized for a few months, but if left unattended, will generally spread and grow in other parts of the body rapidly. Melanomas are occasionally spotted on routine eye examinations, as they can form in the retina, but like most internal cancers, unless spotted through a routine examination, they may not show symptoms until the spread has taken place.

RECOMMENDATIONS

- *See* **Cancer, Cancer of the skin** *and* **Operations and surgery**.
- *Specific attention may be paid to the herbs Astragalus (containing the alkaloid swainsonine), and Chaparral, both of which have been shown through scientific studies to have an effect on this type of cancer.*
- *Research is currently underway to produce a vaccine prepared from melanoma cells that triggers a body response to attack melanoma generally. It is in its early stages yet, and we watch with interest.*

PAPILLOMAS

A papilloma is a growth of surface cells that is differentiated from a wart simply by having a more-vascularized core of tissue (*see* **Warts**).

PRICKLY HEAT

This is a condition characterized by itchiness in association with small, uninfected pimples that can occur anywhere on the body. Most commonly found in fair-skinned individuals in hot conditions, prickly heat is exacerbated by humidity. The cause is overheating, which triggers a histamine-like chemical release in conjunction with a blockage of the sweat glands.

RECOMMENDATIONS

- *See* **Sweating, Hives** *and* **Heatstroke**.
- *The homeopathic remedy Sol (a remedy made from sun energy), potency 6, taken every 10min, can be markedly effective.*
- *Apply Aloe-vera gels or lotions if the area of prickly heat is small, otherwise take the maximum amount of Aloe vera as recommended on the product.*
- *A complementary medical practitioner with expertise in this area may suggest a diagnosis of weakness within the large and small intestine, gallbladder, bladder, thyroid, or adrenal glands.*

RASHES

A "rash" is a lay term used for nearly any skin eruption, but more commonly for a patch of skin that is red. A rash may also be inflamed and hot, flat or raised, dry or wet, and associated with other symptoms, or not.

Many infections—either topical (local) or systemic (through the system)—can be associated with a rash. Measles, chickenpox, and German measles (rubella) are common examples of infections that are not too serious. However, a rash caused by a bacterium such as streptococcus, as in association with a "strep" throat, or meningitis, as found on the thighs of infants in particular, is a much-more-serious condition.

Contact dermatitis (inflammation of the skin due to an irritant) is frequent, such as in the rash from a stinging nettle or from a chemical at work, or a rash may be associated with an allergy, be it from contact, ingestion, or inhalation. Insect bites can commonly create a rash, especially ticks or fleas. A heat rash may be associated with excessive exposure to sun.

More-serious conditions such as blood-clotting disorders or leukaemia may present as a rash. A rash is a form of superficial inflammation. Irritation or damage to cells creates a release of chemicals such as histamine that encourage bloodflow, which in turn brings in white blood cells for defense and nutrients for repair. A rash is generally a warning or healing process, and rarely the end stage of a serious condition. "Heed the warning and encourage the repair" should be your motto for any rash.

The Eastern philosophies consider a rash to be associated with excess heat in the system, and underlying causes should be illustrated rather than paying special attention to the rash. Homeopathy considers skin to be a very important organ of excretion. Disease conditions move from the inside out, and they are often at the end point of resolution when a skin rash appears. Incorrect treatment may suppress the underlying condition, inhibiting repair.

RECOMMENDATIONS

- *Please refer to the relevant section if a cause is known for the rash.*
- *A rash may be soothed by cold applications.*
- *A homeopathic remedy may be selected according to the site and type of rash by reference to your preferred homeopathic manual or a homeopathic practitioner.*
- *Calendula or Urtica cream should be applied to an area that is irritated.*
- *An oat poultice, made by soaking oats in water for a few minutes and compressing, can draw heat from an area.*
- *An application of a strong camomile tea, or oats soaked in camomile as above can be soothing.*
- *Drink plenty of water to flush the system. This should be neither too hot nor too cold, because the former puts extra heat into the body, and the latter causes the body to respond by producing more heat.*
- *A persistent rash with no obvious cause should be reviewed by a doctor or dermatologist to rule out underlying disease. Special attention should be paid to rashes that are not red or not improving after 48hr. Refuse treatment with steroids or other drugs until alternative treatments have failed.*
- *Investigations such as blood tests may be necessary and, at an extreme, a biopsy of the rash may be of benefit to the dermatologist.*

RAYNAUD'S DISEASE

Raynaud's disease, named after a French physician, is characterized by repeated episodes of pallor, and blueness or redness of the fingers, toes, or both, usually induced by cold or emotion. The condition may be secondary to many diseases, but most often to chronic arterial-occlusive disease such as diabetes, arteriosclerosis, or the smoking-related Buerger's disease.

The condition, which is not uncommon, is often noted simply by an individual digit going a different color, most commonly white. It is caused by the arterial supply being obstructed, which is usually due to nervous control of the artery, either from within its own nerve plexus or from the central nervous system. Other than the condition being painful or indicating an underlying disease, the problem is not serious, although in severe cases, gangrene or ulceration may occur due to a lack of blood supply for a prolonged period.

The fingers and toes represent different organs, humors (elements), and systems, depending upon which of the Eastern philosophies you study. Most correlate to some degree, and the Ayurvedic principle, shown in diagrammatic form opposite, gives an example.

RECOMMENDATIONS

- *Infrequent Raynaud's phenomena require no medical investigation, but persistent or painful episodes should initiate a consultation to rule out any underlying disease.*
- *Commonsense attitudes such as wearing gloves or warm socks, and not gripping objects for too long, must be remembered.*
- *Avoid smoking—this causes peripheral vascular constriction. Alternatively, an alcoholic drink daily or just prior to an event liable to trigger Raynaud's disease will help to encourage peripheral dilation.*
- *Vitamin E (100iu per foot of height) taken in divided doses throughout the day may encourage vascular potency.*
- *Spicy food, especially cayenne pepper, taken regularly may reduce occurrences. Cayenne*

HANDS—the Ayurvedic associations

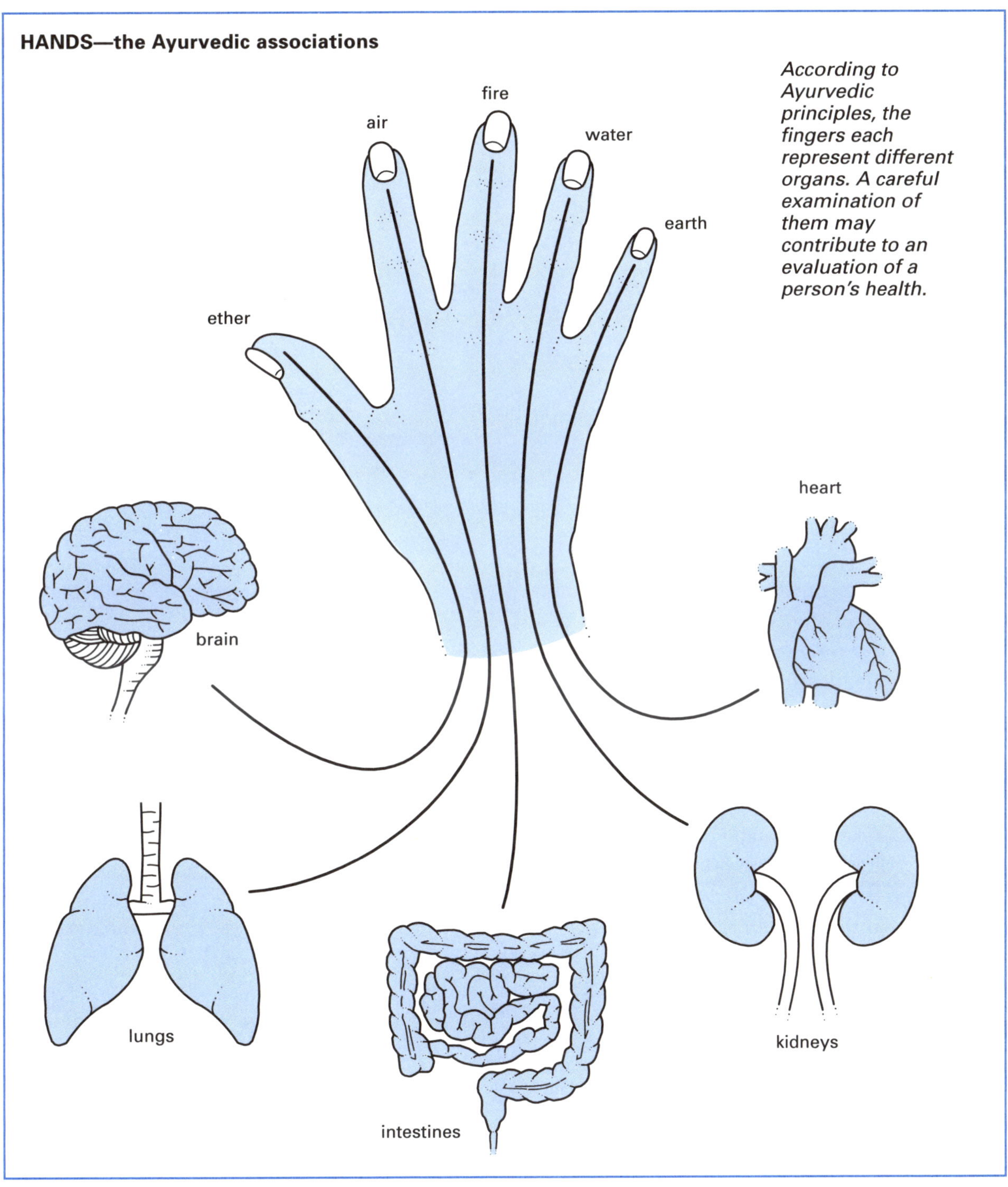

According to Ayurvedic principles, the fingers each represent different organs. A careful examination of them may contribute to an evaluation of a person's health.

capsules may be used if spicy food is not enjoyed. The dosage should be as recommended on the product bought, but if no effect is forthcoming, then double the dose, being wary of any sensation of burning in the stomach: if this is present the treatment cannot be used.

- *During an attack, you may increase circulation by swinging or rotating the arms and legs.*
- *Many homeopathic remedies are of benefit and*

suitable. Choices should be made according to the symptoms by referring to your preferred homeopathic manual. For frequent sufferers who may have burning or aching digits, keep the remedy Cactus 6 in your pocket, and take a dose every 15min until the problem resolves.

- *Biofeedback and meditation training can have a swift effect, and should be practiced daily, regardless of the condition, for those whose problem is severe.*
- *Pallor or pain that is unresolved after a few hours should be examined by an emergency doctor. Paralysis or intolerable pain should be dealt with swiftly. Drugs for peripheral dilation may be administered in acute or severe, chronic cases.*

SHINGLES

Shingles is an aggressive, painful, blister-like rash that can occur in any part of the body, but tends to travel along a band of skin associated with a particular branch of the nerve, and only occurs on one side of the body.

A diagnosis of shingles is best made by a doctor because other conditions may mimic shingles. Once a firm diagnosis has been made, then complementary medical treatment should be considered before the use of orthodox antiviral drugs. These drugs are creating the development of resistant strains. Any herpetic lesion that is internal or is associated with delicate organs such as the eyes should be monitored by a hospital doctor; these are the exceptions to the use of orthodox antiviral drugs.

Shingles is caused by a herpes virus called *Varicella zoster*. The virus, typical of herpes viruses, settles in a nerve root, and travels along the nerve and its branches, causing pain and inflammation, as well as blisters on the skin. The sensitivity is a guideline to the diagnosis, because it is extremely painful initially.

RECOMMENDATIONS

- *See* **Herpes simplex**.
- *Applications of ice wrapped in silk and then applied can be extremely relieving for a few moments.*
- *Analgesic relief with regular drugs is acceptable in the acute phases due to the potentially intense pain.*
- *The homeopathic remedies Rhus toxicodendron, Kali muriaticum, Ranunculus, and the specific nosode Variolinum can all be used at potency 30 or lower every hour for three doses, and then every 2hr in an acute phase, reducing to four times a day once the initial attack is subsiding.*
- *Applications of Calendula or Urtica urens creams can be applied regularly, and are often soothing.*
- *Coffee applied to active lesions may relieve pain and shorten the life of the rash.*

SKIN DISCOLORATION

Discoloration of skin is usually a temporary change caused by an alteration in bloodflow: too little makes the skin go pale, too much makes it go red. Physiological causes, such as embarrassment and excess heat, need to be balanced against pathological causes such as rashes. People may take on a slightly-greenish hue in association with motion sickness. (I have absolutely no idea why this is, and would be grateful if somebody who has some information on this would let me know.) Brown discoloration may occur through changes in estrogen levels, and may be noted during pregnancy or the menopause. The latter are often known as liver spots, but have nothing to do with the functioning of the liver.

Certain metabolic disease processes may alter the skin color in a more permanent manner. An excess of iron may stain the skin brown, and jaundice may cause yellowing.

Tinea nigra

This condition, also known as pityriasis nigra, which is common in the East and the Americas, and is characterized by a black or dark-brown coloration, predominantly on the trunk, neck, or palms. It is created by a fungal infection, and specific antifungal creams are needed to destroy it.

Tinea versicolor

This is a chronic, superficial fungal infection of the skin, which is caused either by a fungus known as *Trichophyton* or *Malassezia*. These fungi cause smooth-edged, usually round or oval lesions of pale skin. The fungus affects or destroys melanocytes (which color the skin) and creates pale lesions. It is usually transmitted from towels or by skin contact, and is common in the Mediterranean and west-coast beaches of America.

RECOMMENDATIONS

- *Apply a selenium-containing shampoo to the lesions three nights in a row. Wash off in the morning. At any suggestion of an irritation, wash the shampoo off and discuss other treatments with a complementary medical practitioner or physician.*
- *Take selenium—20mg per foot of height in one dose with the evening meal.*

SKIN GRAFTING

The skin, because of trauma or burns, may need to be replaced by a skin graft. A patch of skin approximately the size of the area that has been damaged is removed from a healthy area, ensuring that the basal (the growing layer) level of cells is removed. This must be accompanied by some subcutaneous tissue to encourage new blood-vessel growth into the area to feed the basal cells.

RECOMMENDATIONS

- *See* **Operations and surgery**.
- *Once the graft has taken, application of Arnica- and Calendula-based creams would be beneficial.*
- *See* **Eczema,** *and follow the guidelines for supplemental and herbal support.*

URTICARIA

Urticaria is the medical term for hives and nettle rash. It is a condition characterized by the appearance of intensely itching welts, or weals, usually with a raised center and surrounding red skin. They appear in the area where an irritant may have come into contact with the skin, or in crops, widely distributed over the body surface if the reaction is created by the ingestion or injection of a toxin. Urticaria generally disappears within a day or two.

RECOMMENDATIONS

- *See* **Hives, Rashes,** *and* **Itching skin**.
- *Immediately apply a solution made up of ice water with a tablespoonful of baking soda per 16 ounces of water.*
- *Use the homeopathic remedy Urtica urens 6 every 10min until a more-suitable remedy, if necessary, is found through your preferred homeopathic manual.*

VITILIGO

This is a skin disease characterized by the loss of pigment, leading to the presentation of white patches. These are highlighted by hyperpigmented areas around the edges, in many cases.

Vitiligo occurs in many cases in association with certain diseases, including hypothyroidism and pernicious anemia. Occasionally the body forms antibodies against its own melanin-forming cells (melanocytes), but the most common cause is skin fungi. Nutritional deficiencies may cause vitiligo, especially in children.

If no underlying condition is found, then preventing this disease process is unlikely. The Eastern philosophies consider the loss of normal color in skin or hair to be an indication of a profound lack of vital force. I am not sure if this is a fair assumption, because most prematurely gray individuals do not seem to fare worse in longevity or health stakes than others. Without underlying disease, vitiligo is not likely to cause long-term health problems in other areas.

RECOMMENDATIONS

- *Take a multi-B-complex supplement at four times the recommended dose for one week, and then twice the recommended amount for a further month.*
- *Beta-carotene supplements (2mg per foot of height) should be taken twice a day for one week, and then daily for three months. At this level, yellowing of the skin is not likely, but if there is any suggestion, or if pregnant, reduce the dosage by half.*
- *Hair, sweat, and blood analysis should be undertaken to assess mineral deficiencies, which should be corrected by taking twice the daily recommended dose for one month.*
- *Any deficiencies should lead the individual to a nutritionist to discuss whether their diet is poor or their absorptive capacity weak. Digestive enzymes may be required, but this really should be determined by a professional.*
- *Any underlying condition must be treated.*
- *Topical antifungal creams should be tried. Naturopathic ointments may be recommended, but in my experience do not show good results.*

WENS

A wen is actually a sebaceous cyst that most commonly appears on the scalp (*see* **Sebaceous cysts**).

XANTHELASMA

These are yellowish, raised plaques that occur around the eyelids, and result from lipid-filled cells in the skin. They were considered to be an indication of raised cholesterol and higher risk of atheroma; this is not strictly true in most cases, but may be a sign of raised fats in the blood.

The orthodox world cannot explain why these form in this particular area of the body, although the most reasonable hypothesis suggests that it is a thin area of skin, and therefore has smaller vessels, which may become blocked with fatty deposits. A more-holistic consideration is the fact that small-intestine and stomach meridians connect in this area, and are responsible for the absorption of fat.

RECOMMENDATIONS

- *Xanthelasma may be a reflection of lipid (fat) levels, so triglyceride- and cholesterol-blood levels are worth measuring.*
- *Review the diet and reduce fat intake.*
- *Ensure that good hydration is encouraged by drinking at least 8 ounces of water per foot of height, and double that if xanthelasma has formed.*
- *Application of Arnica-based creams may help break down the stores, and in severe cases, laser therapy may be available.*
- *The homeopathic remedy Calcarea carbonica taken at potency 6 taken twice a day for two weeks and repeated in one month if no effect is forthcoming, is recommended by one source.*
- *Consult a complementary medical practitioner for an overview of your constitution, which may be showing a tendency to retention.*

The Nervous System

BELL'S PALSY

Named after the doctor who first described it, Bell's palsy is a paralysis of the muscles, usually unilaterally on one side of the face, due to trauma or inflammation of the facial nerve, which exits at the base of the skull and travels across the face. It is often associated with trauma, strong drafts (such as those experienced by hanging the head out of a moving vehicle), viral infections, and very rarely, more-sinister causes such as tumors.

Bell's palsy may resolve within a few days, while other palsies may never repair completely.

RECOMMENDATIONS

- *Consult a homeopath for a suitable remedy.*
- *Consult a cranial osteopath for treatment.*

- *Use vitamin B_1 (100mg with each meal) for three days only in combination with lecithin (1000mg with each meal), a multi-B complex, folic acid (400μg), and extra vitamin B_{12}, all for one week.*
- *If resolution is not forthcoming within a few days, discuss the matter with a medical practitioner for investigations via a neurologist.*
- *Having established that the cause is not serious, and if homeopathy and osteopathy have failed, consider acupuncture, with or without the concurrent use of Chinese herbs.*
- *Until discussed with an acupuncturist or Shiatsu practitioner, avoid rubbing the area, as this may worsen the matter.*

NERVE DAMAGE

A damaged nerve may cause pain, paralysis, paresthesia (altered sensation), or an alteration in perception in any of the five senses. The effects will depend on which nerves are damaged, and treatment is adjusted depending on the site.

Nerves are divided into those in the brain and spinal column, known as the central nervous system, and those on the outside of these areas, known as peripheral nerves. Every part of the body is innervated except for thickened skin, hair, and nails, but very often, their surrounding parts compensate by being extremely sensitive.

Nerves are further divided into motor and sensory, which control movement and sensation, respectively. A further subdivision is made in the motor nerves: those that are under our control and those that are not. The *autonomic* (noncontrolled) nervous system governs the beating of our heart, our nonconscious respiration, our involuntary bladder valves, etc. You may come across the terms *sympathetic* and *parasympathetic* nerves, which are part of this system and act in opposition to each other. For example, the parasympathetic nervous system slows down the heart, whereas the sympathetic nervous system speeds it up. Adrenaline and noradrenaline are the most common catecholamines, or neurotransmitters, that affect the sympathetic and parasympathetic system in different ways. The ins and outs of biochemical control are complex, and not particularly relevant when treating damaged nerves on a self-help basis.

Treatment must depend on the actual problem and, as always, the underlying cause of the nerve damage must be alleviated where possible. The principal causes are:

- Direct injury—injury to a nerve may be partial damage or a partially or completely severed nerve.
- Deficiency—the nerves are made up of proteins and specialized fats, as well as vitamins and other nutrients; very common deficiencies are vitamin B_{12}, folic acid, and essential fatty acids.
- Disease processes—multiple sclerosis (MS), other sclerosing diseases, infections, and metabolic disorders such as diabetes or hypothyroidism. Specific infections such as tetanus, polio, and shingles are notorious for causing either pain or paralysis by damaging the nerves.
- Toxicity—alcohol, drugs, smoking, and agrochemicals are all culprits. Lead, mercury, aluminum, and (rarely nowadays), arsenic are all known to cause nerve damage and, interestingly, an excess of vitamin E may cause problems.

We are told by the orthodox world that nerves do not regrow. This is not strictly true, and some nerve transmission may be reconstructed even in a completely severed nerve if the opposing ends are joined either naturally or by a surgical technique. More importantly, the body has the ability to grow new nerves or retrain other nerves to innervate the area that the damaged nerve has ceased to affect.

NEURALGIA

This is the medical term for nerve pain, and is most commonly associated with trigeminal neuralgia or sciatica (*see* **Trigeminal neuralgia** and **Sciatica**).

RECOMMENDATIONS

- *Pain relief with orthodox drugs may be a necessary first-line treatment because of the severity of nerve pain associated with injury.*
- *The homeopathic remedies Hypericum, Arsenicum, Ranunculus, Aconite, and Iris should all be reviewed in your favorite homeopathic manual.*
- *Any loss of movement or change in sensation, such as numbness or tingling, should be reviewed by a medical practitioner for a firm diagnosis. Remember that many neurological symptoms are not due to nerve damage, but are associated with muscular or vascular conditions.*
- *These supplements may be utilized in the following doses per foot height, divided with meals throughout the day: manganese 0.5mg, Magnesium 100mg, lecithin 200mg. If there is no improvement within a couple of days, please contact a complementary medical practitioner initially, and consider specific deficiency tests through blood or hair analysis.*
- *Take twice the recommended daily allowance of a multivitamin-B complex. Chromium (40µg per foot of height in divided doses) can be taken with food three times a day.*
- *Extract from the common oat (Avena sativa) can be taken as a fluid extract—1 teaspoonful with water every 3hr.*
- *Acupuncture and mild electroacupuncture treatment can be instantly relieving, and help healing.*
- *Marma massage and other Ayurvedic-derived techniques, such as neurotherapy, can be of benefit.*
- *Any persistent neurological symptoms or obviously badly damaged nerves must be analyzed by a neurologist, and investigations such as neuroconductive tests or magnetic-resonance imaging (MRI) should be carried out in the case of large nerves.*
- *Alexander technique, yoga, and Qi Gong may all help in the redevelopment of innervative areas.*

NUMBNESS

Numbness is known in medical parlance as paresthesia. It describes a sensation of partial or local anesthesia, or a deficiency of sensation. The term can be used for a psychological experience, but this is not strictly medical.

Numbness occurs because of interference with nerve function, and is generally caused by injury, inflammation, infection, or disease, affecting the nerve directly or interfering with the blood supply.

RECOMMENDATIONS

- *Persistent numbness should be examined by a doctor with possible referral for investigations through a neurologist. Conditions such as multiple sclerosis (MS) and diabetes may initially present as numbness and, especially in the case of the latter disease, early diagnosis and treatment can make a profound difference in the long term.*
- *See **Neuralgia** and also **Atheroma** if a compromised bloodflow is associated.*
- *Several homeopathic remedies are indicated, and referral to a homeopathic Materia Medica or a homeopath is recommended. The remedies Argentum nitricum, Gelsemium, Lycopodium, and Rhus toxicodendron are all commonly found in a home-remedy kit, and can be used at potency 6 every 3hr until a suitable remedy is selected. Please refer to your preferred homeopathic manual for an initial choice.*
- *Numbness may be an indication of a deficiency in minerals or vitamins, especially vitamin B_{12}. Blood and hair analysis are recommended before supplementation.*
- *Osteopathy and chiropractic may relieve pressure if the numbness is coming from a structural origin, such as a misaligned spine or cramped muscle.*
- *Numbness may be associated, as may any neurological disorder, with a stagnation of Qi (energy). Acupuncture and Shiatsu may relieve this, as may specific Chinese or, preferably, Tibetan herbal treatments.*

PAIN

Pain is a localized or diffuse sensation, ranging from discomfort to agony. It is caused by stimulating special nerve endings known as pain fibers. Trauma or disease irritates these nerves, either directly or through the release of chemicals, which include arachidonic acid (AA) or substance P. There are four stages in pain recognition. Mild stimulation or the presence of only small amounts of these chemicals may create an itch or irritation, but as the stimulation increases, pain occurs. This process is known as *Initiation.*

Next comes *Transmission.* The ends of these fibers send off chemical impulses along the peripheral nerve into the central nervous system in the spinal column. On the way, the chemical messages pass through junctions known as synapses between nerves. Some of these connections are equivalent to checkpoints. A certain amount of chemical messenger has to be accrued before the next nerve will transmit. These junctions are known as pain gates. Once these pain gates are overcome, transmission terminates at the pain centers in the brain.

The third stage is *Recognition.* The pain centers are connected to the consciousness, and send in pulses to create an appropriate response. The fourth and final stage of pain is *Response.* Initial response is by reflex, and further response is conscious.

Once the pain center has been stimulated, impulses are sent out, generally causing constriction of the muscles in the area, thereby creating reflex recoil. This moves the part away from any external cause. The next response is a conscious one. Movements such as shaking or gripping may be of benefit by changing the level of compression on the affected nerve endings. While this almost-instantaneous action is taking place, the brain is releasing endorphins, the body's natural opiates, which begin the process of pain relief by acting on the pain centers, pain gates, and nerve transmission.

Pain relief is achieved by decreasing sensitivity at a local level through pain-relieving compounds from specific white blood cells and nerve fibers. The peripheral nerves and central nervous system are affected by pain-relieving chemicals.

It is important to understand that pain is not an enemy. The orthodox world has studied and engineered antipain compounds, which are of course the best-selling and most profitable of drugs. Indeed, pain relief is perhaps one of the major things that doctors can achieve for the patient. The holistic view, however, is to establish the cause of the pain and deal with that to achieve a longer-lasting effect. The drug companies might prefer us to take regular painkillers for a splinter we may find in our hand, whereas a sensible physician would remove the splinter.

A recent study and publication by a pain-control specialist has shown that the use of orthodox pain-suppressing drugs may actually enhance and increase the duration of pain. The hypothesis is that artificial, painkilling drugs suppress the body's own painkilling response. The more drugs that are taken, the more the suppression. Chronic pain treated with drugs may relieve after an initially painful six-week withdrawal period, and the individual will be left with a reduced need for painkillers.

The body creates pain for three reasons:

- *Pain as a warning.* If we stick our hand near a fire, pain receptors tell us to stop. If we drink coffee and create dyspepsia through acidity, it is the body telling us not to drink coffee. Interestingly, pain is often absent in serious disease processes such as cancer, diabetes, or AIDS until it is too late.
- *Pain as a repair process.* Pain initiates reflex responses. Not only does this move a body part away from the noxious stimulus, but it also creates a reflex within blood vessels. A stimulated pain nerve will send an impulse to the spinal column, and a reflex reaction will return an impulse to the surrounding vessels. These will dilate, allowing more blood into the area carrying more oxygen, white blood cells, and nutrients for repair. Pain is associated with inflammation, and inflammation is this increased bloodflow which

causes heat, swelling, and redness. Inflammation and pain are actually healing processes, and should not be inhibited unless they are interfering with the healing, which may occur if the response is too great.

- *Pain without purpose.* There are conditions where pain is no longer of use from the point of view of warning, nor does it need to continue, because the repair process is already underway. Serious injuries and the late stages of a disease process do not benefit from pain. In these late diseases or injuries, the consciousness of pain is incorrect. Referred pain, one that is sensed in an area that is not injured, falls into this category. The pain in a "phantom" limb (after amputation) is an example. More commonly, we may feel pain down our leg from a trapped nerve in the back, which is a referred pain acting as both a warning and a repair process, but is in fact in the wrong place.

It is important not to treat pain as a problem, but as a symptom. Even the orthodox world tends to avoid suppressing pain until the cause is established. Pain relief should be aimed at decreasing the sensitivity of local, peripheral, or central-nerve receptors, but also anything that increases sensitivity. Animal fats (which contain high levels of amino acids, caffeine, and stress chemicals, such as adrenaline) all sensitize the nervous system.

RECOMMENDATIONS

- *Always establish the cause of pain. Seek medical advice and diagnostic techniques if uncertain.*
- *Examine the cause, and discern whether the reason is a warning or a repair. Heed the warning and encourage the repair before initiating pain-relieving treatment.*
- *Be wary of the side effects of orthodox painkillers. Specific compounds can be reviewed in chapter 10. However, mild, orthodox pain relief from aspirin, Tylenol, or Tylenol with Codeine can be considered if the side effects are not contraindicated.*
- *Acute pain may be treated with naturopathic medication, but do not assume that these are necessarily free from side effects or safe. The following compounds can be used with safety topically, but ingestion is best prescribed by a herbalist, because the quality and quantity of any active ingredient within a herbal extract can never be certain: clove and thyme (oil or powdered extract) can be very useful on open wounds, especially gum and tooth pain; wintergreen, willow, and meadowsweet all contain salicylic acid (aspirin), but there is no benefit to using this rather than the over-the-counter form and, for the reason mentioned above, no quantities are given here.*
- *Homeopathic remedies are numerous, but do not act in the same way as an orthodox or herbal painkiller. A dose of a remedy will not have an instant effect, but will increase the painkilling response and help to diminish the consciousness if the pain is of no use. Homeopathic remedies encourage healing, so if a pain is warning or repairing, a remedy may actually worsen the discomfort initially. Referral to your preferred homeopathic manual will aid selection. Arnica 6 can be taken for any pain every 10min until an accurate homeopathic selection is made.*
- *Consider structural correction through osteopathy, chiropractic, or Shiatsu if the pain is due to a structural defect. Cranial, spinal, pelvic, and joint misalignment is a common cause of nerve entrapment.*
- *Cranial osteopathy may be very beneficial, especially if the pain is persistent.*
- *Transcutaneous electrical nerve stimulation (TENS) is the passing of a mild electrical impulse through the nerves, which can stimulate the pain-relieving chemicals.*
- *Acupuncture may be instantly relieving and curative, as may acupressure. Specific points may be illustrated by a practitioner of acupuncture or Shiatsu, and acupuncture or acupressure books.*

- *Long-term pain may be alleviated by taking the following compounds in divided doses throughout the day at the following amounts per foot of height: eicosapentenoic acid (300mg), D,L-phenylalanine (300mg), and vitamin B_1 (10mg per foot of height with three meals a day for three days, and then once per day only).*
- *Capsicum (in the form of hot peppers in the daily diet) and camomile (as a strong infusion) may be beneficial for long-term pain.*
- *Pain is subjective, and therefore techniques such as hypnotherapy, relaxation, and biofeedback will benefit.*

RESTLESS-LEGS SYNDROME

This is a condition that is characterized by a crawling, itching, and sometimes painful sensation in the legs and thighs, which is relieved by moving the legs, either by shaking or walking. The condition rarely has an association with serious underlying neurological disease, although an imbalance in the central nervous system's neurochemistry is hypothesized.

Other than being an uncomfortable situation, and—as it usually comes on half an hour into sleep, thus an infrequent cause of insomnia—this condition is not serious.

There is certainly a relationship to stimulants, especially caffeine and other compounds that affect the nervous system, such as nicotine and alcohol. Drug withdrawal may be the cause, and it is important to remember that withdrawal may not necessarily be associated with a complete cessation of use from a high level. Missing out on a nightly "joint" when this is a regular habit may create withdrawal and withdrawal may come into effect around midday for those who drink heavily each evening. There is hereditary correlation, and pregnancy may trigger the condition. This latter aspect has led to the investigation of deficiencies, and folic acid and iron are frequently found to be deficient in those who suffer. It is important to establish why these deficiencies have occurred; if there is a malabsorption syndrome, deal with that rather than just supply the supplement.

Anxiety and stress may be relevant, causing the production of chemicals that interfere with calming processes.

RECOMMENDATIONS

- *Investigate (through blood and hair analysis) any mineral and vitamin deficiency, and correct this through supplementation by taking three times the recommended daily dose in divided portions with food throughout the day. Pay special attention to iron, folic acid, and vitamin-B-complex deficiencies. (Please see a nutritionist if you are pregnant.)*
- *Regular exercise, preferably in the evening, may reduce excessive stress-chemical production at night.*
- *Practice a meditation technique or Qi Gong, yoga, or Tai Chi.*
- *Please refer to your homeopathic manual for a suitable homeopathic remedy. There are many choices, depending upon the symptom picture.*
- *Consider reviewing the section on detoxifying diets if a toxin or drug is taken regularly, or has recently been stopped (see **Detox diet**).*
- *Misalignment of the spine may put pressure on nerves, and osteopathy and massage therapies may benefit.*

RESTLESSNESS

Restlessness is not a serious medical condition, but most of us will struggle with the symptoms at some time in our lives. It is usually associated with boredom, and when a clear correlation is apparent, the answer is to relieve the inactivity.

The difficulty is that we are often unaware of our spiritual, psychological, or physical boredom, and restlessness can interfere with our normal functions.

Restlessness is the chemical effect of stress neurotransmitters on the nervous system. Treatment needs to be geared towards removing excess-stress chemicals, and repairing any deficiencies that might be placing the nervous system under pressure.

RECOMMENDATIONS

- *Isolate any obvious cause of a spiritual or psychological emptiness, and fill it with activity, mental exercise, meditation, or prayer.*
- *If there is no apparent reason for restlessness, then consider counseling or hypnotherapy to isolate a subconscious craving.*
- *Remove all neurological stimuli, such as caffeine, cigarettes, excess alcohol, or other drugs, all of which, directly or indirectly, will overstimulate the nervous system.*
- *If restlessness comes and goes, consider any correlation to foods eaten, because food allergy may be relevant.*
- *A persistence beyond the above measures may be suggestive of a nutritional deficiency, and blood and hair analysis of vitamin and mineral lack should be undertaken under the guidance of a complementary medical practitioner.*
- *Cranial osteopathy may be a temporary treatment.*

TRIGEMINAL NEURALGIA

Trigeminal neuralgia is a sudden, severe, lancing pain that affects the forehead, cheek area, or jaw on one side of the face. The pain is caused by irritation of the trigeminal nerve, which senses pain from three main branches that travel from each of these areas. The irritation is usually from an area of trauma at the angle of the mouth, the side of the nose, or in front of the ear, but may occur because of inflammation along the nerve pathway or even the presence of a tumor.

Trigeminal neuralgia

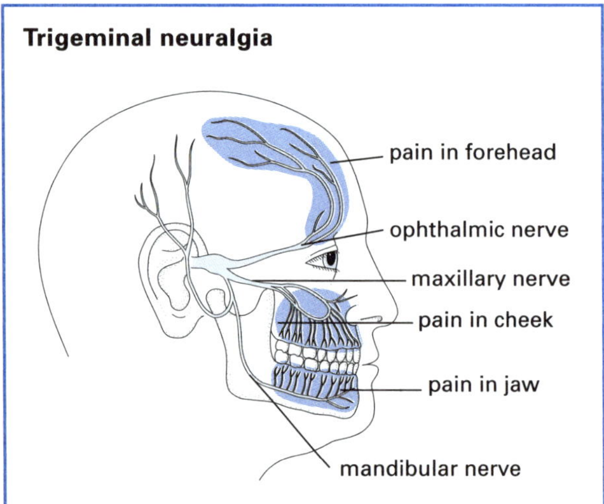

RECOMMENDATIONS

- *A firm diagnosis needs to be established by a doctor or a neurologist, and any underlying serious condition ruled out.*
- *See* **Neuralgia**.

PSYCHOLOGICAL MATTERS

AGORAPHOBIA

Literally, a fear of open places or spaces, although also more commonly used to described the fear of leaving home. This condition is more common than one would expect, and mostly affects women.

Mild cases can be dealt with most efficiently by homeopathy, but if the condition is disrupting normal life and is unresponsive to basic treatment, then counseling is recommended. Agoraphobia is commonly associated with a past event, which once examined, is usually treatable.

RECOMMENDATIONS

- *Review and try the homeopathic remedies Anthemis nobilis, Anarcardium, and Lycopodium. These remedies should be used at potency 200, one dose each night for seven nights.*
- *In acute situations, Aconite and Arsenicum album can be used at potency 6, four pills every 10min.*
- *Use D,L-phenylalanine (50mg per foot of height) with each meal.*

- *See a psychotherapist with a specialty in hypnotherapy, neurolinguistic programming, or eye-movement desensitization.*
- *Avoid situations that cause the anxiety while you are having treatment.*
- *Avoid stimulating foods at night, especially cheese, chocolate, and spices.*
- *Alcohol can offer a temporary relief, but may lead to persistent use and possible dependence in the same way that a drug such as a beta-blocker might. Avoid both.*

ANXIETY

Anxiety, like any emotion, is a necessary survival factor. No anxiety means no apprehension of potential danger. Nature does not encourage this. Anxiety is not a negative emotion, unless it overpowers normal function.

Anxiety can be acute or chronic: acute anxiety will occur in relation to frightening or worrying events; chronic anxiety is persistent and pathological if it has no logical foundation. Being anxious about, for instance, a loss of job or failing relationship is not wrong, and would be best dealt with through counseling and some basic homeopathic remedies.

RECOMMENDATIONS

ACUTE ANXIETY

- *Consider the following homeopathic remedies at potency 6 every 10min: Arsenicum album or Pulsatilla for anxiety at night, Sulphur for anxiety on awakening; Aconite, Causticum, or Ignatia for anxiety with fear; Aconite or Baryta carbonica for anxiety with fever. As always, it is best to review a homeopathic manual when choosing.*
- *Weak, sweet tea or camomile tea is beneficial, because anxiety can be associated with low blood sugar.*
- *Learn and practice a breathing and relaxation technique.*

CHRONIC ANXIETY

- *Visit a homeopath for a suitable remedy.*
- *Consider counseling if the anxiety levels are altering your daily life.*
- *Relaxation or meditation techniques are essential.*

COMPULSIVE OR OBSESSIVE DISORDERS

Compulsive/obsessive disorders are a group of psychological complaints characterized by repetitive actions of nonessential or useful activities. They can be looked upon as uncontrollable physical habits. The most-common examples are frequent washing of hands, counting to a certain number before entering a room, or performing a task or checking behind the door every time a person enters a room. Minor compulsions/obsessions, such as checking under the bed before sleeping, are not serious, and are quite common. Treatment only needs to be considered if disruption or antisocial behavior is occurring.

RECOMMENDATIONS

- *These are not conditions that are easily treated by self-help. Seek guidance through a counselor. Neurolinguistic programming and behavioral-modification techniques are very effective, as might be eye-movement desensitization.*
- *Homeopathic remedies can be utilized, but need to be prescribed by a homeopath, and should be used in conjunction with counseling.*

DEPRESSION

Everybody will experience depression as part of the normal cycle of emotions. Depression should not be treated except when the sadness, melancholy, or dejection is unrealistic, or is out of proportion to the apparent cause.

If one can accept that the human being is an energy source, of which some is material (body), some is mental function (mind), and the remaining part is emotion or being (spiritual), then depression must be looked at on all three levels. Depression manifests in all levels, and treatment needs to be directed to correcting the imbalance.

Manifestations of depression

- Mental—increased or decreased levels of activity, an inability to sleep or an excessive desire to stay asleep, an inability to concentrate or memorize, and prolonged periods of physical overactivity or inactivity.
- Spiritual—indifference to yourself or those around you, decreased ability to enjoy that which was enjoyable, a sense of inadequacy, worthlessness and, very often, guilt, a decrease in libido, recurrent thoughts of how much better things would be if one were dead.
- Physical—weight loss or weight gain, unexplained physical weakness, persisting feelings of tiredness and lack of energy, and increased or decreased appetite.

Medically speaking, four or more of the above symptoms are required to be defined as depression, and these have to persist for longer than a few days.

Endogenous and exogenous depression

The terms endogenous (created from within) and exogenous (caused by external influence) are really academic, because they overlap to such a great extent. I do feel, however, that it helps to have a good understanding of why a depression may not be the fault of will power; also, being able to define whether a problem is endogenous or exogenous is essential in recommending treatment. Years of psychotherapy may not affect an endogenous depression, whereas the most potent drugs will not provide a cure for an allergic, exogenous depression.

Endogenous depression

The causes of endogenous depression are:

- A lack of the nervous system's natural "happy juice," such as serotonin and dopamine.
- An excess of the CNS-depressive chemicals.
- Deficiencies in the nutrients necessary for the production of "happy juice," such as tryptophan, phenylalanine, vitamins B_6, B_3, and lecithin, to name but a few.
- Hormonal deficiencies, particularly in thyroid hormones and cortisol. Female hormonal fluctuations of estrogen and progesterone can have profound effects on mood.
- Hypoglycemia (low blood-sugar levels), which is often associated with a diet high in refined carbohydrates.
- Seasonal affective disorder (SAD) (*see* relevant section).
- Postnatal depression created by the fluctuation of female hormones.

Exogenous depression

The causes of exogenous depression are:

- Depression created by life events, such as bereavement, job loss, and relationship breakup.
- Direct, toxic effect from chemicals such as nicotine from cigarettes, aldehydes as the breakdown products of alcohol, and the effects of most "come downs" from recreational drugs.
- Specific, doctor-prescribed drugs such as steroids, antibiotics, and those drugs that may have a depressing effect on the thyroid gland or on sugar levels.
- Food allergies.
- Environmental pollutants, whether inhaled or ingested through food.
- Infections, most commonly viral, but very often overlooked are fungal and parasitic infections.
- A lack of exercise, which prevents the production of the body's natural opiates—endorphins and enkephalins.

RECOMMENDATIONS

- *If negative feelings persist for longer than a few days and seem to be inappropriate, then discuss the matter with your preferred complementary medical practitioner.*

- *Further discussions with a counselor are recommended if the feelings persist. Recourse to an orthodox medical practitioner, unless they are strongly holistic in their outlook, should be considered only as a last resort, because all too often, the only weapon in their armory is drug treatment.*
- *Preferably under the guidance of your complementary medical practitioner, consider using the following supplements at high doses, depending on the quality and quantity of the appetite through the depression: an essential amino-acid complex that includes tryptophan (minimum 2g per day) and D,L-phenylalanine (minimum 700mg per day). (There is some controversy about the safety of tryptophan following reports of toxicity when given at high doses. Consult a knowledgeable nutritionist); vitamin-B complex at up to ten times the daily recommended dose; vitamin C, folic acid, and magnesium at three times the recommended daily allowance.*
- *Avoid refined carbohydrates and any oversweet foods.*
- *Consider the coinciding times of depression with specific foods, either by maintaining an accurate dietary journal or by having a food-allergy test through blood, vega, or bioresonance tests.*
- *Have a good look at your lifestyle, and eliminate smoking, caffeine, alcohol, and other drugs until the depression has eleviated. Ensure that you have a good balance between your mind/body/spirit existence. Not enough exercise, not enough time spent in meditation or prayer, or indeed an excess of physical or mental activity will allow energy to flow from one level to the other, leaving deficiencies that can manifest as depression.*
- *Review any orthodox medication, including the oral contraceptive, which might be a depressant.*
- *If problems persist, ask a family practitioner to check for thyroid, cortisol, and blood sugar levels. A complementary medical practitioner or doctor should also check for persisting infections such as glandular fever or other such manifestations of Epstein-Barr virus or candidiasis. Chronic-fatigue syndrome (CFS) should be ruled out.*
- *Consider the possibility of postnatal depression or seasonal affective disorder (SAD).*
- *Nutritional deficiencies need to be corrected, as mentioned above, but please do not forget to drink 8 ounces of water per foot of height per day, because chronic dehydration may manifest itself as depression.*
- *Encourage the production of endorphins and enkephalins through exercise.*
- *Regular aerobic exercise is important, but daily work with Qi Gong, Tai Chi, or yoga may be curative for depression.*
- *Homeopathic remedies at high potency (1M or above) are potentially curative, but need to be selected based on all the symptoms of depression. Consult a homeopath.*
- *Herbal treatments are effectively drug treatments. The body may deal with the naturopathic drugs better than orthodox compounds, but I still see the two as similar—dealing with the feeling and not the underlying cause. St. John's wort (Hypericum) has come to prominence following the publication of a trial in a well-respected medical journal, but it is only one of hundreds that are well established as being antidepressive, following hundreds of years of observation and hundreds of small studies. Avoid their use except as a penultimate recourse, and take under the guidance of a naturopath.*
- *If all else has failed, then consider the use of drug treatment. Chemicals such as Lithium carbonate are well established and, if monitored, safe enough in conditions such as manic depression.*

ELECTRIC SHOCK TREATMENT (ELECTROCONVULSIVE THERAPY—ECT)

Many people are surprised to find that ECT is not only still performed, but is quite common. Certain psychiatrists still hold with this as an effective treatment for severe depression that is unresponsive to drug therapy, despite the potential risks to life, long-term memory, and any other brain function. Believe it or not, ECT at one time was used to change personality traits such as aggressive behavior or suicidal tendencies. It was even used as an aversion therapy towards homosexuality. Fortunately, we have moved forward.

RECOMMENDATIONS

- *Electroconvulsive therapy must only be considered when all other avenues have been exhausted.*
- *Ensure that all complementary medical avenues have been explored, because orthodox medicine often overlooks the possibility of deficiencies and food allergy.*

EMOTIONS

Emotion is a normal expression of feeling, and venting of any emotion is essential to long-term well-being. Suppression of emotion, and the consequential maintenance of high levels of adrenaline in the system, may be responsible for conditions as diverse as rashes and cancer. Eastern philosophy considers emotion to create internal heat, which needs to be expressed and eventually will be.

Emotion is only a pathological matter if it is expressed out of proportion to what triggered it. It is also unwise to allow emotion to be expressed as a secondary emotion. This means that if you are unhappy about an event, but then feel anger towards being unhappy, the emotion is a secondary emotion. Feelings about feelings are generally not productive, and can lead to inner psychological turmoil.

RECOMMENDATIONS

- *If you do not feel in control of your anger, or if your anger is directed towards another emotion, organize a consultation with a psychotherapist to establish the best type of therapy.*
- *Review a homeopathic manual, and use potency 200 of the remedy that most matches your emotional state nightly for ten nights.*
- *Learn a meditative technique and practice this daily with the yoga or Qi Gong techniques suitable for your emotional state.*
- *Initiate regular body-work treatments, such as massage or Shiatsu, which are marvelous at dissipating unwanted emotional chemicals.*

MANIC DEPRESSION (BIPOLAR DEPRESSION)

Everybody has moodswings. Those of us who have uncontrollable changes in our behavior pattern, from overexcitement, overactivity, and sleeplessness to periods of depression, marked lethargy, and apathy, are termed manic-depressive or bipolar-depressive.

While there is a tendency for this condition to run in families, true manic depression is generally a neurochemical imbalance caused by the brain tissues making either too much or too little "happy juice."

Certain factors—hormonal, drug or food stimulants, hypoglycemia, or food allergy—may heighten emotions, and thereby turn what would usually be regular moodswings into a type of manic depression. Pregnancy and premenstrual syndrome (PMS) very commonly cause marked shifts in moods, because of the sensitivity of the individual to the estrogen and progesterone levels. This is not manic depression, although some beleaguered husbands may think so!

RECOMMENDATIONS

- *If moodswings are apparent and life-disturbing, discuss the matter with a psychotherapist to establish whether manic depression is a likely diagnosis. Counseling in itself may be beneficial, and neurolinguistic programming may help to train an individual to recognize the early signs of either end of the emotional scale and teach control methods.*

- *Eliminate alcohol, caffeine, refined foods (especially sugars), cigarettes, and recreational drugs.*
- *Have a food-allergy test performed, or keep a very accurate journal listing the foods eaten and the mood felt. See if there is any isolated food or food groups that trigger either emotional state.*
- *Deficiencies in zinc, B-complex, calcium, magnesium, or the active substance in lecithin known as phosphatidylcholine may all be relevant, and taking four times the RDA (recommended daily allowance) may make a difference. This should be done as a trial for two weeks, and if an improvement is noted, the information should be taken to a complementary medical practitioner with experience in this area to analyze your diet or consider why absorption is not taking place.*
- *Amino-acid deficiency, especially tryptophan and phenylalanine, is common.*
- *Yeast infections in the bowel, especially Candida, may create the deficiencies that lead to bipolar depression, as well as producing chemicals that enhance the condition. See* **Depression** *for the downside of this condition, and* **Hysteria** *for the manic part.*
- *As a last resort, psychiatric administration of the drug lithium may be necessary.*

STRESS

Stress is an ever-increasingly popular term that is invading our language and life. Medically speaking, stress is a group of chemicals known as catecholamines and steroids. The better known are adrenaline (epinephrine) and noradrenaline (norepinephrine). The body's natural steroids—cortisol being the most prominent—have a marked influence on the system, and are produced in response to stress.

Stress may be psychologically induced, as common usage of the word conveys, but the chemicals are also produced through physical discomfort from overexercising, excessive tiredness, and unfavorable environmental conditions (too hot or too cold). The stress chemicals may also be produced as a response to toxicity from pollution, ingestion of toxins, or food allergy.

It is worth differentiating between stress and pressure. Every animal reacts better if there is a certain amount of adrenaline in the system. A challenge or an exciting prospect may produce a small amount of stress chemical, which will create a certain amount of "drive" to perform a function. This is a good thing. In fact, I would go so far as to say that without pressure, we may not fare so well. Stress is an overproduction of adrenaline and other stress chemicals.

Stressors (as stress chemicals are collectively known) have evolved with us, and are the principal reason why most animals survive. If other hormones had as strong an influence as stress chemicals, emotions other than fear and a need to fight would have become prominent. For example, if sex hormones exerted a stronger influence than adrenaline, then our distant ancestors might have carried on making love despite the arrival of a saber-toothed tiger. Those of our ancestors who had a stronger adrenaline response would run away. Those who did not would finish the job, and probably be killed.

Natural selection has therefore provided us with a very sensitive anxiety response. We are no longer confronted by saber-toothed tigers, and life-threatening situations are few and far between, but we all have to face anxiety, ranging from "where will we get our next meal?" and "will we have a roof over our head?," to battles with our partners, bank managers, and other road users! Our brain recognizes a stressful situation, and tries to produce the relevant amount of adrenaline for it. Going into an unhappy job every day will produce a certain amount of adrenaline; being confronted by a masked, knife-wielding mugger will produce more. However, the latter event that produces a large amount of adrenaline immediately may be matched by the production of lower levels in response to less anxiety over a longer period of time. The long-term effects of persistent low-level stresses are well established, and can cause an array of diseases and conditions, ranging from angina to ulcers. There are considered to be three stages in a stress reaction.

Initial response or alarm reaction

Faced with a dangerous situation, the level of stress hormones will rise, causing two fundamental changes. Adrenaline and noradrenaline will open up blood vessels to the brain, heart, lungs, and muscles, thereby encouraging oxygenation and nutrition to the organs that need to think, oxygenate, and move the body. Cortisol and other steroids will flood the bloodsteam with glucose, providing energy. In combination with catecholamines, the blood supply to those organs not needed in a fight is then reduced by closing their arteries. Kidney and liver function will slow down and, more noticeably, a lack of blood to the skin will make us go pale, a lack of blood to the bladder will make us want to pass urine, and a lack of blood to the bowel will make us register a need to defecate. In extreme shock, we may go white, urinate, and soil ourselves.

This so-called "fight-or-flight" response increases the heart rate and the strength of heart contraction; increases the rate of breathing, increases sweat production (which lowers body temperature and eliminates the byproducts of metabolism that will have increased under the pressure of adrenaline); and effectively prepares us for action.

Comedown or resistance

The second stage is the comedown or resistance reaction. Here, the body is no longer primed for action, but is dealing with the abundance of chemicals and changes within the physiology of the body that have taken place.

Exhaustion

At some point after the resistance reaction an exhaustion phase may manifest. Under extreme stress, the body may faint or even die. This is characterized by those who have noticed that helping an injured animal may initially be tolerated, but by the time the animal has been placed in a box and taken to the vet, it will have died. The initial fear was so great that when its life was "spared," the resistance and exhaustion phases led to severe, biochemical changes causing its death. It is rare to see this in human beings, but all of us will have experienced the "anticlimax" and exhaustion following anxious or nerve-wracking events, such as exams or a first date!

The important aspect from all of this discussion is to appreciate that stress is a chemical reaction, not a psychological state of mind, although the latter produces the former. Stress does not have to be manifested in sleeplessness, trauma, or wide, staring eyes, but can be produced without symptoms by a low, persistent rate of stress-chemical production. Stress creates excess energy or extra activity for the brain, heart, lungs, and muscles, and exhaustion of these organs will lead to a predilection to disease. Conversely, the organs from which blood is taken may become deficient in nutrients and oxygen, and may also be led to illness.

Stress management

We all undergo periods of anxiety; it is part of existing and attempting to "better" ourselves. We, as human beings, would not function or succeed if we were not pushed by catecholamine, cortisol, and other stressors. It is important, however, to differentiate between being under pressure and being stressed. Most successful individuals, whatever their field, will achieve because of pressure. This drive should be focused on the appropriate

Aromatherapy

Massage with aromatherapy oils is particularly beneficial for relieving stress. The soothing effect of body work combines with the relaxing qualities of aromatherapy oils such as lavender.

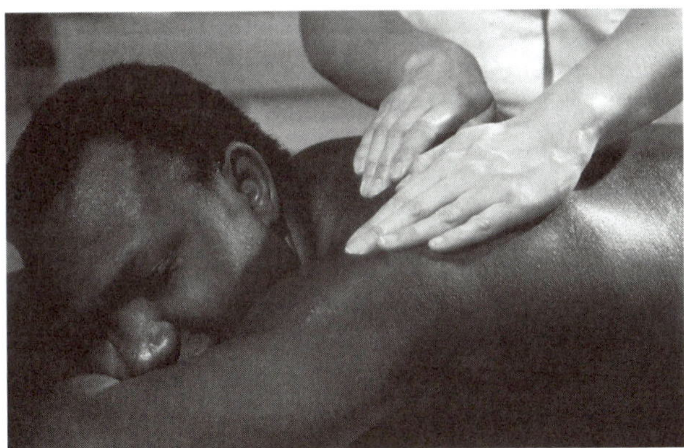

event, and not be transferred elsewhere. An employee angry with their boss should not take it out on their partner, friends, or children. This act of transference is the main indicator that the drive has moved from being pressure to being stress. The stress chemicals are in abundance, and are telling the body, mind, and soul that it is in trouble. Trouble rarely comes in small bursts, according to our evolutionary development, and therefore a problem at work is carried through to home. It is important to learn how to reduce stress-chemical production, and use up any excess chemicals in the bloodstream.

How to differentiate between pressure and stress is difficult. I think the answer may be simply to ask "am I happy?" or "can I accept this particular situation?" If the answer is "no" to either, then you are under stress and not pressure. If stress is present, then you run the risk of any number of conditions and diseases. It is argued by those with a strong meditative or spiritual belief, that all physical ailments, except those created by age (and even that is often debated), are caused by an excess of stress chemicals.

RECOMMENDATIONS

- *Be happy or at least at peace with the activities and emotions in your life. If you are not, sit with a counselor and discuss the reasons.*
- *Learn a relaxation or meditation technique regardless. These produce antistress chemicals that will either act as a treatment or as a preventative measure. Practicing for a few minutes a day is better than nothing at all, although ideally 1–2hr a day should be set aside for meditation. (I have been accused of supporting a concept of "spiritual aerobics!")*
- *Consider physical causes of stress by establishing the presence of food allergies through blood tests, and by avoiding these stressors.*
- *Ensure a healthy environment, both at work and home. Avoid pollution and dirt, and consider the effects of radiation (see* ***Radiation****).*
- *Stress chemicals produce free radicals that are both damaging to cells and carcinogenic.*
- *Take the following supplements (at the doses given per foot of height, divided throughout the day with meals) if under stress or if the diet does not have five portions of fruit and vegetables each day: beta-carotene (2mg), vitamin C (1g), vitamin E (100iu), selenium (40mg), coenzyme Q10 (5mg), and pycnogenol (grapeseed extract); maximum recommended dose on a good, natural product.*
- *Try supplementation with the amino acid D,L-phenylalanine, 150mg per foot of height in divided doses throughout the day. If available, tryptophan can be taken at the same dosage but*

due to an unsubstantiated fear following problems because of faulty manufacture, this amino acid is no longer available as a supplement without a doctor's prescription. Tryptophan is available to nonvegetarians in meat, fish, and turkey, and to everyone through cottage cheese, milk, bananas, peanuts, and lentils. Dried dates, interestingly, have a high proportion.

- *Specific homeopathic remedies, and herbal and antioxidant treatments, are available but most of those that can be bought off the shelf are the wrong potency, or are too low in concentration to be efficacious. Stressed individuals should be under the care of a complementary medical practitioner.*
- *Ginseng and adrenal gland extracts may be selected off the shelves, and taken at twice the daily recommended dose for one week and then reduced to the recommended levels according to the packaging if an effect has been noticed within the first seven days.*
- *Exercise burns up stress chemicals. Overexercising, however, may stress the body further. Set an exercise program within your capabilities, and slowly but gently increase activity. One session with a gym master or personal-fitness instructor will solve your problems.*
- *Body work of any sort is beneficial. Human touch is soothing, and produces chemicals that counteract stresses. Most practitioners are in the field because of a need or an ability to heal, and healing energy will counteract stresses.*
- *Aromatherapy using lavender oils, or other more-specific extracts, depending upon the individual's personality and stress, will act as a pheromone (airborne chemical), and stimulate relaxation chemicals.*
- *Bach flower remedies chosen according to the symptoms of the individual will give benefit.*
- *Sound therapy has been researched, and whether it is simply listening to music or sitting in acoustic chairs, which pass a vibration through the system, relaxation chemicals are promoted to counteract stresses.*

Chapter 6

Middle Age and Onwards

Chapter 6

Middle Age and Onwards

I have chosen not to include a chapter in this book for old age. Complementary medical treatments are less beneficial in old age, because we are reaching a time when our vital force is diminishing, and repair is difficult. Treatments in old age are palliative (relieving) rather than curative.

It is better to establish health in our latter years by working on health concepts from a younger age. It is never too late to change habits and lifestyles, and the advice given in this chapter will, I hope, encourage all of us to review our health at the beginning of the problems associated with aging, rather than after the damage has set in. Provided that no major damage has taken place, then the aging process can be pleasurable, healthy, and prolonged.

The process of aging is dependent on two factors. The first is the loss of vital force, this undeniable energy that keeps cells repairing and replicating. The second is the maintenance of good nutrition and oxygenation to all the cells in the body.

The presence of vital force is a much-debated point, and the Western scientific view is unlikely to agree with the Eastern philosophical view. Libraries could be dedicated to the books and journals that have been written on the principle of vital force. Proponents of meditation, and mind/body-energy workers, would argue that it is feasible and easily possible to pull in life force from the universe to maintain health and youthfulness. Indeed, many yogis take in very little nutrition, and yet maintain a very healthy lifestyle on the energy they absorb from the cosmos. This is beyond most of us in the West, who do not have a nonmaterialistic attitude or the time to practice the more-dedicated spiritual techniques required.

A more-Western orientation of aging would be to assume that the byproducts of metabolism, the free radicals absorbed or produced, the decrease in essential hormone production, and the natural process of clogging the arteries—thereby reducing the oxygen and nutrients to cells—all lead to aging.

RECOMMENDATION

- *See* **Arteriosclerosis**, **Antioxidants** *and* **Free radicals**, **Stress**, *and* **Meditation**. *Mastering and abiding by the rules of these areas is the simple answer to slowing the aging process and avoiding the diseases associated with old age.*

General

BLOOD CLOTTING AND CLOTS

The medical term for a blood clot is a *thrombus*. The formation of a thrombus is known as *thrombosis*. A thrombus differs from a clot because it forms within the cardiovascular system, and is a danger because it may occlude a blood vessel or become loose and travel to a vital organ, causing obstruction at that distant site. If a thrombus moves, it is known as an *embolus*.

A thrombus should form only if a blood vessel is ruptured, which allows the blood to flow into tissues or become exposed to air, thus triggering the clotting mechanism. The formation of a clot is dependent upon a cascade reaction involving 13 different chemical substances, one causing the activation of the next. The absence of one of these prevents or slows down clotting, sometimes to a fatal degree. The best-known condition is hemophilia, which is the absence of factor VIII. Factor IV is calcium, and a deficiency in the availability of this mineral may influence clotting.

RECOMMENDATIONS

- *Any tendency to bruise or bleed more easily or for longer than expected should be investigated by a physician, who will perform tests for the clotting times and factors.*
- *Complementary medical work should be based on the findings. Homeopathy in particular should be considered.*
- *If there is no obvious reason for a clotting deficit, consult a Chinese, Tibetan, or Ayurvedic physician, who will look at the problem from the view that the blood is "too thin," and attention will be paid to correcting this through lifestyle changes, nutritional supplementation, herbal medication, and acupuncture.*
- *See* **Coronary thrombosis**, **Deep-vein thrombosis**, *and* **Pulmonary embolism** *if necessary.*

DEATH AND DYING

This is a subject that could fill a library of books, and indeed has. This short section will talk about dying rather than death, because dying is very much a part of our cycle, and it is as necessary to have a "healthy" lead up to death as it is to be healthy prior to conceiving.

Spiritually speaking, death may be considered an endpoint or a beginning. The importance is not about establishing which it is, but being at peace with whichever decision you as an individual make. Whether you end on the right side of Jesus, in the house of Allah, or reincarnate to continue your lessons, a belief is a great help in stemming the fear that is associated with dying. Indeed, one can be at rest as much with a religious belief as one can with believing that we are "fodder for worms." You should work toward a sense of conviction throughout life, and in doing so, you will remove the fear of death.

The fear of dying is often not associated with the actual endpoint, but more with the fear of pain and discomfort that is associated with this final act. Dying comfortably and without pain, anxiety, or distress to the individual or those around is the necessary goal.

Death often arises swiftly through accident or rapid-disease process, but all too often, death is a process spanning over days, months, or even years. Through that time, the human being goes through a variety of emotions best described by Dr. Elisabeth Kübler-Ross.

Denial

Initially, we will deny the possibility of what we have always known to be an inevitability. However strong our conviction toward a religious or spiritual belief, fear of the unknown will create an option for us. Do we continue to follow our lifelong belief, or not? Indeed, we have had options all through our life, and our mentality is not geared toward having no choice. We therefore tend to deny the possibility of this event.

Anger

Anger is due to the inevitability of death, but tends to be reflected or transferred to the body, the person, or those close at hand.

Bargaining

The individual will bargain with themselves, their lifestyle, or their God, often as a backlash against the second stage of anger: "Perhaps, because being upset has not worked, from now on I will be peaceful and understanding of the situation and then it may go away."

Depression

There will come a point when the true realization occurs that this particular chapter of existence is drawing to a close, and depression will set in. Regrets over actions and thoughts not realized, and the feelings for those who will be left behind all come into play, creating anything from mild to severe depression.

Acceptance

Most of the time, those going through the stages

of dying will reach acceptance. It is a suitable endpoint, and preferable to all the other emotional states because it invariably brings a level of calm, both to the individual and to those close by.

Each stage may take a few hours to a few months to travel through and, like climbing a step ladder, we can slip or climb from one level to another, but overall we generally move toward acceptance. There is no easy way of dealing with death in the short term, and it is perhaps better to consider dying from an early age.

It is a failing in the West that the loss of the extended family has removed most of us from being around the dying. For those who are dying, there is the pleasure of having the exuberance of youth running around outside the bedroom, and for those for whom death is far off, it becomes less frightening when it is no longer part of the great unknown. In the West we have made death into a taboo subject, rarely discussing it in anything but morbid terms, and often ending short discussions with "I really do not want to talk about that." Death and dying must be brought back into our social structure at an earlier age if we are to deal with this important part of our life.

RECOMMENDATIONS

- *Start at a young age to discuss openly death and, when possible, spend time with those who are dying, to experience the event.*
- *Understand the levels of denial, anger, bargaining, depression, and finally acceptance, and relate that understanding to those around you.*
- *Constantly work on your own spiritual beliefs concerning death. By all means, change your attitudes, but it is important to have a belief, whether it is considering death as a final endpoint or the start of a new life.*
- *Contend with outstanding practicalities. Deal with personalities who may find your death traumatic, and also clear your own conscience by saying what needs to be said to those to whom it should be said. If possible and should time allow, fulfil as many ambitions as possible, both practical and emotional.*
- *Discuss dying with a bereavement counselor and ensure that you are conscious of the good and bad points of your leaving this life.*
- *Focus your attention on being comfortable and pain-free. Discuss this with orthodox doctors and complementary medical practitioners, because most alternative disciplines will have potentially useful techniques.*
- *The homeopathic remedy Arsenicum album can be offered by homeopaths as a remedy that challenges the body when it nears death. If vital force can be redirected and be of help in comforting the individual, Arsenicum album will contribute. If the vital force is absent, the demand by Arsenicum album will not be met, and the end will be smoother and less traumatic than it might otherwise be.*

Euthanasia

Although attitudes are changing throughout the world, and in certain parts of Europe and Australia, medically assisted euthanasia is now legal under certain circumstances, taking your own life is illegal. Most religions create a taboo around euthanasia, and different Eastern philosophies have different views and values. Japanese society has its infamous hara-kiri, which is an accepted, expected, and honored tradition under the right circumstances. The concept of reincarnation, however, suggests that suicide or euthanasia will prevent the necessary pain, sorrow, or discomfort that the soul needs to endure to avoid having to come back and learn the lesson next time around. Medically speaking, it is sometimes hard to place the spiritual aspect above the level of physical suffering found in those who have had painful strokes, or who are struggling with neurological conditions such as motor-neurone disease or multiple sclerosis, or those in social circumstances that may be beyond human endurance.

RECOMMENDATIONS

- *Always discuss thoughts of euthanasia with counselors, and not with friends and family.*
- *Contact your National Euthanasia Society.*
- *Hunt around, and you will find doctors or healthcare professionals who will be able to advise you on successful euthanasia techniques. Some may even be willing to assist, despite the legal risks. I have chosen not to include in this book the preferred and most successful technique.*

HORMONE-REPLACEMENT THERAPY (HRT)

Hormone-Replacment Therapy has been promoted in such a way that both the public and the medical profession assume that it is a necessary treatment course for any woman going through the menopause. However, much research since the 1960s leads to the conclusion that the use of hormones creates dangers that outweigh the claimed advantages.

The orthodox world would unhesitatingly encourage the use of hormone-replacement therapy, but initially, alternative treatments can alleviate the problems without entailing the potential risks and side effects of HRT.

Osteoporosis and cardiovascular disease (such as heart attacks and strokes) are not the inevitable outcome of going through the menopause, and protection against these conditions is discussed in the relevant sections of this book.

Along with vaccinations, the promotion of HRT is in my opinion one of the most devastating and misleading of the orthodox medical world's health guidelines. The medical profession seems to consider the menopause to be a "deficiency disease." It compares the lack of female hormones to that of thyroid or insulin deficiencies, which is simply not true. Four-fifths of the world's population will not have access to artificial HRT. It is ironic that this so-called "third-world" population also have strikingly lower levels of osteoporosis, heart disease, cancer, and menopausal symptoms, which HRT is supposed to protect against.

Japan and Africa have negligible amounts of osteoporosis, cardiovascular disease, and stroke in comparison with the West, due to healthier lifestyles, nutrition, and more exercise. All of these are very relevant to the disease processes that HRT supposedly helps to prevent.

Frankly and factually, the processes of aging that the Western orthodox medical world would have us believe are due to our lack of estrogen and progesterone are simply not reflected in those societies that have not been targeted for HRT use. Most, if not all, of the serious conditions, and a majority of unpleasant symptoms, are created by factors other than female hormone depletion. Nutrition, lifestyle, and exercise are far more relevant than hormone levels.

Hormone-replacement therapy is not well proven, either in safety or efficacy. The pharmaceutical industry and many doctors may be unaware of scientific studies published in reputable medical journals that state that HRT has risks, and is not as effective as we have thought.

Initially, HRT was brought forward to remove the unwanted symptoms that the Western woman found uncomfortable. That is not to say that women from less-developed countries do not suffer similarly, but here in the West, we are brought up to believe that any symptom is unnecessary and should be removed, regardless of the reason why it may be there. Most uncomfortable sensations are either a warning or a repair process, and if the underlying cause is diagnosed and treated, the symptom often goes away. Unfortunately, after a few years it was found that 50 percent of women who used HRT to alleviate menopausal symptoms stopped using the preparations because of unwanted side effects or ineffectiveness of the treatment. The pharmaceutical companies experimented with different levels of various estrogens and progesterones, and claimed that the newer preparations were far more effective. My experience—and that of my senior colleagues—supports latter-day studies showing that many women are still struggling with side effects, including continued periods.

The next stage was the pronouncement that HRT prevented osteoporosis. Many widely promoted studies showed that the use of artificial estrogen prevented bone loss. Unfortunately for the HRT supporters, a large study of women in Framingham, Massachusetts, is proving that shorter studies are not accurate, and in fact are flawed. Only women who have been taking HRT for more than seven years show any appreciable difference in bone density and, because these women are at far-greater risk of developing estrogen-dependent cancers, the risk of more-serious conditions outweighs any benefits. What is more, if women stopped their treatment after ten years, they would have the same fracture risk as the population who had not used HRT. Because most women may be advised to use HRT at around the age of 50 years, and most hip fractures (the greatest risk of osteoporosis) tend not to occur until the mid-seventies in age, one can immediately see the pointlessness of using HRT for this condition.

The industry went on to "prove" that the use of HRT protects against coronary heart disease, stroke, and raised-cholesterol levels. I am afraid not. The Framingham study mentioned above suggests that the risk of heart disease is actually increased, and contradicts the findings of numerous studies.

Up until 1993 the main studies supporting HRT as a protection against vascular disease were found to be markedly flawed. An example of this in one of the major trials is described in medical circles as "selection bias." A large group of women were divided into those who would receive HRT and those who would receive a placebo. Neither group would know what they were taking. For "ethical" reasons, all women in the group taking HRT who had any risk factors—i.e. health problems or genetic predispositions to diseases that were associated with estrogen or progesterone—were eliminated, but this same factor was not taken into consideration in the control group. What this meant was that those taking HRT were already at a much lower risk for cardiovascular disease than the control group. When the results came forward they were (not surprisingly) markedly in favor of HRT being a protector of women from heart attacks and strokes. The debate continues, but I have yet to see any new trials that are supportive of HRT in these conditions. In fact, a recent *British Medical Journal* article showed no significant benefit from HRT in cardiovascular disease over a 10-year period.

The latest suggestion is that HRT may protect against certain bowel conditions, but I think even the pharmaceutical industry is aware of this being a weak selling-point.

The risks of HRT

The availability and promotion of HRT has led to doctors neglecting or avoiding the necessary discussion about changes in our diet and the exercise we take, as well as the potentially damaging effects of smoking, alcohol, and drugs. Menopause has become a trigger for doctors to prescribe either estrogen-only preparations or the estrogen/ progesterone combinations.

To understand the risks, it helps to know what the sex hormones are doing. Principally, estrogen and progesterone stimulate cell division, especially in the inner lining of the uterus, breast tissue, and ovaries. This is achieved by increasing the blood supply to these tissues, by improving the strength of blood vessels and opening them up. These are exactly the reasons why people develop headaches, migraines, and cramps.

The hormones also increase the clotting ability in the blood by making platelets adhere more readily, and they also detrimentally raise fat levels in the blood. This combination in the slower blood flow in dilated arteries leads to blood clots, heart attacks, and strokes.

Putting aside the ineffectiveness of artificial HRT, there are also the frank risks of taking these artificial chemicals. Despite discussions with gynecologists and scientific specialists in this area, I am still very confused by what appears to me to be a simple logical argument. In the *British National Formulary*, the official publication of the Royal Pharmaceutical Society of Great Britain that lists all the drugs available, there are 27 contraindications and 17 side effects of the use of the oral contraceptive pill. Hormone replacement therapy, made from predominantly the same chemicals, lists only seven contraindications, but practically similar side effects. For some reason, when women reach the age when HRT can be prescribed, all the side effects that they may have had from the contraceptive pill a year previously are no longer a risk. Doctors (and I include myself in this) are actually told, for example, that the oral contraceptive pill should not be used by women with high blood pressure before menopause, but at menopause this combination of artificial hormones may actually benefit hypertensives because of the "protective" effects against heart attack and stroke. It does not make sense. I frankly find it indefensible, and cannot understand why our professors persist in refusing to see the wood for the trees.

As well as the inefficiency and lack of efficacy of HRT, there are actually proven risks that each individual must take into account before embarking on a course of treatment.

Cancers

Uterine (endometrial) cancer was found to be seven times greater in women using HRT. This was at a time when estrogen was being used without progesterone to "oppose" it. The orthodox medical world rapidly announced that the use of progesterone negated these results, but they failed to mention the continued risk of uterine cancer, which was still three times greater, despite the use of progesterone.

RISK OF BREAST CANCER WITH HRT

Years on HRT	Cases of breast cancer between ages 50 and 70	Extra breast cancer in HRT users
None	45 per 1,000	nil
5 years	47 per 1,000	2 per 1,000
10 years	51 per 1,000	6 per 1,000
15 years	57 per 1,000	12 per 1,000

Breast cancer is also increased by the use of HRT. Studies suggesting protection by HRT are promoted by the pharmaceutical companies, contrary to the evidence of large studies showing that combination HRT (estrogen and progesterone) increases the risk of breast cancer to four times that of non-HRT-using women if it is taken for over six years.

Certain trials have shown that estrogens and progestogen (artificial progesterone) increase other cancers, such as cancer of the ovaries, cervix, pituitary gland, liver, and the skin (melanomas).

The reason why these are not well documented is because money is not available to put into trials that repeat negative results.

Thrombosis (blood clots), strokes, and heart disease

Every doctor will advise a woman that the contraceptive pill can cause blood clots, most commonly deep-vein thrombosis in the legs. Any past history or family history of blood clots, high blood pressure or obesity, history of strokes, or other cardiovascular problems all contraindicate the use of oral contraceptive pills (OCP). If the OCP is known to cause problems, there is no reason to believe that because a woman ages, the chemicals will alter their functions.

One of the main hypotheses supporting HRT against heart and vascular disease is the effects of HRT on reducing cholesterol. The trials, according to eminent research scientists, have all been flawed, and are based on the assumption that lowering cholesterol levels will alter rates of cardiovascular disease in postmenopausal women. None of this has been conclusively proven. What is more worrying is the continued promotion of these unsubstantiated studies, despite the evidence of large followup studies showing that HRT is *not* effective in reducing cardiovascular problems, and in fact may increase risks.

Osteoporosis—see Osteoporosis

Other side effects

Specific problems—such as skin conditions, jaundice, vomiting, stitches—and physiological disturbances such as depression and irritability can all be caused by HRT. One study in the U.K. showed that there was an increase in suicide in groups using HRT. What is more distressing is that symptoms of menopause may be worsened or initiated by HRT. I occasionally see patients who have unique symptoms such as muscular aches and pains or abdominal spasms, and neurological symptoms such as dizziness and "pins-and-needles." I cannot categorically state that these have been caused by HRT, but the symptoms improve when the treatment stops.

There has been reported in one study a sixfold increase in asthma in women who use HRT.

Natural estrogens and progesterones

There is a bandwagon rolling to support natural female hormones. These are plant derivatives that actually contain exactly the same types of sex hormones as the human body, as opposed to the artificial chemicals in HRT that only resemble ours. Natural estrogens from plants, known as phytoestrogens, are much less potent than artificial hormones, but the body seems to respond to them if their application is appropriate. These estrogens are obtained from hops, fennel, celery, soya products, and rhubarb, all of which can be fed comfortably into the diet. Extracts from specific plants can be obtained from healthfood stores as "food products" because no medical claim can be made. It is interesting to note that Japanese women who have a much higher level of soya products in their diet (in addition to no red meat or saturated fat) have negligible levels of osteoporosis or heart disease.

Natural progesterone has risen in popularity on the back of the work of a doctor called John Lee in the U.S.A. Dr. Lee was unimpressed by the efficiency and effects of estrogen, and looked toward decreased progesterone as a possible cause of menopausal problems. His research and personal experience suggested, and has since shown, that a bulk of symptoms that women complain of, and the diseases such as osteoporosis that are associated with aging, may be due to the lack of progesterone, and not estrogen. There is much evidence to support this. As the pharmaceutical industry cannot patent a natural compound, there is no point in experimenting or studying natural progesterone, and so most of Dr. Lee's work has not been repeated.

Natural progesterone has been extracted from the Mexican yam (other sweet potatoes do not contain it), and needs to be administered transdermally (through the skin) because, like any complex chain, it is unlikely to survive the digestive system intact. Natural progesterone does not seem to have an effect on the hot flushes and sweats that are the main disturbing feature for most women going through the menopause, but it may have an effect on all the other symptoms. Most encouragingly, it has a profound effect on osteoporosis (*see* **Osteoporosis**).

Estrogen-dependent tumors, most commonly found in the breast, may benefit from these phytoestrogens. A study in a top London hospital is currently ongoing, and it would appear that these plant estrogens may lock into estrogen receptors, thereby preventing the stronger body hormones from exerting an effect. There may be some risk that the plant extracts will actually encourage estrogen-sensitive tumors, but the experiments to date are encouraging. It may be that premenopausal women should use phytoestrogens and natural progesterones as protection factors in any estrogen-related condition.

Types of HRT

The estrogens are taken as a tablet, patch, an implant, or a gel. Any woman who still has her uterus (i.e. has not been subjected to a hysterectomy) must take regular progestogen (artificial progesterone), which is usually taken as a tablet. The progestogen blocks the estrogen effect. Usually, the progestogen is taken for 12 days, but many women suffer the progesterone side effects, which are principally fluid retention, headaches, skin reaction such as acne, and other premenstrual syndrome symptoms. Women who have gone through the menopause and have not had a period for at least 12 months are offered the combined preparation, which is taken continuously. These do not cause periods to occur, which is certainly a favorable option. Another option is to take an estrogen preparation and progesterone, say four times a year, giving a bleed every three months. This is offered to those women going through menopause who may still be having infrequent periods. I mention this for information and not as a support of their use. In fact, my views are quite the opposite.

Dosage of HRT

Hormone-replacement therapy is mostly given orally or via skin patches. These may be combination pills, or estrogen with short courses of progesterone to encourage a period or offer "protection" from the unopposed estrogen. Implants are becoming more popular, but their safety is highly questionable. For a start, the ovaries, adrenal glands, and fat stores (these actually make estrogen) can all produce hormones at fluctuating rates for years after the menopause. An implant delivers a set dose regardless of the amount that is made by the body naturally. This can cause overdoses, which will lead to all the risks and side effects listed above.

RECOMMENDATIONS

GENERALLY

- *Avoid the advice of your doctor, who will be encouraging the use of HRT.*
- *Work with a complementary medical practitioner if the signs and symptoms of menopause are disturbing.*
- *Obtain relevant blood tests to establish menopausal status.*
- *Consider urinary protein tests and bone densitometry ultrasound to establish a baseline for osteoporosis.*
- *See* **Arteriosclerosis** *with regard to the better dietetic regimes and supplemental treatments to protect against cardiovascular disease.*
- *If you are currently using or considering the use of HRT, consult a complementary medical practitioner with experience in this area.*
- *See* **Osteoporosis**, **Stroke** *and* **Heart attack** *to establish the alternatives to help protect against these conditions in latter years. These techniques are as useful as any positive aspects of HRT.*
- *Consider the use of natural-hormone creams, available through specialist complementary practitioners and all doctors, if they are willing to read the information and prescribe them.*

MALE MENOPAUSE

Many men notice changes within themselves, ranging from fatigue, depression, and irritability to reduced sex drive and impotence, after they get to the age of 40 years.

The term "male menopause" has been coined, but rarely is there a drop in testosterone or other male hormones (androgens) in the bloodstream. Replenishment with testosterone may increase sexual interest somewhat, but most other symptoms are unaffected. It is more likely that stress, combined with arteriosclerosis, accounts for most of the symptoms.

RECOMMENDATIONS

- *See* **Stress** *and* **Arteriosclerosis**.
- *Increase exercise and relaxation/meditation techniques.*
- *Consider the development of food allergy and be tested.*

MENOPAUSE

Menopause is the physiological cessation of menstruation, which usually occurs between years 45 and 55 of a woman's life, and most commonly within two years either side of the age at which the individual's mother went through menopause. Colloquially known as "the change," and medically termed the climacteric, this period of transition commonly lasts 2–5 years, but can be noticed for up to 20 years.

Thought of as a diminution in the estrogen levels produced by the ovaries, menopause is actually a drop in the levels of estrogen and the cessation of production of progesterone. Most of the symptoms of menopause are created by the loss of both progesterone and estrogen, and their effects on the blood vessels, which tend to dilate and cause bloodflow changes, and also on the nervous system directly. These effects cause:

- *Psychological symptoms*—mood swings, short temper, depression, anxiety, usually lowered, but occasionally raised libido, and insomnia.
- *Physical symptoms*—hot flushes, sweats (especially at night), water retention, fat deposit increase, headaches, aches and pains, malaise and lethargy, and cystitis-like symptoms.
- *Physical signs*—loss of breast tissue, vaginal dryness, osteoporosis (bone thinning), and skin changes such as water retention, fat deposit increase, change in texture, wrinkling, and dark "staining".

These symptoms (and the pharmaceutical industry) make menopause sound like a disease process, which of course it is not. Many men who do not have such a dramatic drop in hormone levels will also have many of these symptoms. It is a natural change, and one that has been going on since the human race began.

Seven out of ten women will have some or all of these symptoms for a short period, say up to six months, but one in two will have some or all of these symptoms for anywhere up to five years. There are, in fact, three stages of menopause:

- Premenopause—where periods are still regular and present, but any of the above-mentioned symptoms may set in.
- Perimenopause—where the periods become irregular.
- Postmenopause—no more periods. It is fairly arbitrary as to how long a woman must go without a period, but generally 6–12 months without a period would suggest that the postmenopausal stage has arrived. Periods recommencing after that are unusual, and need to be reviewed by a gynecologist.

Follicle-stimulating hormones (FSH) is the hormone produced by the pituitary glands that promotes the development of eggs in the ovary. Levels of FSH will rise in an attempt to stimulate eggs in the ovaries, but if the normal cycle does not actually take place, then the negative-feedback mechanisms that suppress FSH production are not activated. The levels therefore remain high, and can be measured scientifically to define menopause.

Other investigations that can be undertaken at the time of the menopause include saliva and blood tests for estriol and estradiol, the main estrogen subgroups. Progesterone and testosterone levels may also be informative, as may the levels of dehydroepiandrosterone (DHEA), as discussed later.

A urine test can be carried out for two proteins (pyridinium and deoxypyridinium) excreted in the urine as a byproduct of bone metabolism. Raised levels of these proteins indicate increasing bone loss, and preventive measures can be taken if necessary (*see* **Osteoporosis**). We can also perform bone-density ultrasound scans, and I recommend this at the beginning of menopause for comparison every two years. Unlike the orthodox use of x-rays of the spine and hip, these techniques are simple and harmless. Analysis of the body levels of calcium, vitamin D, and toxins that may affect bone structure (such as fluoride) can be performed through blood, cell, and hair analysis. These may or may not be indicated, depending on each individual.

RECOMMENDATIONS

FOR HOT FLUSHES, SWEATS, PALPITATIONS, AND HEADACHES

- *Try vitamin B_6 (100mg with breakfast), vitamin E (400iu with breakfast and supper), inositol (1000mg with each meal), zinc (30mg before bed), gammalinoleic acid (1g with each meal), and calcium and magnesium (both at 200mg with each meal). If the symptoms are improved, then reduce the doses of these vitamins one at a time until you find the minimal, required dosage. You may not need to take all of these.*
- *Clary sage essential oil and Aloe vera essence can be used in the bath or inhaled by wafting the aroma from a bottle held three or four inches away from the nose.*
- *Aloe vera taken at night and before meals may be beneficial.*
- *The Chinese/Tibetan herb dong quai (1g with meals) can be used, as may Siberian gingseng (50mg with each meal).*
- *Review from your preferred homeopathic manual the remedies Belladonna, Lachesis, Amyl nitrate, and Veratrum viride. The right remedy should be taken at potency 12 or 30 every 2hr for five days, and then whenever symptoms come on.*
- *Eliminate stimulatory foods such as alcohol, caffeine, and spicy foods. Stop smoking or taking any other drugs, because these will contribute to flushes and sweats.*
- *Low blood sugar (hypoglycemia) and adrenaline will sensitize the system, and make all symptoms seem worse. Learn a meditation or relaxation technique, use counseling or psychotherapy, and strictly avoid refined sugars if not eaten with other complex carbohydrates or proteins.*
- *The following botanical (plant) extracts may be considered, and taken in divided doses per foot of height during the day just before meals: glycyrrhiza from licorice (half a teaspoonful of fluid extract), and Agnus castus (0.5ml of tincture or the maximum dose of a capsule or pill preparation). Other herbs have been shown to be useful, but should be prescribed by a herbalist.*
- *Natural progesterone or estrogen creams can be used, but need to be prescribed by a specialist in this field.*
- *Symptomatic relief has been shown to be obtainable through osteopathy, Shiatsu, and acupuncture.*
- *Massage, and especially aromatherapy, may well be of benefit.*
- *Only if symptoms are unbearable and success is not forthcoming after following the above recommendations should an individual consider using HRT.*

SENILE DEMENTIA

Senile dementia is a chronic, progressive mental disease caused by a loss of brain tissue in association with aging. There is a characteristic failing in memory (usually short and midterm), and a loss of other intellectual functions.

RECOMMENDATION

- *See* **Alzheimer's disease** *for treatment options.*

THROMBOSIS—*see* Blood clots

The Head and Neck

THE EARS

DEAFNESS

Deafness or loss of hearing is a very debilitating condition. It may vary from mild loss of particular pitch or notes to a complete inability to hear sound. At whatever level, it creates social difficulties, and any help that can be obtained can make a substantial difference to an individual's well-being.

Deafness is discussed in this chapter because aging creates a certain amount of hearing loss, often within sociably acceptable levels, but of course it can occur at any age.

Acute or sudden deafness must be treated as an emergency, and should be reviewed by a specialist. Deafness can be divided into two groups: conductive and neurological (perceptive).

Conductive deafness

Sound is transmitted from the external ear canal through the eardrum and the ear ossicles, into the vestibular canal, which houses the ends of the auditory-nerve fibers. This part of the ear can be considered the conductive part. Trauma, obstruction, infection, and bone diseases such as arthritis of the ossicles can all be a cause of a loss of hearing.

Neurological (perceptive) deafness

Deafness that occurs because of damage to the neurological system may occur through trauma or infection in the vestibular canal, or neurological disease (for instance, tumors such as cholesteatoma), trauma, or infection along the auditory nerve to the part of the brain that registers sound. Congenital or hereditary deafness may occur because of malformation or damage to any aspect of the brain or ear.

RECOMMENDATIONS

- *Establishing the cause of deafness is paramount, and any diminution in hearing should be checked by a doctor, who should refer you to an ear specialist.*
- *Obstructive causes should be removed if possible. Obstruction may occur because of fluid*

Conductive Deafness—Ear and Brain Section

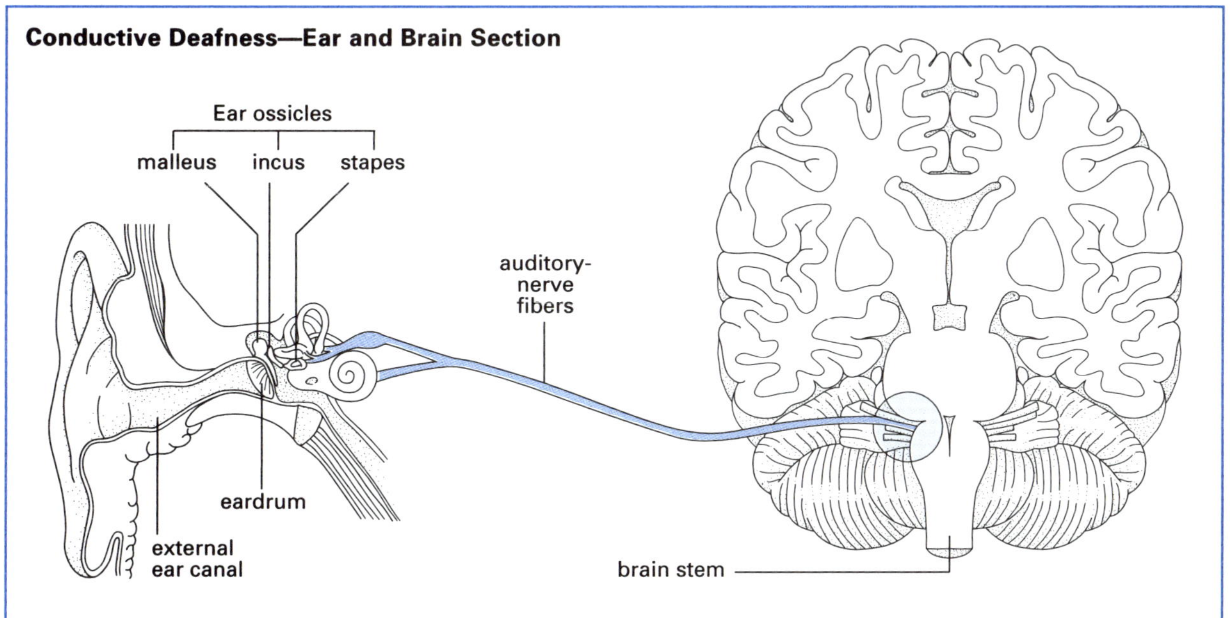

Obstruction or infection in the external ear canal or in middle ear, containing the ear ossicles, may obstruct sound waves and prevent them from being translated into impulses in the auditory-nerve fibers.

in the middle ear (infected or not). For treatment see **Otitis media** *and* **"Glue" ear**.

- *Conductive deafness though damage or arthritic conditions in the ear ossicles may respond to naturopathic treatment, but this needs to be specific, and a visit to a homeopath and a herbalist is recommended.*
- *Do not hesitate to use hearing-aid appliances. If naturopathic treatments do not help and no surgical procedure will benefit, then the use of hearing aids can make a profound difference.*
- *If specific problems, such as cholesteatoma, labyrinthitis, or glue ear are the cause of deafness, please refer to the specific section in this book.*

THE EYES

CATARACTS

The lens at the front of the eye, along with the hair and nails, has no blood supply. It extracts its oxygen directly from the atmosphere to maintain its well-being. Half of all of us after the age of 65 years will struggle with opacity or clouding of the lens. The symptoms are blurred vision, seeing things through a fog, scattering of sunlight, or car headlights at night, and a change in your perception of color. If the cataract is not arrested, it can lead to blindness, generally repairable by surgical procedure.

Cataracts develop at varying speeds, and can be associated with certain disease processes. Diabetes and malnutrition can lead to earlier and speedier development of cataracts.

Once a cataract has set in, it is difficult to remove it medically; however, the following recommendations can (and do) slow down the progress.

RECOMMENDATIONS

- *Any problem with the eye must be checked by your doctor and, if necessary, an ophthalmic specialist.*
- *Antioxidant therapy, particularly beta-carotene and vitamins C and E, helps to prevent the oxidation process and the worsening of cataracts. These can be found in yellow, orange, or dark-green vegetables, or can be taken in specific amounts depending on your size and age. Discuss this with a complementary medical practitioner (see* **Arteriosclerosis***).*
- *The homeopathic remedy Immature cataract 200 should be taken as three doses, one each night, every two months.*

Cataracts

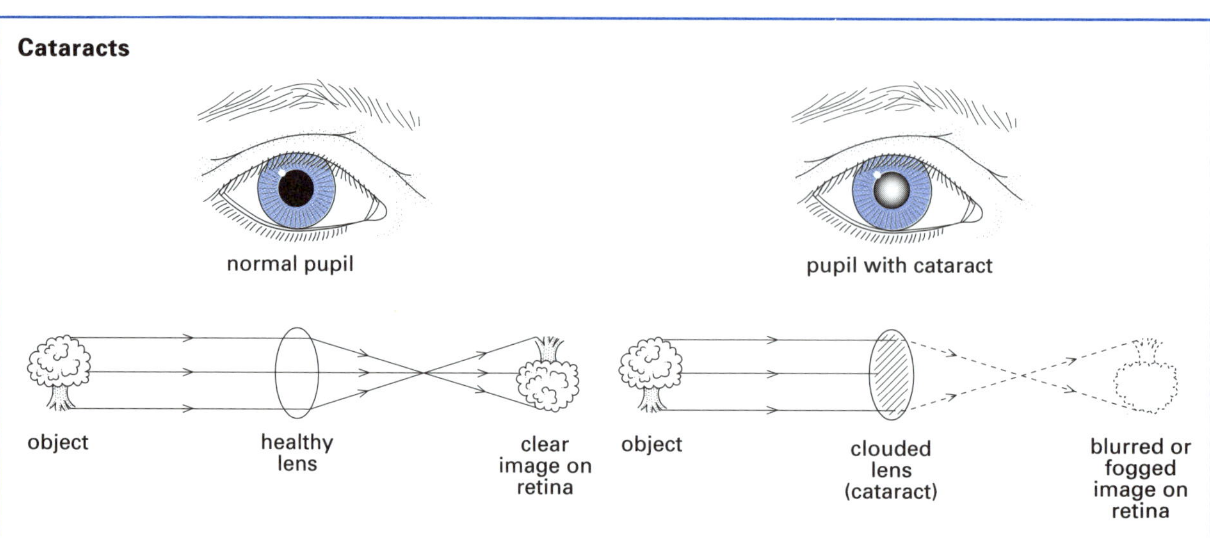

Cataracts have many causes and are a common occurrence in old age.

They cause clouding of the lens in the eye and a resultant blurry image on the retina.

- *Once a cataract has set in, several homeopathic remedies may be indicated depending on the symptoms, and a consultation with a homeopath is warranted.*
- *There is an Ayurvedic concoction by the name of Triphalat that is available from Ayurvedic distributors. Boil a teaspoonful in a cup of water for 3min. Once cooled and strained thoroughly, the eyes should be bathed using an eye bath twice a day.*
- *With any problem of vision, learning to see rather than look can restore sight even in the blind. This sort of differentiation requires specialized training, and books on Bates' eye technique and therapists should be referred to.*
- *Surgical techniques are forever improving. Frequent consultations with your ophthalmic surgeon will advise you on the necessity and best times to operate. Lenses are now replaced, and although they do not have the same visual acuity as your natural lens, they are generally safe and effective. See* **Operations and surgery** *before undergoing any surgery.*

ECTROPION

In this condition, the lower eyelid loses its muscular tone and droops. This exposes the inner lining or conjunctiva, leading to dryness, discomfort, and potential infection. The loss of the lower-lid integrity also means that tears are not contained in the eye, and tend to fall down the face.

RECOMMENDATIONS

- *This problem usually requires surgical repair.*
- *Until repair is performed, use Euphrasia-fluid extract in diluted form—two drops to 10ml of boiled water—and bathe the eye four times a day.*
- *Homeopathic remedies suitable for the symptoms can be considered at potency 6, four times a day, and may be chosen from the following: Borax, Mercurius, Aconite, Pulsatilla, and Euphrasia.*

ENTROPION

This is the converse condition to ectropion, whereby the muscles of the lower eyelid contract, causing the eyelashes to press on the eyeball, resulting in conjunctiva, causing irritation and inflammation, thus allowing for infection.

RECOMMENDATIONS

- *As for ectropion, the problem is usually treated surgically.*
- *Euphrasia-fluid extract—two drops in 10ml of boiled water—can be used as an eye bath four times a day.*
- *Homeopathic remedies suitable for the symptoms can be considered at potency 6, four times a day and may be chosen from the following: Aconite, Rhus toxicodendron, Arnica, and Hamamelis.*
- *See* **Conjunctivitis***.*

MACULAR DEGENERATION

The macula is found at the center of the retina at the back of the eye. It is a conglomeration of rods and cones—the nervous system's receptors for light—and is responsible for fine vision.

Macular Degeneration

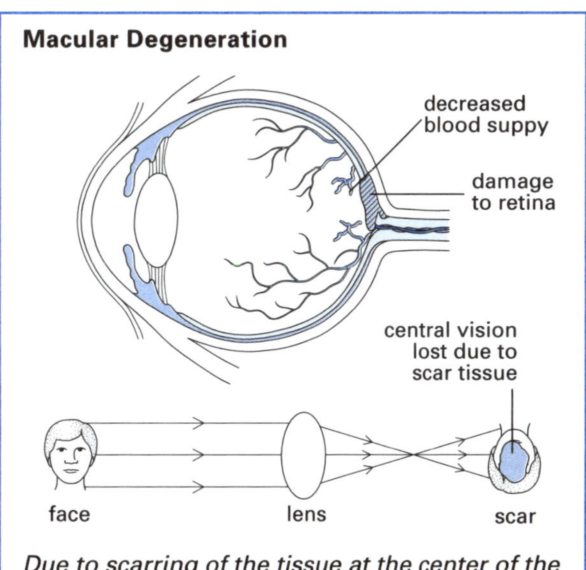

Due to scarring of the tissue at the center of the retina, sight loss is experienced at the center of the field of vision.

Macular degeneration is the medical term used when this area is damaged, usually by receiving a decreased blood supply through natural aging, arteriosclerosis, diabetes, or high blood pressure.

Other than sophisticated laser surgery, which may benefit some people with this problem, there is no orthodox treatment.

RECOMMENDATIONS

- *A diagnosis of macular degeneration can only be made by a specialist, and regular monitoring is of use to know the level of deterioration, although the individual's vision will of course be the benchmark.*
- *See* **Arteriosclerosis**, *and ensure that you follow the dietetic and supplementary guidelines.*
- *Vitamin C (1g three times a day), vitamin E (400iu twice a day), selenium (200µg daily), beta-carotene (3mg twice a day), zinc (10mg three times a day), and pycnogenol (20mg twice a day) can all be used. These treatments should be taken for at least six months, and your eye specialist will be able to tell you if deterioration has ceased.*
- *Two herbal compounds have been shown to have specific predilection for blood vessels in the eye, and studies have shown that these can halt the progress or even improve the deterioration in vision: Ginkgo biloba (24 percent heterosides)—40mg three times a day; and blueberry extract (25 percent anthocyanidin)—80mg three times a day.*
- *Nutritionists may be able to advise you on the use of higher potencies, and homeopaths may be able to administer constitutional or specific visual remedies, depending on the symptoms.*
- *Medically-qualified practitioners can offer intravenous infusions of selenium (200µg) and zinc (10mg), twice a week for one month and then weekly. This treatment is done in conjunction with taking the amino acid taurine orally, up to 1g three times a day.*

PRESBYOPIA

This is a condition of vision, commonly noticed after the middle 40s, but beginning in late childhood. It is due to the diminished elasticity of the lens, so that the individual has difficulty in focusing on near objects and reading fine print.

The condition is the same as hypermetropia (long-sightedness), but is caused by a different process.

RECOMMENDATION

- *See* **Myopia and hypermetropia**.

PTERYGIUM

Pterygium is a growth of tissue from the white of the eye (sclera) that grows across the cornea.

This overgrowth is considered to be caused by excessive exposure to sunlight, but an association with some other factor is probably necessary, because most people do not develop this problem even if they are in the sunshine. Mineral deficiencies, especially zinc, may be relevant.

RECOMMENDATIONS

- *Mineral analysis and correction of any deficiencies may halt the progress.*
- *Dark glasses should be warn in extremes of sunlight by those who have a tendency to develop this condition.*
- *Surgical removal is a simple procedure for an ophthalmic surgeon.*

PTOSIS

A ptosis is a prolapse or "falling down" of an organ or part of an organ. It is generally applied to the drooping of the upper eyelid. This usually occurs because of damage or inflammation to the nerve (part of the third cranial nerve—the oculomotor nerve). In one particular condition, known as Horner's syndrome, the eyelid droops, the eye appears sunken, and the pupil constricts.

Damage to the neuromuscular junction in rare conditions such as myasthenia gravis needs to be considered, although ptosis may simply be a result of aging.

RECOMMENDATIONS

- *Ayurvedic facial-massage techniques may benefit the condition.*
- *Acupuncture may have a profound effect. The topmost acupuncture point for the bladder rests by the eyelid, and bladder-energy weakness may be responsible.*
- *See* **Nerve injury**.

THE MOUTH

RECEDING GUMS

Receding gums, if left unattended, will lead to the loss of teeth and persistent discomfort, and visits to the dentist to deal with infection. Care of the gums is essential from an early age to avoid this happening as we age and go through years of bacterial attack on these very-exposed tissues.

RECOMMENDATIONS

- *See* **Gums, care of.**
- *The avoidance of refined sweet foods is extremely important.*
- *Dental cleaning on a daily basis with a good toothbrush action, as well as a three-monthly visit to the dental hygienist, is recommended.*
- *Vitamin C (500mg per foot of height in divided doses during the day with food) and zinc (5mg per foot of height before bed) are relevant supplements.*
- *Other nutrients are essential for healthy gums, and should be obtained by eating at least five portions of fruit and vegetables per day. The chewing of fiber is also a relevant factor, because it encourages bloodflow, and thereby oxygen and nutrients reach the gums.*

THE CHEST

ANGINA

Angina is the medical term given for pain caused by lack of oxygen to a part of the body. It is most commonly associated with pains in the chest created by a lack of oxygen to the heart muscle. This oxygen deprivation is generally caused by arteriosclerosis forming in the cardiac-blood vessels, but may be caused by spasm in these arteries or by damaged cardiac muscle. The chest pain of angina is generally described as a grip in the center of the chest, occasionally associated with radiation to the back, up to the neck and jaw, and down the left arm. Angina is most commonly associated with exertion, and can come on with walking, climbing stairs, and even lovemaking. More-rigorous exercise will of course initiate discomfort as well. There is often an associated shortness of breath.

Chest pains that are nonresponsive to resting, or experienced while sitting or lying down, are termed *unstable angina*, and require immediate attention. Another form of angina, known as *Prinzmetal* angina, is created by constriction of the coronary vessels, with or without underlying atheroma changes.

RECOMMENDATIONS

- *Every chest pain that is not easily relieved, or that recurs, must be attended to by an orthodox doctor.*
- *Once angina has been diagnosed, medications will be recommended by the orthodox practitioner, ranging from glycerine trinitrate (GTN), placed under the tongue or administered as a spray, to more-aggressive cardiac drugs. Take the treatments, and then obtain curative advice from a complementary medical practitioner.*
- *In the case of cardiac problems, it is better to be treated by a medically-qualified complementary practitioner, or with your cardiologist or doctor in close attention. Do not stop taking cardiac drugs without medical support.*

- *Angina is most often created by blockage to the heart arteries (see* **Arteriosclerosis** *and* **Cholesterol***).*
- *Obtain advice from a nutritionist, herbalist, and homeopath, because all can give sound judgments and offer good treatments.*
- *Use antioxidants (see* **Arteriosclerosis** *and* **Antioxidants***).*
- *Consider the Ornish or Pritikin diets (see chapter 7).*
- *Exercise to just before the point of discomfort is encouraged, but yoga and Qi Gong are the preferred methods of activity. Walking and swimming are mandatory.*
- *To reiterate, I do not recommend self-medication other than antioxidants for cardiac conditions.*
- *The orthodox world will offer surgery of some sort if the condition is not controlled by drugs. Be very wary, and please read the section below on coronary-artery bypass procedures.*

Coronary-artery bypass procedures

If the coronary arteries are blocked by atheroma, and drugs are failing to open the arteries enough to allow a sufficient bloodflow, then the orthodox world is left with no other option than some form of surgical procedure. There are two types.

Angioplasty

This literally means "plastic surgery of injured or diseased blood vessels," but is now in common use for the technique that inflates a balloon within the occluded artery. The specialist inserts a long tube into the femoral artery in the groin, and then feeds it up through the aorta and into the coronary (heart) blood vessels with the use of specialized x-ray equipment. Once in place, the balloon at the tip of this tube is inflated and stretches the occluded artery wall, breaking down the atheroma, and hopefully removing the occlusion.

There are dangers in this procedure, because the balloon may rupture the vessels, so the technique is done only in specialized units. A cardiac surgeon and emergency operating room must be immediately on hand. The procedure remains controversial, because long-term studies and data suggest that the technique is less safe and no more efficient, than coronary-artery bypass grafting.

Coronary-artery bypass grafting (CABG)

Until recently, CABG has been considered the most beneficial of complex surgery. A recent report in *Heart*, one of the top medical journals, has shown that CABG is not all that successful in the long term. The heart is exposed by a cardiac surgeon, who finds the occluded vessel, and literally bypasses the blockage using a short piece of the patient's own vein (taken from the leg). The procedure is risky, but undoubtedly has a profoundly successful effect in the short term. Sadly, it would appear that the procedure does not lead to a longer length of life in the majority of cases.

RECOMMENDATIONS

- *Consider all alternative possibilities, both orthodox and complementary, before considering any form of surgery.*
- *The orthodox world is quick to condemn chelation therapy (see below) but small studies are suggestive of it being a suitable alternative to the not-so-successful surgical techniques.*
- *See* **Operations and surgery***.*

Chelation therapy

Chelation is a word derived from *Chela*, which is Greek for a crab or a lobster's claw. It illustrates the way certain compounds may interact with others to form a bond. It is used in medicine to describe compounds that bind toxic compounds, especially heavy metals and the cholesterol deposits found in arteries, and known as atheroma.

Medical chelation uses a compound called ethylenediaminetetraacetic acid (EDTA). Chelation has been used to treat atherosclerosis, high blood pressure, angina, occlusive-vascular disease, porphyria, rheumatoid arthritis, and cancer. There is good scientific reasoning and research to show how EDTA may work, but controversy still exists. I suspect that this controversy is due to the potential for the use of EDTA in many conditions that dominate and are vastly beneficial to the pharmaceutical industry. If EDTA was proven to be an effective treatment for the conditions that I have mentioned above, billions of dollars of profit would be wiped out. The compound EDTA cannot be patented, so the necessary research has come to a grinding halt.

RECOMMENDATIONS

- *The use of chelation therapy in any of the above-mentioned conditions should be considered.*
- *Chelation/EDTA therapy must be used before coronary-artery surgery is considered, in my opinion.*
- *Ensure that the provider of chelation therapy is a fully qualified doctor, or has had many years of experience in this treatment. Specific tests must be made on liver and kidney function throughout the treatment course, because there is evidence of EDTA being toxic.*

ASTHMA IN POSTMENOPAUSE

Asthma and its treatments are discussed earlier. However, it is worth noting that the use of hormone-replacement therapy (HRT) has been shown to increase the possibility of asthma attacks in postmenopausal women.

RECOMMENDATIONS

- *If you have started on HRT and suspect the beginnings or notice a worsening of current asthma, consider stopping HRT.*
- *See* **Hormone-replacement therapy**.

CHRONIC BRONCHITIS

Chronic bronchitis is defined by having a minimum of three months' continual green, or at least infected, production from the lungs via a cough. As we age, our cough may not be strong enough to remove the infection, and physiotherapy may be required to help bring up the product. Chronic bronchitis is more frequent in smokers and people who have spent their lives in polluted areas. It is caused by infection setting in when the little hairs that usually remove bacteria from the lungs (called cilia) have been destroyed over the years.

RECOMMENDATIONS

- *See* **Bronchitis**.
- *Place yourself under the care of a medically-qualified complementary practitioner.*
- *Inhalations of lavender essential oil (five drops in a bowl of water, four times a day) can be very relieving. Eucalyptus oil and Olbas oil can be used, but should not be used in conjunction with homeopathic remedies.*
- *Homeopathic remedies are essential. They need to be chosen depending on your constitution and symptoms.*
- *Beta-carotene (2mg with each meal), zinc (10mg at night), and vitamin C (500mg with each meal) can be taken, but discuss higher doses with your complementary practitioner.*
- *Regular visits to a physiotherapist will help to clear the chest through the technique of chest-clapping.*
- *Ayurvedic, Chinese, and Tibetan practitioners have a selection of herbs that can ease breathing problems, and they will use chest-cupping (a technique of removing congestion from the lungs by applying a vacuum to the chest wall).*
- *If there are good and bad days, note your diet accurately for two weeks to see if you have any obvious mucus-producing foods in your diet. If you see any obvious associations, avoid these foods.*

EMPHYSEMA

Emphysema is the medical term for the enlargement of the air spaces in the lungs caused by destruction to the tissue of the lung walls, known as the alveoli.

This loss of lung tissue means that less oxygen can be absorbed, and carbon dioxide is stored in these enlarged spaces, causing breathlessness and a characteristic enlarging of the chest, usually known as barrel-chest.

Emphysema

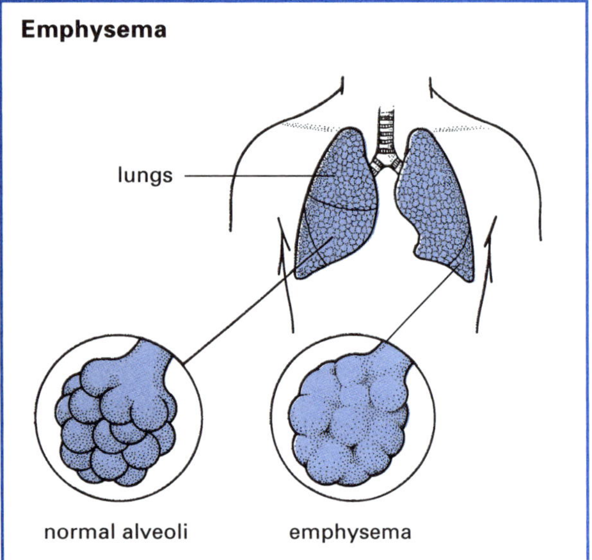

The breakdown of the lung walls in the alveoli—the small air sacs in the lungs—results in fewer larger alveoli, and a subsequent loss of breath.

A certain amount of emphysema will develop in all of us as we age and our body loses the ability to replace destroyed lung tissue, but very often, emphysema is brought on at an earlier age, and to distressing levels, by smoking and recurrent infections in people with chronic bronchitis or even poorly treated asthma.

Once lung tissue has been destroyed, it is unlikely that the body will be able to replace it, so spotting emphysema early and preventing its progression is the best treatment.

RECOMMENDATIONS

- *Any persisting shortness of breath should be reviewed by a doctor.*
- *If emphysema is suggested, either on clinical examination or by chest x-ray, treatment should be initiated immediately.*
- *Stop smoking, and remove the patient from smoky, polluted, or dusty environments.*
- *Any individual who may have lung damage by particle intake should be given the homeopathic remedy Pothos fetidus 200, one dose a day for five days.*
- *Breathing exercises from Buteyko, yoga, or Qi Gong should be taught and utilized daily to encourage energy flow into the chest, as well as oxygen intake and carbon-dioxide removal.*
- *The following vitamins should be taken at the given doses per foot of height to encourage membrane stability and protect against infection: beta-carotene (2mg), vitamin E (20iu), vitamin C (500mg), and zinc (5mg). All should be taken in divided doses during the day except for zinc, which should be taken as one dose before sleep.*
- *In advanced emphysema, acupuncture may be of some benefit.*
- *The use of oxygen delivered by mask or nostril prongs can be organized by your general practitioner at home.*

EMPYEMA

Empyema is the medical term for the presence of pus in a cavity or body space. It is most commonly referred to in association with pus in the lung cavity, and is usually a secondary event following a severe chest infection, pneumonia, or pleurisy (infection or inflammation of the external lining of the lungs).

RECOMMENDATIONS

- *Pus in any part of the body is a serious condition that requires an orthodox assessment and the possible use of antibiotics. There may be a need for surgical intervention to drain the infection from the lung cavity.*

- *Once the problem has been dealt with from the acute-emergency angle, then discussion with a complementary medical practitioner can be considered.*
- *If antibiotics are used, take high doses of Lactobacillus acidophillus concurrently, or the equivalent—around 2 billion organisms—before each meal.*
- *Homeopathic remedies can be used on the basis of the symptoms, but specifically Hepar sulfuris calcarium 6, which is a remedy renowned for removing trapped pus or abscesses from the system. Take it every 2hr regardless of any other medical intervention—it may work by itself.*

PNEUMONIA

Pneumonia is a severe chest infection that has developed to involve the lung tissue and air sacs (known as the alveoli), as opposed to just the bronchial tree as in bronchitis. The symptoms are a persistent cough with (more commonly) or without the production of colorful sputum, shortness of breath and shallow breathing, fever, rigors (shaking) and—if the lining of the lung is affected—pain from pleurisy. Chest x-ray will show patchy, white, cloud-like appearances, and a stethoscope will reveal absent breath-sounds if the congestion is marked, or crackles and wheezes in the area of infiltration.

Pneumonia, like bronchitis, is most common in smokers, and is common in individuals whose immune system is weak. The common causes are viral and bacterial, but noxious gases, fungal infections, and parasites may all trigger pneumonia. Pneumonia is particularly risky in the elderly because of the marked reduction in oxygen absorption. It is the fifth leading cause of death in the Western world.

RECOMMENDATIONS

- *See* **Bronchitis**. *Medical advice should be sought swiftly if pneumonia is suspected. The vitamin-supplement dosages are the same as for bronchitis.*
- *An acute pneumonia in the immunocompromised, the very young, or the elderly should be treated with antibiotics after a sputum sample has been taken, if the following alternative options do not seem to be benefiting within 24–36hr.*
- *Encourage expectoration by using inhalations of Lavender, Olbas, and Lobelia. Their fluid extracts should be dropped into steaming water and inhaled.*
- *Seven drops of Lobelia with seven drops of licorice in a cup of warm water should be taken four times a day by an adult, and may also be used by a child, but needs to be taken in half dosage under the age of 14 years.*
- *Echinacea or Hydrastis (Golden Seal) can be taken in a powdered form at two times the recommended dosage on an over-the-counter medicine.*
- *Bed rest is recommended, because exertion will increase oxygen demand.*
- *Reduce refined-sugar intake because it promotes bacterial growth.*
- *Increase water intake to dilute down mucus and allow easier removal from the lungs.*
- *Osteopathy will open the inevitable contraction of the chest-wall muscles.*
- *Acupuncture can be immediately relieving.*
- *Eastern physicians may use a technique called cupping, which is a vacuum technique placed around the chest and back to pull blood to the surface.*

PSITTACOSIS

Psittacosis is a chest infection that can often develop into pneumonia, but is usually acquired by human beings from birds, particularly parakeets, parrots, and pigeons. Other pets and farmyard fowl may also spread this condition, which is also known as "parrot fever." It is caused by a parasite similar to *Chlamydia,* that can cause venereal disease.

The infection is found in the droppings of the birds, and bird cages and hen-houses are common sources of infection. The condition is not confined to middle-aged people, but the elderly, who frequently keep pets, are more prone because of their diminishing immune capabilities. Young children and professionals in contact with birds may have more exposure, but a better defense.

RECOMMENDATIONS

- *Wear a mask when cleaning bird-soiled areas.*
- *See* **Chest infection** *and* **Pneumonia**.

The Digestive System

DIVERTICULAR DISEASE

Diverticulosis and diverticulitis

The colon or large intestine has a muscular layer running along its length, and bands of muscle that circumvent it. In combination, these muscles contract to form peristaltic waves that push the feces onwards towards the rectum before expulsion.

A tendency to weakness along the muscle wall—either hereditary or due to a prolonged, low-fiber diet which does not allow the bowel to exercise its muscle and keep it firm—lets small pouches of the mucosal lining to protrude through the muscular layer in a form of herniation.

Diverticular Disease

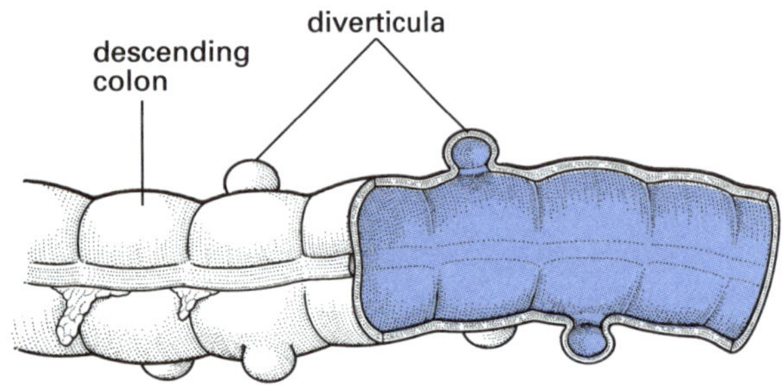

Weakness in the intestinal muscles causes diverticular, small bulges in the intestinal lining to protrude. This may lead to inflammation and the discomfort associated with diverticulosis.

This condition may be symptomless or cause mild discomfort. If feces get trapped in the diverticula it will cause swelling and inflammation, which in turn can lead to infection. When this occurs. the condition is known as diverticulitis.

Diverticulosis may need no attention, but diverticulitis, which is characterized by much stronger cramping pains, tenderness on palpation, a tendency to alternate between diarrhea and constipation, and rarely, bleeding, needs to be dealt with effectively. Prolonged and untreated diverticulitis can lead to colon abscesses, with the risk of perforation and peritonitis. These are serious and potentially fatal conditions. A fever associated with these symptoms should sound alarm bells, because it is probable that infection has set in.

RECOMMENDATIONS

- *Establishing the diagnosis of any abdominal pain should be done by a physician. A suspicion of diverticulosis or diverticulitis may lead to further investigations, such as ultrasound, barium enemas, and colonoscopy. As always, whatever precautions can be used to protect against investigation should be reviewed in the relevant section, but diagnosis is important when treating abdominal conditions.*
- *Discuss your diet with a nutritionist, paying special attention to increasing fiber. The orthodox world is quick to encourage the use of bran or other specially extracted fiber, but this tends to bind salts and electrolytes such as calcium and magnesium that are necessary for strengthening bowel muscle and is therefore not as effective as natural fiber from fruit and vegetables.*
- *Avoid any herbal treatments that may encourage bowel motivity, because this may worsen symptoms.*
- *Diverticulosis/itis is often associated with dehydration, and adequate fluid intake is essential.*

- *The juice of two carrots, two celery stalks, and three ounces of cabbage made up to 8 ounces of fluid with water should be taken after breakfast.*
- *Homeopathic and herbal medicine can be used based on the symptoms, but are best prescribed by specialists in the field.*
- *Ensure the use of a good Acidophilus or other yogurt-based bacterial combination taken with each meal. Correction of any abnormal bowel flora can be rapidly beneficial.*

THE UROGENITAL SYSTEM

ATROPHIC VAGINA (DRYNESS)

As women go through the menopause, the estrogen/progesterone effect on the cells that line the vagina is diminished, and the mucus secretion disappears. This leads to a dryness that can be both irritating and painful on intercourse.

Certain products that contain natural estrogens can be beneficial, as well as supplements and topical applications.

RECOMMENDATIONS

- *Increase your intake of soya products, including soya milk (up to 16 ounces per day), tofu, fennel, celery, ginseng, alfalfa, licorice, and aniseed. When available, eat rhubarb.*
- *Hops are an excellent source of phytoestrogens, and can be taken as real ale or as supplements.*
- *Vitamin B_6 (50mg) can be taken with breakfast and lunch.*
- *Unmedicated lubricants are preferable to estrogen creams, if they are effective. If not, use over-the-counter ointments. They do not seem to be particularly harmful. Calendula-containing oil-based creams are preferable.*
- *A persisting problem can be dealt with by using natural-estrogen extracts topically, and this needs to be discussed with your complementary medical practitioner.*
- *The use of hormone-replacement therapy can be a last resort for unrelenting conditions (see* **Hormone-replacement therapy***).*

ERECTION DIFFICULTIES

Erection problems in middle age and upwards are due predominantly to poor control of the blood circulation, either through damage to the blood vessels or through prostate enlargement causing pressure on the nerves or the blood vessels (*see* **Prostatism and prostate enlargement**). Other potential treatments for erection difficulties are discussed in chapter 4 (*see* **Erection failure**).

INCONTINENCE

Incontinence is very much an age-related condition. As a child, incontinence is a matter of training, and is to some degree anxiety-related, but with older age, it is predominantly due to weakening muscle control. Prolapse of the uterus or the bladder makes things worse. Incontinence

Incontinence

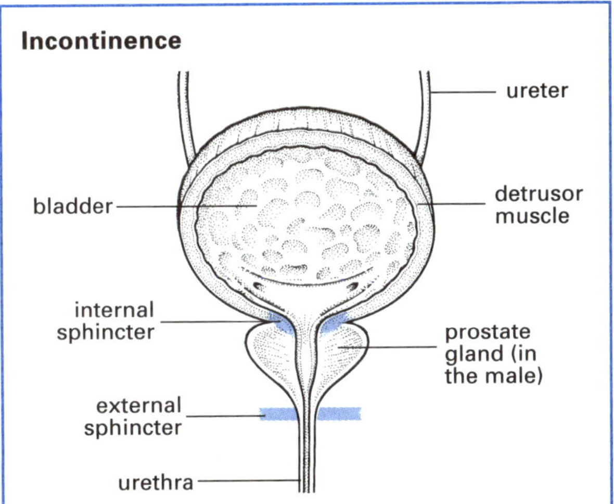

The main cause of incontinence is a weakness of the sphincter muscles, which act as valves to the bladder. Infections of the urinary system may also be a contributory factor.

can occur following pregnancy, and a condition known as stress incontinence defines the loss of urine with increased intra-abdominal pressure (such as coughing and sneezing) in association with a weakened bladder valve.

Incontinence is associated with the weakening of muscles that act as valves; treatment is aimed at strengthening these muscles through exercise, naturopathic medicines and, if other measures fail, surgery. Certain drugs can be used to relax the bladder muscle-wall contraction and thereby reduce the pressure, but this is making no attempt at curing the underlying weakness; is temporary at best; and more often than not, is pointless.

Incontinence—an inability to hold the urine—may be created by urethra or bladder infections (cystitis), and is temporary. Misalignment of the lumbar or sacral vertebrae may put pressure on the central nervous system (CNS), and the part that controls the bladder and its valves.

Incontinence needs to be differentiated from urgency. In urgency, there is a need and sometimes uncontrolled desire to pass urine, which may lead to incontinence. This can occur because of a problem with the bladder muscle (detrusor), but is more commonly found with mild inflammations following intercourse, or with infections of the urethra or bladder.

RECOMMENDATIONS

- *Take a first-morning urine sample to your doctor or laboratory to ensure that there is no infection and that therefore the problem is temporary.*
- *Consult a yoga practitioner for specific pelvic-floor exercises.*
- *Homeopathic remedies have been cited in the past as being helpful in incontinence, although in my experience, remedies by themselves have not been effective. The choice should be made by a qualified homeopath, who would need to consider the constitution in association with the symptoms.*
- *Avoid drinking large amounts of water or fluid at any one time, and get into the habit of passing urine regularly, regardless of any urgency.*
- *External pads are a social and hygienic requirement. Ensure the use of a Calendula-based cream and unmedicated talcum powder to protect the surrounding skin from irritation.*
- *Hypnotherapy and biofeedback techniques can affect mental control over the external pelvic muscles that control urine release.*
- *Acupuncture may be of benefit.*
- *Osteopathic techniques may relieve the problem if a neurological cause is suspected. Osteopathy is particularly effective during pregnancy.*

PROLAPSE

Uterine prolapse is found most frequently in women who have had many pregnancies, and in an increased number of women in the West whose pelvic-floor muscles are not well exercised.

Prolapse of the Uterus

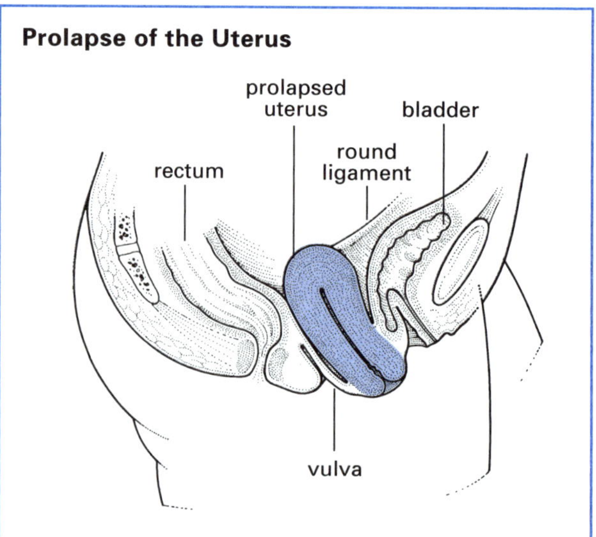

Prolapse occurs because the ligaments around the uterus that hold it in place become stretched, and the muscles involved in supporting the uterus become weak. The outcome is that the uterus falls through the vaginal cavity.

The size and symptoms of this condition vary from an increased frequency and desire to urinate because the uterus is pushing on the bladder, to uncomfortable intercourse, or actually visualizing the cervix at the entrance of the vagina. In severe and untreated cases, the whole uterus may fall out, and is often manually replaced by the patient.

RECOMMENDATIONS

- *Obtain a gynecological opinion.*
- *Gynecologists can insert special ring supports that fit in the top of the vagina and hold the uterus in place. This is a perfectly acceptable treatment for mild cases.*
- *In mild cases, yoga techniques for strengthening the pelvic-floor muscles are a must.*
- *More-severe cases may need surgical repair (see* **Operations and surgery***).*

PROSTATE

The prostate is an organ that surrounds the neck of the bladder and the beginning of the urethra in the male. It is composed of muscular and glandular tissue surrounded by a distinct capsule. Its function is to act as an involuntary valve to the urinary outlet, and also to provide 40 percent of the fluid (or semen) in which sperm receive nutrition.

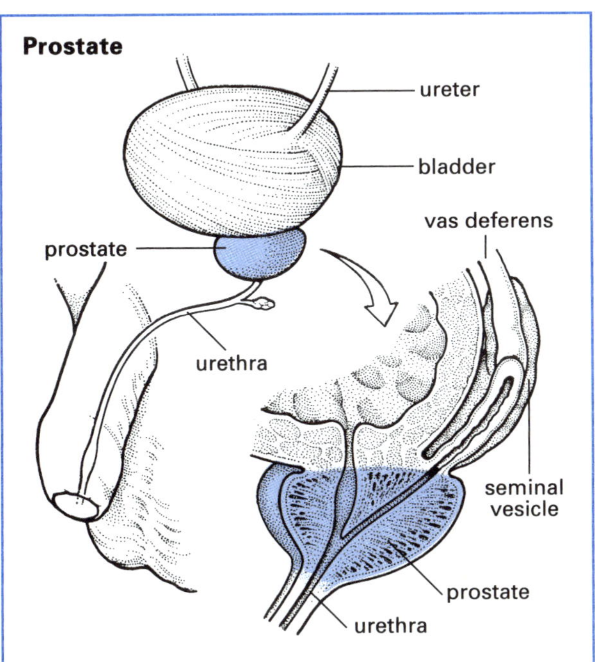

The prostate is the seat of the lowest point of energy in the male in most Eastern philosophies, and therefore has a central role in the provision of energy to the system. A block or weakness in energy flow will lead to prostate disease.

Prostatism and prostate enlargement (hypertrophy)

This condition is characterized by a difficulty in passing water, frequency of urination, excessive dribbling after urination, as well as a frequent desire to pass urine. The symptoms are created by prostatic enlargement, and will occur to some degree in all men over the age of 40 years. In approximately 10 percent of cases over the age of 70 years, the enlargement is so disturbing that treatment is necessary.

Prostate enlargement is primarily caused as a natural result of continually using a muscle for many years, but in some people, an excess of a hormone known as DHT (dihydrotestosterone), which has a testosterone or masculine effect on the system, is produced in excess. This actually causes cells in the prostate to multiply. A deficiency in zinc and essential fatty acids is known to be involved in those who produce too much. Excess cholesterol is broken down, and these metabolites are known to produce excess growth in the prostate, and even cancerous changes.

RECOMMENDATIONS

- *Symptoms occurring before the age of 40 must be checked immediately by a physician, but after the age of 40, it may simply be part of the aging process.*
- *A sudden onset of symptoms may be caused by prostatitis (see below).*
- *A yearly rectal examination (a physician can feel the shape, size, and texture of a prostate by*

pushing forward) is a wise precaution, and blood tests may be recommended if there is any doubt that this condition is benign hypertrophy.

- *Early symptoms of prostatism or changes noted following examination should lead to prophylactic treatment, as described below.*
- *Increase zinc-containing foods such as meat, liver, seafood (especially oysters), wholegrain wheat, pumpkin seeds, and eggs. Organic foods are best because trace metals in agricultural chemicals may remove zinc. Certain pesticides actually increase the levels of DHT, and it may be these that are responsible for the ever-increasing numbers of prostatic enlargement that we are finding nowadays. Cholesterol-containing foods must be kept to a minimum, and high-cholesterol levels should be actively reduced.*
- *Increase oily-fish intake to at least three times a week by eating salmon, herring, mackerel, etc.*
- *Remove diuretics such as caffeine, alcohol, and refined sugar, and replace with water. Initially, symptoms will worsen as the bladder adjusts to carrying more dilute urine, but this will pass.*
- *Specific therapy should include the following nutrients taken in divided doses per foot of height with meals: eicosapentenoic acid (300mg), flaxseed oil (half a teaspoonful), and vitamin E (100iu). Zinc should be taken before bed at a dose of 5mg per foot of height.*
- *The supplemental use of the following amino acids in divided doses throughout the day should be taken: gycine, glutamic acid, and D,L-phenylalanine, all at 40mg per foot of height.*
- *Try the herb Saw palmetto (20mg per foot of height in divided doses twice a day), and a herb called Pygeum africanum (10mg per foot of height in divided doses twice a day). Ginseng taken as a dried root (2g per foot of height) may have a profound effect. All of these doses should be reduced as improvement occurs.*
- *The compound Lycopene and soya proteins may be effective in dealing with prostatism, as they have a strong effect in prostatitis.*
- *The orthodox world will consider drugs known as Alpha-blockers or drugs that inhibit testosterone production since these can chemically reduce the size of the prostate. Surgery known as trans-urethral section of the prostate (TURP) is now undertaken using sophisticated equipment, but can leave the individual impotent. Use these only if the alternatives do not work.*

Prostatitis

The prostate can develop inflammation through infection tracking up the urethra, through trauma, or excessive sexual activity. The symptoms are that of prostatism and/or severe continual pain, often worse on passing urine. The discomfort may appear anywhere from the tip of the penis to the kidney area in the back, but most often can be pinpointed in the area between the scrotal sac and the anus.

RECOMMENDATIONS

- *Diagnosis should be made by a physician's examination. The prostate will be extremely painful if pushed.*
- *Urine and semen samples should be taken for accurate diagnosis of the infection, in case an antibiotic is required. These should only be considered after alternative methods have failed, because long courses are often required.*
- *Please follow the supplemental advice given for prostatism (see* **Prostatism***).*
- *The homeopathic remedy Sabal serrulata, taken at potency 30 four times a day until a more-suitable remedy is selected by a homeopath, may be curative.*
- *Sit in a bath of comfortably hot water up to hip level. Using the bath's shower-head, apply 30-sec bursts of cold water to the perineal (that part*

AMERICAN UROLOGICAL ASSOCIATION SYMPTOM INDEX

Questions to be answered	AUA symptom score (circle one number on each line)					
Over the past month, how often have you had a sensation of not emptying your bladder completely after you have finished urinating?	0	1	2	3	4	5
Over the past month, how often have you had to urinate again less than 2hr after you finished urinating?	0	1	2	3	4	5
Over the past month, how often did you find that you stopped and started again several times when you urinated?	0	1	2	3	4	5
Over the past month, how difficult have you found it to postpone urination?	0	1	2	3	4	5
Over the past month, how often have you had a weak urinary strain?	0	1	2	3	4	5
Over the past month, how many times have you had to push or strain to begin urination?	0	1	2	3	4	5
Over the past month, how many times did you most typically get up to urinate from the time you went to bed at night until the time you got up in the morning?	0	1	2	3	4	5
Sum of 7 circled numbers (AUA symptom score)	0x	1x	2x	3x	4x	5x

(score: 7 or less = mild symptoms; 8–19 = moderate; more than 20 = severe)

between the scrotum and the anus) area, repeating the process ten times and remembering to heat up the bath water in between.

- *Echinacea and Hydrastis (Golden Seal) used at three times the quantity recommended on an over-the-counter preparation should be administered.*
- *Vitamin C (1g per foot of height taken in divided doses with food throughout the day) should be added to those supplements advised in the section on prostatism.*
- *Please note that the above recommendations may need to be taken for up to three months to avoid recurrent or chronic prostatitis.*
- *Ginseng (2g per foot of height in divided doses with meals throughout the day) may be beneficial.*

Prostate cancer

Cancer of the prostate is an increasingly common problem. It is possible that the increased incidence is due to better techniques of discovering cancer, which is performed through a blood test for a chemical released from inflamed or cancerous prostate cells called prostate-specific antigen (PSA). This blood test is often done on routine screens, and whenever somebody complains of prostatism. Confirmation can be made through ultrasound and biopsy.

There is strong evidence, however, that many men who develop prostate cancer have no problems with it. Although it can be aggressive, and spread to the bones and other parts of the body, there is a suggestion that many do not.

Treatment is quite aggressive, using surgery that can leave men impotent or without good bladder control, or estrogen-like drugs that can produce side effects, including breast growth and loss of libido.

RECOMMENDATIONS

- *See* **Cancer**.
- *Discuss matters fully with an orthodox specialist in this field, and question the need to do anything.*
- *Regardless of there being symptoms, follow the supplemental recommendations under* **Prostatism** *and* **Prostate enlargement**.

RETENTION OF URINE—*see* Urination and Prostatism

UTERINE CANCER (ENDOMETRIAL CANCER)

Uterine cancer usually presents as an unexplained bleed from the vagina, but can be a difficult cancer to diagnose since it may produce no symptoms until late in its growth. Like any cancer, it needs to be under the direct care of specialists in both orthodox and alternative medicine (*see* **Cancer**).

Cancer of the uterus occurs most frequently in women who have not been pregnant (nulliparous), and we know of a sixfold increase in uterine cancers in women using HRT for more than seven years. Individuals falling into either of these categories must be checked regularly by a doctor, using ultrasound, specific blood tests (if available), and complementary blood tests, such as the Humoral Pathological Laboratory Test or Vega/bioresonance.

A regular visit should be made to a complementary medical practitioner who uses pulse, iridology, or other alternative-diagnostic techniques to spot the problem before it sets in.

RECOMMENDATIONS

- *See* **Cancer**.
- *Do not ignore any bleed or discomfort in the lower pelvis or vagina. Obtain advice from orthodox and complementary medical practitioners.*
- *Provided that the underlying cause of the development of a cancer is dealt with, operative procedures are often necessary and curative. In the case of a cancer of the uterus spotted early, hysterectomy may be curative, and considered appropriately.*

STRUCTURAL MATTERS

ACHES AND PAINS

Aches and pains in middle age may be associated with arthritis (*see* **Arthritis**). Unlike the aches and pains we get when we are young, those of middle age and upwards are usually due to underuse and previous injury.

RECOMMENDATIONS

- *Ensure good rehydration—an intake of at least 32 ounces per day.*

- *Calcium, magnesium, and copper, found in deep-green, leafy vegetables, root vegetables, meat, fish, and chicken must all be taken regularly to supply these minerals.*
- *A multimineral supplement is useful if taken at twice the recommended dosage.*
- *Qi Gong and yoga keep the muscles stretched and active, and should be used in conjunction with regular exercise, such as swimming or walking.*

ARTHRITIS

Arthritis is the medical term for inflammation of a joint. Arthritis is divided into *acute* and *chronic*, depending on the longevity of the discomfort. Pain may be a dull ache, or a sharp-and-severe pain. The joints may be inflamed and deformed, or show no external changes at all.

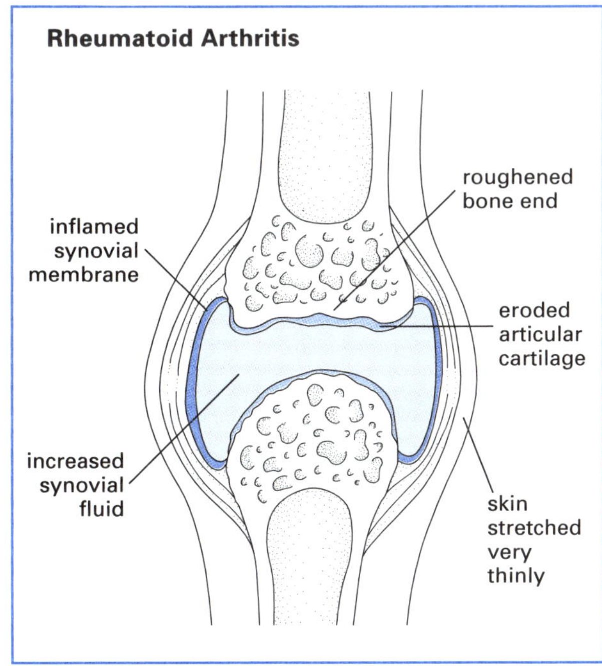

Rheumatoid arthritis and *osteoarthritis* are the most-common forms. Rheumatoid arthritis is an autoimmune disease, whereby the body attacks its own joints. It is uncertain why this happens, but the possibilities are discussed in the section on autoimmune disease (*see* **Autoimmune disease**).

Osteoarthritis is an aging process, created simply by wear and tear on joints. Individuals who have athletic and active lives often struggle with osteoarthritis more so than those who are sedentary, because of repeated small injuries to the joints. It is worth noting that studies have shown that smoking worsens arthritis. Another study has shown less arthritis in women who wear gold.

Acute arthritis

Acute arthritic conditions are triggered by infections such as viruses, bacteria, and other parasites, but certain drugs, and (of course) injuries can all cause an acute attack.

RECOMMENDATIONS

- *Ice wrapped in a towel applied to the joint reduces the inflammation temporarily, without influencing the healing ability of the body. If ice does not ease the discomfort, try a heated application instead.*
- *Homeopathic remedies, such as Arnica if the joint is better for resting, or Rhus toxicodendron if the joint is better for motion, and warm applications should be used.*
- *Application of an Arnica cream several times a day can be beneficial.*
- *As a general rule, rest the joint until improvement is certain.*
- *Persisting discomfort in a joint should be reviewed by a complementary practitioner with knowledge of osteopathy, chiropractic, and especially acupuncture, which can be instantly relieving.*
- *Avoid anti-inflammatories and cortisone injections, because these will remove the pain but allow movement, which in turn can increase the damage. Anti-inflammatory treatment can also prevent healing from taking place.*
- *Painkillers with low anti-inflammatory effect, such as Tylenol and Tylenol with Codeine, may be*

used to take down the pain. If this and the naturopathic recommendations are not working, then consider using anti-inflammatories.

Chronic arthritis

This is a persistence of pain in a joint or joints. The causes can be loosely divided into: persistence of injury or infection, rheumatoid arthritis, other autoimmune diseases, and osteoarthritis.

Pay special attention to the possibility of food allergies, which should be tested for in all cases of arthritis.

Osteoarthritis is the progressive decay of joints that is associated with overuse and aging. All joints will have some evidence of osteoarthritis as we age, and all joints will show some stiffness. Treatment can be useful at all stages of arthritis from stiffness to pain.

RECOMMENDATIONS

FOR ALL CHRONIC ARTHRITIS

- *Take selenium (100µg twice a day), vitamin C (1g three times a day), vitamin E (200mg twice a day), and Evening Primrose Oil (2g with each meal). These can all be reduced as improvement is forthcoming.*
- *Vitamin B_5 and vitamin B_3 (both at 25mg per day) can be taken, but not at night.*
- *Chicken cartilage is a Russian treatment. The cartilage from a chicken carcass should be eaten once a day. This includes the mobile part of the breastbone, and the cartilage of the wing and leg joints. There is currently no preparation of this, and a helpful butcher or chicken farmer needs to be approached.*
- *Copper bracelets may be effective, but only if the level of copper is normal in the body. Each individual has his/her own normal copper level, so a copper bracelet needs to be used with copper supplements to be effective.*
- *Six drops of rosemary and camomile essential oils can be added to a bath, or can be applied directly if mixed into almond oil. Sesame oil can be effective by itself when rubbed in, and may be even more effective if the oil is slightly heated with cayenne or ginger.*
- *The juice of an avocado, daily or eaten whole, may be protective.*
- *Homeopathy is undoubtedly useful, and the choice of remedy should be made on the symptoms of the arthritis. A homeopathic prescriber is best utilized, but attention can be paid to the remedies Rhus toxicodendron, Bryonia, Apis, and Pulsatilla.*
- *Test for hydrochloric-acid production in the stomach and, if low, supplement with hydrochloric-acid tablets.*
- *Wear gold next to the skin in the form of jewelry, such as a wedding ring.*
- *Reflexology, especially in conjunction with massage, is beneficial.*
- *Yoga and Qi Gong are of long-term benefit.*
- *Aspirins, NSAIDs, and steroids are first-line orthodox treatments, and should be left until last because of the high incidence of side effects.*

RECOMMENDATIONS

FOR RHEUMATOID AND AUTOIMMUNE ARTHRITIS, OR OSTEOARTHRITIS SHOWING JOINT DESTRUCTION

- *Use the recommendations above.*
- *Glucosamine sulfate (500mg) can be taken with each meal. Chondritin (500mg) may be used as well.*
- *Avoid members of the solanum plant family, specifically potatoes, peppers, and tomatoes.*
- *Avoid all tobacco, which is a solanum.*

- *If improvement is not forthcoming, avoid wheat, corn, and animal proteins (including cheese, milk, and eggs), and consider food-allergy testing.*
- *I have noticed that tea may exacerbate arthritic conditions, and should be avoided for three or four weeks, and then reintroduced as an experiment if an improvement has been noted. If the discomfort returns, then tea may be a culprit.*
- *A six-day, water-only fast has shown efficacy in acute arthritis affecting chronic sufferers. This should be done under complementary medical supervision.*
- *Orthodox treatment is not curative. All drugs are geared towards relieving the pain, but not helping to improve the structure of the joint. They should be used only as a last resort.*
- *Under medical supervision only, use 10g of fish oil per day. Patients and their clinicians must be aware of a slightly increased risk of brain hemorrhages, and the white-blood-cell count must be monitored. This treatment should only be encouraged in very severe and unrelenting arthritis.*
- *If the above do not show improvements, then surgery may be considered as an option for large joints.*

BUERGER'S DISEASE AND INTERMITTENT CLAUDICATION

Named after an American physician, this disease process of aggressive arterial occlusion is found at any age, although it is more common in middle age, and is associated with smoking. Arteriosclerosis (*see* **Arteriosclerosis**) with associated inflammation, especially in the arteries of the lower limb, causes severe pain that is worse on walking. This is known as *intermittent claudication*, which may occur in nonsmokers. The occlusion of arteries can be so severe that the outcome, especially in those who continue to smoke, is often amputation. The occlusion can occur in arteries other than in the leg, and more-serious operations may be required if occlusions occur in the bowel.

RECOMMENDATIONS

- *Stop smoking (see* **Smoking** *and* **Cigarettes***).*
- *See* **Arteriosclerosis***.*
- *See an acupuncturist, and obtain electro-acupuncture in preference.*
- *Regular massage can be most beneficial.*

CIRCULATION

As we age, the body has a tendency to clog up its arteries with depositions of cholesterol and other unavoidable chemicals. This reaction, created by the body's own defense system, is discussed in the section on arteriosclerosis (*see* **Arteriosclerosis**), and is aided and abetted by mast cells, which are specialized white blood cells that collect unwanted molecules, such as cholesterol and free radicals, and then bind to the nearest surface, taking the dangerous compounds out of the circulation. This process is inevitable, and is necessary for the well-being of delicate organs such as the brain.

Care of the circulation should start at an early age with the avoidance of cholesterol-containing foods, and with daily exercise, good breathing techniques, and proper nutrition full of antioxidants. Unfortunately, this advice is not well heeded, and the ravages and difficulties occur in our latter years.

RECOMMENDATIONS

- *See* **Arteriosclerosis***.*
- *Cayenne capsules, or a level teaspoonful of turmeric in a cup of heated milk, three times a day, may help peripheral circulation in those who have cold hands and feet.*
- *At the first sign of circulatory difficulties, use common sense by wearing hats, gloves, and warm footwear.*
- *Internal circulatory difficulties, such as the clogging of the heart arteries, may not be noticeable until a very late stage. If symptoms*

occur, please refer to the relevant section in this book and contact your complementary medical practitioner immediately.

- *It is never too late to exercise, and yoga, Qi Gong, and Tai Chi are the best forms.*

Aneurysm

Aneurysm is the term given to an artery that loses its integrity from a source other than an injury. Broadly speaking, an aneurysm can be a weakness within the arterial wall, or "dissecting," where the inner lining of the artery ruptures but the outer lining holds, causing a swelling in the arterial wall.

If not surgically treated, aneurysms can be fatal when they occur in arteries in the brain, other vital organs, or the aorta (the main vessel from the heart). Sudden abdominal or chest pain, a sledge-hammer-like blow to the head, sudden blindness, or neurological symptoms (paralysis, pain) must all be treated as an emergency, and reviewed by a surgeon.

RECOMMENDATIONS

- *Aneurysms are difficult to diagnose and any sudden pain should be seen by a medical practitioner.*
- *There is no complementary treatment other than support for pre- and postoperative care.*
- *On your way to hospital or awaiting the doctor's arrival, use Aconite 6, 12, or 30, one dose every 10min.*

DUPUYTREN'S CONTRACTURE

This condition, named after the French surgeon who put it into the medical books at the turn of the 19th century, is a painless contracture of tendon or tendons in the palm of the hand. This causes the fingers to curl inwards, and creates an inability to fully extend them. It occurs most commonly in the third and fourth fingers, chiefly in adult males, and there is no known cause as far as Western medicine is concerned. The acupuncture-energy meridians point out that the tendons most commonly affected are those of the heart, pericardium, sexual function, and the triple heater (triple burner). These meridians or energy channels are most affected by heat, such as created by excess adrenaline or stress, smoking (inhaling smoke at around 100 °F), and by emotional upsets. As Dupuytren's contracture can often take years to form, I have often found it to be associated with longstanding suppression of emotion in smokers.

RECOMMENDATIONS

- *In the early stages, assessment and change of emotional deficiencies may stop the progress.*
- *Gentle massage three times a day with Arnica creams may prevent further deterioration, and may even alleviate the problem.*
- *Osteopathic, chiropractic, acupuncture, and Shiatsu techniques may all stretch the tendon and prevent worsening, if not actually improve the situation.*

ANEURYSMS—Common and Dissecting

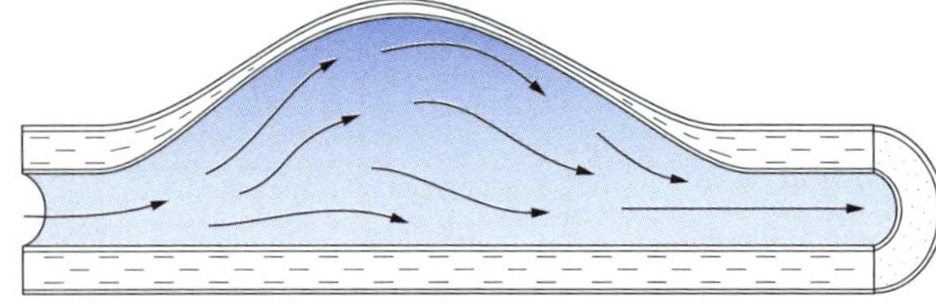

A

A shows a common aneurysm where the middle wall of the artery is weakened.

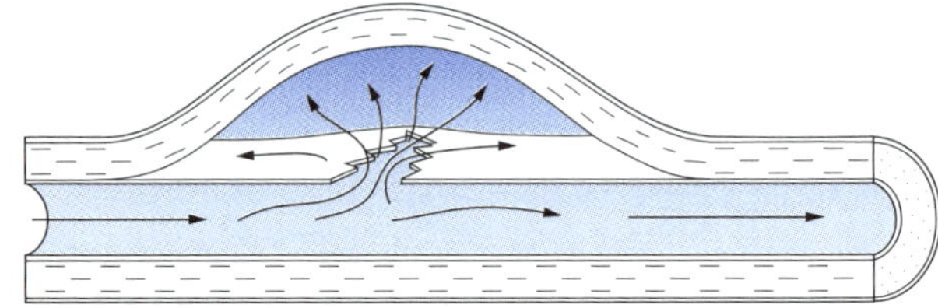

B

In B, a dissecting aneurysm, the inner wall is torn, allowing blood to flow through.

Dupuytren's Contracture

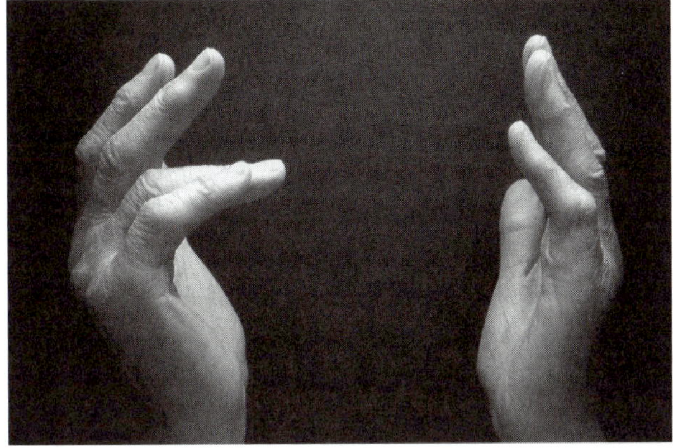

- *If the fingers are becoming useless, then an operative procedure, best performed by plastic surgeons or orthopedic surgeons who specialize in hands, is an effective technique that may solve the problem for several years, but it can recur.*

FRACTURES AND BROKEN BONES

See **Fractures.**

Bones in the elderly often heal more slowly, and it is very important to maintain a calcium and magnesium intake along with the remedies *Calcarea phosphorica* and *Symphytum*, as mentioned in chapter 4.

Bones heal better if they are active, and gentle exercises as taught by Alexander technicians or yoga teachers are very important to prevent arthritis setting in rapidly. The possibility of osteoporosis must be excluded (*see* **Osteoporsis**), and healing time will be improved.

Hands-on healing can be most beneficial in this age group.

MYASTHENIA GRAVIS

This is a disorder characterized by a fluctuant weakness of certain voluntary muscles. Those muscles most commonly affected are found in the face and neck, and this condition tends to affect women twice as commonly as men, and it tends to form in older people. Hyperthyroidism, thymus gland problems, or cancer may be associated with the condition, and need to be ruled out by a physician.

The problem occurs because of an autoimmune (body attacking itself) attack on certain receptors in the muscles, which prevents the nerves from transmitting their orders.

RECOMMENDATIONS

- *Homeopathic constitutional remedies may be chosen by an experienced homeopathic practitioner. The remedies Natrum muriaticum and Silica may be of marked benefit.*
- *See* **Nerve injury**, *and use the supplements recommended there, and* **Autoimmune disease**.
- *Acupuncture may be beneficial.*
- *Tibetan medicine, much geared toward energy flow through the nervous system, may have some answers.*

OSTEOARTHRITIS

Osteoarthritis is the term given for the age-related loss of cartilage and subsequent bone damage to the ends or joint aspects of bones. The condition is due to wear and tear, and may therefore come on before the usual onset at the age of 60 years, particularly in athletes or in the persistently overweight.

RECOMMENDATION

- *See* **Arthritis**.

OSTEOPOROSIS

Osteoporosis is the decrease in bone tissue, leading to structural weakness and increased risk of fracture. The bones that are most commonly affected are the spine, hips, and ribs.

Symptoms are usually absent until osteoporosis is severe, when backaches or structural changes, such as a decrease in height or "hunchback" deformities occur. Spontaneous fractures, or breakage following minor accidents, are the result of osteoporosis.

The density of bone will decline in all of us,

both male and female, generally after the age of about 40. This is partially because of a decrease in exercise, which maintains bone integrity, but also because of the loss of estrogen levels in women and of calcitonin—a calcium-level-controlling hormone made in the thyroid glands—in both sexes. Decreasing levels of stomach acid, and skin- and bowel-membrane changes, all lead to diminished blood levels of calcium, magnesium, boron, and vitamin D, all of which are essential to the production of bone. A diet too high in protein can encourage loss of calcium through the urine, and is probably one of the major causes of the condition in the Western world. Other dietary factors are undoubtedly relevant, as is borne out by the fact that osteoporosis is very much a condition affecting the West, as opposed to in Africa and Japan, where the incidence is negligible. The aging process is by far the most-common cause of osteoporosis, but other conditions must be ruled out before age-related osteoporosis is treated.

Alcohol, steroids, and a few prescribed drugs can all cause osteoporotic conditions. Paralysis or other causes of decreased movement—such as arthritis, lung or heart disease—will also reduce bone density. Certain congenital conditions, malnutrition, and a variety of glandular (endocrine) diseases can all cause osteoporosis.

Postmenopausal osteoporosis is not, as the pharmaceutical industry would have us believe, solely created by a diminution in estrogen. In fact, estrogen has a very small role to play in maintaining bone density, whereas other hormones such as progesterone and dehydroepiandrosterone (DHEA), actually help build bone. Several trials show categorically that weight-bearing exercise is as beneficial, if not more so, as estrogen replacement. This is borne out by the fact that the risk of fracture in a male is equal to that of a female after the age of 70. A good diet containing all the necessary supplements is also essential.

Most of us make the assumption that bone density is governed by the levels of calcium, and to an extent this is true. However, calcium is trapped in the bone on a network or matrix of protein fibers. Osteoporosis is as much due to a deficiency in this matrix as it is due to mineral deficiency. Interestingly, high-animal-protein diets have an adverse effect, whereas vegetarian diets, which are heavy on vegetable protein, seem to be protective.

One important factor has come to light recently. It appears that osteoporosis is more profound in individuals who underwent malnutrition before the age of the menarche (start of the periods). It would appear that the foundation of bone density is laid at this early age. This has led to the suggestion that cow's milk is a must for children. This is incorrect since milk is not a good dietary source of *absorbable calcium*, and is a food that many humans are actually allergic to (*see* **Milk**).

Investigations

The orthodox medical world is quick to promote the use of x-ray investigations of the spine and hip to measure bone density. While the levels of radiation are low, bear in mind that 3 percent of the population carry a gene that is sensitive to radiation, and may become cancerous. There may be times when x-rays are necessary, but as a routine screen, noninvasive and simple tests are available.

Urine

Urine testing for two proteins called pyridinium and deoxypyridinium—principal proteins involved in the bone matrix that trap the calcium—should be carried out, because an increase in levels of these proteins may suggest an osteoporotic tendency.

Ultrasound

An ultrasound of the heel bone (calcaneus) has been shown in comparative studies to be as effective as radiological (x-ray) investigation. Ultrasound is harmless (unless used excessively in pregnancy), and is therefore preferable.

Densitometry—Scan of Spine

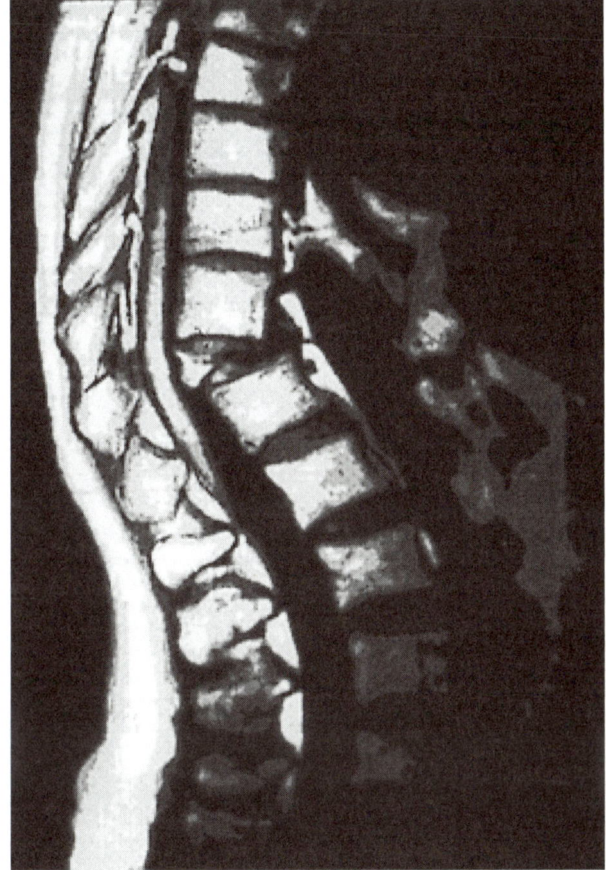

Densitometry scan of a normal lumbar spine. This technique measures the density of the bone, and is used in the assessment of osteoporosis.

Other tests

Minerals as trace elements can be analyzed by a simple blood and hair analysis, and deficiencies of calcium, magnesium, zinc, copper, silicon, and boron can be established, all of which are known to be integral in the formation of strong bones. Orthodox sources may suggest that increasing these minerals in the diet will have no effect, and they are absolutely right if you take an artificial form of any of these, and give it to an individual without the others. Many trials have shown that natural forms of mineral supplementation, especially those in a combined (chelated) form, will be absorbed rapidly, not only in the bloodstream, but also effectively into the bones themselves.

Vitamins B_6, C, D, and K are all essential for bone growth and stability. These levels can be tested in the blood. The absorptive capacity of these, and all the necessary minerals and proteins, is dependent on an intact bowel. Low-stomach acid, poor pancreatic function (*see* **Gastrograms** and **Pancreatic Exocrine Tests**), and bowel-bacterial integrity are all very important.

Bowel conditions such as celiac disease or the less-severe gluten (a wheat protein) sensitivity, Crohn's, other inflammatory conditions, and the leaky-gut syndrome must all be considered as possible causes of osteoporosis. These may all be tested for.

The levels of phosphorus and its derivative phosphate are balanced in the bloodstream by the kidneys. Phosphorus encourages the kidneys to eliminate calcium. Phosphates are found in most foods, but especially in carbonated drinks and meat products. Is there a correlation, I wonder, between the high incidence of osteoporosis in developed countries, and their intake of carbonated drinks and burgers?

There is much press at this time discussing the use of natural progesterone (extracted from the Mexican yam). Dr. Lee, a gynecologist from the U.S.A., has spent over a decade studying the effects of progesterone on osteoporosis and other menopausal problems. His conclusions are that progesterone, not estrogen, is more effective in maintaining bone density. His work needs more study, but theoretically, he is correct. The use of natural progesterone is becoming more popular, and studies over the next few years should help to decide if this is a preferred method of maintaining bone density and avoiding osteoporosis.

RECOMMENDATIONS

- *Prevention is the best form of cure. Ensure—especially in children—a good source of calcium and other relevant minerals. Soya, fish, nuts, and deep-green vegetables, such as spinach, collard greens, and broccoli, are all excellent sources.*

OSTEOPOROSIS PROFILE

Reference:	DJ1J ASSB C90	Age:	72
Patient:	Mrs. Jo Public	Sex:	Female
Doctor:	Dr. Mustafa Consult	Date:	10/02/91

SERUM:	Result	Units	Reference Range
Alkaline phosphatase:			
Total	= 109	units	40 – 190
Bone	= 24	units	35 – 90
Tartrate-resistant acid phosphatase	= 2.6	units	1.5 – 4.3
Inorganic phosphorus	= 0.93	mmol/l	0.8 – 1.4
Calcium	= 2.46	mmol/l	2.25 – 2.75
Copper	= 22.0	μmol/l	12.5 – 25.0
Manganese	= 14	nmol/l	9 – 25
Vitamin C	= 1.1	mg/dl	0.4 – 2.0
WHITE CELL:			
Zinc	= 5.7	μg/10–6	5.4 – 8.2
RED CELL:			
Magnesium	= 2.03	mmol/l	2.8 – 3.00
24-HOUR URINE:			
Volume	= 1900	ml	
Phosphorus	= 38	mmol/24 hours	15 – 45
Calcium	= 3.1	mmol/24 hours	2.5 – 7.5
Zinc	= 3.70	μg/24 hours	220 – 590
Hydroxyproline	= 11.00	mg/24 hours	up to 13

These tests include essential nutrients of known importance in the development and maintenance of bone. Changes in the excretion of calcium and phosphorus occur in some types of bone disease, and increased urinary zinc and hydroxyproline are found in osteoporosis. Recent research demonstrates changes in bone alkaline; phosphatase levels in osteoporotic women.

This profile does not replace the measurement of bone density.

Comments on Results

There is a reduction in bone formation (low bone ALP) with a normal resorption rate (normal TRAP). This is consistent with mild bone loss.

Milk and milk products such as cheese are not necessarily a good source, although yogurt is excellent.

- *Orthodox hormone-replacement therapy should be avoided, as should your doctor, whose first-line treatment will be HRT, unless all other avenues under the guidance of a complementary medical specialist have failed.*
- *Increase proteins from vegetables rather than animals, and if osteoporosis is noted, switch to a predominantly vegetarian diet.*
- *Meat products are particularly high in phosphorus, which increases calcium excretion, and should therefore be reduced. Carbonated drinks contain a marked level of phosphates, and must be avoided.*
- *Ensure an adequate intake (around 1,000–1,500mg) of calcium each day from the sources listed in chapter 7 (see* **Calcium***), rather than milk.*
- *Avoid excesses of protein, alcohol, tobacco, and caffeine. Specific osteoporosis formulae are available, all of which combine the necessary co-factors needed for good calcium absorption. A nutritionist would recommend particular brands.*
- *Remember that calcium is directly linked to vitamin D, and up to 200iu should be taken on a daily basis if there is any sign of bone thinning. Higher doses may be necessary via your complementary practitioner.*
- *Use of DHEA (dehydroepiandrosterone) may be prescribed under medical supervision, along with natural-progesterone creams to increase bone density.*
- *Increase weight-bearing exercise. Thirty to forty minutes of walking each day is a minimum for those with osteoporosis, but 20min of work in a gym or as a racket sport three or four times a week is good for maintenance.*
- *Supplementation of the following may be beneficial, but it is best to check your levels before self-prescribing. Overdosing is not possible on the recommended dosages, but the supplementation is not necessary if levels are not proven to be deficient. The following supplements should be considered and taken in divided doses per foot of height throughout the day: calcium (150mg), magnesium (150mg), copper (500µg), manganese (4mg), silicone (200µg), boron (500µg), and zinc (5mg before bed).*
- *The following vitamin supplements should be taken in divided doses per foot of height with food throughout the day: vitamin B_6 (10mg), folic acid (50µg), vitamin D (100iu), and phylloquinone (vitamin K_1), 200µg).*
- *Blood and hair analysis for mineral deficiencies, phosphorus, fluoride and strontium toxicity, and calcitonin should be taken as the baseline, and monitored on a yearly basis or treated as required. Please note that strontium, while toxic in excess, is necessary for good bone strength, and deficiencies should be remedied.*
- *Plant estrogens (phytoestrogens), natural progesterone, and specific herbal treatments should be considered in osteoporosis, but should be prescribed by a complementary medical practitioner.*

POLYMYALGIA RHEUMATICA (PMR)

This condition describes an inflammatory process that affects the muscles. It is characterized by stiffness, pain, and limitation of movement of the hips and shoulders, in particular. General malaise, weight loss, night sweats, and fevers may also be associated. The condition is often association with inflammation of blood vessels.

Arterial inflammation may be found in 50 percent of cases, and if left untreated can develop into neurological problems if it affects the arteries in the nervous system or brain. This may include blindness or stroke. Polymyalgia rheumatica is considered an autoimmune disease—one where the body's immune system attacks itself. This generally occurs after a prolonged, subclinical allergy, usually a food intolerance or an incorrect response to a viral, bacterial, or other infection. A full constitutional view, taking into account the well-being of the individual from birth onwards, is necessary to speed up the process of repair and prevent further autoimmune disease settling in. The Eastern philosophies would look upon this particular condition as being a stagnation of energy (Qi) and excess heat in the blood.

RECOMMENDATIONS

- *Any unexplained loss of power or pain that persists must be reviewed by a doctor.*
- *Investigations will show a raised ESR (a test for the sedimentation rate of red blood cells) and other changes.*
- *If there is any evidence of inflammation of the arteries (as diagnosed by a physician), then steroids should be used.*
- *Plant extracts that include steroids are used by experienced herbalists and Chinese-trained physicians, but the quantity is variable depending upon the distilling process from each plant, and although available, I think that in PMR with arterial involvement, conventional drugs should be used.*
- *In cases where arterial involvement is not present, herbal treatment under the guidance of an expert may be beneficial, and should be continued until the patient has been symptom-free for at least three months. A trial period without treatment may allow symptoms to return, in which case the treatment should be recommenced for at least another three months.*
- *The condition is an autoimmune syndrome (see* **Autoimmune disease***).*
- *Yoga and Qi Gong, acupuncture, and massage will all help the muscle groups, and help move the stagnant Qi.*
- *Allergy testing is essential, and correction of the diet, aimed at removing allergens and heat-creating foods such as caffeine, alcohol, spicy and refined foods must be adhered to strictly.*

THE NERVOUS SYSTEM

MOTOR-NEURONE DISEASE

This condition—which is medically known as progressive, spinal muscular atrophy—is a progressive wasting of individual muscles or groups of muscles due to the degeneration of nerve cells and pathways affecting the spinal column and the parts of the brain that control muscle movement. It is a particularly distressing disorder, because it slowly and relentlessly diminishes an individual's ability to move, swallow, and communicate, but leaves the thought process, awareness, and pain receptors intact.

The condition, which can strike at any age, usually occurs after the age of 50, and can progress to an incapacitating level within two years, but it may take up to 15 years to reach its endpoint. Usually, individuals will die from infection because of an inability to breathe properly, allowing bacteria to settle into the lungs. The cough and gag reflexes eventually disappear.

There may be a genetic factor, but an infective or toxic cause is most likely. The condition has been known to be triggered by deficiencies in vitamins, specifically vitamins B_{12}, B_6, and E.

I do not recommend self-help in this condition, because aggressive treatment is best suited, and a course should be set and monitored by an experienced medical practitioner.

More so than with other neurological conditions, a philosophical attitude must be taken, and I believe the question needs to be asked: "What lessons can be learnt on a spiritual or karmic level by being struck with a condition that slowly moves an individual to a position of total dependence?" More so than many conditions, the question of euthanasia arises in patients who have this condition, and full and frank discussions must be undertaken on a spiritual level as soon as motor-neurone disease is diagnosed.

RECOMMENDATIONS

- *A full blood and hair analysis for deficiencies in vitamins, nutrients, and amino acids, and toxicity from heavy metals and agrochemicals (including pesticides) must be undertaken.*
- *Assessment of digestive capabilities, both stomach-acid and pancreatic-enzyme production, must be assessed.*
- *Deficiencies of vitamins and amino acids (the breakdown products of proteins) must be plugged.*
- *A herbalist should assess the possible benefits from herbal medicines, especially alfalfa, broom, and mushroom or toadstool derivatives.*
- *A homeopathic consultation with an expert is essential.*
- *Yoga and Qi Gong training, along with the Alexander technique, may maintain neurological and muscular control for longer.*
- *Specialized Ayurvedic and Tibetan massage techniques, such as Marma and neurotherapy, must be undertaken.*
- *Tibetan medicine, based considerably on energy flow through neurological pathways, may have some answers.*

PARKINSON'S DISEASE

Parkinson was an English physician in the 18th century. He described a clinical state that has taken on his name. Parkinson's disease is characterized by an expressionless face, infrequency of blinking, a poverty and slowness of voluntary movement, rigidity of muscles with a rhythmic 3–4 per second tremor that is more pronounced at rest, a stooped posture, and a wide-legged walking stance. This latter symptom is caused by a loss of the normal-postural reflexes. The condition is characterized by a shuffling walk, and the initiation and cessation of movements are impeded. Crossing a road may, in extreme cases, be difficult, because timing is important, and being able to stop is difficult. Memory loss and an inability to concentrate are prominent symptoms.

Parkinson's disease may occur in middle or later life, due to the degeneration of cells in the brain that produce a chemical called dopamine. Dopamine has a pronounced effect on the control of muscles and posture. Parkinson's disease may occur as a sequel to encephalitis or poisoning from certain drugs.

Aluminum has been cited as a potential cause of the destruction of that part of the brain that produces dopamine. Other chemicals, including pesticides, are suspected, but are yet to be proven as causative agents. Most chemicals are destroyed in the liver, and so Parkinson's disease may be a consequence of liver weakness or deficiencies in antioxidants, which are also responsible for the breakdown of toxic compounds. Nutritional deficiencies may lead to a reduction in dopamine, so a long-term, poor diet may be a trigger to the condition.

RECOMMENDATIONS

- *Any neurological symptoms that persist must be reviewed by a specialist, and a firm diagnosis made.*
- *Orthodox drugs are geared towards correcting the loss of dopamine (**see* **Anti-Parkinson's drugs***). These drugs seem to lose their effect after a few years, and are therefore not started by most neurologists until the disease process is inhibiting normal function. The alternative treatments below should be tried as soon as possible, and orthodox treatment delayed as long as possible.*
- *Consult with a complementary specialist with experience in the field for measures of toxicity, nutritional deficiencies, and liver function. These need to be corrected.*

- *Particular attention should be paid to blood-cell copper levels, and this should be corrected by taking an absorbable copper supplement at a level of 1mg per foot of height.*
- *Bioresonance techniques may be beneficial in helping to illustrate any underlying cause of the destruction of dopamine-producing brain cells.*
- *The amino acid tyrosine should be taken (400mg per foot of height) in divided doses throughout the day. L-Methionine is another amino acid that should be taken at a level of 1g per foot of height.*
- *High-dose antioxidants should be considered if there is any level of toxicity.*
- *Any specific toxins that may be isolated should be treated by their homeopathic equivalent at a potency of 30, twice a day for one month, and the levels later remeasured. If there is no diminution, then repeat using potency 200 twice a day for two weeks.*
- *Cranial osteopathy, osteopathy, polarity therapy, yoga, and Qi Gong may all have a beneficial effect on reducing the symptoms and delaying the progression of the disease.*
- *Marma massage and neurotherapy, both Ayurvedic disciplines, can be beneficial.*
- *If the disease is progressing, Tibetan medicine should be employed under the care of a Tibetan-trained physician.*
- *We watch with interest the outcome of trials of implanting dopamine-producing cells from pigs into brain tissue, and the use of electric implants that stimulate the cells that make dopamine.*

STROKE (CEREBROVASCULAR ACCIDENT, CVA)

A stroke denotes the onset of a neurological deficit, most frequently the paralysis of one side of the body, with or without an effect on the contralateral side of the face. This weakness may develop within minutes, and is usually associated with an arterial problem, or may develop over a much longer period of time, even months, which may be indicative of a disease process (most commonly a tumor). Ninety-five percent of strokes are caused by a lack of oxygen, due to a blood vessel in the brain being blocked by a clot, closing up because of atheroma, or (rarely) going into spasm through some neurological or chemical influence. Atheroma may also cause a fragility in the blood vessel, which leaks, causing a hemorrhage that then clots and obstructs bloodflow beyond that point.

Thus, most strokes are cerebrovascular accidents, either hemorrhagic (caused by bleeding) or infarctions (caused by blockage). A stroke is further classified by considering whether the event is completed or still evolving. Finally, in categorizing stroke, the type and severity of the neurological problems will give a clue as to where the arterial damage occurred. This is mostly of diagnostic value, because the treatment is the same and based entirely upon the deficit.

Any condition that can lead to vascular damage will predispose to a stroke. High blood pressure may burst the small vessels in the brain, although the mechanism to protect brain blood pressure is one of the most evolved mechanisms in the human being. Atheroma, and the eventual clogging up of the arteries, with the increased tendency for a clot to form in such blood vessels, is much more likely to cause a stroke, and small emboli (clots from other parts of the body) may fire off atheroma plaques in other vessels, or come from diseased heart valves to occlude the arteries. Preventing any of these factors is the primary concern in fighting stroke, and even if a stroke has taken place, active therapy against these conditions may prevent a worsening or recurrence of the problem.

Stroke is the third most common cause of death in the Western world, after heart disease and cancer. It is, however, the commonest cause of severe, chronic disability, and happens to two out of every 1000 people each year. Three-quarters of this number are over the age of 65, and the event is twice as common in black as in white persons. It is worth looking at these figures, because conditions such as hypertension are actively fought, regardless of the risks of side effects of these drugs. Very simply (and not absolutely accurately) these figures suggest that one in 500 adults at the age of 65 or more will have a stroke. We are told that if one has hypertension the risk is six times greater, which brings the risk to one in 83 people. While this is a marked increase, the chances are still 82:1 that an individual with high blood pressure will *not* have a stroke. I mention this simply because so many people are frightened by their high blood pressure because of the risk of stroke, but the chances are still low even if the problem is not treated. More people on antihypertensive drugs will end up having a stroke than those who do not use such drugs, but this matter is discussed more fully in the section on hypertension (*see* **Hypertension**).

Prevention is the key word in stroke, because full recovery from neurological deficit is rarely possible. Most individuals who have anything other than a major stroke will have some degree of recovery. If the correct treatment is undertaken, an indication of the repair process can be gleaned at about three months, when 90 percent of lost abilities will have returned.

Immediate first-aid and orthodox-emergency medicine reduce the risk of death, and a knowledge of cardiopulmonary resuscitation is always advisable, because a stroke may affect breathing and cardiac response.

RECOMMENDATIONS

- *Avoidance by correct control of atheroma and hypertension at an early age is the best form of treatment (see* **Atherosclerosis** *and* **Hypertension***).*
- *Consider the macrobiotic diet (see chapter 7).*
- *Full assessment by a neurological specialist is mandatory, and push the point to discover whether the stroke is caused by a hemorrhage or an occlusion (or both). Treatment varies depending on the cause.*
- *Treatment of a stroke is dependent on the cause. There is strong recommendation for the use of prophylactic aspirin, because this prevents clotting, but of course will make the situation worse if the stroke is caused by a hemorrhage. Many people are mistakenly taking aspirin because they have heard that it reduces the risk of stroke, but it may do the opposite.*
- *Stop taking the oral contraceptive pill if you are at risk, or have a family history of cardiovascular disease or stroke. The pill increases the risk of blood clots.*
- *Physiotherapy is an integral part of rehabilitation, but all forms of Eastern medicine—principally Chinese, Tibetan, or Ayurvedic in origin—have physical, acupuncture, and herbal treatments that have been used for thousands of years with great effect. Do not ignore Western-therapy techniques, but use them in conjunction with an experienced Eastern-medical practitioner.*
- *Herbal treatments such as Ginkgo biloba are frequently recommended, but increasing bloodflow in the brain of those who may have a tendency to hemorrhagic strokes is unwise.*

TRANSIENT ISCHEMIC ATTACKS (TIA)

A transient ischemic attack is a temporary neurological deficit, usually comprising a dimming of vision, a lack of power or movement on one side of the body, numbness, dizziness, and difficulty in speaking, that usually lasts 10 minutes or less, but may last as long as 24 hours. These attacks are usually related to a temporary blockage in a blood vessel in the brain, caused either by spasm of an already atherosclerotic vessel or by an embolism (traveling blood clot or other matter). The longer the attack, the more probable it is that the effect was caused by an embolism.

Recovery is usually complete, but transient ischemic attacks usually recur, and may be a warning of an impending stroke. Recommendations for treatment are as for **Stroke**, but also *see* **Atherosclerosis**.

TREMOR AND TREMBLING

A tremor is a regular, rhythmic oscillation of a part of the body, caused by alternate contractions of muscles either side of a joint. Trembling is simply an exacerbation of a tremor affecting a larger part of the system, such as an arm or leg.

Anything that affects the nerves or the neuromuscular junction will potentially cause a tremor, and the most common causes are the toxic effect from alcohol withdrawal (delirium tremens), caffeine, or other stimulatory drugs such as amphetamines or cocaine. An excess of thyroxine or adrenaline (such as in extreme nervousness) may cause such problems, and may indicate underlying conditions such as hyperthyroidism or adrenal tumors. Other symptoms, such as sweating and weight loss, are usually associated.

Neurological diseases such as Parkinson's disease (which can cause a tremor when resting) or stroke, which may affect the coordination centers, can be differentiated by causing an unintentional tremor (one that does not disappear on intentional movement, such as picking up a pen). Fevers may trigger trembling or tremors, because the body uses muscular movements to increase its temperature to kill off the bugs.

A twitch is the involuntary contraction of a single muscle group, and is usually an indication of an entrapped nerve or peripheral, neurological damage. A twitch is known medically as a fasciculation, and may be an indication of more-serious neurological conditions such as motor-neurone disease.

RECOMMENDATIONS

- *Any shake that is not associated with an obvious cause such as nervousness, or excess drug intake or withdrawal, should be reviewed by a doctor for a firm diagnosis.*
- *Treatment should depend upon the underlying cause, and reference should be made to the relevant section in this book.*
- *The homeopathic remedy Agaricus muscarius may be taken at potency 30 four times a day until a diagnosis is made. Trembling due to nervousness may benefit from Ignatia 6 taken every 15min, or Argentum nitricum may be used instead.*

Psychological Matters

ALZHEIMER'S DISEASE AND SENILE DEMENTIA

Alzheimer's disease is the process of premature senile dementia. Treatment for both of these conditions is similar.

Tomograph of brain—Alzheimer's disease

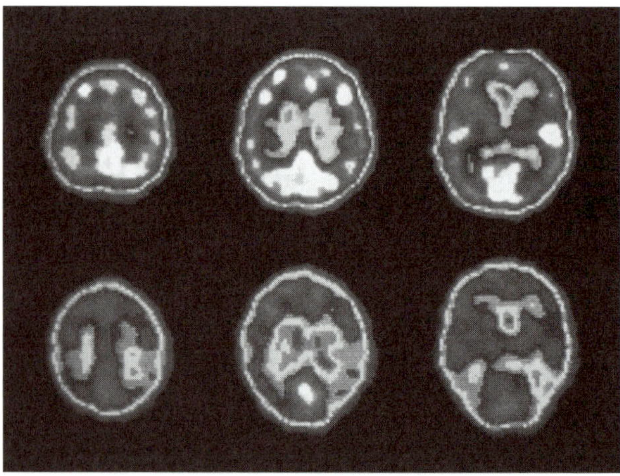

Tomograph scans of a normal brain (top row) and that of an Alzheimer's patient (bottom row). The brighter colors in the normal brain show higher brain activity.

The principal cause of dementia is reduced bloodflow through clogged arteries, preventing oxygen and nutrients from reaching brain tissue. Viruses, environmental toxins such as aluminum, and underusage of mental faculties are other causative factors. There is also a genetic predisposition to early dementia.

RECOMMENDATIONS

- *Conversation and debate are essential stimulants. Crossword puzzles, listening to the radio, and reading educational books also help. Television and nonstimulating reading are arguably part of the cause of the increasing levels of dementia.*
- *Proper concern towards keeping cholesterol levels low and reducing arteriosclerosis/atheroma is essential (see* **Arteriosclerosis***).*
- *Daily intake of antioxidants (see* **Antioxidants***) is necessary, either through diet or supplementation. Vitamin C, in particular, has been shown through trials to benefit cognition in Alzheimer's disease—take 1g with each meal.*
- *Ginkgo biloba—the standard dose is 40mg with each meal—has shown some benefit, and also several Ayurvedic and Tibetan herbal mixtures, best prescribed by specialists in those fields.*
- *Craniosacral osteopathy can increase bloodflow to the brain, and may be of great benefit.*
- *It is worth noting that dementia is not necessarily so much a problem for the patient as for the relatives. If your life is affected by another with dementia, seek support from a group or counselor.*

"ANNIVERSARY REACTION"

"Anniversary reaction" can occur at any age, but is more common as we pass through middle age into our advanced years. Anniversary reaction is, as it suggests, a sadness, anxiety, or depression that occurs on the anniversary of a shock.

It is usual for all of us to have some memory of unhappy events brought back to us by reaching a certain date. Severe depression can occur, however, which needs treating.

RECOMMENDATIONS

- *Homeopathic remedies are excellent in this area, but need to be given at high potency and after full consultation with a homeopath.*
- *Counseling, preferably with a bereavement counselor, is nearly always beneficial.*

BEREAVEMENT AND GRIEF

Generally speaking, we will all have to undergo a grief reaction from the loss of a loved one. Bereavement is an inevitability as we progress to our latter years. I discuss bereavement in this chapter because, beyond all other ailments that we contend with as we age, the loss of our loved ones and friends is a deep pain that is unresponsive to medicine.

The grief associated with the death of those close to us generally follows a typical pattern. We all suffer the emotions and feelings of denial, anger, compromise, depression, and acceptance.

The length of time that we go through each of these emotions varies, depending on the circumstances. Denial is usually short-lived, perhaps no more than a few days, whereas anger (either towards those who the individual feels are to blame for the death, or self-guilt because the individual did not do enough to prevent the death) can last for years. The depression may be mild and short-lived, or deeply ingrained and persistent. Suicidal thoughts, and possibly even attempts, may occur.

Everyone will have their own way of dealing with bereavement, but most people will have memories and reactions that can recur possibly for the rest of their lives. The so-called "anniversary reaction" is a sense of emotion that occurs on or around the anniversary of the death (*see* **Anniversary reaction** and **Death and dying**).

RECOMMENDATIONS

- *Turn to friends and family. There is no shame in venting emotions.*
- *If close support is not available or not helping, then consult your family practitioner or complementary*

therapist, and have a session with a bereavement counselor. It may be necessary to attend for a few sessions.

- *Immediately on hearing bad news, use the remedy Arnica 200, one dose every 4hr. If a sense of fear or "What is going to happen to me now?" is the initial reaction, use Aconite 200 at the same dosage. Once the initial shock has subsided, use Ignatia 200, one dose on waking and one dose on retiring. If physical symptoms manifest—such as skin rashes, indigestion, and flu-like symptoms—then use Natrum muriaticum 200, one dose three times a day for one week.*
- *The Bach flower remedies can be used to great benefit: Elm and Larch for those who do not know what to do; Pine if guilt is the overwhelming emotion; Sweet chestnut and Star of Bethlehem if desolation and suppressed emotions are present.*
- *Physical body work such as massage, using selected aromatherapy oils, can be most beneficial.*

CONFUSION

Confusion in the elderly is often due to the natural process of brain-tissue diminution (*see* **Alzheimer's disease** and **Senile dementia**).

Confusion can, however, be caused by metabolic changes, such as an inability to control sugar levels, poor nutrition, fevers, and illnesses such as coughs, colds, and flu, or drug reactions such as those found in people taking sleeping pills or antidepressants. Other drugs such as antibiotics can cause confused states.

RECOMMENDATIONS

- *Rule out any infectious or drug cause by visiting your doctor.*
- *Ensure good nutritional input by balancing the diet or visiting a nutritionist or dietician. Please consider using the macrobiotic diet (see chapter 7).*
- *Encourage adequate oxygenation of the brain by using a breathing technique, best taught by a yoga or meditation teacher.*
- *If the problems persist, consult a naturopath or homeopath (see **Alzheimer's disease** and **Senile dementia**).*

MEMORY LOSS OR IMPAIRMENT

The formation of memory is a complex matter, involving input and recollection processes dependent on brain chemicals (neurotransmitters) and pathways being intact.

Memory Loss Diagram

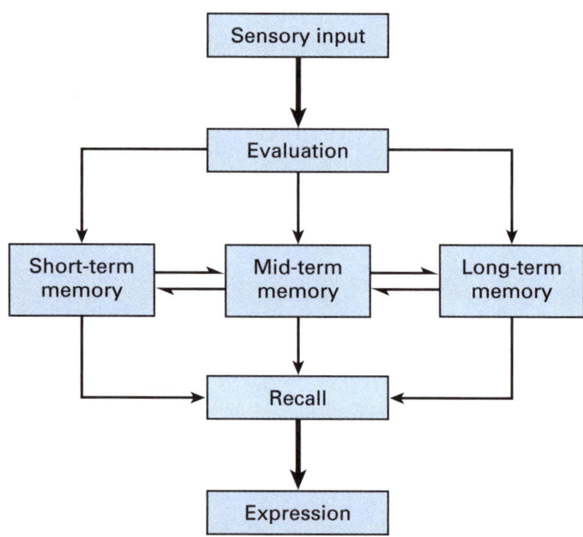

As can be seen by the diagram (above), it is important to isolate the area where the memory problem lies. Difficulty in the input—i.e. the senses of sight, hearing, touch, smell, and taste—can lead to incorrect assessment. Once the brain has assessed the situation, it will decide whether to store the event in short-, medium-, or long-term memory stores; for example, the brain will register the color of a tie that somebody was wearing at a meeting. This is not considered to be an important factor in survival, and therefore will probably be stored in short-term memory. After a while, the chemicals that have been formed and stored in one part of the brain will be broken down, and that memory will be erased. Medium-term memory will register, say, the directions to a party, but if the venue is unlikely to be visited again, this too will be erased. Long-term memory will have neurotransmitters and pathways formed for important matters, or those laid down in youth when the brain is at its most receptive. As the diagram shows, short-term can pass into medium-term, which in turn can be logged into long-term memory.

Recall from any memory center is an important part of memory function, and then the ability to express it finalizes the pathway. How often do we all sit there complaining that we know the answer, but just cannot bring it to mind?

Any condition that interferes with the pathways, the formation of neurotransmitters, or the actual parts of the brain that retain facts and events, can cause an impairment or loss of memory.

Fatigue, whether caused by overdoing things or by a disease processes such as hypothyroidism, will create an increase in the production of adrenaline or other catecholamines. Anxiety, nervousness, and fear will all produce these chemicals as well. Catecholamines are principally there to save our lives, and tell the brain to focus on life-threatening situations rather than memorizing. A poor example would be trying to memorize the recipe for a cake while watching a lion move stealthily towards you. How often have we forgotten items on a shopping list given to us by our partner when we were heading out of the door on a busy day? The catecholamines actually redirect information through different pathways, and therefore disrupt the information being fed into the memory centers. Hypoglycemia (low blood sugar) can have the same effect by increasing stress chemicals, but also diminishes the function of the brain, which exists only on its supply of glucose.

Toxins such as alcohol, drugs of abuse, smoking, agrochemicals (including pesticides), and specific foods to which individuals may be allergic, can all put chemicals in the system that interfere with both the production of neurotransmitters and the pathways.

Damage to the brain or the pathways through trauma, stroke, or tumor may affect memory. Decreasing the amount of brain tissue, as in Alzheimer's disease or senile dementia, and decreased oxygenation and nutritional supply by a narrowing of the arteries (atheroma), will all interfere with memory by destruction of tissue or nerve pathways.

RECOMMENDATIONS

- *Temporary memory loss is most commonly caused by poor concentration or toxic intake, such as alcohol. No treatment is necessary, but caution is advised on intake and stress levels.*
- *Memory loss or impairment that is persistent needs to be assessed by a specialist to isolate the cause. Special memory tests and CT scans of the brain may be employed. Remember that orthodox neurologists may not consider agrochemicals, food allergy, or low blood sugar as a cause of memory loss.*
- *Deficiencies in proteins, zinc, vitamin B_{12}, folic acid, and lecithin are common in the elderly, the stressed, or the unwell who have decreased appetites. Deficiencies in fat intake caused by strict and incorrect dieting may also create a problem. Deficiencies should be measured and corrected.*
- *Blood and hair analysis for the detection of deficiencies and heavy-metal toxicity should be undertaken. Lead, aluminum, and mercury may all be culprits in memory loss.*
- *Relaxation techniques and counseling, if necessary, should be considered in stressed individuals.*
- *Exercising the brain through intellectual reading, crosswords, debate, and puzzles is essential, especially in older age.*
- *Ensure that hypoglycemia is not an issue* *(see* **Hypoglycemia***).*

- *Avoid smoking, excess alcohol, and drug abuse. All drugs will create potentially long-term damage to neurotransmitter production and pathways.*
- *Homeopathic remedies may be of benefit. High-potency Plumbum (lead), Mercurius, and Alumina may all be beneficial if heavy-metal poisoning is found to exist. The homeopathic remedies Anarcardium and Sulphur may be useful at potency 200, taken daily for five days if the ability to remember names and words is a problem.*

PART TWO

Chapter 7

Nutrition

Chapter 7

Nutrition

Introduction

There is a plethora of books on nutrition lining the shelves of every book and healthfood store. They all have their merits and failings, and I would not presume to comment on the expertise of my colleagues and their interpretation of a healthy diet.

I do feel, however, that there is no set diet that is good for everyone. To suggest that Eskimos, who spend their lives eating blubber, would fare well on a macrobiotic diet, or that New Guinea tribesmen, whose diet differs markedly from that of Parisians, would do well to change their habits would be incorrect. Trial and error is principally the best way to isolate your preferred dietetic regime.

This short chapter cannot encompass a fraction of the knowledge we have about nutrition, but attempts to point out some essentials and the basics of which an individual should have a grasp. Sadly, despite the brevity of this section, it magnifies a thousandfold the instructions that the average doctor is given on nutrition through their medical training. Diet is not only about calorific input and output, nor about balance of nutrition. It is to do with these factors, plus an understanding of the vital force imparted from foods, the spiritual and psychological connection with nutrition, and the need to return to instinct when choosing and preparing food.

The Eastern philosophies consider all food to have a variety of energies, some more prominent than others. All foods have a balance of masculine and/or feminine energy, or a mixture of both. Foods contain different categories and states of our universe, specifically space, air, fire or heat, earth, wood, metal, and water. Food is sweet, bitter, sour, salty, or spicy, and may be hot, warm, or cold.

The choice of food should be based on the requirements of an individual at any time in relation to the balance of all these energies. It is not hard to do, and if left to instinct, the body (when healthy) will automatically balance and absorb its requirements.

RECOMMENDATIONS

- *When choosing your diet, put aside the orthodox concept until later and focus on the energy requirements.*
- *Keep in touch with your instincts. Eat what you feel like eating, but ignore unhealthy cravings. If the desire is for a piece of chocolate, then the body is suggesting a desire for sweetness and energy—have some fruit. If the craving is for pasta, make it wholegrain.*
- *Balance temperatures. On a hot, sunny day, enjoy a salad; in the depths of winter prepare hot soups. The rule of thumb is that raw and steamed are cooling; stewed, baked, and stir-fried are warming, and deep-fried, roasted, grilled, and barbecued are heating. (Barbecues in the summer? An occasional aberration is an enjoyable cheat!)*
- *Balance raw and cooked foods, depending on the amount of environmental heat. Even a hot summer's day requires some heating foods, but a predominantly raw diet is best. Predominant is the operative word.*
- *Try to balance all flavors throughout the day, or even at each meal. The salt of a fish can be balanced by the sour of the lemon. The spice of an Indian meal is often counteracted by the bitter of aniseed from seeds at the end.*

PSYCHOLOGICAL AND ENERGETIC CONSIDERATIONS TOWARD FOOD

All holistic practitioners consider there to be a mind–body connection. The energy of one directly influences the energy of another. Science is beginning to pick up on energy wavelengths that may affect the nervous system, and therefore influence both the mind and the body. Energy is provided through the sun, the air we breathe and, of course, the food we eat. Our psychological attitude toward our food is (both theoretically and in my experience) relevant to the benefit we derive from our nutrition.

RECOMMENDATIONS

- *The kitchen. The place of preparation must be comfortable, convenient, and happy. It generally is, and it is not coincidental that people migrate into the kitchen at parties. Very often, family gatherings are only found around food, and ensuring a clean, hygienic, bright, and airy kitchen is an essential prerequisite to deriving the most from nutrition.*
- *Putting aside time to eat. All day we expend energy, and like a car we occasionally need to stop to refuel. Short, rushed meals are equivalent to putting small amounts of petrol in the tank—the car will only run for a short period. The longer we spend eating, the more benefit we derive. Unlike the car analogy, it is not about quantity, but about the time spent in a mental and physical state of absorption rather than usage. Set aside time in the day to eat with no disturbance allowed.*
- *The Chinese state that "the stomach has no teeth." Chew food well to lessen the work of the digestive system.*
- *The Chinese believe that we should work slightly cold and slightly hungry. Ingesting too much food overburdens the system, and requires energy to process all the matter. Eastern philosophies describe it as creating stagnation, and as we return to our daily function after a meal, our energy is split between function and digestion.*
- *Feed the body appropriately for its requirements. A big breakfast for a busy day, a lighter lunch because half the day is done, and a light supper because we are about to rest.*
- *Believe in the concept of energy within food. Eat foods with vital force. Organic food from the environment imparts energy from that part of the world in which you live. Preserved food is food contaminated with chemicals or radiation that kill bacteria. These kill life. These kill energy in food. Avoid anything with preservatives, additives or foods that have been "nuked" by microwaves. Remember that all foods that are on the shelves of our supermarkets may have been irradiated as part of the food industry's attempt to prolong the "sell-by" date. As a general rule, avoid anything that has a "sell-by" date longer than the time that you would keep that product in the fridge if you had prepared it yourself.*

PREPARATION OF FOOD

Many so-called primitive races who have maintained contact with their spiritual past consider all foods to have an energy. A hunter will apologize and pray to the victim of the arrow or spear. The circle of life so popularized by wildlife programs is taken to its spiritual conclusion by such predators. This attitude is not easily transferable into modern Western culture, because the killing of our animals is now done at arm's length and by a third party. The availability of our fruit and vegetables is also limited by our busy schedules and lack of space. In an ideal world, we would all eat the produce from the soil on which we live, because the balance of nature provides what we need, depending on our environment. According to Eastern philosophies, honey produced in sunny countries such as Australia will contain more fire or *pitta* energy than the honey manufactured by the bees of the cooler climate of, say, England. And within England, the pollens that the bees eat in Surrey are different from those in Lancashire, and as our immune system is geared towards those in our own atmosphere, it will therefore deal with the honey from our region better than from elsewhere. Hot climates produce foods suitable for the digestion of humans adapted to heat, to such an extent that chilis are eaten in hot climates, and cucumbers more so in cold climates. These balance the external and internal (body) heat when extremes exist. As seasons change, so does our instinctive input. Soups and stews fill our table through the winter months, providing heat to balance the cold, and salads and fruits become more prominent to counteract our hot summers.

If allowed to eat by instinct, and not by time constraints and availability, the human body would set its own pattern. The food eaten should be chosen and prepared by instinct, and with respect. Eastern philosophies remind us of the interchange between different life forces, and that the lion at the top of the food chain will eventually be the food for the grass.

RECOMMENDATIONS

- *Food should be selected by instinct, smell, and on how it looks. Over- or underripe foods should be avoided.*
- *Once obtained, food should be stored correctly and as soon as possible.*
- *The area where food is prepared should be clean and comfortable. A kitchen where the cook is unhappy will create an energy that passes into the food and those who eat it.*
- *The water supply to clean and prepare food should be as purified as possible by the use of filters (see* ***Water****).*
- *In a family, touching the food should be encouraged, but the hands should be cleaned with unmedicated soap prior to commencing.*

EATING

Eating is not just about obtaining calories. It is about energy and communication. The wonderful phrase "table culture" was introduced to me recently, and is something that many parts of the world excel in, while others substantially lack.

The fast-food and TV-dinner concept is removing a very important time of "herd communication." Children learn manners, and improve their vocabulary and grammar around a table, and bonding is much increased at meal times. It is worth remembering that the human body derives pleasure from both input and output. The time spent eating and drinking should be maximized (and to balance the paragraph, elimination should be allowed to take as long as is required).

All the senses should be brought into play whenever possible. The sight of well-prepared food is stimulatory to the gastric juices, as are the smells. Texture is dependent upon good cooking, which in turn is dependent upon experience and patience. Taste, while the sense that most associate with food, is actually the last to come into play.

If any one of the senses is not pleased by a particular food, then that food should be avoided.

RECOMMENDATIONS

- *Spend time with your food. Make it a time of worship, because you are only what goes into you, and your nutrition is a major part of that.*
- *Ensure cleanliness of food, preparation surfaces, utensils, and especially hands.*
- *A pleasant environment for the preparation and eating of meals. Homemakers may spend much of their lives in the kitchen, and therefore a corresponding amount of energy should go into making it a homely and comfortable place.*

HIGH-FIBER INTAKE

The variety of food groups and types of nutrients are discussed in various parts of this chapter, but perhaps most important—because it is frequently overlooked—is the necessity for a high-fiber intake.

High-fiber foods are principally those that are difficult to digest because of their cellulose content. The human gut is not adept at breaking down cellulose and so this compound—found in most plants—remains in the gut and acts as a cleanser and detoxifier. Cellulose acts as a sponge, absorbing many compounds but particularly excess fats and cholesterol. The "roughage" acts much like a pipe cleaner, and scrapes adhesive debris off the bowel wall. This is extremely important in the colon, where waste products and toxins are stored.

Fiber gives bulk to the feces, which allows the muscle wall of the colon (large intestine) to maintain its strength. This encourages the fast removal of waste products and oxygenation to the bowel itself, considerably reducing the risk of disease.

Fiber will swell in the presence of fluids, and can be a very useful appetite suppressant, with no side effects. Pumpkin and sunflower seeds are an extremely useful aspect of any weight-reduction program, supplying fiber that swells in the stomach to give an impression of fullness. Fiber-containing foods are, simply: vegetables, fruit, wholegrains, nuts, and seeds.

DESIGNING AN IDEAL DIET

There are thousands of books declaring the ideal diet. Frankly, there is no such thing, because everybody is different and will have their own vision of ideal. Attitudes and body types vary to such an extent that what is good for one person may not necessarily be healthy for another. To persuade an Eskimo that a high-fiber, vegetarian diet is liable to be his best bet when an Eskimo might never actually see a vegetable is as pointless as advising the heavily meat-eating Argentines to exist on a vegan diet.

The Eskimos are an extreme example of the adaptability of the human race. Most races should gear their dietetics around individual instincts and the produce of their environment. Our instincts are suppressed by unnatural, "man-made" produce such as refined sugars. A carrot is sweet, but how many of us remember that? Spend five days away from any refined sweetness, and that quality of the carrot will return. Put a piece of chocolate into an infant's mouth and watch its rejection. By the age of two years, however, the hidden sugars in many processed foods will have changed this natural instinct.

ESTABLISHING YOUR IDEAL BALANCE

The preceding tips now have to be balanced with more-orthodox advice.

Principally, a diet has to be balanced between carbohydrates, proteins, and fats. Nutrients are absorbed from all of these groups, and an understanding of which type of food falls into which group is essential. Ideally, we should have our diet made up as follows.

- Vegetables and fruits should make up 50 percent of the diet.

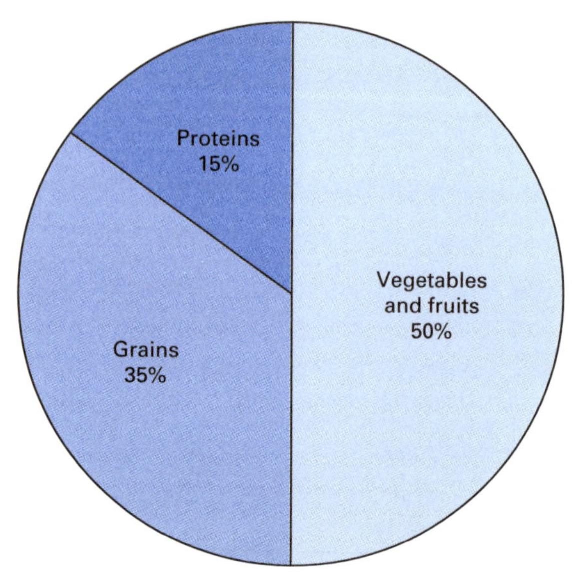

- Grains should make up 35 percent of the diet.
- Proteins should make up 15 percent of the diet.

More simply, half of our diet should be fruit and vegetables, and we should eat twice as much grain as protein. There, that saves you reading any more books on nutrition! The following are just details.

Vegetables and fruits

Balance is the order of the day, but it is best to eat one type of fruit at any sitting. Vegetables may be mixed. Vary vegetables by their color, having deep-green, light-green, yellow, white, and red vegetables in a 5:4:3:2:1 ratio over a seven-day period. (White vegetables refer to potatoes. Yams and sweet potatoes are in between the yellow and white groups.)

Fruits should generally be raw, although an occasional apple pie or stewed prune is enjoyable and nutritious. Vegetables should be a 50:50 mix of cooked and raw. Lightly steamed and/or stir-fried vegetables can be considered a mix of both.

Grains

Wholegrains include wheat, oats, barley, rye, corn, brown or wild rice, and the myriad of lesser-known but equally available complex carbohydrates, such as millet, buckwheat, and spelt. Potatoes and other starchy vegetables partially fall into this group.

Proteins

Many people are under the impression that meat, fowl, and fish are the best sources of protein. While they certainly are a good source, animal protein is harder to break down, digest, and absorb than vegetable proteins. Beans, lentils, soya products, and nuts are all high-protein foods. Animal products such as yogurt and cheeses fall halfway between the two, as far as ease of absorption is concerned.

Water

Most diet and nutrition books frequently make mention of water, but none, I feel, emphasize that without good hydration, all other advice becomes pointless. No biochemical process works without water, and therefore the balancing of nutrition is futile unless good hydration is obtained and maintained.

The minimum requirement is 8 ounces per foot of height, and additional water must be taken in for any excess sweating, caffeine, or alcohol intake, and the ingestion of anything artificially sweet. (*See* **Water** at the end of this chapter.)

The ideal balance

The type of food may vary, but the balance should remain within narrow guidelines. Any dietetic regime should be based around: 60–70 percent complex carbohydrates; 20–25 percent protein; 10–15 percent fat.

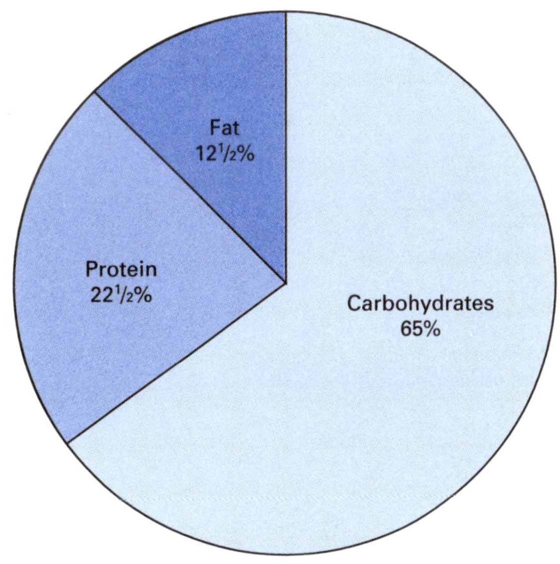

All the food groups should be as free from additives and preservatives as possible, and eaten as fresh as is feasible. Each food group contains specific nutrients, and all the vitamins, minerals, and trace elements must be taken in regularly. They contain good- and bad-quality nutrients, and the lists below clarify the contents. It is very important to note that many foods combine different groups. For example, cheese contains both fat and protein, lentils contain protein and

Food Groups

Predominantly protein
Poultry (skin removed)
White fish (skin removed)
Shellfish
Eggs
Low-fat yogurt
Low-fat dairy produce

Protein and fat
Red meat
Pig meat
Cheese
Yogurt
Milk
Cream
Ice cream
Oily fish
Fish with skin

Protein with carbohydrate
Soya
Lentils
Beans
Seeds

Predominantly carbohydrate
All refined grains
Potatoes
Fruits
Most vegetables
Sugars, including honey and maple syrup
Herbs

Carbohydrates and fat
Avocado
French fries
Chips
Cakes
Cookies
Sauces

Predominantly fat
Oils
Butter
Margarines
Vegetable-oil spreads
Lard
Dripping

Protein, carbohydrate, and fats
Nuts
All wholegrains

carbohydrate, avocados contain carbohydrate and fats. All of these have a variety of different nutrients, and none are particularly good or bad, provided that they are taken in moderation and in balance.

This term "imbalance" keeps coming up in both holistic medicine and health maintenance. If nature provided us with simple foods neatly categorized, we would probably not have any problems, but nature is not black and white; there is a lot of gray. Foods are rarely only protein or only carbohydrate, and it is important to understand what we are eating. The shortlist on this page gives a rough guide to the balance existing within major foods, and I hope it will be a simple list from which to create an individually suitable diet plan.

Use the list, without becoming in any way obsessive, to try to balance all meals according to the 65:22½:12½ ratio mentioned on the previous page. Failing to do so at each meal can be corrected on a daily basis. For example: a heavily protein-biased breakfast of eggs and bacon can be counterbalanced by a vegetable or fruit lunch, and a baked-potato supper. A toast-and-honey breakfast with a fruit lunch would entitle the diner to a slightly more protein-orientated supper, such as fish and vegetables.

Maintaining a balance is extremely important. It is incorrect to assume that removing fats is the best way to lose weight, because many essential vitamins and fatty acids will soon become deficient, and craving will set in, leading to an eventual overwhelming desire to eat what is missing. Similarly, the concept that red meat is "bad" for you can lead to deficiencies in amino acids if a correct balance of other protein-containing foods is not allowed to redress the situation.

TOXINS AND FOODS LACKING QI

Foods that inevitably contain toxins, or foods lacking in vital force or Qi (*see* **Weight loss**) are:

- Fried foods.
- Foods containing refined sugars, such as chocolates and sweets.
- Jellies, marmalades, and preserves with added white sugar.
- Foods made from refined flour, including white bread.
- Inorganic meat, and pig products in general (pigs are mostly fed on waste from human tables).
- Caffeine-containing compounds (coffee, strong tea, chocolate, and many carbonated drinks), fruit drinks and most preprepared juices (most contain extra sugar, regardless of the labeling, because manufacturers are allowed to replace an estimated amount of sugar that may be lost in the manufacturing process—*see* **Fruit juice**).
- Any smoked food, where the fumes come from a chemically-treated charcoal.
- Any alcohol product.
- Any products with added salt.
- High-fat foods such as pizzas, burgers, French fries.
- Mass-produced eggs or poultry.
- Any food with additives or preservatives.
- Any canned foods, and any colored or flavored foods.

This advice is not about being overzealous, it is about avoiding foods that are known to cause illness and disease. I am now amazed at the lack of nutritional knowledge I had, despite a medical training and a wise father with an interest in the subject. It is the same for most of the people I meet. This is by no means our fault. Responsibility must lie in the poor level of education, and a high level of promotion by the food industry.

Eating healthily is not encouraged, and not made easy. There are few organic butchers and vegetable suppliers, and those that exist have to have expensive products to make ends meet.

Water is an extremely important part of diet. I discuss water further in its own section, so it suffices here to say:

- Ensure a purified-water source for drinking and the preparing of food.
- Drink at least 8 ounces per foot of height in divided doses throughout the day.
- Remember that fluids other than water, such as juices and infusions, are *not* water. These can be taken in addition, but not *instead* of plain and simple water.

COOKING UTENSILS

The type and cleanliness of cooking utensils is of paramount importance in protecting one's nutrition. Not only will food remnants on cooking utensils encourage the growth of bacteria, but also the ingestion of chemicals from dish-washing liquids may be harmful.

All detergents have been known for a long time to be potentially carcinogenic, but little is said or done to encourage adequate rinsing. A happy balance needs to be struck between the right amount of cleansing solution to rid the utensils of food debris, and a thorough rinsing. Most machine washes are adequate, but the addition of a "rinse" compound to make utensils more shiny should be discouraged.

Avoid using pans that contribute chemicals to the water or fats in cooking. Aluminum is the most notorious, and may be cited in neurological conditions. Avoid cooking in tin cans, as is often seen on camp sites. Stainless steel is a safe material. Nonstick surfaces are safe, provided they stay in the pan. Change such utensils regularly and immediately if any chip or wear and tear is noticed.

YIN AND YANG FOODS

Put simply, the Yin is the fluid of the body, which acts as our fuel reserve, and lubricant within the system. The Yang is the heat or fire within the system. While Yin is the fuel, the Yang is the spark that ignites it.

Most conditions of ill health are created by an excess or deficiency in one or the other. A commonsense assessment of the disease process can give clues as to the dietary requirements based on Yin and Yang. While all foods contain Yin or Yang, many have a balance, and are not considered either one or the other predominantly. Below is a list of foods that can be used to aid a speedier recovery.

Yin foods

Yin foods tend to be sweet and cooling. They create dampness—for example, milk products that produce mucus—and are principally foods with a variety of nutrition within their substance. Yin foods include:

- Most fruits, especially apple, pineapple, other citrus fruits, pears, and watermelon.
- Eggs, oysters, rabbit, duck, and pork.
- Tofu, yam, tomatoes, asparagus, kidney beans, and peas.
- Milk and cheese.
- Honey (an excellent method of supplying Yin).

Yang foods

Principally these foods are warming. They are foods that benefit from cooking, and are pungent, strongly flavored foods. Herbs and spices are generally Yang. Yang foods include:

- Most herbs and spices, but particularly ginger and garlic.
- Lamb, lobster, and shrimp.
- Nuts, especially the chestnut and walnut.
- Offal, such as kidney.
- Clove and nutmeg (these have particularly powerful Yang effects).

Specific diets

ANTI-*CANDIDA* (ANTI-YEAST) DIET

I am not a great supporter of the anti-*Candida* diet. Generally, yeast overgrowth in the bowel occurs because of a diminution in the bowel's normal flora due to poor diet, the injudicious use of antibiotics, and the unintentional ingestion of antibiotics through meat products that have been processed and include antibiotics within their fibers.

Recommendations against *Candida* include long periods of abstinence (I have read suggestions ranging from three months to a year) from sugars and yeast-containing foods, which principally rules out bread and beer, fruits, milk, cheese, alcohol, and many condiments, such as caffeine, ice cream, lentils, pumpkin, potato, and peas.

It is ridiculous.

For those of us who may have the time to prepare steamed vegetables and limit our diet to one that avoids most convenience foods, the concept is okay, even if it may deny any "naughty" treats, but I sense that most people cannot function like this.

It is better to reduce substantially the foods that particularly stimulate yeast growth, such as refined sugars, caffeine, and high-fat foods, and perhaps cut down on yeast products such as leavened bread and mushrooms (which, apparently, encourage yeast growth), and at the same time use an anti-*Candida* therapy.

Trying to kill *Candida* with potent drugs can lead to the growth of resistant strains, but inhibiting their multiplication will result in their dying off from old age and not being replaced. There is less risk of resistance developing, and the outcome within three months (the general lifespan of a yeast cell) is similar to a vigorous and restrictive dietary existence. Details are discussed in the section on *Candida* (see **Candida**).

Yeast-supporting foods to avoid, but not necessarily to exclude, are as follows:

Bread (unless yeast-free)	Dry fruits
Cow's-milk products	Grapes
Mushrooms	Vinegar
Tomatoes	Salt
Wine/champagne	Caffeine
Apples	White sugar
Pears	Artificial sweeteners

THE BUDWIG DIET

This is a specific anti-cancer diet designed by Dr. Budwig to contain several anticancer nutrients.

The basic mixture consists of one tablespoonful of pure-virgin, cold-pressed, unprocessed flaxseed oil (flaxseed oil), and half to one cup of low-fat cottage cheese. This combination of fatty acids and sulfur-rich protein can be taken alone or as a mixture. Add natural flavoring or other food ingredients to suit you own taste. Eat this mixture three times a day.

The recommended diet

- Fresh fruits—three or four medium-sized portions daily.
- Fresh vegetables—four to six cups. Several tablespoonsful of flaxseeds and/or two tablespoonsful of the oil can be used in the salad dressing or on the vegetables; be sure to include cabbage, broccoli, and maitake mushrooms.
- Unprocessed wholegrain breads and cereals—3–4 cups or portions.
- Fresh fish—4–8oz. An excellent source of omega-3 fatty acids is rainbow trout (preferably the coldwater variety).
- Fresh meat and poultry—organic (without hormones), low-fat, and animals that have been fed food without pesticides or antibiotics.
- Liquids—bottled water or water purified by reverse osmosis. Sixty-four ounces a day are recommended, but do not worry if this is not manageable. Place one glass of your favorite juice in a 32-ounce bottle and fill the remainder with water. It is a cheat, but makes drinking easier.
- Fresh-fruit juices—citrus fruit should not be taken within several hours of the flaxseed oil/cottage-cheese mixture.

Eating any processed oils will counteract everything you are trying to do. They should be treated as poison, as should all fried foods. Eliminate as much sugar as possible from the diet. Remember that honey is primarily sugar, and prepared foods must be devoid of all artificial preservatives or chemical additives. Artificial sweeteners are absolutely forbidden.

THE DETOX DIET

All water should be bottled or filtered, preferably by reverse osmosis (*see* **Water**). If you are hungry during the day, please have some of the pumpkin and sunflower seeds usually reserved for the end of the afternoon.

Choose your favorite herbal teas, and try to drink between 16 and 32 ounces per day, but not within half an hour of any meal.

Day 1

Between waking and breakfast
Sixteen ounces of water

Breakfast
Up to one to two pounds of washed grapes

Between breakfast and lunch
Sixteen ounces of water

Lunch
Any steamed vegetable, but only one type

Between lunch and late afternoon
Sixteen ounces of water

Late afternoon
A handful of mixed pumpkin and sunflower seeds

Between late afternoon and supper
Sixteen ounces of water

Supper
Four ounces of bran or rolled oats, with two teaspoonfuls of lemon juice and apple juice/water mix for moisture, preferably soaked all day

Day 2

Between waking and breakfast
Sixteen ounces of filtered or bottled water (water to be taken between meals, as on day 1)

Breakfast
Two mangos, papayas, or other "exotic" fruit

Lunch
Any steamed vegetable, but only one type

Supper
Up to one to two pounds of potatoes (only pepper may be added, although the potatoes may be had in any form, but with no butter)

Day 3
Water to be taken as on day 1

Breakfast
Up to two grapefruits

Lunch
Any steamed vegetables, but only one type

Supper
Eight ounces of live yogurt, with one type of fruit and two teaspoonfuls of honey (two tablespoons of an unsweetened oat cereal may be added)

GERSON DIET

The Gerson diet is part of a regime that includes coffee enemas, iodine and potassium supplements and the preparation of vegetable and fruit juices. This diet is low in fat, low in animal protein, high in complex carbohydrates, and contains large amounts of organic fruits, vegetables, and whole-grains. Salt is excluded, and foods higher in potassium are increased.

Thyroid supplements may also be administered; initially, raw liver juice was prescribed, but this has been withdrawn because of bacterial growth within the substance.

Max Gerson, a physician born in Germany but who emigrated to the U.S.A., discovered this treatment because he was using sililca techniques for dealing with tuberculosis. It is difficult to come up to the rigorous scientific standards when using a dietetic technique, because other therapies may be in use at the same time. However, both the National Cancer Institute in America and a study published in the *Lancet* accepted that this required further study, and may be "a way forward" in cancer care. There is currently a retrospective study of more than 5,400 patients underway, which we hope will bring forward some answers.

The Gerson therapy is undoubtedly of benefit to confidence and mood, general well-being, faster healing after operative procedures, and reduction of pain.

RECOMMENDATION

- *This is probably the most researched and proven anticancer diet, and can be used safely, and hopefully effectively.*

THE HAY DIET

Dr. Hay devised this concept in the 1920s. He hypothesized that because the human race developed as both hunters and gatherers, it was unlikely that we would eat both animal protein and carbohydrates at the same time. He further suggested that the stomach and digestive tract were therefore geared toward digesting one type of food at a time.

Food combining, better termed as food non-combining, regimes have developed from his hypothesis.

Quite simply, protein foods, including soya and lentils, should be eaten separately from carbohydrates such as rice, potatoes, and wheat. Vegetables may be mixed with either group, but fruit needs to be separated from other foods by at least one hour.

The reasoning is simple. Protein requires longer to digest, and is therefore held in the stomach in the presence of acid for a longer period than other food groups. Keeping starch in the stomach for too long causes much higher liquefaction of the carbohydrate into glucose, which will then be absorbed at a much-more-rapid rate once it enters the small intestine. This, in turn, causes a much greater insulin production, which leads to a reflex hypoglycemic state, causing tiredness, among many other biochemical changes. The increased availability of glucose can also encourage yeast growth within the intestine along with its inherent problems.

Vegetables are carbohydrates. Fruit, with its high content of fructose (fruit sugar), will actually ferment in an acidic environment, and the alcohols produced can affect the body directly, and also enhance the growth of yeasts through the rest of the bowel. It should therefore be eaten separately to ensure quick passage through the acid of the stomach.

Many books have been written on the subject, but in principle the preceding rules should be followed, and an attempt should be made to have one protein meal, one starch meal, and one purely vegetarian or fruit meal a day. The fruit/vegetable meal encourages alkalinity, and this diet can therefore be used very effectively as a Detox regime. For the best benefit, have two days per week purely on fruit and vegetables.

HYPOGLYCEMIA DIET

See also **Hypoglycemia.**

Allowables

- Vegetables—any
- Fruits—any, but with exceptions below
- Juices—any unsweetened cranberry or vegetable juice is allowable (fresh/squeezed fruit juices)
- Beverages—herb teas, decaffeinated coffee, and coffee substitutes (once on the road to recovery, you may sweeten your drinks with honey if desired. Remember, use honey only in mild cases or after the initial program is relaxed.)

On rising

A small bowl of yogurt or half a grapefruit

Breakfast

One egg and half a slice of bread only (it may be toasted) with herb tea

Two hours after breakfast

A snack of two handfuls of either raw nuts or a mix of sunflower and pumpkin seeds

Lunch

- Salad (large serving of lettuce, tomato, vinegar and oil dressing)
- Vegetables if desired
- Slice of bread or toast with butter
- Dessert—*see* below for allowable foods
- Beverage

Two hours after lunch

As after breakfast, or two pieces of fruit

Two hours before dinner

A light snack of raw nuts, cheese, celery, or other vegetables stuffed with cheese

Dinner

- Soup, if desired (not thickened with flour)
- Vegetables
- Liberal portion of meat, fish, or poultry
- Beverage

Two hours after dinner

Dessert—*see* allowables below

Every 2 hours until bedtime

A small handful of nuts or fruit

- Desserts—fruit, unsweetened yogurt, or carob-sweetened snacks

Food and drinks to avoid

- Alcoholic and soft drinks, such as club soda, dry gingerale, whiskey and liquors
- Sugar, chocolate, candy, and other sweet foods, such as cakes, pies, pastries, custards, puddings, and ice cream
- Caffeine: ordinary coffee, strongly brewed tea, and beverages containing caffeine
- Decaffeinated drinks
- Grapes, raisins, plums, figs, dates, and bananas (all high in sugar)
- Donuts, jams, jellies, and marmalades (all high in sugar)
- Wines, cordials, cocktails and beers (the alcohol content is high in carbohydrate)

MACROBIOTIC DIET

The Macrobiotic Diet was created by a Japanese teacher who wrote under the name of Georges Ohsawa. He integrated Eastern and Western cultures, and created a ten-stage diet, designated from −3 to +7. The −3 Diet consists of 10 percent each of cereal or grains and soups; 30 percent each of vegetables and animal products; 15 percent salads and fruits; 5 percent "desserts," and very little to drink. As the number climbs, the diet changes, and at the +3 stage, the individual is on 10 percent soups, 30 percent vegetables, and 60 percent cereals. I believe that it is necessary to sit with a macrobiotic nutritionist, or have a patient attitude toward a good book to appreciate fully the holistic sense of macrobiotic dieting.

Studies have been made on macrobiotic diets with regard to blood pressure, cholesterol levels and estrogen metabolism. Most studies have been made in either treatment or prevention of chronic disease, although the success of the macrobiotic diet on blood pressure and cholesterol supports its use in conditions associated with these components.

RECOMMENDATIONS

- *This is undoubtedly a safe and healthy diet.*
- *Special attention to this regime should be considered by those with high blood pressure or raised cholesterol levels, those with family histories of strokes or heart disease, and smokers.*

ORNISH DIET

The Ornish diet was developed by Dean Ornish, a doctor from San Francisco. This diet is strictly vegetarian, allowing no meat or animal protein except for the whites of eggs. The aim is to provide less than 2,000 calories a day, mostly from carbohydrates, with less than 10 percent coming from fat.

This diet is encouraged for those with cardiovascular disease, particularly angina (heart pain), raised cholesterol, and arterial occlusion. Studies for such conditions have proven successful under rigorous scientific standards.

PRITIKIN DIET

Named after Nathan Pritikin, this is a vegetarian, high-complex carbohydrate-and-fiber diet that is specifically low in cholesterol and fat. It is prescribed in association with 45 minutes of daily walking.

It is possible to obtain books on this diet, although the Pritikin Center in California recommends that a patient attends a 26-day program to adjust to their new type of living.

Good, scientifically based studies showed that this diet was of great benefit in patients with cardiovascular problems, and can be considered of use in non-insulin-dependent diabetes, provided that it is initiated early on in the diagnosis.

VEGAN DIET

A vegan is a vegetarian who excludes all protein and other products of an animal origin. There is an ongoing debate as to whether or not a human being should eat meat. We have digestive enzymes capable of dealing with animal protein, and incisor teeth may be relevant to the kill. One may argue that these teeth are only for defense, and that the protein-digesting enzymes are designed for vegetable proteins, so it is hard to pin down exactly what nature intended. The fact of the matter is that the human being has developed into an omnivore (subsistence on a wide variety of food). Anthropologists point out that the human being is extremely adaptable, and the Eskimo who may never see a vegetable, for example, is capable of surviving on meat alone, whereas many populations are principally vegetarian.

Being vegan is an extremely intricate art, and requires a good knowledge of how to obtain adequate amounts of protein from vegetable sources. Many vitamins, such as vitamin B_{12}, are found predominantly in animal products, and deficiencies are common in uneducated vegans. It may take several years, but eventually most vegans will fall into deficiencies if they don't take supplements.

As a cleansing process, vegan diets are extremely useful. Provided that specific allergy is not noted to gluten or other proteins found in grains, vegan diets are inevitably healthy if taken for a short period of time. Six weeks, I believe, is a maximum, without at least a 10-day break of animal product intake.

The choice of becoming an educated vegan is up to an individual, but I think that it is more suited to those who have a smaller bone and muscle structure, such as the Asian races.

RECOMMENDATIONS

- *Avoid the long-term regime of a vegan diet as a general rule.*
- *Ensure that adequate vegetarian protein is ingested. Beans, pulses, lentils, and tofu must be taken in sufficient quantities on a daily basis.*
- *Smaller bone and muscle mass may predispose to a better tolerance of a low-protein diet.*
- *Discussion with a nutritionist or strict adherence to a vegan guideline book is necessary, and is beyond the scope of this book.*
- *Every six months, have a blood and hair analysis to establish vitamin and mineral status.*

SPECIFIC FOODS AND NUTRIENTS

There is a lot of disinformation put out by various groups, whose motivation is the profit factor. I think it necessary to make mention of some of the more-common and possibly dangerous pieces of advice that are fed to us by "the powers that be" through the media. The following covers some of the most-commonly-asked questions and misunderstood foods within the common diet.

ACID/ALKALINE FOODS

The body works at a pH (the measurement of acid/alkaline levels) of 7.35–7.45. Any movement outside this range is strongly resisted by the body—specifically the kidneys and lungs—which battles to correct the balance by breathing faster or eliminating hydrogen and other charged particles through the urine. A food is not judged to be alkaline by its own pH, but by the effect that it has on the body.

Acid-forming foods	Alkaline-forming foods
Animal protein	Most vegetables
Most grains	Most fruits
Most nuts	Salty fish
Plant seeds	Soya
Sugar	Almonds and brazil nuts
Honey	Millet and buckwheat
Coffee	
Dairy products	
Most berries and tomatoes	

A common misconception is that milk is alkaline. If it is unpasteurized it has a neutral quality, but generally, the actual alkalinity in the milk itself causes the stomach to produce more acid, and therefore acidifies the system.

Acid production is dependent upon the quantity eaten: the less we fill ourselves, the less acidic we are. Not mixing foods, as in the Hay diet or other food-combining disciplines, generally moves food out of the stomach quicker, thereby reducing acid production and creating a tendency towards alkalinity.

ACIDOPHILUS

Acidophilus is the best-known yogurt bacteria, although there are many other types, including *Probifidus* and *Bifidus*. These bacteria encourage and promote the growth of the human bowel flora, in particular, *Escherichia coli*. There are bad *E. coli*, and if an infection of one of these is found, then acidophilus and its cousins should not be taken.

There are many different strains on the market, some found in yogurt, others in powder or capsules. I currently recommend a French brand *Lactibiane*, which reconstitutes from a dehydrated form when mixed with water, and which, when drunk, decreases the stomach acidity, allowing the acidophilus to reach the intestine. Other brands must be in acid-resistant capsules. Not much gets past the high-acid levels in the stomach, which is a good thing, and one that nature intended. Acidophilus is no different, although slightly more resistant, than other organisms. Small amounts of acidophilus will escape into the alkaline intestine if enough yogurt or powdered acidophilus is ingested but I doubt that these will have any profound effect on the colon 30 feet away where the bulk of *E. coli* lives. Where possible, take the compound with or after a meal in an attempt to avoid the abundant acid.

ALCOHOL

Alcohol is fun. It is not nutritious, and is probably harmful if taken in excess, and any suggestions that it may actually be protective of conditions such as atheroma or atherosclerosis are probably true, but the risks overrule the benefits. In any case, it is probably not the alcohol that is protecting, but the nutrients taken in coincidentally.

It is hard to define a safe level of alcohol, but as a rule of thumb, if you do not feel the effects psychologically, then the body is probably dealing with the amount you have taken. Unfortunately, this rule of thumb diminishes in accuracy if you constantly drink enough to get drunk, and then find yourself needing more. Here, the body is simply becoming tolerant. For those not addicted, a method by which a safe level can be assessed is to not drink alcohol for approximately three weeks, eat a light meal, and drink a small amount of alcohol 10 minutes later. Repeat this every 10 minutes and as soon as you feel relaxed or merry, then that is your limit. One or two drinks is usually found to be the level. Once this is established, that amount of alcohol in a day is not likely to do you any harm whatsoever.

If you wish to exceed your tolerance level, bear in mind that it takes the liver approximately two days to recover from the insult of being tipsy or drunk. Try to give the liver that amount of time between alcohol binges, and never drink to a point where your coordination is clearly embarrassing. Regardless of how you feel, coordination is insulted by anything over your personal tolerance level, as established from the technique above, and no important manual tasks should be undertaken. Driving is an important manual task! Our body cannot deal with an impact at any speed above that of a walk without some damage occurring. Driving, even at 30mph, is well beyond the body's capability to deal with should it suffer an impact, and consequently driving at any speed is a life-threatening condition. Do not drink and drive.

ANTIOXIDANTS AND FREE RADICALS

Free radicals are negatively charged particles that are known to affect the genetic strands within the cells, triggering a potentially cancerous change. These negative ions also damage cell surfaces in blood vessels, thereby encouraging clot formation, which in turn attracts calcium and cholesterol to form obstructive plaques.

Antioxidants (incidentally, nothing at all to do with oxygenating of a molecule or cell) bind with free radicals and remove their danger. The antioxidants are vitamins A, C, and E, selenium, grapeseed extract, coenzyme Q10, and—to a lesser extent—zinc. Many different plant extracts contain some or all of these components, and therefore have antioxidant activity; we are also constantly being advised by our nutritional scientists of newer and stronger antioxidant compounds.

Free radicals are found in animal products, fried foods, and any fat exposed to heat, oxygen, and light. Barbecued and smoked products are particularly full of free radicals. Anything smoked, including tobacco and engine fuels, provides free radicals.

Five portions of fresh fruit and vegetables will protect the average adult, provided that excessive free radical intake is not encouraged, otherwise, daily supplementation from as early an age as possible is recommended.

ARTIFICIAL SWEETENERS

When artificial sweeteners were first developed in the 1950s, the compounds (known as cyclamates) were found to be linked to cancer. These were replaced by saccharine, which petered out due to similar fears. These were replaced by a compound called aspartame, which is made from the amino acid phenylalanine, another amino acid, and an alcohol. Phenylalanine is the precursor to serotonin, one of the body's natural calmers, and an increased production of this due to extra availability of its precursor leads to a diminution in other relaxation neurotransmitters, such as dopamine. This can have mild effects on the nervous system, which may or may not be noticed. The alcohol may actually cause a hangover effect, and it is known that large amounts of aspartame can even cause seizures. This compound may also be considered as foreign matter, and set up an immune response or food allergy. Rashes and itching are not uncommon. Might it even be responsible for the increase in asthma that is being seen in the West? I think it might.

Insulin levels are principally governed by the levels of sugar in the system. There is a possibility that aspartame, which is over a thousand times sweeter than sugar, molecule for molecule, may trigger insulin production via a reflex caused by recognition of sweetness by the taste buds. Do not use artificial sweeteners as a general rule.

BEVERAGES AND DRINKS

Water, and water alone, is what the body utilizes in the form of fluids. The body knows exactly what to do with water, and can place it in the right compartments (cells, tissues, or blood vessels) swiftly and easily. Anything mixed with the water has to be separated, and this requires energy, which in turn utilizes water, thereby decreasing the availability for the rest of the body. Very diluted fruit juices and herbal teas may not cause the body too much trouble, but anything sweet, caffeine- or alcohol-filled, or flavored artificially requires processing, which is a strain on the system.

Milk is discussed as a separate entity later on in this chapter (*see* **Milk**), but is a wholly inadequate method of obtaining hydration (*see* **Dehydration**).

These facts do not mean that enjoyable flavors cannot be imbibed. Select and enjoy from a vast number of herbal teas, and fresh fruit and vegetable juices, with the knowledge that they will have cleansing and nutritious effects, but do not assume that they will be a substitute for water.

Artificial drinks such as colas, fruit drinks, and carbonated, highly artificially sugared drinks are not just not good for you, but they are actually *harmful*. They dehydrate, put pressure on the biochemistry and organs in the body, and stimulate the nervous system. The same can be said for caffeine and alcohol, but multiply the damage by ten. If you are going to enjoy these "sins," match every glassful with at least the same amount of water, preferably half an hour before or after imbibing.

BOWEL FLORA

As soon as we are born, we start to swallow bacteria from our environment. We pick up flora as we travel down the vaginal vault from the uterus and continue to pick up bugs from the inevitable kisses and close contact with parents, relations, and friends. Breastfeeding also passes bacteria into the system. Those that require oxygen tend not to survive within the intestine, but the outcome is the development of 10^{14} anaerobic bacteria per square centimeter of bowel content. Fewer live in the stomach and the upper part of the small intestine, but the numbers increase the lower we go.

These flora are essential for the breakdown of indigestible foods, the release of nutrients from plant cells, and the provision (as biproducts of their own metabolism) of vitamins and trace elements. Our body is very dependent on bowel bacteria, for example, for the production of vitamin B_{12}.

The majority of these bowel flora are *Bifidolactobacillus. Eschericha coli* (abbreviated to *E. coli*) and *streptococci* strains make up the rest, with a smaller, fluctuating group known as enterobacteria. Within the bowel, these bugs are of great use, but outside they can be dangerous, since they multiply rapidly, and may produce a considerable amount of toxin, which is harmlesss within the bowel, but potentially harmful elsewhere. There are thousands of different strains, only a few of which are particularly harmful.

Maintenance of healthy bowel flora is a prerequisite of health, and many conditions—from allergies and all their associated conditions (such as eczema, asthma, and hay fever) and arthritis, to chronic conditions such as cancer—may be associated with poor bowel function, which in turn is caused by or creates gut "dysbiosis." This term indicates incorrect function or proliferation of the wrong sort of bowel flora.

Conditions such as irritable-bowel syndrome and the "leaky-gut syndrome" are, in my opinion, invariably linked with gut dysbiosis, and more chronic conditions such as Crohn's and ulcerative colitis may also be related.

Living within the confines of the gut are a myriad of yeasts, fungi, and other parasites that are kept at bay through what is known as competitive inhibition. There is only a certain amount of food available, and if the bowel flora is in abundance and healthy, it eats most of the nutrition available. This means that the "bad bugs" have a limited food supply and cannot, therefore, multiply at any great rate. If the bowel bacteria are insulted, their competitive edge diminishes, and yeasts such as *Candida* can flourish. The ingestion of antibiotics from doctor's prescriptions, or inadvertently through foods (particularly processed meats), nitrates and other food additives, and the preservatives we have in our foods, all kill off the bowel bacteria, but do not affect the yeasts and fungi.

A normal balanced diet should not challenge the bowel flora, but the regular use of yogurt bacteria in supplemental form is strongly advised when the Western diet is the predominant intake (*see* **Antibiotics** and **Acidophillus**), because these encourage the "good bacteria."

CAFFEINE

Caffeine is a marked stimulator of the nervous system, and is found in abundance in coffee, tea, soft drinks, chocolate, and other cocoa products, and a myriad of over-the-counter drugs used for anything from the common cold to stomach upsets.

Initially, caffeine's stimulation of the nervous system gives a "buzz" of increasing energy, concentration, and a sense of euphoria. Caffeine is, at the end of the day, an adrenaline-like compound. Caffeine's effect is to raise blood-sugar levels, giving a short-term supply of available energy.

Decaffeinated coffee is rarely completely free of caffeine, and the chemicals used to remove the compound may themselves be stimulating, and are potentially carcinogenic (cancer-causing). It is also worth remembering that most coffee-making countries will be treating their coffee plants with pesticides and insecticides, and these are going to be fed into your system as well.

Coffee causes cancer? I am afraid so. There are

associations between caffeine and cancer of the pancreas, prostate, and bladder. It is also known that caffeine may be associated with miscarriage, diabetes, hypertension, and I hypothesize that it may create a food-allergy state leading to asthma, eczema, and hay fever. In fact, I place caffeine at the top of the list of health hazards, even above smoking and the eating of refined foods.

Give it up absolutely and totally. There is no benefit in it whatsoever. If you find the thought of actual withdrawal difficult, then you are addicted, and the long-term effects of any addiction are going to be detrimental to your well-being. Ask for help with the same determination that a heroin addict might should he choose to withdraw from his drug.

CALCIUM

Calcium is found throughout the body, either as a structural or biochemical necessity. Calcium is the main component of teeth and bones, and is the reason that muscles can contract. It is very difficult to be calcium-deficient, because it is spread throughout the foods we eat. It is a fallacy to assume that milk is an essential aspect of calcium intake, or that a lack of milk will create calcium deficiency problems such as osteoporosis. In fact, the majority of the world's population do not consume milk products, and are intolerant or unable to utilize the calcium in milk. The incidence of osteoporosis (thin bones) is highest in countries that consume the most milk (*see* **Osteoporosis**).

Calcium is found in abundance, and in an easily absorbable form in sesame seeds, kelp, almonds, meat, poultry, fish (especially salmon), and most deep-green vegetables. These foods should be used regularly, especially in young children and teenage girls, the latter of whom will benefit from reduced osteoporosis if their calcium levels are high when the bones are forming.

CARBOHYDRATES

A carbohydrate is an organic substance containing carbon, hydrogen, and oxygen. That tells us nothing, unless we happen to have done a degree in chemistry! Put simply, sugar molecules such as glucose are built up into chains, and at some arbitrary point, when five or six carbon atoms are present, a carbohydrate is formed. As these chains get bigger, compounds such as cellulose are formed, and around these the addition of proteins and nutrients attach, creating plants. Change the molecular configuration slightly, add in one or two other compounds, and starch is born. Carbohydrates encompass plants and their products, such as potatoes, berries, fruits, and anything sweet. We should derive up to 70 percent of our energy from carbohydrates, the remainder coming from protein (20 percent) and fats (10 percent).

CHOLESTEROL

Studies over the last 30 years have shown cholesterol to be a danger if it is found in excess. There are several types of cholesterol. The three better known are high-density lipoproteins (HDL), low-density lipoproteins (LDL), and very-low-density lipoproteins (VLDL). The LDL, VLDL, and another fat-containing protein called apolipoprotein attach to damaged areas within arteries to help them repair (and they also carry fats to the tissues). Unfortunately, this process has a poor control mechanism, and the over-repair process causes plaques to form, which eventually clog up the artery. The HDL acts by blocking LDL action, and takes fats to the liver for processing. Putting it simply, HDL is "good" cholesterol, and LDL is "bad." Doctors will look at the total cholesterol: HDL/LDL ratio, and the risk ratio is discussed below.

Raised cholesterol and tryglyceride levels have been brought to prominence because of the discovery of lipid (fat)-narrowing agents, which were a sellable and patentable drug regime. There is no doubt that raised cholesterol levels will increase the chances of heart attacks and strokes, but what the orthodox medical world neglects to tell the patient is that the risk of the use of these drugs may outweigh the benefits. The drugs have many serious side effects, including a propensity to severe depression, thereby increasing the risk of suicide. Some of the lipid-lowering agents also inhibit the production of certain essential heart nutrients, such as co-enzyme Q10. Cholesterol is required for the cell membrane of nearly all tissues in the body, and is also required for the production of adrenal hormones, which govern our stress and water balance, for coating our nerves to allow correct conduction, and for all our sex hormones. Admittedly, the level at which treatment is recommended for raised cholesterol has been rising, but the dangers of cholesterol need to be put into context with other factors that encourage cardiovascular disease, such as smoking, the oral contraceptive pill, poor exercise, and diet.

Raised cholesterol by itself does not suggest danger, because the amount of the protective HDL is the relevant factor. A term known as the "risk ratio" is calculated by dividing the total cholesterol level by the HDL level. If the figure is above 5 for a man and above 4.4 for a woman, then the cholesterol levels are relevant to health. If below these figures, the levels are not relevant. For example, a total cholesterol level of 6mmol/l with an HDL level of 2mmol/l gives a risk ratio of 3, despite the cholesterol level being above 5.2mmol/l, which is a typical "upper level" of normal (*see* **Atheroma**).

Cholesterol needs only to be considered dangerous when other factors are considered, such as deficiencies in certain vitamins, minerals, and amino acids, all of which are mentioned below in the recommendations. An excess of cholesterol in the diet is occasionally relevant, although most cholesterol is made by the liver at the body's request. The following foods should be reduced, not only because of cholesterol but also because they can form free radicals, which are (probably) much more involved in arteriosclerosis, heart attacks, and strokes.

High-cholesterol foods

- Red meats
- Offal—especially kidney and liver
- Cheese
- Cow produce (except specially prepared low-fat)
- Shrimps
- Pork

Those who have read about the evils of cholesterol may be surprised to see that eggs and avocado are not included in this list. Eggs, while having a high-cholesterol content in the yolk, actually promote a rise in HDL and, in any case, a combination of cholesterol with the lecithin in the white of the egg while digestion takes place in the acid environment of the stomach causes the cholesterol to bind with the lecithin and not be easily absorbed. Avocados actually contain no cholesterol. They are a high-fat food, and are not useful if triglyceride levels are high or someone is trying to lose weight, but a small avocado will not be harmful in comparison to, say, a slice of bacon.

So, in a nutshell, cholesterol and other lipids are not the dangers that the orthodox medical world says they are. The real problem lies in deficiencies and other factors that damage blood vessels, and high levels of LDL may enhance the problem.

RECOMMENDATIONS

- *A regular check on cholesterol levels is advisable, but please put it into context with the co-risk factors mentioned below.*
- *Consider the Ornish or Pritikin diet.*
- *Avoid smoking, caffeine, stress, oral contraceptives, refined sugar, pollutants, and additives.*
- *Consider using the macrobiotic diet.*
- *Those with a family history of heart disease, atherosclerosis, or strokes should consult with a complementary medical practitioner, and special attention should be paid to levels of copper, chromium, and magnesium, a low level of which will predispose to problems.*

- *Ensure that the diet is rich in vitamin C, niacin (vitamin B_3), vitamin E, and the omega-3 and omega-6 essential oils. This can be done by enjoying mackerel, herring, salmon, or halibut three times a week. Vegetarians should consider taking supplements of these oils. Three to five portions of fruit or vegetable each day will cover the vitamins.*
- *Avoid the high-cholesterol foods listed in the text above, which may increase cholesterol levels.*
- *The body will create more cholesterol to wrap around cells to hold in water if an individual is dehydrated. Ensure that adequate amounts of water are drunk each day (see* **Dehydration***).*
- *Increased liver activity from an input of toxins or an excess of stress (the liver has to work harder to break down excess adrenaline) should be avoided. The faster the liver works, the more cholesterol it makes.*
- *If cholesterol levels are raised and reduction in dietary sources has proved inefficient at bringing the levels down, then consider taking the following supplements in divided doses per foot of height three times a day with food: vitamin C (1g), vitamin B_3 (niacin, 20mg), vitamin E (150iu), copper (500µg), magnesium (100mg), chromium (50mg), L-carnitine (150mg), and N-acetylcysteine (250mg). This all gets a bit complicated, and it might be simpler to discuss the matter with a complementary medical practitioner. More simply, take garlic capsules (200mg per foot of height per day, divided into three doses with food).*
- *Not only because it can reduce cholesterol levels, but also because of its protective factor from the damage that cholesterol may cause with other cofactors—reduce your stress by changing lifestyle or meditating.*

FASTING

Fasting is becoming an increasingly popular activity, which can range from a total fast where nothing passes the lips, to a variety of semi-fasts, ranging from an intake of water and fruit juices to fruits and vegetables.

The benefits of a fast are manifold. Time without imbibing allows the mouth a period to cleanse through its natural saliva, which contains many antibodies and cleansing chemicals. The parietal cells of the stomach (which produce hydrochloric acid), the pancreas, liver, and gallbladder are allowed a rest from the production of their digestive juices. The bowel muscle wall will not contract as frequently, and the colon will be given some time to evacuate the feces that can build up and adhere to the large intestinal wall.

The liver—the chemical factory of the body—can spend time on cleaning the blood rather than digesting new foods, and the kidney can filter out some of the longer-lasting toxins in the system. The fat stores that contain some of the body's toxins that may have been stored there to avoid circulating them will discharge some of these toxins into the bloodstream, and be dealt with better by the less-pressured liver and kidneys.

The islets of Langerhans, which produce insulin in the pancreas, will also have a rest. So, all in all, a body should benefit from some time away from food consumption. However, like all good things, there is often a reverse side. A total fast excludes all food, but must include water at a level of 16 ounces per foot of height per day. Water-restricted fasts must be followed only under the supervision of an experienced naturopathic physician, and are only beneficial in certain treatment protocols.

I am not a great supporter of total fasts because I think that the cleansing effect can be achieved without starving the body. I prefer semi-fast diets, and recommend the one below as a general guideline.

There is no set fasting technique that suits everybody. Individuals with any tendency to hypoglycemia (low blood sugar) will not benefit from a complete fast. Others, who lack nutrients, or who have malabsorption syndromes or chronic debilitating diseases such as cancer or AIDS may in fact make their situation worse with a complete fast.

The Eastern philosophies view each individual as having too much or too little air, water, earth, wood, or metal, and therefore a fast for someone deficient in any of these humors may once again be detrimental.

RECOMMENDATIONS

- *Except under expert advice, any fast must include a suitable amount of water intake.*
- *Specific semi-fasts may be tried on a trial-and-error basis over a 24-hr period. If the individual feels better, then a second day may be even more beneficial. Do not fast for more than 48hr unless advised by an expert.*

A semi-fast diet

A short time on a semi-fast diet may help you feel generally better, and it can be a great pick-me-up if you are chronically tired. It is better to start the diet on a day when you do not have to exert yourself physically.

Day 1
Drink freshly squeezed or pressed fruit and/or vegetable juice at approximately four-hourly intervals. Quench your thirst with mineral water or herb tea, and make sure you drink at least 64 ounces of fluid during the day. Some suggested juices are apple, orange, grape, pineapple, grapefruit, blackcurrant, mango, cranberry, carrot, beet, and celery.

Day 2
As for Day 1, but add up to one pound of grapes and three bananas. Only eat as much as you want.

Day 3
Add raw and lightly cooked vegetables, and any other fruit to anything you want from the previous days.

Day 4
Anything you want from previous days and add wholegrain cereals, nuts, and seeds.

Day 5
As for Day 4, but add fish.

Day 6
As for Day 5, but add offal, poultry, or game.

Day 7
Return to your diet as discussed with a nutritionist.

FATS

Fats are good for you; in fact, fats are essential to our well-being. That is not the impression we would get from the media, although explanation of the concept of good and bad fats is becoming clearer.

Fat is only a problem if it exceeds more than 15 to 20 percent of our diet. Having said that, it is important that the fat that we eat is "good" fat—containing the sort that we can utilize—and has associated with it the vitamins known as the fat-soluble vitamins that cannot be found in water-based foods.

Firstly, let us understand the different terms that we so frequently read about.

- *Essential fatty acids (EFA)*—are those that humans cannot synthesize, and must therefore be obtained through the diet. Fats are made up of fatty acids, which are principally carbon, hydrogen, and oxygen molecules joined together in a variety of combinations.
- *Triglycerides (TG)*—are three fatty acids joined together, which vary in their length and carbon:hydrogen ratio. Dietary fat is mostly composed of triglycerides. These are found in both animals and vegetables.
- *Phospholipids and glycolipids*—these are triglycerides that contain phosphorus and other molecules. These are important constituents of biological membranes, blood plasma, and most

cell walls. Nervous tissue is made up of a type of phospholipid known as sphingomyelins, and it cannot function without them.

- *Cholesterol and its derivatives*—cholesterol is in fact a steroid. Are we not generally led to believe that steroids are bad? Absolutely so, if they are artificially manufactured (although certain conditions require steroid treatment), but in fact life depends upon them. Cholesterol is the starting point for hormones of the adrenal glands and sex glands, vitamin D, and the bile acids, all of which are essential to life. Cholesterol is discussed elsewhere (*see* **Cholesterol**).
- *Vitamins A, D, E, and K*—are all fat-related vitamins that do not dissolve in water, and can only be found in fats.
- *Saturated and unsaturated fats*—if a fatty acid chain has all of the carbon atoms linked together with a single electromagnetic link, it is said to be saturated. If the chain is joined by more than one bond, it is unsaturated. The fewer the links, the harder it is to break down the chains, making saturated fats more difficult to utilize as energy (because it is the breaking of the bonds that releases energy) and increasing the tendency for the body to store these poorly utilizable fats. The more saturated the fat, the easier it binds together, and a simple way to understand whether a compound is heavily saturated or not is by its solidity at room temperature. Beef, pork or lamb fat is hard, butter less so, and olive oil is a fluid. There are more saturated fats in animal proteins than in vegetables.

Fats—strong and weak bonds

SATURATED	$(CHO)_x—(CHO)_y$
UNSATURATED	$—(CHO)_x=(CHO)_z$
POLYUNSATURATED	$(CHO)_a=(CHO)_b=(CHO)_c—(CHO)_d—$

- It is important to remember that many fats are necessary and good for us, particularly those known as the omega-3 and omega-6 oils found in fish oils, eicosapentenoic acid (EPA), ,and flaxseed. Getting the point? Saturated fats are "bad," unsaturated fats are not.
- If a fatty-acid chain has many bonds, it is said to be polyunsaturated, and having more bonds is weaker as a chain, and thus more readily broken down. As a general rule, these are therefore healthier, and are recognized by remaining a liquid at room temperature, as mentioned above. Polyunsaturated fats also have the additional benefit of being cholesterol-free, and although this is not necessarily a good thing (see **Cholesterol**), as a general rule, low-cholesterol foods are liable to do us less harm.
- *Hydrogenated fats*—unfortunately, there is another twist in the tale, and this is the term *hydrogenated fats*. A hydrogenated fat is one that has had additional hydrogen ions added to it, usually by being exposed to heat and altering its natural structure. An otherwise "good for you" polyunsaturated fat may become harmful by being heated. Much to our misfortune, the food-processing industry takes healthy, polyunsaturated vegetable oils and processes them in such a way that they are exposed to high temperatures, oxygen, and light (the latter two also hydrogenate fats) and sell them to us proclaiming great health benefits.
- *Trans-fatty acids*. Lastly, we are hearing about products that are free of *trans*-fatty acids. These are altered forms of the EFAs, altered by the heat and oxygen exposure of processing. *Trans*-fatty acids cannot be used by the body, and actively interfere with the biochemistry of one of the body's protective compounds, known as prostaglandin E_1.

So where are we? We should not eat animal fats, including butter, because of its saturated status and cholesterol, but we cannot eat the vegetable oils that are provided to us because the processing of these otherwise healthy polyunsaturated oils is generally hydrogenated. Unfortunately, these are the facts.

We need to reduce the amount of fat in our diet to an absolute minimum until the "powers that be" can produce an easily available, *non-treated* polyunsaturated fat. At the moment, these are called "cold-pressed" and are available in health-food stores and some supermarkets.

If you have trouble finding fats and oils that are polyunsaturated, cold-pressed, non-hydrogenated, and low in or without *trans*-fatty acids (and you really have to have your thinking cap on when you buy your spread for your morning toast), you may choose to give up. Do not do this. Persevere. The "good stuff" *is* available, and at the end of the day, if you have small amounts even of the most-refined and dangerous compounds, your healthy body will deal with it efficiently, and extract the necessary EFAs and vitamins. Purified supplements can be used on a daily basis, and eating the occasional oily fish (such as salmon, mackerel, herring) will provide the necessary requirements. Remember that the body must have fats to survive, and bad is better than none!

Synthetic fats

Recently, there has been research into production of a fat that carries the taste and flavor associated with the food group, but does not have the capability of being stored in fat stores. The food industry is looking forward to the fortune that such a food product may confer, since it would allow everyone to enjoy their ice-cream sundaes and fried foods without worrying about weight.

Be very wary. There have been no long-term studies, and we have little idea of how the body will react to this extremely artificial substance. Like genetically engineered food (*see* **Genetically altered food**), this is a compound that should be avoided for at least the next 20 years. Then, if no adverse affects have been reported, we may be able to use it. Be very sceptical about "scientific studies," because those that show negative aspects are not likely to be published. Millions of dollars have gone into the production and assessment of this food, and the food industry is not going to give up their profits easily.

FOOD ADDITIVES

The body has developed an enzyme and biochemical system over millions of years of evolution. We are the most complex of organisms and, some would say, the most successful on the planet. This is because we learned and developed abilities over a long period of time, allowing us to deal with most things that nature threw at us. Now our bodies are compromised by an array of unnatural chemicals that are changing at an alarming rate. Our evolutionary capabilities to deal with these compounds cannot keep up, and in an attempt to defend ourselves, we are storing these additives, preservatives, insecticides, pesticides, household chemicals, and airborne pollutants, which are known in many cases to alter our genetic material and trigger diseases as serious as cancer. Wherever possible, just do not eat or use them.

FOOD ALLERGY AND INTOLERANCE

See **Allergies.**

It is important to differentiate between food allergy and food intolerance. An *allergy* is a blood response to a foreign body. A substance that is in the bloodstream that does not belong to the body will have immunoglobulins produced against it. These immunoglobulins, more commonly known as antibodies, attach to foreign matter, and make that particle more recognizable by the white cells that ingest such invaders. An *intolerance* is less well defined by the orthodox world, but holistically would be considered to be a substance to which the body responds badly in any number of ways, such as nausea and vomiting, skin rash, diarrhea, frequent urination, and any other eliminative process. I believe an intolerance to be an energetic confrontation. All cells in the body resonate at a particular frequency, and any foreign molecule whose electrons resonate in such a way as to inhibit or block the body's natural resonance is going to create an intolerance. The orthodox attitude to intolerance is discussed below.

In my opinion, food allergy and intolerance is far more prevalent than even holistic practitioners (as a general rule) consider. Symptoms of food allergy/intolerance may be mild, or may even trigger serious disorders such as diabetes and cancer.

The orthodox world divides allergy into four major components, type one being anaphylaxis and type four being delayed-allergy response.

The development of allergies/intolerance

The bloodstream should have in its flow only compounds that are made and derived by the body, or those that are absorbed through the lungs and bowel (and to some extent the skin). The latter organs filter out unwanted particles and, in the case of the digestive system, break down foods into the smallest of components, such as amino acids and peptides (small chains of amino acids), basic nutrients, small chains of carbohydrates, and fatty acids. When these reach the bloodstream, they are not considered to be viruses or bacteria, and the immune system leaves them alone. If any of these break down, or selective mechanisms are inhibited or fail, the larger molecules are absorbed, the body cannot differentiate between them and invading organisms, and sets up an allergic response. In the case of intolerance, even some small peptides may carry a resonance or vibration that is harmful to the body, but these do not set up an allergic response.

Any action or reaction that inhibits the protective or digestive mechanism can lead to a prolonged, possibly lifelong allergy or intolerance. Most commonly, bowel infections or the use of antibiotics that inhibit the body's natural flora and damage the delicate bowel membranes can lead to larger molecules being absorbed through the intestinal wall in a process that is now termed the "leaky-gut syndrome" (*see* **Leaky-gut syndrome**). Literally, the bowel inflames and loses its selectivity, causing larger molecules to be absorbed. Pollutants and inhalants such as cigarette smoke cause inflammation in the lungs, and allow larger molecules to enter the bloodstream; commonly inhaled components such as pollen and pet hair will follow, and potentially set up an allergic response. The skin is subjected to more cosmetics and chemicals than it used to be, creating more-inflammatory responses such as eczema, which in turn allows compounds into the bloodstream to trigger allergic or intolerance responses.

It is therefore important to understand that allergies and intolerances are not about the causative agent, but are reflections of our lifestyle, habits, and environmental pollutants. We should establish an idea of those foods that may be creating problems. To do this requires some form of investigation or testing, and the choices are listed in the section on allergy testing.

The terms allergy and intolerance have become somewhat synonymous in the holistic world. This is a sad reflection of the lack of education in science that many complementary medical practitioners receive, through no fault of their own. The independent colleges should pay more attention to the basics of psychology, but that is another discussion.

An intolerance is simple: a lack of capacity to endure or an oversensitivity to a compound. This is generally created by a direct chemical reaction between a food and chemicals or cells in the body, which is mediated by a chemical release from the tissues that are intolerant. This is quite a separate concept from an allergy, which is an acquired condition initiated by exposure to a compound (known as an allergen) that creates a blood-cell response to produce histamine-like chemicals or immunoglobulins (antibodies).

It is quite possible to be intolerant without being allergic, and have allergies without intolerance. An example is somebody who drinks coffee and eats wheat, and creates an acidic indigestion or an irritated skin. There may be no changes in the bloodstream or white blood cells of the tissue, and the person is therefore intolerant, but not allergic. Alternatively, the immune system may produce antibodies against a compound with no symptoms being exhibited whatsoever.

The differentiation between intolerance and allergy is only relevant if allergy testing is undertaken, because many people are surprised when allergy tests come back as negative, despite frank reactions occurring.

Applied kinesiology (muscle testing), and all

bioresonance computers and techniques are testing for intolerance. Hair samples, often tested in the alternative world by the unproven techniques of the pendulum or radionics, only show levels of compounds that have been eliminated, and therefore suggest an intolerance within the system. Blood tests are the only method of registering allergy.

FRUIT JUICE

Fruit juice is without doubt one of the best and healthiest products available to human beings. Fruits are nature's vitamin suppliers, eaten by most herbivores in preference to any other foods. Each fruit contains a variety of vitamins, nutrients, minerals, and even proteins, which make it a vital part of the food chain. In juiced form, they are easily available, not hard to digest, and easy to transfer across the bowel membrane.

The above statement applies to fresh fruit or fresh fruit juices. Read on . . .

Juices that are prepared, processed, packaged, and provided to us through the stores are at best—from a nutritional point of view—worthless, and at worst, harmful. Without many exceptions, they have added sugar. Even those that state "no added sugar" may have up to six teaspoonfuls of refined glucose added. I am not sure of the political mechanics, but it is something like this. The food manufacturers (a very powerful industry) claim that the manufacturing process removes sugar that would otherwise be present. Adding sugar back in (albeit, not exactly the same sort that is taken out) is merely replacing the fruit's own store. There is, therefore, no added sugar. The governments believe this, and we and our children are subjected to refined, artificial-sugar additives in these "natural" fruit juices.

To conform to most hygiene standards, fruits from which juices are made are generally put into contact with some form of preservative. The fruits themselves are mass produced, and most often, artificially chemically encouraged to grow larger (often at the expense of flavor). Many chemicals are added to remove the unpleasant flavor of the skin and seeds that are all pulverized in the juice-making process. One of these chemicals is formaldehyde, a chemical used for preserving bodies!

Many vitamins are denatured or altered through the process, especially vitamin C, which alters when exposed to air. The addition of artificial vitamin C at a later stage is the food industry's answer, but this is not absorbed as well as orange's original vitamin C, because it imbalances the proportion of bioflavonoids that are needed to help absorption.

In conclusion, freshy extracted and immediately drunk fruit juice is one of the best forms of nutrition, as opposed to the easily available artificial fruit juices that are sold to us in the belief that they are of benefit. At best, our body will deal with the chemical poisoning and high-sugar content that we take in, and at worst it will not. There is a dramatic increase in the West of diabetes, especially in the age group under five years, and I suspect that the increase in white sugar through fruit juices is a primary factor in this finding.

GENETICALLY ALTERED FOOD

Over the last decade, the enormously powerful food industry and its political lobbyists have been researching, producing, and promoting genetically altered food. Scientists have methods of altering the genes in the nucleus of the cells of the foods that we eat. This provides the foods with abilities such as faster growth, yeast and fungus resistance, and even insect repellence. Lauded as the first step towards eliminating worldwide food shortage (a farce, as there is plenty of food; it is just not distributed as it should be, because of the poor profits involved), the technique is, in principle, a good idea. The problem lies in the inability of the scientific world to assure us that the techniques (chemical and radiation) used to alter the food genes will not carry on their effect within the human body. There is also the fear that the genetically altered genes may, in some way, incorporate themselves into our own cells and alter the function. A manmade (super-bionic) tomato or soya gene may instruct a liver cell to produce chemicals that the plant cell would make.

RECOMMENDATION

- *Until we have had 10 or possibly 15 years of well-controlled studies on animals and volunteer human populations, avoid genetically altered foods.*

GLUTEN AND GLIADIN (GRAIN PROTEINS)

These two proteins are found predominantly in wheat, but also in varying amounts in other grains. They are accepted as the main cause of allergic, intolerant, or inflammatory responses in the human being, often caused by introducing wheat too early in an infant's life, the large quantity of grain that is eaten, or the diminished ability in the human gut to break down these complex protein molecules.

Gluten sensitivity manifests in a condition known as Celiac disease (*see* **Celiac disease**), and it is probable that other proteins such as gliadin may cause similar problems, although a specific disease process has yet to be attributed to them.

MILK

Opinion is divided as to whether milk is of great benefit—only to calves, or a wonderful multi-faceted food?

The proteins casein, lactalbumin, and lactoglobulin (the milk proteins) are known to be the cause of allergies, and are not easily broken down by the human gut. If a protein is not well broken down, it can be absorbed in its entirety, and the body will recognize it as a potential virus or bacteria, and produce an antibody response. If the partially broken-down protein resembles the proteins within our body, then this immune-system response may well attack our cells.

Milk sugar (lactose) is not well tolerated by many races. 90 percent of Filipinos, 50 percent of Indians, and approximately 8 percent of the U.S.A. and the U.K. populations do not have the necessary enzyme to break it down. To these people, this makes the sugar useless as an energy source, and encourages fluids to stay in the bowel, leading to dehydration.

Homogenization, a process to "sterilize" milk to ensure safe consumption, leads to the production of a chemical called xanthine oxidase, which destroys a compound in the blood called plasmogen, which in turn leads to the loss of a protective factor in the arterial walls. This, in turn, encourages atheroma.

Milk is often considered to be a major source of calcium, and indeed the calcium content of milk is very high. Several studies, however, show that the calcium in milk is not easily absorbed into the bloodsteam, and does not increase calcium levels as profoundly as we would assume (*see* **Calcium**).

Milk has been related to a myriad of symptoms and conditions, including problems associated with mucus, such as respiratory infections, ear, nose, and throat problems, sinus congestion, asthma, colitis, acne and eczema, arthritis, heartburn, and ulcers, to name but a few.

Milk has found its way into our diet, and a majority of us enjoy a breakfast cereal (despite its acid-forming tendencies, especially when we liberally add refined sugar). It is an integral part of breakfast, and alternatives are hard to find: goat's and sheep's milk have a distinctive taste that may not be acceptable; soya has a grainy texture; and fruit juices on cereals simply do not work for those of us who are accustomed to cow's milk. It is worth, however, trying to prepare a "milk" from a variety of nuts and seeds by following the instructions below:

- Try almonds, cashews, hazelnuts, sesame, pumpkin, or sunflower seeds.
- Soak overnight in enough water to cover the seeds by at least half an inch.
- The next morning, pour the soaked seeds and water into a blender and pulverize. (Discard the overnight water that the almonds have been in,

as the taste is not pleasant.) If the solution is too thick, add more water.

- If the flavor is not to your taste, add a spoonful of honey or blend in raisins earlier on in the preparation.

I do not think that milk is a good food. If it does not cause obvious symptoms, then there is probably no harm in drinking it, but organic milk (to avoid homogenization) is a prerequisite for anybody whose family has any cardiovascular disease. I do not recommend it as a food for young children, preferring—despite recent scares—formula preparations and weaning onto a wholesome diet.

NITRATES

Of all additives and preservatives, one of the most prominent of those found in our food are the nitrates. They are used to color and preserve foods, especially meats. It has been found that these destabilize the body's oxygen supply, with potentially fatal results if eaten in sufficient quantities.

Blackouts are uncommon, but can occur because of a drop in blood pressure due to nitrate ingestion. As usual, the orthodox world has set a safety level of 200ppm in any food, and thereby suggest that taking in 190ppm is safe, but 201ppm is not. There is, as always, a gray area, and some people are more sensitive than others. Beware, and avoid any foods containing nitrates.

SALT

Salt is made up of two elements: sodium and chlorine. It is the sodium component that is particularly relevant, because this small molecule controls a multitude of biochemical processes, but principally maintains the bloodstream and tissue-fluid integrity.

Dehydration of the body, blood pressure, and permeability of nearly every cell in the body is dependent on sodium, and fortunately, sodium is found in nearly everything we eat. The problems arise with *excess* salt. Salt is essential, and must never be considered toxic unless taken over and above the necessary requirement.

The vital essence of sodium has encouraged our evolutionary development to make the taste of salt a great pleasure and even a comfort. Our mind–body connection knows that salt is essential, and therefore likes to take it in and encourages this by making it taste nice.

Unfortunately, not only does our mind–body connection know this, but so does the food industry. The outcome is an abundance of salt in everything that is manufactured for mass production and sale. Go for a browse through a supermarket alley and find me a product that does not have salt added, and you will bring me a natural food or one that sells poorly.

RECOMMENDATIONS

- *Avoid adding extra salt to meals, and limit any addition to cooking. It may take up to two weeks, but a diet with no salt added will become tasteful after the excess has been removed.*
- *Look closely at any bought product and reduce the intake of naturally salty foods, such as sea fish.*

SOYA

There is a lot written and discussed concerning soya, the bean originally grown in the East. Commonly found in its natural form—soya sauce, tofu, and soya milk—it contains protease inhibitors, isoflavins, and other chemicals, all or any of which may act as an anticancer and anti-atheroma compound.

Soya has been the main vegetable crop to be experimented with using gene-altering or genetic-tampering techniques. Ensure that any products containing soya come from a natural, organic source and do not contain genetically altered substance (*see* **Genetically altered foods**).

Soya products contain chemicals called phytoestrogens. These chemicals are known to inhibit an enzyme that converts not-so-active, estrogen-like compounds into the more-potent estradiol. These chemicals also occupy receptor sites on cells. Both of these reactions stop estrogen from acting and exhibiting its effects.

The Japanese and Chinese have used soya in large quantities as part of their normal diet, and show no detrimental estrogen effects. In fact, soya may be responsible for the lowered levels of breast cancer in the Japanese race. It is suggested that some property of soya combines with estrogen receptors and prevents estrogen from affecting the growth rate of particular estrogen-sensitive cancer cells. The paradox occurs because we use soya for its estrogen-like effect in menopause, but use it as an estrogen blocker in cancer.

Until clearer evidence is available as to whether or not soya works as a weak estrogen, an estrogen blocker, or both, enjoy it as a food, but do not consume it in excessive doses unless you are an estrogen-sensitive cancer risk.

It may be wise not to use high quantities of soya products in infants and children, following studies in animals in New Zealand around 1994. There have been no studies performed on human beings, and therefore there are no known risks, only assumptions. It is worth noting that the levels of estrogens that a fetus is subjected to *in utero* are probably much higher than any level caused by soya-food products.

Soya is a valuable protein source and essential in vegan diets. It is always worthwhile spending time with a nutritionist if any particular diet format is to be used where a balance may be compromised.

SUGAR

Sugar is a carbohydrate (*see* **Carbohydrates**). In its natural form, it is enjoyable to taste, and a swift and excellent source of energy. Sugar, whether in the form of glucose or fructose (fruit sugar), or a variety of combinations, is usually found in nature in association with a variety of other nutrients, and is bound up with larger molecules. This means that the body, at the same time as absorbing sugar, is also absorbing useful building blocks, and does not absorb the sugars too quickly because a considerable amount of digestion is necessary to break down the complexes to get at the sugar molecules.

All of this is lost with refined sugar. The complexes are already broken down, so the glucose is absorbed rapidly. This creates a fast-insulin response, which causes sugar levels to be stored as fat more swiftly, and blood-sugar levels to drop, thereby providing only short bursts of energy. All the nutrients are stripped so the body gets a sudden surge in energy, but no building blocks are necessarily there to do the building. Refined sugar is much sweeter than natural sugar, and the taste buds accommodate rapidly, taking away the pleasure of the sweetness of, say, a carrot or an apple. Very swiftly do we "hook" ourselves—and especially our children—to non-nutritious sweetness, much against the preferences of nature. Sugar is not bad for you. In fact, it is extremely good, but not if refined.

The mechanism of insulin production leads to states of hypoglycemia, with its myriad symptoms: fatigue, depression, irritability, muscle weakness, shakiness, headaches, and even asthma. Diabetes is encouraged, arteriosclerosis is propagated, and blood pressure is elevated. Sugar requires vitamins and minerals to be utilized, and high doses of white sugar keep the metabolism going but, without a nutrient supply, deficiencies will arise. Worst of all, perhaps, refined sugar makes us fat, along with all of the social and health implications that this brings. Believe me, I have only scratched the surface of the metabolic and health dangers of refined sugars. (*See* **Hypoglycemia, Diabetes,** and **Weight loss.**)

SPICY FOODS

Like all food groups, spicy foods have their place. They are generally eaten in hot climates where they raise the body temperature, making the external heat comparatively less intense.

Those in cooler climates who enjoy spicy foods should eat them only in moderation, and preferably with a cooling (raw or lightly steamed) food to compensate. Excess heat in the system, according to Eastern philosophies, will arise

VITAMINS—Dosage and Toxicity

Vitamin	Maximum permissible dosage	Toxic signs and symptoms
Vitamin A	Infants 10,000iu Adults 50,000iu	Appetite loss, headache, blurred vision, unusual bleeding, dry, cracked skin, loss of hair, muscular stiffness, and pain
Vitamin B group	*See* individual compounds below	
Niacin (vitamin B_3)	100mg	Flushing, headaches, cramps, nausea, vomiting and burning or itching skin
Niacinamide	100mg	As above
Pantothenic acid (vitamin B_5)	Not tested	Occasional diarrhea
Pyridoxine (vitamin B_6)	200mg*	Numbness, tingling and other sensory nerve effects
Riboflavin (vitamin B_2)	No toxic effects	
Thiamine (vitamin B_1)	No toxic effects	
Vitamin B_{12}	No toxic effects	
Beta-carotene	No toxicity recorded up to 250mg per day	
Biotin	No toxic effects reported	
Vitamin C	10g per day, except under supervision	Nausea, diarrhea, flatulence
Vitamin D	1,000iu/kg of body weight	Nausea, vomiting, appetite loss, diarrhea, headache, excessive urination, constipation, pallor
Vitamin E	800iu	Severe weakness and fatigue, may worsen hypertension
Folic acid	15mg	Abdominal distension, appetite loss, nausea and vivid dreams
Vitamin K		No side effects if given orally

**There is controversy about this dosage and legal guidelines may state that 10mg or more is toxic. This continues to be a contentious issue.*

from excessively spiced foods, and there are problems associated with inflammation. (*See* **Yin and Yang foods.**)

VITAMINS

Vitamins are a group of organic compounds that are present in variable, minute quantities in natural foods, and are required for normal growth and maintenance of life. As a rule, the human is unable to synthesize these compounds, thus encouraging the term "vital" to be part of the name. Vitamins are generally needed only in small amounts, and have no calorific value, therefore they do not furnish energy, but are essential for transformation of nutrition into energy and the regulation of most—if not all—biochemical processes in the body.

It is not necessary for the individual to have much of an understanding of vitamins, despite what the popular press and complementary medical journals might suggest. A balanced diet containing five portions of fruit or vegetables, not overcooked, in association with unrefined carbohydrates, protein, and a small amount of the right sort of fats, will not lead people into deficiencies. The body is remarkably good at absorbing what it needs from the most unlikely sources, and if food is eaten by instinct, most vitamins will be taken in as required.

For that reason, no more is mentioned in this section on this vast and fascinating subject. Every condition that would benefit from vitamin supplementation will have recommended dosages or guidelines within the text of this book. The recommendations are based on "natural" products that, sadly, tend to separate individual supplements from their coenzymes and other compounds that help their absorption. I therefore strongly recommend the use of natural-food-state vitamins. These are available, and are made by extracting all the nutrients from a natural source and not separating them.

Vitamin toxicity

As more knowledge filters through to practitioners of complementary medicine concerning the beneficial effects of high-dose vitamin therapy, it is necessary for practitioners and individuals to be aware of possible side effects or toxicity.

Principally, it is difficult to overdose on a vitamin, especially if it is a natural-food-state vitamin as mentioned above. I have listed here the maximum permissible amounts that can be taken on a daily basis, and some of the signs and symptoms to watch out for if taking vitamin supplements.

WATER

The importance of water is discussed in the section on dehydration (*see* **Dehydration**, because it is the most important part of this book).

The quality of the water that we take in is of extreme importance to our health. It is very rare that natural sources of water are available, and most Western societies are now drinking water that may have been recycled up to seven times. Water should arrive from the skies to fill our lakes and reservoirs in a pure state, but of course air pollution is altering that factor. Atomic fallout is creating radioactive clouds and earth, through which the rain must pass. Pesticides, insecticides, and other agrochemicals are filling our soil and rivers, and finding their way into the food chain. The water companies (under governmental regulations) in many parts of the Western world are treating our water with chemicals, traces of which find their way into our nervous systems. The less-developed countries have water contaminated by feces because of a lack of recycling plants, and overpopulation is making matters worse.

Sounds gloomy, does it not? We have to rely upon the strength of our body's constitution and on our immune system to deal with the toxins that we inevitably take in. Bottled water has its critics, but is probably safer than most tap water. Human cells are found in occasional samples, but I dare say that these would be found in tap water too. One arguable criticism of bottled water is its mineral content. While the body does need minerals, the absorption of these is energy-consuming, and a water that actually tastes salty is probably best avoided. All bottles are now labeled, and anything with a sodium content over 5mg/l should be replaced with one with less.

Filtration systems that can be fitted under the kitchen sink certainly remove a lot of the contaminants, and none more so than the reverse-osmosis filters that are beginning to come into circulation. These are, at the time of writing, expensive, but are worth it for those who can afford them. The more we buy, the more will be produced, and the more the price will come down and be affordable by the masses.

Water has extremely special properties that are not fully explained by physics, and it is one of the prominent features and categories in Eastern philosophies of medicine. Homeopathy will probably be found to have its "unscientific" effects and success based on the unique properties of the electrons within the water molecules.

Drink plenty, and drink it pure.

YOGURT BACTERIA—*see* **Acidophilus.**

Chapter 8

Diagnostic Techniques

Chapter 8

Diagnostic Techniques

If there is one area of modern medicine that has to be lauded, it is the advance in diagnostic investigation and technique. Whether it is through indirect means, such as a blood test, or direct visualization through ultrasound or endoscopy, the ability of today's doctors to diagnose a problem is incomparable with the options available even only 50 years ago. Computers are creating an ever-more-rapid advance on our diagnostic capabilities.

Unfortunately, in this technological rush, much bedside manner and clinical diagnostic abilities seem to be diminishing. It is quite feasible for a doctor to make accurate diagnoses without touching the patient, and with the advent of television-screen consultations, the doctors need not even be in the same country.

From an orthodox point of view, this may not be a problem, because diagnosis is generally superficial, with most concern being paid to the immediate cause of a symptom rather than any long-term, underlying cause of an illness. The holistic view has to be that modern diagnostic techniques need to be integrated with clinical examination, experience, intuition, and "sixth sense." This abstract concept is probably closely linked with an individual's healing ability. There is no lack of evidence that healing exists, and even the most interventional surgeons may have part of their success manifested by their innate (but not consciously accepted) healing ability.

A holistic physician will take a patient through four stages of examination:

- observation
- listening
- touching
- investigating

There should be no difference, whether you are visiting an acupuncturist or a yoga teacher. These four stages should be considered to the best of the practitioner's ability.

Some aspects of a diagnostic consultation may be awkward for both the practitioner and the patient. Complementary medical practitioners integrate observation far more into the diagnosis than orthodox physicians, and it is not unusual to find the consulting room of an osteopath or chiropractor without a screen behind which a patient may undress. The practitioner may sit and watch, which can be quite embarrassing and unnerving for a patient. A sensitive therapist will explain the reasons for doing so, but as many do not, I have done so in the sections below.

Questions will be asked, the answers to which may not even be known to your spouse or best friend, and the concept of even discussing these matters may be at least embarrassing and at most shocking. The relevance of some questions will defeat immediate logic, but a practitioner with a knowledge of mind–body energy and medicine will need to know your state of mind, even if you only have a fungal infection of your toenail. Questions about gynecological matters may be asked when the complaint is about depression. There is generally a reason for these connections, even if they are not apparent.

An examination should be complete. Every part of the body is linked directly or indirectly with every other part, and any practitioner using meridian or Hara diagnoses (*see* **Hara diagnoses**) will examine the abdomen, back, and limbs, even if the problem is associated with the nostril. Intimate examination is generally not required unless the problem is associated with that area. Traditional Chinese practitioners, especially those of a particular school, may not allow any conversation from the patient. The little ivory statuettes often found as ornaments here in the West were originally designed for the patient to point to the part that hurts or is afflicted. The practitioner would, from tongue and pulse diagnosis only, make a full diagnosis and offer treatment. This too may be done in silence, simply writing out the script and handing it to the patient, who takes it to an assistant. This attitude is not accepted by the Western patient, and with so much media coverage of alternative medicine, individuals are quite rightly asking questions, and demanding to know the basis of the suggested treatment.

RECOMMENDATIONS

- *Do not hesitate to ask a practitioner why they are watching, asking, or examining any part of your mind–body space. No practitioner should object, although some may prefer silence.*
- *If you do not "click" with your practitioner, either discuss your difficulties or change your practitioner. Healing is far more likely to take place in the hands of someone you like and trust.*
- *Do not be turned off by the thought of examination and investigation. Burying your head in the sand (the ostrich syndrome!) may delay the diagnosis of an underlying condition, and hinder the choice of a correct treatment program.*
- *Leave your inhibitions at home. Discuss your condition fully and frankly, and answer any questions, however odd or irrelevant they may seem.*

OBSERVATION

All healthcare providers will start their examination as soon as you enter the consulting room or they meet you in the waiting room. They will be watching the way you walk or how you sit, establishing any obvious structural irregularity. Attention will be paid to the quality of the hair, skin, and eyes, and even to the choice of the color of clothes. Sallow or pale complexion, jaundiced eyes, and the way that an individual may walk into a consultation, perhaps with a limp, are examples of how an initial observation will guide the practitioner to diagnoses. A psychological case of depression or anxiety may be reflected in somebody choosing to wear black, and even the type of clothes may be covering up anorexia or obesity.

Aura reading

The aura is a fuzz around the body. Anybody can be taught to read an aura. There is nothing mystical or magical about this. There is a skill in associating what is seen with underlying illness, but this too is taught and learned through experience.

Most of us are subconsciously aware of an aura, and this manifests in several ways. We have all walked into a room and instantly "clicked" with someone as our auras match. Auras have a sense of a color (and some aura readers can see this), which is why some people suit certain colors. We all have an awareness, especially of those close to us, if something is not right with an individual. It is not just about their lack of a smile or a glint in the eye, it is a feeling or sensation that we cannot explain. Instinct would be a suitable label. While the aura is generally seen within a few inches of the body, its ability to transmit may have no boundaries. An instant attraction across a room is liable to be the joining or meeting of two sympathetic wavelengths, and the term "telepathy" may also be part of the aura. Have we not all experienced an absolute certainty of the telephone being about to ring, only to find that your best friend calls that instant.

The aura is yet to be measured to the satisfaction of the orthodox scientific world. As it is part of the vital force, I doubt if we will be able to measure this field of energy in the near future. Kirlian photography is the process of taking pictures of energy radiating in spikes from the surface of the body. Unlike highly sophisticated orthodox-medical technology, which can measure heat, the Kirlian photograph can sense not only temperature, but also other electromagnetic fields. This is the closest, I believe, that we may get to converting the energy of the aura into a two- or three-dimensional picture.

Those who read auras are capable of seeing colors, and use this to establish general health, or they compare the aura to the superficial points known as meridians or energy channels that travel through the body.

A "black" area is often seen above the head in depression because energy (often discussed as "white light") fails to pass through the chakra and reach the top of the body. If an aura is diminished along a meridian, a dip will be noticed.

Aura reading is a useful tool when considered with other diagnostic techniques, but should not be an acceptable form of diagnosis on its own.

Learning to read the aura

The first step is to be able to visualize it. Take a cardboard box and line it with a black material. Place the box on a table with a candle behind it, and close the room off from external light as much as possible. Training should start at night.

Place your hand in the box, and it should appear to have a small fuzz around it. This may only be half an inch or so in width, and may in fact blend in between the digits. If nothing can be seen, light another candle and continue to brighten the room from behind the box until this fuzz is noticed. Try to focus on the energy layer and appreciate the amount of defocusing that is necessary. When you feel confident, start examining other parts of the body using the same principle of keeping the candle light shielded from the area examined.

Next, ask a friend or relative if you can examine their hand, and after a short while you will be able to focus the eyes immediately on an aura by meeting somebody in a darkened room. Eventually, with practice, auras can be seen in any light, although in a darkened room will always be easier.

You may see or sense a color in an aura, and this color will generally reflect the individual's health. If they are well, then this is probably the color of their aura. If they are not, then the color may change as they improve (or get worse). There is no color that is healthier or unhealthier, but as a general rule, brightness reflects well-being. There is some correlation with the colors green and yellow producing a soothing effect on the brain (as established through electrical brain tests), but whether this means that a yellow/green aura is a healthy one, I cannot comment.

To use this technique in a diagnostic manner requires an individual practitioner to correlate the aura with energy meridians or channels, and also to have a sound anatomical knowledge.

The eyes

The color of the sclera (the whites of the eyes) and the general sparkle can give both orthodox and instinctive clues. Do not be turned off or embarrassed by a practitioner who seems to be staring intently at your eyes. *See* **Iridology** for a discussion of the iris.

Medical practitioners will examine the back of the eye, known as the fundus, with an ophthalmoscope. Blood vessels are clearly visible at the back of the eye, and give the observer information on the patency (openness) of vessels in general. High blood pressure causes the arterial wall to thicken, and this shows up under an ophthalmoscope as a "railway track" appearance.

The tongue

'Show me your tongue" is a popular phrase among TV doctors, and is occasionally muttered by orthodox practitioners. The tongue's color, moisture, and the amount of fur may convey a little knowledge to a Western-trained physician, who will simply use this to confirm a previously considered diagnosis.

Ayurvedic, Chinese, and Tibetan practitioners will all pay marked attention to the tongue, and the table (p. 549) gives some examples of the use of tongue observation for many different conditions. In Ayurveda, the main organs of the body are actually mapped out on the tongue, and patches may represent an energy lack or excess within an organ or system.

Tongue Diagnosis

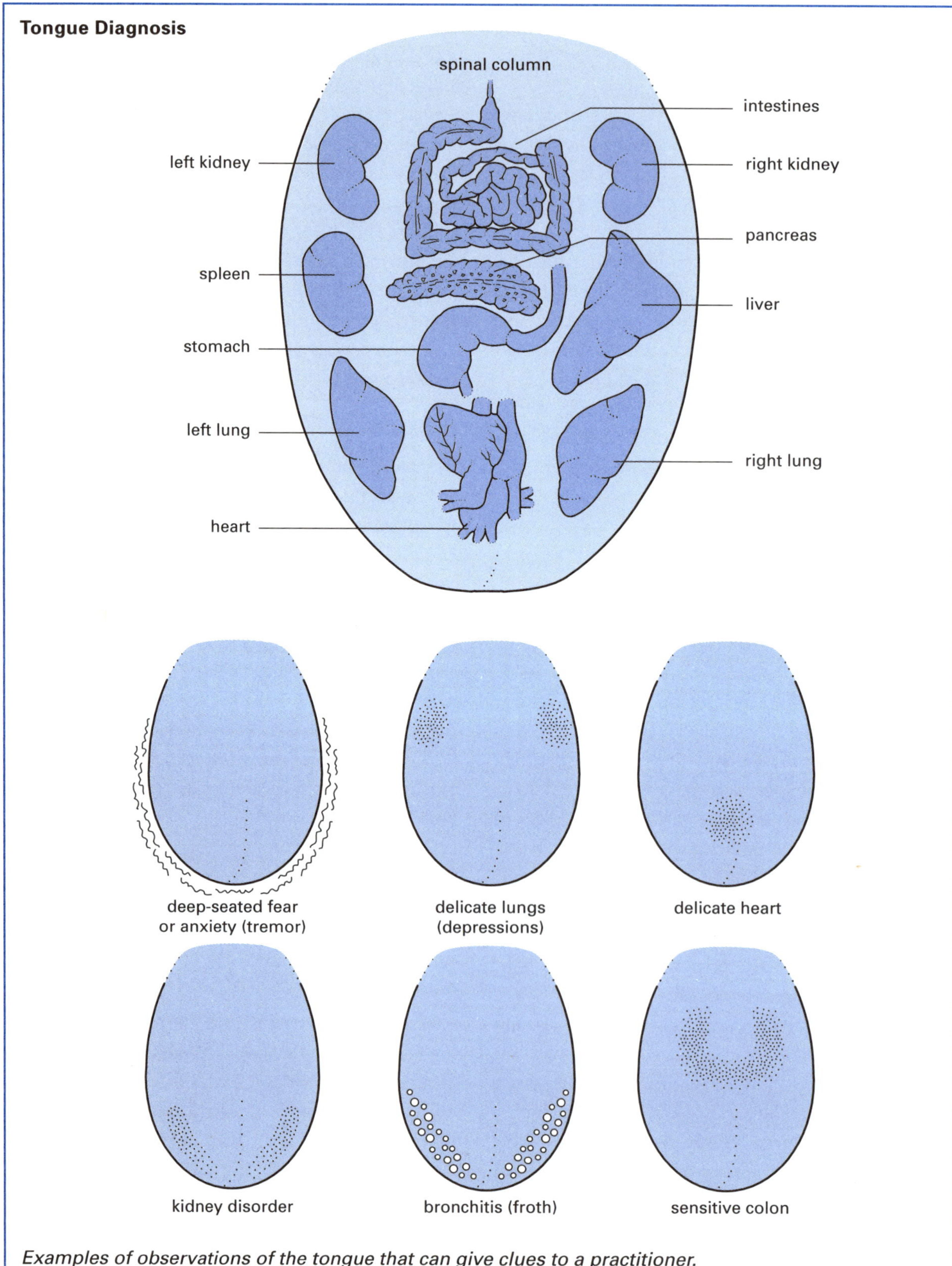

Examples of observations of the tongue that can give clues to a practitioner.

Clinical Examination of the Tongue

Color

Very red	Imminent or present fever
Red and dry	Inflammation of the brain and/or of its membranes, inflammation of stomach, intestines, or organs within the chest
Red, glossy	Excess heat
Pale	General exhaustion and anemia (loss of vital fluids)
Bluish	Poor circulation, anemia, scurvy, heavy-metal poisoning (especially mercury)
Yellow	Gallbladder and liver afflictions
Dark Brown	Oral bleeding
Black	Liver/spleen weakness, dysentery and serious viral infections, abscesses

Humidity

Moist or excessively damp	Exhaustion
Dry	Excessive heat and psychological disturbances, especially anxiety, but also depression

Temperature

Hot	Excess heat
Cold	Lacking heat, cancer
Cold + fever	Impending death

Coating

Often normal	After sleep, tobacco, and tea/coffee
On the tip	Phthisis
One-sided	Unilateral disease, liver, spleen
Patchy or map	Stomach affliction
Thick, white	Upper-respiratory tract, stomach
Leathery	Enteritis, hepatitis, tonsillitis

Form and size

Small	Cachectic diseases
Sudden shrinkage	Inflammatory disease of lungs or liver, formation of abscesses, general exhaustion
Gradual diminution	Obstinate disease, cranial problems
Broad	Calcium/vitamin D deficiency, lymphatic or abdominal afflictions
Narrow, pointed	Internal inflammations
Thick, swollen	Calcium/vitamin D deficiency, lung complaints, gastritis, catarrhal problems, mercury poisoning

Consistency

Hard	Congestion, inflammation in upper torso
Soft	Catarrhal or chronic mucus afflictions, gastric problems, mercury poisoning

Cracks and fissures
(Usually normal, but may indicate swelling)

Dry and bleeding	Severe illness
Down the middle	Back or spinal problems

Movement

Lack of, or trembling	Central nervous system problem, high fever, septicemia, motor-neurone disease (MND)
Uncontrolled	Normal
On extension	Points to side of central nervous system lesions

Other areas of examination

The Eastern philosophies will pay attention to most parts of the body in their observation of a patient. Ayurvedic and Tibetan physicians can glean a lot of information from the face. Examples are: dark circles under the eyes—deficient kidney Qi; puffiness—kidney/spleen; uneven features—long-term Yin/Yang imbalance.

The hands tell many stories. The color of the nailbeds, ridging, or discoloration of the nails themselves, the dryness or moisture and the muscularity of the hands, give many clues. The feet are equally informative.

The structure of the back, and the balance of the shoulders and the pelvis, are all important clues to the possible underlying cause of disease.

RECOMMENDATIONS

- *When visiting a practitioner, avoid wearing make-up or nail varnish, and select clothes that you would normally wear. Do not try to appear to be what you think a physician would expect, but when you enter the consulting room be your normal self.*
- *While basic cleanliness and hygiene must not be shirked, do not apply deodorants or strong-smelling cologne or aftershave. The smell of an individual can be demonstrative of any underlying illness, and part of observation is body odour.*

LISTENING

Orthodox doctors are taught that 90 percent of diagnoses are concluded from the history of the condition and the story the patient tells. Eastern philosophies, as I mentioned with regard to experienced Chinese physicians who only take the pulses, often pay little heed to the patient's complaint, and concentrate on the signs and diagnostic techniques through observation and palpation (touching).

It will come as no surprise to find that I think a mix and balance of the two is the answer. There is no doubt that listening to a story will lead to an understanding of the condition, especially of its origins, provided that the right questions are asked. It is important not to assume that an illness originated from when the patient first started to feel symptoms. The onset of a headache may be because of drinking the night before. The symptoms of cancer or diabetes may only become apparent at the last stage of the disease.

I feel that it is also important for a patient to express his/her concerns, and the way that this is expressed should give the practitioner clues as to how to respond and answer a patient's concerns. A tearful report should not be answered by a brusque response. A patient who is clearly a matter-of-fact type who gives clear and concise symptoms probably does not want to hear about the ethereal imbalances within his/her Qi. A symptom report is not just about the symptoms, but also about assessing the needs of the individual.

From the patient's point of view, therefore, it is important to present the problem in his/her own way and not as the patient would expect the practitioner to want it. Try not to be an "Oh, and another thing . . ." patient. A holistic physician is interested in the "whole," and it is important for all the symptoms to be made available, however irrelevant they may seem to the individual. A good practitioner should elicit all the information needed, but sometimes serious symptoms are not owned up to by the patient, and may be so removed from the reason for the consultation that a practitioner may not ask. An example is a patient of mine who sat with me for 40 minutes while we discussed all the possible underlying causes for her insomnia. As we were parting company I heard the dreaded comment, "Oh, another thing, doctor, I have been passing blood whenever I have gone to the toilet for the last three weeks." Needless to say, I worked late that day.

Use of instruments

The stethoscope is a prerequisite for the archetypal physician to wear around the shoulders. In fact, most doctors will tell you that the stethoscope is of limited use in diagnosis, except for a cardiologist. Very few treatment protocols change because of the findings from a stethoscope examination. A physician can tell whether a lung is well-congested or a bowel is blocked by listening directly with the ear. The stethoscope makes things easier or confirms diagnosis. Modern machines can allow us to hear and monitor heartbeats within a fetus, and can certainly be beneficial in obstetrics.

RECOMMENDATIONS

- *If you do not think that your practitioner is listening to or hearing your complaints or symptoms, then make mention of this and be satisfied with the explanation, or change your practitioner.*
- *Make a list of complaints, because even the smallest factor may make an enormous difference in the ability to diagnose or prescribe. This is particularly the case in homeopathy.*
- *A copy of your list handed to the practitioner on entering the consulting room may make things easier for you both.*

TOUCHING

A lot can be gleaned from physical examination. The orthodox world uses the term "palpation" for the pushing and poking that goes on over the abdomen, and a doctor will tap around the chest and abdomen to test for the amount of air contained. This is called percussion. Congestion in the lungs will sound like a dull thud, whereas excess air in the bowel will sound much like a drum. Stretching joints, and pushing on painful areas in the musculature and skeleton of the body, will tell a physician a lot about injury and inflammation. All of this is a necessity and, while mildly invasive, should be allowed regardless of how remote the examination may be from the area of discomfort. Examination of the lower back and upper thigh is essential for a pain in the foot, for example, and is very important in making a firm diagnosis. The neck may be the reason for cramping in the calves. This is known as referred pain.

Eastern-trained physicians will utilize all these Western approaches, but then have a few tricks of their own. Observation by physicians over thousands of years has suggested that different parts of the body reflect energy flow through the system as a whole. Acupuncturists plant their needles in the points through these meridians or energy channels, and Shiatsu practitioners and reflexologists apply pressure to alter the flow of energy. Shiatsu practitioners study the hara; reflexologists study the reflex points in the feet and hands; and applied kinesiologists will test muscle groups to monitor their strength or weakness, which varies depending on the compound that the body is in contact with.

Hara diagnosis

The Japanese have developed their art of healing from a clear and distinct belief in energy flow through the system. Their practitioners have noted and taught for thousands of years the ability to diagnose by the excess (Jitsu) or deficiency (Kyo) of various systems or organs in the body. Each organ or system is represented by a position on the abdomen or back, and is described in the diagrams below. Gentle application of pressure will either be resisted (Jitsu), or allow the practitioner to push in with very little resistance (Kyo), and this represents the energy within the organ. Specific abdominal pains may or may not be related to the energy area, and muscles on the back that are pulled may have nothing to do with the system or organ, either. A practitioner who uses this together with pulse technique, tongue diagnosis, and such like can pick up the subtle differences that will tell whether the deficiency has been longstanding or is acute. As a general rule, the pulses may change rapidly, but Hara changes are slower. This may account for why a Shiatsu

Hara diagnosis

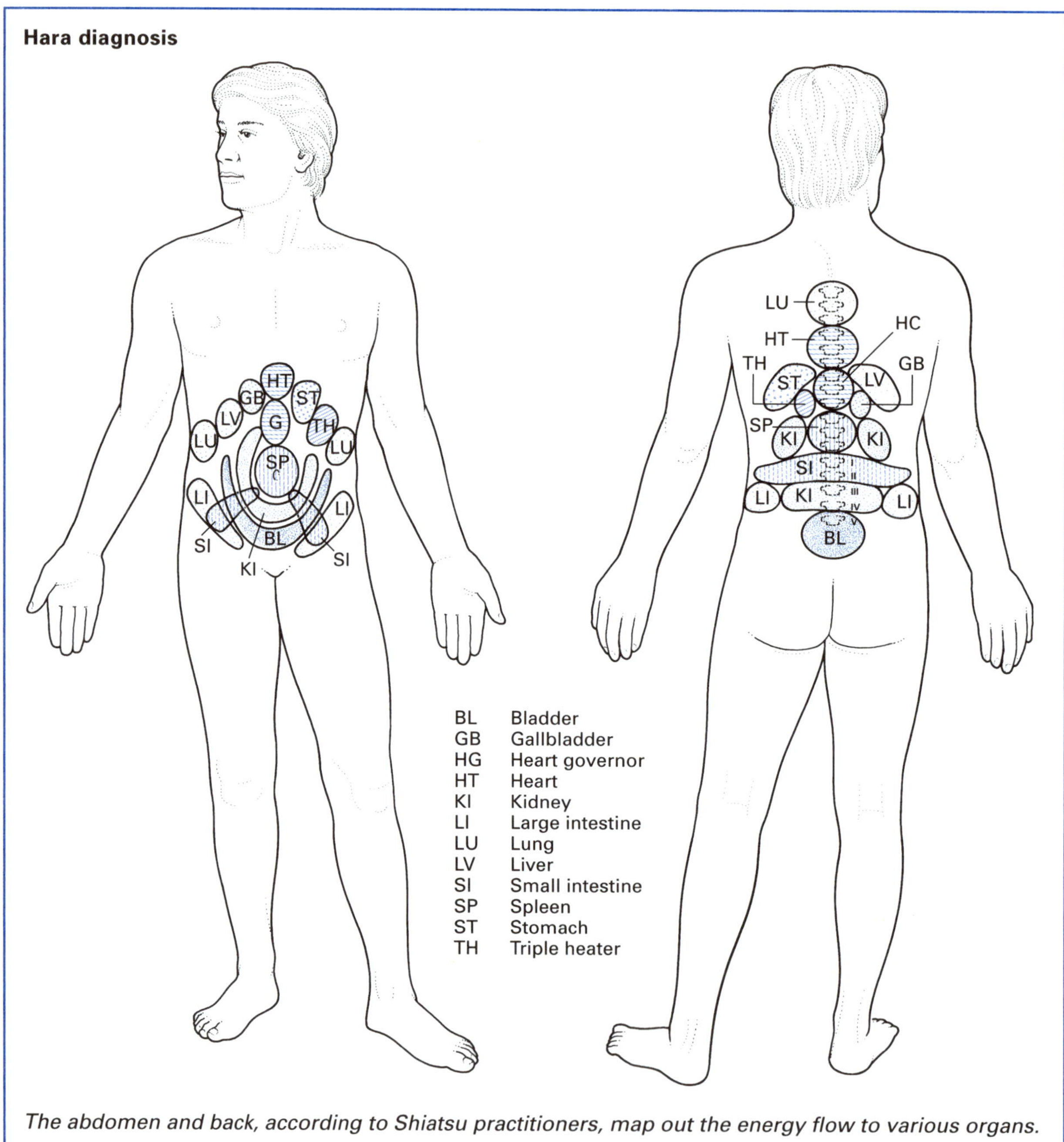

The abdomen and back, according to Shiatsu practitioners, map out the energy flow to various organs.

practitioner may pick up one set of strengths or weaknesses, whereas a pulse-taker will pick up another within an hour or so of examination, or even at the same time.

It is also relevant to note that pressure on a Shiatsu point or on a weakened or excessive pulse point may actually be a treatment or therapy, and therefore alters the energy flow quite markedly.

Pulse taking

The orthodox world considers the pulse in the wrist an accessible point to test for a variety of cardiac functions. We are able to tell the rate of the heart, the rhythm and (with experience) glean some idea of the arterial pressure. The feel of the artery may give clues as to the development of arteriosclerosis, but beyond this, the orthodox world goes no further.

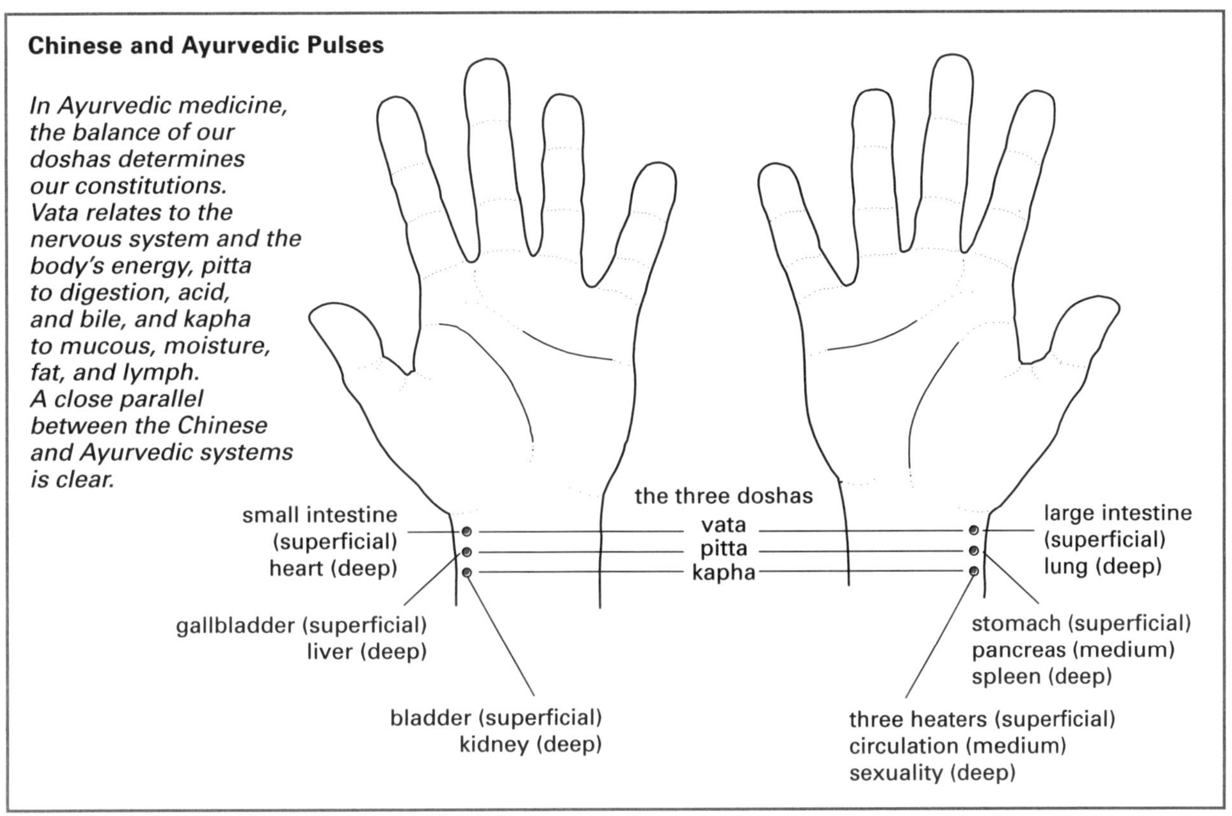

Ayurvedic, Tibetan, and Chinese philosophy believes that different systems and organs reflect their intrinsic vital force in different parts of the body. The wrist is an extremely accessible pulse point, and is the most documented of areas for practitioners to learn how to measure the energy in the system. In principle, all these disciplines share the same fundamental beliefs, but have different names and ways of describing the energies.

The Eastern philosophies believe that the body is made up of humors, organs, systems, and elements. The practitioner will be checking for pulse rate, missed beats, and "quality." An orthodox training will teach about a "full" pulse, or a pulse with a double beat, for example, and correlate this with the function or structure of the heart. An Eastern-trained practitioner might describe the pulse as full or empty, having excess fire, or damp, or as being thready.

The practitioner, using whichever technique he or she has been taught, and possibly by correlating different philosophies in one pulse-taking technique, can perform the examination with the patient sitting or lying. It is important that no part of the body is crossed (legs or ankles), and that nothing that affects the pulse rate has been ingested. This includes caffeine, alcohol, and refined sugars in particular, but also excessively spicy foods or those that may cool the body, such as an iced drink or ice cream.

While the orthodox pulse-taker is interested only in the function of the heart or the influence of chemicals on the heart rate, the Eastern practitioner will take this into account, but also consider the effects on a much-broader diagnostic scale.

The Chinese philosophies believe that the pulses reflect not only the physical, but also the emotional and psychological states. You may hear a practitioner describing a "weak spleen" or a "full liver," which will not necessarily correspond to the normal, orthodox function of that organ.

Another Eastern philosophy suggests the following psychological and spiritual correlations with the organ pulses.

ORGAN PULSES	POSITIVE ATTITUDE	NEGATIVE ATTITUDE
Lung	tolerance	disdain, prejudice, contempt
Liver	happiness	unhappiness
Gallbladder	love	rage, fury
Spleen	faith in future	anxiety about the future
Kidney	sexual security	promiscuity
Large intestine	self worth	guilt
Circulation/Sexual function/ Heart protector	renunciation of past, generosity, relaxation	jealousy, regret
Heart	love, forgiveness	anger
Stomach	contentment	disappointment
Triple Heater	happy	depression, loneliness, grief
Spleen	joy	sorrow, sadness
Bladder	peace, harmony	restlessness, impatience

Taking your own pulse

In each wrist, there is a bony prominence about two finger widths up from the wrist crease on the side of the thumb (*see* diagram below). (A) Place the third finger of the opposite hand on this lump, and move inwards slightly. A pulse should be felt. (B) Place the second and fourth fingers either side, and press as lightly as is necessary to establish a pulse in all fingers. Push down deeply with each finger in turn and then altogether, and you will be feeling the superficial and deep pulses characteristic of Chinese pulse-taking.

Taking Your Pulse

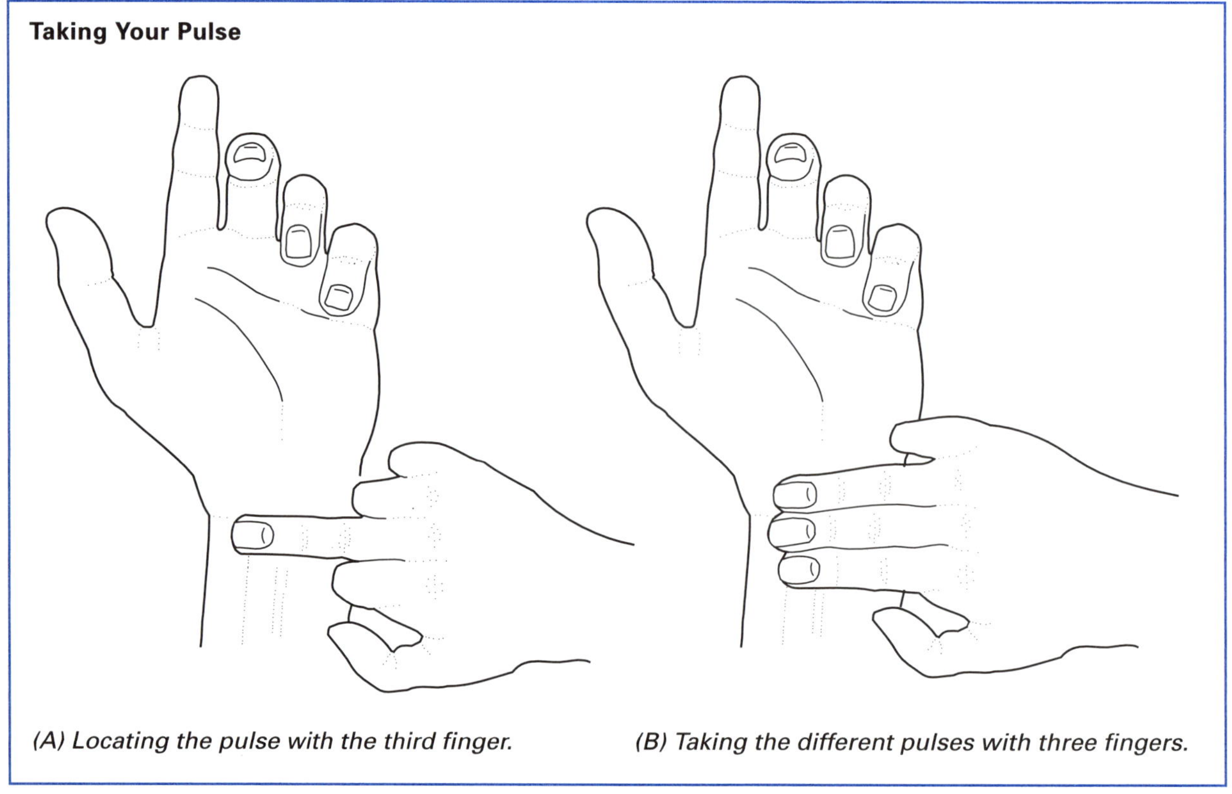

(A) Locating the pulse with the third finger.

(B) Taking the different pulses with three fingers.

Ayurvedic physicians state that the right-hand side of the body is the masculine side, and gives out energy, and the left-hand side, of the body is feminine and receives energy. Imbalances in specific organs or humors can be detected by comparing each point with all of the others, and a generalized weakness in one set of pulses as opposed to those of the other wrist may represent a general lack or excess of masculine or feminine energy. Masculine energy represents aggression, achievement, drive, and ambition, whereas feminine energy represents nurturing, love, homemaking, tolerance, and acceptance. All of us have a balance, and we should all strive for an equality of energy. Pulses change through the day, depending upon the amount of energy that is used. Kidney energy is said to be an energy store, and should be diminished towards the end of the day. Each point represents a spiritual, psychological, and physical aspect, and therefore, when you hear a practitioner talking about kidney energy, it does not necessarily mean the possibility of kidney problems. Lung energy may represent sadness and grief, stomach energy the ability to absorb a concept, and gallbladder energy about digesting facts.

The subject is both fascinating and immense, and can take a lifetime even to attempt to understand and practice accurately.

Reflexology—The Foot

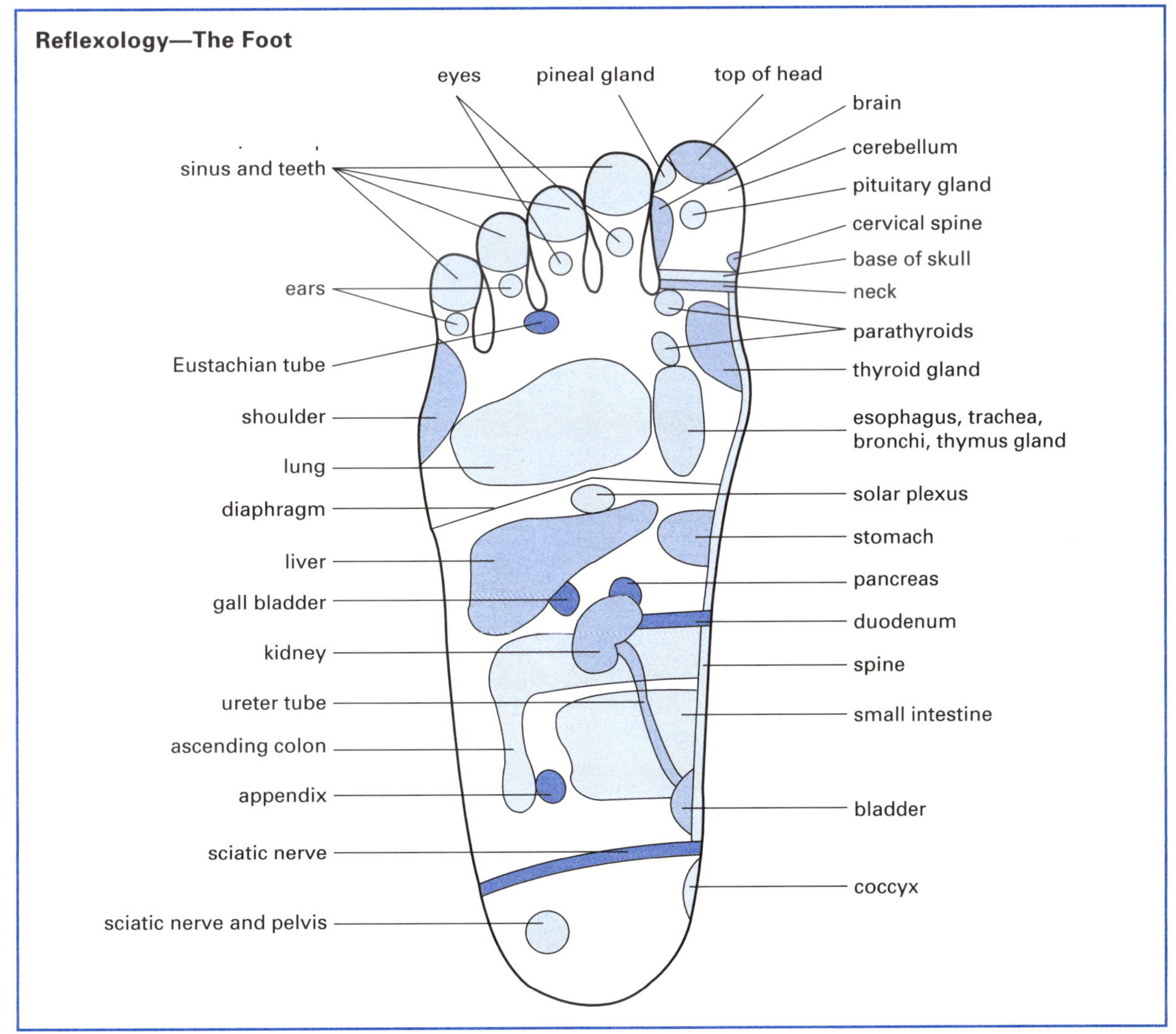

Reflexology—The Hands

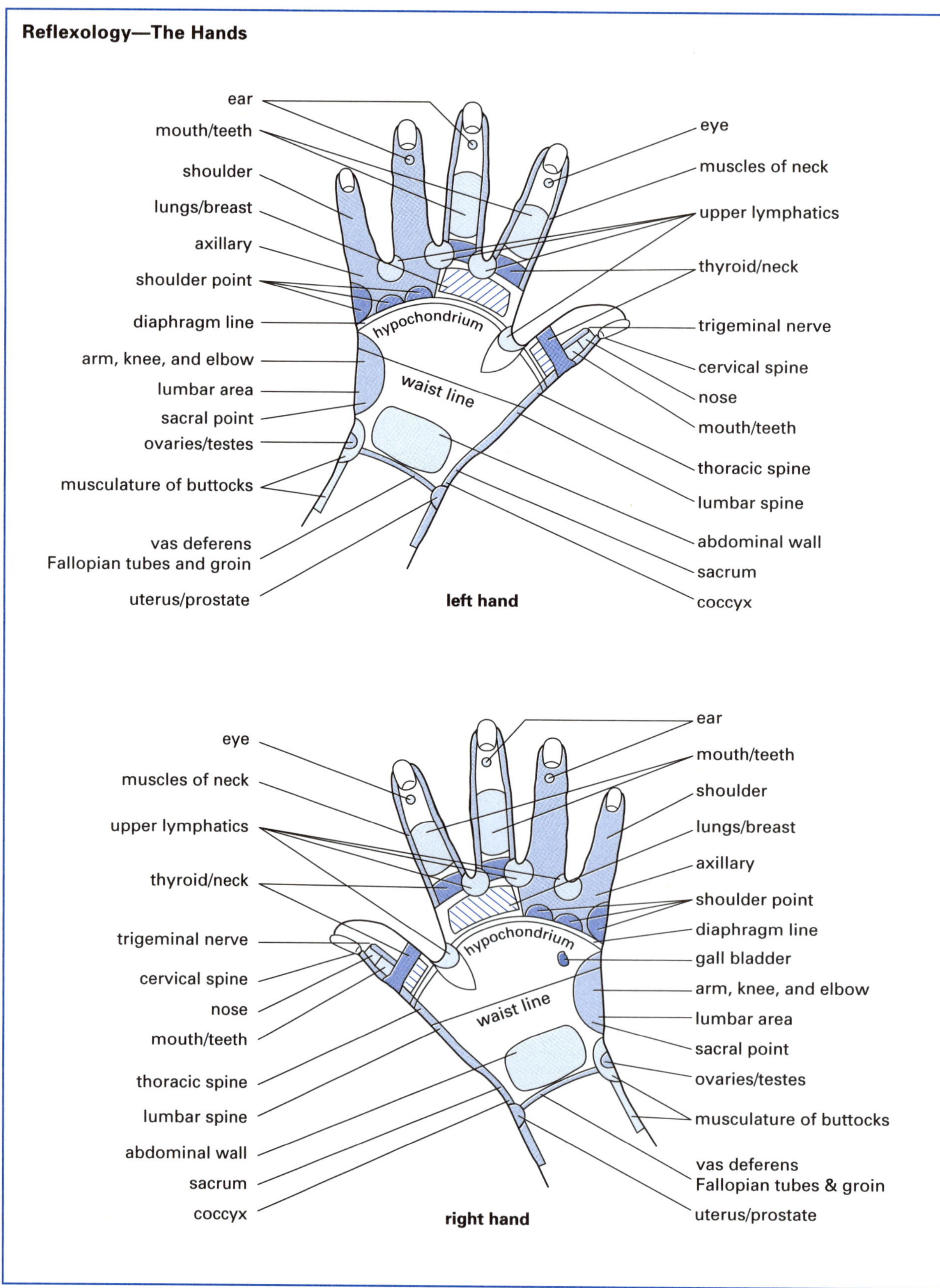

Reflexology

Gentle pressure applied to the feet and hands may give vital information about the underlying areas of weakness from an energetic point of view. Training is academically quite simple, but experience is what counts. There may be very subtle differences in the texture of the tissue where the energy point lies, and a lump or pain is not necessarily reflective of weakness in the system or organ. The diagrams on pages 555 and 556 give a basic representation, and gentle self-manipulation may be useful in self-treating.

RECOMMENDATIONS

- *Overcome any concept of shyness before you enter a complementary medical practitioner's rooms. Physical examination will include pulse-taking and pushing on acupuncture points throughout the body.*
- *A complementary medical examination, while it may be informal, should never be invasive. Any internal examination or examination of the breasts, anus, or genitals should only be performed with a member of the same sex chaperoning the practitioner, and present throughout the entire examination.*
- *If a practitioner uses the pulse technique, ask for their findings and discuss them on the basis of their spiritual, psychological, and physical meaning.*

Investigating

What does that young doctor mean on the TV series *ER* when he blurts out, "We need a CBC, Chem 7 and lytes, LFT, drug screen, AP, and Lat, swab, and call the OR tell'em we'll need a room STAT"? Answer: He is asking for blood and urine samples to be taken and sent to the laboratory for testing, ordering various x-rays, asking for an operating room to be prepared, and raising next year's health-insurance premiums by 15 percent. He is, however, also gleaning the information that he will potentially need to save a life.

Most investigations are warranted, and are without argument, modern medicine's gift to health. Understanding the balance of certain minerals in the bloodstream tells us the state of the kidneys and liver; sugar levels tell us the state of the pancreas; the level of white blood cells tells us how the immune system is functioning—the list goes on. There are many sophisticated tests that an individual may only come across if they become unwell, but a certain array of investigations may be used as a screening process, and might even be encouraged to enable a healthcare provider to monitor the well-being of the patient. I list below some of the basic tests that may be of benefit, or be mentioned, to give the lay person a guideline to what information is being sought. The main problem with investigations is the concept of a "normal" range of results. Normality is measured by testing a large number of people and drawing up a standard deviation curve.

What this means is that the top or bottom 3 percent of any group are automatically considered too high or too low. This may not be the case,

Standard Deviation Curve

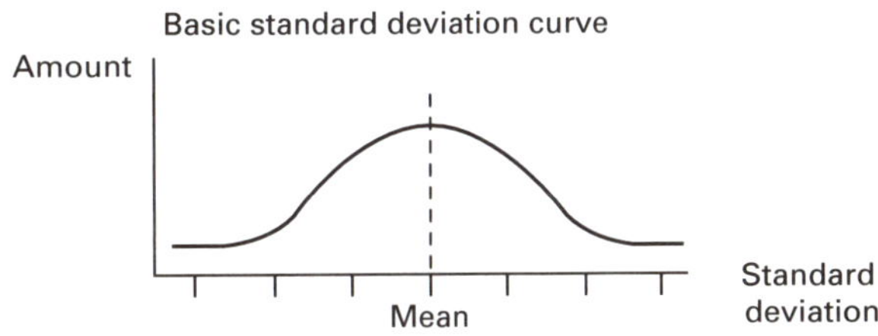

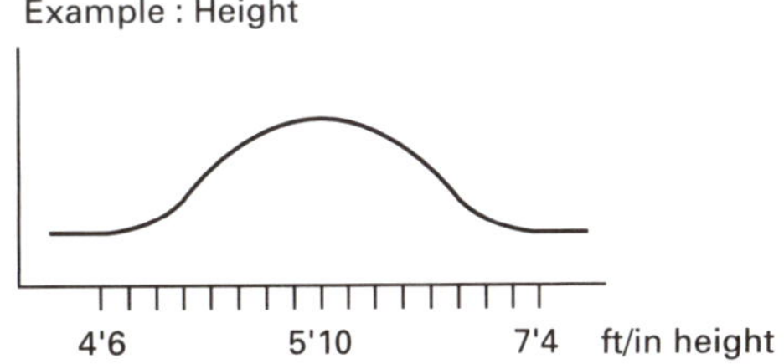

While "normality" might be a reasonable reflection of a population as a whole, it can be very misleading when applied to an individual.

and a result that suggests an abnormality may in fact be perfectly normal for the individual. Also, someone with a result within the "normal" range may in fact be quite abnormal. For example, if a hemoglobin level of 11.5 is found, the orthodox world would say "normal." But if that person *should* have a level of 15, then it is considerably lower than it should be, and yet may not be treated.

There is no black or white in health. The orthodox medical world tends to lose sight of that gray area, and may rely too heavily on results. Investigations should be integrated into a full clinical setting, story-taking and examination, and not viewed on their own merits.

Blood tests

Medics have been studying blood since the advent of the microscope and possibly before. High-power magnification and computers have now made the observing and measuring of the components of the bloodstream extremely easy and swift. Almost anything can be measured, ranging from the number and type of red blood cells to the presence of pesticides or other toxins. The following gives an insight into some of the more-common tests.

Cholesterol and triglycerides

Triglycerides are small molecules of fat that are absorbed via the digestive system, or made up in the liver. Measurement of both of these components can tell us about fat metabolism, intake, and risks, such as of developing atheroma, which may lead to high blood pressure and strokes.

Cholesterol is subdivided into several groups—high-density lipoproteins (HDL), low-density lipoproteins (LDL), and very-low-density lipoproteins (VLDL) are the most common. All forms are needed for survival, but as a general rule, too much LDL is dangerous (*see* **Cholesterol**).

Electrolytes (also known as urea and electrolytes, or Us and Es)

Atoms with positive or negative charges are known as electrolytes. These include sodium, potassium, and calcium, which are positive, and chloride and bicarbonate ions that are negatively charged. The balance of these electrolytes controls the amount of fluid in our system, and the levels are maintained by the functioning of the kidneys, and the amount of water and nutrients that we take in. Measurement of these electrolytes, which should be within narrow bands, enables a practitioner to assess water balance and kidney function.

Urea is the byproduct of protein metabolism, and is a compound that gives the name to urine. Measurement of urea enables a practitioner to assess kidney function, and is usually assessed with a specific protein known as creatinine, which is maintained as a normal level only if the kidney is functioning properly.

The ESR

The erythrocyte sedimentation rate (ESR) is a nonspecific test for a variety of conditions. The investigation is performed by placing a blood sample in a tube, and measuring the speed with which the red blood cells settle. This sedimentation should run at a rate of about half an inch/hour but alters under various conditions. Pregnancy may cause the ESR to "rise" (from around half an inch to anywhere up to an inch). Destructive conditions such as arthritis or cancer may cause the ESR to rise higher, and certain inflammatory conditions may actually cause the ESR to exceed four inches. An ESR rises due to a decrease in the viscosity of the serum in which the blood cells survive. A healthy bloodstream reacts similarly to placing a coin on the top of a pot of honey, as opposed to on a glass of water.

Full- or complete-blood count (FBC, CBC)

This test measures red and white cell numbers, and also microscopy is used to examine the shape, size, and color of the cells. This can give information about the presence of anemia, how the red blood cells are taking up iron, B_{12}, or folic acid, the number and type of white blood cells (the body's

BLOOD VALUES REPORT

Hematology	Sample Values		Male Range
Hemoglobin	14.9	g/dL	13.0–17.5
HCT	44.3		38–52
Red-Cell Count	5.14	× 10^12/l	4.5–6.3
MCV	86.3	fL	76–97
MCH	29.0	pg	27–33
MCHC	33.6	g/dL	32–36
RDW	15.3		11.0–17.5
Platelet Count	194	× 10^9/l	140–440
White-Cell Count	6.0	× 10^9/l	3.6–11.5
Neutrophils	52%	3.12 × 10^9/l	2.0–7.5
Lymphocytes	36%	2.16 × 10^9/l	1.0–4.0
Monocytes	8%	0.48 × 10^9/l	0.0–1.5
Eosinophils	3%	0.18 × 10^9/l	0.0–0.4
Basophils	1%	0.06 × 10^9/l	0.0–0.2
(Comment: *All cell populations appear normal.*)			
ESR	2	mm/hr	0–11
Biochemistry			
Sodium	138	mmol/l	135–145
Potassium	4.0	mmol/l	3.6–5.0
Chloride	109	mmol/l	98–111
Bicarbonate	25	mmol/l	18–31
Urea	4.6	mmol/l	2.9–7.0
Creatinine	78	umol/l	60–125
Bilirubin	8	umol/l	2–22
Alkaline Phosphatase	43	iu/l	30–95
Aspartate Transferase	17	iu/l	10–35
Alanine Transferase	26	iu/l	8–45
HBD	88	iu/l	70–135
CK	73	iu/l	33–186
Gamma GT	23	iu/l	5–50
Total Protein	66	g/l	60–80
Albumin	38	g/l	32–50
Globulin	28	g/l	23–39
Calcium	2.25	mmol/l	2.20–2.60
Phosphate	1.12	mmol/l	0.65–1.55
Uric Acid	327	umol/l	159–475
Random Blood Glucose	6.1	mmol/l	3.5–7.9
Triglycerides	1.68	mmol/l	0.50–2.10
Cholesterol	4.42	mmol/l	Optimum<5.20
HDL Cholesterol	1.14	mmol/l	0.8–1.9
HDL % of total	26	%	20 and over
LDL Cholesterol	2.52	mmol/l	Up to–4.0
Iron	22	umol/l	11.0–32.0
Endocrinology			
Total Thyroxine (T4)	83	nmol/l	58–154
Thyroid-Stimulating Hormone (TSH)	1.32	miu/l	0.35 –5.00

blood-borne immune system). A differential count refers to the types of white blood cells, and can tell a practitioner whether an infection is bacterial, viral, fungal, or absent. Excessive white blood cells are usually present in infection or more-serious conditions such as leukemia. In the latter case, the cells look different, as well as being in abundance.

Liver function tests (LFT)

If liver cells are damaged, their contents spill into the bloodstream, and can be measured. The liver also produces proteins known as albumins, which indicate the state of function rather than the level of damage. Tests for these albumins are all grouped together, and are known as LFTs. Conditions such as hepatitis, alcoholism, and cancer affecting the liver will all alter the LFTs by damaging the cells. Different intracellular chemicals come from different parts of the cell, and the extent of the damage can be measured by defining which liver enzymes are actually present in the bloodstream. Some chemicals exist in the substance of the cell, whereas others live within the nucleus or brain of the cell. These latter chemicals are not released unless severe cell damage has taken place, so measuring the amounts in the bloodstream is as important as measuring their presence.

Thyroid function tests (TFT)

Thyroid function tests measure thyroxine, which is the main hormone produced in the thyroid gland, and another form of thyroxine called triiodothyromine (TH3). TH3 is produced in smaller amounts, but is far more important in its effect. The levels of these two hormones indicate the function of the thyroid gland.

Also measured is the controlling hormone, known as thyroid-stimulating hormone (TSH), which comes from the pituitary gland (*see* **Thyroid**).

Toxicity tests

A few laboratories are sophisticated and forward-thinking enough to be checking blood samples for toxins. Most chemicals can be detected, but may require special requests. These few laboratories actually have panels to test for heavy metals, pesticides, insecticides, and other environmental toxins. Any neurological condition or chronic problem, such as postviral-fatigue syndrome or even cancer, needs to be assessed from the toxicity point of view.

Other tests

Most known compounds can now be assayed (assessed) through blood testing. Levels of glucose, iron, toxins, prescribed drugs, and special chemicals produced by particular inflamed tissues can all be isolated, and used in the process of assessing organ function, body deficiencies, and toxicity.

SPECIMENS AND SAMPLES

Urine samples

Urine is the filtration product of the blood, which in turn picks up toxins from around the system. Measurement of the toxicity and contents of urine gives a clear indication of the state of the body. In days gone by, simple examination by visual assessment, microscopy, measurement of density, and even taste were of great advantage to the physician. Nowadays, computers have given practitioners insights into the very functioning of the body's cells.

A basic urine analysis measures the acidity, water level, presence of sugar or glucose, and certain biochemical products manufactured by the liver. Measurement of these latter compounds—bilinogen and urobilinogen—is a simple, noninvasive method of assessing the health of the liver. Basic analysis also includes checking for red and white blood cells and protein, none of which should be found in the urine because they are an indication of ill health.

Ketones are breakdown products of fat metabolism. They show up in the urine if there is any suggestion of starvation or poor fat-sugar-metabolism control.

URINALYSIS

Urine Chemistry	
pH	7.0
Protein	+ (0.30g/l)
Glucose	Negative
Ketone	Negative
Blood	+
Microscopy	
WBCs	>100/hpf
RBCs	Not seen
Casts	Not seen
Epithelial cells	+
Crystals	Not seen
Organisms	++
CULTURE	No bacterial growth

First-morning urine samples are generally preferred for assessment of the body's metabolism, but for any suggestion of infection, a midstream urine (MSU) is preferred. This reduces the chances of contamination of a sample by bacteria that may have bred at the opening of the urethra, and in the male, elements of seminal fluid that may pass into a sample with the final contractions of the urethra. Such samples undergo what is known as culture, microscopy, and sensitivity (CMS). The sample is looked at under a microscope, and then a portion is placed in a laboratory dish containing a special medium that allows bacteria to grow. If any bacterial growth occurs, it is known as a culture, and then different antibiotics are placed on the dish to see which ones kill the bugs. This technique allows physicians to assess which antibiotics a particular breed or strain of bacteria are resistant to, and then select out those that are effective in killing the bugs. A bacterium is said to be "sensitive" to these agents.

Other samples

A sample of any excretion or discharge may be collected either directly into a sample pot or using a swab. These are then provided to a laboratory or technician who will prepare them (known as "fixing"). Certain stains may be applied to color particular bacterial agents or the presence of other compounds, and a variety of technical assessments may be used.

Anything that is coughed up or spat out is collectively known as a sputum sample, and certain skin samples may be taken by gently scraping the skin—known as skin scrapings. Other areas may be swabbed by a medical "ear bud," and as one bible for the junior doctor describes, "there is no body cavity that a sample cannot be taken from by using a long needle and a brave attitude."

Biopsy

Biopsy is the sampling of a tissue for examination under a microscope, or for some other test. Theoretically, any part of the body can be biopsied, but the risk/benefit ratio has to be examined. Tissue biopsy from the skin, or needle-aspiration from a cyst can be done in the doctor's surgery, but other tissues need to be biopsied under anesthetic. Local anesthetic is used for muscle biopsy of organs that are more easily accessible with a long biopsy needle and an acceptable level of experience. General anesthetic is required if brain-tissue samples are required, or if a suspicion of cancer is high, in which case a further procedure may be required, wherein the tissue sample is sent to the pathologist immediately and a report is produced swiftly to enable the surgeon to proceed with the operation if necessary. This is common in suspicious breast lumps during lumpectomy.

Biopsies are generally to be considered necessary, because they can create a firm diagnosis, and allow a treatment protocol to be accurately prescribed.

ORTHODOX MEDICAL TECHNOLOGY

Blood-pressure measurement

Blood pressure is measured using a sphygmomanometer. An inflatable "cuff" is placed around the upper arm and air pumped into it until a level of 250mm/Hg is reached, as seen on the dial. This pressure occludes the underlying arteries. The practitioner places the end of the stethoscope over the front of the elbow and listens. Nothing should be heard.

The air is slowly released from the cuff, and as the pressure drops there comes a point when the strength of the heartbeat overrides the pressure in the cuff, and blood is squirted down the arteries. This blood hits the wall of the artery with a thump, which can be heard through the stethoscope. As the cuff pressure continues to drop and less impedance ensues, the bloodflow becomes smooth and the thumping stops. Cardiologists

Sphygmomanometer

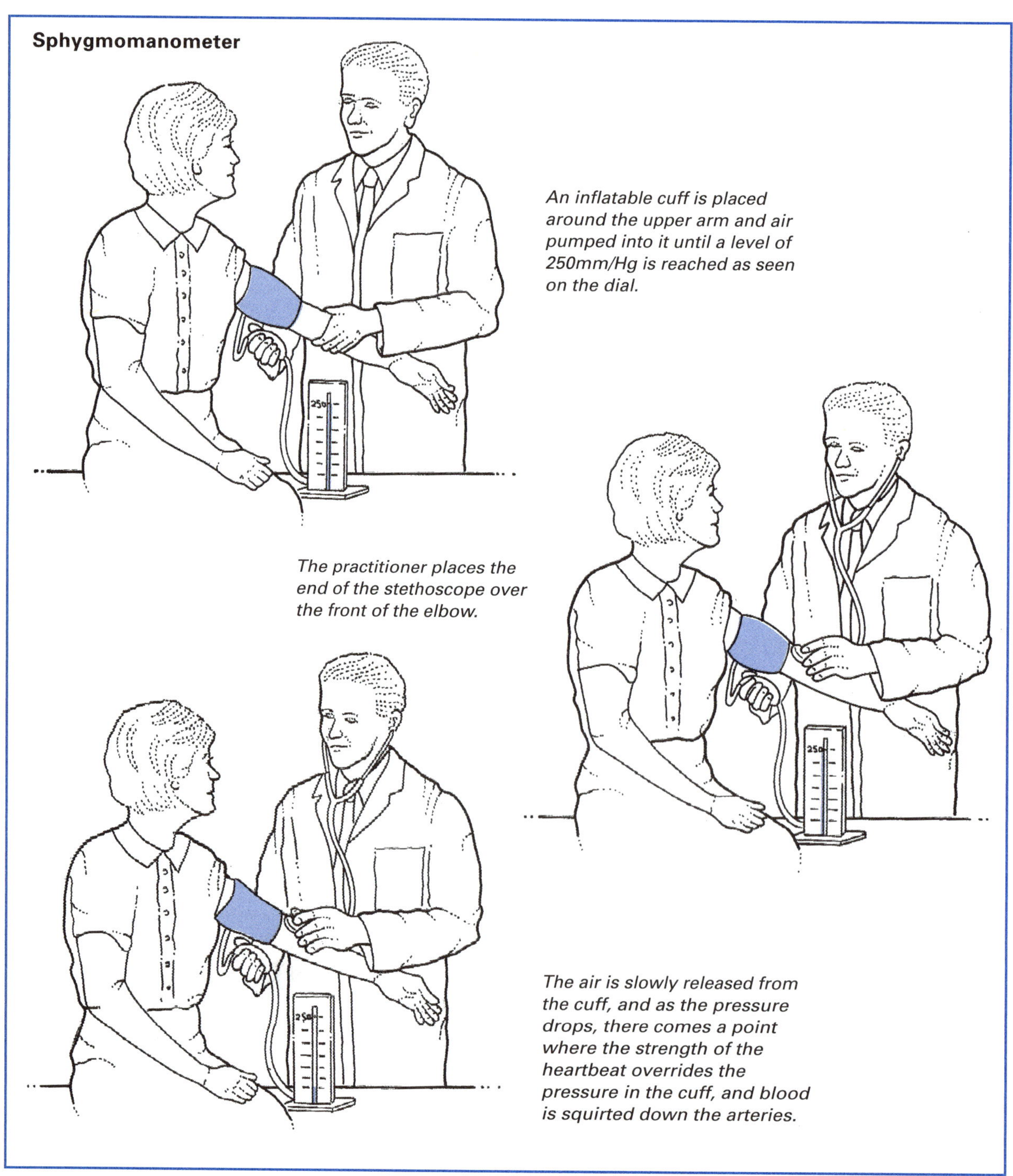

An inflatable cuff is placed around the upper arm and air pumped into it until a level of 250mm/Hg is reached as seen on the dial.

The practitioner places the end of the stethoscope over the front of the elbow.

The air is slowly released from the cuff, and as the pressure drops, there comes a point where the strength of the heartbeat overrides the pressure in the cuff, and blood is squirted down the arteries.

teach us that there are five sound stages, ranging from stage I—the initial thump—to stage V—a return to silence.

Simple and 24-hour blood-pressure machines

Sensitive computers are now being used to take blood pressure, and can be bought at any medical outlet. These generally comprise a finger-sized cuff that slips over a digit and measures the underlying pressure in the arteries. These are fairly accurate, and can be used to check an individual's blood pressure at different times throughout the day.

Twenty-four-hour blood-pressure measurements are of benefit in diagnosis if sporadic symptoms such as dizziness or blackouts are associated with blood pressure. A small computer is carried for 24 hours with cords attached to the body to measure blood pressure. A patient records the time of any symptoms, and this is compared by computer with the blood-pressure measurements. It is worth noting that many individuals who may have high blood pressure when visiting the doctor's office (white-coat hypertension), or at times of stress, may spend much of their time with normal blood pressure, and incorrectly be prescribed treatment. Many hypertensives have normal blood pressure during the night, which suggests to a holistic physician that the stress of consciousness is the underlying cause, and that a relaxation or meditation program may be of benefit rather than drugs.

Doppler test

C. J. Doppler was an Austrian physicist who noticed that sound (and light) waves change if bounced off something that is moving. This is a very simplified description of what is known as the Doppler principle. A Doppler machine emits a sound wave that bounces off moving blood within a vessel, and can show the speed of flow. As this is very dependent on the patency of the vessel, this technique can be used as a noninvasive investigation to check for arteriosclerosis or occlusion within arteries.

Electrocardiogram (ECG, EKG)

An ECG is the measurement of electrical conductivity in the heart muscle. For an explanation of the origin, initiation, and travel of these electric impulses, *see* **Heart, irregular beats**.

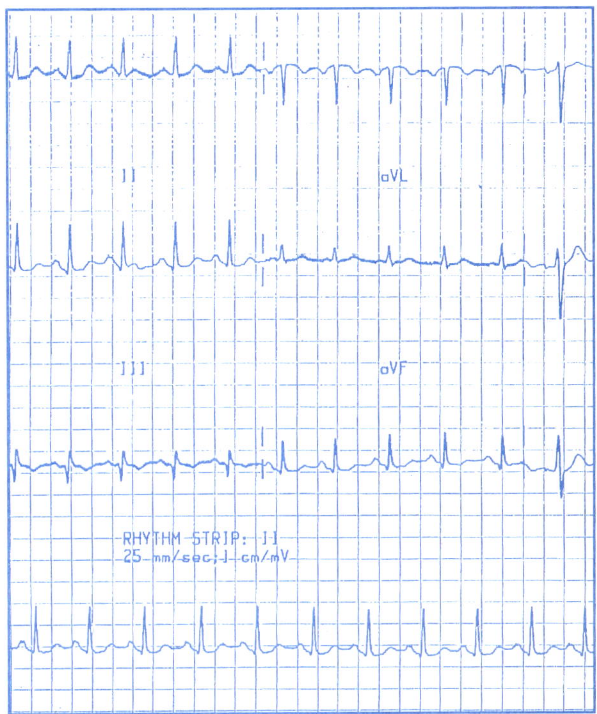

An ECG is a noninvasive technique that can be of great benefit in diagnosing heart diseases. There is no reason to avoid such an examination, although results need to be correlated with symptoms, as with all investigations.

An ECG produced while somebody is on a treadmill is known as a stress ECG, and shows the electrical conductivity when the heart has an increased need for oxygen. This test can be very useful in demonstrating cardiac-muscle disease, because any injury from a heart attack, for example, will damage some of the heart muscle and prevent conduction through that part.

Electrodes are placed around the heart and on both wrists and ankles, because the electrical impulse will be picked up even at distances. The computer within an ECG will correlate all the information from all the cords and print out a pattern that requires a certain amount of expertise to interpret.

Holter monitor

The Holter monitor is a small box that attaches to the side of an individual and is connected to cords that are placed on the chest. The monitor will record the heartrate and electrical pattern over a 24-hour period. The individual notes down any periods of cardiac symptoms, such as chest pain or tachycardia, and any associated heart irregularity can be ascertained.

Electroencephalogram (EEG)

The brain conducts its function through the transmission of chemicals from one nerve to another. This process releases electricity, which can be measured by placing electrodes around the scalp. An EEG can demonstrate not only function, but also structural changes or damage within the brain. Very useful in conditions such as epilepsy or in diagnosing tumors, the EEG is a safe and effective method of diagnosis.

Magnetic-resonance imaging (MRI)

Over the last decade a technique of visualizing internal organs and structures has been developed using magnets rather than sound or x-ray. The technique is complex, and computer imaging from the information sent by powerful magnets, which surround the body part to be investigated, is required.

The MRI has its critics, suggesting that the imaging is not all that accurate in certain areas of the body (the prostate or the coronary arteries), and it is often necessary to use "dyes," which are magnetic substances that may cause problems that we have yet to determine. These dyes are, however, far safer than the known damage created by the CT-scan dyes containing iodine *(see* **Radiography**).

Magnetic-resonance imaging usually involves the patient being passed into a body-sized tube and being asked to keep absolutely still. While claustrophobic, the technique is not in any way invasive or painful, but may take up to an hour to complete a full-body scan. These MRI scans are extremely sensitive and can be used in place of CT scans *(see* **Radiography**) in many if not most investigations.

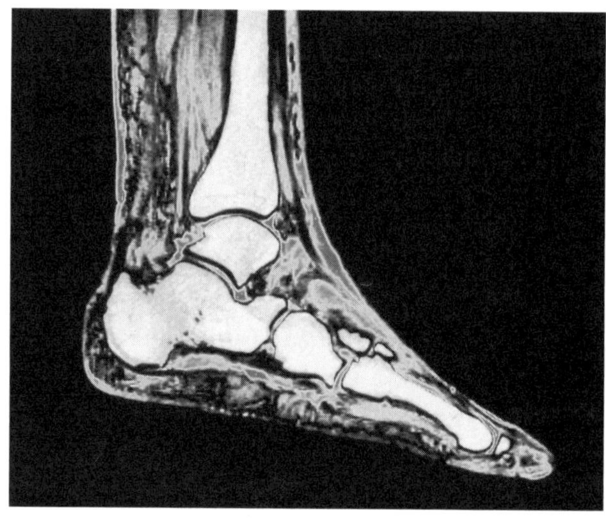

MRI scan of a woman's ankle (age 58).

Magnetic-resonance imaging may impart certain dangers as we now begin to see that magnetic energy may disrupt electromagnetic function in the body, but at the moment it is safer than x-rays. If confronted with a need for hi-tech investigation, always ask whether MRI would be available and as accurate.

Radiography (x-rays)

Radiography (colloquially and commonly now known as x-rays) is the most common, and potentially most damaging, of modern medicine's investigations.

X-rays are very high-frequency waves that pass through most compounds. A radiogram is basically a photograph created by x-rays hitting a wave-sensitive plate. As x-rays are passed through the body, the denser the tissue, the more x-rays are absorbed. The less-dense tissue allows more x-rays to pass through, which hit the plate and show up as a white/gray area. Bones, being dense, are seen as white on an x-ray, because no x-rays hit the plate, whereas air space in the lungs is seen as black, because all the x-rays hit the plate. X-rays are harmful, there is no debate over that whatsoever. The argument concerns whether the amount we receive through an investigation is harmful or not (*see* **Radiation**).

Angiography

Angiography is a frequently used x-ray technique. A radio-opaque dye is injected into the bloodstream and x-rays are taken of the arteries that are suspected of being diseased or narrowed. This technique is popular, but has its critics. Some rarely-repeated studies have shown that angiography is open to misinterpretation, or actually imparts false information. Unnecessary operations are therefore conducted. This, combined with the potential risk of an x-ray, should make angiography a last-choice investigation rather than a first choice, but overall it is likely to be of benefit in the right case.

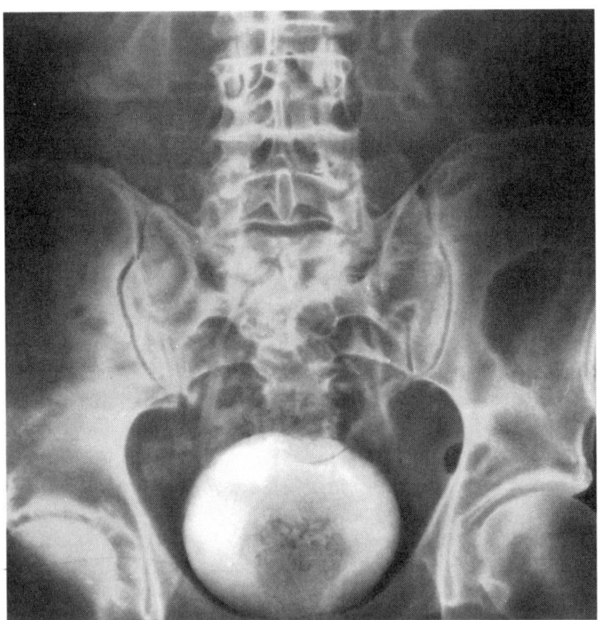

Cystogram—a specialised x-ray to show up bladder deformities.

Myelography

Myelography is an x-ray technique used on the spinal column that also uses radio-opaque dyes. When injected into the spinal column to show disc lesions, a percentage may cause inflammation leading to persistent pain and problems with movement. The dyes themselves may be toxic to the kidneys, and may have a direct effect on the nervous system, leading to paralysis. Dyes used for CT scans contain iodine, which is known to be toxic to the thyroid gland if taken in excess. The trouble is, everyone is different, and nobody is certain how much is too much for any individual patient. Try other techniques of imaging before allowing dyes to be used.

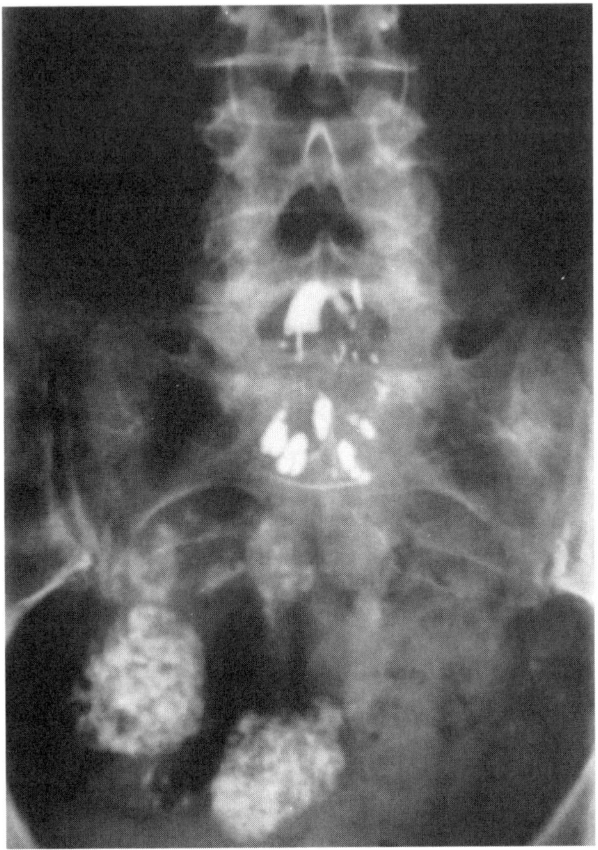

X-ray of the spine two years after undergoing myelography showing oily contrast material (as white patches) still present in the spinal cord.

Densitometry

Bone-density scanning (densitometry) is becoming popular, and while it carries a low risk of x-ray exposure, the scan itself is not a particularly reliable investigation. A variety of studies have suggested that the accuracy is questionable and that bone density can change, depending on such factors as movement and recent diet, so that gen-

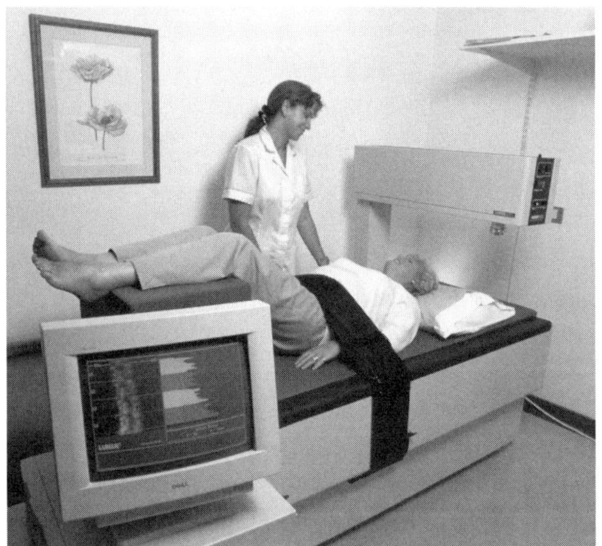

Bone-density scanning for osteoporosis.

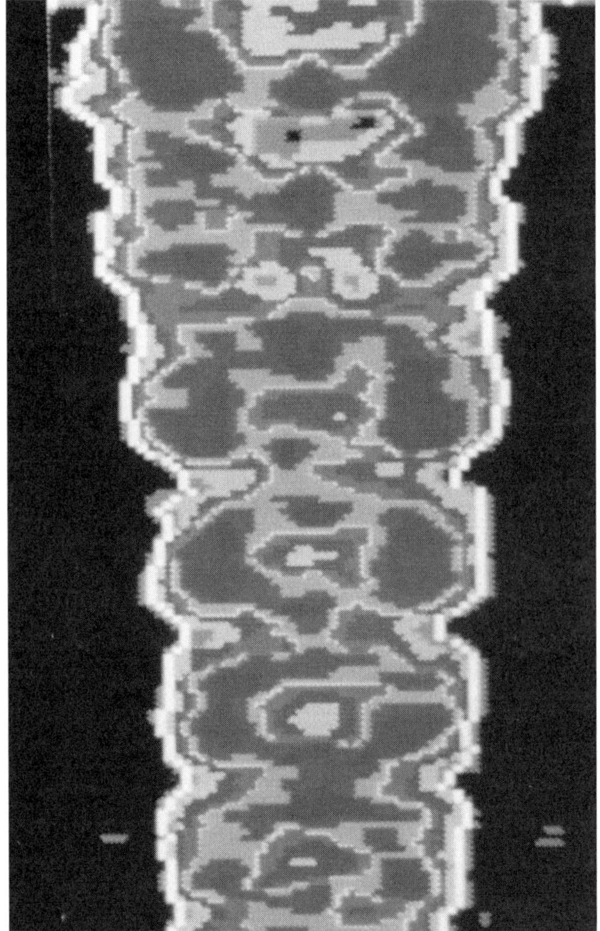

Densitometry scan of the spine, used to measure mineral density of bone in the assessment of osteoporosis.

eral or yearly screening is not reliable. One study followed up a group of 1,000 women who were considered to be at high risk of osteoporosis via a scan, only to find that they had fewer hip fractures than the control group. Neither group were given any orthodox treatment.

There are other alternatives *(see* **Osteoporosis**) for measuring bone density and, in principle, these other ultrasound techniques can be done with safety.

Computed-axial-tomography (CAT or CT)

Computed-axial-tomography (CAT or CT) scans are formed by passing an x-ray image through a computer that is highly sensitive, and therefore produces much more detailed pictures. These scans use a three-dimensional picture, thereby giving the physician an idea of the depth and size of a tumor with far more accuracy than a two-dimensional x-ray film.

A CT scan provides an enormous amount of radiation, especially if the procedure is repeated because of movement of the patient, error within the computer system, or because the technique is being used to monitor a changing situation.

While extremely accurate, many of the results can be obtained through magnetic-resonance imaging, but with lower risks. Also, CT scans are

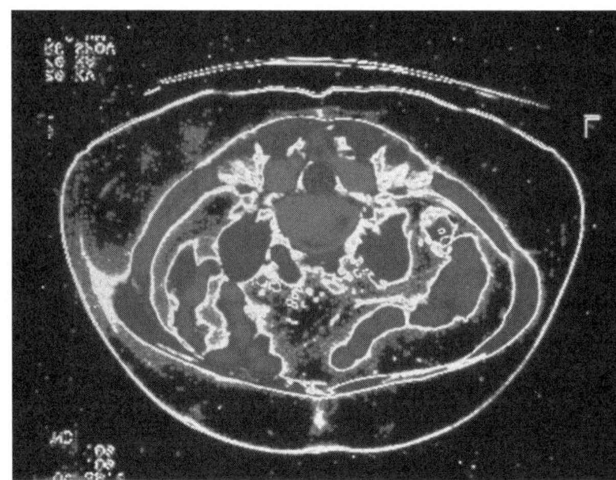

Computed-axial-tomography (CAT) scan of the spine, kidneys, and intestines (female).

often used, despite the fact that whatever the results, no change in treatment is likely. It simply gives a prognosis.

Ultrasound

Ultrasound or sonography has been developed over the last 30 years within the medical fraternity. The principle has been around a lot longer, and was used by geographers to chart the depth of oceans. The principle is simple. A sound wave is emitted from a transmitter into tissues, and rebounds back to a receptor lying next to the transmitter. A less-dense tissue will reflect fewer sound waves, whereas a solid object will bounce back all of the waves. This information is transformed into a visual picture by a computer, much like a radio will pick up inaudible radio waves and transform them into sound through mechanical means.

One trial has shown that using ultrasound eleven times in a pregnancy may produce babies that are small for their age, but otherwise no other detrimental effect has been demonstrated. I suspect that because the fetus is a highly sensitive state of being, the ultrasound is disturbing, and creates a stress response rather than having any direct, detrimental effect upon tissue growth.

Ultrasound can be used for most diagnoses, except for organs such as the brain, which is encased in a solid shell, or organs that are too deep in the body to be imaged without other organs being in the way. Basically, problems may be imaged and a diagnosis made on any part from the neck down with the use of ultrasound. Bone density can be measured without x-rays using this method.

Ultrasound machines vary in size, but the actual transmitter/receptor is rarely larger than a mobile telephone, and is placed over the area to be investigated. A sound-transmitting gel is applied to allow a freer movement and less interference from the skin surface. Ultrasound diagnosis rarely takes more than a few minutes in the hands of a skilled technician, and reports can be read immediately.

ALTERNATIVE DIAGNOSTIC INVESTIGATIONS

If Madame Curie had listened to the derision piled upon her, we would not have x-rays. Her experimentation carried the price of her life, because she died from the effects of radiation. She is the most well-known example of scientists who have come up with ideas in medicine that have been doubted, ridiculed, and ostracized. However, because of their determination, we have an astounding array of investigative procedures.

Today, there are investigations that have been born out of sound scientific and medical hypotheses, but are finding it difficult to attract funding *because* the techniques may be very accurate and inexpensive. This would suggest that they would be popular, but indeed the financial state of play in medicine inhibits study and research into new techniques. I list below some of those that I believe have a future. This is partly because the study and research carried out so far is positive, or because I have used them in my practice for anywhere up to 12 years. In one or two cases the investigation has been around for many decades, but has been either suppressed or vilified to such an extent that it is only recently that it has been able to gain some credibility.

I stress that the techniques below are not well established from a scientific or double-blind viewpoint, and therefore should not be considered suitable diagnostic techniques if used by themselves. But, in conjunction with other orthodox techniques, or when current investigative procedures are inadequate, they may be of benefit.

ALLERGY TESTING

Orthodox medicine uses the skin to reflect the possibility of allergies more so than it does the use of blood tests. These prick or scratch tests seem to be sensitive to allergens found in the air (airborne), but are generally less sensitive than blood tests for food allergy.

It is important to distinguish between an intolerance and an allergy (*see* **Food Allergies and Intolerance**, and **Allergies**).

I also recommend that, before food-allergy testing is undergone, a physician with knowledge of the leaky-gut syndrome is consulted, because allergies may alter rapidly due to this condition, making some of these expensive tests irrelevant within a month of eliminating the foods (*see* **Leaky-gut syndrome**).

Self-testing

Select the five foods you most enjoy, the five foods you most crave, the five foods you eat most, and the five foods that you eat through convenience rather than through enjoyment. These foods may overlap, and you may have a list of 10 or so that are the most likely to be culprits if you suspect food allergy or have persisting ailments.

I am often confronted with quizzical looks when I bring forward this paradox that the foods you most desire are those that are liable to cause problems. It is important to remember that a body, when it is not well, will encourage reactions, because reactions are usually curative. The body, not being a perfect machine, when it realizes it is unwell, will ingest foods that create either a bodily reaction or a psychological sense of well-being in order to encourage a reaction or suppress psychological angst. This is why we eat foods that are not good for us, and we tend to move towards alcohol and drugs to escape our awareness of illnesses.

Eliminate these foods for one month and note the changes. If improvement is forthcoming, then reintroduce each food one at a time over a week, and see which foods are more aggressive towards your well-being. Over a period of time, you may be able to assess that you can eat certain foods if you take them only on a weekly basis, whereas others will create a reaction immediately and persistently.

Self-testing through exclusion-diet regime

There are certain hypoallergenic diets based on foods that are rarely the cause of allergies/intolerances. In my experience of having tested hundreds of individuals, I do not agree with this principle. One popular hypoallergenic diet enforces patients to eat only lamb, rice, watery vegetables, apples, virgin olive oil, goat's products, and honey. I have come across many patients who have had allergies to these foods and, as you can see, the diet is extremely restrictive.

I prefer people to experiment and find regimes such as the Hay diet (food noncombining diet), stone-age diet, or any specific diet picked off the shelf. Find one that suits you and makes you feel better, stay on it for 4–6 weeks, and then reintroduce suspected culprits one by one each week; the reactions will occur much more quickly, and be noticed within a few days.

Food-allergy tests

Applied kinesiology or pulse testing

These techniques are reliant on the sensitivity of a practitioner. In principle, a food compound is placed in the patient's mouth or on the body, and a muscle group such as the shoulder muscles are tested for strength. A food that disagrees with the patient will momentarily create a weakness, which can be assessed by the practitioner. A similar response is noted in the pulse, which will either speed up or slow down in response to the compound.

These tests have been well substantiated in trials, but one has to bear in mind the skill and sensitivity of the individual practitioner. At its extreme, practitioners have suggested that if a patient simply reads the name of a compound, the muscles or pulse may alter. This has not been proven through any trials that I have come across, but I know practitioners and popular healers who are very successful with these techniques.

Hair analysis

A sample of hair is taken and tested against preprepared antibodies. In principle, the body will eliminate foods that it does not like, and the hair has been established as containing (within its keratin fibers) unwanted molecules of foods. The antibodies will then react with these foods, and can be measured. I am not particularly convinced by the accuracy of this test, because certain molecules may not find their way into the hair particles, as the skin is only a secondary mechanism for toxin removal, and the hair is merely an adjunct to that. Chemicals in shampoos may also alter the structure of the food molecules or even remove them, thereby leading to false results.

Be wary of hair analysis being performed by some energetic or dowsing technique. While the use of energetic measurement and the pendulum (the more-popular technique for dowsing tests) is well established, the patient is once again dependent upon the skill of a practitioner and not any scientific reasoning.

Blood analysis

Food-allergy cellular test (FACT). This is the development of a simple hypothesis. Most tests for food allergy are done on immunoglobulins, specifically IgG4 and IgE. These are made by specific types of white cell, and can alter in the bloodstream, depending on the hydration of the person and when they last ate the food. However, the bloodstream carries memory cells, which are white cells specifically geared to remembering past infections. These do not vary to the same degree, and may recognize a food allergen years after it has been eaten. Therefore, FACT is more sensitive than other food-allergy tests.

Radioallergosorbent test/procedure (RAST/RASP). This is a specific blood test to check for IgG4 or IgE antibodies in the bloodstream, and has been surpassed by the enzyme-linked immunosorbent assay (ELISA) (*see* below).

The test for IgG4 or IgE must, in my opinion, be combined: IgE is a fairly short-lived response, but IgG4 tends to last in the bloodstream for a few weeks. A small study done by myself compared very accurate IgE testing with IgG4, and the results were quite different. I do not wish to get bogged down in the science, but it is important to have both immunoglobulins tested, and as these tests are quite expensive, do not waste your funds on an assay that covers only one.

There is no doubt that this test will pick up an allergic response in the bloodstream, but there is no guarantee that the allergy is relevant to an individual's illness. Being strongly allergic to eggs may simply make the patient sneeze once a day, and may not be the underlying cause of their chronic-fatigue syndrome. Conversely, a mild allergic response may be the cause of a cancer. It is important, therefore, to have these tests reviewed by a complementary practitioner who has a strong understanding and overview of the patient's case.

Enzyme-linked immunosorbent assay (ELISA). This is a common-enough term in medical circles. It is a method by which blood is mixed with specific chemicals that bind in a particular way with certain blood components, especially immunoglobulins (antibodies), which can then be detected by a sensitive, computerized machine. The RAST (*see* above) is still available in some laboratories, but has been surpassed by the more sensitive ELISA test. This is the best technique for assessing food allergy.

RECOMMENDATIONS

- *Having selected your choice of food allergy testing, do not hesitate to sit with a complementary practitioner for an overview.*
- *Do not place total emphasis on a food allergy result, because a healthy body may well be able to deal with any food allergy, given an underlying level of good health.*

Electromagnetic testing

The Voll and Vega machines have been surpassed in recent years by American/German computers that pass electromagnetic frequencies through the body, and in many cases through the acupuncture meridians, and measure frequency fluctuations when the body is confronted by food and other compounds. These machines do not test for allergy (as explained before), but are in my opinion profoundly efficient in testing for intolerance, which may also cover allergy.

A patient sits with the practitioner who will connect him/her to the computer, and a painless electromagnetic impulse is sent through the system. Different compounds are applied to the patient, or the computer and the energy flow will diminish or enhance, depending on the beneficial or adverse effect of the food. This is a simple and relatively inexpensive technique, which I think is highly accurate in the right hands.

Bioresonance

A scientist in the 1930s by the unusual name of Royal Rife created a device that was capable of sending energy waves through a body. He noted that this created changes that were beneficial to health. Over the last six decades, scientists and technological-research companies with an interest in his original work have developed more and more sophisticated transmitters associated with complex computers. Research and studies have been done into the concept of disease having a particular energy wavelength or resonance, and this fact has been well established for many bacteria, viruses, and conditions such as cancer.

It has been shown that sending a wavelength that antagonizes or blocks the natural wavelength of a condition can kill the organism or diseased cell. Much of Royal Rife's work was destroyed by a fearful medical fraternity, and since then, there have been several stories of practitioners having their records confiscated, and doors are closed with regard to the availability of finance for research purposes. Other techniques such as Vega and Voll tests have supported the theory.

Nowadays, machines are capable of diagnosis by comparing wavelengths picked up from a body to wavelengths stored in the memory of the computer. If an individual resonance matches, say, tuberculosis, then a diagnosis of a tubercular-like condition can be made. At this juncture, firm diagnosis is difficult, but the process can be used to support an orthodox finding or help to steer a practitioner in the right direction.

The computer has a set treatment program for particular diseases that have individual resonances, and this is correlated with the body's own natural wavelengths, computed, and sent back into the patient.

The two systems that appear most advanced and which work both diagnostically and as a treatment technique, are the BiCom and the Quantum CI computers. Their availability is becoming much more widespread and, in the right hands, they are of great benefit to diagnoses and healing.

Vega and Voll tests

Two machines named after their inventors, the Vega and Voll, were the basic forerunners to more-sophisticated bioresonance computers. The same principle is used, whereby a small electric current is sent through a patient and an electricity-sensitive machine. A sensitive gauge measures the flow, and different compounds are put into the machine to see if the electricity is hampered or enhanced. Many practitioners still use these machines with great accuracy, but the process is much slower than the computers available nowadays.

GASTROGRAMS AND PANCREATICOGRAMS

A gastrogram is a measurement of the amount of hydrochloric acid produced by the stomach, and a pancreaticogram measures pancreatic enzyme release. At the moment, the assessment of this is an invasive procedure requiring samplings from the stomach. However, a noninvasive method is being developed that involves nothing more than drinking a particular solution, which is measured

BIORESONANCE REPORT

Primary Diagnosis: *Leukemia*
Secondary Diagnosis: *None*

Additional Complications: *Does not appear to be energetically reacting to her Leukemia*
Possible Causes of Disease/Nosodal Suggestions: *Multiple psychological stress and also a lot of house renovations, good possibility of Geopathic stress also*
Alersodal: *Molds and Dust . . . aromatic hydrocarbons*
Isodal or Toxic Possibilities: *See summary*
Nutritional Problems: *Fatty-acid deficiency possibly enzymes also*
Behavioral Problems: *None noted*
Trauma: *None noted*
Stress: *Psychological*
Perverse Energy Exposures: *Reacts to radiation exposure*
Inherited Tendencies or Disorders: *See report*
Mental Problems or Emotional Clinging: *None noted*
Sarcoidal Suggestions: *None noted*

Patient report

High items on Main screen
C:19 Fatty-acid deficiency
Soponaria . . . sore throat
Catalase ID'S free-radical Ca risk
Belladonna
Nux Vom.
Coxsackie . . . virus
Hepato liq.
Tinea . . . Fungus

Auricle . . . ear
Gelsemium
Dulcamara
Lecithinase

Kidney liq.
Algin Radiation
Aesculus Hipp.
Lyco
WBC Weakness and defiency
Diethylstilbesterol
Grass
Miasm Cholera
Miasm Allergy

C:14 Fatty acid
Carbonic anhydrase
Zingiber . . . for digestion
Aconite . . . Mental anguish
Sycosi
Chromosome 16 Q Cataract, MPS
Dysentery
Passiflora
Lymph, Spleen, Mammary

Nutrition
Vit. F
Internal enzymes 80
Minerals 86

Allergy screening
Food allergy 109
Inhalant 98
Animal hair 88
Dairy sens 124
Grains 105
Pollen 104
Sulfites 123
Molds 96
Sugar 110

Specific allergens
Tomato
Pollens
Grass
Dog

Energy screening shows possible reaction to geopathic stress

Other remedies
Alkaplex G
Bone C Dent
B12 and Liver
Adreno neucleo

MNX anterior pituitary and E
Enzastatin

Homeopathy
113 Nux Vom.
Uranium 106
Dulcamara 109
Gels 109
Lyco 105
Lobelia 91
Myristica 97
Uva Ursi 101
Iris Vers 89
Machine recommends Nux vom as most similar at this time

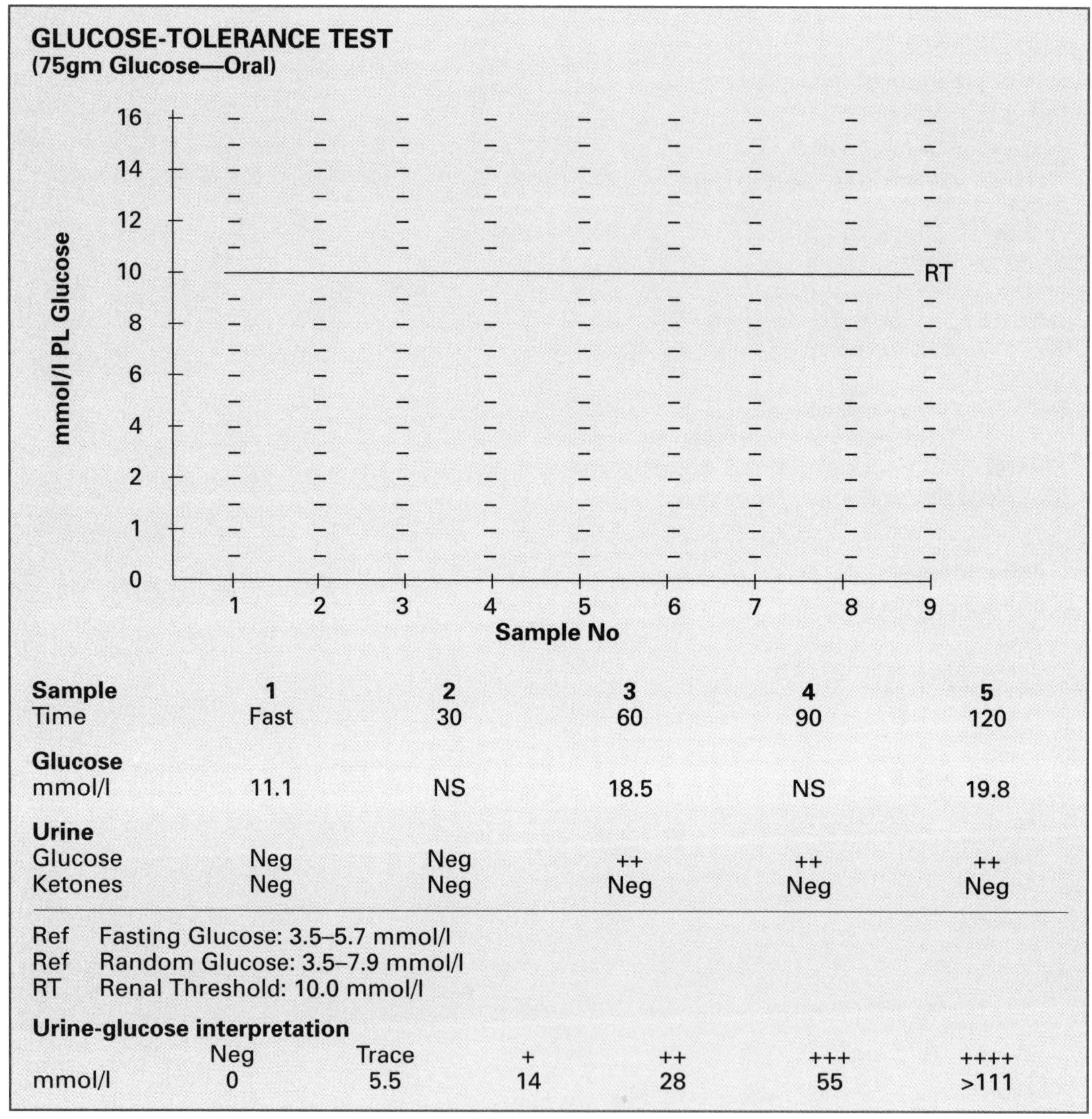

Sample	1	2	3	4	5
Time	Fast	30	60	90	120
Glucose					
mmol/l	11.1	NS	18.5	NS	19.8
Urine					
Glucose	Neg	Neg	++	++	++
Ketones	Neg	Neg	Neg	Neg	Neg

Ref Fasting Glucose: 3.5–5.7 mmol/l
Ref Random Glucose: 3.5–7.9 mmol/l
RT Renal Threshold: 10.0 mmol/l

Urine-glucose interpretation

	Neg	Trace	+	++	+++	++++
mmol/l	0	5.5	14	28	55	>111

by an external monitoring machine. Many bowel problems and dyspeptic symptoms may be associated with a lack of hydrochloric acid rather than an excess, and this simple test can illustrate this.

GLUCOSE-TOLERANCE TEST (GTT)

This test is generally used to show a tendency towards diabetes. The holistic practitioner can also use the GTT to confirm a hypoglycemic state (*see* **Hypoglycemia**). An individual is given a 75ml loading dose of a glucose solution after having fasted for at least 6 hours. Blood samples are taken every 30 minutes for 2.5–5 hours to establish whether or not the body's sugar control is being maintained. The blood-sugar level should rise initially and then drop as insulin levels rise to combat this change. The sugar level should drop below the normal threshold at which blood glucose is maintained, and then rise again as the insulin levels drop.

GUT-PERMEABILITY TEST

Fraction	Molecular weight	Dose (Mg)	Recovery in urine (6-hour collection) Mg	%	Reference range
1	198	4.0	1.3	31.5	26.6–33.4
2	242	9.0	2.7	30.2	26.5–31.6
3	286	39.0	11.2	28.7	25.2–29.4
4	330	96.0	25.7	26.8	21.1–25.0
5	374	157.0	35.6	22.7	17.9–22.0
6	418	171.0	30.4	17.8	12.5–16.2
7	462	176.0	18.0	10.2	6.4–10.8
8	506	145.0	7.8	5.4	3.6–6.0
9	550	105.0	1.9	1.8	1.0–2.4
10	594	67.0	0.5	0.7	Up to 1.4
11	638	31.0	0.1	0.2	Up to 0.7
	TOTAL	**1000.0**	**135.2**	**13.5**	**10.0–13.3%**

Comment

Some increase in permeability, up to molecular weight 450.

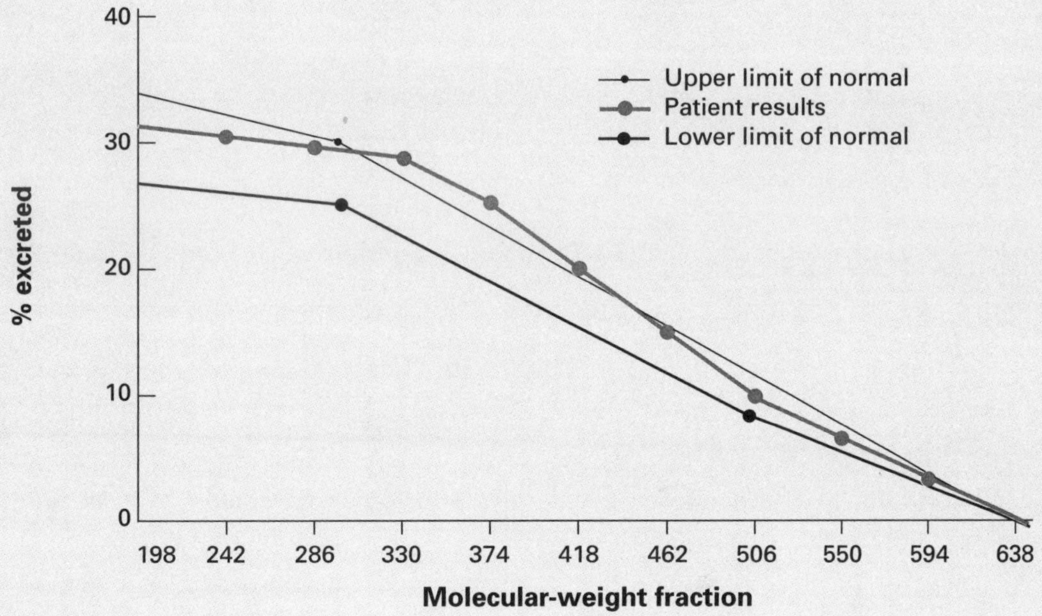

Upper limit of normal
Patient results
Lower limit of normal
% excreted
Molecular-weight fraction

GUT-PERMEABILITY TEST

This investigation is being pioneered at a laboratory in London. Brilliant in its simplicity, it is a test to assess the permeability of the intestine, and is particularly important in establishing leaky-gut syndrome (LGS), which may be responsible for food allergy that can lead to so many disorders.

A patient expels the first-morning urine, and follows this by drinking a solution that contains a range of molecules of different sizes. Depending upon the gut permeability, these molecules are absorbed into the bloodstream. The kidney will filter these, and a collection of urine can be assayed to measure the size of the molecules that were absorbed. If larger molecules are found, then a leaky gut can be diagnosed, and curative treatment obtained.

At this time, the availability of this test is limited, but access to it is being increased, and I believe this will be one of the most important tests available.

HAIR-MINERAL ANALYSIS REPORT

Reference: SHB/ASJD/N91 **Sample Date:** 10-02-1998

Age: 30

Sex: Male

Height: 5'2"	**Shampoo:** Baby	**Conditioner:** None
Weight: 204lbs	**Bleach:** None	**Highlight:** None
Hair color: Black	**Perm:** None	**Tint:** None

	Reference range:	Results: (Parts per million)	Reference Range: Low – High	
Calcium	200–600	442		Ca
Magnesium	30–95	38		Mg
Phosphorus*	100–210	187		P
Sodium*	90–340	202		Na
Potassium*	50–120	34		K
Iron*	20–60	27		Fe
Copper	10–40	18		Cu
Zinc	150–240	196		Zn
Chromium	0.60–1.50	0.56		Cr
Manganese	1.0–2.6	1.1		Mn
Selenium	1.5–4.0	2.8		Se
Nickel	0.40–1.40	0.66		Ni
Cobalt*	0.10–0.70	0.19		Co

**Clinical significance of hair concentration of asterisked elements has not been established.*

Toxic Metals	Accept	Raised	Toxic	Results	Acceptable – Raised – Toxic	
Lead	<15.0	15.0–40.0	>40.0	8.9		Pb
Mercury	<2.0	2.0–5.0	>5.0	0.55		Hg
Cadmium	<0.5	0.5–2.0	>2.0	0.21		Cd
Arsenic	<2.0	2.0–5.0	>5.0	0.11		As
Aluminum	<10.0	10.0–25.0	>25.0	5.2		Al

Ratio:	Normal:	Result:	Ratio:	Normal:	Result:
Ca/Mg	6.1:1	12	Zn/Pb	>10:1	22
Ca/P	2.6:1	2.36	Zn/Cd	>400:1	933
Na/K	2.3:1	5.94	Se/Cd	>3.4:1	13
Zn/Cu	8.5:1	11	Se/Hg		5.09

HAIR ANALYSIS

A tablespoon amount of hair may be used for two investigations.

Mineral and toxic metal analysis

Hair analysis for mineral deficiency or excess has a well-established scientific background, but it is poorly used in orthodox medicine because of the marked underestimation of mineral deficiency or toxic excess as a cause of disease. Samples can be put through a simple analysis to give a clear indication of mineral problems.

Food intolerance

I am highly sceptical of the use of hair analysis in food intolerance/allergy testing (*see* **Allergy testing**).

HUMORAL PATHOLOGICAL LAB TEST (HLB Method)

NAME: **DATE:**

Interpretation:

Notice: These interpretations are based on Newtonian Laws, and have been developed by Heitan, Legard and Bradford (1930). It is widely used in the biggest Cancer Research Institute of U.S.A., the Bradford Institute, and in various Institutes in Europe.

Results could be altered by the influence of Antioxydants, chemotherapy, or radiation therapy. To have an exact reading, it is advisable to refrain from the above mentioned for two weeks, otherwise, slight alterations in the results are possible.

SYMPTOMS	RESULT	SYMPTOMS	RESULT
oxidation leading to allergies	✓	Vitamin-C deficiency	✓
Anaemia of qualitative origin		oxidation MS origin	
oxidation leading to arthritis		Heinz bodies	✓
lack of ability to assimilate food		Hypo-Calcemia	
asthma cellular origin		Physical stress	✓
degenerative state I, II, III, IV		increased acidity in stomach	
Dehydration of kidney	✓	congested lymph system	
Free-radicals activity		Psychological stress (catecholamine)	✓
oxydation patterns indicating fungus	✓	indications for hormone imbalance	

Next proposed Humoral pathological control in six weeks

HUMORAL PATHOLOGICAL LABORATORY TEST (HUMORAL LABORATORY BLOOD TEST)

The HLB test, I am sure, will be one of the most beneficial investigations in the future of holistic medicine. It, like so many great ideas, was based on a simple observational fact, which is that blood—its cells, plasma, and serum—change and react in relation to chemical factors released from diseased tissue.

A pinprick of blood is placed as four drops on a microscope slide. This is placed underneath a high-power microscope that magnifies the blood up to 1,500 times. The pictures produced are entered into a computer, which compares the samples to thousands of other samples taken from known conditions. Deficiencies, poor oxygenation, and the presence of chemicals from cancer cells are just examples of the huge bank of conditions that any sample is compared to. The computer prints out the possible diagnoses and, if programed correctly, may offer advice on treatments that have been successful and have returned abnormal blood back to a normal status.

The availability of this test is increasing but at present it is available in only a few centers. Again, please contact the 101 Group (address on page 661).

Humoral Pathological Laboratory Blood Test

Normal blood cluster

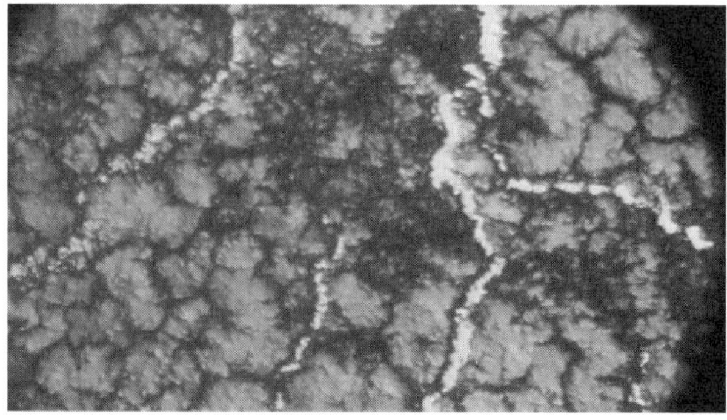

Lymph and bowel toxicity

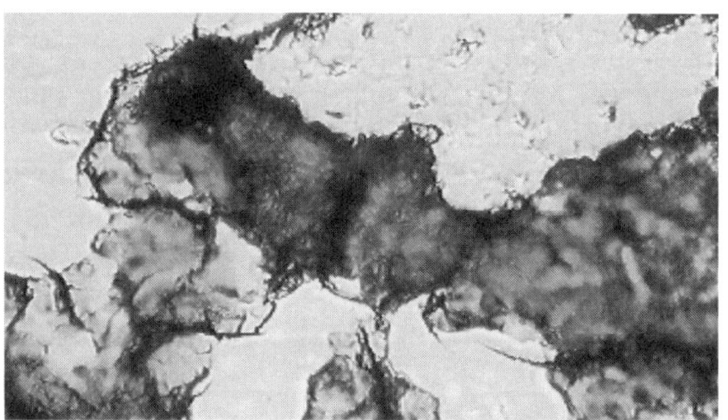

Strong oxidation

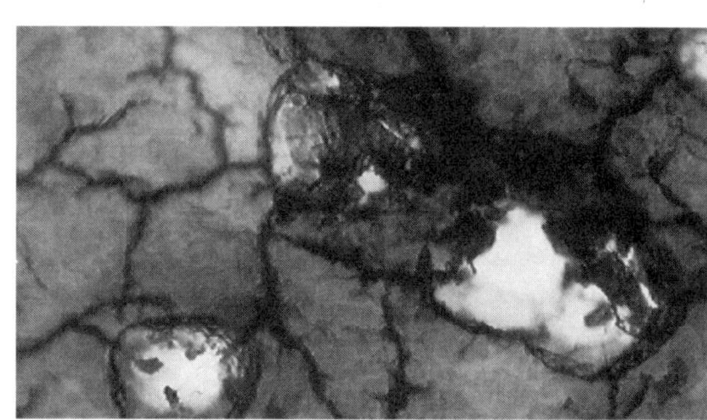

Fungi in blood

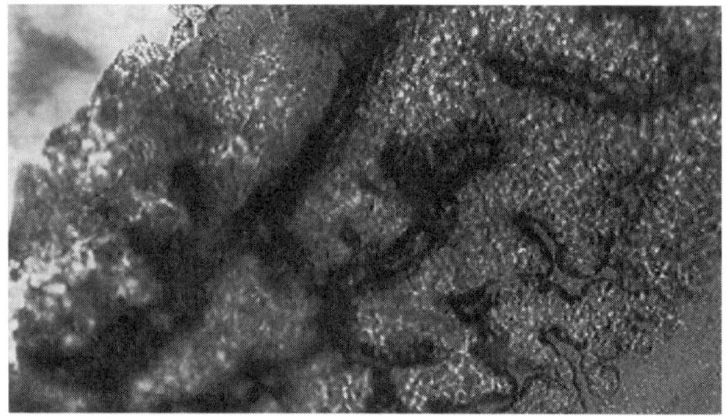

Fungi-infested blood

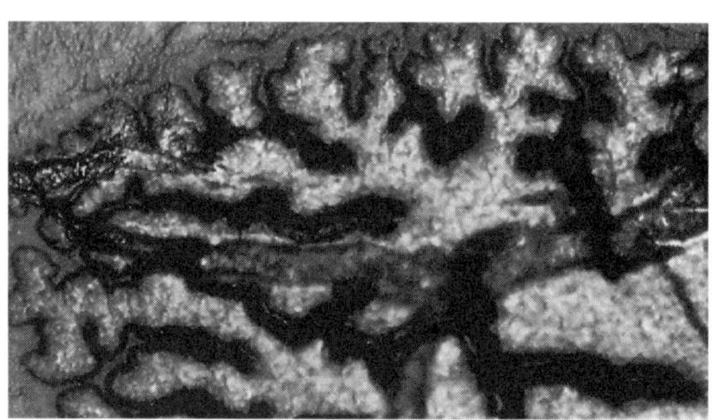

Fungi in blood

Adrenalin stress

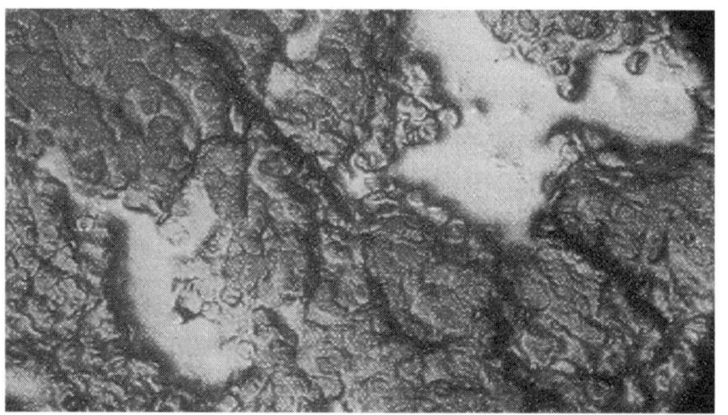

Blood from cancer case

Iris Topograph

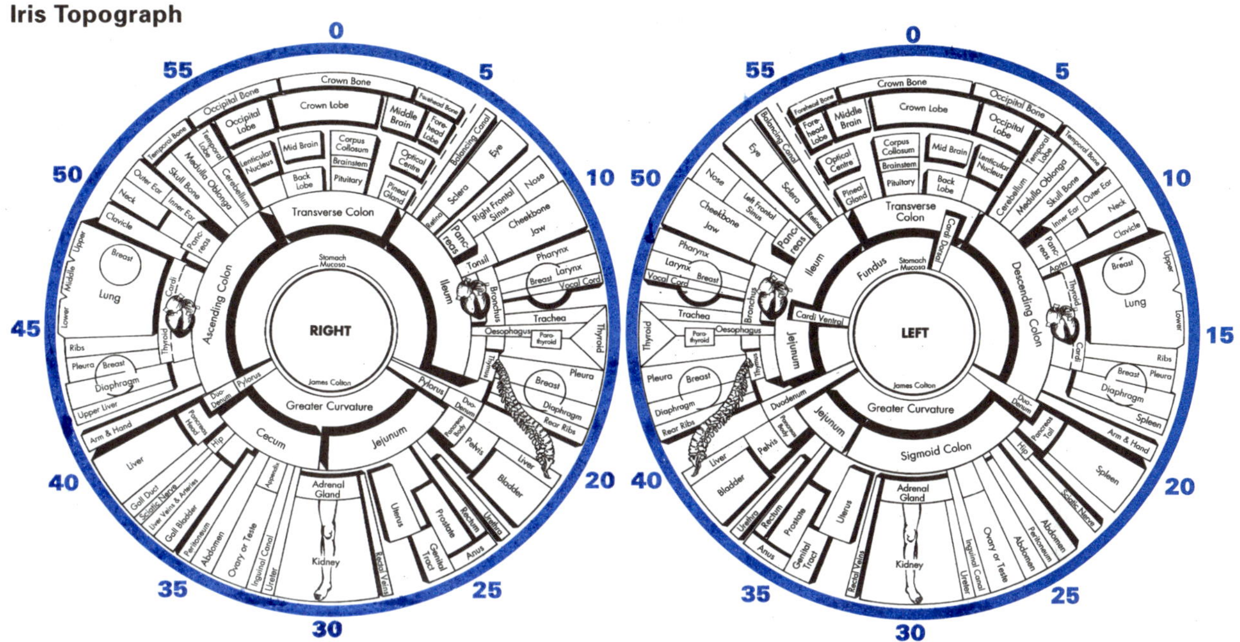

IRIDOLOGY

Iridology is the study of the color and patterns on the iris of the eyes. This technique has been in use for thousands of years, and probably has its origins in the East. However, a Hungarian doctor, Ignacz von Peczely, studied the possibility of the iris being a mirror of the body's health following changes he noted in an owl's iris while repairing its broken leg.

Until recently, study of the iris and diagnosis has been made by practitioner observation, aided by a special magnifying camera that photographs the iris for study. Cameras can now be attached to computers, which do the diagnosis from thousands of comparable iris studies logged in their memory banks.

I was surprised to find that few studies have been done to compare the accuracy of iridologists or their computers with orthodox diagnosis. I would assume that this would be a simple, comparative

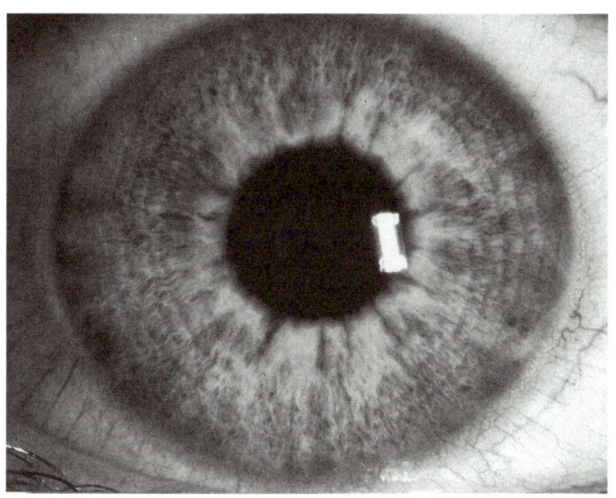

Tendency to rheumatism and arthritis. Stress rings. Pseudoparathyroidism—excess calcium in the stomach.

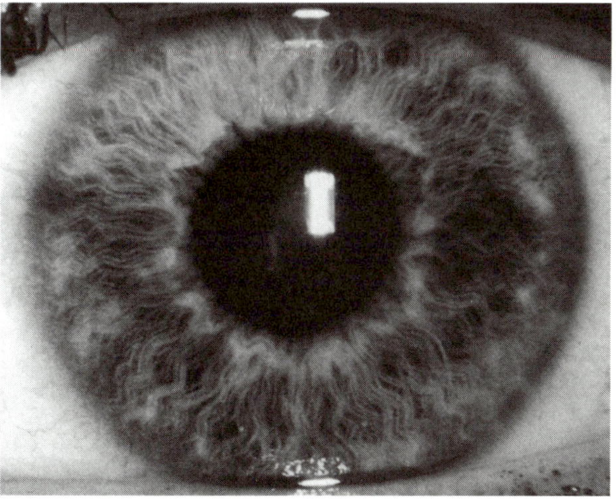

Tendency to toxicity of the lymph glands. Spots showing difficulty with metabolism—overweight. Left-hand side (15°)—weakness of the lungs—asthma.

study, and can only assume that finances are hard to find. I am sure that research will be done in the future to show firmly where iridology may be of benefit. As a diagnostic technique in conjunction with other tests and clinical observation, iridology can be a great eye-opener!

KIRLIAN PHOTOGRAPHY

The Kirlian photograph technique takes "pictures" of the aura (*see* **Aura reading**). Initially created as a diagnostic technique by a Russian engineer, Semyon Kirlian, the original equipment consisted of an electric coil, an aluminum plate, and photo-sensitive film covered by glass. Modern-day cameras, based on the same principles, send a high-voltage charge that measures energy release when part of

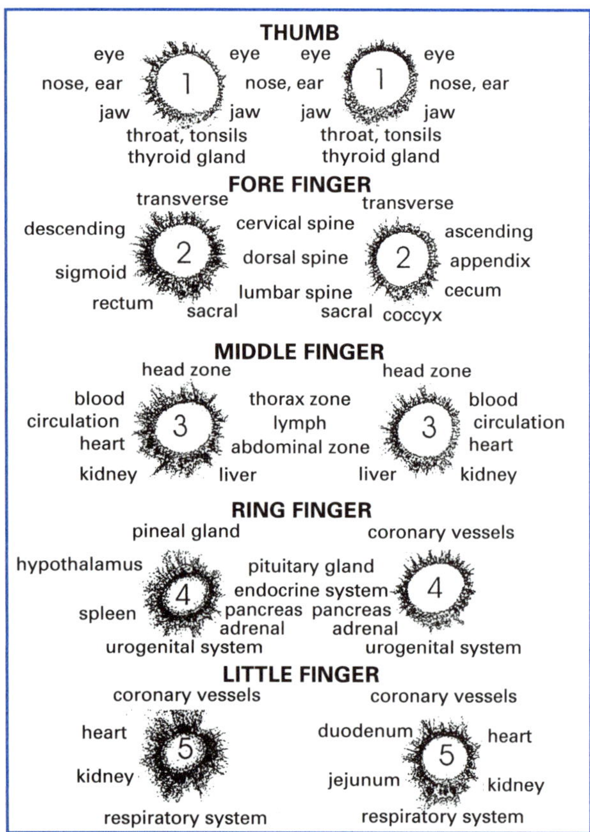

The computer-derived Kirlian images`, above right, are of the fingers of a patient with chronic-fatigue syndrome. The print-out, below right, is significantly worse as the patient has had flu. Above is a table used in diagnosis.

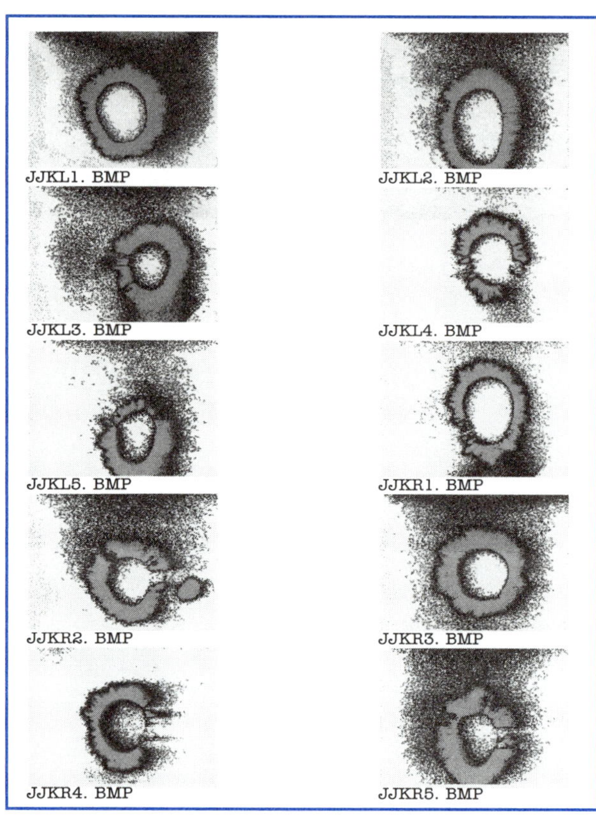

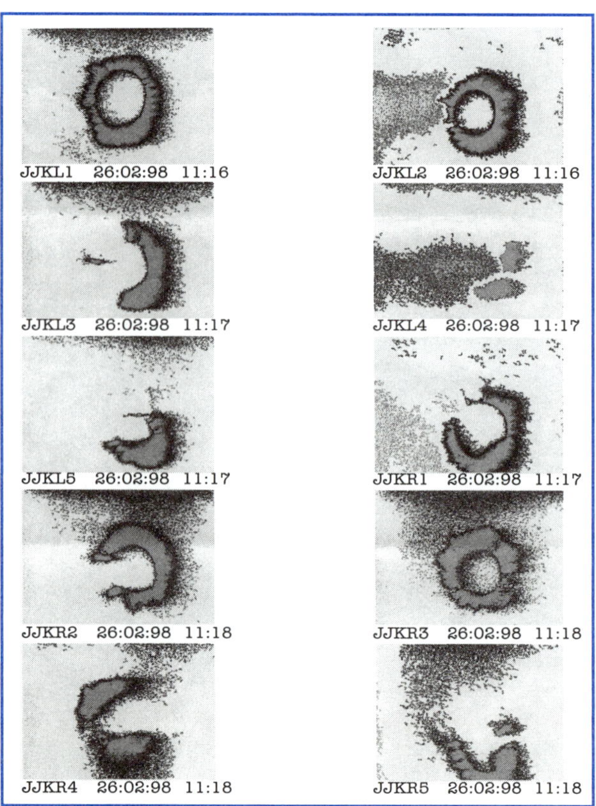

the body is placed in contact with it. Whole-body auras are now taken without actual contact.

An individual's aura will change depending on their health, and certain patterns are correlated with certain diseases. As with iridology, I wonder why a clear correlation has not been made between certain patterns and particular diseases, but I do know that trials are underway in continental Europe and the U.K. I suspect that auras will not correlate to specific diseases, but will alter depending on an individual's response to a particular disease process. Until proven otherwise, Kirlian photography should only be used in conjunction with clinical assessment and other investigations. *See also* **Aura reading.**

PANCREATIC EXOCRINE TESTS

See **Gastrograms and pancreaticograms.**

It is of immense benefit for a complementary medical practitioner to know the individual patient's ability to digest foods. Many conditions may be associated with deficiencies that may be due to a lack of digestive capability rather than insufficient ingestion of a particular compound that is deficient. The orthodox world pays little attention to this factor and, until recently, practitioners of complementary medicine had to use their clinical judgment and experience to assess the possibility that a patient is not digesting properly. A noninvasive test that involves the patient doing no more than swallowing a particular fluid to assess digestive capabilities and enzyme production is available at this stage, but patients need to visit the laboratory in London, and there is currently limited availability and a long waiting list. Availability will, hopefully, become greater. Practitioners rather than patients should contact The 101 Group for information if they feel a patient would benefit (*see* page 661).

Chapter 9

Alternative Therapies

Chapter 9

Alternative Therapies

This chapter provides a synopsis of the different alternative therapies that bind together with orthodox medicine to give us the choices that make up holistic medicine.

Choosing Your Healer

Most main branches of complementary or alternative medicine have a regulatory body, or a college to which a practitioner may be affiliated. Some are more officious than others, but all demand a basic standard of technique and stipulate a certain amount of time spent in training to be able to join.

Unfortunately, many healing arts do not have any form of association, and there is currently no legal requirement to have studied the subject that a practitioner may claim to practice. I believe that this will change in the near future. For now, however, the best method of choosing a practitioner is through word of mouth. Qualifications do not necessarily ensure that a practitioner has healing qualities, but if they have helped someone, they are likely to be able to help others.

If you cannot find somebody in this manner, then select a practitioner from a reputable clinic. It is unlikely that a practitioner who is not safe or effective will flourish within a group. Other practitioners will hear any detrimental information, and either correct the failing, or recommend to the clinic owners that the practitioner is not suitable.

A waiting list is usually a good sign. You need to ask how many days a week that an individual may work with patients. I know of a practitioner who has a remarkable reputation, based on a six-month waiting list. He only works one day a week! Most practitioners should expect a six-day waiting list!

Good practitioners are busy practitioners who, as a rule, do not need to advertise. Accepting that everybody has to start somewhere, and that advertising is a method of getting one's presence known, an advert may represent an unexperienced or failing practitioner. An advertisement may be drawing your attention to a new field of practice or a unique technique, but selecting a practitioner by this method may not be the best. It is better to go on articles that you may read, because journalists are generally quite scrupulous, and have experience. Always, however, look for the political motive in anything that is being written about complementary medicine. I may be overzealous in my belief that the orthodox world would not like to see complementary medicine flourish, but I do feel that many articles on the subject are overcritical, and do not compare the downside of orthodox medicine when criticizing an alternative technique.

At the end of the day, you need to be comfortable with your chosen practitioner. If the area in which they work, the room in which they practice, or their character feels uncomfortable, then look again. Trust your instincts.

ACUPUNCTURE

Acupuncture is one aspect of Chinese and Tibetan medicine. (*See* **Chinese and Oriental medicine.**) Using acupuncture outside of the full discipline of these medical philosophies can be likened to using physiotherapy and no other treatment when dealing with orthodox medicine.

Acupuncture is thought to have originated from the observations by Chinese physicians of their warriors who had been stabbed, speared, or injured in battle. Specific wounds seemed to create changes, depending on their placement superficially in the body.

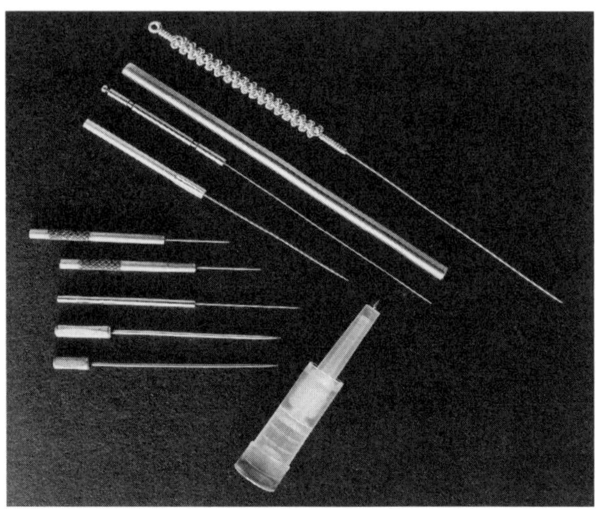

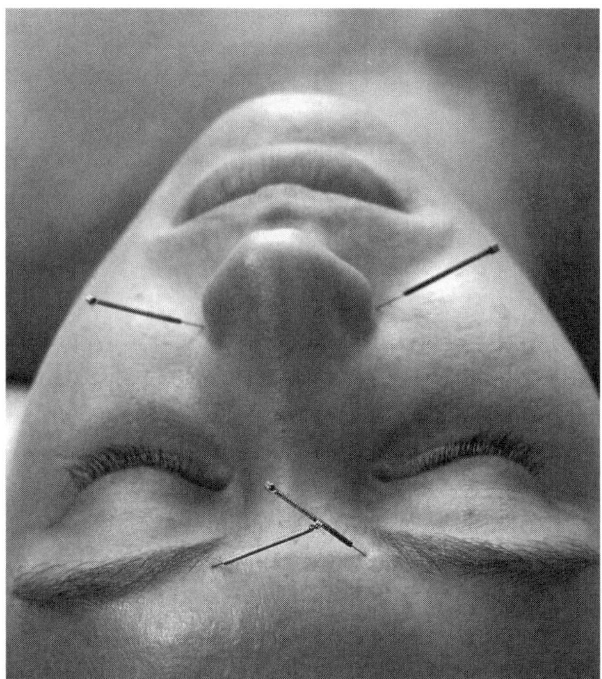

There is a large variety of acupuncture needle designs (above). *A patient receives treatment for hay fever* (right). *An acupuncturist inserts needles to "tonify" the kidneys* (below).

The West has adopted the attitude that the placing of very thin needles at strategic points around the body causes the release of endorphins and enkephalins—the body's natural opiates—to create pain relief and a "feel-good factor." While there is definitely evidence for the release of these chemicals, it only occurs at some of the known acupuncture points, and is only one part of the acupuncture principle.

In truth, and perfectly scientifically provable on the basis of observation, the acupuncture points are stimulatory areas along energy lines, known by the Chinese as meridians, and by the Tibetans as channels. The Tibetans have many points along known nerve routes, whereas the Chinese have little correlation with these. Stimulation of these points increases, decreases, or varies the energy in these lines. These channels or meridians represent organs or systems within the body, mind, and soul of a human being.

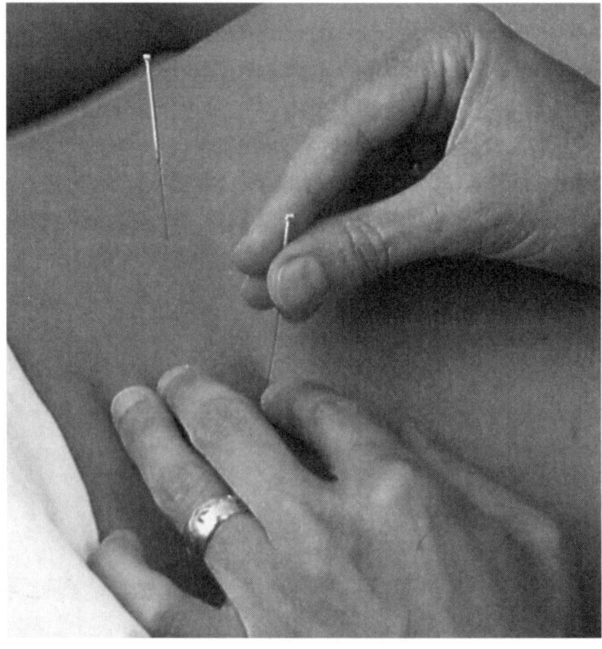

Acupuncture treatment consists of inserting fine needles into the skin to correct the imbalances or disharmony discovered in your meridians or channels. The acupuncturist will first ask you questions, and then examine you in ways that other medical systems may not find important. For example, he may feel the palms of your hands and look at your tongue. He will also feel your pulses at both wrists. On the basis of his understanding of the "symptom picture," he will decide where to place the needles, the depth to which they need to be placed, the application of heat, and the need to apply movement to the needles (*see* **Pulse taking**).

Acupuncture/Acupressure Meridians

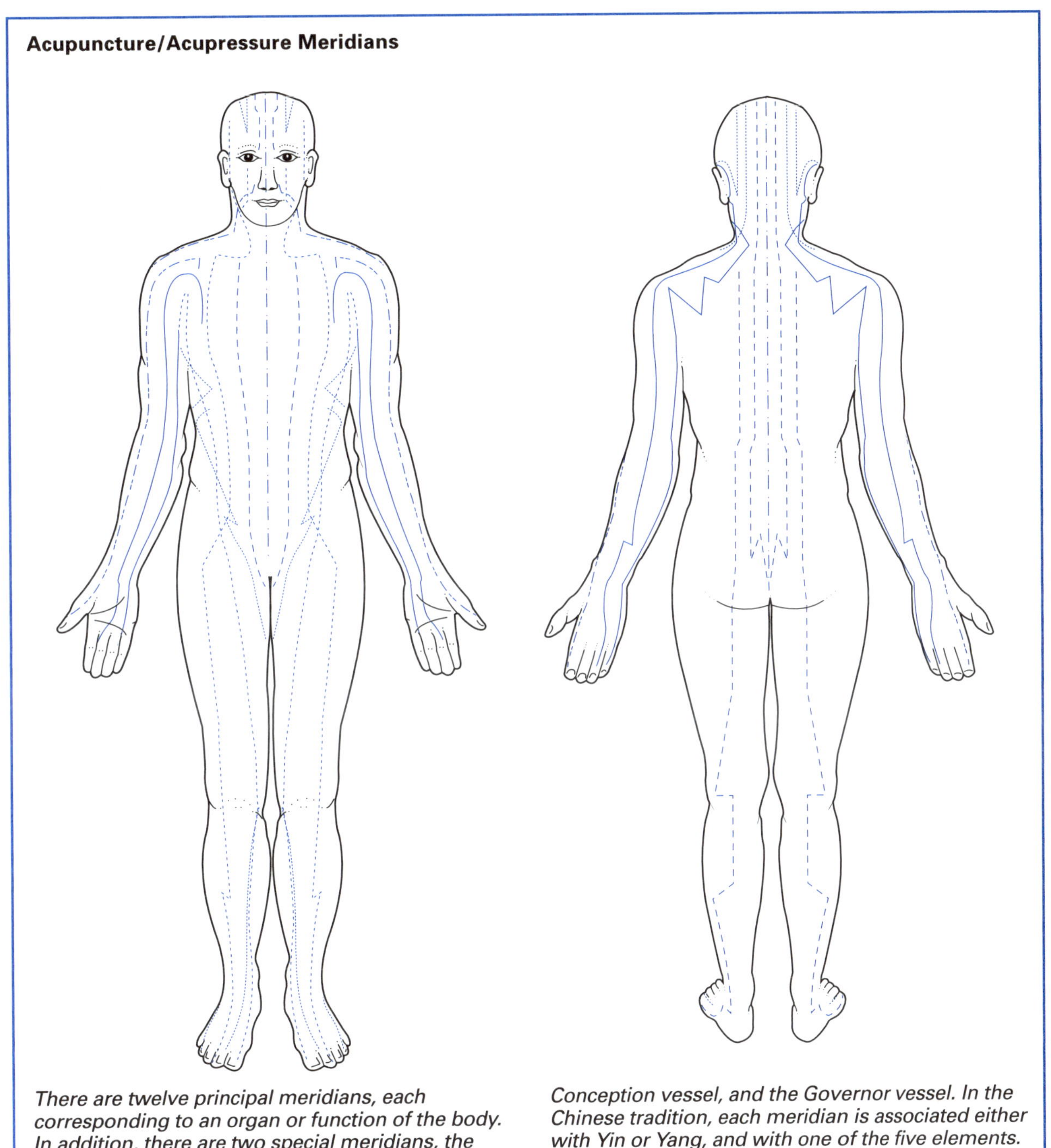

There are twelve principal meridians, each corresponding to an organ or function of the body. In addition, there are two special meridians, the Conception vessel, and the Governor vessel. In the Chinese tradition, each meridian is associated either with Yin or Yang, and with one of the five elements.

ACUPRESSURE

Acupressure is an ancient healing art based on the same principles as acupuncture, except that instead of needles, only finger or thumb pressure is used to harmonize the flow of energy through the body. There is evidence that acupressure was used even earlier than acupuncture, when the Indians first documented some basic principles of massage over 5,000 years ago. The Japanese have advanced this therapeutic application of massage, and from it developed the technique now known as Shiatsu.

Application of pressure, either gentle or deep, to specific pressure points can stimulate the meridians or channels in the same way as acupuncture. Unlike acupuncture, it can be performed at home, either as a self-treatment or to treat other members of the family. If you know the right pressure points to use, it makes an effective first-aid measure for pain or cramps. Acupressure massage will also boost the immune system, relieve stress and fatigue, and treat many common ailments. It is effective for chronic conditions including insomnia, joint pain and stiffness, and acute ailments such as indigestion and headaches. In addition, acupressure will release lymphatic blockages and help relieve "knots" in muscles.

The points and meridians, which correspond to those in acupuncture charts, are pressed for at least 20 seconds with the thumb, middle, or index finger, whichever feels most comfortable. This pressure may be varied in intensity according to the condition being treated. For example, for fatigue or lack of energy, the point needs to be stimulated; this is achieved by applying deep, clockwise pressure. To sedate a point for pain or stress-related conditions, somewhat lighter, anticlockwise pressure is applied. When the person you are treating feels slight discomfort or tenderness under pressure, you will know that you have found the exact point. Points on the body will usually need firmer, more-prolonged pressure than those on the face.

ALEXANDER TECHNIQUE

The Alexander technique was developed in the 1890s by an Australian actor named Frederick M. Alexander, who found that he could correct his voice loss by adjusting his posture. He realized how his poor habits of movement had interfered with the body's healthy functioning, and that learning to move well, and with the head and neck correctly aligned, he derived many beneficial effects, not just on his voice, but on his general health. From his observations, he was able to formulate the Alexander technique, which he taught to other actors and singers, and then to a wider public.

Today, specially trained teachers all over the world help people to improve their health and well-being by changing the way they use their bodies in everyday activities. They teach how to hold the body and breathe more efficiently, which oxygenates the body better. Realignment of posture is necessary in all of us. Unless you are already practicing a physical technique, the chances are that I could ask you at this moment to sit up straight. In doing so, you would probably find that you have been slumped, and can increase your height by about two to three inches. This "slumping" closes up the chest, and may block the energy channels that flow through the body. The technique aims to change these poor habits of posture, movement, and thought permanently, replacing unconscious tensions with thoughtful movement.

Practicing the Alexander technique offers a wide range of health benefits. In addition to reducing stress, and improving the voice and breathing, it may improve lung conditions such as asthma, and persistent postural problems causing, for instance, low-back pain. The technique has been shown through trials to lower blood pressure, and has even been shown to deal with psychological problems such as depression and insomnia.

The Alexander technique should be taught within a course of ten lessons, followed by occasional extra lessons. Visiting the teacher regularly is a bit like having piano lessons—you practice if you know that you are going to be assessed!

ANTHROPOSOPHICAL MEDICINE

Anthroposophy, derived from the Greek words meaning man and wisdom, is the spiritual and mystical teachings of the Austrian philosopher and scientist, Dr. Rudolf Steiner (1861–1925). His ideas have been particularly influential in education, but they also inspired a new approach to healing. Anthroposophical medicine is practiced mainly in continental Europe, although there are doctors and clinics in other parts of the world.

Steiner realized that the human being was not just a physical or biochemical organism, but contained "etheric" and "astral" bodies. These were unmeasurable energies that made up our emotions and "vital force." Steiner used the term "ego" to define our spiritual core. Steiner's concepts harmonize with Eastern philosophy: he believed that the body is made up of earth, water, fire, and air, which are connected through the digestive and movement structures, the sensory system, and the rhythmic system. The physical and etheric energies control digestion and movement; the ego and the astral body control senses; and the rhythmic system controls the circulation and breathing.

Steiner believed that health was governed by a balance of all of these. He had a holistic view of healing, and warned of the limitations of scientific medicine. He saw healing primarily as an art, and the patient as a human spirit finding its way amid its relationships with the body, with other people and with nature, and not simply as an object separated from everything else in the universe. Steiner simplified illness into inflammatory and degenerative conditions, but wished to stress the meaningfulness of each illness by putting it into the context of the individual's biography and surroundings.

Treatment is by altering spiritual and emotional consciousness, through diet, exercise, and remedies. Healing possibilities are enriched by artistic and other therapies, such as painting, eurythmy, sculpture, and music. Anthroposophical medicine uses a mixture of herbal, mineral and homeopathic remedies.

APPLIED KINESIOLOGY—*see* Kinesiology

AROMATHERAPY

Aromatherapy is the use of plant extracts, known as essences or essential oils, to treat a range of common ailments, and also for their effect on the emotions and mental well-being. There are about 30 oils commonly used, ranging from basil and bergamot to lavender, rose, sage, and tea tree.

Aromatherapy oils with herbs and other ingredients.

These highly aromatic oils can penetrate the skin when used in the bath or in conjunction with massage (when dispersed in a carrier oil), but more probably have a greater therapeutic effect through inhalation, when they are absorbed into the body through the nose and lungs.

Aromatherapy is one of the most ancient of the healing arts, and has been documented from the East for thousands of years. The ancient Egyptians used aromatic substances in medicine (and for the mummification process) as far back as 4,500 BC. It was not until the 20th century, however, that the healing powers of essential oils were studied and fully appreciated.

Some of the oils are expensive to buy (a huge number of plants is needed to make just a small amount of oil), but only a few drops are needed to provide an effective treatment, so a little goes a long way. Provided the right oils are used in the correct quantities and are not ingested (unless on the advice of a qualified therapist), the techniques are safe. Many of the oils may be used in combination, which will increase the beneficial effect. For relaxation and to enhance your mood, choose the oil whose fragrance you prefer.

The most successful results have been seen in wound healing, treating skin problems such as acne, PMT, poor circulation, respiratory disorders, and headaches, and other stress-related disorders. Some of the most useful oils include: eucalyptus (for colds, flu, and rheumatism), tea tree, pine, or lemon (for sore throats, colds, flu, and bronchitis), lavender (for eczema, acne, minor wounds, insomnia, and tiredness), and geranium (for skin problems, neuralgia, sore throats, and tonsillitis). There are many good books available, listing the main essential oils and their uses.

One of the most effective ways of using aromatherapy oils is to place a few drops into the water of an oil burner. As the water heats up the aromatic vapours are released.

ART THERAPY

A branch of psychotherapy (*see* **Psychotherapy**), art therapy is used as a means of understanding emotional and psychological problems, and gaining release from them. People know intuitively that creative self-expression is a way of healing oneself, and artistic expression is one such way of doing so. No artistic skill is needed, but through the creative process itself, many problems can be addressed, including depression, low self-esteem, and relationship difficulties. Art therapy is especially effective with severely disturbed people who find it difficult to express their feelings verbally.

An art therapist, through interpreting the meaning of the art produced by the client or patient, can uncover problems that may be deeply buried and that might otherwise take years of regular counseling to uncover. The therapist hopes to come to an understanding of the client, and thereby help him or her towards making fresh discoveries about the self and about life. The process of creating something through visual means can help people to detach themselves from feelings or problems that might be difficult or impossible to express verbally, or that are otherwise too overwhelming to deal with.

Art therapy utilizes color and patterns using pencils, crayons, paint, and any other colorful medium to try to bring whatever is lying in the subconscious to the visual consciousness. Collages, sculpture, paintings, and drawings can all express unexpected angst in the artist in a very immediate way, and this method often bypasses the self-censoring process with which we may block out disturbing feelings and thoughts.

The British Association of Art Therapists is an expanding group, and registered art therapists can be found throughout the U.K., U.S.A, and many other countries. Art therapists will differ in their interpretive approach depending on their school of thought, which could be Freudian or Jungian, or might put more emphasis on interpretation of the artwork by the clients themselves.

AURICULAR THERAPY

Like many parts of the body, the ear reflects and maps out the rest of the body. The diagram below shows the many acupuncture points found on the external ear (*see* **Acupuncture**). Auricular therapy generally involves the insertion of acupuncture needles into these points, but can deal with most health matters (usually in conjunction with more-mainstream treatments) by acupressure. Points are located in the ear by pressing with a fine, blunt

Auricular Therapy

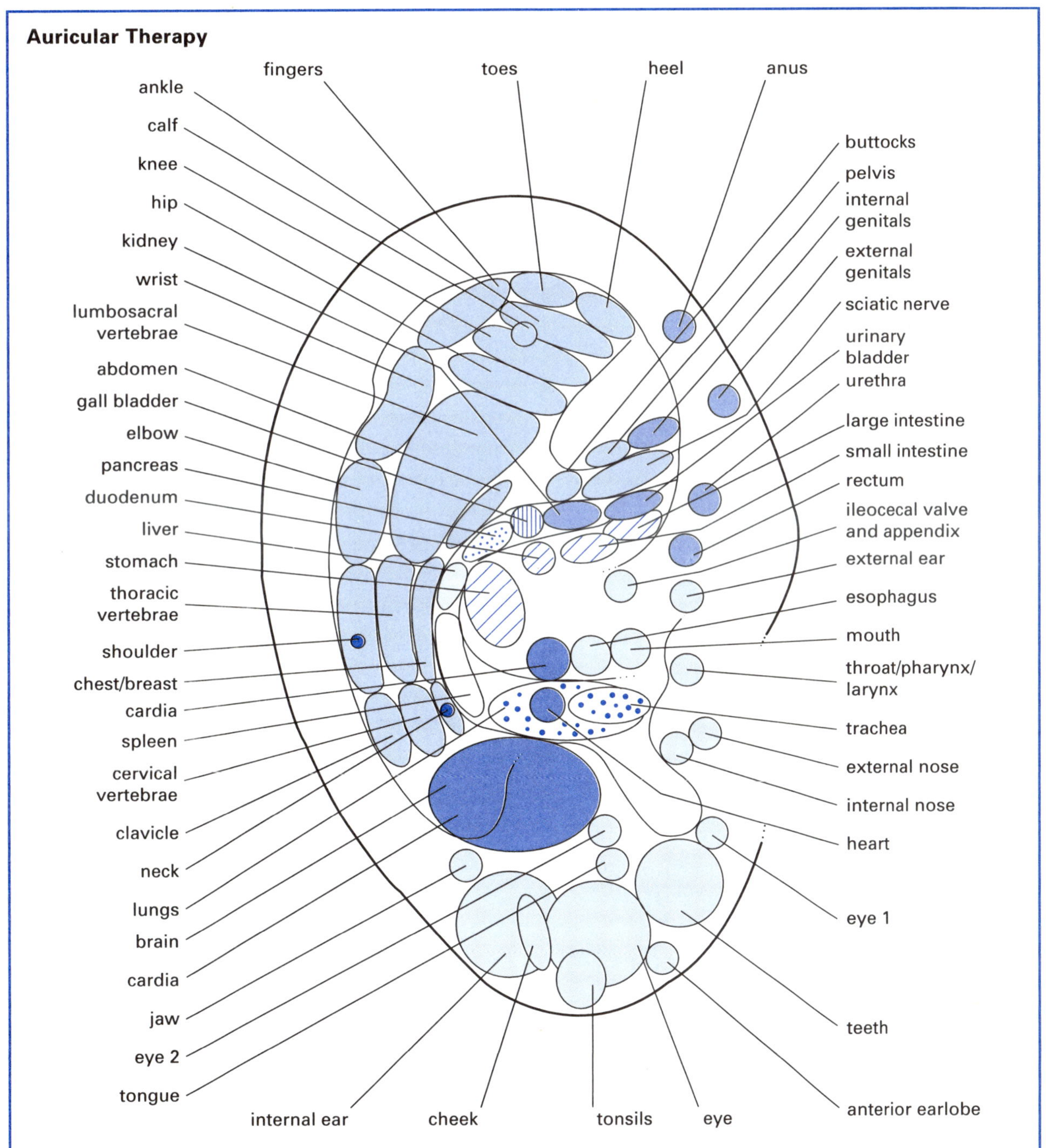

In auricular therapy, the ear may be seen as a map of the body, each area corresponding to an organ or structure.

instrument to locate sensitive spots, or by using an electrical sensor. There are more than 120 points on each ear, and for treatment to be effective, it is important that they are located exactly.

The point is then stimulated by acupressure or with small acupuncture needles. The needles remain in place for about 15 minutes, and are manipulated now and then. Some therapists may use electrical stimulation, which is not painful, and experiments are now being tried using laser. Continuous treatment, lasting several days, may be obtained if the the therapist, using acupressure, attaches a small press needle or seed with adhesive tape to the point in the ear. During treatment, a dull or tingling sensation may be felt in the ear or on the same side of the body.

Auricular therapy is particularly useful for treating addictions (such as help with giving up smoking) and for pain control. Respiratory disorders, musculoskeletal disorders, and chronic conditions such as arthritis and skin problems have all been shown to benefit from this treatment.

AUTOGENIC TRAINING

The word "autogenic" is derived from the Greek for "coming from within" and is principally a self-relaxation/hypnosis technique. Devised in Berlin by Dr. J. Schultz in the 1920s, the training consists of learning a set of six simple exercises designed to induce deep relaxation, and thereby promote self-healing. The exercises include the repetition of certain phrases to bring on feelings of general warmth, an abdominal glow, a feeling of heaviness, and heartbeat and breathing control. Schultz also recommended a technique for cooling the forehead.

Autogenic training involves learning how to control the body's involuntary nervous system, and needs to be taught by a specially trained therapist. It can be used to treat many disorders, from anxiety and tension to asthma and tendonitis. Autogenics is an effective alternative to using tranquilizers or sleeping pills. It is not only an excellent self-help addition to the treatment of any chronic condition, but also one of the most-positive antidotes to everyday stress. By practicing the exercises for only a few minutes, you can release yourself from the stresses in your life, and allow the body to restore itself and become more resistant to illness. Its long-term effects are to lower heart-attack risk factors such as high blood pressure and high blood cholesterol, and to improve emotional balance and willpower.

AYURVEDA

Ayurveda is a word derived from one of the oldest known languages, Sanskrit, and means the "knowledge of daily living." There is mention of Ayurveda in the Vedas, the world's oldest literature, which suggests that this healing system has been practiced for over 5,000 years.

Ayurveda considers human beings to be part of the "whole," indivisible from all else. There are many authorities who define Ayurveda in different ways, but in principle, it is a way of life rather than a medical doctrine, and includes spiritual, emotional, social, and physical concerns. As much importance is given to sleep as to activity, to diet as to ablutions and hygiene, and to exercise as to meditation.

Ayurvedic medicine cannot be separated from a consciousness of one's entire lifestyle. Ayurveda is only properly practiced if the individual is willing to change all aspects of activities creating ill-health. The current fad of using Ayurvedic remedies is like taking painkillers for a badly injured limb. It is only one part of the necessary treatment to regain function.

Ayurveda is based on three principal forces known as the *tri-dosha*. *Vatta* represents air and space; *pitta* represents fire and water; and *kapha* represents water and earth. All these overlap to some extent, and none can survive without the other. For example, fire cannot burn without air, and without some substance (earth) to burn. Water becomes stagnant without air, and fire cannot be controlled without water. Different emotional states and physical activities fall into these categories. Movement and breathing are vatta, temperature and digestion are pitta, and energy and stability are kapha. Emotionally, dreams and intentions are represented by vatta (head in the clouds), ambition and drive by pitta ("he is all fired up"), and nurturing and forgiveness are covered by kapha (nesting and nurturing).

All people are made up of all doshas, but usually one or two predominate. Most books on Ayurveda help individuals to understand their constitutional type, and knowing this can help balance the tri-dosha. People who are predominantly vatta/pitta may benefit from having more kapha, for example. All foods have their own elements. Chilies and hot soups are generally pitta, whereas red meat is predominantly pitta and kapha. Knowing one's constitutional dosha allows a diet to be set for that particular body type.

Ayurveda is a complex philosophy, made more so by the use of Indian terminology, but once the basics have been grasped, the commonsense attitude and approach are simple, and can have a profound effect on well-being. Unfortunately, in the West, the necessary dedication to an all-round lifestyle is not easily formed or followed and, I think, Ayurveda is probably only of benefit to those with time to dedicate to their health, and not to those looking for a "quick fix."

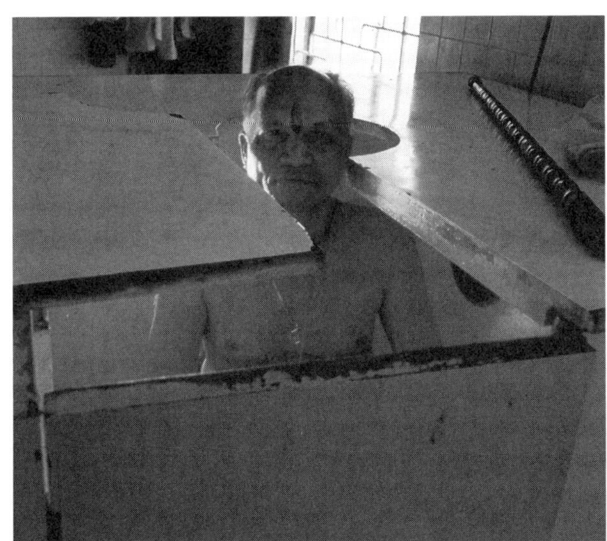

Steam baths are one of the five Ayurvedic purification therapies. The three doshas—vatta, pitta and kapha—are brought to a balanced state, thus promoting well-being.

BACH FLOWER REMEDIES

These are herbal remedies derived from flowers. They promote healing by reducing negative states of mind (seen as the cause of disease) and increasing positive emotions. Physical problems are thought to derive from a mind/body energy imbalance that nature can correct through its effects on plants when they are taken in the right combination. The remedies are extracted from the flowers and buds of common plants by the action of sunlight or heat, and preserved in brandy.

The system was devised by Dr. Edward Bach (1886–1936), a pathologist and bacteriologist, who, following an illness of his own in the early 1900s, discovered that plants contain compounds or energy that affect the psyche. He found that different diseases seemed to be linked to different temperamental types, and classified these types into seven main groups, each with a habitual negative emotional state. These states are indicated by a key word or phrase, and are: loneliness, fear, uncertainty, lack of interest in the present, over-sensitivity, despondency, and overconcern for others.

Working intuitively, Dr. Bach set out to find plants that made these negative states positive, and eventually found 38 in all, ranging from agrimony to willow. For the purposes of prescribing, he further subdivided each state of mind so that, for example, under the heading "uncertainty," aspen acts on fear of the unknown; cherry plum on fear of losing control; and rock rose on terror or self-abandonment. Under the category of "over-sensitivity," agrimony acts on worry and anxiety hidden under a brave face; centaury is for weak will and a "doormat tendency," and holly works for jealousy and anger.

The remedies should therefore be selected to correspond to the state of mind and the personality. The experience of a practitioner may be helpful if you find it difficult to decide on the appropriate remedy. Since they are completely safe for any age, the remedies are commonly used for self-help at home, particularly the "Rescue Remedy," which is a mixture of five of the flower remedies and can be used after a shock or in an emotional crisis.

BATES METHOD FOR EYES

The Bates method of eyesight training, named after Dr. W. H. Bates, an eye specialist of New York, is a natural way of improving and maintaining eyesight, using particular exercises to relearn proper habits of vision. Dr. Bates published his bestseller, *Better Eyesight without Glasses*, detailing these exercises, in 1919. He argued that perfect vision was the product of completely relaxed eyes, and that it was misuse of the eyes that led to defects of vision.

Bates' methods found many advocates, including the writer Aldous Huxley, who as a young man could hardly see to read. Huxley's book, *The Art of Seeing*, explains how he was helped by this method. Followers of the method, found throughout the world, argue that the exercises benefit people of all ages, however poor their eyesight. Many practitioners of other complementary therapies use the Bates method during treatments.

There are seven main exercises which should be practiced daily. They can be learned easily by obtaining a book or, more simply, by consulting a Bates' practitioner, who will usually recommend a course of weekly training sessions. The exercises aim to relax tension in the eye muscles, and include "palming," covering the eyes with the palms of the hands for ten minutes two or three times a day; "splashing," splashing the closed eyes repeatedly with warm and then cold water, morning and evening; and "shifting and swinging," consciously imitating the minute shifting movements of the eyes around objects. Bates also believed in blinking frequently, once or twice every ten seconds. In addition, he considered the importance of diet, supplements, and homeopathy in maintaining the health of the eyes.

BEHAVIORAL THERAPY

This is one of the four main branches of psychotherapy (the others are the psychoanalytic, the humanistic and the cognitive). Sometimes known as stimulus/response psychology, the behavioral approach is based on "learning theory" which grew out of research with animals. Basing his work on Pavlov's earlier studies of conditioned reflexes in dogs, the American psychologist B. F. Skinner (b. 1904) made further studies of animal behavior from which he developed his "laws of learning," the theory of reinforcement on top of conditioning.

Behaviorists emphasize how the environment "conditions" us to behave in certain ways, and that we modify our behavior to suit our surroundings. In principle, anything that we do is reinforced by a reward or punishment. We tell a joke and people laugh, so we tell it again. We chatter in the theater, everybody stares at us with a scowl, so we do not do it again. Behavioral therapy uses this simple fact to encourage correct behavior, and discourage bad behavior. A good example is a disruptive child who manages to attract the attention of his parents by misbehaving. If the parent ignores the child, the behavior goes unattended (the equivalent to not being rewarded), and the child's attitude will change.

Since all behavior is learned, behaviorists argue that undesirable behavior can be unlearned and replaced by more desirable behavior. Behavioral therapy is particularly useful for phobias, breaking habits, obsessive–compulsive behavior, and even bed-wetting. The most successful and widely used form of the therapy is desensitization or flooding for specific phobias: in the first method, the patient is lightly hypnotized, relaxes deeply, and imagines a progressively more-frightening series of fearful stimuli; in the second, the patient confronts the most-frightening stimulus, either in reality or imagination, for 20 minutes or so.

BIOFEEDBACK

Biofeedback is a method of monitoring minute changes in bodily functioning by means of various, small electronic machines. The machines are attached to an individual via electrodes and may be used to measure heartrate, brainwave patterns, body temperature, or respiratory rate. This information—about the autonomic nervous system—shows the level of relaxation or arousal in the body, and can be used consciously to influence bodily processes that were once thought to be beyond voluntary control. Biofeedback is not itself a therapy, but is used in conjuction with the teaching of relaxation or meditation techniques, often including breathing and visualization therapy. By being able to monitor your level of relaxation, it is possible to learn how to change your physiological responses, and vice versa.

The machine will register certain bodily activities by a high-pitched sound or a dial. In response to a reduction in the stress response in the body, the dial will register a lower level, or the high-pitched sound will become low-pitched. The technique reinforces an individual's success with their relaxation method. Biofeedback training may be given in groups or on a one-to-one basis. It aims to accelerate the process of learning how to relax or meditate, so that you can quickly become independent of the machines while using the knowledge gained from them.

Biofeedback can be used to treat stress-related conditions such as insomnia, anxiety, fears, raised blood pressure, and asthma. It is also useful, in conjunction with cardiovascular drugs, for controlling an irregular heartbeat. Migraines and muscular tension can be soothed with meditation techniques, and biofeedback can reinforce this. It has also been found to be effective in relieving chronic pain, and for retraining muscles if their function has been lost after an illness or accident.

BUTEYKO THERAPY

A scientist in Russia by the name of K. P. Buteyko has spent his life showing that breathing can alter the acid/alkaline levels in the bloodstream by adjusting the oxygen and carbon-dioxide levels. In principle, hyperventilation (overbreathing) causes a depletion of carbon dioxide (CO_2). Low levels of CO_2 cause blood vessels to spasm, and tissues to be deprived of oxygen. This can, in theory, create any disease process, ranging from arthritis to ulcerative colitis. The body's metabolism will often slow down in response to this decreased CO_2 level. By counteracting this, the Buteyko breathing technique can be very beneficial in increasing energy and reducing weight.

Buteyko therapy aims to retrain breathing patterns to increase the oxygenation of the blood and tissues. Asthma is particularly susceptible to Buteyko breathing methods. Research carried out in Australia, showing a remarkable response in asthmatics using drugs to control their problem, is soon due to be published. There has been some delay, and I wonder if this is a block by the orthodox medical world, who would lose millions of dollars if a breathing technique were found to be more effective.

The Buteyko method needs to be taught over a number of sessions, generally given on a daily basis over a few days. Buteyko teachers have been fed information suggesting that this method of breathing may affect many different maladies, and those that I know have been (in my opinion) overzealous in suggesting that patients "throw away their crutches" (including stopping prescribed medication) sooner rather than later. It is best to follow a Buteyko method under the guidance of an independent physician or complementary medical practitioner.

The Buteyko method is based on training an individual to breathe less deeply than most Eastern breathing philosophies, and this creates a direct confrontation. I think that the answer lies in following the advice of yoga, Qi Gong, or meditation teachers, while relaxing, exercising, or meditating, but perhaps incorporating the Buteyko concepts into regular life.

CHELATION THERAPY

Chelation is the bonding together of a toxin, usually a metal, into another molecule. Nature has many compounds that chelate, but chelation therapy uses a chemical called ethylene-diamine-tetra-acetic acid (EDTA). This is used to remove heavy metals and toxins from the bloodstream.

This compound, given by intravenous drip, is used in the orthodox world to bind with metals such as mercury and lead that may be ingested or inhaled unintentionally. Chelation therapy was first used in the 1940s to treat lead poisoning. Physicians also noted several decades ago that EDTA treatment was useful in opening up blood vessels, possibly by reducing the calcium deposits or plaques of arteriosclerosis (atheroma).

Chelation therapy may be of benefit in removing industrial toxins that we take in through our food and from pollution. A session of the therapy takes about three hours, and is usually administered a few times a week over two or three months. Chelation therapy is now being used in combination with oxygen and high-dose vitamin therapy in fighting cancer. Treatment is only licensed to fully qualified medical practitioners, because EDTA may be toxic, and specific amounts must be given depending on certain kidney functions.

CHINESE AND ORIENTAL MEDICINE

The ancient traditions of Eastern medicine have developed over many centuries. While there are differences between them in terms of methods of diagnosis and treatment, they all have the same basic philosophy. This has its foundation in a belief that the body is controlled by energy, and not by anatomy or physiology as it is in the Western tradition. The human body is seen as a microcosm of the universe, governed by the same energy and the same five elements. This energy or life force flows through the body in channels or meridians, and ill health is a disruption of this energy flow. The body, like the universe, is made up of five elements through which cosmic energy is manifested: ether, earth, water, fire, and air in Ayurvedic medicine, and earth, wood, metal, fire, and water in Chinese medicine.

In Chinese medicine, there is an emphasis on balancing the life force, known as *Qi* or *chi*. Good health is maintained when the opposing principles of the chi, called Yin (negative) and Yang (positive) are in balance. Ill health is seen as a disturbance of this balance, or disharmony, so that the life force cannot flow freely through the body. Treatment is aimed at strengthening Yin or Yang or eliminating excess Yin or Yang. This is done by various methods, from making lifestyle changes via nutrition, diet, exercise, and meditation, to herbal remedies and bodywork, which includes manipulation and acupuncture/acupressure.

Medicinal herbs are a small part of Oriental medicine, and vary depending on the plants grown in the area. Thai and Vietnamese medicine, for example, differ from Cambodian or Tibetan in the plants used, although the underlying belief system is similar. The Chinese use a different meridian chart from the Tibetan one, which follows much more closely the routes traveled by nerves.

Like Ayurvedic medicine, Chinese, Tibetan, and Oriental medicine should be considered only if a total lifestyle change is possible and acceptable, because these disciplines do not have a "quick-fix" answer.

Chinese medicinal herbs and sliced horns ready for weighing and packing.

CHIROPRACTIC

Chiropractic, derived from the Greek words "kheir" (meaning hand) and "praktikos" (meaning practical), is a manipulative technique which corrects the alignment of the bones of the spine in order to treat a wide range of health problems. By adjusting the position of the spinal bones and joints, and thereby the muscles and nerves attached to them, mobility is restored, and pain relieved.

The system was devised in the United States at the turn of the century by Dr. David Daniel Palmer (1845–1913). Palmer was a gifted healer who discovered the power of spinal manipulation. By adjusting spinal vertebrae, he cured one patient of deafness, and treated heart disease in another. He became convinced that the displacement of vertebrae caused disease, and developed a theory that displaced or "subluxed" vertebrae restricted the spinal nerves, blocking the flow of nervous energy through the body. Although some of Palmer's ideas are no longer seen as correct today, many research studies in recent times have confirmed the therapy's effectiveness. In particular, an eight-year clinical trial, published by the Medical Research Council in 1990, clearly established the superiority of chiropractic over hospital treatment for lower-back pain.

Chiropractors generally work on musculoskeletal problems such as back and neck pain, or complaints created by structural misalignment such as headaches, migraines, sciatica, and sports injuries. It is not only very effective for mechanical problems causing pain in the joints, muscles, ligaments, discs, and nerves in the back, but it has also been used to improve asthma and other breathing problems, to lessen allergies and alleviate digestive disorders. One chiropractor has recently published a short study of nine patients with tinnitus (ringing in the ears), and claims some success. It may be that manipulation of the neck can benefit many different internal problems.

Chiropractic has much in common with osteopathy (*see* **Osteopathy**). Osteopaths use similar manipulative techniques, but have a much broader training in physiology, and they manipulate soft tissues as well as the skeleton. Chiropractic, in well-trained hands, is a safe and extremely effective treatment.

CLINICAL ECOLOGY

Clinical ecology, also called environmental medicine, developed from research into allergies in the early twentieth century. I believe that it was Hippocrates in the 5th century BC, who suggested "let food be your medicine, and medicine be your food." Most practitioners of holistic medicine would agree that the bulk of our ill health stems from that which we put into our bodies. This includes not only food itself, but with it the persistent and almost-unavoidable ingestion of agrochemicals (such as pesticides, fungicides, and weedkillers), as well as airborne pollution from gas and diesel fumes, and household-cleaning compounds. All these environmental factors are very likely to be detrimental to our well-being, weakening our immune system, and making us susceptible to allergies and intolerances.

Clinical ecology takes this into account, and pays special attention to the probability of the development of intolerances and allergies to toxic substances in foods that we commonly eat. Symptoms may well be associated with leaky-gut syndrome in most cases, and irritants and allergens may create any number of illnesses, including respiratory problems, digestive disorders, infertility, headaches, and migraines, and even cancer.

Using techniques ranging from applied kinesiology, iridology, bioresonance, and blood tests, a clinical ecologist will try to isolate problem foods or toxins. The practitioner uses elimination diets, desensitization techniques, and any other preferred naturopathic treatments—such as herbal medicine or homeopathy—to remove these. Practitioners will also suggest changes in lifestyle to avoid exposure to environmental irritants, such as dust, pollen, and chemicals. Mild forms of sensitivity or intolerance may respond well to antioxidant supplements, as well as to drinking filtered tap water.

COLONIC IRRIGATION AND ENEMAS

Colonic irrigation, also known as colonic hydrotherapy, is becoming an increasingly popular technique for clearing out the bowel. Water is passed through a tube into the bowel via the rectum, and used to flush out the bowel contents. Most people report feeling distinctly refreshed and more energetic after having the procedure. The principle is that many toxins build up in the colon, where they may fester or even be absorbed into the bloodstream, and the individual invariably feels better for having these removed. The physical benefits commonly reported include relief from constipation, diarrhea, bloating and wind, intestinal pain, skin problems, stress, and general sluggishness. Many practitioners also offer advice on nutrition as well as other therapies, such as massage.

I remain somewhat doubtful about colonic irrigation. I have often seen pictures of the remarkable amount of debris that is removed following the procedure, but I wonder what it was doing there if the individual was having regular bowel motions. What is more, during my time in hospital, I have seen many colons that have been prepared for colonoscopy or bowel surgery that look immaculately clean once the scope has been passed. The bowels are generally cleansed by taking large amounts of water and a potent laxative 12 hours before the procedure. It appears to me that a fast with some fiber and a natural laxative may be just as effective as the artificial technique of flushing a fluid the wrong way around the colon.

Colonic irrigation and enemas have their place, especially if the bowel is stagnant for any medical reason and, provided that the technique is performed under the watchful eye of an experienced practitioner, is not particularly dangerous. A series of four to eight irrigations is usually recommended, and each procedure takes about half an hour. There are tales of bowel rupture if colonics are performed on individuals with a friable colon, but I dare say that the incidence is far less than for those undergoing colonoscopy in an orthodox hospital.

COLOR THERAPY

Colors affect the mood and emotions, and can therefore influence health. Many studies have shown that color can have a profound effect on the function of brainwaves and on the levels of circulating stress hormones, such as adrenaline and cortisol. Color therapists use color or colored light to treat illness. At a simple level, green has been shown to be calming, and is actually used as the main wall color in most hospitals. Blue light is also calming and lowers blood pressure, while red light is stimulating and increases blood pressure.

The use of color to aid healing involves the whole spectrum of colors. The therapist may diagnose the color a person needs by noting which colors they like and dislike, by looking at their "aura" to see what color it is, and by taking a medical history. When the colors most suited to an individual have been identified and isolated, the therapist will administer the treatment in various ways. For example, you may be bathed in colored light, or asked to eat food of a certain color. Some therapists will advise you to change the color of your home environment, or to wear clothes of a particular color.

It is difficult to use color therapy as a self-help treatment without detailed advice, and a practicing color therapist or a simple book on the subject is recommended. It is certainly worth exploring as an adjunct therapy to other treatments.

COUNSELING—*see* Psychotherapy

CRANIOSACRAL THERAPY

Craniosacral therapy, effectively a branch of osteopathy (and similar to the technique of cranial osteopathy), supports the view that the skull bones (cranium) are not completely fused and immobile. Whereas the orthodox world considers the only mobile joints involving the skull to be at the point where the cranium attaches to the spinal column and at the jaw, this is in fact not the case: minute movements are measurable all over the skull. The craniosacral therapist considers this movement to be relevant because the covering of the brain—the dura—will move with the skull bones. Movement will therefore apply pressures to the brain, and thereby affect the entire nervous system.

By exerting very light pressure on the cranium, the therapist treats the whole craniosacral system, which also includes the membranes and cerebrospinal fluid that surround the brain and spinal cord. Firstly, the cranial pulse is palpated, to give information about the condition of the craniosacral system, and then the skull bones are gently manipulated in order to release any distortions. These can be the result of the cranial bones becoming misaligned or jammed after birth, injury, or even dental work. Pain anywhere from the head all the way down the spinal column can arise, and gentle traction of these bones, by releasing the internal tensions, will relieve it.

Any problem involving neurological supply may be created by cranial misalignment and successfully treated by this form of therapy. In principle most, if not all, health problems will have some neurological involvement, and therefore craniosacral therapy may benefit most conditions. It has been found to be particularly useful in treating chronic pain, migraines, sinusitis, certain eye problems, twisted spines, and joint stiffness. Craniosacral therapy works with the body's own healing ability to improve the functioning of the nervous system and brain, and so enhances general health and well-being.

CRYSTAL AND GEM THERAPY

The ancient belief that certain stones and crystals have healing properties has been held by many cultures. For example, the American Indians were given special stones at birth which were thought to have particular powers. We now know that all objects have a vibrational action: the electrons in the most "dead" of substances are vibrating and maintaining an equilibrium within the molecules. It is theorized that gems and crystals give off a frequency that can affect the human body's resonance, and may indeed be curative. This theory may combine with color therapy (*see* **Color therapy**), and be of benefit as an adjunct to more mainline treatments.

Many practitioners today use the energies emitted by precious and semiprecious stones to enhance the body's ability to heal itself. Different stones are considered to have different therapeutic powers. For instance, a green stone (such as an emerald) will have a stress-reducing effect, while jade has long been used in traditional Chinese medicine to treat disorders of the kidneys and bladder. Quartz and amethyst crystals are thought to be particularly powerful. The healer will either place the stones around the patient, or give them to be worn or carried. Crystals placed in a room are also felt to have a positive effect on the atmosphere.

Crystals can also be used in color therapy, using a special lightbox. Light shone through different crystals will intensify their healing energy and give an array of colors that stimulate different parts of the brain. Electro-crystal therapy involves transmitting pulses of high-frequency electromagnetic energy through crystals and onto the part of the body to be treated. Gem essences or elixirs may also be taken, so that the healing energy of the stones is absorbed directly into the body.

DANCE THERAPY

We are all aware of how body movements can relate concepts and express feelings. When trying to communicate with a speaker of another language, for example, sign language and gestures are invaluable. Eastern cultures, especially the Indian and Balinese cultures, integrate movement and dance very much more than the West into their lifestyle. Most tribal cultures have long included dance as part of their way of life, not only to express feelings, but also as a means of reaching a higher level of consciousness. Both performing and watching such movements is known to be relaxing and transforming.

Dance therapy aims to release the natural flow of bodily self-expression in each individual, concentrating on natural, spontaneous, and unrestricted movements rather than on formal dance patterns. Dance therapists support and motivate their clients to use this healing art form to connect to their unconscious mind, and many are integrating the possibility of an association with the stretching of meridians or energy channels that allow the vital force to move more freely.

A wide variety of situations are appropriate for this therapy. Music may or may not be used. Sometimes the creative aspects of dance are emphasized, sometimes the therapeutic aspects. It can be useful for people who would otherwise find it difficult to talk about their feelings, and is effective for most forms of psychological illness, mild or serious. Theoretically, physical illness affecting mobility, such as Parkinsonism, may benefit from the movement of Qi. Physical symptoms related to stress can also be helped by dance therapy.

Dance therapy takes many different forms and approaches. Eurythmy, an art of movement to music and speech developed in the Rudolph Steiner schools to foster the children's sense of rhythm, and Gabrielle Roth's Five Rhythms freestyle dance, are both forms of therapy designed to encourage self-expression and creativity.

DOWSING

Dowsing is the use of an instrument, be it pendulum, rods, or a fork-shaped stick, that picks up some presently immeasurable energy. At the end of the 19th century, it was realized that, if dowsers can locate the sites of water, metal, and other substances under the ground, then they ought to be able to locate the sites of disease in the body in the same way. Tests were carried out, mainly in France, and it was discovered that they could. The orthodox world continues to be sceptical, but as we delve more into quantum physics, I would not be surprised if—in the near future—we find some justifiable explanation of why a pendulum should swing or a divining rod rise or fall in a different pattern, depending upon the substance over which it is held. The process does not seem to work if the instrument is attached to an inorganic (non-living) object, raising even more doubts in the scientist.

In the medical use of dowsing, there seems to be an interplay between the energy of the practitioner and of the patient, or a sample of the patient's hair or blood. The pendulum or divining instrument merely reflects this. It is a bit like attaching a voltmeter to two ends of a battery: there need to be two opposing or different energies to create a movement.

Dowsing may also be used to determine the most-effective treatment against the disease. The success of the technique relies largely on the skill and sensitivity of the practitioner, rather than on the instrument used. Some dowsers do not need to use a pendulum at all, but simply by holding their hands over the patient's body, will be able to sense a change in vibration or heat, and thereby detect the site of an illness. Healers, in this way, are in fact dowsers.

This is a diagnostic technique that may be useful in conjunction with more-orthodox techniques, but should not be relied upon by itself. This is not because I doubt the efficacy of the technique, but because the assessment is very subjective, depending upon the practitioner.

ENZYME-POTENTIATED DESENSITIZATION (EPD)

Those doctors who practice enzyme-potentiated desensitization would probably be surprised at my putting this treatment into a section on alternative therapies. I do so simply because at the time of writing, this is not a well-established therapy, even though the first treatments were carried out at St. Mary's Hospital Allergy Clinic in Oxford, England, in 1966.

The principle of desensitization is based on a release of a chemical called beta-glucuronidase by specific white blood cells involved in the immune response. This beta-glucuronidase is attached to a known allergen, and kept next to the skin for several days, or injected into the system. The body becomes tolerant of the allergen, and any allergic response is reduced.

Enzyme-potentiated desensitization is currently licensed only for use in asthma by the NHS, and the scientific experts in Oxford are adamant that the technique should not be used for anything else. This is because they do not want "cowboys" to use the technique incorrectly and discredit the work. If this treatment is successful, billions of dollars will be wiped off the pharmaceutical companies' profits because of the decreased necessity of asthma drugs and any other compounds used in allergic-responsive conditions. We await the future with interest.

FELDENKRAIS METHOD

Moshe Feldenkrais (1904–84) was a Russian physicist and engineer who came to England in 1940. He theorized that from infancy, our brain develops patterns of movement. Bad posture or gait in a parent could therefore be passed onto a child, and this incorrect structure can have an effect on the neurological and muscular systems. His exploration of the dynamics of movement in the human body led to the development of his movement method.

The Feldenkrais method teaches gentle sequences of movement, which aim to reorganize previous patterns of action so that the body may be used more effectively. Feldenkrais believed that the body and mind were connected and profoundly affected one another, and that changing negative habits of movement and posture would not only enhance physical well-being, but also have positive influence on the mind and emotions. As with the Alexander technique, pupils learn how to change their restrictive patterns and habits of movement using an awareness technique, and this leads to an increased sense of relaxation and a reduction in stress that benefit the mind as well as the body.

The method is taught in two ways: in a group class called "awareness through movement," the teacher guides students verbally through a series of slow exercises, carried out at first while lying down so that the strain on the body is minimized. Then, in an individual lesson called "functional integration," the teacher guides the student by means of touch, in conjunction with gentle manipulation and massage. Individual lessons are particularly beneficial for those with disabilities or painful injuries.

Anyone can gain from the Feldenkrais method. It is helpful in cases of chronic pain, and helps recovery from physical trauma. Because it is such a gentle therapy, it is suitable for stroke patients and children with cerebral palsy. The method is very popular among athletes and those in the performing arts.

FENG SHUI

The Eastern philosophies, but particularly the Chinese and Japanese, believe strongly that the universe is connected through immeasurable energy. This *Qi* emanates from all living organisms and permeates all matter. The forces of the universe, the movement of water, light, wind, and everything else in the natural world—all these things have an energy that has an influence on everything else. The scientist who recently suggested that the flapping of a butterfly's wings in the Amazon may cause a storm in Central America was merely validating an age-old concept.

Feng Shui, meaning "wind and water," evolved from these ancient principles, and is concerned with the movement of energy in one's immediate surroundings. It is the art of establishing the correct position for the body to be in at particular times of the day, so that negative energy can be curbed, and positive, healing energy increased. (This is a gross oversimplification, but nevertheless describes the technique practically.) The position of the desk at work, the bed at night, and the height of trees around the house all come into play, with a need to understand and vary colors and the shapes of household objects. Nearby water, visible or underground, is also significant. Water is associated with difficulty, and the flow of water can create ionic (charged particles) changes that strongly influence an individual's Qi.

More books are becoming available on Feng Shui, but practical advice from an expert is always the best. He or she can look at your personal space and give advice on all aspects of placement for optimum harmony, seeing the good and bad spaces for different areas of life within your home or office so that relationships, health, wealth, children, career, and creativity may all be enhanced.

FLOTATION

The body and mind are constantly under "sensory attack." In the West especially, it is very difficult to obtain a state of sensory deprivation. We are constantly surrounded by noise, sights, and smells, and we are generally touching something all the time, even if it is merely the ground through our feet or our clothes that are in contact with our bodies.

A good meditation technique can remove us from our senses, but an easier method is the Flotation Tank. This is a bath or pool containing a concentrated saline solution deep enough to allow the body to float, and enclosed in a capsule or cubicle. Floating in a high concentration of salt gives an individual greater buoyancy, allowing the body to be completely and effortlessly suspended, and thereby relaxing all the muscles. The uniform surroundings thus created for the body by the water markedly reduce the sensation of touch. The tank is usually completely dark (although those who fear claustrophobia can benefit from a gentle light), is soundproof, and should have no strong odor. The whole effect is of a warm, cozy environment that feels inviting and safe. By minimizing stimulation of all the senses, any tensions and anxieties can easily be let go. The feeling of deep relaxation that occurs usually endures for some time—up to several days—after the float.

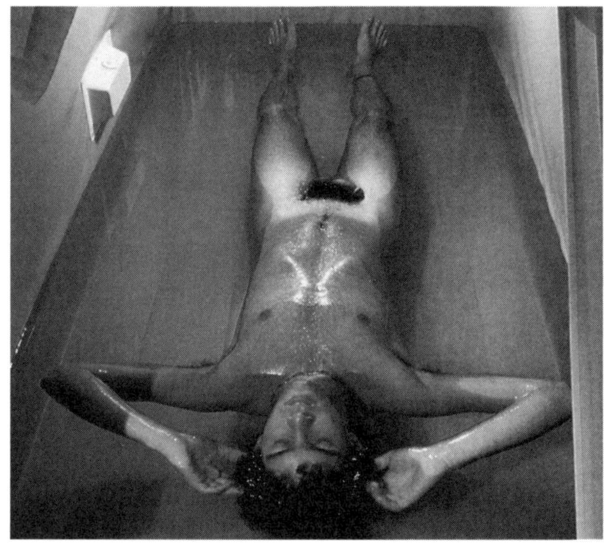

The water in this flotation chamber contains Epsom salts heated to body temperature. Silence is usual, although soothing sounds may be channeled through underwater speakers.

This is a safe therapy, which has been shown by research studies to lower high blood pressure and the level of stress-related chemicals in the body. It can also help reduce pain, because it stimulates the production of endorphins, the body's own pain-reducing hormones. Those who find other relaxation methods such as meditation difficult often find that floating is the answer, since it is passive and requires no effort. It can be used either as a substitute for meditation or as a way of stimulating the ability to meditate.

GEM THERAPY—*see* Crystal and gem therapy

GERSON THERAPY

Gerson therapy was developed by Max Gerson, a German who emigrated to the United States. He initially treated tuberculosis through a low-salt diet, and then modified his recommendations for treatment of more-chronic conditions, especially cancer. He believed that his regimes reversed the conditions that were necessary to support the growth of malignant cells. He promoted the elimination of toxins, protected and supported the liver, and paid special attention to the balance of sodium and potassium in the body. Gerson therapy also encourages the use of thyroid supplements containing iodine and potassium, but is principally a set dietary regime.

The diet proposes fresh, raw juices of vegetables and fruits taken regularly, in conjunction with a restricted fat-and-salt intake, a high intake of complex carbohydrates, and a low proportion of protein foods. Coffee enemas are part of the treatment and, if organic liver is available, raw-liver juice is prescribed. The diet is a strict one, and the regime, which also involves counseling, demands commitment on the part of the client.

The guidelines on diet now officially recommended by governments for optimum health follow the Gerson principles, and the therapy has been shown to enhance mood and well-being, promote faster healing of wounds, and relieve pain. Research supports the Gerson concept as an anticancer therapy, but because there is no element within it that would create profits for a pharmaceutical company, little money goes into further studies (*see* chapter 7).

GESTALT THERAPY

This is a form of psychological therapy that creates a strong self-awareness. It is based on the idea that an event not experienced by both logic and emotion is not completely experienced, and causes an imbalance that leads to behavioral problems. A simple example is that of a child brought up in an abusive household. The conscious mind may make excuses for why he/she is being beaten, but to do so, feelings of hurt and despair must be pushed aside. If this is done successfully, then this trait carries over into other emotional experiences, and the child will grow up suppressing and unable to express feelings.

The founder of Gestalt therapy was Fritz Perls, a Freudian-trained psychoanalyst who became disenchanted with psychoanalysis. His aim was to enable people to learn from their own experience to acknowledge previously denied or suppressed feelings. Rather than paying attention to *why* clients behaved in a certain way, he was more interested in *how* they behaved, and what that behavior meant to them. He was more attentive to nonverbal than verbal cues, and insisted that clients take responsibility for their behavior and feelings. He also wished to help people see the effects of their behavior on others, and this is why Gestalt therapy takes place in groups, sometimes called encounter groups.

A hallmark of Gestalt therapy is "talking to the empty chair." The client is asked to imagine that a person to whom they wished they had expressed certain feelings is sitting in the chair. They then have an opportunity to express those feelings. They may also be asked to place a part of themselves—for example an emotion or characteristic that they find uncomfortable—in the chair, and then have a dialogue with that side of themselves. Other techniques include the highlighting of negative internal "messages," also making clients speak always in the present tense and in the first person, in order to increase self-awareness. Interaction between the members of the group is encouraged, as is the discarding of inhibitions, although the leader of the group also aims to keep the environment safe and unpressured.

HEALING

All forms of treatment are healing, whether they are surgical, chemical, or holistic therapies, such as acupuncture or chiropractic. The term itself, however, describes one of the oldest forms of medicine, and means the technique of "the laying on of hands" by healers who see themselves as the medium for a healing energy. Healing is thus a form of energy therapy based around some immeasurable force. Healers see the source of this force in various ways: some feel that it is a universal psychic energy that passes directly from them into the patient, while others believe that the force is divine in origin, and that they are the conduit through which it flows. Faith healers believe that it is the power of God working through them, and this kind of healing has a long Christian tradition. Healing can be effective regardless of personal beliefs; much more important are the quality of communication between healer and patient, and the patient's receptivity and desire to get well.

The healing technique used may involve physically placing the hands on the body, or by holding the hands over but somewhat away from the body. Practitioners can sense or feel a lack of energy, and may focus their attention upon the energy centers or chakras. Some practitioners will actively vibrate their hands, and others may go into a form of trance while they communicate with the "spirit" or energy source that is transmitting the energy. Healing may also be performed or transmitted without any form of contact, as the practice of radionics shows.

Subjects react differently to healing sessions, which usually last for about half an hour. Some people feel a tingling, or a sensation of heat or cold under the healer's hand. They may feel better immediately, or need a series of sessions before noticing an improvement.

Healers report a sense of changes in their own energy field while healing, and research has shown that the effect of a healer's hand is similar to that of a strong electromagnetic field. Other measurable physical changes in healers include a common pattern of brainwaves that occurs during the healing process.

Every medical philosophy or therapy is utilizing healing energy, and none can be considered any better than any other. There may be, however, a cumulative effect, should a healer also prescribe homeopathy or practice osteopathy.

HELLERWORK

This is a form of bodywork founded in the late 1970s by Joseph Heller, an engineer. Based on the ideas of Ida Rolf, with whom Heller had worked closely (*see* **Rolfing**), its purpose is to provide the individual with a sound foundation for good health by structurally realigning the body through movement and massage. It offers an education in the principles of movement that will help maintain and improve this balance, once achieved. The goal, however, is not only to produce physical results, as with Rolfing, but by emphasizing psycho-emotional aspects of the therapy, to empower clients to grow, change, and improve their total well-being.

The therapy usually consists of eleven 90-minute sessions of deep-tissue bodywork and movement "re-education." Specific to Hellerwork is dialogue between client and practitioner to explore the mind–body connection, and uncover where unconscious thoughts and feelings may have created restrictive patterns in the body. The bodywork is a deep form of massage that concentrates on the interstitial or connective body tissues, rather than the muscles or the skeleton itself. The aim is to release toxic and tension buildup, releasing stored stress and restoring balance. The client is also taught how to move in ways that increase body awareness and improve posture, so that everyday movements become easier, freer, and smoother. Each session concentrates on a different part of the body and the emotions related to it, starting with the outer parts of the body such as the arms and legs, and going on to the "core" areas deep within the body. Final sessions deal with the whole body, integrating all the work done previously.

By balancing the mind and body, Hellerwork aims primarily to prevent rather than treat health problems. Practitioners claim that the method relieves aches and pains, increases relaxation, and improves general mobility and flexibility. Many medical conditions also respond well to this therapy, including headaches and migraine, chronic fatigue, disorders of the musculoskeletal system, respiratory problems such as asthma, and stress-related conditions.

HERBAL MEDICINE

There are two sides to herbal medicine. The first is the pharmaceutical aspect, and the second is the innate energy within the plant itself. In the West, the therapeutic use of herbs is very much based on their chemical effects, and there is much research to suggest that the pharmaceutical benefits of herbal medicines are greater than those of orthodox drugs. Being naturally occurring chemicals, they seem to be broken down by the body

The shelves of a well-stocked herbalist and (above right) *a selection of pills, capsules, preparations, and teas made from the herbs.*

more efficiently and with fewer side effects than seems to be the case with many artificially made drugs. Because they create fewer toxic metabolic byproducts, these chemicals can be broken down by the the liver and kidneys more easily.

A herbalist may follow the Western tradition and use plants native to Western Europe, or follow the Eastern philosophies, and use traditional herbs from China or India. Eastern traditions seem to take into account both the chemical aspects of plants, and also the energy within the plant cells and its structure. More emphasis is placed upon the plants" masculine/feminine, Yin/Yang, and the earth/water/fire/air aspects.

Plant extracts contain steroids and other drugs, such as salicylic acid (aspirin), and thereby work in exactly the same way as over-the-counter drugs. Injudicious use or overuse can be just as harmful as regular drug-taking, and may act by suppressing symptoms rather than dealing with the underlying cause, which is the principle of holistic medicine. The notorious success of Chinese herbs in eczema is an example of this. Most herbalists are scrupulous about sticking to the concept of natural medicine, but many are not. The Eastern philosophies will rarely prescribe a herb without looking at the lifestyle as a whole, but I have noticed that many practitioners of Eastern medicine are simply providing remedies with little or no insight into the person as a whole. Such herbalists should be avoided.

There is occasional "bad press" concerning herbal medicine. Very recently, a major London hospital reported six deaths among people using Chinese herbs for skin problems. The media made out that these deaths were caused by unlicensed practitioners and that the whole of alternative/complementary medicine was a risk. In fact, all six cases were related to people overdosing on the compounds and should have created no more of a stir other than to press for the correct labeling of prescriptions. It is worth putting this piece of information into context by understanding that over 2,000 deaths were caused by over-the-counter (unprescribed) medicines in 1994. There are no statistics to show the number of deaths caused by prescribed drugs that are taken incorrectly. Basically, herbal medicine is safe when prescribed in the right dosages by the right practitioner.

HOMEOPATHY

The term homeopathy is derived from the Greek words "homo" meaning "like," and "pathy" meaning "illness." It is based on the idea that an illness that produces certain symptoms can be cured using a substance that produces the same symptoms in a healthy person. The term "like cures like" explains this treatment in a simple manner.

The founder of this system was Christian Samuel Hahnemann, a respected German physician practicing in the latter part of the 18th century. He noticed that individuals with aggressive symptoms of illness seemed to recover better than those who had only a mild response. He initially experimented by using the bark of the chinchona tree on individuals who had what we now know to be malaria. This bark caused the same symptoms as malaria, and when given in minute quantities, seemed to stimulate the body's symptoms, which in turn defeated the affliction. Hahnemann was unaware of the existence of microbes, but he stuck to this basic observation and experimented on himself, friends, and patients and built up what is now known as a *Materia Medica* of plant, mineral, and animal extracts that exhibit symptoms similar to diseases. He found that using large amounts of a compound actually poisoned a system, but that using very small amounts would stimulate the body's own defenses and enhance reactions that were in themselves curative.

To his surprise, and to the disbelief of scientists today, he found that by shaking the original substance vigorously in water, he could dilute down the compound much more. With the advent of modern scientific techniques, we can actually measure the amount of a substance within a solvent, and in most homeopathic remedies over "potency 20," there are no molecules of the original substance left. This defies the Law of Mass Action, and therefore science discredits homeopathy as being a placebo effect. There are, however, over 160 papers on homeopathy published in reputable medical journals, all of which show a positive effect. Of these, 22 stand up to the most-vigorous scientific standards, but the orthodox world still disbelieves the effects.

The work of a Professor Benveniste from Paris has suggested that water may have the ability to imprint upon its electron structure the electron energy from another substance. Professor Benveniste is a scientist and not a homeopath, and has been ostracized from the scientific world because of his findings. He goes to great lengths to point out that he has no homeopathic bias, and that he is only reporting his own scientific experiments. He is currently considered a maverick, but his work is probably the most important alternative study taking place at the moment. I, personally, wish him success, and hope that he can find the funding necessary to continue his experiments.

Homeopathic remedies prepared by vigorous shaking, known as succussion, are diluted 10 or 100 times before being succussed again. Each time this happens, the potency increases a number. Most remedies come in potencies of 6, 7, 10, 12, 30, 200, 1,000 (better known as 1M), 50,000 (LM), or 100,000 (CM). Remedies and their potency often have the letters X or D after the potency number, and these denote a dilution of 1 in 10, whereas the letter C denotes a dilution of 1 in 100. These letters should not be confused with LM and CM, which represent the number of times a remedy is diluted, as described above. There is generally little difference in an X or a C dilution. The lower the potency, the more physical the effect; and the higher potencies are generally reserved for psychological aspects of a patient.

A homeopath chooses a remedy based on a symptom picture of the person as a whole. There are, for example, over 400 remedies that have a fever, of which 200 will include sweating, 50 include flushing, 25 include trembling or shaking, 10 will be thirstless, 7 associated with diarrhea, etc. The more symptoms presented, the more likely a remedy will be accurately prescribed.

A homeopath will also look at the constitution of an individual, which describes the temperament and personality of the person when well. A homeopath needs to have an understanding of where a patient needs to be returned to when choosing medication accurately. If one person is naturally a sweaty type, then remedies that are particularly dry may move the individual away from their constitution and slow down the healing process.

Homeopathy is a complicated matter, and modern pharmacies try to simplify it by advising that, for example, Arnica is good for bruising, Belladonna for fevers, and Pulsatilla for earache. Homeopathy cannot be prescribed in this way, because it must take into account the whole person, and not just the symptom. Unless homeopathy is prescribed correctly, it often fails. This gives the practice a higher level of failure than it deserves.

Homeopathy can be safely used in any condition where the vital force of the individual is strong or intact, because a remedy will create reactions of healing from within. Homeopathy should not be used where the body is particularly weak, because the underlying energy may not be strong enough, which at best will render homeopathy useless, or may worsen an individual's health by using up the remaining energy more quickly.

HYDROTHERAPY

Water has many properties that are poorly understood by science. It is the only natural compound that is lighter when it is solid than as a liquid (i.e. ice floats). Water is also considered a universal solvent, which means that it will eventually break down any compound immersed within it. (Homeopathy is beginning to have some scientific justification based on the intrinsic electronic movement within water molecules.)

Hydrotherapy is the use of water to promote healing. It may be used as a liquid or steam, taken internally or externally, either by immersion or by inhalation, and taken hot or cold. The water may have a high level of salts, or be extremely pure, depending on the reason for its use.

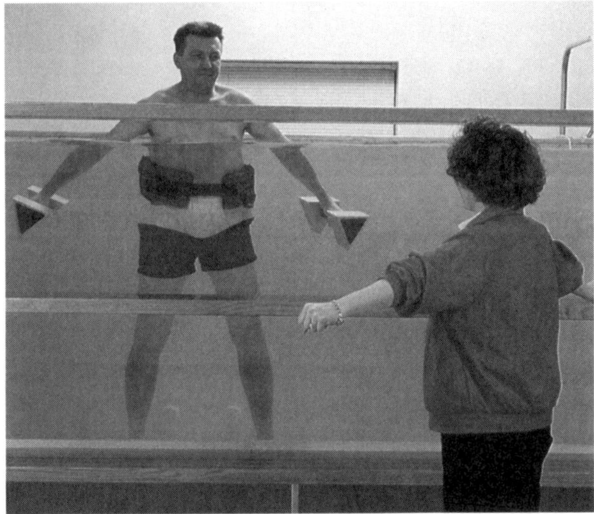

A patient exercises with weights in a hydrotherapy pool in order to build up strength and improve joint mobility.

The healing benefits of water have been known for thousands of years, and are well documented in ancient literature. Roman baths, probably the most famous centers for water therapy, were built at the sites of natural springs, often where the water was hot or minerally rich. The popularity of the spa was at its height in Europe during the 18th and 19th centuries, and hundreds of towns became famous for their waters. Water is now a popular therapy in health farms and hospitals throughout Europe, and the increasing number of whirlpools, hot tubs, and jacuzzis in hotels and sports clubs is testimony to the immediate and beneficial effects of immersion in water.

Therapies include wrapping, baths, douches or showers, sitz baths (where only the lower part of the body is immersed), and steam or Turkish baths. Herb-and-mineral baths and sea-water baths (thalassotherapy) are also used. Sprays and steam may be used externally, and inhalations with or without essential oils may be of benefit (*see* **Aromatherapy**). Hot water is used to stimulate and then relax, while cold water invigorates. Alternate use of hot and cold water stimulates blood and lymph circulation, tones tissues, and relieves congestion. Sitz baths are used in this way to treat pelvic and abdominal disorders, liver and kidney problems, and constipation and piles. Hydrotherapy is also beneficial for people with physical disabilities, since the buoyancy of the water allows an increased range of movement.

Hydrotherapy is one of the safest and cheapest ways of relieving common ailments, and is therefore ideal for self-help treatment. Exercising in water brings relief from aches and pains, increased relaxation, and greater flexibility, and also promotes fitness and a sense of well-being.

HYPNOTHERAPY

The word *hypnosis* is derived from the Greek word "hypnos," meaning "to sleep." It was brought into common parlance by Scottish surgeon James Braid in the 1840s. Hypnotherapy techniques were used with operative procedures before the use of anesthetic, and had developed from the theories of a Dr. Mesmer from 60 years before.

Hypnotherapy is the production of a trance-like state that is not dissimilar to daydreaming. In effect, the consciousness leaves the body, which continues to be controlled and protected by the subconscious. An example is thinking of a beach in Rio while driving a car. Driving demands a lot of concentration and coordination, but can be done without thinking about it. If a child were to run in front of a car, the subconscious would not have the ability to avoid it. The consciousness is called back into the body, which deals with the situation, and Rio is forgotten!

I divide hypnotherapy into two techniques. The first is suggestive, and the second is "part." In both techniques the individual is taken into a deep relaxed state through imagining a comfortable and enjoyable place. The suggestive hypnotherapist will then plant an idea into the subconscious, such as that an onion is an apple or a cigarette is nauseating. When the consciousness returns, the subconscious holds this concept and the individual will bite into the onion with relish (as often seen in shows), or may wish to stop smoking (as is seen in therapeutic hypnosis). "Part" hypnotherapy is geared toward discussing matters with the subconscious, and finding out which part of the individual's past has triggered the unnecessary or unwanted psychological problem. Part hypnotherapy should not be undertaken by those who cannot afford or intend to follow through with the psychological support that is often necessary when something deeply buried comes forward and which can markedly affect their life. Suggestive hypnotherapy is safer, but may not be quite so effective. I would like to stress that these definitions are my own, and would need to be explained to a hypnotherapist to find out which form of treatment they intend to use.

KINESIOLOGY

Kinesiology is a manipulative therapy, based on diagnosing imbalances or deficiencies in nutrition or energy flow by testing the strength of muscles. Applied kinesiology was developed during the 1960s by Dr. George Goodheart, an American chiropractor. He discovered that massaging the neurolymphatic reflexes strengthened muscles. He linked his discoveries with oriental medical ideas of the Qi, or vital force, which flows through the body and can be stimulated by using pressure points. To this extent, kinesiology is not very different from acupressure.

Goodheart was more convinced that the technique's effectiveness was based on spinal reflexes, but whatever the underlying cause, he found that one stimulated muscle can affect others in a different part of the body. This idea has since been expanded, and it has been noted that the strength

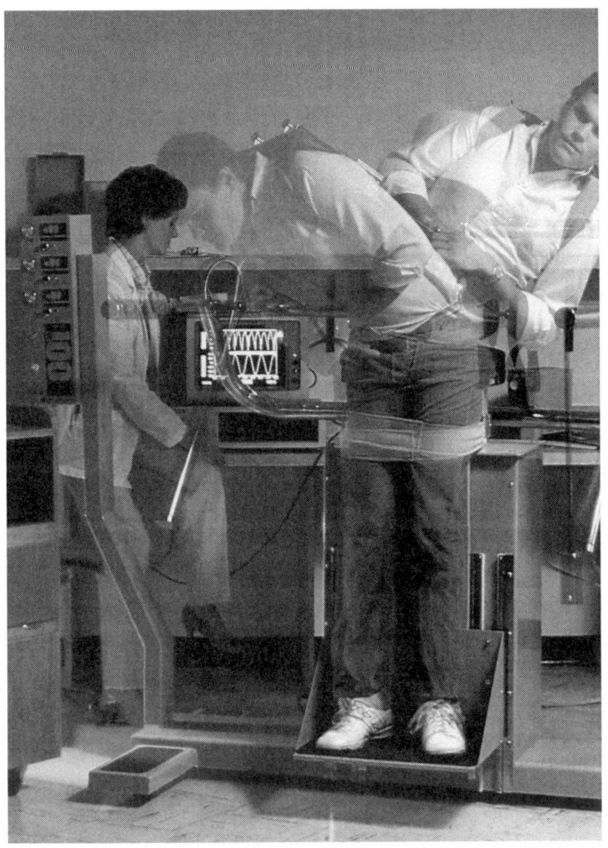

A volunteer undergoing kinesiology tests. A computer displays the flexion of the spine from left to right as the subject performs bending movements.

of a muscle will vary momentarily in response to the body coming into contact with a product to which it is intolerant or allergic, as well as responding in a positive way to compounds in which it may be deficient.

A practitioner will test a muscle group (either trying to force apart opposed index finger and thumb, or testing shoulder muscles by having the patient hold out the arm as it is pushed down), while the patient has a variety of different foods placed on the tongue, one at a time. Some kinesiologists have taken the step of simply placing a compound on the abdomen or even only using the homeopathic form. Theoretically, the resonance of a substance is passed into the watery solution when it is prepared as a homeopathic remedy. Even further removed is the belief that the thought of a compound will affect the muscular energy. Some practitioners simply ask an individual to read a list of compounds one word at a time and test the muscle group. Even the word "yes" as opposed to "no" can strengthen or weaken a muscle group. Used in conjunction with more-orthodox diagnostic techniques, kinesiology can be a very supportive diagnostic investigation. Its therapeutic effects are based on acupuncture and acupressure.

KIRLIAN PHOTOGRAPHY

This is high-frequency photography used to produce a photograph of the "aura" of energy that surrounds a person. Semyon and Valentina Kirlian, who discovered and developed the method for diagnostic purposes, found that photographs made using this technique showed differences in the energy field of healthy and diseased subjects. It is said that a healthy person emits a strong aura, while a person with disease—whether manifest or latent—emits a weak aura. Any imbalances requiring treatment will be identified after interpretion of the aura by the practitioner.

Under strictly controlled conditions, a Kirlian photograph of the two hands of the patient is usually taken. The resulting print will show a furry effect surrounding the outline of the hands, with flares of energy and areas of blockage that can be used to diagnose certain illnesses (*see* **Kirlian photography**).

LIGHT THERAPY

Light has a direct effect on the workings of the body and on our moods. When the sun comes out, our spirits rise, and we feel more energetic, while insufficient light can lead to depression and lethargy. Light is known to stimulate the pineal and pituitary glands, which correspond to the highest two chakras (energy centers) in yogic medicine. There is much scientific evidence to show that certain chemicals, such as melatonin, are produced or suppressed by sunlight. Melatonin controls our sleep patterns, but an excess can lead to depression and tiredness. Seasonal Affective Disorder (SAD), a depression that occurs through the winter, can easily be improved by subjecting an individual to bursts of full-spectrum light. This mimics natural sunlight, exposure to which increases the amount of serotonin (the "feel-good" hormone) produced by the body.

Light therapy is used to treat a range of other problems associated with hormone imbalance. Menopausal and premenstrual problems, infertility, and loss of libido have all responded well to light therapy, which works directly on the eyes stimulating the pineal gland in the brain. The body needs sunlight in order to manufacture vitamin D, essential for maintaining the health of the bones and skin. Skin disorders such as acne, eczema, and psoriasis, as well as the debilitating bone disease osteoporosis, may all benefit from light therapy. In these cases the light is shone on to the skin as well as the eyes. Light therapy is also used to boost the immune system and improve blood circulation.

Each session of therapy involves lying on a couch under an overhanging light, and lasts for about 45 minutes. For acute cases, a weekly session is usually recommended at first. People usually respond very quickly to the therapy, and after a few sessions find that they only need "top-up" sessions occasionally.

Light therapy is also part of crystal therapy (*see* **Crystal and gem therapy**).

MAGNETIC THERAPY

The earth has its own electromagnetic field, aligned to the poles, and the cells of the human body also have subtle magnetic forces. Conventional medicine uses electromagnetic energy in imaging equipment, harnessing this force (MRI scans) for diagnosis, and also in order to influence the body's own electrical currents to promote healing, particularly of fractures. Complementary therapists claim that ordinary magnets can also do this, and many are beginning to use magnets as part of a healing program.

The body has many electromagnetic energies traveling through it, which are measurable or assumed (as in Eastern meridian channels), and magnetic therapy is particularly well known in Japan. The use of powerful magnets placed close to the body for a short or long period of time can influence bloodflow, improving the oxygen supply to the area being treated, and stimulating the metabolism and speeding the elimination of waste products. Magnetic therapy may be used as a self-help treatment, and many magnetic products, such as shoe insoles, mattresses, pillows, and car-seat covers are available. A practitioner will suggest the most suitable items for your needs, and show you how to use them. Special supermagnets may be used for specific points on the body, often over lymph nodes or acupuncture points.

At this time, we still await some reasonable trials or studies of magnets being used in treatment. If a practitioner has had some experience or training, then I can see no risk, except that I would avoid magnetic therapy in conditions that might have been triggered by electromagnetic energy, such as cancer.

MARMA THERAPY

A Marma point is defined in Ayurvedic medicine as a site on the body where flesh, veins, arteries, tendons, joints and bones meet. There are 107 of these "vital points" throughout the body, and it is believed that an injury to any one of them—such as a puncture wound, burn, or impact injury—will lead to permanent damage or even death. Marma therapy is an ancient form of massage, which uses the fingers to stimulate the Marma points, thereby promoting physical and mental healing and well-being.

The Ayurvedic system emphasizes the preventive aspects of healthcare, and part of this is Marma massage, which increases bloodflow to the neuromuscular junction of each point, and tones the surrounding muscles. Results of a Marma massage include increased levels of energy, reduced stress, and freedom from tension and anxiety.

There are also many medical applications for Marma massage. It has been shown to be of particular benefit to stroke victims, because it can clear away obstructions that delay information being communicated between muscles, nerves, and brain, and thus help the brain relearn the use of the parts of the body paralyzed or debilitated by the stroke. Other symptoms that are alleviated through Marma massage include muscular aches and pains, light-headedness, numbness and tingling in the extremities, and a metallic taste in the mouth, as well as stress-related conditions.

The Marma therapist also checks the acidic levels of the tongue with a litmus paper (a healthy result is 60 percent alkaline to 40 percent acid), as well as the muscle and nerve reflexes. A course of between two and six weekly sessions is usually recommended in order to restore full physical and mental health. Stroke victims usually need more treatments, often to be carried out over several months.

MASSAGE

Massage is the manipulation of the soft tissues in the body—particularly muscles—in order to promote relaxation and healing. There are many different massage techniques, and some practitioners may use or base their technique on different body therapies such as Shiatsu, Rolfing, or physiotherapy, while others use a more-intuitive approach. All branches of massage are effective, either in removing cramps, pain, and tension from the muscles, or in stimulating the lymph glands (part of the body's immune system) to eliminate toxins.

The massage session usually takes place at a health center or at the home of the therapist, but in some circumstances, the masseur will come to your home. Some practitioners work with the client lying on the floor, but most will use a massage table. The therapist will work with oil on their hands, to facilitate the smooth, flowing movements of their hands over your skin. A variety of strokes are used, including kneading, rubbing, pummeling, circling, and stroking, using fingertips, thumb or the whole hand.

Choosing a massage technique or practitioner is very much a subjective decision. It is worth experimenting with different types of bodywork until a preferred technique or practitioner is found. Some therapists employ more-vigorous techniques than others. There is some concern that massage should not be employed in cancer, because this may spread the tumor, although there is no evidence to back this up. I think it wise to avoid lymphatic-drainage techniques in a cancer that is known to have spread through the lymphatic system, but massage that employs acupressure such as Shiatsu should be fine.

The use of aromatic essential oils in conjunction with massage brings together two forms of healing therapy, combining the benefits of massage with those of the oil, which acts directly on the bloodstream (*see* **Aromatherapy**). Whichever type of massage you choose, the experience is pleasant because it feels nurturing, soothing, and relaxing, and at the same time is often invigorating. Its benefits are often felt for hours or even days afterwards, especially when used as part of a program for combating stress.

MEDITATION

Meditation is a way of transcending the everyday level of consciouness by emptying the mind of conscious thoughts and concerns. It involves training your awareness so that your mental processes come under conscious control. There are many forms of meditation, but their goal is always to enhance physical and mental well-being.

Meditation has been practiced for at least 3,000 years. Most of the forms we know today are of Eastern origin, and are associated with spiritual practice, but for most people in the West, meditation is seen as a simple self-help technique for which no religious beliefs are necessary. The practical advantages of meditation are that it can be performed in any comfortable place where you will be undisturbed for 20 minutes or so, and that any sitting or lying position that suits the individual may be adopted.

There are two stages in the meditative process:

the first is physical relaxation, and the second is focusing and emptying the mind. Concentrating on your breathing is an ideal way of doing this, as it makes you focus on something calming, which also blocks out other thoughts and quietens the mind. Some people find it more helpful to repeat a single word or mantra, or focus on a single

Any comfortable position that aids relaxation is suitable for practicing meditation.

object, such as a flower or a candle. Whatever the method used, breathing should be unforced and slow, with the stomach gently rising and falling and the shoulders staying still. When you are relaxed, close your eyes and continue to concentrate on each in-and-out breath, excluding all other thoughts, until you gradually become more and more relaxed, eventually reaching a trance-like state. At this point, the mind is calm, yet alert; the brain is producing an even pattern of alpha and theta brainwaves, which is the "relaxation response." You have reached a state of the utmost balance and harmony, and let go of all tensions.

Research has shown that regular meditation for about 20 minutes, once or twice a day, lowers blood pressure, and relieves depression and anxiety. Other benefits include improved concentration, creativity, and memory, and increased energy levels. Meditation has also helped people overcome addictions to drugs, such as tranquilizers and alcohol.

Meditation is discussed more fully elsewhere in this book (*see* **Meditation**).

MUD THERAPY

Immersing oneself in mud for its medical benefits is a form of hydrotherapy (*see* **Hydrotherapy**). Mud contains high levels of vitamins and minerals, small amounts of which will be absorbed through otherwise impregnable skin. There is certainly external benefit, and mud therapy may be useful for treating skin conditions such as acne, eczema, and psoriasis. The internal benefits are suggested but not well documented, and it is probable that the small amounts that are absorbed are dealt with by the efficient liver and kidney before any therapeutic benefit can be experienced. The nerves in the skin may well set up reflex responses through the spinal column.

Mud therapy is an excellent form of treatment, particularly for dermatological conditions, but is not easily available, since very few mud spas exist. The Moor in Austria is one highly regarded spa, based beside a boggy lake and marshland that is home to hundreds of unique medicinal herbs whose lipids, enzymes, minerals, and vitamins are dissolved in the water and mud of the lake. These have been shown to have many healing properties when applied to the skin, and their anti-inflammatory quality makes Moor treatment particularly useful for rheumatism and arthritis. Research into the benefits of mud therapy is currently going on, and the results look promising.

Products from the Moor and from other spas are now becoming available for use at home, either in the form of powders, or in tubs and tubes. Ideally, the mud should be applied to the skin as a soft paste, but since this is an extremely messy procedure, it is probably better to use a liquid mud extract in the bath. Follow the instructions on the container, and soak in the hot bath for about 20 minutes. Afterwards, take a shower and get into a warm bed. You will sweat as the impurities and toxins in the body are drawn out.

MUSIC THERAPY

The ability to appreciate and respond to music is an inborn quality in human beings. Rarely is this ability affected by disability, injury, or illness, and it is not dependent on music training. For people who find verbal communication difficult, particularly those with mental illness or physical, learning, or sensory disabilities, music therapy offers a safe, secure way of releasing feelings.

Fundamental to music therapy is the development of a relationship between the therapist and client, in which music becomes the basis for communication, and a way of promoting change and growth. There are different approaches to the use of music in therapy, depending on the needs of the client, as well as the preferred style of the therapist, but they all involve playing, singing, and listening, either in group or individual sessions. The therapist does not teach the client to sing or play an instrument, but encourages improvization with percussion and other accessible instruments, as well as the voice, in order to explore the world of sound and create a personal, musical language. By responding musically, the therapist supports this process, and encourages positive changes in behavior and well-being.

Music therapists work with adults and children of all ages, in hospitals, special schools, day and community centers, and in private practice. Involvement in creative music-making is particularly useful in psychological treatments for children with behavioral problems, language impairment, and birth defects, since it promotes physical awareness and develops attention, concentration, and memory. For people with emotional difficulties, music therapy allows the safe expression of otherwise repressed or "difficult" feelings. By offering support and acceptance, the therapist can help the client work towards emotional release and self-acceptance. Increasingly, music therapy is being sought by people who do not have any specific difficulties, but who would like to enhance their creativity and gain insight into themselves and their ways of relating to others (*see* **Sound therapy**).

NATUROPATHY

"Naturopathy" is a broad term used to describe a multidisciplinary approach to illness and health. Its practitioners have expertise in a variety of medical therapies, and follow many of the same principles as the Eastern approach to medicine. Ayurvedic, Chinese, Tibetan, and other Eastern philosophies of medicine all share a view of life and health that looks at the whole person rather than at just the symptoms. Naturopathy is the Western equivalent, in which a fundamental idea is that the body has the power to heal itself through its "vital force," and that illness is a reaction to disharmony and imbalance in the body.

The aim of naturopathy is to help the body to regain health by restoring its natural balance rather than by addressing specific symptoms. Indeed, modern research confirms the naturopath's belief that many symptoms, such as fever and inflammation, do have a healing function. The naturopath teaches the patient how to help to boost the body's own defenses, mainly through giving advice on lifestyle adjustments and diet. A healthy, wholefood diet, fresh air, an unpolluted environment, exercise, adequate rest and sleep, a reduction in stress, and a positive mental attitude will all strengthen the body's immune system, and enhance its self-healing abilities.

Naturopaths see themselves as teachers as much as healers, believing that everyone should take personal responsibility for their own health. The body will heal itself and fight off invading organisms when its homeostatic balance is reinstated. The methods used to do this emphasize good nutrition with vitamin supplements, exercise, bodywork, relaxation, and breathing techniques, all of which work with nature rather than against it. Natural medicines (herbal or homeopathic) are also used in naturopathy. Theoretically, a homeopath who spends time on adjusting the lifestyle of an individual is practicing naturopathy. Naturopaths have training in some form of bodywork, often osteopathy. Fasting, massage, and hydrotherapy are also important features of naturopathic therapy.

Most health problems, acute or chronic, may be treated by naturopathy, and many research studies have shown that naturopathic methods are an effective alternative to conventional medical treatment. The therapeutic value of a healthy lifestyle—a vital part of the naturopathic philosophy—is now being confirmed by modern research and is widely accepted.

NEUROLINGUISTIC PROGRAMMING (NLP)

Neurolinguistic programming is a form of psychotherapy that was developed from the work of several well-known therapists in the 1970s. It accurately describes its principle within its own name: the nerves (neuro) are affected by language (linguistic) and, like a computer, can reprogram the thought process. Basically, NLP reorganizes how people think, and allows emotions to flow in a way that they perhaps have never previously done.

The technique depends for its success on the patterns of communication in the relationship between therapist and client, rather than on the particular theories about therapeutic change held by the therapist. The practitioner approaches each client as a unique individual, noting the minutiae of the client's behavior and body language, in order to understand that person's mechanisms of perception. For example, by observing changes in pupil size, direction of gaze, head movements, and breathing, the therapist can identify whether a person is using visual or auditory recall. The therapist can then communicate with the client in the appropriate way, encouraging rapport.

NLP can be used to change deeply-buried emotional states, and is therefore generally practiced by experienced psychotherapists who can deal with what changes are necessary. Practitioners are often trained in hypnotherapy, allowing access to the deepest areas of the subconscious. The client learns some of the skills used by the therapist, such as mirroring, reframing, disassociation, and anchoring.

Anchoring is the recalling of good or positive experiences, and using them as resources for the future, so that they can be superimposed on a situation that has unpleasant feelings, and make those bad feelings less potent. In this way, clients increase awareness of how their thoughts, beliefs, and values influence how they perceive the world, and that they can learn new thought patterns in order to make changes to unhelpful ways of functioning, and thereby increase personal happiness. NLP is a method of thinking and acting more effectively in order to succeed in any area of life, whether it is work, relationships, self-esteem, or creativity.

NEUROTHERAPY

This form of treatment is new to the West. It is a branch of Ayurvedic medicine, utilizing all aspects of prayer/meditation, dietetics and nutrition, and exercise and lifestyle changes, in conjunction with a specific form of therapy involving the meridians of the body.

A neurotherapeutic practitioner will lay the patient on the floor and, while bearing most of their body weight on two chairs beside the patient, will apply pressure on the back through the feet. Particular trigger or acupressure points will be pushed by specific parts of the practitioner's feet, thereby stimulating reflex responses and sending energy from the practitioner's reflexology meridian points directly into meridians in the patient's back. This treatment is yet to become well established, but can be useful for an array of conditions, either on its own or in conjunction with more mainline treatments.

ONANI

Onani is a form of medicine practiced in northern India and Pakistan. It is principally derived from Ayurvedic medicine, but also includes ideas based on Greek and Arab sources. Onani differs from Ayurvedic practice in some of the medicinal herbs prescribed, and it also incorporates the therapeutic use of minerals.

OSTEOPATHY

Osteopathy is a manipulative technique in which the bones, muscles, ligaments, and nerves are restored to their proper alignment and functioning. It is probably the most widely used of the complementary therapies, and certain states in the U.S.A consider an osteopath to have equal training to a doctor.

Osteopathy was devised by an American doctor, Andrew Taylor Still, at the end of the 1800s. In principle, Still felt that the disease process occurred because of structural misalignments. He postulated that when vertebrae slip out of position, the nerves around them become oversensitive and affect surrounding tissue. This in turn affects blood circulation, and since the blood carries substances to protect against disease, the blocked circulation leads to illness. His theories can be well supported, because poor structure may obstruct bloodflow, nerve conduction and, from an Eastern perspective, Qi or energy flow.

A treatment session—which lasts about half an hour—involves using various manipulative techniques, depending on the condition being addressed. You may be asked to take up a variety of positions while the practitioner pushes, pulls, and applies pressure to your back, head, arms, or legs in a number of ways. It is not usually painful, but may sometimes feel a little uncomfortable. The number of treatment sessions needed will depend on the severity of the problem.

Many people consider osteopaths to be "bone crackers" but this is simply not the case. Osteopathy is geared towards work on soft tissues and bloodflow through manipulation. This rarely includes "cracking" the spine. Many people only think of an osteopath when dealing with a structural problem such as an ache or a strain, particularly of the back and neck. There is no doubt that osteopathy is probably the best form of manipulative medicine for such structural problems, but that is not where it ends. Osteopaths, often in conjunction with other forms of complementary medicine, can deal with all health problems, including headaches and migraine, digestive complaints, respiratory difficulties such as asthma, glue ear and sinusitis, and gynecological conditions. Osteopathy may even be able to prevent surgery, in some cases of injury.

OXYGEN THERAPY (INCLUDING HYDROGEN PEROXIDE AND OZONE THERAPY)

There is much scientific evidence to support the belief that disease may stem from poor oxygenation of cells. Oxygen therapy is about increasing the availability of oxygen to the body tissues. Pedantically, we may argue that breathing techniques and oral supplementation with antioxidants are actually oxygen treatments, and we would be right. However, oxygen therapy is generally the term used for intravenous therapies. Ozone (which is three molecules of oxygen attached together) and hydrogen peroxide (two molecules of oxygen with two molecules of hydrogen) can be introduced directly into the bloodstream, and increase the availability directly.

Oxygen has been shown to be of some benefit in cardiac disease, vascular disease, including strokes, and cancer. Work is being done at the moment on HIV and AIDS. Theoretically, enhancing oxygen intake may be of benefit to any condition.

There are risks, however, and intravenous work should only be carried out by qualified medical practitioners, or those with experience in emergency resuscitation. It is not so much the oxygen itself that could cause a problem, but the fact that the introduction of any chemical directly into the bloodstream can alter the biochemistry rapidly.

Low-oxygen treatments

Athletes are known to travel to high places to train before major events. This is because of the rarefied atmosphere. Training at that level encourages the body to make more red blood cells to carry more oxygen, because there is less available in the air. When the athlete returns to sea level, normal atmospheric oxygen appears (to the increased number of red blood cells) to be in abundance. The athlete will potentially benefit by having the oxygen availability increased. There is some evidence coming from the former Soviet Union suggesting that short bursts of low-level oxygen each day (delivered through a machine) may trigger a similar response.

Low blood-oxygen levels at the time of radiation treatment may enhance its effects. It appears that cancer cells are much more susceptible to radiation in the presence of low oxygen, whereas the normal body cells seem to be more prepared to fight its effects. This theory has been put forward following several studies in both Eastern Europe and France, but the treatment is not yet widely available. I hope to put the theory into practice through a trial in the very near future.

POLARITY THERAPY

Polarity therapy is a holistic system of healing that draws on elements of both Eastern and Western medicine to promote well-being. The body is seen to be made up of universal energy or *Qi*, which forms both the material and spiritual universe. The structure and function of the body is underpinned by a system of energy fields that are in constant motion, and it is believed to be the disruption or stagnation of this energy that leads to illness. Developed in the late 19th century by Dr. Randolph Stone, an osteopath, chiropractor, and naturopath working in the U.S.A, polarity therapy combines different healing techniques to bring about the state of balance and health in the body, mind, and emotions.

There are four aspects of polarity therapy: body awareness, posture and balance, which are all retrained; cleansing diets and nutritional advice; awareness and counseling skills; and stretching exercises, with specific bodywork based both on superficial and deep touch. Touch and manipulation are used to relieve stagnation and encourage energy to flow round the body. Since poor nutrition and digestion may often be a factor in physical problems, detoxifying diets are prescribed, followed by a health-building dietary regime. The patient's state of mind has a direct impact on physical health, and so counseling is used when the practitioner feels that negative thoughts are impeding energy flow. Stretching exercises, or "polarity yoga," are prescribed to release and harmonize energy.

Polarity therapy is not designed to treat specific symptoms, but to encourge healing through rebalancing the flow of energy. It requires some effort on the part of patients, who are asked to take responsibility for their own health. Polarity can be used to benefit many conditions, including allergies, ME, respiratory disorders, cardiovascular problems, and aches and pains caused by stress. It may be used either by itself, or in conjunction with other forms of more medicinally oriented therapies, such as herbal medicine or homeopathy.

PSYCHONEUROIMMUNOLOGY

Scientific evaluation of the components of the immune system in the bloodstream have been shown to alter in response to psychological or emotional changes. Most emotions are associated with chemicals that are released within the structure of the brain. These chemicals trigger impulses along the central nervous system that then travel out to the peripheral nerves, and exert an influence on the tissues of the body. The immune system is no different; the thymus (which produces the T cells) and the bone marrow (producing other white blood cells) are particularly influenced.

The fact that the personality and emotions affect the nervous system, which in turn affects the immune system, is the basis of psychoneuroimmunology. Poor stress-management skills and negative emotions are immune-suppressing, and predispose the subject to infection and ill health. Studies show that people who remain healthy in spite of stressful life experiences have a more positive attitude to life in general than those who succumb to frequent illness.

Psychoneuroimmunology is a diagnostic therapy, combining modern scientific knowledge with psychotherapy. It aims to help prevent illness or aid recovery from existing ill health by positive emotional counseling and methods of mind control, including visualization and guided-imagery techniques. A sense of control and happiness, relaxation, and a positive outlook are among the desired outcomes. The therapy has proved helpful for people with cancer and AIDS, and is often highly effective for those with less-serious health problems.

Psychoneuroimmunologists may also use any other healing technique or medicinal therapy, but always work on the principle that a "distress-free" state of mind is essential for strong immune function, since the psyche, through the neurological system, affects the body's defense mechanisms.

PSYCHOTHERAPY

The use of conversation and discussion to illustrate, understand, and sort out underlying psychological problems is a vast subject. The broad term psychotherapy is used to denote a wide variety of methods to deal with emotional problems. It covers everything and anything from counseling (listening and giving basic advice) to psychoanalysis (deep-seated therapy to establish underlying causes of psychological imbalances stemming from childhood). There are four main branches of psychotherapy: psychoanalytic, humanistic, cognitive, and behavioral. Within these branches are many more types, or "schools" of psychotherapy, but all of them (some of which are discussed in more detail in this chapter) use talking to stimulate and support the process of achieving mental health.

Psychotherapy is not only suitable for people in crisis or conflict, but can also be used as a method of achieving personal growth and realizing full potential. Undergoing therapy requires that you make the choice to do it yourself (rather than being pressured by someone else), and that you are open to change and to new feelings and experiences. A basic rule of thumb is to trust your psychotherapist or counselor and to let him or her use whichever therapy is felt to be the most suitable. A few practitioners have training in more than one type of psychotherapy, and these are probably the practitioners with whom to work. Whatever theories or techniques they may espouse, all the psychotherapies have one aim in common—that is, to enable their clients to understand themselves and their relationships with others, and to explore new ways of behaving and dealing with conflicts and difficulties.

QI GONG

The Chinese word for vital force or energy is *Qi*, pronounced chi. *Gong* means "working with." Any energy therapy is therefore Qi Gong. The phrase is, however, used mostly to define a vast number of sets of movement that allow energy to flow freely through the body. The Eastern philosophies believe in meridians, or channels containing energy that supply the life force to organs and systems. Qi Gong is about moving this energy by following particular patterns of movement and exercise.

Qi Gong's system of exercises, positions, and breathing techniques is even more ancient than yoga, originating in China more than 5,000 years ago. Like yoga, Qi Gong is aimed at integrating the mind and body so that a state of harmony is achieved, but unlike yoga, it concentrates on moving energy within the body rather than externally. The exercises relate to the acupuncture or pressure points found on the meridians of the body through which the vital energy flows. There are seven basic exercises with hundreds of variations, and all are suitable for health and relaxation. Different sets of movements concentrate on different body organs and systems, and they may be used to alleviate specific health problems, such as arthritis and digestive or circulatory disorders.

Ba Duan Jin—a form of Qi Gong

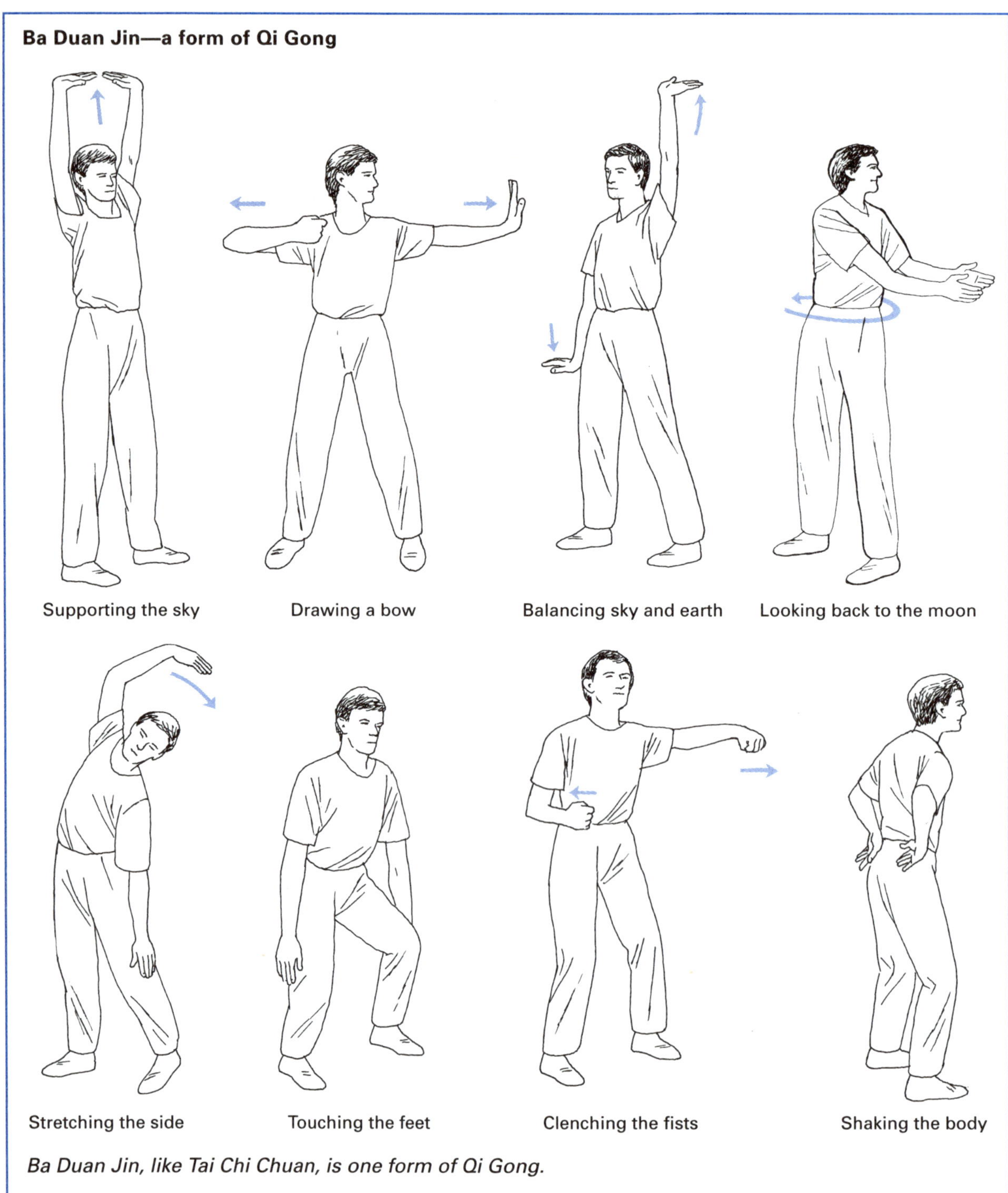

Ba Duan Jin, like Tai Chi Chuan, is one form of Qi Gong.

The breathing exercises may be used to relieve asthma and other breathing difficulties. Both sports injuries and low-back pain can be healed without strain by the exercises, which strengthen the muscles and improve general mobility and flexibility.

Remedial Qi Gong is taught on a one-to-one basis in one-and-a-half-hour sessions, and exercises are chosen on the basis of the problem or problems to be addressed. Ten sessions are usually recommended, and these will involve general bodywork, breathing exercises, and relaxation. You will be expected to practice at home between sessions. People who practice Qi Gong regularly make rapid progress, and invariably find that their health, stamina, energy level, and alertness improve, along with their sense of inner power, well-being, and joy in life.

RADIESTHESIA

Radiesthesia, meaning "the perception of radiations," was developed by a Swiss priest, Abbé Alexis Mermet, at the turn of the 20th century. It is a form of dowsing at a distance for medical purposes, whereby the practitioner responds to changes in the energy field produced by patients using a pendulum and charts. The success of the technique, however, depends more on the skill of the therapist than on the instruments used. The practitioner works by detecting and correcting the disharmonies or distortions in energy patterns, often from a great distance. One of the great advantages of the technique is that the hidden causes of disease, which may be undetectable by other methods, can be discovered and treated.

If you decide on radiesthesia treatment, you need never meet the practitioner. You simply send a medical questionnaire giving your symptoms and case history, along with a sample (called "a witness," which might be a spot of blood or a lock of hair), to the therapist. He or she will place the sample on a diagnostic instrument, mentally tune into you and pose mental questions about your health, and then hold a pendulum over the instrument in order to receive the answers. Healing energies are then focused on you from a distance (*see* **Dowsing**).

RADIONICS

Radionics is, like radiesthesia, a technique of healing from a distance, and the two therapies are often used in conjunction with each other. As with radiesthesia, the principle is based on a universal energy flow connecting all living things. Radionics was developed early in this century in California, but banned in the U.S.A during the 1960s. Since the 1950s, the U.K. has been the world center of radionics, but there is poor scientific research on the subject. The therapy does seem to be particularly effective for certain conditions such as asthma and allergies, however, and many practitioners are extremely popular, which suggests some success. Toxins in the body that are not detectable by conventional means can be identified and dispersed by radionics, as well as radiesthesia.

There is certainly no danger in the therapy other than the convictions of the practitioner, who may try to persuade a patient to stop or avoid other treatments that may in fact be successful. Be wary, but by all means use this treatment of distant healing in conjunction with other forms of therapy.

REFLEXOLOGY

The body has many energy lines running through it, known as meridians or channels. Different parts of the body reflect these channels, which supply energy to the organs and systems. The entire body can be mapped out on pressure points on the feet as is shown in the diagram on page 555. In reflexology, the area of the foot (the "reflex point') that corresponds to the body organ is palpated for diagnostic purposes, and then, if treatment is needed, massaged in order to stimulate the healing energies.

The origins of reflexology go back to the time of the ancient Egyptians, and the art was also practiced by healers in ancient Greece and China. Use of the therapy in the West was developed in the early 20th century by two Americans, Dr. William Fitzgerald and Eunice Ingham. Fitzgerald proposed the theory that 10 zones of communication run the length of the body from head to toe, and that stimulating an area of the foot in one zone affects other parts of the body along the same zone. Eunice Ingham developed his ideas, and her research on thousands of pairs of feet confirmed his findings.

Treatment is carried out with the patient lying or sitting barefoot, either on a couch or a reclining chair. A session typically lasts 30–40 minutes. The reflexologist uses the thumbs, fingers, and hands to isolate any points that are particularly empty (the finger falls into them easily) or full (generally a tender lump). By this means, diagnosis of internal energy weakness can be made. It is important not to confuse a reflexologist's comment that the kidney is weak with any suggestion that the kidney has a disease process. As in pulse-taking, the comment reflects the energy of the system and not the physiology. The therapist will then seek out and treat any painful areas with a compression technique, which clears congestion in the corresponding organ by improving lymphatic, blood, and nerve circulation. It is thought that the sensitive lumps felt beneath the skin are crystalline deposits, and it is not uncommon to feel some pain during massage as these deposits are dispersed.

Reflexology can help almost any condition, especially if used in conjunction with other, more-mainstream procedures. It is a highly effective way to detoxify the body and treat a wide variety of health problems, including skin disorders, digestive and menstrual problems, "glue" ear, and colic in children, urinary and kidney disorders, migraine, and chronic aches and pains. A recent study showed that reflexology helped knee operations to heal more quickly. Further trials need to be done, but in principle reflexology is safe, pleasurable, and undoubtedly of benefit.

ROLFING

Rolfing is a body therapy named after its founder, Dr. Ida Rolf, an American biochemist who suggested that many health problems are caused by poor posture. The principle of improving the body's alignment in order to enhance well-being is not dissimilar to that of the Alexander technique, but Dr. Rolf devised a complex manipulative technique in order to realign the body's structure so that it can work with, rather than against, gravity. This she termed structural reintegration. Deep massage of the body's connective tissues and muscles realigns the system, encouraging energy flow, circulation, and better nervous conduction.

Rolfing is a deep massage, sometimes using the elbows or knuckles, that can be uncomfortable or even painful, but undoubtedly has great benefits. Rolfing stretches the pliable connective tissue, or *fascia*, of the body. If it has contracted, it will have adhered to neighboring structures, impeding freedom of movement, and the proper functioning of the organs and other structures of the body.

Treatment usually consists of a course of ten hour-long sessions spread out over a period of time that is dependent upon the response of the patient. Each session builds on the last one, and works on a different part of the body, starting with areas where the muscles are close to the surface, and moving onto deep-tissue work in later sessions. The Rolfer may take photographs at the beginning and end of the course to document the changes that happen. The effects of a course of Rolfing include increased vitality, a better range of movement, and visibly improved balance and ease of posture. Relief of chronic structural aches and pains also results. It is not, however, a treatment for a particular ailment, but a system of preventive therapy.

SHIATSU

Shiatsu is a combination of massage and acupressure that has derived from the Japanese use of Chinese medical philosophy. The word "Shiatsu" means "finger pressure" in Japanese. Stretching meridians and manipulating acupuncture points can feed vital energy, or *Qi*, into organs and systems within the body to create health. The therapy is becoming increasingly popular in the West, as people come to realize the importance of maintaining their own health and reducing stress.

This is my favorite form of bodywork, because it incorporates the concept of Qi, acupressure, and massage. A session with a Shiatsu practitioner consists of first learning the case history of your complaint, and then taking the pulses. A diagnosis is then made by palpating the abdomen, the so-called "Hara" diagnosis. The abdomen is seen as a map of the body, which is a guide to the energetic state of the person, and the relative strength or weakness of the body's major systems. The process, which takes about five minutes, can tell the therapist which meridians to work on to rebalance the energy flow through the body. Treatment takes place with the client lying fully clothed on a mat or futon on the floor. The practitioner applies sustained pressure that varies in intensity to the appropriate points, using the hands, elbows, knees, and feet. Gentle manipulation may also be used to loosen joints and stretch the meridians, the energy pathways. Shiatsu treatment takes about an hour or so, and is deeply relaxing.

Used in conjunction with other forms of alternative or orthodox treatment, Shiatsu will make people feel better and speed up the healing process. Shiatsu also helps to maintain health by toning up the body's energy and promoting relaxation. Shiatsu can be used safely in all conditions and with all ailments, including cancer, because lymphatic drainage is only a part of the treatment program and can be put aside.

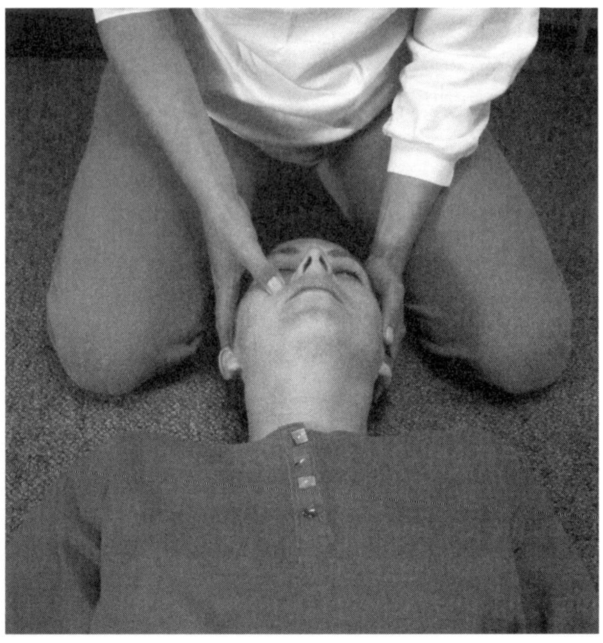

Shiatsu facial massage.

If you know the right pressure points to use, Shiatsu can be used as self-help first-aid treatment to use on yourself or your family to relieve pain or cramps.

SOUND THERAPY

Sound is an energy. The human body is made up of energies, and therefore sound affects the body. This principle has been known for thousands of years, and its health-promoting aspects have been harnessed through the use of singing, chanting, and making music from instruments. Sound is our principal method of communicating and expressing, and works directly on the nervous system which branches into every part of the body.

Sound is used through chanting to create vibration within the main chakras or energy centers in the body, but can also be used in conjunction with movement, as in dance therapy. The theory is that everything in the universe is in a state of vibration, including human beings. There is a natural resonance or frequency of vibration for each part of the body, and certain sound waves directed towards specific areas can affect the frequency of these vibrations, and thereby restore the energy balance.

Many different practitioners will use music and chanting as part of their therapy, and even doctors' waiting rooms may play music as part of the holistic approach (*see* **Music therapy**). Sound therapy may involve the voice, music, or a variety of tonal sounds, and sometimes all three combined. Sound therapy may utilize special machines that transmit "healing vibrations." A special chair known as the acoustic chair has been developed, and is undergoing trials for a variety of conditions. Sound can be used in any condition as an adjunct to other therapies, or in the form of chanting, as part of daily life and for maintaining health. It is an effective therapy for use with the mentally and physically disabled of all ages.

T'AI-CHI CH'UAN

Abbreviated frequently to Tai Chi, this is one group or set of movements among a vast number of exercise protocols that make up Qi Gong. Tai Chi can be practiced at any age, and allows the free flow of Qi through the meridians and channels, many of which are utilized by acupuncture.

Tai Chi works on the body and mind at the same time, relaxing the muscles and calming the nerves. The exercises consist of flowing movements that are performed slowly and gently, and each exercise begins and ends with standing still for a few seconds. It has been described as "moving meditation." The emphasis is not on strength or exertion, but on balance, grace, concentration, and becoming centered. The knees are kept bent, and the body's weight slowly shifted from one foot to the other, while the hands make careful circling and pushing gestures. Attention is also paid to the breathing.

As well as helping to promote and maintain good health and well-being, Tai Chi is often recommended as a therapy for those suffering from high blood pressure, tension, anxiety, and heart complaints, because of its relaxing effect on the body and mind (*see* **Qi Gong**).

VISUALIZATION

The mind has a powerful influence on the body. Whether this is through psychoneuroimmunology (*see* **Psychoneuroimmunology**), or through a direct mind/body connection as the Eastern philosophies suggest, the mind can be used to cure problems. Visualization, or forming meaningful images in the mind, is a visual approach to meditation that can have a therapeutic effect in several ways, especially in conjunction with hypnotherapy.

Most of us will note that a pain is far-less severe if we are happy or doing something we enjoy, rather than sitting around focusing on a discomfort. We can harness this positive mental attitude to overcome stress and other problems by using visualization techniques. Imagining yourself in beautiful surroundings (a sunlit forest or a wide sandy beach, for example) while using relaxation and breathing techniques has the power to counteract negative thinking, anxiety, fear, and low self-esteem. It can also be used to defuse a stressful situation, such as going to the dentist; the use of positive imagery can help us to overcome apprehension, and help us to face challenges.

Just as the mind can override psychological problems, the same energy can be used to heal physical complaints. Visualization is a taught technique that trains the body to visualize the destruction of a problem. Forming a clear image of the part of the body in need of healing can cause actual improvement to take place. An example would be to imagine a small man with an axe chopping away at a tumorous lump. A hose can be imagined to be flushing out the sinuses, and a tailor to be stitching up a hernia. See the part of your body that needs healing or strengthening becoming strong and whole again. In cases of infection, you could see the white blood cells in your bloodstream as attacking warriors destroying disease organisms, with new, healthy cells multiplying in their place.

As a therapy on its own, it may have limited value, but in combination with other more orthodox or mainstream alternative therapies, it can speed up healing. It is now increasingly used in this way in many hospitals and clinics, alongside conventional treatment.

WATER THERAPY—*see* Hydrotherapy

YOGA

Yoga is a system of movement which has been practiced in India for 5,000 years. Yoga is derived from the Sanskrit word for "union" and is principally geared towards uniting the spiritual, mental, and physical aspects of the being. Yoga works on the body, mind, and soul, and is part of an entire philosophical system, the ultimate aim of which is enlightenment and union with the divine. Different branches of yoga have different names, depending on the part of the "being" that they affect.

- Hatha yoga—works on the physical aspects by using postures and exercises in conjunction with breathing techniques. This is the most popular branch, and is what the West considers to be yoga.

- Raja yoga—is a series of techniques that focus on understanding the mind and how it exerts its control over the body.
- Jnana yoga—focuses on intellect, academia, and the understanding of the whole through meditative techniques.
- Karma yoga—concerns itself with the "reason for being" and moral concepts.
- Bhakti yoga—is that part of the being that focuses on a devotional or religious aspect.
- Tantric yoga—is a branch of Hatha yoga that incorporates sexual union between two consenting individuals. Certain sexual positions are formed, and held in conjunction with spiritual meditation.

The camel position.

Yoga can be used as a way of relaxing and keeping fit, as well as a meditation technique. All the different types involve learning breathing techniques, and adopting and holding different poses, such as "cobra," "tree," and "corpse." The poses stretch and strengthen the muscles and ligaments, increasing suppleness, and also stimulate the internal organs. Yoga has been found to benefit certain diseases, particularly arthritis, asthma, backache, high blood pressure, and digestive disorders such as irritable bowel syndrome. It is also a very effective way of dealing with stress.

Lotus position.

Yoga is not just about standing on your head, but is an integrated mind/body activity that connects the material with the ethereal. Books and tapes can introduce people to the basics of Hatha yoga, but a teacher with experience is required to access the true benefit of other forms of yoga.

ZEN

Zen is a Japanese school of Buddhism, of 12th-century Chinese origin, teaching that contemplation of one's essential nature to the exclusion of all else is the only path to pure enlightenment. It is a philosophy of life, promoting self-discipline through insight, self-awareness, and mindfulness, both of the self and others. Buddhism, simply put, sees the body and personal identity as a "block" to spiritual enlightenment.

Zen meditation helps an individual to understand that the soul or spirit is a separate entity from the body, and that illness or disease is merely a process attached to the material world, and not to the self. It encourages a joyful acceptance of the impermanent nature of existence, leading to contemplation of the "reality of emptiness," and complete freedom and transcendence of suffering. Concern for others and the development of compassion are also crucial aspects of the Buddhist philosophy. Of the many approaches to Buddhism, Zen is antirational, teaching an acceptance of ordinary life and encouraging direct experience. Zen influences daily life through *zazen* (meditation), and encourages correct nutrition, hygiene, and exercise.

Zen is perhaps the most well-known form of Buddhism in the West. More information can be obtained from Buddhist Centers which show how Zen practice can be suited to modern living. They offer meditation and study programs through classes, workshops, and retreats.

ZONE THERAPY

Dr. W. H. Fitzgerald, the founder of reflexology, divided the body vertically into ten zones, and isolated the acupressure points within them (*see* **Reflexology**). Pressure applied creates changes throughout the entire body. Whereas reflexology uses points on the feet, a zone therapist works throughout the whole system, using reflex areas all over the body. Pressure is applied to a point corresponding to an organ elsewhere. For example, there is an acupoint on the inner forearm just below the wrist, used for nausea and motion sickness (and utilized commercially in "Sea Bands" worn on the wrist as a preventive measure). Both the fingers and the toes have several points that help the head area, and pressure on the medial edge of the little finger will relieve headaches and a stiff neck. The hand reflexes mirror the position of those on the feet, and are very convenient for self-help treatment.

Chapter 10

Drugs

Chapter 10

Drugs

"If you have to take drugs, here are some facts you should know . . ."

A trial reported in the *British Medical Journal* in November 1996 showed that research sponsored by pharmaceutical companies performed in general practice does not appear to generate a high level of scientifically valid or clinically relevant findings. A report by WHAT DOCTORS DON'T TELL YOU in their journal *Proof* states that 80 percent of drugs are not proven to be safe. The BMA paper also stated that 27 percent of the trials paid for by the pharmaceutical companies were never published, which raises the probability that unsuccessful trials are not put forward in the hope that the next trial on the drug will show the treatment in a better light.

Despite the use of the terms "complementary" and "holistic," many people and doctors consider unorthodox treatments to be alternatives to the use of regular drugs. This is not the case. The best treatments can come in many guises, both orthodox and naturopathic, and good medicine is all about knowing which to use and when. There are many situations throughout this book that illustrate the need to use orthodox medicines. The biggest difficulty is answering two questions:

- If drugs are dangerous, why are they prescribed?
- Why doesn't my doctor know this?

The answers are simple. The pharmaceutical industry accepts that there are dangers, which is why they print side effects and contraindications on the packaging of drugs. The pharmaceutical industry is a business, not a caring profession, so they do not draw attention to the dangers, only to the positive aspects. Doctors are aware of the dangers, but are limited as to what else they could prescribe. Only 1,000 out of the 120,000 doctors in the U.K. have any complementary knowledge, and most of those are trained in only one technique, such as acupuncture or homeopathy. General practitioners cannot be blamed for prescribing antibiotics if they think that an infection is present, because there is little else they can give. In this chapter, I shall discuss some of the major drug groups and point out their negative aspects. This does not mean that they should not be used in specific cases, but illustrates how alternatives should be looked at before rushing into using them.

It is important to remember that many drugs are withdrawn after passing safety tests. I tried to obtain the number of such withdrawals, but (surprise!) no one had that statistic. I tried to contact various pharmaceutical companies to request this information with regard to their own products—my calls were never returned. I say this to ensure that the reader accepts that my comments are accurate to the best of my knowledge at the time I write this, but they are only my opinion.

ACCUTANE (ETRETINATE)

This is a powerful and toxic, antiacne drug based on a derivative of vitamin A. The side effects take approximately two minutes to read out, and this drug is generally only prescribed by a hospital consultant. Try every avenue to treat acne other than with this drug.

ADRENALINE

Adrenaline is a naturally occurring hormone made in the adrenal glands. It is used as a drug to treat allergic reactions in such events as insect stings, medical-drug reactions, and hypersensitivity to certain foods, most commonly eggs and peanuts. The most serious form of allergy reaction is called anaphylaxis, where the bronchial tree tightens up, the blood pressure rises, and the heart beats excessively fast.

Adrenaline needs to be given by injection, and strengths of one part adrenaline to 1,000 or 10,000 parts of water are available through a doctor, and should be kept in the house if anyone has had a strong reaction to anything at all in the past. Adrenaline is given by subcutaneous injection into any muscular part of the body, and is very easy to administer.

AIDS DRUGS

Zidovudine, also known as azidothymidine, and therefore referred to as AZT, was manufactured many years ago as an anticancer, chemotherapeutic agent. It was too toxic for use, and therefore never marketed. Wellcome, the pharmaceutical giant, discovered that AZT was detrimental to the human-immune-deficiency virus (HIV).

In fact, the initial trials suggested very little about its curative aspects, and shortly after its release onto the market, it was suggested that if taken early (after HIV infection and before AIDS had started), patients would live longer and delay the onset of AIDS. There was evidence to support this, but a more-recent and conclusive study—the Concorde Trial—has shown this not to be the case, and in fact, early use of AZT may be detrimental in the long term.

The pharmaceutical industry are now suggesting that AZT, in combination with other drugs, such as didanosine (DDI) and zalcitabine (DDC), is everything they thought AZT was ten years ago. This time, they say, the combination is definitely delaying the onset of AIDS.

New groups—known as protease inhibitors and nucleosides—are coming forward, and seem at this time to be as effective (if not more so) as AZT.

It is very difficult to elicit accurate figures concerning the effectiveness of AIDS drugs. Official reports vary from hospital to hospital, but my personal experience and those of the holistic physicians with whom I work is that the majority of patients using AIDS drugs do not use them for long because of side effects and, on a more-sinister note, the majority of AZT users do not do very well, and have problems eventually.

Azidothymidine is highly toxic, and may well be damaging to the immune system, which goes against the holistic view of AIDS and its treatment.

ALBUTEROL/SALBUTAMOL—*see* Asthma drugs

AMPHETAMINES

Amphetamines are rarely prescribed, except by hospital physicians in a few specific types of disease. Amphetamines are, however, commonplace as a drug of abuse. Uppers, speed, and reds are examples of the varying forms of amphetamines. Derivatives of amphetamines were popularly prescribed as diet pills. Unwise physicians may continue to do this, but they lead their patients into risky territory.

Amphetamines act by stimulating adrenaline receptors, thereby exciting and keeping the user awake. These are exceptionally dangerous drugs. Their direct effect on the adrenal system can lead to heart attacks, strokes, and burst blood vessels due to increased blood pressure. The body does not remove these artificial stimulants easily, and dependency can occur quite quickly.

ANALGESICS

Analgesics can be divided into nonopioid analgesics—which include aspirin; Tylenol; other aspirin-free analgesics, such as Bromo-Seltzer, Aspirin-Free Anacin, Alka-Seltzer Advanced Formula, etc.; and other nonsteroidal anti-inflammatory drugs (NSAIDs), which are discussed in their own section.

If modern medicine has come up with anything particularly worthwhile, it is the ability to numb most pain. All the drugs have side effects, but principally, these are clearly labeled and short-lived. The second group of analgesics are known as opioids, and these are discussed in their own section.

ANESTHETICS

The development of anesthetics has come a long way since biting the bullet and strong slugs of brandy. Ether was a godsend in comparison to the pain relief offered by the barber surgeons. No physician would encourage the use of anesthetics if surgery can be avoided, but on the whole they are safe and necessary. The orthodox world accepts that they are dangerous drugs, but rarely has anything to say about protecting patients from the effects.

Anesthetics have strong effects on both the nervous system (causing it to lose consciousness) and the liver, as does any toxic compound. Anybody who is going under anesthesia should consider this, and use naturopathic compounds to support both the liver and nervous system (*see* **Operations and surgery**).

ANTACIDS

The stomach produces acid to initiate the breakdown of ingested food. The stomach has a lining that produces a thick, protective mucus, which prevents the very high acid content from breaking down the stomach wall. A variety of illnesses and poor lifestyle can lead to the breakdown of this mucous membrane, which in turn leads to discomfort and pain. Many people also have hiatus hernia (*see* **Hiatus hernia**), which allows acid to reflux up into the esophagus and cause a burning sensation.

Antacids fall into two categories:

- Compounds that neutralize the acid (alkalis)—calcium, magnesium, and aluminum salts.
- Drugs that stop acid production—such as cimetidine, ranitidine, and omeprazole.

These treatments are very much geared towards blocking the symptoms by reducing the acid rather than looking at the cause of the damaged mucosa, the reflux, or the excess production of acid. They are not harmful to any great extent if taken for a short period of time, but continual use suggests that the cause of the problem is not being dealt with, and this can lead to difficult and dangerous illnesses.

ANTIBIOTICS

Antibiotics are produced to fight bacterial infection. The drugs may be bactericidal—where bacteria are killed—or bacteriostatic—where the treatment prevents the germs from multiplying. There are many antibacterial compounds in nature—garlic, ginger, and honey being three very common ones. Manufactured antibiotics come about through the fabled tale of Sir Alexander Fleming and his accidental discovery of penicillin at St. Mary's Hospital, London. This simple drug collected from mold has undoubtedly been the forerunner of a group of medicines that have saved lives and relieved discomfort beyond all imagination. Sadly, their misuse has now led to far-greater dangers.

The problem lies in the fact that bacteria, like any organism on the planet, will fight tenaciously to hold onto life. Bacteria multiply at an astounding speed, and through this process create slight changes as their genes copy themselves. As one bacterium splits into two, minor changes occur in the genetic make-up, and because of the billions of these divisions occurring every minute, there eventually comes along a bacterium whose genetic make-up is resistant to the antibiotic that kills the rest of its colony.

In the presence of an antibiotic, this resistant strain finds that it has more food to eat because of the loss of its brothers and sisters. It is unaffected by the antibiotic, multiplies more quickly, and within a short space of time, the colony is made up predominantly of this resistant strain. As new antibiotics are developed to kill this new strain, it too mutates, and once again develops resistance. We are now faced with strains of bacteria that are resistant to most antibiotics, and in the case of some strains of tuberculosis and the so-called "flesh-eating" staphylococcal infections, we have no antibiotic to kill them.

This state of affairs has come about because of

the injudicious choice of antibiotics made by doctors, who "best guess" without taking a sample of the infection for analysis, and because of the distribution of antibiotics to Third-World (and some First-World) countries that allow them to be bought over the counter without a doctor's prescription. All doctors are beseeched at medical school by their professors of microbiology never to prescribe an antibiotic unless a sample of the bacterium has been sent to a laboratory, grown or cultured, and tested against a range of antibiotics. On an individual basis, the use of an antibiotic in a patient who has a strain of bacteria that is even partially resistant will lead to a resistant strain developing, and possibly a more-difficult infection to treat.

Despite my comments above, do not hesitate to use an antibiotic in a condition that your doctor considers serious. Ensure that your physician is as certain as he can be, clinically, that the infection is bacterial. You can request a culture and antibiotic sensitivity test before using an antibiotic, and then having established with your doctor whether or not delaying the start of the antibiotics is dangerous, consult a complementary practitioner for the use of an alternative. Bromelain has been shown to increase the absorption of antibiotics, but should be prescribed by a complementary practitioner.

A second misunderstanding about antibiotics is the assumption that even if they are ineffective, they are not harmful. This is simply not true. An antibiotic is indiscriminate. It does not focus its attention on the "bad" bugs. It will attack all bacteria. Our bodies are entirely dependent on our own bacteria for survival. Skin bacteria are essential to defend against unwanted invaders, as well as being essential for the maintenance and integrity of the skin. Our ears, eyes, mouth, nasal passages, bronchial tree, and lungs are all coated and protected by our own "commensal" bacteria. Our alimentary tract, from our lips to our anus, is covered with bacteria (even in the high acid content of the stomach), which collectively have a vital role to play in our well-being.

These bacteria compete with unwanted bugs for food and prevent their multiplication; they kill many other bacteria and also viruses; they break down food to allow proper absorption; and produce chemicals that are both protective and nutritious to our systems.

Without them we die. Most people who use antibiotics will feel some side effects, ranging from tiredness and lethargy to diarrhea and thrush (*Candida*). These symptoms are all due to the unwanted destruction of our own body flora.

A course of antibiotics can have a profound effect on the bowel bacteria. The effect on large numbers of bacteria can lead to the loss of the protective effect, and can prevent nutrients being absorbed (through lack of breakdown of food, or production by the bacteria themselves). This can lead to a mild malnutrition, which in turn enhances the depressed immune system that allowed into the body the infection for which the antibiotic was being used. A vicious circle is started up with recurrent infections occurring, leading to more antibiotics, *ad infinitum*.

Remember to focus on the fact that an infection represents a breakdown in the body's immune system, and is not the fault of the germ. If an antibiotic is taken, protect the bowel flora by using high doses of *Lactobacillus acidophilus*. Loss of bowel bacteria allows fungal growth such as *Candida*, and an anti-*Candida* treatment should be followed while taking the antibiotics. Assume that your bowel flora have been affected, and that you are not absorbing as well as you should. Take a high dose of a multivitamin/mineral supplement.

ANTICANCER DRUGS

There is no doubt that these drugs can be lifesaving, and have their place in holistic medicine. Their mode of action varies, but in principle they tend to stop fast-replicating cells from doing so. This is usually done by interfering with the chemistry or the chromosomes of the cancer cells. Unfortunately, no cancer drug is that specific, and they will have effects on other cells. The stronger ones will stop the cells in the bowel, hair follicles, and bone marrow from behaving normally, because all of these are fast-replicating cells as well.

If there is any big disappointment concerning cancer drugs, it is that they are used in various combinations and quantities by different cancer specialists. Very few protocols are clearly defined and set up. We are still in a very early stage of anticancer drug development, and many patients today are unwitting guinea pigs.

As in most pharmacological developments, anticancer drugs are geared towards killing the cancer and not dealing with the cause. It is imperative that anybody using an anticancer drug sees a specialist in complementary medicine for the best advice on how to avoid the side effects, help build up the body's immunity, speed up the removal of the toxic drugs once they have performed their action and, most importantly, isolate the possible causes of the cancer and treat them (*see* **Cancer**).

ANTICOAGULANTS

The blood system has a complex and fascinating cascade—one reaction triggers another in a course of approximately 15 different stages—that allows the blood to clot. This process is essential to prevent blood loss if any vessels are damaged externally or internally, but it can become a problem if clotting occurs within a blood vessel. If this does occur, anticoagulants can be life-saving.

Anticoagulation therapy can only be initiated by a physician, and should never be stopped without specialist approval. The most common anticoagulants are heparin, which works swiftly but is generally used only in the short term, and warfarin and coumarin (benzo-α-pyrone), which are used for longer-term prescribing.

ANTIDEPRESSANTS

Volumes have been written about the pros and cons of antidepressants. *See* **Depression** to understand the continual abuse of these drugs by individuals, and the doctors who prescribe them. Discussion on each group and type of antidepressant would require a book this size again, so those using antidepressants should discuss the matter with a medically qualified practitioner of alternative medicine to learn the full pros and cons.

There is no antidepressant of any variety that does not have a myriad of side effects. When diazepam (most commonly taken as Valium) was first produced in the 1950s and considered to be the "housewife's miracle," the public and doctors were told that side effects were few and minor. It now takes over two minutes to read out the list of the side effects that have been registered on this one drug alone in the last 40 years.

As I have explained in the section on depression, the use of antidepressants has its place in truly endogenous depression. When an individual is incapable of producing his/her own "happy juice", and alternative measures have failed, then these drugs can alter a life very much for the better—perhaps more so than any other medical invention.

ANTIEMETICS (ANTISICKNESS DRUGS)

If the body is feeling sick, it is generally an indication that the individual has taken something in that it needs to throw out, or it is busily processing a toxin, and does not need anything else going in to detract from that biochemical process. Once the cause has been established, it is better to use homeopathic medication to encourage a cure rather than a drug that stops the sensation of nausea.

In cases where nausea is part of a treatment course, such as anticancer drugs or radiation, antiemetics are essential to allow the appetite to be maintained. Not eating during serious illness will not allow the body to repair as well as it should. The use of antiemetics is also permissible if it is for short-term use, such as for travel sickness.

ANTIFUNGAL AGENTS

See **Antibiotics.**

The body is coated internally and externally with

fungi. It sounds awful but, like the bacteria in the body, they are essential to our well-being. They prevent foreign fungi (which may be very toxic to our system) from gaining a foothold by what is called competitive inhibition. Fungi thrive on sugars and other nutrients, and our own fungi are not harmful to us. If we kill them off by the use of antifungal agents or poor diet, unhealthy fungi will find themselves with more food to eat because of the absence of the "good guys" and will multiply quicker, producing their toxic effects.

Yeasts are fungi. The most infamous is monilia, more commonly known as *Candida*, which produces the symptoms of thrush. Thrush is controlled due to the phenomenon of cross-species competitive inhibition. To put it more simply, antibiotics and unhealthy lifestyle kill off our own fungi and bacteria, leaving more food for the tougher varieties. *Candida* lives in a high percentage of our bodies (up to 50 percent of women will carry *Candida* vaginally) and will not cause us a problem unless we destroy its competitors. This is why people in immuno-compromised states and those who have taken antibiotics can end up with thrush.

As in the case of antibacterial agents, resistant strains occur, and we are seeing more virulent, aggressive, and faster-replicating yeast and fungi species developing due to the overprescribing of antifungal and anti-*Candida* preparations.

ANTIHISTAMINES

When the body is irritated or invaded by a foreign substance, special cells release histamine. This chemical causes the arteries in the area to open up, allowing more blood to travel to the damaged part and thereby allowing the white blood cells, vitamins, minerals, and other necessary factors for healing to reach the area quickly. Unfortunately, this increase in bloodflow is experienced as inflammation, which is irritating to the nerves and causes redness, rashes, itching, and pain.

The complementary medical view is that if this is encouraged, the problem will be dealt with swiftly in a healthy body. The orthodox view is to take away the irritation by blocking the healing effect of the histamine release. Antihistamines, while effective and (if taken in the right doses) not particularly harmful, are in fact preventing the body's natural healing mechanism. Antihistamines have several side effects, but predominantly cause drowsiness, and should therefore not be taken while driving or using machinery.

ANTI-PARKINSON'S DRUGS

Parkinson's disease is created by a lack of a neurotransmitter called dopamine in the central nervous system. Treatment is by replacing this with a compound called levodopa, which, when given in the right quantities, is a safe drug to take. Another drug, called dopa-decarboxylase inhibitor, prevents natural dopamine from being broken down. The two in combination help people with Parkinson's disease, and can be a very effective treatment.

The problem lies in the fact that the body gets used to these compounds, and after a few years may no longer respond. New drugs are constantly being brought in, such as deprenyl, amantadine, and pergolide. All are beneficial, but avoid the use of these drugs until alternative avenues have not succeeded. Use these drugs as late in the condition as possible, because resistance to their efficacy will develop, and lead to a decrease in usefulness after five to ten years.

ANTIPYRETICS

As a general rule, fever is considered by holistic practitioners to be a friend. Most bacteria and viruses do not fare well at higher temperatures, while the body, although it may not feel too comfortable, can generally survive fevers up to around 103°F. The best-known antipyretics are aspirin and Tylenol. Their mode of action is varied between direct action on blood vessels, the effects on mediators called prostaglandins, and effects on white blood cells that release chemicals that increase the body's temperature in the presence of infection.

The holistic consensus would be to avoid any drug that goes against the body's natural reaction unless the body is losing control. The pain- and discomfort-relieving aspects of antipyretics must be balanced against the potential for these drugs to prevent or slow down the healing response. Occasional use is not likely to be harmful, but a need to use these drugs beyond 48 hours or their apparent ineffectiveness in allowing the body to heal strongly suggests a visit to your healthcare provider.

ANTIVIRAL DRUGS

There are very few effective antiviral agents that can be taken by humans. Killing a virus is not difficult, but the problem is the drugs will kill humans equally efficiently. Acyclovir/Zovirax is the most commonly used antiviral agent against herpes and shingles. This is, without doubt, an effective drug, but probably kills many other viruses that may be of use to the body. It is also unable to penetrate the nervous system well, so it is only superficially effective, and is in no way curative against herpes and shingles, which live in the nerve centers. The body's best defense against antiviral agents is its own immunity, and promotion of this through complementary techniques is a safer and possibly more-effective method of antiviral treatment (*see* **Vaccinations**).

Antiviral drugs are predominantly ineffective unless given in very toxic doses. The concept of an antiviral agent sustains the myth that ill health is created by germs. In reality, the human immune system has the most-efficient antiviral techniques, and correct maintenance and stimulation of this part of our bodies continues to be more effective than drugs.

ANTIWORM (ANTIHELMINTHIC) AND ANTIPARASITE DRUGS

Threadworms and pinworms are very common among schoolchildren, and spread through families very easily. They are generally not harmful, although an excessive number can cause poor absorption, and affect growth and development in children. These parasites lay their eggs at the anus and travel through the gut, usually overnight, to do so. This gives the characteristic itching. Other worms and parasites, such as tropical worms and ameba, can be very devastating and cause serious illnesses.

Most of these live in the gut, at least initially. Early treatment is advisable, and the drugs which are prescribed by doctors stay in the gut and are poorly absorbed. This makes them very effective and nontoxic, although some people can struggle with stomach upsets, nausea, and diarrhea. These drugs should be used if a diagnosis of infestation has been made or if infestation is likely, as in family groups or schools.

ASPIRIN

See **Analgesics.**

Aspirin is being tested as an effective treatment against bowel cancer, because a reduction in the incidence of these tumors has been noted in a group who had been taking aspirin for its anticoagulant and therefore antistroke aspects. We watch and wait for the outcome.

ASTHMA DRUGS

See **Asthma.**

Do not forget that asthma is potentially a lethal condition. Adjusting asthma drugs is not recommended without medical supervision.

There are no orthodox asthma medications that are curative. The pharmaceutical industry has preferred to research into medications that keep asthma at bay, but are not curative. This is a perfectly acceptable situation for an industry that is geared towards profit and not healthcare. Feel no anger towards the pharmaceutical industry on this count; they are very clear in their attitude.

The drugs used in asthma treatment are all geared towards decreasing mucus production and opening the narrowed bronchial tubes. Most are effective, relieving, and (in many cases) lifesaving. Do not underestimate their importance in medicine but do not consider their use in health maintenance. Nearly every branch of complementary medicine will have a treatment for asthma. If one is already being taken, or you are being threatened with the use of asthma drugs, always consult a complementary practitioner before continuing or starting to use these drugs. *Do not stop your use of antiasthma drugs unless monitored by a medical practitioner.*

AZULFIDINE

A salicylic acid or aspirin-based derivative, this drug works as a potent anti-inflammatory agent, used predominantly in bowel inflammation, and particularly ulcerative colitis. Azulfidine definitely has a beneficial effect in inflammatory bowel disease, and may reduce inflammation and prevent operations if taken either alone or in conjunction with steroids.

If prescribed, withdrawal should be under very careful control, and the return of any bowel condition should be assessed immediately.

BARBITURATES

These are rarely prescribed these days, except for specific pediatric conditions. However, they are found in several European-manufactured painkillers, and should be avoided at all costs. Barbiturates are highly effective as tranquilizers and as toxins to the system. There is no need to use them, because far-better and less-dangerous drugs are available for all their potential uses.

BETA-BLOCKERS

Beta-blockers are so called because they block adrenaline beta-type receptors in certain cells around the body. These beta-receptors respond to adrenaline produced by the adrenal glands and nervous system in response to anxiety, shock, and fear.

Beta-blockers are commonly used in heart patients (*see* **Cardiac drugs**), but are also used by people who have palpitations through anxiety, or metabolic diseases such as hyperthyroidism. In themselves, they are not particularly dangerous drugs unless taken in overdose or taken by asthmatics. It is contraindicated to use these drugs if you have any suggestion of asthma.

Once again, these drugs deal with the symptoms and not the underlying cause, and alternative treatments are available, but withdrawal should be done only under medical supervision.

BUPRENEX (BUPRENORPHANE HYDROCHLORIDE)

This is a sublingual, opioid-like painkiller (*see* **Analgesics**).

CALCIUM-ABSORBING DRUGS

There has recently been a surge of interest in drugs that maintain calcium levels in bones. These drugs are not always effective, and need to be taken continuously if any effect is to be maintained. They are often prescribed together with hormone-replacement therapy (HRT). Complementary measures should be tried before resorting to either of these drugs.

More recently, a drug apparently capable of reforming, as opposed to maintaining, bone density has been marketed. Alendronic acid (Alendronate) has only recently been studied, and its long-term effects are poorly known. Like any new drug, I strongly advise against its use, especially as alternatives exist. Cyclic etidronate has been around longer. It has frequently been used to treat osteoporosis, despite a lengthy list of side effects.

CARDIAC (HEART) DRUGS

Cardiac drugs can only be prescribed by medical practitioners. In principle, if you are prescribed them, take them. They may have many side effects and may be unnecessary, but most often they are life-saving. Further discussion on the use of cardiac drugs should be undertaken with a medically qualified practitioner of complementary medicine, or a complementary practitioner in conjunction with the medical doctor who prescribed them.

There are many naturopathic and holistic

medicines and treatments that can be used for most heart conditions, so you may not need to stay on the drugs once a safe and comprehensive holistic view has been taken.

CHLORPHENIRAMINE MALEATE

See **Antihistamines.**

This drug receives a specific mention, because it is one of the more-popular antihistamine ingredients, used for hay fever and urticarial symptoms. Like any drug aimed principally at symptomatic relief, it should be used as a last and not a first choice.

COMPAZINE (PROCHLORPERAZINE)

A very popular antiemetic (*see* **Antiemetics**).

CONTRACEPTIVES—*see* Oral-contraceptive pill

CORTISONE—*see* Steroids

COUGH MEDICINES

A cough is the body's natural response to removing an object, excess mucus or infection from the lung. Cough medicines inhibit this process by desensitizing the nerves that recognize an irritant and, while soothing, will allow the cause of the problem to stay in the lungs.

The general use of these suppressants should be curtailed, unless the patient is losing sleep or coughing so much that bruising and further damage to the lungs seems inevitable. Even then, the cough suppressants should be used sparingly, and the natural-fluid-extract preparations available from healthfood stores and complementary practitioners are supposedly easier for the body to break down than the more pharmaceutically manufactured chemicals.

CYSTITIS PREPARATIONS

The orthodox practitioner will swiftly prescribe antibiotics for cystitis, very often without taking a urine sample to see if the bacteria are sensitive. This is leading to the production of resistant strains of bacteria, which is detrimental to the individual and society as a whole.

Cystitis can be dealt with by altering the acidity of the urine and making it more alkaline. Over-the-counter preparations of alkaline compounds are effective and useful, but expensive. An alternative is the use of baking soda, as described in the section on cystitis (*see* **Cystitis**). Excessive use of the alkalizing compounds can cause other problems, and therefore should not be overused, but I recommend the use of them in preference to antibiotics.

DECONGESTANTS

Congestion of the nasal passages and sinuses is generally a natural body response to the presence of irritants or infection. The swelling and mucus production is there to protect the body from invasion. Decongestants suppress this body healing response, and should therefore only be used in extreme cases. If a patient—particularly a child—is unable to sleep, or if the congestion is such that it is preventing breathing to a dangerous extent, then decongestants should be used.

Decongestants come as oral formulations, nasal sprays, or drops, and all should be avoided with equal effort. Natural decongestants carry the same suppressant activity, but are easier for the body to break down because of their plant origins.

DEHYDROEPIANDROSTERONE (DHEA)

This hormone, found in most cells in the body, is thought to be responsible for maintaining a cell's ability to repair, and maintaining its integrity. Its action is possibly by mediating the permeability of the cell wall to glucose.

This hormone is now extracted and manufactured, and is being touted as a potential elixir of youth. Doctors who have researched it, and those who stand to benefit from its sales, are adamant about its safety and efficacy. So were the doctors who invented thalidomide! My view is that, until further studies are done, this drug should only be taken under the care of a physician who genuinely believes in the curative properties of DHEA, not so much because it will make the drug safer, but they are liable to know of the most recent reports. I am sure that DHEA has its place, but at the moment, not as broadly as certain sources would have us believe.

DEMEROL

Demerol is a commonly employed opioid analgesic. It used to be quite commonplace in childbirth, although like any opiate derivative, it may have a suppressive effect on respiration, and is therefore no longer encouraged because of the risk to the fetus or baby.

Commonly found in the emergency medical bags of doctors, demerol can be used in emergency and for pain, with great relief and safety.

DIABETIC DRUGS

Diabetic drugs should only be taken under the guidance of a qualified doctor, and even then, only after an original prescription by a hospital specialist. The two forms of diabetic drug either stimulate the cells in the pancreas—called the islets of Langerhans—to produce insulin or affect cells generally, and encourage the membranes to let more glucose in.

It is advisable to establish whether diabetes can be controlled through diet and other naturopathic methods, but if not, the use of these drugs is definitely preferable to uncontrolled or high levels of glucose in the bloodstream.

DIURETICS

See **Insulin.**

The kidney has several parts in its miraculously complex make-up. Different diuretics work in different ways, but principally encourage the excretion of potassium, which causes water to leave the bloodstream, and also causes the dehydrating effect of diuretics. There is no doubt that diuretics, along with antibiotics and steroids, have made a profound impact on the survival and well-being of many different types of patient with a variety of conditions. Prescribed by the right people and used in the right way, diuretics are life-saving. When abused (such as in weight loss) they can be surprisingly rapid in creating very dangerous states of health. The abuse of diuretics is a leading cause of death and disease in the list of dangers from prescribed drugs.

Most often used in cases of hypertension (high blood pressure) and cardiac conditions, alternative measures should be reviewed, but prescriptions should not be stopped without the support of a family practitioner or specialist.

DYSPEPTIC DRUGS—*see* Indigestion drugs

EAR DROPS

Antiwax compounds melt the wax buildup in the ear, and are perfectly safe to use. Antibacterial, antifungal, and steroid drops can all be used with some confidence in their safety, provided that the prescription has been given by your physician. Please review the relevant sections, depending on the type of drug being used, and always look for a naturopathic alternative before using them.

EMOLLIENTS

Emollients are principally soothers, smoothers, and hydrators of the skin, and can be used in all conditions that cause scaling or dryness. Those that are unmedicated, such as aqueous cream, and those that are extracted from natural sources are beneficial and safe. They do not claim to be curative, but are generally very soothing, especially in eczema, and can be applied directly or through bathing.

EPILEPSY DRUGS

Antiepileptics work by altering the sensitivity of the cells in the brain. This reduces their firing off an electrical impulse when instructed to do so, incorrectly, by the area in the brain that is triggering the fits. Antiepileptic drugs have side effects, including drowsiness and reduced concentration, but need to be used for at least two years of fit-free life. Being put on and coming off these drugs must be governed by a medical specialist, because sudden removal from the drug can actually trigger fits.

ESTROGENS

Estrogens are a group of hormones manufactured in both males and females, but more so in women. Produced predominantly in the ovaries (testes in males) and the adrenal glands, they affect many different cells in the body. Until the age of puberty, estrogen levels are low in girls; they rise and fall through the normal menstrual cycle, and their production tails off at menopause.

Artificial estrogens are used in the oral-contraceptive pill and in hormone-replacement therapy (*see* **Oral-contraceptive pill** and **Hormone-replacement therapy**). Artificial estrogens, are much more potent than natural estrogens and carry side-effect risks in those who are susceptible. These include minor symptoms, such as headaches, water retention, and mood swings, but may also have an influence on more-serious problems, such as blood clotting, rising blood pressure, and cancer.

The use of any estrogen should be considered with a complementary practitioner who is knowledgeable in this area. Alternative options do exist in the form of oral and topical estrogen compounds derived from certain plants that contain phytoestrols, such as hops, fennel, rhubarb, and soya products.

EYE DROPS AND CREAMS

Optical applications are antibiotic, antifungal, steroidal, or for reducing the pressure in the eye, as in glaucoma. The first three groups can be referred to in the relevant sections, and in principle avoided, if such advice is supported by a medically qualified alternative practitioner. Eye drops to combat glaucoma must be taken, although they do not confront the cause of the condition. Untreated, this condition may cause blindness.

FEVER DRUGS—*see* Antipyretics

FINASTERIDE

This drug interferes with testosterone metabolism, and is an alternative to the more commonly used alpha-blockers in the treatment of benign prostatic hyperplasia. Recent studies have shown that it has reduced the risk of needing surgery by 55 percent, reduced urinary flow obstruction, and reduced one of the main problems, which is urinary retention. The study suggests that it produced no serious adverse effects, but impotence and decreased libido are more serious to some than others.

GAMMAGLOBULINS—*see* Immunoglobulins

GLYCERINE SUPPOSITORIES

Glycerine is a stool softener, and is used by gently inserting a suppository into the rectum. There are no contraindications for this use, provided that they are not needed too often. Persisting hard stool is generally a matter of hydration or poor diet, and referral to a nutritionist would be recommended.

GOLD

Gold is used as an antiarthritic drug prescribed by hospital specialists, and usually after other treatments have failed. It is a toxic drug that should only be considered by those whose quest for relief has failed through basic drugs and extensive alternative treatments.

GOUT DRUGS

The drugs used to combat gout are divided into those for acute and those for chronic situations. Alternative treatments are often very effective in both, while the orthodox drugs are geared towards relieving the pain or cutting down the causative uric-acid crystals by artificial means, paying little attention to the underlying metabolic defect or dietary imbalance. Treatment for acute gout often includes anti-inflammatories (*see* **Non-steroidal anti-inflammatory drugs**).

HAY-FEVER DRUGS—*see* Antihistamines and Decongestants

HEAD-LICE PREPARATIONS

Head lice are a common and irritating infestation that are often amenable to complementary medical treatments. The topical drug preparations have been cited as causing illnesses, possibly cancer, although these compounds have been withdrawn from the market in the U.K. If an alternative treatment schedule does not solve the problem swiftly, then I think the use of these compounds is perfectly acceptable and safe on occasions.

HEARTBURN DRUGS—*see* Indigestion drugs

HEPARIN—*see* Anticoagulants

HIGH BLOOD PRESSURE DRUGS (ANTIHYPERTENSIVES)

See **Diuretics** and **Beta-blockers.**

Treating high blood pressure is discussed fully in the main text. Diuretics and beta-blockers are discussed elsewhere in this chapter, and should be the first-line treatments from doctors and specialists. If complementary methods and these basic drugs do not work, people with high blood pressure will be introduced to calcium antagonists or ACE inhibitors.

Calcium antagonists block the movement of calcium in the muscles surrounding the blood vessels. Calcium is responsible for the tension in these muscles, and thereby the width of the arteries. The narrower the tubes, the higher the pressure.

Angiotension-converting enzyme (ACE) inhibitors block the production of a chemical produced by the kidneys that works directly on blood vessels, again to narrow the lumen. By blocking this enzyme, the blood vessels remain wider, thereby artificially reducing blood pressure.

Both of these drugs have their place in modern medicine for uncontrolled, high blood pressure, but both should be considered only when other treatments have failed, and only under the care of a specialist, initially. Other antihypertensive drugs are being discovered, analyzed, and introduced regularly, and my comments on last-resort and specialist care apply to these as well.

Except in acute and sudden cases of raised blood pressure, alternative treatments should be tried initially, because all these drugs are geared towards suppressing the high blood pressure without any interest in dealing with the underlying cause.

HORMONE-REPLACEMENT THERAPY (HRT) DRUGS

These drugs are principally oral contraceptives, and the pros and cons can be read about in the relevant sections (*see* **Oral-contraceptive pill** and **Hormone-replacement therapy**).

In principle, 50 percent of women who embark on HRT will not be using the medication within the first year. The side effects are pronounced, and efficacy against the symptoms of menopause is limited. The protective benefits against osteoporosis and cardiovascular disease are still poorly evaluated, and need to be balanced against the carcinogenic (cancer-causing) risks of breast and uterine cancer.

The pharmaceutical industry has gone to great pains to promote the lack of estrogen as being the main factor in menopausal symptoms, although there is strong evidence that progesterone is strongly associated, and special reference should be made to the section on the menopause (*see* **Menopause**) where HRT is discussed at great length. Much research continues into HRT, and a new form is being examined, known as a Selection Estrogen Receptor Modulation (SERM). This type of HRT acts on tissues such as bone, but apparently does not affect other estrogen receptors such as those found in the womb, thereby reducing the incidence and risks of cancer. The same, apparently, may be the case for Breast Estrogen Receptors. Unfortunately, these SERMs do not have such a strong effect on the hot flushes and night sweats that encourage people to take such drugs.

HYDROCORTISONE—*see* Steroids

HYDROGEN PEROXIDE

Used most commonly in a diluted topical solution against acne, this molecule containing two oxygen atoms is also found in intravenous techniques for increasing oxygen levels in the blood.

The topical applications are safe, provided that the solution is diluted enough, although they will only treat the symptoms, and not any underlying cause of skin conditions; the intravenous solution can only be administered by doctors trained in the subject, and is therefore of potential use.

HYPNOTICS—*see* Sleeping pills

IMITREX—*see* Sumatriptan

IMMUNOGLOBULINS

The body has a remarkable defense system. Part of its immunity is the production of specialized molecules called immunoglobulins, which attach to invading or foreign matter within the bloodstream to form a larger molecule that is removed from the system by entrapment in lymph glands, or envelopment by white blood cells specialized in recognizing immunoglobulin–antigen complexes. Immunoglobulins are often referred to as antibodies.

Science has been able to replicate very few immunoglobulins, which can be injected into an individual, and generally offer protection against specific diseases (such as hepatitis A) for up to six months. Some complementary AIDS protocols include the use of immunoglobulins, such as gammaglobulin, which can also be used in other immunosuppressive conditions.

Immunoglobulins have their place in modern medicine. If the body is failing to defend itself, then these compounds can be life-saving. There is some anecdotal evidence that immunoglobulins, being foreign proteins themselves, may stimulate an immune response from the body, and problems may be associated with the other compounds that are injected during the manufacturing process. I feel that if an individual is liable to be in a situation where the disease is present, from which the immunoglobulin is due to protect them, there are grounds to use these short-lived treatments.

IMPOTENCE DRUGS

See **Viagra.**

Until early 1998 there were no oral drugs that were legally prescribable to help the formation of erections. Certain combinations of drugs of abuse can be erection- enhancing, but carry potential dangerous side effects. The drugs most commonly used were injected, and work by constricting the venous blood vessels. This allows blood into the penis, but not out, thereby creating an erection. These will last for a few hours, and are not reversible, a little painful to give, and the erections may ache. These drugs can only be offered after review by specialists, and are worth a try if alternative measures have not worked.

INCONTINENCE DRUGS

These are specifically prescribed by specialists, and work by blocking the contraction of the detrusor (bladder) muscles. These drugs should only be used in patients with intractable incontinence. Use only as a last resort.

INDIGESTION DRUGS

Indigestion is a very broad term, covering anything from a sensation of bloating and mild discomfort to severe, acidic, burning pains felt in the epigastrium, the area just below the breastbone. The discomfort can travel up into the chest and throat, and can be associated with diseases such as stomach ulcers, duodenal ulcers, hiatus hernia, and gallbladder problems. Persistent indigestion should be thoroughly examined by a doctor or specialist, and once a diagnosis is made, please review the relevant section in this book. Indigestion medicines fall into two categories:

- Antacids (already discussed; *see* **Antacids**).
- Drugs that prevent acid production.

This latter group, containing common drugs

such as cimetidine, ranitidine, and omeprazole (Prilosec), works by stopping the production of hydrochloric acid (the acid normally found in the stomach) by the special cells lining the stomach wall. These drugs are dealing with the symptom of pain created by an acid burn, and in no way are they working on the cause of the loss of protection that the gut normally produces against acid.

In many cases, a six-week course is "curative," although if the underlying reason for the diminished gut protection is not dealt with, the problem will return, and very often people are kept on a daily or nightly dose of the antacid preparation.

This is not good medicine, and antacids of this nature should only be used if alternative or complementary medical treatments are not working, or if the necessary lifestyle changes—such as stopping smoking, and reducing alcohol and spicy foods—are not taken into consideration. I suspect that over the next 20 years we will see an increase in stomach cancer, because the cause of indigestion is rarely dealt with, as well as other (hopefully) less sinister problems arising because we are not producing enough acid to break down our foods.

Some of these drugs are used in the popular triple and double therapies to fight *Helicobacter pylorus* in conjunction with antibiotics. This once again returns to the principle of the germ theory, where everything that goes wrong with us is caused by a bug rather than our depressed immune system, and is, in my opinion, missing the point. Use triple therapy only after alternative treatments have failed.

INFERTILITY DRUGS

Infertility drugs for both men and women are principally hormonal in character. They stimulate the production of sperm in men and eggs in women. These drugs have considerable side effects, and are only prescribed by specialists.

Try alternative treatments before using these progressive drugs, and if you do you use them, use complementary therapy alongside to help negate the side effects.

INSULIN

See **Diabetic drugs.**

Insulin is prescribed when investigations suggest that the pancreas is unlikely to be able to produce enough insulin, and/or diet and antidiabetic drugs are not working.

Most types of insulin are extracted from pigs, although newer types are obtained from humans. The latter are proving to be more effective, but also have more side effects. Specialists will prefer certain types, and diabetics requiring insulin should follow their advice. I have never seen a case of insulin-dependent diabetes improved to the point that insulin is not required. Alternative therapies may reduce the daily injectable requirement, but under no circumstances should insulin injections be stopped without your doctor's approval.

LABOR AND DELIVERY

One of the few things that doctors can do is remove pain. I am a great supporter of natural childbirth, but for the very small risk that drugs may carry, removing the pain of delivery is (in my opinion) a perfectly safe option to consider.

Pain relief in the first part of labor needs to be minimal so that the mother can be aware of the progression. As the contractions become more severe and frequent, the use of nitrous oxide ("gas") is safe and effective.

If this ceases to be effective, then the mother may be offered an epidural (an anesthetic injected into the lower spinal column) or—more rarely these days—demerol, a painkiller on the same level as morphine. Demerol can cause respiratory depression in the child, and is therefore not commonly offered. Epidurals—when administered properly—are safe, and carry few risks of side effects.

The biggest problem is if the anesthetic travels up the spinal column (the chances of this are reduced to negligible by keeping the mother sitting up), because if the anesthetic hits the lower part of the brainstem, it may stop respiration.

This effect—should it happen—is temporary, and a medically equipped delivery ward will deal with the problem very efficiently.

The use of local anesthetic when repairing any tears, or for an episiotomy if required, should also be taken with no fear of risk.

Use alternative methods primarily, but if in pain, you can feel happy and safe in using orthodox drugs. Ask your complementary medical practitioner for a "washout" treatment for both you and baby if drugs are used.

LAXATIVES

Laxatives are principally of four kinds:

- compounds that increase bulk
- compounds that pull or keep water in the bowel
- drugs that stimulate peristalsis (contractions) of the large bowel
- stool softeners

As discussed in the section on constipation (*see* **Constipation**), these drugs should be avoided if possible. If dietetics and a complementary medical practitioner cannot solve a problem of constipation, then laxatives should be used from as natural a source as possible, and as infrequently as possible. Laxatives that cause gut contraction should be avoided in particular, because the bowel-training habit will alter very swiftly with these.

LEVODOPA—*see* Anti-Parkinson's drugs

LIDOCAINE

This cocaine-like drug is used as a local anesthetic, either with or without adrenaline. Some people have sensitivity to lidocaine, but most have no problems. It is broken down in the liver, which allows the small amount that may be absorbed through its use as a local anesthetic to be tolerable and acceptable. Provided that you have no specific problems with lidocaine, its occasional use is not a problem.

LITHIUM

Lithium carbonate is a drug used specifically in psychiatry for people with psychotic or schizophrenic disorders. It is generally prescribed by psychiatrists initially, and these specialists and general practitioners will monitor levels very accurately, because too little will be ineffective, and too much can be toxic, causing liver and bone marrow problems.

It is a remarkably effective drug, although it carries dangers, and should be used only if other drugs and alternative measures have not proven effective. This is not the safest of drugs, and should be used only under specialist guidance.

L-THYROXINE

This is not strictly a drug, although it is manufactured. It is a combination of an amino acid and iodine, and is used as a supplement in thyroid deficiency. Commonly needed and safe to use in the right dosage.

MALARIAL DRUGS

More accurately termed antimalarial drugs, this group of chemicals is beneficial for travelers, although their use for longer than three months is generally not recommended. The drugs kill the malarial parasites at varying stages of their lifecycle, which includes time spent in the red blood cells as well as in the bloodstream.

Treatment is by quinine, intravenously if the condition is serious, or by tablet if not. Other drugs, such as mefloquine or Sulfadoxine, may also be necessary, and should be used if so advised.

Prophylaxis is with mefloquine, chloroquine, or Sulfadoxine. Mefloquine has recently had some bad press, and ideally should be avoided, but many strains of malarial parasite are now resistant to other drugs, and it is better to try mefloquine and keep a close eye on your general health through your doctor or healthcare provider.

Prophylaxis against malaria is generally safe. The pills are taken once a day or once a week, because the body clears out the drugs within that time frame. If you do not react badly to them, then it is safer to run the risk of the drug causing a problem than to run the risk of malaria.

Homeopathic remedies, specifically Natrum muriaticum, are often mentioned as an alternative. There is no strong evidence to support this, although the use of Natrum muriaticum and vitamin B_6 (100mg per day for an adult) may help the body to fight any malarial infestation.

MAXOLON—*see* Antiemetics

MEBENDAZOLE—*see* Antiworm drugs

METAMUCIL (ISPAGULA HUSKS)—*see* Laxatives and Constipation

MORPHINE

Morphine is the most-potent pain reliever. It is similar to the body's own painkillers—known as endorphins and enkephalins—and also similar in structure and efficacy to heroin.

Morphine is profoundly addictive, not so much psychologically, but certainly physiologically. This means that when its use is stopped, the body will be much more sensitive to pain for a short while. The body does readjust. Morphine is usually introduced when terminal conditions are creating pain that is unrelenting with other painkillers.

I, among other holistic physicians, suspect that the use of morphine is suppressive not only of pain, but also of the body's natural, vital forces. Morphine should only be used when other painkillers are failing to succeed.

MOUTHWASHES

Mouthwashes are principally antiseptic solutions. They kill bacteria, but do not differentiate between the "good guys" and "the bad guys." Our mouths are protected by a variety of useful bacteria that mouthwashes may kill off, leaving us open to unwanted bacterial effects. The loss of bacteria also encourages the growth of fungi and yeasts. Avoid the use of mouthwashes except for short periods under dental or medical advice.

NALOXONE

This drug is given to block the effects of opiates, principally in those who have overdosed on heroin, opium, or morphine. An excess of these compounds can cause respiratory depression, and they are therefore potentially fatal; naloxone plays its part in emergency medicine.

NEBULIZERS

These are instruments that enable patients with lung problems who do not have the necessary skills to use an inhaler to receive inhalations (*see* **Asthma drugs**).

NICOTINE PRODUCTS

Nicotine is a highly addictive compound found in all tobacco. It is conceivable that some cigarette companies might put extra nicotine into their brands to "hook" users.

The pharmaceutical industry has produced nicotine products in the form of patches and chewing gum in an attempt to remove the need for people to obtain nicotine from smoking.

This is simply transferring the addiction from one method of administration to another. However, it is probably better to use a nicotine patch or chewing gum rather than smoking, because you will be protecting the lungs, but dependence on these products maintains the addictive aspect, and is therefore less likely to reduce the cigarette craving in the long term. Many people are allergic to the patches and struggle with nausea when nicotine is chewed. *See* **Smoking**.

NIFEDIPINE

Nifedipine is a cardiac drug, and if prescribed, should be used unless an alternative therapy proves successful, and even then withdrawal should only be under a doctor's supervision.

Nifedipine had some bad press because it was causing suicide and a worsening of symptoms, and cardiac failure in a larger-than-acceptable number of users. Other drugs may be preferable, but this decision must be made with the expertise of specialists.

NITRATES

The most-commonly-used nitrate is nitroglycerine (NTG). This is a potent arterial dilator that has its most beneficial effect on the arteries supplying the heart muscle. It is commonly used in angina and, like any cardiac drug, should be used as instructed unless alternatives can be found.

Like any drug that affects the cardiovascular system, it has side effects, including dizziness, headaches, and nausea, and any such symptoms should be discussed with your doctor.

NITRAZEPAM

This hypnotic drug is more commonly used as Mogadon (*see* **Sleeping pills**).

NITROGLYCERIN (NTG)

This is used as a sublingual tablet, spray, oral tablet, or transdermal patch. It is a cardiac drug (*see* **Cardiac drugs**) that opens up the blood vessels which can instantly reduce the pain of angina. Like any cardiac drug, it should only be used once advised by a medically qualified specialist, and should only be stopped with that expert's approval. It is not curative of heart disease, and a complementary medical view should be obtained in an attempt to remove the necessity of any of these drugs.

NITROUS OXIDE

Nitrous oxide, commonly known as laughing gas, is used as an inhaled painkiller, most commonly in child birth. It is absolutely safe to use.

NONSTEROIDAL ANTI-INFLAMMATORY DRUGS (NSAIDs)

These drugs, as the name suggests, are anti-inflammatory drugs. They are a step up from aspirin, Tylenol and Aleve, and a step down from steroids.

Inflammation is the body's natural healing process, and should only be suppressed as a last resort. Alternative and complementary medical treatment should be tried first before an anti-pain drug is used.

What is more, the British Medical Research Centre recently stated: ". . . (the) high level of prescribing is still not justified," and ". . . the therapeutic role of topical NSAIDs is unclear." This is based on the poor trial evidence there is, and the fact that they showed a "marked placebo response."

Tylenol and aspirin are often as effective as NSAIDs, and seem to have fewer side effects.

NYSTATIN

See **Candida, Thrush,** and **Fungal infections.**

Nystatin (Myeostatin, Myconel, Nystex) is a very popular prescription for candidal or thrush infections, because it kills yeasts but, like any such drug, has a capability of creating resistant strains. Avoid the use of nystatin whenever possible.

OPIOID ANALGESICS (INCLUDING MORPHINE, DIAMORPHINE)

The body produces natural painkillers, the most effective of which is a group called endorphins and enkephalins. These powerful analgesics are produced when the body is in severe pain or has undergone trauma, but can also be produced through heavy muscular exercise. These hormones also carry a sense of euphoria.

"Manmade" opiates have a very strong resemblance to the body's natural opiates, and therefore tend to be handled well by the body. Unfortunately, opiates are addictive, and are usually prescribed only in very severe pain for short periods, or for pain created by terminal disease where addiction does not matter.

The euphoric affect of opiates is well established, but less well documented is morphine's effect on willpower. Very often, opiates are used in terminal diseases, and I have found that the conscious willpower to fight the battle diminishes, as well as a subconscious willpower that I think is very necessary in the fight against disease. It is almost as if the subconscious or the soul shrugs its shoulders and says "well, this is not too bad, why bother fighting?"

Opiates should only be considered when all other orthodox and complementary medical options have been exhausted.

ORAL-CONTRACEPTIVE PILL

When the "Pill" was first produced in the late 1950s, its claims were: socially enormous and medically safe. Nearly 40 years later, the social implications have been supported, and indeed, the number of unwanted pregnancies and the serious complications that go with this—such as terminations (abortions)—will also support its beneficial claims.

It takes over two minutes, however, to read the list of the variety of side effects and dangers that the Pill can create. Although the problems associated with the Pill are less numerous and less risky than the immediate dangers of a termination, and incomparable on a social basis to unwanted pregnancies, the side effects are nonetheless potentially lethal.

There is an increased risk of a variety of cancers with the use of the Pill, although supporters would point out that the Pill also has protective effects. No conclusive trials are advertised against the use of the Pill because of the enormous financial gains made by the pharmaceutical industry from its sale.

The consensus of holistic opinion is against the use of artificially created hormones taking the place of the body's natural cycle. The nature of the Pill's effect is—broadly speaking—to convince the body that it is already pregnant, and therefore does not need to produce the natural fertility hormones. There is little doubt that if other contraceptive methods are usable, then the Pill should be avoided.

If a holistically-minded physician or a knowledgeable complementary medical practitioner has fully pointed out the risks and side effects, and can see no reason why your past history, family history, lifestyle, or general health would make you more prone to the side effects, then I feel that the use of the Pill over a nine-month period (the body's normal pregnancy time) with a 3–6-month break afterwards offers a happy medium.

Please ensure that you read the list of side effects before going on the Pill.

PENICILLIN—*see* Antibiotics

PEPPERMINT OIL

Used as an aromatherapy oil, peppermint can be most beneficial. From an orthodox point of view, peppermint has been found to be helpful in relieving bowel spasm, especially in irritable-bowel syndrome. It has its place in holistic treatments, and if effective, can be used without anxiety, although one must remember that peppermint will negate the effect of homeopathic remedies.

Topically, peppermint oil can be very relieving for hemorrhoids and phlebitis, but remember to dilute the peppermint oil considerably before applying it to the sensitive anal area.

PHENERGAN (PROMETHAZINE HYDROCHLORIDE)

See **Antihistamines.**

Phenergan is the trade name of one of the most-common antihistamines used in the U.S.: promethazine. Promethazine is used all over the world as a first choice for hay fever and other allergic symptoms. It deserves special mention because it is used as a sedative preoperatively, and also for children who are exhibiting sleep-pattern difficulties. This latter use as a sedative is based on one of Phenergan's side effects, which is drowsiness.

Basically Phenergan will suppress symptoms of allergy, and is in no way a treatment or cure. It is best to try to treat the cause of an allergy rather than suppress the symptoms. If necessary, however, it can be used safely if taken short term. The same can be said for its sedative effects; for children, I would recommend that no more than three nights should be affected by promethazine without at least a one-week gap.

PHENOBARBITONE

See **Barbiturates.**

Phenobarbitone is one of the few barbiturates still utilized for certain conditions. It is generally only prescribed by specialists, and only if other, more- effective drugs with less-addictive properties are not available. If you are using a barbiturate, you probably need to, and you should continue to do so unless an alternative treatment is effective.

PHENYTOIN

This is an anticonvulsant or antiepileptic drug. It acts by reducing the sensitivity of neurological cells, thereby preventing the electrical impulses that flash through the brain and cause epilepsy. It is an extremely effective and successful drug, although some side effects are associated.

Phenytoin is usually only prescribed by specialists when no other options are available. Treatment, once started, should be continued until your specialist or general practitioner removes you from the drug. It is worthwhile discussing the underlying problem with a complementary medical practitioner, but stopping any anticonvulsant is a risky business.

PIPERAZINE

Piperazine, along with mebendazole, are the two most frequently used antihelminthic (worms) drugs. Although there is a myriad of herbal treatments that have been used for centuries in dealing with infestation by worms such as roundworms and threadworms, these two drugs are safe and effective.

I recommend the use of these drugs because they are poorly—if at all—absorbed into the system and stay in the bowel, killing the parasites. Very few people have any side effects or problems.

PODOPHYLLUM

This is an antigenital-wart lotion that is painted on topically. A very effective treatment, but the warts may return. Podophyllum is also toxic if used too much, because it damages normal skin. It is important to avoid the area around a wart.

PONSTEL—*see* **Nonsteroidal anti-inflammatory drugs (NSAIDs)**

PREDNISONE/PREDNISOLONE—*see* **Steroids**

PREMARIN—*see* **Hormone-replacement therapy**

PROGESTERONE

See **Hormone-replacement therapy** and **Osteoporosis.**

Progesterone is infrequently used because of the artificial forms being 40 times stronger than naturally made progesterone. Certain conditions require its use, but plenty of alternatives exist for all but the most serious of problems.

Natural progesterone is available in a cream, and may be far more effective than estrogen in many hormone-related conditions, including premenstrual syndrome, breast cancer, osteoporosis, and cardiovascular disease.

PROPRANOLOL HYDROCHLORIDE (INDERAL)—*see* **Beta-blockers**

PROSTAGLANDINS AND OXYTOCICS

Prostaglandins are commonly found in many biochemical pathways within the body, but artificial prostaglandins are principally reserved to induce abortion or labor. These drugs are prescribed by a specialist, and generally have no alternative.

PROVERA

This is a modified progesterone drug that is used by specialists in the treatment of endometriosis and other gynecological problems. It is sometimes used to try to induce periods if they have stopped. Provera has many unpleasant side effects, and should be used only when alternative treatments have failed.

PROZAC—*see* Selective serotonin reuptake inhibitors (SSRIs)

QUININE

Quinine is used in severe cases of malaria, and differs from antimalarial drugs (*see* **Malarial drugs**) simply because it is used as a treatment and not as a prophylactic.

Quinine is the most effective of antimalarial drugs, and that is not speaking too highly. Used in conjunction with complementary therapies, its effects may well be enhanced, but as this is a drug that may save lives, it should not be resisted.

RANITIDINE

See **Antacids.**

Ranitidine is an antacid drug that blocks receptors in the stomach lining that trigger acid production. It is of benefit in relieving symptoms, and supposedly gives the stomach time to repair any damaged membrane.

RETIN-A

This compound, tretinoin, is the acid form of vitamin A. It is a topical application used in acne that causes a drying effect, and temporarily reduces the problem of acne. It is frequently used in association with Accutane (etretinate), again in acne. It is an extremely aggressive topical treatment, and is in no way curative. Avoid if possible.

RIFAMPIN

See **Antibiotics.**

Rifampin is a first-line antituberculosis drug. More and more strains of tuberculosis are becoming resistant to this compound, but it should still be used in the initial fight.

RITALIN

This drug is sold as part of a treatment program for attention deficit disorder (ADD) and hyperactivity disorders. The manufacturers suggest that it should only be used as a last resort, although, especially in America, its use is becoming much greater.

The drug must be prescribed by a specialist, and even then, the safety is questionable. It is known to retard growth, and no trials have been done on long-term therapy. The principle of the drug (methylphenidate hydrochloride, which is derived from amphetamines) is to stimulate the central nervous system, thereby increasing attention. The paradox of the success of a stimulating drug in overstimulated children is unclear, but it clearly stimulates some part of the brain that counteracts the cause of hyperactivity. The belief is that hyperactivity is a compensatory mechanism for a poor concentration ability (*see* **Hyperactivity**).

ROGAINE/LONITEN (MINOXIDIL)

This topically applied drug, minoxidil, has gained fame by acting as a hair-follicle stimulant in male-pattern baldness.

The drug was initially discarded from its original, intended use as an antihypertensive drug because of severe side effects. One of these was hair growth. Some clever scientific expert applied it directly to the skin, and a whole new pharmaceutical angle was born.

Minoxidil works by producing a fine, downy hair growth in over 70 percent of individuals, but less than 15 percent have an acceptable type of hair, and to maintain it they need to continue to use the drug, at approximately $2 a day. The drug is absorbed, and therefore side effects are possible, as well as the compound causing local irritations.

ROHYPNOL

See **Sleeping pills.**

This potent hypnotic receives a mention separate from sleeping pills in general because of its use as a drug of abuse. When taken with alcohol, and the initial soporific effect is fought off, an exciting buzz is said to occur, and a prolongation of time before orgasm during sexual intercourse. This may be so, but the amount of chemical neurotransmitters that need to be produced to override both the soporific effects of the alcohol and this immensely powerful drug are enormous. The drain on the nervous system is intense, and the long-term effects of such abuse are unknown, but certainly not liable to be healthy.

SALICYLATES AND SALICYLIC ACID

These are aspirin by another name (*see* **Aspirin**).

SEDATIVES—*see* Anasthetics and Tranquilizers

SELDANE

This is the most popular trade name for the drug terfenadine, which is an antihistamine (*see* **Antihistamines**).

SELECTIVE SEROTONIN RE UPTAKE INHIBITERS (SSRIs)

The SSRI drugs are relatively new, and work by blocking the breakdown of the body's main "happy juice" neurotransmitter, known as serotonin. If ever a drug was to have a holistic approach, this must be it.

This group is less sedative than its better-known rivals, the tricyclic antidepressants, and have fewer side effects. Fewer side effects does not mean side-effect-free, however, as the group can cause quite-severe symptoms, and has been cited as the cause of marked and severe anorexia. If an antidepressant has to be used, this group is a good starting point, but work as hard as you can to find alternative treatments.

SELSUN, EXSEL (SELENIUM SULFIDE)

Selsun and Exsel are antidandruff shampoos that contain a high quantity of selenium. This is toxic to certain skin fungi, and is used topically. These are extremely effective and safe treatments.

SENNA—*see* Laxatives

SLEEPING PILLS

See **Insomnia.**

There are a variety of different chemical compounds that can be used to put people to sleep. There is no "safe" sleeping pill, because any of them in excess can cause brain damage or death. From a more holistic point of view, sleeping pills are a quick solution for a deep biological imbalance.

Sleeping pills generally work by telling the brain and nervous system that it should be asleep. They override the body's natural chemicals that are being produced to keep you awake for some underlying reason, or take the place of the body's natural "sleepy" chemicals. In both cases, sleeping pills work against the body's natural processes, and are therefore generally contraindicated.

If you use sleeping pills for any length of time, the underlying cause of the sleeplessness will become more deeply buried and harder to deal with, and the body will quickly become quite dependent, and thus take more time to reproduce its own sleeping chemical. As these pills do not stop the production of the compounds that keep us awake, the brain is subjected to both stimulus and suppression at the same time, making the sleep shallow and unrefreshing at a deeper level.

Sleeping pills should only be used under the supervision of a medically qualified and holistic-thinking practitioner. They can be used for up to three nights to break sleep patterns on rare occasions, without too much risk of longer-term problems.

STELAZINE—*see* Antiemetics

STEROIDS

The human body makes its own steroids. These may be anabolic (body stimulating) or catabolic (inhibiting). The body maintains an intricate balance of these chemicals, and different types are produced for different functions, accurately and rhythmically. Steroids that encourage repair are produced through the night when we are sleeping, and those that stimulate activity are produced in abundance in the early hours of the morning. Conversely, those involved in the breakdown of unwanted products and elimination have their set times to be produced at high or low levels. This delicate balance is maintained by command hormones produced in the pituitary and adrenal glands and, provided that we maintain good health, this balance is undisturbed. Steroids have an immunosuppressive action. In the same way that they balance the body's bloodflow, they also prevent overstimulation of the immune system.

As one can see, steroids have many effects, but one of their main methods of action is by constricting blood vessels, thereby decreasing blood-flow. If a body part is injured, the nervous control and histamine release cause arteries to open up to carry the blood into the area, thus bringing in vitamins and other nutrients—white blood cells to kill invaders, and scar-tissue-forming cells to heal damage. The action of steroids is to keep this in balance.

The use of steroids, whether topical or systemic (taken into the body), is damaging from five points of view:

- The delicate balance of healing is disturbed.
- The control mechanisms are blocked.
- The natural healing process is inhibited.
- The steroids themselves are shrouded with side effects, some of them lethal.
- The immunosuppressive action of steroids can lead to recurrent or persistent infections.

The most-common steroids in use in Western medicine are hydrocortisone (a molecule similar to but more potent than the body's naturally produced cortisone) and prednisolone. In the East, many plant extracts contain steroids that are equally potent, equally suppressive, and make a mockery of the concept that natural medicine is safe if injudiciously used or overprescribed. Self-medication with herbs is often dangerous because of this steroid effect.

The orthodox world concerns itself with removing discomfort—often at any price, and with little concern for the underlying cause. For instance, the use of steroids in asthma removes the inflammation in the bronchial tree, thereby opening the passages. In life-threatening conditions this is invaluable, but it does not profess to be a cure. The use of steroids in less-severe cases of asthma is undoubtedly relieving, and often necessary. However, without a complementary medical view, steroids may have to be used in perpetuity or until the body repairs itself regardless of the medication.

When a steroid is prescribed by a physician, *it must not be stopped* except under medical supervision. The inhibition created by steroids on the control mechanisms in the body may stop natural steroid production. Ceasing medication may leave the body without steroids, and this can be fatal. Anyone taking or who has been recommended to take steroids should review the situation with a complementary medical practitioner, and under medically qualified supervision, either withdraw or assess the efficacy of not taking them. The pharmaceutical industry would have us believe that topical steroids are poorly absorbed through the skin, and therefore have little, if any, effect. They do thin the skin if used persistently; they reduce the immunity in the area; and without any doubt, are absorbed in quantities that can affect the system as a whole. One must be particularly wary if using a steroid cream on an area of skin that is weeping or bleeding.

STILBESTROL

This drug is prescribed by specialist units in rare cases now to treat prostate cancer. It has many side effects, and is less used than other estrogens such as fosfestrol (Stilphostrol). Its use should be continued if started unless side effects are noted, in which case the specialist involved should be advised.

STREPTOKINASE

This is an injected drug carried by most physicians and emergency doctors for use within a few hours of a myocardial infarction (heart attack). Streptokinase is also used for deep-vein thrombosis and other clot problems such as embolism. It is considered to increase the chances of survival following heart attack. Further studies are required, but at this juncture it is worth taking.

SUDAFED

Sudafed is an adrenaline-like drug called pseudoephedrine. It is used as a topical nasal decongestant, and should only be considered after alternative treatments have failed for situations such as rhinitis and hay fever.

SUDOCREM

God's gift to diaper rash. This zinc-based, synthetic-beeswax cream acts as a marvelous barrier to infection through diaper rash and open sores. Used in conjunction with an *Arnica* or *Calendula* cream, it will protect while the other heals.

SULFATRIM/BACTRIM

See **Antibiotics.**

These are common antibiotics that are used less because of their toxic side effects. They are popular for urinary-tract infections, and are now used as prophylactic antibiotics against *Pneumocystis carinii*, a common infection in AIDS. Only use these drugs on the recommendation of a specialist, because others are less toxic and just as effective.

SUMATRIPTAN

Initially an injectable drug used in acute attacks of migraine, it is now available orally, but has many side effects and little long-term experience. It should be used only after all other alternatives and orthodox, antimigraine treatments have been tried.

SUN SCREEN

An ever-increasing market is being found for these creams, which contain agents that block ultraviolet light. Their effect is only as a barrier cream, and most people do not apply the lotion thickly enough. This means that the effects are much shorter lived than described on the bottle. Limited exposure to sun, and reference to the section on sunburn (*see* **Sunburn**), should be used in conjunction with sun screens.

TAGAMET (CIMETIDINE)

This is a drug that blocks acid production (*see* **Antacids**).

TAMOXIFEN

Tamoxifen blocks estrogen receptors, and is the first-line hormonal treatment in breast cancer that is sensitive to estrogen. It is also used in postmenopausal women because of an effect other than estrogen blocking (postmenopausal women have low levels of estrogen, and therefore the estrogen-blocking action is not the method of defense). Side effects are rare, but include menopausal symptoms, and it will of course stop the normal cycle.

TEMAZEPAM

This is a benzodiazepine, usually marketed as a sleeping pill (*see* **Sleeping pills**).

TERFENADINE

Until recently, this was the most popular antihistamine because it had a weak sedative effect. It is now known to create marked arrhythmias (irregular heartbeats) and should be avoided.

TESTOSTERONE

Testosterone is only provided by specialists, and for particular conditions. The use of this drug is very limited, and should only be used if other treatments fail.

TETANUS TOXOID

Tetanus toxoid is given if a wound is liable to be infected. Tetanus toxoid is likely to be administered to anyone with a wound or cut that is likely to have been infected by the tetanus-causing bacteria (*see* **Tetanus**).

Its use in serious wounds is sensible, but minor abrasions seem to receive the same dosage, although it is probably safe.

TETRACYCLINES

These are powerful antibiotics with many side effects, and should only be used after a firm diagnosis, culture, and sensitivity have been established on any infection. This is sadly often not done, and many strains of bacteria are proving to be resistant to this antibiotic (*see* **Antibiotics**).

THEOPHYLLINE

This is a second-line antiasthma drug, traces of which are found in black tea. Use it if prescribed, but consider complementary medical therapies to aim at a cure for asthma rather than this drug, which simply relieves symptoms.

THIAZIDES—*see* Diuretics

TIBOLONE (LIVIAL)

This drug is due to be pushed strongly as an anti-osteoporosis drug because of its estrogen and progesterone activity. Initially used to block flushing after surgically induced menopause, the pharmaceutical industry have recently had it licensed for this other use.

Avoid this drug until it has been on the market a little bit longer, in case it comes up with serious side effects, and review the section on osteoporosis in this book (*see* **Osteoporosis**).

TRANQUILIZERS

This term has now been superseded by hypnotics (*see* **Sleeping pills**) and anxiolytics. A tranquilizer is principally a drug that takes away anxiety, and is now synonymous with anxiolytics.

These drugs can be divided into the benzodiazepines and barbiturates. The latter are very rarely used nowadays because of their side effects and rapid addictive qualities. The former are less addictive—but only just. Valium is the most common drug indicated for the short-term relief of severe anxiety. The benzodiazepines can be long- or short-acting drugs, but are being replaced by sustained serotonin reuptake inhibiters (SSRIs), principally Prozac.

TRICYCLIC ANTIDEPRESSANTS

Until recently, tricyclics were a preferred form of antidepressant drug. More recently, the serotonin reuptake inhibitors have surpassed them.

Tricyclics may still be prescribed by psychiatrists who stick with their known, tried, and tested drugs, and if they work and no alternatives are successful, their use should be maintained.

TRYPTOPHAN

Tryptophan is an essential amino acid, and is used by the brain to produce serotonin, one of the body's major calmants and sleep chemicals. L-Tryptophan was a very popular and successful antidepressant, and is found in cottage cheese, milk products, meat, fish, fowl, bananas, dried dates, peanuts, and most other protein-rich foods.

It is now only prescribable by hospital specialists and registered doctors, because it was linked to a potentially fatal blood disease. This was following a contaminated batch supplied by one single Japanese manufacturer. Despite many other trials showing tryptophan to be safe (after all, we are eating it constantly), the pharmaceutical industry took advantage to take this easily available and extremely inexpensive supplement off the market, thereby requiring the increased sales of more artificial and expensive drugs. Sometimes I despair.

TYLENOL

Tylenol is a mild-but-potent analgesic, similar in its effect and strength to aspirin, but with far less anti-inflammatory effect. Because (holistically speaking) inflammation is part of the body's repair mechanism, Tylenol is preferred to aspirin as a first-line pain relief.

However, Tylenol is far more toxic to the liver than aspirin (although aspirin has far-greater chances of causing gastritis or ulcerative conditions in the stomach), and should not be taken too frequently or in excess (*see* **Analgesics**).

TYLENOL WITH CODEINE

A common painkiller containing Tylenol and codeine (*see* **Analgesics**, **Tylenol,** and **Opioid analgesia**).

VACCINES—*see* **Vaccinations**

VALIUM
The most popular trade name for diazepam, the tranquilizer (*see* **Tranquilizers**).

VANCOMYCIN
Vancomycin is an antibiotic that deserves special mention. It can only be given intravenously, and is used as a last resort against multiresistant bacteria. Its use is becoming more needed because of hospital-induced resistant strains, especially of staphylococcal infections. Special mention is given because it is our last-resort antibiotic. We now have resistant strains to this as well. Beware the coming plague!

VASELINE
Vaseline is a safe barrier cream and lubricant.

VASOCONSTRICTORS
These drugs are used as local anesthetics when given by injection, and in the treatment of migraine if vasodilation is considered. Use if needed.

VASODILATORS
Principally, anything that opens up blood vessels is a vasodilator, which includes alcohol. Peripheral vasodilators are used in an attempt to treat Raynaud's disease, and others affect the blood vessels in the brain, and are being unsuccessfully tried in Alzheimer's disease and other dementias. Use only if alternative therapies do not work, because these drugs may be too powerful, causing an overdilation leading to weakness and fainting.

VENTOLIN—*see* **Asthma drugs**

VIAGRA
This drug, released in America in the early part of 1998, encourages the production of a firm erection by influencing a chemical (cGMP) that in turn constricts the contraction of the veins in the penis, as opposed to relaxing the muscles in the arteries. Highlighting the large number of men with erectile problems, this drug has sold more in its first six weeks of availability than any other drug yet produced.

Like all drugs that make it to the market, strict and stringent tests have been performed to monitor its safety. However, at the time of writing, the drug has been associated with the unexpected deaths of 69 men around the world. My advice, as for any new drug, is that the longer it can be avoided, the longer it can be studied, and any long-term side effects can be monitored.

VICKS
Vicks is a collection of painkillers and decongestants under a trade name. The use of naturopathic treatments is preferred.

VOLTAROL
This is a popular nonsteroidal anti-inflammatory drug (*see* **Non steroidal anti-inflammatory drugs**).

WARFARIN
Warfarin is a drug that interferes with the body's clotting mechanism. It takes some time to kick in, unlike heparin, and is given to prevent clotting in deep-vein thrombosis or emboli.

Careful monitoring of blood-clotting time is required, but it may be a life-saving compound. Naturopathic treatments are available, but should only be prescribed by a competent and experienced complementary medical practitioner with experience in herbal medicine.

XANAX
Xanax, a short-term anxiolytic (*see* **Tranquilizers**).

ZANTAC
Zantac is the trade name for ranitidine (*see* **Ranitidine**).

ZIDOVUDINE
Also known as azidothymidine, and best known as AZT (*see* **AIDS drugs**).

Part Three

Glossary

Acute—a term used to describe a disease that is sudden, short-lived, and relatively severe.

Allergen—a substance capable of inducing an immune response and producing an immediate hypersensitivity (allergy).

Analgesia—the relief of pain without loss of consciousness.

Anaphylaxis—a manifestation of immediate hypersensitivity in which exposure of a sensitized individual to a specific antigen results in life-threatening respiratory distress.

Antihelminthic—an agent that is destructive to worms.

Antioxidant—a vitamin-based molecule that neutralizes negatively charged particles (free radicals) in the bloodstream, thus delaying or preventing degradation by oxidation.

Antipyretic—an agent that relieves or reduces fever.

Arteriosclerosis—a group of diseases characterized by thickening and loss of elasticity of the arterial walls.

Asymptomatic—showing or causing no symptoms.

Atopic—allergic response occurring in a site other than the area of contact with allergen.

Aura—an energy "fuzz" around the body that changes color and density according to general health.

Autoimmunity—a condition characterized by a specific humoral or cell-mediated immune response against constituents of the body's own tissues.

Autonomic—self-controlling or functionally independent.

Beta-blockers—drugs that combat hypertension by slowing the heart rate or preventing arterial contraction.

Bioflavonoids— compounds present in plants that maintain the walls of small blood vessels in a normal state.

Bioresonance—the use of electromagnetic energy, in conjunction with a computer, in the diagnosis and treatment of disease.

Calcium channel blockers—drugs that interfere with intracellular calcium flux, and reduce the contraction of arterial muscle, thus acting as vasodilators.

Calculus—an abnormal concretion occurring within the body that is usually composed of mineral salts.

Calisthenics—a system of physical exercises for promoting strength and cardiopulmonary fitness.

CT scan—computed tomography scan: reconstruction of cross-sectional images of the body made by a rotating x-ray source and detector that move around the body and record x-ray transmissions throughout the 360° rotation.

Catecholamines—compounds that function as neurotransmitters.

Chalazion—a small nodule on the eyelid due to chronic inflammation of a sebaceous gland.

Chancre—a hard swelling that constitutes the primary lesion in syphilis.

Chemotherapy—the treatment of disease by chemical compounds selectively directed against invading organisms or abnormal cells.

Chronic—a term used to describe a disease that persists over a long period of time.

Circadian rhythm—a cyclical variation of about 24 hours in the intensity of metabolic, physiological processes and other facets of behavior.

Clinical—founded on actual observation and treatment of a patient rather than theory or basic science.

Commensals—organisms that feed off or within a host organism but do not harm the host.

Complementary medicine—systems of treatment that "complement" orthodox methods, but are not fully accepted by orthodox medical science.

Constitutional remedy—a remedy that affects the whole body.

Contraindicated—a term applied to any condition that makes a particular line of treatment undesirable.

Desensitization—a method of abolishing the sensitivity of a person to an allergen by injecting graded amounts of the same allergen.

Diuretic—an agent that promotes the excretion of urine.

Douching—use of a jet of water to wash a body cavity or opening.

Embolus—a clot or mass formed in one part of the circulation that is moved in the bloodstream to become impacted in another part of the circulation.

Endemic—a disease permanently established in moderate or severe form in a defined area.

Endocrine gland—an internally secreting gland whose function is to secrete into the blood or lymph a substance (hormone) that has a specific effect on another organ.

Endorphins—peptides synthesized in the pituitary gland that have analgesic (painkilling) properties associated with their affinity for the opiate receptors in the brain.

Epidemic—an outbreak of an infectious disease, spreading widely among people at the same time in any region.

Etiology—the cause or origin of a disease or disorder.

Exocrine gland—a gland that secretes into some cavity in the body or onto the external surface of the body by ducts.

Expectoration—the coughing up of mucus or sputum from the air passages.

Free radicals—negatively charged particles capable of free existence in special conditions, usually only for short periods.

Goitrogens—foods that inhibit thyroxine production, thus causing a swelling of the thyroid gland, known as a goiter.

Gynecology—the branch of medicine that deals with functions and diseases of the genital tract in women.

Heimlich maneuver—a procedure used to force an obstruction out of the airway of someone who is choking.

Hematology—the branch of medicine that deals with the study of the blood and blood-forming tissues.

Holistic—the concept of a person being considered as a functioning whole in terms of body, mind, and spirit.

HRT—hormone-replacement therapy, whereby the hormones estrogen and progesterone are taken as a supplement to alleviate the symptoms associated with the menopause.

Iatrogenic disease—a doctor-induced disease, usually occurring as a side effect of prescribed drugs.

Immune—protected against an infectious disease.

Immunocompromised—having the immune response reduced by immunosuppressive drugs, irradiation, malnutrition, or a disease.

Immunoglobulins—proteins that function as antibodies and combine with antigens.

Immunosuppressant—an agent that suppresses immune responses.

Intussusception—the pushing down, or telescoping, of one part of the intestine into the part below it.

Jala Lota—an Eastern technique of nasal washing.

Karma—the force generated by a person's actions that is held in Hinduism and Buddhism to be the motive power for all the rebirths and deaths endured until that person has achieved spiritual liberation and is free from the effects of such force.

Laparoscopy—the insertion of a rigid or flexible device to inspect the abdominal cavity.

Learned response—a biological response that has been learned by association with a stimulus, i.e. a conditioned response.

Lipoproteins—lipid–protein complexes that serve to transport lipids in the blood.

Magnetic-resonance imaging (MRI)—the use of nuclear magnetic resonance of protons to produce proton density maps or images of the human body for diagnostic use.

Miasm—a supposed noxious emanation from the soil or earth, at one time alleged to be the cause of diseases endemic in certain areas, such as malaria.

Neti pot—a small watering can used for nasal washing (Jala Lota).

Nirvana—the state of freedom from karma.

Obstetrics—the branch of medicine that deals with the problems and management of pregnancy and labor.

Orthodox techniques—the tried-and-tested, Western medical techniques for treating the symptoms of a disease or condition.

Palliative—affording temporary relief from pain or discomfort, but not a cure.

Palpation—physical examination by touch.

Palpitation—a subjective awareness of a rapid or irregular heartbeat in the chest.

Parasites—organisms that live on or within a host organism to the detriment of the host organism.

Pathogen—a disease-producing microorganism or substance.

Pathognomonic—indicative of a particular disease.

Percussion—the act of striking with one finger, lightly and sharply, against another finger placed on the surface of the body so as to determine, by the sound produced, the physical state of the part beneath.

Phthisis—a wasting away of the body or part of the body.

Physiology—a study of the functions of the living organism and its parts, and of the physical and chemical factors and processes involved.

Phytoestrogens—natural estrogens from plants.

Placebo—a pharmacologically inactive substance administered as a drug, either in the treatment of psychological illness or in drug trials.

Prophylactic—tending to prevent or protect against disease, especially infectious disease.

Proprietary—any chemical, drug, or similar preparation used in the treatment of disease that is protected against free competition by trademark, copyright, or other such means.

Protozoa—an organism that exhibits both bacterial and viral activity.

Psyche—the human faculty for thought, judgment and emotion.

Qi—according to Eastern philosophy, Qi (or the Vital Force) is an immeasurable energy emanating from all living organisms and through all matter, connecting the whole universe.

Radiography—the making of film records (radiographs) of internal body structures by the passage of x-rays or gamma rays through the body to act on specially sensitized film.

Radiotherapy—theory and practice of medical treatment of disease, particularly cancer, with large doses of x-rays or other ionizing radiations.

Reverse osmosis—purification of water by forcing it under pressure through a membrane that is not permeable to the impurities to be removed.

Sequela—any condition or affliction following or caused by an attack of disease.

Silent—a term used to describe a disease that produces no detectable signs or symptoms.

Subclinical—without clinical manifestation; used to describe an infection or other disease or abnormality before symptoms or signs become apparent or detectable by clinical examination or laboratory test.

Subluxation—an incomplete or partial dislocation.

Symbionts—organisms that live together or in close association for mutual benefit.

Systemic—pertaining to or affecting the body as a whole.

Tens—transcutaneous electrical nerve stimulation: the passing of an electrical impulse through nerves to stimulate the body's pain-relieving chemicals.

Tetracyclines—a group of biosynthetic antibiotics with wide spectrum activity isolated from certain species of *Streptomyces*, or produced semisynthetically by catalytic hydrogenation of chlortetracycline or oxytetracycline.

Tofu—a Japanese food preparation from the soya bean.

Transcendental—beyond human knowledge or independent of experience.

Trichology—the study of hair.

Triple heater—in Eastern medicine, an energy line that controls the head of the body via its influence on the adrenal and thyroid glands.

Ultrasound scan—the visualization of deep structures in the body by recording the reflections (echoes) of pulses of ultrasonic (high-frequency) waves directed into the tissues. This technique is widely used in the diagnosis of disease of the abdomen and heart, and in the management of pregnancy.

Urogenital—pertaining to the urinary and genital systems.

Urology—the branch of medicine that deals with the urinary tract in both male and female, and with the genital organs in the male.

Vessel of Conception—the Chinese meridian or energy line that flows from the top of the head down the midline of the body, connecting the pituitary gland, thyroid, pancreas, and uterus.

Vital Force—according to Eastern philosophy, the Vital Force is the immeasurable "energy for life," or Qi.

Yang—the masculine and positive principle (as of activity, height, light, heat, or dryness) in nature that, according to Chinese cosmology, combines and interacts with its opposite "Yin" to produce all that comes to be.

Yin—the feminine and negative principle (as of passivity, depth, darkness, cold, or wetness) in nature that, according to Chinese cosmology, combines with its opposite "Yang" to produce all that comes to be.

Yoga—a discipline by which the individual prepares for liberation of the self (mind and body), and union with the universal spirit (soul). This is achieved by a system of exercises for attaining bodily or mental control and well being, so that the self may be liberated from all pain and suffering and unite with the universal spirit.

Further Reading

GENERAL

A–Z of Natural Healthcare
Belinda Grant
Optima, 1993

The Alternative Dictionary of Symptoms and Cures
Dr. Caroline Shreeve
Century, 1987

The Alternative Health Guide
Brian Inglis and Ruth West
Michael Joseph, 1983

Better Health through Natural Healing
Ross Tratler
McGraw-Hill, 1987

Choices in Healing
Michael Lerner
MIT Press, 1994

The Encyclopaedia of Alternative Health Care
Kristen Olsen
Piatkus, 1989

Encyclopaedia of Natural Medicine
Brian Inglis and Ruth West
Michael Joseph, 1983

Encyclopaedia of Natural Medicine
Michael Murray and Joseph Pizzorno
Macdonald Optima, 1990

Gentle Medicine
Angela Smyth
Thorsons, 1994

The Greening of Medicine
Patrick Pietroni
Gollancz, 1990

Guide to Complementary Medicine and Therapies
Anne Woodham
Health Education Authority, 1994

The Handbook of Complementary Medicine
Stephen Fulder
Oxford Medical Publications, 1988

How to Live Longer and Feel Better
Linus Pauling
W. H. Freeman, 1986

Maximum Immunity
Michael Wiener
Gateway Books, 1986

Reader's Digest Family Guide to Alternative Medicine
Dr. Patrick Pietroni (ed.)
The Reader's Digest Association, 1991

Will to be Well
Neville Hodgkinson
Hutchinson, 1984

ACUPUNCTURE/ACUPRESSURE

Acupressure Techniques
Dr. Julian Kenyon
Thorsons, 1987

Acupuncture: A Comprehensive Text
J. O'Connor and D. Bensky
Eastland Press, 1981

Acupuncture for Everyone
Dr. Ruth Lever
Penguin, 1987

Acupuncture Medicine
Dr. Y. Omara
Japan Publications, 1982

Health Essentials: Acupuncture
Peter Mole
Element Books, 1992

Traditional Acupuncture, The Law of Five Elements
Dianne Connelly
Center for Traditional Acupuncture, Columbia, 1979

ALEXANDER TECHNIQUE

Alexander Technique
C. Stevens
Optima, 1987

Alexander Technique : A Practical Introduction
R. Brennan
Element Books, 1998

Body Learning
M. Gelb
Aurem Press, 1981

Health Essentials: The Alexander Technique
Richard Brennan
Element Books, 1991

ANTHROPOSOPHICAL MEDICINE

Anthroposophical Medicine
M. Evans and I. Rodger
Thorsons, 1992

AROMATHERAPY

Aromatherapy: An A–Z
Patricia Davis
C. W. Daniel, 1988

Aromatherapy Blends and Remedies,
Franzesca Watson
Thorsons, 1996

The Aromatherapy Book
Jeanne Rose
North Atlantic Books, 1994

Aromatherapy for Healing the Spirit
Gabrielle Mojay
Gaia Books, 1996

Aromatherapy for Pregnancy and Childbirth
Margaret Fawcett
Element Books, 1993

Aromatherapy from Provence
Nelly Grosjean
C. W. Daniel, 1994

The Complete Aromatherapy Handbook
Susanne Fischer-Rizzi
Stirling, 1990

The Complete Illustrated Guide to Aromatherapy
Julia Lawless
Element Books, 1997

The Fragrant Mind
Valerie Anne Worwood
Doubleday, 1996

The Fragrant Pharmacy
Valerie Anne Worwood
Bantam Books, 1995

Health Essentials: Aromatherapy
Christine Wildwood
Element Books, 1991

The Illustrated Encyclopedia of Essential Oils
Julia Lawless
Element Books, 1992

Massage and Aromatherapy
Andrew Vickers
Chapman and Hall, 1996

ART THERAPY

Art as Therapy
S. McNiff
Piatkus, 1994

AYURVEDA

A Handbook of Ayurveda
Vaidya Bhagwan Dash and Acarya Manfred M. Junius
Concept Publishing Co, 1983

Ancient Indian Massage
Harish Johari
Munshiram Manoharial, 1984

Ayurvedic Medicine, Past and Present
Pandit Shiv Sharma
Dabur Publications, 1975

Basic Principles of Ayurveda
Bhagwan Dash
Concept Publishing Co, 1980

The Complete Illustrated Guide to Ayurveda
Gopi Warrier and Dr. Deepika Gunawant
Element Books, 1997

The Handbook of Ayurveda
Dr. Shantha Godagama
Kyle Cathie, 1997

Health Essentials: Ayurveda
Scott Gerson M.D.
Element Books, 1993

Indian Materia Medica: Volumes One and Two
Dr. K. M. Madkarni

Prakrti: Your Ayurvedic Constitution
Robert E. Svoboda
Geocom Press, 1988

Quantum Healing
Dr. Deepak Chopra
Bantam Books, 1989

Return of the Rishi
Dr. Deepak Chopra
Houghton Mifflin Co, 1988

The Seven Pillars of Ancient Wisdom
Dr. Douglas Baker
Douglas Baker Publishing, 1982

The Yoga of Herbs: An Ayurvedic Guide to Herbal Medicine
Dr. David Frawley and Dr. Vasant Lad
Lotus Press, 1988

BATES METHOD FOR EYES

Bates Method
P. Mansfied
Vermilion, 1995

BODY WORK

Bodywise
Joseph Heller and William A. Henkin
Tarcher, 1986

Job's Body: A Handbook For Bodywork
Deane Juhan
Station Hill, 1987

CHINESE MEDICINE

Arisal of the Clear – a simple guide to eating according to Traditional Chinese Medicine
B. Flaws
Blue Poppy Press, 1991

Between Heaven and Earth
H. Beinfield and E. Korngold
Ballantine, 1991

Chinese Herbal Medicine
Richard Craze and Stephen Tang
Piatkus, 1995

Chinese Herbal Medicine, Ancient Art and Modern Science
Richard Hyatt
Wildwood House Ltd., 1978

Chinese Herbal Medicine, Formulas and Strategies
D. Bensky and R. Barolet
Eastland Press, 1993

Chinese Herbal Medicine, Materia Medica
D. Bensky and A. Gamble
Eastland Press, 1993

Chinese Herbal Patent Remedies: A Practical Guide
Jake Fratkin
Institute for Traditional Medicine, 1986

Health Essentials: Chinese Medicine
Tom Williams
Element Books, 1995

Chinese Medicine, The Web That Has No Weaver
Ted Kaptchuk
Rider, 1983

The Chinese Way to Health
Dr. Stephen Gascoigne
Hodder Headline, 1997

The Complete Family Guide to Chinese Medicine
Tom Williams
Element Books, 1997

The Foundations of Chinese Medicine
Giovanni Maciocia
Churchill Livingstone, 1989

The Fountain of Health: An A–Z of Traditional Chinese Medicine
Dr. Charles Windrige and Dr. Wu Xiaochun
Mainstream Publishing, 1994

The Fundamentals of Chinese Medicine
Ellis Wiseman and Zmiewski
Paradigm, 1985

The Practice of Chinese Medicine
Giovanni Maciocia
Churchill Livingstone, 1994

CHIROPRACTIC

Dynamic Chiropractic Today
M. Copland Griffiths
Thorsons, 1991

CLINICAL ECOLOGY

Clinical Ecology
Dr. George Lewith and Dr. Julian Kenyon
Thorsons, 1985

COLONIC IRRIGATION

Principles of Colonic Irrigation
J. Collings
Thorsons, 1996

COLOR THERAPY

Colour Me Healing
Jack Allanach
Element Books, 1997

Health Essentials: Colour Therapy
Pauline Wills
Element Books, 1993

FELDENKRAIS

Awareness Through Movement
Moshe Feldenkrais
Penguin, 1990

FENG SHUI

The Complete Illustrated Guide to Feng Shui
Lillian Too
Element Books, 1996

The Elements of Feng Shui
Man-Ho Kwok and Joanne O'Brien
Element Books, 1991

Feng Shui
S. Rosbach
Rider, 1984

The Feng Shui Handbook
Lam Kam Chuen
Gaia Books, 1995

Feng Shui Made Easy
W. Spear
HarperCollins, 1995

Interior Design with Feng Shui
S. Rosbach
Rider, 1987

FLOWER REMEDIES

A Guide to Bach Flower Remedies
Julian Barnard
C. W. Daniel, 1987

The Bach Flower Remedies: Illustrations and Preparations
Victor Bullen and Nora Weeks
C. W. Daniel, 1964

The Collected Writings of Edward Bach
Julian Barnard (ed.)
Flower Remedy Program, 1987

Health Essentials: Flower Remedies:
Christine Wildwood
Element Books, 1991

Heal Thyself
Dr. Edward Bach
C. W. Daniel, 1931

The Original Writings of Edward Bach
Judy Howard and John Ramsell (eds.)
C. W. Daniel, 1990

The Twelve Healers and Other Remedies
Dr. Edward Bach
C. W. Daniel, 1936

HEALING

The Complete Healer
D. Furlong
Piatkus, 1995

The Healer's Hand Book
Georgina Regan and Debbie Shapiro
Element Books, 1988

Healing Words
Larry Dossey
HarperCollins, 1993

Health Essentials: Spiritual Healing
Jack Angelo
Element Books, 1991

HERBALISM

A Modern Herbal Vols. I and II
Mrs. M. Grieve
Dover Publications, 1971

British Herbal Pharmacopoeia
British Herbal Medicine Association, 1990

The Complete Family Guide to Natural Home Remedies
Karen Sullivan
Element Books, 1996

The Complete Illustrated Holistic Herbal
David Hoffman
Element Books, 1996

The Complete New Herbal
Richard Mabey (ed.)
Penguin Books, 1991

The Complete Woman's Herbal
Anne McIntyre
Gaia Books, 1994

The Dictionary of Modern Herbalism
Simon Mills
Inner Traditions, 1985

The Encyclopedia of Herbs and Herbalism
Malcolm Stuart
Orbis Publishing, 1979

Family Medical Herbal
Kitty Campion
Dorling Kindersley, 1988

The Golden Age of Herbs and Herbalists
Rosetta E. Clarkson
Dover Publications, 1972

Green Pharmacy
Barbara Griggs
Inner Traditions
International Ltd., 1991

Healing Power of Herbs
Michael Murray
Prima Publications, 1992

The Herbal for Mother and Child
Anne McIntyre
Element Books, 1992

Herbal Healing for Women
Rosemary Gladstar
Fireside, 1993

Herbal Medications
Priest and Priest
L. N. Fowler and Co. Ltd., 1982

Herbal Medicine
Rudolf Wess
Medicina Biologica, 1988

The Herb Society's Complete Medicinal Herbal
Penelope Ody
Dorling Kindersley, 1993

Health Essentials: Herbal Medicine:
Vicki Pitman
Element Books, 1994

Herbal Remedies: A Practical Beginner's Guide to Making Effective Remedies in the Kitchen
Christopher Hedley and Non Shaw
Paragon, 1996

Herbs for Common Ailments
Anne McIntyre
Gaia Books, 1992

The Home Herbal
Barbara Griggs
Pan Books, 1995

Male Herbal
James Green
Crossings Press, 1991

Natural Medicine for Women
Julian and Susan Scott
Gaia Books, 1991

Neal's Yard Natural Remedies
Susan Curtis, Romy Frasher, and Irene Kohler
Arkana, 1988

The New Holistic Herbal
David Hoffman
Element Books, 1983

Out of the Earth: The Science and Practice of Herbal Medicine
Simon Mills
Viking Penguin, 1992

Potter's New Cyclopaedia of Botanical Drugs and Preparations
R. C. Wren
C. W. Daniel, 1988

The Power of Plants
Brendan Lehane
John Murray, 1977

Traditional Home and Herbal Remedies
Jan De Vries
Mainstream Publishing, 1986

HOMEOPATHY

The Challenge of Homeopathy
Margery Blackie
Unwin Hyman, 1981

The Complete Family Guide to Homeopathy
Dr. Christopher Hammond
Element Books, 1996

The Complete Homeopathy Handbook
Miranda Castro
Pan Books, 1990

Emotional Healing with Homeopathy
Peter Chappell
Element Books, 1994

The Family Guide to Homeopathy
Andrew Lockie
Hamish Hamilton, 1990

Homeopathic Drug Pictures
Margaret Tyler
Health Science Press, 1970

Homeopathy for Children
Henrietta Wells
Element Books, 1993

Homeopathy for Mother and Baby
Miranda Castro
Pan Books, 1995

Homeopathy: Medicine of the New Man
George Vithoulkas
Thorsons, 1985

The New Concise Guide to Homeopathy
Nigel and Susan Garion-Hutchings
Element Books, 1993

The Woman's Guide to Homeopathy
Andrew Lockie and Nicola Geddes
Hamish Hamilton, 1992

HYDROTHERAPY

The Complete Book of Water Therapy
Dian Dinsin Buchman
Keats, 1994

Hydrotherapy – Water and Nature Cure
C. L. Thomson
Kingston Publications, 1970

Water and Nature Cure
C. Leslie Thomson
Kingston Clinic, 1955

Water and Sexuality
Michel Odent
Arkana, 1990

Water Babies
Erik Sidenbladh
A. and C. Black, 1983

HYPNOTHERAPY

Principles of Hypnotherapy
Vera Peiffer
Thorsons, 1996

Health Essentials: Self-Hypnosis
Elaine Sheehan
Element Books, 1995

MASSAGE

The Bassett Atlas of Human Anatomy
Robert A. Chase
Benjamin Cummings, 1989

Beard's Massage (3rd Edition)
Wood and Becker
W. B. Saunders, 1964

The Complete Book of Massage
Clare Maxwell-Hudson
Dorling Kindersley, 1988

Manipulation and Mobilisation
Susan L. Edmund
Mosby, 1993

Health Essentials: Massage
Stewart Mitchell
Element Books, 1992

Mosby's Fundamentals of Therapeutic Massage
Sandy Fritz
Mosby Lifeline, 1995

The New Atlas of the Human Body
Vannini and Pogliano (trans. R. Jolly)
Chancellor Press, 1980

Tidy's Massage and Remedial Exercises (11th edition)
John Wright and Son, 1968

Visualizing Muscles
John Cody
Kansas University Press, 1990

MEDITATION

The Meditator's Handbook
David Fontana
Element Books, 1992

How to Meditate
K. McDonald
Wisdom, 1984

Teaching Meditation to Children
David Fontana and Ingrid Slack
Element Books, 1997

Teach Yourself Meditation
James Hewitt
Hodder and Stoughton, 1978

NUTRITION

The Complete Book of Minerals for Health
J. I. Rodale
Rodale Books, 1976

The Complete Guide to Food Allergy and Environmental Illnesses
Dr. Keith Mumby
Thorsons, 1993

The Complete Home Guide to All the Vitamins
Ruth Adams
Larchmont Books, 1972

The Doctor's Book of Vitamin Therapy: Megavitamins for Health
Harold Rosenberg and A. N. Feldzaman
Putnam, 1974

The Doctors' Vitamin and Mineral Encyclopedia
Sheldon Saul Hendler, M.D., Ph.D.
Simon and Schuster, 1995

Food and Health
Elizabeth Morse, John Rivers, and Anne Heughan
Barrie and Jenkins, 1990

Food: Your Miracle Medicine
Jean Carper
Simon and Schuster, 1993

Healing Nutrients
Patrick Quillen
Penguin, 1989

Health Essentials: Vitamins Guide
Hasnain Walji
Element Books, 1992

In a Nutshell: Vitamins and Minerals
Karen Sullivan
Element Books, 1997

Nutritional Medicine
Stephen Davis and Alan Stewart
Pan Books, 1987

Raw Energy
Leslie and Susannah Kenton
Arrow Books, 1991

Superfoods
Michael Van Straten and Barbara Griggs
Dorling Kindersley, 1992

Thorsons Complete Guide to Vitamins and Minerals
Leonard Mervyn
Thorsons, 1995

The Vitamin Bible
Earl Mindell
Arrow Books, 1993

Vitamins and Minerals: The Amino Revolution
Robert Erdmann and Meirion Jones
Century, 1987

Which Vitamins Do You Need?
Martin Ebon
Bantam Books, 1974

The Zinc Solution
Derek Bryce-Smith and Liz Hodgkinson
Arrow Books, 1987

POLARITY THERAPY

The Polarity Process:
Franklyn Sills
Element Books, 1989

Polarity Therapy
A. Siegel
Prism Press, 1987

QI GONG AND TAI QI

The Art of Chi Kung
Wong Kiew Kit
Element Books, 1993

Between Heaven and Earth
H. Beinfield and E. Korngold
Ballantine, 1991

Health Essentials: Chi Kung
J. McRitchie
Element Books, 1993

The Complete Book of Tai Chi Chuan
Wong Kiew Kit
Element Books, 1996

The Elements of Tai Chi
Paul Crompton
Element Books, 1990

Embrace Tiger, Return to Mountain
Chungliang Al Huang
Celestial Arts, 1973

Movements of Magic
B. Klein
Newcastle, 1984

T'ai Chi Chuan for Health and Self-Defense
T. T. Liang
Vintage, 1977

Taiji
Chungliang Al Huang
Celestial Arts, 1989

The Way of Energy
Lam Kam Chuen
Gaia Books, 1991

The Way of Harmony
H. Reid
Gaia Books, 1988

REFLEXOLOGY

The Complete Illustrated Guide to Reflexology
Inge Dougans
Element Books, 1996

Reflexology and Colour Therapy: A Practical Introduction
Pauline Wills
Element Books, 1998

The Reflexology Partnership
Adamson and Harris
Kyle Cathie, 1995

Reflexology – The Ancient Answer
Ann Gilanders
Jenny Lee Publishing, 1994

Reflexology: The Definitive Practitioner's Manual
Beryl Crane
Element Books, 1997

Zone Therapy Using Foot Massage
Astrid Goosman-Legger
C. W. Daniel, 1983

SHIATSU

Shiatsu: A Practical Introduction
Oliver Cowmeadow
Element Books, 1998

The Book of Shiatsu
P. Lundberg
Gaia Books, 1992

Health Essentials: Shiatsu
Elaine Liechti
Element Books, 1992

Shiatsu: The Complete Guide
C. Jarmey and G. Mojay
Thorsons, 1991

The Shiatsu Workbook
N. Dawes
Piatkus Books, 1991

YOGA

The Complete Yoga Course
Howard Kent
Headline Press, 1993

The Elements of Yoga
Godfrey Devereux
Element Books, 1994

Preparing for Birth with Yoga
Janet Balaskas
Element Books, 1994

The Yoga Book
Stephen Sturgess
Element Books, 1997

Useful Addresses

Investigations
Where possible, if the text recommends investigations or tests, ask your local doctor or healthcare provider whether they can perform or organize them. If they are unable to do so, which may be the case (especially for the more pioneering or alternative techniques) please contact the following:

General

The 101 Group of Practitioners
87 North Road, Parkstone
Poole, Dorset BH14 0LT
U.K.
Tel: 44 01425 461740

The 101 Group of Practitioners
c/o Best of Both Worlds
13123 Eastbrooke Avenue
Downey
CA 90242
U.S.A.

Bioresonance testing

Scott Moyer
BioElectric Research Group
Box 350
Santa Rosa
C.A. 95402
U.S.A.

GENERAL

Australia

Australian College of Alternative Medicine
11 Howard Avenue, Mount Waverley,
Victoria 3149

Australasian College of Natural Therapies
620 Harris Street, Ultimo,
NSW 2007
Tel: 02212 6699

Australian Traditional Medicine Society
Suite 3, First Floor,
120 Blaxland Road, Ryde,
NSW 2112
Tel: 612 808 2825
Fax: 612 809 7570

Canada

Canadian Holistic Medical Association
42 Redpath Avenue, Toronto,
Ontario M4S 2J6
Tel: 416 485 3071

Europe

The 101 Group Practitioners
87 North Road, Parkstone, Poole,
Dorset BH14 0LT, United Kingdom
(practices in London and elsewhere)

British Complementary Medicine Association
St. Charles Hospital, Exmoor Street
London W10 6DZ, United Kingdom
Tel: 0181 964 1205
Fax: 0181 964 1207

British Holistic Medical Association
Royal Shrewsbury Hospital South,
Shrewsbury, Shropshire SY3 8XF,
United Kingdom
Tel: 01743 261155
Fax: 01743 353637

The British Register of Complementary Medicine
PO Box 194, London SE16 1QZ
United Kingdom
Tel/Fax: 0171 237 6175

The Centre for The Study of Complementary Medicine
51 Bedford Place,
Southampton,
Hampshire SO15 2DT,
United Kingdom
Tel: 01703 334752
Fax: 01703 231835

The Hale Clinic
7 Park Crescent,
London W1N 3HE,
United Kingdom
Tel: 0171 289 4317

The Institute for Complementary Medicine
Unit 15, Tavern Quay,
Commercial Centre,
Rope Street,
London SE16 1TX,
United Kingdom
Tel: 0171 237 5165
Fax: 0171 237 5175

U.S.A.

Alliance/Foundation for Alternative Medicine
160 NW Widmer Place, Albany,
OR 97321
Tel: 503 926 4678

American Holistic Medical Association
4101 Lake Boone Trail, Suite 201,
Raleigh, NC 27607
Tel: 919 787 5181
Fax: 919 787 5146

Holistic Health Association
PO Box 17400, Anaheim
CA 92817 7400
Tel: 714 779 6152

ACUPRESSURE

(*see also* **Shiatsu**)

Australia

The Shiatsu Therapy Association of Australia
332 Carlisle Street, Balaclava,
3182 Victoria
Tel: 0061 395 344780

Europe

ITHMA
PO Box 6555,
London N8 9DF,
United Kingdom

Tony Rusli
82 Ashville Road,
London E11 4DU,
United Kingdom
Tel: 0181 558 9676

Jon Sandifer
PO Box 69, Teddington,
Middlesex TW11 9SH,
United Kingdom
Tel: 0973 338651

Shiatsu Society
Barber House, Storeys Bar Road,
Fengate, Peterborough PE1 5YN,
United Kingdom
Tel: 01733 758341

U.S.A.

Michael Blate
Falknor Books, PO Box 8060
Pembroke Pines, Florida 33023

ACUPUNCTURE

Australia

Acupuncture Ethics and Standards Organization
PO Box 84, Merrylands, NSW
Tel: 0061 296 827882

Canada

Acupuncture Foundation of Canada
7321 Victoria Park Avenue,
Unit 18, Markham,
Ontario L3R 2Z3
Tel: 905 881 5540

Europe

British Acupuncture Council (BAC)
Park House, 206–208 Latimer Road,
London W10 6RE,
United Kingdom
Tel: 0181 964 0222

Richard Field/Andrew Mullen
87 North Road, Parkstone, Poole,
Dorset BH14 0LT, United Kingdom
(practice in London)

The Kailash Centre
7 Newcourt Street,
London NW8,
United Kingdom
Tel: 0171 722 3939

London School of Acupuncture and Traditional Chinese Medicine
University of Westminster,
115 New Cavendish Street,
London W1M 8JS,
United Kingdom
Tel: 0171 911 5000

New Zealand

NZRA
PO Box 9950, Wellington 1
Tel: 00648 016 400

South Africa

Western Cape Su Jok Acupuncture Institute
3 Periwinkle Close,
Kommetjie 7975
Tel: 021 783 3460

U.S.A.

American Association of Acupuncture and Oriental Medicine
1424 16th Street, NW
Suite 501
Washington DC 20036

ALEXANDER TECHNIQUE

Australia

The Australian Society of Teachers of the Alexander Technique
19 Princess Street, Kew,
VIC 3101
Tel: 0398 531 356

Brazil

Association Brasilieria da Tenica Alexander
Rua dos Miranhaas, 333 Pinheiros,
05434-040 Sao Paulo

Canada

The Canadian Society of Teachers of the Alexander Technique
PO Box 47025, 19–555 West 12th Avenue,
Vancouver BC, V5Z 3X0

Europe

Alexander Technique Centre
Richard Brennan MSTAT,
c/o 48 St. Edward's Road, Southsea,
Hampshire, United Kingdom
Tel: 01705 827136

APTA
42 Terrasse de l'Iris, La Defense 2,
92400 Coubevoire, France
Tel: 0033 1409 00623

Danish Society of Teachers of the Alexander Technique
c/o Mr. Marc Grue, Secretary,
Otto Rud's 38 St. th.,
DK-8200 Aarhus, Denmark

GLAT
Postfach 5312, 79020 Freiburg,
Germany
Tel: 0049 76138 3357

ISTAT
PO Box 715, Karkur 37106

Netherlands Society of Teachers of the Alexander Technique
Postbus 15591, 1001 NB Amsterdam,
Netherlands
Tel: 0031 20623 8260

The Society of Teachers of the Alexander Technique
20 London House,
266 Fulham Road,
London SW10 9EL,
United Kingdom
Tel: 0171 351 0828

SVLAT
Postfach, CH 8032,
Zurich, Switzerland

South Africa

SASTAT
5 Leinster Road, Green Point 8001,
Cape Town

ALLERGIES

Europe

Individual Well-being
99 Kings Road, London SW3 4PA,
United Kingdom *(25% discount off by mentioning this book)*

ANTHROPOSOPHICAL MEDICINE

Europe

Anthroposophical Medical Treatment Centre
Park Attwood Therapeutic Centre,
Trimpley Lane, Bewdley,
Worcestershire DY12 1RE,
United Kingdom
Tel: 01299 861 561

Anthroposophical Society in Great Britain
Ruldolf Steiner House, 35 Park Road,
London NW1 6XT, United Kingdom
Tel: 0171 723 4400
Fax: 0171 724 4364

AROMATHERAPY

Australia

International Federation of Aromatherapists
1/390 Burwood Road, Hawthorn,
BIC 3122
Tel: 03 9530 0067

Europe

Aromatherapy Trades Council
3 Latymer Close, Braybrooke,
Market Harborough,
Leicester LE16 8LN,
United Kingdom
Tel: 01858 465 731

International Federation of Aromatherapists
Stamford House, Chiswick High Road,
London W4 1TH, United Kingdom
Tel: 0181 742 2605

International Society of Professional Aromatherapists
82 Ashby Road, Hinckley,
Leicestershire LE10 1AG,
United Kingdom
Tel: 01455 637 987

South Africa

Association of Aromatherapists
PO Box 23924, Claremont 7735,
Tel: 021 531 297

U.S.A.

American Alliance of Aromatherapy
PO Box 750428, Petaluma,
California 94975–0428

American Aromatherapy Association
PO Box 3679, South Pasadena,
California 91031

The Aromatherapy Institute and Research
PO Box 1222, Fair Oaks,
California 95628

National Association of Holistic Aromatherapy
PO Box 17622, Boulder,
Colorado 80308–0622

Nature's Apothecary
6350 Gunpark Drive 500, Boulder,
Colorado 80301
Tel: 001 303 664 1600

The Pacific Institute of Aromatherapy
PO Box 6842, San Raphael,
California 94903
Tel: 001 415 479 9129
Fax: 001 415 479 9121

ART THERAPY

Europe

British Association of Art Therapists
11a Richmond Road,
Brighton BN2 3RL, United Kingdom
Tel: 0171 383 3774

Lisa Elle
87 North Road, Parkstone, Poole,
Dorset BH14 0LT, United Kingdom
(practice in London)

U.S.A.

American Art Therapy Association
1202 Allanson Road, Mundelein
Illinois 60060

AURICULAR THERAPY

(*see also* **Reflexology**)

Europe

British Acupuncture Council (BAC)
Park House, 206–208 Latimer Road,
London W10 6RE, United Kingdom
Tel: 0181 964 0222

AUTOGENIC TRAINING

Europe

British Association for Autogenic Training and Therapy
Heath Cottage, Pitch Hill,
Ewhurst, nr Cranleigh,
Surrey GU6 7NP, United Kingdom

U.S.A.

Mind Body Health Sciences
393 Dixon Road, Boulder,
Colorado 80302
Tel: 030 440 8460

AYURVEDA

Australia

Maharishi Ayurveda Health Centres
PO Box 81, Bundoora
Victoria 3083

Europe

Ayurvedic Company of Great Britain
50 Penywern Road, London SW5 9XS,
United Kingdom
Tel: 0171 370 2255
Fax: 0171 370 5157

Ayurvedic Living
PO Box 188, Exeter,
Devon EX4 5AB, United Kingdom

Ayurvedic Medical Association Great Britain
The Hale Clinic, 7 Park Crescent,
London W1N 3HE, United Kingdom
Tel: 0171 631 0156

Eastern Clinic
1079 Garrat Lane, Tooting,
London SW17 0LN, United Kingdom
Tel: 0181 682 3876
Fax: 0181 333 7904

South Africa

The Himalayan Drugs Company
Tel: 0171 935 0028
(please call for the address)

Maharishi Ayurveda Health Centre
PO Box 5155, Halfway House 1685

South African Ayurvedic Medicine Association
85 Harvey Road, Morningside,
Durban 4001
Tel: 031 303 3245

U.S.A.

American Holistic Medical Association
4101 Lake Boone Trail, Suite 201,
Raleigh, North Carolina 27607

The Ayurveda Institute
11311 Menaul NE, Suite A,
Albuquerque, New Mexico 87112
Tel: 505 291 9698

The Ayurveda Institute
PO Box 282, Fairfield,
Iowa 52556
Tel: 310 454 5531

Dr. Edward Bach Healing Society
644 Merrick Road, Lynbrook,
New York 11563
Tel: 516 593 2206

Ellon (Bach United States of America) Inc.
PO Box 32, Woodmere,
New York 11598
Tel: 516 825 2229

International Federation for Ayurveda
Ayurvedic Medicine of New York,
Scott Gerson, M.D.,
13 West Ninth Street, New York,
NY 10011
Tel: 212 505 8971

Mapi, Inc.
Garden of the Gods Business Park,
1115 Elkton Drive, Suite 401,
Colorado Spring, Colorado 80907

Andrew Weil M.D.
1975 West Hunter Road,
Tucson, Arizona 85737

BACH FLOWER REMEDIES

Australia

Martin & Pleasance
137 Swan Street, Richmond,
Victoria 3121
Tel: 61 39 427 7422

Europe

Dr. Edward Bach Centre
Mount Vernon, Sotwell
Wallingford, Oxon OX10 0PZ,
United Kingdom
Tel: 01491 834678
Fax: 01491 825022

Morris Griffin
Trinders Cottage, Calcot,
Colm St. Denys, Cheltenham,
Gloucestershire GL54 3JZ,
United Kingdom
Fax: 01285 720 931

U.S.A.

Nelson Bach U.S.A. Limited
Wilmington Technology Park,
100 Research Drive, Wilmington,
Massachusetts 01887-4406
Tel: 978 988 3833
Fax: 978 988 0233

BATES METHOD FOR EYES

Europe

The Bates Association of Great Britain
PO Box 25, Shoreham-by-Sea,
West Sussex BN43 6ZF,
United Kingdom
Tel: 01273 342 2090
Fax: 01273 279 9983

Karen Banks
70 Station Road, Finchley,
London N3 2SA,
United Kingdom

BEHAVIORAL THERAPY

(*see also* **Psychotherapy/Stress Management**)

Europe

The Hale Clinic
7 Park Crescent,
London W1N 3HE, United Kingdom
Tel: 0171 631 0156
Fax: 0171 631 3377

BIOFEEDBACK

Europe

Aleph One Ltd
The Old Courthouse, Bottisham,
Cambridge CB5 9BA,
United Kingdom
Tel: 01223 811 679
Fax: 01223 812 713

U.S.A.

Association for Applied Psychophysiology and Biofeedback
10200 West 44th Avenue, Apt. 304,
Wheat Ridge,
Colorado 80033-8436
Tel: 303 422 8894
Fax: 303 422 8894

BUTEYKO THERAPY

Europe

The Hale Clinic
7 Park Crescent, London W1N 3HE,
United Kingdom
Tel: 0171 631 0156

CHINESE HERBALISM

Australia

Australian College of Alternative Medicine
11 Howard Avenue,
Mount Waverley,
Victoria 3149

Chinese and Herbal Centre
1st Floor, 2392–2394 Sussex Street,
Sydney, NSW 2000

Canada

Canadian Holistic Medical Association
42 Redpath Avenue, Toronto,
Ontario M4S 2J6
Tel: 416 485 3071

Europe

British Herbal Medicine Association
Wickham Road, Bournemouth,
Dorset BH7 6JZ, United Kingdom
Tel: 01202 433 691

The Camden Practice
Westhill House, 6 Swains Lane,
London N6 6QU, United Kingdom

Kailash Centre
7 Newcourt Street, London NW8,
United Kingdom
Tel: 0171 722 3939

The Register of Chinese Herbal Medicine
21 Warbeck Road,
London W12 8NS,
United Kingdom
Tel: 0171 224 0803

New Zealand

Holistic Health Centre
CPO Box 2273, Auckland

South Africa

The Herb Society of South Africa
PO Box 37721, Overport

U.S.A.

American Holistic Medical Association
6728 Old McLean Village Drive,
McLean,
Virginia 22101

American Holistic Nurses Association
PO Box 2130, 2133 E. Lakin Drive,
Suite 2, Flagstaff,
Arizona 86003–2130

CHINESE & ORIENTAL MEDICINE

Australia

Australian College of Oriental Medicine
24 Price Road, Lalorama
Victoria 3766

Canada

Ontario Herbalists Association
1565 Carling Avenue, Suite 400,
Ottawa, Ontario K1Z 8R1

Europe

Kailash Centre
7 Newcourt Street
London NW8,
United Kingdom
Tel: 0171 722 3939

Register of Chinese Herbal Medicine
21 Warbreck Road, London W10 8NS,
United Kingdom
Tel/Fax: 0171 224 0803

U.S.A.

American Herb Association
PO Box 1673, Nevada City,
California 95959

CHELATION THERAPY

Europe

Dr. Rodney Adenyi-Jones
Flat H, 21 Devonshire Place,
London W1N 1PD,
United Kingdom

The Arterial Disease Clinic
PO Box 8, Atherton,
Manchester, Gt. Manchester M46 9FY,
United Kingdom
Tel: 01942 676 617
Fax: 01942 260 285

CHIROPRACTIC

Asia

Chiropractic Association (Singapore)
Box 23, Tanglin Post Office,
Singapore
Tel: 65 293 9843/734 8584
Fax: 65 733 8380

Australia

Australian Council on Chiropractic and Osteopathic Education
941 Nepean Highway,
Mornington,
Victoria 3931

Chiropractors' Association of Australia
PO Box 241, Springwood,
NSW 2777
Tel: 61 47 515 644
Fax: 61 47 515 856

Canada

Canadian Chiropractic Association
1396 Eglington Avenue, West,
Toronto,
Ontario M6C 2E4
Tel: 416 488 0470

Europe

Anglo-European College of Chiropractic
13–15 Parkwood Road,
Bournemouth,
Dorset BH5 2DF,
United Kingdom
Tel: 01202 436275
Fax: 01202 436278

British Chiropractic Association
Blagrave House,
17 Blagrave Street,
Reading, Berkshire RG1 1QB,
United Kingdom
Tel: 01189 505 950
Fax: 01189 588 946

Chiropractic Association of Ireland
28 Fair Street, Drogheda,
County Louth, Eire
Tel: 00353 41 305999
Fax: 00353 41 51863

European Chiropractors' Union
The Waldegrave Clinic,
82 Waldegrave Road,
Teddington, Middlesex TW11 8LG,
United Kingdom
Tel: 0181 943 2424
Fax: 0181 977 6626

New Zealand

New Zealand Chiropractors' Association
PO Box 7144, Wellesley Street,
Auckland
Tel: 64 9 373 4343
Fax: 64 9 373 5973

U.S.A.

American Chiropractic Association
1701 Clarendon Boulevard,
Arlington, Virginia 22209
Tel: 703 276 8800
Fax: 703 243 2593

World Chiropractic Alliance
2950 North Dobson Road, Suite One,
Chandler, Arizona 85224-1802
Tel: 800 347 1011
Fax: 602 732 9313

CLINICAL ECOLOGY

Europe

The British Society for Allergy, Environmental and Nutritional Medicine
PO Box 28, Totton,
Southampton, Hants. SO40 2ZA,
United Kingdom

COLONIC HYDROTHERAPY

Europe

Colonic International Association (CIA)
16 Englands Lane, London NW3 4TG,
United Kingdom
Tel/Fax: 0171 483 1595

COLOR THERAPY

Europe

Aura Soma
South Road, Tetford, Horncastle,
Lincolnshire LN9 6QL, United Kingdom
Tel: 01507 533441

Colour & Reflexology
9 Wyndale Avenue, Kingsbury,
London NW9 9PT, United Kingdom
Tel: 0181 204 7672
Fax: 0181 204 7672

The Hygeia College of Colour Therapy
Brook House, Hampton Hill
Avening, Nr. Tetbury,
Gloucestershire GL8 8NS,
United Kingdom
Tel: 01453 832150
Fax: 01453 835757

The Institute for Complementary Medicine
Unit 5, Tavern Quay,
Commercial Centre, Rope Street,
London SE16 1TX, United Kingdom
Tel: 0171 237 5165

The International Association for Colour Therapy
137 Hendon Lane, Finchley,
London N3,
United Kingdom

Know Yourself Through Colour
Maria Louise Lacy,
3a Bath Road, Worthing,
W. Sussex BN11 3NU,
United Kingdom
Tel: 01903 216311

COUNSELING

(*see also* **Psychotherapy**)

Europe

British Association for Counselling
1 Regent Place, Rugby,
Warwickshire CV21 2PJ,
United Kingdom
Tel: 01788 550899/578328
Fax: 01788 562189

Scott Galloway
The Hale Clinic, 7 Park Crescent
London W1N 3HE,
United Kingdom
Tel: 0171 631 0156

The Institute of Stress Management
57 Hall Lane, London NW4 4TJ,
United Kingdom

Lisa Ekke/Kitty Kennedy/Sean Arnold
87 North Road, Parkstone, Poole,
Dorset BH14 0LT,
United Kingdom
(practice in London)

U.S.A.

American Counseling Association
5999 Stevenson Avenue, Alexandrea,
Virginia 22304-9800

CRANIOSACRAL THERAPY

Canada

CST Association of North America
1110 Birchmount Road,
Unit 21,
Scarborough, Ontario
N1K 1S7

Europe

Craniosacral Association
Monomark House,
27 Old Gloucester Street,
London WC1N 3XX, United Kingdom
Tel: 07000 789 735

David Haas
101 Practitioner Network
London and Surrey/Hampshire Practice
87 North Road, Parkstone, Poole,
Dorset BH14 0LT, United Kingdom
Tel: 01425 461740

CRYSTAL AND GEM THERAPY

Europe

Affiliation of Crystal Healing Organizations (ACHO)
International College of Crystal Healing
46 Lower Green Road, Esher,
Surrey KT10 8HD, United Kingdom
Tel: 0181 398 7252
Fax: 0181 398 4237

School of Electro-Crystal Therapy
117 Long Drive, South Ruislip,
Middlesex HA4 0HL, United Kingdom
Tel/Fax: 0181 841 1716

School of White Crystal Healing
Padise Valley, Llangynnin,
St. Clears, Dyfed SA33 4JY
Tel/Fax: 01994 230028

DANCE THERAPY

Europe

Association for Dance Movement Therapy
c/o Arts Therapies Department,
Springfield Hospital,
Glenburnie Road, Tooting,
London SW17 7DJ, United Kingdom
Tel: 0181 672 9911

U.S.A.

American Dance Therapy Association
10632 Little Pateuxent Parkway,
2000 Century Plaza, Suite 108,
Columbia, MD 21044-3265
Tel: 410 997 4040
Fax: 410 997 4048

FELDENKRAIS METHOD

Europe

The Feldenkrais Guild UK
PO Box 370, London N10 3XA,
United Kingdom

FENG SHUI

Australia

Feng Shui Design Studio
PO Box 705, Glebe, Sydney , NSW 2037
Tel: 00612 315 8258

Europe

Feng Shui Association
31 Woburn Place, Brighton,
E. Sussex BN1 9GA, United Kingdom
Tel/Fax: 01273 693844

Feng Shui Network International
PO Box 9, Pateley Bridge,
North Yorkshire HG3 5JN,
United Kingdom
Tel: 07000 336474 / 01423 712868
Fax: 01423 712869

U.S.A.

Earth Design
PO Box 530725, Miami Shores,
Florida 33153
Tel: 305 756 6426
Fax: 305 751 9995

Feng Shui Designs
PO Box 399, Nevada City,
CA 95959
Tel: 800 551 2482

Feng Shui Institute of America
PO Box 488, Wabasso,
Florida 32970
Tel: 407 589 9900
Fax: 407 589 1611

FLOTATION

Europe

Float Tank Association
PO Box 11024,
London SW4 7ZF,
United Kingdom
Tel: 0171 627 4962

FLOWER ESSENCES

Australia

Martin and Pleasance Wholesale Pty. Ltd.
PO Box 4, Collingwood,
Victoria, NSW 3066
Tel: 419 9733

Nonsuch Botanical Pty. Limited
PO Box 68, Mt. Evelyn,
Victoria 3796
Tel: 762 8577

Europe

Bach Flower Remedies
The Bach Centre, Mount Vernon,
Sotwell, Wallingford,
Oxfordshire OX10 9PZ,
United Kingdom
Tel: 0491 834 678

Flower Essence Fellowship
Laura Farm Clinic, 17 Carlincott,
Peasedown St. John,
Bath BA2 8AN, United Kingdom

Healing Herbs
PO Box 65, Hereford HR2 0UW,
United Kingdom
Tel: 01873 890 218
Fax: 01873 890 314

U.S.A.

Dr. Edward Bach Healing Society
644 Merrick Road, Lynbrook,
New York 11563
Tel: 516 593 2206

Ellon (Bach United States of America), Inc.
PO Box 32, Woodmere,
New York 11598
Tel: 516 825 2229

GESTALT THERAPY

Europe

Gestalt Centre London
64 Warwick Road,
St. Albans AL1 4DL, United Kingdom
Tel: 01727 864 806
Fax: 01727 838891

U.S.A.

Gestalt Centre for Psychotherapy and Training
510 East 89th Street, New York 10401
Tel: 212 879 3669

Gestalt Therapy Institute of Los Angeles
Faculty Training Office, Suite 301,
1460 7th Street, Santa Monica,
California 90401
Tel: 909 629 9935

HEALING

Europe

British Alliance of Healing Associations
26 Highfield Avenue, Herne Bay,
Kent CT6 6LN, United Kingdom

David Cunningham
The Hale Clinic, 7 Park Crescent,
London W1N 3HE, United Kingdom
Tel: 0171 631 0156

HELLERWORK

Europe

Bodyworkers
Suite 211, Copergate House,
16 Brune Street, London E1 7NJ,
United Kingdom
Tel: 0171 721 7833

Hellerwork Inc. (Rose-Marie Amoroso)
1 Finsbury Avenue, Broadgate,
London EC2M 2PA,
United Kingdom
Tel: 0171 247 9982
Fax: 0171 247 0082

U.S.A.

The Body of Knowledge Association
3468 Mt. Daiblo Boulevard, Sre. B203,
Ladayetter, CA 945 49 3917
Tel: 510 499 9050

Hellerwork International
406 Berry Street, Mount Shasta,
California 96067
Tel: 530 926 2500
Fax: 530 926 6839

HERBALISM AND HERBAL MEDICINE

Australia

Australian Traditional Medicine Society
120 Blaxland Road, Ryde,
NSW 2112
Tel: 808 2825

National Herbalists Association of Australia
Suite 305, BST House,
3 Small Street,
Broadway, NSW 2007
Tel: 02 211 6437

Canada

Canadian Natural Health Association
439 Wellington Street, Toronto,
Ontario M5V 2H7
Tel: 416 977 2642

Europe

The General Council and Register of Consultant Herbalists
32 King Edward Road,
Swansea SA1 4LL,
United Kingdom
Tel/Fax: 01792 655886

Healing Herb Limited
PO Box 65,
Hereford HR2 0UW,
United Kingdom
Tel: 01873 890 218
Fax: 01873 890 314

The Herb Society
77 Great Peter Street, London SW1,
United Kingdom

National Institute of Medical Herbalists
56 Longbrooke Street,
Exeter EX4 8HA,
United Kingdom
Tel: 01392 426 022

School of Herbal Medicine/Phytotherapy
Bucksteep Manor,
Bodle Street Green,
Near Hailsham, Sussex BN27 4RJ,
United Kingdom

South Africa

South African Naturopaths and Herbalists Association
PO Box 18663,
Wynberg 7824

U.S.A.

American Botanical Council
PO Box 201660,
Austin, TX 78720
Tel: 512 331 8868
Fax: 512 331 1924

American Herbalists Guild
PO Box 1683, Sequel,
California 95073
Tel: 408 484 2441

American Herb Association
PO Box 1673, Nevada City,
CA 95959
Tel: 916 265 9552
Fax: 916 274 3140

Angelica's Traditional Herbs and Food
147 First Avenue, New York,
NY 10003
Tel: 212 677 1549

Herb Research Foundation
1007 Pearl Street, Suite 200,
Boulder, CO 80303
Tel: 300 449 2265

HOMEOPATHY

Australia

Australian Federation of Homeopaths
238 Ballarat Road, Footscray,
Victoria 3011
Tel: 03 9318 3057

Australian Institute of Homeopathy
7 Hampden Road, Artemon,
Sydney, NSW 2064

Australian Institute of Homeopathy
21 Bulah Close,
Berdwra Heights,
NSW 2082

The National Centre for Homeopathy
801 N. Fairfax 306, Alexandria,
VA 22314
Tel: 703 548 7790

Canada

Canadian Society of Homeopathy
87 Meadowlands Drive West, Nepean,
Ontario K2G 2R9

Europe

British Homoeopathic Association
27a Devonshire Street,
London W1N 1RJ, United Kingdom
Tel/Fax: 0171 935 2163

The Faculty of Homeopathy
2 Powis Place, Great Ormond Street,
London WC1N 3HT, United Kingdom
Tel: 0171 837 9469
Fax: 0171 278 7900

The Hahnemann College of Homeopathy
Humane Education Centre,
Avenue Lodge, Bounds Green Road,
London N22 4EU, United Kingdom
Tel/Fax: 0181 843 9220

Homeopathic Development Foundation
19a Cavendish Square,
London W1M 9AD, United Kingdom
Tel: 0171 837 9469

The Homeopathic Trust and Faculty
2 Powis Place, London WC1N 3HT,
United Kingdom
Tel: 0171 278 7900

The 101 Group
87 North Road, Parkstone, Poole,
Dorset BH14 0LT, United Kingdom
(practice in London)

The Society of Homoeopaths
2 Artisan Road,
Northampton NN1 4HU,
United Kingdom
Tel: 01604 621400
Fax: 01604 622622

New Zealand

Institute of Classical Homoeopathy
24 West Haven Drive,
Tawa, Wellington

New Zealand Homeopathic Society
Box 2929, Auckland
Tel: 9 630 9458

U.S.A.

American Foundation for Homeopathy
1508 Glencoe Street,
Suite 44, Denver,
Colorado 80220–1338

American Institute of Homeopathy
1585 Glencoe, Denver,
CO 80220
Tel: 303 370 9164

Homeopathic Academy of Naturopathic Physicians
PO Box 69565, Portland,
OR 97201
Tel: 503 795 0579

Homeopathic Educational Services
2124 Kitteridge Street,
Berkeley,
California 94704
Tel: 800 359 9051 / 510 649 0294

International Foundation for Homeopathy
2366 Eastlake Avenue East,
Ste. 301,
Seattle, WA 98102
Tel: 206 776 4147

National Center for Homeopathy
801 North Fairfax Street,
Alexandria,
Virginia 22314
Tel: 703 548 7790

HYDROTHERAPY

Europe

The British College of Naturopathy and Osteopathy
Lief House, 3 Sumpter Close,
120–122 Finchley Road,
London NW3 5HR,
United Kingdom
Tel: 0171 435 6464
Fax: 0171 431 3630

Tyringham Naturopathic Clinic
Newport Pagnell,
Bucks MK16 9ER,
United Kingdom
Tel: 01908 610450
Fax: 01908 217689

HYPNOTHERAPY

Australia

Australian Society of Hypnosis (ASH)
Austin Hospital, Heidelberg, Victoria 3084

Canada

Canadian Society of Hypnosis (CSH)
Labelle, 7027 Edgemont Drive,
Calgary, Alberta T3A 2H9

Europe

British Hypnosis Research
1 King Street, Bakewell,
Derbyshire DE45 1DZ,
United Kingdom
Tel: 01629 814491

British Society of Experimental and Clinical Hypnosis
Psychology Consultancy,
District General Hospital,
Scartho Road, Grimsby DN33 2BA,
United Kingdom
Tel: 01472 875287
Fax: 01472 875545

British Society of Medical and Dental Hypnosis
17 Keppel View Road,
Kimberworth,
Rotherham, S. Yorkshire S61 2AR,
United Kingdom
Tel/Fax: 01709 554558

The Institute of Stress Management
57 Hall Lane, London NW4 4TJ,
United Kingdom

KINESIOLOGY

Australia

Association of Victoria
PO Box 155, Ormond, Vic 3204
Tel: 03 9578 1229

Europe

Applied Kinesiology Seminars
Eastcott House, Eastcott, Devizes,
Wiltshire SN10 4PL,
United Kingdom
Tel: 01380 813139
Fax: 01380 813078

Body Balance U.K. Ltd.
Kay McCaroll, 12 Golders Rise,
Hendon, London NW4 2HR,
United Kingdom
Tel: 0181 202 9747
Fax: 0181 202 3890

ICAK Executive European
Thea Marshal, 54 East Street, Andover,
Hampshire SP10 1ES, United Kingdom
Tel: 01264 339512

International College of Applied Kinesiology UK
Downsview, New Hall Lane,
Small Dole, W. Sussex BN5 9YJ,
United Kingdom

International Kinesiology College Shifting
PO Box 3347, CH-8031 Zurich,
Switzerland
Tel: 41 1 272 4515

Maya Kraus
The Castle Street Clinic, 36 Castle Street,
Guildford GU1 3UQ, United Kingdom
Tel: 01483 300400
Fax: 01483 400 411

Mr. E. Levin
42 Harley Street, London W1,
United Kingdom
Tel: 0171 935 6202

South Africa

Association of Specialized Kinesiology
14 Osborne Road,
Claremont 7700
Tel: 012 61 8021

U.S.A.

International College of Applied Kinesiology
PO Box 25276, Shawnee Mission,
Kansas 66255-5276
Tel: 913 648 2828

MAGNETIC THERAPY

Europe

British Biomagnetic Association
31 St. Marychurch Road, Torquay,
Devon TQ1 3JF,
United Kingdom

Magnet House
Highworth, Swindon,
Wiltshire SN6 7NA, United Kingdom
Tel: 01793 766001
Fax: 01793 765576

MARMA THERAPY

Europe

The Hale Clinic
7 Park Crescent, London W1N 3HE,
United Kingdom
Tel: 0171 631 0156

The 101 Group of Practitioners
67 North Road, Parkstone, Poole,
Dorset BH14 0LT, United Kingdom

MASSAGE

Australia

Association of Massage Therapists
18A Spit Road, Mosman,
NSW 1088

Society of Clinical Masseurs
PO Box 483, 9 Delhi Street,
Mitcham 3131, Victoria
Tel: 613 874 6973

Canada

Association of Physiotherapists & Massage Practitioners of BC
Suite 103, 1089 West Broadway,
Vancouver, BC V6H 0V3

Europe

Academy of Aromatherapy & Massage
50 Cow Wynd, Falkirk,
Stirlingshire FK1 1PU,
United Kingdom
Tel: 01324 612658

British Massage Therapy Council
Greenbank House,
65a Adelphi Street,
Preston, Lancs. PR1 7BH,
United Kingdom
Tel: 01772 881063

London College of Massage
5 Newman Passage, London W1P 3PF,
United Kingdom
Tel: 0171 323 3574
Fax: 0171 637 7125

Massage Training Institute
24 Highbury Road, London N5 2DQ,
United Kingdom
Tel: 0171 226 5313

Justin Sharma/Alison Underhill
87 North Road, Parkstone, Poole,
Dorset BH14 0LT, United Kingdom
(practice in London)

U.S.A.

Association of Bodyworkers and Massage Professionals
28677 Buffalow Park Road,
Evergreen, Colorado 80439
Tel: 303 674 8478
Fax: 303 674 0859

International Association of Infant Massage
PO Box 438, Elma,
New York 14059-0438
Tel: 1 716 652 9789
Fax: 1 716 652 1990

MEDITATION

Australia

Counselling and Meditation Service
20 Pitt Street, Parramatta, NSW 2150
Tel: 02 891 1628
Fax: 02 891 5675

U.S.A.

Himalayan International Institute of Yoga Science and Philosophy of the U.S.A.
RR1, Box 400, Honesdale, PA 18431
Tel: 717 253 5551
Fax: 717 253 9078

Europe

Himalayan Institute of Great Britain
70 Claremont Road, West Ealing,
London W13 0DG, United Kingdom
Tel: 0181 997 3544
Fax: 0181 991 8090

The International School of Meditation
87 North Road, Parkstone, Poole,
Dorset BH14 0LT, United Kingdom
(practice in London)

The Kailash Centre
7 Newcourt Street, London NW8,
United Kingdom
Tel: 0171 722 3939

MUSIC THERAPY

Europe

Association of Professional Music Therapists
Chestnut Cottage, 38 Pierce Lane,
Fulbourn, Cambridge CB1 5DL,
United Kingdom

British Society for Music Therapy
25 Rosslyn Avenue, East Barnet,
Hertfordshire EN4 8DH,
United Kingdom
Tel/Fax: 0181 368 8879

U.S.A.

American Association for Music Therapy
PO Box 80012, Valley Forge, PA 19484
Tel: 610 265 4006

National Association for Music Therapy
8455 Colesville Road, Suite 930,
Silver Spring, MD 20920
Tel: 301 589 3300
Fax: 301 589 5175

NATUROPATHY

Australia

Australia Naturopathy Practitioners and Chiropractors Association
1st Floor, 609 Camberwell Road,
Camberwell, Vic 3124

Australian Natural Therapists Association (ATNA)
PO Box 308,
Melrose Park,
South Australia 5039
Tel: 61 8 371 3222
Fax: 61 8 297 0003

Federation of Natural and Traditional Therapists (FNTT)
238 Ballarat Road,
Victoria 3011
Tel: 61 3 9318 3057

Europe

British College of Naturopathy and Osteopathy
3 Sumpter Close, 120-22 Finchley Road,
London NW3 5HR, United Kingdom
Tel: 0171 435 6464
Fax: 0171 431 3630

Dr. Harald Gaier
The 101 Group of Practitioners,
87 North Road, Parkstone, Poole,
Dorset BH14 0LT,
United Kingdom
(practice in London)

General Council and Register of Naturopaths
Goswell House, 2 Goswell Road,
Street, Somerset BA16 0JG,
United Kingdom
Tel: 01458 840072
Fax: 01458 840075

U.S.A.

American Association of Naturopathic Physicians
2366 Eastlake Avenue East, Suite 322,
Seattle, Washington 98102
Tel: 206 323 8510

American Naturopathic Association
1413 King Street, First Floor,
Washington DC 20005
Tel: 202 682 7352
Fax: 202 289 2027

NEUROLINGUISTIC PROGRAMMING (NLP)

Australia

The Australian Institute of NLP
c/o Askawn Quality Solutions Pty Ltd,
PO Box 31, Kippa-Ring, Queensland 4021
Tel: 07 3204 0824
Fax: 07 3204 0825

Europe

The Association for Neuro-Linguistic Programming and Rapport Magazine
PO Box 78, Stourbridge,
W. Midlands DY8 4ZJ,
United Kingdom
Tel: 01384 443935
Fax: 01384 823448

Nancy Blake/Ross Myers
102 Park Avenue,
Kingston-Upon-Hull,
E. Yorkshire HU5 3ET,
United Kingdom

Lynne Crawford
The Hale Clinic,
7 Park Crescent,
London W1N 3HE,
United Kingdom
Tel: 0171 631 0156

The Institute of Stress Management
57 Hall Lane, London NW4 4TJ,
United Kingdom

Dominique Radclyffe
87 North Road, Parkstone, Poole,
Dorset BH14 0LT, United Kingdom
(practice in London)

NEUROTHERAPY

Europe

The 101 Group of Practitioners
87 North Road, Parkstone, Poole,
Dorset BH14 0LT,
United Kingdom
(practice in London)

NUTRITIONISTS/DIETETICS

Europe

Cotswold Allergy Clinic
Trinders Cottage, Calcot,
Colm St. Denys, Cheltenham,
Gloucestershire GL54 3JZ,
United Kingdom
Fax: 01285 720 931

Dominique Radclyffe
The Kailash Centre,
7 Newcourt Street,
London NW8, United Kingdom
Tel: 0171 722 3939

OSTEOPATHY

Australia

Australian Osteopathy Association
PO Box 699, Turramurra,
NSW 2074
Tel: 02 4494799

Chiropractors and Osteopaths' Registration
Board of Victoria,
PO Box 59,
Carlton Street,
Victoria 3053
Tel: 61 3 349 3000
Fax: 61 3 349 3003

NSW Chiropractors and Osteopathic Registration Board
PO Box K599,
Haymarket, NSW 2000
Tel: 61 2 281 0884
Fax: 61 2 281 2030

Europe

The Camden Practice
West Hill House, 6 Swains Lane,
London N6 6QU,
United Kingdom

General Osteopathic Council and Osteopathic Information Service
Premier House, 10 Greycoat Place,
London SW1P 1SB,
United Kingdom
Tel: 0171 799 2559

Richard Field/Andrew Mullen
87 North Road, Parkstone, Poole,
Dorset BH14 0LT
United Kingdom
(practice in London)

U.S.A.

American Academy of Osteopathy
3500 DePauw Boulevard, Suite 1080,
Indianopolis, Indiana 46268-139
Tel: 317 879 1881
Fax: 317 879 0563

American Association of Colleges of Osteopathic Medicine
6110 Executive,
Boulevard Apt 405,
Rockville, Maryland 20852
Tel: 301 468 0990

American Osteopathic Association
142 East Ohio Street, Chicago,
Illinois 60611
Tel: 312 280 5800
Fax: 312 280 3860

POLARITY THERAPY

Europe

The Federation of Polarity Training
7 Nunney Close, Golden Valley,
Cheltenham, Gloucestershire
GL51 0TU, United Kingdom

David Haas
101 Practitioner Network
London and Surrey/Hampshire Practice
87 North Road, Parkstone, Poole,
Dorset BH14 0LT, United Kingdom
Tel: 01425 461740

UK Polarity Therapy Association
Monomark House,
27 Old Gloucester Street,
London WC1N 3XX, United Kingdom
Tel: 01483 417714

U.S.A.

American Polarity Therapy Association
2888 Bluff Street\Suite 149
Boulder, Colorado 80301
Tel: 303 545 2080
Fax: 303 545 2161

PSYCHOTHERAPY

(*see also* **Counseling**)

Europe

British Association of Psychotherapists
37 Mapesbury Road,
London NW2 4HJ,
United Kingdom
Tel: 0181 452 9823
Fax: 0181 452 5182

European Association for Psychotherapy (EAP)
Rosenbursenstrasse, 8/3/7
a-1010 Vienna, Austria
Tel: 0043 1 512 7090
Fax: 0043 1 512 7091

U.K. Council for Psychotherapy
167–9 Great Portland Street,
London W1N 5F,
United Kingdom
Tel: 0171 436 3002
Fax: 0171 436 3013

U.S.A.

American Psychological Association
750 First Street NE, Washington,
DC20002
Tel: 415 327 2066

Association for Humanistic Psychology (International)
45 Franklin Street, 315 San Francisco,
CA 94102

International Transpersonal Association
20 Sunnyside Avenue,
A-257 Mill Valley, CA 94941
Tel: 415 389 6912

QI GONG

Australia

Qi Gong Association of Australia
458 White Horse Road, Surrey Hills,
Victoria 3127
Tel: 03 836 6961

Europe

The Institute of Stress Management
57 Hall Lane, London NW4 4TJ,
United Kingdom

Tse Qigong Centre
PO Box 116,
Manchester M20 3YN,
United Kingdom
Tel: 0161 929 4485
Fax: 0161 929 4489

U.S.A.

Qi Gong Human Life Research Foundation
PO Box 5327, Cleveland,
Ohio 44101
Tel: 216 475 4712

Qi Gong Institute
East West Academy of Healing Arts
450 Sutter Street, Suite 916,
San Francisco, California 94108
Tel: 415 788 2227/323 1221

Qi Gong Resources Associates
1755 Homets Road, Pasadena,
California 94122
Tel: 818 564 9751

RADIESTHESIA/RADIONICS

Europe

Confederation of Radionic and Radiesthesic Organisations
Maperton, Wincanton,
Somerset BA9 8EH, United Kingdom

The Radionic Association
Barelelin House, Goose Green,
Deddington, Banbury,
Oxon OX15 0SZ, United Kingdom
Tel/Fax: 01869 338852

REFLEXOLOGY

Australia

Association of Reflexology
2 Stewart Avenue, Matraville,
NSW 2036
Tel: 02 311 2322

Canada

Cecile Myslicki
70 Parkville Drive, Winnipeg,
Manitoba R2M 2H5
Tel: 204 253 9375

Karen Nel
1951 Glenarie Avenue,
North Vancouver V7P 1X9
Tel: 604 986 7121

Europe

Association of Reflexologists
23 Old Gloucester Street,
London WC1N 3XX,
United Kingdom
Tel/Fax: 0990 673 320

Carol Bosiger
PO Box 93, Tadworth,
Surrey TK20 7YB,
United Kingdom
Tel/Fax: 01737 842961

Alberto Carnevale-Maffe
Via Procaccini 47, Milan, Italy
Tel/Fax: 39 2 311116

Ann-Chatrine Jonsson
Varmlandsvagen 438, 12348 Farsta,
Sweden
Tel/Fax: 46 8 942 485

Karine van Niekerk
Frankenstraat 31A,
2582 SE Den Haag,
Netherlands
Tel: 31 70 354 304

Andrea Schippers
Domkeweg 23, 37213 Witzenhausen,
Germany
Tel: 49 5542 71463

Lena Walters
Vale Da Telha, Apartado 173,
Aljezue 8670, Algarve, Portugal
Tel: 351 82 98566

South Africa

Inge Dougans
PO Box 68283, Bryanston,
Johannesburg 2021
Tel/Fax: 27 11 706 4206

U.S.A.

Jill Tonkovich
2222 Kilkare Parkway, Pt. Pleasant,
New Jersey 08742
Tel: 908 892 7566

ROLFING

Australia

Rolf Institute
Pacific Branch Office,
28 Davies Street,
Brunswick 3056, Victoria
Tel: 61 3 383 5045

Europe

The Rolfing Institute
PO Box 14793,
London SW1V 2WB,
United Kingdom

Rolf Institute: European Branch Office
Herzogstrasse 40,
D-800 Munich 40,
Germany
Tel: 49 8939 6802

U.S.A.

The Rolf Institute
205 Canyon Boulevard, Boulder,
Colorado 80302-4920
Tel: 303 449 5903
Fax: 303 449 5978

SHIATSU

Australia

The Shiatsu Therapy Association of Australia
332 Carlisle Street, Balaclava, 3183 Victoria
Tel: 039530 0067

Europe

Paul Lambeth
Albert Cottage, Town Head, Alston,
Cumbria CA9 3SR, United Kingdom
Tel: 01434 381 088

The Shiatsu College of London
Kim Lovelace, Unit 62, Pall Mall
Deposit, 126-128 Barlby Road,
London W10 6BL,
United Kingdom
Tel: 0181 987 0208

Shiatsu Society
Barber House, Storeys Bar Road,
Fengate, Peterborough PE1 5YN,
United Kingdom
Tel: 01733 758 341

Shiatsu Society of Ireland
Greenville Lodge, Esker Road, Lucan,
Co. Dublin, Rep. of Ireland

The Shiatsu Society
14 Oakdean Road, Redhill,
Surrey RH1 6BT, United Kingdom
Tel: 0737 767896

Michael Woolly/Ismail Mazzara
87 North Road, Parkstone, Poole,
Dorset BH14 0LT, United Kingdom
(practice in London)

Japan

Japanese Shiatsu College
2-15-6 Koishikawa, Bunkyoku, Tokyo
Tel: 00 813 3813 7354

Iokai Centre
1-8-9 Higashiuena, Daito-Ku, Tokyo

SOUND THERAPY

Europe

The Hale Clinic
7 Park Crescent, London W1N 3HE,
United Kingdom
Tel: 0171 631 0156

Inner Sound
8 Elms Avenue, London N10 2JP,
United Kingdom

The Tomatis Centre U.K. Ltd
3 Wallands Crescent, Lewes,
E. Sussex BN7 2QT, United Kingdom
Tel: 01273 474 877
Fax: 01273 487 500

T'AI-CHI CH'UAN

Europe

The Institute of Stress Management
57 Hall Lane, London NW4 4TJ,
United Kingdom

The North Pole School of T'ai Chi
83 St. Quintin Avenue, London W10
6PB, United Kingdom

T'ai Chi Union for Great Britain
23 Oakwood Avenue, Mitcham,
Surrey CR4 3DQ, United Kingdom

The U.K. T'ai Chi Association
PO Box 159, Bromley,
Kent BR1 3XX, United Kingdom

VITAMINS AND MINERALS

Australia

Australian College of Nutritional and Environmental Medicine
13 Hilton Road, Beamaris, Victoria 3193
Tel: 03 9589 6088

Canada

Canadian College of Naturopathic Medicine
60 Berl Avenue, Etobicoke,
Ontario M8Y 3C7
Tel: 416 251 5261

National Institute of Nutrition
2565 Carling Avenue, Suite 400, Ottawa,
Ontario K1Z 8R1
Tel: 613 235 3355

Europe

The Council for Nutrition Education of Therapy (CNEAT)
1 The Close, Halton, Aylesbury,
Buckinghamshire HP22 5NJ,
United Kingdom

Health Education Authority
Trevelyan House, 30 Gt. Peter Street,
London SW1 2HW, United Kingdom
Tel: 0171 222 5300
Fax: 0171 413 8900

Institute of Optimum Nutrition
Blades Court , Dodar Road,
London SW15 2MU, United Kingdom
Tel: 0181 877 9993
Fax: 0181 877 9980

Nutritional Science Research Institute
Mulberry Tree Road, Brookthorpe,
Gloucester GL4 0UU, United Kingdom

The 101 Group Dispensary
87 North Road, Parkstone, Poole,
Dorset BH14 0LT,
United Kingdom
(practice in London)

Society for the Promotion of Nutritional Therapy
PO Box 47, Heathfield,
E. Sussex TN21 8ZX, United Kingdom
Tel: 01825 872 921

The Vegetarian Society
Parkdale, Dunham Road,
Altrincham, Cheshire WA14 4QG,
United Kingdom
Tel: 0161 928 0793

U.S.A.

American College of Advancement in Medicine
PO Box 3427, Laguna Hills,
California 92654

VISUALIZATION

(*see also* **Psychotherapy** *and* **Counseling**)

Europe

Holistic Health and Healing Centre
10 Connaught Hill, Loughton,
Essex IG10 4DU, United Kingdom

The International School of Meditation
87 North Road, Parkstone, Poole,
Dorset BH14 0LT,
United Kingdom
(practice in London)

U.S.A.

Academy for Guided Imagery
PO Box 2070, Mill Valley,
CA 94942
Tel: 800 726 2070

YOGA

Australia

BKS Iyengar Association of Australia
1 Rickman Avenue,
Mosman, 2088 NSW
Tel: 2 9969 4052

International Yoga Teachers' Association
c/o 14/15 Huddart Avenue,
Normanhurst, NSW 2076

Canada

Sivananda Yoga Vedanta Centre
5178 St. Lawrence, Boulevard,
Montreal, Quebec H2T 1R8

Sivananda Yoga Vedanta Centre
77 Harbord Street, Toronto,
Ontario M5S 1G4

Unity Yoga International
303 2495 West 2nd Avenue,
Vancouver,
British Columbia VKG 1J5

Europe

British Wheel of Yoga
1 Hamilton Place, Boston Road,
Sleaford, Lincs. NG34 7ES,
United Kingdom
Tel: 01529 306851

Institute of Iyengar Yoga
223A Randolf Avenue,
London W9 1NL,
United Kingdom
Tel/Fax: 0171 624 3080

Kailash Centre
7 Newcourt Street, London NW8,
United Kingdom

Kitty Kennedy
87 North Road, Parkstone, Poole,
Dorset BH14 0LT,
United Kingdom
(practice in London)

Patanjali Yoga Centre & Ashram
The Cottage, Marley Lane,
Battle, E. Sussex TN33 0RE,
United Kingdom
Tel/Fax: 01424 870 538

Sivananda Yoga Vendanta Centre
51 Felsham Road,
London SW15 1AZ,
United Kingdom
Tel: 0181 780 0160
Fax: 0181 780 0128

Yoga for Health Foundation
Ickwell Bury, Biggleswade,
Bedfordshire SG18 9EF,
United Kingdom
Tel: 01767 627271

U.S.A.

International Association of Yoga Therapists
109 Hillside Avenue,
Mill Valley,
California 94941
Tel: 415 383 4587
Fax: 415 381 0876

Sivananda Yoga Vendanta Centre
243 West 24th Street,
New York 10011

Unity in Yoga International
PO Box 281004,
Lakewood,
Colorado 80228

Unity Yoga International
7918 Bolling Drive,
Alexandria,
Virginia 22308

Yogaville
Buckingham, Virginia 23921

ZEN

Europe

The Buddhist Society
58 Eccleston Square,
London SW1V 1PH,
United Kingdom
Tel: 0171 834 3858
Fax: 0171 976 5238

Index

NOTE: The numbers in blue boxes refer to the chapters in which main entries occur. This is to help the reader find the section relevant to any enquiry. For key, see below:

1 Sex, Fertility, and Conception
2 Pregnancy and Childbirth
3 Infancy and Childhood
4 Young Adult
5 Adult
6 Middle Age and Onwards
7 Nutrition
8 Diagnostic Techniques
9 Alternative Therapies
10 Drugs